Powhatan log cabin and court house.

1815 – LAWRENCE COUNTY – 2001

Built 1888

ARKANSAS

Turner Publishing Company

Turner Publishing Company

Turner Publishing Company Staff:
Douglas W. Sikes, Publishing Consultant
Terry Sullivan, Jr., Designer

Copyright © 2001

Publishing Rights:
Turner Publishing Company
ISBN: 978-1-68162-178-4

Library of Congress Control #:
2001091090

TABLE OF CONTENTS

Dedication

Mrs. Robert (Evelyn) Flippo, a woman whose vision will enrich our quality of life for years to come.

Vision, leadership, dedication and determination are just a few of the qualities that describe Evelyn Flippo of Powhatan. Mrs. Flippo, museum curator/program assistant at the Powhatan Courthouse State Park, has been vitally instrumental in seeing the projects at the State Park develop and grow into a historical state park.

The Powhatan Courthouse Restoration Committee was formed as a part of the Lawrence County Development Council. Evelyn served on this committee from the beginning and saw the interest of former Governor Winthrop Rockefeller and a visiting team from Williamsburg, Virginia, provide the momentum to seek funding. Mrs. Flippo helped work for federal grant funding and provided leadership for local fund-raising as matching money. In the meantime, Mrs. Flippo, along with Tommie Tolson of Walnut Ridge, and Glynda Stewart of Powhatan, provided leadership to assemble volunteers to assist them in sorting, filing and preserving the many valuable historical documents in the courthouse. Work on preserving the records was slow and arduous, and volunteers worked in extreme temperatures. The building was deeded to the Arkansas State Parks and Tourism Department by the county and restoration was completed in 1973.

A member of the Lawrence County Historical Society, Mrs. Flippo has been actively involved as a board member and held every office of the society. She is currently serving as Vice-President and has helped with numerous programs and articles for the Lawrence County Historical Quarterly.

She communicated the importance of the Powhatan projects with the Arkansas State Parks and served as liaison for the society in developing the present research room at the Powhatan Courthouse. She worked closely with Dr. John Ferguson and Russell Baker of the Arkansas History Commission in providing proper filing and storage of the historic records. She spent three months helping the Mormon Church in the microfilming of the records.

After serving for fifteen years as a volunteer, Mrs. Flippo was employed in 1984 at the Powhatan Courthouse State Park. Her extensive research provided the information for the panels and exhibits inside the courthouse. Mrs. Flippo has assisted numerous researchers who visit the courthouse each year and has helped people from all across the United States. Dorothy Southern, a researcher from Oklahoma City, Oklahoma, expressed her appreciation for Mrs. Flippo in a recent letter to the society. "Without a doubt Evelyn Flippo ranks right by the side of the late, great Dr. Marion Craig in nurturing and sharing the history of your unique area...she has a loving appreciation of it and has assisted in its being shared broadly. I, for one, have an enormous appreciation of all her efforts. Evelyn and that courthouse belong together; they both possess great and lasting integrity, beauty and character."

Mrs. Flippo has provided many hours of research and historical consultation to the staff of the state parks in their acquisition of the various historical buildings that make up the state

park. Jay Schneider, former park interpreter at the courthouse, has called Mrs. Flippo "a great resource and the rock that Powhatan Courthouse State Park stands on."

Richard W. Davies, Executive Director, Department of Parks & Tourism states; "Evelyn Flippo is Powhatan Courthouse. My earliest recollection of the work on restoring the building and preserving the collection there are inseparable from Mrs. Flippo. She stayed the course, and stayed on us, to assure that a wonderful Arkansas resource has been taken care of properly. We can all thank her for that."

Greg Butts, Director, Arkansas State Parks adds: "At state parks, we like to say we're in the 'forever business' preserving Arkansas' outstanding natural, historical, and cultural resources for generations to come. And anyone that's been involved in a preservation project knows that it may require long term commitment of time, vision, leadership, and energy. For over fifteen years as a department employee at Powhatan Courthouse State Park, and spanning three decades with the Lawrence County Historical Society, Evelyn Flippo has made a lot happen at the park. Thanks to her untiring contributions, a very important part of Arkansas' history will be preserved and shared with generations, 'forever.' We thank her for her dedication."

We gratefully appreciate Evelyn Flippo for her vision, leadership, determination, and dedication to the projects at Powhatan and to the historical society.

Lawrence County Historical Society

Preface

Lloyd Wayne Clark Jr.

Well, it has been a long time getting here, hasn't it? The Lawrence County and Family History Book turned into a much bigger project than we ever imagined. This was made worse by a problem which arose with our original publisher after they had received about 90% of the draft copy and all of the photos. To put it simply, we had to get a new publisher and not lose any of the money, or photos, or copies of items you had entrusted to us in the process. We hope we have done that and do sincerely thank you for your trust and patience. We apologize for the delay but believe we have a quality product you will be truly proud to treasure and show off to your families and friends.

The following pages are devoted to the histories of certain families and individuals who have resided in Lawrence County.

Those included are by choice of that individual or some member of their family. The Society did not place any conditions on who could or could not be included here except that one had to have resided in Lawrence County. Some folks paid a bit extra to have a lengthy article included and some paid a fee to have extra photos included. But, everyone had that option available. No one was denied the privilege of having their family represented.

We are pleased to state that in the index included here are to be found the names and stories of some of the finest families who have ever lived in our county or state. Having good people like these live within our borders has enriched our county.

We are sorry that there are a number of families within our county whose history is not included, who by reason of past and present prominence in county affairs, should have been included. It was their choice that this is the case. We believe we made every opportunity available and advertised and promoted the book effort as much as possible.

We would be very sorry indeed, if there should be found one person who desired to have their family history included who did not know of this opportunity. We ran several advertisements in the papers in Arkansas, sent a flyer to every household in the county, used KRLW radio ex-tensively, and talked to scores of people personally about this effort. We particularly thank The Times Dispatch, *"The Ozark Journal"*, and KRLW radio for their help in promoting the book. In addition to this, the members of the Lawrence County Historical Society and the staff at the Powhatan Courthouse Museum deserve special thanks.

With this in mind, we desire to state once more that the publication of this book was not initiated or promoted as a money making proposition. We did it solely to preserve the rapidly disappearing story of the early days of the "Mother of Counties," Lawrence County, Arkansas.

The "Book Committee" expresses deep and very personal gratitude to everyone who submitted stories, photos, ideas and other items for the book. Your efforts made the book a success. Do read ALL the stories contained herein. There are some funny ones, some poignant ones, some sad ones and some very important historical excerpts.

Lloyd W. Clark, Jr., President
Lawrence County Historical Society

Lloyd Wayne Clark, Jr.
LTC. (Retired) U.S. Army 1969-1991.

Lloyd is a teacher at Walnut Ridge Middle School. He preaches at Alicia Church of Christ. He is married to Barbara Jones Clark and has three children: Jessica Lynn, Jennifer Leah and Kenneth Wayne.

Lawrence County Historical Society

The Lawrence County Historical Society has been a vital organization for the preservation, appreciation, and advancement of the rich history of Lawrence County. The society was first organized in 1964 under the leadership of J.T. Midkiff, Ida Belle Flippo, Marie Penn, Eugene Sloan, and Mr. Croom of Jonesboro. Mr. Midkiff served as the first president and the group continued until 1968.

In 1970 the society was reactivated at the urging of Mrs. Evelyn Flippo, Lawrence County Development Council member, Arkansas State Historian Dr. John Ferguson, and Archivist Russell Baker of the Arkansas History Commission. The restoration of the Powhatan Courthouse was a major Lawrence County project in 1970 and the society took a leading role in seeing this project come to fruition.

The society was instrumental in helping the Arkansas State Parks and Tourism obtain ownership of the building and has been the driving force in seeing the development of the Powhatan Historical District.

The first constitution of the society was revised and accepted at a 1977 meeting with Jerry Gibbens serving as temporary chairman. Mr. Gibbens was nominated to serve as president.

Presidents have been Jerry Gibbens (1977-1978); Viola Meadows (1978-1981); Tom Moore (1981-1984); Evelyn Flippo (1984-1987); Willene Kirkland (1987-1990); Pat Haley (1990-1992); Darlene Moore (1992-1995); and Lloyd Clark (1995-present).

Individuals who have served in officers and director positions through the years have been: Maxine Scott, Dr. Mildred Vance, Lee Hunter, Reta Covey, Frank Shell, Lucia Allen, Rachel Rainey, Revis Casper, Clay Weir, Diane Formby Howard; Glynda Stewart, Carolyn Propst, Richard Spades, Inez Harris, Farris Herren, Jean Guthrie, Jean Jean, Tom Baker, Dalton Henderson, Helen Henderson, Edith Stovall, Karen Holliday, Brent and Maleta Tipton, Charlotte Wheeless, Jerry Joe Ballard, Sue Whitmire, Pat Barnes and Pauline McKamey.

Society members have greatly improved Lawrence County with implementation of the annual Pearlfest (formerly called Pioneer Day) held each September at the Powhatan Courthouse State Park. This event has brought in hundreds of visitors to the area. The society has taken steps in seeing various buildings in the county named to the National Register of Historic Places. In addition

they have supported the restoration of the Walnut Ridge Depot and the Clover Bend Project.

Other outstanding projects include reprinting of the McLeod Centennial Memorial History of Lawrence County; the Arkansas Sesquicentennial activities in the county; an exhibit of pictures of the former one-room school houses in early Lawrence County; a living history presentation at the Powhatan Cemetery; Court room plays and living history reenactments at Pearlfest; historical presentation in honor of the 50th Anniversary of the Walnut Ridge Chamber of Commerce; historical research for displays at the Powhatan Courthouse; and the restoration of the historical buildings at the Powhatan Courthouse State Park.

Outstanding speakers from Arkansas and Lawrence County are featured at the annual Spring Banquet in May. The society prints the Lawrence County Historical Journal (formerly The Lawrence County Historical Quarterly), an excellent collection of historical articles about the county, under the guidance of Helen Henderson, Edith Stovall and Pauline McKamey, editors.

This organization takes tremendous pride in keeping the splendid history of the "Mother of Counties" alive for generations to come.

Historical Society Board Members are, left: Charlotte Wheeless, right: Pat Barnes, above: Pauline McKamey, Willene Kirkland, and Edith Stovall.

In Grateful Appreciation

The Lawrence County Historical Society gratefully acknowledges the outstanding work of our president, Lloyd W. Clark, Jr., for his leadership in all of our historical projects which promote the preservation and appreciation for the rich history of Lawrence County. We especially appreciate his vision, commitment, and guidance with the family history book. Without his leadership, publishing this book would not have been possible.

Evelyn Flippo, Vice President
Pauline McKamey, Secretary
Lisa Phillips, Treasurer
Darlene Moore, Past President

Board Members:
Pat Barnes
Jerry Gibbens
Willene Kirkland
Tom Moore
Edith Stovall
Brent Tipton
Maleta Tipton
Charlotte Wheeless
Sue Whitmire

Historical society officers and board members are: seated, from left: Sue Whitmire; Lloyd Clark, president; Evelyn Flippo, vice-president; Lesia Phillips, treasurer. Standing, from left: Darlene Moore, past president; Maleta Tipton; Brent Tipton, and Jerry Gibbens.

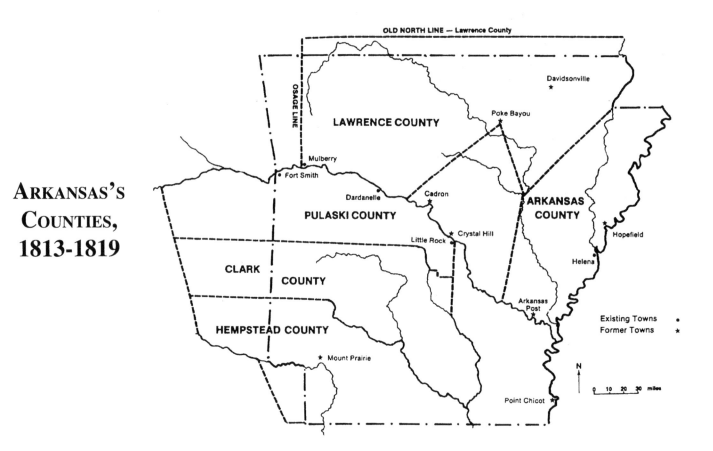

Arkansas's Counties, 1813-1819

OLD NORTH LINE — Lawrence County

OSAGE LINE

LAWRENCE COUNTY

Davidsonville ★

Poke Bayou

Mulberry
Fort Smith

Dardanelle
Cadron ★

ARKANSAS COUNTY

PULASKI COUNTY

Crystal Hill ★
Little Rock

Hopefield ★

Helena

CLARK COUNTY

Arkansas Post ★

HEMPSTEAD COUNTY

Mount Prairie ★

Point Chicot ★

Existing Towns •
Former Towns ★

N

0 10 20 30 miles

Current Arkansas County Map

MISSOURI

BENTON, CARROLL, BOONE, MARION, BAXTER, FULTON, RANDOLPH, CLAY

WASHINGTON, MADISON, NEWTON, SEARCY, IZARD, SHARP, LAWRENCE, GREENE

STONE, INDEPENDENCE, CRAIGHEAD, MISSISSIPPI

CRAWFORD, FRANKLIN, JOHNSON, VAN BUREN, CLEBURNE, JACKSON, POINSETT

SEBASTIAN, LOGAN, POPE, CONWAY, WHITE, WOODRUFF, CROSS, CRITTENDEN

FAULKNER

SCOTT, YELL, PERRY, PULASKI, LONOKE, PRAIRIE, ST. FRANCIS, LEE

SALINE, MONROE, PHILLIPS

POLK, MONTGOMERY, GARLAND, HOT SPRING, GRANT, JEFFERSON, ARKANSAS

PIKE, CLARK, DALLAS, CLEVELAND, LINCOLN, DESHA

SEVIER, HOWARD

LITTLE RIVER, HEMPSTEAD, NEVADA, OUACHITA, CALHOUN, BRADLEY, DREW

MILLER, COLUMBIA, UNION, ASHLEY, CHICOT

LAFAYETTE

OKLAHOMA

TENNESSEE

MISSISSIPPI

TEXAS

LOUISIANA

History Of Lawrence County

Lawrence County History

By Jerry D. Gibbens

Although settled by Bluff Dwellers and Mound Builders perhaps ten thousand years ago, Arkansas was not described, in writing, until Hernando de Soto explored the region in 1542-1543. Prior to the Spanish arrival, the Osage, Quapaw and Caddo had settled on the land. In the seventeenth century, Father Jacques Marquette and Louis Joliet visited the Quapaw villages near the confluence of the Arkansas and Mississippi rivers. Marquette named this region the *Arkansas,* land of the "down-stream people."

The Spanish and the French both claimed possession of the land of the Arkansas before the United States received permanent title during Thomas Jefferson's "Louisiana Purchase" in 1803. Arkansas became a part of the County of New Madrid in Missouri Territory in 1815; in 1836, Arkansas became the twenty-fifth state. To balance the number of free and slave states Arkansas was paired with Michigan. The area adjacent to Arkansas's western border was known as "Indian Territory."

Arkansas was first known as the "Bear State." Prior to the Civil War, the state was characterized by a "rustic, yeoman-farmer society, only occasionally broken by the estate of a plantation owner." Arkansas was a hunter's paradise, with bear hunting the favorite sport. Payton Washburn's painting, *The Arkansas Traveler,* became the most graphic image of the state's citizens. Inhabitants lived close by the Indian territory, and they shared the frontier dislike and contempt for the Indian.

In 1811, the United States opened a road from St. Genevieve, Missouri, southwest through Arkansas to Louisiana. The "military road" passed through Lawrence County by way of Maynard and Jackson, crossed Spring River at or near the Miller ford, went by Denton and Lynn, and crossed Strawberry River. According to Warren McLeod, Davidsonville in Spring River valley, and Smithville were two very important settlements. Davidsonville, on the west bank of Black River, was about two miles above the mouth of Spring River. In 1814, Colonel John Miller and Colonel Robert Smith were engaged in a mercantile business there.

Davidsonville was named in honor of John Davidson who represented the legislature in Missouri Territory. The town was the first county seat of Lawrence County in 1816; Davidsonville was also the first post office in the state—although the mail came only once a month! Davidsonville was laid off in nine blocks. The center block was the court house square with its two-story brick court building. Dallas Herndon's Centennial History of Arkansas, published in 1922, shows a picture of an old log house with the statement that it was the court house at Davidsonville, the oldest court house in Arkansas.

Davidsonville, in addition to the courthouse, had a "jail, several stores and shops, and possibly a few hundred inhabitants." Tradition claimed two or three thousand Citizens were living there; this seems improbable, because in 1830, the population of the territory was only 30,000 and the population of Little Rock was only 600. Another "improbable story is that almost the entire population of the town died within a few days from an epidemic of yellow fever and that immediately following the few survivors burned all the houses and moved away." In 1829, the county seat moved to Jackson on the Military Road.

Smithville, named in honor of Robert Smith who had prospered in business both at Davidsonville and Jackson and had donated the county a considerable sum of money, had its beginning when the county seat was located there in 1837 on land donated by James H. Benson.

Travel to Arkansas was difficult, entailing weeks of discomfort on board a steamboat, or an even more hazardous journey over a primitive wilderness road. The most important of these roads, the "military road," ran from Saint Louis down through the lead- minig district of southeast Missouri to Little Rock and from there to the Red River. The road crossed many unbridged streams and was also short on ferry conveniences. Along the Missouri border, the road was infested with gangs of desperadoes, living in abandoned cabins off the main route. There were no taverns and if the travelers did not wish to camp out at night, they usually had to sleep in a single room with several other tenants, oftentimes in the same bed with another guest.

According to John Gould Fletcher, travel by steamboat was not quite so uncomfortable, but it was equally uncertain because of the difficulties of navigation on the Arkansas River. At most, two or three steamboats a month managed to reach the capital city, after struggling with sandbars and snags in a channel frequently described as "fourfeet, and falling." Stagecoaches were practically unheard of except for a line which ran from Arkansas Post to Little Rock, at first every two weeks and then weekly beginning in 1826.

As the white settlers moved in, the Indians slowly moved out. In 1824, the Quapaws sold their land for six thousand dollars and an annuity of a thousand dollars a year for eleven years. Thus a "good deal of what is now the finest cotton land in the state changed hands at a figure which has been estimated as totaling one dollar per thousand acres." Certainly, the vanishing of the Quapaws was a minor tragedy if we consider the Five Great Tribes: the Cherokees, Chickasaws, Choctaws, Creeks, and Seminoles who were driven en masse from their lands in Tennessee, Alabama, Georgia, Mississippi and Florida to the Indian Territory in the early 1830s.

On June 15, 1836, after an all-night sitting of the House of Representatives in Washington, D.C. , the bill to admit Arkansas as a state was passed and signed by President Andrew Jackson. Arkansans were elated, hanging out their flags and celebrating in Little Rock. The frontier stage of its history was nearly over; and in another fifteen years the tales of big bear, Bowie knives, of enraged buffalo hunters around a lone tree, of frontier brawls and of travelers on lonely roads looking for some shelter for the night became more a matter of folklore than reality.

In 1835, the population of Arkansas was 51,809. By 1840, it was nearly double, the national census showing 97,574. Little Rock, chartered as a city in 1835, had 1,500 inhabitants who were proud of their theater, their three churches, several fine residences, a Federal arsenal, horse racing and an occasional fireworks display.

Statehood marked the beginning of a period of rapid growth that continued until the outbreak of the Civil War in 1861. During this time, the population increased by nearly 860 percent, reaching toward half a million by the war. Arkansas remained a rural state, but the growth in agriculture brought necessary services for the society: mills, gins, and lumbering. During the 1850s, the state even made advances toward solving its persistent transportation problems with the laying of the first railroad tracks.

In 1860, Arkansas had few towns. Little Rock was the largest, with 3,727 inhabitants, followed by Camden, Fort Smith, Pine Bluff, Van Buren, Fayetteville, and Arkadelphia. "Most people lived in the countryside where their days were regulated by nature's clock." Agriculture provided Arkansans with their principal source of income. Farmers produced corn and wheat, and in the rich valleys they grew cotton. By 1860, cotton production had increased to 367,393 bales of "white gold."

In addition to country life and agriculture, slavery was a major component of the state's prewar identity. In 1860, according to *A Documentary History of Arkansas*, there were 111,115 slaves in Arkansas, over 20 percent of the population. Like cotton, most of the slaves were found in the rich valley counties; four counties on the Mississippi River and two on the southern border were more than 50 percent black. "While only 11,481 white Arkansans were slave owners in 1860, and despite the concentration of slaves in the south and southeast, most Arkansans had some stake in the institution, either real or potential."

Following the election of Abraham Lincoln in 1860, South Carolina withdrew from the Union, followed by Mississippi, Florida, Alabama, Georgia, Louisiana and Texas. In February, 1861, delegates from these states created the Confederate States of America. President Lincoln attempted to suppress the "insurrection with force" and the result was a war that lasted four years. Arkansas seceded from the Union on May 6, 1861. Many Arkansans supported the new Confederacy and joined Arkansas military units sent to fight in Virginia, Missouri, Mississippi, Tennessee, and elsewhere.

The war became a costly affair to Arkansans. Military activities in the state were widespread. On March 6, 1862, at Pea Ridge in northwestern Arkansas, the Confederates lost a crucial battle. This defeat opened up all the northern part of the state to Federal troops. In May, the victorious Gen. Samuel A. Curtis went on to occupy Batesville and free the White River for Union operations. The next year Arkansas Post fell to the Federal troops and nine months later, Little Rock fell. Confederate forces fought valiantly and gained victories at Prairie Grove and Camden, but "manpower shortages, inadequate supplies, and sometimes, poor leadership prevented them from taking advantage of their few opportunities." By the end of the war, Confederate forces held only the southwestern corner of the state; Union forces operated practically unrestrained elsewhere. The Civil War in Arkansas "claimed a tremendous personal cost, paid in the lives of men lost in both armies, and in the 'injuries sustained." However, according to Walter McLeod, Lawrence County soldiers were more fortunate than most in that they had homes to which they could return. There was no destruction of property in Lawrence County.

Politically, the decade after the Civil War also saw a continued struggle. Unionists created a government under Isaac Murphy in 1864 and wrote a new constitution. The Murphy government operated until March 1867 when Congress passed laws for a new program of "reconstruction." Under the Reconstruction Act of 1867, a new state constitution was ratified, insuring civil rights for blacks. Republican Powell Clayton was elected governor. Born in Pennsylvania, Powell Clayton was thirty-five years of age. He had come from Kansas in 1862 and had shown considerable courage as a Union officer in the battle of Pine Bluff. Behind cotton-bale barricades, Clayton and his command repelled a violent Confederate cavalry and artillery attack at the close of 1863.

Clayton had married a Southern woman, and with cotton selling at fantastic prices after the war, he had soon become a wealthy planter. Powell encouraged railroad construction, immigration, and education, but Democrats charged his administration with corruption and high taxes. Powell was ultimately elected to the U.S. Senate. But Powell and the Republican regime, however, would only hold power for a few more years. By the early 1870s, the Democrats were again the state's dominant party.

When Sharp County was cut off from Lawrence in 1868 and "carpet baggers" had control of the county, they moved the county seat from Smithville to Clover Bend, which was supposed to be about the center of the county. When the Democrats got control in 1869, they by election-moved the county seat to Powhatan. The courthouse built in 1873, burned in 1885, and the present one was built in 1888. Warren McLeod wrote in 1936, "the old hill on which it stands seems designed by nature for it. On its solid substance the ravages of erosion have but little effect."

In 1870, there were only two towns in western Lawrence County, and the Eastern District was practically unsettled. However, in 1867, Col. W.M. Ponder came from Missouri and located at Old Walnut Ridge where he engaged in farming and saw milling. He owned the land where Walnut Ridge is located. The railroad company agreed to locate a depot there, and he, Lacy Hodge, and a Negro lady "cleared away the bushes and brush from the site for a depot. Col. Ponder built the first dwelling house in Walnut Ridge and was active in the town's affairs until his death in 1904. Other prominent families included the Phelpses, Dowells, Pinnells, Finleys, Rankins, Graffs, Grimes, Lesses, Dr. Minor, Arndts, Dr. Watkins, Charles Coffin, Dr. Camp, and T. J. Sharum. The Lawrence County Bank, the first in the county, was established there in 1890 with Capt. J. M. Phelps as president."

According to Warren McLeod, Hoxie was founded when the "leading men of Walnut Ridge" could not agree with railroad officials on the location for the Kansas City, Fort Scott, and Memphis Railroad. Therefore, the railroad officials moved a mile and a half south. There, Mr. Boas had acquired the land on which Hoxie was built. Mrs. John S. Gibson fell heir, and she and her husband were the "chief promoters of the town's interests." After the Iron Mountain terminal and shops closed in the late 1920s, the town "has not been so prosperous as formerly."

About 1803, Portia was founded by a Frenchman, Joseph Giglonet, who filed a claim to the old Spanish land grant town. After the building of the Frisco Railroad, Portia was a thriving community because of the mills of the Portia Lumber Company. Portia had a newspaper and was a bidder for the county seat. When the mills closed, the town declined. Portia had fine schools and the school was recently restored and currently serves the City of Portia. The grounds are still used for the annual Fourth of July picnic.

Black Rock was founded by Dr. J. W. Coffman and through his influence the railroad depot was located there. The location of Black Rock, only a mile and a half up the river from Powhatan, was the "death blow to that proud old town." Jerry Gibbens in his article, "Sam Payne: Marshal, Murderer, Marshal Again" wrote that Black Rock was incorporated in 1884 and that the town was a "boom town doubling in population from 761 in 1890 to 1400 by 1900, the largest town in Lawrence County. In 1900, Black Rock had eight grocery stores, five hotels, ten saw mills, a weekly newspaper, a school, and a Methodist and Presbyterian church." The town also was the headquarters for three steamboats, and one, the St. Augustine. made daily trips to Pocahontas." Other prominent names associated with Black Rock include the Townsends, Krones, Myers, Moores, Spades, McCarrolls, Freemans, Verklers, Angles, Weirs, Clarks, Smiths, Hills, Williams, Lairds, Coffeys, Kells, McLaughlins, Poindexters, Haileys, Paynes, Dr. Warren, and later Dr. Tibbels, Dr. Cruse, Frank Joseph, Cudes, Callahans, McKinneys, and Oldhams.

According to Warren McLeod, Imboden was begun in 1882 and was developed by Capt. W.C. Sloan, a citizen of Smithville who owned land at and near Imboden. When the railroad station was located there, he gave much time and attention to the development of the town. Capt. Sloan encouraged schools and churches by donating lots and lands for building purposes. By his "liberality and influence," Sloan-Hendrix Academy was located there and under the guidance of Professor J.C. Eaton, many young people were educated. Capt. Sloan organized the first bank at Imobden and built the first bridge across the Spring River. Other prominent families associated with Imboden included the Hendersons, Hatchers, Sullivans, Chessers, Polks, Poindexters, Wilsons, Bacons, Danes, Duprees, Washums, Childers, Ketchems, Porters, Kirkpatricks, Rainwaters, Weirs, Carters, and Taylors.

Other Lawrence County communities included Ravenden. Before the Frisco Railroad was built, Sam H. Ball had helped establish the town when he moved his business there in the early 1880s. William Wilson was also prominent in the town's affairs until he moved to Imboden in the 1890s. Sedgwick, on the Cache River, was the eastern town on the Frisco Railroad and at one time was lively, due to the timber business carried on there by the Culver Lumber Company.

Alicia, the southern town on the Missouri Pacific Railroad, was largely supported by the timber industry. Families associated with the town's history include the McCulloughs, Moselys, Orrs, Allens, Fifes, O'Neals, Lollars, Bushs, Bottoroffs, Lemays, Joneses, Stokeses, Schewgmans, Arnolds, Gibsons, Slaytons and Clarks.

Minturn, six miles south of Hoxie on the Missouri Pacific Railroad, was once the site of a large stave factory. It was the home and business location of A.W. Shirey, the town's leading merchant and an extensive land owner. Warren McLeod wrote that "Shirey was a queer character and the subject of many stories. He was an Odd Fellow and a Spiritualist. He had no heirs and by his will left much property to those two orders. He was murdered, shot at night in his store from ambush. No one was convicted of the crime, though one man suspected of it was tried and acquitted. The litigation which followed his death, partially set aside the will and divided the estate according to the interest of the litigants. The highest monument in Lawrence County marks his grave at Minturn."

Strawberry, originally known as Cathey Town, was surveyed and platted as the Town of Lone Hill. Early settlers included the Crooms, Shavers, Milligans, Penns, Kings, Campbells, Callahans, Greens, Willmuths, Normans, Littles, Sneads, Saffells, Hardins, Steeles, and Hubbards. Jesup, located five miles north of Strawberry on Big Creek, had a cotton gin, a two-teacher school, a church, post office, shops, and homes. Early settlers of the Lynn area were the Lusos, Lingos, Raneys, Goodwins, Ramseys, Prices, Steadmans, Fortenberrys, Adams, Williams, Starrs, Morgans, and Penns.

Soon after the Civil War, a flour mill and wool factory were built at Powhatan. There, farmers could have their wheat made into flour. The wool factory manufactured all kinds of woolens for the family clothing. Many farmers kept sheep, and they could exchange their wool for cloth or sell it.

In 1870, the Western district of Lawrence County had two towns: Smithville and Powhatan. In the Eastern district there were neighborhoods of Old Walnut Ridge, Cross Roads, Lauratown, Clover Bend, and Stranger's Home. Before the railroads came, all freight in and out was handled by steamboats on Black River. Powhatan was the chief shipping point for a large territory. The steamboats also carried passengers. "If anyone was going to Memphis, St. Louis, or New Orleans, he took a steamboat, probably at Powhatan, down Black River and White River and up or down the Mississippi to his destination."

The completion of the Iron Mountain Railroad in 1873 and of the Kansas City, Fort Scott and Memphis Railroad in 1883, induced rapid changes in the county. With railroad transportation, timber became an important business. Col. W.M. Ponder operated a mill not far from Old Walnut Ridge. Minturn, Sedgwick, Black Rock and Portia became "boom" towns. When the timber was gone, the land was cleared for farming.

By the 1880s, horses and factory-made wagons had replaced the old ox-wagon and team. Farmers could also purchase "better farming implements, such as double shovels, cultivators, and steel and chilled breaking plows." The homes were being furnished with factory-made furniture.

In the autumn of 1881, Alice French, Jane Crawford, and her brother Ernest arrived in Minturn, Arkansas, on the Missouri Pacific line, six miles from Clover Bend, where they were met by plantation manager, Col. F.W. Tucker. Jane's father was a shareholder in the five-thousand-acre plantation. Alice French was a rich man's daughter who wrote under the pen name of "Octave Thanet." By 1900, she was one of the five most financially successful authors in the nation.

The Clover Bend plantation and its history absorbed the northern visitors. French pioneers had settled the land when it was part of the Louisiana territory. Spaniards had come later, and part of the plantation was adjacent to what was known as the "Spanish Grant." The first planter had brought slaves and built a small mill and store, and Clover Bend had remained one of a dwindling number of feudal empires. It was eleven miles from the county seat and six miles from the railroad, through what Alice French called the "worst swamp in Arkansas."

Clover Bend was managed by Col. Tucker, a lawyer, marriage counselor, judge, doctor, policeman, and expert in all things except two- he declined to write love letters for the illiterate and he refused to pull teeth." The sharecroppers, black and white, operated under a system of economic bondage wherein plantation land

was rented to tenants who were charged one-fourth of the cotton and one-third of the corn.

Alice French and Jane Crawford stayed in Clover Bend for six weeks, and they decided to make one of the larger cottages into a permanent home where they could return each winter. French wrote in the "Atlantic," "We sleep under two blankets, like the dwellers in St. Augustine, Nice, Algiers, and I dare say all the citizens of the equator that respect themselves." Michael Dougan in his book, *By the Cypress Swamp*, says that Alice French's physical stature "was as imposing as her literary stature. She was six feet tall, weighing 240 pounds. . ." A native of Iowa, she lived at Clover Bend plantation from 1883 to 1909. An article in "The Nation" stated, "There is but one Arkansas and Octave Thanet is its prophet." She was personal friends with Andrew Carnegie, Marshall Field, scores of writers; President Theodore Roosevelt admired her work, calling her a "trump in every way." Thanford, French's Clover Bend house, burned in early August, 1986.

Before and after Octave Thanet, Lawrence County had a literary life. The county has had a newspaper since 1857. The first newspaper was published by Dr. ZP. McAlexander. The paper lasted only a few months until McAlexander joined the Confederate Army. The erstwhile editor was killed in the war. In 1858, Dr. J.W. Townsend started a publication, "The Plaindealer," at Smithville. Ten years later, Dr. Townsend started another paper, The Sketchbook., a Baptist quarterly, which he changed to a weekly in 1877. The weekly paper dealt with religious and civic matters.

A paper called "The Times" was published at Powhatan in the 1870s by J. P. Shotwell. "The Times" was later acquired by George Thornburg who moved the newspaper to Walnut Ridge and published it as "The Telephone." In the 1880s, Thornburg sold the newspaper to G.W. Anderson who moved it to Black Rock at about the same time he moved to Walnut Ridge. In 1890 J.C. Riley came from Kansas to Black Rock and bought "The Blade" from S.J. Howe. Riley sold out in 1919 to F.C. Kirkpatrick. "The Blade" began to decline in popularity, being overshadowed by "The Times Dispatch" which D.A. Lindsey had brought from Pocahontas to Walnut Ridge. James L. Bland acquired "The Times Dispatch" 1910. From 1886 to 1888, the "Portia Free" was published. Imboden has had a newspaper since the 1890s. The first newspaper was titled "Spring River News." "The Imboden Gazette" was established in 1903. "The Imboden Journal" was begun in 1915. Hoxie in 1912 had the "Hoxie Enterprise" and in 1918, Mrs. Gertrude Webb started the "Hoxie Tribune" which ran until 1926 when the railroad shops were closed. Lawrence County has been served by other newspapers.

In 1900, according to Warren McLeod, "The ox-wagon and team were still in common use. Carriages had not come into general use. The family clothing was mostly home-cut and hand-sewed from homespun cloth. Cooking stoves, sewing machines, coal oil lamps, cross-cut saws, factory-made plows, and mowing machines were yet only occasionally to be found. Ice, matches, screen doors and windows, pipe wells, baker's bread, canned goods, excepting oysters and sardines, had not come into use here."

During the first two decades of the twentieth century in Arkansas, Jeff Davis, George Donaghey, and Dr. Charles Brough provided strong leadership as Governor. Although Jeff Davis called himself a "commoner," he was a well-born attorney who used his "demagoguery to fan the flames of prejudice and distrust." During Governor Donaghey's tenure, Arkansas completed the new state capitol building in 1915. Donaghey helped to improve the public schools and the State Board of Education, establishing several agricultural schools and a teacher training program. Donaghey also called attention to Arkansas's notorious convict-lease system but failed to convince legislators to end the practice. Dr. Charles Brough, who moved to Arkansas in 1903, had earned a Ph.D. at Johns Hopkins University in Baltimore. An outstanding educator, orator, and a Christian gentleman, Dr. Brough served Arkansas from 1917 to 1921. Prior to his becoming governor, Dr. Brough taught at the University of Arkansas.

By 1901, Little Rock had a population approaching 50,000, sixty-two miles of improved streets, 1500 business houses, twenty-seven newspapers and periodicals, twelve banks, railroads running in seven different directions, and thriving river transportation. The years of the first World War were dramatic ones for the state and its citizens. Young Arkansans were urged by the Arkansas State Council of Defense on May 22, 1917, and by Governor Donaghey, to register for the military service. The governor also called on Arkansans to buy war bonds. The war years helped move Arkansans into the larger national economic and cultural context.

Arkansas witnessed significant economic growth during the early 1920s. In 1922, the value of Arkansas's mineral products was estimated at $60 million, while the value of all crops and livestock produce was $300 million during that same year. With economic growth and development, many concerned citizens sensed the need to bolster the state's reputation. To accomplish this, the Arkansas Advancement Association took up the challenge and launched a crusade to tell the world about "Ar-kan-saw." The "Bear State" image was abolished; Arkansas became the "The Wonder State." But in October 1929, the American economic bubble burst as the stock market crashed, ushering in a decade of hard times.

In the 1920s and 1930s, cotton was still "king" in Arkansas. Eighty percent of the state's 1, 854,482 people lived in rural areas. Cotton prices plummeted, and with prices low, farmers could not meet their mortgages. Even prior to the Depression, the state's farmers had taken a financial drubbing at the hands of Mother Nature. In 1927, the rainswollen Mississippi overflowed its banks into the Arkansas River, destroying thousands of acres of farmland and drowning countless livestock. Parts of seven states were under water. Nearly 800,000 people were driven from their homes or rescued from housetops, trees, levees, and railway embankments. During the summer of 1930, a catastrophic drought parched land, crops, and men.

In 1933, Governor Marion Futrell, despairing of incurring further state debt, cut back the operating cost of running the state with an austerity program that included a reduction in state services, employees, and salaries. On the national level, Arkansans overwhelmly voted Democratic in 1932, electing Franklin Delano Roosevelt as the thirty-second president.

Immediately, President Franklin D. Roosevelt gave a helping hand to farmers by encouraging them to plow under their already planted crop lands. Crops were destroyed, cattle were slaughtered — and terrible though this logic was, it worked! FDR's New Deal brought WPA projects: gravel roads, canning factories, mattress making, school construction, CCC camps and REA — Rural Electrification Act. Lawrence County homes and lives were radically changed.

On Sunday, December 7, 1941, life seemed tranquil in Lawrence County. But "half a world away the skies had erupted in death and destruction over the U.S. naval base in Pearl Harbor in the Pacific." World War II brought many changes to the county. Within six months of the war's beginning, farmland and timberland north of Walnut Ridge was transformed by the construction of a massive air base which served as home to thousands of servicemen. No event in the twentieth century has made so great an impact on Lawrence County. A Walnut Ridge Army Flying School Museum Committee was formed and efforts are under way to celebrate Lawrence County's contributions during World War II. In January 1947, Southern Baptist College, following a disastrous fire, moved from Pocahontas to the former Air Base facility.

In 1951, radio station KRLW went on the air, opening Lawrence County to a wider world. The station was begun by three Southern Baptist College professors: Rudolph, Lincoln, and Williams.

The 1950's brought national attention with the integration of the Hoxie Public Schools. After the U.S. Supreme Court decision that abolished "separate but equal, public schools on May 17, 1954, the Hoxie Public School integrated voluntarily. The July 25, 1955, edition of Life Magazine stated, "Hoxie, population 1,855, which starts the school term in midsummer to allow farm children cotton-picking time off during the autumn, has taken a bold step to end segregated schools of Negro and white children while other southern communities were busy looking for loopholes in the antisegregation mandate handed down by the Supreme Court. . ." On July 11, 1955, twenty-one blacks enrolled.

Racial problems flared up at Hoxie. In a New York Times Magazine article on September 25, 1955, Cabell Phillips wrote, "This tense, unhappy little cotton town is locked in a make-or-break battle over school integration. . ." Local citizens, outraged by this affront to "white supremacy" have forced the schools to shut. "Now there is a temporary stand off while lawyers for both sides maneuver for a possible court test."

Phillips wrote, "Of the county's 21,000 inhabitants, less than 2 percent of which are Negroes, 18,000 live on farms or in rural villages. Their principal crops are cotton, rice, and soy beans and their median family income (according to the 1950 census) is $1,279 compared with the national figure of $3,073." Phillips ex-

plained that the Hoxie School District was $9,900 in debt and faced "the prospect of going even deeper into the red during the coming year. By integrating, it could save the cost of operating the one Negro school and the salary of its teacher and it could save the tuition and transportation costs of the eight students it would have to send to Jonesboro." Phillips also wrote that "one father is reputed to have offered $100.00 to anyone who would go into the building and beat up Superintendent K.E. Vance, who stands six feet three and weighs 245 pounds. There were no takers."

Hoxie's five member school board—L.R. Howell, L.L. Cochran, Howard Vance, Guy Floyd, and Leo Robert— concluded that integration was "morally right in the sight of God." These five school board members were not self-sacrificing idealists, but ordinary citizens performing their task in the manner dictated by the Supreme Court and their conscience.

Cabell Phillips wrote that locally the "mutterings grew louder around City Hall and the persons of Mayor Mitchell Davis and farmer Herbert Brewer, two local and single-minded foes of integration." Following mass meetings of several hundred residents and a petition with its 1,063 signatures, calling for the school board's resignation, the school board voted to close summer school and reopen on October 24.

The Hoxie school board did not resign. However, in January 1956, Supertindent Vance resigned. "Though the Brewer-led segregation forces captured two of the five seats on the school board in March 1956, they never gained control of the board." In October 1957, Hoxie had twenty-two black students and about 900 white students in grades one to twelve. By February 1958, when two black families with eleven children moved away, only eleven Negroes were left.

However, these problems were minor in comparison to the racial riots in Little Rock on September 3, 1957, when Governor Orval E. Faubus refused to protect the nine AfricanAmerican students who had integrated Little Rock Central High School. President Dwight D. Eisenhower called out the federal troops to protect the African-American students, "bringing instant fame for Faubus and lasting notoriety for Little Rock."

Faubus had begun his Arkansas public life as highway department commissioner in the 1940s under Governor Sid McMath. Faubus was given little chance in his quest for the Democratic nomination for governor in 1954 because his main opponent was incumbent Governor Francis Cherry who had defeated McMath in 1952. However, Jonesboro native Cherry, a poor politician, had alienated some of his supporters.

Faubus had attempted to make use of the race issue which was coming to a head nationally in 1954, the year of the Brown v. Topeka Board ofEducation decision.

Governor Faubus was enormously popular inside Arkansas. Roy Reed in his biography Faubus: The Life and Times of an American Prodigal (University of Arkansas Press, 1997) wrote, "Son of a poor hill farmer with egalitarian and socialist ideals, Faubus was the last governor of the state who could claim a log-cabin

childhood. He used that Populist, "country-boy" image in his campaigns and netted six terms as governor, from 1955 to 1967. In contrast to his stance against desegregation, he often followed moderate lines."

In 1960, Faubus had four opponents, including Lawrence County's Dr. H.E. Williams, President of Southern Baptist College. Faubus called him "Preacher Williams." Faubus's campaign manager was Walnut Ridge's Jim Bland, Sr., owner of the Times Dispatch. Dr. Williams called Faubus a "dictator, tyrant, Caesar Faubus, the Nero of Arkansas, and Benedict Arnold," noting that in three terms, Faubus had appointed a majority of the members of the 124 boards and commissions, including the most important regulatory bodies in the state, among them those that set rates for electricity, gas, transportation, and water. In the end the voters seemed impressed with the governor's claim of a "Proven Program of Progress." Faubus was nominated for a fourth term with almost 59 percent of the vote.

During the 1960s, Lake Charles State Park opened south of Powhatan, largely through the aggressive leadership of Charles Snapp who had served on the Arkansas Game and Fish Commission from 1950-57. Snapp was also responsible for the establishment of Shirey Bay and Rainey Brake. These three "water projects" were part of the Flat Creek Watershed Commission. During this decade county voters, under the leadership of County Judge Brooks Penn, approved building Lawrence Memorial Hospital and Nursing Home; county voters approved moving the county seat from Powhatan to Walnut Ridge. The 1888 Powhatan Courthouse was restored, largely through efforts of the Lawrence County Development Council and the influence of Arkansas Governor Winthrop Rockefeller.

During the 1960s, Arkansas voters became more independent minded, voting for Independent candidate George Wallace for president, Republican Winthrop Rockefeller for governor — the state's first Republican governor since Reconstruction—while electing all Democrats at the at the county and city levels. State voters re-elected "liberal" Democrat William Fulbright as U.S. Senator, the leading dissenter against the war in Viet Nam!

After World War II, life in the county eventually "caught up" with progress elsewhere: paved roads, concrete bridges, indoor plumbing, three-bedroom brick houses, wall-to-wall carpeting, telephones, refrigerators, stoves, central heat and air conditioning, automatic washers and dryers; and in recent years, digital coffee makers, microwaves, cable television, dishwashers, home and business computers, cell phones with "caller I.D.," and ice makers.

With progress, Arkansans have been challenged, especially during Governor Bill Clinton's tenure, to increase our sales taxes to improve our roads, universities, medical school, and our libraries. Lawrence County approved a 1 percent increase in the county sales tax to support Lawrence Memorial Hospital. In 2001, we pay 5.125 per cent state tax, 1 1/2percent county tax; and most cities in the county, including Walnut Ridge, have a 1 percent city sales tax; which, in effect, means we pay over 7 percent for most purchases.

Perhaps the most memorable event of the 1990s was the election of William Jefferson Clinton as President of the United States in November 1991. Arkansans basked in state pride when President-elect Clinton celebrated on national television outside the Old State House in Little Rock with the flags flying and the Philander Smith choir singing in the background.

As we begin the twenty first century, technology has changed the way farmers cultivate their land with cotton pickers, larger tractors, combines with air conditioned cabs, and grain storage bins. Chain saws have replaced the "cross cut saw" and weed eaters have replaced clippers. Fewer families make their living farming, and farms have become much larger. Farmers must be knowledgeable about grain futures, government programs, crop rotation, and marketing. Crop dusting has become big business, and fertilizers and pesticides are unquestioned. Many farmers are "precision leveling" and irrigation is commonplace—a necessity for rice production! At present, we have no cotton gins.

Riding lawn mowers or self propelled mowers and lawn sprinkling systems are evident on farms and in towns. Jacuzzis, hot tubs, and home swimming pools are becoming commonplace. Two and three cars per family are common since several members of the family work in different places. Large numbers of high school students have part-time jobs after school and on the weekend.

Lawrence County follows national trends of larger chains and corporations replacing locally owned businesses. One of our largest county employers, SB Power Tool— originally Skil — then Emerson — came to the county in 1973. In the mid 1980s, the company employed over 1100 individuals. Currently owned by Robert Bosch Corporation, the company employees over 700 people in 1999.

However, the county has exceptions. Jack Allison's Poplar Freeze is still thriving in Walnut Ridge. Alex Lathan has a new grocery store and Angie's Restaurant in Portia. Larry McLeod has a new grocery store in Imboden. The county two's newspapers, The "Times Dispatch" and The "Ozark Journal" are still locally owned. KRLW was sold to a Little Rock firm but is currently owned by the Coker and House families. Walnut Ridge currently has five "convenience gas and sundry" stations and scores of used car dealers. Flea markets and yard sales abound. Mayor J.R. Rogers has restored several downtown buildings in Walnut Ridge.

In 2001, we have two new car dealerships in the county: both owned by the Cavenaugh family. In the last twenty-five years, Walnut Ridge has seen the arrival of Wal Mart, McDonalds, Kentucky Fried Chicken, Pizza Hut, Pizza Inn, Big Star, and Harps. Regions Bank, a national chain, has purchased the Arkansas Bank which had been owned by Bill and Sloan Rainwater. We now have six public schools — Sloan Hendrix, River Valley, Lynn, and Black Rock — in the western district and Walnut Ridge and Hoxie in the eastern district. During the 1940s, Lawrence County had over forty schools.

Other national trends include the "vacant" downtown stores. In Walnut Ridge, we have one clothing store on Main Street. We have become accustomed to driving on our paved roads to shop in large malls, or we shop by catalogs, "outlet malls," or at Wal-Mart. In 2001, Lawrence County has no movie theater, bowling alley, or skating rink. However, in Jonesboro some movie theaters have 15 or more screens. During the 1990s Lawrence Countians have witnessed the closing of our Frolic Shoe Factory and our shirt and golf-bag factory. "Made in America" is no longer an assumption!

Like Americans everywhere, we have become a "throw away" society. We now dispose of our ball point pens, our razor blades, our cigarette lighters, hypodermic needles and tongue depressors. Our babies wear Pampers, and we eat on paper plates and use paper napkins. We wear "quartz" watches- which we discard- and we often replace an item rather than have it repaired. Quilts have largely been replaced with electric blankets; basket making and molasses productions are confined to the "museums." Sadly, we are losing our "waste not, want not" values.

Yet, in the last twenty years, several restoration projects have been completed including the Portia School, Clover Bend Schools, and Walnut Ridge Depot. Major restoration projects in Powhatan include the Imboden-Ficklin house, the county jail, the telephone exchange, the Methodist church, and a $533, 000.00 grant was awarede and restoration has begun on the Powhatan Male and Female Academy by the Arkansas State Parks. These Powhatan projects have been promoted and sustained largely through the efforts of the Lawrence County Historical Society.

Another bright spot for Lawrence County occurred in 1985 when Williams Baptist College moved from junior college to senior college status. The College was renamed for its founder, Dr. H.E. Williams, in 1990. WBC has moved forward with record enrollments, major building projects, and million-dollar gifts. Williams College offers more than twenty majors.

Other recent major projects include the new building for the Lawrence County Library. This effort was led by the Library Board and James Bland, Jr. at the Times Dispatch. Editor Bland was also the honorary Chairman for the Walnut Ridge Depot Restoration Committee. Citizens pledged thousands of dollars for these two worthy projects.

Lawrence County has just completed our first four-lane highway when U.S. 67 between Walnut Ridge and Pocahontas opened in late 1998. The Hoxie bypass on Highway 63 was also completed in 1998. Recently, the Highway 67 bypass around Walnut Ridge was completed.

Two very active organizations emerged in the 1990s: the Lawrence County 2000 Committee which works through the Walnut Ridge Area Chamber of Commerce and is seeking to bring industry to the county; and the Ralph Joseph Leadership group which is training young leaders for the twenty-first century.

With the publication of this Family History book, the Lawrence County Historical Society wishes to thank the hundreds of individuals who have contributed. Lloyd Clark, our President; and Sue Whitmire, our secretary, deserve special appreciation for the many hours they have spent on this project.

Historical Highlights

By Jay Brent Tipton

TRAIL OF TEARS

The Cherokee Indians were removed from Eastern United States to the Indian Territory (present day Oklahoma) in 1838. This national historic event is most often referred to as the "Trail of Tears". One of the routes of this removal ran through Lawrence County and specifically Smithville. A letter written from Smithville on December 13, 1838 recorded a unique insight into the event. An excerpt from the letter states:

"About 1,200 Indians passed through this place yesterday, many of them appeared very respectable. The whole company appears to be well clothed and comfortably fixed for traveling. I am informed that they are very peaceable, and commit no depredation upon any property in the country through which they pass. They have upwards of one hundred wagons employed in transporting them: their horses are the finest I have ever seen in a collection. The company consumes about 150 bushels of corn per day."

"It is stated that they have the measles and whooping cough among them, and that is an average of four deaths per day. They will pass through Batesville in a few days."

Another letter written by G.W. Morris on December 18, 1838 indicates that they arrived in Batesville on December 1, on their way to their new home in the "Far West." Mr. Morris stated that they went into the town at Batesville to get their carriages repaired and horses shod. He also stated that the group began the trail in October 1838, leaving Gunter's Landing on the Tennessee River about 35 miles from Huntsville, Alabama. "...since which time owing to their exposure to the inclemency of the weather, and many of them destitute of shoes and other necessary articles of clothing, about 50 of them have died..."

Mr. Morris's letter would indicate that the Indians moved swiftly through Smithville and Western Lawrence County and were not as prepared as the writer in Smithville observed.

LAWRENCE COUNTY AND THE MEXICAN WAR

During the Mexican War, the regular army troops were withdrawn from the forts on the western border of Arkansas and the Indian Territory. The result was a need for soldiers to protect and defend this area from Indians. Lawrence County men answered a call from the Governor of Arkansas for volunteers to serve in this capacity. Company C, Arkansas Battalion of Infantry and Mounted Rifles was recruited and organized at Smithville (the county seat of Lawrence County

at that time) on June 18, 1846. According to Faye Hempstead (*A Pictorial History of Arkansas from Earliest Times to the Year 1890*), the company had four officers and 69 enlisted that were mustered into service.

The Arkansas Gazette on June 25, 1846, reported that a company of volunteers (mounted gunmen) from Lawrence County led by Captain J.S. Ficklin arrived at Little Rock and took the road for Fort Smith where they are destined for service on the Arkansas Frontier. On June 26, 1846 the Arkansas Gazette reported that a company of volunteers (mounted gunmen) of Conway County reported to the Governor, but could not be accepted because the quota of Arkansas was already filled. This was only one day after the Lawrence County unit was accepted for service. The Lawrence County troops (Company C) Arkansas Battalion, Infantry and Mounted Rifles were officially mustered into U.S. service at Fort Smith on July 6, 1846, and sent to Fort Gibson in the Indian Territory (present day Oklahoma). Several soldiers died while in service at Fort Gibson. The commander of Company C, Captain John S. Ficklin, died on or about December 18, 1846. After his death, 1st Lieutenant A.H. Imboden assumed command of the company and was elected to Captain on January 12, 1847. Company C, along with the other companies of the Battalion was mustered out of service on April 20, 1847 at Fort Gibson. Even though they did not face the Mexican Army, these men served Lawrence County, Arkansas and ultimately the nation by volunteering and remaining at their post. Some of these men made the ultimate sacrifice of their lives and should never be forgotten.

The photograph is reported to be a group of Lawrence County men gathered at New Hope Church in preparation to go to war. Given the

fact that the first church building was built in 1852-53 and that the flag is clearly a United States flag, this is believed to be the Mounted Infantry Company that was involved in the Mexican War in 1846.

LAWRENCE COUNTY AND THE CIVIL WAR

Lawrence County was deeply impacted by America's Civil War. Changes which occurred as a result of the outcome of the war include county seat location, county boundaries, county politics and population shifts within the county. Lawrence County residents were divided, as was the rest of the country. Citizens loyal to the Union were sometimes forced into Confederate service, some fled from the area after being threatened with hanging. Some volunteered to serve in the Federal Army, primarily the 4th Arkansas Mounted Infantry, commanded by Col. Elisha Baxter and the 1st Battalion Six Month's Volunteer Infantry. Most of the county citizenry were loyal to the confederacy and men of military age volunteered for confederate service. More than seventeen companies were organized in Lawrence County. Most of the companies were volunteer units, however, later in the war, several companies were organized by rounding up parolees and other able bodied men into forced service. Company E. of the 1st Arkansas Mounted Rifles, nicknamed "Lawrence County Rifles" was the first unit organized for Confederate Service in Lawrence County. The unit was commanded by Dr. Z. P. McAlexander, a doctor from Smithville. He and many of his command were killed or wounded at the Battle of Wilson's Creek (Oak Hill) near Springfield,

Lawrence County volunteers assembled near Smithville.

Missouri on August 10, 1861. Most Lawrence County companies served in the Trans Mississippi Department, serving mainly in Missouri, Arkansas and Louisiana. Several companies served east of the Mississippi River and fought with distinction in some of the toughest and bloodiest battles of the war, including Shiloh, Chickamauga, Atlanta, and Nashville. According to the Official Record of the War of the Rebellion of the Union and Confederate Armies, there were a few skirmishes in Lawrence County. In June of 1862, a lively skirmish took place on the McKinney farm near Smithville. According to Major S.H. Seley, 5th Illinois Cavalry, the Confederate commander, a Captain Jones and seven of his men were captured. Another report indicates this skirmish occurred in the rain. Skirmishes were also reported on the Spring River and near Powhatan.

During the war, marauders and foragers, referred to most often as Jayhawkers, terrorized the county. Local Homeguards were organized in each township to provide and protect families of soldiers. Former soldiers incapacitated by injuries from the war, boys too young for service and men too old for service were instrumental in the protection of the citizenry.

RAILROADS

The completion of the Iron Mountain Railroad (later the Missouri Pacific) in 1873 induced many changes in Lawrence County. The Kansas City, Fort Scott and Memphis Railroad (Burlington Northern) was completed in 1883. During this period, the economic and political influences shifted from Western to Eastern Lawrence County secondary in part to the railroads.

The railroads brought an infusion of money and investors to the region. It helped decrease the cost of goods and made it easier for travel in the state and connected Lawrence County to other states. Hoxie, Walnut Ridge, Black Rock and Imboden flourished due in part to the railroad industry. The advent of the railroad lead to the founding of new communities and the decline of other existing communities who were bypassed. The population began to shift from Western Lawrence County to the Eastern part.

Dr. J.W. Coffman's influence was responsible for a depot being located at Black Rock just one and one-half miles up river from Powhatan. The placement of the depot at Black Rock was considered to be the "death blow" to the survival of Powhatan as a prosperous town.

ARRIVAL OF TELEPHONES IN LAWRENCE COUNTY

In 1887, the first county telephone system was installed when the local phone system was expanded 12 miles east to Walnut Ridge and 12 miles west to Smithville. James P. Griffin promoted the system and was instrumental in its expansion.

In the early 1890's George W. Anderson, who established the first system in Walnut Ridge, acquired the Powhatan-Smithville-Walnut Ridge system and began to expand the system to connect it with other communities in the county and to install local community exchanges. The first

central office was located in a red brick building that still stands today at the Powhatan Courthouse State Park. Laura Wells, daughter of Dr. John R. Wells was the system's first operator. It is reported that Col. Milton D. Baber made the first paid message over the line from Powhatan when he called Miss Vida Steadman in Smithville.

The Lawrence County Telephone System reached peak prosperity in February 1902 when the system was badly damaged by sleet. It was sometime during this period that the telephone exchange/central office was moved from Powhatan to Black Rock.

Around 1906, the Graceland Mining Company built a telephone line from their mine to Dr. D. B. Rudy's drug store in Smithville. About this time, a telephone company was organized by the citizens of Smithville, managed by Mr. Carlton Dent. The Smithville Switchboard was installed in the home of Mrs. M.E. Fisher and the telephones were installed in individual homes of the Smithville area customers. The operator of the system was Mrs. Fisher's daughter, Miss Ada Fisher. About 1911, Mrs. Lula Fisher Barnett, Ada Fisher's older sister, took over operation of the switchboard and moved it to her home about two blocks east.

Mr. George Anderson called the phone system the "Lawrence County Telephone Company." Prior to his acquiring the Powhatan, Smithville, Walnut Ridge Telephone System, Mr. Anderson established the first telephone exchange in Walnut Ridge. He installed a switchboard and North Electric Company equipment was installed on Main Street where Bloom's Department Store later located. Mr. Anderson had sold stock to T. J. Sharum and F. W. Tucker. The three men expanded the system by installing exchanges at Hoxie, Black Rock, Imboden and Portia. Mr. Anderson served as general manager and the line man.

In May 1912, the Southwestern Telephone and Telegraph Company (forerunner of Southwestern Bell Telephone) bought the Walnut Ridge exchange and installed a new and much larger switchboard built by Western Electric Company.

The next major change occurred in 1925 when a common battery switchboard and the required equipment was installed in Walnut Ridge, which brought the telephone service up to the same standards and the same quality found in the largest U. S. cities at that time.

In 1961, a project promoted by the Imboden-Smithville Lion's Club precipitated the installation of a long distance telephone system at a cost of a quarter of a million dollars. This system was inaugurated in September of that year, at Smithville when W.B. Rudy made the first long distance call. This telephone system opened up an area of telephone service for several who had not had access to phone service previously, Some of the communities which service was provided through the new system of the Southwestern States Telephone Company included Calamine, Cave City, Lynn, Imboden, Jesup, Saffell, Smithville and Strawberry. The inauguration was held at Smithville Methodist Church and over 100 people attended.

Today, telephone service in the county is primarily provided by Southwestern Bell in

Walnut Ridge area and GTE provides telephone service to the Smithville, Lynn, Strawberry and Imboden area. Technology had advanced and cordless telephones, cellular phones, Facsimile "Fax" machines and other devices are widely used throughout the county.

MINING

Lawrence County was rich in mineral deposits and ore mining had a major impact on the early development of Western Lawrence County. An early description stated: "There are several deposits of white carbonate of zinc and several deposits of iron ore also. There are several deposits of lead though it has not been found in large quantities..."

In the 1890's, several men from Iowa decided to invest in zinc mining enterprises in Western Lawrence County near Smithville. The first mine was the "New Era Mine." It was located a short distance northeast of Townsend Cemetery near the Foley Spring. The mine ceased operation in 1912. This mine reopened around 1916 when a Georgia mining firm acquired the mine, tested production and resumed mining operations. They changed the name of the mine to "Red Fox".

The Georgia company used the same kind of machinery (Which was made by King & Company) at the "Red Fox" as was used by the "New Era Mine". Apparently, the company moved the same type of King & Company machinery from a mine that ceased operation on land leased from J. A. (Alec) Miller to a site located about one quarter mile south of Townsend Cemetery on Cooper Creek. Several buildings were erected and this mine was referred to as the "King Jack" mine. This name was chosen because "King" was the name of the machinery and the zinc ore was referred to as "Jack".

There were several other mines located in the county, but all of their production was short lived. There was a mining operation located at Jesup, near the Sharp County line. The "Raney Mine" was located southeast of Smithville. The "Graceland Mine Company" was instrumental in keeping the telephone system in operation and had a phone line at the mine. A newspaper related to mining, *The Homecrofter,* was published in Smithville as late as 1911. The demand for zinc began to decline and the mines ceased operation within a few short years.

THE GREAT DEPRESSION

The Great Depression following the Stock Market Crash of 1929 reached the whole nation including Lawrence County. The Depression saw six banks in Lawrence County close their doors. Businesses closed and farms were sold for much less than they were worth. It was a stagnant time in the county. Most people did not have any money and those who did were afraid to spend it. During the early 1930's, agriculture prices dropped significantly which affected most of the county since it was primarily rural. Hogs were selling for $0.01/pound and other livestock prices were comparable. Also, during that time the weather was very dry, which caused crops to fail, drying up in the fields. Some farmers reported that due to the extended nature of the drought, towns such as Osceola were the closest place to buy hay for their livestock. Many families were quite large and had nothing more than "love." In these desperate times, Lawrence Countians helped one another to survive. The population of the county Poor Farm soared with those who were destitute, elderly and young people who were considered to be mentally deficient and unable to work.

It is recorded that there were as many as 19 vacant buildings in Walnut Ridge during this era and there were several fires which destroyed businesses. James L. Bland had purchased *The Times Dispatch* in 1921 in partnership with David Wilkerson and had been successful. The newspaper's profits dropped during this time, then in 1934, the Sharum Theatre, next door, burned. The newspaper was ruined by fire, smoke and water damage. Mr. Bland relocated the newspaper and reopened. The Bland family has retained ownership and operation of this very successful newspaper to the present time.

Clover Bend Plantation dwindled during the economic hard times brought on by the Depression and it was acquired by the Slayden Brothers. In 1937, the Slayden Brothers sold more than 5000 acres of land to the United States Government for the Resettlement Administration. The old plantation was broken up into farmsteads and Octave Thanet's house was converted into the Farmer's Service Administration's office.

In the late 1930's, the New Deal Era brought about positive changes for Lawrence County through the Civilian Conservation Corps and the W.P.A. (Works Progress Administration). New buildings were constructed at many of the area schools. A rock retaining wall was installed around the Powhatan Courthouse to protect it from erosion and highway traffic. Concrete bridges and other progressive projects helped Lawrence County to recuperate from the Depression Era.

LAWRENCE COUNTY POST OFFICES

Name	Est.	Disc.
Alicia	1873	
Annieville	1890	1920
Ash Flat	1856	
Barry		1852
Bessie	1912	1926
Black Rock	1884	
Bradys		
Broom	1909	1915
Buncombe Ridge	1874	1876
Bush	1886	1886
Calamine	1857	1867
Caney Valley		
Canton	1840	1873
Casper		
Calianda	1875	1877
Clements	1899	1911
Clinton		
Clover Bend	1848	1919
Columbia	1829	
Comanche/		
Commanche	1856	1866
Concord	1880	1881
County Line	1833	
Crowly's	1832	
Cuba	1857	1859
Davisville		
Denton	1894	1954
Dosy	1886	1890
Driftwood	1905	1935
Eaganville		
Eaton	1900	1954
Egypt	1888	
Ethel		
Evening Shade	1847	
Evergreen	1885	1886
Faith		
Fourche Toma/Dumas		
Frisbee	1906	1919
Gum Springs	1860	1866
Havana	1876	1877
Hazel Grove	1851	
Hendersonburgh/Henderson		
Hixes Ferry	1832	
Hope		
Houghton	1854	1860
Hoxie	1884	
Imboden	1883	
Jackson	1832	
Jesup	1894	1954
Kimberly		
Laura Town/		
Lauratown	1860	1954
Lindsey		1900
Linwood	1855	1873
Litha	1891	1891
Lynn	1891	
Martins Creek		1870
Minturn	1873	
Mount Silvan	1851	1866
Murta	1878	1905
Myatt	1846	1866
Oasis	1860	1866
Opposition	1870	1904
Osborn's Creek	1858	1859
Parsonville	1888	1893
Pa Paw		
Paw Paw	1858	186(?)
Pearl		
Popular Hall	1878	1886
Portia	1882	
Powhatan	1843	
Progress	1912	1912
Ravenden	1883	
Red Bank	1846	
Reed's Creek	1838	
Rhea	1870	1872
Richwoods	1903	1913
Riply		
Saffel/Saffell	1901	
Scottsville	1872	1873
Sedgwick	1883	
Sidney	1858	1866
Sloan	1905	1921
Smithville		
Spring River		
Stranger's Home/		
Strangers	1858	1908
Strawberry	1854	
Strawberry Point		
Strawberry River	1832	
Stuart	1905	
Sugar Grove	1851	1866
Surprise	1904	1906
Taylor	1887	1891
Uno	1884	
Valley	1911	1912
Walnut Ridge	1870	
Zincville	1900	1902

Submitted by Russell P. Baker

BLACK ROCK PEARLING AND BUTTON - CUTTING INDUSTRY

Pearling and button-cutting go together like ham and eggs, for in reality, there probably would not have been a button-cutting industry in Black Rock, county of Lawrence, had Dr. J.H. Myers not become interested in pearling.

The 1904 Stockard history describes Dr. Myers as a "scientist, naturalist and business man." It goes on to say that Dr. Myers "having read of valuable pearls being found in clams or fresh water mollusks, began investigating the matter in Black River some two miles above the town of Black Rock. He had only opened a few muckets when a ball pearl weighing 14 grains, fine luster, and pinkish color was found. This was sufficient to start the work right."

This same history credits Dr. Myers with finding the first pearl and with being the first promoter of the button industry in Black Rock. Walter E. McLeod in his history book, *The Centennial Memorial History of Lawrence County*, published in 1936, says that Dr. Myers "may be said to have been the father of the pearling industry on the Black and White Rivers."

During the years 1897, 1898, and 1899 many people began "hunting for pearls." The number steadily increased each summer until cold weather and high water shut down this infant industry. Hundreds of these people "grappled" for muckets by hand putting them in sacks, much like one would in picking cotton

Dr. Myers is quoted as saying, "In 1898, the find was much larger, also the number of hunters. I have seen as many as 500 men, women and children of all sizes and colors on one bar, indiscriminately mingled, wading in as far as they could reach bottom, some opening, others gathering shells. The wealthiest bankers, lawyers, merchants, doctors, etc., their wives and children wading in with the poorest (people), all laughing and singing, working day after day the summer through."

My dad, Samp Hill, recalls as a youngster in the early 1900s, his dad would take them digging or grappling for shells just for the pearls after they had laid their crops by. While talking to him about the pearling and button industry he told me about he and mother taking me grappling for shells when I was a small child. I can remember going to the river and being placed in shallow water on a sand bar with my parents close by, but instead of remembering digging shells, I only remember being tumbled over in my very shallow water by the swift current.

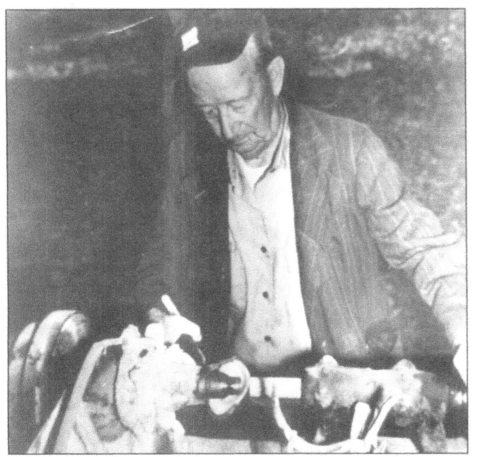
Roy Williams, cutting a button from a mussel shell at the old button factory. Some men would work for weeks and could not master the art of cutting out a button. Photo taken in early 1950s.

By the third year of "pearling" some 150 miles of river was being worked. It was in 1899 that Dr. Myers shipped the first car of shells to Lincoln, Nebraska, for button-making, after learning the shells were valuable for this purpose. Up until this time the shells were thrown away after being opened searching for pearls. "Men from the northern states began pouring in, teaching the people to save the shells and how to boil them (to open them). Some were only shell buyers while hundreds were what they called shellers. It was these men that brought more sophisticated equipment for digging shells and then work could be carried on the year round.

Dr. Myers reported, "as determined by the home banks and express, $1,271,000 was paid out for pearling in seven years." The run down was as follows: paid out for pearls in 1897, $11,000; 1898, $55,000; 1899, $110,000; 1900, $200,000; 1901, $310,000; 1902, $370,000; 1903, $215,000 for pearls and shells.

One of the most intriguing of the pearl stories took place in the spring of 1902. It was then that news reached the streets of Black Rock that a super-pearl had been found on the Julia Dean Bar, located midway between Black Rock and Pocahontas. This bar reached entirely across the river where shellers could wade. The pearl was taken from a large rough shell mussel, known to river people as a mucket, by a man named McCaleb, hence, following the order of the river, it was known as the McCaleb Pearl. Pearls at this time were

bringing a good price and men knowledgeable and those not so knowledgeable became pearl buyers. W.O. Bird, a former druggist and jeweler in Black Rock, was such a buyer. He had an office on Main Street and was one of the more knowledgeable buyers. A dealer by the name of Conner told Mr. Bird about the McCaleb pearl. He, being one of the first dealers to see the pearl, as he was near the bar when it was found. He told Mr. Bird of its size and perfect ball shape. Since Mr. bird wanted the pearl, he and Conner reasoned together and it was decided that Conner would try to make the buy for $1,000 in cash, that is, if he could beat a Memphis buyer to the bar. Mr. Conner had, in his dealings with the river people, made a study of their nature and reactions, particularly in business matters, and believed that with the cash approach, ten $100 bills spread out fan shape before McCaleb, he could get the pearl.

Conner stood in line with waiting buyers. There were five ahead of him including the one in the shack but no sign of the Memphis buyer. From the other buyers, he learned the price was up to $820. The buyer emerged from the shack, he had made a few dollars raise and been refused. The next two buyers in line stepped aside, saying they could do no better. There were only two ahead of Conner now with Holt, a buyer from Newport, waiting after him. The two in front of Conner were worried and ill-at-ease. One at a time they entered and returned to without a word.

As Conner entered the shack a motor boat landed and a stranger came toward the camp. Conner marked him as the buyer from Memphis. Inside the shanty, McCaleb, a bronzed knight of the river, sat by a rough board table. On the table rested a cigar box filled with dirty cotton, in the center lay a handful of clean, white cotton and on this rested the pearl. The box cover was closed as Conner had examined the pearl - this being his third trip to the camp. A revolver lay on the table while two shotguns were leaning against the wall. An old man, a relative of McCaleb, stood by the table. Conner entered, spoke to McCaleb and his male companion, then advanced to the table. In a low tone of voice he talked to the pearler a few minutes; then from his pocket he took 10 crisp $100 bills and laid them fan-shape on the table. McCaleb called the older man, even a woman came to the rim of light and waited. They talked a few minutes, a hushed uncertain silence followed, McCaleb nodded, they raised the box lid, Conner removed the pearl, placing it in a chamois skin bag and put it in the pocket where the thousand dollars had been. He made one request that McCaleb close the box and not let it be known the pearl had been sold until he was well on his return trip down the river.

Mr. Bird took the pearl to St. Louis for appraisal then on to New York where he was advised to join a group of dealers in precious stones on a trip to Paris, France, where the pearl was sold and the people at home were told that it became a part of the royal collection.

What the McCaleb pearl sold for was never known by the people of Black Rock. Mr. Bird returned home, sold all his property and holdings and moved back to his former home in Iowa. He made several trips back to Black Rock to greet old friends and stand in reverie on the bank of the river that mothered the beautiful pearl.

Other valuable pearls have been found in Black Rock but none of the stories so interesting and spell-binding as the one just retold. It is a known fact that a few of the finer pearls from Black River became a part of the crown jewels of royalty in Asia and Europe.

BUTTON CUTTING BECOMES A BLACK ROCK INDUSTRY

This has all been an introduction to the all so important industry to those in and around Black Rock for so many years, button-cutting.

As a result of the interest in pearling and learning the value of shells and for what they were used for a button company was formed in February 1900 by Dr. Myers, Dr. N.R. Townsend, and H.W. Townsend. A small plant was built at Black Rock. The little factory began turning out blanks (rough buttons) cut from shells the following May. This was the first button factory in the south according to Dr. Myers. However, after operating only for a short time, the cutters went on strike and the factory closed. The factory was bought and enlarged by a Davenport, Ohio, pearl button company.

A New York based button company, Chalmers, carried on the button-cutting operation on the river bank at Black Rock for many years in two different locations. First close to the river, which flooded the factory sometimes, and later, somewhat farther from the river's edge and on higher ground. It was here that the tanks and crumbling foundation remained until a few years ago.

The factory employed 64 cutters, five-day men (they graded shells and filled the tanks), one straw-boss, one office girl, and one supervisor when in peak production Their week often consisted of only three days work but there were times when they worked five days a week. There were often many shut downs during a year's time. An example of the shut downs and restarting of the factory is the year 1933. The factory opened January 9, shut down Feburary 11, started March 8, shut down March 30, started May 17 (worked four days a week, nine hours a day), June 12 shop started running 50 hours a week, August 7 shop started eight hours a day. five days a week, shut down September 1, started September 11 (two days), shut down September 20 and didn't start again until January 2, 1934. This tells us the button-cutters life was very insecure at times.

Many of the shells for button-cutting came from the Black and White Rivers in Arkansas but in later years most of them where shipped in by railroad cars from the Tennessee and Wabash Rivers.

The names of the shells used for button-cutting are fascinating.

The shape and texture of the shell helped determine its name. Some of the shells used at the Black Rock factory were Muckets, niggerheads (made most expensive buttons), sandshells (used more for pearl handled knives, etc.), grandma, washboard, cucumber, three ridges, pigtoe (only one found in Black River came from the Tennessee), Maple leaf, and the creeper which was thin as paper.

The little better-than-average cutter in 1933, might make as little as $1.56 as much as $21.45 per week, depending on how many days and on which line the cutter worked. The wage a cutter would make in a year's time with the shut downs, etc. would be about $240.59. The figures are based on a journal my dad kept for the year 1933. He was considered to be just a little above average cutter.

The cutting of buttons is an interesting procedure. After the sheller dug the shells and the shells were boiled out, they were transported to the factory either by rail or sacked and brought by wagon to the local factory. At the factory the shells were loaded into huge storage bins, which could hold 500 tons, waiting their turn to be dumped into one of a dozen 1,000 gallon tanks where they would soak and soften for two weeks in steam heated water.

After softening, the shells were moved by wheelbarrow to a chute leading into the factory grading room, where they were separated according to the size button they would best produce.

Inside the factory workroom, cutters at machines cut buttons in all sizes. The number of the line indicated the size of the button being cut with line 14 being the smallest going up by twos to line 36 which was the largest and about the size of a quarter. The machines had small saws that looked like miniature stovepipes with teeth filed in one end. The shell edge gripped by tongs and pushed against the rotating saw by a wooden peg in a mechanically operated pusher. The result was a pellet-like portion of the shell that could be polished and drilled to become a button. Only one button could be cut at a time. The pellets, already called buttons, fell into buckets below the machine. Once a week, usually on Saturday morning, each cutter would take his weeks work to the grading room. The inspector would then take a quarter of a pound of the pellets and examine them, counting the good ones and discarding those not correct in size. He would determine the percent of acceptable buttons upon the examination of this quarter of a pound. If the cutter's "test" was 308, he had 45 pounds, and he was cutting line 18 regulars, his take home pay would be about $5.43. The cutter was paid 5 to 16-1/2 cents for each 168 (gross) acceptable buttons he cut. The buttons were washed, put in a power shaker to discard all but the correct size buttons, then they were put into a drum with ridges on its interior surfaces where the buttons were polished. After polishing, the smooth buttons were sent to a factory in Amsterdam, New York, which drilled the eyes and placed the buttons on cards.

The Button Factory was a major industry for Black Rock from 1900 to the 1950s. It reached its peak in the mid-40's and finally had to bow out gracefully and give way to the mass produced synthetic button, which could be turned out more quickly and cheaply.

Some of the employees at the old Button Factory included Cecil Meeks, Roy Williams, Sonny Kilgore, Bonnie Williams, Ora Collins, Wade Foster, Frans Peace, Art Kidder, Jim Sutton, Bill Harmon, Ivy Marshbanks, Early Anderson, Albert Barton, Bub Marshbanks, Nate Bunch, Henry Woodson, Esmon Beeler, and Percy Woodson.

There are all kinds of nostalgic memories connected with button-cutting by those of us reared at Black Rock where our fathers made their living at this tedious work. Some of these memories are happy ones; others, when the factory shut down, are not so pleasant to recall, but the former far outweigh the latter.

If you are interested in viewing a button cutter's tools, there are some on display at the Powhatan Courthouse Historical Library and Museum.

This article could not have been written without the invaluable help of Garnet Vance who furnished all the newspaper clippings from which I gleaned my data. Also I want to thank my dad for letting me use his daily journal recording all his years of cutting buttons and for sharing his memories which brought life to this article.

Reprint Lawrence County Historical Quarterly; Fall 1978 "Black Rock Pearling and Button-Cutting Industry" Credit Glynda Stewart

Employees of Black Rock Button Company, Black Rock, Arkansas, around 1900. Photo courtesy of Tom Moore.

A Brief History of the
Walnut Ridge Army Airfield

By Dr. H. E. Williams

In late May, or early June of 1942, while driving to Walnut Ridge from Pocahontas, I saw the first indication that the area was going to have an Army Airfield. It would be engaged in training pilots for the United States effort in World War II. A crew of surveyors was taking measurements along Coon Creek drainage canal, about two miles north of the city of Walnut Ridge, on the east side of Federal Highway 67.

Soon the news media reported the fact that the airport would be built at this location to give basic pilot training in the Vultee B-13 plane, the second stage in training of pilots who would then transfer to advanced training, leading to the final stage for flying bombers, fighters or transport aircraft.

It was reported to the public that approximately 1,800 acres would be taken for the airport in the Mount Zion community, three-fourths of a mile east of Highway 67.

At once, work began on clearing the area of homes and other improvements. Home owners were given a short period of time to remove their buildings off the ground. Failure to do so in the time allowed, resulted in the Army Engineers wrecking or burning remaining structures.

Owners were paid an average of $110.00 per acre for their land, with the promise that they would have the privilege of buying it back from the government at that price after the end of the war.

In a few weeks, the general contractor, said to be from Nashville, Tennessee, arrived and began construction of streets, runways and buildings to house an operation of over 4,000 military and civilian personnel.

Three 5,000 foot runways, in the shape of an "A", were constructed with an average thickness of nine inches. An apron area for parking aircraft on many acres, adjoined the runways. Concrete for the runways and apron was said to have been adequate to pave a standard highway for over fifty-two miles. Streets were constructed of gravel and surfaced with asphalt.

Hundreds of construction people swarmed upon the region, coming from all over the nation. Housing facilities were soon filled and prices for lodging went sky high. Houses which had been renting for $15.00 to $35.00 per month were being rented for $100.00 to $150.00 per month. Even single bedrooms were being rented in private homes for $80.00 per month and up.

Streets and alleys were laid out for the facility and gravel haulers began bringing gravel from the Crowleys Ridge gravel beds. The runways were laid out in the shape of a capital "A". Concrete construction began to lay the concrete for the paving of the runways and aprons.

A water and sewer system was constructed large enough for a community of 5,000 people.

Buildings were arranged for different military personnel, according to their groupings such as officers and cadet pilots. Each group had their own dining room, barracks, etc. Other military personnel such as military police, WACs, etc. had their areas in different parts of the facility.

By 1943, apartments were constructed of tile to be used for officers' families on the north side of Fulbright Avenue, and on the southside for non-commissioned military personnel.

Four huge hangars were constructed on the concrete apron, connected with the runways. Link trainer buildings were built near the flight line for use by pilot trainees in learning to fly "under the hood," on instruments, when visual flight conditions were impossible.

A hospital was constructed to take care of a community of 3,000 people or more.

The chapel was constructed near the center of the facility to provide a place for the ministry of the chaplains. Captain Harry Smith of Georgia, was the first chaplain.

Numerous other buildings for specific uses were also constructed. Most of them were intended for temporary use only. The walls were covered outside with tar paper or asbestos board, which indicated they were to be used for a few years at best.

One of the buildings, a home for the commanding officer, resulted in a special investigation by the War Department. It was being constructed on the northwest corner of the facility, of cut stone; under the claim that it was to be a guest house for military dignitaries who might visit the airport. Walter Winchel, nationally recognized radio newsman, found out about the building be-

ing constructed as a permanent structure on a temporary airport, and made it a special item in his weekly Sunday night network news report. The Truman Senate Committee on Government Waste in the Military, began an investigation and the Army Air Force instructed the commandant to stop using appropriated funds in the building, when it was about three-fourths completed.

The building was a large "U" shaped building containing over 4,000 square feet, with steam heating and attic fans for cooling. After funds were cut off, the commandant had to complete the building by "hook and crook." It was rumored that he sent cadet trainees to work on the building rather than permitting them to pay for their violations of military rules by lying in the "brig." Also much of the needed material that went into finishing the building came from the demolition of the Pocahontas Civilian Conservation Corps camp which was located at Five Mile Spring west of Pocahontas on Highway 90.

The total complement of military personnel at the Walnut Ridge Army Airfield was said to average 3,000 individuals. The civilian workers and civil service personnel complement averaged around 2,000.

A railroad spur was built from the Frisco Railway, running from Hoxie to Poplar Bluff, to the airport's southwest corner. The name of the railway stop inside the operation was named Walport.

The first commandant for the military operation was Colonel Guilette, from Louisiana. He was an officer in the Louisiana Air National Guard.

The Army Air Force trained several complements of cadets all of whom went on to take ad-

WRAAF circa 1944

vance training in heavier aircraft. Some took twin engine training while others went into single aircraft to become fighter pilots. Those who took twin engine training became bomber or transport pilots.

The Army Air Force use of the airport ended in 1944 and it was traded to the Marine Corps for a field in New York state and it became the Walnut Ridge Marine Air Facility. The Marines used the field to train one "wing" of fighter pilots. The plane they used was known as the "Gull-Wing Corsair," a fast and heavy fighter plane. That "wing" was shipped out to the Pacific Theater to finish the war against the Japanese during the last months of the war.

At the end of the World War II, in August of 1945, the airport was designated as a salvage depot for surplus aircraft from all over the world. Over 10,000 planes were flown to the field, said to be the largest number of aircraft ever assembled in one place on the face of the-earth. Many of them were "war weary" planes that had seen rough treatment in the war effort. Hundreds of huge bombers, transports, trainers, and many other types of aircraft soon arrived in late 1945 and early 1946. They were parked all over the airport, until they covered the entire 1,800 acres of land. Hundreds of fighter planes were placed on nose end, in order to provide more room for others. The entire complement of B-32 bombers were flown here from the factory to be salvaged. There were only 73 of these planes made and 67 were brought here. It was said that the plane was intended to be the plane to carry the atomic bombs, but it was said to have had a flaw in the design which resulted in it being unused. They were beautiful new planes of great size, even larger than the famous B-29 bomber.

The War Assets Administration took over the job of disposing of the huge inventory of aircraft. About half of them were sold for military and civilian use all over the world. Several friendly nations put them into use for military operations. Thousands were purchased for civilian use, especially the transports. Slick Airways of Texas bought eight Model F Curtis Transport C-46 planes here and began the first civilian freight service by air in the United States.

Mr. Reynolds, inventor of the ball-point pen, bought a B-26 twin-engine bomber here and made a trip around the world in record time in it. His pilot, Odom, flew the same plane around the world solo. Within two weeks after his return from that flight, Odom came here to secure parts for the B-26 and I met him at the hangar where he got what he needed. Bill Odom was killed in the Akron air races.

The aircraft that did not readily fit into the military and civilian needs of the world, were consigned to be melted into large ingots of aluminum and sold to processors to make needed civilian products such as aluminum roofing.

The melting operation was done by Texas Railway Equipment Company, a subsidiary of the world-wide contractor, Brown & Root Company of Houston, Texas. It was reported that they melted over 5,000 aircraft after they removed components from the planes which were merchantable. This operation took approximately two years.

There were several executive aircraft on the field identified with famous military personnel. I recall that the planes used by Admiral Halsey and General McArthur were flown here. The military personnel who flew them in stripped the interiors of things they could use as souvenirs, as soon as the planes were landed, leaving them in a very destitute condition.

During the last of the war a stockade was erected in the southwest area of the complex for German war prisoners. Few local people ever realized they were here. It was reported that only about 300 were kept in the stockade.

In the fall of 1945, the field was declared surplus and the Reconstruction Finance Corporation took it over for protection of the incoming aircraft and preparation for disposal of the facility. By the spring of 1946, the disposal duty fell to the newly formed Surplus Property Administration.

The United States Congress passed a bill which was designed to make such facilities available to the cities nearby to preserve the runways etc., for civil aviation. They gave first priority to the local city, in each case, provided they could submit a proposal that passed the terms of disposal as set forth in the regulations of the War Assets Administration. I reported the provisions to Bob Surridge, mayor of Walnut Ridge. Since the city, had the first priority on acquiring the property, the board of trustees of Southern Baptist College, through me, submitted a request for a waiver in our favor for 122 acres on the west side of the airport, to be used for the operation of the college. The institution already had secured a "right of entry" for 157 apartment units and six other buildings south of the main entrance. The Walnut Ridge City Council granted the request for a waiver in favor of the college in early May of 1946. Soon after this meeting of the City Council, Mayor Surridge resigned and Mr. E. K. Riddick was selected as mayor. I went to him with a form giving the college the waiver and he asked that I take the leadership role in acquiring the major part of the airport for the city, since I would also be involved in securing a deed to the part needed by the college.

I was happy to take this responsibility and prepared every form and letter incidental to interest of the City of Walnut Ridge and Mr. Riddick signed. I made several trips to Washington in interest of the college and the city. The college paid all of the expenses and we never billed the city for anything.

Deeds were issued to both the city and the college in 1947.

The City of Walnut Ridge appointed an Airport Commission, composed of Irvin Spikes, a member of the City Council, Marlin Wilcoxon, a Walnut Ridge business man and aviation enthusiast, and me, Dr. H. E. Williams, president of Southern Baptist College, (Now Williams Baptist College) to care for the airport. The college took the responsibility of business transactions, collecting funds and accounting for them. The college made no charge for this responsibilty, which continued until the middle of 1952.

Since I had performed all of the efforts to secure both the Walnut Ridge Airport, as well as the Pocahontas Auxiliary Airfield, for the two cities I felt that I had rendered the area a significant service. I realized that neither city would likely have ever been able to build such facilities on their own. (Mayor Newt Pratt of Pocahontas, had asked that I take the initiative for Pocahontas as I also was doing to help Walnut Ridge.)

It is my opinion that these two airfields have truly become "swords beaten into plowshares." No other World War II facility in the region has been turned to better civilian use. Both facilities have become industrial parks where thousands are employed. Also both have been made educational centers where two institutions are engaged in major educational activities. They are Williams Baptist College, an outstanding Liberal Arts Senior college and Black River Technical College.

Note: A Walnut Ridge Army Airfield museum has been created and sits across the road from the modern flight terminal. Visit it to know more about local history and see some tremendous artifacts on display.

Walnut Ridge Regional Airport, 1998

World War I Memories

Catherine S. Richey

World War I was a time of hardship for the families of many of the boys who went away to be a part of the military service. My perspective is through memories of my parents, and from letters written both to and by an uncle, Samuel Moody Pace, who died in France after the war was over. From his letters we know that he was called for his physical examination on February 22, 1918. The postcard is signed by JC Riley, member of local board. By March 31, 1918, he was at Camp Pike, AR, and apparently had been there for some time. It seems he was always being moved to a new base before payday came, so was always waiting for his pay and needing "Dad" to send him a dollar or two to get by on. He mentions that they sign the payrole (sic) on the first of the month, then get paid any time between the 5th and 25th of the month.

He was transferred to Anniston, Alabama (Camp McClellan) and apparently from there moved to the coast and thence to France. An updated postcard came to the family saying "The ship on which I sailed has arrived safely overseas." The organization was F Co., 104th Engineers, American Expeditionary Forces: Sam M. Pace. A letter from Newton Pace to his son, which included a check for $5.00 on the Bank of Black Rock was returned on May 23, 1918 from Camp McClellan, AL. Uncle Moody had apparently been shipped to France before it arrived.

Letters from France came censored and only stating he is at a "small town in France, it is a dull place to stay." He advised his younger brother, Ervie Pace, to join the Navy instead of the Army, stating he would have better quarters there. He writes of being at the front, and having to carry everything he had on his back. He lamented the fact that he was unable to get a watch for his father, who wanted one very much.

After the Armistice, the time was spent in drills and waiting to come back to the "good old U.S.A., as France is not as sunny as you may hear." He was counting the days till they would be able to return home, now that the fighting was over. A letter dated March 16, 1919, from the Chaplain of 104 Engineers, J.B. Hill, notified the family of his death from meningitis on March 14, 1919. He had been ill two days.

Records show that more men died from illness than were killed in the fighting of World War I. All were casualties of war. Both my grandparents, and many others besides, were eagerly waiting for the "mail hack" to come through from Powhatan to Lynn to see the Little Rock newspaper which carried a daily list of casualties, both injured and dead. Grandpa Newton Pace lived where the mail carriers met and swapped their mail, so he got his mail soon. Grandpa Filmore Stewart's, whose oldest son, Roy, was also a soldier, rode a mile out to the main road every day to get his paper. Roy returned safely home following the end of the war. They both lived in the Eaton area.

Some families decided to have their soldiers brought home for burial nearby, and others didn't want to, thinking the soldier in the coffin might not be their son. Some cemeteries have memorials placed for young men who died during war and were buried on foreign soil. Moody Pace is buried in Old Lebanon Cemetery. The Garrett family decided not to have their son, Luther's, body returned after he was killed in the war. It was up to the family.

About 1928, Newton Pace, at left, with his remaining sons: Ervie Pace, who served in WWI in the Navy, Murphy Pace and Richman Pace, who both served during WWII. They are standing in front of the flag which covered Samuel Moody Pace's coffin following WWI.

IN MEMORY OF SEBASTIAN A. (CHUBBY) SPADES
Mayor of Black Rock, 1946

The roster of Arkansas National Guard, Company E, First Battalion, headquartered in Black Rock year of 1909. This company formed in the early 1900's was the first one organized in Lawrence County and many of its members saw action in World War I. The company subsequently moved to Walnut Ridge and was known as Company K during World War II. It is now known as Company A.

Lee McKinney, Sgt.	Rotia Fleming	Lee Martin
Dale Myers, Cpl.	John Fleetwood	Ernest Neil
Lewis Bone, Cpl.	Arthur Finley	Max Pettyjohn
Lee Williams, Cpl.	Lester Gibson	Sam Payne
Bert Angle, Cpl.	John Gibson	Clarence Payne
Rodnay Weir, Cpl.	Roy Hudson	Luther Stone
Max Swindle, Cpl.	S.A. Spades, Captain	John Scott
Ed Middleton	J.R. Carper, 1st Lt.	Walter Seamans
Bide Kroll	Roy Townsend, 2nd Lt.	Albert Smith
John Anderson	Vernon Howe, 1st Sgt.	Leonard Swink
Will Archer	James Jones, Q.M. Sgt.	Ben Stringer
Joe Babb	Luther Clark, Sgt.	Albert Smalley
Ira Babb	Frank Grayson, Sgt.	Robt. Smalley
Roger Brady	Will Rogers, Sgt.	Fred Swindle
Abe Bond	Butler Hudson	Adrian Skillern
Van Bennett	Joe Judkins	Robt. Surridge
John Byrd	Ed Kroll	Harry Williams
Osmer Douglas	Will Matthews	Ed Williams
Charles Davis	W.M. McCullah	Hugh Williams
Harry Ellis	Webster Mendenhall	Hubert Woodward

Communities

HISTORY OF BLACK ROCK

The following history was compiled using information from articles by Reta Goff Covey, C.C. Penny, Mrs. Matthews and others.

In 1846 the area which is now the town of Black Rock was a vast wilderness with a dense, cane break along the river. Wolves, panthers, and other wild animals roamed at will. It was in this desolate area that G.W. McGhehey built the first house. This house was located on the hill northwest of where the depot was later located.

Several years later the land was cleared for farming. In 1882 the Fort-Scott-Kansas City Railroad established a route through the area on land given by Dr. J.W. Coffman. At this time there wasn't a town or even a village. With the railroad came the town of Black Rock. In 1882 Black Rock was nothing but rolling hills on vast land holdings of Dr. Coffman and a few other men. Where Main Street is now there was an orchard, and a log cabin stood where the, old drugstore now stands.

Owen Angle is said to have established the first general store shortly after the railroad went through. Dr. J.W. Coffman established a store in 1883. That same year W.J. and W.B. Matthews put in another store. It was about this time Caldwell and Stout erected a sawmill on Black River near the ferry.

Because of the many rocks with black color, Black Rock was legally named by a Lawrence County court order October 7, 1884, with a population of 277.

When the town was incorporated there were three or four stores, several sawmills (some say about seven), a schoolhouse, and a number of residences.

In 1885 prominent families living in Black Rock included: Dr. J.W. Coffman, S.H. Howe, E.T. Irby, V.P. DeLand, B.S. Weir, W.J. Matthews, Harry Balcume and W.B. Matthews.

Due to the abundance of timber and access to the railroad and river for shipping, the lumbering industry became a step to growth for the town of Black Rock.

In 1885 another sawmill was put into operation by V.P. DeLand of Kansas. His sawmill was located just below the ferry. He also put in a store at this time.

About 1890 George W. Decker and Company established a large sawmill on the river, also a dry goods and grocery store. The mill ran steadily for a number of years and employed about 150 men. His workers were paid in "Decker Brass" redeemable only at Decker store. In 1904 the sawmill was changed into

a stave mill and in 1908 this was moved away leaving the remains of the lumber sheds.

DeLand and Decker were competitors of Mr. Owen Angle.

In 1893 a large sawmill and furniture factory was established by N.F. Coffey and Company. The sawmill was located on the river with the furniture factory located in what is known as the Coffey Addition.

A handle factory was started in 1896 this was located northeast of town.

Since logging and lumbering were such profitable industries and were well established, Black Rock became what is known as a "boom town" in the late 1800s with a population of about 3,000 in 1897.

In 1889 Black Rock had five general stores, eight grocery stores, two drugstores, one hardware store, one millinery store, five hotels, several boarding houses, two meat markets, one wholesale flour store, a bakery and a restaurant, 10 sawmills (seven of which had shingle mills attached), one separate shingle mill, one planing mill, one lumber drying kiln, one heating factory, one lat mill, a wagon felloe factory, one undertaker's store, several mechanic shops, a stone quarry, a weekly newspaper, a schoolhouse, three churches and a population of about 1,000.

Headquarters for three steamboats were located at Black Rock.

The Boulder Publishing Company of Black Rock published a staunch Republican paper of seven columns issued weekly which was first organized August 24, 1888, and edited by J.G. Cash. It was purchased February 2, 1889 and was the only paper published in Black Rock at this time. It was said to be a fearless critic on every course of human events and each issue was replete with interesting matter. George Dent was editor at this time.

Located one mile west of town was Bonita Springs, a noted summer resort where there were mineral springs and a hotel.

In the 1890s the DeLand sawmill, N.F. Coffey mill, and a smaller mill owned by a Mr. McCoy burned.

This loss was estimated at about $75,000. The mills were not rebuilt.

The Bank of Black Rock opened in 1892 with C.H. "Charley" Martin serving as president. The bank was located on the east end of Main Street. The bank was dynamited for the purpose of robbery. Cashier J. Bryan and Marshal John Jones never solved the case. The bank was remodeled and was open until March 4, 1921, when it closed for liquidation.

First National Bank of Black Rock was chartered March 10, 1919 with L.B.

Poindexter, president, and J.M. Metcalf, cashier. This bank was also robbed. The "mid" 1930s a successful robbery included taking cashier, L.B. Sharp, hostage (who was set free unharmed), while the robbers escaped. They were never apprehended. This bank was moved to Walnut Ridge, September 18, 1933, with J.H. Myers serving as president. This bank now operates a window in the bank building on Main Street of Black Rock.

In 1893 the St. Joseph addition was added with other additions as time passed.

In 1896 the Southern Queensware Company was formed by G.W. Decker, C.R. Hansford, J.S. Hansford, J.C. Yancey, Wm. Clayton and S.J Howe. This business was located in Black Rock for the manufacturing of Royal porcelain China, earthenware, encaustic tiles, and enamel brick. This, corporation's capital stock was $100,000 of which $50,000 was subscribed by the corporation. The capital stock was to be divided into 4,000 shares at the value of $25 a share.

In 1897 and 1898, people had begun hunting for pearls. Dr. J.H. Myers found a 14 grain, pink ball pearl in a mussel from Black River. $1,271,000 was paid out for pearling in seven years.

In 1899 Dr. Myers shipped the first car load of shells to Lincoln, Nebraska. Up to then the valuable shells had been thrown away.

The early 1900s (1900-1902) saw the first button factory established by Dr. J.H. Myers, Dr. N.R. Townsend and H.W. Townsend. This was the first button factory in the south according to Dr. Myers. This factory closed after operating only a short time. The factory was bought and enlarged by a Davenport, Ohio pearl button company. Then a New York based company opened the Chalmers Button Factory, about 1909, with Vernon Howe as manager. The factory employed 64 cutters, five-day men (the graded shells and filled tanks), one straw boss, one office girl and one manager, when in peak production. This business was a vital part of Black Rock's economy for 60 years or more. The Black Rock button industry closed completely in 1954. There were a few individuals that continued to cut buttons at their home.

The Box Factory owned by the Duncle Box and Lumber Company was established about 1980 one half mile northeast of the depot. The box factory and sawmill combined employed approximately 50 men.

The M.E. Benson sawmill was erected about 1905.

Also in 1905 a cotton gin was erected in the western part of town.

The electric light plant was put into operation in 1907. At this time the population was about 1500. There were six doctors and five lawyers practicing in town.

Prominent men of the time were Dr. J.W. Coffman, C.H. Martin, A.W. Williams, C. Burns, W.H. Waldron, N.F. Coffey, C. Sloan, Dr. G.A. Warren, C.L. Freeman, E.M. Irby, S.J. Howe, H.V. Wayland, J.B. Judkins and J.H. Townsend.

In 1908 there were five hotels in Black Rock. They were the Cottage, the Commercial, the Ozark, the Frisco, and the Southern. The Southern was the largest with 25 or 30 rooms. The population was given at 1,400 at this time.

Also in 1908 there were three newspapers being published. They were the Telephone which was started in 1902, the Blade which was begun in 1906, and the Black Rock Democrat published by George Anderson in 1908. The first paper to be published in Black Rock was in 1857.

Black Rock was headquarters for a number of boats that ran up Black River sometimes as far as Poplar Bluff, Missouri. The Boll Weevil, The Idlewild and the Ruby Pearl all had headquarters in Black Rock. The 1890s and early 1900s had as many as 15-20 regular packets. They ran mostly from Black Rock to Newport and Pocahontas and sometimes up to Poplar Bluff. Most of the packets were log boats or crosstie boats. They also hauled cotton and corn and brought in building supplies. There were excursion boats which ran from Black Rock to Clover Bend and back. These boats had entertainment on them and there was a little dance floor and food was served. The charge was probably not over 50 cents or a dollar. These boats probably quit running about 1912. Some of the boats carried groceries. People living along the river would meet the boats when they docked and buy their groceries from them.

There was a river "taxi" service that ran from Black Rock to Powhatan, the county seat. Attorneys, as well as clients and witnesses would travel from Walnut Ridge by train and then get a "river taxi" to Powhatan when court was in session. The Angle family owned some of the taxi boats.

The Minnehaha, Columbia, Pocahontas and George Pope were among some of the steamers that ran the river.

Black Rock suffered many severe losses due to fire. 1904 saw the loss of a drugstore owned by C.L. Brown, a dry goods and grocery store owned by M.J. Kelly, the Myers drugstore and several homes near them. This same year the homes of J.Y. Brady, R.H. McCury, and F. Anderson on North Second Street burned. Every year houses were destroyed by fire and were usually replaced with better ones.

In 1912 a fire broke out on what was known as "Rat Row." It leveled that section of town to the ground. The only means of stopping the fire from turning the corner and spreading to homes was to tear down a business owned by Nath Williams. While a group of townsmen worked frantically to tear down the building, others were busy hauling wagon loads of salt to throw on the fire. Their efforts contained the fire to "Rat Row."

The area that is often referred to as the "fruit farm" was once an orchard of 40,000 peach trees. This orchard was located on a hill about a mile south of town. The peaches were hauled into trucks in wagons and then loaded into railroad cars to be shipped to market.

City government has always been a central part of Black Rock's society. Mayors of the city have been: 1887, Sol Isaminger; 1888-89, E.T. Irby; records are missing from 1900-05; 1906, John G. Wells; 1907, Alvin S. Irby; 1908-09, B.S. Weir; 1910, C.L. Freeman; 1911, C.T. Burns; 1912, C.L. Freeman; 1913, B.S. Weir; 1914-15, C.L. Freeman; 1916, E.T. Wayland; 1917, C.L. Freeman; 1918-24, John G. Wells; 1925-26, C.F. Judkins; 1927, J.R. Leonard; 1928-29, W.A. Smith; 1930, P.W. Townsend (at the time Mr. Townsend was the youngest mayor in the state of Arkansas), 1931-32, C.L. Horn; 1933, R.T. Kell; 1934, W.O. Hanshaw (acting mayor); 1935-45, S.A. Spades; 1946, John L. Wilford; 1947-55, J.H. Myers; 1956-58, Cleo Moody; 1959-60, C.H. Starnes; 1961-72, J.H. Myers; 1973-76, Bob Verkler; 1977-82, C.C. Penny; 1983-86, Jakie Hanan.

Unique to Black Rock was that section of town know as "Nigger Hill." It began along the edge of Coffey Lumber Company property and gradually moved up and over the hill that is south of town. The residents had their own school, two churches, and entertainment center. Highway 63 cut through the center of the hill when the new Black River bridge was completed. Many of these people worked in white homes and were often treated as part of the family.

The Methodist church was organized in about 1884. The property on which the church building now stands was donated by J.W. Coffman, Mattie Coffman and R.R. Southland. The land was given to the Methodist Episcopal Church South. The deed was filed in Lawrence County Book of Records on August 23, 1894 and was recorded on August 25, 1884. The church roll today lists many family names that were found in the early days.

The Presbyterian church was organized in 1885. This group no longer is in existence in Black Rock. The Rock Hill Missionary Baptist now uses the building erected by the Presbyterians.

The Church of Christ assembled in people's homes in 1897. The first building was erected in 1910. In 1936 the old building was destroyed by fire and the next year a new building was ready for occupation. This same structure with various renovations and additions is still in use.

The Baptist church was organized in 1889. Their first building was completed in 1890 and is still a part of the renovated building and addition now in use.

Religious groups that meet regularly today in Black Rock are Assembly of God, Baptist, Church of Christ, Methodist, People's Tabernacle, and Rock Hill Missionary Baptist.

In 1884 the first schoolhouse was built. This site later became the location of the W.H.

Waldron residence. The schoolhouse consisted of one large room and was used both as a schoolhouse and a church-house where all denominations united in Sunday school services.

It was about 1907 when the first telephone office was put in upstairs behind the doctor's office. Mrs. Creager was In charge. She lived in quarters where the switch board was located. Josie Dennie worked as an operator for a time. She left to work in St. Louis for a telephone company. Lillie and Mattie Weir trained under Mrs. Creager.

Later two Williams Sisters, worked the switchboard.

Amanda Weir followed as supervisor. The Weir girls and Peggy Hayes' mother manned the switchboard. They kept the position until about 1937. From 1937-40 Mrs. Flora Bryant (sister to Luther Clark) and her girls, Bernice, Audria, and Mary ran the telephone service.

Ruth Weir Davis followed the Bryants and lived where the switchboard was located. She trained several girls who later went to work for Southwestern Bell. The office was discontinued in the late 1950s.

The Post Office was located behind the corner drugstore until the present post office was constructed.

Black River froze over in 1901. For a two month period sleet and snow covered the ground. It was cold enough to freeze the river. Skaters as well as vehicles made great use of the river's frozen condition.

Mines were operated in the area in 1911 by the Powhatan Zinc and Mining Company. Scott Hickman, father of Pete and Harlis Hickman, was foreman of the mine located at the source of one of the city water pumps.

For many years the first two weeks in August were set aside for the annual Black Rock picnic which was held in the Pecan Bottoms. Due to murders and a suicide the annual picnic was canceled. A time or two since a revival of this annual event was tried but never succeeded.

1838-41 saw an Ice Cream Parlor located near the telephone office and was owned and operated by R.C. and Cora Tate. They made their own ice cream and ice cream bars.

The 40s saw five cafes, two barber shops, a furniture store, movie theater, three garages, a shoe store, three beauty shops, two doctors, five

The city of Black Rock as it appeared in the early 1950's. The large building on the left was the old button factory. Almost dead center in this picture in the distance is the old railroad depot.

grocery stores, a drugstore, a stockyard, several rooming houses and two car dealerships going strong in the town.

In 1946 the south side of Main Street was destroyed by fire. Cafes, barbershops and grocery burned. The buildings now standing were constructed of rocks and bricks.

In 1954 Ben M. Hogan Company established operation of a rock crusher. This business is still in operation operating under the name St. Francis Material Company. They employ approximately 50 people.

In 1971 W.W. Smith bought Black Rock Sand and Gravel Company and operated it until 1977. In 1975, they purchased the Verkler Limestone plant. Today they operate both as the Black Rock Sand, Gravel, and Quarries. They employ around 50 people.

The information in this article is as authentic as could be made from the material at hand. If family names are misspelled, please forgive me, these too are as close as I could make them. Dates sometimes varied and I used what seemed to be the most accurate. Someday I hope someone will put a complete history of our little town into book form. There are so many interesting years not fully covered in this article that would make more interesting reading, and our heritage needs to be preserved. Submitted by Glynda Hill Stewart.

BLACK ROCK POST OFFICE

The Black Rock Post Office was established February 4, 1884. The following were postmasters and the date each was appointed:

James W. Coffman - February 4, 1884
Burett S. Weir - December 14, 1888
Sidney J. Howe - December 26, 1889
Burett S. Weir - October 4, 1893
Charles M. Lehman - May 27, 1897
Jay J. Bryan - July 1, 1902
Arthur Deland - June 18, 1903
Sol W. Isaminger - January 16, 1911
Levi B. Sharp - January 12, 1914
Lee W. McKenney - March 3, 1923
Robert W. Moore - May 10, 1935
Cecil L. Horn - December 20, 1944
John Norris Moore - June 19, 1952
Henry L. Clark - May 28, 1957
Mabel Flippo - March 20, 1971
Robert L. Holeman - October 27, 1973
Kathleen S. Moore - December 2, 1978
Joan M. Jacobson - November 21, 1987
Mary K. Brown - December 15, 1990

Brenda J. Prater - July 11, 1992
Deborah A. Mitchener - September 18, 1993
–Debbie Mitchell

BLACK ROCK CAVE

The old Black Rock Cave contained many rooms and was first explored by Earl Peace of Black Rock. It was located along side Highway 25 near the old one-way iron bridge. The first room was a large area containing walls of natural rock and in addition there were several smaller rooms.

On Sunday afternoons it was the order of the day for several young Black Rock boys to take their carbide lights, enter the cave, and write their names on the rock walls. Those boys included brothers Gervase, Luther, and Vernon Peace, Dorse Robertson, Shorty Norris, Bob Long, and Monk Brower.

THE POOR FARM

William Thomas, writer for the Memphis Commercial Appeal, visited Barney Sellers at Black Rock during Barney's annual exhibit. Thomas got an interesting column about the old county farm, or the poor farm, in the 1920's. Here is a portion of his column:

Among the people who browsed through the exhibit this past weekend were two brothers, Jeff and James Watts, who grew up on the county Poor farm, two miles outside of town. Now retired, the brothers had quite a memory to remember and quite a tale to tell:

"Our father, Buster Watts, ran the Poor Farm from 1933 until 1940," said Jeff Watts, who'd driven down from Illinois for his 50th class reunion at nearby Imboden High School. "We lived at the Poor Farm during the Great Depression, and times were hard. People who could no longer support their mothers or fathers would bring them here and drop them off."

"We had as many as 40 people, and we grew all the food on the place. The men smoked, and the women dipped snuff. So we also grew tobacco as an incentive to get them to do their share of the work. My mother kept the books and passed out the tobacco."

"My father got $50 per month for running the Poor Farm. Whenever someone died, dad would go to Black Rock and get the blacksmith to build a pine box for a coffin. It was my job to shave the corpse and dress him. Then my brother and I would dig the grave. Once, we buried two blind men on the same day, and it was all we could do to get the graves dug."

"Most of the people who came to the Poor Farm were simply old and worn-out. But we had one man in his 20's who'd been raised in the insane asylum in Little Rock. He was born tongue-tied, so people thought he was crazy. After they let him out, he was found to be an intelligent fellow."

"The biggest problem we had was keeping the old men from fighting. They'd fight over nothing at the drop of a walking stick. One man would sit in another man's chair, and next thing you knew, they'd be at it."

"There was no entertainment at the Poor Farm. But, on Sunday mornings, a country preacher named Brother King would come and preach a service for $3. Brother King also preached at the funerals. Afterwards, my brother and I would bury the dead in a clay hill behind a grove of cedars. There were no markers for the graves, and no records were kept of the people who were buried there."

Later, I drove out Highway 63 to see where the Poor Farm had been. The buildings, including two big dormitories, are gone without a trace. The state has put in a rest stop, complete with picnic tables and a modern rest room.

Halfway up the hill, past the last picnic table, is a stand of cedar trees. And beyond the cedars, I suppose, are the graves of the people who never got off the Poor Farm alive.
Permission granted by John Blonn.

CACHE TOWNSHIP

Washington Lafayette Rosselot was born February 22, 1852, in Jamestown, Kentucky. His parents were Francois and Nancy P. South Rosselot. Francois was born in Belfort, France, on May 4, 1800, and immigrated to the United States in 1826. Francois was one of Jacques and Susan White Rosselot's 14 children. Nancy was born in Ohio, March 11, 1820, and was the daughter of Thomas and Susannah Rutter South.

Wash lived in Jackson County, Arkansas from 1883 to 1890, and then moved to Cache Township, Lawrence County, Arkansas, and purchased 160 acres in 1891, from William N. and Mary J. Brashere. His wife was Martha Laure Berry, born in 1855. They were wed in White County, Illinois, on May 22, 1873. She was the daughter of John and Sarah Berry of Emma, White County, Illinois.

Around 1897, Wash's brothers, Francis E., born December 18, 1845, and John Alexander, born December 16, 1856, moved to Cache Township, Arkansas, from Burnt Prairie Township,

Black Rock Post Office

Black Rock brothers Luther, Vernon, and Gervase Peace in 1937, whose past time included exploring the Black Rock Cave.

Fred Brandon and his F.W. McNess Wagon in Black Rock, Arkansas in the 1920s.

Carmi, Illinois. This move consisted of Francis E. and Mary Elizabeth Conner Rosselot and three children: William Thomas, born in 1874; Gertrude E., born in 1885; Robert Franklin, born in 1896, and one brother, John Alexander Rosselot, born in 1856. Their entire belongings, consisting of livestock, provisions, clothes, furniture, guns, ammunition and children were hauled overland in ox drawn covered wagons. Traveling by day, weather permitting, and camping by night. This trip took the best part of a month.

Francis Edward and Mary Elizabeth Conner Rosselot purchased land from John and Alabama Darter in Cache Township. One of their sons, Charles Edward Rosselot, born October 9, 1876, had married Miss Margaret Louisa Wagner on November 24, 1897. She was the daughter of John and Texas Josephine Willis Wagner. Charles E. and Margaret moved from Carmi, Illinois, when their oldest son, John Franklin, was two and one half years old in 1904.

When Francis E. Rosselot was 16 years old, he enlisted as a private and served in the Civil War. He was stationed in Memphis, Tennessee, and Vicksburg, Mississippi, in 1863. He mustered out in 1865, at the age of 19 at Helena, Arkansas. His older brother, Fredrick Luellen Rosselot, was wounded at the Battle of Shiloh in April, 1862. At the age of 52 he moved to Cache Township. Francis died at the age of 81 and is buried at Rhea Cemetery, Lawrence County, Arkansas.

The majority of the Francis E. "Ed" Rosselot family have deep roots in the Fender Community. John Franklin "Frank" Rosselot was the oldest child of Ed and Margaret. He married Ima Simmons in 1925, and they bought a farm in the community. They had one daughter, Melba Rosselot Jones, who still resides on the family farm.

There were other children of Edward and Margaret who lived in and reared families in the same area, namely: Violet Nunally, Sylvia Boothe, Clara McCormic, Daisy Dobbs, Ralph Rosselot, who resides in Walnut Ridge, and Jewell Fender. *–Melba Rosselot Jones*

Grandpa and Grandma Rosselot

THE CLOVER BEND BELL

The Clover Bend Bell is a most honored symbol of the writer, Alice French. It dates back to the late 1800s, when she gave it to the Clover Bend Community School. In 1885-90, Alice French placed an order with L. M. Rumsey Manufacturing Company of St. Louis, Missouri, for the striking of a bell suitable for the Clover Bend School. The bell is made of solid brass and weighs about 500 pounds. It has a circumference of 13 feet at the lip and a clapper about 24 inches long.

The bell was shipped from St. Louis to Clover Bend by river boat. This was a regular shipping route and much freight was carried by these boats.

From 1938, when the school left the old two-room building, the bell was used by two Baptist churches and in 1991, was given back to the school community. It was through the efforts of Paul Downum, Paul King, Billy Ed Doyle, and his sons, Steve and Timothy, that the 500 pound bell was removed from the church belfry and brought to the school community center.

It now rests atop the Alice French Bell Pavilion located in front of the community center. The pavilion is attached to the center by a walkway and is surrounded by tablets of gray granite engraved with the names of families who have roots in Lawrence County. Because Clover Bend was the county seat, there are also names of many county and state dignitaries. *–Viola Meadows.*

CLOVER BEND COURTHOUSE

A community established in the early 1800s by a Frenchman named Pierre Le Mieux on the east side of Black River where the river seems to outline a clover leaf, was given the name Clover Bend. The hillock upon which Clover Bend rested was virtually the only desirable place in the area for a settle-

Clover Bend Bell.

ment because much of the area was swamp land. Remote as the settlement was, it clung to existence, and in 1829, steamboats were finding their way to its landing. The settlement was established as an important landing in river travel.

In 1840, Colonel Samuel Robinson, a colonel in the Confederate Army, bought from the United States Government the site of Clover Bend and thousands of acres in that part of the county. Colonel Robinson served in the Arkansas Senate from 1846 to 1850. It was through his powerful influence that the county seat was moved to Clover Bend from Smithville in 1868. The courthouse was situated there for one year until it was moved to Powhatan in 1869.

Because there was a need, Colonel Robinson and his slave force built a ferry for passage across Black River at Clover Bend, and cut a road through the dense forest to Smithville. This connector of the eastern and western sections of the county was called Robinson Road. It fell into disuse after the county seat was moved to Powhatan. Today one of the better fishing bays is located in that vicinity and is known as Robinson Bay. *–Viola Meadows.*

MEMORIES OF DENTON

Slavery was a problem in 1861 in Denton, Arkansas. There were no known battles in the area, but Federal troops raided homes of the area residents. My great-grandmother, Sarah Davis, told how they kept their cured meat hidden in the wood box, so the Jayhawkers would not find it.

We don't have any record of Indians being seen in the Denton area by white settlers, but evidence was found that the Indians had been there before they were moved out by treaty with the United States, about 1810. The cemetery behind the Methodist Church dates from 1830.

Denton developed around the area where the Powhatan-Smithville road and the Military Road, which opened in 1811, crossed. The major influx of settlers into the valley started about 1835 and continued for about 10 years. Denton was a thriving community with 50 or more buildings at one time. A resident of the area, Ceber Denton, circulated a petition for a post office. The Post Office

Clover Bend Courthouse 1868

John and Sarah Ann White Davis

department named the office Denton, in honor of Mr. Denton, and appointed Dave Davis as postmaster in 1894. Other postmasters were Berry W. Field, William P. Dent, John B. Bowers, James T. Turnbow and Everett Moore. The Post Office was discontinued April 30, 1954.

A resident of Denton at that time could find a blacksmith, grist mill, sorghum mill, milliner ship, barber shop, cotton gins operated by oxen, telephone switch board, grocery and hardware store, doctors, brass band, gas station and subscription school.

The New Hope Church, organized in 1844, played a vital part in the community's early days. It has continued to serve the area residents for more than 150 years.

The dwelling behind the school was built for high school student's boarding. Mr. Delania, from Batesville, came to start a high school but failed at his idea.

The second story of the 1881 school building was used by the Masonic Lodge and the Oddfellows Lodge. The building was known as "The Hall."

The mouse trap factory was in the T.C. Jones Grocery Store in the 1940's. I made parts for the traps and operated the store when the Jones were gone.

More details about the history of Denton may be reviewed in the Lawrence County Historical Quarterly, Volume 9, number 4, and Volume 10, number 1. –Maxine Mize

IMBODEN

The town of Imboden was named for Benjamin Imboden, one of the early pioneers who settled here about 1828. He was a descendant of a noble and distinguished clan of Imbodens whose original home was the mountain section of Switzerland. In 1882, the heirs of Benjamin Imboden deeded the land to W. C. Sloan. The railroad survey was made that year. In 1883, the track was laid and the town was laid off by Mr. Sloan and named for Benjamin Imboden.

Some have thought that the coming of the railroad in 1883 was the date for the beginning of the town. But there is evidence that a few houses and a store or two had already been established along the Military Road which crossed Spring River after leaving Old Jackson and proceeding on to Polks Bayou (Batesville). Shortly after the town had received railway service, Captain W. C. Sloan thought the town should be incorporated and thus began the process of governing itself.

Smithville, Arkansas: looking south toward bank; date and people in photo not known.

The records show that on April 7, 1887, a petition to incorporate the town of Imboden was filed with Clay Sloan, Lawrence County Clerk, by W. G. Carter. No action was taken on the first request for incorporation so a second request was made to the Lawrence County Court in its January term, 1889. On Monday, April 9, the court met and approved the incorporation which was recorded on April 15 in the records of the court and signed by W. A. Townsend.

JESUP COMMUNITY

The community now known as the town of Jesup had its beginning along Methodism in the state of Arkansas. Eli Lindsey, a circuit rider, lived about one half mile east of Jesup and held services at his home there in 1815. In 1848, a building was erected of logs near a big spring just south of the present town and it was called Shady Grove. The building was used for both church and school until early 1900.

This community is located in the rolling foothills of the Ozarks and on Big Creek not more than one and one half miles from Strawberry River. There are many types of soil that range from the fertile bottom lands to clay and sandy loam. In the early days people raised their own fruit, vegetables and meats. The major crops were corn and cotton.

Some of the early settlers were the Fortenberrys, Taylors, Finleys and Raineys. As more people came into the area a church and school were erected on the present church site. The first post office established in 1894, was about one fourth mile north of the present town. Jim Simpson wrote to the postal department for a name and it was given Jesup. Mail came from Evening Shade and was carried by horseback from station to station. By 1900, the Sloans, Wassons and Hendersons owned much land here and Will Penn, a carpenter, began construction of buildings at the present town site. There was a big layout of streets, a sawmill, cotton gin, doctor's office, blacksmith shop, church, school and many homes located on main street. Ben Taylor was one

of the early business men, Verdie Mullen was the barber and operator of the general store. The Hillhouse family moved in and purchased section 19. Mail was carried now from Black Rock each day and trucks brought groceries and store supplies from Imboden.

The church was remodeled several times and in recent years the interior has been brought up to pretty modern day furnishings and a fellowship hall was added. It is now known as the Eli Lindsey Memorial United Methodist Church. The stores and post office are now gone, but the Jesup central exchange for GTE is located there. Jesup is still a nice little community to live in. –Kathleen Sisk.

LAURATOWN

According to McLeod's history of Lawrence County, Lauratown was one of the earliest settlements in the county, around 1800. The community flourished. It became a stop for steamboats on the Black River. Mr. John K. Gibson, Sr. purchased several hundred acres from Martin brothers. The settlement was relocated on old Highway 67. There were two large store buildings, one for groceries and hardware; with a pot bellied stove and relocated post office (W. W. Cochran, Postmaster). The other was for feed and grain. A rock building replaced them in 1931.

Part of this article is remembrances of Maxine (Nelle) Bracy whose father was hired to be the bookkeeper for the new farming operation. He slept in the back of the warehouse and took meals at Mrs. Brimhall's. Maxine remembers about 30 houses there. The store had barrels for crackers, beans, coffee, flour, etc. Salt pork stocked on the counter was weighed at time of sale. The cotton gin had a long line of wagons at harvest time. Jim Smith was the gin manager, but several men worked at the gin. An outdoor basketball court was at the gin lot.

Doctors Stephens, Hartman and Robinson were three remembered. When someone died, men gathered and built the casket. Mr. McCord and Ernest Sade were blacksmiths. Charles Phillips had a hamburger stand; later a service station close to 67 Highway.

The mules were housed in a large barn. Clay Halstead was one of the farm bosses who rode horseback over the plantation. Mr. Gibson would sometimes finance a farmer. Fake money called "John Dough" was issued. It could only be used at his business. Children went to school in a two story building known as Bosley School. Masonic Lodge held their meetings there also. Some of the teachers were: Gertrude Robinson, Charlie Grigsby, Rose Conkrell, Nancy Weir, Anna Laura Justus and Roy Smith. The bookkeepers were: J. G. Neece, Walker Smith, Owen Spotts, Frank Kell, John C. Halstead, Truman Moore and Clara Mae Brun.
–Willene Kirkland.

TOWN OF PORTIA

Located in the center of Lawrence County is Portia. Portia is one of the oldest towns. Records in the General Land Office in Washington, D.C. show that Joseph Guignolet confirmed in 1816, Portia to be older than Lawrence County.

In October, 1906, Portia suffered a disastrous fire which destroyed all businesses on the south side of the railroad. The disaster resulted in a town ordinance that all future businesses must be constructed of brick.

At one time Portia stood as the strongest possibility for the county seat. Due to the geographical location and access to rail and waterways. This was considered in 1886. A bid for the seat was made, but was declined when the newspaper, *The Portia Free Press*, published from 1886-1888, by W. S. and S. W. Morgan, antagonized the state's Democrats by printing their populists ideas.

One cannot speak of Portia without mentioning the Fourth of July Celebration. This event has been a part of Portia's heritage for the past ninety years. This celebration started as a political rally since the early settlers of the area were interested in political and governmental affairs. They were well read and versed in civic activities and the discussion of politics was a favorite pastime. July Fourth was the date set for the political rally in Lawrence County and Portia was chosen for its spacious and beautifully shaded grove.

POWHATAN

Powhatan's prominence in Lawrence County's history developed largely because of its early popularity as a port on the Black River. Its earliest development was centered in the oldest part of the city, the bottom lands adjacent to the river. Powhatan began with the establishment of a ferry by its founder James Ficklin.

Powhatan was the local cotton market for a large territory after 1829, when cotton was exported via steamboat from the dock at Powhatan Ferry. By 1853, the population of Powhatan had grown to 500 as plantations and farms were becoming well established in the county. The town was incorporated on January 12, 1853.

When Powhatan became county seat in 1869, a local newspaper, The Times, was published regularly and the town also supported two hotels, Rogers House and Morrison House, and general merchandise shops. Powhatan had become the shipping center for much of the county.

Powhatan in its heyday was described as "a stirring village on the Black River containing wood, flour and saw mills operated by steam; two churches (Methodist and Presbyterian); and a district school. Cotton and livestock were shipped from Powhatan to other ports, and two passenger stages operated daily between Powhatan and Black Rock at a fare of 50 cents. Mail was delivered twice daily from Black Rock.

There was a period of rapid growth and community development in Powhatan shortly after 1869. Three commissioners: Alfred Oaks, Phillip K. Lester and Emanual Good, were appointed to select a courthouse site in 1869, when Powhatan became county seat. Three commissioners: Charles A. Stuart, Charles Coffin and Solomon W. Redding, were appointed by a building committee in 1871.

There was much discontent with the Powhatan site chosen for the courthouse, however, because those attending court from the east side of Black River had to pay ferriage fees, which were later reduced to half-fares by court order to improve the situation. Apparently the commissioners selected the site for the new courthouse with greater concern for its aesthetic appeal than for its accessibility. The terrain was hilly with large boulders. Blocks 8 and 11 proved to be unsuitable for a "public square" similar to those of Davidsonville and Smithville. Nevertheless, the land was purchased from Asa T. and John A. Lindsey and Andrew Balfour for $800 and construction began. The project was financed by the issuing of county bonds in accordance with the Acts of Arkansas, 1871.

Prominent family names in Powhatan included Lindsey, Stuart, Mount, Smith, DeArman, Matthews, Martin, Straughn, Scott, East, Sloan, Baber, Thornburg, Coffin, Redding, Williams, Eudaley, Wayland, Wells, Coffman, Steadman, Flippo and Balfour became well known.

Around 1870 Powhatan quickly became the trade center for many miles around. Merchandise, not only for Powhatan, but for towns to the west, was landed there from a regular line of steamboats going up and down the river and outgoing freight was taken on. The town prospered with shops, a grist mill, woolen mill, newspaper, and a hotel. Another important business carried on at Powhatan was meat packing. Stuart Brothers bought and packed thousands of pounds of dressed hogs to be sold later.

In 1873 a courthouse was built. The two-story brick structure burned in 1885, but country records were unharmed because they were stored in a vault. In 1888 a beautiful Victorian-style courthouse was built and this building served as the county seat for Lawrence County until 1963.

The arrival of railroads and the new bridge, Black River Bridge, constructed at Black Rock were two reasons for the decline in Powhatan's population. In 1968 efforts began to see restoration of the courthouse and in 1973 the building was dedicated. Today it is the center of the Powhatan Courthouse State Park. The Powhatan Jail, Ficklin-Imboden log house, telephone exchange building, and Methodist Church have been restored. The Male and Female Academy is currently under restoration. The town is now a tourist attraction for those interested in history.

SMITHVILLE HISTORY

The oldest post office in present Lawrence County was called Strawberry River, established in 1832, when in Arkansas Territory. In 1837, one year after Arkansas became a state, James Benson gave 50 acres of land for a new county seat and the name was changed to Smithville in honor of Colonel Robert Smith who donated a liberal sum of money to the county when the seat of justice was moved to that location. A courthouse was built behind what is presently the Peoples Bank. The courthouse was a two-story structure constructed of cypress grown in the Black River bottoms. An escape proof jail was erected on the hill south of present day Highway 117. Its floor, constructed of 12-inch hewn logs and 2 x 20 inch slabs, laid one on the other, were nailed with thousands of

The suspension bridge over Black River at Powhatan. The 1888 courthouse is at far right.

square nails. It could not be torn down, but gradually rotted away and was burned in 1925, about 85 years after it was erected. The jail never lodged any notorious criminals, but provided a place for indulgent patrons of the town saloons.

In 1840, the Military Road at Smithville was crossed by a road from the east. Smithville was the primary trade center at this time and saw tremendous growth throughout the time it was the county seat. *The Plaindealer*, a newspaper, was published in Smithville beginning in 1850. Other newspapers published there were: *The Democratic Organ* beginning in 1861, *The Sketchbook, The Mining Microcosm, The Smithville Advocate* and *The Homecrofter*, (The Home, The Farm, The Field, The Mine) printed as late as 1911. Smithville churches included the Baptist Church, established in 1866, the Methodist Church, 1875, and the Presbyterian Church, 1888. The Presbyterians disbanded, but the Baptist and Methodist churches remain active today. Smithville had a school called the Old Solomon School prior to the Civil War and had a public school until 1946, when it consolidated with Lynn due to small numbers of students. The Reconstruction Period following the Civil War proved to be detrimental to the growth of Smithville. In 1868, the county seat was moved from Smithville to Clover Bend. According to the 1870 United State Census, Smithville had a druggist, six dry goods merchants, six physicians, two blacksmiths, two grocers, a printer and a saddler. There were 202 dwellings and a population of 1144. According to *Goodspeed's Biographical and Historical Memoirs of Northeast Arkansas*, Smithville's population had

dropped to 350 in 1880, 12 years following the removal of the county seat to other locations. At that time, Smithville had four general mercantile businesses, a drug store, hotel and livery stable. In 1887, the telephone line from Walnut Ridge through Powhatan to Smithville was established and the first paid message was sent from Powhatan to Smithville by Colonel M. D. Baber of Powhatan to Miss Vida Steadman of Smithville. At one time, Smithville was a mining community with several zinc and lead mines located in the area, however, the mines proved to be unprofitable and were closed. The Citizens Bank was reportedly established in 1901, by some men who were interested in mining. The mines were closed, but the bank survived and flourished. During the Depression, the Citizens Bank remained solvent when the other six Lawrence County banks were liquidated. The bank has reportedly been robbed nine times (1921, 1925, 1945, 1958, 1968, 1969, 1980, 1982, and 1993). Today it is called the Peoples Bank and it is a branch of a much larger institution. Smithville has been the site of several gin companies, the most prosperous being the Smithville Gin Company, founded in 1926 and operational until 1948. It had four stands and one year this company baled over 2300 bales of cotton.

In the post-World War II years, the town was still a prospering business community. It had three general stores, three service sta-

tions, a farmer's supply, cafe, two garages, blacksmith shop, cotton gin, doctor's office and bank. The post office, school, Masonic Lodge and two churches made up the rest of the nonresidential buildings in town.

The present day town has been reduced to a service station, feed supply, grocery/hardware store, cafe, antique store, bank, community center, volunteer fire department and city hall, post office, Masonic Lodge, Baptist Church and Methodist Church.

Smithville was a thriving community for over 100 years, but being passed up by the railroad and major highways was detrimental to the town's commercial growth. It is now a quiet village with a population of 89 and people who are very proud of its legacy.

–Bilbrey Joe Wallis, Maleta Bilbrey Tipton and Jay Brent Tipton.

Minturn, Arkansas, West Front Street, 1910.

Fred Brandon, in front of the hotel at Ravenden, Arkansas, on his mail route in the 1920s.

Men in front of Uncle Jake Casper's Blacksmith Shop in Lynn. Ralph Dawson is the first man in the line wearing a flat cap. Date unknown. Submitted by Clynell Dawson Sandusky.

Business and Industry

THE LIMESTONE INDUSTRY

In 1936, King Cotton had robbed the soils of Lawrence County of its natural minerals to enable the production of crops. At the same time, the pearling industry had been in its glory and the button factory at Black Rock had been making use of the spent muscle shells by cutting fine pearl buttons renowned the world over from the shells.

Wave Ed Verkler, Jr. of Black Rock, a local man, the son of Wave Ed Verkler Sr. and Kate Moore, both with roots going far back in the development of the county, came up with the idea of crushing the muscle shells left after cutting buttons and selling it to the farmers to give the soil new life in the 1950's. He succeeded in doing this, but as the supply of shells diminished, the demand for his product grew and he looked at the possibility of crushing the natural limestone from his farm.

He had started the first limestone crusher for agricultural purposes in Arkansas in 1939, at his farm about three miles north of Black Rock on Stinnett Creek and began crushing the limestone found there. The only other limestone quarry in the county at that time was located at Sloan, on the Frisco railroad about two miles south of Imboden. However, that quarry operated only to cut out rectangular blocks of rock for building purposes. Many of these are still visible around Black Rock.

It was not until probably the 40's, that this quarry began operations to crush the stone, primarily to produce aggregate for their construction company in the construction of blacktop roads. At the same time, one began operations on the western outskirts of Black Rock.

Then, as road construction demanded more and more stone aggregate, more quarries sprang up around the area. As always, some succeeded, some did not. One, which moved in and set up a portable plant primarily to provide aggregate for Interstate 55 near Memphis, converted to a permanent plant and is still operating, though it has changed ownership several times.

In the meantime, the Verklers moved their operation northward about a mile where the supply of rock was more abundant and later sold it, first to W. W. Smith, then Mark Clark, and its now owned and operated by probably the giant of crushing companies, the Vulcan Companies. Two others are presently actively operating, Meridian and Carroll Quarry.

This industry has far reaching economic value to the county in that besides their immediate work force, many gravel trucks are employed in hauling and several trucking companies have spawned from it. Many families have worked at these crushers for over 30 years. The severance tax paid has created much revenue to the state

Dutch Peace, Eva Peace, Nellie Mitchell, and Geo Haynes, in front of Powhatan lead and zinc mine.

and their property taxes have benefited the school districts as well as the other county coffers greatly.

Now, lime for farmland is rather like the muscle shells, merely a by-product of the road aggregate and a minor part of the entire industry.

This is a good example of what one man's initiative and foresight can set in motion when the time is right.

POWHATAN LEAD AND ZINC MINE

A major industry in the Black Rock-Powhatan area was the old Powhatan Lead and Zinc Mine. The mine began alongside Highway 25 and the veins of the mine ran close by the Powhatan Cemetery. Located behind the cemetery was a beautiful Indian Springs adjacent to mine number one. After the Zinc and Lead Mine was closed and the old building located on mine number two was torn down, the town of Black Rock used this mine as a resource for their city water.

MOBIL PIPELINE

The Magnolia Pipeline Company, a predecessor of Mobil, decided in approximately 1946, to construct a 20 inch diameter crude oil pipeline from Corsicana, Texas, to Patoka, Illinois. This line was to supply about 250,000 barrels per day, some would feed to the Lubrite refinery in East Saint Louis and some to the Joliet refinery in Joliet, Illinois, with the remainder moving east to the refinery at Paulsboro, New Jersey.

There are pumping stations at Corsicana and Quitman, Texas; Foreman, Glenwood, Conway and Strawberry, Arkansas; Doniphan and Yount, Missouri. The elevations along the pipeline show the high point, from the Arkansas River to the Mississippi River, is located between Strawberry, Arkansas, and Doniphan, Missouri.

The Strawberry station is located one mile north of Saffell, just off state Highway 25. It was constructed on Lawrence County Road #338

First Limestone operation in Arkansas for production of agricultorial limestone in 1939 Wave Ed Verkler, Jr. operation on Stinnett Creek three miles north of Black Rock.

across from the former Felix Harris residence. The station buildings were constructed from fire resistant materials. The chief engineer's residence was located on the same property, and was a wooden frame house and garage.

Harry Williams was the first chief engineer at the station. He and his family moved there in 1949. The station operation required manning 24 hours per day, seven days per week. This was done by four operating engineers and a yardman to care for the grounds and fill in the extra eight hour shift when the regular operators were off work. The operating engineers were Bob Crouch, Raymond Harris, Joe Neeley and Harold Moore. Henry Yount was the yardman. This crew did not stay the entire time the station was manned. Other engineers who worked in this operation were Bob Bishop and Mark John Hippard. The chief engineers changed a few times over the years with Jerry Jarnisky and Henry Frazier serving in that position.

The Strawberry Station was automated in approximately 1962, and the required staff was reduced. The station is completely automated now and operates by remote from Dallas, Texas. It is controlled according to the volume of crude to be supplied through the line at any given time.

The station and its personnel during the early years provided valuable services to the community where it was located. There was, of course, the taxes to Strawberry schools and the county,

Allen Ray Morrison died March, 1967. Esther Morris died November, 1972.

but most importantly it provided telephone service to the western edge of Lawrence County. The station was required to have a backup communication system with a private line from the Bell Telephone Company out of Black Rock. This Bell telephone was used by nearly everyone at one time or another west of the Strawberry River in Lawrence County. The engineers would often deliver messages when they finished their shift at the station. The chief engineer would, also, deliver emergency messages day or night.

The station has a single 900 horsepower electric motor turning single centrifugal pump producing 600 to 800 psi output pressure. This was to boost the stream of oil over the hump to Doniphan. This kind of electric power was not available from the REA Company in the area. A private line was required from the Arkansas Power substation at Tuckerman. This line was 37 miles long and very difficult to keep in service during thunderstorms.

The personnel lived in the local community near the pump station. Magnolia Pipeline Company had operated company camps, but found it better for families to participate in the community affairs. Strawberry station was the most remote location in the system, however, the families who lived here generally were senior personnel. This pipeline was top of the line technology when it was constructed as it is today. Currently, it provides financial support to the area through taxes.

The pipeline enters Lawrence County in the Southeast of Southeast of Section 32, T15N, R3W from Independence County and exits in Northwest of Northeast of Section 5, T17N, R1W, crossing Spring River at this point into Randolph County. – *Walt Neely.*

Old Walnut Ridge Post Office.

MORRISON DAIRY

Allen Ray Morrison was born February 21, 1890, near Carlisle, Arkansas, Lonoke County, son of Will and Selina Morrison. Esther Puryear was born July 10, 1893, near Carlisle, Arkansas, daughter of John W. and Sarah Puryear. They were married June 24, 1914. They lived in that area until 1925. It was Praire Country. They raised a lot of hay, had cows, sold mile to a cheese factory; raised a little rice. Dad was co-owner of a livery stable. They rented horses and buggies to various people. There were not very many cars then.

In 1924, their first child was born. Allen Glen was very small. They fixed a box and put a pillow inside and set him in the oven to keep him warm. She thought that really helped him to survive.

In 1925, the decided to move to Lawrence County. They moved to the southwest part of Walnut Ridge. They bought a few cows, sold some mile. Later in 1925, they sold the cows. Dad had a good strong team. They went to Biggers where he helped dig a basement for a big gas company building there. They came back to Lawrence and moved west of Hoxie, bought some more cows and sold milk. Their daughter, Anna, was born September 21, 1927. In 1928, they left again, took his team, went to Many Island. He left, hauled large poles to put electricity into Mammouth Springs, Many Island and Hardy area. They came back to Hoxie, moved on the east side of town. They bought more cows and started the Morrison Dairy. In early 1933, they bought 150 acres on Midway Road. The farm had poor drainage and several thickets. As time and money permitted, they improved it. It was just a dirt road. When the road was real muddy, he had a good mule that helped get through the mud holes. He tied the mule to a tree while he delivered milk and he helped daddy to get back home. We finally got electricity out our way and then we got a radio. I don't remember what year, but WPA graveled our road. Later it was blacktopped. It was a great improvement.

Morrison Dairy grew. We usually had 22 or 23 cows to milk. We hand milked them for many years. We usually had one or two men that helped with that and the many other chores. In about 1940, we got electric automatic milkers. That was great! In 1946, they sold most of the cows and quit the dairy business. We have sold milk all over Walnut Ridge and Hoxie. They grew different crops and continued to improve the farm.

This is the way I remember it.–*Anna Ponder*

THE TIMES DISPATCH

The Times Dispatch was established in Walnut Ridge in 1910, when Dave A. Lindsey moved the newspaper to Walnut Ridge from Pocahontas. Three years later, Walter Smith purchased the paper. Then, in 1921, James L. Bland, native of Bigelow in Perry County, and Austin Wilkerson, editor and publisher of the *Newport Independent*, bought *The Times Dispatch*.

Within a short time, the newspaper began a steady climb upward. The following year, Bland bought our Wilkerson's interested in the paper, making him the sole owner of *The Times Dispatch*. With a loan from the W. O. Troutt family, owner of *The Jonesboro Sun*, Bland was enabled to buy new equipment, including a linotype, the first owned by any weekly paper in the state. In those days, the newspaper consisted of four or five handset columns of news per issue, mostly made up of small one paragraph items. In 1946, *The Times Dispatch* bought a used web-fed newspaper press, the first owned by a weekly in Arkansas.

In 1971, *The Times Dispatch* converted to offset printing. Since the newspaper still had an eight page letterpress, and because of an oversupply of newsprint, the first eight pages were printed in Walnut Ridge and the remaining pages were printed at the *Clay County Courier* in Corning. In 1977, the paper began being printed at the *Paragould Daily Press* printing plant. Since 1992, the paper has been printed again in Corning.

James L. Bland Jr. began working with his father at the newspaper office during 1946. In 1951, the younger Bland became editor and later became publisher and general manager. In 1977, the elder Bland was named honorary publisher and Thomas A. Moore was named editor, a position he held until the spring of 1986.

Since 1986, John A. Bland, a third generation of the Bland family, has served as editor, and later publisher, following in the footsteps of his father and grandfather. James L. Bland Jr. continued to serve as business manager and advisor until his death in 1996. Virginia (Mrs. James L. Bland Jr.) is principal owner of the paper and continues to have a role in its weekly production.

The Times Dispatch has been blessed with a number of faithful, longtime staff members, who have contributed greatly to the newspaper's success. In 1997, staff members with *The Times Dispatch* for well over 30 years include: Rennard Cooper, Hope Segraves, Howard Golden and Janice Hibbard.

The Times Dispatch has traditionally been a conservative, Democratic newspaper, with a mission to provide complete news coverage of Lawrence County and to serve as a crusader and primary supporter of Lawrence County and its businesses.

In 1997, *The Times Dispatch* now has a paid circulation of just under 6,000 and averages approximately 28 to 30 pages each week, along with various inserts. –*John Bland.*

Schools

ARBOR GROVE SCHOOL

The first school located in the Arbor Grove Community was a three-room school building. The building burned and a two-room school was built around 1931. Early teachers were Helen Weir, Joyce Lee, Maxine Bracy, Dewell Puckett and Bruce Logan. Arbor Grove School consolidated with the Hoxie Public Schools in the early 1950s. –Maxine Bracy.

BLACK ROCK SCHOOL

In 1884 the first schoolhouse was built. This site later became the location of the W.H. Waldron residence. The schoolhouse consisted of one large room and was used both as a schoolhouse and a church-house where all denominations united in Sunday school services. A few years later another room was added and a partition placed in the original large room making three rooms in all. The 1893-94 graduating class members were Ollie Holloway Eddleman, Allie Propst Pickney and Henry Kelly. This building was used until 1902 when a brick building was constructed.

In the 1920s a two story brick building was built where the present school stands in the St. Joseph addition. That building was razed and replaced with a stone building which burned in the 1933-34 term. Another building was constructed on the same site, which also was destroyed by fire in the 1939-40 school year. It was replaced by the existing stone structure on the same site.

As the years have gone by the school has grown. Renovation of the building constructed in the 1940s as well as the elementary wings added in the 1950s and the 1986-87 school year saw the completion of construction of a new kindergarten through grade three facility, which also houses a central elementary library, nurses quarters and sickroom, speech pathology classroom, office and workroom.

The gymnasium which was built by the WPA was renovated in 1974-75 into what is now the cafetorium. A new gym was constructed ready for use in the fall of 1975.

Black Rock school has produced some outstanding men and women and the town is proud of its facilities and the people who staff it.
  – Glynda Hill Stewart.

BLACK ROCK CLASS OF 1941

The Black Rock High School graduating class of 1941 was the first class to graduate in the present school building. The class went to school in the old Methodist Church in Black Rock due to the fact that the school had burned in 1939. The new school did not have a gym, home economics building, or an FFA building. The class motto was "We Get What We Go After" and the class flower was

Those attending Arbor Grove School (located south of Hoxie) in the late 1930s, or early 1940s, included (front from left): Andrew Ashlock, Jackie Brady, Marie Blackshear, Margaret Ann Jones, Billy Joe Maxie, Billy Wayne Whitlow, Winnie Lou Cole, Patsy Jones, Pauline Brady, Margaret Ann Whitlow, Howard Noblin, Rebecca Brady and Imogene Bookout.
Also, (second row): Nina Jane Brady, Jackie Dobbs, John Earl McCord, Cathryn Turner, Syble Maxie, Bradley Owens, Delta Blackshear, not known, Almeda Alphin and Talmadge Flanagan.
Others include (third row): Norma Jean Turner, Lavon Jones, Coleman Brady, Clarice Whitlow, Margie Blackshear, Lillie Mae Childers, Ray Dobbs Jr., Pearlie Blackshear, not known and Nancy Ann Noblin.
Fourth row includes: A. C. McCord, Myrle Alphin, Geraldine Baird, not known, Maxie Flanagan, Fredreca Brady, Betty Sue King, Lena Fern Turner and Mary Lou Whitlow.
Also, (back): Lawrence Goff, teacher, Lehman Blackshear, Pearl Baird and Julia Van Coffman, teacher. Photo courtesy of Ethel James of Walnut Ridge. Submitted by Leon Blackshear. Names were furnished by Nina Hudson, A. C. McCord and Ray Daniels.

the rose. Dr., Huet from Arkansas State College (now Arkansas State University) gave the commencement address title "Go the Second Mile."

The class motto could accurately describe the class as intelligent, creative, independent, and determined. The class was not happy with the situation while attending school in the old Methodist Church. Mr. Eldon Fair, a teacher, agreed with the students and joined the class to go on strike. The class and Mr. Fair marched down Main Street to the depot and back. The group was met by the school board that made Mr. Fair apologize. Another incident reflected their motto when the class set up tables in the boiler room for the junior / senior banquet prom. A jukebox was borrowed from the Jess Goodrum Cafe for the dance; however, the school board came in on the dance and immediately stopped it. This class did not give up and left their current location for Paragould to finish their dance at the Kingsway Club.

The class trip consisted of riding in cars to Hardy to spend the day on the river. The class consisted of five boys and 10 girls. Evelyn Robertson Flippo was elected high school queen in 1940. Class officers were: President - Noble Richey; Vice

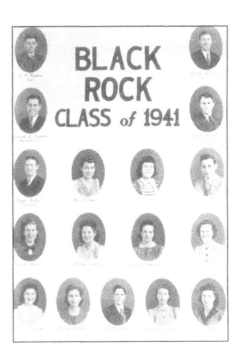

BLACK ROCK CLASS of 1941

Haw Grove School in 1908, grades 1 through 8. Front Row: Earl Rider, Calvin Johnson, Otis Grey, Ernest Grey, Lucien Dawson, Ralph Dawson, Otis Wright, Ben Fortenberry, Marvin Price. Second Row: Cleo Turnbow, Jim Spivy, Roy Price, Frank Turnbow, Oscar Dawson Delia Trentham, Mattie Fortenberry, Mamie Price, Mollie Dawson, Mabel Bristow, Mae Bristow, Delmar Hall, Matra Westerfield, Marylee Fortenberry, Agnes Fortenberry. Third Row: Maggie Bristow, Iva Spivy, Virgie Price, Eva Dawson, Vada Price, Delia Price, Amanda Fortenberry, Ozella Grey. Top Row: Archie Bristow, Cleo Croom (teacher), Arthur Wright, Taylor Dawson.

President - Richard Spades; Secretary - Nan Holloway. Mr. D.K. Vance was class sponsor and Mr. S.H. Kosser was Superintendent. Mr. Kosser's common form of punishment was to have the student walk behind him.

The Senior Play was titled "People Are Funny." Cast members included: Evelyn Robertson Flippo as Jussie Budd - ambitious mother; John N. Moore as Kenny Budd - only son; Edgar Jones as John Budd - husband; Audrey Justus as Helen Budd - oldest daughter; Nan Holloway as Betty Budd - youngest daughter; Rowena Spades as Winnie Wehle - the girl next door; J.L. Starks as Elmer Wehle - father next door; Noble Richey as Jack Whitman - a young man from Chicago; Richard Spades as Arthur Fairchild - a friend of Jack's; Alene Smith as Florence Fairchild - a special guest; Melba Smith as Gladys Bliss - secretary; Helen Aaron as Olga Oguispanski - her traveling companion; Nina Collins as Prudence Paine - an aunt from the country; Aileen Smith as Pamela Pain - her darling daughter.

Class members became businessmen, pharmacists, nurses, museum directors, teachers, engineers, depot agents, college professors, and housewives. Most are retired but a few remain active working in a second career. Class members that are deceased include: Helen Aaron, Aileen Smith, Audrey Justus, Alene Smith, and Noble Richey. Each class member in their own way has made a special contribution to society and will always be remembered as the unique class it was to graduate from Black Rock High School.

BLACK ROCK CLASS OF 1954-1955

Class motto: "Not Finished; Just Begun"

At the last Alumni Association Banquet (July 1998) as a tribute to our fallen warriors: Lena, Eula, and Lavelle, the 1955 Class raised in excess of $500.00 for the BRHS Scholarship Fund, which presently totals more than $10,000 for scholarship assistance to a deserving graduating senior.

When we were freshmen our pick for class sponsor was Farris Herren. In the normal picking order of selection seniors get first choice, juniors second choice, sophomores third choice, and freshmen fourth choice. The upper classmen usually pick the coach, superintendent, agriculture teacher, or commercial teacher. When we were sophomores we had third pick, and picked Mr. Herren. Then when we were juniors with the second pick we again selected Mr. Herren. Then, when we become seniors with the top choice - who did we select? Mr. Herren, of course. He was great to us throughout our school years. Thank you, Mr. Farris Herren.

All of the class of '55 were leaders in their own right. One in particular excelled in jocosity. Every day was fulfillment of high school high jinks. This spirit of unrestrained fun continued until his passing - the "Master of Mirthfulness" was our friend, Mose Lavelle Robertson. Thank you, Mose!

Written by class member Wayne Starnes. Walnut Ridge, Arkansas; cattle / horse ranch manager.

Synopsis of Class members 44 years later:

LENA MCCARROL: Deceased; Secretarial / Bookkeeping lived at Jonesboro, Arkansas.

BILL JUDKINS: Retired from Steel Case Office Equipment, Grand Rapids, Michigan. Current residence Maynard, Arkansas raising cattle.

PATSY WADDELL CLARK: Currently resides at Portia, Arkansas; Bookkeeper for Lawrence County Co-op.

SHIRLEY GAINES GILL: Presently living at Poria, Arkansas; Retired farmer.

GWEN SMITH: Last known address Cincinnati, Ohio.

CHARLES "BUTCH" SMITH: Resides in Lenexa, Kansas; Retired from Swift Packing Company.

BOB DOUGLAS: Resides in Heber Springs, Arkansas: Retired Fence Company Owner.

JOAN FRAZIER TURNER: Resides in Cerritos, California; Housewife.

RILEY MILLIGAN: Currently living at Portia, Arkansas; Retired Garage Owner / Mechanic.

JAMES ROBERTSON: Resident of Black Rock, Arkansas; Retired Military.

SUE CLARK: Resident of Rockford, Illinois; Housewife.

HAROLD JUNYOR: Resident of Taft / Bakersfield, California. Retired Oil Field Worker.

EULA WHITE: Deceased; Housewife; lived in Hoxie, Arkansas.

WAYNE STARNES: Currently living at Walnut Ridge, Arkansas; Retired Federal Government.

HARRY GAINES: Resident of Arnold, Missouri; Retired banking employee.

JIM HOLOBAUGH: Presently residing in Ava, Missouri; Retired school principal / cattle farmer.

LAVELLE ROBERTSON: Deceased; lived at Mount Vernon Arkansas (near Black Rock); Retired heavy equipment operator with Ben M. Hogan and Meridian Companies; Livestock Farmer.

THEDIA GRAY: Resides in Jonesboro, Arkansas; Housewife.

GEORGE BOYD, JR.: Resides in Ravenden, Arkansas; gravel hauler for Meridian Company.

BILLY SMITH: Resides in Walnut Ridge, Arkansas; Retired from Vulcan Company.

NEMA LAWSON: Address unknown.

JOE PONDER: Resides near Little Rock,

JOHN DODSON: Resident of Marion, Indiana; Retired from General Motors; has cattle / farming interests.

DALE SMITH: Resident of Black Rock, Arkansas; Retired farmer.

FARRIS HERREN: Deceased; Retired school teacher and 1955 class sponsor.

M.D. WILLIAMS: Resident of Jonesboro, Arkansas; Retired school administrator; 'Doc' Williams was Superintendent from freshmen through senior year.

—Wayne Starnes

CLOVER BEND SCHOOL

The first Clover Bend School (two rooms) was so crowded, in January, 1938, the school

Main building at Clover Bend School.

board, (Ora Hallmark, Arthur Matthews and Clarence Brand), moved the students to the community center. Head teacher Logan, with a wagon and team and assisted by helpful parents loaded the desks and chairs and school materials and moved to the community center.

The community center buildings were converted into an educational center, establishing the first permanent Clover Bend School in July of 1939. Four small elementary schools (Hopewell, Lauratown, Clover Bend and Duvall) were consolidated to establish Clover Bend's first high school. Some students from Arbor Grove, Minturn, Counts and Coffman came and altogether this made an enrollment of well over 200 students at the new school This was a real asset to the community.

By the end of the first school year, the first graduating class consisted of Marjorie Smith, Marjorie Hallmark and Nova Terry. They graduated in May, 1940.

Numerous school traditions were established in these first years. The student body voted and chose the Eagle as the Clover Bend mascot. Blue and Gold were chosen as the school colors. The school news, *The Eagle Screams*, was first published in *The Times Dispatch*.

High school activities included competitive basketball for boys and girls. Many winning teams and outstanding players were a part of Clover Bend.

The Community Center housed Clover Bend School from its inception in 1939, until its death in 1983, with 44 years of rich and exciting history.
–*Alda Ramsey.*

COFFMAN SCHOOL 1938

This is Coffman School group 1938. The school was located on the road south of Portia, going to Lauratown and Clover Bend. It consolidated with the Clover Bend School soon afterwards. –*Willene Kirkland.*

MT. VERNON SCHOOL

The Mt. Vernon School District, located between Black Rock and Imboden, was formed in March 1852. The first school board members were Edward Holt, N.E. Steadman, L.S. Bobo, and Green R. Jones. These men contracted with James Underwood to build a building of hewed logs 22 by 26 feet long and one and a half stories high. Mr. Underwood would be paid $1,852. Several years later another building was built about one-half mile north and east of the

Coffman School: The students are: Top row: E. A. Medlock, Glen Sharp, Walter Denton, Nail Sharp and teachers, Margie Mullens and Dennis Mullen. Second row: Bill Doyle, Paul Dyle, Paul Weatherford, Grady Medlock, Ennis Hacker, Inez Kirkland, Vera Pratt, Ruby Malone, Corrine Benn. Third row: Nolan Claxton, Park Jeffery, Zane Kirkland, Clarington Vanhorn, Anna Ruth McCall, Jessie Fern McCall, William Denton, Carolyn Jones, Nell Hedrick, Juanita Ballard, Jewel Farmer, Harold Kirkland. Fourth row: Kenneth Oldham, J. O. Kirkland, June Helm, Sue Turnbow, Lois Hacker, Fern Oldham, Yvonne Ussery, Florence Helm, Evelyn Hedrick. Fifth row: James Hacker, Eugene Hendon, Billy Joe Kirkland, Wallace Lew Allen, unknown, Aaron Hacker, Bobby Mullen, J. C. Hendon, Rosa Malone, Clara Mae Benn, Margie Farmer, Kathleen Sharp. Sixth row: front: first four unknown, Claybourne Farmer, Maggie Jane McCall, Gene Hacker, Jimmie Ussery, Judy Medlock, Maxie Trimmer, Inez Townsley, Bonnie Sue Graham, Betty Trimmer and Dennis Lewallen.

Mt. Vernon School, 1922. Bottom Row-left to right: Vela Robertson, Lucy Brandon, Hershel Weir, Rena Beeler, Mildred Woodson, Raymond Beeler, Vernon Robertson, Elsie Roland, Vivian Swindle, ?, Charlie Smith (teacher) and son Bernis. Second row: Gladys Roland, Clara Pickney, ? Milan, Vella Buram, Lucian Weir, Doris Robertson, Ira Long, Cody Long, Earl Long, Raymond Swindle. Third row: Annie Milan, Charis Roland, Bertha Weir, Harry Pickney, Russell Forbes, Jewel Thompson, Esmon Beeler, Andrew Stratton, Hubert Weir, Albert Beeler, Clyde Woodson, T.J. Robertson, Ora Kildow, Alvin Pickney.

building. It was also constructed of logs. In 1892 the Frisco Railroad went through the Mt. Vernon School District. Districts such as Mt. Vernon could vote a one mill school tax and have money to hold 10 weeks of summer school and five months of winter school.

Years later school districts that had railroads began to accumulate extra money and they began to get rid of their log buildings and build more modern facilities. Sometime about 1902 the Mt. Vernon District School Board bought a 10-acre tract of timber land.

On the west end of the tract of land, an area of two acres was cleared to build a one-room school house and play ground. In the summer term of school the boys in the upper grades would play match games of baseball with the Pleasant Hill School District.

Family names who had children attending Mt. Vernon School included John McCarroll, Dan Beeler, Andrew Stratton, Frank Long, Mose Robertson, Bill McLaughlin, Bertha Langing, Will Weir, Pat Kildow, Dock Smith, and Jim Phillips.

First Sloan-Hendrix Academy building, 1899-1923.

Minturn School 1949: Front Row-left to right: Larry Robert, Thaddeus Allen. Second row: Eunice Robert, teacher, Clyde Galbreath, Glenda S. Smithee, Geraldine Knight, Arthurline Carter, Charles Smith, Barbara Whitlow, Mary A. Galbreath, Johnny Galbreath, Cloyce House, Cloyce Smithee, Alice Rains, teacher. Third row: Mattie Lue Carter, Edna Dodd, Glendola Allen, Mazie Simms, Earl Dale Baker, Kathryn Whitlow. Fourth row: Billy Slayton, Jesse Baker, Nancy Ray, Dale Pace, Jaunita Whitlow, Reba Wiles, ? Knight, Geraldine Smithee, Wanda McCarty, Shelby Allen, Jerry Simms, Angie Pace. Fifth row: Freda Baker, Norma Simms, Oneida Simms, Glenda Simms, Frances Allen, Wanda Knight, Freda Wiles, Barbara Wiles, Boyce Smithee, Tom Dodd.

New Friendship School.

Surridge School

In about 1936 the present building was made larger. Concrete steps replaced the former wooden steps. A stage was built inside the building and the school had programs for the community every two or three weeks on Friday nights. About 1948 the one-room country school was forced to consolidate with the Black Rock School District. The building was later used for the Mt. Vernon Church.

School teachers at Mt. Vernon were Julian Smith, John (J.C.) Claud, Lucy Beeler, Virgil Baker, Ruth Price, Clarence Taylor, Frank Noblin, S.H. Kosser, Mrs. Carson, Beatrice Harris, Dula Baker, Ruth Andrews, Jewel Verkler, R.W. "Bob" Moore, Bob Underwood, Farris Herren, Mrs. Stanford, Virginia Smith, Josie Jane Brannon, Grover Davis, and Joe Dent.
Submitted by Julian Smith

NEW FRIENDSHIP SCHOOL

New Friendship School was located in Randolph County and was part of Sloan-Hendrix Imboden School District 45. Students who attended school there are as follows (1932): Mary Agnes Johnson, James Johnson, Joe L. Johnson, Lola Mae Johnson, James Oaks, Tommie Lea Johnson, Fracie Anne Oaks, Selena Oaks, Marvin W. Oaks,

James L. Shockley, Deloise Shockley, Leroy Shockley, Statin Marshall Shockley, Tommie W. Young, Marlin Lee Young, J. L. Johnson, Wanda Lee Johnson, Carl Johnson, Maggie Lorane Johnson, Nina Johnson, Hazel Taylor. This school was for black students.
Submitted by Anna Lue Cook.

POWHATAN MALE AND FEMALE ACADEMY

The first school house in Powhatan was a log building located east of the present building. Andrew H. Imboden, a resident of Powhatan, constructed a building in 1854 in which school terms of two months were held. B.F. Matthews, a native of Georgia, was recruited as school master and he named the school "The Powhatan Male and Female Academy." The Academy continued to serve Powhatan until 1861 when the Civil War stopped everything up to 1865.

After the war classes resumed and the district size increased. In 1871 D.L. Montgomery was hired as an instructor by the School Board of Trustees: Champ T. Stuart, D.L. Richey, and J.E. Thompson. In 1872 George Matthews taught for a three month summer term and three month winter term at $50 per

month salary. Miss Fannie Jackson was hired as instructor in 1874 and was paid $270 from the Black River Township Teacher's Fund by John N. Campbell, Trustee for School District #9.

In 1880, George Thornsburg petitioned the court to allow the courtroom of the Powhatan Courthouse to be used as a school room as there was no school building at the time. Apparently the previous school building burned or was destroyed; there are no records to explain why there was no school.

On October 18, 1889 John A. Lindsey, nephew of James Ficklin, deeded to Powhatan School District #9, Block No. 38 and the present building was erected. School records list 92 students, 35 white males and 57 white females in 1889. J.F. Grant was the instructor. In 1895 Maude E. McGee was instructor to 62 students and in 1896 N.A. Moore taught with an enrollment of 66 students.

The building rests on a stone foundation and has an exterior of wood weather-board siding. There are two class rooms; each room has five large windows and between the two rooms is a folding partition. Heat was furnished by use of wood or coal. The class rooms were furnished with factory built seats and desks. A cistern was dug at the northeast outside corner and enclosed. A well was drilled a few feet east of the cistern and there was a water bucket and all used a common dipper. There is a large bell in the attic which was first used on one of the early steamboats which came up Black River.

In 1911 there were listed 52 males and 68 females and Mr. Walter E. McLeod was the teacher. C.N Casper and Vena Saffell Park were instructors in 1923. Farris Herren taught at Powhatan from 1947 to 1954. Other teachers were Mary Steadman, Bill Swink, Ed Moore, Clara Poindexter, Mrs. R.B. Warner, Sylvia Verkler, Dula Baker, Velma Gray, Pauline Chaney, Eva Williams, R.C. Ingram, Maude Starr Brannon, Annie Alls, Effie Kell Bragg, H.C. Coke, Ruth Hall Cooper, Opal Hall, Lillian Brannon, Rheamona Clark, Mrs. Mason Harris, Raymond Wingo, Edith Madden and Ruth Andrews.

In 1948 came consolidation with Black Rock, but the first six grades were left at Powhatan. In 1955 the first six grades were taken to Black Rock and the building was left vacant. The building was named to the National Register of Historic Places. It is currently in the process of being restored as one of the few one- and two-room schools left in the state of Arkansas.–Darlene Flippo Moore.

Richwoods School, 1955 or 1956. Danny Barr, Danny Ellis, Lloyd Wallace, Alvie Swan, teacher, Darrell Davis, ? Osborn, Floyd Wallace, Cotton Davis, Dwight Ellis, Joan Stone, Butch Stone, Linda Stone, John Jackson, ? Osborn, Linda Parker, ? Brown, Carol Brown, Rita Brown, Larry Dale Richey, Kathy Johnson, Sherman Wallace.

RICHWOODS SCHOOL

Richwoods School, an eight grade school, was located in school district #10. Originally consisting of one room with a second added later, the building was a white clapboard frame with two outhouses. It was designed by Caleb Dillport, who taught there many years, as well as at Clear Lake.

Children at Richwoods began in the Card Class, which usually contained three or four pupils. Featuring cards with pictures and one or two words, the Card Class was followed by the Chart Class, the Primer Class and then first grade.

Behind the school was a large ball field and as Erna Saylors (the daughter of Caleb Dillport) recalled, there were plays and many other activities. "It (Richwoods) was a very happy place to grow up", she added.

After completing all eight grades, those who wanted could complete the last four years of high school at Walnut Ridge.

Among those who taught at Richwoods were: Mr. Brown, Luceal Wooldridge, Caleb Dillport, Clara Russell, Thelma Eskridge, Edgar Stone, Howard Allison, Curtis Davis, Margie Dillport, Alva Swan, Earl Smith and Clyde Smith.

In 1948, residents of Richwoods petitioned the Lawrence County School Board to merge Richwoods School District with Walnut Ridge. After the public hearings required by law, their petition was approved. On January 14, 1949, Richwoods School District #10 was annexed to Walnut Ridge School District #19 by the Lawrence County Board of Education.

Only farm land exists now where the school building once stood.

Submitted by Regina Horton.

WILLIAMS BAPTIST COLLEGE

In June, 1941, Dr. H. E. Williams, pastor of First Baptist Church in Pocahontas, led in the establishment of Williams Baptist College (originally Southern Baptist College) in Pocahontas. For several years Dr. Williams had been building support for the college. The new college, which opened on September 10, 1941, was actually a restoration of Baptist higher education in northeastern Arkansas. Maynard Baptist Academy in Randolph County, Woodland Baptist College and Jonesboro Baptist College had all flourished briefly during the period 1900-1935. Williams College benefited from these pioneering educational efforts; some alumni and friends of the Academy and Jonesboro Baptist were also supporters of the new institution. Significantly, Williams College acquired the large library holdings of Jonesboro Baptist College. Williams College received books and the science department from Mountain Home Baptist College, and books from Central College in Conway and from Missouri Baptist College in Poplar Bluff.

For five years the college experienced steady growth in Pocahontas, but on December 26, 1946, the administration building was destroyed by fire and the college moved to Walnut Ridge. In 1948, a milestone was reached when the Arkansas Baptist State Convention included the college in its budget. In 1968, the ABSC officially adopted the college. The college was accredited by the North Central Association in 1962.

In the spring of 1973, the college trustees announced that Dr. H. E. Williams, who had served as president for 32 years had been appointed President-Emeritus and that Dr. D. Jack Nicholas had been elected the second president of the institution. Nicholas, who had served the college since 1966, as Vice-President and professor of Psychology, led the college to four year status, strengthened the college's endowment and led in several new building programs on campus. Nicholas resigned as president in 1990, and returned to the classroom as Professor of Psychology. He retired in 1997.

In 1991, the Board of Trustees named Dr. Jimmy Millikin, Professor of Religion, as the third president. Millikin served two years and returned to the professorate at Mid America

Seminary. On August 1, 1994, Dr. Gary C. Huckabee, a vice president from Dallas Baptist University, was named the fourth president. After 18 months, he resigned and the board elected Dr. Jerol Swaim as the fifth president in July, 1995.

Dr. Swaim has served the college since 1964, as Professor of History and Vice-President for Academics. Since Swaim became president, the college has received several major gifts to its endowment fund and has completed several major capital projects.

More than 20,000 students have matriculated at Williams. The college currently offers degrees in Art, English, Religion, History, Music, Elementary Education, Physical Eduction, Biology, Psychology, Business, Liberal Arts, Religious Education, Church Music, Pre-Law and Pre-Med.

SLOAN-HENDRIX ACADEMY

Sloan-Hendrix Academy was established in 1899, under authorization provided by the Constitution of Hendrix College, Conway, Arkansas, as an affiliated academy; that is, as an integral part of the Hendrix College System. Sloan-Hendrix was the second of five affiliated academies to be established, but was by far the longest lived. By 1906, only Sloan-Hendrix had survived as an academy affiliated with Hendrix College, but also in that year, affiliation status with the college was terminated. The academy continued to operate, under sponsorship of the North Arkansas Conference of the Methodist Episcopal, South until 1931.

The citizens of Imboden, provided the campus and the money to secure the buildings and equipment needed to meet the approval of the Board of Trustees of Hendrix College. The first campus was located at the southeast end of the town. In 1923, the academy was relocated to a farm on the northwest end of the town.

The academy was almost constantly beset with financial difficulties. Although it was established as an affiliated academy with Hendrix College and continued under the sponsorship and general administration of the church, it received no funds from either of these before 1913. Beginning in 1913, the General Board of Education made annual appropriations for the operation of the school and the North Arkansas Annual Conference of the church included in its annual assessments funds earmarked for the academy. The problem of obtaining sufficient funds became so complex and torturous in the late 1920s, that the school was sold to the Imboden Public Schools, effective in the early spring of 1931.

During its history, 277 students graduated from Sloan-Hendrix Academy. Most of them attended college one or more years after graduation. One hundred and six graduates entered the field of education, 14 entered the ministry and three entered both fields.

For a number of years, after the Imboden School system took over the high school, it was still called Sloan-Hendrix Academy. Later, the name was changed to Sloan-

Students and faculty of the Powhatan Male and Female Academy enjoy a break from classes. The woman teacher at right is believed to be Bessie McLeod. (Circa 1913)

Hendrix Public Schools, under which name it is known today.

In 1941, the Eaton Hall, building constructed in 1923, burned. It was rebuilt in the same walls, but was not renamed Eaton Hall. In 1957, again the three story building burned. A new building was erected south of the site of the old one. The walls of the burned construction were destroyed and a cafetorium, with an attached home economics department was built on that site.

The first gym was erected in 1924. It burned in 1970. A new gym was built that year, also.

As was stated in the academy history, graduates from Sloan-Hendrix High School have entered fields of teaching, law, the min-istry, banking and other business, military, medicine and public relations.

Sloan-Hendrix has been known for its sports record. By having excellent coaches during the years, many trophies have been won and most important is the number of sportsmanship trophies displayed, along with others.

The school has grown to an enrollment of 565 pupils, with 248 of these in the upper six grades. There are 43 members of the faculty and 25 classified employees.

Mr. J. C. Eaton served the longest tenure as the head of the school. He was principal from 1911, until 1927, when a superintendent, J. F. Glover, a Methodist minister, was hired. Mr. Eaton remained on the faculty until 1934, when he resigned after being injured in an automobile accident.

S. B. Wilford, also a Methodist minister, was superintendent when the school was taken over by the Imboden School District. He was followed by Millard Phillips. Other superintendents have been G. S. Butler, H. B. Sallis, Revis Casper, Marshall Matthews, Dalton Henderson, Larry Davis, and Michael Holland, the present superintendent, who has been there since the 1993-1994 school year. Four of these nine superintendents are graduates of Sloan-Hendrix.

The 100th anniversary of the school was recently celebrated.

Submitted by Mrs. Edith Stovall.

Churches

ALICIA CHURCH OF CHRIST

The Church of Christ assembled for worship in 1921 at the Lodge Hall. Among the families attending were Otto Milner, Tom Noblin, Bud House, Will Whitmire, Floyd Pearce, Dr. Gibson, John Shell, the Allens, Kimbroughs, Callahans, Bakers, Nicholsons and Darrs.

The building burned in 1937 and the congregation moved to the schoolhouse for services. The members rented a plot of ground and donated their time to plant and harvest a cotton crop to help finance the building of a new church. This church was finished in 1939.

Ministers serving the church through the years have been L. C. Sears, Noland Lemmons, J. H. Curry, Taylor Davis, L. N. Moody, Donald Layne, Alva Dunham, Bud Whitmire, Steve Prestidge, Arthur Inman and the present minister is Lloyd Clark.

We have approximately 18 members now. The church has been remodeled on the inside. We have a nice fellowship hall in the back where we used to have classrooms. We have a nice nursery and two nice bathrooms.

We meet for Sunday morning and evening services, and on Wednesday evening. We have gospel meetings and we help the Children's Home in Paragould with a monthly donation and coin banks. We also send a monthly donation to the "Voice of Truth" program. *–Joelene Shell.*

ARBOR GROVE FREE WILL BAPTIST CHURCH

It has been passed down that the first religious services were held in a brush arbor about one half mile southeast of the present church in 1885 by a Presbyterian preacher. During these services, a dog ran a rabbit through the brush arbor and Rabbit Roust became the name of the community until a school was built and it was then called Arbor Grove. The religious services were held in the school until 1890, when a church building was erected serving the Free Will Baptist, Methodist, and Presbyterian denominations. Henry Colbert deeded one acre of land where the church building was standing and was to be jointly used by these denominations. Members of these churches furnished labor and material and built a frame church.

The Free Will Baptist was organized in 1890 by the efforts of Jasper Pace and Henry Colbert and the church was called Love Divine Free Will Baptist Church. In 1893, the church belonged to the East Black River Association and reported to have 20 members and A. J. Rowlett as pastor. In 1896, Joseph Hutchins was pastor and he reported 31 members, "the state of religion good, state of union good, degree of interest in public and social meeting good" and $16.25 paid the pastor. In August, 1896, the East Black River Association joined the Polk Bayou Association and Love Divine was in that association until 1950 when it joined the Social Band Association and changed its name to Arbor Grove.

On May 9, 1927, a tornado destroyed the church and a new building was erected by October and services were held in that building until 1989 when the church erected the present building. The present pastor is Brother David Outlaw.

ARBOR GROVE MISSIONARY BAPTIST CHURCH

The Spring River Baptist Association of Missionary Baptist Churches had been in existence about 100 years when the Arbor Grove Missionary Baptist Church was organized in 1927.

This church had the following charter members: Brother Henry Giles Brady, wife (Lee Ann), sons Edd, Dent and Lester; daughters, Allie and Mary; Brother John D. Lee and wife, Jennie Brady Lee; Brother Arthur Lee and wife, Vida Milligan Lee; Mrs. J. H. "Jim" Ratliff; Brother Graham and wife, and perhaps the George McCarroll family, with Brother J. H. Martin as assisting minister-moderator.

These Baptists met in the Duvall school house, a two room school building. Soon after the Baptists started meeting, the Church of Christ began meeting in the other room of this school building. They met at alternate hours, the Baptist at 10 a.m., the Church of Christ at 11 a.m. However, the church prospered and several members were added.

Naturally this arrangement did not prove satisfactory, so a plan was put into action in 1931 to buy one half acre of ground from the Arbor Grove School District. J. G. "Doc" Neece saw the school board members and they consented to sell the one half acre for $20. Then J. G. Neece gave the oak timber to build the framework of the church. The members would have to cut the trees and haul the logs in wagons to nearby Buercklin's sawmill. Immediately work began on the church building by such men as H. G. Brady, Dent, Edd and Lester Brady, A. L. Lee, John Lee, Budgie Little and his father J. B. Little, J. G. Neece, and Tom Oliver. Many of these men were good carpenters and all the work was donated. Then came the time when finished lumber was needed, so the trustees signed a note to the Hoxie Lumber Company for $600 to finish the building.

The congregation began meeting in September of 1931 in this unfinished building with no floor, homemade cypress pews, and heated by two warm morning stoves. The H. G. Brady Crown organ was moved in for services.

The following people were officers and participants in the first service: Walter Griffen, pas-

Alicia Methodist Church, 1912, Mrs. Ruby Owens is on the front row, eleventh person from right.

Arbor Grove Missionary Baptist Church.

Immaculate Heart of Mary Catholic Church, Walnut Ridge, about 1955.

tor; A. L. Lee led the first song, "Sweet Hour of Prayer"; Henry Brady led the first prayer; John D. Lee, Superintendent of Sunday School; J. G. Neece, teacher of the Bible class.

Later, a concrete floor was laid. In 1955, new pews were made by Danny Kopp of Hoxie. The cedar for the ends of the pews came from the Charles M. Bracy farm near Batesville, Arkansas, and was donated by John H. Bracy.

Sunday School rooms were added about 1964. The church was carpeted and bathrooms added in 1976.

The following men have been pastors of the church: Walter Griffen; Edgar Wilkerson, L. D. Bowman, George Pierce, James F. Dew, Paul Goodwin, James Ivy, Gordon Cooper, Milam Cowan, Robert Frazier, A. J. Johnson, Luther Lott, Cecil Lewallen, Bob Miller, John Kaffka, Hershell Lee, Rudy McClanahan, Robert Miller, Otho Norris, Frank Manning, J. H. Martin, Richard Dancer, Joe L. Schultz, and Carl Rider.

Ordained ministers from this church were Gordon Oliver, Clay Oliver and B. B. Sawyer.

Deacons who have served are H. G. Brady, John D. Lee, M. A. Corbett, Arthur Lee, John H. Bracy, Harry Stark and Martin Whitlow.
–Helen Weir.

CATHOLIC CHURCH OF LAWRENCE COUNTY

Mass was celebrated for the first time in Hoxie in 1881, at the home of Mr. and Mrs. S. C. Dowell by Father John E. Weibel, then located in Jonesboro. From then on, for some length of time, it was Father Weibel's custom to visit Hoxie at regular intervals, saying Mass sometimes at the Dowell home and sometimes at the Boas Hotel.

For a number of years, due to Hoxie being a railroad town, the population was transient. For instance, when Father Weibel was making his visits there, it was not at all unusual for him to come on an occasion, make the acquaintance of his parishioners, and the next time find that it was necessary to look through almost the whole congregation before finding one of the old faces. In view of this fact, he found it difficult to maintain the stability necessary for building up the parish and hence too much stress cannot be laid upon the help given to him by the few faithful souls who remained permanently in the town. Chief among these were Mr. and Mrs. S. C. Dowell, Mrs. Mary Boas, and Mr. and Mrs. Pat Whelan. These above mentioned peopled were also the first Catholic settlers here.

In 1886, Father McQuaid followed Father Weibel as pastor of the Catholic Church in Hoxie.

In the pages of the history of the Diocese of Little Rock, Father McQuaid's activities are numerously recorded. Here, as elsewhere, he left his mark of devotion to the faith. It was in 1886, that he erected Hoxie's first church, a beautiful, if rather small, frame building which served the needs of the congregation for 38 years. He also had the property surrounding the church improved and fenced in. This new church was named All Saints' Church.

Father Cattani succeeded Father McQuaid and maintained the parish on the solid foundation which his predecessor had established.

From the time of Father Cattani until 1913, there are no records to indicate the names of the priests attending this mission. It is to be presumed that it was attended at intervals by one of the neighboring pastors.

In 1913, Father Heagney took charge, traveling to Hoxie every two weeks from Little Rock College, Little Rock, where he was stationed. It was during his pastorate that the old church burned. He immediately undertook the building of a new one. By dint of hard work on his part and the generosity of the parishioners and others, he was able to successfully complete the enterprise. The new All Saints' Church was dedicated by the Rt. Reverend John B. Morris on May 15, 1914.

In 1920, Father S. J. Peoples was assigned to Hoxie. The congregation had been steadily growing during those years and by 1923, it had outgrown the old building and it necessitated the building of a new one. In 1924, a half block of ground was purchased in another section of town and a new church was erected at the cost of $20,000. At the same time, a parish hall was built. This new church was named Mary Immaculate Church. The first Mass was celebrated on June 14, 1925.

A Catholic school was established in 1929, through the gift of five lots by Mrs. Anna Boas Gibson and the contribution of an 11 room house by Mr. and Mrs. C. J. Saenger.

Priests serving the Catholic community over the next several years were: S. J. Propus, R. J. Marmon, E. N. Hinckley, R. J. McCauly, Joseph Murphey, John J. Mulligan, L. H. Scheper, Ed. J. M. McCormick, Thomas P. Reynolds, J. M. Walshe, John C. O'Dwyer and George P. Freyaldenhoven.

Reverend Joseph A. King was pastor from 1949 until 1959. During his tenure a new site was located in the neighboring town of Walnut Ridge. On December 11, 1949, the site was blessed and ground was broken for a new church and rectory. The new location on West Free Street was donated by Mr. and Mrs. Henry Baltz. First Mass in the new church was offered by Father King on Sunday, May 7, 1950. The cost of the new church and rectory was $21,000 and was a brick veneer building measuring 106 x 80 feet. Five rooms at the rear of the church served as a rectory for the pastor. The new church, Immaculate Heart of Mary, was blessed and dedicated by Bishop Albert Fletcher on Sunday, October 8, 1950.

Priests following Father King were Louis V. Stemac, John J. Kettler and Robert F. Boyle.

Reverend Robert Dagwell arrived in 1964, and under his direction a parish hall was built next to the church.

The Clear Lake Free Will Baptist Church.

Since 1971, the church has been served by Fathers Francis D. Colavechio, Bernard L. Bolds, Michael Bass, Les Farley, and presently, by Father Clayton Gould.

During Father Bolds' tenure, 1973-1995, the church underwent a complete interior redecoration, a bell tower was added to the property, and, through the generosity of Robert H. Smith, the grounds were landscaped and an Italian statue of the Holy Family was placed in a garden setting.

At the present time, Father Gould celebrates Mass two Sundays each month and the other Sundays are observed by a Word and Communion Service that is conducted by the local Catholic Deacon, Marlin Tate. *–Lucia Warner Allen.*

CLEAR LAKE FREE WILL BAPTIST CHURCH

The Clear Lake Free Will Baptist Church is one of the oldest churches in Lawrence County, having been in existence at least since the late 1800s. In 1904, they had a membership of 117.

In the early years, the church was the scene of big revivals in the summer and they, as well as many other churches for miles around, would have their baptizings in Clear Lake. Sometimes large crowds from several different churches would be baptized at one time. The church met the first 40 years or so in the school house on the banks of Clear Lake. When the new school house was built in 1938, the church began having services there. The Clear Lake School was closed about 1960. The building is now owned by the church. The Clear Lake Church has been affiliated with the Social Band Association practically since its beginning.

Two of the very earliest ministers at the Clear Lake Church were Jesse Burrow, in the late 1890s, and Fred B. Starnes, in the early 1900s. Some of the ministers who have served the church since then have been D. C. Jones, W. C. Lakey, Henry Pauley, Melvin Shelton, L. D. Johnson, J. W. Russell, Thurman Johnson, Jim Surles, James Gosha, D. W. Pinkston, Claud Harmon, Leonard Milligan and Joe Barnett.

On April 19, 1998, Relton Forehand was recognized for having been a deacon of the church for 45 years. *–Joyce Holder.*

CLEAR SPRINGS BAPTIST CHURCH

Clear Springs Baptist Church was built in 1883. The lumber was purchased at a sawmill one fourth mile from Hope Cemetery in Imboden. The school district which was already established had been named Clear Springs after the spring which runs

Clear Springs Baptist Church, original built 1883, rock building erected 1941.

Members standing on front steps of Clover Bend Church.

Fellowship Missionary Baptist Church, 207 Rebecca Lane, Walnut Ridge, Arkansas.

through the countryside. Thus, the church took the same name. In 1886, M. D. Hudson and his wife deeded the land that the church sits on to W. B. Hudson and S. J. Park who were trustees of the church. Mr. Hudson hewed the logs out for the old building. It was said there were no knots in the wood whatsoever. Some of the early family members were the Butlers, Chapmans, Easts, Forresters, Gibsons, Hendersons, Hudsons, Parks, Phillips, Smiths, and Wilsons. Clear Springs is the third oldest member of the Black Rock River Association of Baptist Churches. Tent meetings were held in the grove on the grounds of the old church. Mrs. Susan Hudson who lived near the church, opened her home to visitors who lived far away. When the old building was torn down, William Hudson found shingles with his father's and other friends' names written on them. Unfortunately, they were destroyed when his home burned.

In 1940, the old building was torn down. The school house was used for church services until the new building was completed in 1941. The rock exterior of the building was furnished by Lee Tate. To help pay for the new building, the ladies of the church sold lunches at auctions. The money to finish the building was borrowed from Black Rock Bank and was paid off by donations during homecoming. Labor on the new building was donated by members. Kitchen, bathrooms and classrooms have been added on since. Today there are 50 church members. *–Lovis Stewart.*

CLOVER BEND METHODIST EPISCOPAL CHURCH

The Clover Bend Methodist Episcopal Church, South was founded in 1919. Edwin Mouzon was Bishop of North Arkansas Conference, U. L. Oliver was presiding elder of the Batesville District and E. A. Horn was pastor. Charter member family names were Slayton, Hallmark, Franks, Coats, Schater, Webb and Ford.

Until 1939, the church used the old Clover Bend School on the brake. When the new school-community center was built, the congregation met there one Sunday each month

for about eight years. Walnut Ridge shared their pastor on Sunday afternoon once each month.

The funds for a new building were collected over a period of time. In 1946-47, Chester Goff, a local contractor and assisted by Homer Callahan, carpenter, built the new building. Jeff Brand Sr. donated the land.

Clover Bend had been on charges with a number of small community churches, i.e. Arbor Grove, Black Rock, Portia, Lauratown, Minturn, Strangers Home and Hopewell. They were with Paragould and Batesville Districts. Furnishings for the new building were given by the District from the closed Success church. Members refinished the beautiful oak furniture for a most impressive sanctuary.

The church was dedicated in 1947, by District Superintendent A. N. Storey. The trustees were O. H. Hallmark, Homer Callahan and C. H. Brand. Patsy Hallmark was pianist.

In 1987, Clover Bend closed its church doors and joined with Hoxie United Methodist Church. They took with them the furnishings and their sanctuary. Hoxie converted it into a beautiful fellowship hall.*–Viola Meadows.*

CLOVER BEND MISSIONARY BAPTIST CHURCH

The Clover Bend Missionary Baptist Church was established in 1938, with a meeting being held in the home of Mr. and Mrs. A. L. Lee. Known charter members were: Mr. and Mrs. Harvey Jean, Mr. and Mrs. A. L. King, Mr. and Mrs. A. L. Lee and Mrs. Ruth Morgan.

Since there was no church building, Sunday School classes were held in the Agricultural Building and preaching services were held in the school auditorium once a month. Other denominations also used the school buildings.

In 1945-46, the original church building was built for approximately $515. Earl Rider deeded the church three acres of ground

across the road from his house, near the high school. Arthur Lee was master carpenter and Harvey Jean, A. L. King, Earl Doyle, Allie Frazier, Earl Rider and probably others, helped build it. All of them donated their time.

In the late 60s, a new brick church was built next to the original one. The old church was purchased and moved to the Freda Buchanan farm.

Some of the remembered pastors were: Edgar Wilkerson, Paul Goodwin, James Ivy, Sidney Cook, Bob Faulkner, Luther Lott, Herman Bonner, Robert Miller, Joe Schultz, Melvin Tinker, Gary Woodard, Melvin Landers, Neil Dowling, Brother Teague, Brother Garner and Bob Frazier.*–Clella Horrell.*

FELLOWSHIP MISSIONARY BAPTIST CHURCH

Fellowship Missionary Baptist Church of Walnut Ridge was organized March 23, 1962, through an arm extended by Bold Springs Baptist Church, Strawberry. There were 15 charter members. Elder Woodrow Wilson was Missionary Pastor.

Property on Rebecca Lane was purchased that fall from Miss Rebecca Andrews and a building was erected. It was enlarged in 1969-70, with pastor's study, office, nursery, lounge and additional classrooms. A kitchen area and fellowship hall were later added.

A 40 x 60 foot building was erected behind the auditorium in 1999, for a fellowship hall with full kitchen facilities.

Three churches have been established through an arm extended to: Calvary Baptist Church, Black Rock in 1976, (now disbanded); Calpules Baptist Church, Calpules, El Salvador, C.A., in 1980, under the leadership of Missionary David Dickson, former member of Fellowship; and Pocahontas Baptist Church, Pocahontas in 1988.

Six men have been ordained to the gospel ministry and other Christian workers have gone out from this church.

We have an active Childrens Ministry, Youth Ministry, Women's Missionary Auxiliary and Bus Ministry.

We are affiliated with the Jonesboro Missionary Baptist Association, Arkansas State Missionary Association, and Baptist Missionary Association of America.

Our internet Home Page is http://users.bscn.com/fbc/

Current membership is 365. Pastor is Elder Bob G. Smith, 870-886-5649, and Associate Pastor is Elder Carl Rider, 870-886-5031.

Site of Salem Church, first Baptist church in Arkansas, about three miles west of Maynard, Arkansas.

First Baptist Church, Walnut Ridge, built in 1990.

We are Bible believing, fundamental and premillenial. We welcome visitors to all our services. –Alice Poteete.

FIRST BAPTIST CHURCH IN ARKANSAS

Our ancestor, Reverend Jesse James, was born 1770-1780, in North Carolina, and arrived in Missouri Territory by 1815. In June, 1816, the Missouri Bethel Baptist Association met in Cape Girardeau County, Missouri, and sent Elders Jesse James, Benjamin Clark, and James Philip Edwards as missionaries to Lawrence County, then Missouri Territory, for the purpose of establishing the first Baptist church in present day Arkansas. The Bethel minutes of September, 1818, state the church was constituted that year with 12 members and was represented by Elders Jesse James, Benjamin Clark and Richard Brazil. Dr. J. M. Peck, the famous missionary, stated when he visited in 1818, Elders Jesse James and Benjamin Clark were the ministers and the location of the church was on Fourche 'a Thomas, and the name of the church was Salem. According to the Bethel minutes of 1819, Salem Church was constituted into another church named Union, also located in Lawrence County on Cypress Creek, with 14 members and represented by Jesse James and Richard Brazil. The Bethel Minutes of 1820, state Union Church in Lawrence County was represented by Jesse James (not present), Richard Brazil and Wilis Wilson. Reverend James was again a messenger from Union in 1923, but was not mentioned in later minutes. David Orr, who was sent to Lawrence County by the Bethel Baptist Association in 1828, stated that when he arrived Reverend James was enfeebled and incapacitated for work.

Reverend Jesse James was enumerated in the 1820 reconstructed census of Arkansas Territory for Lawrence County. The *Arkansas Gazette* in an article dated September 8, 1821, states Colonel John Hines and Jesse James were elected to serve a two year term in the House of Representatives from Lawrence County. This was only the second session of the Legislature and it met for the first time in Little Rock on October 1, 1821. Reverend James lived in Columbia Township in Lawrence County very close to the then disputed Arkansas-Missouri line and apparently because of the boundaries he and several other residents of Columbia Township were enumerated in Wayne County, Missouri, in 1830. He

paid taxes in Columbia Township, Lawrence County, Arkansas, for the years 1830 through 1833. In 1832, while not actively a minister, he did perform the marriage ceremony for his daughter Abigail to Jesse Dodd on November 13, 1832, and was listed in Lawrence County Marriage Book A, page 34, as a licensed preacher.

In the early part of 1834, Reverend Jesse James moved his family to present day Saline County, Arkansas. The *Arkansas Gazette* in a news article dated June 24, 1834, records another marriage performed by the Reverend Jesse James in present day Saline County, Arkansas.

The probate records of Saline County, Arkansas, give us an approximate date of the death of Reverend Jesse James. The bill of sale for his estate was dated March 5, 1836.

In 1954, the Arkansas Baptist State Convention placed a marker at the site of Salem Church and in 1993, it was replaced by another monument. The present location of this site is in Randolph County, off Highway 38, about three miles west of Maynard, Arkansas.
–Duane Wilson and Carole Mayfield.

FIRST BAPTIST CHURCH OF WALNUT RIDGE

In 1885, *The Arkansas Evangel* revealed that three fourths of Arkansas' county seats lacked Baptist congregations. In 1888, the Spring River Baptist Association reported that much of the country comprising Lawrence and Sharp counties lacked "Baptist preaching." In 1888, the Arkansas Baptists State Convention met in Jonesboro and Governor James Eagle and other Baptist leaders determined to establish new Baptist congregations in the northeastern part of the state. Governor Eagle, who served 21 terms as president of the Arkansas Baptist State Convention, was twice elected president of the Southern Baptist Convention; Eagle was deeply committed to "home missions."

Governor Eagle provided encouragement and leadership in the Baptist church planting campaign in northeast Arkansas. More directly involved in the founding of First Baptist in Walnut Ridge, Martin and Lizzie Ball of Mississippi, aided by E. P. Minton, another veteran preacher in the Jonesboro area, provided crucial leadership in the first years of First Baptist, Walnut Ridge. A group of 10 or 12 Baptist believers met with Ball at Mrs. Rutha Rhea's home on

September 19, 1889. Mrs. Rhea opened her home to a Baptist congregation. Mrs. Rhea was a 59 year old widow of Moses Boling Rhea, a successful farmer and businessman. Others who attended the first meeting included: George Anderson, Allen Pierce, T. C. Swindle, Dr. M. V. Camp, J. T. McCullough, Sarah McCullough, Mrs. A. C. Swindle, Mrs. Ida Wilson and Miss Van Camp.

In 1889, Walnut Ridge was a frontier town. It did have a small telephone exchange with some 40 customers and it had a train depot, several cotton gins, livery stables, a freight warehouse, and a few stores, but it still lacked a bank. Walnut Ridge had plenty of taverns and Saturday nights were often punctuated by gunshots and angry howls as revelers stumbled from one saloon to another. Most citizens were peaceful and responsible, but overall the town was rough and unsettled.

Reverend Ball was the first pastor, but he left in 1890, taking a position in Fulton, Kentucky. E. P. Minton, a native of Alabama, became the second pastor. Minton was a bold preacher who believed in church discipline. In the late 1870s, he had purged the First Baptist Church of Jonesboro of most of its membership for what he termed "disregard for Christian standards of behavior." During Minton's tenure, he preached every third Sunday and the church met in the two story frame courthouse, the school house, or the Methodist meeting house.

In 1891, Minton was succeeded by W. P. Kime who received the greater portion of his salary from the state convention, $20.83 and one half cent per month." By 1892, the church's membership had risen to 21 and the congregation managed to contribute $80 toward the pastor's salary and $5.50 to "home and foreign missions."

Kime was succeeded by M. D. Bowers, a native of Tennessee. In 1893, Walnut Ridge suffered a disastrous fire, resulting in a loss of over $100,000, a staggering sum. Yet, in 1894, Kime would lead the church in building a frame structure that would cost almost $1000, with Aunt Rutha Rhea contributing about $500 to the project.

The Sunday School greatly benefitted from the new, permanent church home. In 1894, E. P. Minton returned for a second tenure as pastor. Minton was succeeded by J. W. Scott, and later by T. C. Mahan who was pastor until 1901. Shortly before her death in 1903, Ruthie Rhea had given the church her home and three building lots. This was especially helpful when the frame structure burned in 1908, and the church constructed a new meeting house. By 1906, the church had 100 Sunday School pupils enrolled; the church membership was 116.

Charles Elliott was pastor from 1914 to 1917. More than any other pastor he helped to bring structure and organization to the Walnut Bridge church and was instrumental in founding the Black River Baptist Association. During World War I, the church was led by H. E. Kirkpatrick.

In the 1920s, the Walnut Ridge church was forced to cope with the closing of the Missouri Pacific Railroad Yard - a crippling blow to the local economy in 1927. A tornado ravaged the community in the same year. In 1927, the church gave $1700 to the new "Cooperative Program" of state and foreign missions. This represented one fourth of the church's budget. In 1929, the stock market collapsed and the nation descended into an economic recession. That same year the church reported over 370 Sunday School members and G. E. Henry served as superintendent.

Encouraged by the steady growth of the church the deacons recommended that the fellowship construct a new parsonage with the cost estimated at $3500. Ironically, the pastor, W. E. Fuson, never lived in the new parsonage since Fuson accepted the First Baptist Church, Poplar Bluff, Missouri. The church suffered during the depression years and paying the debt on the new parsonage was especially onerous.

The 1940s brought new challenges since Walnut Ridge was jammed with thousands of servicemen who had come to the new "air base" north of town. Members often opened their homes to the servicemen providing good meals and good conversation. In 1941, the church opened a reading room for the servicemen. It was war time and everything was in short supply - flour, gasoline, houses and even Sunday School space!

In February, 1945, D. Blake Westmoreland was called from Morganfield, Kentucky, to be pastor. Westmoreland was immediately popular and brought a great intensity and energy to the pastorate. Within six months of his arrival as pastor, the church committed to a building program. An effective preacher, constant visitor, visionary and planner, Westmoreland also began teaching two mornings each week at Southern Baptist College. Westmoreland resigned after the education building was completed.

In the 1950s, the church built a new sanctuary, a plain, functional building. By 1957, a Sunday School attendance of 325 was commonplace. Blake Westmoreland returned to Walnut Ridge as pastor and served from 1953 until 1957. He was succeeded by William H. Heard, a friend and roommate of Westmoreland's. Heard served the church for nearly a decade.

In 1966, Heard was succeeded by Jim Tillman, an energetic and passionate preacher, who led the church in beginning a new mission, Calvary Baptist, a new kindergarten program, a church nursery, and Tillman began an aggressive college ministry and brought the Williams College community into the fellowship.

Tillman was followed by T. O. Spicer who served for five years. Other pastors have included Frank Shell, 1977-1983; Gerald Bounds, 1984-1987; Ronald Sanders, 1987-1992. During Reverend Sanders' tenure, the church built its present lovely sanctuary at a cost of over $1,500,000. The building program was headed by Jerry D. Gibbens, Larry Sloan and Jeff Teague. In 1998, the congregation had completely paid for the new structure.

In the 1990s, the church was pastored by Dr. Kenneth Moore, 1992-1997. The current pastor is Dr. Sam Roberts who came to the church from a pastorate in Kentucky. –Jerry Gibbens.

FIRST FREE WILL BAPTIST CHURCH

The First Free Will Baptist Church was founded on October 19, 1952, and organized 10 days later with 12 charter members: M. Doyle Boyd, Dorothy Boyd, Henry Glenn Campbell, Lereau Faith Campbell, Leonard Douthit, Ethel Douthit, Katie James, J. D. McKinney, Robert McMullin, Ethel McMullin, Abby Overstreet and Jim Woody. The first service, with 41 in attendance, was conducted by Reverend Glynn Campbell in a renovated store front on West Main Street in Walnut Ridge. Property was purchased from Mrs. Mabel Stanley for the first church building in 1953. The 32 x 50 building contained an auditorium and two Sunday School rooms. Two additions were added onto this building in 1955 and 1958. Reverend Campbell served the church as its first pastor for nine years until September, 1961.

In October, 1962, the church voted to build a parsonage while Reverend Keith Johnson was pastor.

In July, 1976, the church voted to build a new building. Reverend Terry Forrest was the pastor. It was dedicated in June, 1977. The old building was sold and moved. In January, 1980, the church constructed classrooms upstairs in this building.

In July, 1988, the church voted to build a new sanctuary with a seating capacity of 426 and it was completed in February of 1989. The existing sanctuary was converted into a fellowship hall.

The church building has changed both in its location and appearance through the years, but its purpose of bringing people to Christ and magnifying the name of our Lord has remained the same. The church celebrates its 49th anniversary this October with Reverend Steve Trail serving as its current pastor. –Reverend Stephen Trail.

FIRST UNITED METHODIST CHURCH

In the early fall of 1885, a revival meeting was held at a brush arbor in the east end of Walnut Ridge. Following this meeting, the first congregation of the Methodist Episcopal Church, South, of Walnut Ridge, was organized in October, 1995, by Reverend S. D. Evans.

During the first months of the church's existence, members shared a building with members of the Presbyterian Church.

The first church building, a one room frame structure, was erected in 1886, near the corner of East Walnut and northeast Fourth Streets. The parsonage adjoined the church.

In 1921, construction of the present church began, and was completed in 1922, at a cost of $60,000. This debt was retired in 1941. Having sold the first site to the Church of Christ, services were held in the courthouse until the building's completion.

Two lots adjoining the church were purchased in 1952, for $11,000 on which a two story education building was erected in 1955, at a cost of $75,000.

In 1967, the church building was completely remodeled at a cost of $55,000. At this time the front entrance to the church was changed and the side balconies in the sanctuary removed.

In 1979, the congregation launched an extensive $118,000 project which included the renovation of classrooms, the Wesley Room, covered walkways, a new roof, fire escapes, an elevator lift and storm windows to protect the beautiful stained glass windows.

Our church's 100th anniversary was observed on July 7, 1985, with a Centennial Homecoming, potluck dinner, old fashioned Singspiration Service and History Room containing pictures, written articles and memorabilia.

A fire, causing damages of $311,764 occurred May 18, 1996. The kitchen areas and part of the Fellowship Hall were destroyed by flames and the rest of the building received extensive smoke damage. Services were held in the chapel of the education building during restoration.

Annual Conference has been held at Walnut Ridge Church three times. In 1903, Bishop Hoss presided at the annual White River Conference here. We were also hosts in 1923 and 1945. Forty-one pastors have served this church to this date.

–Jimmy Snapp.

HOXIE UNITED METHODIST CHURCH

Hoxie United Methodist, Church, organized in 1903, has come through a tornado; a devastating fire; a railroad strike which took about half of the congregation when workers moved out; integration of schools; a depression; five wars; and a merger. Each event had its impact on the life of the church and necessitated different types of ministry.

In their history of almost a century, Hoxie Methodists have had at least four locations for their place of worship. The 11 inspired charter members for a time met in a little red brick school near the Frisco Railroad west of the Boas Hotel. Later, the group rented a building owned by the Presbyterians.

Walnut Ridge First Free Will Baptist Church.

First United Methodist Church. Walnut Ridge, Arkansas.

Hoxie United Methodist Church, 318 Broad Street, Hoxie, Arkansas.

In 1908, with a membership of 40, they purchased a site at the corner of Broad and Gibson Streets and built a one room wood frame structure.

In 1913, a tornado ripped through the town and left the church badly damaged. The persevering members, now numbering 70, repaired the sanctuary and added two classrooms. Four years later they built a wood frame parsonage beside the church. In 1927, all the church buildings and furnishings went up in smoke, along with six residences down the street.

Methodists don't give up easily. They used their church insurance and what money members could borrow to build a modern brick sanctuary and a six room wood frame parsonage.

As the congregation grew to some 150 members, members saw the need for additional classrooms, a fellowship hall, a kitchen and a new brick parsonage completely furnished.

In 1987, when Clover Bend chose to merge their church with Hoxie, they moved their building, and it became a nice fellowship hall and classrooms.

Change in every facet of life continues to challenge congregations to seek guidance for the best ways to meet the needs for ministry. Methodists want to be a part of that ministry.
–the History Committee, Hoxie United Methodist Church, Frances Tennison, Jean Jean and Helen Weir.

IMBODEN FIRST BAPTIST CHURCH

It is recorded that the gospel was preached by a Baptist preacher in what is now Imboden in the year 1877. Brother B. F. Holford testified in 1919, that "he preached his first sermon in a log cabin at this place 42 years ago, before there was any town or railroad here." A church was organized in the year 1893, with six known members.

In 1897, Brother W. P. Kime preached from his special car on a side track near the depot. It was during this series of meetings that a church building site was selected for the First Baptist Church of Imboden. The location was the corner of Second and Elm Streets on land donated by Captain W. C. Sloan. The frame building was dedicated in May of 1900.

In 1927, the building was destroyed by a tornado. A native stone edifice was erected on the same site. This building was destroyed by fire late in 1940.

Property was then purchased on Highway 63 and another rock edifice was erected in

Imboden First Baptist Church.

1941. The church bell that had been used on the original location was placed in front of this building. An addition was added and dedicated May 7, 1961.

Today there are 228 resident members. The house of worship is a brick building located next to the rock structure on Highway 63. It was erected in 1972, with a formal dedication service being held June 4, of that year.
–O.H. McKamey.

IMBODEN UNITED METHODIST

The Methodist Episcopal Church, South, in Imboden, was organized in 1884. The first minister to the parish was C. W. Roane. The Imboden Church was part of the Hoxie Mission which included Hoxie, Portia, Black Rock and Hopewell. Later, the Hopewell circuit was formed and a parsonage was built at Hopewell. The first pastors of the Imboden charge lived at Hopewell. The charter membership was 13 women and one man.

The first church building was erected in 1895, on Second Street across from the first town hall or a block west of the present building. The building was 40 x 60 with 15 foot ceilings.

Quoting from a letter received from Mrs. J. C. Poindexter on January 7, 1952, "J. S. Sullivan, the only male member of the church, had to make great sacrifices and surmount difficulties to get the building up and comfortable enough to use. T. A. Bowen was the pastor. H. C. Skinner was the Presiding Elder."

Mrs. Poindexter continues, "When W. M. Wilson came on the work in November of 1898, the membership was still small, one adult member had been added. An open saloon was on Main Street and other evils were

Imboden United Methodist Church.

in the town at the close of 1899. Hendr. Academy had been built at the cost of $11,0(and was in debt $3,600. Mr. Sullivan hadn recovered from sacrifices he had made in building the church a few years before. Therefore, he didn't take an active part in the academy enterprise. It was left up to Brother Wilson and Dr. Poindexter to do something. They decided the thing most needed was a revival. After much research, worry and prayer, they secured the services of W. H. Evans of Dallas, Texas, with the understanding that he would stay on the job as long as they thought it necessary. At the end of 24 days of revival, 67 had been added to the church. The saloon keeper had been fined for keeping open on Sunday which resulted later in voting liquor out of town and the debt on the academy had been paid off. Dr. A. C. Miller, President of Hendrix College, came to the revival and while he was here he made a proposition to Mr. W. C. Sloan who had already donated very liberally, that if he would pay the deficit of $3600 and free the school, it should wear his name. Mr. Sloan accepted the proposition and saved the school and it became Sloan-Hendrix Academy."

One Sunday morning in the early spring of 1921, as the Reverend James F. Glover was finishing reading the scriptures, Mr. Charlie Chambers entered the door and announced "the church is on fire." The announcement was accepted very calmly. As the congregation filed out of the burning building, each one carried something of value. The men returned to carry out the pews, the pulpit, the lighting fixtures, the chancel railing and the carpet from the choir loft and the aisles. Even the windows were removed from the frames. At last the bell rope was cut, placed around the stove and it was dragged from the building. To answer the question of why didn't the congregation extinguish the fire? There was no fire department in the town and the nearest water supply, 'a cistern', was a block away.

The Board of Trustees purchased the property on Main and Second from the Dwyer family and the construction of the new church soon began. It was completed in 1922.

Early Imboden United Methodist Church.

Landmark Missionary Baptist Church.

1936 Lauratown School/Church (same building).

Through the years the Methodist Church has served the community needs in times of happiness and in times of despair. Today the Imboden United Methodist Church prayerfully and expectantly accepts the mission of a caring, sharing, redemptive fellowship in ministry for Jesus Christ. The congregation shall proclaim the gospel of Jesus Christ, extend life and fellowship of the church and in Christ's name lovingly reach out and serve others within and beyond the community. –Edith Stovall.

LANDMARK MISSIONARY BAPTIST CHURCH

Portia Landmark Missionary Baptist Church is one of the oldest established churches in the Spring River Association in Lawrence County. The church is located at 204 Lawrence Street in Portia.

Records of the church date back to 1875. The church was organized at the home of Austin Henry, and members worshipped for a brief time at Portia First Baptist Church. The church moved to the old Coffman School in June, 1876, and later moved to the church building in the Crossroads Community. Records indicate the congregation was locked out by seven "board Baptists" and they built a second house of worship in November, 1914.

The first pastor recorded was Elder B. H. Holford in 1876. Some of the members mentioned in these minutes were Brother Elam Hall, Mrs. S. E. Thorn, Elder W. E. Sherrill, Alex Little, S. M. Prince and Will Brummitt.

Minutes of June 20, 1912, (Saturday night before the third Sunday) reflect the pastor's annual salary was $150. The church property was valued at $800. The minutes recorded an increase in membership of 50 people and a decrease of seven "by exclusion." On September 29, 1912, James Anderson deeded property for a new church site. The new church was built in January, 1928, with the entire congregation raising money, including the donation of cotton crops with all members helping pick the cotton. Revivals were first mentioned in the records in 1924, donations to missions in 1943, support for an orphanage in 1944, and in 1942, worship offerings were first mentioned "so that each may have an opportunity to help in the Lord's work."

Mr. and Mrs. J. H. Miller donated land for the present church, which was completed in 1958. In 1982, Fred and Clara Bell Kellow and James and Louise Hacker donated additional land to extend church boundaries. The church added two classrooms in 1991. The old church bell was erected on again in 1996, and a much needed fellowship hall was added in 1997.

Though small in number, we hope to remain a shining light laboring in the Lord's work. Our current pastor, Brother Leon Jones and his wife Brenda, invite you to join us in worship.
–Brenda Warren.

LAURATOWN METHODIST CHURCH

The organized date of the Lauratown Church is not known, however, information for this article will be taken from a church registry dated 1900 through 1947, and Quarterly Conference records dating 1932 through 1940.

Lauratown Church was on the Strangers Home circuit along with Arbor Grove, Clover Bend and Strangers Home. It was in the Batesville District of the North Arkansas. Later, it was changed to the Paragould District.

Lauratown Church used the same building as school. Located about one half mile north and one fourth mile east of Lauratown Store, where the road turns north again. Several trees and a small cemetery where several members of the Myers family were buried was on the grounds. These tombstones have been removed.

Fred Starling family built a home at this location after it ceased to be used as a church/school. Following pastor served the church are: Reverend Maynard, A. C. Clovers, J. M. Thrasher,. M. R. Paine, E. A. Horn, W. S. Story, W. M. Hamilton, C. L. Martin, G. A. Moore, J. E. Buchanan, Luther Love, Owen Love, W. T. Watson, L. R. Ruble. Presiding elders names available are: Reverend Skinner, Williford, Wade, King, Jefferson, Sherman, C. W. Lester and Conner Morehead.

Names on the church register: J. B. Liles, Effie Hartsell, Owen Smith, J. T. Hall, Ida Madden, Grace Smith, H. G. Harksell, Mary Owen, Lucille Lady, Lou Liles, W. H. Owen, Harold Lady, J. T. Shaw, Don Gibbs, Jesse Grissom, Mattie Shaw, Emily Gibbs, Florence Grissom, J. M. Jeffrey, J. W. Cole, Ruby Grissom Camp, Mary Jeffrey, N. C. Cole, Mable Cochran Bratcher, Evaline Jeffrey, N. J. East, Lloyd Cochran, Sallie Gipson, E. Comes, Charles Phillips, Will Davis, Minie Cochran, Jim Smith, Sallie Hall, Katie Hartsell Sharp, Syble Smith, Matt Dodd, Ruby Jeffery Little, Olene Jones Baker, Puss Wade, Gertie Smith, Freda Jones Buchanan, Sallie Owen, Mollie Spotts, Agla Moody, Monro Neil, Hazel Osburn King, Tice Hamil, Em Hamit, A. J. McCall, Homer McMillen, A. M. Barlow, Besie Cochran Phillips, Jan Green, E. McPike, Blanche Spotts, Lula Simmons, Rodie Neil, Sue Spotts, Olly Sawiers,

Emma Hartsell, Fern Spotts, Jack McCall, Olivia Cunningham, Enid Cooper, N. J. Foster, Resia Horton, Vida Milligan, J. P. Foster, Ellia Brimhall, Ruby Jeffrey, Curtis Wilson, Katie Hamil, Ola Colahaw, James Benson, Myrtle Comer, Grace Miligan, Bamma Halstead, Arvilla Hamil, Alice Sawyers, Fannie Goodwin, Lillie Cunningham, Bill Whitiker, J. W. Webb, W. H. Davis, James Franks, Bowen Osburn, A. C. Conner, Fred Sawyears, James Sherman, Etta S. Padan, Cora Raney, Tommy Goodwin, Myrtle Cunningham, Essie Milligan, James Sherman, E. H. Vores, Mary Franks, Henry Sallings, Sylvia Freer, Betty Riley, Sally Sallings, Bryan Johnston, Ester Milligan, Ben Moody, B. C. Marst, W. W. Cochran, Halbert Moody, John Mason, Owen Spotts, Roy Grissom, Stella Mason, Fern Spotts, Kathryn Grissom, J. T. Shafer, Leona Osburn, Emit Phillips, Annie Foster, Beulah Osburn Ratliff, Mire Phillips Kwotts, Alice Freer, Blanche Osburn, Lilie Williams, Lasey Moody, Silvda Medlock, Marie Halstead, Ferd Grissom, Altha McCall, Kathleen Halstead, Cecil Grissom, James Webb, Pearl Foster, Mable Ruth Grissom, Parter Milligan, Innis Foster, Ruby Goodwin, Lena Milligan, Gladys Hersley, Irene Goodwin, Homer Milligan, Imogene Justus, Artie Madden, I. O. Kirkland, Lillie Callshaw, Delilah Kirkland, Harie Lawhorn, Willene Baker, Arlan Sanders, Eva Freeman, Chas Goodwin, Ollie Davis, Mary Phillips, Rudolph Sharp, H. E. Sharp, A. T. McCall, Zola Osburn, Willie Baker, Homer Davis, Della Davis, Ollie Davis, Emit Phillips, Neil Sharp, Glen Sharp, Kathleen Sharp, Irma Lee Spotts, Ernest Malone, Addie Malone, Mary McKinney, Oscar Kirkland, Ila Kirkland, Billy Joe Kirkland. –Willene Kirkland.

LEBANON PRESBYTERIAN CHURCH

Sessional records of Lebanon Presbyterian Church indicate the church was established May 30, 1852, in a settlement a few miles east of Smithville (Eaton), in Lawrence County. The meeting was held in a school house on that date at 10 o'clock in the morning. There had been preaching on the morning and afternoon of the previous day.

The following persons presented letters of dismission from their churches and were united in public confession of faith of the Presbyterian Church.

Those listed are: James Blackwell and his wife, Elizabeth Melissa; Benjamin Blackwell and wife, Elizabeth H.; Sarah M. Blackwell; An-

Old Lebanon Church, 1852.

thony Cozort and wife, Mary Ann; Lusene Cozort, their daughter; Burgess Thomason; Miss Eliza Anderson; and James H. Johnston and wife, Elizabeth.

On this date John Calvin, infant son of Benj and Elizabeth Blackwell, was baptized.

Four acres of land was given to the church in December of 1852, by Burgess Thomason. It was the corner part of his property in S17 R2 T16, pretty much where the present building is located.

There have been numerous stories told about the church and cemetery which is next to the church. As early as 1851, there are known burials, though these graves are not marked with engraved stones. George Thomason, who was the father of Burgess Thomason; Mary Ann Cozort; Elizabeth Blackwell; and Sarah Blackwell Casper died in 1851, as well as Burgess Thomason's wife, Nancy. They are both buried in the very oldest part of the cemetery. Their deaths occurred before the church was established.

The building, which has been moved at least twice, is built of logs and was originally put together with wood pins whenever possible. There is a loft which is said to have been intended for slaves when they came to services with their owners. It is not known if any ever attended.

The Lebanon School District 51 met in the log building until about 1911-12. After that the building was used for many things, from a store and post office, hay barn, and cattle shed. A new school building was built about a half mile southeast in the woods.

The cemetery, now called Old Lebanon Cemetery, is located on Highway 25, between Lynn and Eaton, about 10 miles west of Powhatan. There are probably a thousand graves in this cemetery, dating from at least 1851, til the present time. Veterans from many wars, starting with the War of 1812 and all wars since are at rest in this quiet place on the hillside.

A homecoming, which started as Graveyard Working Day, is held every year on the third Tuesday in August. When it started the men came and worked with their tools and hands after they had the crops laid by. In later years the women came along and brought dinner to spread on the ground at noontime. During the 1950s, the cemetery committee was formed. The log building was bought from its owner and moved back across the highway beside the cemetery. The upkeep and mowing are paid for by volunteer donations by people with family buried there. *–Catherine Richey.*

LYNN UNITED METHODIST CHURCH

The Lynn Methodist Church was originally the Raney's Chapel Church and was located two miles southwest of its present location on land donated by Green Raney. Organized in 1894, it had nine members and a Reverend Register as pastor.

Raney's Chapel members included Fortenberry, Osburn, Goodwin, Clinton, Hedrick, Adams, Brannon, Jones, Birmingham, Morrison, Epperson, Segraves, Birdson, Dawson, Newport and Raney.

In August, 1924, the church was moved near its present location in Lynn on an acre of land given by Mr. and Mrs. J. L. Casper and their children: Angy Brannon, Foulata Casper and Homer Casper. (However, relinquishment of dower was not given until 1957.)

Trustees at that time were James Clinton, A. J. Segraves, and W. O. Brannon. Pastor W. S. Tussy worked two years in erecting the building which had a basement. Lynn School held some classes in the church. Nothing remains of this building except indentations where the basement was.

In the 1940s, the Shiloh Church consolidated with Lynn Church. (See history of Shiloh Methodist Church.)

In 1946, the members erected a block building north of the original building. In 1956, an addition was made. In 1957, a plot of ground south of the present church was sold/donated to the church by the Caspers.

Many families donated labor and memorials, but in addition to the Caspers, another family should be noted, the Jeans. Will Jean and son, Elton, did most of the work on the addition in 1956, and donated their labor. Elbert Jean, another son, built the pulpit. The Jean family, which included a daughter, Fay, gave the piano and two choir chairs. *–Lillian Brannon.*

MT. HARMONY FREE WILL BAPTIST CHURCH

Mt. Zion Church was organized August 15, 1878, by John F. Crafton. There were 10 charter members: Sarah Howard, Nancy Wilson, Elijah Vickers, Mary Wilson, Mary Cason, L. L. Wilson, J. B. Wilson, St. T. Hensley, Ezekiel Godwin, John Crafton. The church was located about three and one half miles west of Saffell where the Mt. Zion Cemetery is now. In 1911, Mt. Zion and Harmony merged and became known as Mt. Harmony. In 1912, they had the first service in their new building.

Revivals were held through the years. One held in 1921, had 45 people baptized at the Military Crossing on the Strawberry River. Later in 1947, during a revival, 27 members were added to the church.

In 1946, the church was moved to Saffell. The new building was built on land donated by Mr. and Mrs. Henry Walker. Additions were made to the building during the years as space was needed.

In 1965, the church built a parsonage on one half acre of land purchased from Tom Allen.

The church saw a need for a larger building, so in March, 1979, a new building was completed containing a sanctuary seating 300, three

Mt. Harmony Free Will Baptist Church.

classrooms, nursery, library and study upstairs, 10 classes, kitchen and fellowship hall downstairs. On September 12, 1993, a note-burning service was held.

The Women Active for Christ Organization was established in 1959, and is still active. The church also has a children's church which began in 1986. Many youth have won Bible competitions at the district, state and national levels.

Pastors: John Crafton, George Hassell, W. C. Haley, Jeff Doyle, A. J. Rowlett, H. O. Damons, John E. Willmuth, J. F. Finney, Louis Doyle, H. O. Eagan, C. H. Palmer, Gordon King, John Huskey, Herman Lewis, Obie Eagans, Grady Linebaugh, Lyle Cartwright, Ray Watkins, Lonnie Clark, Oris Doggett, Jimmy Richardson, Terry Forrest, Bernard Roberts, Jerry Smith, David Waltrip, Dennis Artman, Dewayne Goforth, John Freeman, Larry Pounds, John Neal.

Church Clerks: George Hassell, Andy Saffell, A. D. Wilson, J. M. Willioms, W. H. Richardson, Louis Doyle, James M. Turner, Bennie Doyle, Columbus Huskey, Millard Williams, Harold Howard, Bennie Hardin, A. I. Willmuth, Avanell Saffell, Mabel Croom, Lorene Doyle, Ann Doyle.

Deacons: John Wilson, John E. Willmuth, W. Willmuth, J. M. Turner, Joe Williams, Sam Sneed, Bill Callahan, Henry Sides, Wesley Huskey, Luther Croom, Hubert Newberry, Luther Reaves, Harold Howard, Horace Doyle, Gerphus Huskey, Millard Williams, Lowell Eagan, Jerrell Polston, Jimmy Crabtree, Paul Huskey. *–Ann Doyle.*

NEW COVENANT FREE WILL BAPTIST CHURCH

In the early 1900s, the church minded leaders of the community felt a need of having a church organized.

Services were being held in the Fender School building during inclement weather (in the winter maybe once a month). During the summer months, services were held in brush arbors which were constructed in the area of the school.

Early records show the New Covenant Church as being received as a new member church into the Social Band Association in 1909.

Services were gaining interest and the Odd Fellows Lodge was needing a meeting place for their meetings. The ideal thing to do would be to build a building for the dual purposes. A two story building would be ideal, suing the ground floor for church meetings.

In July, 1925, the work began on land donated by Mr. J. G. Richardson. Mr. John Sisson was employed as head carpenter. Mr.

Fender Lodge Hall, 1940s.

New Hope Baptist Church.

Richardson also donated the timber for the rough lumber.

The first load of logs was hauled to the sawmill by Frank Rosselot. Mr. Moore furnished his labor and use of the sawmill.

The following is a partial list of workers: Reenan Carter, Mont and Wiley Dobbs, Monroe, Bob and Perry Segraves, Edd Rosselot, Tom Allison, Pud Hutcherson, Lester Turner, Bob and Joe Reeves, Lucian Stalnaker, George Thompson, Mr. Smallwood and Ervin Holder.

Since the lodge brothers belonged to different denominations, it was decided they take turns having different speakers.

Early preachers included: Brother Abe Lincoln, Brother W. T. Sharp, Brother Ray Hudson, Brother G. M. McGee, Brother Tom Allison, Brother J. D. Doyle, Brother W. T. Shoffitt, Brother R. S. Shelton, Brother Charley Lakey and many others.

In the summer of 1959, the upstairs part of the building was removed. In January, 1966, the first classrooms were started. During the 1970s, floors were refinished, new pews added, bathrooms installed, classrooms lined both sides of the old building along with a fellowship hall. The building was bricked and in 1982, a steeple was built with Billy Segraves and Ralph Rosselot donating their labor.

The New Covenant Church is located in the Fender community, Highway 231, eight miles North East of Walnut Ridge. –*Melba Jones.*

NEW HOPE BAPTIST CHURCH

One of the oldest Baptist churches in Arkansas is located in Western Lawrence County between Denton and Smithville. This old country church was established July 22, 1844, and has been in continual service from its inception. The church records have been preserved in their entirety and contain many interesting facts. On this date nine people gathered at the home of Carney C. Straughan and organized a church of the Regular Baptist Faith and Order by the name of New Hope. During the early years of the church's existence, they met in homes of the membership and at the Flat Creek Meeting House. The

great influx of immigrants into this part of the country in the 1850s, allowed them rapid growth, so they found it necessary to buy land and build a church house. In 1953, Allen Moore agreed to build the church house for $125, to be built by July "no providential thing preventing." It was also reported that the church had 38 living members at that time. The church has built three church houses and each one has had materials used in it from the previous building. The first building was torn down in 1892, and a new one was built which was completed in February of 1893. The present building was erected in 1940, with classrooms added in 1955. A new fellowship hall and basement with educational rooms was completed and dedicated on July 19, 1997. During the first 50 years or more of its existence, New Hope Church was the religious and social center for the country for miles around. The "Rules of Decorum" were very strict. Church discipline was taken seriously and disciplinary action was taken frequently to "exclude" members from the full faith and fellowship of the church. Offenses included anything from swearing, dancing, "playing', drunkenness or adultery to nonattendance. Some members lived as far away as 10-15 miles and had no better way to get there than in wagons, horseback or on foot. If a member missed three consecutive church meetings (held once a month), they risked being excluded.

Nothing went untouched during the Civil War including New Hope Baptist Church. The church records dated October 11, 1862, reflect that a Kentucky immigrant member, Isaiah Wheeler, of the church who was a credentialed preacher and new to the country was arrested at his house being "suspicioned of horse stealing...and taken off by a passel of men and...that he was put to death in a summary manner." The church felt it necessary to erase his name from their church roll, stating that they had suffered much in the "calamity." It was also stated in this record that "it was during the war between the United States the Confederate States and in a very short ˌme after the former in partly had invaded thiˈ portion of the country and that civil law was not used to much ex-

tent, but pretty much under military." It was also stated that the church held it's monthly meetings all during the Civil War even though Federal troops were camped nearby and that these troops attended their services. Company "F" of the 45th Arkansas Confederate Cavalry was organized at New Hope church in early fall of 1864. The exact date is not known, but a roster of the company reveals that several soldiers in the company were members of the church.

New Hope Church has been the location of great revival meetings, picnics, singing schools and community singings. Great baptizings were held following some of these revivals with as many as 30 or 40 people being baptized on the big red bank of the creek behind the church. It is a missionary minded church and has trained numerous clergy throughout its history. Three churches are known to have been missions from New Hope Baptist Church: Smithville, Pleasant Grove at Annieville and Pleasant Hill at Lynn.

Some of the elder members of the church state today that they can remember when families did not sit together during church services, but the men sat on one side and the women and children on the other. They also tell of older gentlemen who came to church every time services were held, but would not come into the building, but stand outside the open windows so they could hear what was being said. Many things have changed throughout the years in relation to New Hope Baptist Church, but one thing remains the same and that is the congregation's desire to serve the Lord. –*Maleta Bilbrey Tipton.*

OAK GROVE CHURCH OF CHRIST

The Oak Grove Church of Christ had its beginning in the early 1930s, when Nate Worlow realized he had no place in the near vicinity to worship. He talked to Brother Bill Harris and they asked Doc Stevens if he would teach a Bible class to begin a congregation in the community. And so the church began meeting in Nate's house, about one mile north of the present church grounds.

Oak Grove Church of Christ, 1998.

Powhatan United Methodist Church.

Richwoods Church.

Among the first families were:

Nate and Sarah Worlow, and their children, John, Bill, Geneviev, and Sarah.

Bill and Jesse Harris and their three children.

Doctor John Henry Stevens and wife, Ethel Mae, and children, John, Lesley, Leon, Marilyn, and Howard.

The Henry Parks family and their three children.

The preacher was Brother Reair Wortham.

Services were conducted at the Worlow home for about two years. Gospel meetings were conducted in a brush arbor across the highway from the present building. The meetings were met with great success as many were added to the church. The people in the community began to desire a place to meet. Brother Joe Webb gave the grounds for the church to be built on. Doc Stevens gave money to get the building started. Sister Dobie Roberts, Sister Cloe Pierce, Brother Henry Parks, Brother O. T. Swindle, and many more families gave labor as such was needed to finish the building. Brother Earnest Rice, Brother Edgar Simpson, and Brother Terry Mullen were active in the procuring of materials and labor to build, out of rough lumber, the first auditorium.

The church grew to an attendance of over 200 in the early 1970's, but now has a much smaller average attendance possibly due to the community being smaller in population. The church's ministry outreach includes "Voice of Truth" on KRLW Radio, "Speaking the Truth in Love" on KAIT television, and services held at Lawrence Hall Nursing Home in Walnut Ridge. The church contributes to publications, "Speaking the Truth in Love" news brochure and "Southern Christian Home" news brochure. The church also gives local aid as needed to families in the community, and gives assistance to Paragould Children's Home and Lawrence Hall Nursing Home.

May God bless those who have so faithfully worked to build and bring the church to its present state today. –*Judy Bonner.*

POWHATAN UNITED METHODIST CHURCH

The Powhatan United Methodist Church was established in 1854. In 1858, Powhatan was part of the Jacksonport District, with 284 members. In 1859, records revealed 181 white members, 49 "probationers", and 14 "colored" members as they were called. From 1858 to 1871, Powhatan was served by pastors William R. Foster, Jonathan Stockham, F. W. Thacker, J. M. Clayton, Moses C. Morris, Josiah Williams and T. Robinson.

The present church building was built in 1874, after John A. and Martha A. Lindsey, his wife; and Asa T. Lindsay and Sallie W. Lindsay deeded the property to Champ T. Stuart, Frances Wayland, William T. Rainey, Henry T. Wickershaw, and Charles A. Stuart, trustees of the Methodist Episcopal Church, South. Many years later the name was changed to Powhatan United Methodist Church.

Colonel George Thornsburg, one of the greatest laymen Arkansas Methodism ever produced was superintendent of the Sunday School at Powhatan around 1890. While at Powhatan, he practiced law and later became business manager of the Arkansas Methodist newspaper. Elisha Theodore Wayland followed as superintendent until 1895.

Powhatan Methodist Church served as the only church in the town until the mid 1880s. Citizens of all faiths attended church at Powhatan and it was the focal point for the town's special events. Weddings, baptisms and funerals of outstanding citizens were held in the church. It was also the scene of quarterly conferences. Church members traveled by foot, in wagon and on horseback to attend church at Powhatan. A wooden board walk on he northwest side of the building led many people up the wooden steps into the church, The church building appears the same today as when first constructed. Prominent family names who were members of the church in-

clude: Matthews, Thornsburg, Wayland, Wickershaw, Jung, Stuart, Wells, Cravens, Saffell, Rowsey, Sloan, Martin, Rainey, Poindexter and Flippo.

The building was named to the National Register of Historic Places in 1977, and in 1983, was the recipient of a matching grant from the Arkansas Historic Preservation Program for restoration. A dedication service was held in October of 1984. The building still maintains the simplistic beauty of its mid 19th century architecture. It stands proud as a reminder of the contribution religion played in the rural life of Lawrence County. –*Darlene Moore.*

RICHWOODS CHURCH

In 1887, J. M. Phelps, Zacheus Phelps, Sr. and Victoria Phelps (daughter of pioneer settler Henson Kinian), his wife, deeded an acre of land to the Methodist Episcopal Church, South for the only church building ever to be erected in the Richwoods Community. This community lies above Walnut Ridge, about five miles from Portia.

This first church, constructed of logs, burned and around 1913, the men of the community built another one, a two-story white frame with a wooden platform extending around the front entrance, where visiting singing groups performed. A lodge hall once occupied the second floor, but when structural difficulties arose, the second story was removed. A large bell, stolen years ago, once stood in front of the building. Beautiful old trees framed the church on three sides.

The church, since it was the only one, functioned as a true community church, allowing preachers of differing beliefs (Baptist, Methodist, Pentecostal) to preach there whenever their circuits included Richwoods. Baptisms were performed at Clearlake.

Lorene Tillman, age 92, who still worships there, recalls that crowds would jam the house; during revivals and horses and buggies were parked at each window and tied along the fence row.

May Arnold Spence, also 92, fondly remembered a man coming through Richwoods and stopping at the church building to show silent movies for a dime admission. "When they heard his "rattlin' ol' buggy," all the children would come flying," she said.

About 20 people still meet for worship on Sunday mornings. Richwoods Church is being considered for inclusion in the Arkansas Historical Register. –*Regina Horton.*

SAFFELL MISSIONARY BAPTIST CHURCH

The Saffell Missionary Baptist Church was organized January 13, 1946. Jerusalem Missionary Baptist Church and Union Missionary Baptist Church extended their hands in organization. The people had been holding services in the old Harmony School House since 1943. Sunday School was started in October of 1945. Brother Albert Garner was the first preacher for the congregation.

Charter members were Brother Joe Smith, Sister Frances Arkansas Smith, Brother Wess Anderson, Sister Leona Anderson, Brother Wess Smith, Sister Eila Howard, Sister Mary Erwin and Sister Beatrice Harris.

Later services were held on the Lane Theater until a church building was completed in 1947. The building was made of field stone and was first used with a dirt floor. Seats were planks on blocks of wood. In later years classrooms were added to the rear of the building.

A three bedroom parsonage was built in 1967, on land donated by Brother and Sister Arthur McLaughlin.

In 1975, the church moved to Highway 25, next to the parsonage. Land for the church building was donated by Brother and Sister Noel Roberts.

Smithville Baptist Church.

Those eight charter members have grown to a church roll of over 150 members. To accommodate her growth the church approved a building program which will add a larger sanctuary to the present facility. The land for the expansion has been donated by Brother and Sister Noel Roberts.

Saffell Missionary Baptist Church has always been committed to spreading the gospel of Jesus Christ unto Salvation. The church presently supports 11 mission works in addition to her dedicated efforts to serve the Lord in Saffell and the surrounding communities.

Saffell Missionary Baptist Church pastors: Cecil Lewallen, 1946-47; J. A. Sheppard, 1948-49; Cecil Lewallen, 1950; T. C. Miller, 1951; B. J. Watson, 1952; M. E. Moore, 1953; Joe Schutz, 1954; Hubert Owens, 1955-56; Joe Schutz, 1957; Bobby Miller, 1958; I. C. Helms, 1959; Naamon Landers, 1960-62; Harold Mann, 1964-64; Kennard Townsley, 1964-66; Remil Layton, 1967-71; J. W. Richey, 1972-75; Jimmy Platt, 1976; Johnny Davis, 1977-80; Dexter Preston, 1981-87; Bill Threet, 1988-92; Greg Bixler, 1993-97; and Keith Wilson, 1998-present.

SEDGWICK BAPTIST CHURCH

According to the records of the Arkansas Baptist State Convention, the church was organized in 1907. Records of the Mount Zion Baptist Association reveal that the church associated itself with this association after its beginning and then in 1925, the church became affiliated with the Black River Baptist Association.

The church first met in the Sedgwick School building and in 1921, the church secured a warranty deed for land on which to build a church. It named the trustees of the First Missionary Baptist Church by which it was then known as J. H. Rhodes, C. N. Whitener, and J. M. Smelser. The church was built shortly after and the membership worshipped in this building until 1972-73, when the present structure was built during the pastorate of Reverend Donald Settles.

Some of the early pastors of the church were the Reverends A. A. Ryan, W. G. Mathis, J. W. Seay, J. M. Casey, W. H. Meredith, Ralph Kerley, Russell Duffer, Ray Hudson, Ira Meadows, D. C. Mayo, J. M. Stevens, C. L. Davis, David Patton, Earl Gorbett, Robert Johnson and J. T. Tippett.

More recent pastors have been Reverends Oda Masters, Claude Applegate, Howard Williams, Sidney Goza, Carroll Fowler, Marley Brooks, Harvey Fowler, Cyril Miller, Donald Settles, Sam Howell, Wayne Faulkner, Bill Ladd, Alvin Harms, Sam Stone, Paul King, Lynsol Richmond, Michael Bradley, Freddie Muse and the current pastor, Reverend Thomy Green. –*Tommie Jean Worlow.*

SHILOH METHODIST CHURCH

Shiloh Class (or Church) was organized by C. W. Rook on June 21, 1885, and was one of the Methodist Episcopal Church, South. It was located on what is now Lawrence County Road 267. Nothing remains of the two room Shiloh School, where the church met.

Ten people are listed as organizing members in 1885. In that same year, 24 more were added, many transferring from Rock Cove, Oak Grove and Shady Grove.

Sometime in the 1940s, the Shiloh Methodist Church consolidated with the Lynn Methodist Church. Active Shiloh members at that time included the Camerons, Jeans, Stewarts and Rainwaters. –*Lillian Brannon.*

SMITHVILLE BAPTIST CHURCH

Smithville Baptist Church was organized September 22, 1866.

They took turns with other denominations meeting in the Solomon School, located across from the Smithville Cemetery.

In 1867, it was voted to share a building with the Masonic Lodge.

About 1870, Captain W. C. Sloan bought a bell in St. Louis to be used by the church and the Masonic Lodge.

The church was a member of Spring River Baptist Association until 1919, when it merged with Black River Association because of a difference of opinion on how to carry out state mission work. Those opposing the plan became known as Landmark Baptists and later Missionary Baptists.

In 1924, the original handmade seats were replaced with seats made by a local cabinet maker.

A new building was dedicated in 1939.

Classrooms and a fellowship hall were added in 1954.

A second addition consisting of a nursery, classrooms and restrooms was completed in 1963. New furniture was placed in the church at this time.

Mrs. Lottie Hoggard gave funds for a baptistry in 1970. A pastor's study, larger fellowship hall, kitchen and classrooms were added at the same time.

Pew cushions, carpeting, stained glass windows and central heat and air are some of the things added in more recent years.

Sedgwick Baptist Church.

As you can see the church has continued to grow over the years with a congregation greatly exceeding the original nine members. –*Janice Lovelady and Beatrice Justus.*

SMITHVILLE UNITED METHODIST CHURCH

The Smithville United Methodist Church was one of three churches organized in the Old Solomon School in 1867.

The Methodist congregation erected its own church building on the present site in 1875. The frame structure faced the west and was furnished with an organ, factory built pews, pulpit, deacon bench, a dozen children's chairs, a bookcase, and light wine carpet covered the chancel and the two aisles. The church bell was purchased in St. Louis in 1886, and shipped by river and is presently functioning. The church was located on donated land; however, the church received a deed to the property on April 2, 1885. The church was dedicated on October 10, 1875. The church has been blessed with many gracious gifts throughout history.

The Presbyterian congregation worshipped with the Methodist until they could later build a church building for their worship services.

The present rock structure was built in 1938, with the sanctuary facing the south. In 1956, one fourth acre was purchased east of the existing structure and a new educational complex was constructed on the parcel of land.

A parsonage was built in the early 1900s, and the minister served the church at Smithville, Rock cove, Flat Creek, and Raney's Chapel. In 1950, Smithville and Imboden were placed on an Imboden-Smithville charge with the minister also responsible for Wayland Springs Camp. Denton Church united with the Smithville Church in 1957.

Ministers serving the church have been: Reverends Phipps, Morris, Thacker, Brooks, Self, Wooley, Mosley, Walker, Wilkerson, Reedy, Register, Kemper, Fain, Copeland, Kelly, Champion, Jones, Glissen, Miller, Mack, Martin, Black, Benbrook, Long, Langston, Glover, Tassey, Gibson, Harris and Williams. Other pastors have been: Stewart, Bounds, Odom, Huggins, Gibbs, Yount, Fair, Watson, Simpson, Beal, Orr, Strayhorn, Yorbrough, Weatherford, Whitfield, Roberts, Clark, Bruner, Stahl, Wilmouth, Wilson, Kirkland, Shelton, Long, Thresher, Klinger, Newberry, Gray and Sims.

The congregation presently consists of approximately 40 members. The church services include Sunday morning services at 11 a.m., Church School at 10 a.m. each week, Sunday evening services one Sunday each month and choir practice each Wednesday evening. –*Maxine Mize.*

SECOND BAPTIST CHURCH

The genesis of the Baptist denomination in Arkansas was in Cape Girardeau County, Missouri Territory, where Bethel Baptist Church had been established in 1806. The Bethel Association was organized there in June, 1816, and sent Elders James Philip Edwards, Benjamin Clark and Jesse

Smithville Methodist Church, erected in 1875, replaced with this building in 1938.

James as missionaries to Lawrence County. They successfully constituted Salem Church in 1818.

In 1819, Salem Church reported that 12 members had been dismissed by letter and that a new church had been established named Union. Union was represented at the meetings by Elders Jesse James and Richard Brazil who were doubtless responsible for organizing it. They represented Union Church at the next two association meetings and reported 14 members in 1818, and 27 in 1820. The congregation had grown to 41 in 1821, but fell to eight in 1822. It was again represented by Reverend Jesse James in 1823, and reported 29 members. The church then apparently became inactive as there were no further reports to the Bethel Association.

We can only conjecture as to the causes of the short lives of these early Lawrence County churches. David Orr and a missionary team surveyed the area in 1829, and reported that they found only "a few scattered lambs", probably a result of the continuation of the westward migration. That movement is characterized by the removal of the extended James and Brazil families to Saline County only a few years later.

No local records of Union Church have survived and neither the identity of the members nor even the location of the church (the Bethel minutes refer to Union as being located on Cypress Creek) has been discovered. However, although details have not come down to us, we know that for a few years, Reverend Jesse James and Elder Richard Brazil ministered to the spiritual needs of those earliest settlers of Lawrence County through Salem and Union, the first and second Baptist churches in Arkansas. –*Carole Mayfield and Duane Wilson.*

UNITED FREE WILL BAPTIST CHURCH

On August 20, 1992, a group of 40 concerned Christians met at the Walnut Ridge Fire Depart-

ment to discuss the organization of a Bible believing church. They decided to have church services there on Sunday, August 23, and did so with 61 present.

Sister Jean Baltz contacted the owners of the former Nazarene Church in Walnut Ridge. Brother Ken Stallings came to Walnut Ridge and met with people at the church. He said they were welcome to use the church for services, free of charge. On Sunday, August 30, 97 people were present for worship.

On Sunday, September 20, Brother Dale Blackwell came to the church as a guest speaker. A business meeting followed the Sunday evening service and the congregation of 111 voted to ask him to serve as pastor and he accepted.

On September 22, 1992, several from the church met with Brother Stallings and others from the Nazarene Church to discuss purchase of the building. In November, the building and land was purchased. The original board members were Brothers Robert Poindexter, Howard Jarrett, Jack Williams, Bill Holder and Earl Borah.

On Sunday, November 22, the church was organized with 90 charter members. The members joined the Social Band Association of Free Will Baptists in January, 1993.

By November, 1996, it was obvious that more space was needed. In March, 1997, final blueprints were approved by the church and on April 30, 1997, a building committee was appointed consisting of Brothers Herman Shaw, Bill Holder, David Baltz, Charles Rickey and Bob Heard.

Groundbreaking occurred on Mothers Day, May 11, 1997, and services were held in the new sanctuary on Sunday, December 14, 1997. On Easter Sunday, 1998, there were 298 present for worship. God continues to bless. –*Brandon Baltz.*

Cemeteries, Clubs and Organizations

HALCUM FAMILY CEMETERY

We might call M.L. Detar, who lives on Fourth Street in Imboden, an archaeologist. However, his excavations were above ground level.

Mr. Detar travels to the East End of Fourth Street on his walks. For some time, he had noticed 'humps' on a lot owned by Mrs. Eva Verkler at Hendrix and Fourth Street. The area had been cleared by a bulldozer in the past year, but the raised portion was not removed.

After obtaining permission, Detar, assisted by Stanley Starling, began to cut into underbrush and vines. Honeysuckle vines had grown into the limbs of a nearby tree. Branches of the tree were cut off with a chain saw while standing in a truck. Thus the Halcum Family Cemetery was uncovered.

A space, approximately ten-by-ten feet, enclosed with a rock, two and one-half feet high, was capped with concrete. In the western side of the wall, two cemetery monuments of the same design are set in concrete. They bear the names John Halcum (born April 11, 1832, died June 20, 1908) and Nancy Halcum (born January 12, 1836, died March 19, 1932). At the top of Mr. Halcum's stone are the words "A Federal soldier of the 8th Regiment of the Tennessee Infantry." Engraved on the stones, above the family names, are buildings of a city and below the names, gates opening into the walled city. Identical people are on each monument an inscription reads: "A precious one from us has gone, A voice we loved is stilled. A place is vacant in our home, Which never can be filled."

It is interesting that the cemetery is listed in Cemetery Records of Lawrence County, Arkansas by Extension Homemakers Council with the names given as John Thomas Halcum and Nancy Brazil Halcum. The location is given as the old Halcum estate, one-fourth mile south of Highway 63 in Imboden.

Some Imboden residents remember John W. Halcum, son of the older couple, who served as town marshal for a number of years and lived on Fifth Street. Other names remembered in his family are his wife, Nancy, and children, Melvin, Nettie, Mae, John T., and Pauline.

It is believed that John W. Halcum is buried in Hope Cemetery in an unmarked grave. One of his sons, Sgt. John T. Halcum (1919-1952), died while in service in Korea and is buried in Hope Cemetery. Ozark Journal, Imboden, AR 3-21-91
 –Pauline McKamey

HOPE CEMETERY

We find an historic area of Imboden when we travel past the Housing Area, cross the Hardin Creek Bridge, and enter beautiful Hope Cemetery.

A new beacon from the past has been shining there for several years. This new monument appeared in the oldest section of the cemetery about six years ago with the inscription, "Benjamin F. Imboden 1971-1852, and wife Polly Hunter Imboden 1795-1848. Settled here 1828 for whom the town was named."

Sloan Rainwater of Jonesboro, a great-great-grandson of Benjamin Imboden, has explained the erection of the monument. When his grandfather, Dr. W.J. Hatcher, passed away in 1904, a vertical monument of white marble marked his resting place. After the death of Dr. Hatcher, in 1944, a double stone was set in the cemetery with both names inscribed and the marble marker was laid aside.

A few years ago two daughters of Mamie Bridges Shannon, another descendant of Benjamin Imboden, visited the cemetery. They were from Oklahoma. They regretted the fact that a number of members of the Imboden family were buried in Hope Cemetery, but no monuments could be found in their honor. Mrs. RS Rainwater, mother of Sloan Rainwater and a first cousin of Mamie Gridges Shannon, suggested the discarded marble stone that originally marked her father's grave be used to honor the Imbodens. The Oklahoma ladies, whose names are unknown at this time, were responsible for having it polished, engraved, and set in place.

Another stone that for some reason has been overlooked by numerators is leaning against a large rectangular pile of stones with a flat top. The top of the leaning stone has been broken off, but the inscription, "Polly, wife of James Couts born Nov. 2, 1801, died Jan'y 1857 in the 56th year of her age," is quite clear, James Couts is known to be an early settler who evidently owned hundreds of acres of land here. In the 1850's he was granted land by the General Land Office of the United

Hope Cemetery, Imboden, Arkansas.

Stone of Polly, wife of James Couts 1801-1857, leaning in front.

Stones in Hope Cemetery, taken from the west.

Benjamin F. Imboden tombstone.

Standing, left to right: Wilma Jones and Clover Bend Preservation Board Members: Viola Meadows, Lavania Baker and Willene Kirkland, Representative Tom Baker.

Hope Cemetery, Imboden, Arkansas.

States located at Batesville and was deeded land by the Hardins, who were also early settlers.

It is believed that the large rectangular pile of stones with the flat top was used as an unloading place for caskets in earlier days. Also, the story that another large pile of stones marks the graves of carpetbaggers, who were killed on a nearby farm due to stealing, has been passed from generation to generation since post-Civil War days.

The cemetery was owned by the town of Imboden until Hope Cemetery Association was formed in 1960 and the land was deeded to the Association. Now each person owning a lot or having given a contribution is a member of the Association. Most of the old records of the cemetery were destroyed by fire. However, in recent years, a record book kept for the town by Bouldin Duvall has been found. It has proved to be of great value in locating many of the older gravesites. Also, a plat of the 1914 section of the cemetery with lot numbers was obtained from the Powhatan courthouse years ago. It is very helpful if an old deed is available with a lot number. Sections of the cemetery are the oldest part located next to the road, the 1914 addition, the 1954 addition, and the new area recently donated by the Rash family.

The visible record of the earliest burials in the cemetery is gradually fading. Either vandalism or the age of the stones - probably both - is responsible for the broken condition of so many. Some are lying flat on the ground - such as the stones for Orleana Duvall, 1824-1871,

and JB Hendrix, 1830-1893. Longfellow's poem on the Hendrix stone is perfectly clear after 95 years. - "Life is real, life is earnest, and the grave is not its goal; dust thou art, to dust returneth, was not spoken of the soul." The tops are broken off of many of the stones that are still standing. It is good that names were recorded by J.W. Jean in a book of the county, "Directory of Cemeteries in Western District," published in 1959 and in the new Lawrence County cemetery records compiled by the Extension Homemakers Council and published in 1960.

The earliest recorded burials were in the 1850's with the Imbodens, Couts, Jay and Jane Bridges in 1952, and another Hendrix stone, BH Hendrix, 1830-1853, being some of the oldest. Another stone revealing an early birthdate is that of Marvin Duvall, 1789-1862.

Other tombstones have stories to tell, but many will remain a mystery. Some are only small stones projecting from the ground with no clues as to the person buried there. They may have been there many, many years. The cemetery was in existence when some of the earliest settlers came to Imboden.

Beginning the year of 1988, veterans are being remembered on Memorial Day, Veteran's Day, and other major holidays with flags purchased by the Stovall, Hackworth, Haney VFW Post 10573. Over 60 graves were marked with the American flags on Memorial Day and Veterans Day. As information is available, more can be remembered. It is known that at least one Mexican War veteran, Robert McKamey, 1788-1870, is buried there and two veterans from the Spanish-American conflict, Earnest Anderson Ray, 18??-1963, and CE Martin, 1873-1954. Others were in service in the Civil War, World Wars I and II, and the Korean and Vietnam conflicts.

Most of the stones in the cemetery face east. I have been told it is traditional in cemeteries for graves to face the rising of the sun. The Encyclopedia Britannica states that as customs were established, Christian tradition preferred the feet toward the east, ready to rise and meet

Christ when He appears. And how fitting that someone in the Estes family planted surprise lilies, which could be called resurrection lilies, in their grave enclosure.

We may see decay in the old sections, but the inscriptions of hope on many of the stones, the expectant position of the stones, the resurrection lilies, all make us know that Hope Cemetery was properly named.

Note: Since 1988, many of the older stones have been repaired and placed in an upright position. –Pauline McKimey

CLOVER BEND HISTORIC PRESERVATION ASSOCIATION

It was in the late 1930's, that the community of Clover Bend had its new start when 92 home sites were carved out of the large farms that made up the area. As the community grew, so did the school, but in 1983, it had dwindled until only three students graduated. Consolidation was the only option. Plans were started to demolish the school buildings. Graduates and friends started a movement to keep the community together. A need was seen to preserve not just the school history, but the rich history of all of Clover Bend dating back to the early 1800s. This could be accomplished by forming a Preservation Association, which could preserve the five buildings, and attain placement on the State and National Register, hold an annual reunion for all former students and residents, and establish a school museum to preserve the memorabilia of the school and the surrounding communities. This has been an on going process, but all of the above have been accomplished.

With Representative Tom Baker and Mr. Don House leading the drive, and with the help of the alumni and friends in Lawrence County, the Clover Bend Historic Preservation Association became a reality. A corporation was formed and a nine-member board of directors was elected to serve. The first board members were: Don House, Viola Callahan Meadows, Lance Phillips, Don Tennison, Eddie Gardner, Kenneth Quarry Jr., Viril Ward Pratt, Tom Baker and Billy Ed Doyle. Others who have served: Eugene Brand, Roger Tinsley, Bettye Whittaker Claxton, Lavania Spotts Baker, Dale Phillips, Chester Warnick, T. M. Herriott, Willene Baker Kirkland, Alda Jean Ramsey, Robert Pratt, Mazie Alls and Robin Whaley. –Alda Ramsey.

LAWRENCE COUNTY CHINA PAINTERS

Maxine Bracy, Helen Henderson, Pearl Looney and Dorothy Cox were members of the Reyno Club and when it became too large, they organized the Lawrence County China Painters Club on July 6, 1973.

China painting started in the 1800's, then it died down and was revived in the 1930's. Pauline Salyer was president and founder of The World Organization of China Painters. She traveled the world painting with renowned artists. In 1960, she organized The Sooner China Painting Club in Oklahoma. It was the first of many clubs to be formed across the United States and foreign countries. The International membership has grown to nearly 7,000 members. The Museum and Corporate Headquarters are in Oklahoma City, Oklahoma. –*Faye Shannon.*

HOME DEMONSTRATION CLUB/EXTENSION HOME-MAKERS CLUB

In July, 1918, Miss Kate Scott came to Lawrence County as an emergency agent to assist women in food preservation. This was the beginning of Home Demonstration/Extension Homemaker Club work.

The first Home Demonstration Agent, Miss Odessa Pearce, came in 1923, and organized a club at Anchor in the Smithville-Denton area of Western Lawrence County. The first Council was formed in 1929, by Miss Gladys Waters.

Early programs included food preservation, baking, and soap making. In the 1930s, the Live at Home Program was popular. Freedom or Victory Gardens were utilized by members during World War I and World War II to supplement food supplies for the family. Civil Defense and Self Medicare Programs were also war time programs.

The Council worked on the Mattress Program, where cotton mattresses were made locally. The Canning Kitchen made available pressure cookers for women to use in canning their produce or meat.

Home Demonstration members saw the need for electricity in rural areas and promoted this project. Club projects have included roadside parks, tree planting, health education, child abuse awareness, clothing and nutrition.

In 1935, under the direction of Geraldine Orrell, County Agent, work began to obtain a county council building. Through the leadership and untiring efforts of Mrs. Ida Belle Flippo, Miss Inez Sitton and Mr. J. F. Sloan and Clarence Webb, County Judge, the building received approval as WPA project after their meeting with Hattie Caraway, Arkansas' first lady Senator in Little Rock. Club contributions and WPA labor enabled the 30 x 60 foot building to reach completion. Mr. J. F. Sloan donated the

native rock and split sandstone used for the construction. Mr. and Mrs. Jim Lewis donated the five acre land site in Powhatan and County Judge C. W. Webb provided support for this project. On May 11, 1937, the council building was dedicated as the first county council building in the state of Arkansas. The building was used until it was destroyed by a forest fire in 1962.

In 1968, Lawrence County members gathered information from cemeteries in the county. In 1982, this information was bound into a book with 90 cemetery listings.

Agents who have led the local Home Demonstration/Extension Homemakers Clubs have been: Kate Scott, 1918; Odessa Pearce, 1923-1924; Lillian Deeden, 1924-1925; Myrtle Leach, 1926; Gladys Waters, 1928-1931; Mable Bickersraff, 1932; Geraldine G. Orrell, 1934-1935; Inez Sitton, 1936-1938; Amy Woolwine, 1938-1940; Ruth Pyle Parsons, 1940-1941; Edna Earle Reynolds, 1942-1945; Novelle Bond Anderson, 1946; Margaret B. Kemp, 1946-1947; Thelma Davidson, 1947; Turnmire B. Carroll, 1947-1968; Dianne Formby Howard, 1969-1980; Gail Wiederkehr Clark, 1975.

Council Presidents from 1919 through 1998 include: Mrs. Tol Wilson, Mrs. Victor Sloan, Mrs. M. F. McKamey, Mrs. C. M. Mason, Mrs. R. L. Flippo, Mrs. Tom Penn, Mrs. L. C. Sloan, Mrs. E. M. Johnson, Miss Lucy Wasson, Mrs. E. B. Andrews Jr., Mrs. J. L. Smith, Mrs. Lee Snow, Mrs. Miles Ponder, Mrs. Jewell Howard, Mrs. V. J. Cameron, Mrs. Max Hollander, Martha Dawson, Marilyn Craig, Maxine Wildrick, Lillian Rooker, Lois Henson, Daphene Starr, Barbara Whitmire, Elaine Stoll, Catherine Richey, Priscilla Walling, Helen Blackburn, Pauline Walker, and Mary Lou Hollehy. –*Gail Clark.*

SMITHVILLE EXTENSION HOMEMAKERS CLUB

Smithville Extension Homemakers Club was organized January 19, 1949, in the home of Helen Rudy. Charter members were: Dula Baker, Mattie Bellamy, Lorene Holder, Secretary and Treasurer; Anna Holt, Gladys Justus, Vice President, Beatrice Perkins, President, Oneida Ratliff, Mollie Richardson, Helen Rudy, Reporter, Lola Russell, Bonnie Starr, Lura

White, Wallece White, Anna Williams and Turnmire Carroll, Extension Agent. Other members: Annie Abee, Hazel Baker, Ella Bratcher, Audrey Brown, Donna Cain, Mae Childers, Sherry Childers, Zora Clements, Minnie Cox, Vee Cummings, Bertha Davis, Leta Dean, Rowena Dickson, Dina Durham, Dora Gay, Cora Gray, Velma Gray, Gertie Helms, Viola Helms, Etta Hillhouse, Jennie Hoffman, Lottie Hoggard, Zula Howard, Mrs. Charles Johnson, Mary Johnston, Harriet Jones, Linda Jones, Myrtle Judkins, Pauline Justus, Leona Karsch, Lonita Klinger Ellen Lewis, Christene Light, Jeffie Long, Ada McClintick, Mary McIntire, Maxine Mize, Lillie Massey, Pauline Moore, Geneva Mullen, Debbie Newberry, Bonnie Perkins, Vida Perkins, Mrs. Conally Potter, Eva Ratliff, Virgie Ring, Lillian Rooker, Mary Rooker, Nora Rudy, Emily Smith, Daphine Starr, Joan Thrasher, Georgia Venable, Claire Wade, Priscilla Walling, Linda Wallis, Grace Ward, Geneva Willett, Maxine Winters, Sena Winters.

Members have learned valuable techniques through Extension Homemakers Club. Worthwhile projects provided by these 74 members and Agents, Turnmire Carrol, Diane Howard and Gail Clark: Furnished doctors office, town clean-up, improvements on old school building, established City Park, landscaped church grounds, health fair, blood pressure clinics, fund raisers, neighborhood watch signs, entertained 4-H Club, "Read To Me", "I Will Tell", recovery pillows, donated to Fire Department, exceptional school, childrens home, St. Jude Hospital, purchased blinds for community center.

Lawrence County Council building at Powhatan, built by WPA and donated labor. The building was destroyed by fire in 1962.

Members of the Lawrence County China Painters Club are: front row, left to right: Lorene Taylor, Maxine Bracy, Louise Ponder, Ehrline Walter, Elizabeth Staudt and Jewell Snapp, president. Back row: Gale Rorex, Edwina James, Wilma McGee, Glynda Stewart, Faye Shannon, Annie Parkinson, Dorothy Rorex and Wilma Jane Penn. Members not present for the picture are: Patrica Corder, Ruth Cox, Maxine Doran, Judy Perdue, Dorothy Pettyjohn. Carrie Mae Snapp, Lela Snapp, Junena Yerke and Willene Kirkland. Associate members are: Ginger Adams, Margaret Brown, Dorotha Turner and Ehrline Walter.

Smithville HDC Group, 1964: Left to right, front row: Geneva Mullen, Pauline Moore, Hazel Baker, Mollie Richardson, Beatrice Perkins, Myra Perkins and Cora Gray. Second row: Bonnie Starr, Bonnie Perkins, Daphine Starr, Lillian Rooker and Ada McClintick. Back row: Anna Williams, Mary Rooker, Dula Baker, Lottie Hoggard and Virgie Ring.

Family Histories Of Lawrence County

John Filmore Gibbens house made about 1912-1915 at Smithville, Arkansas.

ALBRIGHT FAMILY. The Albright family is one of the older and well established families of Northeast Arkansas.

The name "Albright" comes from the German name Albrecht. It is found among those making up the House of Hapsburg.

At the close of the Civil War, E. A. Albright settled on a farm six miles west of Jonesboro. To him and his wife, Oma, were born nine children. The sixth one was Augustus Garland, born March 21, 1876.

Augustus Garland married Annie Dowdy of Florence, Alabama. They lived in Hoxie until their deaths. To them were born 10 children. Their names are: Ruth, Homer, Shannon, Virginia, Hariania, Elmo, Rosemary, Woodrow, Billy Sunday and Gus Jr. —*Gus Albright.*

CHARLES E. ALDRIDGE. Charles Edward was born in 1864, in Missouri. The son of Fredrick and Christine Willey Aldridge, he came to Arkansas as a young man. He married Treny Manning in 1888, in Lawrence County, Arkansas. They were the parents of two children: Lottie and Fritz Aldridge.

After Treny's death in 1899, Charles returned to Missouri, and married his childhood sweetheart, Mary Rhodes Statler. In 1900 they moved back to Lawrence County. Mary had two sons from her first marriage, George and Grover Statler.

Charles and Mary were the parents of three girls: Ruth Aldridge Garner, Edith Aldridge Meadows and Marie Aldridge Orvis.

Edith Aldridge, daughter of Charles and Mary Rhodes Aldridge, Harvey Meadows.

Charles owned a store in Sedgwick for several years. He also farmed between Sedgwick and Egypt. Charles died in 1914, and is buried in the Aldridge Cemetery near Egypt.

Edith Aldridge married Harvey Meadows. They were the parents of three children: Avalee, Neil and Delores. Ruth Aldridge married Jack Garner. They were the parents of one son, Charles. Marie Aldridge married Russell Orvis. They were the parents of one son, Wendell. Lottie Aldridge, daughter of Charles E. and Treny Manning Aldridge, married Grover Statler. They were the parents of seven children: Arnold, Carl, J. C., Harold, G. R., Florine and Juanita. —*Viola Meadors.*

BUREN AND JIM ALEXANDER. Buren and Jim Alexander, sons of Lafayette and Eunice Peoples Alexander. Jim served as Lawrence County Circuit Clerk in Lawrence County in 1931. They had brothers and sisters: Lockie, Jeffie, Ora, Laura and Lillie.

CHARLES BOYD ALLEN AND LINDA ANN DUMONT. Charles Boyd Allen, better known as Chuck, was born in 1964 and lived most of his life in the Land Between the Lakes area. He attended Dover Elementary and Stewart County High School. He was a member of the Stewart County High School band, playing the saxophone and tuba. In 1982 he graduated high school and attended training and technology program in Oak Ridge, Tennessee. At the end of the program he returned to Dover and was hired to work at Dover Products Corporation. In 1987 he joined the United States Navy and became an electronic warfare technician. He became a member of the precommissioning crew for the *USS Wisconsin BB 64* and Iowa class battleship. During the summer of 1989, he went on temporary assigned duty on the *USS Iowa BB 61.* In 1990 he was stationed in Newport, Rhode Island, and in December of that year married Linda Ann Dumont. After getting out of the Navy, he stayed in the New England region to get a job in the electronics industry. In 1995 he got his associates of science degree in electronics and got a job at Cherry Semiconductor Corporation. In the summer of 1997 he got a job with Unitrode Corporation in New Hampshire. Charles and Linda now reside in Weare, New Hampshire with three daughters: Kristen Renee, Bethany Jean and Heather NicClain. —*Chuck Allen.*

JACOB STRALEY ALLISON FAMILY. When Jacob Straley Allison and his wife, Sallie Storey, departed from their middle Tennessee home in 1817, they had no intention of making Lawrence County or Arkansas their home. Fate, with assistance from "Ole Man River," brought about a change in their plans. The Allisons were on a delayed honeymoon enroute to Texas. When they arrived in Memphis the mighty Mississippi was too high for the crossing so they stayed in a hotel and waited for the water to recede. Another guest at the hotel was a Captain Frank Tucker from Clover Bend, Arkansas who managed the Clover Bend plantation for Alice French (whose pen name was Octave Thanet) and her friend, Jenny Crawford. While waiting, Captain Tucker and Jacob Straley developed a friendship which resulted in him taking a position with Captain Tucker. The honeymooners moved to Clover Bend, settled in a small house on Black River and forgot about Texas.

During the next two decades, two noteworthy items were recorded in the Allison family history. One of which was an increase in the family from 2 to 10 members. The other was Jacob Straley began buying up land from the homesteaders until he acquired 1,400 acres between Stranger's Home and Black River.

Goodspeed's *History of Northeast Arkansas,* page 771, published in 1877, provides the following information: "Jacob Straley Allison, a farmer and stock raiser whom Lawrence County can feel proud to claim as a citizen, was born in Burke County, North Carolina, November 12, 1837. He is a son of Bird and Elizabeth Davis Allison, of the same state. The elder Allison was a farmer in North Carolina, until the year 1859, when he moved to Cocke County, Tennessee and from there to Alabama, where he now resides with his wife, very near the age of 100 years. Jacob remained with his parents in North Carolina until he grew to manhood, and then started in life on his own account. In 1861, he enlisted in the 22nd North Carolina Infantry, and served in that company until the close of the war. He took part in the battles around Richmond, at Manassas, Chancellorsville, and the 7 days battle in the Wilderness, the fights and siege at Petersburg, Ce-

dar Creek and others, besides 20 or more skirmishes. He was wounded twice, once through the shoulder, at Shepardstown by rifle balls and had one finger shot off. His service for the cause was brilliant, and there are few that are superior. After receiving his discharge he returned to the state of Tennessee, where he remained up until 1871, when he moved to Arkansas and located at Clover Bend. He first bought some land near Stranger's Home, and has since then added to it on different occasions, until now he owns about 1,400 acres of rich bottom land, with about 200 acres under cultivation. He has 10 houses altogether on his land, eight of them being on the home farm. When Mr. Allison first came to Lawrence County, all he possessed was $90 cash, and two beds, and was in debt to the extent of $100, which he has since paid. He now owns a fine farm, and is considered to be one of the most substantial men in Lawrence County. He was married in 1869, to Miss Sallie Storey, of Tennessee, a daughter of William E. Storey and has eight children by his marriage. William W., Clara and Clarence (twins), Rose, Pearl, Lizzie, Robert E. Lee and Zola. Mr. Allison is a Master Mason, and he and Mrs. Allison are both members of the Eastern Star Chapter. The Allisons lost two of their children in infancy, Clarence and Zola". This is the end of the Goodspeed's information provided.

By the late 1800s, the Allisons were living on their almost totally self-sufficient farm on Surrounded Hill near Stranger's Home. When the children were ready for high school they chose to attend Cave City Secondary School. The male members of the family went on to Arkansas College, Batesville. The females became teachers by taking the teachers examination, securing a license, or attending Galloway College, an all girls' school in Searcy.

Between 1900 and 1910, William W. Allison had lost his wife, Henrietta Owens Allison, and three sons, Carl, Allen and Jack. All were buried in the newly established Allison Cemetery on the Surrounded Hill farm. Max and Clara attended Arkansas College, where Max met and married Wynona Arnn. Clara married George Adams of Moorfield. Both Clara and Max's family lived in Little Rock until their death. They did not have any children. Max and Wynona are interred in the Oaklawn Cemetery in Batesville, where Max's father is buried. Clara and George Adams are interred in Rest Hills Cemetery in Jacksonville, Arkansas.

Clara Allison, the surviving twin, married Hugh K. Gibson of Clover Bend. Clara died in childbirth and baby Hugh died in infancy. There was no record of their interment.

Rose Allison taught in the Lawrence County Public Schools and taught music on the pump organ in her mother's parlor before she married Harry D. Logan, a farmer in the Stranger's Home vicinity. They had five sons, all who attended school in Lawrence County. Bruce, the oldest son, was a teacher before going into business in Walnut Ridge. He served in the armed forces during World War II. He married Ruth Coker of Alicia, they had two sons, Scott who lives near his mother Ruth in Walnut Ridge, and Steven in Columbus, Georgia.

Tom Bernard was elected to the position of Lawrence County Clerk after returning home from World War II. Tom remained in politics and served as county judge before being elected as representative in the state legislature from Lawrence County; a position he held for many years. Tom married Virgie Wilmuth of Swifton, they had a daughter, Barbara Pomeroy, who lives in Monticello, Arkansas. Virgie, who celebrated her 91st birthday, resides in Trinity Village in Pine Bluff.

Wiley Bly's first wife was Marie Selvege from Alicia. They had a son, Laddie, who is a professor at Arkansas State University in Jonesboro, Arkansas. Wiley's second wife was Kitty Gains from Portia. They have three sons, Allen, John and Phillip. All live near their mother in the St. Louis area.

Steven Brooks married Willine Turley; they have a son, Blaine. They reside in Mobile, Alabama. Brooks is one of the surviving grandsons of Jacob and Sallie S. Allison.

Charles Harry, a state policeman, served many areas in Arkansas before he retired in Batesville, Arkansas. He married Katherine Sherrel. They had a daughter, Sherrey Hilburn. Sherrey and Katherine still live in Batesville. The four deceased sons of Rose and Harry Logan are buried in Lawrence Memorial Cemetery in Walnut Ridge with their mother and father.

Pearl Allison met and married Dr. Thomas "Tommy" Laman while attending school in Cave City, where they made their home until he died. The Lamans kept many of the Allison family children in their home during school years to further their education. They were the parents of one daughter, Ruthel, an accomplished musician and graduate of Galloway College. Ruthel's first husband was Alvis Johnson. They had one daughter, Martha Carolyn Allen. After a divorce she married Jesse R. Healsey of Batesville. Ruthel lived to be 90 years old. She is buried in the Cave City Cemetery with her parents.

Elizabeth "Lizzie" married Jess M. Watts. They resided in Lawrence County. The Watts had three children of their own, but helped to raise many children who were left without parents. Their children were Jakie and Maxine, who died at the age of 13 and is buried in the Allison Cemetery by her father.

Wallace Bufford and his first wife, Arlene French, had two children: Robert Monroe and Willene Watts Mitchell. Bufford's second wife was Mildred Ashlock. Their five children are: Lana Leale, Terry and Tammy (twins), Jerry and Lisha Watts Sutterfield. All of the children live in Grand Rapids, Michigan. Bufford and his present wife, Myrtle Lane Watts, reside in Biloxi, Mississippi.

Elizabeth Larue Watts was a former Lawrence County teacher mostly at Alicia. Noel Hall, her first husband, died while they lived in Alicia. Larue later married Hassel A. Marshal of Batesville and inherited the grandchildren she loves and enjoys. Larue lives on Dennison Heights overlooking Batesville and White River. Elizabeth "Lizzie" is buried in the Stranger's Home Cemetery,

Robert E. Lee Allison married Mollie Betty Warren and started their family of six children. Two died in infancy. One was never named and the other was Donald Jacob Lowell, who lived for nine months. They were buried in the Allison family cemetery.

Ruth Allison married Doyne Jackson Steinsiek of Judsonia. They made their home in Jonesboro where Doyne was in the finance, loan and real estate businesses. The Steinsieks had three daughters. Kay Allison married Wayne Snipes Jr. Kay and Wayne died three days apart from natural causes while living in Sachse, Texas, leaving four children: Christopher, Straley, Storey and Jonathan. The children have lived in Jonesboro with their grandmother, Ruth Steinsiek, and their Aunt Betty, who is their guardian.

Betty Josephine married Jan Shaw, a band director from Searcy. Their only child, Misty Lynn Velasquez, lives in Biloxi, Mississippi and is associated with the WLOX television station. Betty is a HUD housing consultant in the southern states area.

The Steinsiek's third daughter is Sally Rona, who married Ron Blake and has one child, Candice. Sally is an assistant professor at the University of Texas at El Paso. Doyne died in 1954, and is buried in Oak Lawn Cemetery in Jonesboro. Ruth continues to work for Childhood Services of Arkansas State University.

Robert Aurelius "Bob" Allison was involved in relocation of the Japanese from the Jerome and Rohwer Internment Camps following World War II. He married Marie Wilson from Newport. They made their home in Jonesboro where they reared a family.

Jo Ann Allison has been involved in training and providing technical assistance to preschool staff throughout the state as director of Childhood Services of Arkansas State University. Jo Ann married Bill Nalley from South Carolina. They have two daughters: Allison Ann Fletcher and Ashley Nalley, both of Jonesboro. Marie continues to live in Jonesboro where she is in business.

Jerry Allison, a conscientious and popular state representative from District 86 in Arkansas is married to Jo Ann Redmon Bailey of Manila. They have two sons: Lance Bailey of Franklin, Tennessee, and Robert "Bobby", who is following in his family's business of "manufactured" homes.

Johnny Warren Allison, a skilled financier involved in banking and manufacturing, and a loyal supporter of Arkansas State University, lives in Conway, Arkansas with his wife, the former Jennifer Sossamon. They have a daughter, Whitney, and a son, Johnny Warren II. Johnny has two daughters by a former wife, Virginia Castleberry. They are Gigi Johnson and Kristin Druery.

Rona Latain Allison, an educator and free lance architect married Milton H. Summerour of Lucedale, Mississippi. During World War II, Rona enlisted in the Women's Marine Corps while her husband was in the Air Force. Rona and Milton did not have any children, but provided educational opportunities for many students who needed assistance in completing their education. Both Rona and Milton are interred in Oak Lawn Cemetery in Jonesboro.

Warren C. Allison was a lieutenant in the Navy during the Normandy invasion in World War II. He married Floella Blackman of Jonesboro after the war. They adopted a son, Michael Warren. Floella and Michael continue to make their home in Nashville, Tennessee. Warren died in 1996. He was cremated, his remains are interred in Wood Lawn Cemetery in Nashville, Tennessee.

The four living grandchildren of Jacob Straley and Sallie Storey Allison are as follows: Steven Brooks Logan of Mobile, Alabama; Wallace Bufford Watts of Biloxi, Mississippi; Elizabeth Larue Watts Marshall of Batesville; and Ruth Allison Steinsiek of Jonesboro, Arkansas.

One great-grandson, Scott Logan, and family live in Walnut Ridge. Scott is the only direct descendant of Jacob Straley and Sallie Storey Allison who has remained in Lawrence County. His brother, Steven, lives in Alabama. *–Ruth Steinsiek.*

ALLS-JONES. The Alls family migrated to Lawrence County, Arkansas, from Tennessee in the 19th century.

My grandparents, Harry Steadman and Virginia Bell Grey Alls, lived in Lynn and raised their family there. Harry's uncle was John Franklin Alls of Lynn. My father, John Benjamin Franklin Alls, was the eldest of Harry and Virginia's children. His siblings were: Minnie Alls, Betty Alls Walker, Blanche Alls Glenn, Deam Holloway Alls, Idell Alls Crum and Harry S. Alls Jr.

My father and his family were raised in the "bottoms" of Black River and later moved to a 160 acre farm just outside of Lynn. My grandfather, Harry, died in 1905, when my father was 11 years

Mr. and Mrs. Ben Alls, Alls farm, July 17, 1929; wedding day.

of age. He became the head of the household at this age. His only brother, Harry Jr., drowned at the age of 18 in Black River. This happened on July 4, 1925, at a community picnic. My father's pregnant sister, Idell, and her husband, Ross Crum, drowned on March 3, 1929, when Black River overflowed its banks.

My father met my mother, Elizabeth Gladys Jones, also of Lynn and they married July 17, 1929, at the Alls family home. He was 28 and she was 19.

My mother's family was quite large also. Her father, W. Stanley Jones, was married to Luilley Butram on March 31, 1897. Their children were: George Winfred, 1897-1899; Gertrude "Polly", born 1899, married Nathaniel Tobe Callahan in 1915; Eva Stella, born May 3, 1901, married first Fred Callahan, second Berry Lingo, third Edgar Lawson, fourth, Marian Shannon, fifth Oscar Davis, sixth Clarence Davis; Modeana, born 1903, married Charles Orrick; John Paul Jones, born June 21, 1905, married first Madaline Simmons, second Pearl Jones, third Liddie Stockton; Ethel, born October 6, died June 9, 1968, married Robert Adair; Snowdie, 1907-1907; William Stanley "Bill", July 19, 1908-November 19, 1977, married Ethel Mae Schales; Elizabeth Gladys, January 27, 1910-December 29, 1998, age 88, married to my father for 53 years; Loucille, born 1911, married first Philip Farmer, second Charles Greathouse; Cora Faye, born June, 1913, married first Richard Palmer Penn, second Frank Brown; Hester, born December 31, 1914, married first Ammon Benton, second B. Mason.

My mother, best known as "Lizzie" to her family and friends, bore two sons while living in Arkansas. My eldest brother, Harry La Vaughn, was born September 19, 1931. The next son, Benny Brooks, was born May 19, 1933.

My parents sold the farm and moved to California in 1939, with Mabel Howard and her family, also of Lynn.

Three more children were born to my parents in California. Two more sons, Danny Delano and Gary Curtis; a daughter, Rebecca Eve was born last.

On April 19, 1958, at the age of 14, Gary drowned in the Pacific Ocean. His body was never recovered.

My father died in 1982, and my mother died on December 29, 1998. They were married 53 years.

My father outlived all his siblings. Mother survived all her siblings except Lucille Greathouse and Cora Penn Brown, who resides in Cave City, Arkansas.

Having visited Lynn several times while growing up, it will always hold a special place in my heart. *–Rebecca Alls Peterson.*

LORINE PHELPS RAINEY ANDERSON was the sixth and last child of Russell and Lorine Rainey and was born on February 13, 1926. The "baby" of the family was cared for by her siblings and especially older sister, Leenell, as her mother's health was so poor during her childhood. Her mother would swing Lorine to sleep and Pop (Russell) would carry her to bed. "Too old - too big, but just a little more spoiling the baby."

Her father was a rural postman who kept Lorine busy painting names on mail boxes and typing route sheets. She checked his car every day for pennies he dropped on the route so they could buy candy from McCarroll's Grocery store. Her mother was noted for church work and Lorine accompanied her to Circle meetings. Lorine's school years were spent having older sister Leenell as teacher in the third, seventh and ninth grades. Lorine's other sisters were Rachel Rainey and Martha Jane Rainey Boyd and her older brothers were: Gilbert and Jack Rainey.

Billie and Lorine Anderson - 1996.

Lorine was editor of the *Bobcat* high school newspaper and received the home economics medal for outstanding student and citizenship awards. She was voted Miss WRHS in 1944 when she graduated. When World War II broke out, Rachel and Lorine often played ping pong at the USO where Rachel introduced Lorine to Billie Neal Anderson from Sulphur Springs, Texas. Billie was honorably discharged in November, 1945, and they were married on December 2, 1945, at Lorine's home at 123 East Walnut Street. Billie Neal was born September 20, 1920, in Hopkins County, Texas, the son of Bert L. and Ethel D. Martin Anderson. After Lorine's mother died in 1946, they left Arkansas in a 1939 Ford, the hood tied down with baling wire, $65 (borrowed), a shotgun and a radio-record player.

Billie and his father, Bert Anderson, formed a partnership in November, 1946, to operate a dairy. They bought 7 Jersey cows and 100 acres of land. The years which followed were hard with Billie putting in many long days and Lorine experiencing farm life from a city girl perspective. Their family included: Marynell, born August 29, 1948; Rachel Ann, born August 31, 1950; and Billie Neal II, born January 18, 1856. Another daughter, Laura, was stillborn in 1954.

Lorine was devoted to her children and spent hours working in PTA groups, 4-H clubs, dairy shows, dress revues, public speaking contests and piano recitals. Based on the number of medals which were won as well as other accomplishments, she was a highly successful and creative mother. She was named Outstanding State Homemaker for Texas in 1963. She was a lifetime member of the Women's Society of Christian Service. The family belongs to the Methodist church. Lorine's interest in genealogy allowed her to become a member of the Daughters of the American Revolution and the United States Daughters of 1812. Traveling was of great interest to the family from childhood vacations to retirement. Billie and Lorine bought a motor home and for 15 years they traveled the country visiting all 48 contiguous states. After 51 years of marriage, Lorine died from brain cancer at her home in Sulphur Springs, Texas on May 10, 1997. *–Rachel Rainey.*

ROBERT S. ANDERSON FAMILY.
Robert "Uncle Bob" Anderson and his new wife, Sarah McCauly Anderson, came from Missouri and Tennessee to settle in the Clear Springs area of Lawrence County in the late 1800s. Robert ran the family farm, raising cotton and also owned and operated a sorghum mill. Folks from around the area would bring cane to Robert's mill to be

processed. They usually paid with a share of the molasses produced. Robert and Sarah attended the Missionary Baptist Church in Clear Springs where Uncle Bob was said to have a fine singing voice. He studied the Bible daily and was completely familiar with the scriptures.

Robert and Sarah raised 10 children: Cora Omie, Granville T., Dolly, Eunice Elizabeth, Robert A., Filmore Sloan, Cliffie Mea, Elsie Ivy, Nadene and Flossie.

Cora Omie was born September 3, 1886. She married Henry Paul East on December 25, 1904. Their children were: Alma Marie, Juanita, Charlene, Ulysses H., Robert Eugene and Herbert.

Granville was born January 3, 1889. He married Eula King in October 1910. They had the following children: Opel, Woodrow Harrison, Helen, Ailene, Avis and Eula Jean. After the passing of Eula, Granville took a second wife, Jessa Anderson. They had two daughters: Lotus L. and Loretta L.

Dolly married Oscar Brady. Their children were: Lorenne, Carson and Paulene.

Eunice Elizabeth was born June 9, 1891. She married Clarence Webster Dent on April 12, 1912. Their children were: Lois Thelma, William Webster, Robert LeRoy, Melba Fern and Darrell Victor.

Robert A. was born June 28, 1893. His wife was Mae Howard; married October 30, 1919. They had five children: Vivian, Beuin, Hubert, Sarah Ellen and Betty Lou.

Filmore Sloan was born January 14, 1897. He married Pearl Amanda Rice. Their children were: Marvella, Margueritte, Delma, Shirley and Phyllis Pearl.

Cliffie Mea was born September 15, 1898. She and her husband, Alva "Pete" McBride, raised B. Christine, Robert Eugene and Bonnie O.

Elsie Ivy was born September 15, 1900. She had a son, Raymond T., with her first husband, Harve Smith. Later, with her second husband, Lex Hankins, she had six more children: Imogene, Thomas, Jay, Sue, Fred and Audrey.

Nadene was born March 6, 1903. She married Oscar Davis. Their children were: Edith, Paulene, O.T. and Mary Catherine.

Flossie was also born on September 15. She shared this birthday with her two sisters, Elsie and Cliffie. She married Jewell Thompson and they had three sons: Jr., Bobby and Joe T.

The family of Robert and Sarah has grown and spread out over the years to include several hundred descendants. Current generations include the following surnames: Brown, Calvert, Campbell, Carter, Cole, Corbett, Culver, Ditto, Faulkner, Gelvin, Hawk, Lunsford, McBride, McCarroll, Milgrim, Nanna, Pinckney, Portugal, Ross, Sheffield, Smith, Thompson, Vaughn, Wallis, Weyland and Webb. Each year they try to reunite at the annual family reunion in Walnut Ridge. *–Jerry Smith.*

CALVIN JONES ANDREWS FAMILY.
Calvin Jones Andrews migrated to Arkansas from Georgia in 1868. Calvin "Jones" Andrews was born in Orange County, North Carolina in 1840, to William and Martha Carroll Andrews. Jones was one of 14 children and in 1845, the family moved to Walker County, Georgia. In March, 1862, Jones married Cynthia Elizabeth "Lizzie" Bowers, daughter of Henry and Martha Bowers. A few years after the Civil War, Jones, wife and three children along with his father, seven sisters and families, and Lizzie's brother and sister (64 in all), came by wagon and steamboat to Arkansas. The family settled in what is now southeast Sharp County just over the Lawrence County line. Calvin Jones died in 1909, and Lizzie in 1916. They are buried

along with his father and several of the family members in the Mahan Cemetery near what was called "Wildcat Corner." Jones' mother and Lizzie's mother and father are buried in Walker County, Georgia.

Jones Andrews was with the Confederate forces during the Civil War and was wounded during one of the many battles he participated in. Jones enlisted in 1861, near Chattanooga, Tennessee, as a 2nd Sergeant in the Tennessee Volunteer Cavalry. He later joined Company A of Colonel Esters Third Confederate Cavalry of Georgia and spent most of the war with this unit. Lizzie Bowers Andrews attended the Girls Academy in LaFayette, Georgia,

Cynthia Elizabeth Andrews

and Jones the LaFayette High School. Both were very aware of the value of education and strongly supported the educational system after they moved to Arkansas and saw to it that their children had the opportunity to attend school. Jones was very active in the Shell Rock School (Wildcat Corner) and one time moved his family to Evening Shade so they could attend schools that offered higher levels of education. Several of their children and later descendants were school teachers.

Nine children were born to the marriage of Jones and Lizzie Andrews: Edward Byron "E. B.", Martishia, William

Calvin Jones Andrews

"Bill", Georgia, Ruby, Sallie, Ferd, Allie and Junie. Georgia, Ruby, Sallie and Allie all died as young children. E. B., a farmer, teacher and member of the Arkansas State Legislature in the early 1900s, married Mollie Childers and were the parents of 10 children. (See a more detailed history on this family elsewhere in this book.) Ferd married Ada Dawson and was a medical doctor in and around Clover Bend where he died in his 1930s. Bill, a successful farmer, married Ada Walden and they had 10 children: Martishia, married Walter Phillips and was a homemaker; Junie, a music teacher, first married a Mr. Kirkland and then M. A. W. Coffee. She died in Louisiana in the 1940s.

Jones and Lizzie Andrews left many descendants in the Lawrence County area, some of the names of these kin: Andrews, Bowers, Due, Mitchell, Mason, Crawford, Wilmuth, Sparks, Pinkston, Presley, McGaha, James, Robins, Wendt, Bush and Phillips. *–David Robins.*

E. B. ANDREWS FAMILY.
Edward Myron Andrews was the first of nine children born to Calvin Jones and Cynthia Elizabeth Andrews. (See their history elsewhere in this book.) Edward Byron Andrews was born in a Confederate Cavalry tent near Valley Head, Alabama, in November, 1864. "By," as he was called, lived in Walker County, Georgia, until 1868, when he came with his family to Arkansas. In the mid 1870s, the family moved back to Georgia, but found out they missed Arkansas and moved back to stay around 1878. In the late 1880s, while teaching school in Ravenden, By met Mollie John Childers and in November, 1890, they were married. Mollie was

E. B. and Mollie Andrews family about 1930. Seated: Edward Byron and Mollie John Andrews. Standing, left to right: Mollie Faye, Myrtle, Jennie, Lucy, Edward "Sam", Ruby, Grover, Lacy, Frank and Marvin.

born in January 1871 to John and Elvira Janes Childers of Ravenden. Mollie's great-grandparents, Isom Childers and John Janes, were some of the earliest settlers in Lawrence and Randolph Counties. Mollie's father died when she was just a baby and her mother married a Mr. Vinsel, he too passed on and she then married Mr. Fuller, a circuit preacher. Later after Mollie married, Mr. and Mrs. Fuller moved to Haskell, Texas, where Elvira Janes Childers Fuller died in November, 1928.

By Andrews represented Sharp County in the State Legislature for the 1905, 1907 and 1909 sessions and was a delegate to the Constitutional Convention in 1918. In the late 1930s, By and Mollie moved from their old home place to Strawberry. Byron Andrews died in 1948, and Mollie in 1953. Both are buried in Forrest Lawn Cemetery in Batesville. By and Mollie were the parents of 10 children, as of this writing only the

Claude and Lucy Andrews Sparks, 1944.

youngest, Mollie Fay Andrews Robins, is living. These 10 children were raised just over the Lawrence County line in Sharp County and attended school at Shell Rock (Wild Cat School), some later also attended Strawberry schools. The 10 children were:

Grover Jones Andrews married Burlie Rubie. Grover worked many years in the dry goods business in Batesville and the surrounding area selling for Barnett Brothers. Grover died in his mid 30s, and his wife many years later. Both are buried in Forrest Lawn Cemetery in Batesville. Grover and Burlie were the parents of four children: Jaunita, Donald, Byron and Grover Jean.

Ruby Elvira Andrews married

Frank and Ruth Andrews.

Arthur Leland Due. Arthur and Ruby spent many years in the educational field and for sometime operated a business college in Moline, Illinois. Over the years they resided in Arkansas, Texas, Tennessee and Illinois. Two children were born to this union: Arthur Leland Jr. and Eileen. Arthur

and Ruby retired to Cave City in the early 1970s, where both died and are buried in the Cave City Cemetery.

Marvin Melvin Andrews married Allie Barnett. Marvin worked for many years for Butler Brothers (Ben Franklin) and lived for a number of years in St. Louis. Three children were born to Marvin and Allie: Marvin Jr., Betty and William E. Marvin and wife Dorothy are retired in Dallas where Marvin worked for an oil company, Betty Gleaton, a widow, owns an independent phone company in Tifton, Georgia, and William E. was killed in a plane crash while in the service just after World War II. Marvin and Allie are buried in Tifton, Georgia.

Lacy Childers Andrews married first Minnie Mize and then Idella Crabtree. Lacy and Minnie lived in Batesville for many years where Lacy was an insurance salesman. They had three sons: Noel, Woodard "Woody" and Deal. Noel passed away a few years ago. Woody is retired and resides in Cave City and Deal lives near Mountain Home. Lacy and Idella are buried in Ward Cemetery near Strawberry and Minnie is buried at Campground Cemetery.

Elizabeth Myrtle Andrews married Lewis Mason. Myrtle and Lewis lived for many years in Swifton where he was postmaster and she also worked at the post office. Myrtle and Lewis had two daughters and a son. J. L. Mason has resided in Stuttgart for many years and was employed in the rice industry. For awhile he lived in Little Rock and was Director of the Arkansas State Prison System; Freida married Hoyt Wilmuth and Billye married Alfred Crawford. Both Billye and Fredia were school teachers. Hoyt and Freida had one daughter and Alfred and Billye had a son and a daughter. Lewis and Myrtle are buried in Tuckerman.

Lucy Andrews married Claude Sparks of near Poughkeepsie, October 24, 1925, and resided in Imboden until 1944 when they moved to Jonesboro. Both were school teachers in early life. He was a grocery salesman and liked to be known as a "drummer." She packed parachutes at Walnut Ridge AAF Pilot School during World War II. Both were very active in First Baptist Church. They had one son, C. E. Sparks Jr., who was married to Anne Weldy of Montgomery, Alabama, in 1952 and became a Russellville, Alabama newspaper owner and publisher. C. E. and Anne have three children: Amy, Joe and Tom. Claude died November 12, 1974, and Lucy on September 2, 1986. Both are buried in Russellville, Alabama. *(Shelbyville News Item, 1925: "Claude Sparks passed through our burg Saturday on his way to Mr. Andrews. Miss Lucy Andrews joined him there and going over to Reverend Edgar Wilkerson's home they were united in matrimony.")*

Jennie May Andrews married S. D. Mitchell. S. D. was a teacher for a number of years in Strawberry. They later moved to Conway, and then Russellville. S. D. and Jennie had one daughter, Mozelle. Mozelle married Jack Nelson and they had two children. Mozelle, now a widow, lives in Little Rock. Jennie and S. D. died in Russellville and are buried in Conway.

Edward Byron Andrews married Irene Campbell. Edward Bryan, known as "Sam," and Irene spent most of their entire married life in Strawberry. Sam was a rural mail carrier until he retired. For many years Sam and Irene enjoyed vacations to the Florida Keys where they loved to fish. After retirement they moved to Mountain Home where they both died and are buried. They had no children.

Frank Ferd Andrews married Ruth Lanell Puckett. Frank and Ruth moved from Sharp County to Lawrence County in 1932, where both taught school at Denton, Post Oak, Mount Vernon and

Powhatan. In 1938, Frank was appointed Deputy Circuit Clerk at Powhatan and later moved to Walnut Ridge where he held county offices until 1948. Their two children, John and Charles, grew up in Walnut Ridge. Frank and Ruth moved to their farm near Powhatan in 1948, and later moved to Batesville where they owned and operated a Ben Franklin store. They retired back to the Powhatan farm in 1980. John married Margery Hall and, after a career as a university professor, they now reside in Fayetteville. They have three children: John Patrick, Carol and Laura. Charles married Ada Jo Hatcher and was a salesman for IBM. At the time of his death in 1985, he and Ada resided next to his parents in Powhatan. They were the parents of four children: Robert, Cynthia, Leonard and Regina. Frank Andrews passed away in 1986, but Ruth still lives on the farm. Frank and Ruth have seven grandchildren and 11 great-grandchildren.

Mollie Fay Andrews married James Lovell "Jim" Robins. Jim and Mollie were married in Smithville in October 1935 and resided in Jesup until 1940. Over the next five years they lived in Black Rock, Hoxie and Walnut Ridge. During that time, Jim taught school at Jesup, Pleasant Hill, Strawberry and Calamine, worked for the welfare department and at a furniture store. Mollie stayed home to take care of the house and the five children. Bobby Lowell, born 1936, married Patricia Gould; Byron Louis, born 1937, married Wanneta Cave; Barbara Ann, born 1940, married Gerald Billions; James David, born 1943, married Janis Hawk; and Martha Jo, born 1945, married Denny Willis, then Joseph Ruiz. From 1945 till 1976, Jim and Mollie lived in Missouri, Arkansas and Tennessee, where Jim either worked or owned furniture stores. In 1976, they retired back to Cave City where they still reside today. They have both been very active in the Baptist church over these many years and her church in Cave City recently honored Mollie for teaching Sunday School for over 50 years. Jim and Mollie have 10 grandchildren and 10 great-grandchildren. –*David Robins.*

RICHARD "DICK" ANTHONY. If one walks or drives through Hope Cemetery in Imboden, it is almost impossible to miss seeing the gravesite of Richard Anthony by the roadway. Flowers, baskets, vases and sprays cover the grave and almost obscure the small tombstone which reveals the span of his life, 1852-1942. The flowers are placed there by those who feel that he should not be forgotten.

His earliest known home in the area was the town of Smithville, located about 12 miles from his burial place. Smithville was a typical frontier town in the Arkansas hills when Richard Anthony came there after the close of the Civil War. It has been stated in the writings of J.T. Alexander that he was the only black man among 200 people in the town.

One wonders why he was the only person of his race in the town since there had been a number of

Dick Anthony.

slaves in the area before the Civil War. Perhaps it was because many had gone to live in the settlement "Little Africa," later called Driftwood, near the Strawberry River. Ex-slaves banded together there at the close of the war.

Born in 1852 it must be assumed that Richard Anthony's parents were slaves and that he grew up as a slave. The place of his birth is unknown. It may be that Anthony was the name of his owner.

The Civil War brought changes in the town of Smithville. W.C. Sloan, who had extensive land and merchandising interests in the Smithville-Imboden area, organized a company of Confederate soldiers and became active in the war. One report by Alexander as to why Richard Anthony came to Smithville was that he "stumbled into the camp of Captain Sloan, breathless, scared and hungry" and later was brought to Smithville by the captain who gave him sustenance and protection.

Richard "Dick" Anthony. It is thought that Dick Anthony came to Smithville with the Julian family who operated a store there for several years and sold it to Fortenberry Brothers in 1889. He worked for W.C. Sloan and later his son-in-law and daughter, Mr. and Mrs. Lucian Andrews. He moved with the family to Imboden and later to Walnut Ridge. He was the first black, and probably the only black, to join a church in Lawrence County with all white membership. He joined Smithville Methodist Church in 1901 along with 19 whites. After Dick's death Mrs. Mollie Barnett Richardson was the only member of the group living for many years. She died in 1978.

Others thought he came to town with a family named Julian who bought and operated a general store, later Hillhouse Brothers store. He lived with the Julians and was often seen around town hauling freight with a pair of little mules.

In about a year the Julians decided to move on to another town, but Richard Anthony did not go with them. Remaining in Smithville, he became the faithful servant of Captain Sloan and the Andrews family. Lucien Andrews, who operated a store in the town, was the son-in-law of Captain Sloan having married the captain's daughter, Leona.

When Richard Anthony came to Smithville, drinking and fist fights were still a part of community life. However, there were churches - Methodist, Presbyterian and Baptist - to lead people to a better way of life. Methodist church history records that in 1901 W.H. "Wild Bill" Evans held a 17 day brush arbor meeting at Smithville. Richard Anthony presented himself for membership. J.T. Alexander states that the evangelist hesitated, but after a speech by Lucien Andrews declaring the candidates integrity and his need for salvation, the church received him officially. He became a regular attendant and contributor.

An accident in the Sloan family caused Richard Anthony to assume another task which was his loving duty for years to come. A little granddaughter of Captain Sloan fell from an upstairs window and as a result, was paralyzed and unable to walk. The small man carried her from place to place. She was Rebecca, daughter of Lucien and Leona Andrews.

When the Andrews family moved to Imboden their faithful helper was willing to accompany them. He had probably begun to feel that he was a necessary part of the household because of the service he rendered in caring for Rebecca.

He seemed to fit into life in Imboden as he had in Smithville. J.T. Alexander records that while living in Smithville, Richard Anthony was "somewhat reserved" and "talked only if someone approached in a conversational attitude." However, a present-day resident of Imboden remembers that "he kidded with the white folks." Those of his own race seemed to look up to him, calling him "Mr. Richard."

He cared for the yard and garden for the Andrews family and continued to transport Miss Rebecca. He would drive her to Sloan-Hendrix Academy with horse and buggy, then carry her to her school seat. In the afternoon he would return with the horse and buggy to transport her to the Andrews home. Some remember that he spent time in town, making many friends. He continued his church attendance, always occupying the same seat in the back of the church.

A love for children seemed to be a part of his nature. He would give candy and chewing gum to the little ones. He wanted to please them and would exude a chuckle if they were pleased with his treats. The boys and girls at school were his friends.

The next move of the Andrews family was to Walnut Ridge. Richard Anthony remained in Imboden this time, staying at the home of the Andrews' daughter and son-in-law, the Tol Wilsons. The small house in which he lived at the rear of the former Wilson home is still standing today on what is now the Ruth Dent property.

Finally the time came when he had to leave the town of Imboden. We can imagine that his small body was bending with age and that he knew he would be the one to be cared for rather than the one who cared for others. He moved with the Wilsons to Walnut Ridge where he resided until his death in 1942 at the age of 90.

What makes his a character that many remember? Certainly it is not fame, position, or money as he had none of these. Perhaps it is the qualities that exemplify character in anyone. He was humble, faithful, loved people and lived a life of service. He loved the Lord and became one of His children. Though his gifts to others were small, he always wanted to present gifts - especially to children. Not only did he love, he was loved in return. The inscription on his monument in Hope Cemetery reads - "Richard Anthony, beloved servant of Leona Andrews, 1852-1942."

(Permission has been obtained from Dula McLeod Baker, niece of J.T. Alexander, and from editors of the *Lawrence County Historical Society* quarterlies to use writings of Mr. Alexander and other historical information found in their quarterlies.) –Pauline McKamey.

COLONEL MILTON DYER BABER.

Milton Dyer Baber (always referred to after his service in the CSA as Colonel Baber) was born on February 3, 1837, at Rumsey, McLean County, Kentucky, the sixth child of the marriage of Charles M. Baber, 1800-1868, and Lucy Harwood, 1800-1867, daughter of Judge Harwood. The Baber family was of English origin and migrated from Virginia to Kentucky.

No authentic data exists as to the nature and ex-

Colonel Milton Dyer Baber was a distinguished lawyer in Lawrence County who served notably during the Civil War.

tent of his education. Pleadings in old court files written in his own hand show that he wrote an attractive and legible hand. He is reputed to have been a great reader and he had an unusually large law library for his time.

He came to Arkansas in 1858. On May 9, 1859, at Smithville, Arkansas, the then county seat, before the Honorable William C. Bevens, circuit judge, Milton Baber was admitted to practice law.

He and Samuel Robinson were elected to represent Lawrence County in the Secession Convention of 1861 which convened March 4, 1861. Although Baber voted for "immediate secession," the majority of this convention decided to submit the question of secession to popular vote. Before this election could be held, Fort Sumter was fired upon in April 1861; the convention reconvened on May 6, 1861, and voted immediate secession. At this reconvention, Milton Baber introduced the resolution confiscating the public lands and other property of the United States in Arkansas.

On June 16, 1861, Baber enrolled at Camp Shaver in Captain Robert Glenn Shaver's Company I, 7th Regiment, Arkansas Infantry, later converted into Company I, 7th Regiment, Arkansas Infantry, C.S.A. He was chosen as First Lieutenant (at this time troops elected the officers to lead). This regiment drilled at General Hardee's headquarters at Pittman's Ferry in Randolph County until the last of August, 1861 when it was ordered to Bowling Green, Kentucky. It protected the rear in the retreat from Bowling Green after the fall of Forts Henry and Donelson, and later participated in the Battle of Shiloh, April 6 and 7, 1862. The Battle of Shiloh is said to be the bloodiest battle ever staged upon the American continent in proportion to the number of men engaged.

The severe losses suffered at Shiloh required a reorganization of the Confederate forces on May 8, 1862, when both Shaver and Baber were sent back to Arkansas for the purpose of coming home and organizing a new regiment. On July 12, 1862, at Smithville, Baber enlisted in and was selected as Captain of Company D, Shaver's Regiment, Arkansas Infantry, subsequently known as Company D, 38th Regiment, Arkansas Infantry, C.S.A. On August 2, 1862, he was promoted to Major and on April 1, 1863, to Lieutenant Colonel. The 38th became a part of Tappan's brigade of Hindman's Army.

During January and February 1864, by order of Lieutenant Colonel Holmes, dated Camden, January 19, 1864, Baber was absent from the 38th on recruiting service in North Arkansas. In his extensive report to the Confederate government, General Hindman referred to "Major Baber" among others as having rendered important services in raising and organizing Arkansas troops. Major Milton Baber participated in the battle of Jenkin's Ferry, April 30, 1864.

In the summer of 1864 he organized and became the colonel of the 45th Regiment Arkansas Cavalry, C.S.A., commonly called Baber's Regiment. No muster rolls of this regiment are now extant, but J.W. Clark was Lieutenant Colonel and George R. Jones, adjutant. The only active service of this regiment appears to have been in Price's Raid through Missouri. The raid started on October 5, 1864, but Colonel Baber was taken prisoner October 22, 1864, in the fighting at Independence, Jackson County, Missouri. He was received at Gratiot Street Military Prison, St. Louis, Missouri, during the five days ending November 15, 1864 (exact days not known), transferred to Johnson's Island, Sandusky, Ohio, November 12, 1864, transferred to Camp Douglas, Illinois, February 17, 1865, where he was paroled on June 20, 1865, and released on June 20, 1865.

Returning home to Smithville in 1866 Colonel Baber was elected prosecuting attorney of the Third Judicial District, but was ousted in 1868 during the reconstruction government. When Clover Bend was made the county seat in 1868 he moved there, but within about a year moved to Pocahontas where he formed a law partnership with W.F. Henderson, under the firm name of Baber & Henderson.

While a resident of Pocahontas, Colonel Baber was very active in the practice of the law. Among other things he obtained title to thousands of acres of tax title land, resulting in a lawsuit with P.K. Lester, holding a conflicting tax title, which was compromised by his conveying to Lester in 1874 of 7,433 acres thereof. He conveyed lands to Cairo & Fulton Railroad in consideration of their establishment a station at O'Kean. He platted the town of O'Kean, but this enterprise was not very successful for that town did not grow as did Walnut Ridge south of O'Kean.

On October 29, 1877, at the age of 40, he married Mrs. Margaret Raney Sloan of Powhatan, then aged 33, widow of James F. Sloan, deceased, daughter of Andrew Jackson Raney. No children who lived to maturity were born of his second marriage. After this marriage, Colonel Baber moved to Powhatan. A few years thereafter, he formed a law partnership with George Thornburg, which continued until Mr. Thornburg moved to Walnut Ridge to begin the publication of the *Lawrence County Telephone*. About 1886 Colonel Baber formed a partnership with R.P. "Frank" Mack, which continued until about 1892. About 1889 Colonel Baber moved from Powhatan to Walnut Ridge, Mack remaining in Powhatan, the firm thereby having a member in each town, the eastern district of the county with Walnut Ridge as district seat having been created in 1887.

From 1882 to 1890 Colonel Baber was a member of the Board of Trustees of Arkansas College, a Presbyterian supported institution in Batesville, Arkansas, now known as Lyons College. The Babers sent her sons and his daughter to Arkansas College in Batesville.

Colonel and Mrs. Baber had a gracious home on what is now the site of Coles Furniture Store. This home burned and a smaller home on site was built for the widowed Mrs. Baber by her children. On July 5, 1893, at his residence in Walnut Ridge, without the warning of any prior illness, Colonel Baber died apparently of heart failure. He was buried in the Smithville Cemetery. The newspaper said of Colonel Baber's passing, "that for a lawyer he was a good man."

Colonel Baber's reputation as a lawyer was based primarily upon his masterful and successful defense of criminal, especially murder, cases. He was an unusually keen judge of human nature. He was conceded to be unexcelled in the selection of juries, the examination of witnesses, and in the presentation of an argument designed to sway and influence the sympathies of juries. Weighing over 200 pounds, about five feet and 10 inches tall, impressive and dignified in appearance, of masterful personality as a trial lawyer, the colonel headed the local bar.

In the bar resolution adopted in the circuit court soon after his death, it was said:

"Therefore, Resolved, that in the death of Colonel Milton D. Baber, the Bar of Lawrence County has lost its oldest, most useful, and most respected member. During his long residence in this State, he occupied many high and responsible positions, always with credit to himself and to the satisfaction of the public, and whether in public or private life, as a citizen, as a friend, as a husband and father, he so conducted himself as to merit, secure and maintain the approbation of the people

and the warmest friendship and affection of those with whom he was most intimately associated." – *Sara Sloan Heckle.*

NOBLE AND JUANITA BAILEY. Noble Bailey was born near Ravenden Springs on May 10, 1925, the youngest child of James T. and Bertie Wells Bailey. His siblings were: Burley, who married Mazie English; Jewell, who never married; Eugene, who married Oma Freeman; Arlene, who first married Millard Blansett and after his death married Luther Cline; Ruby, who married Sol Bradford; and Donal, who married Doris McKinney. Only Arlene, Donal and Noble are living as of 1999. Noble and his siblings are descended through the Wells, Davis, Janes, Wyatt, Black, Ferguson, Griffith, McIlroy and McLain families, all early residents of present-day Lawrence and Randolph Counties.

Noble graduated from Sloan Hendrix High School in Imboden in 1942, having attended school at Ravenden Springs until the school burned in 1940. Jewell, Donal, Noble and their parents moved to Paragould in 1946, to row-crop farm. Then in 1947, they moved to Lunsford, where they remained for several years.

Juanita Rains Bailey was born near Bay in Craighead County on March 17, 1920. She graduated from Bay High School in 1937, and from Arkansas State College in 1954. She married Henry Brown in 1945, and they had one child, Don Ray Brown, born October 3, 1950. After Henry's death, Juanita married Noble Bailey on December 29, 1955. Her mother, Alva Inman Rains, was born and raised in the McIlroy Community in Randolph County and her father, James W. Rains, was born in Kentucky. Juanita and her three younger brothers were raised by their mother's sister, Jane Inman, following the deaths of both of their parents in 1929.

Noble's brother, Gene Bailey, and wife, Oma, and Juanita's brother, Allen Rains, and wife, Lottie, were residents of the Imboden area at various times over the years. Juanita's uncle, James H. Inman, lived in the Walnut Ridge and Black Rock areas for much of his life.

Noble, Juanita and Don Ray moved to a farm in the Finch Community near Paragould in 1962. Then in 1971, they purchased and moved to the Hollander farm located south of Imboden on Clear Springs Road. After living in Imboden since 1976, Noble and Juanita purchased and moved to the Slayton farm on Clear Springs Road in late 1998, where they still reside and raise cattle. Juanita's former brother-in-law and sister-in-law, Laban and Lorene Brown, live nearby on an adjoining farm.

Juanita retired from teaching school in 1982, the last several years of her 30 plus years of teaching being at Oak Ridge Central near Ravenden Springs. Don Ray Brown, his wife, Carolyn, and their children, Stacy and Matthew, live near Pocahontas. Stacy and Matt are presently students at the University of Arkansas at Fayetteville. The Bailey and Brown families have engaged in cattle farming together for many years. *–Don R. Brown.*

JOHN LEE BAIRD FAMILY. John Lee Baird was born December 20, 1868, near Ravenden and died January 2, 1951. He was one of three children born to Andrew Jackson Baird and Sarah Bailey Baird. His grandfather, Leroy Baird, was born in North Carolina and married Fannie. Fannie did not know her last name or correct age because she had been stolen by the Indians that killed her parents. The Baird descendants have been traced back to John B. Baird Sr., born in Scotland and immigrated to the United States by way of Aberdeen, Scotland on the Exchange with Captain James Peacock. He arrived at Staten Island, New York, December 19, 1683.

Margaret Sloan Bowen was born October 28, 1866, and died March 14, 1939. She was one of three children born to Abner Bowen and Martha Frances Gaither. They came from Tennessee.

John and Margaret married on December 31, 1885. They lived near Ravenden and had 10 children: Mary, Anna, Emma, Willie, Homer, Robert, Martha, John, Margaret and Thomas.

Mary Dorothy was born October 20, 1886, and married Ruff Hill. After his death, she married George Gray. She had no children. Mary died April 8, 1972.

Anna Elizabeth was born January 10, 1889, married Joseph Morris. They had three children: Edna, Joseph and John, who lived in Lawrence County until they graduated from high school. Anna died November 18, 1984.

Emma Leota was born July 12, 1891, married Cecil Holder. They had three children: Ruby, Norma Jean and Cleo, who were raised in Missouri. Emma died May 30, 1977, in Dexter, Missouri.

Willie Mae was born August 12, 1893, married Ralph Hepler. They had two children: Imal and Wanda, who still live in Ravenden. Willie died April 26, 1993.

Homer Jackson was born December 27, 1893, married Myrtle Hartgrove. They

John Lee and Margaret Sloan Bowen Baird.

had five children: Howard, Paul, Thelma, Zelma and Anita. Zelma and Howard are deceased. Homer served in World War I and died May 26, 1970.

Robert Lee was born April 26, 1898, married Audrey Arnold. They had three children: Harold, Novaleen and Thomas. Harold and Novaleen are deceased. Robert owned a store in the Richwoods Community. Robert died November 2, 1943.

Martha Francis was born December 25, 1900, married Noah Aumon. They had two children: Nina Pearl and Edwin. Edwin is deceased. Noah and Martha owned stores in Walnut Ridge and College City. Martha died July 20, 1960.

John Hobert was born January 7, 1903, married Jessie Shields. They had three children: Hubert, Ann and Margaret. Hubert is deceased. John later married Clarabell Davis Matthews. Clarabell had two sons: Jack and Earl Matthews. She and John had two children: Regina and Rick. Jack is deceased. John worked for Gregg Funeral Home and other funeral homes. He served in the Army during World War II. John died July 4, 1993.

Margaret Jane was born January 20, 1905, married Millard Anderson. They had two children: Bobby and Darrell. Both children are deceased. Margaret died March 31, 1991.

Thomas Elmer was born February 13, 1907, married Connie Waddell. They had three children: Kathleen, Maydeen and Carl. Tommy and Connie farmed and owned a store at White Oak. Tommy served in the Army in World War II. Tommy died February 28, 1989.– *Kathleen Hattenhauer & Charlotte Wheeless.*

THOMAS E. BAIRD FAMILY. Thomas Elmer Baird was born February 13, 1907, near Ravenden to John Lee and Margaret Baird. He was the youngest of 10 children.

Connie Altonia Waddell was born July 21, 1910, to Henry Boyd and Edna Waddell. She was one of 10 children. Her family lived in the Old Walnut Ridge Community.

Tommy and Connie married November 2, 1929. They lived near Walnut Ridge and had three children: Kathleen, born June 15, 1930; Maydeen, born May 5, 1934; and Carl, born July 25, 1936. Tommy and Connie farmed for several years before purchasing a cafe on Hamburger Hill in Walnut Ridge. After two years, they purchased a general merchandise store in the White Oak Community. In 1940, the Baird Store was a busy place. They sold gas, oil, groceries, medicine, hog feed, and many other items. On the fourth of July, the children in the community gathered at the store to buy and shoot fireworks. At the age of only 10 years, Kathleen worked at the store, pumping gas, filling oil and keeping credit books.

In 1943 Tommy joined the Army leaving Connie and the children to run the store. He was sent to Fort Custer, Michigan, where he received training for overseas duties as a military policeman. He served in the military police in England, France and Germany. He served under General Eisenhower when his new head-quarters were opened in Frankfort, Germany.

During this time, Connie and the children continued to run the store. The food rations and new paperwork for the store brought on by the war created new challenges for the family. Ev-

Thomas E. Baird, Military Police, World War II.

ery night, after the store was closed and the homework done, Connie and Kathleen would write a letter to Tommy. These letters would include all the day's events and the news from Lawrence County. The family eagerly awaited letters home from Tommy.

On January 25, 1945, the family received a box of souvenirs from France including silk handkerchiefs, compacts and a hand-painted portrait of Connie done by a French artist from a photo that Tommy had with him. Also included in the package was a clipping from an overseas newspaper showing a picture of a robot bomb as it was falling. Tommy received an honorable discharge and returned home in 1946.

Connie, Kathleen, Maydeen and Carl Baird awaiting Tommy's return from World War II.

The family continued to run the store until 1951, when they moved to the farm. Kathleen, Maydeen and Carl all graduated from Walnut Ridge High School.

Kathleen married Fred Simmons and had five children: Tony, Mike and Byron Simmons, Cynthia Nichols and Charlotte Wheeless. She has 11 grandchildren and seven great-grandchildren. Kathleen later married Jack Hattenhauer. She was employed by the B.R.A.D. Agency as a Head Start teacher and retired after 30 years. She resides in Hoxie.

Maydeen married Buford Forkum and had two children: Steve and Jason Forkum. Maydeen worked at Lawrence Manufacturing for 27 years. She resides in Walnut Ridge.

Carl married Betty Holt and had two children: Carl Baird Jr. and Sherry Engelken. They have two grandchildren and reside in Jonesboro. Carl was employed at Frolic Footwear for many years and recently retired.– *Kathleen Hattenhauer & Charlotte Wheeless.*

WILLIAM WASHINGTON BAIRD, a farmer, lived on the Star Route, Ravenden, Arkansas, where he died at home on April 18, 1959, 12:00 p.m. He was born in Randolph County, December 11, 1871, to Jack and Sarah Bailey-Baird.

He married first Annie Crawford, October 18, 1894. His second marriage was to Selena Tennessee "Tennie" Hall born February 14, 1882, daughter of George R. and Dilla Hall, March 12,

William Washington Baird's grandchildren, December 31, 1993. Left to right: Thomas Buford Yates, Mima Earlene Yates-Moon, Clifton Eugene Yates, Franklin Delano Yates, George Earl Yates and Buck Edward Yates. Not pictured: William Buel Yates, deceased.

1899, by R. W. Cruse, Justice of the Peace. Tennie died at the birth of twins on March 3, 1900. She is buried in the Williford Cemetery, Sharp County on the left side of her mother. The surviving twins, a girl, Nola Jane, married May 20, 1919, by W. H. Bradford to Lonnie Ben Yates, born January 28, 1895, the oldest of 12 children of John Stokely and Carra Bell Cooper-Yates. Lonnie Ben's great-grandfather was Ben Davis from whose family the Ben Davis Apple came from. (For information on the Ben Davis Apple see *The World Book*, 1926, volume one and the April 16, 1897, Sharp County record.)

Lonnie and Nola's seven children (all born in Williford, Sharp County, Arkansas are:

1. William Bud Yates, born May 3, 1920, married Katherine Lumpkin, died December 27, 1993, Memphis, Tennessee.

2. Burl Edward, born September 9, 1921, married first Mary Magdalene Marion and second Benita "Tina" Perry.

3. George Earl, born January 9, 1923, married Ellen Virginia Taylor.

4. Thomas Buford, born June 25, 1924, married first Hazel Barrow and second Ruth Gentry.

5. Mima Earlene, born February 4, 1926, married Charles S. Moon.

6. Clifton Eugene, born July 27, 1931, married first Wanda L. Rogers and second Deby Elliott.

7. Franklin Delana "Dell", born November 16, 1932, married Marilyn T. Marker.

These six children all live in Oregon. The Lonnie Yates family left Sharp County and moved to a farm near Haynes, Arkansas, for a short time, then on to Helena, Arkansas, where they grew bountiful cotton crops before moving to Oregon in 1947.

As a member of the Powell Butte Christian Church in Redmond, Oregon, Nola Jane Baird-Yates made a quilt for the 13th annual church auction in 1959. Her quilt was bought by John F. and Jackie Kennedy. Her picture with the Kennedys and the quilt has been featured in several central Oregon Ranger magazines and other news articles.

W. W. Baird had one brother, John, and sister, Jane, who married J. H. Smith. After the death of his father his mother married ?? McCrory and had three children: Gibson, Thomas and Sarah Dink, who married Edgar Pack. William W.'s other marriages were: third, Remell Morgan, February 21, 1902, and fourth, Maude Walker on January 30, 1912.

In the 1945 Sharp County tax records it shows W. W. Baird owning 240 acre tracts in section 4, twp 19N R3W with a valuation of 50 dollars each. Randolph County deed records show the purchase June 5, 1947, from E. V. Steep and Anna of 43 acres in section 31, T10NR2W. Family history tells us the "Will Baird Place" was near the Bradford Cemetery. Seemingly he lived all his life in the Ravenden, Ravenden Springs and Williford area. He was known by many as "Uncle Will." He was a foster parent to several children.

William Washington Baird's funeral service was at the Ravenden Church of Christ. He is buried in the Walker Cemetery in Hardy. –*Patsy Yates.*

CHARLES WILLIAM BAKER FAMILY. Times were very hard for many rural Lawrence County families in the early 1900s. Charles William Baker "Willie" was born April 14, 1907, to Columbus Gaston "Lum" and Mollie Potts Baker. They lived in the Lauratown Community near the Black River. (The community was previously known as "Bosley.")

Mollie Baker died in 1910, leaving Lum with two sons. Willie, the youngest, was just three years old. Nearby neighbors, the Jim Smiths, have related stories about the children walking across the field to their house in the morning barefoot

Willie and Olene Baker at 60th wedding anniversary, September, 1986.

and Willie still in his night clothes.

Their father was working long hours in the field leaving the children at home. Sometimes the Smiths had food left over from their breakfast which was offered to the children if they were hungry. A few years went by and Lum married Rose Young from Calamine, Arkansas. They had five boys: Maynard, Eldon, Rudy, Robert and Vernon. Around the same time period Issac Taylor Jones of Strawberry, Arkansas was also struggling to raise his family.

Columbus Gaston Baker and Mollie Baker.

Taylor Jones, September 27, 1875-March 15, 1917, and Mattie Edda Jones, February 20, 1881-

April 22, 1912, were married January 10, 1897. They had six children: Agla, born 1898; Homer, born 1900; Leslie, born 1902; Earl, born 1905; Wilma Olene, born 1908; and Freda, born 1910. Edda Jones died in 1912. Taylor was a farmer and also a fisher-man. Fish were kept alive in the Strawberry River in what was called a "fish trap." He was able to keep his family together until the oldest daughter, Agla, married Ben Moody. It wasn't long before they wanted a place of their own. They

Edda Jones, 1881-1912

moved across Black River to the Lauratown Community. Agla took the two youngest children, Olene and Freda to live with her. As they reached school age, Willie Baker and Olene Jones attended Lauratown school. They were married September 3, 1926. Willie, a farmer, rented land to make a crop. The first two years they lived on the Baker farm on Black River, but flood waters forced them out. From the Baker farm they moved to Clover Bend. Later, they moved to Lauratown to a farm known at that time as the "Ethel Daily Farm."

Olene's grandmother, Mary Francis Hunter Jones, a widow, lived with them until her death in August, 1934. Willie and Olene had two daughters: Agla Willene, who married Billy Joe Kirkland, and Marylin Frances, who married Ray Kinder.

The Depression years were hard years when families had to be self sufficient. They grew all their food. Fruits and vegetables were preserved by drying or canning. Corn was shelled for grinding into meal at the grist mill. Milk, butter, eggs, chicken and pork were all from the farm. About the only foods purchased were sugar and flour. Willie and Olene purchased one of the Clover Bend Farms. Moving into their new home on May 12, 1938, they continued to live in the same location until their deaths. Willie died September 29, 1989, and Olene died March 18, 1991. –*Willene Kirkland.*

DULA DURAN MCLEOD BAKER was born in Smithville, Arkansas on November 7, 1904, to former Sheriff and County Judge, Murdock Cornlius and Ora Alexander McLeod. She departed this life on February 17, 1998, at Lawrence Hall Nursing Center in Walnut Ridge. Her grandparents were Hector and Maggie Davis McLeod and J. Lafayette and Eunissa Peebles Alexander. She was married to Rudy Baker on January 14, 1928, in Black Rock by Dr. Charles D. Tibbles. Rudy preceded her in death on September 2, 1971.

Dula lived in Smithville 88

Dula Duran McLeod Baker.

years and was a devoted daughter, wife and public servant, who loved to help others. Among her accomplishments were: school teacher for 15 years. Teaching at Pleasant Valley (Squint Eye), Anchor, Coffman, Oak Hill, Mount Vernon, Powhatan and eight years at Smithville. A bad case of arthritis forced her retirement from teaching. God, shots and hot baths in Hot Springs made her recovery possible. She taught piano lessons in her home. She was a dedicated Baptist until she gave up her church to join the Methodist church with her

husband. She served God and both churches well with her tithes, teaching, piano and organ playing and in many other ways. She was a graduate of Sloan Hendrix Academy in Imboden and attended Arkansas State College in Jonesboro. She gave to many charities, was a strong Democrat and a 60 year plus member of the Extension Homemakers Club. First she was a member of the Anchor Club and in 1949, helped to organize the Smithville Club. She served in all local offices and also in the County EHC Council. She was hostess for the club's annual Christmas parties for many years. When she was no longer able to attend due to ill health, she was always interested in her club and supported it financially. Smithville EHC is now in the process of buying vertical blinds for the Smithville Community Center kitchen with funds she left for club projects.

Dula and Rudy loved children and though they had none of their own, they enjoyed entertaining youth as well as adults on Halloween and Christmas. They enjoyed traveling to all 50 states. Larry Croom accompanied them on many trips.

Dula served on the Lawrence County Library Board for 13 years and was a Smithville correspondent for the *Times Dispatch* and *Ozark Journal* for 22 years. She wrote seven quarterlies of history for the historical society. She served as City Treasurer and Recorder for many years. In 1968, she retired after 20 years service with the Smithville Post Office, as clerk and postmaster. She was a teller and bookkeeper at Citizens Bank in Smithville. Dula received the Community Service Award in 1987, presented by the Smithville Masonic Lodge. Her success is evident, which she was modest in us telling about. –*Bonnie Perkins.*

EDWARD LATHEL BAKER was born in Kentucky about 1846. His parents were Burdit and Nancy Baker of Tennessee and Kentucky. He married in Independence County, Arkansas, July 9, 1870, to Martishia Evaline Andrews, daughter of William Andrews and Martha Ann Carroll Andrews. She was born in Georgia, August 9, 1848.

The family also lived in Sharp County, Arkansas, as well as Independence and Lawrence Counties. Their two children were: Columbus Gaston, born June 17, 1871, and Laura Adline, born October 21, 1873.

Martishia died October 15, 1876, and is believed to be buried in the Mahan Cemetery. They lived on a farm near by. Edward then married Marilda Gooden. Their children were: John Burdette "Byrd," born October 6, 1878; Girtha Evaline, December 8, 1880; Will-

Edward Lathel Baker.

iam Timothy "Tim", December 31, 1883; Adderson Edward, October 3, 1891, died January 10, 1892; James N., June 18, 1895, died February 2, 1896. According to a newspaper article, Edward died at his home near Lauratown, April 27, 1927, and was buried in the Clover Bend Cemetery. He had served in the Civil War and was a member of the Methodist church.

Marriage of the children:

Columbus Gaston's first wife was Maliah Elizabeth. They had one child, Ellen, born January 5, 1899. Maliah Elizabeth "Lizzy" died.

Second wife was Mollie Potts, born December 25, 1885, to Polk Potts and Rebecca Watson Potts. They married August 24, 1902. Their chil-

dren were: Columbus Melvin, born September, 1905, died September, 1975; Charles William Baker, born April 14, 1907, died September 29, 1986. Thelma, born November 17, 1909, died November 10, 1910. Mollie died August 19, 1910, and is buried in Coleman Cemetery.

His third wife was Rose Young. Their children were: Maynard, Eldon, Rudy, Robert and Vernon. Rose died ????. Columbus Gaston died August 25, 1966.

Laura Adline married Thomas Graddy. Their children were: Edward, Oliver, Dora, Alvie, Elsie, Cecil and Hester. Laura died February 3, 1944.

Byrd first married Annie Berry. His second wife was Jane Taylor. They had four children: Julian, Mildred, Rance and Merle. Byrd died January 30, 1944.

Girth married Kit Polston. She died October 1, 1922. Family unknown.

Tim married Hattie ??. They had two children: Mildred and Edward. –*Willene Kirkland.*

JACOB C. BAKER was born August 21, 1876, in Equality, Illinois, and died January 5, 1969, in Alicia, Arkansas, at the age of 93.

He left his home in Illinois when he was 12 years old. He and his stepmother could not get along. He rode a freight train to Alicia, Arkansas. He helped with the wood and water to make the steam engine train run.

When he got off at Alicia he did not know anyone. The family of John Mosley let him stay with them and work.

He later married a young lady, Emma Jones, October 25, 1877-August 20, 1967. They bought a farm three and one half miles south of Alicia. There they raised their family. They had three boys and two girls: Leroy, born 1909; William "Bill", 1898-1971; Gladys, 1900-1995; Grace, 1903-1993; and Jake, 1905-1969.

Mr. Baker opened a store in Alicia in the early 1930s. One of their sons was Bill, who opened an insurance company in Walnut Ridge for several years.

Leroy Baker's son, Don, bought the family farm in 1971. There are many descendants left in Lawrence County and other places. –*Marie Baker.*

JAMES POLK BAKER FAMILY. The James Polk Baker family can be documented in Lawrence County, Tennessee on February 19, 1835, when James S. Baker, who was born in 1814, married Martha Wasson, who was born May 24, 1817, and died June 1888. She was the daughter of Abel Wasson, born 1783, and Hannah Hill, born September 1777. They were married in 1804. James S. and Martha were the parents of five children. It is unknown when they came to Arkansas. The 1860 census of Conway County shows their eldest son, Jack M., was born in Tennessee in 1838. He was killed fighting in the Civil War. Evaline, born 1844, died December 30, 1922, married William H. Dungan. Sarah, born 1846, believed to have died young as there is no record of her living in Lawrence County, Arkansas. Caroline, born 1850, married W. James Walling. The youngest child, James Polk Baker, born July 4, 1860, died February 8, 1937. He told his descendants of seeing his brother, Jack, ride off to fight in the Civil War and never saw him again. He also remembered his family and others leaving Conway County, Arkansas in the mid 1860s, to move to Lawrence County for safer territory. They burned everything they could not pack on a covered wagon to keep the raiding Jay-Hawkers from taking it. The women came by wagon pulled by oxen and driven by Evaline. The men walked through the woods to protect those in the wagon.

In Lawrence County, Arkansas on December 31, 1884, James Polk married Margaret

Back row, standing: James Polk Baker, father, Bilbrey Steele Baker, Mary Steadman Baker, Bernice Veynoy Baker Hillhouse, Avo Bob Baker, Mattie Naoma Baker Turnbow. Kneeling: Kennard Shelby Baker, Margaret Dee Bilbrey Baker, "Mother," Taylor Rudy Baker.

Dee Bilbrey, born December 31, 1866, in Tennessee, died March 15, 1951. She was the daughter of Mounce Gore Bilbrey, born April , 1841, died 1883. He was the son of Lard Bilbery, born January 27, 1876, and has Edie Gore and the grandson of Isham and Ruth Sellers. Her mother was Rebecca Ann Gragg, born August 17, 1845, in Cooksville, Tennessee, died November 26, 1927. She lived with the Bakers after the death of her husband. James Polk and Margaret Dee Baker lived on a small farm near Smithville. They were the parents of seven children: Bernice, October 10, 1885-November 7, 1962, married Ben Hillhouse, December 2, 1906-October 30, 1950; Kennard, September 12, 1887-May 2, 1957, married Floy Hillhouse, April 2, 1884-June 7, 1975; Avo, October 22, 1889-December 28, 1990, never married; Oma, July 30, 1892-January 28, 1970, married Cleo Turnbow, August 22, 1884-January 17, 1991; Mary, November 26, 1894-November 23, 1970, never married; Rudy, October 17, 1898-September 2, 1971, married Dula McLeod, November 7, 1904-February 17, 1998; Steele, May 18, 1901-September 15, 1997, married Hazel Rudy, August 12, 1908-January 1, 1999. *–Bonnie Perkins.*

ANDREW BALFOUR V

ANDREW BALFOUR V was born January 23, 1816, in Randolph County, North Carolina. In 1835 following the death of Andrew's father, his mother moved the family, by covered wagon, to Adams County in Illinois. In 1843 Andrew is found to be settled in the Black Rock/Powhatan area of Lawrence County, Arkansas, where he was a practicing physician.

His doctor's office, located at the site of the present Telephone Exchange Building in Powhatan also housed his general store.

In later years when a new courthouse was being erected, court was held in Dr. Balfour's store which was rented to the county for $8.33 a month.

During the Civil War, Dr. Balfour served as a Captain in the Confederate Army as a physician with Company D, 13th Arkansas Volunteers.

Dr. Andrew Balfour V Powhatan Cemetery Tombstone.

Records indicate that two brothers of Dr. Balfour, Jesse Henley and Samuel Dayton, were also residents of Arkansas in Lawrence and Baxter Counties.

Dr. Balfour died in April 1884 and is buried in the Powhatan Cemetery. His tombstone reads:

Sacred to the memory of Dr. A. Balfour

Born in Randolph County, North Carolina, January 23, 1816

Died in Lawrence County, Arkansas, March 31, 1884

Cease to do evil.

Learn to do well.

Isaiah 1:16 and 17

A niece, Anna Balfour, who died in 1883, is buried in the grave beside his. She was the daughter of Samuel Dayton Balfour.

Dr. Balfour was survived by one daughter, Mollie Henley Balfour, who resided with him the last year of his life. *–Doris Carter King and Richard D. Carter.*

BALLARD-HOLDER

BALLARD-HOLDER. My roots go deep into the past of northeast Arkansas. As a boy, my grandfather, George Ballard, fought in the War Between the States, delivering mail and water to the troops around Powhatan. I grew up in Coffman, in a drafty, high-ceilinged farm house with porches stretching across both its front and back. In our family were: Poppy and Mommy, (W. M. and Jessie Ballard) and us six girls: Pearl, Lola, Jennie, Minnie-Lee, myself, Ermaneal and Willie-Juanita.

My mother, partly Native-American, was a beautiful woman and my wonderful father was a mess! He picked on us girls and let us pick on him. A farmer, Poppy was also deputy sheriff in Hoxie and Game and Fish Commissioner at El Dorado, so he sometimes had to travel. Once, he returned home from traveling on his birthday, and we girls tackled him, planning to floor him and shove him under the bed. We tackled, all right, and hung on in vain as Poppy lugged us, flapping and flopping, until he could reach the high shelf above the bed and get his (unloaded) pistol! We never did get him under that bed!

From left: Lola, Hennie, Minnie, Clara.

We lived across the road from the three room Coffman School, which doubled as the Baptist Church. Coffman grouped grades 1-2, 3-5 and 6-8. The high school was over in Portia, but high school cost money, because students bought their books in grades 9-12. At Coffman School, three of us Ballard girls played basketball in dresses on the outside court. I was jump center, Jennie and Minnie-Lee were forwards. Back then, the court had three sections: two end sections, where two forwards played against two guards and a center section, where each team's jump center stayed. The year I finished eighth grade, W. W. Miller, the Portia coach (whose boys team surprised the nation by winning the state championship), came and offered to let Jennie and me go to high school free, if my parents would let us play ball in the new indoor gym. Sounded wonderful, until he said we would wear new uniforms with knee-length shorts. Mommy and Poppy said, "No!" Ever since, I have had a sadness in me that I could not finish school.

Strangers, passing through and hoping to sleep in the church, would cross the road to knock on our door for permission; often Poppy would let them stay at our house, which had no indoor plumbing, no running water, and no electricity, but a telephone. (Poppy's official positions required a phone.) Once, a group of midgets knocked and Poppy let them stay with us. I can see Poppy, now lifting a midget and standing him on our table to use that telephone. More than strangers kept life interesting in Coffman, though: it had its share of parties for young people, including square and slow dances (Kent Been and Ben Whitlow played guitar and fiddle music at them). We did not, of course, go dancing alone, but with boys. We loaded into some parent's buckboard, padded with straw and they would take the whole group. Oh such fun! We had fun going to church revivals and singings, too. It was at a Coffman revival, when I was 15, that I met Elmer Holder from Arbor Grove, my future husband. After church, Elmer (age 22) asked to walk me across the road to my house. I let him.

A year later, a wagon load of us went to a singing over in Oak Grove and Elmer, who went in someone's car, met me there. He had gotten us a license and we talked Brother Gordon King, the preacher, into marrying us on Oak Grove bridge. It was July 3, 1932. The next morning, for our honeymoon, Elmer's daddy took us to the train at Portia, and we rode it to Mammoth Spring, got off and were about to walk across the line into Thayer, Missouri, to go spend some time with Elmer's sister when, instead of carrying me across that line, Elmer got behind me and kicked me over it! Oh, so young and happy! All through the years, though, we kept a hush about our elopement, never telling the children about our wedding day. After our honeymoon, when Elmer and I got to my parent's house, I was scared, but when I stepped on the porch, I heard Mommy running down the hall to greet us. She was so glad to see me and everything was all right.

Elmer and I lived in Arbor Grove, near Hoxie, and he farmed with his parents, A. P. (Arson Phipps) and Modena Webb Holder, who were like parents to me. There, in June, 1933, I gave birth to twins, Eugene and Modene. In a few years we moved to Lesterville, on the Lawrence and Randolph county lines, but before too long, Elmer quit farming and took a job working for the Ford Tractor Company in Walnut Ridge, where we settled permanently. Spaced over the next nine years, we had two mores sons and two more daughters: Leroy, Joyce, Linda and Stanley. From 1962, until his retirement in 1976, Elmer was custodian at First Baptist Church.

We celebrated our 50th anniversary at a reception our children gave us in the church. Ten years later, they gave me a 75th birthday party. At my party, I decided it was finally time for us to give them the long-hushed story about our run-a-way wedding on Oak Grove Bridge.

Elmer died January 4, 1984.

I handled the faded images of my youth, grateful that the faces, places and events of those stretching years come vividly to life in me; I see us, still, the way we were back then.

On October 5, 1986, I married Buster Kennedy, who has one son, Marvin. *–Clara.*

JAMES M. BARNETT

JAMES M. BARNETT was born September 9, 1826. Left an orphan at an early age, he was raised in Lawrence County by Mrs. Sally Gibson. In August, 1849, he married Margaret Amanda Finley, who was born September 30, 1827, to James and Jane Dobbins Finley. They were the parents of six children: Martha A.; Mary Ellen married Dr. S. L. Fisher; Nancy Walker married Sevier Fortenberry; Jasper Newt married Lula Fisher; William; and James M. The family lived near Smithville until 1860, when they moved to near Greenfield, Missouri.

James, who was a veteran of the Mexican War, was among the first to join the Confederate Army. He was killed the first year of the war. Two of Mrs. Barnett's relatives started to Missouri to return the family to Arkansas, but were killed on their way, so she loaded her children and some belongings in a wagon and returned to Arkansas. During the war, Mrs. Barnett and about 10 children, representing different families, went to Cape Girardeau, Missouri, in ox wagons to get salt and other articles that could not be obtained near home. They were gone about two months and were constantly in fear of the Yankees.

In 1866, Mrs. Barnett married Joseph Taylor, her brother-in-law. They were the parents of three sons: Reverend Joseph G., who married Ida Estelle McBryde; Benjamin D.; and George.—*Bonnie Perkins.*

ADAH JOSEPH BARNHILL was born in Tennessee in 1857, to Caswell Hall Barnhill, born March 23, 1828, in Blount County, Tennessee and Sarah Jane McDonough, born January 31, 1836, in Knox or Blount County, Tennessee. They married January 12, 1853, in Knoxville, Knox County, Tennessee. They had George Houston and Adah Josephine in Tennessee and Arminta Elizabeth, Leah A. and Sarah Jane "Sally" in Greene County, Arkansas. She died November 21, 1868, the day after "Sally" was born, in Greene County. She is buried in Pruett Chapel Cemetery.

Caswell Hall Barnhill then married Epsy Jane Jones. Born to them: Epsy Arkansas, William Caswell, Jonathan C., David King and Joseph Hall. He died July 2, 1879, and is buried in Pruett Chapel Cemetery.

Caswell Hall Barnhill, father of Adah Josephine Barnhill.

In 1873, Adah Josephine married James Thomas Hicks, 1851-1882, in Arkansas. To this union was born: Mary Lavena, 1875-1908; Charles Ezra, 1877-1880; and Sarah Louisa, 1880-1974.

In 1889, she married Pleasant Green Light, 1831-1889, in Greene County, Arkansas. Their children were: Wake Orville, 1884-1963; Dewitt, 1886-1886; Willie Izora, 1887-1889; Addie Lee, 1889-1922; Tennessee D. "Tennie", 1889-1973, twins.

In 1892, she married Zackarias Taylor Anderson of Alabama, 1850-1910. Born to them were: Robert Edgar, born 1893; Susie Audrey, born 1895; Ella Blanch, born Lawrence County, 1901-1961.

Adah Josephine died December 14, 1911, and is buried at Walcott, Arkansas.

Thomas William Rickey and brother, Charles Louis, came to Lawrence County (near O'Kean) to visit a sister, Lizzie Jane "Jennie" and George Erwin. After some time, they both married here; Charles Louis Rickey to Edie Elizabeth Connelly on January 1, 1899, and Thomas William Rickey to Mary Lavena Hicks on November 20, 1899, in Greene County. George and "Jennie" returned to Ohio.

"Tom Will" and Mary had a daughter, Odessa Gustava, born October 15, 1900. He became ill with cancer and returned to his parents in Scioto County, Ohio, where he died December 22, 1901. Mary and Odessa returned to her mother and stepfather in Lawrence County, near O'Kean, where daughter Willie Felicia Rickey was born, June 21, 1902. Odessa died that year.

Mary did housekeeping in other homes to support herself and baby. She later married John Rummel (born in Germany). They had Josephine Prudence, born December 21, 1904. He left while Josephine was still a baby. Mary died from measles and pneumonia February 4, 1908. Willie was reared by Charles and Edie Rickey; Josephine by Ira and Louisa Hicks Gray.

Willie married William Edward Heral, September 21, 1925. They had Wanda Louise, 1926-1983; Viola Maxine, born 1927; Albert, born 1928; Cecil James, 1930-1987; Rose Mary, born 1931; Alice Lillian, born 1933; Arthur Glen, born 1934; the first three being born in Greene County and last four in Lawrence County. Of the surviving five children, all but Glen live in the same county or adjoining county of their birth. Willie died December 31, 1958, of cancer (as did Wanda in 1983) and Ed died October 16, 1970. They and Wanda are buried at Lawrence Memorial Cemetery. —*Mary Hibbard.*

KENNETH DALE BARTON FAMILY. Kenneth Dale Barton was born March 18, 1930, the son of Albert H. and Ella Davidson Barton. Dale attended Black Rock School and then spent seven and one half years in the Navy and later became a welder.

He married on July 17, 1953, to Allie Jane Pickney, daughter of Harry and Gertie Emmerton Pickney. Dale and Allie Jane had four children.

1. Donald Gene Barton, born July 14, 1954.

2. Kenneth Wayne Barton, born December 13, 1955. Kenneth married first to Debra Mashburn and

Dale and Allie Jane Barton.

they had one child: Shawn Barton, born April 14, 1977. Kenneth married second to Tracy Norlin. They had one child: Travis Barton, born February 24, 1992.

3. Dianna Lin Barton, born January 16, 1957. Dianna married first to Jerry Guilliam. They had two children: Jerry Dale Guilliam, born December 20, 1974, and Kenneth Gene Guilliam, born August 29, 1976. Lin married second to Jackie Eagan.

4. Marie Ann Barton, born May 4, 1964, married Steve Woods. They had two children: Natosha Marie Woods, born December 15, 1980, and Branden Keith Woods, born July 14, 1984.

Dale, Allie Jane and their children all attended Black Rock School and all still live in the Black Rock area. —*Allie Jane Barton.*

DUDLEY BASSETT was born November 29, 1881, near Hardinsburg, Kentucky, in Breckinridge County. He died December 16, 1940, in St. Bernard's Hospital in Jonesboro, Arkansas, after having a stroke earlier in the day. He was married to Laura Mae McClamroch, December 26, 1911. Their children were: Jerry Bassett, born September 17, 1912, Walnut Ridge, Arkansas; and Mary E. Bassett, born October 31, 1914, Walnut Ridge, Arkansas.

Jerry Bassett married Helen L. Moore, August 11, 1949. Their children were: Jerry Dudley Bassett, born July 18, 1950; Richard Barry Bassett, born December 8, 1952; and William Michael Bassett, born March 7, 1956. Great-grandchildren were: Tanner Dudley Bassett, born February 15, 1978; and Brett Michael Bassett, born June 26, 1985.

When Dudley Bassett was about 1 year old, his mother and father left their home in Breckinridge County, Kentucky to live in Arkansas. The other members of the family were his brothers and sisters, Rachel, Alvah, Silas, Nancy, Ida and Hattie. With all their worldly possessions they traveled down the Ohio River to Cairo, Illinois, where they boarded a train on the Iron Mountain Railroad and traveled to O'Kean, Arkansas. From there they went to the Elnora Community, north of Walnut Ridge on the Lawrence-Randolph County line. They went to this area in Arkansas because a relative and some friends from Kentucky had come to Arkansas and settled there.

Census and assessment records reveal that they had moved from the Elnora Community to the Mt. Zion school district in Lawrence County. Their personal property assessments were on the Mt. Zion assessment records of 1886 through 1890. Sometime after 1890, they moved from Mt. Zion to the town of Walnut Ridge. The census records of 1900, show that they lived in Walnut Ridge, Campbell Township. Listed were: Laura, age 54; Hattie, age 22; Dudley, age 18; and Russell Rainey, age 11.

Dudley attended schools in the Mt. Zion and Walnut Ridge schools and at Mountain Home, Arkansas. He completed a business course in Springfield, Missouri, at Springfield Business College. He taught school at Mt. Zion and Portia. Later, he clerked in Walnut Ridge Power & Light Company. He was court reporter in District Circuit Court.

From 1908-1912, he was elected Circuit Clerk, Lawrence County.

From 1913-1916, he was elected County Judge, Lawrence County.

From 1917-1922, he worked at McClamroch Hardware and Furniture Company and Walnut Ridge Wholesale Grocery Company.

From 1923-1932, he was Vice-President, Lawrence County Bank.

From 1932-1936: liquidated closed banks in Swifton, Newport and Walnut Ridge.

From 1937-1940: Manager of White River Production Credit of Lawrence County (now known as Farm Credit Service) of Lawrence County. —*Jerry Bassett.*

BEASLEY FAMILY. Mary Elora Webb married William M. Beasley. They came from Tennessee. William had a brother, Tom Beasley. He lived around Strawberry. His first wife was Ester and they had two children: Paul and Ester. His second wife was named Sally. She had one child named Velmer. Mary Elora's father was an orphan. She had two sisters that married Holder brothers named Arson and Abner. One of the brothers moved to Illinois. William died in a flu epidemic of 1900. William Marian Bealsey II had three sisters: Annie married Otis Creek and had four children: David, Lida, Ida and Vida. They live in Rockford, Illinois.

Ovella married Harve Tolbert. They had four children: Jack, Betty, Virgil and Clarence. They live around the Walnut Ridge area. Diane was the third sister. She died in childbirth. William Marian Beasley II married Jesse Clementine Butler. They had seven children: William M. Beasley, who had three children and lives in Columbia, Missouri; Dorothy B. Jones had four children and lives in Rockford, Illinois; Linda Neitzel lives in Pamona, Missouri and has four children; Joe Trousel (family name) lives in Rockford, Illinois and has four children; the two girls are twins; Henry Cornelius (family name) lives in Rockford, Illinois and has two girls: Patricia Ann Hunt lives in Durand, Illinois and has five children: four boys and one girl; Charles Merrill Beasley has no children.

William and Jesse Beasley were the county farm family for 1945. –Sandra Martin.

BEAVERS FAMILY.
The first of my Beavers family to settle in Lawrence County were Charles and Hannah Beavers. They arrived sometime in the early 1800s. They settled near where the Lone Oak Church and Cemetery are located.

Charles was born about 1828, in Giles County, Tennessee. He served with the Fifth Illinois Cavalry Company K, during the Civil War. He married Hannah in Illinois. They had two sons: John E., born in 1850, and William J., born in 1861, in Illinois. Both sons came with them to Arkansas. John E. Beavers married

Mary Jines Beavers with child, Van Beavers, daughter-in-law, Carrie Street Beavers, grandchildren: Wallace Beavers, Howard Beavers, Dorothy Beavers.

Mary Elizabeth Jines or Joines in Illinois or Missouri. Charles and Hannah are both buried in the Lone Oak Cemetery. Also, an infant Beavers is buried there. Family legend says that John Beavers taught school in the Lone Oak Church and School. John and Mary Beavers had nine children: Edward E., born April 25, 1874, died young; Charles Wesley, born September 7, 1875; Albert E., born November 1, 1877; Annie Bell, born October 8, 1879, died young; Henry Richard "Dick", born February 16, 1882; James Monroe, born July 18, 1884; Jahue Jasper "Jay", born December 26, 1886; Fanny Victory, born December 15, 1888; Van, born March 13, 1894. John and Mary's family moved to the Williford area in Sharp County, where they married and lived most of their lives. Many are buried in the Williford and Baker Cemeteries of Sharp County.

In the mid 1940s, Dick's son, Don, moved to Imboden. Don worked for the Frisco Railroad until his retirement. He and his wife, Irma Christine Galloway, had several children when they moved to Imboden: Irma Jean, Donna, Nancy and Catherine. One daughter, Sarah Beavers, died as an infant and is buried in Potts Town, Mississippi. While living in Imboden other children were born: Richard, Mary Beth and Cindy. About 1956, the family moved to Willow Springs, Missouri, where three more sons were born: John, Timothy and Gregory. They resided in Willow Springs, Missouri, until their death. Don died in 1985, and Christine died in 1997. Both are buried in the Willow Springs Cemetery.

My parents, Howard Beavers and Evelyn Galloway, sister of Christine Galloway Beavers, moved to Imboden in 1946. Their children were: Morris Ray, Clara Darlene and Clarence Van. Roger Lee was born in 1948, and was killed in an automobile accident in Missouri shortly after returning from two tours of duty in the Vietnam war. Robert Eugene was born in 1950. Evelyn died when this child was born. He was raised by Howard's sister, Dorothy Beavers Greenlee. After Evelyn's death, Howard married Wilma Smith Rippee, daughter of Grundy and Nellie McLeod Smith, whose families were early settlers in Lawrence County. Their children were: Danny, Sandra and Judy Anita, who died when she was one day old. Wilma had a daughter by her first

husband, Azril "Jack" Rippee: Brenda Lynn. Jack's family are also early settlers in Lawrence and Randolph Counties. Howard and Wilma have lived in the Annieville Community for many years and are still very active in the Pleasant Grove Baptist Church.

Howard's parents, Jay Beavers and Carrie Belle Street, moved to the Imboden area in late 1948. They first lived across Spring River in Randolph County. Later, they moved to the Annieville Community where they lived until Jay died in August, 1961. Carrie lived with her daughter, Dorothy, and for short periods of time with her son, Howard, until her death in January, 1976.

Evelyn and Christine's youngest sister, Sarah Leona Galloway, married Willie Albert "Bill" Beavers, son of Dick beavers and brother to Don Beavers. They had three children: Charles, Carol Jane and Linda Kay. Bill also worked for the Frisco Railroad until his retirement. They lived in Hoxie and Ravenden for a short time. Then they moved to Willow Springs, Missouri and Memphis, Tennessee. Later, they moved back to Willow Springs, where they lived the remainder of their lives. Bill died in the early 1960s, and Leona died in 1995. They are both buried in the Willow Springs, Missouri Cemetery. –Clara Martin.

BEELER FAMILY.
D.N. Beeler was born in Kentucky in 1867 and married Dora Simmino who was born in Arkansas in 1872. They were the parents of three daughters: Lelah, Edith and Rena; and three sons: Albert, Esmond and Raymond. Albert married Lucy Galbraith and had one daughter, Mary Alta. Esmond married Bessie Ward and had one daughter, Lonnie Faye. Raymond married Elsie Baughman and had three daughters. Raymond was killed during World War II in

D.N. and Dora Beeler with their daughters, Lelah and Edith. The girls are holding china dolls purchased for 98 cents each from Krone's Mercantile in Black Rock, Arkansas.

the European Theater and his family then relocated to California where Elsie's parents lived. Lelah married Shelton Brown and they were the parents of Lima, Newton, Irvin and another son who died during infancy. Edith married T.M. "Mose" Robertson and they were the parents of 11 children: Vernon, Vergil, Shelby, Maudline, Evelyn, Sherman, Nettie, Betty Jean, Bernard, Dora and Lavelle. They also raised three other children from the marriage of T.M. and Verdie Slatton who died during childbirth. Those children were: T.J. Dorse and Vela. Rena married Marvin Holder and they were the parents of two sons, Bud and J.D. The Beelers resided in the Mt. Vernon Community near Black Rock and are buried in the Moran Cemetery. –Evelyn Flippo.

BELL FAMILY.
A Virginia family of Johnsons saw their daughter marry and leave with her husband and her Negro "mammy" for Illinois (by covered wagon). Their daughter had married Charles Bell. Their son, Joe, was not happy in a post Civil War of northern people, who had northern sympathy, so he, having married by then, took advantage of the Iron Mountain railroad's offer of a free boxcar's transportation to Arkansas which

needed people. He brought farming equipment and family in 1909, and bought land on Village Creek in Lawrence County. The descendants are still here. –Lenore Doyle.

WILLIAM RILEY VANDERBILT BENCH.
My father, William Riley Vanderbilt Bench (known to his friends as Van), came by foot from Flippin to Opposition and procured a job from Jacob Jasper Sharp (my grandfather) as a farmhand in 1903, at the age of 18.

Not long after, my mother (oldest child of Grandpa Sharp), Lillie Lee Sharp, age 18, and my dad were married.

This Bench family picture was taken in 1930. Family members are (front, from left): Ruth Jean, Millard Gale "Mickey", Riley, Ralph, Cloyce; (back) Bob Finley (Ethel's husband), Ethel and her daughter, Margaret, Oscar Lester, Bertha, W.R. (father), Lillie Lee (mother) and Alma Holder (housekeeper). We had a sister who died at age of three, Lillian.

They had my oldest sister, Bertha, then Lillian, who died at age three. Then Ethel, mother of Margaret and Marilyn. Next, Oscar Lester.

Before all that, Mother and Dad moved to Walnut Ridge at age 19 and Dad bought the Safety First Barber Shop (5 chairs) and entered several other businesses along the railroad track close to where we lived.

After that, Cloyce came along, then Ralph and Riley. All three graduated from Walnut Ridge High School together and played on the '38 famous Walnut Ridge football team.

And then there was Ruth Jean and myself, who were trained to do a lot of chores taught to us by Father, Mother and the older siblings. This was during the Depression, so Ruth and I had a number of skills, such as keeping the fire going under the kettles so my mother could render hog fat for number one (which was important to Ruth and I) into cracklings to eat or be put into cornbread.

My older brothers butchered hogs and cattle at Dad's slaughter house. The boys, especially Oscar and Cloyce, did much of the butchering on the concrete floors and me on the ladders way up to supervise and out of the way because I was kinda scared, but not too scared.

My mother would cook three big meals a day. Can you imagine the number of biscuits, ham, bacon, beef, chickens, milk, butter, eggs and all the work involved, like my chopping wood for the cookstove.

All of Ruth's and my older siblings told us how good life was until we came along. But that was okay because they watched over us like an old mother hen.

We were happy. We had lots of brothers and sisters who tried to teach us everything. But some things we just didn't have the knack for, like Dad's perfect music pitch (he was song leader at the church for many years), and Ethel, who could hear a tune and play it back on the piano.

Or Bertha, who had the knack of loving people and got her own beauty shop at age 19 in the back of Dad's barber shop. They had shoe shine boys, manicurists and public baths and all those stories! Bertha had some of the customers she started with when she died at 82 (Dad had his one chair in the front of her beauty shop, which she owned).

Or Ralph, who could sing from G to G and was a music teacher. After his retirement, he sang with groups at weddings, etc. (Once was in a barber shop quartet, no less).

Or Riley, who had a knack for mathematics. He used that working for the government testing grain, etc. He also had patience working with his nephews, teaching them a good attitude about things and good sport skills.

Oscar made his living as a butcher and Cloyce as a produce manager directly because of their father's teaching in earlier years.

Ruth and I are the only ones alive at this writing. Ruth worked for the telephone company since the age of 17; was a manager when she retired. I taught school for 30 years at some of my former classmates' amazement.

All-in-all, my mother and father were very much church oriented. I really believe that is why we had so much fun. People who have this much love today are very fortunate indeed.

All five of us boys were in the Army in World War II and came home in one piece to my mother's relief. —Millard G. "Mickey" Bench.

BERRY-MOSIER. The time was December 1927, the year of the Mississippi flood. The place was water-soaked Mound City, Illinois, located on the west bank of the Ohio River, just north of Cairo. I was six years old.

July, 1985, Ozelle Berry Mosier standing in front of the house she lived in 1931-1933.

My father had traded our Model T Ford for a truck and we were moving to Smithville, Arkansas where my grandparents, George and Josie Rennison lived with five of their children. "We" consisted of my parents, Frank and Artie Berry, my brother, Jasper and me, Ozelle. We crossed the Mississippi River at Cairo on a ferry boat into the state of Missouri. To me, the boat was quite large with an enclosed "center room" for, I assumed foot travelers and rest rooms.

After leaving the ferry boat we drove until nightfall, then camped by the roadside, right side if I remember correctly. Early the next morning we resumed our trip to Smithville. My parents spoke of a river we would have to cross on a ferry boat. The river (Black River) came into view and as we drove down a steep incline I saw what I thought was a gang plank for the ferry boat, but where was the boat? We drove onto the gang plank, and it started moving. Believe it or not, this gang plank moved us across the river. To the right was a small town my parents said was Black Rock.

When we arrived at the town of Smithville we did not stop because my grandparents lived west of the town in "the hills." As we continued deeper into the wooded area another surprise awaited us - Christmas Trees in all sizes. Jasper and I jumped up and down with joy, clapping our hands and yelling. In Mound City we only saw such trees at Christmas time, decorated with ornament and candles. Later we learned, in Arkansas, they were called pine and cedar trees.

Another unusual sight, enroute, was large trees lying on the ground with broken roots protruding upward, large holes in the ground beneath these roots. An explanation, given later, was that a man named Forrest Smith became angry one day and said he didn't care "if a tornado came and blowed the whole _____ (oops! my parents didn't allow me to use that word) place away." A tornado did come and nearly blew it away. Later, my parents met this Forrest Smith, who, seemed very nice.

My grandparents lived on a hill overlooking a creek, whose name I do not recall. Could it have been Cooper Creek? On the bank of this creek sat grandpa's blacksmith shop and a sawmill with a huge boiler and piles of logs. He made railroad ties from these logs by sawing them into long, squared pieces, about the length of a fence post.

My two teenage uncles, Claude and Frank, helped at the sawmill, my two older aunts, Delta, 13, and Lavena, 11, played big girl games and helped with the dishes after meals. Mary, age 8, my brother, Jasper, age 7, and I loved to wade in the creek, play in the blacksmith shop or climb over the logs. We loved to climb trees or swing on the grapevines hanging from the trees or were they called muscadine vines? Also, the large flat rocks were wonderful for Mary and I to make play houses on. And oh, the sweet smell of honeysuckle flowers in the evening, when they were in bloom.

My parents bought a farm known as the old Coyle Place, near a hill. Now we had a home, Christmas trees, a hill to slide down with our snowsleds we brought from Mound City, but no snow.

This hill was called Pine Hill and on top of it sat a small building that we learned was a school house, Pine Hill School, the school we would attend. Here was another surprise.

In the Mound City school we had attended there was a room and a teacher for each grade. At Pine Hill there was one room and one teacher for all grades and there was no water pump. Water had to be carried from the spring at the foot of the hill. The "big" boys, during recess, carried a bucket to the spring and brought up fresh water, setting the bucket on the doorstep at the entrance to the school. We all drank from the same ladle and when recess was over entered the building for more lessons.

The desks at Pine Hill were long enough to seat two pupils, instead of one. They had cut marks on them and I learned later, were made by an axe used to hew the planks from logs. There was a front row of seats to sit on during "recitation" and the grades took turns reciting. The blackboard on the wall facing the front row of seats looked like it had been painted on with black paint.

Shortly after we moved into our farm home a strange man stopped by. When he learned that we did not have a cow he brought us one from his farm so we could have milk. That man's name was Jim Peeples.

We moved from Smithville to a community called Richwoods about 1929 or 1930. At Powhatan we had to cross Black River on what was called a swinging bridge. The experience was frightening, but I held tightly to the side of our wagon. Also, at Powhatan some men were building a wall with rocks around a large, beautiful brick building. The building was called The Courthouse.

Another memory is our driving from Powhatan to Black Rock on a road that ran along the side of Black River. Along the right side of this road were some buildings sitting on stilts. These were similar to the fish houses and homes built on the Ohio River at Mound City. On the other side of the road were large vats with steam blowing out at the top of them, and there were all size "sea" shells scattered about.

I was told the men were boiling mussels in those vats for pearls. The mussels came from Black River, my parents said. I didn't understand this type of cooking, but we came to something farther down that was more interesting, a cave. Jasper and I wanted to peek inside, but my father would not stop.

Time passed and it is now 1931. We moved to the town of Smithville and settled into an old one story house built on slant with a low rock wall in front of it. The house had large windows the size of doors, and had storm shutters on each side that could be closed together over the windows during a storm.

There was a front porch the width of the house with a door in the center that opened into a long hallway. This hallway extended to the back of the house with another door opening to a small back porch.

On the left side of the hallway were two bedrooms, each with its own fireplace. On the right side of the hallway were three rooms, the "front room" with its fireplace, a dining room that we used for a bedroom and a kitchen. The kitchen had a chimney for a woodstove and a trap door for inside entrance to the cellar under the kitchen. All the rooms were large.

The cellar had an outside walk-in entrance from the back. Also at the back of the house was a cistern, a well, a large garden space and below it a very important building, the outhouse.

One of my most pleasant memories of school at Smithville was the starting of our school day with the singing of songs. Our teacher, Mrs. Dula Baker, played the piano and taught us the songs, patriotic songs such as Star Spangled Banner, America The Beautiful, Stephen Foster songs, and songs like Yandee Doodle Dandy.

Another memory dear to me is the friendship and love of Mrs. Eslie "Gussie" Cole. One Christmas she made me a beautiful cloth doll which I loved very much and kept for years. The last time I saw Gussie was in July, 1986.

In 1985, my family and I were in Walnut Ridge for a family reunion. Before leaving my family and I drove to Smithville so I could show them the old house where I lived as a child. The owner of the house was Jessie McKnight who remembered me. She invited us in for a tour and let us take pictures. We all enjoyed our visit with Mrs. McKnight and seeing the house.

Oh, how I wish I knew the history of that old house, how old it is, who built the house, who was the first family to live in it. –Ozelle Mosier.

JOHN CAMPBELL BILBREY FAMILY. The Lawrence County Bilbreys are descendants of Isham Bilbrey who was listed in the first United States Census of 1790, in Greenville County, Virginia. He was a patriot and was honored by the Daughters of the American Revolution with a grave marker for his service in Halifax Military District during the American Revolution. His grandson, John Campbell, was the first Bilbrey to settle in Lawrence County, Arkansas.

John Campbell Bilbrey, son of Lard and Nancy Copeland Bilbrey, was born in Overton County, Tennessee on May 27, 1828, and died in Lawrence County, Arkansas on November 12, 1912. In 1850, when he was a young man, he became part of the westward expansion by migrating to Lawrence County, Arkansas as he followed the Ozias Denton family from Sparta, Tennessee. He then married the Denton's daughter, Rutha, on October 30, 1851. They initially settled on lands in Denton. In 1858, he purchased land from John Lingo and settled south of Smithville.

John Campbell and Rutha Denton Bilbrey's children were: Martha L., James T., Mary E., Twins George W. and Andrew J., Cyntha J., Denton L., John M., Josiah H., Samantha J., William R. and Canzada.

Rutha Denton Bilbrey died November 26, 1872, and J. C. married two other times: Mary "Polly" Harrison Alexander in 1873, and Sophia Hughes in 1902.

J. C. Bilbrey heeded the call to serve in the Confederate cause by enlisting in the First Arkansas 30 day Volunteers until they were mustered out of service. He then enlisted in the 38th Arkansas Confederate Infantry, Company D on July 12, 1862. He served in this unit at the rank of Sergeant until the fall of 1864, at which time he enlisted in Company F, 45th Arkansas Cavalry at the rank of First Lieutenant and was paroled at Jacksonport, Arkansas on June 5, 1865. Family legend has it that the mule in the picture above was given him at parole by virtue of the fact that he was a cavalry officer.

Mr. Bilbrey returned to private life and his farming operation. He was a shoemaker and the springs on the creek near where he lived are known as Tanyard Springs. Mr. Bilbrey was active in civic and church matters. He was a member of the Old Bethel Church which belonged to the Pilgrim's Rest Association of the Primitive Predestinarian Baptists. This

John Campbell Bilbrey.

church died down about 1907. John C. Bilbrey, along with his good friend Amos J. Bratcher, erected a frame building on the southern boundary of the Bilbrey farm near the Stoney Point School. They called it New Bethel. The church died out shortly after the death of Mr. Bilbrey and the building was then used as a hay barn.

The descendants of John Campbell Bilbrey still living in the Smithville/Lawrence County area are descended from three of his children: Denton Laird "Dee", who married Susan Felix Kendall; Josiah H. "Joe", who first married Lillie Belle Fields and then Fannie Justus; and Canzada "Ada", who married George Franklin Davis.

Two of his younger brothers, Mounce Gore Bilbrey, April 27, 1841-1883, and Lewis O. Bilbrey, June 22, 1860-?, came to Lawrence County and some of their descendants also live in the county today. –*Maleta Bilbrey Tipton.*

NEWT BILBREY FAMILY. The marriage of Newt Bilbrey and Geneva Culver took place in Portia, Arkansas, on October 29, 1927. The couple returned home to the Bilbrey Community two and one half miles south of Smithville, Arkansas, and lived there the rest of their lives.

Their children are: Madia Marie and Oleta. Madia married Eugene Winters of Smithville in 1947. They had one daughter, Eugenia Marie "Jeannie." Jeannie married Frank Miller of Searcy. They have one son, Chadd Miller.

Oleta married W. A. Wallis of Smithville in 1952, and two children were born to this couple: Bilbrey Joe Wallis and Billie Ann Wallis. W. A. was killed on a horse August 9, 1957. Joe married Linda Milligan of Strawberry in 1973. Their children are: Joseph Heath Wallis and Wendie Alyson Wallis.

Billie Ann married Ron Slusser of Smithville in 1978. They had one daughter, Lea Ann.

Daddy (Newt) was a cattle farmer and mother was a housewife. They taught us to love God, be honest and be the best we could be. They were always very supportive.
–*Newt and Geneva Bilbrey.*

Newt and Geneva Bilbrey

WILLIAM EDWARD "ED" BILBREY SR.
Denton Laid "Dee" and Susan Felix Kendall Bilbrey (daughter of Jarrett W. and Mary George Box Kendall) had 12 children. Their youngest child was William Edward, born February 2, 1908, at Smithville. His mother died of tuberculosis, March 26, 1914, when he was only six years old. Dee never remarried, but he had several older daughters who nurtured and helped to care for Ed after his mother died.

Ed attended school through the eighth grade, which is as far as you could go without having to leave home at that time. He said he "took" the eighth grade three times and that his best

Ed Bilbrey and Gladys Williams during their "Sparking Days."

subject was spelling. He has reminisced that community spelling contests were held for the general public and that he could out spell most. One of the words he often won with was "biscuit." He said that once he even won the contest over his future mother-in-law, Gertie Harrison Williams. He met Gladys Williams, daughter of Ernest and Gertie Harrison Williams, and started to "spark" her after they met at a "candy breaking." Gladys was also from the Smithville area, but she was boarding and attending Sloan-Hendrix Academy where she graduated in 1930. They dated for a couple of years and then married February 8,

Ed and Gladys Bilbrey.

1931. Ed did not only gain a wife, but a life partner. They built their home and farming operation by working side-by-side. They had one son, William Edward Bilbrey Jr. Edward married Mary Carolyn Faulkner, April 27, 1956, and they made their home on the family farm. Edward and Carolyn had two children: Rita Karen and Maleta Sue. Rita married John Hollis Thomison Jr. on October 7, 1977. They have two children: Lindsay Lane and John Hollis III. Maleta Sue married Jay Brent Tipton on October 2, 1982. They have one daughter, Emily Renee.

Ed and Gladys were very industrious people who farmed cattle, poultry, hogs, hay, corn and ran a dairy until their later years. Gladys sewed for her family, making most of

the clothes her granddaughters wore in their youth. She cooked, sewed and gardened in addition to the farming that she did along side Ed and Edward. She always had a lovely yard with a wide assortment of flowers and shrubs. Gladys departed this life July 26, 1997, and is buried at the Smithville Cemetery. Ed still lives on the family farm two and one half miles south of Smithville. –*Maleta Bilbrey Tipton.*

WILLIAM EDWARD BILBREY JR. FAMILY. William Edward Bilbrey Jr. was born the only child of Ed and Gladys Williams Bilbrey of Smithville. In his youth he attended Haw Grove School, where he walked or rode horseback with Jessie Williams Foley, his aunt, who was the teacher. He also attended school at Smithville until it was consolidated with the Lynn School District and that is where he graduated in 1950.

When Edward was about 10 years old, he met a little girl at a funeral. Her name was Mary Carolyn Faulkner, daughter of Lawrence and Taddie Todd Faulkner, of Powhatan. It was this same girl

Seated, left to right: Rita Bilbrey Thomison, Emily Tipton, Lindsay Thomison, John Hollis Thomison III, Carolyn Faulkner Bilbrey. Standing, left to right: Maleta Bilbrey Tipton, Jay Brent Tipton, John Thomison, Edward Bilbrey.

that he married on April 27, 1956. They made their home on the Bilbrey family farm, building their house across the road from his parents. Edward has farmed livestock his whole life and he ran a dairy with his parents for many years. Edward has always had a strong sense of community. He is a Mason and a volunteer fireman. He served for 14 years on the Lynn School Board and he is a past justice of the peace. He has always eagerly helped any of his neighbors who were in need of his assistance. Initially, Carolyn was a homemaker. Since she was a talented seamstress and an excellent cook, she excelled in this role. When their youngest child started to school, she entered the manufacturing world by working at Frolic Footwear. She worked there for many years until she left to work for Skil Corporation where she has been employed for 20 years.

Edward and Carolyn have two daughters: Rita Karen and Maleta Sue. Rita met John Hollis Thomison Jr. of Medina, Tennessee, at Southern Baptist College. They married October 7, 1977. They live in Smithville where he is the mayor and they both teach at Sloan-Hendrix. Rita and John have two children: Lindsay Lane and John Hollis III. Maleta met Jay Brent Tipton of Conway when she was at the University of Central Arkansas and they married October 2, 1982. They also live in the Smithville Community near the Bilbrey farm. Brent is an officer in the National Guard and a rehabilitation counselor for the State of Arkansas. Maleta is an occupational therapist. They have a daughter, Emily Renee. This family carries on in the long time Bilbrey traditions of strong family ties, sense of community, helping neighbors and love for God. –*Maleta Bilbrey Tipton.*

MARION WILLIAM BISHOP FAMILY.

Marion William Bishop was born in Tennessee about 1849, the son of David and Cynthia M. Bishop, born about 1830. Some Bishop descendants believe the family was from Lawrence County, Tennessee. Marion's parents had two more sons, David Washington, born 1849, and died 1928, and James W., 1851-1922, and probably a daughter, Sarah, born about 1855. Marion's father died 1855-1860, and his mother married Isaiah Hutcherson, 1848-1888. Children of Isaiah and Cynthia Hutcherson were: Almira, born about 1860; Thomas, 1865-1954; Nancy, born about 1868; Amos, 1871-1898; and Ducery, 1873-1890. The Hutcherson family moved to Lawrence County, Arkansas in the 1870s. Isaiah, Amos and Ducery are all buried in the Mount Zion Cemetery at College City.

I believe that Marion Bishop is the William Bishop on the 1870 census of Perry County, Tennessee, next door to the Hutcherson family. This William Bishop married Eliza Stephens in Perry County, June 14, 1866. Their children were Sarah Elizabeth, 1868-1926; Mary, born about 1870; and Flora, born about 1872. Marion then married Martha. Their children were perhaps another Sarah, born about 1879; and Laura, born about 1881. In the early 1880s, Marion moved his family to Lawrence County, Arkansas, from Pemiscot County, Missouri. He then married Mrs. Malvina King Hawley, born about 1848, the widow of William Hawley, February 12, 1884. Their children were: Joseph Cleveling, 1885-1967; Lue Victoria, born about 1886, and died 1960; and Bertha Susan, 1888-1972. Family tradition is that Marion and Vina had died by the mid 1890s, leaving their children as orphans.

The children of Marion Bishop all went in different directions as they reached adulthood. The oldest daughter, Sarah Elizabeth Bishop, married George S. W. Butler, born about 1861, on October 16, 1887, in Lawrence County. They were divorced and Sarah then married John Norris, 1880-1950, in Russellville, Arkansas, on April 5, 1900. Sarah died February 15, 1925, in Muldrow, Oklahoma.

Laura Bishop was in Oklahoma before settling in Milan, Kansas. She was first married to McDonald and secondly to Alfred Abbot. Laura died in the 1950s, in Kansas.

Joseph Cleveling Bishop was raised at least part of the time in the household of his half brother, John Hawley. He was married about 1907 to Victoria Malissa, born about 1887. They settled near Ravenden Springs, Arkansas. Joseph died September 14, 1967, at Pocahontas, Arkansas.

Lue Victoria Bishop was apparently raised by the Robert Colquett family and moved with them after 1900, to Caldwell Parish, Louisiana. Here she married George Henry Jackson, 1885-1976, on September 10, 1903. They eventually moved to Kennett, Missouri, where Lue died January 20, 1960.

Bertha Susan Bishop was raised in the household of her half uncle, Thomas Hutcherson, near Russellville, Arkansas. She married James David Riley, 1885-1950, at Scotland, Arkansas, on September 1, 1905. They moved to Tulsa, Oklahoma, about 1915. There were divorced and Bertha then married Robert Anderson. She died November 14, 1972, in Tulsa, Oklahoma.

The history of this family still has many missing pieces. It is hoped that readers will add to and correct this information. *–Gary D. Treat.*

BLACKSHEAR FAMILY.

The Blackshear family originated in Scotland and England. The name is said to mean "In or from a dark wood (forest)." The name has had several spellings over the years. The original spelling was "Blackshaw" or "Blackshawe." Randall Blackshaw and his family

Blackshear family reunion, Hoxie, Arkansas, 1997. Children of Jesse Thomas Blackshear. Left to right in front: Everett, Edith, Pearlie, Margie. Left to right in rear: Bob, Lehman, Maisebell, Leon and Jennie.

are documented to have arrived on the ship "Submission" in 1682, in Maryland. Their path of migration was to New Jersey, Delaware, North Carolina, Georgia, Tennessee, Texas, Missouri, Louisiana and Arkansas. The name changes began with Robert Blackshaw, born August 24, 1677, who converted to "Blackshare" and whose sons, Randall, Thomas and Alexander, changed to "Blackshear." Other changes to "Blacksher", Blackshire and Blackshere have also been noted. These families are documented to have fought in the Revolutionary War, the War of 1812, the Civil War, and other major national conflicts. Their social status has, for the most part, been that of the

Children of Sam Blackshear and Minerva Dewitt. Left to right: Retha, Arthur, Virgil, Rutha, William, Lavina and Gailya. Photo taken at Blackshear reunion, Hoxie, Arkansas.

common man, the farmer. However, there have also been notable accomplishments as statesmen, military and professional (doctors and lawyers).

The first Blackshear to arrive in Lawrence County, Arkansas was Elijah McDonald Blackshear and is documented in the 1860 United States Census as a resident. The family migration to Lawrence County was circular in geographic standards and with the addition of family members. He married Lucinda Hedrick in Tennessee in 1853. The first two children, William and Nancy E., were born in Bolinger County, Missouri. The third, Edward P., was born in Ripley County, Missouri. The fourth, James Albert, was born in Lawrence County in 1862. Although these were difficult times, the family migrated the circle once again, going back to Tennessee where one son, E. M. Blackshear Jr. and daughters, Frances and Rebecca were born. Following those events, the family moved back to the Poplar Bluff, Missouri area by 1880, before settling in the Pocahontas and Lawrence County area by 1883-1884.

The expansion of the Blackshear family in Lawrence County was by E. M. Blackshear's third child, Edward Pinkney Blackshear. This individual married Nettie Catherine Melton, daughter of John and Elizabeth Melton of Pocahontas, Arkansas

Back row, left to right: Unnamed Carr, James Carol Carr, Jesse Blackshear, baby Everett and Jessie Bush Blackshear, Frances Blackshear Carr and husband Wilson Carr, Elvis Allen, Orba Allen and Sallie Carr. Middle row, left to right: Apsy Holmes, Grandma Holmes, Alfred Allen, Ada Allen, Dennis Allen, Ida Allen Holmes and Jim Holmes. Front row standing, left to right: Ervin Blackshear (4 years old), Bertis Allen, Lester Carr, Willie Allen, Geneva Allen, baby Jay Holmes sitting in lap of Ida Allen Holmes, Ray Holmes and Carlon Holmes.

and these two became the parents of James A., Sam, Jesse and Nora Blackshear. These four children in turn were to become parents of 51 children (James 1, Jesse 18, Sam 16, and Nora 16). The four children were separated at an early age by the death of their parents. The families of James, Sam and Jesse moved about in the early 1900s, but came to reside permanently in Lawrence County between 1908 and 1919. The Jesse and Sam Blackshear families are documented by markers at the Clover Bend Historical Society as one of several early families to Lawrence County.

Early residences of Sam and Jesse Blackshear was in the Alicia, Minturn and Arbor Grove area of Lawrence County. Like so many Blackshears before them, they were of humble surroundings and made their living by farming. As with all families of the day, times were hard and survival was difficult. Several epidemics ravaged the communities which resulted in the deaths of Jesse's children, Jesse Thomas Jr., Ruby, Allie and Joyce, who are buried in the Clover Bend Cemetery. Few concessions were expected and few received. Jesse Blackshear bought a farm in the Arbor Grove, Arkansas, area in 1935, and most of his children were raised here. Most of Sam's children have lived out their lives here and several buried here. Jesse's first wife, Jessie Bush, is buried in the Clover Bend Cemetery. Sam and wife, Minerva Dewitt, along with Jesse and second wife, Matra Westerfield Blackshear, are buried in Lawrence County Memorial Cemetery at Walnut Ridge, Arkansas.

The accompanying picture shows families of Jesse Blackshear, Carr's, Holmes and Allens. The photo was taken in 1914, at a family gathering near Alicia, Arkansas. Frances Blackshear Carr was the aunt of Jesse Blackshear who raised him after the death of his parents. *–Leon Blackshear.*

BLAND FAMILY.

James Lloyd Bland, 1898-1987, first child of Aaron Bland and Ida Jane Pruitt Bland, was born in Perry County, Arkansas. He attended school at Bigelow, Arkansas. During World War I, he enlisted in the United States Army in May, 1917, and served overseas. He was discharged February, 1919, with five battle stars, purple heart and Croix De Guerre (unit).

James Lloyd started in the printing trade in 1919, in Bigelow for the *Citizen Press* weekly newspaper and subsequently became business manager of the *Newport Daily Independent*, June 1920, to September 1921. He became owner and publisher of *The Times Dispatch*, Walnut Ridge, Arkansas on October 1, 1921.

Bland was married to Mayme Emmaline Evans, 1898-1963, daughter of John Pleasant Evans and Belle James Evans of Plainview, Arkansas on December 25, 1920. They had three children: James Lloyd Bland Jr., 1921-1996; Mildred Evans Bland, 1924-1988; and Memory Lee Bland, born in 1927.

James Lloyd Bland Jr. served in England during World War II. After the war he returned to Walnut Ridge and went to work at *The Times Dispatch*. He later became editor and publisher, positions he served in for many years. He married Virginia McNabb, daughter of Herman and Nell Lehman McNabb on June 14, 1949. They had three children: James Lloyd Bland III, who died at age 1, Elizabeth Lehman Bland and John Aaron Bland.

Elizabeth "Beth" Bland is married to Paul Girolamo and lives in New York City, where she is a reporter for *Time* magazine. They have two sons: James Paul and John Cullen.

John Bland is now editor and publisher of *The Times Dispatch*, following in the footsteps of his grandfather and father, who died in 1996. He is married to Renee Ann Rainwater, daughter of Bob and Patty Wilcoxson Rainwater of Walnut Ridge. John and Renee have a daughter, Anna Elizabeth Bland.

Virginia Bland continues to work at *The Times Dispatch* and is active in church and community.

Ellen Riddick Simpson and Leigh Ann Riddick, are the daughters of the late Mildred Bland Riddick and late Edgar K. Riddick Jr. Ellen and Leigh grew up in Little Rock and Walnut Ridge. Ellen is married to Harold H. Simpson III, and they reside in Little Rock with daughter, Elspeth Jane Simpson. Leigh is married to Ted Jaditz, and they reside in Rockville, Maryland. Mildred died in 1988, and Edgar died in 1997.

Memory Bland married Frederick S. Balch Jr. of Little Rock and they have five grown children: Beverly Bland Balch Hoofman, Fred III, Anne Balch Ward, Helen Balch Moix and James "Jim" Bland Balch, who all live in Little Rock. Memory and Fred also have seven grandchildren: Will Hoofman, Fred IV and Helen Balch, Seth, Jay and Kate Ward and David Joseph "Jordy" Moix Jr.

—John Bland.

JACK BOAS FAMILY. Jack Boas was the second son of Harry and Ida Jackson Boas. His only brother was Harry Jr. Jack was born in New Mexico where his family had moved to find relief for Harry's asthma. They returned to Lawrence County after only two years. They built their home in Hoxie and it is used today by Jack's widow, Ruby.

Jack was a natural mechanic and followed this trade all his life except for a few years when he was a fireman for Missouri-Pacific Railroad.

Ruby Land married Jack Boas in 1942. She was the daughter of Jess and May Rainey Land. She was a granddaughter to Lewis and Elizabeth Land and James and Sarah Rainey. Sarah later married Jim McCall. All these families had been farmers in Portia.

July, 1956; Jack Boas standing right, accompanied by Richard Choate and children.

Jim McCall was a merchant in Portia. His store, like that of his neighbor, was located in the front part of his house. They were located north of the railroad tracks in Portia.

Ruby had a sister, Fern Land Choate, and a brother, Gus Land.

Ruby and all her family are Methodists. She grew up in Portia and graduated from Portia High School in 1920. She served as church organist for many years at the Methodist Episcopal Church, South in Portia. Ruby remembers when pastor, Eugene Hall and his wife organized the Women's Missionary Society there - WMS was a forerunner of United Methodist Women. She remained active in the Walnut Ridge Methodist Church.

Ruby was talented in fancy hand and needle work. She worked with Lawrence County Welfare Services for over 25 years. She was a part time sales clerk for the Sam Levit Department Store on Main Street in Walnut Ridge.

Ruby lived in the Boas home in Hoxie, drove her own car and managed her own affairs until her death at the age of 97 on September 2, 2000. She and Jack had no children.

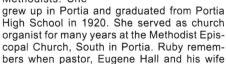

Fern Land Choate, (seated) May Rainey Land, Gus Land and Ruby Land Boas .

Fern Land Choate, Paul Hudson, Ruby Land Boas

LOYD AND MARY BOLEYN. Loyd Bell Boleyn and Mary Ann Furnish were married October 23, 1930, in Lake City, Arkansas. To this union were born seven children. They are:

1. Opal Lee Brewer, December 8, 1931, of Hernando, Mississippi.
2. Edna Marie Boleyn, March 12, 1933-April 3, 1933.
3. Janie Merle Johnson, September 18, 1934, of Memphis, Tennessee. She receive the AA Degree from Southern Baptist College in 1956.
4. Rheba Jean Jones, February 24, 1941, of Bloomington, Illinois.
5. Virginia Ann Gibson, July 25, 1943, of Horn Lake, Mississippi. She attended Southern Baptist College, 1962-1963.
6. Jimmy Loyd Boleyn, June 21, 1947, of Bell Flower, California. He served in the Marines, 1968-1971. He served in Vietnam.
7. Kerry Lynn Boleyn, September 23, 1951, of Sand Springs, Oklahoma. He served in the United States Army Airborne, 1969-1971.

Mary Boleyn and all her children attended school at Childress, Arkansas. The four oldest graduated from the Childress High School. After consolidation Jimmy graduated from the Monette High School.

Loyd was a farmer and did trucking, from 1931 to 1969. He also had the following jobs in Lawrence County in 1929, cleared land around Minturn; helped build the Walnut Ridge Army Flying School, 1943; worked at the Singer Plant,

Trumann in late 1951, and early 1952; and helped lay utility lines in the Briarwood subdivision, College City, Arkansas.

He and Mary moved from Monette to College City in Lawrence County, November 1, 1971. Loyd died September 15, 1991. He is buried in the Nettleton Cemetery.

Mary was a seamstress and did upholstering, 1940-1974. She still resides in College City and is active in the Calvary Baptist Church, Walnut Ridge. *–Mary Boleyn.*

FELAND CALHOUN BONNER. Feland Calhoun "Callie" Bonner married Katie Manning, December 18, 1912, in Izard County, Arkansas. They moved to Lawrence County in the 1930s, and farmed outside of Hoxie. Mr. Bonner was born June 14, 1890, and Mrs. Bonner was born August 11, 1893. They lived in the Hoxie area until his death on August 4, 1969, and her death October 25, 1975. Their children are:

1. Munice Monroe, born October 27, 1913, and married Juanita Nesmith, died December 9, 1987. Children are: Linda and Ricky.

2. Johnny, born July 27, 1915, and died at a very young age.

3. Mary Agnes, born April 8, 1917, and married Henry Edgar Grimes, died January 4, 1990. Children are: Ida, Charles and Henry Edgar Jr.

4. Amos Andrew, born April 27, 1920, and married Sylvia Dan, died December 24, 1997. Children are: Stanley, Eddie, Wilma, Billy, Larry and Ruthie.

Callie and Katie Bonner.

5. Howard Feland, born May 5, 1923, and married Almeda Alphin, died June 1, 1983. Children are: Don, Alma Faye, Jeanette, Betty and Wanda.

6. Floyd Bonner, born November 9, 1925 (twin), died March 29, 1945.

7. Lloyd Bonner, born November 9, 1925 (twin), and married Virginia Smith, died July 11, 1988. Children are: Judy and Ronnie.

8. Ewell Bathes, born October 14, 1928, and married Christine Foster. Children are: Terry and Troy. *–Judy Bonner*

GEORGE WASHINGTON AND MATILDA HALE BOTTOM. George W., 1826-1882, and Matilda Hale Bottom, 1833-1887, and three young children moved from East Tennessee to Missouri shortly before their son, John, was born in 1858. According to his obituary, George was "a warm advocate of and soldier of the Union cause."

Although George and Matilda remained in Dallas County, Missouri, several of their children, some of whom were still minors when their father died, later moved to Lawrence County. following is information about these Lawrence County descendants.

Most from this Bottom family who settled in Lawrence County are buried in the Snow Cemetery north of Walnut Ridge. Also in Lawrence County was a Bottoms family, who were buried in Opposition Cemetery. Probably the two families living close together is what led to some of George's descendants sometimes using the surname Bottom and sometimes Bottoms.

Wash and Matilda's oldest child was James A. "Alex" Bottom who married Jennie Teenor. Their child, Ollie, died as an infant.

William Bottom came to Lawrence County where he worked as a farm laborer. Later, Bill married Mary Jane Elder, the widow of Confederate veteran George Snow. Bill and Mary's son, Charles, died when he was two months old. William died in 1889, while their daughter, Parrie, was still a child, leaving Mary again a widow.

John W. Bottom married Annie Hennessee. Their children were: Clay, Clara and Thomas.

George L. Bottom married Laura H. Thompson. Their children were: Alice, Texas "Teck", Edna, Suda "Sudie", Oscar, Rex and Harry.

Charles Loafman "Doc" Bottom married Flora Jane Medearis. Their children: Robert, Grace and Winnie, died as infants. Lela "Maude" married H. R. Hennessee; Ethel Grey "Trixie" moved to Oklahoma and married R. D. Starbuck. Myrtle worked for 16 years in Washington D.C., where she saw General Pershing's World War I victory parade. She later returned to Arkansas to live with her parents. They also had Savannah Gladys "Van", who married Dr. John C. Hughes and George "Dewey" who married Donna Hurn. Our Bottom ancestor was C. L. and Flora's daughter, Margaret Matilda Jane "Maggie." She married Walter

Left to right: Charles Loafman, Alex, John, Alonzo "Dick" and George Bottom.

"Clifton" Kirkpatrick, son of Hiram Tinsley and Thalia Kirkpatrick. Cliff died of a heart attack soon after retiring from the post office. At the time of her death, Maggie had been widowed for over 20 years. They had two children: Charles and Maggie. Charlie, whose post-teaching career was in the insurance business, married Jan Duncan and Maggie, a secretary and administrative assistant, married Randall Max Snow.

Lonzo Fountain "Dick" Bottom married Wilma Holt Wade. Their children included: Lizzie, Gertrude, Alta, Mary Ella, Jessie, Anna, Lois, Frank, Clarence "Bud" and George.

Margaret "Parrie" Bottom married Joseph D. Hennessee. Children included: Joan, Ressie, Mary, Nell, Chloe, Margaret and Joseph Jr.
–Stephen R. Snow.

JOHN AND JANE BOTTOMS FAMILY. Mary Bottoms, born 1861, died 1871; John Bottoms, born 1862, died 1911; Thomas Bottoms, born 1867, died 1934; Joseph Bottoms, born 1871, died 1955, married Mollie Holder; Elizabeth Bottoms, born 1871, died 1959, married Bledsoe "Bletch" Holder; Sallie Bottoms, born 1873, died 1957, married Henry A. Deyling; and William "Pete" Bottoms, born 1875, died 1937. –Bonnie Perkins.

PHILLIP AND MARY ANN COLBERT BOULWARE. Phillip Boulware, son of Barnett Boulware and Elizabeth Walker, was born about 1837, in Missouri. Phillip married Mary Ann Colbert about 1855, daughter of Henry Colbert and Fereby Richardson. Children of Phillip Boulware and Mary Colbert were:

1. Feby Jane Boulware, born 1856, Missouri.
2. Mary E. "Molly" Boulware, born about 1858,

who married Leander Lafayette Hendrix on July 16, 1874, in Minturn, Arkansas. Children of Mary Boulware and Leander Hendrix are: Arthur Fredrick Hendrix, who married Lizzy Collins; Sylvester Hendrix, who married Effie Payne; Richard Robert Hendrix, who married Lizzie Collins; Rosie Mae Hendrix, who married first James A. Whitford; and second Robert Collins; Artie Lafeyette Hendrix, who married first Lottie Vival Lewis and second Rosie Devenport and third Aslee Hamilton.

3. Nancy E. Boulware, born July 3, 1860, Arkansas, died January 7, 1900, and is buried in Clover Bend Cemetery, Arkansas. She married John Calhoun Hawkins on May 26, 1875, in Arkansas, son of John Hawkins and Margaret. Children of Nancy Boulware and John Hawkins were: Max Hawkins, born Arkansas, died Plant City, Florida; Meg Hawkins, born 1879, Arkansas, died Florida; William M. Hawkins, born February, 1884, Arkansas; Otto Hawkins, born September, 1889, Arkansas; Lou Delia Hawkins, born March 4, 1892, Alicia, Lawrence County, Arkansas, died September 4, 1971, Pekin, Tazewell County, Illinois.

4. Julia Ann Boulware, born about 1861, Arkansas. She married first Grandville Whitlow, August 21, 1879, son of Henderson Whitlow. Children of Julia Boulware and Grandville Whitlow are: Henrietta "Etta" Whitlow, who married Arthur Gaskin, April 10, 1902; and Phillip Whitlow, who married Olie Howard, February 14, 1903. Julia Ann married second Anthony "Andy" Wayne Clark Sr. and third Andy Wayne Clark Jr., son of Andy Wayne Clark Sr. Child of Julia Boulware and Andy Clark Jr. was Lloyd W. Clark Sr.

5. Phillip Boulware was a Confederate soldier in the Civil War from Lawrence County, Arkansas. His record is as follows: Phillip Boleware - Monday, April 6, 1863 - Book F, Page 40- Lawrence County - Marion Township - Jones' Battalion - In service - Mary Ann, 24, wife; Sele Jane, six, daughter; Mary E., five, daughter; Julian, two, daughter. Phillip never returned from the war. He was captured by the Union Army and took the Oath of Allegiance and requested transportation to New York. A probate record - Lawrence County, Arkansas - Page 14 states: Boulware, P. - D. not include - wife: Mary Ann Boulware - Inv.: December 27, 1865. The appraisers stated that the husband of Mrs. Boulware was "supposed to be not living."

Mary Ann Boulware then married George W. Jackson on March 4, 1866, in Lawrence County, Arkansas. Children of Mary Colbert and George Jackson were: Tennessee Jackson, born about 1852, Tennessee; George W. Jackson Jr., born about 1867, Arkansas; Clementine Jackson, born about 1871, Arkansas, who married John Ed Calvin, on September 11, 1892, Arkansas; Ellen Jackson, born about 1873, Arkansas; and Emma L. Jackson, born about 1876, Arkansas.

BOWMAN-WRIGHT. This writer does not know what circumstances brought James H. and Mary E. Bowman to Ravenden. While they were residents they ran a gin and a general merchandise store. For whatever reasons these businesses failed. The Bowmans lived in a modest home on Second Street. The house is still standing, but has fallen into great disrepair. When their businesses failed they moved to Brinkley, Arkansas, where they remained until the death of James. James and Mary are buried in the Moore Cemetery east of Spring River on the old Moore farm. After the death of James in 1927, Mary married John Simmons. This marriage was short lived as Mary died in 1931.

James Bowman's father was Simeon Bowman

and his mother was Martha A. "Mattie" Gadberry. Mary Elizabeth's parents were Adam S. Wright, a founder and minister of the gospel of the Christian Church in West Plains, Missouri. He was also in the Civil War serving first as a private and then as a quartermaster sergeant in the Union Army. Her mother was Rhoda I. Durham. Family conversations down through the years say that Rhoda's mother, Pay Nuby (Newby) was a full blooded Cherokee. The stories say that she was on the Trail of Tears and probably due to the death (or hardship) of her parents she was "taken in/ adopted" by the Durhams.

The Bowman, Wright, Perrin and Lemmons families have been an integral part of Lawrence and Randolph Counties for well over 100 years.

James Henry Bowman was born October 30, 1864, and died May 12, 1927. Mary Elizabeth Wright was born February 5, 1869, and died October 30, 1931. Their children are as follows.

1. Rhoda Maude, December 1, 1891-November 29, 1914.

2. Maggie Alice, August 27, 1895-April 8, 1910.

3. Mary Ellen, March 21, 1890-September 9, 1939, married John Clay Moore.

4. James Wright, February 20, 1894-September 30, 1894, probably buried Evening Shade.

5. Ernest R., September 9, 1899-January 26, 1900.

6. Carrie Ernestine, February 9, 1903-November 11, 1993, married Julian Pickett; probably buried in Friendship Cemetery, Columbus, Mississippi.

7. Lorene L. Perrin, June 27, 1905-January 16, 1993, married Hulet I. Perrin on September 27, 1923. He died October 11, 1985; probably buries in Crittenden Memorial Park, Marion, Arkansas.

8. Lois Evangeline, born June 15, 1907, married Virgil Baker.

9. John Henley, October 17, 1910-April 12, 1977, married Melva McCartney; probably buried in Memphis Memorial Park, Memphis, Tennessee. –Larry and Barbara Perrin.

HAROLD BOYD. Martha Jane Rainey Boyd was born on November 15, 1920, to Russell and Laura Lorine Rainey. Martha Jane had five brothers and sisters, and all six were born at home, 123 East Walnut Street, Walnut Ridge. Her sister, Rachel Rainey, still lives there today.

Martha Jane graduated from Walnut Ridge High School in 1938, and in 1941, from Methodist Hospital School of Nursing in Memphis, Tennessee. She worked in Memphis, Tennessee, Newport, Arkansas and Big Springs, Texas during World War II.

While she was working in Texas, she met Harold Thomas Boyd, from Rowletts, Kentucky. They were married on January 20, 1946, in Walnut Ridge. After living for a short period of time in Kansas, Paragould, Arkansas and Jonesboro, Arkansas, they returned to Walnut Ridge to remain permanently.

Boyd, as he was known to

Harold, Martha Jane, Russ and Virginia Boyd - Easter, 1951.

most people in Lawrence County, worked for Arkansas-Missouri Power Company and the later, Arkansas Power & Light. During the 50s and 60s, the electrical distribution system in Lawrence County was not all that good, which meant when it rained hard, someone's lights were going to go out. The phone would start ringing, and Boyd would be called out. Dewey Vance, Lawrence Warner, Bill Dame, Julian Hart, J. W. Shelton and Dale Davis, to name a few, would be right there helping to get the service back. There was always someone who would call and say their eggs and milk were going to spoil without their electricity. Boyd retired from Arkansas Power & Light in January, 1984. He retired as District Customer Service Manager of Walnut Ridge, Pocahontas, Corning, Rector, Mammoth Spring and the Hardy area.

Martha Jane was a stay at home mom until the early 60s, when Lawrence Memorial Hospital was built. Her duties over the years included emergency room nurse, making rounds with the doctors and supervisor of nursing. She also assisted in countless surgeries, which she enjoyed the most. One winter the rains came and Village Creek overflowed. All hospital workers that lived on the other side of Village Creek had to be taken to work by boat. She retired in June, 1983, after 23 years of service.

Harold and Martha Jane had two children, Thomas Russell and Virginia Rainey. They also grew up at 123 East Walnut Street, before moving to 408 East Georgia Street in 1964, where Martha Jane lived. Both Russ and Virginia graduated from Walnut Ridge High School and attended college at Arkansas State University in Jonesboro. After graduating from college, Russ moved to DeSoto, Missouri to teach school. He moved back to Walnut Ridge to live in 1995. Virginia married in 1972, and moved to New Orleans, Louisiana, where she lives today with her husband, Michael Angelico, and their four children, Robyn and Erin Lockhart, and Julie and Jeffery Angelico.

Harold Boyd passed away on May 5, 1996, at the age of 77, and Martha Jane passed away on March 29, 2000 at the age of 79. –Rachel Rainey.

HENRY GILES BRADY, born April 10, 1857, was the son of Eli Brady, born around 1832, and Sarah V. Dent, born around 1843. Henry married Lee Ann Phillips on February 21, 1884. Lee Ann was born June 23, 1862. Lee Ann was the daughter of William P. Phillips, born April 25, 1822, died February 7, 1888, in Lawrence County and Mary Armstrong on October 21, 1847.

Henry's mother, Sarah, was the oldest of Josiah Dent's daughters. She met and married Eli Brady in Lawrence County. Their children were: William, Henry Giles, Darius, George, Josiah, Burns, Mark, Edie, Allie, Mollie, Ida and Beulah.

The Bradys.

The Brady family was quite a large family. The descendants met quite often for large reunions. They were all Baptist and were great singers.

Henry Giles Brady and Lee Ann Phillips were the parents of eight children: Beutha, James Edward, William Dent, Virginia "Jennie", Sarah Elizabeth "Bessie", Allie, Mary and Lester.

The children were all born in the Annieville Community, but moved to Arbor Grove where they remained. Both Henry and Lee Ann died at home at Arbor Grove and are buried in the Clover Bend Cemetery.

Bertha married Hugh Byers, and they were the parents of three children: a son, Henry R., and daughters, Ida and Edith. Bertha died as a young woman at the age of 38. Her children came and

lived with the grandparents. James Edward, known to all as Uncle Ed, was born October 3, 1887, and was never married and he and his sister, Allie, lived at home with their father until his death in 1940, and then farmed the land in the Arbor Grove Community together for the rest of their lives.

William Dent married Pearl Gray. They lived at Arbor Grove and their children were: Coleman and Jackson and Jessie Colleen.

Virginia "Jennie" became the wife of John Lee. They farmed in the Arbor Grove Community and raised two daughters, Joyce and Jewell.

Sarah Elizabeth "Bessie" married Jewel Gordon "Doc" Neece. Doc established a country store at Arbor Grove. They had two daughters, Helen and Maxine.

Mary married William Harvey Jean and they lived at Clover Bend. They had five children: two sons, William Henry "Bill" and Robert Joseph "Bob", three daughters, Mary Elizabeth, Betty Ann and Alda Garland.

Lester Dunn became the husband of Florence Pritchett, and they had four daughters, Frederica, Nina, Pauline and Rebecca.

Lee Ann Brady died at age 68. The obituaries of the early part of the century were very different from today's obituaries. In her obituary it states she was loved and honored and respected by all who knew her, a lady of wonderful character and noble birth, one whom very few can excel.

When Henry Brady died at the age of 83, there were no phones in Arbor Grove and Aunt Allie rang the dinner bell. Soon relatives and friends came from all around all within the sound of the ringing bell on a quiet April night.
–Brady Family

AUBREY BRANDON FAMILY. Lucy Lavanna Pickney (born February 4, 1913, of Black Rock) married Aubrey Kenneth Brandon (born on October 19, 1910, in Water Valley)

on July 13, 1929.

They had 13 children: Allie May, Freddie Edward, Charlene Clara, Kenneth Hiram, Thomas Gene, Alvin Edward, Emma Sue, Barbara Ann, Joe Dean, Agnes Marie, Audrey Lavanna, Aubrey Kenneth Jr., and Richard Allen.

Aubrey and Lucy

Aubrey Brandon worked in construction in both Arkansas and Michigan. He also worked at the Chevrolet Motor Division. Aubrey passed away in September 1951, and was buried in Michigan. Lucy moved to Black Rock in 1970, and now lives with her daughter and son-in-law Charles and Charlene Clark in Black Rock.

Fred Brandon in front of the Ravenden Hotel at Ravenden, Arkansas, on his mail route in the 1920s.

Photo Caption: Family of Jehu and Fannie Belle (Hoover) Brandon. Taken by their son Hiram Brandon on their farm in Poughkeepsie, Arkansas, summer of 1923. L to R, back row: Jehu Brandon; son, Conrad Brandon; grandson, Glen Campbell (son of Lee and Maud (Brandon) Campbell; grandson, Ado Watkins (son of Charlie and Ethel (Brandon) Watkins); grandson, Aubrey Brandon (son of Fred and Lena (Blansett) Brandon); grandson, Sam Huckabee Jr. (son of Sam and Audrey (Brandon) Huckabee); son-in-law, Sam Huckabee Sr; son-in-law, Charlie Watkins; son Fred Brandon. L-R, second row: Fannie Belle Brandon holding her granddaughter Bonnie McCoy (daughter of Fate and Mary (Brandon) McCoy; daughter, Ethel (Brandon) Watkins holding her daughter Bernetta; daughter-in-law Maud (Tompkins) Brandon (wife of Conrad) holding her son, Ratchford; daughter, Audrey (Brandon) Huckabee holding her daughter, Zelma; daugher-in-law, Nona (Campbell) Brandon (wife of Hiram) holding her son, Hiram Jr.; daughter-in-law, Lena (Blansett) Brandon (wife of Fred) holding daughter Ruby. Sitting on ground, grandchildren: Edwin Campbell, son of Lee and Maud (Brandon) Campbell; L.F. McCoy, son of Fate and Mary (Brandon) McCoy; Nelson Brandon; Thelma Brandon; Gertie Brandon, children of Fred and Lena (Blansett) Brandon; Celeste McCoy, daughter of Fate and Mary (Brandon) McCoy; Mildred Brandon, daughter of Fred and Lena (Blansett) Blandon.

FRED BRANDON. Fred Brandon was a mailman. Fred and his wife Lena lived in the Lawrence County area until 1928.

AMOS J. BRATCHER was born in Grundy County, Tennessee, on December 27, 1842, to Allen and Caroline Bratcher both of Tennessee. They moved to Lawrence County prior to the Civil War and Amos served in the Confederacy until he was captured July 3, 1863, after the fall of Vicksburg, Mississippi. He returned home until 1864, when he enlisted in the 45th Confederate Cavalry to participate in Price's Raid into Missouri. He was captured near Bentonville, Arkansas, and sent to Federal military prison at Alton, Illinois. He was paroled at the end of the war.

Sallie Bratcher Harrison Black and her granddaughter Gladys Williams Bilbrey

Amos Bratcher returned to Smithville, Arkansas. He married Mulissa Jane Ratliff, daughter of Zachariah and Margaret Underwood Ratliff, on February 10, 1868. They lived at Smithville and raised a large family as follows: Lou married Bud Forrest; Addie married Chris Ponder; Josie married Claude P. Cowan; Sarah Jane married Henry

Standing, left to right: Bud Forrest, Lou Bratcher Forrest, Addie Bratcher, Josie Bratcher, Sarah Bratcher, Wash Goff, Mattie Bratcher Goff, sitting left to right; John Bratcher, Laura Bratcher, Fannie Bratcher, Albert Allen Bratcher, Amos J. Bratcher (father), Doshia Bratcher, Mulissa Jane Bratcher (mother), Delia Bratcher, Betty Bratcher Clements, Calvin Clements and Carson Clements.

Harrison and then Henry Black; Martha C. "Mattie" married George Washington Goff; Laura married a Werner; Fannie E. married Charles Werner; Albert Allen (wife's names was Ida); Doshia married Elick Pickett; Cordelia "Delia" married Harry Sullivan; Betty married a Clements; John Z. married Ella R. Pickett; and Amos Lee died as an infant. Amos Bratcher was a farmer and a spiritual man who was very active in his church. Bulletins from the annual meetings of the Primitive Rest Association of the Primitive Predestinarian Baptists indicate that he was a messenger from New Bethel Church. After the death of Mulissa on January 21, 1899, Amos married Mrs. Temperance Cook, December 5, 1901. She also preceded him in death on February 12, 1918. Amos J. Bratcher died July 2, 1926, and is buried in the Bratcher Cemetery north of Smithville near his homestead. Today, many descendants of Amos and Mulissa Bratcher live throughout Lawrence

County as well as surrounding counties in this part of the state.

Sarah Bratcher Harrison Black (see photograph), one of Amos Bratcher's daughters, was the great-great-grandmother of this article's author. The child in the picture is my grandmother, Gladys William Bilbrey, daughter of Gertie Harrison Williams and Ernest Williams. She lived her entire life in the Smithville area.
–Maleta Bilbrey Tipton.

MATTHEW CLINE BRISTOW FAMILY. The Matthew Cline Bristow family located in Lawrence County, Arkansas in the late 1800s. Matthew Cline "Bud", 1855-1943, and his wife, Hannah Ellen Darling Bristow, developed a home place on the Strawberry River a few miles from Lynn where they farmed and operated Bristow Mill Dam. Many of the descendants of Matthew and Ellen still dwell in this area and the home place still stands with its breezeway and attached kitchen.

Matthew and Ellen produced 12 children.
1. Archie Jefferson, 1893-1981, who married Myrtle Orrick.
2. Pelham, who married Coy Boathammer.
3. Grover, who married Elmera Penn.
4. Seborn, who married Cleadee Gleason.
5. Christina "Ena", who married Ralph Dawson.
6. May, who married Barney Justus.
7. Anna who married ?? Gleason.
8. Mable, who married Oscar Dawson.
9. Ora Dell, who married Mitt Mayland.
10. Bertha.
11. Maggie.
12. Larman.

The 1998 Arkansas Democratic nominee for governor, Bill W. Bristow of Jonesboro, is a great-grandson of Matthew and Hannah Ellen.

Matthew Cline descended from the family of John Wesley Bristow, 1835-1903, and Emily Belle Hudson Bristow in

John Wesley Bristow, 1835-1903, Patriarch of NE Arkansas Bristow families.

Sharp County. A Civil War veteran, John Wesley worked in law enforcement in Sharp County and farmed. John Wesley and Emily had moved to Sharp County from Boone County, Arkansas, after the Civil War. John Wesley's parents were Judge Matthew Cline Bristow, 1810-1870s, and Hannah La Salle Bristow from Carroll County, Arkansas. Judge Matthew's parents were Samuel and Lavinia Bristow who migrated to Arkansas from Illinois in 1835. *–Mary Bristow.*

MATTHEW CLINE BRISTOW FAMILY. Matthew Cline "Bud" Bristow, my grandfather, was part of an old Arkansas family. He moved to Lawrence County from Evening Shade and reared a family of 12 children.

Back row: Anna Bristow, Seborn Bristow, Ena Bristow (mother). Front row: Matthew Cline "Bud" Bristow and Ellen (Darling) Bristow.

My mother, Christina Belle "Ena" Bristow, was the youngest. She always talked fondly of her young life on the banks of the Strawberry River. Grandpa operated the grist mill (Bristow Mill Dam) and helped many families during those hard years. His agreement with each person was to grind their grain for a portion of the grain as his fee. He was a very compassionate man. There were a lot of widows and families with very small amounts of grain and many times he would not take his portion, as he knew that they would not have enough to feed their families through the winter

Bristow Mill Dam and Grist Mill near Lynn in the late 1800s and early 1900s. Owned by Matthew Cline Bristow.

if he did. Mother said that he never refused anyone who brought grain the be ground. He was a very good husband and their home had running water in a time when it was unheard of (the early 1900s). For a time he helped run the cotton gin at Lynn. I only have vague memories of it. He and grandma Ellen (Darling) Bristow lived their last years in a little house near Lynn.
–Clynell (Dawson) Sandusky.

JOSEPH BYRON BROWN is my great-grandfather. His mother, Ruth Ann Mullins, came over on the Mayflower as a child. He married my grandmother and moved to Kentucky, later moving to this area. He died accidently at a ripe old age of 90 plus.

He was born March 30, 1861, in El Dorado, Illinois. Since 1884, the poems of Mr. Brown have appeared quite extensively in the periodical press. For a while he was employed on the correspondence staff of the *St. Louis Daily Republican* and was sent by that paper on a tour through Texas and Old Mexico. He next engaged with the *Rocky Mountain News* and in 1883, returned to Morganfield and began the publication of a country newspaper, but soon disposed of that periodical. He then returned to *The St. Louis Republican* and was sent abroad as traveling correspondent for that paper. He sailed from San Francisco to the Argentina Republic, traveled extensively in that country and Brazil. From Rio de Janeiro he voyaged to Capetown, Africa, touched St. Helen's Islands and stopped for some time in the West Indies. His correspondence is a lasting record of this great voyage. After his return home he was appointed to a position in the Signal Service. He next received an appointment as Indian Inspector under Cleveland's administration. After that he was engaged in the mercantile business in Corydon, Kentucky. *–Geraldine Gatewood.*

PARMER SANFORD BROWN FAMILY. Parmer Sanford Brown was born in Herkimer County, New York, about 1831. He was living in Granby Township, Oswego County, New York, when he married Rosetta Davis on July 29, 1849. He worked as a boatman on the Erie Canal in 1850, and later as a farmer in 1860. They had two sons: John Eugene, born 1852, died 1912, in Owosso, Michigan; and Charles Thomas, born 1854, died September 24, 1864, in New York.

In late 1864, in the dead of winter, they followed the Indian trails through Canada, going over ice covered lakes and rivers to Gratoit County, Michigan. In 1868, they settled on a farm near Elsie in Clinton County, Michigan. Before 1873, Sanford and Rosetta took in Madora Page, a 16 year old orphan, to help raise the family.

On February 26, 1873, Sanford married Madora Emily Page, daughter of George Page and Emily Steward, and moved to Dickinson County, Kansas. They homesteaded there until April of 1880, then moved south of Headlee in White County, Indiana. In the fall of 1894, Sanford and Madora moved to a farm on the "flat woods" area of Lawrence County, Arkansas, because of Sanford's health. This farm is the present day Lucus farm on Perry Toles Road. When Sanford returned to Indiana in the summer of 1895, to sell the farm, he became ill and died on September 21, 1895, and was buried in the Mt. Pleasant Ploss Cemetery at Headlee.

Their children were: Bert William, born 1875, married Mollie Delzell; Albert Bruce, born 1876, married Cora Bragg; Sanford Bud, born 1877, married Mary Ragsdall; Estella, born 1880, married Claud Lawson; Arthur McKinley, born 1884, married Mabel Ray; Nancy, born 1886, died at 13; Joseph Alfred; and Parmer Grover Brown, born 1896. All children married Lawrence County women except Bert and Grover. Nancy is buried in the Old Pleasant Grove Cemetery next to Mabel Brown, the oldest daughter of Bert and Mollie Brown.

Joseph Alfred Brown was born in White County, Indiana near Headlee on February 8, 1892. Joe was a farmer and died July 24, 1965, at Chaffee, Missouri, and was buried in Union Park Cemetery, Chaffee, Missouri. He married Nettie Evia Oldham, daughter of Henry Clay Oldham and Sarah Mahala Ketner, on April 11, 1909, at Eaton, Lawrence County, Arkansas. Nettie was born February 14, 1893, at Lynn, Lawrence County, Arkansas, and died December 22, 1988, at Walnut Ridge, Arkansas. She is buried at Old Lebanon Cemetery, Eaton, Arkansas.

Joe and Nettie had the following children: Virgie married Fred Foster, William Parr and Grover Poteet; Virgil Alfred married Mary "Jane" Hibbard; Ray Edgar married Mrytle Frisbee; Ralph Edward married Mattie Gray; Stella Margaret married Claude Kissee; and Molly Nadine Brown married Harold Ingram.

Joe also married Daisy Thompson Calton on July 17, 1935, at Walnut Ridge, Lawrence County, Arkansas. They lived at Marshall and Chaffee, Missouri, and had the following children: David, Tom, Douglas, Paul, James, Mrs. Murial Schaefer.

VIRGIL ALFRED BROWN was born in Marked Tree, Arkansas, the son of Joseph and Nettie Oldham Brown. He married Mary Ellen "Jane" Hibbard, daughter of William Hibbard and Mattie Lairamore, on October 12, 1935, in Walnut Ridge, Arkansas. Mary was born in Bloomer, Arkansas. They had the following children: Virgil Ancil, Alan Dale, Sharon, Jerry, David and Michael.

In 1936, they moved to Randolph County near Lesterville so that Virgil could help Mr. Hibbard with the crops and Mrs. Hibbard could help Jane with her first child. Later, they moved to the Ryburn place also near Lesterville. Virgil and Jane then moved back to Portia to the Hatcher farm. They farmed there until around 1943, moving to the Fender Community near Walnut Ridge. From there, Virgil bought a farm in Lawrence County from Earl Rainwater. They later moved to the Fender Community in Randolph County near O'Kean, staying there until the fall of 1953, then moving to the Pat Jansen farm near Sedgwick in Lawrence County. There they farmed around 300 acres, and the house was very well built. In 1965, they bought a dairy farm near Ravenden and built a house on the farm on flat woods. This farm is located on the old Frisbee place. This dairy was operated until around 1976. They are now living in Paragould, Arkansas.

Virgil Ancil Brown was born in Walnut Ridge, Arkansas. Ancil married Sybil Nutt, daughter of Hose Earl Nutt and Allie Buchanan, on November 3, 1962, in Walnut Ridge, Arkansas. Sybil Nutt was born in Wynne, Arkansas.

Alan Dale Brown was born in Walnut Ridge, Arkansas. Alan married Christine Melim on April 9, 1978, in Kansas City, Missouri.

Sharon Brown was born in Walnut Ridge, Arkansas. Sharon married Donald Greer on July 19, 1958, in Kennett, Missouri. Donald Greer was born in Hornsville, Missouri. They had two daughters and a son. Sharon also married Clayton Dean Timperly on December 9, 1972, in Norfolk, Nebraska. Clayton Dean Timperly was born in Norfolk, Nebraska. Clayton owns and operates Jeter Plumbing in Fremont, Nebraska.

Jerry Brown was born on November 7, 1944, in Walnut Ridge, Arkansas. He died on November 15, 1993, in Jonesboro, Arkansas, and was buried in the Old Military Cemetery, Sedgwick, Arkansas. The cause of death was cancer. Jerry was known for his fishing and the fishing lures that he made. He called them B&Os (Brown & Oliver's). Jerry married Anita Carroll Andrews, daughter of Jesse Andrews and Ernestine Melton. Anita Carroll Andrews was born on July 21, 1948, in Walnut Ridge, Arkansas.

David Brown was born in Walnut Ridge, Arkansas. David married Lorene Beehler on April 17, 1969, in Ravenden, Arkansas. Lorene Beehler was born in St. Cloud, Minnesota.

Michael Brown was born in Walnut Ridge, Arkansas. Michael married Pauletta Wheeler, daughter of Russell and Alline Mills Wheeler, on March 2, 1974, in Paragould, Arkansas. Pauletta was born in Louisa, Kentucky. –Tony Greer.

CHARLIE ELI BRUCE was born March 6, 1908, in Fisk, Missouri. He is the son of May Irene and James Thomas Bruce. He moved to Hoxie when he was a teenager. In 1930, he married Lillian Rosella Emmons, daughter of Jennie Wright and Samuel Davis Emmons of MoArk, Arkansas. Mrs. Bruce had two brothers, Claude and Claredon Emmons; and two sisters, Dollie and

Charlie Eli and Lillian Rosella Emmons Bruce.

Daisy. Mr. and Mrs. Bruce were married for 43 years until her death on October 5, 1973. They had one son, Joy Spencer Bruce; and two daughters, Charlsie R. and Barbara R. Bruce. All three graduated from Hoxie High School. Mr. and Mrs. Bruce had six grandchildren and eight great-grandchildren. Joy Spencer Bruce married Eula White of Portia. They had one son, Spencer Eli Bruce. Charlsie married James F. Little of Brunswick, Georgia. They had one daughter, Kristy Michelle Little. Barbara married Lamar Little of Brunswick, Georgia. They had one daughter, Beverly Little. Later, Barbara married Ted Cabato of Brunswick, Georgia. They had three children, Ted, Melissa and Jeff Cabato.

Mr. Bruce was a painter for 48 years. He worked with his brother, Hartford, for several years and later operated Bruce and Son Contractors for 26 years with his son, Joy Bruce. In his spare time he liked to travel and fish. He had three brothers, George Asher, Horace Bruce and Hartford Bruce; and two sisters, Rachel and Ruth Asher.

Mr. Bruce's father died when he was one year old and his mother died when he was eight years old. When he was eight he lived with his brother for a little while, but his brother's wife was not receptive to him so he ran away from their home. He stayed with different families working for his keep until he was living on his own. When he was a teenager he traveled back and forth through several states riding the rails on various freight trains. He finally settled in Hoxie. In later years he traveled extensively by train as a paying passenger. He had many interesting stories of his early years. Mr. Bruce died February 14, 1987.

His son, Joy Spencer Bruce, lives in Hoxie. His two daughters, Charlsie and Barbara, live in Albany, Georgia. –James Little.

ROBERT BRUCE FAMILY. Robert Bruce of Smithville and Winona Durfee of Saffell, Arkansas were married in August, 1941, in Fort Walters, Texas. Winona was postmaster at Saffell. During World War II, Robert served in the United States Army and served

Adam, Seth and Andrew Bruce.

in the South Pacific including Solamon Islands and the Philippines.

After returning home, Robert and Winona had two sons: Michael, born in 1947, and Wallace, born in 1949. They moved to Powhatan where Robert farmed. Michael and Wallace graduated Black Rock High School and attended college at Southern Baptist, Fayetteville, and Memphis State. Michael currently lives in Jonesboro and has one son, Seth Bruce. Wallace lives in Houston, Texas and has two sons, Adam and Andrew. Robert died in 1990, and is buried in Lancaster Cemetery at Jesup, Arkansas. –Winona Bruce.

WILLIAM CEDRIC AND SUEBELLE PARKS BRYAN. William Cedric and Suebelle Parks Bryan, from Booneville, Arkansas, moved in 1935, to Walnut Ridge to manage the Gregg Funeral Home. Mr. Bryan had served his apprenticeship in Booneville at the Roberts Funeral Home which his father co-owned at one time. In 1948, W. C. and Suebelle co-founded the Bryan Funeral Home in Hoxie, Arkansas.

W. C. was the fourth child, born on October 26, 1909, in Booneville, Arkansas to William Lafayette and Dona McBee Bryan. Suebelle Parks

Mr. and Mrs. William Cedric Bryan, owners and operators of the Bryan Funeral Home, 1970.

Bryan was the fifth of 10 children, born on October 3, 1908, to Granville Winfield and Sena Mutelle Shamblee Parks, also of Booneville. Suebelle taught school for several years before becoming Mrs. W. C. Bryan.

On November 28, 1931, the Bryan's only child, Edith Sue Bryan, was born. The family lived in an apartment inside their business. They were members of the First Baptist Church of Walnut Ridge. Edith Sue graduated from Walnut Ridge High School in 1948. While attending Arkansas State

College in Jonesboro, Arkansas, in 1949, she met Robert "Bob" Frances Warden from Salem, Illinois, son of Harry Clelon and Neva Elizabeth States Warden. Bob was attending college on a football scholarship. On July 4, 1950, Bob and Sue were united in marriage.

Jacqueline Sue Warden was born to Bob and Sue on January 16, 1952. Robert Bryan Warden was born on April 4, 1954. Jackie married J. R. Cox of Walnut Ridge on August 14, 1970. Their children are Matthew Blake, Brett Aaron, Blair Suzanne and Britni Sarah Cox. Robert Bryan married Gayla Ann Ellis of Walnut Ridge on December 28, 1973. Their children are Amanda Michelle and Robert Christopher Warden.

Suebelle Bryan died on June 16, 1977. William Cedric Bryan died on January 14, 1978.

The Bryans were members of the First Baptist Church, Walnut Ridge. –Jackie Cox.

BUCHANAN FAMILY.
Thomas Franklin Buchanan was born in 1820, in Missouri. His wife was Eliza Welty. They moved near Annieville in Lawrence County where Mr. Buchanan was a

Pauline Buchanan, Marie Buchanan, Toler Buchanan, nieces, nephews, in 1970.

farmer. They had five children: Hannah, Henry, Mary, Thomas and Greene. Greene married Louisa Dupuy.

As a child Louisa was on a wagon train of some 20 families, led by her stepfather, William Ledford. Upon rising one morning she put her hand into her shoe to pull out the tongue and a baby snake had climbed into the shoe in the night and she was bitten. Her hand began to swell and as there were no doctors available, an Indian recommended that she be given whiskey to kill the poison.

Green farmed and his wife was a homemaker until his death on Clay Sloan's farm south of Portia in 1908. According to Green's obituary he was remembered for his

Pat and Pauline Buchanan Chaney, daughters Marilyn and Patsy Jo.

generous, congenial and forgiving ways. Green and Louisa had nine children.

1. William "Will" who married Evelyn Decker and served as City Marshall of Walnut Ridge. They had four children: Bryan, Pauline, Marie and Toler.
2. James married Marietta Payne.
3. Joseph "Joe", a deputy sheriff and a store owner married Donna Doyle and they had two children: Clay and Kathleen.
4. Homer drowned in Portia Bay,
5. Addie married James Henry "Jim" Justus who was a farmer in Lawrence County. They had nine children: Roy, Ruth, Paul, Imogene, Jack, Anna Laura, Bill, Geneva "Toots", Thomas "Dick" and Helen.

6. Hattie who married John Wilson and had five children: Mark, Marie, Virginia, Joan and Mary.
7. Ida who married Oscar Kennedy, a farmer and had three children: J. M. "Buster", Mary Mae and Loretta.
8. Maude married Jess Meadows and had four children: Harold, Betty, Jerald and Jo Ann. They raised their family in Hoxie before moving to Michigan.
9. Pauline who married A. L. "Pat" Chaney, a bookkeeper and had two daughters: Marilyn and Patsy Jo.

After the death of Green Buchanan, Louisa had to support four children still left at home. She moved the family to Powhatan and sold goods such as the *Titanic*. The older children eventually married and Pauline was the only child left at home and she entered school at Powhatan. Later, Louisa moved she and Pauline to Imboden where Louisa became the telephone operator for 20 years.

An exciting event of the family was when Hattie and her husband, John, left the state and journeyed into Indian Territory in Oklahoma. No word came from them for some five years and the family had given up hope of hearing from them until they returned to Arkansas.

William "Will" had to walk the streets of Walnut Ridge as Marshall day and night, carrying a gun and for many years was the only one to maintain law and order in the city. Pauline taught school for 45 years in Lawrence County and retired from the Walnut Ridge schools. William, Joe, Addie, Ida, Maude and Pauline all remained in Lawrence County and raised their family here. Both they, their children and grandchildren have contributed to the county as public servants, teachers, farmers, homemakers and businessmen. –Pauline Chaney.

THE BULLA FAMILY HISTORY.
The Bulla ancestors immigrated to America from Ireland in 1786 and settled in Tennessee. William W. Bulla (1811-18647) married a widow, Rebecca Posey Bell, and they had four children together. One son, James W. Bulla, was born in 1864 in Missouri. James married Fanny and had three children: William Edgar (1889-1941), Thomas Lee (1892-1947) and Rose (1895-1927), all born in Lawrence County, Arkansas.

William Edgar Bulla (Ed) married Clara Wadley in 1911 at age 22. He was a farmer and a World War I veteran. Thomas Lee (Lee) married Kate Shinault in 1917. They had a son, Louie Loran, on November 21, 1918. Kate died a week later form the flu. In 1933, Lee married the widow Connie Grubbs, who had three daughters: Beatrice, Ruby and Inez. Together, Lee and Connie had three more daughters: Geneva Lorene in May 1934, Jennie Sue in December 1939 and Lucy Ann in April 1943. Rose Bulla married Lewis Shinault and had three sons, Gene, Jack, and Roy Thomas.

On December 18, 1923, Ed Bulla married Josie (Wilson) Higginbotham (1888-1979), a widow with six children of her own. Her children were Lena, Bill, Connie, Winnie, Ailie and Neece. In August 1925, twin boys Leroy and Troy were born in Lawrence County. The Bullas moved to Poplar Bluff, Missouri, where daughter Nola Mae was born on March 1, 1928. The family then returned to Lawrence County and bought the Ficklin-Imboden log cabin in Powhatan from John and Agnes Holm in 1930. Troy Bulla died May 8, 1937 from a ruptured appendix and Roy Bulla died October 6, 1939 by accidental shooting. Ed was commercial fisherman when he died in 1941. Ed's widow, Josie, continued to live in the log cabin until 1970, when she left to live with Nola Mae and family. Josie Bulla died on July 11, 1979 at the age of 91.

Nola Mac married Troy Staggs on December 2, 1949. They had four children. Julie May was born February 21, 1955 and Pamela Jo was born

January 14, 1956 in Walnut Ridge. The family moved to Brinkley, Arkansas in 1957. Nanette, the third child was born on April 19, 1958 and son Bret was born September 2, 1959 in Brinkley. Nola Mae and all her children still live in Arkansas.
–Nola Mae Staggs.

HOLLIS BURKE FAMILY.
On February 14, 1955, Hollis and Corine Burke, with their six children, moved from Waldenburg (in Poinsett County) to Lawrence County. Hollis had rented the Burrow farm, a rice farm in Whiskerville, northeast of Walnut Ridge.

Cotton was the major crop for that area and rice farming was relatively new. The Burke family lived and worked on this farm until November of 1957. During October and November of that year, Cache River overflowed and covered the fields and roads. When the Burke family moved water was nearly in the house and the furniture had to be carried out over a wooden walkway that had been constructed for that purpose.

Of the Burke children, Glenda, Gloria and LaVita, attended Walnut Ridge School. LaVon and Dwayne went to Fender and Derrell was not of school age.

When the Burke family moved, Glenda had married Ed Romine and they lived in the White Oak Community. Later, Ed and Glenda, along with the Bill Romine family moved to the Burrow farm to farm rice, soybeans and some cotton.

Glenda now lives in Jonesboro and is a reading teacher in Osceola. Gloria owns and operates Gloria's Classic Hair Corner in Walnut Ridge. LaVita, a health care professional, lives near Beebe and LaVon, a special education teacher, lives and works at Newport. Dwayne and Derrell own and operate fish farms in northwest Arkansas.

Terry Romine, Ed and Glenda's older son, is a military chaplain, stationed in Fort Benning, Georgia. Lynetta, their daughter, lives in Jonesboro and works for a realty company. Nathan, Ed and Glenda's younger son, owns and operates a tire business in Hoxie. –Gloria Heard.

GEORGE ROBERT BUSH,
of Clover Bend and Alicia, was the son of Benjamin Bush, a Civil War veteran, was born in Clover Bend, Arkansas, a very successful farmer and landowner. Mr. Bush was very active in all community affairs as well as all farming activities. He was married to Hattie Alphin Bush and they were the parents of Dolph Bush, Rolph Bush, Julia Bush Best, Mildred Bush McLeod, Gertrude Bush Sloan and Ben Robert Bush.

George Bush spent his life in Alicia, a very liked and generous man. The Bush family owned a cotton gin, theater, and general mercantile store in Alicia and a store in Clover Bend, where everyone met and visited many hours. Mr. Bush was very interested in education especially the school at Alicia, where his daughter-in-law, Sibyl Bush, wife of Rolph, taught for many years. Ben Robert Sr. was principal in Alicia and Walnut Ridge Elementary which was later named for him. George Bush was a member of the United Methodist Church and took a very active part in the affairs of the church. Mr. and Mrs. Bush were the grandparents of three: George and Jeannie McLeod and Ben Robert Bush Jr. –Jeanette Bush.

EDWARD F. BUTLER
was born January 8, 1854, in Randolph County, Arkansas. He is the son of John W. and Neoma Perrin Butler. They were in household 1088, township Roanoke in the 1860 census. He married Julie Ellen Forrester

on August 18, 1877, in Randolph County. Julie was born August 23, 1860, in Lawrence County, daughter of Robert and Mary Ellen Nations Forrester. She is the granddaughter of James and Permelia Forrester and Thomas and Martha Weathers Nations. Edward is the grandson of Lafayette Washington and Rebecca Butler and Joab and Rebecca Churchman Perrin.

Edward and Julia were the parents of six children.

1. Rosetta, born June 18, 1878, married Robert Britton McLaughlin, January 30, 1898, died December 22, 1964, and is buried in Hope Cemetery, Lawrence County. He is the son of William Harvey and Sarah Kelly McLaughlin. They had three daughters: Eula Mae, 1899; Nema Edna, 1903; and Emma Pearl, 1920. Nema married Henry Almer Smith, died 1975, and is buried at Oak Forest, Lawrence County.

2. George, born January 2, 1881, died 1882, buried at Fairview, Randolph County.

3. Vennis Viola, born December 10, 1882, married Reverend William Sherman Ward, October 21, 1903, died February 21, 1966, and is buried in Oak Forrest. He is the son of Charles and Mary Songer Ward. They had" Maude, 1906; Doyle, 1908; Orvel, 1911; Edna, 1917, Willene, Pauline and Carl.

4. Naomi, born 1882, died 1891, burned to death.

5. Mary Leona, born June 30, 1885, married 1906, Charles Robert Moore, died July 11, 1976, in Michigan, buried at Fairview, Randolph County. Charles is the son of Mack and Fannie Moore. Their children are: Beulah, 1909; Marvin, 1910; Moses, 1913; Marie, 1915; Jewel, 1917; and Louise, 1919.

6. Malissa Ellen "Tint", born March 31, 1889, married September 13, 1909, Charles Whitaker McCarroll, died December 26, 1975, and buried Fairview. He is the son of Charles Absolom and Ellen Craves McCarroll and grandson of James and Rebecca Forrester McCarroll making Tint and Charles second cousins. They had Velmer Eugene, born 1910, who married Helen Smith.

Edward died April 11, 1889, and is buried at Fairview, Randolph County. Julie died January 16, 1931, and is buried next to her husband. Randolph County Cemetery book has her death at October 4, 1923.

Edward Butler was a first cousin to John C. Carter, who married Susan Forrester, sister to Edward's wife, Julie Ellen Forrester. –*Mary Ann Carter*

HOLLIE CALDWELL. My name is Hollie Jean Caldwell. I was born in Jonesboro, Arkansas, in the Methodist Hospital on September 17, 1984. I have lived in Walnut Ridge, Arkansas, all of my life.

My father is William Vance Caldwell. He was born on December 16, 1958. He has always lived in Walnut Ridge. His parents were David Houston Caldwell of Walnut Ridge. His mother is Wanda Jean Andrews Caldwell. David Hoyston Caldwell was born on July 7, 1979. David Caldwell's parents were the late Elizabeth Campbell Caldwell and william Burten Caldwell. Wanda Caldwell's parents were the late Imagene Andrews and Harry Andrews.

My mother is Lesa Lynn Townsley Caldwell. She was born on June 4, 1957. She has lived in Lawrence County all of her life. Lesa Caldwell's father was William Leon Townsley and he was born November 19, 1932. He was born in Clover Bend. He has always lived in Lawrence County except for when he was in the service. William's father was William C. Townsley. His mother's name was Willie Mae Banner Townsley. Lesa Caldwell's mother was Margaret Ann Spurlock

Townsley. She was born on February 20, 1938, in Walnut Ridge. She also has lived in the Lawrence County all of her life. Margaret Ann Spurlock Townsley passed away on October 20, 1981, in Walnut Ridge. Margaret's parents were Irene White Spurlock and Gilbert Spurlock. Irene Spurlock's parents were William White and Lola White. –*Hollie Caldwell.*

EARL CALLAHAN FAMILY. Earl Lee, 1908-1968, fourth son of Frank and Viola Callahan, was born in Cathy Town (Strawberry) Arkansas. He attended school in Clover Bend, Arbor Grove and lived at home and farmed with his father until he married Goldie Pender in 1929.

Earl's brothers were Floyd, Homer, Claude, Noel, Tol, Jewel and Louis. His sisters were Pearl and Eunice.

Goldie's parents were Joe Pender and Fannie Smith Pender. Her brothers were Omer and Elmer. Her sister was Emma Pender.

Earl and Goldie lived in Lawrence County and farmed for two years, then went to Toledo, Ohio, and worked until the Depression forced them back to Arkansas. They again farmed mostly by the day. Earl joined the Army and served

Earl Lee and Goldie Pender Callahan.

in the military during World War II while the family lived and attended school at Clover Bend.

Their first child, Mable Katheryn, was born while her parents lived in Toledo, Ohio. She attended school in Lauratown, Duvall and Clover Bend. She married Lowell Lamew in Dearborn, Michigan. They had two sons, Lowell Jr. and Charles Ray. Lowell was employed with the railroad. Lowell died and Mable married again and had two more sons. She died in California.

In 1931, Floyd Edward, their first son, was born in Arbor Grove and spend most of his young life in Lawrence County. He served in the US Navy 15 years. He married and lived in Michigan and worked for General Motors.

Joyce Lee, born in 1933, in Lauratown, attended school in Lauratown, Clover Bend and Hoxie. She married Delbert Schuleter. They had four children: Sandra, Debbie, Larry and Gene. She now lives in Ventura, California.

Thomas Earl was born in Lauratown and attended school there and in Clover Bend. He served briefly in the military and while stationed in North Dakota, married Jewell and had two sons, Carey Lee and Jeff. Thomas was killed in a train accident in Hoxie, Arkansas, along with his mother while they gathered for a family reunion in 1970.

Jimmy Dale grew up in Lauratown and attended school in Clover Bend and Hoxie. He married Glenda Ruth Adams in Walnut Ridge in 1955. They have four children: Susan Ruth, Jimmy Scott, Paul Edward and Tracie Rena. Susan has three children: David, Heather Ann and Desiree'. Scott has four children: Judith, Carrie, Linden and Judy. Paul has four children: Castle, Jon Paul, Coty and Paul Jr. Tracie has two children: April, Rana and Brandi.

Jo Ann Barker, 1940, who married Leon Baker, was born in Lauratown. She attended school in Hoxie. She is an LPN and lives in Heritage, Arkansas. She and Leon have five children: Bobby, Leon Jr., Becky Lee, Beatrice Lynn and Billy Leon. –*Viola Meadows.*

JOHN FRANKLIN CALLAHAN FAMILY. John Franklin Callahan was born in Rockford, Illinois to James Nathaniel and Catherine Smith Callahan, August 23, 1880-June 19, 1944. Frank arrived in Lawrence County with his parents, three sisters and three brothers in 1881. They were: Mary, Lavesta, James, Elizabeth, William and Joseph. Minor was born in Strawberry.

Frank married Viola Elizabeth Doyle, 1882-1964, in 1901. Her parents were George Washington and Latisha Wadley Doyle. Her siblings were: John, Jake, George, Joe, Lee, Melissa and Prudence.

Frank and Viola had 10 children. They settled on a farm near Cathy Town where they farmed and had their first six sons: Floyd, Homer, Claude, Earl, Noel and Tol. Frank also worked at the Strawberry Cotton Gin.

In 1914, Frank and Viola and six sons moved to Clover Bend. He farmed John K. Gibson's land in Clover Bend, Lauratown, Arbor Grove and Duvall for the next 30 years. Two more sons, Jewell and Louie, and two daughters, Pearl and Eunice, were born in eastern Lawrence County.

Frank and Viola Elizabeth. Front: Louie, Pearl, Eunice, Claude. Back: Tol, Homer, Floyd, Earl, Jewell and Noel.

Floyd, Earl and Jewell served in World War II.

Their children, spouses and grandchildren are:

James Floyd - Gladys Lane - no children.

William Homer - Lillie A. Robins; William Franklin, Viola Bell, Charles Lindburg and Rosemary.

Henry Claude - Bulah Lawrence; Robert, H. Shirley, Merle Dean, Opal Gerline and Dixie Lou.

Earl Lee - Goldie Pender; Mable Katheryn, Floyd Edward, Joyce, Thomas Earl, James Dale and Joan.

Noel Joseph - Lida Doyle - James Carroll William Jewell

Louis Washington - Ninnie Doyle; Margaret Jean, Harold Franklin.

Prudence Pearl - David Elsworth Pappas Sr.; David Jr., Robert Elswroth, Margaret Beth and James David.

then Pearl and Edward Shultz.

Eunice Melissa - J. D. Overstreet - Shelia Janet, then

Eunice Melissa - Glen Green - Frankie Clarence.

Homer, second son resided in Walnut Ridge until his death. He retired from farming at age 70. He lived most of his life in the Clover Bend area.

Frank was a good farmer. His cotton rows were straight as an arrow. He had one field in the Lauratown farm where he planted cotton rows one mile long. He had a four row cultivator operated by his son, Tol, and pulled by four mules.

Viola was an excellent cook. It is said she, on occasion, would prepare potatoes four different ways to satisfy the taste of the large family.

Saturday evenings often included popcorn. She would move the wood stove cap, place a large three leg pot over the hole and pop the corn. Large black pans of evenly roasted homegrown peanuts were a special treat also.

Viola's mother, Lou Wadley Doyle, lived with this family the last 22 years of her life. She died at age 96 in 1945. –*Viola Matthews.*

HENRY CLAUDE CALLAHAN FAMILY.

Henry Claude was born 1905-1967, in Cathy Town, Arkansas, third son of John Franklin and Viola E. Doyle. His brothers were Floyd, Homer, Noel, Tol, Jewell and Louie. His sisters were Pearl and Eunice Callahan.

Claude attended school in Mt. Harmony, Clover Bend and Arbor Grove.

Claude married Bulah Lawrence in 1924-1988. Her siblings were: Elvis, Alfred, Paul Everette, Nellie, Lalah and Ellie. Her parents were James and Lottie Lawrence of Duvall.

Claude and Bulah Callahan. Left to right: Claude, Dixie on lap, Bulah, Shirley, Dean, Robert, Opal Callahan.

Claude and Bulah farmed one year and then moved to Toledo, Ohio, where their first child, Robert, was born in 1926. They bought a 1928 Whippett car in 1929. The great depression forced them out of work. They returned to Arkansas in the Whippett car and shortly afterwards Shirley was born. They sold the car for 700 dollars, a cow and some hay. Claude worked for 75 cents a day on the Wink Phillips farm. The next year they rented the Kincade farm, bought a team of mules with money borrowed from the U.S. Government. Claude had been a caretaker of government owned mules while farming during the first year of their marriage. In 1938, they bought a farm in Clover Bend from the Farm Security Administration through a program of the Resettlement Act of 1936. By this time they had Merle Dean, Opal Gearline and Lady Faye, 1936-1937. The new house on this farm was special. Claude made flower boxes and placed under the three main front windows and they were the talk of the community. Claude farmed cotton, corn, hay, cattle, chickens, hogs, a large vegetable garden, fruit, sweet potatoes and honey. He bred mules and it was a thriving business. He also worked as a fireman at the Army Air Base in Walnut Ridge.

A daughter, Dixie Lou, arrived in 1944 and in 1946 the family moved to Wayne, Michigan where Claude was employed by Edison Electric Company. He was later in business for himself.

Robert and Shirley each served a tour of duty in the military.

Robert married Avis Metcalf in 1948. They had two daughters, Debbie Van Hull and Stephanie Kerr. Robert had a son, Karson Carpenter. His second wife was Uldene Callahan.

Shirley married Clara Marshelewiezh and they had one daughter, Shirley Gerline. He had one daughter, Vonda Lynn (Oprita) by his second wife,

Evelyn D. Jones. He married Nyoka Callahan in 1997.

Merle Dean married Delores Nesebitt Callahan. They had two sons, Brian and Gary Dean and a daughter, Darlene Marie.

Opal Gearline married Don Milam. They had one son, Gregory Eric and two daughters, Donetta Jo Milam Hammond and Shelley Jean Milam Marowelli.

Dixie Lou married George Lee Armstrong. They had a son, Loren Scott and a daughter, Leah Janette.

Claude and Bulah remained in Michigan until their death. Their children have all married and raised families in the Detroit area.

Robert, Shirley, Dean and Opal attended school in Clover Bend and Robert graduated from Clover Bend High School. Shirley returns annually to Lawrence County and contributes his skills and professional efforts in the preservation of the Clover Bend Historic District. –*Viola Meadows.*

LOUIE AND NINNIE CALLAHAN.

Louie, son of Frank and Viola, was born near Hoxie, March 28, 1919, died January 9, 1994, in Poplar Bluff, Missouri. He was third youngest of 10 brothers and sisters.

Ninnie, daughter of James and Margaret Doyle, was born in Portia, Arkansas, December 9, 1920, and still resides in Poplar Bluff. She is the youngest of nine brothers and sisters. She is also a descendant of the late Ephriam Sharp, state legislator in the late 1800s.

Louie and Ninnie were married March 26, 1938, and had two children, Margaret and Harold. Louie, Ninnie and children lived in St. Louis for a while, then returned to Lawrence County and

Louie Washington Callahan and Ninnie Doyle Callahan. Harold and Margaret, 1950.

farming in 1944, near Lauratown. In 1947, they moved to the Coffman area and in 1949, moved to Alicia. The family moved to Hoxie in 1950, and Louie began working for a building supply company. While at Hoxie both children, Margaret and Harold, finished high school. Louie and Ninnie moved to Jonesboro in 1961, where he worked for N. E. Arkansas Fence Company for two years. They then moved to Poplar Bluff and made it their permanent home.

Regardless of where they lived, Lawrence County has always been home. They have two grandchildren, Michelle Pogue, daughter of Margaret and Sonya Owings, daughter of Harold. – *Viola Meadows.*

MINOR AND MAGGIE CALLAHAN FAMILY.

The story is that Callahan brothers, James, born November 1, 1830, and John, born about 1831, came from around the Chattanooga area. They had a falling out in the 1850s, and parted ways. On February 16, 1862, James married Catherine E. Smith, born March 26, 1846, in Knoxville. He may have fought in the Civil War. James supposedly went to Rockford, Illinois, and later moved to Lawrence County after his brother, John, wrote and told him how good things were in Strawberry. James died February 16, 1889, and Catherine died February 3, 1893.

James and Catherine had eight children: Mary A., born January 4, 1863; Susan LaVesta, born June 8, 1865; James M., born march 17, 1868; William, born December 15, 1870; Joseph R., born July 27, 1873; Liza A., born November 27, 1875; John Franklin, born August, 1880; and Minor Lafayette, born July 25, 1884.

Minor and Maggie Callahan family, May 1920.

Hiram Saffell, born May 26, 1847, married September 31, 1866, Mary Ann Shepard, born 1848, died 1887. They had seven children: Sarah Jane Saffell, born 1868; Melissa Evelyn Saffell married Ephriam Edmond Sharp; Mary Ellen married Milton Horn; Liza A. married first Jim Wilmoth and second Ilie Ward; William Thomas married first Allie Hooten and second Polly Allan; James Oscar married Nellie Wynne; and Maggie Tennessee married Minor Callahan.

Minor Lafayette Callahan, died February 11, 1951, married September 17, 1905, to Maggie Tennessee Saffell, born November 14, 1886, died October 14, 1970. They moved from Strawberry to Portia where they farmed. Their children, all born at Portia, were:

1. Gertha May, September 23, 1906-February 21, 1982, married Fred Marshall, no children.

2. William Melvin Callahan, August 24, 1908-March 11, 1990, married Mildred Butts, no children;

3. Roy Jewel Callahan, April 27, 1911-April 8, 1992, married Louise Lee, two children

a) Nancy Lee Callahan married Oliver Kirkpatrick; children: Wendell Lee married Jackie Urhahn and Virginia Kay married Doug Glastetter; children: Matthew Kyle, Maggie Elizabeth and Mark Lee.

b) Margaret Virginia married first Doug Wolaver; children: Roy S. and Katherine Ann, who married Trent Lee and Margaret married second Grady Osborne.

4. Verma Letha, December 22, 1915-October 29, 1982, married Kenneth Marion Graham; two children

a) Cynthia Kay married Bill Starling; children: Graham married Amy Kelley, child Chandler; Gregory James married Gina Pruitt; and Sarah Elizabeth "Betsy" married Michael Heath Long.

b) Kenneth Michael married first Rebecca Wall; child, Suzanne married Russell Johnson; children: Sean, Shelby, Shannon. He married second to Deborah Spint, child, Trenton Callahan Graham.

5. Harold Hiram Callahan, August 9, 1916-June 21, 1919, married Cynthia Browning; children:

a) Rebecca married David Shipman, child Meagan.

b) Kerry married Mary Jane Sturch, children Kerry Matthew and Harold and Tyson.

c) Cynthia married Cole Warner, child Lashlee.

Minor and Maggie's only descendants now living in Lawrence County are Kerry Callahan and family. –*Cynthia Starling.*

WILLIAM HOMER CALLAHAN FAMILY.

Homer, second son of John Franklin Callahan and Viola E. Doyle was born in Cathy Town, Arkansas in 1904. He attended school at Mt. Harmony and Clover Bend.

Homer married Lillie A. Robins, 1903-1983, on October 18, 1922. She was the daughter of Will and Julia Robins. She attended school in Rangle, Rabbit Roust and Duvall.

Homer farmed as a day hand and share-cropped in his early marriage. In 1937, they were accepted by the Resettlement Program at Clover Bend where they moved with their four children, Billy Frank, Viola, Lindy and Rosemary. Viola, Lindy and Rose graduated from Clover Bend High School. Billy left school and entered the Navy to serve in World War II. He finished his schooling in the Navy and received his training in sheet metal and followed this trade all his life in private business and with larger firms. He married Marie Noblin and to them were born four children, Pamela, Michael, Jeannie and Bill Jr. They were schooled in California and two daughters graduated from Pepperdine University. Michael,

Homer Callahan family. Seated: Lillie Robins Callahan, William Callahan. Left to right: William Franklin, Rosemary, Viola Bell and Charles Lindburg Callahan.

talented in real estate and marketing and Bill Jr. with several patents to his credit, have been successful businessmen. Bill has 12 grandchildren and he died in 1992.

Viola married Howard Meadows in 1957. They have a son, Matthew, who has MBA and BS degrees from University of Arkansas and a MBA from Dallas University. He and his wife, Stephani Morris, manage their own business in Dallas, Texas. Their daughter, Mary Jane with a BA from University of Arkansas, married Richard Pyburn. They live in San Antonio, Texas where Richard is CEO of a medical clinic. Mary is working in Early Childhood Education and they have two children, Ariana and Andrew.

Viola was a home economics teacher in Arkansas. She earned a Fulbright Exchange Teacher Award to India, was an administrator to the American School in Japan. She was Arkansas 4-H Alumni of the Year, the state's Home Economic Teacher of the Year and Arkansas' Vocational Teacher of the Year. Howard was a foreign service officer with the Agency for International Development. They served in Sudan, Libya, Nigeria and Afghanistan. They retired to Lawrence County and Viola works with historic preservation in Clover Bend.

Lindy, 1927-1995, attended University of Arkansas and served in the United States Army in Korea. He returned to California and was associated with Safeway stores until retirement.

Rosemary, an outstanding high school basketball forward, received her BS and MS degrees from University of Arkansas. She taught in Arkansas, did a pilot program in vocational guidance with the State Department of Education before moving to California as State Supervisor in Counseling and Guidance. She directed a graduate counseling program for University of Southern California.

Lillie was active in Eastern Star, Garden Club and Extension Club. She was a beautician and especially talented in hand and needle work. Homer was skilled in carpentry, remodeling their home many times. He helped build the Methodist Church in Clover Bend and served on the Administrative Board. They were

United Methodists and always a farmer. *–Viola Meadows.*

ALBERT CAMERON was the son of William Cameron and Rosa Anna Hauser. Albert married Jennie M. Kincaid in Lawrence County on January 31, 1895. *–Wilma McCarroll.*

WILLIAM A. CAMERON was born in Indiana in 1845. He married Rose Anna Hauser on April 7, 1867. Two boys were born to them: Jason Winfield, September 2, 1869, and Albert, 1874. William took his two boys, boarded a steamboat and went down the Black River toward Powhatan. There he took the boys off the steamboat, entered the Morrison Hotel across from the Powhatan Courthouse. There he remained for a while, driving the stagecoach in the area. He became ill. Before he died, he asked to be

This may be Jason Cameron's brother, Albert Cameron, son of William.

taken across the Black River for burial. Jason and Albert were orphaned again, for their mother died in Hopkins, Indiana. Now the boys were without a father. George Thornburgh, became their legal guardian April 15, 1884.

Jason Winfield went to school in Lawrence County and went on to a college in Missouri.

On his return from college, Jason married Minnie Margaret East. She was only 16, and he was 24. Minnie Margaret East grew up under the old Powhatan Bridge raised by her Uncle Henry East. She was also an orphan at an early age. She played on the Black River bank and among the historic sites.

Minnie Margaret East and Jason Winfield Cameron were married September 17, 1893, at Powhatan by Dr. Wayland.

Jason did not care for the education that he earned at college. Jason and Minnie found an 80 acre farm near Denton, Arkansas. His love of his farm and the lands overruled his college education. He planted every known fruit tree and tilled the lands. They had 10 children and they were happy. Carlyle died at six weeks. Minnie always felt guilty about his death. She was so young, and felt she did not have the knowledge to raise him. Vera Geanette Cameron Stalnaker, Velmar Joe Cameron, Jamie Warren Cameron, Paul Winfield Cameron, Edith Lee Cameron Madden, Luella Cameron Johnson, Linual Cameron, Iverson Clair Cameron, Claretta Cameron Connaughton were other children.

All their offspring have passed away except Edith Lee, who is now 90. Most all their children have followed them in death to the New Hope Cemetery. They had many happy family reunions close to their beloved farm. The site of William A. Cameron's resting place has never been found.

Jason became ill and died of pneumonia at the age of 46, on February 3, 1916. Minnie was a widow at 38. She cared for the children with the help of the older ones as the youngest was only three months old. William A. Cameron, Rose Anna Hauser Cameron, Jason Winfield Cameron, Minnie Margaret East Cameron.

They would be very proud of the foundation that they have laid for descendants. Their children have become anthropologist, contractors, teach-

ers, supervisors, public servants, politic law, medical professionals, farmers, queen of college, and some have made it to the capitol in D.C.

Great-grandparents of William A. Cameron. *–Anna Cameron.*

EDWARD FRANKLIN CARTER is the first son of John W. and Delilah Perrin Carter, grandson of William Carter who came to Randolph County around 1844, and started a grist mill on the Eleven Point River, which later became known as Hufstedler Mill. Edward was in charge of the estate of his father in order to sell above property. Edward was born January 27, 1850, in Randolph County. He married January 9, 1872, to Delilah Jane Scott. She was born June 8, 1852, to William and Sarah Scott. They had eight children.

1. Ida Srailda, born February 1, 1872, who married her first cousin, James Frank Perrin, son of Jasper and Sarah Jane Nations Perrin (Jasper is a brother to Delilah Perrin Carter).

2. Margaret

Mrs. Minnie Cameron.

Blanche, born April 23, 1873, married December 4, 1890, to John Kibler Puckett, died November 28, 1956, buried at Hope Cemetery, Imboden.

3. Florence Ethel, born January 18, 1876, married her first cousin Eli Perrin, brother to James, on February 7, 1894, died June 30, 1955, and buried at Old Union Cemetery, Randolph County.

4. John Harry, born January 18, 1878, married December 29, 1898, to Della Wells, believed to be daughter of Washington and Louisa Haas Wells. He was killed in a fight in Lawrence County. He died June 18, 1910, and is buried at Hope Cemetery, Imboden. John and Della had: Orvel, Audrey, Harry, Stella, Frank and Johnnie.

5. Everett Franklin, born September 17, 1880, married Nellie G. Tanner, June 13, 1901, Lawrence County. He had two sons, Earle and Paul.

6. Agnes Pearl, born October 27, 1884, married Doctor L. B. "Benjamin" Price and died November, 1962. She had two children, Carter and Virginia.

7. Robert Lee, born July 20, 1888, died before 1900, Lawrence County.

Delilah died January 31, 1915, and is buried at Hope Cemetery, Imboden. Edward Franklin died May 12, 1939, and is also buried in Hope Cemetery next to his wife. *–Mary Ann Carter.*

ESSIE FAYE RICHARDSON CARTER was the only child of Mollie Henley Balfour Ivie Richardson and William Drewry Richardson. She was born September 18, 1905, on a farm at Denton near Black Rock, Arkansas.

Although Faye was an only child, her mother had five other children from a previous marriage. (Mollie's first husband died when she was only 35 years old leaving her a widow for four years before her marriage to Faye's father.) Although these sisters and brother were older, Faye felt very close to each of them, especially her brother, Bill, and oldest sister, Elsie.

Faye enjoyed growing up as a farm girl in Denton. Her father, having been a cattle driver at one time, shared his joy of horseback riding with her. In later years she would recall these happy times remembering the names of each of their horses.

Mollie Balfour Richardson and Faye Richardson Carter.

Faye's father became ill when she was in her teens and he died when she was 16. The farm was too much for two women and Mollie and Faye moved to Black Rock until Faye graduated from high school there in 1923. They then moved to St. Louis to live with Bill.

While in St. Louis, Faye met Henry G. Carter. On May 31, 1926, they were married in Waterloo, Illinois. Two of their five children were born in St. Louis. Donald Edward was born in 1927 and Richard Douglas in 1928.

Times were hard during the Depression and in 1930 the family moved to Rector in northeast Arkansas where Henry had grown up and where he still had family. Faye had the task of caring for the family while Henry was away at work. She became a superb cook and homemaker.

The family continued to grow as three other children were born: Doris Jean in 1933, William Neal in 1936 and Carol Ann in 1943. The next few years were especially difficult for the family as Carol became ill with polio and frequent trips to doctors in Little Rock were necessary.

Henry Carter died in 1976 and Faye continued to live in Rector until her health began to fail in 1987 at which time she moved to Mountain Home, Arkansas, to be near Donald's family. She died in 1995 at the age of 90 and is buried beside her husband in the Woodland Heights Cemetery in Rector, Arkansas. –Doris Jean King and Richard Douglas Carter.

John Clinton "Clint" Carter was the third child of John William and Delilah Perrin Carter. He was born October 16, 1856 in the Birdell community, of Randolph County. He was a farmer and helped his dad run the grist mill on the Elevenpoint River, which later became the Hufstedler mill. He married Susan Marie Forrester on March 15, 1877. She was born April 15, 1859 in Lawrence, daughter of Robert and Mary Ellen Nations Forrester. Her father died at Holley Springs, Mississippi, October 1862. In August 1863, Thomas Nations, grandfather, applied for administrator of Robert Forrester's estate. In June 1866, Elijah Forrester, brother of said Robert, applied for guardianship of his two minor nieces. April 1967, Elijah, again goes to court saying that Thomas Nations is wasting the estate of Robert Forrester, and wants to the be the guardian of the girls. It appears he was finally successful, becuase he sells some of Robert's property at different times for them. Their mother Mary Ellen remarries, a John Ewing, on January 8, 1865. She has both the girls in the 1870 cenus of Randolph county and then either marries again, moves, or dies before 1880. John Clint and Susan Marie had ten children. John Robert born December 19, 1877 Birdell, married September 23, 1900 to Johnnie Walter Million daugther of George Washington and Alice L. Peay Million. He died May 1, 1966 and is buried in Oak Ridge, Kennett, Dunkin county Missouri.

Mary Eleizabeth "Lizzie" born June 27, 1879, married September 27, 1902 to Benjamin Franklin Million, first cousin of Johnnie, son of Ambrose Hodge and Susan A. Chesser Million. She died

April 6, 1963 and is buried at Sutton Baptist Church.

Benjamin Franklin born September 12, 1880/2, married May 27, 1905 to Rettie Lea Hunt, daughter of J. Thomas adn Margaret A. Bramlett Hunt. He died Febuary 24, 1963 and is buried Memorial Gardens, Kennett, Dunklin county Missouri.

Alder V. born March 28, 1883, married June 1906 to William Henry Chilton. She died May 10, 1979 Paragould, Green County and is buried at Sutton Baptist.

Dora born September 1, 1886, married December 23, 1905. to George David Kincade son of John R. A. and Mary Elizabeth Sutton Kincade, died March 29, 1961, and is buried at Sutton Baptist.

Eli Burley was born September 21, 1888, married October 9, 1913 Dunklin, Missouri to Lucy Emily Marshall, died September 27, 1953, and buried at Monnett, Arkansas.

Edger William was born November 13, 1890, married April 23, 1916 to Tishie Ann Bates daughter of Benjamin Horace and Louvica Victoria Collier Bates, died September 25, 1918 before son was born, and buried at Sutton Baptist, with son.

Iva Ethel "Ivie" was born March 19, 1894, married November 28, 1911 to William Wesley Baldridge son of Charles R. and Mary C. Haney Baldridge, died January 25, 1986, and buried at Sutton Baptist

Florence Delia was born October 22, 1896, married Ira Tom (Thomas) Sutton, son of Samuel Thomas and Dora B. Cannon Sutton, died October 23, 1980 Norwalk, Los Angeles, California, buried Cypress Susan died January 16, 1931 and is buried at Sutton Baptist. There is no Arkansas death certificate for her so I wonder if she died at Memphis or Popular Bluff at a hospital. John lived long enough to have four generation picture ca 1941: John Clinton, son of John Robert, grandson William Lloyd, and great grandson Bobby Glenn. He died June 27, 1943 and is buried next to his wife at Sutton Baptist. –Mary Ann Vuylsteke Carter.

MARGARET BLANCHE CARTER was born April 23, 1873, Lawrence County. She is the second daughter of Edward Franklin and Delilah Jane Scott Carter, granddaughter of John W. and Delilah Perrin Carter and William and Sarah Scott. John W. ran the grist mill on the Eleven Point River with the help of her father and uncles. She married December 4, 1890, to John Kibler Pucket, son of John and Margaret Pucket. He was born September 5, 1871, Randolph County. They had seven children.

1. Marvin, born October, 1892, died February 12, 1912.

2. Sally, born January 14, 1894, married before 1910, to Rennard Cooper, died October, 1982.

3. Edward Franklin, born March 19, 1896, married Edna Ellen McCarroll, November 14, 1916. She is the daughter of Charles Absolom and Ellen Cravens McCarroll, born October 5, 1897. Edward died November 19, 1983, and is buried Lawrence Memorial Cemetery, Walnut Ridge.

4. Robert Lee, born December, 1897, married Oda Murphy.

5. John Chester, born February 6, 1902, married Ruth May, died March, 1979, Walnut Ridge.

6. Ottie Pearl Puckett, born November 5, 1906, married Earl Surbur, died April, 1987, Madera, California.

7. Kathryn Eunice, born May 5, 1913, married Raymond Storey, died July, 1995, Senath, Dunklin County, Missouri.

John Kibler died February 12, 1949, and is buried in Hope Cemetery, Imboden. Margaret Blanche died November 28, 1956, and is buried next to her husband at Hope Cemetery, Imboden.

DAN AND DEBORAH CASPALL FAMILY. The Caspalls moved from Midwestern Illinois to Walnut Ridge in 1969. Dan Caspall was a young

enthusiastic executive with Vaughan and Bushnell Manufacturing Company, a quality hand tool manufacturer for over 100 years. Deborah Caspall was a young mother of two sons, Joby Dan, 5 and Jayme Jon, 3. The couple's first home in Lawrence County was a company leased trailer situated near the runway at the Walnut Ridge Airport. Dan had been sent by his company to set up a production control system at their newly acquired facility. The job that would supposedly be temporary has lasted 32 years. After one year passed the Caspalls bought a home from the Burt Finch family located in the Highland Addition in Walnut Ridge where they raised their two sons.

During this period of time V & B has expanded and prospered. Dan is currently Vice President and General Manager of V & B and two additional facilities in Tennessee. Due to his engineering expertise, Dan has patented the popular chevron grip on Vaughan hammers, designed automatic loaders for their handle operation and redesigned handles for the popular line of landscaping tools, Groundbreakers.

Mr. Caspall has been active in county affairs. He has served as President of the Chamber of Commerce, President of the Walnut Ridge Booster Club, President of the Walnut Ridge Country Club and he presently serves on the Arkansas Industrial Association Board.

Deborah completed her AA degree at Southern Baptist College and her BSE and MSE at Arkansas State University. Mrs. Caspall has worked as secretary to the Juvenile Probation Officer under General Guntharp and David Foley. She worked as a Head Start teacher and Educational Coordinator for BRAD. Deborah has taught English, reading, geography, career orientation and served as a counselor for the past 23 years in the Walnut Ridge schools.

Mrs. Caspall has been active in community and professional affairs. She was one of the first to be trained as a Red Cross Water Safety Instructor and supervised and taught child and adult swimming lessons at the Walnut Ridge pool. She has served as Vice President of PTA, worked 6 years as United Methodist Youth Coordinator, helped facilitate a Boy Scouts Webelos group as well as actively worked on many fund-raising

Dan and Deborah Caspall and August Rinn Caspall, first grandchild, born September 6, 1998.

drives and benefits. In her professional life, Deborah has served two consecutive terms as President of NEARK School Counselors, State Vice President of Elementary Counselors and currently serves as State Vice President of Middle/Jr. High Counselors. Mrs. Caspall has received the award Outstanding Teach of the Year.

Both Job Caspall and Jayme Caspall graduated from Walnut Ridge High school, Job in 1981, and Jayme in 1983. Job attended the popular kindergarten of Miss Goldie Lane. Jayme went to kindergarten at the First Baptist Church taught by Mrs. Sharon Kennedy, the year before public schools had kindergarten. Both boys participated in a wide variety of school activities. Job graduated an honor student in 1981, and went on to graduate with both a BA in accounting and a MBA for ASU. Job married the former Vickie Brewer from Hoxie. They spent six years in Houston, Texas, where Job worked as a financial analyst and Vickie completed her Ph.D in Pediatric Neuropsychology at the University of Houston. Currently, they live in Collierville, Tennessee and have a daughter, Emma Elise, born June 10, 1999.

Jayme Caspall graduated valedictorian from Walnut Ridge High School in 1983. He received his BA in physics from Hendrix College and his masters degree in Mechanical Engineering from Georgia Tech. Since graduation, Jayme has

Caspall family Christmas, 1993. Job Dan Caspall, Dan R. Caspall, Jayme Jon Caspall, Vickie Brewer Caspall, Deborah Louise Caspall, Lisa Campbell Caspall.

worked as a research scientist in the acoustics department at Tech. Jayme is married to the former Lisa Campbell from Little Rock whom he met at Hendrix. Jayme and Lisa have one child, August Rinn Caspall, born September 6, 1998. They live in Stone Mountain, Georgia. Lisa is a dance instructor and choreographer.

During the time Dan and Deborah have lived in Lawrence County, their lives have meshed with many wonderful people who made this home for a young couple with two young sons to raise. Six years ago Dan and Deborah began a new bold adventure. They purchased a 400 acre farm in Western Lawrence County, the former Paul Howard farm, two miles north of Lynn and started a cattle operation. Everyone who lives across Black River and has met and visited with the Caspalls knows the joy and happiness they feel living on the farm. The wonderful warm neighbors in Lynn and Eaton have been both helpful and supportive. Although the Caspalls are first generation Lawrence Countians, they are proud to be part of the rich history and continue to work hard and make contributions to the community. *–Deborah Caspall*

CASPER FAMILY. My great-great-grandfather, George Casper, was born in 1795, while George Washington was President and was possibly named for him. My great-grandfather, John Casper, was born in 1827, in Rowan County, North Carolina to George and Nancy Leonard Casper. He came to Arkansas in 1853, and settled in Lawrence County near Cypress Creek between Lynn and Eaton, Arkansas. John had three brothers and four sisters, two of his brothers, David and Alexander, came to Arkansas to settle, also. In 1854, John Casper married Sarah Blackwell, a widow from North Carolina. Sarah was a charter member of the Lebanon Presbyterian Church established in 1852. They had a son in 1855, George Washington Casper, my grandfather.

David Casper had a son, Jacob Casper, a well known businessman in the Lynn area who was known to many as "Uncle Jake." Alexander Casper had a daughter, Emma Casper, who later married Jacob. Uncle Jake died sometime between 1940 and 1941.

John Casper enlisted in the Confederate Army in 1863, and was a member of the Seventh Missouri Cavalry. Later, he transferred to the Seventh Arkansas Infantry. He fought in battles at Little Rock and at Pilot Knob. He also fought with General Price in his various raids throughout Missouri. He was paroled at Shreveport, Louisiana at the end of the war.

John's wife, Sarah, died in 1877. In 1879, John married Harriet Harris, also a widow from North Carolina. To this marriage, a daughter, Etta, was born in 1882. Harriet died in 1884, when Etta was only two years old. John Casper married his third wife, Nancy Carolina Tracy, in 1890. Nancy died in 1904. John lived until 1910, reaching the age of 83. Etta married James Stewart in 1910. Their chil-

dren included Harry, Ralph and Verniel Stewart. Etta died in 1974. Her daughter, Verniel Stewart Jackson, lives in Batesville, Arkansas. John Casper and his three wives are buried in Old Lebanon, all descendants of John, David and Alexander Casper from Rowan County, North Carolina.

In 1879, my grandfather, George Casper, married Jane Ketner, daughter of Daniel and Catherine Bour Ketner. Daniel Ketner was the son of David and Mary Izehom Ketner of North Carolina. David's father was a soldier of the Revolutionary War. Daniel Ketner left North Carolina in 1849. He moved to Union County, Illinois for eight months. Then he moved to Tennessee where he married Catherine Bour. He stayed in Weakley County, Tennessee for three years and moved back to Union County, Illinois. In 1858 Daniel came to the Lynn and Eaton area in Lawrence County, Arkansas. In 1863, my great-grandfather, Daniel Ketner, also enlisted in the Confederate Army. He fought battles in Pine Bluff, Pilot Knob, Little Rock and Independence County. He also fought with General Price's various raids through Missouri. He was wounded several times during the war. He was paroled at Shreveport, Louisiana in June, 1865. Daniel Ketner was the father of eight children. Three sons, George, J. Daniel and Jesse Ketner; and five daughters, Mahala, Jane, my grandmother, Margaret, Amanda and Nettie.

George Washington and Jemina Jane Ketner Casper did help populate Lawrence County with eight children and 59 grandchildren. The following are the children and their spouses and grandchildren of George Washington Casper.

1. Ethel Casper and Clinton Richey: Odell, Brooks, Lewis, Homer, Jess, Littie, Virgil, Elsie, Alva and Alpha.
2. Ara Casper and Frank Richey: Eva, William, Orace, Ora, Celia, Daniel, May, Roy, Vernon, Winnie, Elizabeth and Otis.
3. Arry Casper and Tom Atchisson: La Vernia, Ella, Della, Ruby, Orma, Majorie, Velma and Alta.
4. Joe Casper and Ella Richey: Cora, Neva and Ethel.
5. Joe Casper and Mahala Ketner: Roy, Albert, Cecil, Truman, Thurman, Louise, Clara, Margie, L. D., Nadine and Fred.
6. Adabell Casper and John Winchester
7. John Casper and Mary Lee Britton: Revis, Kathleen, Lucy, Ralph, Raymond, Clentis, Geralene, Virginia and Evelyn.
8. Filmore Casper and Verna Lawson: Maynard and Lois.
9. Filmore Casper and Ada Smith: Imoneal.
10. Willie Casper and Hester Eppsion: Sewell, Billie Sue and Joe Pat.

George Washington Casper died in 1900, and never saw any of his 59 grandchildren. Jane lived until 1929, and knew all but 6 or 7 of the grandchildren. Their grandchildren were born over a 33 year period from 1904-1937. Fifty of George Washington Casper's grandchildren were born in Lawrence County. There are 27 grandchildren still living and the following still live in Lawrence County:

Walnut Ridge: Cora Campbell, May Hooten, Fred Casper.

Eaton: Clara Wells.

Strawberry: Margie Harris.

This picture was taken in 1916. My grandmother, Jane Casper (seated in the dark dress) and her children and their spouses (the two back rows). My father, Willie Casper, seated by his mother is not married yet. Twenty-three of her 59 grandchildren.

Lynn: Maynard Casper, Otis Richey, Nadine Goodwin, Billie Sue Penn. *–Joe P. Casper.*

GEORGE WASHINGTON CASPER is the son of John and Sarah M. Thomason Blackwell Casper. He was born in 1855, in Eaton and in 1879, he married Jemima "Jane" Ketner, daughter of Daniel and Catherine Bour Ketner. They lived in the Eaton area and were the parents of eight children. George died in 1900, and Jane lived until 1929. The children are:

1. "Ethel" Oma, 1882-1951, married Clinton Richey in 1904.
2. "Ara" Mahalia, 1885-1964, married A. Frank Richey in 1904.
3. "Arry" J., 1885-????, married Tom Atchison in 1909.
4. J. Joseph "Joe", 1887-1967, married Ellar Richey in 1908, and Mahalia Ketner after widowed.
5. Ada Belle, 1890-1918, married John Winchester in 1912.
6. John D., 1892-1957, married Mary Lea Britton in 1910.
7. R. Filmore, 1894-1983, married Verna Lawson in 1916, and Ada Smith in 1931.
8. Willie V., 1896-1952, married Hester Epperson in 1917.

The family lived mostly in the Eaton and Lynn Community. Five of the eight children and their spouses are buried in the Old Lebanon Cemetery at Eaton. *–Catherine Richey.*

CASORT AND PROPST FAMILY. Anthony Cazort married Mary Ann Thomason both of Salisbury, North Carolina in 1831. They had eleven children: Laura Jane, Alemedia Ann, Sophronia E., Mary M., Margaret L., Clarissa (Clara) Marie, Emma E., Harriett Ellen, George D., Eugenia I., and Belle Cazort. Their daughter Clarissa Cazort (from Salisbury, North Carolina born March 5, 1846) married Henry Caldwell Propst (from Cabarrus County, North Carolina born on October 22, 1842) on July 11, 1875. They together had four children: Margaret Elizabeth, Stephen Alexander, Minnie Ann, and Allie Propst. Their daughter Allie Propst (born Sep-

Clarissa (Clara) Marie Propst

tember 24, 1882, in Smithville, Arkansas) married William Elijah Pickney (born January 1, 1881, in Tennessee) on June 19, 1901. They had eleven children: May Francis, Marvin Elizander, Alvin Caldwell, Jewell William, Clara Marie, Garry Roofus, Lucy Lavanna, Bessie Allie, Charley Woodrow, Freddie James, and Burnis Clay Pickney. –Aurrey Meeks

Aubrey and Lucy Brandon

URA ELIZABETH MCCARROLL CHAMBERS was born in Walnut Ridge, Arkansas on January 31, 1901, to Dr. Horace Rudolph "Dolph" and Pearl Henry McCarroll. She died there August 26, 1964. While attending Ouachita Baptist College, she met H. Noble Chambers. They were married in Walnut Ridge on February 9, 1924. Dr. Chambers attended Washington University Dental School in St. Louis, Missouri and returned to Walnut Ridge where he had a dental practice for 55 years, retiring in 1984. He was born in Augusta, Arkansas, November 25, 1901, and died in a hospital in Jonesboro, Arkansas on September 20, 1985. –descendants of Nathaniel and John McCarroll by John Richard McCarroll and Margaret McCarroll Watson.

CHAPLAIN FAMILY. John Henry Chaplain, about 1794-1858, is found earliest in the militia of Rowan County, North Carolina, during the War of 1812. He moved from North Carolina to Tennessee, then to southern Illinois near Benton. Family history has John Henry Chaplain in Imboden, Arkansas, during the late 1850s. It is believed that he was killed by bushwhackers as he traveled for business, on horseback, between Arkansas and Illinois. His wife, Elizabeth McCluskey Sutton, twin sons, Austin (Allstin) and Aaron (Orin), and daughters, Cynthia and Almanza, remained in Imboden. Family tradition says that they returned to southern Illinois in the 1860s, working a team of oxen to a wagon with a mule at the end of the tongue.

In 1879, John's son, Austin Chaplain, 1854-1918, Austin's second wife, Dorcus Delia "Delila" Eaton, 1850-1927, and his two oldest children relocated from Illinois to Lawrence County in a covered wagon. Austin and Delila continued to reside in Lawrence County and are buried in Hope Cemetery.

Austin's first child by his first wife, Mary M. Waller, was Ora Dell. Ora Dell (Oray A.) Chaplain, 1875-1956, married Henry "Jake" Smith and they lived northwest of Black Rock. Ora Dell and Jake Smith had 10 surviving children: Cora Betty "Bessie" Smith, Mitty Laird, Lark William Smith, Charles H. "Charlie" Smith, Harvey "Harve" Smith, Virgil A. "Virg" Smith, Julian Smith, James Madison "Matt" Smith, Manzie Smith and Marie Baker Large. Eight of these children lived and raised families in Lawrence County.

Ora Dell was very reserved, short in height, and worked in the kitchen the whole day. She always had sugar cookies and biscuits with Karo syrup and peanut butter on the table for visiting grandchildren. Dinner was always ready at exactly 12 noon and Ora Dell rang a large bell that was on the back porch. The bell could be heard for miles along Stinnett Creek, and neighbors timed their day according to this bell. The bell, a hand-cast #2 dated 1868, is still in the Smith family. Ora Dell and Jake Smith are buried in Kelley Cemetery.

Austin and Delila Chaplain's son, John Henry Chaplain, 1877-1963, married Ellen E. Hudson and

their four children are: Austin Chaplain, Ruby Vick Petit, Ruth Dent and Mary Edna "Pete" Jean. A descendant in the Dent family has a rocking chair that came from Illinois in that covered wagon with young John Henry Chaplain in 1879. John Henry Chaplain lived in Imboden and is buried in Hope Cemetery.

Austin and Delila Chaplain's third child was daughter, Dr. Mary Elizabeth "Betty" Chaplain, who married Dr. Britton Eldridge Pickett, moving to Austin, Texas.

Chaplain descendants still live in Lawrence County, now as Smiths, Bridges and Dents. –Donna Christensen.

BURLIE CORNELIUS (B. C.) CHESSER was born December 31, 1889, in the Birdell Community of Randolph County, Arkansas, to John T. and Elizabeth Jane Price Chesser.

Burlie's father died when he was seven years old and his mother remarried only to have the new father abandon the family soon after.

Burlie and his sister, Tish, boarded with their relatives and attended high school at Mt. Harmony. Burlie graduated high school at Pocahontas on May 14, 1915, and then he joined his mother, Lizzie, on a farm near Minturn, Arkansas. He later moved to Sharp County

Burlie and Janie Chesser.

where he attended an academy in Calamine and received his teachers certificate.

Mr. Chesser was inducted into the Army in November of 1918, and was discharged in February of 1919. He returned to the farm near Egypt he and his mother had purchased in 1917. On August 16, 1924, Burlie married Janie Cline in Randolph County, Arkansas, and they returned to Egypt to live. They soon started a family and their first child, Imogene, was born on May 26, 1925. Imogene married Jeep Krietzler and lives in Detroit, Michigan. Ruth was born on November 9, 1926. She married Earl "Red" Hamilton and lived in Detroit for many years. They are deceased.

Clynd "Skint" was born on January 5, 1928. He married Ethel Belk and they live in Jacksonville, Arkansas.

Dorothy was born on July 29, 1929. She lives in Walnut Ridge.

Leslie was born on October 30, 1930. He married Jay Berry. Both are deceased.

Betty Sue was born on June 30, 1935, and died on February 1, 1936.

Jerry was born on September 24, 1937. He married Zetta Marshall and they reside in Jonesboro.

Phyllis Ann was born on October 29, 1941. She married Bill Phillips. She lives with Dorothy in the family home in Walnut Ridge, Arkansas.

Burlie was a gentle man, quiet and kind, and any visitor was quickly welcomed into his home and offered food and drink. Burlie and his sister, Tish, possessed the most remarkable memories. They could quickly connect people, dates, places all by connecting certain events.

Small children always found a wonderful place to play in Burlie's huge barn. On rainy days many hours were spent playing school with a huge trunk of books he stored there. Burlie was seriously injured in August of 1942, when he honked his car horn as he passed a wagon and team and one of the mules became spooked and kicked him in the head

The Chessers farmed until most of the children had gone. Then in 1954, they sold the land to Arnold Statler and they bought a home and moved into Walnut Ridge. They remained here until Burlie's death on November 2, 1968.

Janie later married Alvey Easter, but she passed away on August 7, 1978.

Both Burlie and Janie are buried in the family plot in Lawrence Memorial Park in Walnut Ridge, Arkansas. –Barbara Howard.

JAMES CHILDERS FAMILY. James Childers was born in 1804, in Virginia and on June 18, 1825, married Sarah Carter. In 1828, they sold their land on Copper Ridge along Clinch River in Scott County, Virginia and moved to Lawrence County, settling along the Strawberry River. His parents, Isom and Mary Childers, were also early settlers of Lawrence County and the Childers played an important part in the settlement of the Lower Strawberry Valley. James was prominent in the affairs of the community in Old Walnut Ridge and Powhatan, being chosen to represent the county in the Lower House of Legislature, 1846-1848, and 1858-1860.

Joseph Holmes Childers family. Front row, left to right: Allen, Joseph Holmes, Eliza Josephine, Olen. Back row, left to right: Carl, Hazel Irene, Albert. Taken in the peach orchard.

Their children were: Mary Jane, who married John Campbell in 1846; Ersula married John Blakely in 1845; John was a Methodist minister and they moved to Drew County; John Morgan; Hiram Crockett married Elizabeth Finley in 1856; Hiram was killed in the Battle of Wilson's Creek in 1861; James R. married Sarah Cox, 1857; Isom and Benjamin.

John Morgan Childers, son of James and Sarah, married Seletha Jane Hardin August 5, 1854. Their children were Nancy, Ersula, Mary, James Simon "Jim", who married Martha Hennessee; Joseph "Joe", Sarah, John Crockett "Crock" married Mollie Hennessee, Emma Lou "Em" married J. C. Rains then William Jennings Pryor.

Jim, Joe, Crock and Em were called "The Singing Childers" because of their love of music and God-given ability to sing.

Joseph Holmes Childers, son of John Morgan and Seletha Childers was born May 1, 1862, and died October 9, 1949. On December 14, 1887, he married Eliza Josephine Farrar, born November 18, 1861, died January 31, 1916, the daughter of Reverend Nimrod Farrar and Demarius Jane Yarbrough.

When the tornado of 1929 hit the area it destroyed his house and blew him into a field. His cook stove landed on top of him, crippling him for life. He was a member of the Pleasant Hill Methodist Church in Lorado and was their Music Director for many years. Their children were: Allen, born October 4, 1888, married Clifford Gleghorn; Olen, born March 7, 1890, married Zeffie Ellington; Omer, born 1892, died 1894; Roy, born and died 1894; Hazel Irene; Albert, born May 3, 1899, died August 18, 1988. He never married, remaining with his father until his father's death. He left his impression of Christian influence on many lives; Carl, born August 27, 1901, died September 2, 1916; Hazel Irene Childers, born January 27, 1897, died January 30, 1993, daughter of Joseph Holmes and Eliza Josephine Childers married September 21, 1921, Oliver Ralph Cook.

They were farming near Lorado when the 1929 tornado also destroyed their house, but they and their children were spared. Their children are Joseph Edward Cook, born October 18, 1922, died July 2, 1996, Sergeant in Army Air Corps, World War II, married Ruby Smotherman, had JoEllen, Larry and Dennis.

Juanita Cook, born August 2, 1927, daughter of Hazel and Oliver Cook married October 13, 1944, Harold Eugene Stacy. He served in the Merchant Marines, World War II. Their children are: Linda Elaine Stacy, who married Ronald Coffman and they have Connie, Caren and Rowdy, who has a daughter Jamie. Randy married Monica Gomez and had Jorden, Curtis and Kasey. Michael Douglas Stacy married Patricia Harmon. Their daughter, Michelle, married Dana Dawson and had Trey. Cherly Anita Stacy married Jim Davis and had Staci (has Alissa and Kelsey), Kari and Chad. Cheryl then remarried and has Hillary Rae. Daryl Eugene Stacy married Carol Bruce and has Stefani, Jennifer and Steven. Glenn Edward Stacy married Glenda Deckard and has Anthony, Wade and Aubrey. –Juanita Cook Stacy

SANFORD S. CHRISTOPHER. The families of Sanford S. Christopher and Hannah Matilda Rabun were raised in the hills of Carolina and Georgia. Sanford and Christopher and Matilda Rabun were married on June 18, 1891, in Rocky Face, Georgia. They were part Indian and worked for the rich people. They escaped being driven out when the Indians were forced to relocate further west. Following increased migration of Eastern (white) people to Carolina and Georgia the Christophers and Rabuns were then forced off of the lands, persecuted and their jobs taken by white people. In 1892, the family migrated west. The family consisted of John M. and Hannah Rhodes Rabun, Sanford S. and Matilda Rabun Christopher, son Gaither and three of Matilda's sisters, Mary, Martha and Liza.

The Christophers sold everything they could not take with them and boarded a train heading west at Purdy, Georgia. They arrived at Black Rock, Arkansas, which is as far as they could get with dwindling finances and decided to settle there. They spent their first year on what was then called "Nigger Hill." The hill is located near the west end of the New Black Rock Bridge. Sanford went to work at the Coffey wagon factory. The next year they moved to Denton, where their son, Estes, was born. In 1894, they homesteaded a place on the Anchor School Road near Smithville. Their other children were born near the Anchor School. Two

Left to right: Harvey, Myrtle, Utah, Patricia, Euna, Christina, Ceburn, Bobby, Alpha, Harvey Jr.

children, Franklin and Lloyd, died in infancy. Harvey, Floyd, May, Thelma and Noah were added to the family near Smithville. Gaither and brother Estes marched off to World War I. Gaither was wounded in battle. Gaither married a Dora Mattox, Estes married Eddie Mae

Sanford and Matilda Christopher, 1935.

Stephensen, Harvey married Myrtle Whitlow, Floyd married Lucille King, Mae married Monroe McCalister, Thelma married Luther McCalister and Noah married Lucy Lovelady.

The economic crash of 1929 caused them to lose everything they had including the homestead. During those years, they sharecropped and did day labor for the Wasson family. Immediately after losing the first homestead, they set out to homestead acreage on Quality Creek and proved up on the land in 1932. This was to become Sanford and Matilda's family home. Harvey Christopher now had his eldest son, Ceburn. They moved on to the property a small building for his parents to live in. Later, a log house raising was held by the family which added a larger room onto this building.

Sanford and Matilda saw their parents, John M. and Hannah, some of their children and a nephew, Ransey Rabun, who was killed by lightning, buried in the New Hope Cemetery. Noah, their youngest, joined the Navy when World War II started.

Matilda passed away in 1957, at age 86, leaving 36 grandchildren and numerous great-grandchildren. Most of them live in Lawrence County. Ceburn, the oldest son of Harvey and Myrtle, purchased the old homestead. He has built a modern home and tills the same soil his grandfather worked. –Alpha (Christopher) Palmer and Ceburn Christopher.

JACOB CLARK. Sarah Isabelle, 1831-1923, and Jacob Clark, 1829-1858, were both born in Canada. After marrying, they moved to Kent County, Michigan. This is where their first two children were born: Olive, 1855-1906, and Spencer Leroy, 1856-1946. Jacob was ill and the doctor thought moving South would help his health. They reached Black Rock and bought a farm around 1858. This year a third child would be born, Elva Ann. With Jacob's health he hired a man from Ash Flat to help on the farm, his name was Archie Estes. When Jacob died, it was Archie who took over the farm and helped Sarah raise her family, along with his son, David. The next fall, Archie and Sarah were married. By this time there was trouble brewing between the North and the South. Being right in the middle, it was not uncommon to be troubled by raiders from either side. One day a polite young man asked for dinner for himself and several men. He was so polite and gentlemanly that Sarah prepared a good dinner for them. One man stood guard while the others ate, then he took his turn at the table. Two days later, Sarah found out from a neighbor friend that this same young man had been a former neighbor of hers. His name was Jesse James.

Sarah and Archie had born 11 of 12 children when they joined a wagon train to head West. Sarah and Jacob's farm was at Black Rock and Archie's was at Ash Flat. They must have moved there shortly after marriage, then moved back to Black Rock around 1871, where two of their children were born, Thomas and Jasper Estes. By the

Luther Clark and his seven sons: (back row from left to right) Luther, Chalmers, Chester, Millard and Lavelle. Front row: C. Leroy, Ralph and Victor. Picture about 1934.

(Left)Sarah Isabelle Clark, 1831-1923, mother of Spencer Leroy Clark. (Right) Hubert Clark is standing at the left behind his father, William Henry Clark, the oldest son of Spencer. Standing to the right is Luther Clark behind his father, Spencer Leroy Clark. Luther is the second son to Spencer; about 1920.

time they headed West, Spencer was married and decided to stay behind.

Spencer Clark was a good Christian man (Church of Christ) and a family man. When he was 18 he married Mary Melina Roberts in Black Rock. They had eight children: William Henry, Dora Isabel, Martha Emma, Phoeba Ann, Luther Sherman, Flora Mae, Eva Florence and Sarah Lillian. Spencer's wife, Mary, died in 1909. In 1921, he married Mary Jackson, who died in 1944. Spencer died in 1946, at William Henry's house in Edinburg, Texas. Four of his children stayed in Lawrence County for some part of their life: Martha Emma, Flora Mae, Sherman Luther and Eva Florence.

One of the biggest families within this Lawrence County family was produced by Luther Sherman Clark, born 1889, and Aurora Corbet, whom he married in 1909. Together they had seven sons: Luther Chalmers, Chester Alfred, Millard Morris, Sherman Lavelle, Corbet Leroy, Ralph Roberts and Victor Albert.

It was an annual tradition for this family to meet on Luther's birthday. All but one of the surviving seven sons live in Lawrence County at this writing.

Chalmers, born January 12, 1911, married Ramona Ponder. They had one daughter, Mona.

Chester, born August 8, 1912, married Johnnie Magee. They have two children: Ernie and Betty. Chester and Johnnie reside in Brookhaven, Mississippi.

Millard, born June 26, 1915, married Myrtle Morrison. They had three children: Robert Morris, Betty and William Morris.

Lavelle, born December 17, 1918, married Frances McCarroll. They have one daughter, Barbara. They live in Portia, Arkansas.

Leroy, born January 18, 1922, married Jayetta Rowsey. They have four children: Corbet Leroy

Jr. "C.L." and Philip Rowsey both of Walnut Ridge, Carolyn of Wise, Virginia and Rochelle of North Little Rock. Leroy and Jayetta live in Walnut Ridge.

Ralph, born October 18, 1925, married Betty Lou Aaron. They have three children: Terry, Peggy and Billy. Ralph and Betty also live in Walnut Ridge.

Victor, born June 25, 1930, married Patsy Waddell. They live in Portia, and have four children: Patricia, Vickie, Mary and Vic. —Jay and Dedra Clark, grandchildren of Leroy Clark.

MARY JANNECE CLARK is the daughter of Victor and Patsy Waddell Clark of Lawrence County.

I married and had two children. After my divorce I changed my name and my children's names to Clark. I have a son, Christian Jagger Clark, age five and a daughter, Cierrah Jayde Clark, age three. I am currently teaching at Westside High School in Jonesboro and have been there for the past 10 years.

Christian Jagger Clark, age 5, Cierrah Jayde Clark, age 3 and Mary Clark.

My children are called by middle names: Jagger and Jayde. We live in Bono, Arkansas. —Mary Clark.

VICTOR A. CLARK SR. Mr. and Mrs. Victor A. Clark Sr. of Lawrence County, Portia, Arkansas.

I am Patsy Waddell Clark, the daughter of the late Bryson Waddell and the late Iola Mae McElroy Waddell of Powhatan. As a child, the other children and I used to play in the Powhatan Courthouse because at that time the county had two county seats.

Victor and Patsy Waddell Clark, Portia, Arkansas.

My husband is Victor Clark Sr., son of the late Luther S. Clark and the late Aurora Corbet Clark of Black Rock, Arkansas.

Victor and I have four children: Patricia Rose Clark Tribble of Bono, Arkansas; Vickie Annette Clark Riddle of Pocahontas, Arkansas; Mary Jannece Clark of Bono, Arkansas; and Victor A. Clark Jr. of Walnut Ridge, Arkansas.

Victor and I have 14 grandchildren.
—Patsy Waddell Clark.

Left to right, front row: Victor Clark Jr., Christian Bryson Clark, two years, Judy Clark, Lila Brooke Clark, age nine, Allison Ann Clark, age 11, Heath Williams, age 17 (foster child), Jeffery Scheller, age 17.

VICTOR CLARK JR. Mr. and Mrs. Victor Clark Jr. of Black Rock, Arkansas.

I am the son of Victor and Patsy Waddell Clark, Lawrence County. I am married to Judy Everett Hampton Scheller of Paragould, Arkansas. We have six children: John Hampton, Lacey Hampton, Keffery Scheller, Allison Ann Clark, Lila Brooke Clark and Christian Bryson Clark.

We are foster parents. We have had 16 children to come into our home at this time. Some stayed five days to 20 months.

Victor Jr. is foreman of Delta Consolidated Industries of Jonesboro. Judy works at Lawrence Memorial Home Health Agency at Walnut Ridge.
—Victor Clark Jr.

CHARLES PHILLIPS and Bessie Cochran were married on December 25, 1927. They spent their entire married life in the Lauratown Community, where they owned and operated a service station and grocery store.

Charles was an avid sports fan. He managed the Lauratown baseball teams and was a great supporter of the Clover Bend School basketball teams. He was a member of the Lauratown and Clover Bend School boards. After the schools consolidated, Charles served as president of the Clover Bend Board for several years.

Bessie was a homemaker and worked in their store. She was a member of several community, school and church organizations.

Both Bessie and Charles were members of the Lauratown Methodist Church.

Bessie and Charles were parents of Nina Charline, who married Bill McKnight on April 11, 1955. They were grandparents of Bess Anne and Nina Elizabeth McKnight. Bill and Charline live in Jonesboro and both girls live in Memphis, Tennessee.

After graduating from Clover Bend High School, Charline attended Arkansas State University and retired from teaching in 1993. She taught in Jonesboro schools (south) for the last 21 of her 31 year teaching career.

For several years Bessie's mother, Minnie Cochran, and her two sons, Ray and Millard, lived with Bessie and Charles.

Bessie Cochran Phillips was born June 27, 1902, and died March 10, 1955. Charles Phillips was born October 16, 1897, and died December 20, 1956.—Nina McKnight.

WALTER W. COCHRAN. John Cochran was born in Scotland. His parents came to America and settled in Pennsylvania and later moved to South Carolina. Grandparents of Walter Winfield Cochran were John Cochran and Margaret McClanahan. Margaret was from Ireland. John and Margaret moved to Tennessee and settled in Manny County. Several years later members of the Cochran family moved from Tennessee to Fulton County, Arkansas.

Walter Winfield Cochran's parents were Samuel Lee Cochran and Mollie L. Ross. Samuel was a Methodist minister. He served in the North Arkansas Conference of Methodist Church and was pastor of Gardner Memorial Methodist Church in North Little Rick, at the time of his death in 1909. Walter Winfield was born at Sulphur Rock, Arkansas.

Walter Winfield Cochran and Minnie Smith were married September 1, 1901. They lived at Clover Bend and Lauratown during their married life. Walter and Minnie were the parents of Bessie Cochran Phillips, Lloyd Lee Cochran, Melvin Ray Cochran, Baby Cochran(died at birth), Billy Darrell Cochran, Millard Eugene Cochran and Mabel Cochran Bratcher. They were grandparents of Thomas Dale, Billy

Ray and Teddy Bratcher; Winfield Cochran and Alice Lee Cochran Gregory; Linda Kay Cochran Sims, Mary Cochran May and Garry Cochran and Charline Phillips McKnight.

Walter Winfield was a member of Clover Bend Masonic Lodge and he taught school. He also operated the general store and was post master for Lauratown. The original site for Lauratown was on the banks of Black River.

Minnie Smith Cochran was a sister to Ernest Smith of Clover Bend and Florence Smith Grissom of Clover Bend and Hoxie. After Walter's death Minnie and two sons, Ray and Millard, lived with Charles and Bessie Phillips of Lauratown.

All of the children of Walter and Minnie Cochran are deceased. Seven grandchildren and several great-grandchildren are living descendants.

Walter Winfield Cochran was born September 10, 1878, and died March 1, 1927. Minnie Smith Cochran was born November 7, 1880, and died October 12, 1955. —Nina McKnight.

COFFEL FAMILY. When the 1860 Census Enumerator visited the Coffel household in Cache Township, Lawrence County, Arkansas, my grandfather, James Henry Coffel, was only one day old.

That 1860 household consisted of Phillip Coffel, farmer, age 19, born in Kentucky; Wife Elizabeth, age 20, born in Tennessee; daughter Orlena E., age one, born in Missouri; and

Clara Matilda Kepner Coffel, 1918 era, November 10, 1901-August 18, 1975.

son James H., age one day, born in Arkansas.

Private Phillip Coffel left home to serve in the Civil War for the Confederate States of America. The Civil War years brought a hard life to the families left behind and many became destitute.

Elizabeth Coffel and her children were one of those families and on February 27, 1863, she registered to receive relief from the state of Arkansas. Her registry information appears in Book F in the Circuit Court Record maintained at the Lawrence County Courthouse in Walnut Ridge.

Phillip died during the Civil War, but the actual date and place are unknown. Elizabeth Coffel was listed as head of household on the 1870 Census of Campbell Township, Lawrence County. After that time, she more than likely remarried, but to whom remains a mystery. In Lawrence County an Elizabeth did marry a George Ragsdale on January 26, 1874, but I cannot verify she was Phillip's widow.

On July 23,

Robert Edward Coffell, 1918 World War I, March 21, 1897-May 22, 1977.

1882, the marriage of James H. Coffel and Elizabeth Minton (Menton) was recorded in Book G-211. James used his middle name, Henry, and Elizabeth was known by her nickname, Betty, as reported on my father's birth certificate. Henry and Betty had the following children: William George, John Henry, Bertha and Robert Edward.

Robert Edward Coffel, my father, was born in Walnut Ridge, Arkansas, on March 21, 1897. He was inducted into the United States Army at Piggott, Arkansas, on June 26, 1918. Robert Edward served in Company C, 161st Infantry according to his World War I Honorable Discharge dated July 3, 1919. I am very proud to note that his character was marked as excellent on the discharge paper. Robert Edward served in the Allied Armed Forces in France from August, 1918, until June, 1919, but like so many veterans he never talked about the war.

On July 16, 1919, Robert Edward Coffel and Clara Matilda Kepner, born in Fisk, Missouri, married in Clay County, Arkansas. Robert and Clara raised the following children: Mildred Neoma, Loyd Elwood, Robert Edsel, Wanda Jeanette, Thaddis Wayne, Richard French, Newell Estes and Zelda Mae.

In 1943, for some unknown reason, the family decided to add another 'L' to the end of Coffel. Today, the Coffell descendants of Phillip and Elizabeth Coffel number in the hundreds and the families, though scattered from coast to coast, keep in touch by way of a bimonthly family newsletter and a yearly family reunion.

Since 1998, I have been researching the Coffell surname, and like most genealogists, I have uncovered more questions than answers. If you have any information about Phillip and Elizabeth Coffel, I certainly look forward to hearing from you. –*Zelda Coffel Starr.*

DR. BENJAMIN FRANKLIN COFFMAN,

1837-1923, was a doctor in Robert E. Lee's Army during the Civil War. He married Amanda Eddy. They had one son, Lee.

Lee married Mattie Peebles. They had three sons and one daughter, Milne, who died in a hunting accident at

Dr. B. F. and Amanda Coffman.

age 19, Benjamin Franklin and Edwin Eddy, both killed in automobile accident in 1934, at the ages of 28 and 25.

Their daughter, Bonnie Belle, married Alfred Moore Starr. They had one son, Maurice Gene. Maurice married Daphine Stewart. They had one son, Ben; and one daughter, Patti. Patti married Gary Russell. They have two children, Joshua and Sarah. Ben married Karen Brown. They have two children, Nicole and Allison. – *Maurice Starr.*

HUBERT HOUSTON COLBERT FAMILY.

The Colbert ancestors arrived in Lawrence County about 1837, when Henry Charles Colbert and his first family traveled from Illinois and settled in the Clover Bend Community. On November 5, 1846, Henry Charles married Fereby Richardson. This second marriage produced eight children. They were Taylor Worth in 1847, Lambert, Lavinia, Arkansas, Lucy, Francis, Arizona, Hiram Jackson and Palestine.

Taylor Worth is the grandfather of Hubert Colbert. He married Mary Whitlow who bore

two children, James Monroe in 1874, and Virginia in 1876. Both were born in Dunklin County, Missouri. On June 28, 1885, Taylor Worth married Cora B. Gordon in Lawrence County. They produced four children: Alice, Maggie, Delia and Luther.

On September 30, 1894, James Monroe Colbert married Louretta Jones Hall whose family had earlier migrated from Kentucky. This marriage produced four children: Hubert Houston, 1897; Alice Maggie, 1904; Jeff Davis, 1908; and Anna Jodell, 1916. James Monroe continued the Colbert family tradition of farming. Some of his favorite pastimes were reading Zane Gray novels and going catfishing in Black River.

The Hubert Colbert family was begun in 1921, when he married Beulah Mildred Wilson. During the next nine years, five children were born. These included: Jack, Clifford Ray, Billie Jewel, Gladys and Thelma Louise. The family started out as farm-

Hubert Houston Colbert family. Reading left to right: Ray, Thelma, Hubert, Beulah, Gladys and Jack.

ers in the Lauratown area. About 1937, they moved to Powhatan where Hubert and Beulah Colbert spent the rest of their lives, except for short periods of time during World War II.

Beulah Wilson is the daughter of Alexander C. "Bud" Wilson and Polly Ann Higginbotham. Bud and Polly started out around Sitka, Arkansas, where most of their 10 children were born. Later, they moved to the Clover Bend area.

World War II profoundly affected the Hubert Colbert family. In 1942, after graduating from Black Rock High School, Jack joined the Marine Corps. Within months Ray was in the Navy and Billie Jewel was in the Army. Hubert went north to work in the defense factories. Beulah, Gladys and Thelma remained in Powhatan.

After the war, everyone returned to Powhatan. In September, 1946, Jack went to a university in California. Soon thereafter, Ray married Lois Smith of Powhatan and they moved to DeKalb, Illinois, where they still live in 1999. Along the way, they produced three children: Carol Rae, Cheryl Jeanetta and Clifford Ray Jr. Billie Jewel was killed in action during the invasion of Normandy. In 1948, his remains were returned to Lawrence County for burial in the Powhatan Cemetery. Gladys married "Buster" Croom. They produced four children: Willie Ray, Billie James, Teresa Ann and Michael Houston. Gladys and David Woodson, her second husband, and most of her family members still live in Powhatan and Black Rock. Thelma married Earl F. Davis Jr. of Powhatan. They later moved to DeKalb, Illinois, to work and to raise a family: Ronald Earl and Tonya Louette. After retirement, Thelma and Earl returned to Walnut Ridge. Finally, Jack married Sherrie Durham and they now live in Dallas, Texas. –*Jack Colbert*

JAMES FRANKLIN COLBERT, February 23,

1829-April 23, 1881, was born in Illinois and at the age of eight came to Clover Bend with his father, Henry C. Colbert and Uncle James Colbert. They came down Black River on a steamboat with their children.

James F. Colbert married Sarah Margaret Holloway from Tennessee on July 17, 1855. Their issue: Phoebe Sarah Colbert McCambell, Benjamin Malcom Colbert, William Edward Colbert, James Franklin Colbert Jr., Dolly Savina Colbert Guest, Henry Allen Colbert, Margaret Victoria Colbert Robins and Joseph Sephus Colbert.

William Edward Colbert married Louisa Savannah Kindrick on December 22, 1884, at Minturn, Arkansas. They had six children. Elsie Sarah Colbert Robins Wilson was the only one to survive.

Louisa, always called Lou, was widowed in 1905. She was a good business woman. At her husband's death, she had a nine year old daughter to care for. As the years passed, she owned two farms, a candy kitchen and a grocery store. She also had the responsibility for nieces, nephews, stepchildren and her grandchildren.

William Edward Colbert is buried in the Whitlow Cemetery. Louisa's parents, Sarah Patience Pace Kendrick and Dempsey Kendrick, are also buried there.

William's parents are buried on the Bulcom Ridge area between Lauratown and Arbor Grove in the large walnut grove. Their cabin, built when they first married, is now in the Arkansas Territorial Restoration in Little Rock, Arkansas.

William Edward Colbert was a farmer, blacksmith and built coffins. At a young age, Louisa helped prepare the dead and helped deliver babies. She visited the sick with soup and food for the families. She was always busy traveling with her buggy and horse, Dolly. She was tall, slim and beautiful. She had blue eyes and coal black hair which was never cut. She taught Sunday School in the church where Methodists, Baptists and Presbyterians worshipped together. Her brother-in-law had given the land for the church. She taught a class of 25 boys and girls, ages six-12.

Louisa was married to Thomas Richard Robins, who also was a widower. His first wife was Louisa's niece, Suvanah Colbert. Thomas and Suvanah had two children: Rudy and Lucy Robins. In 1902-3, flu and pneumonia killed Louisa's brothers and their wives. She took into her home five children named Kindrick. She raised a total of 12 children.

JAMES LOGAN COLBERT was born about

1721, in Scotland. He came to America aboard the Prince of Wales, which landed at Darian, Georgia, January 10, 1736. About 1740, he moved to the Chickasaw Nation and married into the tribe. His first wife, a full blood, bore him one daughter. His second wife, also full blood, bore children named William, George, Levi, Joseph and Samuel. His third wife, a half breed, bore children: James and Susan.

The fourth child, Major Levi Colbert, was born in Chickasaw County, Mississippi. He married two full blooded Chickasaw, Mintahoyo and Temsharhoctay. They bore him 17 children. Four of these were adopted. Levi died at Buzzard Roost in Colbert County, Alabama.

Martin, his first child, was born in Chickasaw County, Mississippi and died in Horn Lake, Desoto County, Mississippi. He was educated in Greenville College, Tennessee. He married Sally Allen, daughter of James Allen and Betty Love. His second wife was Louisiana Allen, sister of Betty. Third wife was Sally Oxberry, daughter of Christopher Allen and Molly Colbert.

Henry Colbert, the fifth child of Martin, moved to Illinois, the Chickasaw nation which extended from Alabama, Mississippi, Kentucky and Tennessee. Henry sold his land and lived in Gallatin County, Illinois with his son, James Colbert and family. They came to Arkansas by steamboat down Black River to Clover Bend with three children.

James Franklin Colbert, the first child of Henry C. Colbert, settled at the age of eight in the area of Clover Bend and later in the Bucom Ridge area. He married Sarah Margaret Holloway, July 17, 1855. James Franklin Colbert's mother is unknown. James Franklin Colbert and his wife, Sarah, are buried in Walnut Grove Cemetery at Arbor Grove. Their third child was William Edward Colbert. He married Louisa Savannah Kindrick. Their only child who survived to adulthood was Elsie Sarah. She married Lon Crafton Robins.

PRESTON COLLINS. When Preston's father, Jimmegan, was a boy, over two thirds of the residents of Ozark County, Missouri, where his family lived, fled the bushwhackers and jayhawkers who preyed on them during the Civil War. Preston's uncle, Stephen Collins, with his family, fled to Lawrence County, as Jimmegan's must have, too, since they arrived about the same time.

Nora and Dona Collins.

Along the way, Stephen's family were stopped at Bird Point, Arkansas, by Confederate troops. His three sons, Aaron, David and Stephen, were given a choice: be shot on the spot or join the CSA. They chose to become privates in Company K, 4th Regiment, Missouri Cavalry, CSA.

Preston's parents were Jimmegan Collins, son of Aaron and Anna, and Margaret Hopper, born Indiana. They married in 1867, in Lawrence County. Their children were: Preston, born 1868; and Benjamin, born 1870. Jimmegan apparently died, as by the 1880 census, Margaret had married A. W. Hart and had a new son.

In 1886, Preston married Sarah Suda Moody, daughter of Margaret E. Howell and James David Moody, who lived in Richwoods. Sarah's father fought with the eighth Kentucky Mounted Infantry during the Civil War.

Preston and Sudie had three children: Claude, Nora and Dona. Preston farmed in the Clearlake Community. He died around 1907.

Claude, born 1890, who also farmed, married Mary Mullins. He died in 1969. Nora, born 1894, married Jack Wilson, who died of flu on a World War I troopship, then Ogle Parker. She is buried in Dinuba, California. Dona, born 1898, married Jake Horton of Richwoods in 1916. She died in 1975, and is buried in Johnson Cemetery at Cash, Arkansas. *–Regina Horton.*

THOMAS COOPER AND IBBIE MAHALA WILLIS. Thomas Cooper was born in North Carolina on October 21, 1835. He migrated to Lawrence County where he married Ibbie Mahala Willis on August 20, 1857. Ibbie was born April 6, 1840, in North Carolina. For a short time after they married, Thomas and Ibbie lived in Missouri where their daughter, Nancy, was born in 1858. By the time their second child, Mary Elizabeth "Lizzie", was born in 1861, they had moved to Lawrence County. After their daughter, William and Ibbie had four sons: William Thomas, born in 1862; James W., born in 1865; Moses S., born August 26, 1870; and Robert Jackson "Bob", born September 6, 1874.

Thomas served in the Confederate Army during the Civil War. He was a private in Company G, 1st Battalion Arkansas Infantry. He was captured at the fall of Vicksburg, Missis-

sippi, in 1863. After the Civil War, Thomas remained in Lawrence County where he farmed.

Nancy died young; Lizzie married John A. Rhea, James H. Turner and W. C. Burel; William married Lena Teenor; James married Amanda (probably in Missouri); Moses married Silla Gravett; and Bob married Mae McCarroll. James went to medical school to become a doctor. Moses and Bob both established drug stores in Walnut Ridge.

Thomas died January 7, 1884, and is buried in Mt. Zion Cemetery at College City. After his death, Ibbie was married for a short time to John Rhea McCarroll. Then she married Henry Thomas Snow. Ibbie died September 25, 1911, and is buried next to Thomas in Mt. Zion Cemetery at College City. *– Nancy Matthews.*

CORBETT. Every family likes to trace their family to someone famous. The Corbetts, according to Marion Aral Corbett, are kin to the famous Davy Crockett thru his mother, Julia Wood Corbett, and her father, Bill Wood, who was a first cousin to Davy Crockett.

Marion Aral Corbett, July 26, 1884-November 21, 1958, born at Gainesville, Arkansas, to Marion E. and Julia Wood Corbett, who came to Arkansas from Tennessee. He married Myrtle Howard Corbett, December 14, 1886-September 18, 1967, on September 4, 1910, and lived in Black Rock, Old Walnut Ridge, Lauratown and Hoxie. M. A. Corbett was one of six children: David Corbett, who died around the age of 21; Joe Corbett married Bea Propst; Leota Corbett married Wesley Spikes; Neoma Corbett married Brooks Brinkley; and Aurora Corbett married Luther Clark.

Children of M. A. and Myrtle Corbett were:

1. Marion Daniel, October 28, 1911-May 2, 1981, married Alma Cook. They had two sons: Marion Aral and Donald Ray.

2. Aral Glenn, born June 13, 1913, married Snoda Perry. They had one daughter, Glendola Corbett Worlow and four sons: David Aral, Charles Howard, Ronald Perry and Daniel Joseph. Children all graduated from Hoxie

Marion Aral and Myrtle Howard Corbett.

High School before furthering their education.

3. Lundy Mansfield, October 21, 1915-September 20, 1937.

4. Herbert Wood, October 24, 1917-February 15, 1989, married Cleney Waddell. They had two sons: Larry Eugene and Stanley Bruce. Both sons graduated from Walnut Ridge High School before furthering their education.

M. A. Corbett worked in the box factory, Coffey Lumber Company, button factory (all at Black Rock) and was a farmer. Myrtle Howard rode sidesaddle on a horse to pupils homes to give organ lessons.

Marion Daniel moved to LaHarba, California (near Los Angeles) and was mayor for a time.

Lundy played football at Walnut Ridge High School and University of Arkansas (Razorbacks). He was accidentally electrocuted in his dorm room at the University of Arkansas while fixing a reading lamp.

A. G. Corbett, currently of Walnut Ridge, a farmer, had two sons: David, West Point graduate, and Howard, who served military tours in Vietnam.

Herbert, of Alicia, a farmer, served on the city council and both sons: Larry and Stanley served

as mayor and on the Fire Department. Stanley also served on the council.

Three of M. A.'s grandsons: David, Larry and Howard, were officers in the armed services, concurrently.

Christianity plays a huge part in M. A.'s family as they accept and worship our Lord Jesus Christ and serve Him in various church positions, primarily in the Southern Baptist denomination. *–Larry Corbett.*

VIRGIE WEIR COURTNEY FAMILY. Grammaw Virgie, "Aint" Virgie, Miss Virgie, Ms. Courtney - all names demonstrating loving relationships to Virgie Weir Courtney. She was a "people person," and was able to visit until the last days of her 96 years despite the loss of most of her eyesight.

Born near Imboden on October 15, 1901, Virgie was the daughter of Charles Burette and Zillah Rainwater Weir. After finishing ninth grade at Sloan-Hendrix Academy, she stayed home, as many eldest daughters did, to help her mother raise six other children.

She married Jewel J. Courtney on April 16, 1925, at her parent's home near Imboden. The wedding was delayed a day because the wooden spoke on the wheel of the automobile they were driving to get the marriage license broke and they ran into a ditch. The couple moved to Akron, Ohio, where he worked in a factory and three of their four children were born.

When they returned to Arkansas because their small son was ill, Jewel tenant farmed until 1945. In 1946, he bought a grocery store in Fender, selling it in 1960, to Virgie's brother. A few years later, they moved to Walnut Ridge. Jewel died in 1971, but Virgie lived there until 11 months before her death.

Their firstborn was a daughter, Jewel. "Little Jewel" was born April 25, 1926. She married C. R. Snapp, who worked at Snapp Motor Company. He and Jewel have lived in Walnut Ridge for many years.

Their two daughters: Constance Lynn, born 1947; and Ginger Elaine, born 1949, also live in Walnut Ridge. Both now teach at Walnut Ridge High School. Coni married Billy Davis and had two sons: Blaine, born 1973; and Garrett, born 1978. Blaine graduated from the University of Arkansas and married Nikki Fowler of Hoxie in 1998. They live in Walnut Ridge. Garrett married Leah Wise. They have a daughter, McKenzie, born 1995, and live in Pocahontas.

Ginger married John Bibb. Their children: Johna, born 1978; and Clay, born 1981, were born in Rock Springs, Wyoming. Johna attends Hendrix College. Clay was a member of the WRHS Class of 2000 and is attending West Point Military Academy.

Virgie and Jewel's second child, James Burette "Bud", was born in 1928. He died on dia-

Virgie Weir Courtney, fourth from left, with her father, mother and siblings on her parent's 50th wedding anniversary. Left to right: Burette and Zilla Weir; Jewel Weir; Virgie Weir Courtney; Ina Weir Poe; Cleo, Sloan, Alvin and Jack Weir.

Jerry and Sondra Cox, Deana, Jennifer and Chad; 1985.

John Glover and Mary Melissa Hogan Rice, parents of Dorothy Rice Cox, 1930s.

Jennifer and David Smith united in marriage November 11, 1995.

Deana and John McCormack united in marriage September 19, 1994.

Mary Frances Story Cox, mother of Loyd Cox, 1940s.

Loyd and Dorothy Cox, Jerry, J.R., and Emit and Mary Cox Stone, 1957.

Brett Aaron Cox, 1994.

Chad Cox; 1994.

Loyd and Dorothy Cox, 1950s.

Margaret Rice Cox was born June 4, 1939. Grandparents Will Ed and Mary France Story Cox and John and Mary Melissa Hogan Rice were Lawrence Countians. Jerry grew up in the Owl City Community with his sister, Mary Frances Cox and Loyd Oliver "J. R." Cox. He was a graduate of Walnut Ridge High School. Jerry worked on the family's farm as a teenager, later joining the staff of Cox Implement Company of Hoxie. Jerry attended Arkansas State College.

Jerry Dean and Sondra Sue Blagg of Newport were united in marriage April 5, 1966. Sondra was born November 10, 1941, to Juanita and Orville Blagg of Pleasant Plains and Centerville, respectively. Sondra is a 1963 graduate of Arkansas State College with a degree in Fine Arts. Jerry is Sales Manager and co-owner of Cox Implement Company and Cox, Cox, and Stone Farms.

Jerry and Sondra have three children: Deana Renee', born January 2, 1968; Jennifer Ann, born September 22, 1969; and Chad Jeremy, born February 2, 1976. All three children are graduates of Walnut Ridge High School. Deana was an honor graduate and Chad was valedictorian of the class of 1976. Deana is a 1990 graduate of University of Arkansas and was married on September 19, 1994, to John McCormack, born June 23, 1969. They live in Tulsa, Oklahoma and work for a theatrical promotions organization. Jennifer is a 1992 graduate of Arkansas State University and was married to David Smith, born October 24, 1959, on November 11, 1995. David's son, Andrew, was born September 27, 1991. They live in Walnut Ridge and are engaged in farming. Chad graduated in 1998, from University of the Ozarks with a degree in theatre and married a former Miss Arkansas, Brandy Rhode, in August 2000. –Jackie Cox.

LOYD OLIVER SR. AND DOROTHY MARGARET RICE COX .

Loyd Oliver Cox Sr., fourth child of Will Ed and Mary Frances Story Cox, was born September 23, 1911. Will Ed Cox was born July 2, 1867, and died January 8, 1945. Mary Frances Story Cox was born November 15, 1876, and died June 16, 1952. The six Cox children: Leslie, Edward Lee, Reba, Loyd, and twin daughters, Imo and Jewell, lived in Black Rock before moving to Portia. Loyd attended Portia Elementary School. He helped on the family farm with cotton, corn and sorghum crops and tended the livestock: cows, chickens and hogs.

On December 24, 1934, Loyd and Dorothy Margaret Rice eloped. They kept their marriage a secret until May, 1935, when Dorothy was graduated from Hoxie High School.

Dorothy Margaret Rice was the 13th child born to John Glover and Mary Melissa Hogan Rice. She was born on May 23, 1914, in Salem, Arkansas. John Rice was born November 18, 1859, and died February 9, 1945, and Mary Rice was born August 12, 1867, and died December 18, 1955. John Rice's family lived in Old Lauratown. He and Mary had 13 children: Etta, Samuel, Billy, Lilly, Glover, Arch, Edward, Dora, Horace, Lavadia, Roy, Opal and Dorothy Margaret.

When Dorothy was three months old the family moved to Portia to pick cotton and make a home. They farmed in later years in Clover Bend and in Hoxie around the 1920s.

Dorothy walked two miles to and from school. In the mornings she sold a dozen eggs for 10 cents, a gallon of buttermilk for 5 cents, a gallon of sweet milk for 10 cents, and butter to the railroad workers living in the rail cars at the Railroad Roundhouse in Hoxie. During the summer months after the crops were layed by, Dorothy worked in her sister-in-law's laundry for $3 weekly plus room and board during her high school years. She also played guard on the Hoxie Girls Basketball Team.

Loyd Cox continued to work on farms as work

betes in 1932, and was buried in Holobaugh Cemetery.

Mary Ann, born in 1930, married Leroy Lacy. They had a son, Courtney Leroy, born 1956. Courtney married Nancy Wilson and they had two children: Corey, born 1982, and Nicole, born 1988. He later married Joy Johnson and they live in Batesville. Mary Ann died in 1985.

Carolyn B. Courtney was born January 13, 1933, in Walnut Ridge. She married John Honore'. Residents of Baltimore, Maryland, they are parents of John Courtney, born 1970, of Dallas and Danielle, born 1978, of Washington, D.C.

With the exception of Carolyn's children, who did not grow up in Lawrence County, all Virgie and Jewel Courtney's children and grandchildren are proud graduates of WRHS. Great-grandchildren: Blaine, Garrett, Johna and Clay are also WRHS alumni.

Virgie Weir Courtney died January 10, 1997, well-known and much-loved in Lawrence County. She was a devout Christian lady who believed that life is worth living right. Although she was always up-to-date, she seemed to take with her in death the last vestiges of "old times." –Frances Green.

BRETT AARON COX,

son of J. R. and Jackie Warden Cox of Walnut Ridge, Arkansas, entered this world on January 18, 1976. He is the grandson of Robert Francis and Edith Sue Bryan War-

den of Hoxie and Loyd Oliver and Dorothy Margaret Rice Cox of Walnut Ridge. Brett is the great-grandson of the late William Cedric and Suebelle Parks Bryan of Hoxie; the late Harry Clelon and Neva Elizabeth Warden of Salem, Illinois; the late Will Ed and Mary Frances Story Cox of Hoxie; and the late John and Mary Hogan Rice of Hoxie.

Brett's brother is Matthew Blake Cox and his sisters are: Blair Suzanne Cox and Britni Sarah Cox, all of Walnut Ridge.

Brett was very active in football and basketball from elementary through high school at Walnut Ridge schools. Brett received many awards of recognition for his athletic skills, including All State in football. Brett was elected to serve as President of the Student Council for 2 years and as Vice President of his Senior Class. The Top Cat Award, recognition for leadership and citizenship, was presented to Brett before graduating from Walnut Ridge High School with the Class of 1994.

Brett attended Arkansas Tech University. In 1998, he joined the sales and service staff of Cox Implement Company of Hoxie. Brett is a member of the First Baptist Church, Walnut Ridge.

Brett purchased land in Noland, Arkansas and plans to build a home there in the future. –Jackie Cox

JERRY DEAN AND SONDRA SUE COX.

Jerry Dean Cox, son of Loyd Oliver and Dorothy

was available. Around 1938, they moved into a one room home in the Owl City Community with their daughter, Mary Frances Cox, born February 3, 1937. With a pick axe, saw and team of horses they worked together to clear the wooded area for row crop farming and to make their home. Their second son, Jerry Dean Cox, was born June 24, 1939. Loyd and Dorothy built a new home and continued to farm. Loyd was one of the first rice farmers in the area. Their third child, Loyd Oliver Cox Jr., called J. R., was born September 2, 1951.

In April, 1956, they opened Cox Implement Company of Hoxie. Dorothy served as the bookkeeper while Loyd managed the store. Both continued actively working the farm.

Mary Frances Cox married Emit Ray Stone, son of Dallion and Lena Stone , born March 13, 1938. Emit and Mary became managers of Cox, Cox & Stone Farms in the 1970s. Mary also came to work as bookkeeper at Cox Implement Company when her mother retired from that position. She is a co-owner of Cox Implement Company.

Mary and Emit have a son, Emit Ray Stone Jr., born January 31, 1964. Ray is a graduate of Hoxie High School. Ray and Johnnie Barnhill were united in marriage on June 16, 1984, and have two children: Ben, born January 28, 1988, and Ragan, born June 18, 1991. Ray and Johnnie are both graduates of Arkansas State University. Ray is employed with Cox, Cox & Stone Farms.

Jerry Dean Cox married Sondra Sue Blagg of Newport. Jerry is the Sales Manager and co-owner of Cox Implement Company and Cox, Cox & Stone Farms. Jerry and Sandy have three children: Deana Renee;, born January 2, 1968; Jennifer Ann, born September 22, 1969; and Chad Jeremy, born February 2, 1976. Deana is married to John McCormack. Jennifer is married to David Smith and has a stepson, Andrew.

J. R. is married to Jackie Warden. He is co-owner of Cox Implement Company where he is Parts Department and Office Manager with partnership in Cox, Cox & Stone Farms. Jackie is former owner of Hoxie Florist & Gifts. They have four children: Matthew Blake, born July 3, 1971; Brett Aaron, born January 18, 1976; Blair Suzanne, born March 22, 1978; and Britni Sarah, born October 15, 1980. Blake and Rhonda Cox have three children: Matthew Garrett, born April 6, 1995; Courtney Blake, born September 28, 1996; and Madison Grace, born June 8, 1998. Blair Cox has a son, Caleb Bryan Cox, born June 26, 1998.

Loyd and Dorothy are members of the First Baptist Church of Walnut Ridge. They have retired from farming. –Jackie Cox.

LOYD OLIVER "J.R." AND JACQUELINE SUE WARDEN COX.

Loyd Oliver Cox Jr. "J.R." and Jacqueline "Jackie" Sue Warden were united in marriage August 14, 1970, at the First Baptist Church, Walnut Ridge, Arkansas. Their first date was to the Sweetheart Valentine Banquet in February, 1969, at First Baptist. The church continues to be a major part of their lives.

J. R. was born Loyd Oliver Cox Jr. on September 2, 1951, to Loyd Oliver and Dorothy Margaret Rice Cox of Walnut Ridge. His sister is Mary Frances Cox and his brother is Jerry Dean Cox. He is the grandson of Will Ed and Mary Frances Story Cox and John Glover and Mary Melissa Hogan Rice, all of Lawrence County.

Jackie was born Jacqueline Sue Warden on January 16, 1952, to Robert Frances and Edith Sue Bryan Warden of Walnut Ridge. Jackie has one brother, Robert Bryan Warden. She is the granddaughter of Harry Clelon and Neva Elizabeth States Warden of Salem, Illinois and William Cedric and Suebelle Parks Bryan of Hoxie.

J. R.'s interest in agriculture was evident in high school where he received several awards in FFA.

J. R., Jackie, Britni, Blair, Blake and Brett Cox, 1985.

Blair Cox and son, Caleb Bryan Cox, 1999.

Britni Cox, 1999

Jackie was active in Mixed Chorus and Ensemble, played clarinet and oboe in the Walnut Ridge High School Band, and was a majorette and drum majorette for the band. J. R. and Jackie, an honor graduates, were graduated from Walnut Ridge High School in 1969.

After they married on August 14, 1970, J. R. transferred from Southern Baptist College and Jackie transferred from Hendrix College to Arkansas State University. J. R. received his BSE in business and Jackie received her BSE in elementary and special education in 1974. J. R. joined his family's farming business, Cox, Cox & Stone Farms and Cox Implement Company, Inc. Jackie chose to be a stay-at-home mom. Their children are: Matthew Blake, born July 3, 1971; Brett Aaron, born January 18, 1976; Blair Suzanne, born March 22, 1978; and Britni Sarah, born October 15, 1980.

Blake lettered in football and basketball and was a student council officer. He graduated from Walnut Ridge High School in 1989. Blake married Rhonda Lynn Desgranges from Poplar Bluff, Missouri on June 26, 1993, and graduated from Arkansas State University with a degree in agriculture in December, 1973. Rhonda received a BSE in elementary education in 1993, from Arkansas State University. Blake is employed at Cox Implement Company of Hoxie. Rhonda is a stay-at-home mom with children: Matthew Garrett, born April 6, 1995; Courtney Blake, born September 28, 1996; and Madison Grace, born June 8, 1998. They live in Walnut Ridge, Arkansas.

Brett graduated from Walnut Ridge High School in 1994. Brett received the Top Cat Award for leadership and citizenship, starred in football and basketball and was President of the Student Council for two years. Brett joined the staff of Cox Implement Company in 1998. Brett plans to build a home on his farm at Noland, Arkansas.

Blair graduated from Walnut Ridge High School in 1996. She was a cheerleader, played saxophone in the band and was an officer in student council. Blair attended Williams Baptist College for three years concentrating her studies in art. The fall of 1999, Blair transferred to Arkansas State University to major in graphic arts. Blair has a son, Caleb Bryan Cox, born June 26, 1998.

Britni was a Walnut Ridge High School honor graduate of the Class of 1999. She has started in basketball since the eighth grade, held many club offices, was sophomore and senior class president, and was student council vice president. Britni enrolled at Arkansas State University in 1999, to major in business-marketing.

In 1984, Jackie became the owner and operator of Hoxie Florist & Gifts, Hoxie, Arkansas. J. R. is co-owner of Cox Implement Company, Inc., Hoxie, Arkansas. –Jackie Cox.

MATTHEW BLAKE AND RHONDA LYNN DESGRANGES COX.

Matthew Blake Cox was born July 3, 1971, to Loyd Oliver "J.R." and Jacqueline Sue Warden Cox of Walnut Ridge. Blake is the grandson of Lawrence Countians Robert Francis "Bob" and Edith Sue Bryan Warden and Loyd and Dorothy Margaret Rice Cox and the great-grandson of the late William Cedric and Suebelle Parks Bryan, Will Ed and Mary Frances Story Cox and John and Mary Hogan Rice. Great-grandparents, the late Harry Clelon and Neva Elizabeth States Warden, are from Salem, Illinois.

Blake attended all 13 years of school at Walnut Ridge. He lettered in football and basketball and was an officer in Student Council. He graduated from Walnut Ridge High School with the Class of 1989.

On June 26, 1993, Blake and Rhonda Desgranges of Poplar Bluff, Missouri, were united in marriage. Rhonda was born June 1, 1969, and is the daughter of Jan and Roger Desgranges.

Blake earned a BS in agriculture from Arkansas State University in

Blake, Rhonda, Matthew, Courtney and Madison Cox, 1999.

1993. Blake was employed with Cox, Cox & Stone Farms throughout high school and college. He joined the sales and service staff of Cox Implement Company of Hoxie in 1994.

Rhonda earned a BSE in elementary education from Arkansas State University in 1993. Rhonda has chosen to be a stay-at-home mom with their children: Matthew Garrett, born April 6, 1995, Courtney Blake, born September 28, 1996, and Madison Grace, born June 8, 1998.

The Blake Cox family lives in Walnut Ridge and are members of the First Baptist Church of Walnut Ridge. –Jackie Cox.

CRAIG FAMILY.

Thomas Stansbury Craig came to Lawrence County in 1900, from Evansville, Indiana. He married Addie Peebles from Sharp County in 1906. She was the daughter of Captain Thomas B. Peebles, a captain during the Civil War, and Margaret Cravens Peebles. Four children were born of that union. A son, Tom Craig, married Pauline Penn of Denton, and they had one son, Harold Craig, who resides near Tulsa, Oklahoma, where his mother also now lives. Harold has two sons, John and Jeff Craig. Tom was killed in Italy during World War II.

Their daughter, Ruth Craig, moved with her young son, Dale Masner, to Lake Luzerne, New York, after the death of her first husband, Floyd Masner, to marry Seymour Clews, whom she had met through postal correspondence, and they had one daughter, Jeanne. Ruth died in 1996, in Lake Luzerne. Both of her children live in New York, Dale in Lake Luzerne and Jeanne in Schenectady.

Mary Lee Craig, the only surviving child of Thomas and Addie Craig, married Edwin Baldridge, who died in 1979, and they had four children. Jay Baldridge, who died of a sudden heart attack in 1978, was married to Jackie McLaughlin of Black Rock, who now resides near there and works as a nurse for Lawrence Memorial Hospital. They had two children, Kim and Steve, who both live in Michigan. Charles Baldridge lived in Rockford, Illinois, with his wife, the former Joan Light of Clover Bend. They also had two children, Cheryl and David. Cheryl lives in Illinois and David lives in Florida. Ruth Ann Baldridge is married to Glen Dunahay, has two children, Tracy and Glen, and lives in Jacksonville, Arkansas. Rosemary Baldridge, who works for the Department of Human Services in Walnut Ridge, is married to Paul Mitts, who operates a radiator shop, and they live on the Baldridge family farm place near Hoxie. Mary Lee survives a second husband, O. T. Swindle, and she now lives in Walnut Ridge.

A son, Jesse David Craig, who died in 1994, engaged in farming and lived his entire life, except for a stint in the Army during World War II, on the Craig family farm which his father had purchased at the beginning of this century. The farm is located on Highway 117, about three miles west of Powhatan. He was married for 52 years to Pauline Jones of the Smithville Community and she still lives on the family farm amidst her children and grandchildren. They had four children. Two daughters, Judy and June Ann, died at ages seven years and seven months, respectively. Jesse David Craig Jr., who also has spent his entire life on the family farm and has engaged in cattle and row crop farming, is married to the former Marilyn Harris of Strawberry. She is an elementary teacher in the Black Rock Elementary School. They have three daughters.

Angela Craig is married to Scott Miller and lives in Rogers, Arkansas, where she teaches second grade and Scott is a computer specialist for Wal Mart. Andrea Craig is married to Darren Vancil of Pocahontas, and they also live on the family farm with their two children, Tyler McCarroll and Emma Vancil. Andrea works for Cavenaugh Ford of Black Rock, and Darren is a machinist for Lawrence County Machine Shop in College City. Amanda Craig is married to Chris Kirksey of Walnut Ridge and they live near Black Rock with their son, Trent. Amanda works for First National Bank in Walnut Ridge, and Chris is a deputy for the Lawrence County Sheriff's Department. The youngest child of Jesse and Pauline Craig is Rita Craig. She and her husband, Steve Prestidge, also live on the family farm near Powhatan with their two teenage children, Adam, a college student and part time worker at Dairy Queen in Walnut Ridge, and Allison, a senior at Black Rock High School. Steve is formerly of Jonesboro and is a math teacher for Black Rock School in and the minister for the Black Rock Church of Christ, and Rita is a school counselor for the Black Rock Schools.

Four generations of the Craig family enjoy life on the farm that Thomas Craig and Addie Peebles Craig started out on nearly 100 years ago. –Rita Prestidge.

JESS ROBERT CROW was born in Lawrence County, Arkansas on May 31, 1897, to Joseph Bertha Ballard Crow. On February 7, 1914, he married Anna Rebecca Newman, daughter of John and Ida Buckley Newman. Rebecca was born in Randolph County, Arkansas, on April 18, 1896. Rebecca's mother died when she was 13 years old.

Jess Crow family. Left to right: Jess, Rebecca, Opel, Cleo, Audrey and Louise, believed to be taken in the late 1940s.

Jess and Becky farmed in several areas of Lawrence County never staying long in any one place. Their first child, Opel, was born in 1914. She married Lonnie Colson. She is deceased and is buried at the Markham Cemetery near Egypt.

A son, Cleo, was born on April 21, 1918. Cleo married Agnes Warnick. They are both deceased and are buried in the Straw Floor Cemetery at Jonesboro.

Audrey was born on August 25, 1927. She married George Barker. George is deceased and Audrey lives on Route three, Walnut Ridge.

Louise was born on November 7, 1932. She married Rudolph Gosha and has one son, Bobby. She is deceased and is buried in Lawrence Memorial Cemetery.

Richard and his twin, Lloyd, were born on June 11, 1938, and died one week later on June 18, 1938. They are buried in the Minturn Cemetery.

After the death of her husband, Jess, on May 9, 1965, Becky would remain in her home on Route 3, but would make frequent trips to visit her daughter, Louise, in Illinois. Becky suffered a heart attack and died in Illinois on October 29, 1970.

Becky was a spotless housekeeper and a prize winning cook and made wonderful blackberry cobblers from berries she had picked and canned. She would often share one of the delicious treats with her brother, Johnnie. She was a gentle person, tall, plain and shy. She was rarely seen without her apron and her bonnet on her visits to Johnnie's were always special. They were very close and would spend hours reminiscing of times long past.

Jess and Rebecca Crow are buried in the Lawrence Memorial Cemetery at Walnut Ridge. – Barbara Howard.

CUNNINGHAM FAMILY. Squire Matthew Cunningham, 1779-1826, married Mary Blakely, 1786-1867, in Laurens, South Carolina, on November 28, 1805. The youngest of their 11 children, Samuel Decatur Cunningham, born 1825, served in a Confederate militia in South Carolina during the Civil War. Then moved his family from Laurens County, South Carolina, to Clover Bend, Arkansas in 1873. Samuel married Emily McDowell, born 1824, in 1858, and had three children: Alice Almirea, 1859-1889; John Elford, who died at age 10 in 1873; and William Anderson Cunningham, 1866-1964. Samuel died the February after arriving in Clover Bend and is buried in the Clover Bend Cemetery, along with Emily, died 1889; Earl, an infant of William Anderson's; Alice Almirea and an infant born to Alice. William Anderson married Dora J. Smith in 1891, and had Cecil Ray Cunningham, 1892-1984; Lora Alice, 1894-1989; William Earl, 1896-1898; and Percy Smith Cunningham, 1898-1984.

As the man of the house from early on, William Anderson supported the family. He was a public school teacher when he married. In 1891, having read law under John K. Gibson, he obtained his license to practice law. He served from 1898 until 1902 as Lawrence County Judge as noted on the cornerstone of the county courthouse dedicated

Percy Smith Cunningham　　*William Anderson Cunningham*

in 1898. At one point, William Anderson served as Chairman of the Arkansas Board of Bar Examiners. W. A. also served as President of Planters National Bank in Walnut Ridge. His son, Percy, practiced law with him in the law firm of Cunningham and Cunningham.

The eldest child of William Anderson, Cecil Ray, married Kathleen McLeod and had four children: William Ray, deceased; Betty Jane, died in infancy; Robert, deceased; and Lowell. Cecil Ray served as manager of the State Revenue office in Lawrence County for many years in the 1950s, and 1960s. Lora Alice married Troy Teague, but had no children.

Percy Smith Cunningham, having attended Hendrix briefly before serving in World War I, practiced law with his father for 31 years. In 1921, he established The Cunningham Agency, an insurance office then owned and operated from 1952, until 1965, by Barbara Cunningham. Percy was appointed Circuit Judge in 1952. He was then elected Chancery Judge later that year, a position he held until his retirement in 1970. Percy married Barbara Beryl Fry on July 1, 1932. They had four children: Barbara Lee, Alice Jeanne, Mary Anne and James Percy.

Barbara Broadhurst married to Bill Broadhurst, and had two children: Stuart Judson Wooldridge and Melissa Anne Wooldridge. Alice Jeanne was a member of the faculty at Agnes Scott College in Decatur, Georgia, from 1968 until 1992. From 1978 to 1992 she chaired the Department of Chemistry as William Rand Kenan Jr., Professor of Chemistry. Mary Anne Meacham, married to Bruce Erwin Meacham, had two children: William Wesley Hamilton Jr. and Kelly Elizabeth Hamilton. James Percy Cunningham married Maria de los Angeles Villaseca and had two children: Ian James and Lindsay Alexandra. –James Cunningham.

IMAL DAIL FAMILY. Ralph Hepler, born 1891, arrived in Arkansas at the age of 17 with his parents, Jefferson Hepler and Eva Hinshaw Hepler, and brothers, Harry and Paul. They came by covered wagon and drove their cattle through. It took 11 days to travel from Hickman, Kentucky, to Ravenden, Arkansas, where they settled on a farm just outside of Lawrence County in a community called Kingsville.

The history of the Hepler family in America began in 1748, when Johanne Casper Hepler of Germany arrived in Philadelphia, Pennsylvania with his wife, Suzanne, and two small sons, Jacob and Christopher. He had two more sons, Casper and George, and all four served in the Revolutionary War.

The family had settled in Allentown, Pennsylvania, but Christopher later moved to North Carolina. Ralph was a descendant of Christopher. His son, David, moved to Indiana and later to Kentucky where Ralph was born.

Ralph married Willie Baird and they moved to Lawrence County in the town of Ravenden. They had two children: Imal, who married Richard Dail, and Wanda, who married Cleo Bailey. Both girls are now living in Ravenden and several grandchildren also live there. Imal and Richard had six children: Jack, Janice, Ann, Betty, Larry and Ted. Wanda and Cleo had three children. Their girls: Patricia Jo and Sharon have died, but their son, Randy, lives in Walnut Ridge and is married to Sherry Fiedor and they have two children.

Ralph's brother, Harry, died soon after they arrived here. His brother, Paul, married Bessie Curry of Ravenden and they had one son, Vernon Hepler. Ralph served in World War I and his sons-in-law, Richard Dail and Cleo Bailey, served in World War II. His grandson, Jack Dail, served in the Vietnam war.

The Heplers were charter members of the Ravenden Baptist Church, organized in 1942. Ralph served on the city council for a number of years. Jack Dail has served as Mayor of Ravenden and his wife, Wanda, is now city treasurer. Larry Dail is now serving on the city council.

Grandchildren living in Lawrence County are Jack Dail, who owns Dail's Body Shop in Ravenden; Larry Dail, who is an instructor at Black River Technical College in Pocahontas; and Ted Dail, who lives in Black Rock and is an insurance adjustor for Allstate Insurance; and Randy Bailey, who lives in Walnut Ridge. Dail children who have moved out of Lawrence County recently are: Janice Meada of Colorado, Ann Spencer of Jonesboro and Betty Busby of Pocahontas.

Great-grandchildren living in Lawrence County are: Shane Dail, Angela Dail and Anthony Dail of Ravenden; Jessica Bailey and Marissa Bailey of Walnut Ridge; and Savannah Dail and Nicholas Dail of Black Rock. Three other great-grandchildren have moved out of the county: Keith Foushee of Newark, Rodney Spencer of Jonesboro and Scotty Dail of Tuckerman.

Ralph and Willie Hepler have four great-great-grandchildren: Jason, Kyle and Ian White and Colton Dail. –*Imal Dail.*

ALFORD DARRIS FAMILY. Alford, born Alphonse Hubert, Darris was born January 20, 1889, in Pocahontas, Randolph County, Arkansas, son of Jan Hubert and Francis Catherina Patterson Darris. He had one brother, Antone Alphonse, born January 2, 1998.

Alford married Mary Pauline McCutchen on July 8, 1908, in Lawrence County. They lived in Black Rock in a houseboat on Black River for about 41 years. Alford ran the ferry boat at the mouth of Spring River for several years. About 1949, they moved from the houseboat and built a house on Highway 25 in Black Rock, across from the Black River. The house was made from the lumber of the houseboat. Alford was a commercial fisherman and shell taker. He died March 17, 1963.

Mary was the daughter of James and Mandy Partan McCutchen. She was born April 25, 1891, in Newton County, Arkansas, and died March 16, 1955, at home in Black Rock. Together Alford and Mary had eight children.

1. Francis Evelyn, born August 25, 1910, died May 18, 1958, in a fire in her upstairs apartment above the old drug store in Black Rock. She married William Stinson January 15, 1932. They had two children: William "Billy" Dean and Gladys Louise.

Alford and Mary Darris.

2. James Henry, born July 16, 1912, died November 3, 1992, from drowning in Black River at Black Rock. He married Zelma Margaret Neece on January 15, 1932. Zelma was born September 10, the daughter of Homer Charles and Clara Margaret Richey Neece, 1917, in Eaton, Arkansas. They had 12 children: Betty Jo, Alfred Charles, Viola Magdaline, Joyce Yvonne, Anita Pauline, Henrietta, James Douglas, Bobby Ray, Jerry Wayne, Cathryn Ann, Judy Kay and Peggy Sue.

3. Pauline, born June 7, 1915, died April 1, 1990, in Plymouth, Michigan. She married Lester Scott June 7, 1934. They had two children: Mary Ellen and Freddie.

4. Mary Pearl, born January 26, 1920, died September 3, 1986, married Emanuel L. "Rooster" Woodson on September 18, 1937. They had seven children: Jewell Winston, Charles Henry "Porky", Paul Edward, Johnny, Billy Salvan, James Wesley and Elaine Patricia.

5. Richard Carlson "Dick", born April 30, 1923, died May 23, 1993. He was married first to Crickett. They had two children: Nancy and Rodney; second he married Louise, and they had one son, Richard; third he married Lousie Compton; and fourth he married Doris Bowers-Jackson.

6. Anne Maxine, born January 9, 1926, died December 20, 1987, married Hartman Willis Morse on July 8, 1944. They had seven children: Alveta, Joyce Louise, Nina Ann, Brenda Sue, Hartman David, Tommy Gene and Sandra Leora.

7. Wanda, born September 23, 1929, married Olan Lawson on May 23, 1946. They had three children: Joan Marie, Jack Alfred, Leslie Mark.

8. Jackie, born January, 1932, and died February 11, 1937. –*Cathryn Ferguson.*

REVEREND JAMES HENRY DARRIS AND FAMILY. James Henry Darris was born July 16, 1912, in Walnut Ridge, Arkansas, but lived all his life in Powhatan and Black Rock. He was the son of Alford and Mary Pauline McCutchen Darris. In 1940, at the age of 30, he became a minister of the gospel.

On January 15, 1932, he married Zelma Margaret Neece. Zelma was born September 10, 1917, in Eaton, Arkansas, the daughter of Homer Charles and Clara Margaret Richey Neece. Henry and Zelma had 12 children.

1. Betty Jo, born April 7, 1932, died October 10, 1962, married August 9, 1952, to Paul Eugene Berry, born January 10, 1931, and died December 25, 1962.

2. Alfred Charles, born January 15, 1937, died March 11, 1939.

3. Viola Magdaline, born January 15, 1938, married July 20, 1955, to Charles "Hoody"

Reverend Henry and Zelma Darris

Davidson, born April 17, 1930.

4. Joyce Yvonne, born August 3, 1939, married first May 25, 1957, to John Wayne Higginbotham, born August 1, 1939, and died March 7, 1962; married second December 15, 1962, to Leon Shelton, born November 25, 1939.

5. Anita Pauline, born January 25, 1941, married May 27, 1955, to W. E. Wilson, born December 30, 1935.

6. Henrietta, born December 7, 1944, married August 21, 1959, to Jack Twilla.

7. James Douglas "Sonny", born April 3, 1945, married February 4, 1966, to Patricia Tribble, born October 8, 1946; divorced.

8. Bobby Ray, born January 7, 1948, married July 19, 1969, to Jacquelyn Bond, born February 22, 1952.

9. Jerry Wayne, born September 2, 1949, married November 9, 1968, to Jeanette Pickney.

10. Cathryn Ann, born May 6, 1953, married first July 25, 1969, to Gerald Tribble; married second, June 28, 1991, to Clinton Ferguson, born April 3, 1954.

11. Judy Kay, born January 11, 1955, married March 19, 1976, to Don Reynolds, born September 26, 1947.

12. Peggy Sue, born March 11, 1959, married March 19, 1976, to Carson "Sonny" Haley, born September 3, 1957.

The family lived in a houseboat on Black River in Powhatan for a number of years and then moved to Black Rock where Zelma still lives. Henry loved the river, fishing, shelling, hunting or just getting out in his boat by himself to "as he would say" have a good talk with the Lord. He loved to squirrel hunt and look for arrowheads. He helped people loved everyone. The Lord dealt with him and blessed him and that made him a great man to us. He is greatly missed.

Henry went home to be with the Lord on November 3, 1992, in a drowning accident in Black River at Black Rock. His body was found 250 miles away from home. He is buried in Oak Forest Cemetery in Black Rock. –*Maggie Davidson.*

JERRY WAYNE DARRIS FAMILY. Jerry Wayne was born September 2, 1949, in Powhatan, Arkansas, the son of Reverend Henry and Zelma Neece Darris. In 1959, when he was 10 years old he moved along with his family to Black Rock.

He started picking cotton at the age of three. By the time he was 10 years old he was picking 350 pounds of cotton a day. When he was 15, he along with his dad and brothers, dug for shells in Black River using crowfeet bars or hogging for them. The shells were shipped to Japan to make cultured pearls. Jerry never got to attend school very much; since he had to work to help support his family.

In 1962, when he was 13 years old he was in a car accident and he left teeth marks in his dad's 1954 Studebaker.

In June of 1967, he went to work for Ben M. Hogan Rock Crusher Company in Black Rock and worked there for five years.

On November 9, 1968, he married Jeanette Fern Pickney. She was born on July 28, 1951. She is the daughter of Freddie and Viola Pickney Sr. of Black Rock. Jeanette attended Black Rock School. Jerry and Jeanette had three children.

1. Pam Anette Darris, born August 7, 1969. Pam graduated from Black Rock High School. She also graduated from Black River Vo-Tech with two degrees, one in Accounting and one in Secretarial Word Processing. Pam married first January 31, 1987, to Perry Clifford Leon Gosha, born February 29, 1968, son of Lonnie and Lorene Gosha of Clover Bend. Perry died from leukemia on March 24, 1991, in Lexington, Kentucky hospital.

Pam married second on July 3, 1993, to Dweight Alan Smith, born August 27, 1973,

Front row, left: Hunter, Alyson. Second row: Jerry, Jeanette. Third row: Alan, Pam and Wayne.

the son of Larry and Rhoda Wallis Smith of Hoxie. Alan graduated from Hoxie High School.

Pam and Alan have two children: Hunter Drake, born December 31, 1995, and Alyson Chloe, born September 24, 1997. Pam is currently working at V & B Manufacturing in Walnut Ridge and Alan is currently working at Pools-R-Us in Jonesboro. They along with their two children live in the Walnut Ridge area.

2. Jerry Wayne Jr. was born October 4, 1970, and died October 4, 1970. He is buried in Oak Forest Cemetery in Black Rock.

3. Jacob Wayne was born August 8, 1973. He graduated from Black Rock High School. He also graduated from ICS School with a degree in Computer Programming.

In 1972, Jerry helped his brother-in-law run a fish market in Black Rock. They used Hoopnets, Trammelnets, Trotlines and Snaglines to catch the fish. Jerry has lived and worked most of his life on the Black River.

Jerry, Jeanette and their son, Wayne, still live in the Black Rock area. –Jerry Darris..

CORNELIUS DAVIS. Cornelius (aka Keel), Davis, son of Roswell and Lavenia Davis, born in Tennessee in 1837, came to Arkansas with his family. The family settled in the Denton Community.

In 1858, he married Mary Webb, daughter of John B. and Mary Pearson Webb. Mary died in 1881, after having seven children. Three died as babies. Keel and Mary are buried in Old Bethel Cemetery.

Margaret "Mag" was born in 1860, and married Hector McLeod. They are buried in Old Bethel Cemetery near Denton.

Mary L. "Mollie" was born in 1862, and married Alex Miller. She died after a fall off a porch, both she and the baby she was expecting. They are buried in the Townsend Cemetery near Smithville.

Perditta "Ditta" was born in 1874, and married Filmore L. Stewart in 1895. They lived between Denton and Eaton near Crow Creek most of their lives. They are buried in Old Lebanon Cemetery near Eaton. They had seven children: Roy Foster, born 1896, who married Nettie Weir; Earl Jennings, born 1898, who married Lois Pickett; Leland Stanford, born 1901, married Elsie Field; Cleo Champ, born 1905, who married Mary Pace; Ewell Ottis, born 1914, married several times; and Beulah Lee, born 1917, married Chester Beary.

James Lee "Jim" Davis was born in 1875, and married Julie Hacker in 1895. They had 10 children: Homer, born 1897, married Allie Nunnally; Oliver Davis, 1899-1957; Ernest Davis, born 1902; Rube Davis, 1904-1978; Clara Davis; Lester Davis, born 1910, married Clever Harris; Clida Davis married Mr. Hollowbrooks; Cleda Davis, born 1914, married Ollen Turley; Orville Davis, born 1916, married Glenda Smith; Mabel Davis, born 1919, married Velva Hunt and Robert Jeans.

After Mary Webb Davis died in 1881, Keel married three more times before his death in 1914. He married Margaret Phillips in 1881, six months after Mary's death. In 1897, he married Hannah J. Sharp Mills; then in 1913, he married the widow of John C. Bilbrey, Sophia Bilbrey.

Cornelius served in the Confederate Army, though he had a severely withered leg, and walked with a limp. He received a pension before his death and Sophia received a widow's pension after he died. –Catherine Davis.

RUDOLPH DAVIS was born June 16, 1923 in Powhatan to Gordon Davis and Margaret Elivra "Vira" Hacker Davis. Gordon and Elvira were born in Lawrence country near the Eaton community. Gordon Davis had a large store across from the Powhatan Courthouse and he stocked anything needed by the family and farm. Elvira was a kind,

gracious, loving and God-fearing lady. The Davis family were long time residents of Powhatan and raised Rudolph along with three other sons Oris, Gene, and Earl. Earl continued to live in Powhatan and raise his family; he had a general store where the Powhatan Boat Landing is now. The Gordon Davis home is still standing is inhabited by Cleadus Smith, Jr. and his family.

Rudolph attended school in Powhatan and as a young boy remembered attending many of the trials held in the Powhatan Courthouse. Ruldolph became a minister and preached the word of God for over 61 years. He married his first couple in the circuit clerk's office at the Powhatan Courthouse. Rudolph was an accomplished pianist and gave private piano lessons. He had an excellent memory of the county and poeple that lived from 1923 on. His direct family line is related to the Richeys, Neeces, Coles, Hackers, and Oldhams. His family were great friends of the Rex family, Flippo family, Smith family, and Robertson family. Rudolph labeled these great families as "dear and trusted friends".

His work in the ministry reached people in Missouri and Arkansas. He retired with his wife Mamie in Paragould where he kept in touch with his many friends in Lawrence County. He loved history and one of his favorite possessions was a copy of Walter McLeod's County History which he bought from Mr. McLeod personally. -Rudolph Davis.

GROVER DAVIS. Many of the Davis families presently residing in Lawrence County are descendants of Roswell Davis, as I am. Ross, as he was known, was born in North Carolina. His wife, Lavenia, was born in Virginia the same year, 1805. Ross and Lavenia located their large family of nine children on 160 acres west of Old Bethel in 1852. Roswell and Lavenia's children were: John, Elizabeth, David, Cornelius, Susan, Sarah, Martha, Mary and George Washington.

John, 1831-1904, was a teacher, a shoemaker and my ancestor. He married Martha McCarroll, 1833-1860, on March 26, 1853. She was born near Smithville. They gave birth to five children: Nathan, Frances, David, James Mack and Zachary. Martha died eight days after Zack was born. John joined the Civil War for the Confederacy serving until 1865. He was paroled at Jacksonport, Arkansas. While John was away his children lived with grandparents.

On June 1, 1864, John married my maternal ancestor, Sarah Ann White. She was born August 1, 1842, and died August 8, 1922. John and Sarah had eight children: Mary Adeline, George Franklin (my grandfather), Henrietta Ann, Charles Cornelius, Martha Elizabeth, John Melvin, Suzie Agnes and Barbara Elizabeth. John Davis' home was located one mile west of Denton.

George Franklin Davis was born May 21, 1868. He was an organ salesman and a farmer. He died April 27, 1942, He married Elizabeth Canzada "Ada" Bilbrey on April 4, 1888. Ada was born January 27, 1872, to John Campbell, 1828-1912, and Rutha Denton Bilbrey, 1834-1872, who migrated here from Sparta, Tennessee. George and Ada had two children: Addie, 1891-1978, and Homer. Addie married John G. Penn, 1891-1969, on December 24, 1913. John and Addie were parents of two children: Pauline and Denton. Ada and George are both buried at Old Bethel Cemetery with many of my ancestors.

My father, Homer, was born November 22, 1895, near Denton where he farmed, constructed roads and reared his family until he died on November 25, 1959. He married Nellie Crabtree from Williford, Arkansas, October 18, 1918. She was born March 30, 1896, and died July 14, 1962. They had seven children, four lived to adulthood. I,

Left to right standing: Kyle Neeley, Walt Neeley, Betty Davis Neeley, Larry Burrow, Ann Davis Burrow, Clent Burrow and Cass Burrow. Seated: Grover and Imogene Davis.

Grover, was born November 21, 1919. Maxine was born June 29, 1922. Paul was born September 10, 1924, and Ada Sue February 12, 1927. Ada Sue died April 4, 1957.

I married Imogene Dailey November 18, 1939. She was the daughter of James Washington, 1883-1956, and Ida Lee Jean, 1896-1981, Dailey of Smithville. Jim and Ida were married March 23, 1914. They had four children. Imogene was born January 20, 1919; J. W., 1922-1944; Louise, born 1925; and Jearl, born 1930.

Imogene and I have two daughters. Betty Gene was born July 3, 1941, and Glova Ann was born April 13, 1943. Betty married Walter P. Neeley, born 1937, of Strawberry on August 5, 1961. They have a son, Kyle, born March 18, 1979, in Irving, Texas. Ann married Larry Gene Burrow, born 1942, of Earle, Arkansas, on June 6, 1964. They have two sons, Jakey Cass, born February 3, 1969, and Davis Clent Burrow, born February 18, 1975. My grandsons are the seventh Davis generation in this county. I presently live in Lawrence County near the same location of my Davis ancestors. –Grover Davis

JACOB MALONEY DAVIS was born on December 23, 1859, in Edgar County, Illinois to George W. and Arminda Maloney Davis. The Davis families were farmers and they dreamed of the wild unspoiled land in the west, free for the taking to those who had a pioneer spirit. The Davis families moved continually west for a couple of years, crossing several Illinois counties, finally settling for a while in Moultrie County, Illinois. Here on November 26, 1884, Jacob Davis married Hannah Jane Mills, daughter of James Mills and Nancy Ellen Wiles Mills of East Nelson, Illinois.

The newlyweds and Jacob's parents decided to continue their migration west and for the next several months they traveled with a large wagon train across Illinois and Missouri and then crossed the Missouri River at St. Joseph, Missouri. They continued the long trip across Kansas on their way to Wyoming, but somewhere along the way their plans changed and they settled in northwest Kansas and southwest Nebraska.

On January 15, 1886, Jacob and Hannah's first child, Levi Etna, was born in Sheridan County, Kansas, followed by Myrtle, also in Sheridan County, Kansas.

The families then moved to Hitchcock County, Nebraska. Here Hannah gave birth

Jacob and Ida Davis, 1920s.

to three more children: James in 1889, Frank in 1890, and Mary Elizabeth in 1892. Then Jacob moved his family to a homestead in Hays County, Kansas where tragedy struck. Baby Mary, 11 months old, died of a fever.

Lizzie was born 1893, in Hays County, Kansas. In addition to the death of baby Mary, Jacob's sister, Susan Carolina, age 21, died due to complications of childbirth and at least four other children in the related families died in rapid succession. The Davis families were on the verge of starvation due to several years of drought and then what little crop they had grown was consumed by the grasshoppers. They decided they had given it their best shot and Jacob and his father, George, returned to Illinois.

During their trip east, they received a letter from Hannah. Davis' brother, Michael Mills, and he encouraged them to settle near him in St. Clair County, Missouri. He reported that land was plentiful and fertile, so the family turned south and traveled many months in terrible winter conditions in a wagon pulled by a team of oxen. They finally arrived in St. Clair County, in the Roscoe Township in February of 1896, and in April, Hannah gave birth to another daughter, Susan Arminda. In September of 1898, Hannah gave birth to a son, Dewey, then in January, 1901, she gave birth to Clara Mae, followed by Ada Bell in April, 1903.

Hannah could not seem to recover from the rapid succession of births and she contracted diptheria and died on October 29, 1904, leaving Jacob a widower with several small children to raise alone. Hannah Davis is buried in the Pleasant Springs Cemetery at Roscoe, Missouri.

In June of 1911 Jacob married Mrs. Ida Mathis, a widowed neighbor with three small sons. Soon after their marriage, Jacob and Ida moved their combined family to Lawrence County, Arkansas, settling near Egypt, where they built a home and began to farm. In a few years Jacob sold the farm near Egypt and moved into the Promised Land Community near Big Brown. As his children were all married, he became semiretired and quit farming. In the summer of 1940, he was diagnosed with stomach cancer and he died on June 29, 1941. He is buried in the Arnold Cemetery near Swifton, Arkansas.

Ida remained near her children until her death in August, 1945; she is buried in the Whitaker Cemetery near Walnut Ridge, Arkansas. –Barbara Newman Howard.

JAMES MACK DAVIS FAMILY. James Mack Davis was the son of John Davis and Martha McCarroll who came to Lawrence County from Warren County, Tennessee. John Davis was the eldest son of John Roswell and Lavinia Davis who also came from Tennessee to Arkansas. John and Martha (his first wife) had five children: Nathaniel, Frances Buchanan, David, James Mack and Zackaria. When Martha died in 1860, John remarried a Sarah White and had seven more children. John fought in the Civil War as Private in 45th Arkansas Cavalry. John Davis died on January 8, 1904. John, Martha and Sarah are buried at the Old Bethel Cemetery off Highway 117 in the Denton area.

James Mack Davis was born June 24, 1858, and died May 8, 1894, at the age of 36 in Arkansas. He married Martha Ann Lawson, daughter of Thomas Lawson and Sarah Jones, on February 16, 1882. James and Martha, born August 16, 1865, had six sons: Tom, Charles, John, Garland, Luther and Carl Lucian. James Mack Davis was a farmer. Martha Ann Davis later remarried to J. T. Erwin. They had four or five children. When J. T. Erwin died in 1909, Martha remarried a Jerry Davis (no relation to her first husband), no children from this union. James Mack and Martha are buried at

Old Bethel Cemetery.

Carl Lucian Davis, the youngest son of James Mack and Martha Davis, never knew his father. James died in May and Lucian (as he was called) was born November 6, 1894, in Denton, Arkansas. Lucian married Rittie Mae Webb Pearson,

James Mack, Martha Ann and their sons: Charles, John, Garland and Tom.

the daughter of Rufus Webb and Amanda Josie Richey on January 24, 1914. Rittie Mae was the widow of Henry Pearson and they had one child, Lois Rosetta Pearson. Lois, like Carl Lucian, never knew her father. She was only an infant when he died. Rittie Mae had also experienced the loss of her parents when she was only nine years of age, she was raised by her grandmother, Mary Amanda Singleton Richey. Lucian and Rittie Mae loved all their children equally and brought them up to be good hardworking, moral citizens. Lucian and Rittie had eight children: Faye Etta, Cledia Mae, Lucy Ann, Carl Willard, Rufus Winford, Wilma Maxine (died at age 19), Alvin Taylor and Oleda. Lucian and Rittie worked hard to provide for their family. He was a farmer and had his own sorghum mill. The older children went to the Shiloh School which was within walking distance of their home, the younger children went to Lynn Schools. Their oldest daughter, Faye Etta, related many memories of her childhood. She spoke of walking over rocky cedar glades to get to friend or relative's house, and walking home after church singings. Those were slower more peaceful times it seems. Faye Etta Davis married Otto B. Richey (see ancestry of Otto Bevily Richey). Descendants of James Mack Davis still reside in Lawrence County. –Mada Berrett.

JOHN AND SARAH DAVIS. Memories of Denton. Slavery was a problem in 1861 at Denton, Arkansas. There were no known battles in the Denton area, but Federal troops raided homes of the area residents. My great-grandmother, Sarah Davis, told how they kept their cured meat hidden in the wood box, so the Jayhawkers would not find it.

We don't have any record of Indians being seen in the Denton

John and Sarah Ann Whitt Davis.

area as white settlers, but evidence was found that the Indians had been there before they were moved out by treaty with the United States, about 1810. The cemetery behind the Methodist Church dates from 1830.

Denton developed around the area where the Powhatan-Smithville Road and the Military Road, which opened in 1811, crossed. The major influx of settlers into the valley started about 1835 and continued for about 10 years. Denton was a thriving community with 50 or more buildings at one time. A resident of the area, Ceber Denton, circulated a petition for a post office. The post office department named the office Denton, in honor of Mr. Denton and appointed Dave Davis as postmaster in 1894. Other postmasters were: Berry W. Field, William P. Dent, John B. Bowers, James T. Turnbow and Everett Moore. The post office was discontinued April 30, 1954.

A resident of Denton at that time could find a blacksmith, grist mill, sorghum mill, milliner shop, barber shop, cotton gins operated by oxen, telephone switchboard, grocery and hardware store, doctors, brass band, gas station and subscription school.

The New Hope Church, organized in 1844, played a vital part in the community's early days. It has continued to serve the area residents for more than 150 years.

The dwelling behind the school was built for high school students to board in. Mr. Delania from Batesville came to start a high school, but failed.

The top story of the 1881 school building was used by the Masonic Lodge and the Oddfellows Lodge. The building was known as "The Hall."

The mouse trap factory was in the T.C. Jones Grocery Store in the 1940s. I made parts for the traps and operated the store when the Jones were gone.

More details about the history of Denton may be reviewed in the *Lawrence County Historical Quarterly*, Volume 9, number 4, and Volume 10, number 1.

Submitted by Maxine Davis Mize.

MILDRED ALICE ROBINS DAVIS. My name is Mildred Alice Robins Davis, born July 23, 1915. I am the fourth child born to Clyde Oliver Robins, born February 28, 1886, and Sarah Elizabeth Blankenship Robins, born January 30, 1889. I had a brother and sister, Mona May and Charles Monte, who died very young, and my sister, Novelle Agnes, born October 2, 1913.

Clyde was the first child born to William Edward "Will" Robins, born April 4, 1861, and Julia Alexander Robins, born March 14, 1867. Will and Julia settled on Hoxie Route in a community known as Duvall. My mother died of tuberculosis leaving two babies (I was nine months old and Novelle was 21 months old). Our grandparents raised us and we had a wonderful life growing up with all our cousins, aunts and uncles and being regular "country girls."

When I was 18 years old I met Charles Davis, born October 27, 1900, from Oklahoma, who was a traveling salesman with the *Kansas City Star* newspaper. After a brief courtship we

Charles and Mildred Robins Davis with daughter, Barbara Ann, at age six months.

married in 1933, and traveled from 1933 to 1941. After that we moved to North Little Rock and worked at the Jacksonville Ordinance Plant for four years making bullets for the United States Navy. After the war ended I went to work at Timex in Little Rock. In 1946, our baby, Barbara Ann, born September 18, 1946, arrived and she was such a joy. I quit working and stayed at home with her for several years before returning to work. We lived on West Second Street and then on Park Drive in North Little Rock. Barbara attended schools in North Little Rock all the way through graduation. After attending college and joining the work force she married and gave us three granddaughters: Tiffany, born July 20, 1966; Gina, born April 9, 1969; and Meredith, born November 20, 1972. Charles died in 1970, and I have remained single all these years. In the years that have passed, I now have two great-grandchildren, Christi and Corbin (by Gina and Tiffany, respectively).

I began singing with a group called "Sweet

Adelines" Top of the Rock 26 years ago. I retired in 1981, from Affiliated Food Stores and have kept singing and traveling every chance I get. I am blessed to have my daughter, grandchildren and great-grandchildren all living within 25 miles of me and we all enjoy good health.

After leaving Lawrence County I never moved back, but it will always be my home. I will always remember the days with my Ma and Pa and the love that I was given. –Barbara Pitts.

ROSSWELL AND LAVINIA DAVIS.
Rosswell Davis was born in North Carolina in 1798. His children were all born in Warren County, Tennessee. Ross and Lavinia came to Lawrence County, Arkansas in the early 1850s. Other family members had preceded them to Van Buren County, Arkansas, but it was decided that Rosswell and his brother, James, would settle in Lawrence County. These are the children of Rosswell and Lavinia Davis: John M., born July 31, 1831; Elizabeth, born October 10, 1833; David, born 1836; Cornelius, born December 27, 1837; Sarah C., born 1846; Martha, born 1847; Mary, born 1848; George W., born 1850; and Susan Ann, born 1840.

John M. Davis is my great-grandfather. John's first wife was Martha McCarroll, daughter of James R. McCarroll. She was born 1833, and died on June 18, 1860; buried in Old Bethel Cemetery. Their children were: Nathaniel, born 1854, died 1916; Frances, born 1856; David D., born 1857, died 1923; J. Mack Jr., born 1858, died 1894; and Zachary Taylor, born 1860.

John M. Davis and his second wife, Sarah Ann White, daughter of Abram T. and Barbara White, had these children: Mary Adeline, born 1866, died 1937, married Sam Faulkner; George Franklin, born 1868, died 1942, married Canzada Bilbrey; Henryetta, born 1870, died 1953, married first J. R. Goad, second Thomas Ephram Helms, born 1870, died 1935; Charles C. Davis, born 1874, died 1920, married Floda Field, born 1880; Martha Elizabeth, born 1876, died 1913, married William Cam Helms, born 1873, died 1931; John M. Davis, born 1879, died 1925; Susie Agnes Davis, born 1882, married Daniel Webster Puckett, born 1874, died 1965; Elizabeth Barbara Davis, born 1885, died 1934, married Thomas C. Guthrie M.D., 1880, died 1948.

Martha Elizabeth Davis and William Cam Helms are my grandparents. They had these children: Alvin Leslie Helms, born July 20, 1902; Thomas William Helms, born January 23, 1904; Warren Joseph Helms, March 23, 1905; Ray Helms, born October 23, 1906; Ivey Helms, born August 8, 1908; all dead. William Cam Helms married after the death of Martha, Kate Hancock Riggs, daughter of James Franklin and Mattie Pritchard Hancock and they had these children: Jessie Helms O'Dell, born February 12, 1925; Edward Helms, born and died in 1916; James David Helms, born July 15, 1918; Hosea Wayne Helms, born November 15, 1919; Mildred Helms Shapiro, born April 28, 1924; and Willie Helms Williamson, born October 12, 1925.

One of the interesting things about all of my Lawrence County relatives is that they all originally came from North Carolina and indeed many of them married there. George Helms married Mary Margaret Fortenberry in 1744, in Mecklenburg, North Carolina. Valentine Price married into my Helms in 1834, North Carolina, Susan Ann Davis, daughter of Rosswell and Lavinia, married Wilson Price, son of Valentine and Caroline Hargett Price of North Carolina. The Thomas Presleys of Randolph County married into my Helms in Tennessee, North Carolina and Arkansas and the grandson of Abram T. White, C. Henry White, married Mary Helms "Mollie", daughter of David and Nancy Brown Helms in Arkansas. –Geraldine Fultz.

REVEREND RUDOLPH DAVIS.
see Rudolph Davis.

ISRAEL FOLSOM DAWSON FAMILY.
The first recorded information I have about Israel Folsom Dawson and his wife, Margaret Elizabeth, was the record of their marriage in Lawrence County on March 7, 1867. He was born in North Carolina, the son of Dr. Burrell Dawson. I am not certain of the date of his birth, but according to the 1880 United States Census for Lawrence County, he was 53 years old. When Israel and Margaret married there were already children in the family, but it is not clear if they were his or hers. Children in the family were: Martha Beatle, William David, Selina E., James B., John F. and Charles W. Israel

F. Dawson was the grandmaster of the Smithville Masonic Lodge #29 in 1895. He lived to be a very old age. According to family legend, he died of a wound he suffered during the Civil War which later became cancer. My grandfather, William David Dawson, was his son. He married

Israel Folsom Dawson and Margaret Elizabeth Dawson.

Josephine Harlow on February 10, 1892. They and their six children lived in a large house near Smithville at his untimely death from a heart attack in 1907. He was only in his 40s when he died. My dad, Ralph Dawson, was the sixth child of William and Jo (as she was called) Dawson.

–Clynell (Dawson) Sandusky.

RALPH DAWSON FAMILY.
Ralph Dawson was the son of William David and Josephine Harlow Dawson. They lived in a large house near Smithville. Ralph was 3 years old when his father died of a heart attack in 1907. The young widow had a large family (six children) and not much experience. Ralph could only recall one memory of his dad. He could remember standing on a wood gate eating a banana while watching his dad work cattle. Ralph was reared by his mother and siblings. He married Ena Bristow in May of 1923 when he was 19 and she was only 16. A note of permission to marry was required from her parents due to her young age. They were married in a buggy on the road to the Townsend Picnic. Grandpa Bristow was not happy when they got back to his house. Ena was his youngest and he wanted her to go to college. She never forgot this and worked very hard over the years to finally graduate

Ralph and Ena Bristow Dawson.

when she was better than 50 years old. She received her Bachelor's degree and wanted to go into special education. She always held a teaching job while she raised her four children in a time when women did not work out away from home. When Ena and Ralph were dating, they would sit on a trunk in the parlor and grandpa said to grandma, "Old woman, don't we have more chairs?"

Ralph and Ena's children are: William David Dawson, Ellen Joline Dawson Vande Voorde, Eugenia Clynell Dawson Sandusky and Bertha Ralphaine Dawson Copeland.

It is very hard to describe my dad. He was what is known as a character. He loved to play pranks on us when we were small. I remember one prank, in particular, he played on me many times. He would be plowing back on the river and it was my job to carry fresh water to him. It was very hot and the path was lined with weeds higher than my head. I remember the fear I would feel and then I could hear the tractor and soon would reach him. The water was in a small lard bucket and it would have weed seeds and grasshoppers in it. He would whoop and holler, skim off the top and drink gratefully. Then he would tell me to reach into his shirt pocket, as he had something for me. The first time, it was a penny. The next time he had a "ground puppy" (salamander). I never knew when I reached in there what I would find, but he always coaxed me into checking. He was a very affectionate and good dad. Dad loved the great outdoors and had many stories about his hunting and trapping experiences. He served many years as a deputy sheriff in our part of the Lawrence County. We got free admission to the movies in exchange for dad's services. He took care of any disturbances and arrested trouble makers.

Dad's main contribution to our income was trapping and selling furs and driving a school bus. He entertained the children with his songs and jokes. They loved it and so did he.

One of the stories I loved for dad to tell was when he stepped on a nail and it went all the way through his foot. The doctor came every day for a week and ran a swab with medicine back and forth through the hole. This would have been about 1916. I also loved the story of when the threshers would come through the country and move from farm to farm threshing the grain. All of the farmers worked together. He especially remembered all of the tables built out of saw horses and put together and filled with good food the women had prepared. They too, worked together and moved from farm to farm. This would have been between 1910 and 1920.

Ralph and Ena were very happy until Ena passed away in 1972. Ralph was a very lonely person for the next 20 years. He was very independent until his death in 1992. He has been greatly missed ever since.

–Clynell Dawson Sandusky.

DENISON FAMILY.
About 1918-1920, Floyd Denison came to Arkansas from his birthplace in Red River County, Texas. Floyd was the son of Stephen Denison from Henderson County, Tennessee, and Norma Mayer Denison, born in Kentucky. He worked on farms for hire and sharecropped with landowners. In 1922, he married Dicie Armanda Bell, the daughter of Samuel Houston Bell of Salem and Mary Elizabeth Anderson of Saffell. Mr. Bell died when Dicie was two years old. Mary married several men who also died. Mary eventually married Joe Wadley and they lived with their extended families in the Clover Bend Community. Floyd

Floyd and Dicie Denison at their home in 1972.

and Dicie were married in Monette.

They first bought land in Craighead County. About 1950, they bought the Witt Hall place near

Tafe Dent 7-18-93

Christopher Dent 1-8-95

Kevin Dent 1-31-61

Kevin and Galin Dent.

William Patton Dent, 1855-1938.

Galin Dent University of California, Berkeley, 1995, P.B.K., 2-16-68.

Pleasant Grove - Earliest Dent settlers are resting here. 1998.

Jesse, Joe and Edsel Dent families.

Edsel Dent, November 6, 1927. Veteran of WWII, Korea, Vietnam.

Carla Sue Dent, 7-30-1990.

Jessie Dent 1889-1996.

The W.P. Dent place at Rock Cove. Still occupied 1998. From left: Sons, Clay, Webster and wife Eunice holding first child, Lois. W.P. (Uncle Billy) seated by dog. Youngest son Jesse, Edsel's father standing at far right. circa 1913.

Willis Dent family, Veteran, Vietnam Captain U.S. Army.

Black River. Their sons also bought land in the area. Floyd farmed the land with row crop farming and raised beef cattle until his retirement. In the 1960s, Floyd made a land transfer with their son, Billy. They then moved out to Highway 25 West of Powhatan. That was their home until their deaths. Floyd died in 1974, and Dicie died in 1992.

They had 11 children.

1. Sanford Julius, born 1923, married Francis Pickle. Samp lives in Jonesboro now and has two children and two grandchildren.

2. Cleo Stephens, born 1925, married first in 1945, to Geraldine Vicks; married second in 1969, to Ivaleen Adair Morris. Cleo lives in Lynn and has two children, six grandchildren and five great-grandchildren.

3. Etta Elizabeth, born 1928, married in 1946, to Verlin Adams. Liz lives in Bono and has nine children, about 16 grandchildren about five great-grandchildren.

4. Kenneth David, born 1930, married in 1962, to Clara Lee Morgan, daughter of Theodore and Blanche Morgan of Lynn. Dave lives near Powhatan and has two daughters and four grandchildren.

5. Margie Lucille, born 1932, married in 1948, to Franklin Price. Margie lives in East St. Louis, Illinois and has five children and about six grandchildren.

6. Edward Floyd, born 1933, never married and died here in Lawrence County in 1992.

7. Billy Eldon, born 1935, married in 1956, to Wanda Marie Hinds. Bill makes his home in Walnut Ridge and has four children and six grandchildren.

8. James Huston, born 1937, married in 1963, to Betty Jean Stewart, daughter of Cleo and Mary Pace Stewart. James lives in Fenton, Michigan and has three children and five grandchildren.

9. Melvin Earl, born 1940, married in 1963, to Mary Kathern Morgan, daughter of Theodore and Blanche Morgan of Lynn. Melvin lives in Lynn and has three daughters and two granddaughters.

10. Jerry Wayne, born 1942, died in 1945. He is buried in Craighead County.

11. Linnie Pamela, born 1944, married in 1964, to Lloyd Martz Jr., son of Buster and Hazel Martz of Saffell. Pam lives in Salem and has four children and two grandchildren.

Lawrence County has been good to the Denisons and Lawrence County is a better place for their presence. The love for God, family and country takes first place. Floyd instructed his children to keep their name pure and honorable. – James Denison.

DENT FAMILY HISTORY. The Dent family had its inception into America almost 400 years ago as a result of one Thomas Dent standing on the shores of England and claiming headrights in hte new colonies for Captain John Dent. (Gentleman). 1600-1712

Josiah Hatch Dent's family, direct descendants of John Dent were the first Dents to settle in Lawrence County about 1850. Coming from Tennessee, during this trip the wife and mother died and were buried in Hermantwon, near Memphis. Except for one son, Henry, the family continued their journey into Arkansas where they started new lives. Josiah Dent was born in Rowan County, NC, in 1797 and died in Lawrence County in 1879. He married his first wife Susan Dunn in Murfreesboro, TN, about 1822, and they had 12 children. Except for his wife and oldest son, Henry, they all settled in the Flatwoods District of Lawrence County. The community was later named Annieville, for the Anne's in his life, mother, sister, and daughter. His second wife was the Widow Buchanan and she bore him four children, William I., Emps, Bailey, and Mandy. The four children would carry on the bloodlines of his second family. The bloodlines of those children are still circulating through the generations of this day, over 400 years later. Some of the families still carrying on the Dent lineage are; The Campbells, Phillips, Andersons, Winders, Bradys, Smiths, Moores, Judkins, Hudsons, and many others.

The marriages of the Dent men and their descendents were the springboard from which many generations have risen. Josiah's great-grandson, while doing research years ago said, "There's possibly five to ten thousand of these descendents scattered East to West, North to South, from the palms of Florida to the Red Woods of California and from Alaska to Tamalipas, Mexico, where one descendent owned 15,000 acre ranch."

Josiah H. Dent was the oldest son of Thomaas ?h and Anne (Trott) Dent. He and his nine chil- acquired land in the wooded primitive area ?d "Flatwoods". The township was named Dent, ?er this family. They set aside land for the Pleas-?nt Grove Church, a school and the Old Pleasant Grove Cemetery, still intact today. Josiah, his wife, father, other descendants and friends are buried there. A plan is beign formulated at this time form the preservation of these landmarks and restoration of some of the oldest gravesites and markers. Charle Dent and Edsel Dent will be working with others to formulate and carry out this plan.

Annieville was a thriving community during Josiah Dent's time, with a two-story school, church, store, and cafe on the well traveled road from Imboden to Smithville. The two tin ballot boxes for Dent Township as seen in the Powhattan Courthouse, causes wonder of town population, as other townships had only one ballot box. Elected as County Judge, serving in the late 1860s and early 1870s, Dent was said to be an outstanding man of fairness, good character and good judgement. He was credited with solving justly and equitably many complex problems submitted to him during those days.

The decision of Henry Dent, Josiah's first son to stay in Memphis and not migrate to the undeveloped area of Northeast Arkansas changed many aspects of future Dent ancestry. Memphis had an estimated population of 20,000 at that time, but was a fast growing city and port on the Mississippi. Henry gained solid footing there, and was married to Sarah Gail, cultured daughter of a Baptist Minister. They had five children. They remained in Memphis for many years. Henry later acquired land in Arkansas near the place where his father had settled. He built a beautiful home called "Evergreen". It was a lovely estate on a hill, with landscape among the oaks and cedars. The original house no longer stands bur new owners have rebuilt. Henry Dent's first son George, reared in Memphis, moved to Arkansas and settled in Annieville. He became a shrewd, energetic lawyer with a striking personality. He was a popular individual, a Baptist. He was a Republican who left his mark on the community. Like Josiah, he had two wives but only four children. He is remembered fondly for his involvement in the annual Annieville Picnic that was a July highlight. He organized and sponsored the entire event and was the master of ceremonies.

At the July extravaganza there was music, dancing, concession stands, and barrels of lemonade selling - two glasses for a nickle. The band came all the way from Memphis, the former home of Lawyer Dent. The sound of the bugle by the Bandmaster announced their arrival. Later as 'Old Glory' waved 5,000 happy souls cheered as the band played, "America."

William Tayor Dent (1820-1862) was Josiah's second son. He married Mary Winders, whose family was from Mississippi. They had seven children, William Patton, better known as "Uncle Ben", Albert C, and are the only two on record.

William Patton Dent married Rhoda Phillips. They had five children, two daughters. Clara and Ivie, both died before they were two years old. Their sons were Clay Sloan, Clarence Webster and Jesse Earl. They lived on the land settled by William and Albert, near the Rock Cove School. They set aside land for the Dent Cemetery that is well preserved today, thanks to the Hudson family and others.

Clay Dent, married twice but had no children. Uncle Webster married Eunice Anderson and they had five children, Lois, William W. (Billy), Robert, Melba and Darrell. William's great grandson Tate William Dent is the youngest descendent of the Clarence Webster branch of the family tree. Jessie Earl married Magnolia Crabtree and they had two

sons, Joe Sloan and Edsel Winders. Melba and Edsel are the only two surviving cousins. Edsel married Bernice Swatman and they have two sons, Kevin and Galin, neither being married. Joe Sloan married Velma Lawrence and they have one son Willis Joe. Willis married Joy David and they have three children, Michael, Kimberly and David. David has one son, Christopher Joe Dent. He is the youngest descedent of the Jesse Dent first branch of the family tree.

Charles Dent is a direct descendent of Josiah Dent's second family. Charles is the son of Cecil and Ruth Dent and the grandson of William I. His family retains to this day much of the original Josiah Dent land. Caela Clarke Dent, granddaughter of Charles is the youngest descendent of Josiah Dent second family tree.

Although the Dents have made indelible marks in this country for four centuries and their lines have been passed on to thousands, at the time of this writing there are few left with the Dent name in or near the original settlement of Dent Township of Lawrence County. Listed below are the only ones that could be located:

Name	age	location
Breanna	97	South Carolina
Morgan	96	Ohio
Ean	94	Maryland
Ashley	94	South Carolina
Christopher	88	Missouri
Brian	88	Ohio
William A., Jr.	84	Ohio
Roy Patton, Jr.	84	Missouri

When Captain John Dent set foot on the land of the new world in the 1600s in a place called Colonial Maryland could he have imagined that his ancestors enter the 21st Century and would be writing and talking about his heritage?

In ending this story it is fitting to mention two other Dents who have made their mark on contributing to the history of the family.

Captain Willis Dent, U.S. Army veteran, Vietnam where he served two tours as a supply officer and helicopter pilot. He was awarded the Bronze Star for his service. Dent was the first Vietnam veteran elected State Commander of The American Legion in South Carolina, 1997. Captain Charles Dent, U.S. Army veteran, Vietnam where served one tour. In 1967 he was awarded the Bronze Star medal with "V" Device for heroism in connection with military operations against hostile forces.

The research done for this family history was limited to the direct lineage from Captain John Dent through Josiah H. Dent and the branches of their family tree. Using other pertinent data that was useful and interesting. An apology to all of the Dent ancesters whose names were omitted.

–Edsel Winders Dent

JOSIAH DENT. It all started in 1853, when Josiah Dent came from North Carolina to develop 40 acres of land in Lawrence County that he was given for military service from the United States government. This land grant which I have in hand was signed by President Franklin Pierce on August 1, 1853. He was accompanied or followed to Lawrence County by James T. Dent and William Dent. On July 1, 1859, James T. Dent purchased 120 acres of land and his land grant, which I have in hand was signed by President James Buchanan on July 1, 1859, and the land was in the Clear Springs area of Lawrence County. On May 1, 1860, Josiah Dent purchased an additional 40 acres and this land grant was signed by President James Buchanan on May 1, 1860, and I have it in hand. I believe this land was out toward the Annieville community.

James T. Dent was married to a woman whose name was Empire and they had 12 or 13 children,

several of which died at a very young age. One of their children was Augusta Emmitt Dent, who was my grandfather. His wife's name was Betty. They had five children and the oldest was May, followed by Dolph, Augusta Emmitt Jr. (my father), Harold and Elizabeth. They lived on the farm in the Clear Springs area and the children all attended the Rock Cove School. I have a picture of the Rock Cove School Class of 1910. In this picture are May Dent, Dolph Dent and Gussie Dent (my father). There are also a number of other Dent children and they were descendants of James T., Josiah and William Dent's children.

Augusta Emmitt Dent Jr. (my father) married Susan H. Brady and they had two children, Helen and Buster. After Susan's death, he married my mother, Virginia Dare Macon. They had three children, myself, James E. Dent, Virginia and Ann Catherine. We were raised in Imboden and the last place we lived together was the rock house on the Imboden-Smithville Road near the Jessens. Helen's children, Susan Gail and Delfon L. Scroggs Jr., live in North Little Rock. Buster and wife, Mildred, have a son, Nelson Dent and they live in Mississippi. Virginia Ann married Eugene Romines from Pocahontas and they have two daughters, Sandra and Eugenia. I married Janet Davy in England, UK, we have five children, James E. Jr., Jolene Ann, Jonathan E., Perry L. and Tina Marie. None of Buster, Helen, myself, or my sister Virginia Ann's children have lived in Lawrence County.

–James E. Dent.

DENTON FAMILY. Reverend Richard Denton, born in Yorkshire, England in 1586, was the first Denton of our family to immigrate to America. Reverend Denton was a Puritan minister who came to America in search of religious freedom. He first joined the Massachusetts Bay Colony and later established Christ First Presbyterian Church on Long Island "Denton Green" before returning to England where he died.

Seven generations from Revered Richard Denton family descends from White County, Tennessee, immigrated to Lawrence County, Arkansas. In 1850, Reverend Ozias Denton, a Baptist minister, with his wife, Susanah Walling, led eight of his children, other family members and friends to Arkansas.

Denton children settling in Lawrence County were: James W. and his wife Elizabeth Pennington and their children; Rutha, who married John Campbell Bilbrey in 1851; Cynthia married James A. Wiles; Elizabeth who married Rice Foreman; Lucinda, of whom we have no record; Isaac N. married Sarah Wood; Mary married John C. Holt; and Ozias C. married a girl named Salvia.

James W. Denton was my great-grandfather. His son, William B., my grandfather, was born in White County, Tennessee, and remembered as a small child crossing the Mississippi River on a flat boat into Arkansas.

William B. Denton later moved on to Ash Flat which at that time was part of Lawrence County. He fought in the Civil War, married Martha Rotan Griffith and raised a large family.

Denton, Arkansas, a small community in Lawrence County, was named after Reverend Ozias Denton and his family. They farmed, ran a blacksmith, built a church and as the community grew, Denton Post Office was established.

Revered Ozias and other members of his family are buried in cemeteries in Lawrence and Sharp Counties.

The Denton descendants are scattered now and some are back in England where our story began. –Rebecca Hughes.

HENRY ANTHONY AND SALLIE BOTTOMS DEYLING FAMILY. Henry Anthony

Deyling was born in Ohio on August 11, 1864, died February 18, 1950. He was the son of German born parents, Charles Christopher and Wilhelmina "Millie" Deyling, who lived in Ohio and later in Waseca County, Minnesota. His grandparents were Henry and Mary Deyling of Germany. On February 2, 1892, he married Sallie Bottoms, born August 25, 1873, died October 9, 1957. To this union 11 children were born in the Opposition Community near Ravenden.

1. Ralph Deyling, April 14, 1893-August 14, 1912.

2. Norma Jane Deyling, February 8, 1895-July 26, 1988, married Oscar Neal Lawrason; no children.

3. Willie Beatrice Deyling, May 7, 1897-October 30, 1998, married Webster Perkins; children: Earl Deyling Perkins, who married Mary Irene Taylor; and Paul Laverne Perkins, who married Bonnie Baker.

4. Buell Deyling, February 11, 1900-November 14, 1978, married Ernestine Pickett; children: Rosemary Deyling married Robert Kiawans; Patricia Lou married Charles Beals; and Jeanine married John Basinger.

5. Alva Deyling, December 12, 1902-March 9, 1938.

6. Carlie Elizabeth, April 26, 1905-July 14, 1995, married Kermit Crawford; children: Charles Crawford married Peggy Bryant; and Lawrence Crawford married Marilyn.

7. Mildred Deyling, born October 27, 1907, married Clarence Dale; children: Howard Dale married Dorothy; and Betty Joyce Dale married Bobby Anderson.

8. Josephine Viola Deyling, March 17, 1911-March 29, 1937.

9. Mary Maxine Deyling, January 22, 1913-September 29, 1985, married Ketchel Crawford, divorced, married Foy McNabb. Children by Ketchel Crawford: William Buckner Crawford, Mary Jo Crawford Marchant, Polly Ann Crawford Rodrigues. Children by Foy McNabb: Joseph Randell McNabb, Eula Sharon McNabb Phillips, Frances Carol McNabb Walker.

10. Floy Deyling, December 14, 1914-January 13, 1915.

11. Clair Franklin Deyling, December 9, 1915-January 16, 1984, married Elizabeth Vaccaro; children: Henry Vincent "Hank" Deyling married Linda Coyle; and Mary Deyling married Hickman Ewing. –Bonnie Perkins.

EARNEST DOBBS HISTORY. Dating back to 1890, the Dobbs family consisted of George Dobbs, his wife, Margaret Barnes Dobbs and five children: Ida, William Henry, Mont, Nancy and Lilburn. The family moved from Dalton, Arkansas, to Lawrence County and lived in the Strangers Home Community.

Thomas England and Beckie Deubois England lived near Doniphan, Missouri. Their children were: Mel Vina England Dobbs, Bill England who lived in Walnut Ridge in the early 1960s, and

Quarry Family.

Frances England Harbison who lived in Myrtle, Missouri.

William Henry Dobbs and Mel Vina England were married on December 24, 1896, in Dalton, Arkansas. To this union was born: Edward, Sylvia, Nora, Nellie, Henry, Earnest, Hershel, Delphard and Leonard.

Spring 1936, Earnest and Vida Dobbs.

Coming to Lawrence County in 1913, William Henry and Mel Vina moved their family to Moran, Arkansas, out near what is now called College City. The next year they moved to Strangers Home and farmed for two years before buying an 80 acre farm from Dr. J. C. Neece in the Arbor Grove Community and moved there on December 7, 1917. After seven years they sold that farm and rented 80 acres from Tom Allison for two years. The family then moved to the Charlie Fender farm at M. Zion, now known as the pecan grove out near the air base. In 1928, they moved to the John Lester farm at Moran. They moved in 1934, this

Margaret Barnes Dobbs and second husband La Roix plus children and grandchildren. Grandmother Mel Vina and William Dobbs.

time to Cash, Arkansas and rented the Hilles place from Claude Gregory. In 1935, they moved to the Lamew farm at Clover Bend and stayed three years, before moving to the Sloan farm for four years.

During this time, the children had been leaving home by way of marriage or jobs elsewhere. Earnest had married Mary Mooney on December 4, 1926, in the courthouse at Walnut Ridge by J. B. Allison. To this union came three girls: Pauline, Ruby and Faydell. Mary died in May of 1932.

Earnest remarried on November 22, 1935, to Vida Lee Quarry at Lauratown. Vida was the daughter of James Marion and Mary Frances Howard Quarry; and sibling to Ben, Annie Callahan, Bill, Hiram, Burton, Arthur and Rolla Whitmire Quarry. James Marion was the son of Annie and Dave Quarry and sibling to Jane Quarry and Bud Quarry. Mary Frances was the daughter of Sam Howard and Winney Coker Howard; and the sibling of Mattie Rash, Ollie Phillips, Frank, George and Bill Howard.

Earnest and Vida had nine children: Frances, Barbara, Edward, Darrell, Shirley, Linda, Bonnie, Rickey and Phyllis and all attended Clover Bend School. Barbara graduated from Clover Bend in 1957. Bonnie and Phyllis graduated from Strawberry High.

William Henry finally bought 80 acres from Dr. Neece at Clover Bend "in the bottoms" near Shirey Bay and lived there until 1946, when Mel Vina died. By this time, Earnest's three older girls were

gone. Pauline and Faydell were married and Ruby had died in California in 1941. Earnest and family had returned to Arkansas in 1945, and had been farming with his dad, as well as renting land from Arthur Matthews on Running Water Creek. Earnest bought the farm from his dad, and in 1950, he bought 40 acres from Luther Counts bringing his total acreage to 120. He farmed, raised cattle and sawmilled. He lived there and raised his family until March of 1961, then moved to Strawberry and bought a farm from Nathan Williams. He continued to raise cattle, work at a sawmill, and then for three and a half years worked in a factory at the air base in Walnut Ridge before becoming disabled on September 30, 1970.

In 1972, the farm at Strawberry was sold and the family moved to Lynn. Only Phyllis remained at home at this time. She finished school and was married soon after graduation. Earnest and Vida moved to Walnut Ridge in the early 1980s, where they enjoyed their last years with family and friends. Earnest departed this life January 29, 1984, and Vida joined him on September 5, 1990. They are buried in the Strangers Home Cemetery along with William and Mel Vina Dobbs, and also George Dobbs. –Frances Herring.

PAUL HENRY DOTY JR. was born to Paul Henry Doty Sr. and Helen Phillips Doty of Walnut Ridge in 1951. He graduated from Walnut Ridge High School and Arkansas State University. In 1975, he married Sue Jane Senteney, daughter of LeRoy Senteney and Bobbie Smith Senteney of Weiner, Arkansas.

Paul and Jane had two children: Emily Jane Doty, born 1978, and John Paul Doty, born 1981. Emily is a 1996 honor graduate of Walnut Ridge High School and is currently a junior at Arkansas State University. J. Paul is a member of the Class of 2000 at Walnut Ridge High School.

Paul and Jane are actively involved in farming and were named state finalist in the Young Farmers and Ranchers Award by the Arkansas Farm Bureau in 1975. In 1995 the family was named Lawrence County Farm Family of the Year. Paul helped form Northeast Arkansas Seed Inc. in 1977 and maintained an ownership interest until 1996. Paul served on the Board of Directors of Tuckerman Grain Dryer, Lawrence County Chamber of Commerce, Lawrence County Farm Bureau and First United Methodist Church.

Jane has been active in the First United Methodist Church as well as past Chairman of the Lawrence County Farm Bureau Women's Committee. She has also been active in community and school organizations.

Paul and Jane currently reside in Walnut Ridge. –Paul Doty, Jr.

PAUL HENRY DOTY SR. was born to Elmer Lee and Dora Kifer Doty in 1924, and lived in Otwell and Jonesboro, Arkansas, before moving to Lawrence County. Paul leased land and starting farming in Lawrence County in 1945. In December, 1946, he married Helen Phillips (1927), daughter of George Arthur Phillips and Bertha Skaggs Phillips of Weiner, Arkansas. They moved to Lawrence County in 1949.

In 1951, they purchased a section of wooded land at Minturn. Paul began clearing the land and putting it into rice production. Their land is still farmed by family members.

Paul and Helen had two children, Susan Paulette Doty, born 1949, and Paul Henry Doty Jr., born 1951. They both graduated from Arkansas State University in Jonesboro. Susan married Denver L. Dudley of Jonesboro in 1971. They have two daughters, Sara Dudley Herget, born 1974, and Claire Dudley, born 1979. Paul

Jr. married Sue Jane Senteney of Weiner in 1975. They have two children: Emily Jane Doty, born 1978, and John Paul Doty, born 1981.

Paul and Helen made their home in Walnut Ridge and have been very active in agricultural and community affairs. Paul has been active in the seed business, maintaining an ownership interest in Lawrence County Rice Dryer and Seed Company until 1975, and Northeast Arkansas Seed Company until 1996. He was instrumental in the formation of Farm Service, Inc. Cooperative and served on the Boards of Directors of Farm Service, Inc., Lawrence Memorial Hospital, Tuckerman Grain Dryer, First United Methodist Church, Lawrence County Farm Bureau, and First National Bank of Lawrence County, as well as various other community organizations.

Helen has been very active in the First United Methodist Church of Walnut Ridge as well as various community organizations.

Paul and Helen moved to Jonesboro in 1998, where they currently reside. –Paul Doty, Jr.

DOWNUM FAMILY.

The Downum family moved into Arkansas from Missouri and Tennessee around the turn of the century. John Sidney Downum and his wife, the former Janie Adele Pope, were among them. John's father and mother, Richard Sidney Downum and Mary Elizabeth Vail (or Vale) Downum were there as well. These were my grandparents and great-grandparents.

John and Jane had 10 children who survived past infancy: Dorothy, who died while still a child; twins, Eva and Everett; Alva; Adele; Laviller; Edward; Jesse; Paul; and Wanda. Everett died in his teens. All the other children grew into adults. My father, Paul Howard

J. S. and Janie Downum, Paul, Bonnie, Danny and Gary Downum.

Downum, was the youngest son.

Although my dad dreamed of farming his own land it would take a move to Michigan and laboring in the steel mills before he and my mom, Bonnie Marie Montgomery Downum, had saved enough to buy acreage in the bottom land near Shirey Bay in Lawrence County. This occurred around 1950. There were no luxuries back then, such as indoor plumbing. The house Paul, Bonnie and my two brothers, Danny Neal and Gary Dewayne, occupied was small, with a barn out back for the old milk cow and chickens and to store any extra provisions that they could accumulate.

The work was hard and continuous for everyone on the Downum farm. However, little by little, more land was purchased and by the late 50s, the Paul Downum family had moved to a bigger house on the Lauratown Road in Clover Bend. By this time my sister, Paula Marie Downum Smith, had joined the family. My grandparents, John and Janie, were also living in the Clover Bend area and helped some with the farm work.

In the early 60s, Paul Downum family moved to the house I grew up in and knew as home. My grandparents had lived there and the two households more or less just switched houses. So my family moved on to the Strangers Home Road (Law 543) and my grandparents moved to the Lauratown Road house.

This move enabled my dad to accumulate more land and his farming operation began to prosper and in 1970, we were Lawrence County Farm Family of the Year. He raised cotton mostly, with milo, beans and wheat on the side. In addition, there was the hog barn, with hogs both to sell and butcher, calves to fatten up and butcher, chickens, dogs and cats. Is it any wonder when I was young I wanted to be a veterinarian? Although living on a farm meant hard work summer and winter, I would not have wanted to grow up anywhere else.

In the 70s, my dad branched out into catfish, eventually having approximately 6-7 fish ponds. I loved to go with Dad to feed the fish, especially if it was the floating food because you could see all the fish come up to eat. During the fall, my dad would join together with other men from the community and church to seine the catfish from the ponds. It was unbelievable how many fish came out of those ponds.

The cotton market slowed down so my dad switched from cotton to rice in the mid 70s. This turned out to be a wise decision. There were still the milo, bean and wheat crops, but rice was dad's primary crop. Dad was happiest driving a tractor or walking the levees out in the fresh air and sunshine. I remember him telling me more than once that he had been lucky because he had been able to make a living doing something he loved.

Unfortunately, dad was diagnosed with Lou Gehrig's disease and in January, 1996, passed away. My oldest brother, Danny, passed away in 1984. These two deaths stunned and saddened my family and there are still days where I miss my dad so much it hurts. Life does go on and so does the Downum name.

My mom lives in Hoxie. I, Karen Sue Downum Rivera, also live in Hoxie with my three children: Eric Ramon, Jessica Alexis and Mercedes Sibohan Rivera.

My sister, Paula and her husband, Dennis Smith, now live on the home place and continue to farm the land my dad and mom worked so hard to attain. They and their children, Wesley Adam, Tiffany Marie and Brittany Denise, also have dogs, cats and have added horses to the family farm.

My brother, Gary and his wife, Linda Mitchell Downum, live in Walnut Ridge, along with their sons, Kevin Mitchell and Scott Dewayne. Scott and his wife, Kim Cobble Downum, have a son, Jacob, and one on the way.

My brother Danny's children, Gregory Neal and Cynthia Denise live in El Dorado and Searcy, respectively. Greg and his wife, Tammy, have a son, Zachary, and one on the way and Cyndi and her husband, Chris Matthews, have a daughter, Madison.

Thank you Dad for leaving your family a living legacy of hard work and commitment in the land. I will always be your "Daddy's Girl."

–Karen Downum Rivera.

JOHN SIDNEY DOWNUM

married Janet A. Pope. Mr. Downum came to Clover Bend after living in Tennessee and Missouri. They had nine children: Edward "Ed", Paul, Evert, Alva, Laviller, Adele, Wanda, Jessie and Eva.

Edward "Ed" Benrie Downum married Virginia "Lou" Grigsby, daughter of Jefferson "Buster" Grigsby and Connie Lackey Grigsby. They had four children: Melvin, Barbara Downum Phipps, Kathy Downum Bilbrey, Linda Carolyn Downum Taylor and Donnie "Don" Downum.

Melvin Downum married Janet Ramsy of Chicago. They have five children: Shirley, Jimmy, Mark, Sandra and Sharon, also six grandchildren.

Barbara Downum married Ray Phipps of Egypt, the son of Ray Sr. and Essie Vaughn Phipps. They had one daughter, Andrea Phipps.

They have three grandchildren: Shamle, Alexa and Jassine Trammell.

Linda Carolyn Downum married Berlan Taylor, son of William "Bill" Taylor and Alice Geneva Pickett Taylor of Alicia. They had one daughter, Carolina "Cari" Marissa Taylor.

Kathy Downum married Dee L. "Sonny" Bilbrey, son of Lester and Dottie Bilbrey of Clover Bend. They had one daughter, Tanya and one granddaughter, Emily.

Donnie "Don" Downum married Sherry Downum of Katy, Texas. They have two sons, Steven and Justin. –Berlan Taylor.

JAMES STAFFORD DOYLE JR. AND PRUDENCE JANE BRYANT.

James Stafford Doyle Jr. was born July 27, 1823, in Tennessee. He married Prudence Jane Bryant, born December 7, 1827, on January 22, 1844, in Monroe County, Tennessee. She was the daughter of Moses Bryant and Nancy Ginn. In 1850, James and Prudence were living in Dade County, Georgia, along with his brothers, Pleasant and Isaac.

James and Prudy had four children born in Georgia: Jacob M. in 1845; Isaac in 1847; Melissa Jane in 1849; and Sarah in 1850. After the death of his father in August, 1851, and an infant daughter, Sarah, in September, 1851, James and his family, along with his mother Sarah, joined a wagon train headed to California. The journey was to take them through Memphis and Kansas City. By the time they reached Lawrence County, winter was setting in and they decided to remain here until spring. By the time spring arrived, the family decided to stay in Lawrence County and Sarah received bounty land for her husband's war service.

After settling in the Strawberry area, James and Prudy had six more sons: George Washington in 1852; James Henry in 1853; John Pleasant in 1856; William Bryant in 1858; Jefferson Davis in 1861; and Robert Hiram in 1865. Jacob married Margaret Elizabeth Martin; Isaac married Samantha Higginbottom, then Josephine Hendricks; Melissa married Elam Sides, then Andrew Saffell; George married Lutisha B. Wadley; James married Ester Jane Runyon; John married Sarah Ann Bailey, then Susan LaVesta Callahan; William married Mary Eudora Bailey and Laura Belle "Viola" Daniels; Jefferson married Bettie Ann Hardin, Nancy Jane Dunehew, and Hattie Evelyn Lindsey; and Robert married Susan Abby Horn.

The family were staunch Democrats. James and Prudy's sons and grandsons were active in Lawrence County politics. James Henry was a Justice of the Peace as well as Lawrence County Tax Assessor. Jefferson Davis was County Judge and State Representative. Robert was a deputy sheriff in Catheytown (Strawberry). They were also active members of the Freewill Baptist Church. Many were either ministers, elders or trustees.

After James and Prudy settled in the Strawberry Valley, they remained there the rest of their lives. James died August 9, 1898, and is buried in Ward Cemetery at Strawberry. Prudy died February 17, 1907, and is also buried in Ward Cemetery. Many other family members are also buried in Ward Cemetery including James' mother, Sarah, who died October 16, 1872. –Nancy Matthews.

JEFFERSON DAVIS "J.D." DOYLE

was born in Strawberry on September 21, 1861. At the age of 18 he was married to Elizabeth "Bettie" Ann Hardin on October 3, 1880. She was born on July 15, 1857, and was the daughter of Benjamin A. and Nancy E. Hardin. J. D. and Bettie had James Theodore, Charles Leonirdas, Bertha Barbara Ann, Martha Melissa Katherine, Betty Jane and May.

May was born September 19, 1889. Both May and her mother, Bettie, died on September 19, 1889. They are buried in Ward Cemetery at Strawberry. On April 10, 1890, J. D. married Nancy Jane Dunehew. Nancy was born February 18, 1870, and was the daughter of John Calvin Dunehew and Cassie Emaline Thorpe. Children of J. D. and Nancy were Dona, William Isaac, Telitha LaVesta, Emaline Nancy Prudence, Surilda Belle and Fanny Echo Mae. Fannie was born December 31, 1902. She and her mother, Nancy, died December 31, 1902. They are both buried in Ward Cemetery next to J. D.'s first wife. J. D. then married a third time on March 30, 1903. He married Hattie Evelyn Lindsey. Hattie was born December 8, 1876. They had Jefferson Davis Jr., Harvey Clay, Hattie Evely, Almalisey (Alma Lindsey), Cameron Brooks, Willie, Christine and Jessie Woodrow.

J. D. became an ordained Freewill Baptist minister on August 28, 1889. He performed many of the family marriage ceremonies. For a time he was the pastor at Mt. Harmony Freewill Baptist Church. His first political office was that of Justice of the Peace. In 1908, he was elected as County Judge for Lawrence County. While serving as County Judge, he worked for the improvement of county roads. After he was elected to the legislature, J. D. helped in the establishment of the Blind School in Little Rock. He also worked on the legislation that established what is now known as Arkansas State University.

"The outstanding traits of Judge Doyle were his ruggedness, sincerity, honesty and courage. He was not afraid to take a stand and express his views on any moral or public issue. Of course, such a man had opposition, but he was tolerant and fair toward those on the other side of a question. He made his impression in lasting good to his fellow man." This quote was taken from his obituary.

J. D. Doyle died February 13, 1945, and was buried in Lawrence Memorial Cemetery in Walnut Ridge. He was outlived by his third wife. Hattie Evelyn Lindsey died August 30, 1957, and is buried next to him in Lawrence Memorial Cemetery. –Nancy Matthews.

HERMAN DULANEY FAMILY. Herman Cecil Dulaney was born in 1922 to Perry Thomas and Myrtle Dora Moore Dulaney. He married Ruby Faye Whitlow in 1942. He was a lifetime resident of Lawrence County and will be buried in Lawrence Memorial Cemetery. He is the father of Virginia Kay, Lelia Ann and Regina Mae. –Ruby Faye Dulaney.

Herman and Ruby Faye Dulaney.

Aliene, Myrtle (mother), Herman, Perry (father) and Daisy Dulaney.

MYRTLE MOORE DULANEY is the daughter of William Riley Moore and Tabatha Moore; married Perry Thomas Dulaney; mother of Daisy, Theodore, Andrew "Jack," Herman, Vera and Aliene Dulaney; buried at Lawrence Memorial Cemetery. She also had one sister, Rosetta, who married Chester Dulaney; sisters married brothers. –Ruby Faye Dulaney.

PERRY THOMAS DULANEY was born in Missouri, son of John Alfred Dulaney and Ollie Ussery. He came to Lawrence County in a wagon train. He married Myrtle Dora Moore. He is buried at Lawrence Memorial Cemetery. They were parents of Daisy Marie, Theodore, Hubert Andrew, Hermon Cecil, Vera Virginia and Sadie Aliene. They were farmers. –Ruby Faye Dulaney.

Perry and Myrtle Dulaney.

RUBY FAYE WHITLOW DULANEY was born at Coffman, Arkansas, in 1926 to Benjamin Tolbert Whitlow and Mary Ann Campbell Whitlow. She will be buried at Lawrence Memorial Cemetery. She is the mother of Virginia Kay, Lelia Ann and Regina Mae. She is a lifetime resident of Lawrence County. –Ruby Faye Dulaney.

Family of Herman and Ruby Dulaney. Seated, left to right: Lelia, Virginia Kay and Regina Mae.

DENNY BOYCE DURHAM FAMILY. Denny, the oldest son of Boyce and Martha Ann Penn Durham, was born November 14, 1950, at Walnut Ridge, Arkansas. He was one of the first babies to be born in Dr. Ralph Joseph's new clinic. Denny was raised on the family farm and learned to work at an early age. He attended school at Strawberry for nine years and Lynn until graduation in 1968. His favorite sport was basketball and he looked forward to each and every game, but especially those games with Clover Bend, Black Rock and Strawberry. After graduation he married Martha Jean Hunter and they had three sons: David Scott, John Martin and James Andrew "Andy."

Denny and family spent several years working in Texas, Arkansas and Missouri doing telephone construction. Over the years he has owned and operated Imboden Auto Sales that has included rebuilding and selling vehicles. The business has now changed to Imboden R.V.'s where he keeps a large inventory of recreational vehicles. He became a licensed agent for Shelter

Andy, John, Denny and David Scott Durham.

Insurance and worked for a few years for his dad before building his own agency in Imboden. David Scott, born November 6, 1968, married Kellie Huskey, born July 17, 1973, and they have three children: Shea, born December 30, 1994; Cameron, born October 17, 1996; and Rachel, born July 10, 1998. David has a Agri Business degree from Arkansas Tech and is employed by Townsends of Arkansas as field manager over laying hens and pullets and Kellie is employed by the Arkansas Bank. John Martin, born August 14, 1970, married Libby Duckworth, born June 3, 1970, and they have one child, Morgan, born July 8, 1996. John is employed by Hytrol of Jonesboro and Libby is a homemaker. Andy is single and enrolled in college.

Denny remarried Kelly Wayne in 1991. Kelly has two sons: Brian Wayne, born August 28, 1977, and Jason Wayne, born March 28, 1981. Brian is in medical school and Jason is a senior at Sloan Hendrix and still lives at home. Denny has another son, Adam Durham, born June 18, 1982, who lives in Illinois and attends high school there. –Martha Ann Durham.

JIMMY TERRY DURHAM FAMILY. Jim, son of Boyce and Martha Ann Penn Durham, was born at Walnut Ridge, Arkansas, February 5, 1954. Jim was the farmer who had all the bad luck with whatever animal he tried to raise. He was also accident prone. He was squeezed by a power lift on the tractor, swallowed a steel ball bearing, was shot by his brothers while hunting and was burned badly while burning the trash, but still grew to be the tallest in the family and was left with no disabilities. He attended school for five years at Strawberry and then came to Lynn in the sixth grade where his mother was teaching her first year. After graduation he started telephone construction in Texas. He also worked some in Missouri and is in his 20th year for General Telephone Company as an installer/repairman in

Lacy, Shawn, Jim, Ladell and Christy Durham.

Pocahontas, A
at Farm Servi
months. He ov
that he built h
Jim mar
1983. Ladel
born July
marriage

kansas. He was also employed ... e in the Lynn store for several ... ed cable TV in Knobel and Okean ... self, but later sold.

... ed Ladell Loggins, January 7, ... had a daughter, Christy Mitchell, ... , 1975, that became part of that ... They lived at McCrory, Judsonia and ... onville while working for GTE. They had ... aughter, Lacy Ann, born July 20, 1983, and ... on, Shawn Michael, born February 9, 1986. The children are both active in school, sports and beauty pageants. Ladell graduated from Williams Baptist College with a degree in elementary education and she now teaches in the River Valley School District at Poughkeepsie. Jim has served for several years on the River Valley School Board and served one term as president and is now serving as secretary. Jim spends most of his spare time coaching pee wee basketball teams. – *Martha Ann Durham.*

JUSTIN SLOAN DURHAM. This poem was written for Justin Sloan Durham, son of William Sloan Durham and Dina Sloan Durham. It was written by Dina, with God's help, she knows, for it was written only hours after learning of her son's death and upon returning from seeing and feeling him laying still and cold on a sterile hospital table inside a funeral home and being asked what she wanted put in the paper for her son's memorial.

Justin Sloan Durham, April 27, 1980-July 2, 1997.

Justin's life, at only 17, was taken on July 2, 1997, in a tractor roll-over accident near Portia while working for Penn Brother's Land Leveling. Justin was born with farming in his blood, he absolutely loved it and loved what he was doing working for Jim and Joe Penn, they could do no wrong in his eyes. Jim's son, Chris Penn, and Justin were closer than even brothers and those two became inseparable. The Penns thought very highly of Justin also, and they, as well as others, had commented in amazement at the knowledge Justin had about tractors, other equipment, and farming in general, but why wouldn't he? This child had been around and on farm equipment all of his life. He drove his first tractor around age 8, raking, baling, or shedding hay; by age 9 he was actually paying for his own tractor, not a toy, but a John Deere 4630, using money from his cow herd started with a calf his granddad, Boyce Durham, gave him when he was born.

Justin had a very outgoing personality and was well like and loved by many. He was a very compassionate person, always aware of his blessings, wishing to share with others, going out of his way to speak to the elderly and young alike, and offering a helping hand when needed. This was made evident in the crowd that came to say good-bye to Justin and show their love for him and the family. Over 1000 people came to the small town of Strawberry. There was a line from the front of the church extending past the intersection in town and beyond.

Justin will always be loved and missed by those who knew him. The family wishes for all who read this to send up a prayer that God will continue to use Justin's life here to lead others to Him. –*Dina Sloan Durham.*

IN LOVING MEMORY OF JUSTIN SLOAN DURHAM
JULY 2, 1997

Our Justin,
The Lord must have
great plans for you:
to take you from us before
we thought we were through,
You were our firstborn child
Made us laugh, Made us smile,
Gave us love, joy and now tears,
In your short loving 17 years.

Your great ambition for life
at age four,
Was to be a preacher and farmer,
like those you adore.
Not many a soul
can reach life's goal,
In only 17 years,
without a firm hold.
The Lord gave you that hold,
though we didn't know,
For a preacher and a farmer,
he made you so.
You are our blue-eyed,
blond-haired, firstborn son;
Seems your life was over
before it had begun.
But those of us
who know our Lord,
Know that's not so -
there is much more!
We love you Justin,
our firstborn son.
We realize your life isn't over;
it's just begun.

Mom and Dad
Courtney, April and Calie
–*Dina Sloan Durham.*

MICHAEL DURHAM FAMILY. Michael, son of Boyce and Martha Ann Penn Durham, was born March 5, 1953, at Walnut Ridge, Arkansas. His beginning came about after a few changes. Dr. Ralph Joseph loved horse racing and was in Hot Springs on this exact date so Mike was born at Dr. Elder's clinic. The power went off so he transferred to Dr. Joseph's clinic the next day. Mike lived and worked on the farm while attending school at Strawberry and Lynn. He graduated from Lynn in 1971. After graduation he completed auto mechanics training at the Searcy Vocational School and

Amanda, Michelle, Becky and Mike Durham.

worked on a farm and also for Yarnell's Ice Cream. He then decided to do telephone construction working in Missouri, Arkansas and Texas.

Mike met Becky Jo Tolbert, born July 15, 1953, his seventh grade year at Lynn and they dated until their marriage, March 10, 1973. Becky tells the story that Mike never formally proposed to her, but that he bought the engagement ring, came to see her, asked her into the bedroom, closed the door, and held out the ring and asked, "would you like to have this?" They began their life together in Athens, Texas, where Mike was doing contract work for Continental Telephone Com-

pany. By 1974, his brother, Jim, had formed Durham Communications and was working in Newton, Texas. Mike and Becky came to work and on July 5, 1974, Mike was doing a connect on a power pole and came in contact with 7620 volts of electricity that changed his life. He spent most of the next three years in hospitals in Beaumont, Texas and Memphis, Tennessee, where he underwent 26 surgical procedures that made it possible for him to live. He is handicapped, but lives a good productive life. Their first child, Becky Michelle, was born March 31, 1975. She married Mitchell Evans, born March 29, 1973, on April 14, 1995. Michelle is the customer service representative for Craighead Electric and Mitchell is tool and die change-over employee for Waterloo in Pocahontas. They are expecting their first child, April 20, 1999.

Amanda Suzanne was born March 13, 1977. Amanda is single, lives at home, attends Arkansas State University and will graduate in the spring of 1999, with an associate degree in radiology. She plans to specialize in radiation therapy. This family has a bond that is not often seen in most families and that may have been a result of knowing how fortunate they were that Mike was able to receive the medical care that not only kept him alive, but left him looking great. Dr. Robin Stevenson, Methodist Hospital in Memphis is to be given credit for all the plastic surgery. He not only provided medical help for Mike, but he also opened his heart and his home to him. They exchanged visits over the years that grew from the many months that he cared for him medically.

Becky, the daughter of Jack and Jo Tolbert, was born in Portia and attended her first six years of elementary school there. She came to Lynn in the seventh grade and stayed there until graduation in 1971. In May of 1972, she graduated from LaVera Beauty School in cosmetology. She worked in Cherokee Village for one year. Becky is not only a homemaker, but she manages the beef cattle farm.

Mike and Becky enjoy traveling. They are both members of the Lynn Church of Christ.
–*Martha Ann Durham.*

WILLIAM BOYCE AND MARTHA ANN PENN DURHAM. Boyce, son of Claude and Annie Smith Durham, was born February 12, 1929, at Jesup, Arkansas. He has lived in Lawrence County all of his life. He attended school at River View, Squint Eye and Strawberry. He graduated in 1947, from Strawberry High School. He then enrolled at Arkansas State for the next year and half, living in the home of Hubert and Virginia Coke. Boyce has remained a farmer all of his life and he has raised broilers, managed laying hens, operated a grade A dairy, farrowed hogs, grew beef cattle and raised a variety of crops. He became a licensed Shelter Insurance Agent in 1960, and still helps with the agency. He is now retired after working 44 years for the Rainwater family in what has been known variously as the Citizen Bank, Lawrence County Bank and The Arkansas Bank. Even though he says he is retired he finds never ending wood

Boyce and Martha Ann Durham.

working projects with the latest being a cabin on Lake Charles where he has built many unique projects from wood sawn from the family farm that was blown down in the tornado of March 5, 1996. He also spends a lot of time doing all the things that his four sons have going that need "dad."

On March 16, 1950, Boyce married Martha Ann Penn, the daughter of Dennis and Syble Casper Penn. Martha Ann was born in Wauchula, Florida, where her grandparents, Homer and Annie Boatenhammer Casper lived. She soon came to live at Lynn, Arkansas and attended all 12 years of school there. She married during her sophomore year, but returned to graduate in 1953. They had four sons: Denny Boyce, November 14, 1950; Michael Blaine, March 5, 1953; Jimmy Terry, February 5, 1954; and William Sloan, March 20, 1957 (see history for each son). They all married and settled in the area. They gave their parents 14 healthy and lovely grandchildren. On July 2, 1997, Justin, the oldest son of Sloan and Dina, was killed in a tractor accident. This was the most tragic event in their lifetime. He is buried on the family farm.

Martha Ann enrolled in college at Arkansas State after getting the boys in school. She completed a BSE and MSE degree in Elementary Education. She taught sixth grade at Lynn for 29 years. Later, she became certified to teach gifted education and did that for six years before retiring in 1995. She is now a Shelter Insurance Agent. Antique cars have intrigued Martha and she has a nice collection that she shows in the area.

Boyce and Martha are both members of the Lynn Church of Christ where they attend regularly. Martha teaches an adult ladies class. Boyce has served as a commissioner on the Cooper Creek Watershed, secretary for the Lawrence County Cattleman's Association, and a board member for the Arkansas Bank. Martha is a member of Delta Kappa Gamma where she served two terms as president. She also served two terms as a commissioner on state committees for Governor Clinton and Jim Guy Tucker in Little Rock.
–Martha Ann Durham.

WILLIAM CLAUDE AND ANNIE BELL SMITH DURHAM.
Claude, the son of George Washington and Carrie Hooten Durham, was born February 4, 1903, on his parents farm in the Jerusalem Community near Strawberry, Arkansas. Claude's brothers and sister include: Elmus, Ed, Everett, Audie and Maudie. They attended grade school at Jerusalem. Claude continued his education at Strawberry and was a member of the first graduating class of 1925. He was member of the football, baseball and basketball teams. He once told of the time a group of boys walked to Imboden to play football. When time came for the game some of the boys were missing and were later discovered down by the railroad tracks watching the trains go by. Claude remained an avid fan of the Ranger basketball teams throughout his life. In 1933, he obtained a teacher's permit, signed by R. S. Rainwater, county superintendent and for a number of years taught at Belmont, Union and Penn rural schools. His teaching career ended in 1940, when he became a full time farmer. Education was still very important to Claude and he served several terms on the Strawberry School Board. He was proud to have his children graduate from Strawberry High School.

In July of 1928, Claude married Annie, daughter of L. B. and Ada Sparks Smith. Annie was born August 29, 1902, at the Henderson Place near Jesup. She attended school at Shady Grove and Jesup. Later, she boarded with the L. H. Kaiser family in Imboden and attended Sloan Hendrix Academy.

Durham family, standing front: Terry. Back row from left: Kathleen, Claude, Annie, Boyce.

In 1921, she returned to Jesup where she worked in the post office and general store for Verdie Mullen. It was at this time that she met and married Claude. Their first home was the house adjacent to her parents. This house became known as the "Weaner House" as it was the first home for so many young married couples. Claude and Geneva Hillhouse Mullen were perhaps the last couple to live there.

Claude and Annie are the parents of Boyce, born February 12, 1929, who married Martha Ann Penn in 1950. They are the parents of Denny, Mike, Jim and Sloan. Kathleen, born December 3, 1930, married Jack Sisk and had Larry and Debbie. Terry, born June 17, 1937, married Lillian Harris and their children are: Teresa, Mitchell, Mark, Kevin and Karen.

In January of 1938, Claude moved his family from Bricky Hill to the Kaiser farm south of Smithville where he lived until his death, July 5, 1961, in a farm related accident.

Annie was lunchroom manager at Strawberry school from 1946-1956, before beginning an upholstery job that had formerly been a hobby after learning the trait from Homer Casper, Martha's grandfather. She continued working and was active in church and community affairs until May 19, 1994. She fell in her home, broke a hip and was bedfast for 14 months. With the care of family and friends she was able to remain at her country home until her death, September 6, 1995.

Claude and Annie were members of the Eli Lindsey Methodist Church and were buried at Lancaster Cemetery. –Kathleen Sisk.

WILLIAM SLOAN DURHAM FAMILY.
Sloan, son of Boyce and Martha Ann Penn Durham, was born March 20, 1957, at Walnut Ridge, Arkansas. He was raised on the farm and it really stuck in his blood. He became the only true farmer out of the family. He attended his first and second grades at Strawberry and came to Lynn in the third grade. He was scared to death when he

Caley, April, Courtney, Dina, Sloan and Justin Durham.

changed schools and Mrs. Clar[...] teacher that first year at Lynn. S[...] scared and she told him one day [...] ate him she would put salt and p[...] and that seemed to relax him. Befo[...] from Lynn, Sloan was already wo[...] jobs, running a large hog operatio[...] chased his first farm at 17. In 1975, h[...] Texas to do telephone construction for a[...] time. He also tried carpentry as a trade, but farm[...] ing seemed to hold the most interest for him. He now owns and operates, with his sons help, several acres in the Black River bottoms which he row-crops. He owns land in the Smithville area where he raises beef cattle, hay and grain. He has also operated a chicken litter business for several years, cleaning out chicken houses and spreading the litter as fertilizer. He ran these businesses in conjunction with his farming operation.

Sloan married Dina Gail Sloan Durham, daughter of Jack and Suzanne Cornelius Sloan of Black Rock, June 18, 1976, and have four children: Justin Sloan, blonde hair, blue-eyed, born April 27, 1980; William Courtney, dark, curly hair, green-eyed, born September 13, 1983; April Shanel, blonde, curly headed, blue-eyed, born on her mother's birthday, April 13, 1986; and Kalie Blair, dark haired, green-eyed, February 6, 1990.

Dina attended Southern Baptist in Walnut Ridge and Arkansas State University in Jonesboro, studying art and English while working for Boyce and Martha in their Shelter Insurance business for 13 years, mothering, as well as teaching Sunday School, substitute teaching, volunteering as a Cub Scout leader, 4-H leader, Tot-Teen leader, sewing and crafting for family and friends, teaching clogging and performing for local events.

On March 5, 1996, the family farm was hit by a tornado destroying fences, 10 out buildings, including the big, red, "landmark" barn built over 75 years ago by Sloan's grandfather, Claude Durham. With the bad came the good; neighbors poured out helping to repair and build back; yet only a little over a year later a tragedy struck that changed them and the surrounding community forever. On July 2, 1997, Justin, who attended Lynn School, kindergarten-seventh, transferred to River Valley his eighth grade year, where he received several FFA awards and athletic awards, lost his life at age 17 in a tractor roll-over accident while working for Penn Brother's Land Leveling in Portia. Yet, even with the unimaginable, came blessings, for in Justin's short life, he had made an impression on many, with his friendly, mischief, and Christian ways. The line at his visitation stretched nearly half a mile in people. Many who may never have come to know our Lord, within hours of last good-byes to Justin, rendered obedience to Christ in baptism or were brought back to Christ, and are now living a life, that only such a tragedy such as this could bring about. Family and neighbors poured out to help ready a 100 year old, dormant cemetery on the family farm just across from the family home to lay Justin to rest. Hundreds of people gave of their time and money to set up the Justin Sloan Durham Agriculture Scholarship; enough money was raised so that the scholarship will continually fund itself.

The family struggles to go on, and only in faith, do so, for the loss of a child one does not get over, the gapping hole is not healed by time, one only learns to live with the pain. If you are reading this and have all your children, discount your trivial complaints, count your blessings and thank your Lord. If you are reading this and have lost children, remember God's promises; we will see them again, if we live faithful, for they are not gone, only gone away.

Sloan, along with Justin's spirit and Courtney's help, continues to farm and raise cattle, for he knows that this is what Justin would want him to do. The family attends church at the Strawberry Church of Christ where Sloan, Dina and Courtney are members. Sloan is a deacon and teaches a Sunday School class. Dina is a Title I aide, working with children at the River Valley (Strawberry) School. She also serves as president of the PTC and AGATE, and also teaches classes at church. Courtney attended school at Lynn, K-6, but enrolled at River Valley School his seventh grade year, where he plays basketball and was voted All Conference in 1999. April, who attended Lynn, K-3, transferred her third grade year. She is a beautiful, curly-headed, blonde, excelling in academics, basketball and loves to read. Kalie, a real beauty, too, attends River Valley also, she, too, excels academically and loves to play basketball. The family asks for continued prayers always, that the Lord continues to use them and Justin's life to lead others to Christ.

–Dina Sloan Durham.

THOMAS EAST. Although Thomas East did not live in Lawrence County very long, members of his family contributed to the beginning of the county and many of his descendants still live there and in its neighboring counties.

Thomas East was born about 1790 in Laurens County, South Carolina, the son of Shadrack and Mary (Hundley) East who moved to South Carolina from Halifax County, Virginia. Thomas was the youngest son. His father died when he was a child and his mother remarried to John Sinclair. After his older brothers died and his sisters were married, the land of his father was sold.

Thomas probably married in South Carolina and soon after the birth of his first son, Shadrack, he moved with others of his family to Lincoln County, Tennessee. He later sold his land there to one of his brother-in-laws, William Milner, and moved to Giles County. He lived in Giles and many of his children were married there. Thomas sold his land there in 1851. By 1852 he was in Lawrence County and was testifying for his son, Shadrack, in a lawsuit. In 1855 he obtained a lease of land from James R. Taylor to make a crop with the aid of his son. There was a dispute with Taylor and Thomas went to court to get his share of the crop. Among those who signed his bond were his sons, Shadrack M. and Robert Allen East, who had just moved there from Mississippi. The case was settled in 1856 and nothing more is known about Thomas. His wife, Nancy, and his son Don moved to Webster County, Missouri with Shadrack's family. Since no estate was involved and no probate has been found for Thomas, it has been difficult to find names of all his children. Besides his three sons, S.M., Robert A. and Dona F., there were three daughters who married brothers: Susan married Ruel Pace; Eliza married Abner Pace; and Martha married Sion/Cion Pace. One daughter, Margaret Catherine "Kitty," married Archibald Campbell McDougal in Mississippi. All these families later moved to Texas. These families were in Tishomingo County, Mississippi, in 1850 along with Robert Allen whose first wife, Charlotte Mitchell, died there. A son of Robert Allen corresponded with some of their descendants. Another daughter, Nancy, married Reuben Seagraves in Giles about 1851 before moving to Lawrence County. After the death of Reuben, she married Thomas J. Robertson.

The youngest son of Thomas, Don F. East, remained in Missouri with some of the children of Shadrack after Shadrack returned to Arkansas. Many of the children of Shadrack and Robert Allen East married and continued to live in Lawrence County.

EDMONDSON. William R. Edmondson, born in 1821, in North Carolina, and his wife, Amanda, moved from Gibson County, Tennessee. The Lawrence County 1850 census listed the family and children: William M., age 13; John B., age six born in 1853, in Walnut Ridge; and Zachery, age two. The 1860 census listed the children as: William M., John B. and James B. William B. died in 1865.

John B. Edmondson and Emma M. Wylie, born in 1860, were married August 31, 1879. John B., Emma and Amanda, John's mother, age 53, were living in the Campbell Township of Lawrence county in the 1880 census. Their children were: Rosa, Zola, Maude, Oscar B., born March 3, 1887, and Edgar. Edgar married Ina Moore. Their children were: Inez Campbell and Ramona Benson.

Rosa Edmondson married Jim Penny. Their children were Raybon, Atha, Emily, Horace and Morris (twins).

Zola Edmondson married Monte Wyatt. Their children were: John Newton, 1918; Tommy, 1919; and Robert, 1923. Zola taught school in Lawrence County. She later married James W. Lee. Their children were: Emily, Edna Ruth and Charles Lee. Later, Zola moved to Wardell, Missouri to teach. Maude, who was blind, and Emma, their mother, lived with Zola.

Oscar B. Edmondson married Willie Myrtle Moore, born 1893, in Walnut Ridge. Their children were: Preston Moore Edmondson, June 11, 1914; Emma Regina and John Henry. Preston married Opal Mae Irvin, born January 17, 1918, in Dyer County, Tennessee. Their children are: Billy Mack and Sandra. Billy married Jean Colwell in 1960. Their children are Alan Mack, William Scott and Lee Ann Grady. –Jean Edmondson.

DR. JOHN BYRON ELDERS "JB" came from a line of physicians, starting with his grandfather, G. W. Nicholas Elders M. D. of Hematite, Missouri. Nicholas Elders had a brother-in-law, four sons, three grandsons, one nephew, one grandson, and one great-grandson, all physicians.

Young Byron Elders first came to this county in 1910, at the age of one. His parents, Dr. John Wesley and Grace Seat Elders, moved to Alicia in that year from Hematite, Missouri. His older sister, Dottie, was three at the time and their home was next to the Clyde Campbell family. The Elders later moved to Walnut Ridge and lived on Southwest Second Street. Byron recalled having a "bicycle shop" with young Sterling Wood, behind the house that stood where the Elders Clinic would be. When Byron was 12, the family moved to Harrisburg, where the senior Dr. Elders would spend the remainder of his life. He died in 1949.

Byron Elders attended Harrisburg schools as did Dottie. After attending Jonesboro Baptist College in 1927-1929, he enrolled in the College of Medicine in Little Rock, and graduated in 1935. In 1934, Byron married Lucille, daughter of Thomas Monroe and Catherine MacIntosh Hogue of Winchester, Drew County, Arkansas. The couple moved to Stockton, Georgia in 1935, and their only child, John Byron Elders Jr., was born that year during Byron's internship.

Dr. Elders and family moved to Paragould then Walnut Ridge, serving as a State Health Officer. He was among the doctors attending the sick among refugees from the Mississippi flood of the late 1930s, at a tent city set up on what is now Jonesboro High School grounds. After enlisting in 1941, Dr. Elders served in Europe as a company commander of a Medical Aid Station, and was discharged in December, 1945, as a captain. During this time, Lucy and young John were moved about the country, finally returning to Walnut Ridge.

Byron started private practice in Walnut Ridge in 1946, and remained in practice there until his death in 1984. His first office was located in a back room of Sexton Drugs, which was then located where Hart Accounting is now. After a brief time back in Harrisburg sharing an office with his father, he returned to Walnut Ridge and

Dr. J. B. Elders

set up an office in a second floor on the south side of West Main. His next location was in the house which stood where he would open his clinic in 1950.

The Elders Clinic offered general and maternity services and overnight care until the opening of Lawrence Memorial Hospital. Over 1000 babies were born during those years, and many photos of those children are still displayed in the back hall of the clinic building. It has been said the Dr. Elders delivered over 5000 babies in his career.

During his time at Walnut Ridge, Dr. Elders was a member of the Methodist Church, Kiwanis and retired from the Arkansas National Guard with a rank of lieutenant colonel. He and Lucy traveled widely in later years, visiting all 50 states, and many foreign countries. Lucy was very active in church matters, loved to paint and was much missed when she passed away in 1987.

John Elders Jr. graduated from Walnut Ridge High School. He married Bonnie Wyatt, daughter of John and Marie Ivins Wyatt, in 1962. Their only child, Greg Elders, was born in 1963. John and Bonnie are retired and live in Walnut Ridge. Greg Elders M.D. is married to the former Stacey Nosari. Residing in Mountain Home, Arkansas, they have four young children. –Greg Elders.

ENGELKEN FAMILY. Fred Wilburn Engelken, wife Barbara Jean Engelken, and son Robert Dale Engelken moved to Walnut Ridge from Little Rock in 1958, after Fred was transferred as a field representative with Retail Credit Company (now Equifax). Robert was born in Poplar Bluff, Missouri, on November 14, 1955, and other sons, Stephen Wayne and Jeffrey Scott were born in Walnut Ridge on April 29, 1958, and March 4, 1966, respectively.

A descendant of 19th century German immigrants, Fred was born in Doniphan (Ripley County), Missouri on November 18, 1931, to Louis Paul Engelken and Violet Elzy Engelken and graduated from Doniphan High School in 1948. He has one brother, James Engelken of Doniphan. Barbara was born on January 1, 1938, in St. Louis, Missouri to Jack Baggett and Kathleen Brooks Baggett, but moved to Doniphan at an early age. She was raised by her mother and her stepfather, Oscar Emmons, and graduated from Doniphan High School in 1955. She has one sister, Carol Emmons Kersting, of St. Louis. Barbara and Fred were married in Doniphan on March 5, 1955. After local employment and membership in the Missouri Army National Guard, Fred and family moved to Fort Benning, Georgia with the National Guard. Subsequently, Fred accepted the position with Retail Credit Company in Little Rock, Arkansas before being transferred to Walnut Ridge.

With typical happy small town childhoods in Walnut Ridge including Little League baseball, Cub/Boy Scouts, school activities, and lots of hunting, fishing and arrowhead hunting, Robert and Steve graduated from Walnut Ridge High

School, Robert as valedictorian in 1974, and Steve in 1976. Both attended Arkansas State University in Jonesboro from where Robert graduated in 1978, with a Bachelor of Science in Physics degree and Steve graduated in 1980, with a Bachelor of Science in Business Management degree.

Robert married Sherry Diane Baird of Walnut Ridge on August 13, 1977. Sherry was the daughter of Carl Edward Baird and Betty Holt Baird, the granddaughter of Tommy Baird and Connie Waddell Baird of Walnut Ridge, and brother of Carl Edward Baird Junior, born in 1957, and graduated from Walnut Ridge High School in 1975. Sherry was born on June 6, 1958, in Jonesboro, Arkansas, graduated from Walnut Ridge High School in 1976, and subsequently attended Arkansas State University.

Robert attended graduate school in electrical engineering at the University of Missouri-Rolla and received the Master of Science in Electrical Engineering degree in 1980, and the Ph.D in 1983. He joined the Arkansas State University Department of Engineering faculty in 1982, and is currently a professor of Electrical Engineering there.

Robert and Sherry have two sons. David Robert was born in Rolla, Missouri on October 6, 1981, and Daniel Alan was born in Jonesboro, Arkansas on July 19, 1985. Both currently attend Westside Public Schools in Jonesboro.

Steve married Robin Lynn Whitmire of Hoxie on May 26, 1979. Robin was the daughter of Brooks Whitmire and Virginia Robinett Whitmire of Hoxie and had two brothers, Scott and Greg. She was born on July 17, 1958, graduated from Hoxie High School in 1976, and subsequently attended Arkansas State University, graduating with a Bachelor of Science in Business Management degree in 1981.

Steve has been employed with S-B (Skil-Bosch) Power Tools (former Skil Corporation) of Walnut Ridge since his college days and is currently Materials Manager for the Walnut Ridge plant. Robin is currently working at Douglas Quikcut of Walnut Ridge and is also very active in local drama productions.

Steve and Robin have two sons, Stephen Michael was born in Jonesboro in 1982, and Benjamin Andrew was born in Jonesboro in 1988. Both attend Walnut Ridge Public Schools.

Fred, Barbara and Jeff moved to Neosho, Missouri in 1980, after Fred accepted a position with the Federal Defense Contract Administration Service. They subsequently lived in Wichita, Kansas and Arkansas City, Kansas before moving to Joplin, Missouri, where they currently reside. Fred retired from the federal government in 1994, and currently works with Barbara as a home-based production contractor to Outlet Sports (formerly Lohman Game Calls) of Neosho, Missouri.

After attending elementary school at Walnut Ridge, Jeff attended school at Neosho and Wichita, graduating from Wichita Public Schools in 1984, and subsequently attended colleges in Wichita and Joplin. He is currently employed with Montgomery Ward of Joplin. He married Jodie Backerman of Carthage, Missouri on May 28, 1988, and has two daughters, Brittney, age 9 and Emilee, age 7.

Although now disappeared, the Engelken family still has strong ties to Walnut Ridge and Lawrence County and frequently gathers in Walnut Ridge for visits with friends and family and outdoor recreation. The family will always consider Lawrence County as part of its roots.
–Robert Engelken.

VIRGIL A. S. ERWIN was born July 20, 1836, in Tennessee, married about 1862, in Arkansas to Rebecca Anderson, daughter of James and Susan Anderson of Lawrence County, Arkansas.

Virgil died June 20, 1880, and is buried in Gardner Cemetery in Sharp County, Arkansas. Rebecca died November 26, 1909, and is buried in Old Jerusalem (Little) Cemetery, Lawrence County, Arkansas.

Family legend says that Rebecca was very angry with Virgil and refused to be buried in the same cemetery as he. Their children were:

Susan Emily Mary Erwin, September 18, 1863-August 25, 1935, married October 29, 1885, in Lawrence County, Arkansas to James L. Wright.

James J. Erwin, 1865-about 1905.

Samuel M. Erwin, March 17, 1867-December 9, 1916, married January 26, 1890, to Mary A. Brandon.

Malinda Erwin, 1868-about 1880.

Left to right: Odessa, Emily Mary, and Mary Wright.

Wade H. Erwin, August 10, 1869-September 11, 1947, married March 13, 1895, to Mary R. Massey.

William Anderson Erwin, April 9, 1827-November 9, 1955, married about 1902, to Nannie Mary Little.

David Elisha Erwin, May, 1876-1947, married March 27, 1904, to Mattie Ellen Baker.

Alfred R. Erwin, born about 1877, and married August 9, 1899, to Ida Brannon.

Theodore Thayer Erwin, July, 1878-1960, married April 17, 1907, to Mary May Baker.

Lee Al Erwin, born November, 1883, and married January 28, 1906, to Lee Robinson.
–Barbara Wright Miller.

WADE HAMPTON ERWIN, December 4, 1810, Tennessee-December 12, 1880, married before 1832, Malinda Kincade, born September 24, 1815, in Tennessee, daughter of Clingon Kincade. She died April 30, 1877. Both are buried in Gardner Cemetery, just over the county line into Sharp County, Arkansas.

Having come from Tennessee, the Erwins are in the Independenc County 1850 census and in 1860, are in the Lawrence County census. Their children were:

Matthew, born about 1832.

Virgil A. S., born July 20, 1836, Knox County, Tennessee, and died June 20, 1880, buried Gardner Cemetery; married Rebecca Anderson.

Samual Huston, born September 17, 1837, in Tennessee, and died October, 1905, married Susan E. Gardner, February 21, 1867.

Sherwood R., born October 27, 1838, in Tennessee, and died December 31, 1921, married September 5, 1859, to Matilda R. Gardner.

Thomas C., born 1840, and died before March 1, 1878, married on June 24, 1866, Mary Elizabeth Mullens.

William H. Erwin, born 1843, in Tennessee.

Doctor Franklin Erwin, December 23, 1845-March 29, 1884, married Nancy Rachel Brooks and Virginia D. Judkins.

James M., born 1848, married about 1870, Susan C.

Marion M. Erwin, June 8, 1849-August 2, 1909, buried in Auvergne, Jackson County, Ar-

kansas, married April 3, 1873, to Catherine A. Wright in Lawrence County, Arkansas.

Theresa B. Erwin, born 1852.

Malinda A. Erwin, born 1854.
–Barbara Wright Miller.

JOHN T. EVANS FAMILY. John T. Evans, son of Thomas Jefferson and Miriam Rainey Evans, was born in Tippah County, Mississippi, on June 23, 1837. The family moved to Batesville, Arkansas, in 1851.

During the Civil War, Thomas Jefferson and one of his sons, David F., joined the Union forces. John originally joined the Confederate forces, then changed sides. After his Union unit disbanded, he went to Illinois until the war was over. He then settled in Lawrence County, Arkansas. He married the former Mary E. Hargett, born about 1839, in North Carolina, and died after 1910, on May 3, 1868. Mary, her father, Jason Hargett, and some of her siblings moved to Arkansas in 1857, from Union County, North Carolina. Mary, at the time of her marriage to John, was a widow with one daughter named Fannie, born 1864, and died about 1892. (See Fannie Craige Lenard's story elsewhere in this book.) By 1890, John and Mary had a farm of 70 acres under cultivation. He was one of the best farmers in Lawrence County, specializing in fruit orchards. Mary and John were the parents of a daughter, Miriam Emmeline, and a son, John William. Emmaline, born 1870, in Arkansas, married Lewis A. Richey, born 1867, in Arkansas; she died in 1955 in Duncan, Oklahoma. In 1888, they had several children according to the Lawrence County, Arkansas, Black River Twp. 1900 census: Fannie Ella, born 1888, Arkansas, died 1961, in Eaton, Lawrence County, Arkansas; William M., Thomas; Sidney H.; James H.; and Horice C. By the 1910 census Dover F.; Floy W.; and Lum H. were also in the family. Also shown in the 1900 household were Emmeline's mother, Mary E. Evans, widow; and nephew George Craige.

According to Brenda Bush, a great-great-granddaughter of Emmeline's, Fannie Ella married W. A. McElyea, born January 15, 1884, Eaton, Arkansas, and died June 15, 1958, in Eaton, Arkansas. They had a son named Louis Weldon, born August 10, 1916, in Eaton and died December, 1990, in Rockford, Illinois. Louis married Joyce Madge Gilbreth, who was born on December 28, 1920, in Portia, Arkansas, and now resides in Willow Springs, Missouri. Louis and Joyce had four sons: Louis Weldon McElyea Jr., born December 23, 1938, in Powhatan, Arkansas, and now resides in Venice, Florida; Daryl McElyea, who resides in Oklahoma; Terry and Gary (twins), who now reside in Willow Springs, Missouri. Louis Jr. is the father of Brenda McElyea Bush of Henderson, Kentucky. –Sheila Farrell Brannon.

LAWRENCE FAULKNER SR. William Samuel Faulkner, son of Thomas and Elizabeth Carver Faulconer, of Missouri, moved to Lawrence County and settled in the Flat Creek/Denton area. He married Mary Adeline Davis, daughter of John and Sarah White Davis, February 4, 1886, and had several children: William Roy, Thomas Claude, Amelia, Lawrence and Agnes. Sam Faulkner's names was spelled Faulconer when he came to Lawrence County and it is uncertain when and how the spelling was changed to Faulkner; however, the name is spelled both ways on their marriage license. Lawrence, the subject of this biography was born June 20, 1899, at Denton and married a Powhatan girl, Taddie Mamie Todd, daughter of Pete and Effie May Lay Todd, on April 23, 1921. They raised their family in the Powhatan area. Their children were: Clyde William, Joe Calvin, Vivian Lucille, Lawrence Jr., Mary Carolyn and Glenda Sue.

Clyde William married Martha Sanders. There were no children born to them and after her death, he later married Sally. Clyde died August 26, 1995.

Joe Calvin married Betty Jean Chappell. They had three children: Joe Maurice, who died at a young age; Linda Kathryn; and Phillip Alan, who married Lana Dement. They have two sons: Phillip Joseph and Zachary Paul.

Vivian Lucille died as an infant.

Lawrence and Taddie Todd Faulkner.

Lawrence Jr. married Carolyn Burns Myers. He has a step-son. Randall Wayne Myers married Marcia Westmorelan.

They have a son, Tristan Randall Myers.

Mary Carolyn married William Edward Bilbrey Jr. They have two daughters: Rita married John Hollis Thomison Jr. and they have two children: Lindsay Lane and John Hollis III; and Maleta Sue married Jay Brent Tipton. They have a daughter, Emily Renee.

Glenda Sue married Stephen Michael Bierk. They have two children: Todd Michael and Kelly Sue, who married Barry Roberts.

Lawrence Faulkner Sr. served several years on the Powhatan School Board and was active in local political affairs until his accidental death in November 30, 1954. Taddie continued to farm with the help of her children. She then moved to Walnut Ridge where she lived until she died January 22, 1991. –*Maleta Bilbrey Tipton.*

JAMES FINLEY. Among the earliest settlers in Lawrence County was the James Finley family. James was born in 1791, possibly in Georgia. He died in November, 1852.

He married Nancy Jane Dobbins in Missouri. The family moved to this area in 1816, coming from Kentucky. They settled on the Strawberry River three miles southwest of Smithville and about four miles above the Taylor Mill.

They were the parents of 11 children, and were known as the "Seven Sisters Family." The children were:

1. Joseph married Nancy Childers Stuart.
2. Jasper married Lucinda Mann and moved to Texas after the Civil War.
3. Mary "Polly" married Joseph Fortenberry.
4. Sarah Walker married James Taylor.
5. Harriet married James Fortenberry.
6. Margaret Amanda married James M. Barnett, who was killed in the Civil War. She then married Joseph Taylor, her brother-in-law.
7. Martha was the second wife of Joseph Taylor.
8. Lucy married John Steadman.
9. Nancy married James "Jim" Henderson.
10. John may have died in Missouri.
11. Newt may have died in Missouri.

This family is one of the four pioneer families honored on the four-family monument, located near the Strawberry River. –*Bonnie Perkins.*

SHERROD LEWIS FISHER. Dr. Sherrod L. Fisher, the son of Frederick Fisher and Elizabeth McWhirter Fisher, was born in Maury County, Middle Tennessee, May 30, 1836. His parents were among the first settlers of Middle Tennessee, and the father was in the mercantile business, known

as Fisher's Stand, for a number of years on the Duck River. He came to Jacksonport, Arkansas in 1851. He studied medicine under the guidance of his brother, John P., and in 1857, he began practicing medicine in Wild Mountains of Izard County, Arkansas, where panthers, bears and other wild animals were numerous.

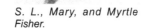
S. L., Mary, and Myrtle Fisher.

Later, he practiced medicine in Randolph County, where he enlisted in the Confederate Army in June of 1861, and served in Colonel Lowe's regiment, Price's brigade, as assistant surgeon. He was wounded twice during the war, the last time begin riddled by a bomb shell at Kansas City on Price's raid. He then returned home and after recovering, he resumed his practice at Smithville, Lawrence County, Arkansas.

He was married November 15, 1866, to Miss Mary Ann McKnight, who was born in Lawrence County, Arkansas, in 1846, and died August, 1872. They were the parents of three children: Martha L., who married J. N. Barnett; Charlie F.; and Gertrude, who married John Morgan. On October 10, 1875, he married Miss Mary Ellen Barnett, who was born January 14, 1852, to James M. and Margaret A. Finley Barnett. They were the parents of two children: Ada L., who married John Wesley Raney and Myrtle Amanda, who married William b. Rudy. Dr. Fisher died June 23, 1898. –*Bonnie Perkins.*

G.W. AND TENNESSEE (DAVIS) FLIPPO. G.W. (George Washington) Flippo, born in 1856, was the son of William Flippo who came to Lawrence County in the early 1800s from Lawrence County, Tennessee. G.W. was married to Tennessee Ann Davis, born in 1856, a first cousin of the Confederate President Jefferson Davis, on January 22, 1882.

The Flippos resided in the Flat Creek Community several years before moving to Powhatan. G.W. and Tennessee moved into a two story home overlooking Black River at Powhatan. The home was located on a hill within sight of the Powhatan Courthouse. Mr. Flippo served as mayor and for many years was the jailer at the Powhatan jail. He had a watermelon farm where his produce was

G.W. and Tennessee Flippo with their sons, William Rector "Will" and Robert L. Jr. "Luther" on March 16, 1901. The Flippos operated a boarding house in Powhatan for many years.

shipped commercially to St. Louis by the boxcar loads. Tennessee cooked meals for the lawyers and judges that were in court at Powhatan. Their house was a popular boarding home for the lawyers and judges who attended court regularly at Powhatan. The couple raised Minnie Flippo (daughter of Jack Flippo - G.W.'s half brother), who helped Tennessee with the cleaning, cooking and serving of boarders at their home. The Flippos attended the Methodist Episcopal Church, South which is now the Powhatan United Methodist Church.

G.W. and Tennessee were the parents of twins, a boy Eddie and a girl Addie, who died shortly after birth. Later, two sons were born while the Flippos resided in Flat Creek: William Rector "Will," born in 1886 and Robert Luther, born in 1889. Will worked as the desk clerk at the Lawrence Hotel in Walnut Ridge. In 1905 he moved to Crittenden County where he served as tax assessor for 24 years and became a prominent landowner and owner of Lion Oil Company in Turrell. He married Bessie Stalls of Memphis. Will and Bessie were the parents of Willie Mae (Flippo) Shaw, teacher and librarian in the Turrell Public Schools.

Luther remained at Powhatan and became a prominent businessman, justice of the peace and worked on the Powhatan ferry. He married Ida Belle Matthews, daughter of William and Lavenia (Martin) Matthews. Luther and Ida Belle operated a mercantile business and in 1920 Ida Belle became postmaster of Powhatan serving in that capacity until 1961. Luther and Ida Belle were the parents of William Woodrow "Billy," a Lawrence County game warden; Robert Luther Jr. "Bobby," a farmer and Lake Charles boat dock operator; and Marjorie Miriam "Sis," a housewife.

G.W. Flippo died in 1931 and Tennessee continued to live in Powhatan until her death in 1941. Both are buried in the Powhatan Cemetery. – *Darlene Flippo Moore.*

LUTHER AND IDA BELLE FLIPPO. The Flippo family name has long been associated with the town of Powhatan. Luther and Ida Belle Flippo have played a special part in Powhatan's history.

Luther was born on August 22, 1893, at Flat Creek to G.W. and Tennessee Flippo. He moved with his family at a young age to Powhatan. He became a prominent businessman, justice of the peace and worked on the Powhatan ferry. He married Ida Belle Matthews, daughter of William and Lavenia (Martin) Matthews. Ida Belle was born on January 4, 1891, at Powhatan.

Luther Flippo.

Luther and Ida Belle operated a mercantile business and purchased the building known as the Telephone Exchange Building in 1920. This was the same year Ida Belle became postmaster for Powhatan. In the back of the building was the post office and in the front was a general store.

In the 1930s the Flippos moved the store and post office to a building located on the side of the Powhatan Courthouse grounds facing Highway 25. Ida Belle served as postmaster until her retirement in 1961. The Flippos were known to extend credit to needy families through their store especially during the Depression knowing that some of those debts would never be repaid. Many times the Flippos would take food to those in need in the community. They were highly respected and extremely civic minded.

Mr. Flippo was known for his sense of humor and love of playing checkers. Mrs. Flippo was a kind-hearted and gracious lady. She was an outstanding community and county leader. She was

Ida Belle Flippo

very active in 4-H and Home Demonstration Club. Her deep faith in God was demonstrated in her devoted work at the Powhatan Methodist Church where Ida Belle and Luther were members. She served as pianist, Sunday School teacher and treasurer for many years. Her devotion to the maintenance of the Powhatan Cemetery was evident in the many hours she gave to clean up work and the planting of shrubs and flowers for beautification of the cemetery. (Her grandfather, B.F. Matthews, donated the land for the cemetery.) Mrs. Flippo was instrumental in helping the Home Demonstration Clubs in Lawrence County obtain a Community Building at Powhatan. She envisioned the restoration of the Powhatan Courthouse and Powhatan Male and Female Academy and worked unceasingly towards that goal until her death in 1971.

Luther and Ida Belle were the parents of William Woodrow "Billy," Robert Luther Jr. "Bobby" and Marjorie Miriam "Sis." Billy married Mable Jones of Black Rock and was a game warden for Lawrence County. They had two children, Carolyn and Merilyn. Bobby married Evelyn Robertson of Black Rock and was a farmer, World War II Army veteran and boat dock operator on Lake Charles. They had four children, Suzanne, Darlene, Robert M. and Miriam. Sis married Monroe Jones, was a waitress and had three children, Leanne, Lantie and Linda. She later married Bill Elliott where they operated a trucking business.

Luther died on July 16, 1968, and Ida Belle died on June 7, 1971. Both are buried at the Powhatan Cemetery. *–Darlene Flippo Moore.*

ROBERT L. "BOBBY" FLIPPO JR.

entered the service in February 1942 and after obtaining basic training at Camp Robinson, was assigned to a quartermaster unit at Oakland, California. He sailed for Australia in July 1942 and subsequently saw service in New Guinea, landing at Buna on Christmas Day 1942. In Buna he endured some of the fiercest battles in the South Pacific.

Bobby was sent into the Philippines and served there until August 19, 1945, when he was released from duty with a port company and an early return to the United States with an honorable discharge from the service. He came home tired and worn from the ravages of war, but never forgetting those who had made the supreme sacrifice especially those from his home town of Powhatan: Alton Stewart and Billy Jewel Colbert.

Mr. Flippo was a veteran who shared with his family the extreme pride he felt for his country. He was always appreciative of those who

served in the Korean and Vietnam wars and he knew the sacrifices they made in blood, sweat and tears to secure the freedom Americans sometimes take for granted.

His daily life exemplified the dignity, patriotism and reverence for the blessings of freedom and liberty.

Robert L. "Bobby" Flippo Jr.

ROBERT L. "BOBBY" AND EVELYN FLIPPO.

The Bobby Flippo family is the fourth generation of the Flippo name that has continued to play a significant part in the history of Powhatan and Lawrence County.

Bobby was born November 22, 1914, to Luther and Ida Belle (Matthews) Flippo in Powhatan. He grew up in Powhatan where he attended school then went to Black Rock High School, graduating in 1933. He married Evelyn Robertson, daughter of T.M. "Mose" and Edith (Beeler) Robertson, on November 24, 1945. Evelyn was born on October 28, 1922, at Mount Vernon, outside Black Rock. She was raised in the Mount Vernon Community and attended school there, later graduating from Black Rock High School in 1941 and attending the University of Illinois.

Bobby entered the Army in 1942 and served in the Philippines during World War II. Bobby and Evelyn purchased the George Jung farm outside Powhatan where they raised four children: Suzanne, Darlene, Robert Matthews and Miriam Robertson. The Flippos were named the Arkansas Balance Farming Family in 1952. Mr. Flippo farmed for several years until several acres of his property was purchased for Lake Charles. Mr. Flippo operated the commercial boat dock on Lake Charles. Evelyn did substitute teaching and worked as a clerk in the post office. She was active in the Powhatan Home Demonstration Club.

Bobby and Evelyn served as 4-H leaders for many years and their four children were all active 4-H members. They participated in the local, state and national activities and were selected to represent Lawrence County and Arkansas at the National 4-H Citizenship Conference in Washington, D.C. Robert and Miriam were State and National 4-H Scholarship recipients.

Suzanne, Darlene and Robert received Bachelor's degrees from Arkansas State University, and Miriam received a Bachelor's degree from University of Arkansas in Fayetteville gradu-

The Robert L. Flippo Jr. family: Miriam Flippo Smith, Robert M. Flippo and Robert L. Flippo; (seated) Suzanne Flippo Hager, Evelyn R. Flippo and Darlene Flippo Moore.

ating magna cum laude. Suzanne, Darlene and Miriam received Master's degrees from Arkansas State University.

The Flippos have been very active in the preservation of Lawrence County history and all have worked toward the restoration projects in Powhatan, especially the Powhatan Courthouse. They were participants in the Mother of Counties Pageants in 1964, 1965 and 1976.

Other civic commitments have included support of the Black Rock Boy Scouts, Black Rock School, Powhatan Cemetery Association, Lawrence County Development Council and the Lawrence County Historical Society.

The family are all active members of the Powhatan United Methodist Church serving in various leadership roles. Evelyn is the director of the museum at the Powhatan Courthouse State Park. She is sought nationwide for her expertise in historical and genealogical research. Suzanne is a kindergarten teacher at Bay Public Schools and the mother of two children: Jesse David and Holly Suzanne Hager. Darlene, high school choral director at Walnut ridge Public Schools, is married to Thomas A. Moore, director of communications at Arkansas State University and they are the parents of Matthew Thomas Moore. Robert is an associate with Blackwell Baldwin Ford in Bentonville and is also a real estate agent. Miriam is vice-president of Blackwood Martin/Cranford Johnson Robinson Woods, an advertising firm in Fayetteville and is married to Randell Smith, senior vice president and general manager of national accounts at Tyson Foods.

Bobby died on January 8, 1987, and is buried at the Powhatan Cemetery next to his parents. The Flippos continue the family tradition of supporting the preservation of Lawrence County history. *–Darlene Flippo Moore.*

FOREHAND FAMILY.

The Forehands came to this country from Ireland about 1700, living in North Carolina, Kentucky, Tennessee, Mississippi and Missouri before moving to Randolph County, Arkansas, about 1875. In 1902, Raleigh Greene and Eliza Jane Griffith Forehand and children, Della, Cordia, Minnie, Lura, Maude, Elmer and Almus, became Lawrence County residents when they moved from Dalton to two miles north of Portia where he farmed.

Della married Jess Archer. Their son, Cyril and wife, Roberta Allen, had four sons: Ronald, Bill, Jack and Jerry. This family returned to Randolph County in the 1940s. Cordia married Tom White. Their children were Leonard, Carmel and Marie. This family moved to Delaplaine, Greene County in 1917. Minnie married Charlie Lane. Their children were Vada, Elsie Jane and Lavoyde. While living in Clay County, Charlie died in an auto accident. Minnie returned to Portia and lived there until her death. Vada married Fred Buercklin, postmaster at Portia. They had one son, Tommy. Vada lived at Portia her entire life.

Lura married Sam Madison, a banker at Portia. Lura died when her children, Opal and Alton, were quite young. Alton graduated from West Point, became a captain in the US Army, was captured at Corregidor, and died in a prison camp in Japan during World War II.

Maude married W. E. Archer, Sheriff and County Judge of Lawrence County. They lived in Walnut Ridge until their deaths. Their son, Howard, and wife, Trell Parrish, had one son, Don. Elmer and wife, Millie had four children: Gerald, Don, Eugene and Juanita. They moved to Tulsa, Oklahoma, in the 1930s.

Almus married Cratie Starnes, daughter of Fred and Mattie Burrow Starnes. They lived and farmed in the Clear Lake Community their entire married life. Their children are Liberty, Relton and

Joyce. Liberty married Chester Pulliam. Their children are Dennis and Karen. Dennis and wife, Dixie Eno, have three children: Kevin, Steven and Lee Ann. Kevin married Kristi Washington. Their children are: Ashley, Eleanor and Caroline Susannah. Steven married Allison Davis. They are parents of Joshua. Karen married David Patterson and their daughter is Kerri.

Relton married Loyse Pulliam (Chester and Loyse's parents were Layman and Amy Pulliam). Their children are: Janet, Jo Carol and Harold. Janet married Jim Surles. Their son is Jonathan. Janet is now married to Daryl Cox. Jo Carol married Michael Phillips. Their children are Amy and Craig. Harold married Renee Pinkston. Their daughter is Cameo. Harold is now married to Teresa Boyd.

Joyce married Edward Holder, son of Redman and Viola Holder. Their daughters are Sharon Kay and Beverly. Sharon Kay married Kevin Hinchey. Their children are Sara, Malia and Stephen. Beverly married Herbert Shatzen and their children are Ellen, Jill and Hannah.

Descendants of Raleigh Greene and Eliza Jane Forehand living in Lawrence County in 1998, are Liberty Pulliam, Dr. Dennis and Dixie Pulliam and Lee Ann, Karen Patterson and Kerri, Relton and Loyse Forehand, Harold and Teresa Forehand and Cameo, and Mike and Jo Carol Phillips, Amy and Craig. Relton, Harold and families live in the Clear Lake Community and continue to carry on the farming tradition of their ancestors. –Joyce Holder.

CHARLES FORRESTER

CHARLES FORRESTER was born 1827, in Smith County, Tennessee. He is the son of James and Permelia Forrester. He was with mother and stepfather Nevil Wayland in the 1840 census of Lawrence County and in household 581 in 1850, two households away from his mother. He was already married to Mary Jane Robertson, daughter of Moses Robertson. She was born 1831, in Arkansas. They had two children. Narcissa J., born after the 1850 census was taken. Charles died before Mary Jane, who has died before March 28, 1859, when her brother, Thomas J. Robinson, got guardianship of Narcissa and Charles. Narcissa is in the household of Jacob Johnson in 1860. Elijah Forrester takes over guardianship by 1869, of Charles. Mary Jane died before February, 1859, when Andrew J. Cravens was appointed administrator of her estate.

Their second son, Charles R., was born 1852, and living with his uncle, Elijah Forrester, in 1870, Randolph County. It states he is eight years old, but must mean 18 years since he had died before 1860. He married Sarah Louisa Jane Weir in 1875. She is the daughter of James and Sarah Sloan Weir. They had eight children.

1. John Sloan, born 1876, married Ida Jane McCarroll, February 7, 1909. She was the daughter of Charles Absolom and Ellen Cravens McCarroll. They were second cousins. He died in 1941, and is buried at Fairview, Randolph County. They had a son, Charles Jewel, born 1912.

2. Laura "Lou", born 1878.

3. Burrett S., born 1880, married Selma George 1899, died 1959, buried Kelley, Lawrence County. They had a son, Odis D., born 1913, and maybe others.

4. Thomas, born 1882, married Anna Bell, died 1941, and is buried Lawrence Memorial. They had two children: Agnes, 1916, and Jerry, 1938. It seems that the age difference is so great, they either had several in between or Jerry is a son of their son. All are at Lawrence Memorial Cemetery.

5. Eudora, born 1884.

6. James R., born 1886, married October 12, 1911, to Tavner Ellis, died 1945, and is buried Oak Forrest, Lawrence County.

This family has given us problems. If anybody can help fill in data, please contact: Mary Ann Buylsteke Carter, the submitter.

Mary Jane Forrester's death date not included: Administrator February 28, 1859, Andrew J. Cravens appointed Inv. March 24, 1859. Heirs: Narcissa and Charles R. Forrester, minors.

Guardian March 28, 1859, Thomas J. Robertson, an uncle of Narcissa and Charles was appointed their guardian.

Charles R. and Narcissa J. Forrester (minors).

Guardian: in 1862, Thomas J. Robertson was guardian of both these heirs of Jane Forrester, deceased date of appointment not included. By 1869 Elijah Forrester was guardian of Charles.

Thomas, born 1812, Alabama, married Martha Weathers, about 1816, son of Thomas, about 1755, and Nancy Nations. Thomas and Martha had five children.

1. Mary Ellen, born 1839, Lauderdale, Alabama, married Robert Forrester, June 21, 1858, in Lawrence. He was born 1833, in Tennessee or Lawrence County, Arkansas, son of James and Permelia Forrester. Mary Ellen and Robert Forrester are in household 1353-1860, Lawrence with daughter, Susan Marie, born April 15, 1859. They have another daughter, Julia Ellen, born August 23, 1860. Robert goes off to fight for the Confederate cause. He was in Company C, 1st Arkansas Battalion, Cabell's Brigade, Battle of Corinth and Hatchie Bridge wounded October 3-5, 1862, died 15th at Holly Springs, Mississippi. Thomas Nations, father or brother of Mary Ellen Nations Forrester, applied for administrator of said Robert's estate in August, 1863. Elijah Forrester, brother of the deceased, goes to court, June, 1866, to apply for guardianship of his two minor nieces. In April., 1867, Elijah goes to court stating that Thomas Nations is wasting the estate of said Robert Forrester and wants to be guardian of his nieces' estate. It appears he was finally successful because he sells some of Robert's property at different times for the girls. Mary Ellen married John Ewing, January 8, 1865, in Randolph County. They are here in household 81-1870 census with both Forrester girls and a son of their own, Napolean. By the 1880 census Susan had married John Clinton Carter and Julie had married Edward Butler with no signs of John and Mary Ewing.

2. Sarah Virginia, born about 1840, married Lafayette Crim/Grimm, June 14, 1866, Randolph County, Arkansas.

3. Robert, born about 1842, enrolled September 10, 1861, at Camp Price, Northeast Arkansas, Company A, 8th Arkansas Infantry.

4. Martha, born about 1846, married John A. Fry, January 14, 1866, Randolph County.

5. Thomas, born about 1848, married Permelia Poindexter, June 1, 1864, Randolph County. She is the daughter of Dandridge and Julia McDonald Poindexter. He marries second Charlotte "Lottie" Darter before 1873, in Lawrence County. Charlotte is the daughter of Hezekiah and Hannah Darter. Charlotte was married first to Wren Tisdale, July 23, 1865. They had James R. Tisdale, 1867; Emily Emma Tisdale, September, 1869; and William Tisdale. Thomas Nations in household 27-1880, married to Charlotte with two Nations children and one Tisdale child: John Shepherd Nation, born 1873, and Ella V. Nations, born 1874. Charlotte marries for the third time to George F. Weir, February 9, 1887. They are in household 26, Dent township in 1880. Thomas Nations either dies or they are divorced. George Weir was born 1849, married first to Martha J. Smith in 1871, died 1903, and is buried at Kelley Cemetery. George and Martha had five children: Margaret, born 1872; James F., born January 24, 1874, married Dora McLaughlin; William H., born Janu-

ary 24, 1876, married Dodie V.; Julie Elizabeth, born 1878, married James Laird; and George Robert Weir, born 1878, married Amanda Laird. George Weir marries the third time to Georgia Ann Dent, September 22, 1901. She is the daughter of William and Mary Dent.

Thomas Sr. marries Elizabeth. He died before September 9, 1873. –Mary Ann Carter.

ELIJAH FORRESTER

ELIJAH FORRESTER was born about 1826, in Smith, Tennessee. He was the son of James and Permelia Forrester Wayland. He moved to Lawrence County with his parents about 1830s, before coming to Randolph County. He entered the military in Smithville on June 18, 1846. He was a private in Company C, Gray's Battalion, Arkansas Volunteers in the Mexican War. He married Elizabeth Mitchell December 23, 1847, in Randolph County. Elizabeth was born in 1826, in Tennessee, probably Grainger County, to William F. Mitchell and Margaret Churchman. (I believe Margaret was a sister to Rebecca Churchman Perrin, mother of Delilah Perrin Carter and Naomi Perrin Butler. These two ladies were the mother of his two nieces, Susan and Julia Forrester's husbands, John W. Carter and Edward Butler.)

They had five children: James A., 1849; Martha P., 1851; Margaret J., 1852, married J. W. Burrow; William "Bud" Mitchell, 1855; and Mary Elizabeth, May 22, 1863. James Arthur dies either in Arkansas before going to Texas, or in Texas before 1860. William married Margaret Amanda Sharp. She was born 1856, daughter of Levi and Margaret Mcgeehee Sharp. They had 12 children, three of whom died young: Elijah Napoleon, November 9, 1877, married Leona Wells, June 25, 1904, died September 23, 1912, is buried Masonic County, Randolph County; Levi A., born December 24, 1879, married Mary C. East, December 23, 1905, died January 10, 1961, is buried Linwood, Paragould; Cordelia, born March 16, 1884, married John Million, October 2, 1904, died December 29, 1968, and is buried Masonic County, Randolph County; William, born September, 1881, married Louise Lucas, died 1961, buried Little Rock; Benjamin Frank, born July, 1885, married Ina Ward, 1914, died August 7, 1961, and is buried Oak Forrest; Grover Cleveland, born October 1, 1888, married Johnnie Janes, August 16, 1914, died September 16, 1967, and is buried Memorial Park, Jonesboro; Mary Isabel, born February 16, 1891, married Henry Simington, March 17, 1914, died May 16, 1985, and buried at Cross Cemetery; Emma, born April 22, 1895, married B. Frank Pettyjohn July 17, 1917; and Claudia O., born August, 1897. Mary Elizabeth, born May 22, 1863, in Imboden, married William Parker, June 18, 1885. He was born October 14, 1858, in Lake County, Tennessee. They had four children: William Arthur, buried beside his mother at Imboden; Robert Thurman, born October 5, 1888, married Grace Prow, died December 20, 1954, and is buried at Hillcrest Cemetery, Mountain Grove; Ida Mae, born May 5, 1890, married Walter Ward Tucker, February 17, 1906, and died April 22, 1973; and Marvin William, born April 12, 1893, married Nora Spurlock, December, 1917, died December 23, 1952, in Burbank, California. Mary dies April 12, 1893, and is buried at Imboden. The family moves to Mountain Grove, Missouri, where William dies November 11, 1913. Elijah died before July 11, 1882, and his wife, Elizabeth, after then because she tries for a land grant since Elijah fought in the Mexican War, but she dies before 1900 census. –Mary Ann Carter.

JAMES FORRESTER

JAMES FORRESTER, born in South Carolina or Tennessee. Elijah, his son, says he was born in Smith County. He entered the military for the Mexican War. James married Permelia before

1820. They moved to Lawrence County in the 1830s. James must have died before September 3, 1837, because Permelia married Navel/Nevil Wayland at that time in Lawrence County. She is listed in the 1840 census under his name with M 1 (15-20) Robert I (10-15) Charles 2 (15-20) Elijah and Absolom, F I (5-10) Sarah I (10-15) Anastasia I (15-20) Rebecca and I (0-5) a Wayland daughter or Forrester daughter who died before 1850.

James and Permelia's children are: Absolom, 1820; Rebecca, September 10, 1821; Elijah, 1825; Charles, 1827; Anastasia, 1829; Robert, 1831; and Sarah, 1835, last two born in Arkansas. Permelia is listed in household 579-1850 census Lawrence County, Spring River township under Wayland with four of her seven children. It was very hard finding this family especially since they were under Wayland and not Forrester.

Rebecca married James McCarroll, born November 11, 1817, Caldwell County, Kentucky, and lives in household 240 Randolph County with five of their six children: William, 1842; Andrew, 1843; John, 1846; Martha, 1847; and James, 1849. Charles was born in 1854. Elijah lived in Randolph household 513, married to Mary Elizabeth Mitchell and one son, James, 1849. Mary is the daughter of William and Margaret Churchman Mitchell of Grainger County, Tennessee. Elijah entered the military at Smithville, June 1846, Mexican War, Private in Company C, Gray's Battalion, Arkansas Volunteers. Charles is listed in household 581, Lawrence County under Foster married to Mary Jane Robertson. Robert married September, 1852, in Randolph County to Rosetta Manson, daughter of William and Elisabeth Crabtree Manson. He married June 21, 1858, Lawrence County to Mary Ellen Nations, daughter of Thomas and Martha Weathers Nations. They are in household 1353, Lawrence County with one daughter, Susan Marie, born April 15, 1859. Later, having their second daughter Julia Ellen, August 23, 1860. Permelia is in household 1351, Lawrence County with two daughters, Rebecca and Sarah, and five grandchildren. Absalom and Anastasia have either died, married or moved away. Elijah is in Kauffman, Texas with four children: Martha, 1851; Margaret, 1852; William Mitchell, 1854; and John, 1856. Charles has died before 1860, and his wife, Mary, also before February, 1859, because her brother, Thomas Jefferson Robertson, is legal guardian of their two children Narcissa, 1850; and Charles, 1852. Elijah Forrester becomes Charles' legal guardian in 1869. Sarah married James Turman of Kentucky and is in household with mother and sister Rebecca. Robert enters the Civil War and died from wounds, October 15, 1862, Holly Springs. Elijah Forrester finally becomes administrator of Robert's estate for his two nieces. By 1870, Permelia has either died or remarried because she has not been found. — *Mary Ann Carter.*

REBECCA FORRESTER, born September 10, 1821, in Tennessee, daughter of James and Permelia Forrester. They came to Lawrence County in the 1830s. Rebecca is listed in the 1840 census of Lawrence County with her mother and stepfather, Nevil Wayland. She married James A. McCarroll before 1850, in Lawrence County. James was born November 11, 1817, in Caldwell County, Kentucky. He died before 1860. They are in household 240 in Randolph County with five children: William, 1842; Andrew, 1844; John, 1846; Martha, 1848; and James, 1849. By 1860, Rebecca is a widow, and living with her mother in household 1351 in Lawrence County. Her son, John, has also died, but has a son, Charles, born July 23, 1854. William or James are not in the 1870 census. Andrew J., born September 4, 1843, married October 12, 1868, to Lucinda J. Milam of Tennessee. They have five children.

1. Robert, 1869.
2. Charles Wiley, born July 24, 1870, married Susan Angeline Ulmer, February 16, 1914. She is the daughter of John and Elizabeth Richey Ulmer. They had three children: Annie, 1915; Catherine, 1916; and Eugene, 1917. Charles died August 18, 1947, and is buried at Davis A.
3. John Henry, born June 21, 1871, married Minnie Roberson, 1893, and had 10 children: Darett; Clarence, 1895; Nancy, 1900; Clara, 1902; Beatrice, 1903; Notra, 1910; James Abb, 1916; Juanita, 1920; and Verlon, 1922. He died 1938, and is buried Davis A.
4. Mary, 1873.
5. Lucinda, born January 16, 1880, married before 1901, James A. Melton. They had six children: Mary, 1901; Franklin, 1903; Myrtle, 1905; Bertha, 1907; Henry, 1909; and Pearl, 1911. Lucinda died February 24, 1915, buried Brockett Cemetery, Randolph County.

Martha Pernesa Jane, born August 15, 1847, married James Pharoh McLaughlin October 13, 1872, He is son of Archabald McLaughlin. They had five children.

1. Thomas, born 1873, married Margaretta, 1896, and died 1938. He is buried at Fairview Cemetery, Randolph County.
2. Virginia, born 1878, not in 1900 census.
3. James, 1880, married after 1910, to Mary H. He died in 1949, and is buried at Fairview. They had Virginia, 1914; Bernard, 1915; and Samuel, 1916.
4. William, born 1882, married Johnnie after 1910, died 1954, and is buried Kelly Cemetery, Lawrence County.
5. Cora Rebecca, born 1885, died 1947, and is buried in Fairview Cemetery.

Charles Absolom, born July 22, 1854, married Ellen N. Cravens, January 10, 1875. He died April 21, 1937, and is buried at Fairview. They had six children.

1. Clara Rebecca, 1875, married before 1902, William Campbell Starr. Their children are: Claude, 1901; William, 1903; Virginia, 1906; John, 1909; Millard, 1911; and Lyerl, 1914.
2. James Andrew, born 1878, married Laura Weir.
3. John Ellison, 1880, died 1967, buried Black Rock. He married Virgil Ward.
4. Ida Jane, born 1882, married February 7, 1909, to John Sloan Forrester, her second cousin. He is the son of Charles and Sarah Weir Forrester. They had a son, Charles Jewell, born 1912. She died 1968, and is buried in Fairview Cemetery.
5. Robert Frank, born 1884, married Johnnie Ward. They had Lillian, 1914; Flossie, 1916; and Mollie, 1918.
6. Charles Whitaker, born 1886, married Mallissa Ellen Butler, second cousin, on September 13, 1909. They had Velmer, 1920. He died 1969, and is buried in Fairview Cemetery.

Rebecca was not on the 1880 census.
—*Mary Ann Carter.*

ROBERT FORRESTER is the fifth child of James and Permilia Forrester. He was born about 1833, in either Tennessee or Lawrence County, Arkansas. His father died before September, 1837, because his mother, Permelia, married Nevil Wayland on the third. They are in the 1840 census under Wayland and Permelia is again a widow by the 1850 census. She is in household 579, Spring River Township, with four of her seven Forrester children. Robert was listed as 19 years old and born in Arkansas. In 1860, after he was married to his second wife, he was listed as 27 years and born in Tennessee. He married Rosetta Manser, September 30, 1852, in Randolph County. She must have died because he married Mary Ellen Nation on June 21, 1858, in Lawrence

John Clinton and Susan Marie Forrester.

County. She was the daughter of Thomas and Martha S. Weathers Nations. She was born in Alabama. They are listed in household 1353, next to his widowed mother, Permilia, in Lawrence County, 1860. They had one daughter, Susan Marie, born April 15, 1859. They had another daughter, Julia Ellen, born August 23, 1860. Robert joined the military and fought in the Civil War as a private. He was in Company C, First Battalion. He appears on a list of killed, wounded and missing of Cabell's Brigade, in the Battle of Corinth and Natchie Bridge, Mississippi, wounded October 3-5, 1862. He died near Holly Springs, Mississippi, October 15, 1862, from the wounds.

In August of 1863, Thomas Nations applied for administrator of the estate of Robert Forrester. In June, 1866, his brother, Elijah Forrester, applied for guardianship of his two nieces of the late Robert Forrester. In April, 1867, Elijah again went to court saying that Thomas Nations was wasting the estate of said Robert Forrester and asked to be the administrator of the girls' estate. It appears he was finally successful, because he sold some of Robert's property at different times for the girls' welfare. Susan Marie married March 15, 1877, in Randolph County to John Clinton Carter. He was born October 15, 1856, in the Birdell Community of Randolph County. He was the son of John W. "William" and Delilah Perrin Carter. They had 10 children: John Robert, Mary Elizabeth "Lizzie", Benjamin Franklin, Ader, Dora, Ider, Eli Burley, Edgar William, Iva and Florence Delia. They lived in Birdell, Roanoke Township. They were of the Baptist faith. Susan died January 16, 1931, and John, June 27, 1943. They are buried at Sutton Cemetery, Randolph County. Julia Ellen married August 18, 1877, in Randolph County to Edward F. Butler. He was born January 8, 1854. He was the son of John W. and Naoma Perrin Butler. Naoma and Delila were sister, daughters of Joab and Rebecca Churchman Perrin of Grainger County, Tennessee. They had six children: Rosetta, George, Vennis Viola, Naomi, Mary Leona and Malissa Ellen. They lived in Imboden, Spring River Township. They were of the Baptist faith. Edward died April 11, 1889, and July, January 16, 1931. They are buried at Fairview Cemetery, Randolph County. —*Mary Ann Carter.*

FORTENBERRY FAMILY. The Fortenberrys were among the original settlers of Lawrence County, arriving from southeastern Missouri between 1810 and 1815. This pioneer family included Jacob Fortenberry, 1789-1862, who settled on Reeds Creek at the site of present day Lancaster Cemetery; Jacob's parents, James Leath and Margaret Fortenberry; and Jacob's siblings: Margaret Raney, Mary Taylor and Henry Fortenberry and their families. Margaret and Samuel Raney settled on Coopers Creek - later the Turnbow farm. Mary and William Taylor settled on Strawberry River where the Taylor Mill stood until 1983, about two miles east of Jesup, and Henry settled on Dota Creek, now in Independence County.

Per Stanley Arnold, genealogist, the Fortenberry family came from Germany (name was Falkenberg) via Sweden in the late 1500s, and settled in New Jersey about 1650. (*The Fortenberry Family of Northeastern Arkansas*, Stanley W. Arnold Jr., 1992.) The journey to Arkansas over the next 150 years took the family to Virginia, the Carolinas, Tennessee and finally, Missouri soon after the Louisiana Purchase in 1803.

Sevier and Nancy Walker Barnett Fortenberry, 1845-1931.

The Fortenberrys became a large family. Several moved to Texas after 1850, including five of Jacob and Nancy Taylor Fortenberry's children. Their other three children, Taylor, James and Matilda Childers, lived all their lives in Lawrence County. Walter McLeod wrote in 1936 "The Fortenberrys have been and are among Lawrence County's most respected citizens. They are outstanding for their industry, thrift, independence and general respectability." (*Centennial Memorial History of Lawrence County*, Walter E. McLeod, 1936.)

The continuance of the Fortenberry family name in Lawrence County was mainly through Taylor Fortenberry, 1813-1865, oldest son of Jacob and Nancy Fortenberry.

Sevier Fortenberry, 1845-1931, son of Taylor and Jane Cravens Fortenberry, served in the

Mary (Polly) Fortenberry Penn.

Confederate Army, Sevier Fortenberry married Walker Barnett, whose mother was from the Finley family, also Lawrence County pioneers. Sevier and Walker began their life together in 1871, on the Strawberry River, one mile downstream from the Lynn-Strawberry Bridge. Later, they lived two miles southeast of Smithville on the David Wagster farm (now Webster Goff's farm). In 1889, Sevier and Walker moved to Smithville, buying the Jim Sloan home. Sevier and his brother, Jacob, took over the ownership/operation of the Fortenberry Mercantile Company. Sevier and Walker were charter members of the Smithville Cumberland Presbyterian Church in 1896.

Sevier and Walker's children included James (Uncle Jim) Taylor Fortenberry, 1875-1945, politician, farmer and assistant professor; Newton (Uncle Newt) Fortenberry, 1884-1971; and Dot Fortenberry, 1892-1962, who owned the Ford Company in Imboden with their brother-in-law, Herman Kaiser. Newt and Dot also farmed and Dot was Imboden Postmaster. Other children were Mattie, Jane, Fred, Crete and Mae Fortenberry Kaiser, 1880-1973, whose daughter, Mary Crabtree, now lives in Imboden.

This Fortenberry sketch based upon the Fortenberry Family in Arkansas, by John and Maxine Fortenberry, Little Rock, Arkansas, 1997.
–John Fortenberry.

CLARA MAE DAVIS FOSTER

CLARA MAE DAVIS FOSTER was born on January 17, 1901, at Roscoe, St. Clair County, Missouri, to Jacob Maloney and Hannah Jane Mills Davis, former residents of Moultrie County, Illinois.

The Davis family moved frequently, traveling from eastern Illinois through Missouri, Kansas, and Nebraska. Their plan was to migrate to Montana or Wyoming, but after losing their crops to the drought and then the grasshoppers in the mid 1880s, they returned east. They began their trip east, but after entering Missouri, they went to St. Clair County, where Hannah's brother, Mike Mills, had settled. Hannah Davis died there on October 29, 1904, of diptheria, leaving Jacob with sev-

Charley and Clara Foster, 1930.

eral small children including Clara and her infant sister, Ada. Hannah is buried in the Pleasant Springs Cemetery at Roscoe, Missouri.

Jacob later married Mrs. Ida Mathis, a widowed neighbor with three sons.

In the spring of 1911, Jacob moved his family by covered wagon and an oxen team to Craighead County, Arkansas, west of Egypt. Here they built a home and homesteaded. The family remained until the 1920s, when they moved to a farm south west of Sedgwick, Arkansas.

On March 26, 1921, Clara Davis married Charley Foster. Charlie died of pneumonia on April 18, 1942.

Jacob Davis died at his daughter's home on June 22, 1941, and is buried in the Arnold Cemetery near Swifton.

Clara never remarried and continued to farm alone. She later bought a farm near Sedgwick and with the assistance of her nephew, Dowell Foster, and his wife, Virgie, she continued to farm until her retirement in the mid 1950s, when she sold her farm and moved into Sedgwick.

Clara never had children of her own, but delighted in the frequent visits of her many nieces and nephews, many who simply rode the school bus to her home and made the trip to the field in search of her. They were always treated with bread pudding, apple butter or some other wonderful treat; then they were privileged to be able to listen to her radio, before climbing the steps into her high feather bed.

Clara was a talented seamstress and quilted beautiful quilts. Fall visits to her home were usually rewarded with gifts of fancy snuff glasses and delicious peanuts she had grown and roasted herself. She was a simple woman, and always wore her long hair in a braid wrapped around her head underneath the always present bonnet.

Clara Davis Foster died in Sedgwick on January 22, 1985. She is buried beside her husband, Charley, in the Arnold Cemetery near Swifton, Arkansas. –Barbara Howard.

FREEMAN FAMILY

FREEMAN FAMILY. Relatively new to Lawrence County, Arkansas, the Freeman clan arrived between 1915 and 1917. Heading south from Ozark County, Missouri by horse drawn covered wagon, Willis Garfield Freeman, his wife Della and their eight children crossed the Black River at Powhatan, Arkansas.

The story handed down from one generation to the next alleges that the ferryman at the Black River crossing joked with the couple about having so many children that they could easily lose one. This is exactly what happened. Once the ferry pulled away from the shore, Della and Willis noticed their son, Lester, throwing rocks into the river from the west bank. The friendly ferryman thought the couple were continuing the jest and didn't tend to believe them at first. Finally, upon convincing the ferry operator that they really had left one of their children behind, the ferry returned to the shore to rejoin the playful youngster with his family.

A week after the wagon train began; the Freeman clan made their first home in Lawrence County in the Strangers Home Community near Alicia. Making a living by farming, the large family continued to expand with the birth of two more children.

The original members of the settling family included:

Willis Garfield Freeman, born March 20, 1882, in Thayer, Missouri, died February 12, 1960, in Jonesboro, Arkansas.

Della L. Workman Freeman was born March, 1885, in Ozark County, Missouri.

They were married in Missouri in 1899. Their children were:

1. William Isaac Freeman, born December 20, 1901, in Ozark County, Missouri, died June 14, 1989, in Walnut Ridge, Arkansas.

2. Arie B. Freeman "R.B.", born August 21, 1903, in Missouri, died June 11, 1968, in Hoxie, Arkansas.

3. Jesse Claude Freeman, born February 24, 1905, in Missouri, died March 29, 1991, in Walnut Ridge, Arkansas.

4. Estel N. Freeman, born December 4, 1906, in Missouri, and died 1923, in Arkansas.

Willis Garfield and Della L. Workman Freeman. Apprx. 1920.

5. Josie Ann Freeman, born December 3, 1908, in Missouri, died July 30, 1950, in Steele, Missouri.

6. Dorothy Freeman, born April 9, 1911, in Missouri, and died in 1917.

7. Lester Freeman, born February 9, 19193, in Missouri, died February 27, 1991, in Swifton, Arkansas.

8. Doshe Chloe Freeman, born February 21, 1915, in West Plains, Missouri, and died October 14, 1995, in Walnut Ridge, Arkansas.

9. Lesley Arno Freeman, born July 10, 1917, in Alicia, Arkansas. Currently resides in Paragould, Arkansas.

10. Cecil Harding Freeman, born February 19, 1923, in Arkansas, and died January 25, 1950, in Jonesboro, Arkansas.

Many descendants of the original family have since migrated across the United States, mostly in search of gainful employment. There are currently Freeman descendants in the Illinois, Arizona, Massachusetts, California, Georgia, Tennessee, Michigan, Alabama, Indiana and South Carolina. A copy of the most recent family tree is available at the Lawrence County Historical Powhatan Courthouse. The latest edition includes the original settlers through their great-great-great-grandchildren. Attempts to research the Freeman family tree further into history have been hampered due to lack of information and records that were destroyed during the Civil War. Strangers Home remains the family cemetery and a good source of family history.

Freeman descendants who currently reside in Lawrence County include:

William Troy Freeman of Walnut Ridge and Bobby Gene Freeman of Ravenden, who are the descendants of William Isaac Freeman.

Lesley Reginald "Reggie" Freeman of Black Rock, descendant of Lesley Arno Freeman.

Jerry Lee Moore of Portia, Glenda Gereline Moore Johnston of Portia, and Billie Gail Moore Dunlap (Lawrence County Clerk from 1989-present) of Walnut Ridge, who are the descendants of Doshe Chloe Freeman Moore.

There are also several great and great-great-grandchildren living in Lawrence County.

The annual Freeman family reunion is held in Lawrence county at an Arkansas State Park each year on the Sunday of Memorial Day weekend.

—Judith E. Freeman on May 18, 1999.

Willis Garfield Freeman and his first wife, Della L. Workman freeman, approximately 1920. —*Judi Freeman.*

ISAAC FRISBEE FAMILY. Isaac Frisbee was born in Tennessee. He died about 1880, and is buried at Dent Cemetery, Lawrence County, Arkansas. According to the 1880 census, he was a physician; his father born in North Carolina; mother Tennessee. Children: Louiza C., born 1853, Kentucky, married Henry Phillips; Robert L.; Erwin P.; Isaac Lonnie; and Nancy A. Frisbee.

Robert L. Frisbee, born August 8, 1859, Missouri, died July 21, 1938; and is buried at Friendship Cemetery, Lawrence County, Arkansas; he married Martha Matilda Fuller in 1879. She was born August 31, 1861, Kentucky; and died April 21, 1937, at Lawrence County, Arkansas. Robert and Matilda did not have children.

Erwin P. Frisbee, born about 1863, in Arkansas, married Martha Fannie in 1885. She was born November 23, 1868; she died November 11, 1946; and is buried at Friendship Cemetery, Lawrence County, Arkansas. Chil-

Ray E. and Myrtle Frisbee Brown.

dren: Ada Belle; Myrtle, born about 1904, Arkansas; and Dennie, born about 1905, Arkansas.

Isaac Lonnie Frisbee, born August 16, 1867, Missouri, died January 9, 1930; he is buried at Friendship Cemetery, Lawrence County, Arkansas; he married Josephine Louisa Ratliff, daughter of Zachaeus Ratliff and Martha Margret Underwood, on March 10, 1887. Children: Lillie; Cleo T.; Garlin, born September 10, 1895, Arkansas, died October 28, 1895; William, born about 1898, Arkansas; Elmer Isaac; and Earnest B.

Nancy A. Frisbee, born about 1872, Missouri, married Thomas J. Rice on August 25, 1893, in Lawrence County, Arkansas.

Ada Belle Frisbee, born about 1894, in Lawrence County, Arkansas; buried at Sharp Cemetery, Lawrence County, Arkansas; married a Mr. Barker.

Lillie Frisbee, born about 1892, in Lawrence County, Arkansas, and married Royal B. Wood; born August 15, 1911, in Lawrence County, Arkansas.

Cleo T. Frisbee, born June 24, 1893, in Lawrence County, Arkansas, died October 13, 1971; buried at Friendship Cemetery, Lawrence County, Arkansas; he married Lora Patterson on March 13, 1921, at Lawrence County, Arkansas; she was born April 29, 1894, died October 4, 1973; she is buried at Friendship Cemetery, Lawrence

County, Arkansas. Children: Virgil, born June 15, 1915, at Lawrence County, Arkansas, died June 15, 1915; buried at Friendship Cemetery, Lawrence County, Arkansas.

Elmer Isaac Frisbee, born about 1903, died about 1932, in Lawrence County, Arkansas; he is buried at Friendship Cemetery, Lawrence County, Arkansas; married Hettie Rexroad, daughter of Jake and Bertie Honey Rexroad, on December 24, 1919, at Lawrence County, Arkansas; Hettie was born June 26, 1901; she died April 24, 1970, at Lawrence County, Arkansas; she is buried at Friendship Cemetery, Lawrence County, Arkansas. Children: Myrtle Ethel; Cruse Lavern, born March 28, 1925, died March 12, 1986, buried at Friendship cemetery; Henrietta. After Elmer died, Hettie married a Mr. Hon.

Earnest B. Frisbee, born October 15, 1903, at Lawrence County, Arkansas, died May 6, 1980, at Lawrence County, Arkansas; he is buried at Opposition Cemetery, Lawrence County, Arkansas. He married Alene V. Lawrence, born October 20, 1906, died December 29, 1989, at Lawrence County, Arkansas; he is buried at Opposition Cemetery, Lawrence County, Arkansas. Alene was the daughter of Lucius and Lizzie Pickett Lawrence.

Myrtle Ethel Frisbee, born January 2, 1922, at Walnut Ridge, Arkansas, died January 2, 1990; she married Ray Edgar Brown, son of Joseph Alfred Brown and Nettie Eva Oldham, on April 23, 1937, at Walnut Ridge, Arkansas; Ray was born September 1, 1919, at Marked Tree, Arkansas; he died April 12, 1992. Both are buried at Lawrence Memorial Cemetery, Walnut Ridge, Arkansas. Children: Joe, Jim, Bonnie, Carolyn, Evia, Henrietta and Terry. (Also see Ratliff and Underwood families.) — *Bonnie Smith.*

JOHN L. FRY FAMILY. John Leondus Fry was born August 9, 1863, near Ravenden Springs, Arkansas, in Randolph County. His parents were Leonidas "Lee" and Nancy Jane Jones Fry.

Lee Fry was born June 13, 1836, in Tennessee. His mother was Martha Fry. His father is not known. Jane was born in Arkansas in 1836. The names of her parents are unknown. Martha Fry was born in Tennessee in 1813. She had seven children all born in Tennessee.

About 1854, the family left Carroll County, Tennessee, and went to Missouri. They stayed there a few years before moving to Randolph County, Arkansas.

Lee and Jane were married July 10, 1859, in Randolph County. They had 10 children, who all married and lived in the Ravenden Springs area for most of their lives.

Martha Fry married Peter Puckett in October of 1862. Martha died sometime between 1890 and 1900.

The second son born to Lee and Jane was named John Leondus. The spelling of his father's name varied from Leonidas to Leondus. The family pronounced it Lee-on-dus.

John L.'s first wife, Laura Barber, died young, leaving him with two small sons, Will and Tom. John L. married Mary Ladyman on December 24, 1888. They had five children: Jessie Mae, Herbert, Almus Witt, Gussie and Vera Blanche. Almus died as an infant and Gussie died in her late teens.

Jessie married Robert Woodson. Herbert's wife was Maizie. They settled in Texas. Vera married Clarence Lawson.

As a young man, John L. was a teacher in the hill country around Ravenden Springs. In his 40s, he began his ministry for the Church of Christ. He was well known for his fiery debates for the gospel.

He was also a lawyer, handling mostly civil cases. He made two unsuccessful bids for representative of Lawrence County. He served as Lawrence County Surveyor for a time, but his life's work was preaching. John L. moved to Lawrence County in the early 1920s. He purchased a large portion of land which is now in Northeast Walnut Ridge. He donated the land for the first Church of Christ in Walnut Ridge. Mary died in 1928. She is buried in Lawrence Memorial Park. In the early 1930s, John L. married Ella Gilmore, a widow. She survived him many years, living to be over 100 years old. John L. died January 1, 1939. He is buried at Lawrence Memorial Park in Walnut Ridge. His many descendants are spread from New Jersey to California.

Mary Ladyman was born March 1, 1869, in Ravenden Springs, Arkansas. She was the daughter of Benjamin Ladyman and Cathleen Hall. Ben was born in Tennessee and Cathleen was born in Missouri.

The Ladymans came to America sometime before 1778. They were in Maryland until about 1810, before moving into North Carolina. From about 1830, until around 1854, they were in Tennessee.

They left Weakley County, Tennessee, and lived in Missouri for a while prior to moving down to Randolph County, Arkansas. —*Diane Neldon.*

GAINES. The first Gaines immigrant, Thomas, came to America in 1641. He is the son or grandson of Sir John Gaines of Brecon Brecons, Wales.

Thomas settled in Virginia. There were several Gaines families in the area, so it is difficult to know which ones were the ancestors who eventually came to Lawrence County.

The Gaines ancestors moved into North Carolina and then into Tennessee. William E. Gaines was born in Tennessee in 1823. His father was Wilson and his mother Catherine. They had about 10 children; William was the third son.

By the early 1800s, they were living in Weakley County, near the Kentucky border.

William E. married Elizabeth R. Maxwell about 1849. She was born in Tennessee in 1832. William's sister, Susannah, married Joseph Ladyman.

About 1853, William E. and his family, his brother, Ira, Susannah and her family, the Ladymans and the Maxwells all left Tennessee. They stopped in southeastern Missouri for a few years. Ira married there and William's first son, John Wilson, was born in Stoddard County, near Dexter on December 6, 1854.

By 1860, the whole assembly of Gaines, Maxwells and Ladymans had moved to Randolph County, Arkansas.

William E., Ira, and Joseph Ladyman joined the Confederate forces at Pocahontas in 1862.

Elizabeth died about 1865-66. William married Elizabeth Wells, a widow with four children, in December of 1866.

William and his second wife both died in the early 1870s, leaving John W. to raise his younger brothers and sisters. He did not marry until they were grown up. On February 19, 1885, he married Louticia Jane Bell, in Davidson Township of Randolph County.

Between 1860 and 1900, the family moved from Randolph County, Arkansas to Oregon County, Missouri, several times.

John and Lou had seven children that reached adulthood. Ollie Adolphus and Elzada Jane married brother and sister, Beulah and John Hall; Edward Allen, married Effie Ring; Everette Roy married Carlas Beavers; Nola Edna and Maudie Ella married brothers, Troy and Lee Davis; and Cecil Lloyd, married Melva Woodson.

In the early 1900s, the family moved into the Richwoods Community of Lawrence County. For many years all the children and their families lived in the Richwoods and Portia area.

About 1925, John, Lou and Cecil moved to Walnut Ridge. Lou died in 1934, and John died in 1936. They are buried in Jenkins Cemetery.

Elza and John Hall settled in central California. Everette and Carlas lived in Arizona before moving to California, also. The other Gaines children remained in and around Lawrence County for the rest of their lives. –Bobby and Sharon Schmidt.

CECIL GAINES FAMILY. Cecil Lloyd Gaines was born March 30, 1908, near Portia, Arkansas in Lawrence County. He was the son of John Wilson and Luticia Jane Bell Gaines. Cecil married Melva Mae Woodson on August 25, 1928.

Melva was the daughter of Robert Franklin Perry and Jessie Mae Fry Woodson. She was born September 17, 1913, in Lawrence County, Arkansas.

Cecil and Melva lived in several places around the county as they struggled to raise their large family. Cecil worked at a variety of jobs. At one time he was a mechanic at Webb's Garage in Walnut Ridge. He also worked for the Smith Brothers as a bulldozer operator, he dug stock ponds all over the hills. For several years before he retired, he worked for the city of Walnut Ridge as the trash truck driver.

Cecil was an excellent hunter, he would bring home game for every shell he took with him, he didn't believe in wasting ammunition. Cecil played a little music; guitar and harmonica. His loved of music was inherited by most of his children, with some of them playing instruments and some being singers.

The family moved to Walnut Ridge in 1953. They lived next door to Melva's Aunt V and her husband, Clarence Lawson. There were many good times with Melva's sisters and various cousins and friends. The "gang" would gather at V's house for coffee and fun several times a month.

Melva stayed home and "rocked the babies." She had a green thumb and always had a beautiful plants. She sewed some for the girls and herself. Melva loved to read and passed this love down to most of her children. She taught Sunday School at the Missionary Baptist Church and she was active in the Senior Citizens group before her health failed. Melva had a good sense of humor and loved to dance when she was young. She lived by her own rule, "if you can't say something nice about someone, don't say anything at all."

Melva and Cecil had 11 children.

1. Lloyd Beauford, born 1929, married Vivian Corey; children:
   a) Virginia Lee married Marty Peterson (divorced).
   b) Nancy Ann married Charles Neuman, children: Christopher, Lauren and Catherine.
   c) Patricia Sue married Grant Cunningham; children; married Brian Pulson; Corey and Anna.
   d) Kenneth Lloyd married Elysia Bowman.
2. Bobby Allen, born 1931, married Joan Carey; twin sons:
   a) Robert Allen Jr. married Lynda Fuller; child: Jessica.
   b) Roger Lee, born and died 1953.
3. Rexie Ray, born and died 1932.
4. Jerry Lawson, born 1939, married Sandra Lomas; children:
   a) Shelly Jo Ann married Timothy Winegar; children: Daniel, Christian and Ethan.
   b) Jeffrey Lawson.
5. Sharon Jean, born 1942, married Bobby Schmidt; children:
   a) Theresa Kaye married Michale Brinkman; children: Adam and Vanessa.

b) Lorita Denise married Michael Hunt; children: Melissa married Steven Darrah; child: Katelin; Jeremy and Matthew.
   c) Marcy Ann married Jeffrey Brinkman; children: Jamie and Nicole.
   d) Paula Suzanne married Brian Thienes; children: Kimberly and Michelle.
   e) Kevin Robert married Tania Driver; children: Kevin Jr. and David.
6. Linda Faye, born 1947, married Ed Clifford (divorced); children:
   a) Edward Arthur Jr.
   b) Christina Suzanne married Bill Scott; child: Trevor.
7. David Woodson, born 1949, married Trudy Wynn, no children.
8. Diana Mae, born 1952, married Don Neldon (divorced); children:
   a) Brandon Heath; child: Keegan, Joshua Neil.
   b) Twins; Don Benjamin and John David.
9. Rodney Gale (twin), born 1954, married Doty Blackwell; children:
   a) Rodney Eric.
   b) Lisa.
10. Randall Dale (twin), born 1954, married Linda Middlecoff; child:
   a) Michael Allen married LaDonya Riggs; child: Gage.
11. Vicki Renee', born 1957, married Sam Brandon (divorced); children:
   a) Samuel.
   b) William.
   c) Jedidiah.

Lloyd died February, 1996, in Winnebago, Illinois. Vicki died January, 1995, in a traffic accident near Pocahontas, Arkansas.

Cecil passed away July 17, 1980, in Walnut Ridge and Melva followed him April 4, 1991, in Walnut Ridge. They are buried at Lawrence Memorial Park. –Sharon Schmidt.

GARDNER FAMILY. According to family records, John H. R. G. Gardner, 1810-1876, migrated from Tennessee in 1841, to Lawrence County. In 1830, in Tennessee, he married Susan Evens, 1813-1894; and in 1833, was ordained an elder in the Baptist faith at Hickory Creek United Baptist Church in Knox County, Tennessee. John H. R. G. and Susan were the parents of eight children. After reaching Arkansas, the Gardners bought many acres of land which they farmed, growing hundreds of fruit trees. Although all three sons of the Gardners served with the Confederate Army during the Civil War, the family owned no slaves. One son, Josiah S., born 1842, died in January of 1863, of gunshot wounds received in the Battle of Murfreesboro. Like his two brothers, he enlisted with the First Arkansas Volunteers in 1861, and later served with Company E, 11th Arkansas Infantry Battalion.

Quoting from a Jackson County Historical Society publication, "Elder Gardner and his family, along with most families, suffered hard times during and immediately after the Civil War. With the first bale of cotton he was able to produce after the war, Elder Gardner started for Jacksonport, where he was able to sell the valuable commodity and purchase some of the things he had lost during the war. For his wife, he bought a beautiful set of china. Three pieces of this same set have made their way back to Jacksonport. They were generously given to the Jacksonport Courthouse Museum by Elder and Mrs. Gardner's granddaughter, Beulah Shaver Murphy."

Elder Gardner died in 1876, at age 66. A quote from his obituary states, "Elder Gardner was one of the first to raise the Baptist standard in Arkansas, having preached successfully for 33 years, 32 years pastor of Bold Spring Church. He was a bright star of the church, esteemed by all, faithful

in all his ministerial life. According to his memorandum book, he baptized about 2700 persons. He was not only a good preacher, but among one of the best pastors; has been moderator of different associations for 27 years, and was one among the best men." He is buried in Sharp County. His wife, Susan, died in 1894, at age 81.

Robert B. was born in 1836, in Tennessee and was the first son born to John H. R. G. and Susan Gardner. He served in the Confederate Army during the Civil War, enlisting first in 1861, in Company E., First Arkansas Volunteers. His last enlistment in July, 1862, was with Company B, 38th Arkansas Infantry. Robert and his wife, Mary A., were the parents of 10 children. Their seventh child, John Lee Gardner, was born February 16, 1874. John Lee, who died of pneumonia at age 30, was my grandfather. He was married to Sarah Ann Raney in 1896. (See Raney History.) – Yvonne Saeger.

JERRY D. GIBBENS FAMILY. When I was born on August 20, 1942, the United States was at war with Japan and Germany. My parents, William Amon, born June 27, 1908, and Lorene Mae McCarroll, born January 3, 1914, were living in Randolph County in the Spring River Community. My earliest memories are living on a farm near Imboden in a large Victorian, two-story house with a wraparound porch. I recall my mother learning to drive our black 1938 Plymouth. One day she told my sister, Shirley, and me that she would drive us to the highway, a half mile away, to get the mail and that we would wash the car in the creek between our house and Highway 412. After washing the car, the Plymouth would not start and Mother cried and said her driving days were over. When my father came in from working, he took his horse and pulled the Plymouth out of the creek. He insisted that mother continue with her driving!

Other early memories include driving on the gravel road to Powhatan, crossing the wooden bridge, shopping in Walnut Ridge at Krogers, smelling the coffee beans roasting and the

Jerry and Barbara Gibbens, seated. Julie and Sarah Gibbens Glenn, standing.

cashews toasting at the "Dime" store. One day at the Sterling store, Mother bought me a porcelain pig flower pot and I insisted on carrying it. Just outside the door of the store I dropped the pig and broke it. Mother was so kind, slightly scolding me, but she returned and bought me another pig, which she later gave to my older daughter, Julie - starring a pig "collection."

I was seven years old when our house was wired for electricity. I remember listening to a battery operated radio, sitting by a kerosene and later an "Aladdin" lamp, watching mother wash her clothes on a rub board, carefully rinsing the clothes twice, running them through the "blue" water, and starching everything except the towels! Mother washed on Monday and ironed on Tuesday. Every Sunday we had a starched tablecloth and napkins and mother "set the table" in her best china and flatware. We often hosted the preacher from the Mount Vernon Church or we ate lunch with my grandparents, John and Virgie McCarroll, in Black Rock. Every Sunday was a family reunion with my Aunt Jessie, Aunt Gussie, Uncle Vernon, Uncle John and all my cousins.

My mother was and is a "classy" lady who created beauty from leftovers or scraps, making pillow cases, shirts, skirts, draperies and underwear from our feed and flour sacks. She looked at pictures in the Sears catalog and made dresses or suits and she slip covered chairs and sofas. She wall papered, made a garden and canned blackberries, pickles, green beans or corn. Mother dried our peaches and apples on a tin sheet of roofing material and we had "fried pies." Daddy grew peanuts and popcorn and butchered hogs and "salt down" our meat in the smokehouse. We always had lots to eat, warm, stylish clothes to wear and though we lived an isolated life in rural Arkansas, I never felt poor. Mother always had a hillside full of chickens and we always milked several cows, selling our cream and bartering our eggs at Dee Cude's grocery store for sugar, flour, tea and coffee. In the summer, I picked blackberries and in the fall when school dismissed I picked cotton, buying my school clothes.

I started school when I was five at Mount Vernon. My teacher was Mrs. Carson. Since mother had taught me to read, "Miss Carson" quickly promoted me to the second grade. The next year my parents sent Shirley and me to Black Rock School where I graduated at age 16 in 1959. At school I dreaded when the county health nurse came and gave "shots" for polio, whooping cough, or smallpox, but mother always insisted that we "line up" and get whatever shot was being given. My parents encouraged me to be involved in school activities and provided me with money for school trips to Little Rock, Memphis or Jonesboro. They also bought me a piano and gave me piano lessons with Mrs. Pattye Townsend, another "classy lady" who smiled and encouraged me. I was a voracious reader and loved when the "bookmobile" came to the public schools with a new supply. I am thankful that I was 14 when we bought our first television.

When I entered Williams (Southern) Baptist College in 1959, I met Barbara Mitchell from Stone County, Arkansas. After I graduated from Arkansas State University in May, 1963, and after Barbara graduated from the University of Central Arkansas, we were married on August 10, 1963. We taught in the Arcadia Valley Schools in Ironton, Missouri, until 1967, when I accepted a position at Williams Baptist College and Barbara began teaching fourth grade in Walnut Ridge. I am the chair of the Division of Arts and Sciences at WBC and Professor of English. Barbara retired after 34 years of teaching in 1998.

Barbara and I have two daughters: Julie Anne, born February 10, 1967, a graduate of Williams Baptist, Ouachita Baptist University, and the University of Arkansas School of Law. She is a corporate attorney with Wal Mart in Bentonville. Sarah Elizabeth, born August 2, 1970, is also a graduate of Williams Baptist and has a Master's degree in Physical Therapy from the University of Central Arkansas. Sarah married Ronald James Glenn in March, 1995. They live in Mountain Home and are Physical Therapists at Baxter County Hospital.

Barbara and I have witnessed many changes in life-styles and technology. Having been born during World War II, our lives have changed dramatically. We were fortunate to grow up in strong Christian families. We received excellent educations in rural schools and small colleges. We have appreciated visiting in all the 48 contiguous states and in having visited Europe six times. *–Jerry Gibbens.*

JOHN FILMORE GIBBENS FAMILY. John Gibbens was born in 1800, and his wife Martha in 1802, in North Carolina. John and Martha moved from Rowan County, North Carolina, in 1835, to Shelby County, Tennessee and to Lawrence County, Arkansas, in the 1840s. They were the parents of seven children: William C., born 1827; Andrew Jack, 1829-1878; Jesse P.,

John Filmore Gibbens house made about 1912-1915, at Smithville, Arkansas. At left: Lillie Gibbens Massey; Delia Gibbens Norman; Robert Gibbens; Missouri Isabella Helms Gibbens; twin sons, Robert Amen and William Amon; and John Filmore Gibbens.

1831-1889; Ann J., born 1832; Martha, born 1834; Mary, born 1835; and Robert, born 1838.

Andrew Jack married Elizabeth McKnight, born October 29, 1838, in Arkansas in 1857. She died May 6, 1910. Andrew and Elizabeth were the parents of four children: John Filmore, October 29, 1858-April 8, 1931; Salena E., born 1860; Nellie Belle, born 1870; and Robert Franklin, 1874-April, 1944.

John Filmore married Missouri Isabella Helms, born January 17, 1867, on February 16, 1896. They were the parents of four children: Delia, Lillie and Robert and William. John Filmore died April 8, 1931; Isabella died on August 31, 1949. They are buried in Parks Cemetery near Smithville. Their large family portrait hangs in the Powhatan Courthouse Museum.

John Filmore raised a small patch of tobacco. First he burned a brush pile and planted his seeds in the ashes. The whole family chewed and smoked tobacco, including Grandmother Elizabeth and Isabella. John read the Bible and attended the Missionary Baptist Church. John and his brother, Robert, raised cotton, had cows and hogs, and planted cane. They made sorghum molasses. John and Robert belonged to the Odd Fellows Lodge at Annieville.

The Gibbens family always attended the annual Annieville picnic where they enjoyed the swings drawn with mules. Each year a band of 15 or 20 people, led by George Dent, marched through Smithville. The Gibbens children reported buying a two foot long whip and ball on a rubber string. The rides were five cents.

The Gibbens family did not drink tea, but they enjoyed coffee, buying green coffee beans, roasting the beans and grinding their coffee. Their "typical" meal consisted of dried beans, cornbread or biscuits, gravy, salted pork meat, smoked in the smokehouse, and vegetables. They raised a large garden and canned food during the summer. Isabella grew grapes and brewed her own special brand of wine - always used medicinally!

The Smithville Community had telephones; each family paying dues, after the men had built the poles and installed the line. Mrs. Barnett was the telephone operator. John Filmore and Isabella never owned a radio or automobile, but they homesteaded a section of land. They purchased a pump organ and Delia and Lillie played.

At Christmas time, the Gibbens family did not put up a tree, but they did sing carols and they had

fruit and nuts and visited with their extended family. Lillie and Delia received dolls one Christmas after their "Aunt Sis" tried playing Santa Claus, but the girls recognized her "bad finger nail." The family often killed turkeys and squirrels.

John and Isabella's daughter, Delia, was born November 27, 1896. She died January 28, 1965. Delia married George Norman on January 5, 1915. Their children were: Shelby, 1916-1983; Ethel, born 1918; Eva, 1920-1997; Georgia Evelyn, born 1923; Helen Ilene, born 1927; and Charles, born 1935.

Lillie, born February 9, 1898, married J. Robert Massey on April 6, 1930. Lillie died on December 25, 1991, and Robert died in June, 1959. They are buried in Parks Cemetery near Smithville. On January 6, 1936, they became parents of twin daughters: Erma and Edna. Erma married Ewen Frisbee and they are the parents of three daughters: Joyce, Imogene and Judy. Edna married Gene Dixon and they have two daughters: Linda and Lisa.

Robert Amen married Freddie East on December 3, 1932. Robert died November 30, 1987, and Freddie died December 4, 1978. They are buried in Parks Cemetery near Smithville. Their son, Bobby Joe Gibbens, born August 25, 1933, lives in Hendersonville, North Carolina, with his wife, Viola, and they are the parents of three children: Ronald, Gina and Dennis. Their second son, Charles Jesse "C.J." Gibbens, was born October 9, 1936, and lives in Sycamore, Illinois. C. J. is married to Donna and they have three children: Leslie, Sheri and Larry.

William Amon married Lorene Mae McCarroll, born January 3, 1914, on December 23, 1936. They are the parents of two children: Shirley Mae, born February 25, 1939, was married to Carl Hester. She has a son, Chip Ford; and Jerry D., born August 20, 1942, is married to Barbara Mitchell and they are the parents of two daughters: Julie Anne, born February 11, 1967, and Sarah Elizabeth, born August 2, 1970. William Amon died October 29, 1972, and is buried in Oak Forest Cemetery in Black Rock. *–Jerry Gibbens.*

JOHN SHEPHERD GIBSON, better known as Shep, was the second of three sons of John H. and Sarah Gibson. Born in Arkansas on September 16, 1876, his first marriage was to Clara Rhea. They had two daughters, Lou and Juanita, but Clara died in 1907, before she was 25.

Mary Gillihan, a native of Viola in Fulton County, was born August 30, 1877. She was the daughter of Edmund Riley and Martha Franks Gillihan. After teaching school for several years, she moved to Black Rock to work in a mercantile business, Farmers Union Store, which was owned by Bob Rice, husband of Mary's sister, Nancy.

While working at the mercantile, Mary met Shep, who was also working there. They married on February 18, 1912, when she was 34 years old and he was 35. They had three children: Lorine, born 1913; Herman Nelson, born, 1916; and Bonnie Marie, born 1919.

Shep had several occupations. He was a photographer, a farmer, a hotel operator, a property landlord and a taxi driver at various times during his life. He

John Shepherd and Mary Gillihan Gibson.

made commercial photographs in the Black Rock area, during the early part of the century. He farmed 160 acres of row crops and pastureland near the Clear Springs Community, growing cotton, corn and cane, and raising hogs and cattle. He always found time for fishing, too, and often sold his larger catches.

Mary was a housekeeper and canned garden produce. She kept her canning on long shelves in the hallway which ran through their house. The couple seemed to manage money well. They paid 1,000 dollars cash for a brand new Ford Model T in the 1920s.

In about 1922, the couple heard about the prosperity of Hoxie due to the new railroad roundhouse. They moved there and borrowed money to buy the City Hotel. They operated the hotel and paid it off in about 15 months. They sold it for a profit, invested in some rent houses, and then moved back to Clear Springs. They managed the rental property, sold produce and engaged in other activities over the next several years.

Shep died in 1947, and was laid to rest at Holobaugh Cemetery. Mary lived until 1964, and was laid to rest at Oak Forest Cemetery.

–Tom Moore

JAMES GILBERT, born 1828, in Alabama, married Francis Jane Lawrence, born 1830, in Alabama are in Lawrence County, Arkansas in 1880. James is a farmer. Apparently this family had been in Arkansas in about 1860, as the older children were born in Arkansas and the younger children born in Missouri. Their children:

1. Thomas Gilbert, born about 1852, in Arkansas or Alabama, wife named Missouri.

2. Manerva J., born 1856, in Arkansas; married August 31, 1876, to James H. Gibbens.

3. George W. Gilbert, born about 1860, in Arkansas.

4. Sarah Ann Gilbert, born January 13, 1861, in Arkansas, married November 30, 1882, to James Lykrugious Hoffman Sr., son of Christopher M. and Catherine Bishop Hoffman. James, died in 1894. Sarah had her youngest son, James L. Jr., after her husband's death. Sarah then marrying second to Andrew Jackson Holder.

5. Elijah B. Gilbert, born about 1863, in Arkansas.

6. Silus W. Gilbert, born about 1865, in Missouri.

7. Maudora Gilbert, born about 1867, in Missouri.

8. Allie M. Gilbert, born about 1869, in Missouri, married February 17, 1889, to J. D. Stainaker in Lawrence County, Arkansas.

9. David J. Gilbert, born about 1871, in Missouri.

10. Cora Bell Gilbert, born about 1873 in Missouri, married January 8, 1893, to Joseph A. Matthews in Lawrence County, Arkansas.

11. James Gilbert, born about 1879, married

Sarah Gilbert Hoffman Holder, family and stepchildren.

September 24, 1899, married Zellie Davis in Lawrence County, Arkansas.

Any help with this family would be greatly appreciated by the submitter.

–Barbara Wright Miller, 211 W. Michigan Avenue, Clinton, Michigan 49236.

GLENN FAMILY. Although the Glenn family did not arrive in Lawrence County until after 1880, the tragic saga of their migration began before the Civil War. In 1857, Austin H. Glenn and his family of 10 children moved from Tennessee to Hunt County, Texas. A preacher and avowed unionist, Glenn's antislavery sentiments were not popular in eastern Texas, where feeling ran high both for and against the southern cause.

On a chilly night in March, 1863, Glenn was dragged from his home, "tried" and hanged on the banks of the Sabine River. Through the night, the Glenn women boiled water to throw on the attackers if they returned. It was their only defense. At dawn, Austin Glenn was hastily buried near the family home and the entire family fled Hunt County. According to family history, the little caravan did not stop until a wagon broke an axle in Arkansas.

Once they reached the relative safety of the union state of Missouri, three of the Glenn sons immediately joined the northern army. Two would be wounded in union service near Fort Smith. The third would be killed in the battle of Bayou Fourche, near Little Rock. The fourth and eldest son, Elias Turner Glenn, continued east with his own family, his mother and the three teenage girls. The family finally settled in Hamilton County, Illinois.

In 1875 Elias T. Glenn took out a federal land grant in Arkansas and shortly thereafter, moved to western Lawrence County. There he met and married his second wife, Margaret J. Foley. This union would result in six children, with some descendants still living in Lawrence County. Elias Glenn was a Baptist minister and both he and his wife placed a premium on education. In turn, many of their children, and their children's children, became teachers in Lawrence County schools for several decades.

The Glenn family was accompanied by their sister, Rhoda Glenn Mitchell, her husband, John, and three Mitchell brothers. While John farmed, Rhoda also became a Lawrence County teacher. A tiny, but firey redhead, Rhoda was known for her particularly harsh, no nonsense approach to teaching. She was also the family's ex-officio historian, whose letters provided much of this family history.

Rhoda Glenn was 16 years old at the time of her father's hanging. She never discussed the incident in her writings or in person. However, until her death in Imboden in 1926, she was violently against all things pertaining to the confederacy and the Southern cause.

–Fred Mitchell Odom. Much of the information was obtained from letters written by Rhoda Glenn Mitchell to various relatives. Some of these letters still exist, the most recent dated 1924.

JOHN P. GOODWIN was born June 4, 1825, in South Carolina to Wyche Goodwin. His first wife's name is unknown. The family moved to Jefferson County, Alabama, around 1830, where John had one brother, Lewis, born. His mother apparently died in the mid 1830s, and Wyche married Mariah Sharp. Wyche and Mariah had at least eight children, stepbrothers and sisters to John P. and Lewis. About 1851, they moved to Lawrence County, Arkansas. Many descendants of these children still reside in Lawrence County around the area of Lynn.

John P. Goodwin.

In 1848, probably in Jefferson County, Alabama, John married Monima Davis. Monima was born in South Carolina around 1826. In 1851, they moved to Lawrence County to the Smithville area where they remained for the rest of their lives. There were five children born to this marriage: Mary Elizabeth, 1850; Nancy Elander, 1852; and Martha Emily, 1863. The other two children died young and their names and birth dates are unknown. Mary married Henry Wagster and Nancy married Thomas S. Robins. Monima Goodwin died in the very early 1900s, and in 1904, John married Mrs. Mary Johnson of Poughkeepsie. This marriage did not last very many years and John moved back to Smithville where he died in December, 1919. Monima, John, Martha and Elizabeth are all buried in the Smithville Cemetery. Nancy is probably buried there, but has no marker. Nancy died in 1876. All five of John and Monima's children preceded them in death.

Monima Goodwin

John Goodwin served with an Arkansas regiment in the Civil War and was paroled at Jacksonport in 1865. For most of his life he was a carpenter; he built furniture and wooden coffins for local burials and for a St. Louis casket company. He was active in the Baptist church at Smithville and was a Mason. I have in my home a fine chest of drawers that I made, probably in the 1880s. I was told by Dula Baker and Cleo Turnbow, long time residents of Smithville, that Aunt Monima made some of the best ginger cookies they had ever tasted and that they often visited them to have some of the cookies. –David Robins.

R.V. GOSS (1867-1922) FAMILY. The story begins at the close of the Civil War. James Wilson Goss had fought on the Confederate side. According to family information, he was mustered out of the Army at Richmond, Virginia. When his son was born in Birmingham, Alabama, June 1, 1867, he said, "Name him Richmond Virginia."

Little is known of the early life of Richmond Virginia Goss. However, we do know that he married Mary Elizabeth Crawford, 1867-1939, in Carbon Hill, Alabama, on September 18, 1890.

Five daughters were born into this family. They were: Mabel, 1892; Gussie, 1894; Lois, 1898; Olive, 1900; and Eunice, 1902. Gussie died in 1895.

Many moves were made in their lifetime. The first was from Carbon Hill, Alabama, to Jasper, Alabama, then to Loss Creek, Alabama. The next was to Amory, Mississippi, then to Verona, Mississippi. After moving from Verona, Mississippi, to Okolona, Mississippi, the family was bothered with malaria. Mr. Goss said, "We will hunt the hills."

First, Mr. and Mrs. Goss made a trip to Knoxville, Tennessee, prospecting, but they did not like that area as a place for their family to live. Then they heard of property for sale at Imboden, Arkansas. They made a trip by train, by way of Memphis, to Imboden. They found a river, hills, a good school, churches, a bank, two drug stores and a hotel. According to daughter Lois, they were "thrilled to death." They moved to Imboden in 1909.

R.V. and Mary Elizabeth Goss. September 1922.

The first house in which they lived was the Nemnich house on Main Street in Imboden. Mr. Goss opened a shoe store on the same street.

Many family memories are associated with the Nemnich house. Perhaps the most exciting was the big fire at the boarding house across the street at Christmas. Landers Lumber Company was built at this location after the fire. Another outstanding event was viewing Halley's Comet at this time.

Mr. Goss became restless. He wanted a place for his prize chickens and bees. He purchased a farm across Spring River and built a house on it. It is the Burrel Cude house today.

The girls attended Sloan-Hendrix Academy and the Grade School in Imboden. Later, Mabel married Oscar McKamey and Olive married Dr. Edwin Dunn. Lois married Grover Bowers at the Spring River farm in 1916.

A sad event occurred when Martin Goss McKamey, the first grandchild, died of pneumonia on November 20, 1917. Some feel that his passing was the reason the grandparents wanted to move again. The couple and daughter, Eunice, moved to Brooksville, Florida, where R.V. Goss died November 23, 1922. Mrs. Goss returned to Imboden. She passed away March 20, 1939. –Pauline McKamey.

THE W. THOMAS GRADDY FAMILY. Tom Graddy, March 19, 1869-May 18, 1949, married Laura Adaline Baker, October 21, 1873-February 3, 1944, daughter of Edward Baker and Martishia E. Andrews. Their children: William Edward, Oliver, Dora, Alvie, Elsie, Cecil and Hester. Oliver married Minnie Warren. Norene, Kenneth, Wendell and Jerry made up their family. Dora married S. A. Hammond. She died in April, 1919, leaving two small daughters: Opal and Ruby. The grandparents, Tom and Laura, raised the children. Arvil married

The Tom Graddy Family.

Edna. Elsie married a Bergin. They had one son, Lilburn. Cecil married Rettie. Hester married Bernita Spotts. Three daughters: Jean, June and Jill make up their family. –Willene Kirkland.

A. B. GREEN FAMILY. As the school color, green is synonymous with Hoxie. The name "Green" also has a long and colorful association with the town.

Arthur Bynum Green, 1882-1969, was born in Southeast Missouri, one of James and Hester Green's eight children. His siblings were sisters: Myrtle and Eunice (twins), Ola and Audrey, and brothers: Sam, Ben and Harold. James Green drowned in Current River when A. B. was quite young.

As a grown man, A. B. settled in Hoxie after living in Randolph County. He married Nettie "Sally" Coats of Lyndon, Tennessee, and they had two children: Lillian in 1905, and Herbert Eugene in 1908. Lillian was a member of the third graduating class from Hoxie High School in 1924. She completed nurse's training and became one of Lawrence County's first county health nurses, later marrying Harolan Trice, co-owner of Trice Brothers Furniture in Paragould.

Herbert finished school in Grady, Alabama, where the family moved briefly during the Depression. He married Julia Mae Hughes, 1914-1987, of Alicia in 1934. Her parents were the long time Alicia mayor, Wilson Simpson "W.S.," 1872-1953, and Kate Carson Ruffner Hughes, 1875-1927.

From left: A. B. Green, Jim Green and Herbert Green in front of the family grocery store in the late 1940s, along with Edward Rice, the barber and Jim Steed.

The Greens were well known in Hoxie because they operated A. B. Green and Son Grocery on Main Street across from the railroad. The store was in business approximately 40 years, closing in the mid 1960s. Like his father, Herbert was an ardent Republican and active in the Methodist church. He died suddenly in 1957.

Herbert and Julia Mae had four children: Thomas Eugene, born 1935; Julia Ann, born 1938; James William, born 1940; and Robert Joseph, born 1950. Tom served 30 years in the United States Army, attaining the rank of colonel. He married Patricia Heilig, and after several postings at army bases, they lived in Springfield, Virginia, before retiring in Florida. They have two sons: Tom Jr., born 1965, of Burke, Virginia; and Art, born 1969, of Wilmington, North Carolina. Their daughter, Sheila Marie, died in infancy.

Judy married Joe Belk, the son of Harry and Mary Belk. Joe and his brother, Charles, were dairy farmers like their father, but converted to farming rice and soybeans. Judy and Joe raised four children: David, born 1960; Carol Ann, born 1962; Mark, born 1965; and Laura Lynn, born 1967; all Hoxie graduates.

David, Carol Ann and Mark live in Jonesboro. David and his wife, Susanne DeRossitte Belk, have a son, Jayson, born 1999. Mark and his wife, Jill Ritter Belk, have two daughters: Kaitlyn, born 1993; and Kristyn, born 1998. Laura Lynn and her husband, Richard Wilcox, have a daughter, Megan, born 1993; and a son, Jordan, born 1994, and reside in Mountain View.

Jim married Mary Frances Weir. Both are graduates of Hoxie High School. They taught school together at Hoxie for many years, retiring in 1995. They have a son, James William Jr., born 1963; and a daughter, Gwendolyn Anglee, born 1973, who are also Hoxie graduates. Jimmy and his wife, Valarie Kegley Green, have two daughters, Sarah, born 1994, and Olivia, born 1996, and reside in Walnut Ridge. Gwen lives in Oxford, Mississippi.

Bob married Naomi Annabelle "Annie" Reagan Hufstedler. They live in Jonesboro and have a son, Robert Joseph Jr., born 1981. –Francis Green.

GRIGSBY. In 1979, a Grigsby family reunion was held at Natural Bridge, Virginia. Three hundred people from 28 states attended. They formed a National Grigsby Family Society and meet every three years in a different state.

This meeting was to celebrate the 200 year anniversary of Soldier John Grigsby's arrival in the Shenandoah Valley in 1779. While in Virginia, we received proof John Grigsby and his brother, James, came to America in 1660, from England. They settled in Stafford County, Virginia.

The Grigsbys prospered and at one time owned seven plantations. They helped organize the Presbyterian church.

Gradually the Grigsbys started moving West.

We have traced our ancestors back to the following:

Dempsey Grigsby, born calculated May, 1799, in Kentucky. On May 16, 1820, he married Cassanda Harrison, born 1805, in Gibson County, Indiana. Their children were: Wesley, John Harrison, Alexander, Betty, Thomas, Emeline, Perline and Julia. Cassanda died calculated 1831.

On March 15, 1833, Dempsey Grigsby married Thursey Stapleton, born calculated 1812, in Gibson County, Indiana. Their children were: Carolina, George, Joseph, William and Charles. Thursey died between 1880-1900, in Cloud County, Kansas. Dempsey died February 16, 1875, in Wapella County, Iowa.

John Harrison was born November 2, 1822, in Gibson County, Indiana. On March 16, 1843, in VanBuren County, Iowa, he married Frances Fallis, born September 30, 1827, in Kentucky. Their children were: Cassanda, William, George, Nancy, John Harrison II and Luanne. Frances died January 18, 1916, in Lawrence County, Arkansas

Sarah Whitlow Grigsby

and was buried at Calvin Crossing Cemetery. John Harrison died November 15, 1876.

John Harrison II was born September 22, 1859, in Lawrence County, Arkansas. On August 26, 1880, he married Sarah Whitlow, born July 24, 1860. Their children were Murta and Harry

John Harrison Grigsby

Sylvester. Sarah died November 22, 1889, and is buried in Whitlow Cemetery.

On July 13, 1890, John Harrison II married Julia Hoard, born July 24, 1865, in Lawrence County, Arkansas. Their children were: Virgin, Lena, Dewey and Clay. Julia died October 11, 1901, and buried in Whitlow Cemetery.

On May 13, 1903, John Harrison II married Addie Paxton, born February 23, 1871, in Lawrence County, Arkansas. Their children were: Charlie, Edna and Albert. Addie died October 16, 1911, and are buried at Calvin Crossing Cemetery.

On August 8, 1912, John Harrison Grigsby II married Susie Harris, born about 1873, in Lawrence County, Arkansas. Their only child was Jess. Susie died in 1949, and is buried in Arnold Cemetery in Jackson County, Arkansas.

John Harrison Grigsby II died May 2, 1917, at Alicia, Arkansas.

Harry Sylvester Grigsby was born April 28, 1889, in Lawrence County, Arkansas. On March 14, 1909, at Minturn, Arkansas, he married Dona Bell Turner, born June 20, 1889, in Corinth, Mississippi. Their children were: Myrta Gladys, Irene Estella, Eunice Esther and Harry Jr.

Harry Jr. died 1921, and is buried in Florida. Dona died 1924, and is buried at Calvin Crossing Cemetery. Myrta died 1974, and is buried in Michigan. Harry Sylvester died 1978, and is buried in Calvin Crossing Cemetery.

Dr. and Mrs. Thomas Campbell Guthrie resided in Smithville where Dr. Guthrie practiced medicine.

DR. THOMAS CAMPBELL GUTHRIE, April 6, 1880, and his wife, Elizabeth Davis Guthrie, April 27, 1885, lived for many years in the town of Smithville, Arkansas. He doctored the rich and poor alike and travelled many miles to see the sick and injured. Dr. Guthrie was the son of Riley M. and Mary C. Guthrie. Elizabeth Davis Guthrie was a sister to Susie Pickett. Dr. and Mrs. Guthrie had two sons, Dr. Noble Guthrie and Thomas Guthrie.

Dr. and Mrs. Guthrie are buried in the Smithville Cemetery. –Mrs. Ruth Andrews.

RALPH HELPLER FAMILY. Ralph Hepler, born 1891, arrived in Arkansas at the age of 17 with his

parents, Jefferson Hepler and Eva Hinshaw Hepler, and brothers, Harry and Paul. They came by covered wagon and drove their cattle through. It took 11 days to travel from Hickman, Kentucky to Ravenden, Arkansas, where they settled on a farm just outside of Lawrence County in a community called Kingsville.

The history of the Hepler family in America began in 1748, when Johanne Casper Hepler of Germany arrived in Philadelphia, Pennsylvania with his wife, Suzanne, and two small sons, Jacob and Christopher. He had two more sons, Casper and George, and all four served in the Revolutionary War.

The family had settled in Allentown, Pennsylvania, but Christopher later moved to North Carolina. Ralph was a descendant of Christopher. His son, David, moved to Indiana and later to Kentucky where Ralph was born.

Ralph married Willie Baird and they moved to Lawrence County in the town of Ravenden. They had two children: Imal, who married Richard Dail, and Wanda, who married Cleo Bailey. Both girls are now living in Ravenden and several grandchildren also live there. Imal and Richard had six children: Jack, Janice, Ann, Betty, Larry and Ted. Wanda and Cleo had three children. Their girls: Patricia Jo and Sharon have died, but their son, Randy, lives in Walnut Ridge and is married to Sherry Fiedor and they have two children.

Ralph's brother, Harry, died soon after they arrived here. His brother, Paul, married Bessie Curry of Ravenden and they had one son, Vernon Hepler. Ralph served in World War I and his sons-in-law, Richard Dail and Cleo Bailey, served in World War II. His grandson, Jack Dail, served in the Vietnam war.

The Heplers were charter members of the Ravenden Baptist Church, organized in 1942. Ralph served on the city council for a number of years. Jack Dail has served as Mayor of Ravenden and his wife, Wanda, is now city treasurer. Larry Dail is now serving on the city council.

Grandchildren living in Lawrence County are Jack Dail, who owns Dail's Body Shop in Ravenden; Larry Dail, who is an instructor at Black River Technical College in Pocahontas; and Ted Dail, who lives in Black Rock and is an insurance adjustor for Allstate Insurance; and Randy Bailey, who lives in Walnut Ridge. Dail children who have moved out of Lawrence County recently are: Janice Meada of Colorado, Ann Spencer of Jonesboro and Betty Busby of Pocahontas.

Great-grandchildren living in Lawrence County are: Shane Dail, Angela Dail and Anthony Dail of Ravenden; Jessica Bailey and Marissa Bailey of Walnut Ridge; and Savannah Dail and Nicholas Dail of Black Rock. Three other great-grandchildren have moved out of the county: Keith Foushee of Newark, Rodney Spencer of Jonesboro and Scotty Dail of Tuckerman.

Ralph and Willie Hepler have four great-great-grandchildren: Jason, Kyle and Ian White and Colton Dail. –Imal Dail.

JOHN AND KATHERINE HALBROOK arrived in America in 1682, on the ship Maryland Merchant from Bristol, England. John arrived in 1733, in King George, Virginia. John and Katherine were the parents of Joseph Halbrooks, who died in 1752, in Westmorland County, Virginia. Joseph was father to William Halbrooks.

William Halbrooks and wife, Susannah of Surry County, North Carolina, were the parents of William Halbrooks Jr., who married

wife, Margarate. William died about 1874; Margarate died February 17, 1766. William and Margaret were parents of W i l l i a m Halbrook III, born March 3, 1874.

W i l l i a m Halbrook III married Sarah Davis in 1906, and he

Jewell Nunnally and Gladys Murry Scott.

provided for his family by farming. William and Sarah had Elizabeth Halbrooks in 1819, in Wilson County, Tennessee. Elizabeth married John Cowger in 1945.

John Cowger was the son of Adam Cowger and Keziah Davis Cowger. Adam Cowger was a blacksmith in Wilson County, Tennessee. He and Keziah married on December 29, 1817.

John Cowger, a veterinarian, and wife, Elizabeth, moved to Mt. Vernon, Illinois, where he died in 1856, and she died in 1900. Elizabeth and John Cowger were the parents of Zelda Cotton Cowger, born July 1, 1857, in Mt. Vernon, Illinois.

Zelda married Matthew Winston Britton in Mt. Vernon, Illinois. Matthew, like his father, was a farmer. He was born to Johnathan and Sarah Britton on March 22, 1852, in Vandalia, Illinois. Johnathan Britton was born in 1821, in Benton County, Tennessee to Thomas and Sarah Oglesby Britton, and like Johnathan, Thomas was also a farmer. Johnathan and Sarah married in 1836. Johnathan died February 13, 1887, in Powhatan, Arkansas. Sarah Britton was born in 1823, in Tennessee. She later died in 1856, in Illinois at the age of 33.

Matthew and Zelda Britton were parents to Ina Silverine Britton in Mt. Vernon, Illinois. Ina married Albert Fletus Murry in 1903. Ina died in Jonesboro, Arkansas; Albert died in Illinois in 1898. Ina and Albert Murry were parents of Jewell Murry, who was born in Illinois. Jewell married Yancy Nunnally in Eaton, Arkansas on September 1, 1918. –Loretta Carpenter.

WILLIAM HAROLD HALEY, 1897-1993, born in Denton, Arkansas on August 17, 1897, was the son of James Barney Haley and his wife, Ora Lula James. His father owned the Haley Real Estate Insurance Brokerage Firm and Boarding Home in Black Rock, Arkansas. His mother was a daughter of Dr. William Henry James, an 1870's Smithville-Powhatan physician.

As a lad, he attended the New Hope Church at Denton with his family. His mother died when he was five. He began his education in the Denton Grammar School. Thereafter, he attended the Sloan-Hendrix Boys Academy at Imboden, Arkansas. In 1914, he transferred to a boarding school in Salem, Missouri. During the train trip to Salem, a pickpocket lifted his tuition fees. He voluntarily washed the school dishes until his father telegraphed additional funds. After graduating high school, he furthered his education by attending Chillicothe Business College in Springfield, Missouri.

He was a World War I Army Infantry veteran; then enlisted four years in the U. S. Marine Corps. He was recognized for his business acumen and assigned to the Payroll Department at the Quantico, Virginia, base. He devised a systematic pay plan to pay the returning Fifth and Sixth Regiments who had not received compensation in World War I.

When stationed at the Naval Powder Factory, Indian Head, Maryland, he met Hazel O. Willett, a native. Subsequent to his honorable discharge from the Marine Corps, they were married in 1923, and they settled in the area and had four children.

He began his civilian career in Civil Service with the U. S. Government and became a supervisor of the Supply Department at the Naval Powder Factory (The powder produced there was used in the Big 10-Inch guns on the battleships in World War II). He served as an executive officer for the National Federation of Federal Employees. He collaborated on the active passage of the Federal Employees Retirement Bill. He served in many civic organizations, including the Masons. He became a 32nd degree Shriner.

Mr. Haley was one of five men selected from the Naval Powder Factory to establish the Naval Ordnance Depot in Shumaker, Arkansas. He returned to the state of his birth as an administrative assistant to the base commander in charge of the Supply Department. Haley created the Employee Classification System for over 100 civil service employees. A street (Haley Street) was named in his honor on the base.

William Harold Haley

Following retirement from civil service, he returned to Lawrence County to manage his father's cattle and land interests. He was a cofounder of Lake Charles. He served faithfully for 25 years under the Lawrence County Soil and Water District. He was elected by the landowners to serve as secretary and treasurer to the Improvement District Board of the Flat Creek Watershed. He received support

William Harold Haley

from the Arkansas Game and Fish Department for a wildlife refuge in the Black River bottoms. In his 90s, he created a collage representing the Lake Charles projects. This work is on view at the Powhatan Courthouse Museum.

He was the family's historian. He compiled a family book of historical accounts. His lineage can be traced to about 1700, English-Scottish antecedents with participants in the American Revolutionary War, the War of 1812 and the Civil War.

He was a member of the Hoxie American Legion Post. He received a 50 year pin from the Black Rock Masonic Lodge. The Arkansas Travelers' Award and the State Flag were presented to him. In 1990, age 93, he attended the Indian Head, Maryland Centennial to be honored as one of the three oldest living past employees of the Naval Powder Factory. His name is designated in granite near the entrance to Lake Charles State Park and outside the restored Iron Mountain Depot.

He died April 18, 1993, in Walnut Ridge, Arkansas. He was buried with the highest military honors (15-gun) salute. *–Genevieve Haley.*

EDWARD (EDNA) MORGAN HALL FAMILY.
Edna was born October 9, 1887, in Powhatan, Arkansas, the son of Thomas and Ella McAnvia Hall. He was the youngest of six children. They lived on a farm west of Powhatan. Thomas farmed and was in the lumber business. They bought the old hotel in Powhatan in 1924, and ran it for several years. When the Black River Bridge was being built at Powhatan, the workers stayed there and Ella cooked for them.

Edna married Ruth Nancy King October 28, 1917. She was born April 2, 1903, in Eaton, Arkansas, daughter of William and Fannie Rainwater King.

Edna and Ruth had four children.

1. Paul Pershing Hall, born June 12, 1920, in Powhatan, married Sarah Jane Woodson in 1947, the daughter of Dick and Etna Woodson. Paul died in March, 1995, in West Virignia and is buried there. They had two children: Randy and Sherry.

Top: Ruth and Edna Hall. Bottom from left: Paul, Charles, Brooks, Glenda.

2. Charles Clay Hall, born June 13, 1923, in Hoxie, Arkansas, married Julia Berniese Holder on September 26, 1942, in Black Rock, Arkansas. She is the daughter of Waymon Lester and Zanna Augusta Holder. They had three children: Charles Jr., Bob and Ronnie.

3. Brooks Harold Hall, born December 25, 1928, in Powhatan, married first to Gloria Jean Carson in July 1948, in Walnut Ridge, Arkansas, the daughter of Carl and Nellie Carson. Brooks married second to Elinor Elrod on June 20, 1984, daughter of Ray and Anna Jones of Jonesboro. They had two children: Jeanne and Rickey.

4. Glenda Sue Hall, born April 9, 1931, in Powhatan, Arkansas, married Raymond Hall Willis, May 8, 1948, in Black Rock, the son of Houston Lafayette and May Francis Pickney Willis. They had three children: Joanne, Jamey and Jerry.

Edna worked for the Missouri Pacific railroad in the early 1920s. They lived in Hoxie until 1924. He was laid off due to the depression. They moved back to Powhatan where he farmed.

Edna and Ruth went to Michigan in early 1948. He worked in a factory in Plymouth, Michigan. They returned that fall to Arkansas.

Edna was stricken with lung cancer in early 1959. He died November 1, 1959. He is buried in the Powhatan Cemetery.

Ruth moved to Portia in 1963. She now lives in Lawrence Hall Nursing Home in Walnut Ridge. She is 95 years old. *–Joanne Fields.*

HARDIN-WADE FAMILIES. Thomas B. Hardin (Harden) and Lenora Wade were married on January 11, 1888, in Taylor, Sharp County, Arkansas. They lived in the Jesup and the Driftwood area of Lawrence County.

Thomas' parents were Alfred and Jane Hardin. They came to Lawrence County in the late 1870s, from Sevier County, Tennessee. Alfred was born in North Carolina in 1829. Alfred and Jane Birchfield were married September 13, 1855, in Blount County, Tennessee, and their children were: Nancy, Thomas B., Moses, Mary, John, James and Fanny, who were all born in Tennessee. Jane's parents were Moses and Ruth Birchfield of North Carolina and Tennessee. Alfred made his living by farming.

Lenora's parents were Asa D. and Mary Wade and came to Lawrence County from Sharp County in the 1880s. Asa D. was born in Virginia in 1829, and Mary Verdin was born in Missouri in 1832. They were married in Pope County, Arkansas on March 16, 1848. Their children were: Phebe, Mary,

Tom and Nora Wade Hardin family.

Benjamin, Matilda, Thomas, Lenora, James, Lucy and Even and they all were born in Arkansas. Asa D. owned a cotton gin, lumber mill and a store in the Evening Shade area and owned the mill west of Lynn on Strawberry River, better known as the Beverage Mill, for a short time before his death in 1886.

Lenora Wade was married to J. F. Medlock on November 21, 1880, in Sharp County and they had two children: Bertha and Cordia. Bertha married Jess Murphy and Cordia married Charlie Parks. J. F. passed away and Lenora then married Thomas B. Hardin and their children were: Mary, Florence, Elsie and Beulah. Mary's husband is James Edward Ingram and Elsie was married to Walter Foster and later she married Doson Goad. Florence and Beulah passed away at a young age.

In the first decade of the 1900s, Thomas was stricken with tuberculosis and died leaving Lenora and the children to make a living farming in the Driftwood Community. One of Thomas' brothers moved on the farm to help and he also developed tuberculosis and died. This left Lenora and children again doing the field work without the help of a man. They moved to the Coffman area with Lenora hiring men to plant and raise the farm crop. After a few years, Lenora and Elsie moved to Portia and open a cafe and a general store. Elsie operated the store until she retired in the late 1950s. Elsie also wrote the Portia news for *The Times Dispatch* for many years. *–James Whitlow.*

JOSIAH HARNED was born March 18, 1817, in Orange County, Indiana, and died December 14, 1873, in Sharp County, Arkansas. His first wife, Judeth French, was born October 19, 1826, in Kentucky and died November 8, 1867, in Sharp County, Arkansas.

Josiah Harned is listed in Lawrence County, Arkansas, tax records in 1848. Josiah Harned and Judeth French married about 1844. Josiah enlisted in Company D, 7th Arkansas Infantry on July 26, 1861. He was discharged December 17,

1861, because of a broken arm. He reenlisted in Company H, 45th Arkansas Cavalry.

The children of Josiah Harned and Judeth French Harned were:

1. Mary Jane Harned, born September 25, 1844, in Tennessee.

2. Lydia M. Harned, born February 26, 1848, in Lawrence County, Arkansas. Lydia married Will Bragg about 1868.

3. Thomas J. Harned, born June 9, 1850, in Lawrence County, Arkansas.

4. William Harned, born September 6, 1852, in Lawrence County, Arkansas, died November 17, 1881, and is buried in Marcus Hill Cemetery.

5. Tandy C. Harned, born July 26, 1858, Lawrence County, Arkansas, died December 23, 1941, in Faulkner County, Arkansas. He is buried in Marcus Hill Cemetery. Tandy Harned married first Arminda L. Garrett, November 23, 1879, in Faulkner County, Arkansas. Tandy Harned married second Dovie "Doris" Sneed, November 13, 1934.

6. Margarett Malissa Harned, born May 2, 1860, in Lawrence County, Arkansas. Margarett Harned married Reuben H. Ware. Margarett Harned and Reuben H. Ware were divorced January, 1878.

7. Josiah Harned Jr., born January 2, 1867.

Josiah Harned married second Lucy Mariah Susan Thomas about 1869. Lucy was born December 12, 1835, in Pennsylvania and died January 28, 1912. Lucy is buried in Spotts Cemetery, Sharp County, Arkansas.

The children of Josiah Harned and Lucy Thomas Harned were:

1. Charles Houston Horned (both Charles and his sister, Rosa, spelled the last name Horned instead of Harned). Charles Horned was born April 15, 1872, in Sharp County, Arkansas, and died July 15, 1937, in Sharp County, Arkansas. Charles is buried in Babe Collins Cemetery, near Wirth, Arkansas. Charles married first Sarah Fleming, November 20, 1890. Charles Horned married second, Mary Manervy Huckabee, born September 1, 1880, in Sharp County, Arkansas, and died November 3, 1919. Mary Huckabee Horned is buried in Babe Collins Cemetery near Wirth, Arkansas.

2. Rosa Horned, born about 1873, married first E. O. Carver, November 20, 1890, in Sharp County, Arkansas. Rosa married second Andrew J. Duncan, May 8, 1897, in Sharp County, Arkansas.

–Joseph Harned.

JOHN HARRIS was born about 1815, in Tennessee. This is stated in the 1880 census of Yell County, Arkansas. He states that his parents were born in South Carolina. The person that John married first is unknown, but the marriage produced a child named John, born about 1854, in Arkansas.

In the 1870 census of Lawrence County, Arkansas, John is listed with wife, Elizabeth, his son, John Jr. and her two daughters by her first marriage to John Nunnally. Her daughters by John Nunnally were Florence and Nancy Nunnally. He is listed in that census also as a farmer and justice of the peace. They lived in Strawberry Township.

There were other Harris families living in Lawrence County at the same time that John and his family resided there, but we can find no connection. We can not trace John Sr. back to any other place of residence before Lawrence County. We have not found a John Harris listed anywhere in Arkansas with a child John at the right age to be our ancestor. Nor

have we been able to find a family in the Tennessee census that could be John with his parents, but we hope that through endeavors such as the printing of this county history, that we can make family connections that will help us in our search for the Harris families ancestors. –Shirley Perez.

WILLIAM JOHNSON HATCHER FAMILY. William Johnson Hatcher M.D. was practicing medicine in Imboden when it became a town in the 1880s. He practiced medicine from as far north as West Plains, Missouri to as far south as Jonesboro, Arkansas. W. J. Hatcher was one of the members of the first graduating class of Vanderbilt Medical School. He was born June 10, 1851, in Williamson County, Tennessee. Moving west to Imboden, he married Susan Virginia "Johnnie" Bridges in 1875. Johnnie was the granddaughter of Benjamin Imboden. Together they had six children: J. Octavis, Wright Woodard, Virginia, Lou, Irene and Ida.

J. Octavis and W. W. followed in their father's footsteps. Octavis moved to New Mexico and practiced medicine until his death in 1931. He had two children: Bill and Lewis. W. W. practiced his profession in Imboden all of his life. He married Sarah Kathleen Hill, granddaughter of P. K. Lester, in

William Johnson Hatcher M.D.

1912. They had two sons: Wright Hill and William Lester of Jonesboro.

Virginia married R. S. Rainwater and they produced two sons: R. Sloan Jr. of Jonesboro and William I. of Jonesboro. Ida married Cleo Ball and also had two sons: Cleo Jr. and Octavis.

Wright Hill Hatcher lived in Walnut Ridge most of his life. He was the district manager for the Lawrence County Soil Conservation Service. He married Jessamine Huff of McCrory in 1937. They had two children: Milton Wright of Mountain Home and Victoria Reid of Walnut Ridge. Vicki married Philip Clark in 1968. Wright and Jessamine are also survived be five grandchildren: Philip Jayphen, Dedra Victoria, Amanda Kathleen, Lindsey Merritt and William Wright.

–Philip Jayphen Clark, grandson of Wright Hatcher.

JOHN CALHOUN HAWKINS AND NANCY E. BOULWARE HAWKINS. John Calhoun Hawkins, son of John and Margaret Hawkins, was born June 9, 1850, in Mississippi and died October 13, 1917, in Arkansas. He married first Nancy E. Boulware, May 26, 1875, in Arkansas, daughter of Phillip Boulware and Mary Colbert. He married second Lucinda Howdeshell, April 5, 1903, in Minturn, Marion County, Arkansas. Children of John Hawkins and Nancy Boulware were: Max Hawkins, born Arkansas, died in Plant City, Florida; Meg Hawkins, born 1879 in Arkansas, died in Florida; William M. Hawkins, born February 1884 in Arkansas; Otto Hawkins, born September 1889 in Arkansas; Lou Delia

Hawkins, born March 4, 1892, in Alicia, Lawrence County, Arkansas, died September 4, 1971, in Pekin, Tazewell County, Illinois.

Max Hawkins married Clyde Hawkins, daughter of Charlie Hawkins and Luella Grigsby. Children of Max Hawkins and Clyde Hawkins were: Vada Hawkins; Maxine Hawkins; Everett Hawkins; Robert Leon Hawkins, died 1980.

Meg Hawkins married Joe Covington, September 15, 1895, in Lawrence County, Arkansas. Children of Meg Hawkins and Joe Covington were: Lonzo Covington; Maude Covington; Gladys Covington.

Otto Hawkins married first Pearl Goodman, January 24, 1915, in Lawrence County, Arkansas, and second Willie Matney, April 29, 1939, in Lawrence County, Arkansas and he married third Pearl Lowe, March 2, 1962, in Lawrence County, Arkansas. Children of Otto Hawkins and Pearl Goodman were: Price Hawkins; Irene Hawkins; Paul Hawkins; Lucille Hawkins; Geneva Hawkins.

Lou Delia Hawkins married first John Howard Turner, January 18, 1909, in Minturn, Lawrence County, Arkansas, son of Henry Ross Turner and Lou Estella Lane. Children of Lou Hawkins and John Turner were: Jewel Zerue Turner, born January 1, 1912, in Alicia, Lawrence County, Arkansas, died March 6, 1993, in Pekin, Tazewell County, Illinois; Ruby Bell Turner, born June 17, 1914, in Alicia, Arkansas; John Huston Turner, born August 8, 1917, in Arkansas, died December 10, 1941, in Jonesboro, Arkansas; Dora Bernice Turner, born May 8, 1922, in Alicia, Lawrence County, Arkansas, died May 13, 1985, in Pekin, Tazewell County, Illinois. Lou Delia married second Bob Bolin and third Harry Boyer in Pekin, Tazewell County, Illinois. –James Whitlow.

MARTHA THELMA MCCARROLL HAYNES, who was born in Walnut Ridge, Arkansas, on January 2, 1904, to Dr. Horace Rudolph "Dolph" and Pearl Henry McCarroll. After graduating from Ouachita Baptist University, she taught Latin at Pine Bluff High School for 15 years before moving in 1936, to San Antonio, Texas, where she taught English and Spanish. She was married on September 8, 1926, to James H. Haynes, who was born on October 20, 1898, and died in Pine Bluff, Arkansas on May 18, 1967. He is buried in Pine Bluff, Arkansas. She died in San Antonio, Texas on July 3, 1960, and was buried in Lawrence Memorial Park Cemetery in Walnut Ridge, Arkansas.

–Margaret McCarroll Watson.

HEALEY FAMILY. Spencer and Nancy Duskey Healey migrated to the Lauratown and Clover Bend area of Lawrence County, in the early 1890s from Clinton County, Indiana, with their five sons: Alzora "Zode", Dolzora "Dol", Clifton Roscoe "Towne", Everett Arnold and Emmett Earl. Three additional sons born in Lawrence County were Lee Troy, Claude William and an infant who died. Two firstborn sons, Martin and Milton, died at young ages in Tipton County, Indiana.

Spencer was the son of Michael and Rebecca Price Healey. Nancy was the daughter of Jehiel and Martha Alexander Duskey.

Of the seven living sons, Zode, Towne, Everett and Emmett married and reared families in Lawrence County. Dolzora did not marry.

Alzora "Zode" married Betty Goza on December 2, 1906. They had two children, Earl, and an infant who died young. Earl and his wife, Willie Malone, and their children resided in Powhatan, Eaton and Portia.

The Spencer and Nancy Healey Family - Twins Alzora and Dolzora, Spencer, Claude, Nancy, Clifton, Everett, Lee, Tom Fisher (half brother of Nancy) and Emmett Healey; around 1898.

Clifton "Towne" married Lena Scott on April 4, 1908. Their three children were Ora, Oles and Harry.

Everett married Geneva Spivey on October 22, 1911.

Emmett married Ivie Spivey on October 31, 1909.

Geneva and Ivie Spivey were the daughters of Julius and Lucy Wade Spivey. Julius migrated to Lawrence County in the 1870s from Kentucky. He was married to Lucy Wade on November 14, 1886, in Lawrence County. Lucy Wade was the daughter of Asa D. and Mary Verdin Wade who came to Lawrence County in the 1880s, by way of Pope and Sharp Counties in Arkansas.

Everett and Geneva Healey had seven children: Uel, Teddy, Emma Jean, Buster, Eunice, Marie and Billy Joe. They resided in the Lauratown and Clover Bend Communities.

Emmett and Ivie Healey had eight children: Hazel, Ruby, Ola Faye, Cecil, Jessie, Calvin, Emmett Paul and Bobby Gene. They resided in the Clover Bend and Lauratown area and moved to Sedgwick in January, 1924.

Hazel married Roy "Jake" O'Connor and they had eight children: Loeta, Louise, Joe, Glenn, Franklin, Benny, Joyce and Dale. They resided and farmed in Sedgwick and Portia.

Ruby married Joe Worlow, the son of John William and Catherine Woodward Worlow, in Sedgwick on January 2, 1932. They resided in the Oak Grove and Arbor Grove communities before moving west of Sedgwick in January, 1945, where they have farmed and reared their six children: Joline, John Earl, Glendon Ray, Tommie Jean, Jerry Winston and David Randall.

Ola Faye died in 1930, at age 16.

Cecil died as an infant.

Jessie married Duane Bales. Their five sons are Warren, Ronald, Steve and twins, Kevin and Kelly.

Calvin married Lorene Neal. Their two daughters are Rheamona Faye Healey Reithemeyer and Linda Gale Healey of Sedgwick.

Emmett Paul Healey married Joyce Meyers. Their four children who were born in Lawrence County are Shirley, Paula, David and Cynthia "Cindy."

Bobby Gene Healey married Inus Rush. They reside in Sedgwick.

Claude Healey married Etta Scott in Lawrence County in 1917. After the death of his wife and young daughter in 1918, he moved to Mississippi County, Arkansas.

Lee Healey married Sarah Arlena Deaton in Lawrence County in 1916. They resided in Mississippi County, Arkansas. *—Tommie Jean Worlow.*

HEARD FAMILY HISTORY. Because of a disagreement with authorities over the amount of tithe (taxes) owed, John Heard, Earl of Tyrone, left Ireland. He immigrated to Hanover County, Virginia, in 1718.

John's son, Thomas, served as captain in the Virginia State Troops in the Revolutionary War. Thomas' brother, Stephen, was the first governor of Georgia and his home served as the seat of government for a time. Heard County in Georgia was named for him.

Thomas' son, Hubbard Peeples Heard, was married the second time to Sara Prince from Russell, Arkansas, thus bringing the Heard family from Georgia to White County, Arkansas. He died in 1866. His son, Hubbard Jr., was a successful agriculturist and stock raiser in White County. He joined the Third Arkansas Confederate Cavalry in the early part of 1861. His regiment took part in 65 engagements and of the 104 men who started out, only eight returned. He was in the siege of Corinth at Beauregard's retreat into the river, at the

Left to right: Drew Heard and Brady Heard, sons of Rob and Toni Heard.

Battles of Shiloh, Thomas' Station, Missionary Ridge; also at the capture of Knoxville and many others where he was in constant fighting for 60 days.

Hubbard Jr. was taken prisoner near Holly Springs and taken to Cairo, Illinois, where he was kept for nearly three months. He was then exchanged with nearly 1100 Confederate soldiers. After peace was declared, he returned home and to his farming interests. He died in 1907 and was buried in the Judsonia Cemetery in a grave marked by a Confederate tombstone.

Hubbard P. Jr. was the father of six children, one of whom was Joseph William, who in turn is the father of Joseph Neal. Joseph Neal "J.N." was born in 1912 in White County and was married to Gracie Ellen Lamb of Lawrence County in 1941. He was engaged in strawberry farming in White County and in 1945 moved with his family to the Oak Hill Community in Lawrence County.

J.N. Heard and son Bob Heard, 1943.

Joseph Neal fathered six children: James Robert "Bob," Linda Kay, Kenneth Joe, twins Teddy Harold and Terry Carroll, and Marsha Ann.

In 1951 J.N. moved his family to Hoxie and opened Heard's Fruit and Fish Market. After 23 years on Highway 63 in Hoxie, the business was relocated to a site about three miles west of Hoxie due to the construction of a Highway 63 bypass. He and his wife operated the store until 1977 when his son, Bob, and his wife, the former Shirley Warner, bought the business.

Bob and Shirley have two sons, James Robert Jr. "Rob" and Jeffrey Scott. Rob is married to the former Toni Sullinger from O'Kean and are the parents of twin sons, Brady Scott and Drew Taylor.

This brings the Heard family history up to the present time. *—Bob Heard.*

TOM HEDRICK. The Hedricks came to America from Germany and settled first in Pennsylvania and thus became some of the first "Pennsylvania Dutch" in this country. From there they migrated south into Kentucky and west into Missouri and Arkansas. From this group came George Hedrick, who married Mary Pennington in Kentucky and became the father of May Burton Hedrick and several other children.

Our Lawrence County Hedricks were descendants of May Burton Hedrick, who married Winnaford Jennings on February 21, 1830, in St. Charles County, Missouri. To "Burt" and "Winnie" were born nine children.

1. George, born 1830, married first Elizabeth Scott and second Melvina Mitchell, who was a half sister to Elizabeth, George's first wife.

2. Cordelia, born 1833.

3. Thomas Crockett, born November 18, 1835, in Missouri, died January 26, 1906, in Imboden, married first Lucinda and second Rebecca Jane Kelley.

4. Shelton, born 1836, in Missouri, died 1866, married Elizabeth Roberts, April 17, 1856.

5. Joseph, born 1840.

6. Jesse, born 1844.

7. Isabel, born 1849.

8. John, born 1851.

9. Burton Jr. who was also called "Burt", born 1856, married Fannie E. A. Smith, October 26, 1881.

Shelton Hedrick was the grandfather of "Bert" Hedrick who lived for so long in Imboden. Bert married Addie Underwood and had Louise and Joe. Thomas Crockett, Shelton's brother, married first Lucinda and had two girls, Eliza and Mary. These girls went through life being known as Lyde and Sally. "Lyde" married Andrew Jackson Smith and many of their descendants still live in and around the area. "Sally" married Ed Slayton and moved out of the area. Then Lucinda died and Tom Hedrick married Rebecca Jane Kelley, daughter of John W. Kelley and Nancy Lawson. The Kelley Cemetery is on the old Kelley home place and the graves of John and all three of his wives are located in the Kelley Cemetery.

Tom and "Granbecky" had nine children.

1. John Burton Hedrick, born December 7, 1877, in Imboden, died March 12, 1951, in Forrest City, married first Kate Wayland, November 21, 1899; married second Myrtle Blackwell, November 3, 1911, in Hoxie.

2. Addie Lou, born May 9, 1874, in Imboden, died February 13, 1924, in Marked Tree, married Charlie E. Dent, December 17, 1891.

3. Sarah Abigail, born September 11, 1876, in Imboden, died June 18, 1949, in Naperville, Illinois, married Leander Eaberry Sovereign, December 16, 1893.

4. Thomas Clay, born April 25, 1880, in Imboden, died February 21, 1965, in Flint, Michigan, married Sarah Brown, January 28, 1886.

5. Mary Edna, born October 16, 1881, in Imboden, died October 16, 1960, in Elgin, Illinois, married William Addison Hudson, March 21, 1900, in Black Rock.

6. Nancy Octavia, born February 1, 1883, in Imboden, died February 1, 1958, in Harrisburg, Arkansas, married Charlie Taylor, October 6, 1901.

7. Juddy Jackson, born January 1, 1886, in Imboden, died August 12, 1969, in Tracy, California, married Stella Leona Parsley, January 29, 1905.

8. Daisy Belle, born July 24, 1889, in Imboden, died May 29, 1976, in Heber Springs, Arkansas, married William Walter Smith, October 15, 1905.

9. Georgia Velma, born October 31, 1891, in Imboden, died October 24, 1918, in Marked Tree, Arkansas, married Charles F. Davis, November 25, 1905. Georgia and Charlie both died in the flu epidemic of 1918, and died only a day apart.

Thomas Crockett Hedrick served in the Civil War and Rebecca drew a widow's pension. She needed it, for she raised her grandchildren who were left orphaned when her daughter and son-in-law, Georgia and Charlie Dent, died in the flu epidemic.

These were church going, hard working, loyal and dependable farm people. They raised their children to have the same sturdy moral fiber they possessed in such abundance. Those of us who descend from these Hedricks are proud to proclaim our heredity. We only hope those who follow us will be as proud to claim us for theirs! – *Dale MeMasters.*

GEORGE "G.W." AND GERTRUDE "GERTIE" GRACE LEE HELMS. George

Helms, September 13, 1879-May 9, 1970, was born in Lawrence County, Arkansas, son of Leaton, 1850-September 28, 1884, and Emerline Helms, July 23, 1846-January 6, 1934, grandson of Wyatt, 1826-1875, and Elizabeth Helms, 1829-1893, and great-grandson of Archibald, 1800-1853, and Elander Helms, 1804-1880, of Mecklenburg County, North Carolina.

After his father, Leaton, died in 1884, George spent all his time working on the farm to help feed the family. He taught himself to read and cipher. On September 9, 1900, G. W. married Gertrude "Gertie" Grace Lee, November 30, 1882. She died May 23, 1966.

He became an ordained Baptist minister on October 21, 1916. Friends say George gave a good long sermon. He would ride a mule on circuit, be gone a week, and return with a pail of molasses as payment for services. In 1914, the sale of intoxicants was prohibited in Lawrence County. George lived most of his married life on the Cooper's Creek farm near Smithville. George rented out the good land and he and boys farmed the bad patches providing for the large family. The family subscribed to the newspaper, *The Kansas City Star,* and had a telephone by 1920. Between 1920-1927, a massive road building and road improvement project brought big changes and more people to the area.

George and Gertie raised 11 children, all of whom survived infancy. The children are:

G. W. Helms family: Back row, left to right: Bertha, Mary, Sherman, Carl Wyatt. Front row, left to right: Genevie, Frank, Lillie, George holding Leora, Gertie holding Isham; date 1921. Inset: Charles, date 1927.

Sherman, March 22, 1901-November 21, 1989, Smithville Cemetery, Lawrence County.

Carlton, February 12, 1904-October 26, 1995, Smithville Cemetery, Lawrence County.

Wyatt, born September 26, 1905.

Mary E., September 27, 1907-October 10, 1953, Townsend Cemetery, Lawrence County.

Bertha I., October 29, 1909-October 17, 1940, Townsend Cemetery, Lawrence County.

Genevie E., born November 26, 1911.

Frank, November 17, 1913-March 15, 1995, Matthews County, Missouri.

Lillie M., born May 4, 1916.

Leora M., March 8, 1918-November 18, 1962, Cisco, Illinois.

Isham C., July 15, 1920-April 9, 1993, Pine Crest Memorial Park, Alexander, Arkansas.

Charles F., born October 14, 1922.

During his life, George owned partnerships in a cotton gin and a general store in Smithville. Isham and Charles became Baptist preachers after their father. All of the children married and have had successful lives. George and Gertie are buried in the Townsend Cemetery, Lawrence County.

Related marriages are Willett, Reynolds, Flippo and Bilbrey.–*Richard Walters.*

DAVID AND NANCY BROWN HELMS. David

Helms was born in Jackson County, Tennessee, the son of Wyatt and Elizabeth Helms, grandson of Archibald J. and Elender Helms of Mecklenburg County, North Carolina. He was a farmer, an ordained Baptist minister and the husband of Nancy Brown Helms, daughter of Powell and Sarah Brown, Lawrence County, Arkansas. Wyatt Helms, David's father's siblings were: Hiram, born 1823, North Carolina, died Jackson County, Tennessee; Jenkins, born 1828, Mecklenburg County, North Carolina, died after 1880, Buffalo Valley, Putnam County, Tennessee; Leaton, born February 8, 1832, died August 24, 1904, Lawrence County, Arkansas, Townsend Cemetery; Lavinia, born 1836, in Tennessee, died October 9, 1883, Lawrence County, Arkansas; Emily, born 1839, Tennessee, died 1875, Arkansas, Lone Oak Cemetery; Lena Harriett, born 1844, Jackson County, Tennessee.

They spend much of their early child rearing years in Sharp County, Arkansas. Their later years were in Powhatan Township in Lawrence County. David fought with Shavers Infantry in the Civil War. He died January 13, 1896, and is buried in Powhatan Cemetery. Nancy died after 1909, and is buried next to her husband and close by her parents, Powell and Sarah Buchanan Brown.

David comes from a long line of "Primitive Baptists", beginning in Anson and Mecklenburg Counties, North Carolina, where early Helms founded the "High Hill Baptist Church" in Helmsville, North Carolina, present day Monroe, North Carolina in the mid 1740-50 time period. David's siblings were: Elizabeth, born 1847; Leaton, born about 1850; Catharine, born 1853; Marylind, born 1854; Emily, born 1856; Amanda, born 1860; Samantha, born 1862; Louvenia, born January, 1863; and Annie Hester, born 1866.

There are published stories about David digging a well for the school, stopping to harvest his crops and when he came back to finish the well, it had filled with greasy water. Unfortunately, the well was down hill from a cemetery. David had to fill the well back in. David and Nancy had the following children: James K. Polk, born 1869; Thomas Ephram, born March 18, 1870; William Cam, born march 3, 1873; Sarah, born 1875; Joseph Helms, born 1878; Mollie, born 1880; and Belle Helms, born 1883. William Cam Helms was my grandfather, who married first, Martha Elizabeth Davis, daughter of John M. and Sarah Ann White

Davis. Martha died in childbirth on June 6, 1913. William and Martha had these children: Thomas, Warren, Leslie, Ray and Ivey Helms. William next married Kate Hancock Riggs on March 29, 1914, daughter of James Franklin and Mattie Hancock. Their children were: Jessie Evelyn, Edward died at birth, James David, Hosea Wayne, Mildred and Willie Mae Helms.

Several books have been written about our line of Helms from North Carolina by Gerald C. Helms of Weddington, North Carolina, and we are all currently researching the origins of the Helms Brothers, George Sr., Jonathan and Tilman Helms and finding new cousins all the time on the internet.

Related marriages in Lawrence are: Davis, White, Brown, Holder, Gee, Marshall, East, Cameron, Bagley, Fletcher, Huey, Ward, Goings, McKinney, Cunningham and Price, to name a few!–*Geraldine Fultz.*

LEATON HELMS FAMILY. Leaton Helms was born in 1850, in Jackson County, Tennessee, son of Wyatt Helms, born in 1826, in North Carolina. Leaton's mother was Elizabeth, born in 1829. Leaton's grandfather, Archibald Helms, was born about 1800, in Mecklenburg County, North Carolina.

Leaton had nine siblings: David, 1845-1896; Elizabeth, born 1847; Catharine H. Goings, born 1853; Marylind H. McKinney, born 1854; Emily, born 1856; Amanda H. Cunningham, born 1860;

Center: Prescilla Emmerine. Back Right: John Filmore Gibbens holding twin son, William. Second row seated: Missouri Isabella (Helms) Gibbens holding twin Robert.

Symanthia H. Holder, born 1862; Louvinia H. Holder, 1864-1918; and Annie H. East, born 1866.

Leaton married Precella Emmerine Young, 1846-1934, on January 31, 1865, and they had six children: Sarah E. Helms Hallmark; Missouri Isabella, 1867-1949, who married John Filmore Gibbens; William Albert Helms, 1872-1949; Mary Emily Helms, born 1873, who married Charles Lee; James D. Helms, born 1876; and George Helms, 1879-1970.

George married Gertie Lee, 1882-1966, in 1900, and they were the parents of 11 children: Sherman, born 1902; Carlton, born 1904; Wyatt, 1905-1927; Mary H. Reynolds, 1907-1953; Bertha H. Reynolds, 1909-1940; Geneva H. Willett, born 1911; Frank, born 1913; Lillie H. Flippo, born 1916; Leora H. Bilbrey, born 1918; Isham, born 1920; and Charles, born 1922.

Wyatt Helms died in 1875, the first person buried in Lone Oak Cemetery. His son, Leaton, died on September 28, 1884. He and his wife, Pricella Emmarine Young Helms, who died on January 6, 1934, are buried in Lone Oak Cemetery near Smithville, Arkansas.

Many descendants of Archibald and Leaton Helms reside in Lawrence County. –*Jerry Gibbens.*

LEATON AND PRESCILLA EMERINE GO-INGS YOUNG HELMS. In the year 1850, President Zachary Taylor died and Millard Fillmore became President of the United States. In Arkansas, settlers had swarmed to settle on free land made available with the Arkansas Donation Law of 1840. Also, former military men were collecting land grants of 160 acres each. Among those pioneers were Archibald, 1800-1853, and Elander, 1804-1880, Helms of Mecklenburg County, North Carolina, who settled in the rolling Ozark foothills northwest of Smithville near Little Creek. Archibald's son, Wyatt, 1826-1875, of North Carolina and wife, Elizabeth, 1829-1893, of Jackson County, Tennessee, carved a homestead from the oak forest and settled nearby for protection from bandits and the occasional Indian who wandered the area.

Left to right, front row: Carl, Wyatt, seated Emerine and Gertie holding Bertha, Mary. Left to right, back row: William James, George, Sherman, on porch Isabella; date 1910.

Leaton Helms, 1850-September 28, 1884, second son of Wyatt and Elizabeth Helms, was two months old when the family settled in Lawrence County. He was born into a family of prosperous farmers whose worldly possessions included cows, saddles, 32 hogs and assorted farming tools. Soon the telegraph line would snake from Memphis to Little Rock, 1860, and train tracks were heading north from Batesville to Lawrence County. Editor's note: We are not aware of a railroad from Batewville to Lawrence County. Cotton was the "cash" crop and you could see it planted in all the empty spots; even fence rows. It provided money for sugar, coffee, flour and shoes.

In 1861, Arkansas seceded from the Union. Leaton was finally allowed to go to the war in 1864. He probably served near his uncle and namesake, Leaton Helms, 1832-1904. Being a lad of 14, he became a "horse holder" for the officers of the Confederacy. The war years were hard and the Helms nearly starved. Arkansas was cut off by the Union army and salt

Left to right: Leaton Helms' girls: Sarah Hallmark, Isabella "Belle" Gibbens, Mary Lee; date, 1910.

and sugar were not available. Nearby Big Lick Hill became critical as a natural source of salt. After the war Leaton married Prescilla Emerine Goings Young, July 23, 1846-January 6, 1934, on January 31, 1865, settling near his father. Wyatt had become a Baptist circuit preacher and it was good to have Leaton and his family near while he was gone. One evening in the 1870s, Wyatt was riding a horse through the woods and, seeing a strange moving light, followed it to a large oak tree where the light disappeared into the ground. Wyatt took the guiding light as an omen and directed that he be buried at that place. Shortly thereafter, Lone Oak Cemetery was established when Wyatt died and a nice gravestone was erected with the inscription, "The first to be buried here by a guiding light in 1875. We Shall Live Again." In 1893, when Leaton's mother, Elizabeth, died, she was buried beside Wyatt, her husband.

In 1880, Leaton got in a ruckus involving United States Marshals, moonshine stills, and vigilantes in which one man was killed. After this Leaton became a Baptist preacher at Lone Oak School/Church. It is said that he devoted the rest of his life to converting the people in that "reckless territory" west of Smithville. Leaton and Emerine had eight children: Mary Jane, 1865-1879, buried Lone Oak Cemetery, Sharp County; Sarah,, born 1866, Missouri; Isabella, January 17, 1867-August 31, 1949, buried Parks Cemetery, Lawrence County; William "Willie", 1872-1949, buried Lone Oak Cemetery, Sharp County; Noah, born/died 1872, buried Lone Oak Cemetery, Sharp County; Mary, 1873-1955, buried Lone Oak Cemetery, Sharp County; James, 1878-1943, buried Lone Oak Cemetery, Sharp County; and George "G.W.", September 13, 1879-May 9, 1970, buried Townsend Cemetery, Lawrence County. In 1884, Leaton contracted German measles and with a raging fever went to swim in the creek to cool off. He died shortly afterwards. Times became very hard for the young widow with six children. In 1927, she was granted a Confederate Widow's Pension of four dollars per month. Leaton was buried in 1884, and Emerine in 1934, in Lone Oak Cemetery, Sharp County, which is across the road from Lone Oak Church, Lawrence County.

Related marriages are Hallmark, Gibbens and Lee. –Bonnie Walters.

WYATT AND MARY TENNESSEE WILLETT HELMS. Wyatt, born September 26, 1905, was born in Lawrence County, Arkansas, third son of George, September 13, 1879-May 9, 1970, and Gertie Helms, November 30, 1882-May 23, 1966, grandson of Leaton, 1850-September 28, 1884, and Emerine Helms, July 23, 1846-January 6, 1934, great-grandson of Wyatt, 1825-1875, and Elizabeth Helms, 1829-1893, and great-great-grandson of Archibald, 1800-1853, and Elander Helms, 1804-1880, of Mecklenburg County, North Carolina.

As a child, Wyatt was often kept home to work in the fields. One day he placed a bullet on top of the stove at "Squint Eye" school and let it heat until it shot a hole in the roof. Both the teacher and his father tanned him severely.

Wyatt was married to Mary Tennessee Willett, August 17, 1906-December 2, 1996, at the Cooper's Creek farm by George Helms on September 25, 1927. The depression hit the family hard. Wyatt dug shells in Black River for the button factory as well as farming, cutting wood to sell, and hiring out for labor. In 1938, he was bedridden with typhoid fever for

six months. In 1939, he moved his family to the Cache River "bottoms" in Egypt where they lived and farmed with Mrs. Mary Lee Caraway who was a sister to Gertie. Mary Caraway was a learned lady who insisted on having electricity as soon as possible, getting a radio, and she bought a car so Wyatt could drive her around.

Left to right: Arrie Edna Norris Willett, Lindy Helms, Wyatt Helms, Mary Willett Helms. Front: Bonnie Helms Walters; date 1947.

Wyatt and Mary had children: Hiawatha Lindberg "Lindy", born June 23, 1928; Bonnie Wyatt, born August 3, 1944; and Roy Lee, born and died 1946, buried in Townsend Cemetery, Lawrence County. World War II created different hardships. Wyatt couldn't get rationed tires, shoes or sugar. They traded eggs, butter and chickens for sugar, coffee and gas stamps. Then the boll weevil appeared and heralded the end of cotton as the "cash" crop.

In 1947, the family moved to the San Joaquin Valley of California where Wyatt farmed in cotton, grapes and almonds. When the children were grown, Wyatt and Mary returned to Smithville in 1974. Mary was buried in 1995, in Townsend Cemetery, Lawrence County. Wyatt is five feet, nine inches tall with gray hair, fair skin and blue eyes at age 93.

Bonnie married Richard E. Walters on September 17, 1965, in Amarillo, Texas.–*Richard Walters*

HENDERSON FAMILY. The story about the Hendersons in Arkansas is rooted in the beautiful Spring River land that has been owned by the family since 1858.

Arkansas had been a state for only 21 years when Samuel T. Henderson decided to sell his lands near Rogersville, Tennessee and move west into the Imboden area of Lawrence County. In September, 1857, Samuel, age 44, his wife Amanda, age 45, and their eight children left the security of their home for new opportunities and adventure in the fledgling state of Arkansas. There are no records of the route or length of their journey, but the approximately 500 mile trip was probably made with horses and wagons. The children's ages ranged from 21 to one and a half.

The family first settled in a small log house just west of the present Hope Cemetery in Imboden. After a few months Samuel bought a farm across Spring River from James Couts for $4,200 in gold. The early years were building times and although the family loved the land and the settlement, life could be hard. Amanda died in October, 1861, and their newborn son died a few days later.

As the community grew so did tensions in eastern states, as conflicts between slavery advocates and abolitionists split the nation. The War Between the States deeply affected the Henderson family as it did many others in the area. Eldest son, George, enlisted in a Confederate Arkansas Infantry Regiment in August, 1861. He was 27 when he was killed in a battle in Franklin, Tennessee. Young Samuel, age 21, was killed December, 1862, in the battle at Prairie Grove, Arkansas. William was wounded May, 1864, captured and sent to a prison camp in Illinois.

After father Samuel's death in 1871, the farm was divided between the remaining heirs. Simon Bolivar, a son who was 22 at the time, purchased all the shares of their farm within a few years. This was quite an accomplishment during the hard economic times of the Reconstruction Era.

Simon Bolivar and the youngest son, Arthur G., were the only children of Samuel and Amanda who continued to live in the Imboden area. Bolivar married Belle King and they built a home on the lot where the Dalton Henderson home now stands. They had two sons, Marvin, 1880; and Clay. Dalton Henderson, Bolivar's grandson, told of the loving attention he received from his grandpa, of frequent fishing trips to "grab suckers," and of riding with him on their farm to salt cattle. He wrote, "Grandpa loved music and fiddled for many square dances. He taught a Sunday School class of teenage boys in the Methodist Church and he was a leader in the project to build the first bridge crossing Spring River at Imboden."

Arthur went to medical schools in Missouri and New York City and settled in Imboden with his bride Frances Wright. They had a son, Samuel, and a daughter, Mary Elizabeth, 1900. Much has been written about Dr. A. G. Henderson, 1851-1947. He served citizens of the area for 68 years as a caring, compassionate physician, retiring at age 92. He was very active in the Methodist Church where he taught the men's Sunday School class for 62 years. Gardening was a special interest to him and he planted and cultivated a garden each year. His great love of peaches resulted in many orchards he planted.

Mary Elizabeth married Cleo Hill and they had four children: W. C. Jr., Dorothy, Herbert and Mary Lynn. They spend several years in Imboden before moving in the 1940s. After Cleo died Mary returned and lived in the area until her death in 1995.

Marvin, Bolivar's son, was a quiet man with a keen mind for mathematics. He married Celeste Dalton from Dalton, Arkansas in 1905, and they built the stately home that still stands at 606 W. 3rd in Imboden. Two sons were born to them: Dalton, 1907, and Ralph, 1914. Celeste was very active in community affairs. Her leadership was important in the Methodist women's organization, W.S.C.S. and the Altruian Club. She was a gracious hostess and accomplished homemaker.

Dalton and Helen Henderson, 1990.

Marvin continued to farm the old family land until his death in 1967.

After Dalton's graduation from Hendrix College he returned to teach at Sloan Hendrix. There he met Helen Kimberlin from Tuckerman who was a newly hired teacher. They were married March, 1930. After four years with jobs in other areas they returned to Imboden with their infant daughter, Anna Beth. In 1953, Beth married Eli Abbott. Their two children are Helen Kim Abbott-Harris and Scott Dalton Abbott. They have one grandson, Alex Dalton Abbott.

Ralph married Nova Glenn Freeman in October, 1938. A son, Ralph Bernard, was born to them in 1940, in the old Simon Bolivar house. They have lived in Little Rock since the 1940s. Bernard had two children, Julia Henderson Chavis and Bret Henderson and one grandson, Justin Henderson.

Dalton and Helen worked as a team in the Imboden school system for many years. Both were dedicated to the importance of education and both sincerely cared about each of their students. The Methodist Church and their faith were a central focus in their lives. Each of them served in many positions in their church throughout the years. Dalton and Helen loved the small town and the land as did the first Hendersons in 1857. And they shared their pride and love of family.

With Helen's death in September, 1998, the last person to carry the Henderson name is gone from the town. But one descendant of Samuel and Amanda still lives in the area, Dorothy Hill Gabriel, granddaughter of Arthur. The farm and a home are still owned by Ralph Henderson and Beth Henderson Abbott, who still feel the tug of those roots laid down so many years ago.–*Beth Abbott.*

JAMES "JIM" HENDERSON, probably the son of Alexander and Anna Henderson, was born about 1835. In March 1852 Wesley Taylor was appointed guardian of James and John F. Henderson, heirs of Alexander Henderson. James married Nancy Finley, daughter of James and Nancy Jane Dobbins Finley, March 16, 1853.

They were the parents of the following children: Alexander married Lena Dawson (second wife); Margaret married Rufus B. Hillhouse; Anna Bell married Dr. D.B. Rudy; Laura married John F. Brady; Loring G. married Virginia Almeda Byars; and one infant.

James died about 1864 and his brother, John F., was appointed administrator of his estate. His brother, John F., 1836-1872, married Margaret Sloan and is buried in the Henderson Family Cemetery which is located one mile south of Jesup, Arkansas. His sister, Susan, 1831-1865, married first Benjamin B. Sloan and second William C. Sloan. –*Bonnie Perkins.*

HENDERSON. William, 1780-1825, and Mary Henderson, 1782-1837, came to Lawrence County, Arkansas in the early 1800s. They settled on land near Jesup and Smithville, which in 1850, adjoined the Sloan farm. They had at least two children: William Alexander, 1805-1839, and Mary. William was murdered August 6, 1825, in Lawrence County, Arkansas.

William Alexander and Anne Halbert were married about 1823. Their children: Mary J., 1825, married Joseph Taylor; William Henderson married Elizabeth; James Henderson married Nancy Finley, and settled near Marked Tree, Arkansas; Susan Elizabeth Henderson married first Benjamin Barce Sloan and second Captain William Comfort Sloan (both were sons of Fergus); and John Franklin Henderson, 1885-1872, married Margaret Rosanna Sloan, 1839-1908.

John and Margaret Sloan Henderson settled on a farm near Jesup. He was a farmer. John served in the Confederate Army. His death at the early age of 36 was the result of his Army service. Their children were: Charles Franklin, 1858-1889, married Eva L. Wadley; William "Will" Clinton, 1860-1935, married 1901, in Black Rock, Ella Lorena James, daughter of Dr. William Henry James, 1844-1894, and Temperance A. Wesson James, 1841-1884; Elizabeth Caroline "Lizzie" C. married W. C. Wallis; Rosana Zanie, 1866-1941, married Sloan Wyatt; Lude Blon, 1868-1962, married first William Bates, second Frank Mills and third Reverend Southworth, Walter, 1870-1871; and John V. Jr., 1872-1873, born after his father died.

During the Civil War, Margaret Sloan Henderson had to make coffee in a wash kettle for the Union soldiers. She also had to feed them. During the war, the Sloans and the Hendersons

buried bales of cotton. After the war, they dug them up and took them to St. Louis and traded them for merchandise which they brought back to Arkansas and sold.

Margaret was a spunky small woman with a very small foot. After the death of her husband, John, Margaret remarried four times. It has been recalled that as long as the good Lord took them, she would too. She married second Alfred Oaks, who had been married to her sister, Ann, who was killed by a servant; third Mr. Goad; fourth Mr. Vinson; and fifth Mr. Church. They separated and Margaret took the name Vinson back. She is remembered as Grandma Vinson. A son-in-law, Frank Mills, built her a house in Ravenden where she spent her remaining years.

John F. and Margaret's son, William Clinton Henderson, married Ella Lorena James, daughter of Dr. William Henry and Temperance Wesson James. They lived on the corner of the main intersection in Imboden; where Highway 62 and 63 now separate used to be their garden, spring house, stables and barn. Their house is no longer there. Uncle or "Pa" was blind for the last 24 years of his life, but continued to be an astute businessman. He would sit in the corner of his front porch and speak to all who passed, calling them by name. He knew them by their walk. Most days, someone would take him to town in the morning and go and get him in the afternoon. This was a highlight of my memories, when I was with my grandparents. The Henderson were quite a self sufficient household. They raised their fruits, vegetables, chicken and livestock (including a cow). It was like a farm in the middle of town.

They had two children: Margaret married Earl Ernest Wheeler and Willorena married William David Beseau. Their descendants are scattered from Arkansas to Texas, California, Hawaii and Missouri.–*Vivagene Wheeler Handley.*

HENDERSON FAMILY. William J. Henderson, son of Father Henderson and Mother Henderson, was born in Alabama-Tennessee about 1836.

He married Martha Witcher Springer in Tennessee, 1851. Martha was born in Tennessee about 1836. She was the daughter of Father Springer and Mother Springer. In the 1910 census, William was in the Army.

William J. Henderson and Martha Witcher Springer had the following children:

1. William A. Henderson died about 1954, in Fillmore, Ventura County, California. He married Elizabeth Crim in Ripley County, Missouri, September 9, 1880. Elizabeth was born about 1854.

2. Lincoln Henderson married Sarah A. Pulliam in Ripley County, Missouri, March 5, 1885. Sarah was born about 1865.

3. Sarah E. Henderson married Mark Holland in Ripley County, Missouri, April 26, 1883. Mark was born in Macon County, Tennessee, November 13, 1861. He was the son of Wiley Saltlick Holland and Sarah Rush. Mark died July 20, 1954, at age 92 years. Mark died July 20, 1954, at 92 years of age.

4. Rachel E. Henderson.

5. Alexander F. Henderson married M. A. Holland in Ripley County, Missouri, September 21, 1888. M. was born about 1868. She was the daughter of John Martin Holland.

6. Thomas Jefferson Henderson.

7. Adam Lynn Henderson.

8. John Egle Henderson married Matilda about 1876. Matilda was born in Tennessee about 1857.

9. Andrew W. Henderson "William J." was born in Macon County, Tennessee, April 15, 1856.

He married Sarah Louise Holland 1882. Sarah was born in Macon County, Tennessee, July 30, 1866. She was the daughter of Wiley Saltlick Holland and Sarah Rush.

Andrew W. Henderson and Sarah Louis Holland had the following children:

1. Wiley J. Henderson. Wiley died March, 1911.

2. James Lafayette Henderson died November 12, 1978, in Randolph County, Arkansas. He married four times. He married Florence Houston in Randolph County, Arkansas, 1911. Florence was born about 1888. Florence died 1913. He married Martha Bellah in Spring River, Lawrence County, Arkansas, May 17, 1914. Martha was born about 1890. He married Dealey Davis about 1924. Dealy was born about 1894. He married Viola about 1930. Viola was born about 1898.

3. Benjamin Henderson married Emma Petitt about 1910. Emma was born about 1890.

4. Alma Henderson died October, 1901.

5. Mary Elizabeth Henderson was born February 8, 1884.

Mary Elizabeth Henderson (Andrew W., William J.) was born in Tucker, Ripley County, Missouri, February 8, 1884. Mary died October 11, 1965, in Pocahontas, Randolph County, Arkansas, at 81 years of age.

She married Francis Marion Sharp in Spring River, Lawrence County, Arkansas, about 1910. Francis was born in Spring River, Lawrence County, Arkansas, February 12, 1880. He was the son of William Thomas Sharp and Martha A. Holder. –David Berlin.

HENSON/CASH. Stephanie Carole Henson was born September 8, 1973, at the Randolph County Medical Center in Pocahontas, Arkansas. She is the daughter of Charles Henry Henson and Peggy Ann Rice, both of the Lawrence County area. Stephanie has one brother, Timothy Owen Henson, born November 17, 1970, and one sister, Tanya Jene VanHoozer, born September 11, 1987. Her grandparents are Troy and Mildred Jones Henson of Lawrence County and Aubrey Owen Rice and Virginia Lytle Meriwether of Lawrence County.

Stephanie graduated from Beebe High School in 1991, and went on to obtain a BS in Psychology at Arkansas State University in Jonesboro in 1996. Stephanie is currently a homemaker residing in Pocahontas, Arkansas with her husband two children.

Gregory Reid Cash and Avery Jensen Cash.

On May 26, 1996, Stephanie married Gregory Claud Cash of Trumann, Arkansas. Greg is the son of Claud V. and Joan Sugg Cash. Claud is owner/operator of Lawrence County Tractor in Hoxie. Greg is currently manager of Pocahontas Tractor and Supply in Pocahontas and Assistant Manager of Lawrence County Tractor in Hoxie. On January 10, 1997, their son, Gregory Reid Cash, was born. His sister, Avery Jensen Cash, followed on May 13, 1999.

Greg and Stephanie Cash currently reside in Pocahontas, Arkansas. Stephanie enjoys painting, drawing and golf as hobbies while Greg is an avid hunter, fisherman and golfer. The family is actively involved in the First Baptist Church of Pocahontas as well as other community activities, including Circle of Friends, Beta Sigma Phi and Rotary Club. –Stephanie Cash.

W. E. HERAL FAMILY. William Edward Heral was born June 8, 1893, in Siebert, Kit Carson County, Colorado, to William Sherman and Rosina

Maud Chamberlin Heral. Their other children were: May Augusta "Gussie", 1895-1971, married Frederick Oglesby; Carrie Emma, born 1897, married Arden Bolton; Charles Franklin, 1899-1903; Arthur Raymond, 1902-1982, never married; Dacie Ruth, born 1903, married Charles Baremore; Rosie Alice "Dollie", 1907-1992, never married; Grace Marie, born Lawrence County, Arkansas, near Murta Junction, 1909-1970, never married.

Most of W. E.'s life was spent in and around O'Kean, but just outside O'Kean lies both Lawrence and Greene Counties. From Greene County he entered World War I where he served in France as a military policeman, he was honorably discharged at Camp Pike, Little Rock, Arkansas, on July 31, 1919.

W. E. first married Ila Mae Holder. She and their baby both died. After he returned from the war, he married Dora McKnelly. Their son, Edward Delbert, was born in 1922. Dora died Feb-

W. E. and Willie Heral family: Cecil, Mary, Wanda, Maxine, Willie, W. E. holding grandson Edward "Jr.", Glen, Delbert, Lillian and Ray.

ruary 24, 1923, when Delbert was only four months old. He was reared by his grandparents, Thomas and Edith Mann McKnelly. Delbert married Emma Rothe, then Margie Rogers.

On September 21, 1925, at Walnut Ridge, W. E. married Willie Felicia Rickey, daughter of Thomas William and Mary Lavena Hicks Rickey. They first lived in Greene County where was born to them: Wanda Louise, 1926-1983, married Charles Bode; Viola Maxine, born 1927, married Albert Lance; Albert Ray, born 1928, married Margaret Boozer. They moved to Lawrence County where their last four children were born: Cecil James, 1930-1987, married Jaunita Getson; Rose Mary, born 1931, married Bill Hibbard; Alice Lillian, born 1933, married Howard "Joe" Snow; and Arthur Glen, born 1934, married Lucille. Their grandchildren: Edward "Jr.", Mildred, Joann, Thomas, Dean, Jean (twins, Patricia, Bob, Kenny, Sue, Gary, Deborah, Eugene, Lanny, Darlene, Tammy, William, Albert Ray, 1972-1993, Jim, Wayne, William K., Gaye, Rebecca Faye (stillborn), Marilyn, 1951-1996, Tim, Jon and Thomas.

In early life, timber work was his occupation. The family re-

William Edward Heral. World War I Uniform.

members him hewing railroad ties with a broad ax. Later he farmed. In 1936, the family moved to Randolph County, one mile from O'Kean, where they lived until 1956, when they moved into O'Kean. He served as Mayor of O'Kean from 1959 to 1961.

W. E., Willie, Wanda and Rebecca are buried in Lawrence Memorial Cemetery. Howard and Marilyn are buried in Snow Cemetery in Lawrence County. –Lillian Snow.

CARL HERRING FAMILY. Carl Herring and Frances Dobbs were united in marriage on September 23, 1954, at the Powhatan Courthouse with Raymond Goza officiating.

Carl is the son of William Earl and Bessie Lee Rutledge Herring. The Earl Herring family lived in the Lauratown and Clover Bend Community. Carl's siblings are J. E., A. C., Earl Gene, Jimmie Dale, Howard Gordon, Rose Lee, Ima Lorraine, Dollie May and Patricia Ann Herring. Dollie, Jimmie and Howard attended school at Clover Bend.

Frances is the daughter of Earnest Daily and Vida Quarry Dobbs. The Dobbs family lived at Clover Bend in the Shirey Bay bottoms (once known as the Counts Community). Siblings of Frances are: Pauline, Ruby, Faye Dell, Barbara, Edward, Darrell, Shirley, Linda, Bonie, Rickey and Phyllis.

Carl and Frances raised their family in Lawrence County. The children attended school at Clover Bend and Walnut Ridge. Laverne lives in Jonesboro and works at the Human Development Center. Carleen lives in Walnut Ridge and works at the Hair Tech Beauty School. She has a daughter, Tonya, who attends school at Walnut Ridge. Lester and wife, Linda, live at Imboden. He is the Walnut Ridge City Water Superintendent. His wife, Linda, works at Skil. They are raising two children. Their daughter, Amanda, is going to Black River Technical College, while son, Joshua, attends school at Sloan Hendrex. Cheryl lives in Jonesboro and works at the Human Development Center. Cynthia and husband, Todd, live in Walnut Ridge. Cynthia is a nurse and teaches CNA classes. Todd is a mail carrier for the Walnut Ridge Post Office. Their children are: Michael, Brandy, Matthew, Andrea and Rafe. They attend school at Walnut Ridge. Michael lives with his grandparents, Carl and Frances Herring, and attends school at Sloan Hendrix. Brenda and husband, Rickey, live in Okinawa, Japan. They are in the Air Force. Their children are: Lisa, John and Justin. Mary and husband, JR, live at Clover Bend. Mary teaches school at Swifton, while JR works at Harp's in Walnut Ridge. Their children: Bret, Adam and Ty, all attend school at Swifton. Carl and Frances now live at Imboden. Carl is finally getting to enjoy retirement, while Frances has a few more working years to put in at Kids First in Pocahontas. –Frances Herring.

Bessie, Earl Herring Family.

A group at a barn raising around 1912, in the Clover Bend area. John Waite and wife, Rebecca Francis Tucker, Four of their children-Pearl, Loma, George, and Bill.

HERRIOTT. John Waits and Rebecca Tucker Herriott moved from Agnos, Arkansas, in Fulton County to Lawrence County in 1909. They moved to a spot almost directly across Black River from what is now Old Davidsonville State Park. The children were: Theodore, Pearl, Frank, Lon, George, Willie and Loma. It was a long trip in a wagon. Pearl, who was 13 at the time, walked behind the wagon and led the milk cow. The trip took almost two weeks and Rebecca was not a happy traveler. She was leaving the only life she had ever known.

The Tuckers had homesteaded at Agnos and she had many relatives there. John had been raised at Wiseman in nearby Izard County. His father was acting county sheriff and was shot while apprehending a criminal. The Herriotts could be traced back to their immigration to America from Scotland in 1685, but John was dreaming of rich soil where the farming would be easier. When they finally arrived at their destination, they had to live in a one room cabin with a dirt floor. The first winter was harsh; one of their neighbors had slept so soundly during the cold night that his feet had frozen. You had to get up to stoke the fires in those old cabins in zero weather. They survived the first winter and made their way to the Clover Bend-Lauratown area where the soil was rich and the crops grew tall.

Though John and Rebecca never owned land of their own, John was a hard worker and they had a good life. The home now boasted two big square rooms with a fireplace at each end. There was a hallway and a side room that made a cozy kitchen. The children heard John and Rebecca sing as they cooked breakfast together for their brood. The children grew up and some of them married people from that area.

Pearl met Frank Garrett at the Portia picnic in 1913. They were married in December of that year. Frank Garrett was from the other side of Black River near Powhatan. He worked for Captain Tucker who ran riverboats on Black River. Frank and Pearl later moved to the Lynn area where they lived until their deaths. They had four children who lived to adulthood; one son, Luther, was killed in action in Italy during World War II.

Theodore, Willie and Loma all married locally and farmed in the area until their deaths. Lon, who was the hunter of the family, married and moved to Searcy. George enlisted in the Navy during World War I. While in the Navy, he made quite a name for himself as a boxer. After his discharge, he came home to live with the family. He never married.

John died suddenly one damp fall day in 1928, on his way to the store. He was found dead sitting by a tree. He was 60 years old. Frank never married. He eventually bought a farm at Pocahontas on what is now Holsher Lane. He cared for his mother until her death in 1938. He remained on this farm until his death at the age of 90.

John, Rebecca, George and Loma are all buried in Clover Bend Cemetery, Theodore and Willie are in Lawrence Memorial at Walnut Ridge. Frank is in Randolph Memorial Gardens. Pearl is buried in Old Lebanon near Lynn and Lon is buried at Searcy. Although it seems just a short trip to us today, Rebecca never got to go back to her beloved Agnos even for a visit. *–Bonnie Smith.*

JOHN E. HIBBARD was the son of George Washington Hibbard and Mary Ellen Gollihar. He was born August 10, 1876, in Randolph County, Arkansas, Gravesville Community, having 10 brothers and sisters.
1. Joseph Adam, 1874-1964
2. John E. Hibbard, 1876-1921
3. James Franklin, 1878-1950
4. Love S., 1880-1888
5. Jennie M., born 1883
6. Emily Anna, died 1957
7. William Nathaniel, 1888-1970
8. Sarah Elizabeth, 1889-1965
9. Georgie Thomas, 1893-1973
10. Mayme Ellen, 1897-1971

John wed Emma De McMillon, February 18, 1897. She was the daughter of Alfred Tillman McMillon and Mary Elizabeth Lawson, born 1877, Powhatan, Black River Township, Lawrence County, Arkansas.

From the union of John E. and Emma Dee were:

Daily Albert, 1899-1970

Earl died in infancy, Lawrence County, Arkansas.

Ray died in infancy, Lawrence County, Arkansas.

Stella Mae, Lawrence County, died about 1903.
Pauline, 1905-1944, wed Dock Warren.
Charles Marks, 1907-1969.
Irene Inez, born 1914.
Terence, about 1916, died age 2 weeks.
Living in Richards, Lawrence County, Arkansas, John died in 1922, with Emma Dee moving to Hoxie. She died in Little Rock, Pulaski County, Arkansas in 1939, and is buried there.

This family has a long lineage to Lawrence County.

W. N. and Mattie Hibbard family in 1934. Front row: George, W. N., Leon, Mattie, Bill. Back row: Marshal, Betty, Ruby, Jane and Cousin Joe Lairamore.

W. N. HIBBARD FAMILY. William Nathaniel Hibbard, 1888-1970, was born at Attica, Randolph County, Arkansas. After completing school at Maynard Academy, he moved to the Ft. Smith area and married Mattie Lee Lairamore in Keokuk Falls, Oklahoma (1911). Over the years they lived in several communities in Arkansas and Oklahoma. In 1929, they traveled by covered wagon to the Plains of Texas. Drought forced a move back to Charleston, Arkansas. In 1933, with two covered wagons and over a period of one week, they moved to Old Walnut Ridge. W. N., Mattie

and their younger children were members of the Old Walnut Ridge Baptist Church, where he served as Sunday School Superintendent for many years.

While he farmed at Old Walnut Ridge, much of his life was spent in the mercantile business. In the 1950s and 1960s, W. N. and sons, Bill and Leon, owned and operated O'Kean Mercantile Company. He also served as Mayor of O'Kean in 1954-1957.

He was a descendant of Joseph and Delilah Walker Hibbard. Joseph died during the Civil War. He is buried in Jefferson Barracks National Cemetery. Delilah and children moved from Fulton County to Randolph County after the war ended. Their children were Leuisa Jane, born 1844; George Washington, 1846-1927, married Mary

W. N. and Mattie Hibbard in 1934.

Ellen Golihar (W. N.'s parents); Joseph, 1847-1853; William Elison, 1850-1901, married Martha Collier; Robert, 1851-died young; Nancy, born 1852, married Abijah McDaniel; Emily, 1854-1941, married James McDaniel; Sarah, born 1857, married Robert Belew; Samuel Love, 1859-died young.

W. N.'s siblings were Joseph Adam, 1874-1964, married Rebecca Chastain; John, 1876-1921, married Emmadee McMillon; James Franklin, 1878-1950, married Anna Belew; Love, 1880-1888; Jennie Mae, 1883-1931, married James O'Neal; Emily anna, 1885-1957, married George Johnson; Sarah Elizabeth, 1889-1965, married Newton Chastain; George Thomas, 1893-1973, married Nellie Chastain; Eatham, 1895-1895; Mayme Ellen, 1897-1971, married Burley Weatherford.

W. N. and Mattie's children were Andrew Buel, 1912-1929; Thomas Marshal, born 1913, married Jessie Mae Cole and after her death Laura Ruhl; Ruby Lucille, 1915-1959, married Claude Waddell; George Milford, 1918-1987, married Mildred Going; Mary Ellen "Jane", born 1921, married Virgil Brown; Betty Lou, born 1923, married Darrell Holder; William Nathaniel Jr., born 1925, married Mary Heral; Johnny, 1927-1927; Clifton Leon, born 1928, married Sue Jones.

Grandchildren are: Marshal's: Thomas Nathaniel, Anita Faye, Kenneth Wayne, Brenda Dale; Ruby's: Edna Lea, Hope, Carroll Jullian, Paul Gene, Kelly Boyd, Mona Sue; George's: Homer Milford, Ronald George, Duane Gerald; Jane's: Virgil Ancil, Allen Dale, Sharon Alene, Gerald Eugene "Jerry", David Anthony, Michael Wayne; Betty's: Charles Richard, Bennett Darrell; Bill's: William Keith, Barbara Gaye, Rebecca Faye (stillborn); Leon's: Randal Leon, Rhonda Gail and Nathan Lee.

Family still residing in Lawrence County are Leon and Sue, Virgil Brown, a resident of Lawrence Hall - grandchildren: Edna Lea

W. N. and Mattie Hibbard in 1961; 50th Wedding Anniversary.

and Arliss LaMew, Hope and Billy Segraves, Kelly and Joyce Howard Waddell, Ancil and Sybil Nutt Brown and Nathan Hibbard. Other descendants in the area are: Jane and part of her family and Betty and family in Paragould; Bill and Mary in O'Kean. Marshal and George moved to California in 1939, and have families living there.

Jim and Annie and John and Emmadee Hibbard both have many descendants in Lawrence County. *–Bill and Mary Hibbard.*

ROBERT HICKS FAMILY.
Robert William Hicks is a descendant of W. E. Hicks and A. J. Slayton. His parents were T. W. and Freda Slayton Hicks. He was born on January 15, 1934. He married Patsy Ann'E Robert on January 22, 1952. Patsy's parents were Frank Robert and Gracie Ann'E Smith Robert. She was born on January 22, 1935. Their descendants include: Robin Willene Hicks Blakeney, Donna Ann'E Hicks Pinkston and Joseph William Hicks.

Robin married David Blakeney on January 22, 1977, and her descendants are: Joshua David, Robert Bryon and Laura Allison Blakeney. Donna married Michael Pinkston on December 19, 1987, and her descendants are Steven Michael and Stephanie Ann'E Pinkston. Joe married Melanie Burns on May 19, 1989. His family includes Audrey Jane and Gracie Mae Hicks.

The Robert Hicks family all reside in the Hoxie-Walnut Ridge area. They are farmers, teachers, business owners and are active in the church, school and community. *–Donna Hicks.*

Front row: Audrey Lane Hicks, Gracie Mae Hicks, Robert Hicks, Patsy Robert Hicks, Melanie Burns Hicks, Joe Hicks, Robin Hicks Blakeney, Robert Blakeney, Donna Hicks Pinkston, David Blakeney, Stephanie Pinkston, Steve Pinkston and Mike Pinkston. Not pictured: Ali Blakeney and Josh Blakeney.

WILLIAM ELMER "W.E." HICKS FAMILY.
The Hicks family settled in the Pugh area of Owl City in 1921. Luther Pugh came 10 years earlier and contacted his sister's family in West Tennessee to come to Arkansas because land was cheap. Luther Pugh's descendants were Imo Pugh Shackleford, Mary, Pugh Eskridge, Vera Pugh Floyd, Glaydis Pugh Smith, Virginia Pugh Eskridge and Etta Wanda Pugh Kail. Mr. Pugh donated land for the first school house known as Pugh School in that community. His sister was Ethel Pugh Hicks. She married William Elmer "W.E." Hicks in 1908, and their descendants were Verna Hazel Hicks Gilmore, Thomas William "T.W." Hicks and Adrin Roberta Hicks Dulaney.

Verna married Hubert Gilmore in 1930, and their descendants are Garland Gilmore and Lesha Ann Gilmore Prater. T. W. married Freda Slayton on November 4, 1931. Their descendants are Robert William, James Harold and Joann Hicks Hagar.

The Hicks brothers farm and have a flying service that is in the Pugh and Owl City area to this day. T. W. Hicks farmed with his sons until his death.

The descendants of W. E. and Ethel Hicks include: Gilmores, Hagars, Blakeneys, Pinkstons and Praters that create the 5th and 6th generation of

T. W. Hicks, W. E. Hicks, Ethel Pugh Hicks, Roberta Hicks Dulaney, Verna Hicks Gilmore.

farmers. One of the areas they farm includes the original 40 acres that was purchased from Jewel Robert by W. E. Hicks back in 1921. *–Donna Hicks.*

HILLHOUSE FAMILY.
An early reference to the name is documented in 1547, Ayr County, Scotland, parish records. The South Carolina branch (Scotch-Irish) emigrated from County Derry, Ireland, around 1744. Lawrence County Hillhouses are descendants of Eli and his wife, Mary Dean, arriving in Arkansas around 1812. They had five children: Atlantic, Lavira, Serbira, Aarron and Rosetta. Serbira and W. B. Marshall had a son whom they named Jasper Newton, February 22, 1832-February 12, 1902. He took his mother's family name of Hillhouse. Jasper served as County Clerk of Lawrence County, County Judge and then as a teacher for the remainder of his life. He built the first frame school building in the county and in 1850, he traveled to St. Louis where he purchased two bells: one for the school and one for the Methodist church. On February 3, 1874, he married Ann Eliza "Daught" Wasson, August 24, 1847-February 16, 1935, and they set up housekeeping on a farm one and one fourth miles south of Smithville. They had four children: Benjamin Milton, May 15, 1875-October 30, 1950; Lockey Geneva, June 17, 1879-1881; Sydney Ralph, February 8, 1882-March 21, 1958; and Floy Louise, April 2, 1884-June 7, 1975.

Ben married Bernice Venoy Baker on December 2, 1906, and moved to Jesup where he started the Hillhouse Brothers general store. He was a successful farmer, merchant and trader. Syd never married and lived at the original farm home near Smithville with his mother. In addition to the Hillhouse Brothers Jesup store, he and Ben opened a store in Smithville. The brothers held extensive farming interests in Lawrence County and Southeast Missouri. Floy married Kennard Baker on January 20, 1912. The Bakers bought a farm near Batesville and for many years Kennard was employed at the Batesville Cotton Compress. Floy was active in the Rural Women's Missionary Society and the Moorfield Women's Home Demonstration Club. They did not have any children.

Ben and Bernice's children are: Rebecca Jane, April 1, 1908-June 4, 1996; Helen Avo, born January 5, 1910; Willie Louise, November 5, 1912-February 23, 1928; Glenn Marshall, March 25, 1914-September 14, 1986; Ray Baker, born June 24, 1916; and Geneva Deanne, November 15, 1918-February 10, 1998.

Jane married Lo Byron Holt on August 20, 1926. They moved to Missouri where Lo farmed and worked in a general store. Jane was employed as a postal clerk. They had two children: Rebecca Daphine, born August 8, 1927; and Evelyn Louise, June 3, 1929-March 29, 1976.

Helen married Benjamin Clyde Robins on May 26, 1929. In 1935, they relocated to Phoenix, Arizona, where Clyde worked as a federal inspector of citrus and vegetables. Helen was a bookkeeper and personnel manager. In 1975, she returned to

Arkansas and now resides in Batesville. They had one child, Ferna Alene, born October 1, 1930.

Glenn married Charlene Kunz on April 9, 1942. After World War II, Glenn and Charlene moved to Southeast Missouri where he purchased land that he farmed. Their children are: Glenn Marshall Jr., born August 17, 1943; Patricia Ann, born March 13, 1947; Marilyn Jane, born November 16, 1948; and Margaret Louise, born November 17, 1955.

Ray married Nelsene Brewer on January 21, 1940. Shortly after their marriage they also bought land in Southeast Missouri which Ray farmed. Their children are: June Louann, born June 9, 1941; James Sydney, born September 1, 1944; Johnny Ray, born August 30, 1946; Jana Lee, born March 14, 1949; Benjamin Michael, May 17, 1951-February 14, 1969; and Lisa Ann, born October 22, 1957.

Geneva married Claude Durham Mullen on June 1, 1947. Claude worked as a rural mail carrier. Geneva was postmaster and clerk at the Jesup store. They had one child, Deanna Sue, born October 27, 1948.

In addition to the above listed grandchildren, Ben and Bernice have 19 great-grandchildren, 15 great-great-grandchildren and one great-great-great-grandchild. *–Helen Robins.*

HILLHOUSE FAMILY.
John Hillhouse, born 1744, was of Scotch-Irish descent and a captain in the Revolutionary War. He was the son of William Hillhouse, who moved to York District, South Carolina, from Ireland.

John married Margaret Chowkes and they were the parents of 12 children, one being named Eli, who married Mary "Polly" Dean. Eli and Polly moved from South Carolina about 1812, to a farm near Strawberry River in Smithville, Arkansas. Eli died between 1820 and 1825. His wife, Polly, was murdered the summer of 1831, by one of her Negro slaves who was trying to gain his freedom. He escaped in a boat going down Strawberry River, but was captured, brought to trial, convicted and put to death by hanging. This was the first legal execution in Lawrence County.

Eli and Polly were the parents of five children, one being Sebira, the mother of Jasper Newton Hillhouse, born February 22, 1832.

At the age of 20, Jasper Newton was elected as Lawrence County Clerk and served for four years. He also served four years as County Judge.

The greater part of his life, however, was devoted to public teaching. After retiring from public

Benjamin Clyde and Helen Hillhouse Robins; taken in approximately 1943.

Jasper Newton and Ann Eliza Wasson Hillhouse with their children: Floy Louise, Benjamin Milton (center) and Sydney Ralph; taken in approximately 1893.

teaching he continued to teach school one half day weekdays in his home. He was known to be highly educated in those days and owned a large library containing many classics. He married Anne Eliza Wasson, born August 24, 1847, who was the daughter of Finis and Sophia Wasson of Smithville.

Jasper Newton and Anne were the parents of four children. (see previous history for photo)

1. Benjamin Milton Hillhouse, May 15, 1878-October 30, 1950.

2. Lockie Geneva Hillhouse, June 17, 1879-September 15, 1880.

3. Sydney Ralph Hillhouse, February 8, 1882-March, 1957; was never married.

4. Floy Louise Hillhouse, April 2, 1884-June 7, 1975, married Kennard Baker, the son of James Polk Baker and Margaret Bilbrey. They had no children.

Benjamin Milton Hillhouse and Bernice Vernoy Baker, October 28, 1885-October 30, 1962, married December 2, 1906. They were the parents of six children.

1. Rebecca Jane Hillhouse, April 1, 1908-June 4, 1996, married Lo Byron Holt of Smithville.

2. Helen Avo Hillhouse, born January 4, 1910, married Clyde Robins of Strawberry.

3. Willie Louise Hillhouse, November 4, 1912-February 23, 1928.

4. Glenn Marshall Hillhouse, March 25, 1914-September 14, 1984, married Charlene Kinz of Wyatt, Missouri.

5. Ray Baker Hillhouse, born June 24, 1916, married Nelsene Brewer, daughter of the late Nels and Nellie Brewer of Batesville.

6. Geneva Deann Hillhouse, November 15, 1918-June 10, 1998, married Claude Mullen of Strawberry.

Helen Robins resides in Batesville. She and Ray Hillhouse are the only remaining living children of Ben and Bernice Hillhouse.

Ben Hillhouse and Syd Hillhouse were equal partners in what was known as "Hillhouse Brothers." They owned two general merchandise stores in Smithville and Jesup in Lawrence County. These stores being in small communities served the citizens with a multitude of supplies from "eggs to caskets." A corner of the store in Jesup was used as a United States Post Office where Ray Hillhouse served as a United States Postmaster, along with managing the store until he and his wife moved to Mississippi County, Missouri, to take over the farming operations owned by Hillhouse Brothers. Other holdings of Hillhouse Brothers, included a cotton gin and the buying and selling of livestock. They also owned extensive farmland in Arkansas and Missouri.

Mr. and Mrs. Ray Hillhouse live in Charleston, Missouri, where they raised six children. They are the grandparents of six and have one great-grandchild. Ray is retired from farming, but assists his son, John, in the operation of farming approximately 2,200 acres which they own in Mississippi County, Missouri.

1. John Ray Hillhouse married Nancy Bryant and they have one daughter. Nancy is also the mother of two sons.

2. James Sydney Hillhouse married Pam Lietke and they have two sons. They live in Windsor, Colorado and own the architectural firm of Hillhouse Associates, Inc. James is an architect.

3. June Hillhouse Slinkerd of Destin, Florida, is employed by the Destin Beach Club condominium complex. She has two sons and one grandchild.

4. Jana Hillhouse Lee of Dania, Florida is an Executive Assistant with Paper Partners, Inc. She has one son.

5. Lisa Ann Hillhouse resides in Charleston, Missouri.

6. Benjamin Michael Hillhouse died in an automobile accident in 1969, at the age of 17.

Jasper Newton Hillhouse, Anne Eliza Wasson Hillhouse. Children: Benjamin Milton Hillhouse, standing left, Sydney Ralph Hillhouse, standing right, Floy Louise Hillhouse, girl seated on left. – *Ray Hillhouse.*

FRANK HOELSCHER (HOLSCHER) HISTORY.

Frank H. Holscher was born on April 16, 1839, it is believed in Alten Melle, Lower Saxony (Niedersachsen), Germany (Prussia), to parents Franz Heinrich and Maria Gertrude Tettinghof Holscher. After spending some odd 20 years in Amsterdam, he sailed for America, arrived on June 20, 1886, and eventually settled in Imboden. Two of his brothers also came to America: Dave "David" and Henry B. With his brother, Dave, and others, he helped build a small Catholic church in Imboden in 1888. He also married Mary "Marian" Helenam Heitz there on April 9, 1888. Mary had been born on June 18, 1868, in Toledo, Ohio, to parents Ludovican "Louis" and Helenam Sarah Kauz Heitz. Frank and Mary's first child died at birth, but a second, Mary Elizabeth (Schaechtel), was born in Imboden on August 13, 1890, (died 1986). Shortly afterwards, the family moved to Randolph County and eventually settled on a farm in Shiloh Township west of Pocahontas not far from the Eleven Point River. Five other children followed: a son who died at birth; Clara (Bauer, Mills) in 1895, died 1986; Agnes, in 1897, died 1914; Joseph Henry, in 1897, died 1989; Anna Mary (Sorg), in 1903, died 1998; Catherine (nicknamed Katie), in 1909, died 1953. Frank also applied for naturalization as a United States citizen and was granted this on July 29, 1902. By this time, his last name was spelled Hoelscher which was the Americanized version of the original Holscher name with the umlaut over the "o". Frank passed away in 1929, and Mary in 1949, in Pocahontas. Many descendants of these early Hoelschers still live in that county.

Frank and Mary's son, Joseph, stayed on the original family farm on what is now Hoelscher Lane west of Pocahontas. He married Martha Melissa McCoy, 1894-1977, in 1921, and had six children: Paul, 1926-1935; James Edward Sr., born November 11, 1927; William; Robert; Leo; and Christine.

James Edward served in the Marines in World War II and later in the Army Reserve and National Guard plus attended the University of Arkansas in Fayetteville, obtaining a BS and MS in Agronomy. He married Madonna Elaine Thennes, born May 16, 1925, on September 6, 1952, in Pocahontas. They had five children: Linda Elaine, born November 16, 1954; James Edward Jr., born August 22, 1955; Joseph Matthew "Joey", born December 26, 1956; Elizabeth Ann "Betty", born November 11, 1958; and Edward Michael, born May 21, 1960.

After the Korean War and finishing college, James Sr. went to work for the County Extension Service in Northeast Arkansas and eventually with the USDA Soil Conservation Service where he was stationed in Walnut Ridge in the early 1960s, moving into a new home at 804 SW 5th Street. His wife, Elaine, who had graduated from St. Vincent's Infirmary and the University of Arkansas School of Medical Sciences in Little Rock as a registered nurse, worked as a RN at the Lawrence County Memorial Hospital during this time. The family attended the Immaculate Heart of Mary Catholic Church in Walnut Ridge and the oldest children began public schools there. Soon though, James Sr. was transferred to Nashville in the southwest corner of the state. Their children graduated from high school in Nashville in Howard County and attended the University of Alabama in Fayetteville.

Linda Elaine Sanders, school counselor, now lives in Tulsa, Oklahoma, with husband, Jimmy, and son, Jason, premed student at Oklahoma University in Norman, Oklahoma, born March 1, 1978.

Clockwise, from center: Frank H. Hoelscher, Mary Elizabeth (Schaechtel), wife Mary (Marian) Helenam Heitz, Anna Mary (Sorg), Joseph Henry, Clara (Bauer, Mills), and Agnes. Daughter Catherine not born yet. (about 1905.)

James Edward Jr., drinking water plant lab supervisor, lives in Fayetteville, Arkansas with daughter, Catherine, freshman at the University of Arkansas, Fayetteville and member AR National Guard, born December 22, 1979.

Joseph, fire department supervisor, lives in Baldwin, Kansas, with wife, Lorri Jo, and children: Leah, born November 16, 1986; Noah, born November 23, 1989; and Eli, born May 10, 1991.

Elizabeth Ann, former Army Intelligence Specialist and now postal service, lives in Fayetteville, North Carolina.

James Sr. and Elaine moved back to Pocahontas to part of the old Frank Hoelscher farm in the early 1980s. Joseph Henry, his son James Sr. and his son Edward Michael, all passed away in 1989, and are all buried at St. Paul's Cemetery in Pocahontas. Elaine still lives in Pocahontas with friends and family. –*James E. Hoelscher Jr.*

HOFFMAN FAMILY.

Christopher Hoffman, born 1814, in White County, Tennessee and Catherine Elizabeth Bishop, born April 9, 1822, in Montgomery County, Virginia, married about 1846, in Tennessee, moving to Lawrence County in 1851.

William C. Hoffman, born 1848, died before 1860.

John C. Hoffman, born October 19, 1949, in Tennessee, died April 11, 1889, married Louise Ellen Monihan, August 21, 1873, in Lawrence County; children: Amanda "Mandy", Madison W., Arthur and Charlie Hoffman.

Daniel Hoffman, born 1851, Arkansas and married January 2, 1873, to Hannah Jane Long, born 1852, in Tennessee. They had one daughter, Mary "Mollie" Hoffman, born 1874, and died before 1919. Mollie married on January 18, 1891, to Thomas H. McEntire, their children were: Rector Louis, Lolly Melvin, Jessie, Hurl "Jody", John, Horace and Alvin McEntire.

Sarah Minerva Hoffman, born January 20, 1854, in Lawrence County, died May 1, 1945, married August 27, 1876, Thomas Franklin Buchanan and they had seven children: Effie Lester, Ella A., Oral B., Hugh Emerson, Ora J., William T. and Bill William Buchanan.

Josephine Hoffman, born 1855, and died before 1870.

James L. Hoffman, born September 12, 1856, in Lawrence County, Arkansas, and died July 2, 1894, married November 30, 1882, to Sarah Ann Gilbert, born January 13, 1861, and died November, 1935, daughter of James and Francis Jane Lawrence Gilbert; four children:

1. Clara Bell Hoffman, November 4, 1883-September 13, 1972, married September 28, 1899, William H. Hales, 1879-April, 1960; children were: Viola Hales Floyd, Pauline Hales Sommerfeldt, Marcella Hales Janske, Martha Ann Hales Davis, Maxie Hales, Ralph Hales and Harrel Hales and Clarence Hales.

2. George Washington Hoffman, born May 5, 1887, in Imboden, married Ruth Gatlin on August 30, 1915, and died February 2, 1951; children: Sue, James and Mary Sue Hoffman.

3. Elizabeth Catherine "Lizzie" Hoffman, February 26, 1891-1929, married September 15, 1912, to Abe Meredith Decker.

4. James L. Hoffman Jr. was born September 18, 1894 (after father's death), and died January 21, 1977. On February 23, 1921, he married Christena Octavious Sudduth, June 23, 1901-January 12, 1990, burial in Lawrence Memorial. Their children: Marguerite L., born December 13, 1921, married November 14, 1938, Rector Eli Wright, son of Ira Lee and Mollie Tolbert Wright; J. L. Hoffman, born April 12, 1925, and married November 11, 1944, Della Jane Wooley, daughter of Virgil A. and Ottie Ballard Wooley; Jack LaMar Hoffman, born May 12, 1929, and married May 18, 1950, Margaret Marie Amos, daughter of Isom and Bertha Bates Amos; Billy Joe Hoffman, born August 31, 1931, and married July 24, 1965, Vivian Hollans McMullen, daughter of W. E. and Mary Chesser Hollans.

Joseph Hoffman, born about 1858, died very young.

Francis C. "Fannie" Hoffman, September, 1861-1901, married September 4, 1887, to William James Ellis and had six children before her death: Adolphus, Ida O., James F., Sarah E., Artie L. and Henry Shafter Ellis.

Any one wishing to exchange or correct information may write submitter: Barbara Wright Miller, 211 W. Michigan Avenue, Clinton, Michigan 49236.

HOLDER FAMILY. Thomas Holder was born about 1785. Thomas Holder and Nancy had the following children.

1. Isaac Holder.
2. Abner Holder was born in South Carolina about 1804. He married Linda in Georgia about 1830. Linda was born in North Carolina bout 1803.
3. Bennett W. Holder was born about 1805.

Bennett W. Holder "Thomas" was born in South Carolina about 1805. Bennett W.? Holder and Sally had the following children:
1. Henry J. Holder, who died October 24, 1901.
2. Patsey Martha Holder, who died 1867. She married James McKinney in Jackson County, Alabama, 1838. James was born about 1826.
3. Thomas Holder died 1911. He married Nancy Jane Gibson in McNairy County, Tennessee, 1850. Nancy was born in Tennessee about 1828. Nancy died after 1900, in Spring River, Lawrence County, Arkansas. Nancy died after 1900, in Spring River, Lawrence County, Arkansas.
4. William M. Holder died May 7, 1922. He married Patricia Sarah Halstead in McNairy County, Tennessee, March 11, 1849. Patricia was born about 1831.
5. Sally Holder.
6. James Holder married Malinda Jane Halstead. Malinda was born about 1836.
7. Nancy J. E. Holder.
8. Joshua A. Holder married Mary Jane Hambleton in Spring River, Lawrence County, Arkansas, March 18, 1858. Mary was born about 1840.
9. Lucy Holder died after 1910. She married Bennett C. Washam in Spring River, Lawrence County, Arkansas, May 17, 1857. Bennett was born about 1842.
10. Bledsoe Holder was born about 1834.

Bledsoe Holder was born in Jackson County, Alabama, about 1834. He married twice. He married an unknown person in McNairy County, Tennessee, about 1852. He married Elizabeth in Spring River, Lawrence County, Arkansas, about 1852. Elizabeth was born about 1834. Bledsoe Holder and Elizabeth had the following children:
1. Nancy J. Holder.
2. Sarah Holder.
3. William T. Holder died 1900. He married Mary J. Hair in Spring River, Lawrence County, Arkansas, February 29, 1872. Mary was born about 1856.
4. Andrew J. Holder.
5. Marion A. Holder.
6. James S. Holder died September 10, 1938. He married Sarah Mashburn in Spring River, Lawrence County, Arkansas, January 31, 1889. Sarah was born about 1865.
7. Bennett R. Holder died December, 1880.
8. Henry J. Holder.
9. Martha A. Holder was born about 1858. Martha married William Thomas Sharp, August 26, 1875. *–David Berlin.*

HOLDER FAMILY. The Holder family first came to Lawrence County in 1854, when Bennett Holder, 1805-1886, moved his wife, Sarah, and their 11 children from McNairy County, Tennessee. Bennett Holder had volunteered twice in the second Seminole Indian War, for which he received a government land grant of 80 acres. He was mustered in as a private in Company I of North Alabama Volunteers on October 26, 1837. After the six month term, he was honorably discharged at Fort Mitchell on April 12, 1838. Bennett volunteered again and mustered in on June 7, 1838, as Third Corporal of Alabama Infantry Volunteers in Belfont, Alabama. After 40 days he was honorably discharged at Gunter's Landing on July 7, 1838.

Bennett is buried with many Holders in the cemetery at the Friendship Methodist Episcopal Church South. After Sarah died, Bennett married Pernicia Jane Smith Blackwell Ellison. He was 58 and she was 35.

Andrew "Jack" Jackson Holder and Sarah Gilbert Hoffman Holder; about 1925.

Bennett and Sarah's son, Thomas, 1828-1920, fought at the Battle of Prairie Grove, Arkansas, in Company D under Colonel Robert Shaver on December 7, 1862, along with three of his brothers: Henry J., James and Joshua. Thomas was wounded and later discharged at Little Rock. He and his wife, Nancy Jane Gibson, had 15 children.

Thomas Holder and Nancy Jane's son, Andrew "Jack" Jackson Holder, born April, 1858, married Harriet Davis on July 31, 1879. They had six children. After Harriet died, Andrew "Jack" Jackson Holder married Sarah Gilbert Hoffman, the sister of Harriet Davis. Andrew "Jack" Jackson and Harriet's son, Thomas Wesley Holder, 1880-1938, married Audrey Belle Clements. They had nine children. Audrey was the daughter of Samuel Harrison and Sallie Berry Johnson Clements. Samuel was pastor at the Lone Oak Baptist Church and a veterinarian. Audrey is buried in Pearl, Illinois, and Thomas Wesley is buried just 30 feet from his great-grandfather, Bennett, in the cemetery of the Friendship Methodist Episcopal Church South. Thomas Wesley and Audrey had nine children.

Thomas and Audrey's son, Calvin Dolye Holder, 1903-1982, married Clara Belle Pruite, 1907-1985, in Jonesboro on August 24, 1925. They had one son, Harold Luther. Calvin was a farmer as were his ancestors, but gave up farming and moved to Flint, Michigan, to work.

Calvin and Clara's son, Harold Luther Holder, the author of this story, was born December 18, 1930, four miles east of the Friendship Methodist Episcopal Church South. I remember my mother telling me how she walked the four miles to the church in all kinds of weather. She had a beautiful voice and sang alto in the choir. Most of the church members today are Holders or related in some way. Though there are still many Holders living in Lawrence County, most have moved to other parts of the country. There are two Holder Roads in Lawrence County and a Holder Street in Walnut Ridge. Holders have been and still are in all professions: the military, farming, business, law, medicine, writing, teaching and politics. William "Bill" Holder has been, for many years, the Lawrence County Treasurer. *–Harold Holder.*

HOLDER FAMILY. Bennett and Sally Holder were born in South Carolina about 1805. After their marriage, they lived in Franklin County, Tennessee, Jackson County, Alabama, and McNairy County, Tennessee. They had several children, one of whom was Thomas. While the family was living in McNairy County, in about 1849, Thomas married Nancy Jane Gibson. In the 1850s, the Holder family came to Lawrence County, Arkansas, settling in Union Township which later became Spring River Township. Thomas was in the Civil War with Robert G. Shaver's regiment of the 38th Arkansas Infantry, Company D, serving with them at the Battle of Prairie Grove, Arkansas.

Thomas and Nancy had 13 children, one of whom was William J. "Billy" Holder. William J. married Luvina Helms, daughter of Wyatt and Elizabeth Helms. They lived their entire married life in the Spring River Township and had nine children: Samantha Albertine, Henry, Effie, Martin, Jesse, Redman Daniel, Dellia and Willie. Samantha, Martin and Willie all died at an early age. Redman married Viola Ward, daughter of Charles and Mary Songer Ward. They had seven children: Ruby who died in infancy, Lucille, Almer, Louie, Pauline, Charles William "Bill" and Edward. In 1933, Redman and Viola moved to the Richwoods Community where they lived until 1952; they moved to Pocahontas where they lived until their deaths.

Lucille married Wilson "Bill" Davis. Their children are Billy Ray, Kathern, Don, Darrell, Dale and Ricky. Almer Louie married Eva Simpson. Their children are Gale and Daphene. Pauline married Johnie Stone. Their children are Linda, Joan, Larry, Brenda and Gary. Pauline died in 1965, in a car-train accident. Floyd married Georgia Woodard. Their children are Kelly and Barbara. Charles "Bill" married Billye Woodard. Their daughters are Debra and Denise. Edward married Joyce Forehand. Their daughters are Sharon Kay and Beverly.

Almer Louie served in the U.S. Army during World War II and Floyd served during the Korean Conflict.

Descendants of Redman and Viola living in Lawrence County in 1998, are Lucille and Bill Davis, their children, Kathern Richardson, Darrell, Dale "Cotton" and Ricky Davis and families and Pauline's daughter, Joan Stout. –Joyce Holder.

WILLIAM THOMAS "BILL" AND SAMANTHA HELMS HOLDER.

William Thomas "Bill" Holder was the son of Bledsoe Holder and Elizabeth Gibson. Bledsoe and Elizabeth had moved to Lawrence County about 1856, and settled in the Opposition area where William was born in March of 1857. William had two older sisters, Nancy Jane and Sarah A., a younger sister, Martha Ann, and six younger brothers: Andrew Jackson, Bletch, Bennett, Henry James, Charles N., John "Pony" and one unnamed. Nancy married David Richard McEntire. Sarah married Benjamin F. Ragsdale. Martha married Rev. William T. Sharp. Andrew married Harriett Davis and Sarah Davis. Bletch married Elizabeth Ann Bottoms. Henry married Lucy Washum. Charles married Mary Gilbert and Florence Burk. John married Emma McBride.

William married Samantha Helms on July 27, 1879, in Opposition. Samantha was the daughter of Wyatt and Elizabeth Helms. Her family had also migrated to Lawrence County about 1855. Samantha was born in 1861. She was from a family of 10 children, many of whom are profiled in this book. William was a farmer and they lived their entire lives in Spring River Township.

William and Samantha had a daughter, Etta, born in October, 1888. It is possible that they also had another daughter who was born after 1880, and died young. They also had three sons, Ervin Richard born in November, 1890; Robert Clifton born January 6, 1891; and Clinton Wyatt born January 7, 1893. Etta died from a snakebite in 1901. Ervin married Lester Moore and Alpha Bell Rosselot and had a total of 10 children. Robert married Susie Pickett and they had five children. Wyatt, as he was known by, married Telitha LaVesta Doyle, the daughter of Jefferson Davis Doyle and they had seven children.

Samantha died in 1893, when her youngest child was about two months old. She is buried in Friendship Cemetery next to her daughter, Etta. William later remarried. He married Mrs. Nettie Allen on August 12, 1897. William died in 1900, and is buried in Friendship Cemetery next to Samantha. Nettie is also buried in Friendship cemetery. After William's death, his sons went to live with an uncle, Charles Holder After they were grown, all three sons married and raised their families in Lawrence County. –Nancy Matthews.

HENRY BENNETT HOLDER FAMILY.

Henry "Bennett" Holder, 1882-1968, was born at Black Rock nearly two months after his father's death. His parents were Henry Bennett, 1856-1882, and Sarah Elizabeth Sharp, 1852-1950. She was a descendant of the Solomon Sharp, 1795-1839, family - some of the earliest settlers in Arkansas and from which Sharp County is named. She later married James "Matt" Smith. Widowed again, she lived much of her 98 years with Bennett.

His siblings were Katie Bell, 1874-1959, married James Hathcoat; Mollie, 1876-1959, married Joseph Bottoms; Arson Phipps, 1877-1963, married Modena Webb; Albert Edward, 1879-1969, married Martha Webb, later Sarah Burrow Chappell; and Vinnie, 1880-1881.

In 1901, at the age of 19, Bennett married Mary Jane Dunegan, 1884-1963, from the

Batesville area. They bought a farm and moved to the Opposition Community near Ravenden. He was a farmer and one of the early leaders in the Opposition Church of Christ. Ten of their 11 children were born there. Although successful, he tired of the hill country and moved his family to flatland near Walnut Ridge.

Henry Bennett and Mary Jane Holder, 60th wedding anniversary, December 19, 1961.

He would later often comment, with his unique wit and humor, that he "tried to raise his older children on a rock pile." He moved in a wagon, but since Mary was near delivery with their last child, she was put on a train at Ravenden to Hoxie.

Their children were: Thurman, 1903-1967, married Anna Fain; Ida Lee, 1905-1980, married Joseph Sandefer; Roland, 1907-1952, married Millie Kirby; Katie May, 1909-1988, married Elmer Nicholson; Alma, 1911-1992, married Earle Smith; Bennett Franklin, 1913-1917; Mary Agnes, 1914-1934; Josephine, born 1916, married Reginald Allen, later Andrew Motes; Geneva, born 1918, married Dowell Ramer; Henry Bennett "Junior", 1919-1986, married Ruth Teel; Darrell, 1922-1980, married Betty Hibbard.

Bennett was a successful farmer near Walnut Ridge and a staunch Democrat. Election time would find him in the heat of the process fighting for his favorite candidate. He and his family were faithful members of Main Street Church of Christ where he served as an elder for over 30 years.

Grandchildren are - Thurman's: Wanda Lee, deceased; Raymond Corbett, deceased; and Mary Etta. Ida Lee's children: Bobby Glynn, deceased; and Marieta Faye. Roland's children: Billy Ray and Ronnie. Katie May's children: Marguerite, Madge, Deloris and Kenneth. Alma's children: Patsy Karen. Josephine's children: Marcia, Judith, Marie and Jacquline. Geneva's children: Alma Jean and Janet Lee. Henry Bennett "Junior's" children: Michael Wayne and Scott Keith. Darrell's children: Charles Richard and Bennett Darrell.

Family residing in Lawrence County in 1999, are daughter Geneva Ramer, daughter-in-law Ruth Teel Holder; grandchildren Don and Patsy Smith Cooper, Scott and Becky Roberts Holder. In the area are daughter-in-law Betty Hibbard Holder, grandchildren Richard and Janis Redwine, Bennett and Jodie Statler, Michael and Lisa Gipson Holder, in Paragould. Gary and Janet Ramer Overstreet in Pocahontas, and George and Alma Jean Ramer French in Monticello and Little Rock.

In the late 1920s, and early 1930s, Katie May, Ida Lee, Josephine, Thurman and Roland went to Michigan. Thurman and Roland worked for Ford Railways and lived in Detroit. Daughter-in-law Anna Fain Holder still lives there. The daughters lived in Flint and worked in automotive industries. They all have families living throughout the country, mainly, North and Northeast. Daughter Josephine Motes now lives in Edgewater, Florida.

Bennett's siblings, Arson and Albert, Katie Hathcoat and Mollie Bottoms have many descendants in Lawrence County. –Betty Holder.

HOLLAND FAMILY.

William Holland was born in Virginia, August 23, 1805. He died September 1, 1883, in Gatewood, Ripley County, Missouri. He married Minerva Ann Scott in Kentucky about 1829. Minerva was born in Barren County, Kentucky, May 2, 1810. She was the daughter of John William Scott and Francis Wood. William and Minerva had the following children:

1. Sarah Melinda Holland married Martin Hudson in Macon County, Tennessee.
2. James Mitchell Holland married Elizabeth Pedigo. He died April 5, 1861.
3. John Martin Holland married Nancy McDonald.
4. William H. Holland married Cyrena Fanny Mungle.
5. Henry Holland.
6. Mary Frances Holland married John W. Meador.
7. Manerva Ann Holland died August 6, 1947.
8. Scott M. Holland married Sarah Frances Gum. He died April 20, 1913, in Gatewood, Missouri.

Wiley S. Holland, born April 3, 1831.

9. Wiley S. Holland was born in Macon County, Tennessee, April 3, 1831. He married Sarah Rush in Macon County, Tennessee, November 9, 1851. Sarah was born in Macon County, January 6, 1832. She was the daughter of Joshua Rush and Elizabeth Springer. He married Nancy F. Tipton in Ripley County, Missouri, April 24,1913. Wiley was a lieutenant in the Union Army during the Civil War. He was wounded in the left leg at Solomon's Grove, Fayetteville, North Carolina during Sherman's March. Wiley and Sarah had the following children.

1. James Frederick Holland married Sarah L. Campbell in Ripley County, Missouri, August 5, 1883. He died January 3, 1907.
2. Mary Elizabeth Holland married Russell L. Pulliam in Ripley County, Missouri, July 1, 1877. She died July 3, 1879.
3. Manervia Frances Holland married Barnabas A. O'Neal, May 31, 1874, and second married Kenner about 1889. She died in 1904.
4. William John Holland died October 10, 1860.
5. Clark Holland married Sarah Holcomb, January 12, 1899. He died July 25, 1952.
6. Martha Ann Holland married John Louis Pulliam, February 15, 1887. She died in Dewar, Oklahoma, April 7, 1970.
7. Thomas Randolph Holland married Lucy McCauley, May 30, 1900. He died April 15, 1962.
8. Wiley Benjamin Holland married Zilpha Jane Pulliam, April 1, 1894. He died July 23, 1961.
9. Samuel Lafayette Holland married America Mahalie Holcomb, January 12, 1899. He died May 2, 1961.
10. Mark Holland was born in Macon County, Tennessee, November 13, 1861. He married Sarah E. Henderson, April 26, 1883. She was the daughter of William J. Henderson and Martha Witcher Springer. He died July 20, 1954.

11. Sarah Lousie Holland was born July 30, 1866. She married Andrew W. Henderson, son of William J. Henderson and Martha Witcher Springer. –David Berlin.

HOLOBAUGH. David Green Holobaugh, 1813-1861, and his wife, Elizabeth Ann Winders, came to Lawrence County, Arkansas, in 1845, from Shelby County, Tennessee. David was of Pennsylvania Dutch (German) ancestry, being the son of John George Holobaugh and Margaret Innes of Rowan County, North Carolina, near the town of Salisbury. The parents of John George Holobaugh were George Holobaugh and Susanna Savitz.

James Harvey Holobaugh, born April 7, 1851, died October 13, 1889, in Black Rock, Arkansas.

Relatives from Rowan County, North Carolina (Winders, Dent, Park and Gibbens) also came to Lawrence County. Other close relatives, John Mathis Hollabaugh, George A. Hollabaugh and James Calvin Hollabaugh came to Pope, Searcy and Washington Counties in Arkansas, respectively.

David Holobaugh and his wife took up land and lived near Black Rock and Imboden. He was a farmer, deputy sheriff and road overseer.

Seven children were born to this union: Susan A., John David "Bud", Green Paul, James Harvey, Mary M., Narcissa Ellen and Lucinda Elizabeth Holobaugh. John David and Green Paul left Lawrence County in 1864, when Union troops marched through the area. John joined the service and was part of a Missouri unit. Green was too young for the service and eventually went to Texas and died there in 1892. Narcissa Ellen married Stephen Jasper Park and lived in the Portia area. Lucinda Elizabeth married William Park, brother of S. J., and moved to Roseburg, Oregon.

James Harvey Holobaugh, 1851-1889, married Mary Susan Grizzle and located in the Clear Springs Community between Black Rock and Imboden. Jim and Susie had the following: Martha Anna, William Stephen "Bill" John David, Charles Henry, Leila E., Myrtle E., Jennie Winders and Jessie J. Holobaugh.

The writer of this sketch is a great-grandson of William Stephen Holobaugh, 1877-1920, and his wife, Martha Ellen Cravens. Martha was a daughter of Jerry N. Cravens and Cynthia Johnson. Bill and Martha lived in Lawrence and Randolph Counties and became the parents of Ruth, Betty, Willie, James Harvey, Robert Karr, Jennie Sue Hardin, Ines Marie, Christine, Nettie Mae and Pauline Holobaugh. W. S. "Bill" Holobaugh was a farmer. Martha Cravens Holobaugh lived in Pocahontas and Ft. Smith until her death in 1967.

James Harvey Holobaugh, 1904-1974, had a barber shop in Black Rock for a few years before moving to Pocahontas about 1938. He continued to barber until his death. His wife, Irene Foster, was a daughter of Wade Hampton Foster and Lou Forrester of Black Rock. Three children were born to Jim and Irene: Wil-

liam Harvey "Bill", Betty Lou and Joan Holobaugh.

Robert Karr Holobaugh, 1907-1993, and wife, Beulah Moore, lived in Black Rock many years, where he was a building contractor and carpenter. They had the following children: William Robert, Walter Charles, Mary Ellen, Patsy Ann, James Moore and Gene Larry Holobaugh.

In recent years, at least two members of the David Holobaugh family still live and serve in Lawrence County, one being a past county sheriff and the other a bank official. –*William Holobaugh Rogers.*

HOLT-NORRIS FAMILY. Mary Ann Holt born on November 11, 1835 in Lauderdale county Alabama moved to Lawrence County Arkansas with her family before 1850.

Mary Ann met and married Thomas Norris, born in 1830 in Arkansas, who worked in the local grocery store. Mary and Thomas Norris married in Lawrence County on July 4, 1852. To htis union these known children were born in Arkansas; Martha Jane, 1854; Thomas Jefferson (Jeff) 1855; Laura F., 1859; Sarah A., 1861.

The was between the states came in the process of all wars people die. Thomas Norris was one of many persons who died.

–*Nelta Depree Evans*

RICHARD JASPER HOOTON, son of John Riley Hooton and Nancy Penn, was born March 27, 1855, in Strawberry, Lawrence County, Ar-

The family of Richard Jasper Hooton and Sarah Jane Bearden Hooton; about 1908. Front, left to right: Bertha, Burlie, Richard Jasper "Uncle Dick", Sarah Jane "Aunt Jane", Tom White, husband of Margaret Hooton White holding Opal. Back: Nora and Will, children of Jeff J. Hooton, Louisa (Campbell-Slayton), Jim, Vicie, Slayton, Joe, Ross, Richard.

kansas. He died in Tipton, Oklahoma, March 8, 1926, and is buried in City Cemetery. He was a farmer and member of the Church of Christ. Dick and Sarah Jane Bearden were married on July 18, 1874, in Lawrence County, Arkansas.

Jane was a daughter of John Bearden and Caroline Wilson, born May 22, 1857, in Lawrence County and died December 20, 1943, in Pocahontas, Randolph County, Arkansas. She was buried in Lancaster Cemetery, Strawberry.

All 13 children were born in Lawrence County. John Riley lived briefly in 1877, and Cora Uphenia in 1893. Joseph Jefferson "Joe", July 9, 1875-September 4, 1950, wed Laura Belle Harris and had a son, Otis, who died young. Joe and Otis lived with Dick and Jane.

Nancy Abby Hooton, June 5, 1878-January, 1905, married Oscar Freeman. Her one child died young and she suffered an epileptic seizure and died of burns.

Margaret Caroline, September 14, 1880-

July 5, 1942, and husband, Thomas Franklin White, had children: Tishie Ellen married Virgil Raymond Moughler and Lora Jane married William Leo McKnight. Cnorous White married Barrett Noblin and all three of the sisters had children and lived in Flint, Michigan, in 1969.

Jane, November 2, 1882-January 1, 1964 wed Burlie B. Slayton and arrived in Tipton Oklahoma with a son, Enos Eber, and daughter, Velma, was born November 3, 1912, and died February 13, 1922, there. Eber had no children and died about 1990, in Oklahoma.

Richard Bandy Hooton, December 30, 1885-March 5, 1971, and Hattie Pyland went to Brea, California, and one of their four children was born there. Bennie Lambirth lives there.

Martha Louisa, March 21, 1888-February 24, 1966, married first Thomas Campbell and second Seph Slayton. Louisa and Tom had Vivian, Lillian, Eber, Wanda and Velma. Vivian, Lillian and Velma live in Walnut Ridge.

James Franklin, March 9, 1890-May 13, 1956, wed Viola Vicie Lemmons in Randolph County, Arkansas; he died in Tipton, Tillman County, Oklahoma. They had three sons and a daughter, Pauline Kohler. Pauline lives in Electra, Texas.

Burlie Levi "Dock" and Bertha Lou Tishie were born September 22, 1897. Dock married Laura Pettyjohn and lived in Memphis, Tennessee, many years. Their daughters, Anna Lee Weber and Mary Sue Posey, live in Texas where Aunt Laura celebrated her 100th birthday last year. Richard lives in Pine Bluff, Arkansas.

Betha and Irvin Sutton wed and lived in Reyno, Arkansas, where Irvin died in 1930. Their daughters are: Janelle Tomlin and Eunice Spurlock. Janelle left a daughter, Debra Lynn. Eunice Spurlock lives in Kilgore, Texas and has two sons and two daughters. –*Flo Hooten Gates.*

ROSS HOOTON. William Ross Hooton, a son of Richard Jasper Hooton and Sarah Jane Bearden, was born March 12, 1894, near Strawberry, Lawrence County, Arkansas, and died February 6, 1976, at Newport, Arkansas. He married Thena Minnie Della Bowers, September 4, 1896-June 8, 1976, in Pocahontas, Arkansas, on December 31, 1915. They are both buried in Masonic Cemetery Pocahontas.

Herbert Hillman, born December 4, 1916; Reba Jolene, born June 25, 1918; and Ralph Lavoy, born February 13, 1920, were born in Pocahontas before the family moved to Oklahoma.

Glyn Bowers Hooton, born June 6, 1922, in Altus; Don Riley, November 4, 1923, in Cordell; Etta Flodelle, born September 26, 1927; and Elizabeth Sue, born January 15, 1930, in Tipton, joined the Hooton family.

They returned to Arkansas and lived in the Walnut Ridge area where William Ross Hooton Jr. "Dub" arrived on May 9, 1933, and Nada Jane on June 27, 1934.

They moved to Pocahontas in 1935, and lived there until 1944. They moved to Kansas, Mississippi, Arkansas, Texas and back to Arkansas, where Ross and Della both died.

Ralph, Glyn, Don and Dub all served in the United States military and returned safely home. Don died in an automobile accident. The rest of the family married and gave Ross and Della 20 grandchildren. Most of them have reproduced. Hillman, Jolene, Ralph and Don are buried in Pocahontas.

Hillman married Leila Felts and Jacque Wolverton before the move to New Mexico. His

Golden Anniversary - December 31, 1965 - Pocahontas, Arkansas. William Ross and Della Bowers Hooton. From left: Flo Gates, W. R., Jr., Ralph, Jolene Smith, Hillman Hooton, Betty Smith, Glyn and Nada Stenberg.

children were born in Arkansas. James Lynn died in California and is buried at Walnut Ridge. Jean lives in New Mexico and Dwight in Georgia.

Jolene married Buel Smith and had five children. He and his daughters, Suanne Walker, Beth Smith and Kay Gowen, and their families are in Searcy, Arkansas. His sons, Rick and Steve, and their families live in Houston, Texas.

Ralph and Thelma Babb have three sons, Fred, Ted and Kenny, and all live in Arkansas. Fred and Ted have families.

Glyn and wife, Lottie Gramling, live in Paragould, after many years in New Mexico. Their children, born in Arkansas, Jane Townsend and Gaye Childress, live in Denton, Texas, and Vance Hooton in Albuquerque, near their families.

Flo and Denzil Gates have lived in many places with the Air Force and retired to Midwest City, Oklahoma. Their daughter, Debra Eileen "Debbe" King, is in California.

William Ross Jr. "Dub" married Nadine Blalock in San Antonio, Texas and now lives in Lufkin. He has two sons, W. R. III "Bill", in Pennsylvania and Don in Arizona.

Nada and E. V. Stenberg were married in San Antonio, Texas and had two sons, E. V. Jr. "Butch" and Timmy. Stan and Timmy died early and Butch and his family are in San Diego, California. *–Flo Hooten Gates.*

MELVON CORNELIUS "JAKE" HORTON,
son of Minnie Trimble and Thomas M. Horton, was born in Richwoods in 1896. His dad, Tom, left Marshall County, Tennessee in 1882, with his brothers James, William J. and his twin, Benjamin C., about 20 years after their father, John N. Horton, (4 Tennessee Cavalry) died during the Civil War. They lived in Ash Flat till 1886, before moving to Richwoods.

Tom died around 1898 (the last time he appeared in the tax records). Jake's sister, Salina, born 1898, died as a child. On December 21, 1904, Minnie Horton married James M. Sagely. They had two children, Leola, known as "Tincey" and Virginia Melford, known as Jack.

Jake attended all eight years of school at Richwoods, and then worked for Sam Dillport, a farmer in the Richwoods Community. In May, 1916, he married Dona Collins, daughter of Preston and Sara Suda Moody Collins, from the nearby Clearlake Community.

When their daughter, Agnes, was two years old, Jake and Dona moved to Egypt, Arkansas, where Jake farmed. Later they moved to Cash. At Egypt, their house was demolished by a tornado. Afterwards, the family lived in an old school house for a while.

The couple's children were: Agnes, Ruby, Cletus, Carthel, M. C. Jr., Mary Sue, Oberdean,

The Jake Horton Family: Seated: Jake Horton and Dona. From left, first row: Cletus, Mary Sue, Bobby, Oberdean, Billie and Helen. From left, second row: Ruby, Carthel, MC and Agnes.

Bobby, Helen and Billie June.

Jake led singing in the Church of Christ over 42 years, for worship services, gospel meetings and funerals all over Northeast Arkansas and in the bootheel of Missouri, and for funerals. He taught all his children to sing and they performed throughout the area at his direction. In addition, he taught music schools, and played the organ and piano. Jake died in 1979, and Dona in 1975. Both are buried in Johnson Cemetery at Cash. *–Carlyn R. Horton.*

ROY GOLDMAN HOUSE
was born on November 5, 1913, in Mt. Vernon, Arkansas, to Martin George "Bud" House and Sara Ellen S. Hembry House. He moved to Alicia with his father and brother, Ora, following the death of his mother, who died on December 6, 1916. He grew up in the Alicia Community and attended school at Alicia and Strangers Home.

He married Edna Opal McNutt on November 21, 1932. They were married 63 years and were parents of five children: Helen Juanita Crumpton was born August 25, 1933; Wanda Lee Moon, born April 2,1936; Jack B., born October 29, 1938; Glen D., born February 1, 1941; and J. W., born March 14, 1944.

Roy and Edna began their married life living in the Strangers Home Community and farmed. They were active in the Alicia Church of Christ and they, and several other church members, raised and harvested crops to build a new church building. He served as an elder in that church until he moved to Walnut Ridge in 1959.

Following their move to Walnut Ridge, he began working for Inman Lumber Company and remained there until his retirement in 1981. He served two terms as justice of the peace, district four and was treasurer for Main Street Church of Christ until ill health forced his resignation in 1996.

He loved Alicia and Strangers Home. Many leisure hours were spent with lifelong friends playing checkers and horseshoes, or friendly "horseplay" at Allens Store in Alicia and Strangers Home

Wedding Day, Roy and Edna House, November, 1932.

General Store. He and his friends at Allens Store formed the Alicia No-Shave Club during World War II, vowing not to shave until the war ended. These men formed a friendship that continued until death separated them.

When his health began to fail, he expressed a desire to make a "one way trip to Strangers Home." He was laid to rest there in the Strangers Home Cemetery following his death on March 2, 1997. His widow, Edna, died in 1999. *–Wanda Moon.*

ALVIN VAN CALVIN HOWARD,
born at Saffel, Arkansas, 1883, to William Griffith Howard and Sarah E. McLaughlin Howard. Their children were: Joseph W. Howard, born in Kentucky in 1868; Andrew J. Howard, born in Kentucky in 1869; William L. Howard, born in Arkansas in 1870; General Fillmore Howard, born in Arkansas in 1873; Sarah W. Howard, born in Arkansas in 1874; Mahalia J. Howard, born in Arkansas in 1876; John Howard, born in Arkansas in 1880; Alvin Van Calvin Howard, born in Arkansas in 1883; and Oliver Howard, born in Arkansas in 1891.

Alvin Van Calvin Howard married Maggie Eagan in 1901. Maggie Eagan was the daughter of Henry O. Eagan and Jennie Eagan. Their children were: Elsie, Inez, Claude, Arbelle, Audie Mack, Jack, Jaunita, Hazel, Pauline and Joe Deral Howard.

Alvin Van Calvin Howard made a living as a farmer and sawmill worker. He lived most of his life in Lawrence County. Mrs. Jones, the mother of Wendel Jones of Clover Bend, Arkansas, told me that she and Mr. Jones went to Minturn, Arkansas to buy supplies and when they got back home they discovered that they had lost a 20 dollar gold eagle. She said they were worried sick. She said, she and Mr. Jones went outside and heard a team of horses coming down the old muddy road and that Van Howard got down off his wagon and handed Mr. Jones the 20 dollar gold eagle he had found at the store, stuck in a wagon track where Mr. and Mrs. Jones had parked their wagon while loading their supplies at Minturn.

Alvin Van Calvin Howard died at age 59 at Haynes, Arkansas, 1942. *–Billy W. Howard.*

HAROLD JOSEPH HOWARD,
son of John Alexander and Stella Crooms Howard, was born on December 22, 1907, near Strawberry, Arkansas. He attended grade school at a country school called Jonesboro. In 1926, when a high school opened in Strawberry, he transferred there, where he was a member of the track team.

Mr. Howard took his first teachers' examination at Imboden, Arkansas, and was granted a second grade teachers certificate.

Mr. Howard went on to finish high school; he attended Jonesboro A and M College and received a state wide teaching certificate.

Mr. Howard began to teach school in 1930, and in 1931, married Miss Eula Smith, who was born November 11, 1911, at Strawberry.

Mr. Howard taught school for 10 years, but 40 dollars a month was not enough income to support a family, so he quit teaching school and went into the mercantile business. He owned a store in Sharp County for three years; then he opened a store at Saffell, which he ran for the next 43 years, retiring at the age of 70. During that time, they worked an average of 80 hours a week, opening the store at six o'clock and staying open until eight or nine at night, and later if it was Saturday and the movie was playing in town.

Activities for country boys were varied, but

if it was too wet to plow the boys cut sprouts or built terraces to prevent the hill land from washing. Harold and his brothers, Rufus and Talmage, fished and hunted rabbit and squirrel. They liked to coon hunt because in 1920, coon hides were a premium price and they had good hunting dogs so they would catch five or six coon a night.

Mr. Howard was converted and baptized in the Strawberry River and he remembers that 25 or 30 people were also baptized that same day.

Harold and Eula Howard are the parents of one daughter, Eleanor (Mrs. G. A. Perrin) of near Saffell. Also, two grandchildren, Mike Perrin of Oklahoma City and Mrs.. Teresa Rose of Cave City. Teresa has taught in the Strawberry school system for many years. She is the mother of two sons, Shawn and Dustin Rose.

Mrs. Eula Howard passed away of breast cancer on November 27, 1965. Mr. Howard continues to live in Saffell, surrounded by friends, loved ones and wonderful memories.
–Barbara Howard.

JOHN ALEXANDER HOWARD

JOHN ALEXANDER HOWARD was born October 24, 1879, the seventh child born to William Griffith and Sarah E. McLaughlin Howard. The Howard and McLaughlin families had migrated to Western Lawrence County from their homes in Calhoun County, Kentucky, in the fall of 1868.

The families staked a homestead in the Reeds Creek Township, near Strawberry, where they cleared land and built cabins and farmed for the remainder of their lives. Family stories told how the family had to fight bushwhackers as they lay in wait to rob or kill the settlers as they traveled through the swamps and tall cane breaks of north eastern Arkansas. The families made it safely through the swamps and staked a homestead in the Reeds Creek area near Strawberry, where they cleared land and built cabins and raised large families.

John's mother, Sarah, is a charter member of the Mt. Harmony Freewill Baptist Church at Saffell, Arkansas.

John grew up on the family farm and after his father's, William, death in 1898, of meningitis, he continued to live at home and helped his mother on the farm cared for his younger siblings.

A few years later, Sarah Howard remarried only to be widowed shortly afterward.

In January of 1907, John married Stella Croom and they began a life and a family together.

The Howard family farmed several different areas near Strawberry and John later bought some of the land he was farming and here he and Stella lived out the remainder of their lives.

John and Stella Howard raised five children: three sons, Harold J. Howard, Rufus and Talmage. Also, two daughters, Gladys (Mrs. Ivorn Har-

John Alexander Howard

ris) and Myrtie (Mrs. Homer Bell).

As her health deteriorated, John's mother, Sarah, came to live with the family, and she delighted in sitting for long periods of time in her rocking chair with young Harold in her lap. Sarah Howard died in 1910, and she and William Griffith are sleeping in the Mt. Zion Cemetery near Saffell, Arkansas.

Through the years John and Stella continued to farm and to raise their growing family.

After their children had all left home, John remarked that he wished that all the children were back at home again. He stated that he would find a way to feed all of them someway.

John Alexander Howard died on February 10, 1949, at the age of 69. He was a farmer and a member of the Odd Fellows Lodge.

Stella continued to live near her children until her death on May 10, 1976. Both are buried near three of their children in the Ward Cemetery at Strawberry, Arkansas.
–Barbara Howard.

JOSEPH EDGAR HOWARD

JOSEPH EDGAR HOWARD was born August 25, 1906, near Strawberry, Arkansas. He was the youngest child of Joseph Warren and Sarah Dukes Howard.

The Howard family traveled to the "bottoms" to pick cotton. One fall the family was living in the Crossroads Community when Warren contracted pneumonia and died on November 7, 1918. After Warren's death, Sarah returned to the Denton area of Lawrence County and worked tirelessly to care for her children. Sarah died August 18, 1936, while living in the home of her daughter and son-in-law, Roscoe and Fannie Osburn. Sarah and Warren are buried in the Clover Bend Cemetery.

Joseph Edgar Howard and Ira Evelyn Justus were married on September 20, 1927, in Smithville. Ira was the daughter of T. Y. and Estella Justus and lived in the Denton Community.

Edgar and Ira Howard were farmers and began married life on the Osburn farm. Their first child, Marie, was born here June 11, 1928.

Their second child, Lavon, was born on September 9, 1933, while the family lived on the Holt farm. Ed

Edgar and Ira Howard family, 1941-42.

later moved his family to Imboden in the "Cedar Glade" and here their last child, Vernon Lee, was born on November 2, 1938.

Edgar and Ira farmed two years on the Buster Williams farm in the Fairview Community and then moved to Walnut Ridge and farmed for several years for Dr. Hatcher in the Richwoods area.

Marie married J. B. Sharp and had begun a family when Ed and Ira quit farming. In 1950, they sold all their machinery and stock and moved to Auburndale, Florida. They remained there for several years and in 1957, returned to Lawrence County where Edgar worked for Norman Welch at his service station near College City. They later moved to the Air Base and Edgar worked for the city. Ed, as he was called, loved a practical joke and could take one as well as put one out. He had a gift of

gab and never met a stranger. Family stories are told of Saturday trips to Walnut Ridge and how Ed would still be at the car talking to friends when the family returned hours later.

J. B. Sharp died in February of 1988, and in May, 1990, Marie married Ralph Jarrett of Walnut Ridge, She and J. B. raised six children.

Lavon married Barbara Newman in September of 1957, and has lived in Wichita, Kansas, for 36 years. They have four daughters and eight grandchildren.

Vernon Lee has lived in Texas since 1964. He married Barbara Sanders and they have two children and one grandchild with a second on the way. They are divorced and Vernon has remarried.

Edgar suffered a fatal heart attack on January 23, 1963, while walking to work in the cold. Ira continued to live in Lawrence and Randolph County until her death at Pocahontas on March 4, 1979. They are at rest in the Lawrence Memorial Cemetery. –Barbara Howard.

EVAN HUDSON

EVAN HUDSON. In the state of North Carolina, Evan Hudson was born in 1808, his wife, Mary, in 1813. Their first two children were also born there. Joshua was born May 25, 1833, died July 2, 1913, in Logan County, Arkansas; he married Almira Gibson; Elizabeth, born 1834, married Lundy C. Price. In the 1840 census of Smith County, Tennessee, Evan Hudson was listed as between 30/40, male under five, male five/10, his wife, 20/30, female under five feet, and female five/10. Six children were born in Tennessee: Lucinda, born 1837, married Hugh Garside; James Franklin, born 1838, married Mrs. Mary Ann Holt Norris; Benjamin Washington, born 1842, died November 7, 1918, in Denton County, Texas, married Sarah Elizabeth Harmon and then Mary L.; Mary Ann, born 1847, died 1911, in Yell County, Arkansas; she married James Thomas Ross; David, born 1848, married Elizabeth Case, and then Mary H. Murphy; Elijah, born 1849; Martha J., born 1852, in Lawrence County, Arkansas. Mary died before the 1860 census, where they lived in Strawberry Township. Evan married Mrs. Alzira Buchanon on April 7, 1864. William was born 1865; Nancy, born 1866, and died 1882, in Denton County, Texas; and James C., born 1870, in Texas.

At least two of Evan's sons joined the Confederate Army in Lawrence County. Joshua was in Shaver's Regiment, Company D, 7th Arkansas Infantry. He was wounded in the Battle of Shiloh and released. When he was well enough, he returned to his unit until the war was over. His wife, Almira, received a pension, application #24228. Benjamin Washington Hudson was in Company D, 38th Arkansas Infantry. He has a CSA headstone, where he is buried at Graham-Argyle Cemetery.

After the war was over most of the stock was gone and farms destroyed. In the spring of 1867, the Evan Hudson family, including Benjamin and Lucinda, with her husband, Hugh Garside, and R.

James Thomas and Mary Ann Hudson Ross, with David Washington and Robert Evan, their sons, c. 1894.

L. Lane, who had been captain of Company C in Joe Shelby's command, and his family, headed for Denton County, Texas. In July, 1867, they passed through Denton, enroute to Springtown in Parker County. They pitched camp at the Matthews home in Wise County, expecting trouble with the Indians. Sonney Thomas and Andy and James Elkins had encountered the Indians and fled to the Blackwell house and then to the Matthews house. At the break of day on July 15, 1867, about 100 Commanche Indians swooped down on them. J. H. Matthews and Polk Matthews were wounded. All of their horses and mules were driven off, and they were left without teams and money. After the Indian storm was over, they secured some ox teams, and 10 wagon loads of Lanes, Matthews and Hudsons moved back to Argyle, in Denton County, Texas.

This story taken from *History and Reminiscences of Denton County* by Ed F. Bates.

Evan was not in the census of 1880, where his wife, Alzira, was with her three children in Denton County, Texas. Children of Evan Hudson were found in Arkansas, Texas and Oklahoma. –*Ina Howard Willingham*.

HUDSON - WITTEN FAMILY. Mary Ellen Hudson born on May 8, 1868 at Smithville, Lawrence County, Arkansas to James Franklin Hudson and Mary Ann (Holt) Norris.

Mary Ellen married April 11, 1885 at Sunset, Montague County, Texas to a widowerIsaac James Witten. Issac's first wife Elizabeth J. Sipes died a vineyard, Jack County, Texas in 1884 leaving him two small children. Thomas Franklin born August 19, 1880 and Mary Elizabeth born February 17, 1883. Isaac James Witten was born on January 6, 1858 in Camden County, Missouri to Isasc Mullins Witten and Nancy Emeline O'Donnell.

Mary Ellen, had a ready made family. She and Isaac James decided the family wasn't large enough, and to this union these children were added.

1. Isaac Albert born February 24, 1887 in Waco, McLennan County, Texas, died November 5, 1960. He married Gracie Ethal Chapman October 20, 1907.

2. Nancy Annie Frances born March 9, 1889 in Sunset, Montague County, Texas died Devember 1982 in Lindsay Garvin County, Oklahoma. She married on April 28, 1908 to Reason Davis.

3. Lillie May born April 12, 1891 in Healdton Indian Territory, Oklahoma, died May 24, 1973 at Modesto, Stanislaus County California. She married on January 16, 1911 in Tucumcari, New Mexico to Ovie Orene Dupree. Georgia, born April 18, 1976 in Clinton, Custer County, Oklahoma, son of Charles Anderson Dupree

and Martha Elizabeth Gleaton. Children are; Martha Ellen October 21, 1911 - August 1965, Nancy May Orene November 4, 1913 - living, Isaac Anderson (I.A.) October 30, 1915 - December 25, 1996, Viola Christan January 25, 1921 - June 9, 1985, Ruth Marie June 16, 1924 - living. Her second marriage was to James Hanley no children.

4. Johnie Orvil born May 3, 1893 in Healdton Indian Territry, Oklahoma, died in August 1951, at Raton, Colfax County, New Mexico and was buried at Butler Cemetery, Custer County, Oklahoma. He married on January 2, 1919 to Bessie Henderson (1902-1959).

5. James Hubert born February 15, 1895 in Healdton, Indian Territory, Oklahoma. He married Tracy Bates on September 3, 1918. Tracy was killed instantly in a car crash near Alice, Jim Wells County, Texas, James was injured, on April 20, 1946. James' second marriage was to Georgie Cook on March 2, 1949.

6. Gracie Leona Pearl born on December 18, 1896 in Healdton, Indian Territory, Oklahoma and died March 16, 1965 in Oklahoma City, Oklahoma. She married Walt McIntire. Her second marriage was to Fred Rasmussen.

7. Oscar T. was born on January 9, 1900 in Marlow, Indian Territory, Oklahoma, died Octover 14, 1966 in Oklahoma City, Oklahoma. He married Ida Grace Hicks.

8. Jessie Josephine born in 1902 in Marlow, Indian Territory, Oklahoma, died on September 14, 1996 in Clinton, Custer County, Oklahoma. She married Durard Jackson Frazier on November 19, 1921 at Bulter, Custer County, Oklahoma. They had two children; Mary Lucille born on January 21, 1923 and died November 27, 1946, Billie Jack who is still living. The three Frazier family members are buried at the Butler Cemetery in Custer County, Oklahoma.

9. Elija Barksdale born on August 25, 1904 in Marlow, Indian Territory, Oklahoma, died August 1, 1966 in Kansas City, Wyandotte County, Kansas. He married Annis Turner.

Isaac James died July 13, 1935 in Oklahoma City, Oklahoma and Mary Ellen died at her home in Hobart, Kiowa County, Oklahoma on April 20, 1946. Both are buried in the Clinton Cemetery, Custer County, Oklahoma.

–Nelta Dupree Evans

WILLIAM J. HUDSON, born 1811 in Missouri, was Sheriff of Lawrence County, 1854-1856. He married Lavina Marshall, born 1814, in Arkansas, on September 1, 1841. He also married Sarah Eddy on June 3, 1866. William and Lavina's children were: Madison, born 1844, in Arkansas; Amanda, born 1845, in Arkansas; William Butler, born 1850, in Arkansas, and died 1887; and Labira, born 1850, in Arkansas.

The third child, William Butler Hudson, was married on January 25, 1872, to Mary Susan Dent. Mary Susan, born 1852, in Arkansas, died 1927, was the eighth of 11 children born to Josiah Dent and Susan Dunn. William Butler Hudson and Mary Susan's children were:

Back Row: Left to right: Gracie Leona Pearl; Oscar T., Johnnie Orvil Witten. Front row: Isaac James, Elijah Barksdale, Mary Ellen (Hudson) Witten, Jessie Josephine, c. 1910.

Sydney Hudson on left and Webster Dent on right at Imboden.

1. William, born 1874, who married Edna; children were: William Jr., Octavia, Evelyn, Lillian and Opal.

2. Herbert Giles, born March, 1877, who married Retta; child was Helen, who married Irvin Jackson.

3. Sydney Trott, 1878-1937, married Cythia Mabel Rowland; children were:

a) Mary Susan, born 1912, married Owen Beach, child was Owen Beach Jr.

b) Clara R., born 1914, married Forrest Holloway, children were: Joyce Ann and Forrest Jr.

c) Edward Rose, born April 9, 1918, married Joyce Mae Wood, child was Beverly Edrath.

d) Dorotha, born January, 1917, married George Sullivan, children were Sydney George, Peggy and Ann.

e) Paul Butler married Syble Hulet, children were: Bryan, Randy and Mark.

f) Calvin Coolidge.

g) Virginia Vaughn married William Johnson. Their children were Stephan and Jill.

h) Louise, born 1935, married first Depriest, married Joe Ryals, child was Marty Ryals.

4. Ellen E., born September, 1880, married Henry Chapin.

5. Laura, born March, 1885, married Clay Weir. Their children were: John, Marie and Clay Jr.

6. Fannie married Mose Weir. Their children were Nell and Clara.

7. Joseph, born April, 1886, married Minnie Brown.

In 1886, Madison D. Hudson and wife deeded land the Clear Springs Baptist Church sits on to William Butler Hudson and S. J. Park, church trustees. This site is off Highway 63, north of Black Rock. The original church building was made of logs hewn by W. B. Hudson. Some of the early families attending Clear Springs were the Hudsons, Hendersons, Parks, Phillipses, Smiths, Wilsons, Forresters, Chatmans, Gibsons, Easts and Butlers. When the original building was torn down in 1940, William Hudson found shingles with his father's and other friends' name on them. A new building was completed on the same site in 1941.

Josiah Dent, who was born December 27, 1797, in North Carolina, and Susan Dunn were the parents of: Thomas, born 1826, in Tennessee; James, born 1827, in Tennessee; Charles, born 1828, in Tennessee; Sarah Virginia, born 1835, in Tennessee; Susan, born 1839, in Tennessee; Ellen, born 1840, in Tennessee; George, born 1842, in Tennessee; Mary Susan, born 1852, in Arkansas; Hannah, born 1852, in Arkansas; Green, born 1854, in Arkansas; and Thomas, born 1855, in Arkansas. –*David N. Lee.*

HUTCHERSON FAMILY. The Lawrence County Hutcherson family members are direct descendants of Dr. Robert Lee Hutcherson, who moved from Kentucky to Delaplaine, Arkansas, in February of 1901. Dr. Hutcherson and his wife, Essie, had one child born June 21, 1912, who they named Rupert Leon Hutcherson. In 1933, Rupert Hutcherson married Namah Floyd, daughter of Guy and Sophia Floyd of Lawrence County, Arkansas. In 1940, Rupert and Namah Hutcherson gave birth to Robert Lee Hutcherson and they continued to live in Greene County, Arkansas, until 1947; at that time, Mr. Hutcherson was teaching school in Delaplaine, Arkansas.

Rupert Hutcherson resigned from teaching and moved his family on October 15, 1947, to Walnut Ridge, Arkansas. Mr. Hutcherson opened a furniture store at the corner of 115 Walnut Street, which became known as

Hutcherson and Norwood Furniture. Mrs. Sophia Floyd and Guy Floyd had divorced and she had married Dave Norwood. They ran this store successfully for several years while Robert Hutcherson was off attending school. In 1966, Rupert Hutcherson suffered a massive heart attack, so Robert Hutcherson decided to go into business with his mother, buying out his grandmother, Sophia Norwood, and they changed the name of the business to Hutcherson Furniture.

Also, in 1966, Robert Hutcherson married Paula Howard, daughter of Rufus and Pauline Howard. Robert and his wife, Paula, have three children: Robert Lee, born October 28, 1966; Holly Sue, born November 5, 1968; and Kara Beth, born October 10, 1970. At the present time, they still live in this area. In 1994, Hutcherson Furniture burned and therefore, Robert Hutcherson retired and maintains an office in Walnut Ridge for his personal business. –Bobby Hutcherson.

HUTCHERSON FAMILY. According to records found, John Jeffery Hutcherson lived from 1762-1829. His son, Jessie Hutcherson, was born in 1809, and died about 1836. Jessie married Rebecca Eddington on December 9, 1823. Their son, Robert A. Hutcherson, was born in 1833, and they moved from Rockingham County, North Carolina to Clinton, Kentucky, where Robert Lee Hutcherson was born in 1868. In 1899, Robert Lee Hutcherson attended medical school in Tennessee and received his degree in 1901, and moved to Delaplaine, Arkansas, in Greene County. While there, he met Essie Johnson, who was a school teacher and they married in 1910, giving birth to Rupert Leon Hutcherson on June 21, 1912. Rupert grew up in Greene County and attended Arkansas State University and married Namah Floyd on February 14, 1933. They lived in Greene County until 1940, and at that time Robert Lee Hutcherson was born on August 18. Mr. Rupert Hutcherson was employed at Delaplaine High School until 1947, at which time he moved his family to Lawrence County, settling in Walnut Ridge and opening a retail furniture business. In 1966, Robert Lee Hutcherson married Paula Sue Howard on January 22. They have three children: Robert Lee, born October 28, 1966; Holly Sue, born November 6, 1968; and Kara Beth, born October 10, 1970. To our knowledge, there are no other living descendants of our family and as of this date, Robert and Paula Hutcherson still live in Walnut Ridge. Rob married Jill Sanders on February 13, 1999, and they reside in Little Rock, Arkansas. Holly married Dr. Jeff Hall on March 15, 1997, and lives in Jonesboro, Arkansas. Kara married Drew Guinn on January 10, 1994, and they live in Paragould, Arkansas. At the present time, the only two grandchildren Robert and Paula have are Casey and Megan. –Bobby Hutcherson.

EDMOND INGRAM FAMILY. Edmond and Latitia Ingram came to Arkansas in the mid 1850s, living first at Clover Bend and then moving to the Milligan Campgrounds Community on Reeds Creek in Big Creek Township by 1860. Edmond and Latitia were born in Tennessee and lived in Paris, Tennessee before moving to Lawrence County. Their children were Sarah and Samuel, who were born in Tennessee and Christopher and John, who were born in Arkansas.

On December 24, 1860, Edmond married Margarett Potter by Justice of the Peace, G. R. West. The children from this union were William and Laura.

Edmond's third wife was Edy Milligan, who's first husband, George R. West, had died. Edy's parents were John and Eda Milligan, who helped start the Milligan Campground Cumberland Presbyterian Church in 1826. The children were James, Enoch, Alpha and Fenes.

Edmond served in the Confederate Army with the 38th Arkansas Infantry. He died of pneumonia in 1876, and is buried in the Milligan Campground Cemetery. Edy lived until 1914, and is buried at the Milligan Campgrounds.

Enoch was born on March 3, 1868, near Strawberry and was married to Tennessee Baker on October 16, 1887. Their only child, James Edward, was born on August 15, 1888, and Tennessee died sometime between 1888 and 1891, of tuberculosis. Enoch's second wife was Sissy Williams and they were married on January 28, 1892. Their children were Queen, Joe Bob, Ella Mae, Claude, Shelby, Charlie and Herschel. Sissy passed away on April 6, 1911. Nora Head became Enoch's third wife on July 5, 1911. Their children were Edia, Imogene, Geneva, Millie and Neal.

Enoch was raised in the hill country of Lawrence County, but in the early part of the 1900s, he moved his family to the rich fertile delta land in Eastern Lawrence County. The family farmed in the Coffman Community where Enoch served on the Coffman School Board and went to Coffman Free Will Baptist Church. He later on lived on the Sloan farm four miles west of Hoxie and later lived at Sedgwick.

Enoch passed away on June 17, 1952, and is buried at Crossroads Cemetery.

James Edward's "Eddie" wife was Mary R. Hardin of Portia. They were married on October 13, 1910, by A. C. Benn, Justice of the Peace. Their children were Burton Edward, Beulah Ester and Wilma Adrain.

Burton was born in 1911, and died in July, 1928, from appendicitis.

Beulah married Milton Sprinkle in Newport, Arkansas in the early 1950s, and their only child, Jimmy Lee, died when only three days old. Beulah was a beautician and Milton was a truck driver and later worked at a local tool handle factory.

Wilma married Johnny Whitlow of the Arbor Grove Community. They were cotton and soybean farmers on the 200 acres that belonged to his dad. Johnny and Wilma later bought 140 acres of the farm.

Eddie was a farmer on the Sloan farm most of his life. He served on the Surridge School Board and lived in Hoxie with his daughter, Beulah, the last few years of this life.

Mary passed away in 1942, and Eddie passed away in 1950, and both are buried at Crossroad Cemetery. –James Whitlow.

EDMUND INGRAM AND 2ND WIFE MARGARET BARNETT. Edmund Ingram was born 1828, in Paris, Tennessee, and died January 15, 1876, in Strawberry. He is buried at Milligans Campground Cemetery. He apparently came to Arkansas from Tennessee in the late 1850s. His ancestry is not known. In 1870, he resided in Sharp County, Arkansas. His first wife was Myrtle and they had children: Sarah E., Samuel Houston and John Wess. Myrtle died before 1860, and Edmund married Margaret Barnett on December 27, 1860. Margaret was probably the widow of J.B. Potter of Lawrence County. Family tradition is that she was part Cherokee Indian. Edmund and Margaret had three children.

William Granville Ingram, 1865-1955, family photo taken about 1910. Left to right: Maggie, Charles, William Granville, Oscar (above), Dolphus "Doc", Cora, Laura (above), Margaretta Graddy, Vida and Lilly.

1. Betty.
2. Laura Ingram, born 1862.
3. William Granville Ingram, May 22, 1865-November 3, 1955.

Margaret died and Edmund married third wife, Edy Milligan on December 24, 1865, in Strawberry. They had children: James Perry, Enoch E., Edy, Jane Alpha and Fenes.

Vida Isabella Ingram Jones, 1906-1996, with son, Leslie Crooms Jones, about 1930.

William Granville Ingram, 1865-1955, served as sheriff for Lawrence County. He married Margaret Etta Graddy, who was born March 19, 1869, in Dyersburg, Tennessee, and died June 15, 1962, in Flint, Michigan. She was the daughter of Samuel A. Graddy and Martha A. Briant. William and Margaret married in Evening Shade. They had the following children.

1. Charles, born March 8, 1896, in Strawberry, married Louise Sallings in 1920. Louise was born January 29, 1897, in Walnut Ridge.
2. Dolphus "Doc."
3. Oscar.
4. Laura.
5. Cora Jane, born August 9, 1902, in Lauratown. She married on July 26, 1921, in Black Oak, to Harry Morrow, who was born June 17, 1897, in Maynard, Arkansas.
6. Maggie May, born October 2, 1900, in Lauratown. She married Ambrose Ponder in 1921, in Black Oak.
7. Lillie Ingram.
8. Vida Isabella Ingram, who was born August 23, 1906, and died 1996. She married Leslie Crooms Jones of Strawberry.
9. Ula.

Vida Ingram, 1906-1996, married Leslie Jones, 1906-1984, and lived in Lauratown until 1937, when they moved to Little Rock. They had two children.

1. Leslie Jennings Jones Sr., born 1929, married Katherine Elizabeth Parker, 1948-1970, and had three children: Karen Ann, born 1949; Leslie Jennings Jones Jr., born 1952; and Jani Elizabeth, born 1957. Leslie worked in the car sales business and moved to Austin, Texas, shortly before the death of Katherine in 1970. He is now retired and married to Ramona Montgomery. Leslie has five grandchildren and Ramona has two.

2. Marietta Jones, born 1932, who married Roy Miller and had two children: David, born about 1959; and Scott, born about 1963.

For more information on Leslie Crooms Jones see "Descendants of Isaac Taylor Jones" and "Descendants of James Marion Jones." –Patricia Funk.

NMAN. Alvin Inman moved to Lawrence County in 1952, and purchased a small 40 acre

Alvin and Daisy Shaver Inman.

rm in Walnut dge, Arkansas, Evergreen ad, farming un-i his death at age 58. He was the son of Mordicai Inman and Sarah Frances Nelson Inman of the Ingram Community in Randolph County, Arkansas. He was born on May 19, 1899, and had three sisters and three brothers:

Napolean Bonaparte (N.B.), 1891
Rebecca Louiza, 1893-1969
James Henry, 1895-1968
Alva, 1896-1929
Alvin, 1899-1957, wed Daisy Shaver.
Sarah Jane, born 1901
George C., 1904-1904 (four months)

Alvin wed Daisy C. Shaver on January 2, 1916. She was the daughter of Jacob Seburn and Alice Lou Carter Shaver of the Palestine Community in Randolph County, Arkansas. Daisy had five sisters and four brothers. They were:

Carter, 1886-1925
Ruby, 1888-before 1910
Minatry, 1890-1969
Marvin, 1892-1957
Melvin, 1893-before 1910
Daisy, 1896-1969
Mazie, 1899-approximately 1987
Thalia, 1901-1980
Mary, 1904-1980
May 1906-????

From the union of Alvin and Daisy came eight children, two boys and one girl died in infancy. Surviving are five girls.

Willow Naoma, 1923-1998
Emma Jean, born 1925
Frances Lou, born 1926
Lois Jane, born 1931
Rebecca Priscilla, born 1934

Rebecca married Billy Joe Warren on January 5, 1949, in Marked Tree, Arkansas, in Poinsett County and this is how the Billy Joe Warren family began. –Brenda Warren.

JOHN WALLACE IRVIN, January 30, 1884-August 24, 1937, and his wife, Eva Lee Pugh, February 2, 1892-April 22, 1971, moved from Dyer County, Tennessee, with their children: Vivian Heape, born May 6, 1913; Tharland Mack, March 4, 1915-February, 1995; and Opal Edmondson, born January 27, 1917. They purchased a farm on Highway 91 South near her sister, Ethel (Mrs. Willie Hicks), and her two brothers, Luther and Jim Pugh. Hoxie Flying Service is located on the home place. Children born after their arrival in Lawrence County were: Venita Smith, born February 6, 1919; John Wallace Jr., born January 22, 1923; Mary Kathryn Williams, born November 4, 1925; Ewell Wilbert "Jack", born February 23, 1928; and Evalene Bright, born October 3, 1931. –Jean Edmondson.

IVINS. Henry Clay Ivins and his wife, Mollie Minerva Webb Ivins, moved to Lawrence County shortly after the turn of the century. He had lived with his family near Flora, Illinois, before then, and decided to move after a bear hunting trip to this county. He bought land and settled on the current Floyd farm on Highway 91 South, near the Oak Hill Community. His children, John, James Arthur, born 1888, Effie Jane, born 1886, and Fred, born 1892, came with him. Two older daughters, Liz and Mamie, remained in Illinois.

Henry and his family set to work clearing land and running a sawmill while the timber lasted. He then set up one of the earliest rice farms in the county before 1910 (see article by Lila Floyd, Times Dispatch, Walnut Ridge, September 14, 1994), using the old steam engine from the sawmill days to pump water. That engine was still on the land until the 1930s.

His children, Effie and Arthur, each married; Effie to Archie Ball and Arthur to Dorothy Lamb, daughter of Samuel and Jane Lamb. Arthur and Dorothy had seven children that survived to adulthood: Harvey, Minnie, Mamie, Maggie, Marie, Muriel and Myrtle. Arthur farmed and was a country preacher. He died in 1964. Dorothy died in 1974. Fred married Pearl Kisling and had two daughters, Viola Ivins Bellah and the Ruby Edith Ivins Aaron. Fred was killed in 1945, in this county.

Henry Clay Ivins, Mollie Minerva Ivins and John Ivins (standing).

Harvey married Ruth Warner and had eight children, the family moving about the country. Minnie married Leon Hubbs and has lived most of her adult life in Orange County, California. Mamie married Cleo Rainwater, and some years after his death in 1973, married Conley Doyle. Maggie married the late Walmer "Diddle" Burns and lives in the Oak Hill Community. Their children are: Sammy Burns of Hoxie and Jeanette Phipps of Jonesboro. Marie married John Wyatt (see Wyatt history, this book) and also lives at Oak Hill. Their children are: Bonnie Elders of Walnut Ridge, Darrel Wyatt of Florida and Ted Wyatt of near Tulsa, Oklahoma. Muriel married Phil Parks and lives in Jonesboro. Myrtle married Jack Weir and had five sons while living in Rock Falls, Illinois. Jack was killed in an auto accident, and later, Myrtle married Roger Schultz. They now live in Jonesboro. –Greg Elders.

CECIL JAMES. A native of Black Rock, Cecil James was born in 1906. He resided in a small home on the banks of the Black River. Being a member of a poor African American family during this period, Cecil started working at the age of 12. His primary occupation became that of the ferry operator. He sepnt many a day implementing the safe passage of travelers and commerce across the stirring waters of the Black River. This occupation was not without its dangers however. Cecil James was almost killed in an accident involving his ferry and a steam boat. Mr. James was transporting travelers cross river when a steam boat approach-

ing at a fast rate made contact with the mooring cable that secured the ferry. Cecil scarcely escaped with his life when the cable snapped.

Mr. James recollects that scarcely a night would pass when the sounds of violins and piano

Cecil James

music couldn't be heard from a passing steam boat. He remembers grand boats as the "F.W. Tucker" and the "City of Miskogi" which he refered to as the "grand boat" over three stories tall and detailed with tall stacks and fresh paint.

Cecil aslo recollects working for a time at Verkler Bros. Saw Mill. He was in the employment of Jim Sloan and Waive Verkler Jr. while there. Cecil James said that the button factory was also a big business in town and that Cecil spent many afternoons wading the shallows of the Black River for shells.

Today Mr. James resides in Harrisburg, Arkansas where he is close to his family. He is now 94 years old, rich in both memories and friends.

DR. WILLIAM HENRY JAMES was born January 11, 1844, at Humboldt, Tennessee, to Dr. John William James and Mrs. Lucinda James Nee McWhirter. His father, born in 1819, in Virginia, moved to Tennessee as a young boy. Later he received a doctorate from Vanderbilt University Medical College in Nashville. His mother was born 1817, in North Carolina, and died in 1860. The James', both of Scottish origin, were blessed with five children.

William Henry James

William H. James came to Arkansas with his parents in 1858. His father had a successful practice, served as a Baptist minister and built a grist mill which led to the establishment of the James Mill in the Arkansas Settlement near Memphis. James Mill is listed on Arkansas state road maps at exit 14 Highway 55.

William H. James enlisted in the Arkansas Confederate Army at age 17, as a member of a Cavalry (mounted rifle) regiment. He was severely wounded in the Battle of Bentonville, North Carolina, while making a charge upon the enemy. His near death experience and traumatic recovery in an Atlanta hospital did not deter him from his ethical beliefs. He would be on the battlefield again in one of the bloodiest major engagements of the Civil War, where 10,000 Confederate men suffered at Stones River (Murfreesboro), Tennessee. He must have been under divine care for he was only slightly wounded. He served until the close of hostilities, when he surrendered at Jackson, Mississippi. As a Confederate soldier he had to restore his original status as a citizen of the United States by taking the Oath of Allegiance.

The influential part of his education took place after the Civil War when he accepted his doctorate in 1869, from the Missouri Medical College in St. Louis. From there he traveled to the Smithville-Powhatan areas to start his practice.

Dr. James married Temperance Adela

Wesson, a Virginia aristocrat, who brought to this union her freed slaves who chose to stay with her after their emancipation. Dr. and Mrs. James had five daughters, whose first name initials are the vowels.

He stayed in touch with former alumni of his medical society, and frequently traveled by train to St. Louis attending medical institutes. On occasion his family accompanied him to experience the Victorian social season. He was also a territorial doctor who kept a livery boy on call day and night. A young James Barney Haley came to live on the James' estate as an employee and rode with the doctor as a bodyguard whenever attending to a sick person in the dangerous Black River bottoms.

In addition to a large practice, James managed a large farm under cultivation, a large tract of timberland, engaged in sawmilling, mineral mining and entered into the mercantile business. In 1879, he formed a partnership with F. M. Wayland who managed his firm of James & Wayland, merchants and lumber dealers. For novelty, he raised black sheep called Karakul.

Temperance Adela James with five daughters, about 1884. Ada, Ula, Ora, Ida and Ella James.

The sheep had curved horns and long hair that touched the ground. He even had some strutting peacock birds. His residence with office was located on Flat Creek, near Denton.

The Goodspeed Publishing Company, *Biographical Memoirs of Northeast Arkansas*, featured Dr. William H. James and regarded him as one of the most successful men in Lawrence County, both for his business acumen and professional qualifications as a successful physician and a man of fine physique.

He died March 1, 1894, from advanced pneumonia. James Barney Haley married one of the daughter, Ora L. James, and they were the parents of William Harold and Thomas Holt Haley.

After the death of his wife, Temperance, Dr. James married Virginia Brady of Annieville, Arkansas, and they had five more children. One of his grandchildren, Dr. James Taylor Bridges, followed in his grandfather's profession. –*Genevieve Haley.*

JANES/ARMING. John Janes was born in 1744, in Virginia. He was in the Revolutionary War and was wounded in the Battle of Yorktown. He married Margaret Arming of Virginia. They had 12 children.

About 1800, the family came from Virginia to what is now Missouri. They came down the Ohio River in canoes to near St. Louis. He was denied a land grant there.

In 1809, the family came from Missouri to what is now Lawrence County, Arkansas, but was then the territory of Missouri. In 1809, they settled on what is now Janes Creek, which was named after him since he was the first settler in that part of the country. Lawrence County was later divided and that part of the county where he settled became Randolph County. They owned land south of Highway 90, along Janes Creek. He and some of his sons owned land from there to near Imboden, Arkansas.

John built a horse powered grist mill. This was the first mill in that part of the country. The mill was later changed to water power. Descendants remained in this area and some (with different surnames) still are in the same area.

Their children were: John, 1785-1844; Joseph, 1788-1830; Jarrett, 1787-1848; Massack, 1794-1844; Elvira; John T.; William H., 1875; James; Henderson and Benjamin. –*James R. Forrester.*

JANES/BOWEN. James Janes was born April 7, 1818, in Ravenden Springs, Lawrence County, Territory of Missouri, to John Jones and Margaret Arming Janes. He died February 19, 1879, in Lawrence County. He married Lucinda Wyatt, born about 1824, in Arkansas on January 20, 1842, in Lawrence County, Arkansas.

They had six children: Hardy, born 1843, Lawrence County, Arkansas; Lydia Carolyn, born December, 1845, in Randoph County, Arkansas, died December 18, 1911, married Hugh Wells; Elvira, born December 4, 1848, in Randolph County, Arkansas; James F., born October 29, 1853, in Randolph County, died December 14, 1879, married Mary Francis Phillips; Marion B., born July 7, 1856, died December 14, 1879, in Randolph County, married Lizzie A. Buster; William Lafayette, born October 8, 1858, in Randolph County, died July 15, 1947, in Oregon County, Missouri, married Mary Standley.

His second marriage was to Martha Bowen.

James and Martha Bowen, born April 30, 1831, were married in 1859. They had five children: Margaret O., born July, 1861, died 1889, married George Galbraith; Thomas A., born February, 1863; Julia B., born August, 1865; John Henderson, born March, 1872; Martha D., born November, 1874.

–*James R. Forrester.*

JANES/HENDRIX. William Ervin Janes was born December 22, 1864, near Imboden, Arkansas, to John Janes Jr. and Mary Black on the John Janes farm near Imboden, died June 22, 1899. The house was a log house with two bedrooms on one side and the kitchen on the other with a "dog trot" between.

He married Eugenia Hendrix on March 15, 1890. Eugenia was born, near the "point" where Black River and Spring River run together, to Isaac Brown Hendris and Henrietta Rhea Hendrix, September 3, 1867, and died January 20, 1958. They owned a farm there.

William Ervin and Eugenia had five daughters. They were:

1. Ina was born January 24, 1892, died December 12, 1984.
2. Iva was born January 24, 1892.
3. Eva was born February 11, 1894, died November 12, 1912.
4. Johnnie was born September 11, 1895, died November 26, 1984.
5. Minerva E. was born April 26, 1898, died February 11, 1997.

Ina married Albert William Davis. Albert was born September 23, 1891, died January 27, 1973. They had seven children.

1. Herschel, born October 8, 1911, died October 9, 1996, married Mary Miller.
2. Harry, born April 8, 1914, died 1967, married Lois Puckett.
3. Susie Aquila, born June 29, 1916, married Clifford Savage.
4. Walter Eugene, born February 17, 1919, died July 3, 1941, married Katie Decker.
5. Eva Inez, born November 25, 1921, married Glen "Pat" Verkler.
6. Albert O'Neal, born May 15, 1926, married Katherine Holder.
7. Lewis Ray, born December 10, 1930, died September 26, 1955.

Iva married Charles B. Ward. Charles was born November 28, 1890, died March 17, 1961. They

had one son, Alvin Ward, born February 22, 1915, who married Ruth Propst.

Johnnie married Grover Cleveland "Cleve" Forrester. Cleve was born October 1, 1888, died September 16, 1967. They had seven children.

1. Mack Hendrix, born June 23, 1915, died January 7, 1999, married Ina Mae Grable.
2. Grover Gerald, born November 17, 1916, died January 13, 1919.
3. Johnnie Geraldine, born October 11, 1918, married James Faulkner.
4. Hazeldine Amanda, born March 6, 1921, died January 22, 1988, married David Hazel.
5. James Ray, born October 24, 1926, married Loretta Moon.
6. Cleveland Edward, born July 26, 1930, died December 5, 1984, married Jane Pitman.
7. Katheryn Lucille, born February 3, 1936, married first Leon Deloach and second Onus Millsap.

Minerva E. married Oscar W. Davis. Oscar was born March 11, 1895, died December 3, 1977. They had eight children.

1. Dewani Leon, born Sept. 29, 1916, died Dec. 3, 1977, married Mary Anna Winchester.
2. Oscar Olwin, born January 5, 1918, died January 28, 1924.
3. William Earl, born April 29, 1923, married Minnie Jane Lemmons.
4. Odessa Faye, born March 25, 1925, married J. T. Davis.
5. Stella May, born December 21, 1928, married Charles Toye.
6. Dorothy Luella, born December 28, 1932, married James R. Decker.
7. Frank Ray, born March 6, 1936, married Marzell White.
8. Virginia Irene, born April 7, 1937, married Richard Kirley.

–*James R. Forrester.*

JANES/RHEA. John Janes was born September 7, 1785, in Virginia to John Janes and Margaret Arming Janes. He married Margaret Rhea, born October 19, 1795, in Virginia, died May 16, 1833, in Lawrence County, Arkansas.

He was a farmer along Janes Creek in what is now Randolph County, Arkansas. He and Margaret had six children: James, born April 7, 1818, died February 19, 1879, in Lawrence County; John Jr., born October 27, 1835, in Lawrence County; Tom; Rube; Merry, born January 14, 1843, in Lawrence County; and Marion B., born July, 1857, and died in Lawrence County.

–*James R. Forrester.*

JOHN JANES FAMILY. John Janes I (also called John Sr.), for whom Janes Creek was named, was one of the earliest settlers of Lawrence County. He was born in Virginia about 1745, was a veteran of the American Revolution, and died in Lawrence County, Arkansas (now a part of Randolph County) in 1826. John I, wife Margaret Arming and their small children traveled down the Ohio River and settled near St. Louis on the Merrimac River prior to 1800. Then in 1809, the entire family moved to Lawrence County (then in Missouri Territory).

John I is a fifth generation descendant of William Janes, who emigrated from England to present day Connecticut in 1637. Most every Janes in the United States today can be traced to this same William.

John I and Margaret had at least nine children. They included:

1. John II (also called John Jr.), who first married Mary Black, daughter of David Black, an early settler on Elevenpoint River at what is today called Black's Ferry.
2. Joseph, who first married Nancy Black, sister to Mary.

3. Samuel, whose widow Jane was living in Sharp County in 1870.

4. Jarrett, who first married Margaret Stevenson.

5. Masack H., who married Nancy Stevenson.

6. Elizabeth, who married William Black, brother of Nancy and Mary.

7. William L.

Most of the Janes descendants in Lawrence and Randolph Counties today trace back to either John II or to Elizabeth Black. William L., Jarrett, Massack and Joseph moved to Southwest Arkansas and have descendants throughout southern Arkansas and Texas.

John II was the father of at least 10 children. He was born about 1785, and died in 1844. Jarrett E. was his oldest son. Jarrett E. married Elizabeth Sloan in 1840, and he died in 1850. Elizabeth later married Jarrett E.'s younger brother, William B. James first married Lucinda Wyatt, daughter of Abraham Wyatt. Following Lucinda's death, James married Martha Ann Bowen.

John II (who like his father was sometimes referred to as John Jr.) lived with his older brother, James, for several years after the death of their father. John III first married Mary Wells, daughter of Thomas Hutchinson Wells. Following her death, he married Mary Wayland. His sons, Ervin and Rufus, settled on the lower Spring River near Imboden. Many of Ervin's descendants reside in the Imboden area today.

–Don R. Brown.

J. W. JEAN. "Sixty Years Ago" by J. W. Jean (1970-Imboden Journal).

When I was 22 years old, I was summoned on the Petit Jury and I served every other term until I was 65 years old. I helped try every kind of case, from a misdemeanor to murder.

One case I served on was a case of two teenagers who were indicted for disturbing religious worship. The late Joe Judkins was the defense lawyer and Bob Whitlow was the prosecuter's witness. On cross examination, Mr. Judkins asked when the disturbance took place. Mr. Whitlow replied that they were in the back of the house. Then Mr. Judkins asked Mr. Whitlow in what part of the house he was in when the alleged disturbance took place. Mr. Whitlow replied that he was in the Amen corner. The lawyer then asked him to explain what he meant by the Amen corner.

Mr. Whitlow told him it was about one seat from the pulpit. Mr. Judkins asked in what part of the service did the alleged disturbance take place and Mr. Whitlow answered that it was during prayer. When asked if he was down on his knees when it happened, he answered that he was.

Mr. Judkins then asked the witness to explain how it was that he, Mr. Whitlow, being in one end of the house, down on his knees praying, how he could see and recognize the defendants, who were at the other end of the house. Mr. Whitlow readily replied, "The Bible says watch and pray, Mr. Judkins." That was all, the defendants were found guilty and fined $10.00 and the costs. –J.W. Jean.

WILLIAM HARVEY JEAN FAMILY. The progenitor of the Jean family in Lawrence County was John Wesley Jean, 1829-1904. John Wesley was a descendant of William Jean, an Episcopal minister. Two of William's sons served in the Revolutionary War. Two other sons were Methodist ministers.

John Wesley married Elizabeth Little in 1847, and they were the parents of 10 chil-

The Harvey Jean family in 1940.

dren. They moved from Tennessee to Lawrence County in the 1860s, and one child was born in Lawrence County. Three of his children settled in Lawrence County. They were William Samuel, who married Emily Cozart; Martha Ann, who married John Darter; and Joseph, William Harvey Jean's father. Joseph Jean, 1853-1903, married a Lawrence County resident Mary K. "Mollie" Morgan in 1883. Mollie Morgan was the daughter of Randle and Mary Morgan. Joseph and Mollie lived at Denton and were the parents of five children, all born at Denton. They were Emma, Virgie and Birdie (twins), William Harvey and Lee Ann. They were farmers and attended the New Hope Baptist Church. In the early 1900s, they returned to Tennessee and it was there in 1903, that Joseph died. Harvey (as he was known) was only 12 years old, yet he took over the responsibility of his family. Working at whatever jobs he could find at his young age, he managed to take care of his mother and young sister. He, his mother and sister, returned to Arkansas where he worked with his Uncle John Morgan. He served in World War I and after being discharged from service, became a farmer.

In May of 1922, he married Mary P. Brady, bringing her to his home located on the banks of Black River at Clover Bend. They became the parents of five children. These were happy years, but lean, since they lived through the 1930s depression. To supplement his farming income, he drove a truck for the Slayton brothers. After the United States Government purchased land and created small farms, Harvey Jean was one of the first group of farmers to qualify for the purchase of a farm. In May of 1938, they moved to their new home. Harvey Jean died in February, 1969. Mary was killed in a car-train accident at Minturn in 1972.

They were survived by their children: William Henry "Bill" Jean. Bill was born in 1923, and died in 1985. Bill was married to Faye Hackney and they had three sons.

Mary Elizabeth Jean, 1925-1981, was married to James Tanner. They were the parents of two sons and two daughters.

Robert Joseph "Bob" Jean, born in 1927, married Mary Lou Moore, and they are the parents of two sons.

Betty Ann Jean, born in 1933, married Delphard Pope and they are the parents of one son and two daughters.

Alda Garland Jean, born 1936, married Harold Ramsey and they are the parents of two sons.

Mary and Harvey have 40 grandchildren, great-grandchildren and great-great-grandchildren in 1999. –Alda Ramsey.

BILL AND EDNA VERN JOHNSON and their 10 year old son, Harloyd, moved from Hot

Springs, Arkansas, to Lawrence County in August, 1946, so Bill could attend Southern Baptist College. Bill worked as a city bus driver in Hot Springs and Edna worked in the Army and Navy General Hospital laundry.

They moved into the Walnut Ridge Army Flying School officers apartment complex, which the college had arranged to use for student housing. Bill attended Southern Baptist College from September, 1946, through May, 1950.

Bill was born April 14, 1903, the son of Thomas Paul Johnson, a farmer, who was born in Saline County about 1834, and Gertrude Harris, a housewife, who was born in Yell County about 1836. Edna was born November 25, 1910, the daughter of Samuel Ford, who was born August 30, 1882, and Laura Medlock, who was born February 17, 1883.

Bill and Edna had each been married before, and lost their spouses. Bill married Velma Ella Nethercutt, March 7, 1925. They had one child, Billy Harloyd, born August 19, 1935. Velma died April 18, 1940, from an infection following an appendectomy. Edna Vern Ford married Lilburn Hefley about 1925. They had two children: Mary Lee, born September 15, 1928; and Lilburn Harold, born January 11, 1930. Harold died at age five with spinal meningitis. His father, Lilburn, was killed in a hunting accident before Harold was born.

While attending Southern Baptist College full time, Bill served as pastor of churches at Poynor and Myrtle, Missouri and later, the First Baptist Church at Edgemont, Arkansas. He worked as a carpenter for the college. Edna worked for the Walnut Ridge Cleaners for several years as a seamstress, and later for Van-Atkins.

After graduation from Southern Baptist College, Bill continued to pastor churches in northeast Arkansas, including Ravenden and Old Walnut Ridge, and worked for the college maintenance department. Bill and Edna bought a house at 902 Southeast Second Street in Walnut Ridge on August 19, 1950, and lived there until about 1953, when they moved to a church parsonage near Tyronza, Arkansas. Old Harloyd, who was then a senior at WRHS, worked and stayed at the Walnut Ridge Airport water plant. Bill and Edna moved back to College City in 1955. In 1956, they built a new house in College City.

After retirement in 1968, Bill enjoyed spending time in his woodworking shop, and continued working part time for the college maintenance department for several years.

Bill died November 8, 1983, and is buried in the Gravel Hill Cemetery near Benton, Arkansas. Edna lived in College City until June, 1990, when she entered Walnut Ridge Convalescent Center. She died July 28, 1997, and is buried in the Antioch Cemetery near Hot Springs, Arkansas. –Harold Johnson.

B. H. "HAROLD" AND JANIE JOHNSON.
Billy Harloyd Johnson and Janie Merle Boleyn met in 1953. Harloyd was in his senior year at WRHS, and working at the Walnut Ridge Airport Water Plant (which served the airport and college). Janie was a freshman at Southern, and was working in the cafeteria. They began dating in the fall. Janie liked the name "Harold" more than Harloyd, so he soon became "Harold." "Harold" and Janie were married July 2, 1954, by his dad, the Reverend Bill Johnson.

Harold was born August 19, 1935, in Saline County, near Paron, to Bill Johnson and Velma Ella Nethercutt Johnson. His mom died when he was four, and he lived with his grandmother, Jessie Ann Hutchingson Nethercutt, near Benton. His dad later married Edna Vern Hefley, and he lived with them in Hot Springs. The family moved to Walnut Ridge in 1946.

Janie was born at Childress, in Craighead County, September 18, 1935, to Loyd Boleyn and Mary Ann Furnish Boleyn. Janie's dad was a farmer and school bus driver for the Childress School. Her mom was a housewife and full time mother. Janie graduated from Childress High School in 1953, as Valedictorian.

Harold and Janie lived in College City after they were married, and both worked for Ace Manufacturing Company. The company made speaker baffles, then later, shipping pallets and finally, suitcases.

They had two daughters born at Dr. Joseph's Clinic. Pamela Jane, born November 22, 1956, only lived about 12 hours. Debra Jane was born December 26, 1947.

A career in aviation took Harold and Janie to Malden, Missouri, in 1955, as a link trainer instructor. Later, they lived in Tulsa, Oklahoma, and Memphis, Tennessee, where he worked as ground and flight instructor. Harold was employed by Southern Airways in 1965. He flew DC-3s, Martin 404s and Douglas DC-9s.

On November 10, 1972, Harold's flight was hijacked by three gunmen. The ordeal lasted about 28 hours, before ending in Cuba. Harold was shot during the flight, but continued his copilot duties. In 1973, he checked out as captain on the DC-9.

Harold and Janie moved back to College City in 1967. They operated a flying school, restaurant and aircraft service at Walnut Ridge from 1967-1970. He served as mayor of College City from January 1, 1970, to January 18, 1977, and July 21, 1989, to August 1, 1995.

Janie earned her private pilot's license in 1968, and currently works as marketing manager for a company in Memphis. Their daughter, Debra, a 1976 graduate of WRHS, became a USAF pilot, and flew T-37s, T-38s and KC-135s. She currently flies with the USAF Reserves and is a pilot for United Airlines. – *Harold Johnson.*

ETHEL "BERNICE" MCCARROLL JOHNSON

was born in Walnut Ridge, Arkansas on December 14, 1914, to Dr. Horace Rudolph "Dolph" and Pearl Henry McCarroll. After graduating from Ouachita Baptist College. Bernice taught English at Walnut Ridge High School and Draughn's Business School and later worked as a private stenographer. She was married in Newport, Arkansas on March 18, 1944, to Richard Benjamin Johnson, who was born in Little Rock, Arkansas, August 19, 1913. They are the parents of three sons.

Richard Benjamin Johnson Jr. was born in Jonesboro, Arkansas on April 22, 1945. On May 17, 1969, in Sherman, Texas, he was married to Nancy Philips Everhart, born in Rochester, New York, on March 16, 1947. Dr. Johnson and family live in Houston, Texas, where he has a medical practice specializing in cancer diagnosis. Mrs. Johnson is a Presbyterian minister. They are the parents of two children: Evan McCarroll Johnson and Meridith Gray Johnson.

James Noble Johnson, who was born in Orange, Texas, on January 30, 1947, was married in Edinburg, Texas on June 26, 1971, to Linda Mae Southwick, born in Edinburg, Texas, on January 19, 1949. He is an attorney in Austin, Texas. They have one daughter: Margaret Ruth Johnson.

Philip McCarroll, who was born in Beaumont, Texas on July 17, 1949, was married in Philadelphia, Pennsylvania, on November 27, 1983, to Virginia Catherine Stokes, who was born in Philadelphia, Pennsylvania, on April 22, 1948, and died of cancer in Tyler, Texas, on January 9, 1987. She is buried in Philadelphia. On April 13, 1990, Dr. McCarroll married Lynn Davis in California. They have four children: Sarah, Kristi and Richard Davis and Russell Johnson. They live in Dallas, Texas, where Dr. Johnson is an anesthetist in private practice.

After living in Orange, Texas, for many years where they had a printing business, they moved to Dallas, Texas in 1998.
–*Margaret Watson.*

CHARLES O. JONES was born at Clover Bend on June 17, 1875. He was married to Mae Bonner. Charles, as he was known, was a farmer and cotton ginner in the Minturn and Clover Bend area. He and Mae had a son, Rudy, who was born April 11, 1903, at Clover Bend.

Rudy moved with his family to Minturn in early life. He married Grace Griffin on January 14, 1923. Rudy farmed with his father. Grace worked 32 years as the Minturn Postmaster. Rudy and Grace had a son, Charles Franklin "Jack" Jones, born on September 17, 1923.

Jack married Wilma Bilbrey in 1946. Their three children are Larry, born February 27, 1948; Jackie, born October 26, 1954; and Mary, born November 23, 1959.

Larry Jones married Marta Easterly in 1973. They have one son, Andrew, born on December 3, 1980. Larry and Andrew now farm on some of the same land that their great-grandfather and great-great-grandfather once farmed. Andrew is the fifth generation of Jones to farm on this land and the sixth generation to live in Lawrence County. –*Larry Jones.*

HOMER JONES FAMILY. Homer Stanley Jones, November 21, 1899-April 1, 1979, married Minnie Bell McKnight. They lived most of their lives in the Lauratown area. Their four children are: William Hollis, Kenneth, Joe and Janice.

William Hollis is deceased. He had four children.

1. Sandra Kaye married to Troy Martin, now lives in Corning, Arkansas; one daughter.
2. William Homer now lives in Chattanooga, Tennessee; one daughter.
3. Michael Wayne now lives in Rockford, Illinois.
4. Linda Ann Jones Maggio; one child

Kenneth is deceased. He had two stepsons. Kenneth's widow, Patsy, lives in Paragould.

Joe now lives in Searcy, Arkansas. He teaches at Harding University.

Janice "Jan" lives in Walnut Ridge; one son, Steve. She was married to Wayne Swartzlander, now divorced. –*Sandra Martin.*

ISAAC TAYLOR JONES. Isaac Taylor Jones was born September 29, 1875, and died March 15, 1917. He married Frances Edda Jones (no relation apparently), born February, 1881, and died about 1909, on January 10, 1897, in Lawrence County. She was the daughter of Zachary Taylor Jones and Mary Frances Hunter. Zachary Taylor Jones line descended from James Jones of Tennessee to Ambrose Jones to Zachary Taylor Jones of Jackson County. Isaac and Frances resided in Strawberry. Family tradition says that Isaac was a fisherman and a ferry operator, probably on the Strawberry River.

The descendants of Isaac Taylor Jones and Mary Frances Jones were:

1. Leslie Crooms Jones, who was born in Strawberry, May 9, 1902, and died in Little Rock on June 12, 1984. He married second Vida Isabella Ingram, 1906-1996, of Lawrence County on December 12, 1924, in Portia. She was the daughter of Sheriff William Granville Ingram and Margaret Etta Graddy. Leslie and Vida resided with their two children in Lauratown until 1937, when they moved to Little Rock. Their son, Leslie Jennings Jones, born 1929, is retired in Austin, Texas. Their daughter, Marietta Jones Miller, resides in Little Rock. There are five grandchildren and five great-great-grandchildren.

2. Mary Agla Jones, born November 1, 1897, died April 22, 1912. She married Benjamin Moody, born April 22, 1889, and died March 8, 1954. They had one child, Halbert, who resides in Little Rock.

3. Homer Stanley Jones, born November 21, 1899, married Minnie McKnight. Their children were: Hollis, Kenneth, Joe and Janis. These people lived in the Lauratown area.

4. Earl Jones, born October 29, 1905, and died June 2, 1925, in Lawrence County.

5. Wilma Olene Jones, born February 22, 1908, in Strawberry and died March 18, 1991, in Jonesboro. She is buried in Walnut Ridge Cemetery. She married Charles William Baker, born April 14, 1907, in Lauratown and died September 29, 1989. They had Agla Willeen Baker, born 1928, in Lauratown and now resides in Imboden. Willeen married Billy Joe Kirkland, 1927-1986.

6. Nina Elfreda "Fredda" Jones, born August 21, 1910. She married Clay Buchanan. Their children were:

Children of Isaac Taylor Jones, 1876-1917. Left to right: above Agla, Leslie, Olene, Homer, and Earl; about 1908.

Leslie Crooms Jones, 1902-1984, with wife, Vida Isabella Ingram and children: Leslie Jennings Jones and Marietta Jones. Photo taken in Walnut Ridge about 1937.

Leslie Crooms Jones, 1902-1984, about 1930.

Jeanne, Mary Lou, Joe Taylor, Don and Randy. Freddy and Clay lived in the Lauratown/Clover Bend area.

For ancestors of Isaac Taylor Jones see "Descendants of James Marion Jones." For ancestors of Vida Isabella Ingram Jones see "Descendants of Edmund Ingram."

JAMES MARION JONES was born in Arkansas or Tennessee in 1845. His father was born in Tennessee and is unknown. In 1860, he was an orphan with property worth 600 dollars and asked Wiley C. Jones (relationship unknown) to act as guardian. Wiley was appointed guardian, October 11, 1860. Also signing was James R. Burns.

On August 2, 1869, he married Caroline Jane Raney, who was the widow of Joseph Ward. Caroline and Joseph had children: Samuel, born 1858; Margaret, born 1860; Julia, born 1862; and Frances, born 1868. Carolyn Jane was the daughter of Radford Ellis Raney and Huldah Morris. The Raneys were one of the first families along with the Fortenberrys and Taylors of Lawrence County. The Morris' are descendants of John Alden and Pricilla Mullins of the Mayflower. Caroline died December 15, 1883, and James married second wife, Mary J.

James Marion Jones resided in Strawberry, Lawrence County since 1870. He died October 23, 1889, in Strawberry. He left behind second wife, Nancy and at least five minor children. Uncle Morgan C. Raney applied for Letter of Administration for the heirs of James on November 19, 1889. Uncle William P. Raney was appointed guardian of the children on October 4, 1892. Hiram Croom and W. E. Jones signed the guardian bonds. The petition for appointment of guardian says that son, James, was an epileptic and that all four boys were in Texas on October 4, 1892. It also stated that there was property to divide among the heirs.

Isaac Taylor Jones, 1876-1917, about 1915, son of James Marion Jones.

Children of James M. Jones and Caroline Raney were:

1. John Morris Jones, born October 20, 1878, and died July 10, 1937. He married Matilda Little and became a prominent clergyman in Oklahoma and served in World War I. Their children were: Lloyd Raymond, John Webster and Matilda Jewell.

2. Isaac Taylor Jones, born September 29, 1875, and died March 15, 1917. He married Frances Edda Jones (no relation apparently), born February 20, 1881, and died about 1912, on January 10, 1897, in Lawrence County. She was the daughter of Zachary Taylor Jones and Mary Frances Hunter. Mary Francis Jones' line descended from James to Ambrose Jones of Jackson County, Arkansas.

3. William Ellis Jones, born April 17, 1871, and died November 14, 1942. He married Julia Ann Croom on July 15, 1890. Their children were Eula Byron, Don Shelby, Hiram Croom, William Aubry and Julia Florence.

4. James M. Jones, born 1872.

5. David Ashley Jones, born April 11, 1874, and died December 8, 1936, married Emily Sadona Pollard on June 11, 1899. Their children were Denton Aric, Naomi, Gladys May, Mary Ruth, James Pollard and Ima Nell.

6. P. Mathew Jones, born 1880, and died before 1889.

7. Green Childers Jones, born July 1, 1881, and died May 28, 1910. Green married Mary Alva Rushing on August 15, 1909. Their child was Geneva Childress.

8. Baby girl Jones (who was probably a daughter of Mary).

Some of the descendants of Isaac Taylor Jones and Mary Frances Jones were Leslie Crooms Jones who was born in Strawberry, May 9, 1902, and died in Little Rock on June 12, 1984. He married second Vida Isabella Ingram of Lawrence County on December 12, 1924 in Portia. She was the daughter of Sheriff William Granville Ingram and Margaret Etta Graddy. Leslie and Vida resided with their two children in Lauratown until 1937, when they moved to Little Rock and he worked for the Livestock and Poultry Commission for the state. Their son, Leslie Jennings Jones Sr., is retired in Austin, Texas. Their daughter, Marietta Jones Miller, resides in Little Rock. There are five grandchildren and five great-grandchildren.

For more on Isaac Taylor Jones see "Descendants of Isaac Taylor Jones." –Ann Jones.

S. A. D. JONES. This picture about 1901, is of my parents, Stephen Arnold Douglas Jones, Laura Jones and their daughter, Cora Lee Jones, (my oldest living sister) born September 30, 1900, on the Jones Mill Dam farm two and one half miles south of Smithville.

Cora clerked in dad's store until his sudden death in 1917, then in the Syd Hillhouse Mercantile Store at Smithville until her marriage to James I. Gray in 1923. They lived on a farm near New Hope Church until her husband's death in 1952. She then clerked in the Jeff Matthews Store at Smithville for several years until she fell and broke her hip several years later.

She now lives in Hoxie and maintains her own apartment. Her husband, Jim, was a veteran of World War I and was injured in service. Cora was organist almost one half century at the Smithville Methodist Church. Her daughter, Wylleen Gray Crider, and her husband, Dexter Crider, live in Hoxie where he was Superintendent of Schools and she was employed as a bookkeeper.

Cora's son, Stanley Gray, and wife, Ida Mae Stokes Gray, live in Jonesboro where he works for the post office and is also a part time surveyor. He served in the Korean War and was wounded in battle on the front lines.

My dad is the picture was born on the farm by the Mill Dam on Strawberry River in 1860. He was named after Stephen Arnold Douglas, the United States Senator, who debated with Lincoln before the latter became president.

My dad's father, Wiley C. Jones, came with his parents, Mr. and Mrs. Elbert Jones, from Georgia and Alabama and settled on the farm on Strawberry River in the 1830s.

Wiley C. developed the mill dam whereby he harnessed its energy to power a rolling mill, carding mill, a cotton gin, a grist mill and a sawmill. He also cut ice in the river in winter time and stored it in sawdust in an ice house for use in summer.

His multiple enterprises along with his farming operations required a number of employees and he had customers from throughout Lawrence and surrounding counties.

Although the old dam is no longer intact, a few yeas ago, one could observe some of the large boulders from its construction as well as large pieces of discarded machinery.

Wiley C. was a charter member of the Methodist Church in Smithville. He served as a captain in the Confederate Army in the Civil War Between the States. He was captured by the Union Army and escaped by swimming the Mississippi River. He returned to Lawrence County and recruited more soldiers before he returned and rejoined his company.

After the war ended, he returned to Lawrence County and developed all the enterprises on the Jones Mill Dam farm. He also owned land in Sharp County and property in Ravenden Springs. He and my grandmother are buried in the Smithville Cemetery.

My dad and mother were married in 1894, near Opposition where her parents, the Carl Christian Frederickson and Matilda Gilbert Frederickson were farm homesteaders. My maternal grandfather came to this country from Denmark.

My father (S.A.D. Jones) entered the mercantile business by starting his own store in Smithville about 1900, which he expanded three times by adding to his store building and stock of merchandise until his sudden death from pneumonia in 1917. He hauled his merchandise from Imboden and Black Rock with a team and wagon. Elizabeth, my sister, and I accompanied him to the railroad depots many times.

One of our biggest childhood thrills was when mother hitched our horses to our buggy and took Elizabeth and me down to Denton to see the circus. There was no daytime performance so mother paid the circus manager to let us see the elephant and some of the animals. The elephant broke loose and they had to chase it over the field to corral it.

Another childhood thrill for us was when dad took us on the steamboat ride on Black River and we observed the huge paddle wheel plowing through the waves.

My dad and mother were very active in the Smithville Community and in the Methodist Church where he was a long time steward and Sunday School superintendent and where mother taught Sunday School classes.

My dad was an original shareholder in the Smithville Telephone Company.

My parents are buried in the Smithville Cemetery. Mother died suddenly of a heart attack in 1915, and dad died in 1917. We four children were orphaned early by their deaths (age 6, 9, 12 and 14), but the four of us stayed together and lived in our old home place until it burned about 1920, then moved into dad's old store building.

My other two living sisters, Wyllie Vera Peavey and Sarah Elizabeth Jones now retired from many years of secretarial work and motel renovation and operation now live in Wichita, Kansas. Vera and her husband, Ernest, maintain their own apartment there as does Elizabeth. Vera was like a mother to Elizabeth and me after our parents' deaths.

My wife, Mildred Irene, my son, Stephen Michael, and I live in Jefferson City, Missouri. I am retired as the state wide Director of the Accident Prevention Program of the Missouri Division of Health after 21 years. My wife is retired from the Missouri Department of Revenue.

I served as a sergeant in a railway battalion in Europe for four years during World War II.

Our son, Stephen Michael, is currently a

post graduate computer student here in the local university.

This is a brief history of the three people in the picture and of their parents, their children, grandchildren and ancestors.
 –Wyllene Crider.

WILLIAM EDWARD JONES, born March 11, 1888, was the son of James Alec Jones and Caldonia Shockley. On October 16, 1910, he married Bertha Tyler, born June 16, 1889. She was the daughter of Booker Tyler and Rosetta Land.

"Will" and Bertha raised their eight children farming around Running Water Creek, out from Walnut Ridge. In the 1940s, they moved to Illinois for several years before returning to Arkansas.

The children of Will and Bertha were: Lehman, born August 20, 1911, who married Opal Marshall. Lehman passed away October 24, 1974. Opal lives in Walnut Ridge.

James Gerald, born June 29, 1914, married Lelia Horsman. James passed away May 29, 1994. Leila resides in Imboden.

Juanita, born September 10, 1918, married Burl Gray. Both are deceased.

Oneida, born August 26, 1920, married Benson Cole. Both are deceased.

Billy Joe, born November 17, 1926, married Malissie Herrin. Both are deceased.

Vera, born June 13, 1922 was first married to Charles Boehmer; later she married Joe Mendolia. Vera died November, 1981.

Billy Gene, born March 3, 1931, married Darlene. Gene passed away about 1992, in Illinois.

Many grandchildren, great-grandchildren and great-great-grandchildren live in Lawrence County today. *–Leon Jones.*

STEPHEN JUSTUS, 1790-1875, came to Smithville, Arkansas, from Jackson County, Georgia, between 1837 and 1839. He had six children: John M., William H., Ira Newton, Elizabeth, Caroline and Jane Justus, before arriving in Lawrence County. Stephen married Jane Ragsdale Williams, widow of William Williams, in Lawrence County on March 9, 1843. They bore James A., Francis Marion, Rebecca, Benjamin H., Mary and Isabella Justus. Stephen was the County Coroner from 1844-1846.

Stephen's third son, Ira Newton Justus, 1827-1899, or "Newt", was a carpenter like his father. He married Rebecca Matthews on January 8, 1850. They bore Jasper E., William Whitfield, Mary C., George C. and Molly Justus. He married Margaret Hornback on February 27, 1861. He married Mary Gibbons on December 26, 1867. They bore Thomas Yancy, Martha E., Emmit R., Elizabeth and Fanny Justus. Newt was conscripted into Freeman's Missouri Cavalry before General Price left on his ill fated raid into Missouri. He was held captive in Springfield for the duration of the war. Mary Elizabeth Gibbons Justus lived to be 102 years old and drew Confederate pension.

Newt's third son, Thomas Yancy or "Bee", January 11, 1872-February 18, 1943, married Chrissy Estella Matthews, September 26, 1878-January 28, 1958, on August 25, 1893. They bore Lillie May, Odessa Calodia, Elsie Blanch, Yancy Matthews, Ira Evaline, Jessie Pauline and Eli Newton Justus.

Thomas' oldest son, Yancy, August 29, 1901-February, 1984, married Della Mandy Winters, October 12, 1902-August, 1978, on December 14, 1924. They bore Freed Faye, Austin (stillborn), Thomas Dale and Gail MacAuther. Yancy ran the cotton gin in Smithville and was the town blacksmith. Children loved him and hated him at the same time.

He teased everyone. Yancy was the king of practical jokers. As a child, Yancy dropped his blind cat from the loft of the barn onto the back of their work mule. The mule destroyed everything in sight and "Bee" destroyed Yancy's backside.

Yancy's second son, Dale Justus, born July 28, 1931, was the terror of Smithville. He was redheaded and befreckled from head to toe. Dale was so redheaded the rooster used to attack him when he walked across the yard. The rooster met a violent death and was eaten for supper one summer evening.

Dale was the first to leave Smithville. He left the hills to play football for Walnut Ridge High. He became the student body president and a track/football star. He was offered a football scholarship from Paul Bryant while the "Bear" was coaching at Kentucky. Instead, Dale received a Purple Heart in Korea. He returned from the war to win the biggest battle of his life involving a black-haired brown-eyed Egyptian. Her name was Sue Sammons and they were married October 17, 1954. Sue Sammons Justus, born November 29, 1934, was the Egypt Homecoming Queen and lettered in basketball. (I've seen her play and that does not speak well for the Egypt Bulldogs.) They bore Joe Dale and Jay Dean Justus. Dale and Sue Justus moved from Lawrence County in 1963.

Jay, born July 22, 1959, is the family historian and married the perfect wife in Dolores Ann Gard, born February 13, 1965, on May 12, 1984. They bore Jared Newton, born April 9, 1991, and William Stephen Justus, born August 17, 1994. The families of Jay, Dale and Mac Justus presently reside in Hot Springs, Arkansas. *–Jay Justus.*

JOHN THOMAS KEITH FAMILY. John Thomas Keith was born in Tennessee on January 29, 1886. He was the son of William H. and Jennie Keith.

The Keith family migrated to Randolph County, Arkansas, in the late 1800s, and later they moved to Craighead County.

The 1900 Craighead County, Arkansas, census finds the family living in the Little Texas Township, west of Egypt.

William and Jennie Keith became the parents of nine children, with one dying in infancy.

The Keith family farmed for several years in the Egypt area and William became a very prominent landowner.

In March of 1909, Jennie Keith died from the complications of childbirth, leaving William to raise their large family.

In the spring of 1912, John's father leased out the Egypt farm and moved the family back to Randolph County, where he purchased farmland in the Skaggs Community. William planned to sell the Egypt farm, but he contracted "the fever" and within a week in mid November of 1913, both William and John's brother, Robert, died.

John Keith had not moved to Randolph County with the family, but instead had remained at Egypt to oversee the farm and to feed the remaining live-

Maggie and John Keith.

stock, and he had fallen in love with Margaret Rebecca McQuay. Maggie, as she was lovingly called, was the daughter of prominent local physician, Dr. Jimmy McQuay. John and Maggie were married on June 26, 1913.

The new family settled in the Promised Land area of Lawrence County. Here they farmed and started their family.

John Keith was a hardworking, no non-sense man, serious and solemn and very quiet by nature. John farmed for many years; then he went to work for the East Texas Pipeline Pumping Station near Egypt. He worked in the station for a time, but later he walked the pipeline five miles in both directions five days a week to look for leaks.

Maggie, meanwhile, raised her growing family. Most Sundays would find her busy preparing Sunday dinner and always cooking extra food for the company that usually dropped in. Maggie always graciously invited the visitor to come in and "have a bite" knowing that it would mean less food for her family the following week.

There are wonderful, warm memories of the love shown by this mother and many a small child stood peeping over the tabletop waiting anxiously for her chocolate fried pies and the huge cookies that she made by the dishpan full, as if by magic. Maggie was a gentle woman and many lives are richer because of her.

John and Maggie are the parents of seven children.

1. James, the eldest, married Bonnie Conner. They lived, farmed and raised a large family in the Bono, Arkansas area.

2. Juanita "Neti", married Earlie Lawson. They also lived and farmed in Lawrence County; both are residents of a Walnut Ridge nursing home.

3. Dean Keith married Othella Browning and they farmed in the Bono area. Dean is deceased.

4. Earnestine is a twin to Dean. She married Chester Shrable. They have lived in St. Louis for many years. Chester is deceased.

5. Ruby married Henry Buff. They also lived in St. Louis. Henry is deceased.

6. Billy married Imogene Wynne. Billy died in October of 1955, at age 23.

7. Ivonne married Kenneth Thompson. They farmed in the Evergreen Community. Kenneth is deceased. Ivonne and her son, Bobby, continue to farm in the same area. *– Barbara Holder.*

WILLIAM JESSE KEITH was born in Tennessee on March 8, 1892, to William H. and Jenny Keith. There are conflicting stories concerning the Keith family, but by using available public records and interviews with his sister Jenny in 1996, I will try to document my grandfather's life. I first find the Keiths on the 1900 Craighead County, Arkansas census at the time the family was living in the Little Texas Township, west of Egypt.

Jennie Keith was only 13 years old when William married her. No one can verify her last name, but believe it was either Cane or Kane, census records say she was from Missouri. No marriage records were found.

I do know, that before 1900, and before moving to the Egypt area, the Keiths were living in Randolph County, Arkansas.

In July of 1912, Jesse married Mattie Steadman. She was a young widow with a small daughter. Mattie died the next spring from complications of giving birth to a son who was called Little Joe Keith. The boy was raised by his Steadman grandparents, and was lost track of in the 1940s.

On January 28, 1914, William Jesse Keith married Susie Davis in Craighead County, Arkansas.

William Jessie Keith and Susie Davis on their wedding day.

The young family began their lives together on the Davis farm near Egypt. On January 17, 1915, Susie gave birth to their first child, a daughter, Pearl Mae, and on September 10,1916, she would give birth to a second daughter, Gladys Marie.

Jesse Keith was a handsome man, family pictures show him always dressed up with a tie and the ever present hat sitting lopsided on his head. He loved to hunt and spent many nights in the Cache River bottoms hunting and trapping. On one such trip he became wet and caught a chill, which developed into pneumonia and on November 3, 1918, he passed away, leaving Susie near death herself from the flu and also pregnant with their third child. He is buried in the Arnold Cemetery near Swifton, Arkansas. Susie recovered from her illness and her brother, Dewey Davis, took her and her children into his home at Minturn and here she stayed until after Minnie Viola was born on February 1, 1919. Susie later married George Parker and he helped raise Jesse and her children.

Pearl Keith married Bunk Kisling on February 3, 1931. Bunk is deceased. Pearl lives in Hoxie.

Gladys Keith married Johnny Newman on February 17, 1934. They are both deceased.

Minnie married Mack Seels. They live in Hoxie, Arkansas.

William Jesse Keith had a large family, many who remained in Lawrence County all their lives. His brothers, John and Charley, farmed in the Promise Land Community of Lawrence County for many years.

John Keith married Maggie McQuay.

Charley Keith married Vickie Prater.

Jessie had another brother, Robert, who died a few days after their father in November, 1912, in Randolph County, Arkansas. He also had a sister, Cricket, who disappeared when she was 16 years old, never to be heard from again.

Jesse also had three sisters who survived him. Rosie married George McDaniels. George died in the flu epidemic. Rosie then married Tillman Grooms of Egypt. They moved to central Florida in the early 20s. Both are deceased.

Minnie Keith married Willie Hendrickson. They are deceased. A son, Kenneth, lives at Saffle, Arkansas.

Jennie Keith was the family baby. Her mom died when she was six months old. She lived in the home of her sister, Rosie, and husband, Tillman Grooms, until her marriage to Jess Daniels. Jennie passed away in 1997, at age 89, and was an enormous help to me in my research.

Susie Davis Keith Parker passed away in July, 1946. She is buried in the Aldridge Cemetery near Egypt. –Barbara Newman Howard.

LEVI W. KELL FAMILY. Levi William Kell was nine years old when his family moved to Arkansas in 1860. He was born in Tennessee on July 2, 1851. He is listed in the U. S. Census of 1870, as living in Lawrence County in the Spring River Township with his parents, Robert A. and Elizabeth Rodgers Kell, and his siblings, Lucinda, Sarah Jane, Josiah "Joseph", Serena, Mary Belle and James N.

For 35 years, Levi served as deputy sheriff of Lawrence County. He died on May 30, 1930, at the age of 78. In his obituary, Levi is remembered as "a pioneer of the county." The obituary also noted that "his natural ability, coupled with his high moral principles soon marked him as one of the county's truest, most able officers."

Levi married Nancy Jane Alexander on December 19, 1872. Nancy's maternal grandfather, George Washington McGhehey, served as a County Judge of Lawrence County between 1852 and 1868. Levi and Nancy had a total of 11 children, only six living past childhood. They were: Johnson Hatcher, Rufus Tandy, Minnie Florence, Effie Belle, Levi Homer and Georgia Adelaide. Nancy died on November 23, 1917. Levi and Nancy are buried in the Kelly Cemetery near Imboden.

Johnson Hatcher "Hatcher" was born in 1875. He married Mattie McLaughlin, and they had nine children: Melvin Clyde, Willie, Helen, Frank, Vernon, Edith, Ken, Johnson and Wilson. George Clyde Kell, a professional baseball player, who was inducted into the Baseball Hall of Fame in 1983, is a grandson of Hatcher and Mattie. His father was Melvin Clyde Kell.

Rufus Tandy, born in 1879, was ordained as a minister of the General Assembly of God Church in 1923. He married Margaret Propst and they had five children: Agnes, Lillina, Ernest, Hazel and Leo.

Minnie Florence was born in 1881, and married William Albert Judkins. They had seven children: Marie, Fannie, Lucille, Florence, Faye, William and Aileen. Soon after her marriage, Minnie and her husband moved from Arkansas to Ohio.

Effie Belle, who was born in 1891, died just three weeks after celebrating her 100th birthday in September, 1991. She married W. Henry Bragg and had six children: Elsie, Gladys, Nancy, Ruba, Joyce and William Henry Jr.

Levi Homer "Homer" was born in 1893, and married Ora Buchanan. They had three sons: Hubert, Alva and Lester. Homer worked as a blacksmith and carpenter, helping to build Fort Leonard Wood MO.

Levi W. Kell family, about summer of 1916. First row, kneeling, from left: Vernon Kell, Marie Judkins, Fannie Judkins, Pauline Kell, Fay Judkins, Florence Judkins, Hazel Kell, William Judkins and Ernest Kell. Second row: Helen Kell, Frank Kell, Agnes Kell, Clyde Kell, Lillian Kell and Willie Kell. Third row: Mattie Kell (holding Edith), Hatcher Kell, Levi W. Kell, Nancy Kell, Rufus T. Kell (holding Leo) and Maggie Kell. Fourth row: Ora Kell, Homer Kell (holding Hubert), Effie Kell Bragg (holding Gladys), Addie Kell, Henry Bragg (holding Elsie), Abb Judkins (holding Lucille) and Minnie Kell Judkins.

The youngest child of Levi and Nancy, Georgia Adelaide "Addie", was born in 1899. She married Ernest C. Hughes and had five daughters: Blanche, Georgia, Ernesteen, Ruth and Shirley.

Through the years, the descendants of Levi and Nancy Kell have continued to grow and the family is now spread across the country. But many of the descendants have chosen to stay close to their ancestor roots and remain in the Lawrence County area, where a family reunion is held each fall. –Edith Stovall.

KELLEY FAMILY. Marvel Kelley was born in Morgan County, Georgia. He married Sarah Ann Cockerham, April 5, 1813, in Morgan County, Georgia. She was the descendant of the Cockerham and Spencer families who helped found Jamestown, Virginia. We know of five children born to Marvel and Sarah, or "Sally", as she was known. In the Goodspeed's history of this area he says there were eight children, but we only know the names of five.

1. Eli Marion Kelley, born March, 1823, in Walton County, Georgia, died July 22, 1905, in Butler County, Kansas, married Elizabeth Jane Reynolds in 1846, in Jackson County, Alabama.

2. Marvel Kelley, born 1827, in Walton County, Georgia, married Sarah Reynolds in 1848, in Jackson County, Arkansas.

3. John W. Kelley, born December 19, 1830, in Georgia, died November 17, 1923, in Lawrence County, Arkansas, married first Nancy Lawson, December 19, 1851, in Jackson County, Alabama; second to Mary Ann Lawson, a sister of his first wife, January 31, 1867, in Imboden, Lawrence County, Arkansas; and third to Cynthia Cravens.

4. Levi Kelley.

5. Minerva Kelley.

John W. Kelley moved first to Dent County, Missouri and it was there his first wife, Nancy Lawson, died. John brought his orphaned children and came to Lawrence County, Arkansas to be near his in-laws, the Lawsons. He then married Nancy's sister, Mary Ann. Children of John and Nancy are:

1. Sarah M. Kelley, born 1853, in Alabama, died March 4, 1887, in Lawrence County, Arkansas, married William Harvey McLaughlin, January 14, 1877.

2. Rebecca Jane Kelley, born April 26, 1855, in Alabama, died January 16, 1929, in Marked Tree, Poinsett County, Arkansas, married Thomas Crockett Hedrick.

3. William W. Kelley, born 1856.

4. Mary Ann Kelley, born January 9, 1859, in Missouri, died November 26, 1939, in Lawrence County, Arkansas, married James Crittendon Smith, November 2, 1886, in Lawrence County, Arkansas.

5. Marvel Jackson Kelley, born September 12, 1860, in Dade County, Missouri, died March, 1945, in Lawrence County, Arkansas, married first Abigale Baird, November 29, 1883, in Lawrence County, Arkansas, married second Sarah A. Moore, January 5, 1890, in Lawrence County, Arkansas.

6. Nancy Kelley, born 1865.

Child of John W. Kelley and Mary Ann Lawson: Andrew Kelley, born 1868, Lawrence County, Arkansas, died August 20, 1887, in Lawrence County, Arkansas.

Child of John Kelley and Cynthia Cravens: Johnnie Kelley, born June 14, 1889, in Lawrence County, Arkansas, died November 23, 1960, in Lawrence County, married William McLaughlin.

Many of these are listed elsewhere in this history with their spouses and the families they raised. The Kelley, Lawson, McLaughlin, Smith and Hedrick families are so entwined it is impossible to keep the threads straight, at times.

John W. Kelley settled and built his home on Highway 63 near Imboden. The Kelley Cemetery contains a lot of the Kelley family and allied families. It is located on ground, which was part of the Kelley home place.

John served in the Civil War, or as his descendants called it, the War of Northern Aggression, enlisting in Colonel Mitchell's Company F, 8th Missouri Infantry, which was, of course, a southern unit. He served until the fall of 1864, when he contracted the dread smallpox disease. This put an end to his service.

Many people in Lawrence County can trace their lineage through this family. –Dale MeMasters.

DANIEL KETNER FAMILY.

Daniel Ketner, farmer and stock raiser, was a son of Dawalt Ketner of Rowan County, North Carolina. Dawalt Ketner married Miss Mary Eisenhower on January 17, 1819, in Cabarrus County, North Carolina; their son, Daniel, was born November 26, 1825. Dawalt is the son of a George Michael Ketner II, who was born in Berk County, Pennsylvania. The Ketner family came to America in 1733, on the Charming Beauty.

Daniel's mother died on April 24, 1846. Daniel remained with his father until he reached the age of 24 years. In 1849, Daniel moved west and settled in Illinois. He labored on a farm in Union County for 18 months, and then, thinking the prospects brighter for him, he moved to Tennessee, where he married Catherine A. Bour, born in 1835, in North Carolina.

After his marriage, he settled on a farm in Weakley County, Tennessee, where he remained three years, and then moved to Union County, Illinois, residing there until 1858. He then came to Arkansas and bought 80 acres of new land, which he cleared and put under cultivation. Meeting with success in his new home, he bought more land on different occasions. His home place consisted of 160 acres, with 55 acres cleared and another of 73 acres, of that, 35 acres ready for cultivation.

In 1863, he enlisted in the Confederate Army and served until the final surrender. He served in Company G; 38 Arkansas Infantry as a private. His name is on a prisoner of war list which has him being paroled at Shreveport, Louisiana, on June 8, 1865. He was in the battles at Pilot Knob, Pine Bluff, Little Rock, Independence and Price's raids through Missouri. Family legend has it that Catherine was raped by Carpetbaggers and Daniel took the children, but kicked Catherine out. He then married a Sophia Cozart, but she left him and would not live with him. Daniel divorced her and married a Mrs. Mary J. Lawson, a widow lady of Tennessee, in 1883.

He is the father of seven children by his first marriage: George Henry Ketner, John Daniel Ketner, Jesse Alex Ketner, Sarah Mahala Ketner (wife of Henry Clay Oldham, son of Jackson Henderson Oldham and Sarah Ann McCarroll), Jane Ketner (wife of George Caspar), Margaret Ketner (wife of James Nunley), Amanda Ketner (wife of Elihu Davis), and there was also one child by a third marriage, Nettie Ketner.

Mr. Ketner was a member of the Old School Presbyterian Church and also of the Agricultural Wheel, while Mrs. Mary Ketner attended the Baptist Church.

Catherine A. Bour Ketner died on March 12, 1898, and is buried in the Clover Bend Cemetery in Clover Bend, Arkansas. Daniel and Mary J. Ketner both died on October 12, 1902, and are buried in the Old Lebanon Cemetery in Eaton, Arkansas.

SIMEON KIDDER FAMILY.

The Simeon Kidder family moved by rail boxcar from Elkart County, Indiana, about 1890. Simeon Kidder and Emma Mary Cole were married at Waharuska, Indiana, in 1860. To this union were born six children: Ronald, Arthur, Harvey, Franklin Chester, Myrtle and Nellie. Myrtle married Robert "Bob" Propst and lived her life in and around Black Rock, Arkansas. She has many relatives still living in Lawrence County and in Arkansas.

My mother, Nettie Fern Kidder was born at the Sutton Place on Coffey Creek in Lawrence County on February 12, 1905. She was the daughter of Franklin Chester Kidder and Nettie Charity Robertson. My mother's mother, Charity, died soon after her birth. Franklin Chester Kidder would marry a widow, Elizabeth Felkins (Ghormley) in that same year.

Frank and Lizzy would move to Baca County, Colorado, in 1914 where he and his brother, Harvey, had homesteaded some land. Franklin Chester and Lizzy had five children. Nettie Fern grew to womanhood in Baca County, Colorado, and would marry Lewis Lester Davis on January 2, 1923, at Wiley, Colorado. To this union were born nine children: Nettie Elizabeth, Theodore Ellsworth, Wilma Fern, Lewis Eugene, Laura Ellen, Ernest LeRoy, Joyce Juanita, Beatrice Eileen and Sarah Christina. Sarah Christina at age 6 in 1950 and Theodore Ellworth died in 1992.

My mother always had a fond remembrance of her childhood in Black Rock, Arkansas. She always wanted dad to "take her back to Arkansas." Dad did once in 1932, but said the black snakes were too much for him. Mother talked of learning to play the piano, Christmases, a Negro doll and many other experiences that she had there in Black Rock.

They moved to Lincoln County, Colorado, where four of the children were born. Later, they moved to Elbert County, Colorado, where two more children, Eileen and Sarah, were born.

I was born in 1937 on the "Peterson Place" in Lincoln County, Colorado. I presently am 61 years old.

Lewis Lester Davis died January 27, 1973. Nettie Fern died August 13, 1984. –Ernest L. Davis.

RAY KINDER.

Marilyn Baker, daughter of Willie and Olene Jones Baker of Lauratown, married Ray Kinder of Swifton, March 28, 1953, in Walnut Ridge by Reverend Glynn Campbell. They were the first couple Reverend Campbell married. They lived in Walnut Ridge, Paragould and in 1964, moved to Swifton and opened Ray's Super Market where they remained until Ray was forced to retire because of poor health in 1993. They have four children, three girls and one boy.

1. Vickie was born in 1955. She is married to Steve Henderson and they have two sons: Chad, 18, and Shaun, 16. They live in Jonesboro.

2. Tony was born in 1958, and he has one daughter, Autumn, by his first marriage. Autumn is 19 and has an 18 month old son. Tony lives in Swifton.

3. Cindy was born in 1960. She is married to Deral Duncan and they have two children. Destiny is 14 and Blaise is four. They reside in Swifton.

4. Misty was born in 1970. She married Donald Cates, July 1,. 1998. She lives in Bentonville, where she teaches school. –Marilyn Rinder.

KING HISTORY.

The United States census of 1850, taken on August 5, 1850, for Bracken County, Kentucky, listed the King family. The father was William D. King, age 47, born in North Carolina, and the mother was Nancy S. King, age 47, born in Virginia. There were seven children listed on the census report: John W., Joseph, Elizabeth, Nancy J., Mary, Martha and Lewis.

Nancy S. King died on February 13, 1859, and is buried in Old Town Cemetery at Kirklin, Indiana. The death and burial of William D. King is unknown. John W. King was born in Kentucky in 1833, to William and Nancy King. John married Luvise Blackburn on June 18, 1855, at Clinton County, Indiana. John served as a private in Company G of the Indiana 86th Regiment Infantry of the Union Army during the Civil War and died at Murfreesboro, Tennessee, on July 8, 1863, and is buried in the Stones River National Cemetery at Murfreesboro, Tennessee.

John and Luvise had four children: America, William Joseph, born March 15, 1858, Terrissia and Nancy. Luvise married William Dotson on February 19, 1869, and they moved to Alton, Missouri, in October, 1871. William Joseph "Joe" King moved to Arkansas and met Josephine "Josie" Williams from the Clover Bend area. They married on February 18, 1891, in Lawrence County. They moved to Alton, Missouri, where they had five children: Burgain, Maud, Gladys, Maxine and Clyde.

Joe and Josie moved from Alton, Missouri to the Richwoods Community in Lawrence County between 1906 and 1910. Joe died in January, 1922, Josie died February 9, 1937. They are both buried in the Sanders Cemetery at Richwoods. Clyde married Odessa "Dessie" Wright. They continued to live in the Richwoods Community and had two daughters: Genendol and Barbara. Dessie died in February, 1937. Clyde married Alice Rock in September, 1939. Alice had a daughter by a previous marriage named Virginia. Clyde and Alice had three children: Edith, Bonnie and Donnie. Clyde died on February 25, 1970, and is buried in the Whittaker Cemetery in Lawrence County. Alice King, as well as all six children, are still living, five of which are living in Lawrence County: Genendol Atkinson, Walnut Ridge; Barbara Disher, Indiana; Virginia Meriwether; Edith Passalaqua; Bonnie Walton; and Donnie King, all live at Hoxie. –Don King.

BILLY JOE KIRKLAND FAMILY.

Billy Joe Kirkland, October 25, 1927-April 19, 1986, son of Joseph Oscar Kirkland and Betty Bell Burdick Kirkland and Agla Willene Baker, daughter of Charles William Baker and Wilma Olene Jones Baker, were married by Methodist minister Reverend Lloyd Conyers in Walnut Ridge, Arkansas, on June 1, 1947. They lived in Blytheville, Arkansas, where Bill was employed.

The 1940s had a much different life-style than today. Our country had just gone through several years of World War II. Many of our friends and neighbors had served in the war, several did not return. It was common to see crocheted curtains over the front door windows that spelled out "V for Victory!"

The world moved at a much slower pace. In small communities, men gathered to sit on benches, visit, play checkers or whittle a piece of wood. We do not see this much today. No new cars were made during the war because manufacturing plants were needed for defense vehicles. When new cars were produced again, car dealers used a list of people interested in buying to see who would get the next new car.

The war caused many things to be rationed. Coupon books were used to purchase coffee, sugar, even shoes. Nylons were nonexistent. Today we hear the word "recycle" as if it was a new word. Those of us who lived during the 1930s and 1940s, remember when recycling was a way of life. Flower sacks were made into everything from dresses, aprons, pillowcases, tea towels, napkins, etc. Whenever bed sheets wore thin in the middle, they were split down the center, the outer edges were then sewn together. This added years of life

The Billy Joe Kirkland family. Seated: Willene, Billy Joe and grandson, Stephen. Back: William, Teresa and Michael in 1985.

to a sheet. The same was true of men's shirt collars whenever they became frayed. The collar was removed, turned over and re-stitched.

Newspapers, magazines and catalogs did not accumulate as they do today. Most people received only one weekly newspaper and a Sears catalog twice a year. Many farm families papered their walls with newspaper. When a new catalog arrived, the old one was sometimes used by children to cut out paper dolls, before it was removed to the outhouse.

After a few years, Bill entered the ministry of the Methodist Church. Serving churches in the following Arkansas towns: Blytheville (Promised Land), Lake City, Black Rock, Lynn, Smithville and Imboden.

Willene worked for Southwestern Bell Telephone Company. They had two sons: William Joseph (named for both grandfathers) and Michael Anthony. William is unmarried. Michael married Teresa Salyards of Pocahontas, Arkansas. They have three children: Stephen, Spencer and Whitney Michelle.

Perhaps we have lived in a time that has seen more changes than any other time in history. Example: Our mode of travel has gone from wagons to cars and planes. We have even seen a man on the moon. The technology has been unbelievable - radio, TV, computers and phones that are voice activated - to name a few. Just a wonderful time to have lived. *–Willene Kirkland.*

J. O. KIRKLAND FAMILY. Joseph Oscar Kirkland, born September 11, 1884, to Isaac Newton Kirkland and Eliza Jane Workman Kirkland in Ozark County, Missouri, married Betty Bell Burdick, daughter of Elijah Franklin Burdick and Elizabeth Rosenberger Burdick, born January 8, 1897, Wright County, Missouri.

They farmed in the Strangers Home Community. Their family: Mildred Mae, born March 23, 1915; Ralph, May 19, 1917; Mabel Inez, January 3, 1920; Harold Stephen, March 4, 1925; Billy Joe, October 25, 1927; Jarrell Oscar, August 2, 1929. Betty died in March, 1930.

Oscar's brother, Zack Kirkland, died within a few weeks, leaving a widow and children. It seemed logical to put both families together and raise them as one.

Oscar married Zack's widow, Ila Rowe Gadberry Kirkland, May 31, 1930. Ila had two sons, Wayne Gadberry and Zane Tildon Kirkland. This arrangement worked well since Oscar needed someone to care for his family and Ila had no means of support for her family.

Oscar and Ila had two daughters: Delilah June, July 18, 1931; and Lanita Jane, April 19, 1935. Lanita died at age three.

In the late 1930s, the family lived a short time in the Coffman Community before moving to the Martin farm in the Lauratown Community.

Mildred and Inez married brothers, Mildred married Henry Harris; four children: Delores, Jimmy, Carol and Tommy.

Inez married Dave Harris; one son, David.

Both couples lived in New Jersey until after World War II. Dave and Inez then returned to Lawrence County.

Ralph married

Oscar and Ila Kirkland.

Geneva Wenfry; one son, Danny. Ralph served as an infantryman in World War II, saw action in "Battle of the Bulge" and the North African Campaign.

Harold married Pearl Baird; four children: Marsha, Mary, Larry and Lori. Harold served in the Marines during World War II.

Billy Joe married Willene Baker; two sons: William and Michael.

Jarrell married Betty Golden of St. Louis, Missouri; two daughters.

Wayne married Stephie Pickellock of New Jersey; one son, Wayne Jr.

Zane married Doris Austin. Zane and Phillips are their children.

Delilah married Claude Hall; three daughters: Claudia, Cathy and Darlene.

In addition to the parents, all of the siblings have died. *–Willene Kirkland.*

MICHAEL ANTHONY KIRKLAND was born August 19, 1956, in Mississippi County, Arkansas. His parents were Reverend Bill J. and Willene Kirkland.

Since Michael's father was a Methodist minister, the family lived in several locations of Northeast Arkansas including Craighead, Lawrence, as well as Mississippi County.

He met a young lady, Teresa Salyards, while she was a nursing student at Methodist Hospital in Memphis, Tennessee. Teresa is the daughter of Lloyd and Irene Salyards of Pocahontas, Arkansas. They were married December 22, 1978, with Reverend Bill J. Kirkland and Reverend Bill Gray performing the ceremony.

Three children complete the family unit.

Stephen Michael, born January 13, 1982, in Craighead County, Arkansas. Stephen's present interest is "hunting" for whatever is in season: deer, squirrel, quail, etc. He also likes "real cool" cars.

Spencer Lloyd was born December 24, 1986, in Baxter County, Arkansas. Spencer is an avid gardener; and is knowledgeable in many plants and their care. He takes pride in sharing with neighbors from his garden. Learning to play music also holds his interest.

Whitney Michelle was born September 1,

Michael and Teresa; children: Stephen, Spencer and Whitney.

1989, in Springfield, Missouri. Books, dolls and Beanie Babies, along with playing with the family cats, fill most of her time. *–Willene Kirkland.*

KIRKPATRICK FAMILY. Edmund Singleton Kirkpatrick, born February 22, 1810, in Jackson County, Tennessee, son of John, born 1786, Chester County, South Carolina (War of 1812). Edmund's paternal grandfather fought in the American Revolution. John's second wife, Sarah Tinsley, must have raised Edmund. His mother died in childbirth with his sister, Margaret, just before his first birthday.

Edmund married Annie Barnett Woodome in Perry County, Illinois, before moving to Independence County, Arkansas in 1835, when he was 25. He had already fought in the Black Hawk War at Kellogg's Grove. His horse had been killed beneath him.

In 1836 they settled on Reed's Creek in Lawrence County. He farmed his considerable property while raising his family there. He was a brick and stone mason. He built some of the now oldest homes in Batesville. He was a Missionary Baptist preacher at Reed's Creek from 1839 until his death in 1876. He and Annie had 10 children, seven lived to adulthood. They were: Dr. John Newton "J.N.", Civil War veteran and physician in Randolph County; Hiram Clinton, Civil War; Alfred Riley, Civil War; Milton Francis, Civil War; James Edmund, Civil War; William Tinsley; and David D., Civil War.

Edmund married Elizabeth Goatcer Smithee after Annie's death. They had one child to live to adulthood. Eva J. Edmund died in 1876.

David Kirkpatrick married Mariah Lawrence Sullivan. They had the following children: Franklin, her child from previous marriage, George, Andrew and Mary.

David was a preacher at Cedar Grove Baptist Church, Independence County. After Mariah's death he married Margaret S. King, daughter of James and Mary Lawrence King, about 1874. They had the following children: Willie, Amanda "Minnie", James E. and Mariah. David died about 1885.

His son, James E., married Annie Lacks, daughter of Eli and Belva James Lacks in 1894. They lived in Cedar Grove. They had the following children: Virgie, George, Mary, Esther, Martha, now at age 98, and James. James E. died in 1950, with burial in Jackson County, Arkansas. Annie died young in 1909, age 33, and is buried in James Cemetery at Cedar Grove beside her parents.

Esther married Toney Ray, son of James Nathan and Julie Hager Ray in Egypt, Arkansas in 1916. They made their home in Jackson County, Arkansas. They had the following children: Mildred, Vernia, James, Milvin, Dorathy and Paul. Esther died in 1955, buried same cemetery as her father, James.

Mildred married Edmond Flowers, son of Columbus H. and Clara Anderson Flowers, in Newport, Arkansas in 1933. They were married 62 years before his death. They had the following children: Martha, Raymond, Donald, Ronald and Carolyn.

Mildred is now 80 years old and still lives in their home in Newport, Arkansas.

–Carolyn Flowers Tucker.

BOYD KIRKSEY FAMILY. Boyd Anderson Kirksey, born September 7, 1917, at Mena, Arizona, and the late Mary Lou Collins Kirksey, born December 9, 1925, at Wirth, Arkansas, moved to Hoxie in September, 1949, from Thayer, Missouri. Boyd was transferred to Hoxie while working for the Frisco Railroad. He is a World War II veteran, having served in Europe and Africa as a member of the 2nd Armored Division.

Boyd and Mary were married February 22, 1946, at Mammoth Spring, Arkansas. Mary died September 25, 1995.

Boyd was one of the original members of the Hoxie Fire Department, organized in 1954. He was active in the Hoxie Lion's Club and a board member of the Hoxie Community Center. He is a member of the American Legion and the V.F.W.

Boyd and Mary had three children: James Edward, born November 18, 1946; Sharon Kay, born March 26, 1951; and Patsy Anita, born December 9, 1954.

James married Freida Lynette Miles of Memphis. They have two children: Leah LaWanda, born October 6, 1969; and Chrsitopher Edward, born September 17, 1974. Leah married Rod Martin of Arkadelphia and now lives in Little Rock.

Chris married Amanda Craig of Powhatan. They have one child, Christopher Trent, the most beautiful baby in the world, born December 18, 1996.

James owns and operates Prichard Kirksey Rentals in Walnut Ridge.

Sharon married Thomas Robert of Walnut Ridge. She has taught at Swifton School for over 20 years. They reside in Walnut Ridge.

Patsy is employed with Wal-Mart. She has been a Wal-Mart associate for over 15 years. She lives in Jonesboro. –*Jim Kirksey.*

JACK AND LINDA (DOBBS) KREPPS.
Lawrence County was home to this couple for several years in their early lives. Jack was born in St. Louis, Missouri, and moved to Arkansas before he was 6 months old. His parents were Arthur Krepps from St. Louis and Mildred Thatcher Krepps, Gray, who was from Jonesboro. Jack's family included Jim Krepps, Bill Krepps, Gary Gray, Gail Gray, Beth Gray, Tom Gray and Dianne Gray. Jack attended schools in Hoxie, Walnut Ridge, Black Rock and Imboden. Jack's stepfather, James Gray, was a career serviceman in the Army and the family traveled a lot. Jack quit school during his senior year in Missouri to return to Arkansas. After working at a sawmill for a few months, he took night classes at Southern Baptist College, now known as Williams Baptist College. He began working at Selb Manufacturing Company in 1963, discovered that he liked the tool and die business, and decided to make that his career.

Linda Dobbs was the daughter of Earnest Dobbs and Vida (Quarry) Dobbs, and was born and raised in the Clover Bend Community until the age of 13, when she moved to Strawberry with her family. Other siblings were: Pauline, Faydell, Frances, Barbara, Edward, Darrell, Shirley, Bonnie, Rickey and Phyllis Dobbs.

Jack and Linda were married in December of 1964 and Linda finished school through Cave City High School. They lived in Walnut Ridge for two years - Jack worked at Selb and Linda worked at Frolic Footwear. In 1966 they moved to St. Louis where Jack worked for Comet Tool and Die Company. After two years of city life they moved back to Arkansas and settled in Sharp County and that is where they have lived and raised their family since 1969.

The family has owned a 170 acre farm on Strawberry River in Sharp County since 1978. Their family includes Jacqulyn Ruth, Jonathan Glenn and Jarrod Grant Krepps and son-in-law, Kal Korkis, originally from Strawberry. Jack also owns and manages a machine shop. Linda is a registered nurse. Jacqulyn is at Williams Baptist studying to be an elementary school teacher. Jonathan is in his third year of engineering school at University of Missouri at Rolla. Jarrod has just begun his studies in preparation to go into the ministry. Kal works for Canal Barge Company on the Mississippi River. –*Linda Dobbs Krepps.*

JOHN WILLIAM LABASS FAMILY.
John William LaBass Sr. was born about 1750 in France and died November 12, 1826, in Lawrence, Arkansas, probably near Davidsonville on the Black River. He married Louise Mary Janis Sr. before 1790 in Arkansas. She was the daughter of Anthony and Mrs. Frances Janis, a prominent French family living near Lauratown, on a Spanish Land Grant. Antoine Janis states in a document from the Powhatan Court House that John LaBass, formerly known as John Fayce (probably his name in France.) (Various spellings of Fayac, LeBask, LeBasque are listed in documents by Josiah H. Shinn and Marion Stark Carlk, MD.) John could not read or write.

Excerpt from *Early Days in Lawrence County* by W. E. McLeod. John LaBass was one of five Frenchmen owning the original settlement rights to land on which Davidsonville, Arkansas was founded. John Sr. and Louise Janis settled on the Black River as early as the 1790s. It is believed these five Frenchmen were scattered from Clay County to Clover Bend in Lawrence County and were there years in advance of other white settlers, perhaps as early as 1760. From *Pioneers and Makers of Arkansas* by Josiah H. Shinn, John Fayac (LaBass) had lived for years prior to 1800, at the Fort on the White River. Less than 500 souls inhabited the District of Arkansas in 1803. The 1810 census gave a population of 1,026. This land was part of the Louisiana Territory and Arkansas Post was the name of the settlement.

At John's death in 1826, his will listed the following children: John William Jr., Jacob, Mary and Mary Ellen. Administrators were his brother-in-law(s), Peter LaMew and Henson Kenion. The estate was valued at $200 and a list of property exists today that was made out by Lalta Logan, William Russell and George Berry. Mary married a Willmuth, Jacob has no records, Mary Ellen married Eliza Gocia and John William Jr. has considerable family documentation.

Second Generation

John William LaBass Jr. was born November 5, 1811, in Old Black River, Arkansas and died September 15, 1885, and is supposed to be buried in the Old Campbell Cemetery in Strawberry, Arkansas alongside his daughter, Eliza Jane and her husband, James Patrick McLaughlin. John William enlisted in the Blackhawk War and served with Captain Jesse Bean and the United States Rangers in 1832, at Ft. Gibson, Indian Territory, now Oklahoma. In 1833, he was given 120 acres in Lawrence County near Batesville for his service. In 1851, he was given an additional 40 acres and in 1853, another 80 acres. In 1864, he enlisted in the Civil War, in Captain Taylor A. Baxter's 4th Arkansas Mounted Infantry, USA, Batesville, Arkansas.

In about 1840, John married Malinda, her last name could have been Harris, census records show she was born in Tennessee and living in the LaBass household was a young man named Harris, also born in Tennessee. They had three children before Malinda died during childbirth in 1851. Morning Frost Corbitt witnessed the death. The children were: Eliza Jane, Francis and John. John died young, Eliza Jane married James Patrick McLaughlin and John did not return from the Confederate Army after the Civil War.

In 1851, John married Volumnia Frost, daughter of Gabriel Frost and Louvisa Tyler Husley, daughter of Peter Tyler. Louvisa was widowed from Allen Hulsey in 1827, and married Gabriel Frost in 1829. Volumnia Frost LaBass was born September 22, 1830, and married John William LaBass Jr., July 29, 1851, by Reverend J. Gardner. The LaBass homestead was a 157 acre property at the southwest corner of Section 30, Township 14, Range 3 West four miles southwest of Strawberry, Lawrence County, Arkansas. From 1871 to 1876, John William was the postmaster at Hazel Grove, near Strawberry. The homestead was sold to Charles McLaughlin and in 1986, he owned the property and was still living in Strawberry.

Third Generation

John William LaBass Jr. and Volumnia reared five boys and two girls. One other son died at an early age.

1. Mary E. LaBass was born November 9, 1854. She married William Lafayette Stogsdill in 1883, in Independence County. She married Green Aaron Fortner about 1900. Mary died on July 10, 1941, and is buried in Blackjack Cemetery near Muldrow, Oklahoma.

2. Anne LaBass, 1856-1926. On November 29, 1885, she married E. Jeffrey Huggins. Anne is buried in Arlington Cemetery near Sprague, Oklahoma. Their children are:

a) Cora Huggins, born April 12, 1888, died March 17, 1976, buried in Turlock, California. She married Elmer Cope about 1910, and later married Phil Hill.

b) Samuel Huggins, born about 1890, died 1913, in Lincoln County, Oklahoma after being shot by a jealous ex-husband of his lady friend.

c) William Arch Huggins Sr., born December 15, 1894, and died November 1983. About 1913 he married Elizabeth Albright and later a lady named Maud.

d) Maggie Huggins was born February 27, 1898. She died in 1974 and is buried in Paden, Oklahoma. In 1913, Maggie married Tom Bird.

e) Tennessee Mae Huggins was born February 28, 1898, and died September 5, 1968, in Turlock, California. In 1913 Tennie married Walter Hopkins.

f) Mattie Mae Huggins was born on April 19, 1900, and died August 11, 1969, in Oklahoma City, Oklahoma. In 1917, Mattie married Julius Xray Giltner, later Stanley Dotson and later Jesse Pratt.

After E. Jeffrey Huggins died in 1900, Anne LaBass Huggins married Henry Freeman in about 1905. They had twin boys born in 1908, one died at birth and the other, Clarence, lived until he died in 1960, in San Francisco, California. Clarence never married. He had a unique career as a billboard artist. He painted the billboard picture full-size on paper on the floor that was then pasted on the billboard.

3. John J. LaBass was born December 26, 1857, and died March 16, 1920. He is buried in the Box, Oklahoma Cemetery. In 1881, he married Margaret M. Robertson in Lawrence County. She was born October 7, 1866, and died June 9, 1904. She is buried in the Arlington Cemetery near Prague, Oklahoma.

a) William Frank LaBass, born October, 1883.

b) Mary E. LaBass, born March, 1886, and died in 1970, in California. She married Calvin Williams.

c) Charles Alexander LaBass, born February, 1888. Charles died in California. He married Alma Macmen Acuff in 1925, in Arkansas.

d) Viola LaBass, born May, 1891, in Oklahoma. She married Mr. Healey.

e) Homer Henry LaBass, born February 17, 1893, I. T., Okfuskee, Oklahoma. He died July 31, 1942, in Los Angeles, California. Homer married Ella Maude Diacon about 1912, and later a lady named Audrey.

f) Claude Earl LaBass, born May, 1894, in I. T., Oklahoma. He died in 1962, in California. He was married twice, first to Bertie and then to Helen.

g) George Oceola LaBass, born February 2, 1897, in I. T., Grady County, Oklahoma. He died on February 14, 1982, in Neosho, Newton County, Missouri. George married Bonnie Christina Butler on May 7, 1930, at Chickasaw, Oklahoma. He later married Violet Pollock.

h) Pearl LaBass was born in 1901, and married Mr. Stouder.

i) Ellen LaBass was born in 1903.

On July 28, 1910, John J. married Nellie Lue Blanche Attebery. Nellie was born November 15, 1864, in Clarksville, Red River County, Texas. She died January 6, 1953, and is buried in the Oakdale Cemetery, Paden, Oklahoma.

a) William Albert Stovall was raised by John and Nellie after his parents died. William was born February 28, 1904, in Haworth, Oklahoma and died on August 20, 1944, in Oklahoma City, Oklahoma. He married Maudie Lee Powell and later Laura Iva Holden.

b) Orville LaBass was born after 1910, and died in 1974.

4. Charles A. LaBass, born March 22, 1858. He died May 23, 1926, and is buried in the Oakdale Cemetery in Paden, Oklahoma. Charles married Margaret A. Drake on August 5, 1880, in Sharp County, Arkansas. For many years Charles was the Town Marshal of Paden, Oklahoma. Charles and Margaret had three children.

a) Ida Jane LaBass, born February 22, 1881, and died February 28, 1883.

b) John Theodore "Ted" LaBass, born January 23, 1884, at Black River, Arkansas and died August 23, 1952, in Beaumont, California. Ted married Ethel Myrl Wallis on July 15, 1919, in DePew, Oklahoma. Myrl was born on December 9, 1896, in Missouri and died on January 10, 1968, in Beaumont, California.

Ted and Myrl had two daughters: Margaret Jacqueline LaBass (Lambert, Fainer), 1920-1978, and Lois Lee Ruth LaBass (Rubright, Chapin), born in 1921, and living in California in 1999.

c) Otey M. C. LaBass was born on January 26, 1893, and died November 19, 1894.

5. Salon LaBass was born in May, 1860, and died before 1880.

6. Nicholas Hannibal LaBass was born March 17, 1864, and died on February 23, 1938. He is buried at Box, Sequoyah County, Oklahoma. On March 13, 1886, near Calmine, Jackson County, Arkansas, Nicholas married Lucinda Elizabeth Hoggard. Lucinda was the daughter of William H. Hoggard and Laura Elizabeth Goin. They had the following children:

a) Eliza Jane Kathern LaBass, born February 11, 1887, married Frank Hood in 1901.

b) Mary Helen LaBass, born March 27, 1882, married Dock Cooper.

c) Margaret Ann LaBass, born April 24, 1889, married Alva Matthews. She died in Vian, Oklahoma.

d) Thursa Vallie Permilia LaBass, born December 4, 1891, and died September, 1892.

e) Julia Ellen LaBass, born January 28, 1891, and died in Vian, Oklahoma. She married Wylie Davis.

f) Dovie Lee LaBass, born October 13, 1894, and died July, 1895.

g) Ada Bell LaBass, born February 26, 1895, died February 26, 1983, in Vian, Oklahoma. In 1914, Ada married William H. Ritter.

h) Gracie Maze LaBass, born February 2, 1896, and died in September, 1897.

i) John William LaBass II, born December 23, 1898, and died in September, 1899.

j) Bess Adele LaBass, born December 2, 1900, in Long, Oklahoma. On November 3, 1917, Bess married William Emmett Briley.

k) Effie Emma LaBass was born August 22, 1902. She died January 19, 1949, in Live Oak,

California. Effie married William Luther McFarland on October 16, 1923.

l) Essie LaBass was born in 1906, in Oklahoma. She married J. Virgil Courtney and L. W. McFarland.

7. Alexis Mitchell LaBass. "Sea" LaBass. Sea was born February 4, 1872, in Lawrence County, Arkansas. He died on September 30, 1917, in Muldrow, Oklahoma and is buried in the Maple Cemetery, Maple, Oklahoma. Sea married Mary Elizabeth Taylor on September 16, 1894, in I. T., Muldrow, Oklahoma. Their children are:

a) Tersie Bertha LaBass, born July 29, 1895, and died July 7, 1933. Tersie's parents both died very young. Tersie was only 22 years old when her mother and father died. There were eight children at home from a few weeks of age to her, the oldest at 22. She decided to try and keep the family together on a farm in very hard times. With the help of neighbors, she was able to raise the children. It took a terrible toll on her and she died in 1933, at the age of 38.

b) Troy John LaBass, born March 19, 1897, and died June 14, 1983. He is buried at Duck Creek Cemetery near Mounds, Oklahoma. In 1921, Troy married Alice Jane Morgan.

c) Huey V. LaBass, born June 24, 1900, and died in 1912. He is buried in Maple Cemetery.

d) Alta Jane Amanda LaBass, born January 17, 1903. Alta died in 1998. In 1921, Alta married Charles Riggs.

e) Jessie Lillian Anglatine LaBass, born January 29, 1907, and died in June, 1996. In 1931, Jessie married Claude Jones.

f) Johnie Lola Agnes LaBass, born October 10, 1909. In 1942, she married Carl Nelson. In 1950, Johnie married Edwin E. Arndt. Johnie is 90 years old in 1999, lives by herself in Gerber, California and is enjoying life.

g) Frank LaBass, born December 5, 1911, and died December 7, 1995. He is buried at Duck Creek Cemetery near Mounds, Oklahoma. In 1922, Frank married Nellie Scott. In later years, he married Thelma Faye Jackson and a few years before he died, Emma Brooks. Frank loved to sing and had an extensive collection of religious songs.

h) Cleatus Beatrice LaBass, born March 7, 1914, and resides in Placerville, California. On June 16, 1940, Cleatus married Edgar Louis Allen. Ed was a police officer with the Los Angeles Police Department until his retirement when he and Cleatus moved to Placerville. Ed died in 1998, and Cleatus has her home that she shares with her daughter, Judy. She thoroughly enjoys her two grandsons and her great-grandchildren. Occasionally, Cleatus and Johnie spend a few days with each other.

i) Atlas Ulysses LaBass, born October 15, 1916. In 1947, Atlas married Katheryn Lucille Catt, and they currently reside in Indiana with their daughter, Kay Ann.

8. Frank Lincoln LaBass, born March 7, 1874, and died November 28, 1952. He is buried in Blackjack Cemetery near Muldrow, Oklahoma. In 1895, Frank married Dovie Angleine McKenney. They have the following children:

a) John William Austin LaBass, born August 28, 1896, and died April 19, 1965. He is buried in Blackjack Cemetery near Muldrow, Oklahoma. He never married.

b) Ernest B. LaBass, born October 21, 1899, and died November 1, 1981. In 1931, Ernest married Ruby Easter Lewis.

c) William Houstin Larkin LaBass, born December 10, 1901, and died June 2, 1992. He is buried in Blackjack Cemetery. In 1923, William married Ola R. Jenkins.

d) Goldie Geneva LaBass, born December 23, 1903. She was married to S. Elzie Thrasher. According to Goldie's sister, Ruby, living near

Muldrow, Oklahoma, Goldie is enjoying taking cruises and living in Washington state.

e) Ruby Fern LaBass, born November 17, 1907, and was married to Charles William Champion in 1934. They were later divorced. Ruby had a career of teaching school and working in the aerospace industry prior to her retirement and moving back to her home in Muldrow, Oklahoma. Ruby is a sincere joy to be around.

f) Robert Raymond LaBass, born August 22, 1914, and died May 20, 1976. He is buried in Blackjack Cemetery. In 1940, Robert married Ina L. East.

g) Velma Ruth LaBass, born June 6, 1917. She was married to Bill Durham. She currently lives in Ft. Smith, Arkansas near her daughter.

Family group sheets of descendants are available with considerable narrative stories. Reference sources are also available. Please contact Lois LaBass Chapin.

—Les and Lois LaBass Chapin.

LILLIE LUISA MANNING FRY LAMB. Lillie Luisa Manning became the bride of Benjamin Olden Fry in 1905, in Lawrence County. Ben and Lillie were both born in Lawrence County in 1885, and 1886, respectively. Ben was the son of William and Martha Fry and the grandson of John and Sara Fry. His siblings were Ella Fry Manning, Emma Fry Wynn, Silva Fry and a half-brother, John Fry. Lillie's parents were William and Hettie Trotter Manning. Her grandparents were Francis Marion and Emily Kitchens Manning. Her siblings were Emily Manning Lamb, Frank Manning, Daniel Wayne Manning and Bertha Manning Williams.

Soon after marriage, Ben and Lillie began farming. They were probably helping his father who owned a farm in eastern Lawrence County. A year later their first child, Allen, was born. He died before their next son, Lonel Francis, was born. In 1909, their son, John Bailey, was born.

In the winter of 1911, Ben's father and mother became sick with pneumonia. Ben cared for them until their deaths. Within a few weeks he also died.

At age 25, Lillie became a widow with two sons, age two and four. She inherited a farm and trust fund for her sons, but had no one to help her farm. She moved in with her parents who had two children, ages 10 and 13, still living at home. This was a very difficult time for all involved. The two families tried to make the most of a bad situation. Within a year of Lillie and her sons moving in with her parents, her father died. At this time, the mother and daughter were single mothers each having two children to take care of. No one seems to know when Hettie, Lillie's mom, died. Some family members think she only lived a few years after husband, William, died.

In 1913, Lillie married Samuel Jackson Lamb. Samuel had two previous wives who had died.

Left to right, back row: Lonel Fry, Samuel Lamb, Lillie Lamb, Johnny Fry. Front row: Thedford Lamb and Gracon Lamb. c.1919.

He had six children, two of which were teenagers and still living with him. His children were Dorothy Lamb Ivans, Noah Lamb, Leonard Lamb, Clayburn Lamb, Nellie Lamb Manning and Myrtle Lamb.

Lillie became a midwife. Many people in Oak Hill and surrounding communities called on her to deliver their babies. She was known as Aunt Lillie. She made a statement saying that of all the babies she delivered, only one was named after her: Lillie Mae Lamb, the daughter of Leonard and Mattie Lamb. Lillie and Samuel had three children: Thedford Lamb, Gracon Lamb and Pauline Lamb Hudson. Samuel died in 1928. Aunt Lillie continued delivering babies. Lillie's oldest son, Lonel and his family, took care of the farming duties until Thedford was old enough to take over. Later, Gracon was in charge of the farm. Lillie died in 1961. –Geraldine Fry Brewer, granddaughter of Lillie.

RUBY ELIZABETH LAWRENCE LAMBERTH FAMILY.
Ruby Elizabeth Lawrence was born July 12, 1911, in Fulton County, Arkansas, the daughter of Richard Ruben and Martha Elizabeth Thornton Lawrence.

On December 31, 1927, Ruby married Charles "Dock" Cornelius Brandon in Fulton County. Dock was born in 1891, died in 1955. They had one child: Quinton Vero, born May 16, 1932, married December 23, 1954, to Joyce Lorene Hatfield.

On November 1, 1933, Ruby married John Benjamin Williams, born April 20, 1909, died August 29, 1973. They had two children: Anna Fay, born September 18, 1934, married August 20, 1954, to Luther Thomas Finley, born August 6, 1927, died March 11, 1994; and Rethel Virginia, born November 21, 1936, married J. W. Hill, born April 7, 1928.

On January 13, 1941, Ruby married James Thomas Raney, born 1894, died 1943. They had two children: Alis James, born July 20, 1942, married March 12, 1965, to Linda Fay Corbit; and Gail Dee, born March 14, 1944, died September 5, 1960, from a drowning accident at the age of 16.

Acquilla and Ruby Lamberth.

On November 23, 1946, Ruby married Acquilla "Peg" Osborn Lamberth, born September 16, 1899, in Jonesboro, Arkansas, the son of John and Rebecca Lamberth.

When Acquilla was 11 years old, he and some more children were playing on the church steps and Acquilla fell off and broke his leg. It set up gangrene and he had to have his leg amputated at the knee. When he was older he wore a wooden peg leg with a wide leather belt and strap that fastened to the upper part of his leg. He was nicknamed Peg.

He did not drive a car, but he had a red Farmall tractor that he drove wherever he wanted to go.

For many years he worked for Craighead Electric Company and retired at the age of 55.

Peg and Ruby had five children.
1. Rosa Marthalene, born March 2, 1948, married June 29, 1967, to James Edward Thomas, born February 7, 1948.
2. Vesta Kay, born March 20, 1949, married September 16, 1967, to Bobby Ray Smith, born November 18, 1941.
3. Sharon Gay, born September 12, 1950, married October 11, 1967, to Jerry Byron Broadway, born February 11, 1948.
4. Boyce Osborn, born April 22, 1952, died July 2, 1952, at the age of three months.
5. Nona Ruth, born October 19, 1953, married January 26, 1970, to Michael Gene Richey, born November 16, 1949.

Acquilla died December 23, 1970, at the age of 71. Ruby died March 15, 1998, at the age of 86. She, along with Dock, James, Boyce and Acquilla "Peg", are all buried in Oak Forest Cemetery in Black Rock. –Vesta Smith.

LAMEW (LEMIEUX) HISTORY.
One of the first settlers in Lawrence County was Pierre LeMieux, 1743-1817, who is common ancestor the many LeMieux descendants in Lawrence County today. The name was Anglicized in the mid 1800s, to "Lamew." Originally from Quebec, Pierre LeMieux and his wife, Victorie Marie, accompanied his father-in-law, Antoine Janis, 1741-1816, into the Black River country in the last decade of the 18th century. Janis obtained a land grant from the Spanish authorities at Arkansas Post and was living on that grant, which was in the Portia area, by 1799. In the Lawrence County Deed Record Book, 1815-1817, there is an entry dated September 28, 1816, wherein Pierre LeMieux deeded to Lewis deMun for 40 dollars an improvement made by him in 1800, on Big Black River, 15 miles north of "the

Darcus Wyatt Whitmire, daughter of Callie Lamew Wyatt Bennett.

Currants River, which place has been known by the French under the name of Petit Barrel and by Americans, generally, as Peach Orchard." In a four page essay on the LeMieux and Janis families, W. R. McLeod states that this was the first known settlement in what was later to become Lawrence County. Pierre had apparently by that time moved to what is now Clover Bend, and is mentioned in Goodspeed's History of Arkansas as the head of a French settlement there.

Pierre had a large family, including his son, Peter, 1799-1860, who lived his entire life in Lawrence County. Peter's wife was Matilda and she was a native of Mississippi. Among their progeny was Joseph Lamew, 1833-

California Ann "Callie" Lamew, 1877, age 16, great-granddaughter of Pierre LeMieux.

1870, who became a landowner of some wealth before his death from tuberculosis at an early age. In 1860, he married Elizabeth O'Laughlin, 1836-1878, a native of Indiana. Joseph and Elizabeth raised three children during the Civil War period, two of whom survived childhood. They were California Ann "Callie" Lamew, 1861-1943; and William Lafayette Lamew, 1866-1939. Stories of the war years were handed down through the family by Elizabeth and her daughter, Callie, including tales of starving Federal soldiers stripping orchards and taking food wherever they could find it.

Joseph Lamew's will left over 421 acres of land to his wife and children, including 107 acres "known as the Peter Lamew farm in the county of Lawrence in the state of Arkansas." This farm was in the Clover Bend area.

Both Callie and William Lamew spent most of their lives farming in Lawrence County. William married Nancy Cagle in 1890, and they raised a family in Clover Bend. Although he later lost his farm and moved his family to Light, both he and Nancy are buried at the Clover Bend Cemetery.

Callie first married John D. Wyatt, 1851-1883, and the marriage produced two children surviving to adulthood: John Lehman Wyatt, 1883-1968, whose daughter, Ruby Wyatt Ratliffe, still lives in Imboden; and Darcus Wyatt, 1881-1965, who married France Whitmire. Darcus and France had nine children, seven of whom survived childhood. They were: Minnie Whitmire Mullen, Frank Whitmire, Kate Whitmire Perry, Lucille Whitmire Harris, Gladys Whitmire Felts, Thelma Whitmire and Geraldine Whitmire Koerbel Altis. Gladys Felts, Thelma Whitmire and Geraldine Altis still live in Lawrence County. In 1886, Callie married John Franklin Bennett and from that union five children were born: Edna Bennett, who married John Mullen; Hattie Bennett, who married Garfield Slayton and whose children, Emmet Slayton and Grace Slayton Estes, are still residents of the county; Jessye Lee Bennett, 1891-1987, who married Matt Vinson and moved to Memphis; Earnest Bennett, 1894-1962, who married Mary Robert; and Frederick Bennett, 1895-1958. Earnest and Frederick were World War I veterans. Callie Bennett is buried at Calvin Crossing Cemetery, as are several of her children and grandchildren. –Susan Briner.

JOSEPH MELVIN LAWRENCE FAMILY.
Joseph Lawrence was born May 20, 1842, the son of Thomas and Elizabeth, born respectively in North Carolina and Georgia. This family had 14 children and many of them migrated along with their parents from Tuscaloosa County, Alabama, just prior to 1860. Thomas died soon after settling in Independence County, Arkansas.

Joseph was a farmer who had bought and homesteaded many parcels of land. The family still has some of the original land grant papers in their possession. Even a part of the old original home place in Lawrence County is still standing.

Joseph married several times; whether from love or the genuine need to have a mother for his children. His first wife was Mary Jane Wells; they lived in Independence County near Convience. They had four children, with only three surviving. Jodie married Pearl and lived in Lawrence County. Beulah Leona married Buddy Holder and also lived in Lawrence County. Fannie married William Montgomery and raised her family around Cave City. Mary Jane died in 1876.

Joseph then married a Mrs. Sarah Durham.

His third wife was Martha Fort Foster, widow of William Foster, who already had two daughters. These girls were Susan Elmira, who married David Crick and Sarah Ann who married James Jenkins. Joseph and Martha had four children. The oldest was Lucius "Luke" Kellum. He married Lizzie Matilda Pickett and had four children; Leonard who married Opal Watts, Alene who married Ernest Frisbee; Beulah who married Claude McGoldrick; and Nina who married Lyle Clements. All of them had children except Beulah and she very lovingly claimed us all!

The next child was William Cecil who married Ara Adne Grant. They lived and raised their family near Friendship. Maxfield married and moved to Oklahoma. The family at this time moved to the Friendship area. Martha was carrying Minnie. Minnie was born November 16, 1886, and Martha died shortly afterward because of complications of childbirth.

In March of 1889, Joseph married Susan Foster and their children were: Austin, Maude, Buster, John and Lottie. Austin married Talitha Jane Fort and had several children. Maude married Oliver Simpson, had several children and lived in Bartlesville, Oklahoma. Buster married Josie Campbell, had several children and lived near Friendship. John married Maude Jines, had two girls and made their home in Hot Springs where he had a business. The youngest child was Lottie. She married Wallace Smith and died young after having two children that never reached maturity.

Joseph was living with his son Luke, when he died April 10, 1912. He, two of his wives and several children, are buried at the Friendship Cemetery, south of Ravenden. This was a large complicated family and it took very courageous and strong people to have the very special relationships they all had. –Carolyn Lawrence.

MARTHA ELIZABETH LAWRENCE AND FAMILY.

Martha Elizabeth was born July 18, 1893, in Fulton County, Arkansas, the daughter of Hosea Lee and Cora Ann Reynolds Thornton. Martha married March 4, 1909, in Elizabeth, Arkansas to Richard Ruben Lawrence, born April 15, 1889, and died January 4, 1927, in Amagon, Arkansas, in Jackson County. He died from double pneumonia and is buried in Johnstown Cemetery there.

Martha moved to Black Rock in 1945, to live with her daughter, Viola. She lived with her in Black Rock until 1982, when she lived in Lawrence Hall Nursing Home in Walnut Ridge until her death on October 16, 1983. She died from lung cancer. She is buried in Oak Forest Cemetery in Black Rock. Martha and Richard had six children.

1. Ruby Elizabeth, born July 12, 1911, married four times; first on December 31, 1927, to Charles "Dock" Brandon, born 1891, died 1955; second on November 1, 1933, to John Benjamin "Ben" Williams, born April 20, 1909, died August 29, 1973. Ruby married third on January 13, 1941, to James Thomas Raney, born 1894, died 1943; and fourth on November 23, 1946, to Acquilla Osborn "Peg" Lamberth, born September 16, 1899; he died December 23, 1946.

From left: Viola, Mary Ann, Bud, Ruby and their mother, Martha Lawrence.

2. Bud, born July 9, 1916, married September 25, 1937, to Josephine Violet Thrasher, born February 4, 1920.

3. Mary Ann, born February 22, 1919, married three times; first on February 2, 1939, to Jesse Marchant, born November 9, 1919; he died November 18, 1989. Mary Ann married second on November 4, 1941, to Jesse Skidmore, born October 30, 1917, died October 15, 1984, and third on August 3, 1990, to Green Lee Slater, born January 7, 1912.

4. James Avis, born July 15, 1921, died July 12, 1923.

5. Violet Viola, born June 21, 1924, married first October 4, 1941, to Teed Sanders, born July 5, 1924, died July, 1980; married second on May 21, 1947, to Freddie James Pickney Sr., born February 2, 1921.

6. Talmage Lee, born August 16, 1926, died January 16, 1949.

Martha worked hard all her life, working in the fields farming, picking cotton, doing laundry for others and being a midwife in her early years. There were no doctors around for miles so they would come and for her to deliver their babies. She worked hard and received little money to support herself and her six children. Her husband was away most of the time and then died at an early age leaving her to raise their children alone. She lived a full life and loved her family dearly. She was also seven-eighths of Cherokee Indian blood. She died at the age of 90 years, two months and 28 days. –Pam Smith.

LAWSON. Prior Lawson was born in 1803, in North Carolina, the son of Thomas Lawson from Scotland. He married Rebecca Hopkins on January 9, 1822, in Wilson County, Tennessee. This couple moved to Jackson County, Alabama and had eight children of whom we have knowledge. All were born in Jackson County, Alabama.

1. Nancy Lawson, 1836-1866, married John W. Kelley, December 19, 1851. The descendants of this couple are listed elsewhere in a separate article.

2. Pleasant Lawson, born 1830.

3. Andrew William Lawson, December 4, 1836-April 11, 1923, in Lawrence County, Arkansas, married first unknown and second Mary Ann Griffith.

4. John V. Lawson, born 1838.

5. Teletha Elizabeth Lawson, born 1839, married first Stanwich Smith and second James K. P. Miller, January 25, 1881.

6. George Washington Lawson, born 1841.

7. Louisa Lawson, born 1830.

8. Mary Ann Lawson, 1828-October 8, 1882, Lawrence County, Arkansas.

Nancy and Mary Ann were both married to John W. Kelley and there is a separate article about the Kelley family. Pleasant married Sarah L. Perrigan, July 23, 1852, in Alabama.

John V. Lawson came to Lawrence County and was here by 1866, when he married Lydia Ann Jones, September 6. John and Lydia had four children.

1. John H. Lawson, born 1867.

2. Mary A. Lawson, born 1870, married Andrew J. Fleming, had one son, Raytha E., who married Lucy Kendricks.

3. Pryor D. Lawson, born 1872.

4. Cora Belle Lawson.

Teletha Elizabeth is buried in Oak Forest Cemetery, Black Rock, and has a tombstone, the stone has no dates! In the 1870 census they are in Lawrence County in Black River Twp., and the first three children are listed as born in Missouri and Andrew as born in Arkansas. In 1880, they are still in Lawrence County, but Teletha is still listed as a Smith. There is a Thomas P. Jenkins

listed in the household as a son. Did Teletha marry again to a Jenkins and if so, why did she resume her Smith name? Or did the census taker just get it wrong? It is a puzzlement. Children of Teletha and Stanwich Smith:

1. Carter Smith, born 1856, Missouri.

2. John V. Smith, born 1864, Missouri.

3. Mary J. Smith, born 1866, Missouri.

4. Andrew C. Smith, born 1869, Arkansas.

George Washington Lawson married Eliza J. Griffith, December 2, 1866, in Lawrence County. She was the daughter of David and Catherine Griffith. George W. was a carpenter, according to the 1900 census of Lawrence County and Eliza was listed as a medicine vendor. George and Eliza had one child, Andrew W.

Prior and Rebecca's son, Andrew William, and his first wife, name unknown, had five children.

1. Lucy Lawson, born 1859.

2. Margaret Loucinda Lawson, born 1868.

3. Allen Lawson, born 1873.

4. Walter Washington Lawson, January 2, 1876-March 31, 1952, married Nettie Ragsdale, December 25, 1898, and they had four children: Marvin, Ina, Eda and Harley.

5. Claude F. Lawson, December 20, 1877-December 15, 1951, married Estella Brown, May 28, 1899. Andrew W. and his second wife, Mary Griffith, had two children.

a) Ida B. Lawson, born 1872, married J. D. Killough, March 9, 1893.

b) Ada Lawson, born May, 1880.

Much more could be written about the descendants of these Lawsons if space permitted. They were wonderful and they left a goodly heritage. – *Dale Hinshaw McMasters.*

LAWSON. In 1785, Tom Lawson came to America from Ireland at the age of eight. He married Nervil Spurgen and had one son, William Preston Lawson, who was born September 10, 1840, in Georgia. Nervil died March 1, 1848. Their son, William Preston Lawson, married Josie Collins and fathered William Price Lawson on February 7, 1870; Peter Merriman Lawson on February 17, 1872; James Riley Lawson on September 29, 1874; Thomas Ashberry Lawson on March 11, 1878; and Wiley Elexander Lawson on April 27, 1883.

William Preston Lawson later married Mary Melissa Shelly and fathered Preston Hall Lawson on February 11, 1890; Leona Bell Lawson on April 7, 1894; and Jewell Dewey Lawson on July 23, 1898.

William Preston Lawson's father, Tom Lawson, evidently died in Georgia. Later, William Preston Lawson moved to the Beaver Dam area of Missouri. His son, William Price Lawson, was born in the Poplar Bluff, Missouri area and married Sarah Collins. He fathered Bernard Lawson; Jefferson Columbus Lawson, born March 11, 1893; Otto Lawson, died at age 14; Nora Annis Lawson, born July 9, 1898; and Rosia Mae Lawson, born July 6, 1902. After Sarah's death, William Price Lawson married Leona Jones on February 4, 1906, in Biggers, Arkansas. He moved from the Poplar Bluff, Missouri, area to the Agnos, Arkansas, area before moving to Lawrence County, Arkansas, where he lived most of his adult life, settling in the Clear Lake-Richwoods Community.

Jefferson, Nora and Mae Lawson all remained in Lawrence County, marrying and raising families.

Jefferson married Ola Norris and fathered Effie Mae Lawson on September 24, 1910; Ervin Oakley Lawson on September 4, 1913; Earnie Lawson, died 1920; and Earlie Lee Lawson on July 28, 1918.

Ola died and Jefferson married Ada Bell Coach and had one son, Bernard Goldman Lawson. Ada died and he married Sleety Manning. She gave birth to a daughter, Vera Lawson. After divorcing Sleety, Jefferson married Mae Elizabeth Lamb and fathered Lavonda Berniece Lawson, Lola Arda Virginia Lawson, J. C. Lawson, Peggy Sue Lawson and Richard Uzell Lawson.

Jefferson's three living children by Ola Norris, Effie, Ervin and Earlie, have lived their entire lives in Lawrence County.

Effie married Trammel Wynn and had Talmage, Cleveland, Edwin, Melvie Dean, Willie Dean (twins), Echol, Velma and Tommy Wynn.

Ervin married Lon Alta McQuay and had Elanzo, Lois, Oakley, Spurgen, Billy, Randall, Ronald and Altheia Ellen Lawson.

Earlie married Esther Juanita Keith, daughter of John and Margaret McQuay Keith, and they are the parents of Lutisha, Leon, Joan, Sue and Cathie Lawson.

Effie and Trammel and Earlie and Juanita farmed and raised their families in the Little Brown Community of Lawrence County.

Ervin and Alta and family farmed southwest of Sedgwick where they still reside. –Earlie Lawson.

ANDREW GLEN LAWSON FAMILY.

Glen Lawson was born March 1, 1923, the son of Randall and Laura Smith Lawson. Glen lived all his life in Lawrence County. Glen had four brothers: Randall "Pat", Thurman, Paul and Lowell. They were all raised around the Powhatan area where Glen met Ruby Pearl Helms. She was born July 19, 1923, the daughter of Cleo and Josephine Oliver Helms.

Ruby had seven sisters and three brothers, most of whom moved to California and still reside there.

Glen farmed around the Portia area and one year things were so bad when the cotton crop ended and the debts were paid he only had a dollar and some change to make it through the winter. He went to work on heavy machinery. Later, he and Ruby had three sons.

Glen and Ruby Lawson.

1. Cleo Jackson, born October 24, 1942, died January 15, 1986. Jackson married Judy Allen of Saffell and they had two children: Stephen and Dawn. Jackson was a state trooper in Arkadelphia for 18 years and was a Mason.

2. Randall Roy was born October 2, 1945. He married Joyce Louise Morse. They had five children: Denneshia, Randall Jr., William "Billy", Dewayne and Jonathan "Johnny."

3. Ronnie Glen, born 1950, died 1958.

Glen and Ruby built a small house at Denton where they raised their children. In 1966, Glen bought his mother's house and moved to Powhatan. Glen went to work as deputy sheriff of Lawrence County. When sheriffs changed, Glen changed jobs and became the county road foreman. He retired from that after suffering a heart attack. Later, he took on the job of mayor in Powhatan. He worked hard and received federal funding to build the community center that is dedicated to his honor along with others that helped including Ruby, who served as an officer. Glen owned the ground where the building and parking lot now stands. Glen died not getting to see the building finished or the roads paved. Glen was also a Mason.

Ruby was also a hard worker. She planted and tended a huge garden, canned and froze most of the food they ate. She and Glen owned and op-erated what is now the Powhatan Landing, also the cafe in Black Rock that is now called Barb's. Later, Ruby went to work at Frolic Footware. She held an office under Glen; she worked at the new Wal-Mart store in Walnut Ridge as department manager where you could hear her laugh many aisles away. The store won the friendliest store award that year.

Ruby's greatest love was her sons. Ruby died in June of 1988, and Glen died December 29, 1976. Both are buried in Oak Forest Cemetery in Black Rock. –Randall Lawson.

J. C. AND MARY SNIDER LAWSON.

J. C. Lawson, a lot of people referred to him as "Uncle Clint." He lived most of life in the Eaton Community, born 1876, married to Maggie Snider, died 1973. They had seven children: Odessa, Alva, Albert, Bessie, Fred, Opha and Coy. Three of them are still living at this writing.

He owned a country grocery store and station for several years. The store was located on Cypress Creek, the Cedar Grove Church is just across the road.

From left to right: Opha Lawson Richey Hugg, Coy Lawson, Fred Lawson, Albert Lawson, Alva Lawson, Odessa Lawson Wright, J. C. Lawson, Bessie Lawson Richey.

He had a brother, Henry Lawson, that lived across the creek from them. He was married to Maggie's sister, Amanda. They had four children: Homer, Vela, Verna and Ottis, all deceased. They had several grandchildren and great-grandchildren.

J. C.'s sons ran the store and a post office that was in the store, and Alva did the farming. (J. C. owned some Black River bottom land.)

At the end of 1945, J. C. bought some bottom land and a country store and station at Calvin Crossing, and Alva moved his family to Calvin, and lived there until they retired in 1966. He died in an auto accident at Walnut Ridge in 1987.

Albert moved with his family to Strawberry and ran a grocery store there. He is living at Walnut Ridge at this time.

Fred ran the store at Eaton until they closed it, and he started farming. Later on he had a bad wreck and he was never the same afterwards. He died in 1998.

Bessie lives at Popular Bluff.

Coy went to college at Conway, taught

J. C. Lawson's (Avis's Grandpa) store at Eaton, Arkansas.

school and sold school books. He lives at Fairfield Bay on Greers Ferry.

J. C. never owned or drove a car. He went on horseback. He made his living "mule trading", whatever that means. In his later years he did a lot of "hitchhiking."

At the time of his death he was survived by his seven children, 36 grandchildren, 91 great-grandchildren and 11 great-great-grandchildren, and now there are many, many more.

Way back in the 1930s, Maggie started having a dinner to celebrate their birthdays, hers was the 12th and his was the 13th of June. Their descendants still meet at that time of the year for a family reunion.

They had a grandson, J. D. "Jack," that was injured in a diving accident that broke his neck. He lived a little more than 30 years confined to his bed and wheelchair. He died at the end of 1995.

Mr. and Mrs. Lawson are buried at the Old Lebanon Cemetery. –Aris Holloway.

JENNIE SUE LAWSON FAMILY.

Jennie Sue Lawson, daughter of Ollie Woodson and Ernest Lawson, was born November 27, 1927.

Her first marriage was to Herman L. Green. Children of Jennie Sue and Herman are:

1. Olan Lee Green, born May 1, 1943, married in 1964, to Mohanna Lou Issac. Children are:

a) Billie Conway Green, born 1964, married Lisa and they have three children: Brittany, Chantel and Brock Olan.

b) James Leroy Green, born 1967, has six children: Jamie, Jeff, Mario, Joshua, Devon and Shelley.

c) Tabitha Green, born 1968, married Brian, and had one son named Jordan.

2. Ollie Sue Green, born June 13, 1964, first married Leonard Robert Bernhardt. Ollie Sue and Leonard's children are:

a) Lori Lynne Bernhardt, born March 10, 1965, married Mark H. B. Townsend. Lori and Mark's children are: Joseph Benjamin, Kyrstin-Leigh Susanne and Andrew David Townsend. Lori later married Melvin Andrew Hale.

b) Leonard Robert Bernhardt Jr., born April 10, 1966.

Jennie Sue and sisters visiting their Aunt Johnnie Meeks family. Pictured are Jenny Sue, Tuffy, Johnnie Meeks, Tina, Shirley, Faye, Nema, and Bob.

c) Jeni Lynn Bernhardt, born November 28, 1968, married Harry Edward Leonard and had one child, Troy Edward Leonard. Jeni later married John Allen Daily and they have two children: Rebecca Lynn Daily and Brandon Michael Daily.

Ollie Sue Green married February 15, 1972, to Bernard Thomas Coady. Their children are:

a) Bernard Jacob Coady, born September 30, 1972, died September 30, 1973.

b) Michael Patrick Coady, born August 10, 1975.

c) Adam Bernard Coady, born February 8, 1976.

d) Ryan Susanne Coady, born February 23, 1980.

e) Anren Joseph Coady, born October 6, 1981.

3. Linda Kay Green, born June 27, 1950, married April 13, 1967, to Richard Dean Amberg. Linda and Richard's children are:

a) Richard Lee Amberg, born October 27, 1967, married Michaeline Eaustachio, and had one child, Colton Lee.

b) Joshua Paul Amber, born October 7, 1972, has two children: Nichole Lynn and Parker James.

Jennie Sue Lawson's second marriage was to Ernest Glines Jr. Their children are:

1. Debra Ann Glines, born August 8, 1953, married in 1971, to Michael Anthony Carvso. Children are:

a) Anthony Michael Carvso has one child, Brook Lynn.

b) Nicholas Paul Carvso, born January 11, 1980.

2. Ernest Edward Glines, born April 15, 1962. Names of Ernest's children are:

a) Melissa Kay Glines, born October 6, 1992, died December 28, 1992.

b) Stephen Ray Glines, born August 31, 1993.

Jennie Sue Lawson's third marriage was to John R. Polic, born May 30, 1923, and died March 14, 1981. Jennie Sue Lawson Polic lives in Springfield, Illinois. –Jenny Polic.

OLLIE WOODSON LAWSON FAMILY. Ollie

Woodson, daughter of John Riley Woodson and Minnie Bell Horton, was born in December 1902. She married Ernest Lawson, born in 1889. The names of Ollie and Ernest's children are:

Eula Mae "Sis" Lawson family at Woodson reunion at Lake Charles.

1. Eula Mae Lawson, born September 28, 1924, married on March 26, 1943, to Lester Huskey, born July 12, 1917. Eula Mae "Sis" and Lester have one daughter: Judy Ann Huskey, born September 30, 1947, married Billie Marler, born May 31, 1947. Judy has one daughter: Kimberly Dawn Marler, born January 7, 1974. Eula Mae "Sis" and Lester live in Kennett, Missouri.

2. Olan Lawson, born July 31, 1922, married May 23, 1946, to Wanda Darris, born September 23, 1929, and have three children: Joan Marie, born March 13, 1948, Jack Alfred, born November 26, 1949, and Leslie Mark, born March 25, 1951.

3. Jennie Sue Lawson, born November 27, 1927.

4. Minnie Lou Lawson, born November 27, 1927, married in Hernando, Mississippi, on August 18, 1944, to James Carroll Murley, born December 20, 1923. They had six children: Ernest Jeffery Murley, who has one daughter, Jenny Mitchell; James Nelson Murley, who has one son, James Christopher; Michael Joseph Murley; Timothy Wayne Murley, who has two daughters: Leslie Kay and Lynsie Paige; Mark Alan Murley, who has three children: Amy Mitchell, Tabitha Ann, Alan Bruce; and Jacqueline Yvette Murley Rivera that has two sons: Benjamin James Rivera and

Alexander Rivera. Minnie Lou lives in Houston, Texas.

5. Ernestine Lawson, born 1931, married the first time to Veal Russell and second marriage was to Harvey Glisson on August 24, 1974.

6. Lucille Faye Lawson, born March 24, 1933, married first time to J. W. Hill, had two children. Linda Ann Hill, born August 16, 1950, who married Larry Stivens, had one daughter Lucinda A. Stivens, born February 5, 1968, who married Darrel Parris, had two children: Bryan and Kelly, Robert Ray Hill, born May 3, 1952 (adopted by Paul Raymond Guntharp and went by the name of Robert Ray Guntharp) married Tricia McKee, had one son, Robert Ray Guntharp Jr. and two children from Tricia's other marriage, Ritchey Gagnee and Adrian Gagnee.

Lucille married the second time to Paul Raymond Guntharp on September 10,1 954. They had two children: Myra Gail Guntharp, born August 20, 1955, who married Michael Myers, had two children: Michael Paul Myers and Benjamin Issac Myers; and Becky Lou Guntharp first married Russell Benton, had two children: Matthew Christopher Benton and Chelsey Amanda Benton. She married second time to Daniel Edward Blanchard. Lucille "Tuffy" and Paul Guntharp live in Beebe, Arkansas.

7. Norma Jean Lawson, born in 1936, married John Warner.

Ollie Woodson died January 7, 1939. –*Eula Mae Huskey.*

PRYOR LAWSON was born in North Carolina about 1806. He went to Jackson County, Alabama about 1820. His wife, Rebecca, was born about 1800, in North Carolina. They had at least seven children. Mary, born about 1826, Pleasant, born about 1830, Nancy, born about 1833, John, born about 1835, Andrew, born about 1837, Delilah, born about 1839, and Washington, born about 1841.

Mary either had an illegitimate son, Lorenza, born 1845, or he was the son of an Indian named Gopher. She then apparently married a Woodson and had a son, John Riley, born 1853. Nancy married John Kelly. Nothing more is known of Pleasant and Delilah. The other children, John, Andrew and Washington, along with Mary and her two sons, Pryor and John and Nancy Kelly's family all moved to Dent County, Missouri before 1860.

The entire extended family moved to Lawrence County, Arkansas about 1864. They settled near Powhatan.

Nancy died soon after the move and John Kelly married her sister, Mary. In 1870, Pryor and John Riley Woodson are living with John Lawson and his family. He had married a widow, Lydia Griffith Jones, who had two daughters, Frances Emilene and Caledonia Jane. A few years later, Frances and John Woodson are married. Andrew and Washington marry and settle in the area.

John and Lydia had four children that are known: John, born 1864, Mary, born 1870, Pryor David, born 1872, and Cora Bell, born 1879.

Pryor died sometime between 1870 and 1880. Mary died in 1882. John Lawson died September 8, 1905.

Pryor David "P.D." married Lulu E. Mullen, December 22, 1898, in Lawrence County. He moved his family to Texas and a son, Clarence Elmore, was born March 8, 1901. Lulu died between 1901 and 1908. They went back to Arkansas and P. D. married a 15 year old named Eliza McBride. They had a daughter named Annie.

Clarence married Vera Blanche Fry, November 4, 1922. "V", as she was known, was born December 7, 1901, the daughter of John L. and Mary Ladyman Fry. They had one child, John Pryor "J.P.", born September 12, 1923. J. P.

served in World War II. He made a career out of the Air Force. J. P. married Irene "Arlene" Little on May 12, 1946. They lived in several different places, but Lawrence County was always home. They had one child, Laura Blanche, born February 7, 1947.

Laura Blanche married Wiley Norris Watson on June 13, 1965. They have two children: Heidi Marietta, born March 31, 1966, and Gary Lawson, born April 11, 1968.

J. P. died July 25, 1972, in Peculiar, Missouri of a heart attack. He was working at an Air Force base near there.

Clarence died October 11, 1975, and "V" soon followed him on December 9, 1975. They are buried at Lawrence Memorial Park.

Heidi married Robert Lee Rogers. They had one son, Robert Eugene, born September 1, 1993. Heidi and Robert later divorced.

Laura and her family live in Tucson, Arizona. Arlene lives next door to them. –*Sharon Schmidt.*

RANDALL ROY LAWSON FAMILY. Randall was born October 2, 1945, at Portia, Arkansas, where his dad was a farmer. He was the son of Glen and Ruby Helms Lawson. Randall's dad moved to Denton when Randall was a small child. There he built a small house on Highway 117, which was still gravel. When Randall was nine they moved close to the Denton ranch where Glen owned several acres. Randall was raised on this farm where he had several horses that he rode and trained. He attended school at Lynn, Arkansas, and gradu- ated in 1964. Dur- ing that year, he met and on Octo- ber 22, 1964, married Joyce Louise Morse. She was born March 12, 1948, in a dry docked cabin boat on the banks of the Black River, the daugh-

Randall and Joyce Lawson.

ter of Hartman and Annie Maxine Darris Morse.

Joyce is a graduate of Black River Vo-Tech in computer programming. She quit school in the ninth grade at Black Rock and went back at the age of 40 to take her GED and finish school.

Joyce's dad, Hartman, was said to be the de- scendant of a full blooded Englishman and a full blooded Cherokee Indian. I guess that explains their love for nature. Joyce lived her first years in Powhatan and Black Rock across the road from Black River. She spent many hours playing on its banks. Later in life she moved to Michigan, Florida and finally home again where she met her sweet- heart, Randall.

Randall and Joyce raised five children.

1. Deneshia, born July 22, 1966, married Elden Helms and had two sons: Wesley, born May 2, 1995; and Jared, born July 21, 1997.

2. Randall Jr., born June 29, 1968, married Ruth Ann Burrow on December 17, 1998. They have one son, Jacob Steven, born April 17, 1997.

3. William "Billy", born October 21, 1971, mar- ried Jeri Shearon. They have one son, Billy Jr.

4. Dewayne, born April 4, 1973, married Chrissa Hoffman. They have two children: Zachariah, born April 17, 1997; and Moriah Grace, born August 3, 1998.

5. Jonathan Paul, born February 4, 1977, married Amanda Manning. They had one son, Isaac Paul, born July 10, 1994. Johnny died January 28, 1995, at the age of 17. It was said that he had the largest funeral at Greggs Fu- neral Home with literally hundreds attending. He is buried in Oak Forest Cemetery in Black

Rock. Amanda remarried to Michael Thurman and has a daughter, Katlyn Leeann, born April 12, 1996.

All of Randall and Joyce's children attended Black Rock School.

Randall and Joyce still live in Powhatan. Randall is a construction superintendent for Michelle Ex. in Paragould, Arkansas. He has helped build roads all over Arkansas and parts of Missouri. He is said to be one of the best motor patrol operators in these parts. –Deneshia Helms.

ARTHUR LITTLETON LEE AND VIDA MAE MILLIGAN LEE FAMILY.

The earliest history we have of the Lee family was 1766, when William Lee was born in the British Colony of South Carolina. He was 15 years old when America came into being. After marrying and living in Alabama for about 20 years, they started moving west, first to Kentucky, then to Tennessee in Old McNairy County. In 1802, William and Mary had a son, David Lee. David married Ellender in early 1830s, and in 1849, Sargent Wisdom Lee was born. He married Sarah Margaret Browder in 1877, and they moved to Arkansas, settling in Strawberry. They had six children, three who lived to adulthood: John David Lee, who married Jennie Brady; Marilla Lee, who married William McCall; and Arthur Littleton Lee, who was born at Clover Bend, March 9, 1889. He married Vida Mae Milligan in 1913.

Arthur L. and Vida M. Lee.

The Milligan family history began in Ireland in 1751, with the birth of John Milligan I. In 1771, he came to America and lived in Virginia. In 1799, John II, one of 10 children, was born. After his mother's death, he left Virginia and settled in Arkansas. In 1818, he married Eda Jeffery and shortly after their marriage, moved to Lawrence County. In 1826, John and Eda helped organize the Milligan Camp Ground Cumberland Presbyterian Church. That year he surrendered to the ministry and was licensed the following year. He was ordained as a minister in 1840, and pastored at Milligan Camp Ground for many years. Reverend John and Eda had 13 children. Their last was Andrew J. Milligan, born in 1844. He married Mary Smithee and they had seven children. Their third child was William Porter Milligan, born in 1874. Porter married Eleanor Watson in 1893, and they had eight children. Their third child was Vida Mae Milligan, born at Strawberry, January 16, 1898.

Spending their entire lives in Lawrence County, they were farmers and Arthur was also a carpenter. They were charter members of the Missionary Baptist Church organized at Arbor Grove and then at Clover Bend. They were always active in church, school and community activities. Arthur and Vida had six children.

1. Hazel Margrette Lee, January 7, 1914-May 5, 1916.
2. Vivian Eleana Lee, March 28, 1915-May 8, 1985.
3. Pearl Lee, March 23, 1918-May 9, 1926.
4. Arthur Earl Lee, March 28, 1921-September 9, 1996.
5. Roxie Mae Lee, born March 29, 1927.
6. Clella Anne Lee, born January 5, 1933.

After only 13 years of marriage, they had lost two children, Hazel and Pearl, to pneumonia; then one year later, on May 9, 1927, a tornado destroyed their home and other buildings at Arbor Grove, severely injuring Vida, Vivian and Roxie. With faith and determination, Arthur and Vida rebuilt their home and continued living and farming in the Arbor Grove Community until 1938, when they moved to Clover Bend. They were one of the pioneer families of the FSA Project and Arthur helped build many of those houses and barns. Besides helping farm, Vida canned fruits and vegetables, was an excellent seamstress, and made beautiful quilts for her family.

Vivian attended Hoxie High School and married Earl M. Doyle in 1932. They had David, Bobby and Jeannette. After his death in 1964, she married Paul King in 1973. Earl Lee graduated from Walnut Ridge High School in 1938, and married Jessie Elliott in 1943. They had Saundra, Jacquelyn, Arthur Earl and James Leslie. Roxie graduated from Clover Bend High in 1944, and married Walter Rickard in 1947. They had Keith, Roger, Kerry, Lori and Melodie. Clella graduated from Clover Bend High in 1950, and married Lee Horrell in 1951. They had Scott, Kimberlei, Kelli and Kristi.

Arthur and Vida celebrated their 50th anniversary on March 9, 1963, and Vida died in her sleep January 7, 1965, at the age of 66, at their home. Arthur continued farming until he was 78. He then sold the farm, but continued living in their home. When he was 86, he married Moree Prince. They continued living at Clover Bend until their house burned while they were at church on Sunday evening in 1978. They moved to Hoxie and Arthur died at Walnut Ridge, December 16, 1982, at the age of 93.

Arthur and Vida had 16 grandchildren, 32 great-grandchildren and 11 great-great-grandchildren. They and many of their family members are buried at the Clover Bend Cemetery. –Clella Horrell.

FANNIE CRAIGE LENARD.

Fannie Craige was born to Mary E. (maiden name Hargett) and her husband in 1864, in Lawrence County, Arkansas. (See the John T. Evans story elsewhere in this book.) We do not yet know Fannie's father's name. Craige seems to be the name of Fannie's first husband. She and Craige had a child named George Craige, born about 1883.

Fannie's second marriage was to William Henry Lenard, November 19, 1856-December, 1901, son of David L. and Mary B. "Polly" Moss Lenard of Christian Twp., Independence County, Arkansas, on February 17, 1884. Fannie's son, George, later changed his last name to Leonard. George was Bessie Leonard Reeves' father. George and his family lived in Hardy, Arkansas, and later moved to Kansas City, Missouri, where George died in 1944. Bessie and her husband, Norman Reeves, had three children: Norman Leonard Carlat, Freda Bell and Rosalie.

Fannie and Henry Lenard had at least three children of their own: Della, Walter and Bertha, September 6, 1890-December 25, 1976. Henry already had a daughter, Lillie, and two stepsons by a previous marriage. I don't know what happened to Della and Walter, but Bertha married Eugene S. Farrell, January 23, 1888-March 22, 1970, on May 9, 1909. They had six children: Oather, May 20, 1910-February 23, 1997; Julia Hazel, July 25, 1912-July 19, 1993; V. L., born at Saffell, Lawrence County, Arkansas on January 29, 1915; Katie Mae, died at birth, 1918; Eugene Roy, born October 25, 1923; and Ernestine "Tena", born August 23, 1926. The family followed the sawmill traffic along the rivers in Lawrence, Jackson and Independence counties and eventually settled in Dermott, Chicot County, Arkansas in 1933. Most of the family is still in the Dermott area.

Lillie's daughter, Cora, by her first marriage to Sylvester Allen, married Austin McKee. They had several children and after living in the Bradford, Arkansas area for many years, moved to a small community outside Indianapolis, Indiana. Lillie's daughter from her second marriage to John Brinkley, Opal Brinkley Pierce Swain, lives in Daytona Beach, Florida and has a son, Bill Pierce, who lives in Katy, Texas.

Submitted and written by Sheila Farrell. Sources: Goodspeed's History of Arkansas, 1890; family group sheets; marriage records; census records; personal family knowledge. –Michael Brannon.

LEWIS FAMILY.

John Wesley Lewis was born May 20, 1885, in Kentucky or Tennessee, to Jim and Tilda Belle Starks Lewis. He arrived in Lawrence County in 1894, in a covered wagon pulled by oxen with a wagon train headed for Illinois. His parents took sick with flu and stopped west of Black Rock and both soon died there.

Their other children, Jess, Tom, Joe and Becca, were taken in by neighbors. At nine years of age, John was the oldest child and went to live with Joe Madden near Portia. He never attended school and

Lewis family in 1934, left to right: Arvella, Homer, Pearl, Henry, Ollie Belle, Lucy and John.

ran away at 16 looking for work. He slept in fence rows. Near Strangers Home a woman fed him and sent him to Henry Hartsell at Lauratown who gave him a job and home. He worked there until 1915. John married in 1906. A son, Homer, was born June 29, 1907. His wife and infant daughter died in 1909.

John and Lucy Vena Nunally married September 3, 1911. Lucy was born September 1, 1891, the first child of Hosea and Ollie Clark Nunally at Powhatan. Her siblings were Roy, Jess, Emma and Myrtle. Three daughters were born to John and Lucy: Pearl Mae, August 10, 1912; Arvella, October 14, 1922; and Ollie Belle, August 12, 1931. They farmed near Lauratown for nine years. In 1924, they bought wooded land four miles south of Clover Bend in Black River bottom. They built house and barn and cleared more land each year. After floods in 1927-28, they moved to Bald Knob. In 1934, they returned to farm, but all buildings were gone and land back in woods. They rebuilt and started over. Homer and wife, Lela, had two children, Paul and Pauline. He worked in Chicago and retired in Portia where he died in 1990. Pearl married Henry Winfrey in 1932. They had two sons, Robert Wesley and Chester Henry. They homesteaded a farm on Shirey Bay, but moved to Flint, Michigan in 1945. Pearl retired from Hurley Hospital. She died in 1992. Henry retired from General Motors and died in 1988. After school at Clover Bend, Arvella married Hershell Harley "Dick" Choate in 1941. They had three children, Roger Dale, Emma Ruth and Vastina. They farmed on Shirey Bay and moved to Flint, Michigan in 1946. Both retired from General Motors. Dick died in 1970. Arvella returned to Lawrence

County and married Preston Shipman. Preston died in 1984, and Arvella now lives in Grayling, Michigan. After graduation at Clover Bend in 1950, Ollie Belle attended business school in Little Rock. She married Ansle Dean Simmons in 1958. They had one son, William Craig. She retired from United States Department of Agriculture and Dean retired from Arkansas State Highway Department. They now live in Conway.

Through good times and bad John and Lucy always worked together with a spirit of optimism and good cheer. Lucy died in 1957, and John died in 1962. –Ollie Simmons.

LINEBAUGH FAMILY AS OF FEBRUARY 2, 1999.
Grady Benton Linebaugh was born May 2, 1921, to Theodore Edward and Myrtle Mae Groves-Linebaugh near Imboden. He lived there with his six brothers and sisters until he married Juanita Kathleen Sharp, born May 18, 1924, of Walnut Ridge on April 12, 1946. The first of their four children, Wayne, was born in that same year. Gale followed in 1948, Larry in 1950, and Debbie was the last, born in 1954. Grady worked for John Deere, Smith Implement until 1984. Juanita was a homemaker and passed away with cancer in 1986. Grady preached in many Free Will Baptist churches in Lawrence County from 1950-1998. He remarried Mabel Crooms and moved to Jonesboro in 1987, where he presently lives. All of these children live in Lawrence County: Wayne in Walnut Ridge, Gale in Hoxie, Larry in Hoxie and Debbie in Hoxie.

Wayne was married to Linda and they bore two daughters: Shelly and Susan. He divorced and remarried Renee and bore two more daughters: Chelsey and Sydney. Gale married Juda and they bore a daughter, Cindy. Larry married Betty and they bore three daughters: Melanie, Valerie and Jenny. Debbie married Rodger and they bore three children: Jordan, Bobby and Kathleen. Grady has three great-grandchildren, all girls, as well. Shala was born to Cindy; Maddison was born to Shelly; and Baylee was born to Melanie. –Melanie Inman.

LOOKOUT LONG
moved to Reeds Creek Township, Lawrence County, around 1887, from Dade County, Georgia. Born in Davidson County, Tennessee, in March, 1853, Lookout was one of three children of Asa Long and Melissa Bryant. He was named for Lookout Mountain, Tennessee. He became a father figure to his siblings, Clakey, born in 1865, and Sarah, born in 1868, since their father, a Confederate veteran, died in 1869.

Lookout married Louvina Jane Long, January, 1858-December 28, 1909, on January 25, 1874, in Dade County. They were first cousins, since Louvina's father, Presley Castleberry Long and Asa were brothers. He was a farmer and in 1885, served on the jury when his brother Clakey and wife, Sarah Castleberry, were going through divorce proceedings.

Lookout Long.

When Lookout moved to Arkansas, Clakey went with him. He farmed and was in the cotton gin business. Lookout died in October, 1933. I have not been able to find out where he or Louvina were buried. They had the following children, the first six born in Georgia, the rest in Arkansas:

1. Monroe Anderson, November 1, 1874-September 21, 1930, is buried in Ward Cemetery in Lawrence County. He married Dora Saffell, March 5, 1879-February 3, 1966, in Saffell, Arkansas. They had six children: Essie died young; Fatha died young; Alberta "Bertie" married Tom Hennessey; Elzie Dennis, first married Vercie Martz, second Eula Hooker; Alma married Henry McGinnus; and James Restes married Marie Victor.

2. Robert Russell, born in Georgia either in 1875, or 1878 (census/family Bible), died March 2, 1956. He is buried in Brawley, California. Russell's wife, Annie and his daughter, Vina, were killed by a tornado on April 10, 1929, in Lawrence County.

3. Fanie, November 24, 1876-August 8, 1965, married John H. Willmuth on January 13, 1898. Fanie had at least one child, Margaret, born in 1898.

4. Leta M., May, 1882-December 10, 1964, is buried in Oaklawn Cemetery, Batesville, Arkansas. The cemetery book for Independence County lists her birth 1886.

5. Asa, born 1883, married Girtrue Pucket in Sharp County at age 33. He resided in Grange. He was called Ace. Ace left his family and no one knew where he was until he died somewhere close to Lockhart, Arkansas. He had one child, Elmo.

6. Lena I., November, 1884-July 27, 1943, married George Sharp. Lena had at least one child, Delia.

7. Canzada E. "Zodie", October, 1887-September 5, 1935, is buried in the Willmuth family cemetery west of Saffell. Zodie married David Willmuth on February 13, 1910. She had six children, four boys and two girls. There are two small children buried near her, Lookout Willmuth, September 26, 1919-August 20, 1920, and Arretus Willmuth, March 3, 1917-November 3, 1919.

8. Ada, born October, 1889, married Scott Lockey on February 4, 1914; no children.

9. Hosea H., October 19, 1891-November 18, 1963, is buried in Mount View Cemetery, Sharp County. He was a World War I veteran, Company F, 49th Infantry, married Myrtle McGinness on June 10, 1917. He had about nine or 10 children.

10. Zona, born September, 1894, in Shelbyville, Sharp County, died December 5, 1959. She is buried in Oaklawn Cemetery, Batesville. Zona married George Wilkerson. They had two children, one boy and one girl: Dallas and Dimple. –Judith A. Bailey.

JOHN LUCE
was Baptist, farmer and had a sawmill; dark complexion, grey eyes, medium height, and he had a 201 acre farm. He sold the old Luce homestead about 1845, for 500 dollars and removed to Arkansas. The homestead then became known as the McCullough place, bought by David A. Action in 1892, for 10,000 dollars. John was born 1802, Muhlenberg County, Kentucky. He was the son of David and Elizabeth Carter Luce. He married Nancy Galloway, March 17, 1828, in Rockport, Spencer County, Indiana. She was born 1815, in Kentucky to Pleasant Galloway. They had Mary, William, Abner Franklin, born 1829, Spencer County, Indiana, married November 11, 1858, Mary Elizabeth Skidmone. He died in 1890, in Hallton, Shackleford County, Texas. Elizabeth Caroline, born April 30, 1833, Spencer County, Indiana, married William Askew, who died in 1885 at Evening Shade. James Luce, born about 1838, married Sarah Ellen Walden, Houston County, Texas. Nancy, born 1841, married Isaac Elson Sharp; she died 1879 at Evening Shade. John moved with his niece, Elizabeth Everton and Josiah VanMeter Richardson and

nephew, John William and Matilda Richardson Carter from Spencer County, Indiana, to Lawrence County, Indiana, in about 1844. Daniel, born 1845, and Minerva about 1847, married Nathan Hildreth. Nancy died 1850, in Lawrence County and John married Julia Gist in 1851. They had two children: Thirza/Therisa, born September 15, 1858, married Samuel Daine. Martha, born September 15, 1858, married Thomas Donnell. John died in 1861, Lawrence/Sharp County. Julia died May 11, 1900, in Izard County. –Mary Ann Carter.

MADELINE MARTIN.
My first visit to Lawrence County was in 1978. My dear mother-in-law had often expressed her wish to revisit her birthplace, Black Rock. I promised as soon as our boys were old enough to take care of themselves, I would drive her there. My husband, the youngest of her four sons, bought a small motor home in May of that year and off we went for three months to explore, with Madeline as my 75 year old navigator.

Tom Thumb wedding at First Baptist Church about 1907 or 1908. Left to right: Clarence Wayland, Madeline Martin, Charles Penny and Beulah Wayland, cousin of Clarence.

Mom's great-grandfather, Josiah and wife, Mary, came to Lawrence County from Troy, Missouri, after a few years in the California gold fields. He established a mercantile on Main Street, eventually called "Martin and Son." Their two children, both born in California, became lifetime residents. Son John Henry married Nancy Leticia Talullah McLeod and had one son, Charles Henry. Daughter Rosanna married Charles Lehman and had two daughters, Cora and Mamie. John Henry continued the business, purchasing Josiah's share at his death in 1897. "Lula" died in 1880, and young Charles was raised by his grandmother, Mary. John died young also, in 1899.

Charles married Elizabeth Luticia Williams in 1901. Two daughters were born in Black Rock, Madeline in 1902, and Elizabeth in 1908.

In 1892, the Bank of Black Rock opened on the east end of Main Street with Charles Henry, "Charley" Martin as president. He retained controlling interest in the

Black Rock School about 1909.

capital stock until selling about 1917, when he was named Federal Bank Examiner in the Eighth and Twelfth Reserve Districts. In 1918, Charley moved the family to San Diego, California, where he continued in the banking business until his death in 1949. A son, Charles Henry Martin II, was born in 1918.

Madeline finished school in San Diego and attended Pomona College. She married Dr. Charles William Brown in 1925, raised her family and served her community in many ways.

Dr. Brown died in 1961, and in 1965, Madeline married Reverend Roland Fiske in Los Angeles. He sadly passed away eight months later.

Mom's 1978 trip "back in time" brought her together with childhood friends and acquaintances. Many names escape me now, but I remember Sloan, Coffee, Myers, Townsend, Kelley and Charles Penny, who owned and was remodeling the building that once housed Mom's Uncle Albert Williams' drug store on the corner of Third and Main. We also met and enjoyed relatives, Evelyn and Bobby Flippo.

We visited the First Baptist Church she attended with her family and her grandmother, Eliza Watkins Daugherty Williams. The building that was home to Charles Henry's first bank was interesting, as was the Powhatan Courthouse Museum and the property where the Martin home stood before it burned. Then there was the site of the old button factory. We still have a shell with button holes drilled and Charles Henry's pearl tie tack.

These were dear memories that stayed with her always. Mom passed away in 1988, but the photo album from our trip will keep Lawrence County alive for future generations. –*W. Yvonne Brown.*

MATTHEWS. According to family tradition, my second great-grandfather, John Westley Matthews (Mathis), was born in Tennessee in 1840. He deserted his family in Arkansas, and later died at Kingfisher, Oklahoma, between 1904 and 1908. His mother's name was Katherine Morris. He married Mary Tennessee in Tennessee, in 1863.

Mary Tennessee was born August 21, 1843, at Smith County, Tennessee. She died September 15, 1919, in Walnut Ridge, Lawrence County, Arkansas, where she was buried. Her mother's name was Matilda Phillips. Both mothers were born in Tennessee.

In the 1900 census, Lawrence County, Arkansas, Campbell Township, Mary Tennessee lived in a rent house with her grandson, who was single and at school. She was a married head of household who had 10 children and four were living.

Milton Granville "Pat" Matthews, 1885-1953, with wife, Birdie Mae Miller Matthews, 1895-1991.

In the 1870 census, Logan County, Russelville, Kentucky, I found information on four of these children. Matilda C., born in 1864, in Tennessee; William Washington, born in 1865; Mary, born in 1867; and John, born in 1869. The last three were born in Kentucky.

Other children known to be in the family include: Rachel Ardelia, born 1872, in Kentucky, Chris C., born 1874, and a "Uncle Jack" who could be John as the names are often interchanged.

I have not been able to locate any information on John or Chris C. I'm told Uncle Jack died in Kansas City, Missouri. "Little Mary" married and remained in the area.

Rachel Ardelia married three times; Mr. Orr, Mr. Wells and George W. Anderson. Mr. Anderson owned a newspaper which was published as the *Telephone* at Black Rock. Rachel lived in both Black Rock and Imboden, Arkansas. Her children were: Duncan, Donald, Derrell and Dorris Anderson. Of these children we only know that Dorris moved to Spokane, Washington.

William "Wash" Washington married Melissa "Alice" Jones, December 27, 1888. They remained in the area and had a family of eight children. Of those eight children William Arthur "Happy" Matthews is the only one who has family still living in the area.

The oldest child, Matilda C., had a son, "Pat", born in Walnut Ridge on January 22, 1885. He never knew his father. Matilda's second marriage on January 3, 1889, in Lawrence County was to John Hoover, born in Indiana in 1840. They had one son, Ed Hoover, who was born at Walnut Ridge on October 16, 1889, the day Matilda died. She had contacted a contagious illness, now believed to be tuberculosis and may not have been strong enough to recover from the illness and childbirth.

Matilda's oldest son, Pat, was four years old at the time of her death. He had contacted the same illness. A former slave, Matt Harris, who did day work in the neighborhood, wrapped him in a blanket, took him home, treated and cured him. At a later date, he took a name from his mother's family, Milton Granville Matthews. Some people say Matt raised him, but on the 1900 census he is listed as living with his grandmother, Mary Tennessee. He never forgot Matt's kindness. When he visited relatives in the area, he always stopped to eat at her house. –*M. Mobbs-Gutierrez.*

B.F. MATTHEWS FAMILY. One of the early pioneers of Lawrence County was Benjamin Franklin "B.F." Matthews. Born in Danielsville, Georgia, on August 12, 1823, he was the fifth of 10 children to Allen Matthews and Margaret Pickens Elton Matthews, residents of Gainesville, Georgia. Other children were: Nancy C., Phineas D., Mary E., Allen E., Elizabeth, Jefferson, Margaret E., William and Sarah E.

Allen Matthews was a distinguished lawyer and the oldest of seven children of William and Rachel (Wakefield) Matthews of South Carolina. William was a planter, founder of the Sandy Creek Presbyterian Church, an American Revolutionary soldier and Representative and Senator in the Georgia Legislature, 1805-1830.

B.F. Matthews married Catherine McElroy on October 24, 1844, at Hickory Flats, Georgia and were the parents of 10 children. The first five children born in Georgia included daughters Josephine Louise, 1846 and Sarah Elizabeth, 1847 both born in Auraria, Phineas, the eldest son, was born in Cartersville in 1849. Two other sons, John Franklin, 1851 and William, 1853 were born in Rome.

The remaining children were born in Powhatan which were Thomas Benjamin, 1860; Henry Elton, 1862; Margaret Catherine "Kittie," 1864 and Georgia Ella, 1868.

After correspondence with Andrew H. Imboden, who had built a school in Powhatan, B.F. moved his family to Powhatan on April 28, 1854. He became the first school master at the Powhatan Male and Female Academy, which opened on May 1, 1854. After the school of three months was out, B.F. built a Ferryman's house for Lindsay on the east bank of Black River.

Benjamin Franklin "B.F." Matthews was a prominent businessman, landowner, county official and teacher in Powhatan.

B.F. was a prominent businessman, landowner and county official. In 1855 he entered in partnership with a man named Werner in a Wagon and Blacksmith Shop. He joined with George Wright in a mercantile business in 1867. After the partnership dissolved, B.F. kept the business and it grew to over $50,000 worth in 1872. He sold the remnants of goods to E.T. Wayland in 1888. He also operated a saw mill on Flat Creek. In 1873 he devoted himself to a land business and by 1876 had acquired over 4,000 acres of land.

In 1856 Alfred Gay was elected County Surveyor and appointed B.F. his deputy. After procuring an instrument from Lindsay and surveying for about a year, B.F. resigned the deputyship. He continued to survey and enter lands until 1861 when the Civil War stopped everything for five years. B.F. and Ham Richey went to Pocahontas to join a regiment of the Confederate Army stationed under General Hardy. Only those men who had a certificate of health were accepted. Ham was accepted, but B.F. was refused.

Lawrence County elected B.F. as sheriff from 1862-1864 and appointed him sheriff from 1864-1866 after the elected candidate did not qualify to serve. In the fall of 1870 he was appointed deputy sheriff to assist in assessing and collecting taxes.

B.F.'s wife, Catherine, died on October 31, 1871, at Powhatan. His second wife, Mary, died on January 12, 1893. He served as a commissioner when the Powhatan Courthouse was constructed in 1888. He donated the land for the Powhatan Cemetery and served as the census numerator for the 1880 census.

Lovingly called "Uncle Frank" by his Georgia relatives, B.F. was highly respected in Georgia and Arkansas. He was an extremely intelligent man that left an impact on the town of Powhatan. Of his 10 children, two daughters, Sarah Elizabeth married F.M. "Francis" Wayland and Mary Alice married Theodore Wayland, sons of Reverend Jonathan Wayland.

Two sons married into prominent Lawrence County families. Phineas married Belle E. Raney, daughter of Jackson and Julia F. (Chadwick) Raney and William married Lavinia Martin, daughter of F.G. Martin. The Martins were well known manufacturers of wagons, farm implement stock and hard wood lumber. William and Lavinia had a son, Frank, who died in infancy and four daughters: Beulah, Bessie, Marjorie and Ida Belle.

B.F.'s daughter, Margaret Catherine "Kittie," married Clay Sloan, son of James F. Sloan, one of the sons of Fergus Sloan, another prominent family. Kittie and Clay lived at Powhatan until moving to Black Rock in 1900 to rear four sons, Lawrence, Eugene, James F. and Ralph M.

B.F. died on January 14, 1909, and was laid to rest in the family plot at the Powhatan Cemetery. –*Darlene Moore.*

LAVINIA MARTIN MATTHEWS "LITTLE GRAN" REMEMBERED.

She was a tiny figure: four feet, 10 inches tall and weighing less than 90 pounds. Gentle in manner, soft in speech, few in words, modest in dress, she reigned over our family - that is to say, she "served" our family for three generations.

Orphaned when so young, so small, she stood on a box to wash the dishes. She took care of two brothers. Widowed, she reared her four daughters (a son died in youth). On the death of a daughter, she raised her three orphaned granddaughters. Then on losing another daughter, Little Gran sheltered yet another family of four young children.

So, she "mothered" three sets of children other than her own.

Gracious and genteel, Venie (her sobriquet) was adored and admired by all she met. Her days and nights were spent in caring for her own. She is, for me, the ultimate example of womanhood at its best, the ultimate example of the Christian life. Her Bible was always at hand.

Lavinia Martin Matthews.

    —Inez
Rowsey
Schubert, granddaughter.

WILLIAM AND LAVINIA MARTIN MATTHEWS.

William Matthews was born on December 29, 1853, in Rome, Georgia, to B.F. and Catherine McElroy Matthews. He moved with his parents to Powhatan at a very young age in 1854. He was raised in Powhatan and later settled there.

Lavinia Martin Matthews, born in 1857 in Powhatan, was the daughter of the prominent Powhatan businessman F.G. Martin. F.G. and his brother, Josiah, were very successful in the wagon manufacturing business at Powhatan for many years. F.G. later sold out to his sons, J.A. and J.W. Martin, who later expanded the business to include the manufacture of farm implement stock and hard wood lumber.

William met Lavinia and their marriage united two prominent and well established families from Powhatan. William followed in his father's footsteps as a land surveyor. He served as Lawrence County Surveyor from 1898 to 1900 and for a longer term from 1902 to 1916.

Lavinia was a housewife and a very devout

William Matthews was a well known resident of Powhatan and Lawrence County Surveyor.

Christian. Walter McLeod in his book, *Centennial Memorial History of Lawrence County* described her as "one of those unselfish women who seemed to live wholly for others."

William and Lavinia were the parents of five children. A son, Frank, 1888-1890, died as a toddler and a daughter, Beulah, 1885-1932, never married. Marjorie Matthews, 1895-1930, married

William F. Rowsey, well known Lawrence County official. They were the parents of William "Bud" Rowsey, Frank Rowsey, Mary Rowsey Boucher and Inez Rowsey Schubert. Bessie Matthews, 1883-1920, married Jack Lemay and from this union were born three daughters: Juanita Lemay, 1909-1920, who died as an infant; Frances Lemay Beck; Ruth Lemay Rowsey; and Marie Lemay Clay. Ida Belle Matthews, 1891-1971, married Robert L. "Luther" Flippo and they were the parents of William Woodrow "Billy" Flippo, Robert L. "Bobby" Flippo Jr. and Marjorie Miriam "Sis" Jones Elliott.

William and Lavinia were very active members in the Powhatan Methodist Church known during their time as the Methodist Episcopal Church, South. They raised their family in this church and were active in community service as well.

William died in 1918 and Lavinia remained active caring for several grandchildren and nieces and nephews until her death in 1936. They were laid to rest in the family plot next to William's father, B.F. Matthews, at the Powhatan Cemetery. – *Darlene Moore.*

MATTIX FAMILY.

Edward and Elizabeth Bond Mattix, early settlers of Lawrence County, were born in North Carolina and married March 31, 1805, in Wayne County, Kentucky. They lived in Harrison County, Indiana from approximately 1806 to 1820. In March, 1821, Edward and Elizabeth began to sell their Indiana land, apparently in preparation to move. In February, 1822, they sold the remaining land and with other family members emigrated to northeast Arkansas Territory, settling on Eleven Point River in Lawrence County, seven miles northwest of Pocahontas. This land is now in Randolph County. The Bureau of Land Management has documentation showing Edward purchased land in Lawrence County, Territory of Arkansas in 1824 and 1826.

Records for the early years in Arkansas are scarce, but we do find Edward named guardian for Jarrett Seats, son of Benjamin, deceased at the October, 1827, Lawrence County Court. Edward's son-in-law, Lawrence Thompson, and John Hinds posted security.

Both Edward and Elizabeth are presumed to have died after 1850, as they are not found on any census records after the Arkansas 1850 census. According to family lore, they are buried "across the river" from their property in Water Valley.

Their children were:

1. Edward, born about 1804, married Charity Robertson, daughter of James and Sarah.

2. Jane, born February 10, 1806, Harrison County, Indiana, married Lawrence Thompson, May 15, 1822, Harrison County, Indiana, died December 23, 1836, Lawrence County, Arkansas. Jane is buried in Sweet Moments Cemetery, north of Jonesboro.

3. Margaret Ann, born October 30, 1808, Harrison County, Indiana, married David Hines (Hinds), February 22, 1827, Lawrence County, Arkansas and Dr. Autrey, died March 12, 1861, Cook County, Texas.

4. Cynthia, born March 21, 1813, Harrison County, Indiana, married Nimrod Capps, June 3, 1830, Lawrence County, Arkansas. Cynthia died March 10, 1866.

5. Elizabeth married George W. Cochrain, November 29, 1832, Lawrence County, Arkansas.

6. Cinderella, born June 6, 1815, Harrison County, Indiana, married first Edward Bennett, second Robert James Rodgers, died February 15, 1889, Venice Hills, Tulare County, California.

7. John, born about 1820, married Polly Hucheson, May 5, 1843, Lawrence County, Arkansas.

8. Matthew, born about 1823, Randolph County, Arkansas, died September 18, 1945, Randolph County, Arkansas.

9. David, born about 1828, married Elizabeth West, May 31, 1847, Randolph County, Arkansas.

10. Esther, born 1830, married Lorenzo Dow Hatcher, May 5, 1842.

CHARLES ABSOLOM MCCARROLL

was born in Randolph County on July 24, 1854. Charles was the son of James McCarroll, born November 11, 1817. James was married to Rebecca Forrester, born September 10, 1821. James died in 1858, and Rebecca died March 19, 1889.

Charles "Boob" had three brothers: Andrew, Frank and Bob. His sister, Jane, married James McLaughlin. Andrew, Frank and Bob fought in the Civil War. Frank was wounded in the Civil War and never returned. Andrew and Bob returned and reared large families.

Charles' father, James, died when he was four years old. In 1875, Charles was living with his mother, Rebecca, when he married Narcisus Ellen Cravens, born on October 3, 1855. Miss Cravens was the daughter of Andrew J. Cravens, born on January 18, 1816, and Narcisus Ellen Wells. Andrew Cravens lived two miles north of Black Rock in the Mount Vernon Community. He was a very wealthy farmer and stockman and owned several slaves. At the end of the Civil War, the Cravens slaves were freed and they took their master's name and lived in the Birdell Community. Andrew and Narcisus Ellen are buried on the farm. They supposedly buried gold on their land during the Civil War, and grave diggers searched in vain for the Cravens gold, but no one has found it!

Charles and Ellen lived in the Spring River area of Randolph County and were the parents of 12 children: Clara Rebecca, James, Andrew, John Ellison, Ida Jane, Robert Franklin, Charles Whittaker, George Washington, Hugh Homer, Edna Ellen, and two daughters who died in infancy.

Clara Rebecca, born August 28, 1876, married William Campbell Starr, born November 1, 1869, in 1901. Their children were: Claude, born October 1, 1901, died March 22, 1973; Elmo Starr, born November 25, 1903, died February 22, 1975; Virginia, born August 30, 1907; John, born February 3, 1909; Charles Millard, born March 23, 1911; and Lucille, born April 16, 1913. Clara died in 1967, and William Campbell in 1938. They are buried in Fairview Cemetery in Randolph County.

James Andrew McCarroll, born February 19, 1878, married Laura Weir in 1903. James Andrew died on January 10, 1952. Laura died in 1983. The couple had no children and are buried in Lawrence Memorial Cemetery in Walnut Ridge.

John Ellison, born January 10, 1880, married Virgie Ward in 1912. They were the parents of five children: Lorene, born January 3, 1914; Jessie

Charles Absolom McCarroll and Ellen Narcisses Cravens McCarroll. Photo taken in the fall of 1916.

Marie, born May 14, 1915; Vernon Octavius, born August 22, 1918; Gustavia, born February 20, 1923; and John Albert, born October 31, 1928. John died in 1967, and Virgie in 1979. They are buried in Oak Forest Cemetery in Black Rock.

Ida Jane, born May 25, 1882, married John Sloan Forrester in 1909. John died in 1841, and Ida on December 26, 1968. They had one infant child, Charles Jewell, who died in 1912. They are all buried in Fairview Cemetery in Randolph County.

Robert Franklin, born April 24, 1884, married Johnnie Ivie Ward in 1912. They were the parents of Lillian, born November 3, 1913; Flossie, born October 23, 1915; Willie, born June 15, 1917; and Frances Marvene, born September 27, 1923. Robert died in 1928, and is buried in Imboden Cemetery. Johnnie died in 19??.

Charles Whittaker, born April 8, 1886, married Ellen "Tint" Butler in 1909. They had one son, Velmer Eugene, born September 15, 1910. Charles died in 1969. Ellen died in 1975. They are buried in Oak Forest Cemetery in Black Rock.

George Washington McCarroll, born April 7, 1892, married Mary Pearl Davis in 1915. Their children were: Mildred Lucille, born September 12, 1916; Edward Lee "Jack", born February 20, 1920; Marshall Warren, born January 29, 1923; Charles Ray, born March 25, 1925; and Melba Ruth, born December 3, 1926. George died in 1980. Pearl died in 1978. They are buried in Oak Forest Cemetery in Black Rock.

Hugh Homer, born February 18, 1894, married Martha Mazilla Brown in 1914. They were the parents of Mary Juanita, born June 2, 1917; Charles Leon, born March 3, 1920; and Eva Jewell, born June 2, 1928. Homer died in 1979, and is buried in St. Petersburg, Florida.

Edna Ellen, born October 5, 1897, married Edward Franklin Puckett in 1916. They were the parents of Lois Rheamonia, born October 10, 1917; Franklin Robert, born April 29,1920; Margaret Imogene, born November 15, 1922; Notra Fern, born October 22, 1925; Freda Mae, born March 9, 1931; and Robert Dale, born June 24, 1939. Edna died in 1996, and Edward in 1983. They are buried at Lawrence Memorial Cemetery in Walnut Ridge. –Jerry Gibbens.

HENRY RELTON MCCARROLL was born in Walnut Ridge, Arkansas, on August 6, 1905, to Dr. Horace Rudolph "Dolph" and Pearl Henry McCarroll. He died February 27, 1972, in Hawaii while there to present a paper before a medical meeting. He graduated from Ouachita Baptist University and Washington University Medical School, St. Louis, Missouri, where he was on staff of Barnes Hospital for many years. He also served on the staff of Shriner Hospital for Crippled Children. Dr. McCarroll was active in North American Orthopedists and served as President of this organization for one year. He was invited to give lectures on congenital dislocation of the hip before many medical groups. He married in Chicago, Illinois, November 29, 1934, Nina Elizabeth Snyder, who was born in Iowa. They were the parents of three children.

Henry Relton McCarroll Jr. was born in St. Louis, Missouri, on December 19, 1936, married in Montreal, Canada, on May 24, 1969, to Barbara Ann Reed, who was born in Canada on February 9, 1942. They have two children: Michelle Lynn McCarroll and Nicole Renee McCarroll.

Sandra Beth McCarroll was born in St. Louis, Missouri, on May 5, 1938, was married in St. Louis, Missouri on October 14, 1961, to David Joe Hunsaker, born in Girard, Kansas, on May 22, 1937. They have three children: David Scott Hunsaker, Stephanie Lynn Hunsaker and Eric Christian Hunsaker.

David Lawrence McCarroll was born in St. Louis, Missouri, on November 19, 1943, was married in Charlottesville, Virginia, on November 27, 1974, to Roberta Ann Rankin, who was born in Hopewell, Virginia, on August 23, 1945. They had one child: Sarah Elizabeth McCarroll.

–Margaret Watson.

HORACE RUDOLPH "DOLPH" MCCARROLL, the son of William Henderson and Elizabeth R. "Betty" McGee McCarroll, was born in Denton, Arkansas, August 25, 1871, and died in San Antonio, Texas, March 4, 1937. On December 13, 1899, he married Pearl Henry, who was born May 23, 1879, to William Andrew and Martha Thorn Henry Sr. in Walnut Ridge, Arkansas, where Pearl died on January 14, 1964.

Pearl was a sister of William Andrew "Drew" Henry Jr., who was married to Iora "Elsie" McCarroll, daughter of John Henderson McCarroll. Dolph was first a school teacher and then he graduated from the University of Tennessee Medical School, Memphis, Tennessee. In 1900, he opened his office in Walnut Ridge where he remained in practice until the last year of his life. Both are buried in Lawrence Memorial Park Cemetery, Walnut Ridge. They had six children, all of whom did undergraduate work at Ouachita Baptist College (now university). The children were: Ura Elizabeth McCarroll, Martha Thelma McCarroll, Henry Relton McCarroll, William Harroll McCarroll, Margaret Connell McCarroll and Ethel Bernice McCarroll. –Margaret McCarroll Watson.

JAMES MCCARROLL FAMILY. James McCarroll was born on September 2, 1797, in Spartanburg County, South Carolina. He died on July 16, 1872. James married Mary Beasley, daughter of James Beasley and Sarah. Mary Beasley was born on June 7, 1801, in South Carolina, died on July 24, 1863, in Lawrence County, Arkansas. They had the following nine children:

1. George Washington McCarroll was born on July 13, 1822, in Smithville, Lawrence County, Arkansas. George died about 1870, in Smithville, Lawrence County, Arkansas. George married Mary Ann R. Thompson.

2. Sarah Ann McCarroll was born about 1823, in Smithville, Lawrence County, Arkansas. She died about 1861, in Lynn, Lawrence County, Arkansas. Sarah married Jackson Henderson Oldham, son of Tyree and Nancy Oldham, on June 22, 1846, in Lynn, Lawrence, Arkansas. Jackson Henderson Oldham Sr. was born on February 1, 1813, in Madison County, Kentucky, and died on September 9, 1886, in Lynn, Lawrence, Arkansas. (See Oldham family.)

3. Thomas McCarroll was born on August 9, 1824, in Smithville, Lawrence County, Arkansas. Thomas died on February 2, 1904, in Imboden, Lawrence County, Arkansas. Thomas married Jane Balfour Dean.

4. Mary McCarroll was born on October 26, 1826, in Smithville, Lawrence County, Arkansas. She died on January 23, 1927, in Black Rock, Lawrence, Arkansas. Mary was buried in Old Bethel Memorial Cemetery, Denton, Arkansas. Mary was married to Thompson Mason Oldham, oldest son to William and Ann Wilkerson Oldham, and James N. Davis.

5. Nancy J. McCarroll was born in 1828, in Smithville, Lawrence County, Arkansas. She died in August, 1862, in Lawrence County, Arkansas. Nancy married Jeremiah Brady.

6. Zebedee B. McCarroll was born in 1830, in Smithville, Lawrence County, Arkansas. Zebedee died in December, 1870, in Clover Bend, Arkansas. He married Mary Deliala Mitchell Strickland.

7. James B. McCarroll was born in 1831, Smithville, Lawrence County, Arkansas. He died on May 8, 1861, in Smithville, Lawrence County, Arkansas. James married Mary Oldham, the oldest daughter of Jackson H. Oldham Sr.

8. Martha McCarroll was born on January 18, 1833, in Smithville, Lawrence County, Arkansas. Martha died on June 19, 1860, in Denton, Lawrence, Arkansas. Martha married John Davis.

9. John Rhea McCarroll was born on December 24, 1834, in Smithville, Lawrence County, Arkansas. He died on October 30, 1892, in Smithville, Lawrence County, Arkansas. John Rhea married Elizabeth Davis, Ibbie M. Cooper and Mrs. Emily Rutledge.

10. William Henderson McCarroll was born on June 8, 1839, in Smithville, Lawrence County, Arkansas. William died on October 3, 1877, in Smithville, Lawrence County, Arkansas. William married Elizabeth R. "Betty" McGhee.

11. Melissa J. McCarroll was born in January, 1841, in Smithville, Lawrence County, Arkansas. She died in August, 1912, in Eaton, Lawrence County, Arkansas. Melissa married Jackson Henderson Oldham Sr. on October 13, 1862, in Lawrence County, Arkansas after her sister died, and had 11 children by him.

(See the Jackson Henderson Oldham family and The Descendants of Nathaniel and John McCarroll written by the late John Richard McCarroll of Waco, Texas for more information.)

NATHANIEL MCCARROLL was born in Surry County, North Carolina, on September 27, 1765, and died in Lawrence County, Arkansas in early 1835. He was married in Spartanburg County, South Carolina in the mid 1790s, to Martha ??, who was born in South Carolina about 1756, and died in Lawrence County, Arkansas, near the time of Nathaniel's death in 1835. The notice of deaths in Lawrence County, Arkansas, which appeared in the Arkansas Gazette dated April 6, 1835, showed "Nathaniel McCarroll and his wife, both of advanced age, died recently."

The identity of Nathaniel McCarroll's parents has not been determined for certain, but it appears that his father was John McCarroll, who died in Spartanburg County, South Carolina, on March 5, 1800. The will for this John McCarroll did not contain the name of his wife, but it named three sons: Nathaniel, John and Thomas; and two daughters: Genrot and Ruth. It also appears that this John McCarroll was the son of Nathaniel McCarroll, who died in Surry County, North Carolina in 1779. His will names his wife, Elizabeth: two sons, Thomas and John; and one daughter, Mary.

It is not known just when Nathaniel McCarroll moved from North Carolina to South Carolina, but he stated to the county court of Independence County, Territory of Arkansas, on January 7, 1833, that in 1781, he was living in Spartanburg County, South Carolina, when he was called into the Revolutionary War. After the war ended he remained in Spartanburg County, South Carolina until 1807, when he moved his family to Caldwell County, Kentucky. He remained in Caldwell County until 1815, when he moved his family to Missouri Territory and settled in the area that later became Lawrence County.

The first Arkansas tax list of 1819 to 1829, names Nathaniel McCarroll as a property owner at the time. He settled on Cooper Creek about two miles south of Smithville, Arkansas, on what was later known as the J. N. Hillhouse place. He and his family were among the earliest settlers on the Strawberry River. His farm was about three miles north of the famed "Old Taylor Mill", which was built on the Strawberry River about five miles south of Smithville. He continued to live in this area of the northeast Arkansas Territory where he became a very prominent and highly respected member of the community.

In January, 1833, he appeared before the Independence County Court, which approved his application for a Revolutionary War Pension. Before death came to Nathaniel and Martha McCarroll in early 1835, they owned two of the finest farms in Lawrence County. One consisted of 160 acres and the other 80 acres. The division of Nathaniel's property was made between his sons, James and Thomas, his daughter, Elizabeth Steadman, and his grandson, John McCarroll Jr., in right of his father John McCarroll, deceased. On November 12, 1990, the Jonesboro Chapter, Daughters of the American Revolution, marked the grave of Nathaniel McCarroll in Old Bethel Cemetery, Lawrence County, Arkansas.

—Margaret McCarroll Watson.

NATHANIEL AND JOHN MCCARROLL FAMILY.
A John McCarroll died in Spartanburg County, North Carolina, on March 5, 1800. His will contained the names of three sons: Nathaniel, John and Thomas; and two daughters: Genrot and Ruth. It also appears that this John was the son of Nathaniel McCarroll who died in Surry County, North Carolina in 1779. His will shows a wife Elizabeth; two sons, Thomas and John; and one daughter, Mary.

Nathaniel McCarroll was born in Surry County, North Carolina, on September 27, 1765, and died in Lawrence County, Arkansas, in early 1835. He was married in Spartanburg County, South Carolina, in the mid 1790s, to Martha, who was born in South Carolina in about 1765. Both died prior to April 6, 1835. Nathaniel was called to serve in the Revolutionary War in 1781, while living in Spartanburg County, South Carolina. After the war, he remained there until 1807, when he moved his family to Caldwell County, Kentucky. He remained in Kentucky until 1815, before coming to Arkansas. The first Arkansas Tax List of 1819 to 1829, names Nathaniel McCarroll as a property owner on Cooper Creek, about two miles south of Smithville, Arkansas on what was later known as the J. N. Hillhouse place. Nathaniel's farm was about three miles north of the famed "Old Taylor Mill' which was built on the Strawberry River about five miles south of Smithville. Nathaniel and Martha McCarroll are thought to be buried in the Hillhouse Cemetery.

Nathaniel's children were: Thomas, born 1795, South Carolina, died 1844, Arkansas; James, born 1797, South Carolina, died 1872, Arkansas; Elizabeth, born 1799, South Carolina, died 1853, Arkansas; John, born 1800, South Carolina, died 1825, Arkansas; Martha, born 1812, Kentucky, died 1890, Arkansas.

John McCarroll was born in Surry County, North Carolina, in about 1770, and died in Lawrence County in Arkansas Territory between July 29, 1833, and the end of that year. He was married in Spartanburg County, South Carolina, in the early 1790s, and had three young sons when his wife died in Spartanbury County or in Caldwell County, Kentucky, between 1800 and 1815. He married again in Spartanburg County, North Carolina or Caldwell County, Kentucky, before 1817, to Nancy, born in South Carolina in 1793. John and Nancy moved to Lawrence County in Arkansas Territory between 1818 and 1820, settling in the Spring River area, north of where Nathaniel had settled a few years earlier. This part of Lawrence County later became Randolph County.

John's children were: William, born 1791, South Carolina; Nathaniel W., born 1793, South Carolina, died 1843, Arkansas; John M., born 1795, South Carolina, died 1844, Arkansas; James, born 1817, Kentucky, died 1877, Arkansas; Martha, born 1821, Arkansas, died before 1860, Arkansas; Mariah, born 1823, Arkansas, died 1857, Arkansas; Jane, born 1825, Arkansas, died before 1860, Arkansas; Esther, born 1827, Arkansas; Margaret, born 1829 Arkansas.

More information can be found in *The Descendants of Nathaniel and John McCarroll* written by the late John Richard McCarroll of Waco, Texas.

WILLIAM HARROLL MCCARROLL
was born December 4, 1907, to Dr. Horace Rudolph "Dolph" and Pearl Henry McCarroll. He died in Denver, Colorado, on November 11, 1981, and is buried in Ft. Logan National Cemetery. On October 21, 1944, he graduated from Ouachita Baptist College and the University of Tennessee Medical School. He was house surgeon in the Nix Hospital in San Antonio, Texas. In 1940, he graduated from the graduate school of Aviation Medicine and in 1945, from the Army's Command and General Staff School. From 1941 to 1957, he was a military hospital administrator. During World War II, he served as an Army Air Force surgeon at Pearl Harbor and in the South Pacific Theater of Operation, and was awarded two silver stars. He served in Japan during the occupation. At the time of his death, he was a retired Air Force Colonel.

He married Ellynne Margaret "Lynne" Burns, who was born in Denver, Colorado, on June 14, 1911. He and Lynne had no children, but Lynne had children by her first husband, who died during World War II. They were: Richard B. Kenehan of St. Louis, Missouri; John C. Kenehan of Denver, Colorado; and Patricia Cook Woodson of Houston, Texas. *—Margaret McCarroll Watson.*

ZEBEDEE B. MCCARROLL FAMILY.
Zebedee, son of James McCarroll and Mary Beasley, was born in 1830, in Smithville, Lawrence County, Arkansas. He died in December, 1870, in Clover Bend, Arkansas. He married Mary Deliala Mitchell Strickland, born in 1827; died 1853, on January 11, 1853. She was a daughter of Robert L. and Sarah Mitchell. They had one child: Mittie Mary Ann McCarroll.

Mittie McCarroll was born in 1853, in Alicia, Lawrence County, Arkansas. She married George Washington Byrd, born April 19, 1851, died January 10, 1904; buried Clover Bend Cemetery Lawrence County, Arkansas. Mittie died 1929, buried Stranger's Home Cemetery, Lawrence County, Arkansas. They had the following children: William Jefferson, Margaret D., James Ambrose, Lula Emmaline, Frank Tucker, Georgia Ann and Andrew Alexander Byrd.

William Jefferson Byrd, born 1876, married Hattie Alphin. William died 1905, Clover Bend, Lawrence County, Arkansas.

Margaret D. "Lillie" Byrd, born 1877, married Joseph Gibson. Margaret died 1898, buried Clover Bend, Lawrence County, Arkansas.

James Ambrose Byrd, born March 6, 1879, married Katie Bush, December 2, 1886-November 3, 1975, buried Stranger's Home Cemetery, Lawrence County, Arkansas. James died June 12, 1908, buried Clover Bend Cemetery, Lawrence County, Arkansas. Their child: Ruby Byrd married Willis Owens, September 13, 1904. Ruby and Willis' children: Ben Edwin, Mary Kay and James Carroll.

Lula Emmaline Byrd, born December 21, 1887, married January 12, 1903, Leonard Walker Hinton, born December 10, 1882, son of J. A. Hinton and Elizabeth Caroline Teter, and died January 7, 1965. Lula died September 9, 1979. Both are buried Stranger's Home Cemetery, Lawrence County, Arkansas. Their children: Leola, Leone, Imogene Walker, LeRue, Mary Colleen and Elizabeth.

Leola, born October, 1910, died as a child, buried in Anniston, Calhoun County, Alabama.

Leone Hinton, born November 4, 1911, Alicia, Arkansas, married Everett Martin Lawrence, born December 5, 1906, son of John Walter Lawrence and Tina Fort, and died 1963, Oklahoma; buried Perkins, Oklahoma Cemetery. One child: Ann Carolyn Lawrence, born Alicia, Arkansas, married July 26, 1959, Billy Ray Jennings.

Imogene Walker Hinton, born April 16, 1915, in Alicia, Lawrence County, Arkansas, married July 12, 1941, to James Bomar Ryall. Their children: James Bomar Jr., married December 27, 1968, Linda Marie Pritchett; Emma Scudder married June 30, 1967, in Selma, Alabama, to James George Gammons; and Sally Byrd Ryall married November, 1974, James Ralph Cullinane II.

LeRue Hinton married Ouida Kelly. Their children: Sandra Kay married Robert Arthur; and Warren Hinton.

Mary Colleen Hinton, born January 7, 1923, Alicia, Lawrence County, Arkansas, married James Newsum and died 1996, in Georgia. They had six children: David, Daniel, Jennifer, Jan Keller, Jeremy and Joel.

Elizabeth Corrine Hinton, born August 28, 1925, Alicia, Lawrence County, Arkansas, married September 23, 1945, Charles Clay Robb, born July 29, 1923, and died December 1, 1993, Arena, Wisconsin; buried Arena, Wisconsin. They had five children: Charles Hinton married March 10, 1979, to Amy Wendorf; Susan Kay married April 7, 1969, in Arena, Wisconsin, to Bruce Allen Baker; Samuel Ray married August 16, 1975, Celeste Spalding; Dwain Alan married first Jo Ellen Husom and second July 18, 1981, to Susanne Marie Accola; and Elaine M. Robb married October 23, 1982, to Daryl Wayne Miller.

Georgia Ann Byrd married first John Franklin Davidson, then she married Ben York.

Andrew Alexander "Judd" Byrd, born May 11, 1894, died June 18, 1962, Alicia, Arkansas.

He is buried in Stranger's Home Cemetery, Lawrence County, Arkansas.

Frank Tucker "Tuck" Byrd married Lutie Williams Spikes. Their children: Mabel, Vernell, Ruby and Frankie. *—B.R. Jennings.*

MCKAMEY.
According to Leona McKamey Karsch, 1879-1969, daughter of Robert Jr. and Susan Ann Bragg McKamey, 13 families left Anderson County, Tennessee, in 1858, and migrated to Lawrence County, Arkansas. Some remained in Lawrence County and others went to Texas.

Robert McKamey Sr. and his wife, Jemima Parks McKamey, were among these families. Perhaps at the same time, seven of their 10 children came. Some were married and had families of their own. William McKamey had married Betsy Courtney in Tennessee in 1850, James Luttrell McKamey married Rosanna Galbraith in 1858, Jane McKamey married Houston Courtney in 1855, Catherine McKamey married Luke L. Dail in 1856, and Malinda McKamey married James Brown in 1857. Martha was probably 16 and Robert was 13 in 1858. William drowned in Spring River when 36 years of age. His wife, Betsy, and three children returned to Tennessee.

Robert McKamey Sr. and Jemima first settled on Hardin land, later known as the Alcorn Place, which is owned by C. C. Rorex today. Robert McKamey Sr. then purchased a farm on Spring River.

Political unrest in Tennessee, preceding the Civil War, has been given as the reason for the migration to Arkansas. When 18 years of age, Robert Jr. joined the Union forces serving in the Sixth Missouri Volunteer Cavalry. His older brother, James Luttrell, served in the same unit.

Photo taken at Robert and Susan McKamey's Fiftieth Wedding Anniversary Celebration, October 15, 1923.

Seated: Robert McKamey and wife, Susan Ann Bragg McKamey. First row: John B., Anna, Leona, Maida, Ora, James L. Back row: Abb, Robert, Oscar, Millard; October 15, 1923.

After the war, he married Barbara Wells and lived on land in Randolph County for four years. After his parents died in 1870, he purchased the family farm from the heirs of Robert Sr. and Jemima. Some of the heirs were living in Arkansas and others were in Tennessee.

Robert Jr.'s first wife, Barbara, died leaving two small children, Margetta and Emily. He then married Eliza Bragg, who drowned a month after their marriage, while riding her horse through a swollen creek flowing into Spring River. His third marriage was to Eliza's sister, Susan Ann Bragg, who was the mother of their 13 children. The children were: James L., John B., Ann Eliza, Leona, Robert, Maida, Abb and Anna (twins), Oscar H., Ora, Millard F., and two infants who died at birth. Ann Eliza died when nearly five years of age.

After World War II, O. H. McKamey, a son of Oscar, purchased the farm from three aunts who had possession at that time. They were Leona McKamey Karsch, Ora McKamey Guthrie and Anna McKamey.

Once a large family, the only descendants living in Lawrence County in 1998 are: O. H. McKamey; his children, Tim McKamey and Susan Ann McKamey Hawkins and a grandson, Anthony Hawkins. A sister, Hope McKamey Sloan, lived in Pocahontas and a granddaughter, Anita Hawkins Dickson, lives in Jonesboro. *–Pauline McKamey.*

ARCHIBALD MCLAUGHLIN FAMILY.
Archibald McLaughlin was born in July, 1825, in Tennessee. He married Perlina Easter Duvall, daughter of Maureen and Jane Bouldin Duvall on December 14, 1847, in Grainger County, Tennessee. They lived in Tennessee and Kentucky before coming to Lawrence County. Their four children were: James B., born May, 1849; George Washington, born February 20, 1852; William Harvey, born December, 1857; and Amanda Jane, 1860. After Perlina's death in 1868, Archibald married her sister, Jemima Duvall, and had three more children: Columbia, Francis and Eliza.

Archibald and Jemima deeded land for a building for the Hopewell Methodist Church, located three miles south of Imboden.

SECOND GENERATION

James McLaughlin married Mary Jane McCarroll. George married Mary Martha Moore. Their children were: Dora, Martha Jane, Nellie, Jennie and Alva Morris. William McLaughlin married Sarah Kelley. Their children were: Robert Britton, Mary Dollie and William Jackson. Amanda Jane McLaughlin married James Rogers. Their child was Emma Rogers.

THIRD GENERATION

Dora McLaughlin married James Frank Weir and Charles D. Woodyard. Her children were: Bowen and Millard Weir and Dalton and Taylor Woodyard. Martha Jane McLaughlin married Johnson Hatcher Kell on December 14, 1897. Their children are: Clyde, William, Helen, Frank, Vernon, Pauline, Owen, Herschel, Edith, Kenneth, Johnson Hatcher Jr. and Wilson. Nellie McLaughlin married Girt Jones. Their children were: Amelia and Lois Jones. Jennie McLaughlin married Walter Hedrick November 6, 1901. Their children were: Mae, Myrtle, Lola, Alvin, Marvin, Charlotte, Walter Jr., Robert and Charles. Morris McLaughlin married Clara Woodyard. Their children were: Elizabeth and Hubert.

Robert Britton McLaughlin married Rosette Butler on January 30, 1898. Their children were: Nema, Eula and Emma Pearl. Dollie McLaughlin married William Raleigh Black August 3, 1895. William Jackson McLaughlin married Minnie Propst August 12, 1895. Their children were: Mabel, William, Calvin, Marie, Raymond Albert, Margaret Lois, Eugene and Geneva.

Picture made in fall of 1916. Back row: Walter Hedrick, Hatcher Kell, Mattie (Martha Jane) McLaughlin Kell, holding Edith, Gert Jones, Nellie McLaughlin Jones, Charles D. Woodyard holding Dalton, Dora McLaughlin Weir Woodyard, Millard Weir. Second row: Jennie McLaughlin Hedrick, holding Charlotte, Zack Moore, George W. McLaughlin, Mary Martha "Mollie" Moore McLaughlin, Thursie Moore Weir, Clara Woodyard McLaughlin, "Alva" Morris McLaughlin, Melvin Clyde Kell. Third row: William Washington Kell, Vernon Kell, Lola Hedrick, Frank Kell, Mae Hedrick, Jewel Woodyard, Helen Kell. Front row: Myrtle Hedrick, Lois Jones, Marvin Hedrick, Beth McLaughlin, Alvin Hedrick, Pauline Kell, Amelia Hones, Cleo Woodyard. –Edith Storall.

FOURTH GENERATION

Clyde Kell married Alma Perrin in August, 1921. Their children are: George Clyde, Hatcher Franklin and Everett Lee "Skeeter." William Kell married Marie Graham February 1, 1922. Their children are: Billy Gene and Patricia. Helen Kell married Thomas Hatcher Smith September 28, 1920. Their children are: Eva Inez, Gail Cleveland, Vernon Kell, Terrell Herschel and Beryl Thomas. Frank Kell married Joyce Duvall June 12,

1929. Their children are: Betty Estelle and Franklin Theodore. Vernon Kell married Pearl Lyons August 23, 1930. Their child was Gerald Lyons Kell. Edith Kell married Austin Andrew Stovall December 22, 1942. Their children are: Austin Andrew Jr., Martha Jane and Nancy Janelle. Kenneth Kell married Jerry Thompson June 13, 1942. Johnson Hatcher Jr. married Dorothy McDonald October 28, 1945. Their children are: Kevin and Mark. Wilson Kell married Betty Sue Harris November 10, 1951. Their children are: Cynthia and Herbert Wilson Jr.

Nema McLaughlin married Henry Almer Smith December 18, 1921. Their children are Marshall Laverne and Alma Jewel. Mabel McLaughlin married Wilbur Hanshaw September 20, 1924. Their children are Victor Hull, Wilma Jean and Rethea Ann. William H. McLaughlin married Dorothy Hill May 23, 1957. Their child is Judie McLaughlin. Calvin McLaughlin married Anna Smith May 14, 1930. Children are: Calverine, Jeroline, Carolyn, Marion and Calvin Eugene. Marie McLaughlin married David Willett December 24, 1930. Their children are: Jackson David, William Lloyd and Harold Wayne. Eugene had one son, Dean. Geneva married Arthur Girard. *–Edith Stovall.*

MCLEOD FAMILY. In the year 1857, Murdock McLeod and wife, Barbara Matthews McLeod, and their 10 children, came from Harnett County, North Carolina to Arkansas. They landed by boat at Powhatan, Christmas week.

Parents of Murdock were John McLeod and Mary, both born in Scotland and died in America. Parents of Barbara were Simon Matthews and Elizabeth. He was born in Virginia, died in North Carolina.

In 1858, Murdock, Barbara, children and slaves moved to the Coffman farm east of Black River, two miles south of Portia. The fall of 1858, they moved to the west side of the Black River and bought the Dodson farm near the site of the Old Bethel Church, which is known as the McLeod farm. Murdock died there in 1861.

James McLeod, born in 1834, married Jane Webb. They had children: Barbara, William F., Mary Ladona and John H. He and his family lived on part of the McLeod homestead. He died in 1926, living the last three years of his life back at the old home place with Hector and wife caring for him.

John Archibald, born in 1837, served in the Confederate Army and married Lucy Christian Dodson in 1866. Lucy was the widow of the his friend and army companion who died in the war. She had three children by her first marriage and one John Simon by John.

Simon, born in 1845, served in the Confederate Army and in 1868, he married Sally C. Judkins. They located three miles east of Smithville. Nine children were born to them: Walter E., Maggie, Lettie, Bessie, Joseph H., Luther H., Eva Ann and Lawrence S.

William, born in 1850, married Harrriett Guthrie, settled near New Hope Church at Denton. Their children were: Cora, who died young; Tommie; and Emmett. After the death of Harriett, William married Sarah Estes and they had Cora Emma, John Cleveland, Charles, Jimmy A. and Edna.

Alexander married Jane and settled at Imboden. They had three children: Milton, Lee and Cora. After Jane's death that year and Alexander's the next year, Hector took Milton and Lee to raise and John A. took Cora.

Hector was born in 1854, and married Margaret Davis in 1878. They had four children: Leona, Henry, Cornelius "Neil" and Nellie; plus they took care of Barbara until her death in 1888.

Barbara and Murdock had four daughters born in North Carolina: Elizabeth in 1835; Christina in 1838; Nancy in 1841; and Mary in 1848. All four daughters died in 1865, in eight weeks from the first to the last.

Two descendants of Barbara and Murdock have been to Scotland to see the McLeod Castle on the Isle of Skye. Frances Price Mills, a third great-granddaughter of Murdock and Barbara, and John David Garrett, a fourth great-grandson, both from Lowell, Arkansas, have had the opportunity to view it with their own eyes, which both enjoyed.

–JoAnn Bradford Garrett.

BURTON H. AND PEARL JANE WHITTAKER MEADOWS.

Burton H. Meadows was born in Olney, Illinois, in 1892, the son of George H. and Mary Jane Fleming Meadows. His widowed, then newly married, father moved to Sedgwick, Arkansas, Lawrence County, in 1886, with Burton's sister, Iola, and brothers, Robert and Clarence. He later married Pearl J. Whittaker in 1903.

Pearl J. Whittaker Meadows was born near Sedgwick in 1885, the daughter of John F. and Laura Bell Crow Whittaker. She married Burton H. Meadows in 1903.

Burton and Pearl Meadows on their wedding day.

The young couple settled on a subsistence type farm near Sedgwick. They reared a family of 12 children.

Roy E. Meadows married Delphia Smelser. They had two children, Phillip and Roy Jr. He worked as a counselor for the Lawrence County Welfare Office and later became an official with the Arkansas Employment Security Division.

Cecil E. Meadows married Millicent Adams. They had two children, Margaret and Evelyn. He was a Baptist minister in Arkansas and Texas.

Ruth M. Meadows married G. Anderson Hopkins. He taught in elementary one room schools in Lawrence County in early life, later taught and retired in Illinois. She had no children.

Edith C. Meadows married Avin E. Johnson and had three children, Avin Jr., Ronald and Jane Ellen. They owned and operated employment agencies in Texarkana, Little Rock and North Little Rock, Arkansas.

Lorine M. Meadows married Ira E. Meadows and had two children, Ira Jr. and Donald. She was a licensed practical nurse in St. Louis.

Esther B. Meadows married Abner B. Osterhus and had two children, Carol Ann and Carl. She was a licensed practical nurse in St. Louis. She was a twin to Lorine.

Hazel M. Meadows married Lawrence Coleman and had two children, Betty and Ruth Ann. She was a hospital dietician in St. Louis.

Harold T. Meadows died at the age of 19 years. He was the twin of Hazel.

Effie I. Meadows married Cullus D. Auman and had three children, Markham, Sharon and Linda. She was a realtor in California and Virginia.

Howard W. Meadows married Viola B. Callahan and had two children, Matthew and Mary. He was an agriculture advisor with the United States Agency for International Development in Sudan, Libya, Nigeria and Afghanistan.

Juanita P. Meadows married Dr. Robert E. Haughey and had eight children: Patricia, Robert Jr., Stephan, Bonita, Danielle, Mark, Phillip and Beth. She was a homemaker in McKeesport, Pennsylvania.

Naomi C. Meadows died at age 11 months.

This was a strong family unit. It stayed strong throughout the years. As children, they worked together, played together, went to school together and went to church together. Amenities were limited: no electricity, no indoor plumbing, no television, but life was always interesting. A party air prevailed during the evenings. The aroma of home-grown roasted peanuts, popcorn and other treats were common during winter evenings. Outside games and activities were enjoyed until dusk during the warmer months. –Viola Meadows.

CLARENCE E. AND MILLIE CHAMPION MEADOWS.

1880, the son of George Harper and Mary Jane Fleming Meadows. Clarence came to Lawrence County in 1886, with his widowed, then newly married father, and his sister, Iola, and his brothers, Burton and Robert.

Clarence married Millie Champion. She was born in Winicome, Wisconsin in 1878, to John and Alica Alyea Champion. Millie was a nurse working in Willow Springs, Missouri when she married Clarence. They settled in Sedgwick where Clarence farmed with his father and served several terms as a deputy sheriff in the county. He also ran the ferries across Black River at Black Rock and Powhatan for three or four years.

Clarence and Millie were the parents of three children of their own, one adopted son and one foster daughter.

Clarence E., Millie and Harvey Meadows.

Harvey E., son of Clarence E. and Millie Meadows, was born in Sedgwick in 1905. He married Edith Aldridge in 1924. Harvey farmed with Clarence and was a mechanic. He moved to Jonesboro, in Craighead County, Arkansas in the 1940s, working as a shop foreman for Lacey Motor Company. He and Edith later moved to California until his retirement when they moved back to Jonesboro.

Edith Aldridge Meadows was born in Sedgwick in 1960, and was the daughter of Charles and Mary Rhodes Statler Aldridge.

Harvey and Edith reared three children: Avalee Meadows Dickson, Richard Neil Meadows and Delores Meadows Bobbitt.

Avalee married James P. Dickson and had one son, James E. "Jim" Dickson. Jim is an attorney in Jonesboro and is married to the former Candace Baker. Avalee is retired from Citizens Bank of Jonesboro.

Richard Neil is retired from the Air Force and lives in Biloxi, Mississippi.

Delores married Jerry Bobbitt. Jerry is retired from farming. They reside in Jonesboro. Jerry and Delores are the parents of two children, Jerry Jr. and Susan Bobbitt Austin. Jerry Jr. is married to the former Sherry Burns and is a farmer in eastern Craighead County. Sherry is a business teacher. They are the parents of a daughter, Kelli Elizabeth, and a son, Jonathan Allen. Susan Bobbitt is married to Tony Austin. Susan is in business and Tony is a state trooper. Susan has a daughter, Susan Ashley Lewellen.

Alice Meadows married Wiley C. Graham. They are the parents of five children: Martin, Clarence, Glyndon, Janet and Lynn.

Leora Meadows died young. Harold Meadows died in 1924. Melvin Meadows (adopted) is married and lives in Tennessee where he is a minister. Lizzie Belle Fry married Lawrence Gilbery and lives in Glyndon, Minnesota. They are the parents of five daughters.

Clarence E. Meadows died at the age of 98. He and Millie are buried in Lawrence Memorial Cemetery. –Viola Meadows.

GEORGE HARPER MEADOWS

was born June 27, 1849, in Richland County, Illinois to John H. and Mary Elizabeth William Meadows. George H. moved to Sedgwick in Lawrence County in 1886. He remained there until his death February 29, 1936; rearing a large family and becoming one of the best known and substantial citizens. He was a member of the First Baptist Church in Sedgwick.

George H. was a farmer, at one time he owned all the land between the Old Military Cemetery and the railroad to the Cache River. He made a living without growing cotton, making only two cotton crops in his lifetime. He bought the Culver Home, a big house that Mr. Culver, who owned the lumber company, had built. George and his family lived there until his death.

George Meadows family.

George H. was first married to Mary Jane Fleming. Four children were born to this union. They were: Iola Meadows Bailey, Robert "Bob" Meadows, Clarence E. Meadows and Burton H. Meadows. After his first wife died, George H. married Mary Frances Rye the third day of May, 1886, in Olney, Illinois and eight children were born to this union. They were: G. A. Meadows, Flossie Meadows, Alma Meadows Worlow, Charles C. Meadows, Gertie Meadows Champion, Gail Meadows, Raymond Edward Meadows and Lula Meadows Baldridge Hughes.

George Meadows home. Standing in yard, left to right: Lula Meadows Edward Meadows, Mary F. Rye Meadows, Reverend Merideth.

George H. and Mary Frances Meadows are buried in the Old Military Cemetery at Sedgwick.

George has grandchildren and great-grandchildren living in Lawrence and Craighead Counties. –Viola Meadows.

HOWARD W. AND VIOLA C. MEADOWS FAMILY.

Howard was born June 20, 1919, on a farm near Sedgwick to Burton and Pearl Whittaker Meadows. He attended the Union (Ponder Switch) Elementary School, graduated from Walnut Ridge High school, attended Arkansas State College,

The Richard Pyburn Family. Left to right: Richard, Andrew, Ariana, Mary Meadows Pyburn.

Jonesboro for two years, served over three years in the Army Air Force, received an agriculture degree from the University of Arkansas and taught veterans on-the-farm agriculture in Lawrence County from 1949 to 1957.

Viola was born September 26, 1925, on a farm at Duvall to Homer and Lillie Robins Callahan. She attended Duvall, Lauratown, Arbor Grove and Hoxie schools and graduated from Clover Bend High School. She received Bachelor of Science and Master of Science Degrees in Home Economics from the University of Arkansas. She has taught in Black Rock, Hoxie and Clover Bend High Schools. She was a Fulbright Exchange Teacher to India and a teacher and administrator for the American School in Japan, Tokyo.

Howard and Viola were married at Walnut Ridge in 1957. After a brief assignment with the

Howard Meadows, Mary Meadows, standing, Viola Meadows, seated Matthew on floor.

United States Department of Agriculture in Osceola, Arkansas, they accepted a position with the United States Operations Mission and departed for Khartoum, Sudan, in January, 1959, where Howard served as an agriculture advisor to the Sudanese government in remote southern Sudan. They lived in this tropical rain forest for over two years.

They were next assigned to Libya and lived the next two years in a Sahara Desert oasis, Sebha, in Fezzan Province, about 500 miles south of Tripoli. From there they went to Nigeria for four years, two years in a village named Gombe and two years in the northern capitol of Kano.

Their final foreign assignment was Kabul, Afghanistan. They spent over six years in this spectacular and fascinating country. Their children attended school there and became attached to the area. The family retired to a farm near Imboden, Arkansas in 1974.

Viola and Howard have two children: Matthew Marion and Mary Jane. Matthew was born in Osceola, Arkansas and accompanied his parents to Sudan at the age of six months. Viola taught him at home during the outpost assignments, he attended a British established school in Nigeria, an American school in Kabul, finished high school in Imboden and acquired

a BA degree and an Electrical Engineering degree from the University of Arkansas. He earned an MBA degree in Dallas.

Mary was born in the Belgian Congo. This was the nearest place with reasonably adequate medical facilities during our Sudan assignment. Her schooling paralleled that of Matthew and she received a Journalism degree from the University of Arkansas.

Matthew lives in Dallas, Texas, with his wife, Stephanie, daughter of Ross and Priscilla Morris of Dallas. Mary lives in San Antonio, Texas with her husband, Richard, and their two children: Ariana and Andrew. Richard's parents are Archie and Lillian Pyburn, Keansburg, New Jersey. –Viola Meadows.

BILLY GERALD MEEKS FAMILY. Billy Gerald "Carrot" Meeks, son of Cecil Curtis Meeks and Johnie Caldonia Woodson Meeks, was born in Black Rock, Arkansas, on October 11, 1943. He graduated from Black Rock High School in 1961. He married on August 20, 1966, to Lyndell Janette "Tooter" Ethridge, daughter of Pat and Iva Ethridge, born in Corning, Arkansas, December 28, 1948. She attended school at Swifton, Arkansas, and later went to ASU and Southern Baptist. Billy Gerald and his brother, Winston, contracted and built houses for a number of years. Then Paul Propst took him flying and he was hooked, selling his home and five acres of land that was completely paid for. He began taking 150 flying lessons from Frank Wilson of Walnut Ridge, Arkansas, in a Cessna airplane. After completion, Tooter gave up her job as a licensed practical nurse working at Lawrence County Family Clinic with Dr. Rob Lowery, and they moved to Pennsylvania so he could attend a special flying school, taking 50 hours of flying at 100 dollars an hour.

Billy and Britt Meeks working a helicoper business

His first job was in South Bay, Florida, in 1979, and in 1980-1981, he was flying in Plainsville, Wisconsin, for Rebbas Flying Service. He started flying in Arkansas for Gene Grant, just out of Jonesboro. He bought a wrecked helicopter from Illinois in 1980, and for three yeas, kept it in the old red barn down by Black River, owned by his sister, Faye, and her husband, Eldon Shannon, working on it every spare minute. He started his own business in the spring of 1983, as Southern Helicopters with a Bell 47 D-1 Helicopter. He now has two setups one in Black Rock and one in Delaplaine. He buys and sells helicopter parts and works for Agricultural Business spraying rice, beans, wheat pasture, pollinate corn, sprays for weevil and then goes out of state spraying alfalfa. Tooter is the secretary, bookkeeper and go-fer for the business. Two children: Bobby Glen Foster, born May 3, 1965, at Little Rock, Arkansas; and Gerald Burton "Britt" Meeks, born at Newport. Britt has helped his mom and dad, learning about the helicopter business since he was 14 years old. He helps now by driving the truck with a nurse-rig and a helicopter landing pad on top. Bobby lives in Delapaine and Carrot, Tooter and Britt live at Black Rock, Arkansas.

BOYD WINSTON MEEKS FAMILY. Boyd Winston "Pedro" Meeks, son of Cecil Curtis Meeks and Johnie Caldonia Woodson Meeks, was born September 4, 1941, at Black Rock. He graduated from Black Rock High School in 1960, married

Family of Boyd Winston "Pedro" Meeks.

December 15, 1962, to Gaynell Elaine Bragg, born September 10, 1944, at Ravenden, Arkansas. Pedro and Gaynell Elaine had three children.

1. David Warren Meeks, born November 15, 1963.

2. Susan Michelle Meeks, born November 29, 1966, married Johnnie Lee Snyder on May 1, 1986. They have three children: Amber Nycole Snyder, born June 13, 1985; Johnnie Lee Snyder Jr., born January 1, 1989; and Ashley Dawn Snyder, born February 1, 1991.

3. Elaine Janine Meeks, born March 10, 1969, who married Rocky Warren Gann and they have two children: Nathan Lee Gann, born October 7, 1988; and Ryan Warren Gann, born February 26, 1991.

Pedro and Gaynell raised their family in and still reside in Ravenden, Arkansas.

CHARLES DAVID "RUNT" MEEKS, son of Cecil Curtis Meeks and Johnie Caldonia Woodson Meeks, was born April 8, 1929. Runt was born and raised in Lawrence County. At this time in history, Herbert Hoover was inaugurated as the 31st president of the United States and gasoline was only 10 cents a gallon. Runt served his county in the United States Navy for four years, but spent most of his life in Black Rock. He married on August 29, 1963, to Della Jean Jones, daughter of Violet and Charles Goad, born in Black Rock, May 23, 1947. Runt and Della have three children.

The family of Runt Meeks.

1. Charles David Meeks Jr., born February 26, 1964, married Rhonda McKinley of Atkins, Arkansas on June 24, 1995, and they have four children: Michael Wayne Meeks, born June 9, 1990; Bryan David Meeks, born October 25, 1992; Crystal Nichole Meeks, born March 29, 1995; and heather Danielle Meeks, born January 6, 1998. Charles Jr. works in Russellville and he and his family live in Atkins where his wife, Rhonda, works as a CNA for a nursing home.

2. Kenneth Gene Meeks, born January 11, 1967, served four years in the United States Navy and now lives at Black Rock. He works for Hytrol in Jonesboro, Arkansas.

3. Gary William Meeks, born February 17, 1973, married Candi Cobble of Alicia, Arkansas on August 20, 1993, and together they have one child, Whitney Mischerie Meeks, born January 26, 1995. Gary and his family live at

Smithville and he works in Jonesboro for Hytrol. Candi is attending Black River Technical College at Pocahontas to become an LPN.

Charles David "Runt" Meeks died July 16, 1998, of lung cancer and is buried in Oak Forest Cemetery.

Della Jean Jones Meeks still lives in Black Rock.

CURTIS WAYNE MEEKS FAMILY.

Curtis Wayne Meeks, son of Curtis Cecil Meeks and Johnie Caldonia Woodson Meeks, was born at Black Rock in Lawrence County April 23, 1946. Curtis is known to everyone as Moe Meeks, getting this nickname when he was a young lad. He graduated from Black Rock High School in 1965, receiving a basketball scholarship in his senior year to Southern Baptist College. He married Syrena Butts in June of 1971, and they had one daughter, Sharice Alyn Meeks, born January 13, 1970. She was married June 2, 1991, to Stephen Keith Beavers, born April 29, 1969, and they have one son, Zachary Stephen Beavers, born December 13, 1992, and one daughter, Alexandra Shea Beavers, born March 29, 1996. Sharice has one half brother named Scott Holmes. She and her family live in Higden, Arkansas, down by Greers Ferry. Moe has operated his own backhoe business for the past 20 odd years and lives at Black Rock, Arkansas.

The Sharice Meeks Beavers family.

FRANKIE WILBORN MEEKS FAMILY.

Frankie Wilborn Meeks, son of Cecil Curtis Meeks and Johnie Caldonia Woodson Meeks, was born September 8, 1935. At the age of 12 he was riding to Jonesboro in an A Model car at the high speed of 20 miles an hour, helping Tommy Brower paint houses, worked at Woosley's Saw Mill in 1949, getting paid 25 cents an hour. He began his career in construction for Ben Hogan in 1951. Frankie met the love of his life, Betty Earlene Dail in 1953, while engaged in a snowball fight at Black Rock School, was married December 24, 1953. Betty is the daughter of Earl and Leona Holland Dail of Ravenden, Arkansas. Frankie and Betty have three children.

1. Cheryl Dawn Meeks, born April 13, 1956, married Darrell Davis, and had one daughter, Jennifer Lea Davis, born May 31, 1972. She is a certified nurse's assistant and works at retirement homes; she lives in Walnut Ridge. Cheryl married the second time July 6, 1974, to Michael Chastain, son of Robert and Grace Chastain. She has one daughter, Misti Dawn Chastain, born September 14, 1976, who graduated from school and enlisted in the Army. She married on August 28, 1997, to Eric Seyl, son of Roger and Diane Seyl; they have two sons: Michael Tristan, born December 14, 1996, and Dustan Rodger, born April 23, 1998. Misti and Eric are both stationed in Hawaii. She is an M.P. and attends college. Cheryl Dawn Chastain has been employed at S-B Power Tool Company for 20 years, as a setup in the molding department. Michael works for Morgan Buildings as a dispatcher and management assistant. They live in Black Rock.

2. Frankey Wilborn Meeks Jr., born March 1, 1960, married May 13, 1983, to Gracie Snyder, daughter of Junior and Vernie Snyder; has two children: Derek Lee, born June 12, 1987, and Ariel Chantail, born February 8, 1991. Frankey has

Frankie Wilborn Meeks family.

been employed at S-B Power Tool Company for 20 years as a service and export group leader. He is a master scuba diver and dive master and will be a scuba instructor. Gracie is a licensed cosmetologist and electrologist; she owns and operates her business by their home in Black Rock.

3. Jimmy David Meeks, born January 30, 1963, joined the National Guard after high school; married March 27, 1986, to Robin Ivy, daughter of Jess and Bonnie Ivy. They have five daughters: Erica Haley, born September 29, 1982; Bridgett Nicole, born February 22, 1987; Holly Shea, born December 26, 1988; and twins Sheena Rena and Shawn Larae, born June 30, 1990. Jimmy is employed at Waterloo Industry at Pocahontas as a setup and works on automobiles at home in his shop. Jimmy and Robin took their daughters and ran to the hills of Williford to live. Frankie Wilborn Meeks retired from Atlas Construction of Jonesboro as a heavy equipment operator in 1998. Frank and Betty live in Black Rock, Arkansas.

MEEKS FAMILY.

Herschel Lamon Meeks son of Cecil Curtis Meeks and Johnie Caldonia (Woodson) Meeks was born December 13, 1931 in Black Rock. He married on October 1, 1960, Audrey Lavanna Brandon. She was born December 16, 1944 to Audrey Brandon and Lucy (Pickney) Brandon. Herschel worked in construction until 1980, then went to work at the Skil Corporation in Walnut Ridge, where he is presently employed. Herschel and Audrey have six children.

1. Tresa Lea Meeks was born on May 6, 1961. She married January 9, 1982 to Gary Lynn Clark. He was born on February 6, 1954. They have two children: Gary Lynn Clark II, born December 15, 1985 and Joshua Alan Clark born July 7, 1988. Tresa is a school teacher at Batesville Kindergarten Center. Gary works in Aerial Crop Dusting for AAC Flying Services.

2. Herschel James Meeks born December 20, 1962. He married July 17, 1982, to Robyn Arlene Tyler who was born on July 7, 1965. They have four children; Herschel Curtis Meeks Born on August 28, 1983, Rusty James Meeks born August 28, 1985, Bryan Edward Meeks born February 23, 1987 and Lara Arlene Meeks born March 8, 1989. Herschel works in aerial crop dusting for AAC Flying Service.

3. Ricky Lamon Meeks born May 26, 1964. He married July 7, 1984 to Debra Marie Cooper, who was born February 24, 1966. They have three children; Ricky Lamon Meeks Jr. born 2, 1985, Dustin Allen Meeks born May 19, 1987 and Blake Evan Meeks born February 18, 1989. Rick is a Aerial Crop dusting pilot for AAC Flying Service.

4. Lisa Lavanna Meeks born April 9, 1966. She married on December 21, 1985 to Barry Bryan Bryant who was born on August 21, 1964. They have three children; Elizabeth Ann Bryant born on June 1, 1988 and a set of twins, Victoria Lea Bryant and Stephanie Bryant born on February

Frankie Wilborn Meeks family.

18, 1990. Lisa is a Service Team Representative for the Schneider National in West Memphis, Arkansas. Barry is an estimator for Mercury Printing in Memphis, Tennessee.

5. Rita Jean Meeks born November 16, 1976. She married July 20, 1996 ot Norman (Brad) Bradley Dickson born May 2, 1974. Rita is a student at Arkansas State University seeking a degree in Early Childhood/Elementary Education. Brad is a Social Service Director at Woodbrair Nursing Home Harrisburg, Arkansas.

6. Donna Darlene Meeks born on March 8, 1980. Married December 17, 1997 to Johnathan (John) Wayne Augustine born January 16, 1976. John is a Roof Contractor with B&J Roofing in Hoxie Arkansas.

Herschel Lamon Meeks has one daughter from a previous marriage, Betsey Lynn Meeks born May 20, 1957 in St. Louis, Missouri. Betsey is married to Louie Paul Phillips and they have one daughter, Shanna Phillips.

Herschel and Audrey reside in Black Rock, Arkansas.

JIMMY DEAN MEEKS FAMILY.

Jimmy Dean Meeks, son of Curtis Cecil Meeks and Johnie Caldonia Woodson Meeks, was born December 28, 1947, in Lawrence County. He graduated from Black Rock High School in 1968. Jim played basketball and his team won the county and district tournament, but they were defeated in the regional tournament. He went to work at Hogan's Rock Crusher in 1969, and retired from there in 1997. He married on November 4, 1972, to Ada Marie McDowell, born March 15, 1949. They have two daughters.

The Jim Meeks family.

1. Carla Michelle Meeks, born February 28, 1982, married Jonathan Morris Littlejohn, born December 20, 1977, son of Brenda and Larry Ashley of Bono. Carla and Jonathan have one son, Dylan Eugene Littlejohn, born October 11, 1997, and are expecting another son in July of 1999, whom they are going to name Caleb Blaze Littlejohn.

2. Jessica Nichole Meeks, born August 20, 1987.

Jim and family live at Black Rock.

JOHNIE CALDONIA WOODSON MEEKS FAMILY.

Johnie Caldonia Woodson, daughter of John Riley Woodson and Minnie Bell Horton Woodson, was born January 23, 1910, at Black Rock. Her daddy deciding to make her into a little tomboy, built a box and nailed it on his cultivator and took her with him in the fields as he was making a couple of cotton crops at Portia. By the age of three, she could drive a team of horses around the farm. In 1914, World War I broke out and her half brothers, Percy and Henry, had to go serve their country so they sold all of their goods and moved to Marvel, Arkansas, to be close to them.

Cecil and Johnie Meeks.

They lived at Gum Stump when her daddy died at the age of 65. They moved back to Black Rock and lived on their Uncle Fred's place. She went to school and after getting promoted to the third grade, she and her sister, Hazel, got a pair of white shoes that laced up almost to the knees and wore them to school and everyone laughed at them so she threw her pain away and quit. Hazel said she was going to fight to go to school and she did and finished the eighth grade. At nine years of age, Johnie was plowing and busting middles in the cotton fields. When she was 13 she was walking down the railroad tracks and fell in love at first sight with Cecil Curtis Meeks and married him six months later on November 5, 1924.

Cecil was a native of Black Rock, born October 1, 1902, son of Frank Meeks and Addie George Meeks, who was married November 16, 1901, in Lawrence County. Frank was 22 years of age and Addie was 17 years old. Cecil spent 20 years working at the button factory as a button maker and was getting paid 15 dollars a week in 1934. The factory completely shut down in 1954, and he worked as a custodian for the Black Rock Public School, retiring in 1973. Johnie and Cecil reared 10 children.

1. John Riley Meeks, who only lived one day.
2. Otho Curtis Meeks.
3. Charles David Meeks.
4. Herschel Lamon Meeks.
5. Melba Faye Shannon.
6. Frankie Wilborn Meeks.
7. Shirley Charlotte Williams.
8. Boyd Winston Meeks.
9. Billy Gerald Meeks.
10. Curtis Wayne Meeks.
11. Jimmy Dean Meeks.

Cecil Curtis Meeks died March 20, 1975, of cancer. Cecil, Johnie, and sons are buried at OakForest Cemetery in Black Rock. Johnie was a member of The Life Pentecostal Church and lived at Black Rock until her death in early 2000.

OTHO CURTIS MEEKS FAMILY. Otho Curtis Meeks, son of Johnie C. Woodson Meeks and Cecil Curtis Meeks, was born December 28, 1926, at

Otho "Mick" Meeks with his brothers and sisters. First row: Jimmy Dean Meeks, Frank Wilburn Meeks, Shirley C. Williams, Melba Faye Shannon and Otho C. Meeks. Second row: Bill G. Meeks, Boyd Winston Meeks, Curtis Wayne Meeks, Herschel L. Meeks and Charles D. Meeks.

Black Rock, Arkansas, and died September 16, 1977. He served his country in the United States Army, Navy and the Merchant Marines, was married twice and leaves no children. His widow, Ozella Meeks, lives in Conway, Arkansas. –*Ozella Meeks.*

HENRY SCOTT MILLER FAMILY. Horatio Miller came to Arkansas, 1822-1823. His son, Joseph Edward Miller, was born in Crittendon County, Arkansas, and died 1898. He was the father of Henry Scott Miller, who married Sarah Hill, the daughter of John Hill and Louisa Brown. Research has determined that Louisa Brown was a direct descendant of Pocahontas. Children of Henry Scott Miller were:

1. Etta Sparks. Her children were Lois Shaver, Claude and Lela Arnold.
2. James. His children were Clara Belle Kellow, who had one daughter, Linda. She and her daughter still live in Walnut Ridge, Arkansas.
3. Leonard (now deceased) had son Kenneth and daughter, Audine.
4. Louise. Her children are daughters Jane, Jean and Jim Hacker who live in Portia, Arkansas.
5. John, who had no children, died in his teens.
6. Mollie had one daughter, Eulois Kendall.
7. Belle has three sons: Ewin, Eugene and Orus McKnight.
8. William Scott. His children were daughters, Wilma and Lois (died soon after birth).
9. Thelma Willeen married to Aubrey J. Hough, had two sons: Aubrey J. Hough Jr. (lives in Little Rock, physician at University of Arkansas Medical Center) and William Arthur, attorney, chief of legal division at Savannah, Georgia Office of Corps of Engineers. Willeen remarried after Mr. Hough's death, to Charles F. Adams.

The Henry Scott Miller Family.

10. William Scott Miller Jr., attorney, married Imogene Puckett and had two sons: Gary Miller, attorney, Houston, Texas and Alan Miller, attorney, Dallas, Texas.

Sarah Miller died when William Scott was about two years old and Henry Scott remarried. His second wife was Josephine Foley. Their children were:

1. Charles David, whose children were: Verna, Marie, Wayne, Charles David Jr. and Sybil. Charles David and Charles David Jr. are deceased.
2. Christina had two daughters: Nellie and Ruthel.
3. Frederick had one son, William. He lives in Little Rock, Arkansas.
4. Robert, who had daughters Roberta, Gladys, Joan, Judy and son, Danny.
5. Luther had no children. His widow lives at Portia, Arkansas.
6. Delcie had one son who died in infancy.
7. Edith had one son, James Marvin Kennedy, who lives in Walnut Ridge, Arkansas.
8. Walter, no children, died in his early 20s.

All of the children of this union of Henry Scott and Josephine Foley are now deceased. Several children were born to this union who did not survive.

William Scott Miller was tax assessor in Lawrence County with an office on the second floor of the Powhatan Courthouse in the 1930s. – *Willene Adams.*

JOSEPH EDWARD MILLER was born April 16, 1832, died November 22, 1898, and served in the Confederate Army. He married Mary Webb, born July 27, 1837, died August 24, 1915, on January 4, 1853, in Lawrence County. She is the daughter of Jessie Webb and Miss Jones. Both are buried in the Townsend Cemetery.

The Miller family lived between Smithville and Townsend Cemetery near a natural spring and an old oak tree. (Last time I was there the spring had been disturbed due to road construction.) There are still old timbers and a stone fireplace there that belong (I have been told) to the Millers.

My great-grandmother, Amanda Miller Willett, said she remembered helping Alec, her brother, keep the deer out of the garden. Amanda's spinning wheel is on display in the Powhatan Courthouse, donated by Vada Milligan Bowers.

Per family tradition, when Joseph came home from the Civil War no one knew who he was when he came walking up the road, until the family dog recognized his owner. According to war records, Joseph was in the hospital at Monroe, Louisiana in 1863. He was a private in Company D, 38th Arkansas Infantry, Shaver's Regiment under Captain Baber.

There is a Miller family Bible out there somewhere. If you know of it, please contact me. I would love a copy of the family information.

The children of Joseph and Mary are:

Sarah Elizabeth "Betty", born 1853, married Jesse Goff.

Amanda Melissa, 1855-1945, married Henry David Willett of Kentucky. They are buried in the Townsend Cemetery.

William Robert, 1857-1922, married Pocahontas "Polka" Hill, second Addie Burris.

Henry Scott, 1859-1942, married Sarah B. "Puss" Hill, second Josie Foley.

James Alexander "Alec", born 1861, married Millie Davis, second Rena Helms.

Mary Jane, born 1866.

Henry David Willett and Amanda Melissa Miller Willett.

Joseph Edward "Tobe", 1868-1898, married Melinda Petty.

Alabama "Belle", born 1870, married John Crawford.

Lily Minerva Josephine, 1870-1950, married Richard Bellamy, second W. G. Lewsaw.

Blanchie LaVella "Ella", born 1872, married Whit Justus.

John H., born 1880.

Joseph's parents are Horatio S. Miller, 1800-1861, Elizabeth "Betty" ???? (Wright? per family tradition). Their children were:

William L, 1824-1853.

Milton, 1830-1858.

Joseph (above).

Thomas M., 1836-1863, during Civil War.

Amanda "Eliza", 1838-1890, married Drewry Richardson.

My line comes down through Horatio, Joseph, Amanda Melissa, who married Henry Willett, their daughter Virginia "Ginnie" Victoria, who married Ernest Asro Milligan (they are buried in Lebanon Cemetery, Sharp County), their daughter, my mother, Rosetta, who married Coy M. King. Their children: Sherry Stolp and Karen Brown.
–*Karen Brown.*

ROBERT FRANKLIN MITCHELL, a direct descendant of John Mitchell, who was a lowland Scot of Stirlingshire, Scotland, migrated to Chester County, Pennsylvania, in 1687.

Robert Franklin "Frank", was born 1848, in Ashmore, Coles County, Illinois, and died in 1910, in Walnut Ridge, Arkansas, married Louisa Ann Hensley in 1870, in Coles County, Ashmore, Illinois. Robert Franklin and Louisa Hensley Mitchell moved from Coles County, Illinois to Old Walnut Ridge, Arkansas, in 1882.

Frank Mitchell's occupation was bookkeeper. His clients included the T. J. Sharum Enterprise and other businesses of the community.

Frank's wife, Louisa, born 1847, in DeMossville, Pendleton County, Kentucky, died in Walnut Ridge, in 1887. Louisa Hensley's family history is documented and may be found in the LDS center in Salt Lake City, Utah. She had many proven English ancestors, as well as French Huguenot (French Protestant), whose pedigree has been thoroughly researched and recorded. Louisa's first Huguenot ancestor who migrated to Virginia Colony was Gabriel Maupin, arriving with his family at Yorktown in 1700, eventually settling in Williamsburg, Virginia, where he died in 1720.

Louisa's patriot ancestors were Daniel Mullins of the French and Indian War and Gabriel Mullins and Joel Berry in the Revolutionary War.

R. F. or Frank and Louisa Mitchell were the parents of: Nettie, born 1871; Mabel, 1873-1899; Millie Jane, 1876-1947; Sarah Margaret "Maggie", 1879-1945; Phobe Anne, 1881-1921; and Myrtle Mitchell, 1883-1919. All the children except Myrtle were born in Ashmore, Coles County, Illinois. –Lester Robinson.

MIZE FAMILY. My grandfather, William Cimsey Mize, was born in Alabama, July 4, 1875, to L. Singleton and Henrietta Justus Mize. He was the second son of four sons and one daughter born in Alabama. One additional son and daughter who lived were born at Lynn, Arkansas, Lawrence County. Two additional children died and are buried at Milligan Camp Grounds Cemetery.

Left to right: Charles Polston, John Pelenley, Fred Polston, Aaron Polston; note size of logs.

James Singleton Mize, August 23, 1883, Alabama-November 11, 1910, Lynn, Arkansas, buried Milligan Campground Cemetery, Lawrence County.

Mize Sawmill where L. Singleton and sons worked.

Logging operation where William C. Mize worked.

He moved to Lawrence County, Arkansas, with the rest of his family sometime after December 15, 1882, when L. Singleton applied for patented land at Huntsville, Alabama, per authority, May 20, 1862. (I have the patent description.)

In the Lawrence County, Arkansas, 1900 census he is listed with his wife, Estella Birmingham and brother, George Herbert mize, age 13. My grandfather and grandmother were married February 14, 1889.

In the late 1800s, and early 1900s, timber was much in demand so L. Singleton and his sons, Will, Riley, Singleton and Herbert, all worked at Mize's sawmill or in the logging portion of their business. Grandfather's brother-in-law also worked at the mill, and possibly other family members.

My father, William Carroll Mize Sr., was born October 16, 1901, at Driftwood/Lynn, Arkansas, as were his sisters, Verna and Olive. Dad told me many stories about the logging and sawmill business. He said his dad had numerous yokes of oxen which they used in their logging operation and around the sawmill. He said his dad was considered a "bullmaster" and had a very soft voice and almost never raised his voice because his long bull-whip could almost talk with the popper on the end.

My grandfather and grandmother were hard workers like most of the people in that area. They had bought a farm and had built up a large amount of oxen, mules, horses, wagons, cattle and other farm items. Dad remembers when trees had a diameter so large that a crosscut saw had to be rotated around to cut the tree down. He also said men would sometimes have to stand in flat bottom boats fastened to the trees to cut the trees in sloughs.

Estella Birmingham Mize died December 18, 1915, and is buried in Union Cemetery with other Birminghams. Will Mize died February 22, 1919, and is buried in Dry-Creek/Pleasant Hills Cemetery. He has a Woodmen of the World headstone. –William C. Mize, Jr.

WILLIAM CROCKETT MIZE AND IRMA RUTH MITCHELL. William Crockett Mize and Irma Ruth Mitchell were married February 21, 1924, at Powhatan, Arkansas. Both were born in Powhatan. W. C. Mize was born October 22, 1902, and died July 7, 1980. Ruth Mitchell was born October 13, 1905, and died October 21, 1992.

W. C. and Ruth Mize, around the 1940s.

Seven children were born to them: Nona Ruth Mize, born July 20, 1951, died January 10, 1969; Norma Jean Mize Justus, born September 12, 1943, living in Little Rock, Arkansas; W. C., born August 24, 1938, died October 17, 1939; Bobby Dean Mize, born July 5, 1932, living in Rolla, Missouri; Earl Dent Mize, born April 22, 1930, died May 3, 1985; Glenda Mae Mize Glenn, born March 25, 1926, living in Lynn, Arkansas; and Wanda Alice Mize Glenn, born May 30, 1924, living in Plant City, Florida.

William Crockett was the son of Joe Shelb Mize, born November 6, 1865, and a sheriff of Lawrence County, Arkansas. Joe Shelb's father was Christopher Newton Mize, born October 20, 1838, in Habersham County, Georgia. Christopher's father was Howell Mize, born 1801, in Georgia. Howell Mize's father was Zachariah Mize, born 1751-1775, in Virginia.

William Crockett's mother was Alice Kirkpatrick, born July 25, 1881. Her father was Joseph Francis Kirkpatrick, born in 1837, or 1839, in Kentucky.

Irma Ruth Mitchell's father was Willis Laughette Mitchell, born April 30, 1864. Willis' father was William Park Mitchell, born December 25, 1836, in North Carolina. He was a deputy sheriff in Lawrence County, Arkansas. William Park's father was William Mitchell, born 1807, in North Carolina and married Sarah Ross there.

Irma Ruth's mother was Alice Sharp. Alice was born October 17, 1874, in Lawrence County, Arkansas. Her father was John James Sharp II, born 1846, in Lawrence County, Arkansas. John James II was the son of John James Sharp I, born in 1816, in Lawrence County, Arkansas, and died in the Mexican War in 1845. John James I was the son of Solomon Sharp. Solomon was born about 1792. He was in Lawrence County by 1823. He and his wife, Amy Sharp, had several slaves. Solomon died in 1839, in Lawrence County, Arkansas. –Norma Mize Justus.

BEN H. MOODY FAMILY. Native to Lawrence County, Ben and Agla Moody spent their lifetime there except for one brief period of a few years they spent in California in the late 1920s.

Ben Moody was born in 1889, named after President Benjamin Harrison. He was a small farmer and sharecropper who raised cattle and tilled the soil. His brother, A. J. "Andrew" Moody, farmed on a larger scale (mostly cattle) in "the hills" near Jesup and Strawberry.

Mary Agla Jones Moody was born in 1897, and died in 1977. She was the daughter of Taylor Jones and Mary Francis Jones. Taylor Jones was a fisherman by trade. Ben and Agla Moody were married December 16, 1916. He was 27 and she was 19 years of age. After the Ben Moodys returned from California, where they lived briefly, they purchased a home in the Clover Bend area when the Federal Government made it possible for persons with limited resources to purchase a house. Ben Moody purchased a 40 acre tract when it was built and later purchased one half of another adjoining

Ben and Mary Moody.

unit where he farmed until his death. Ben Moody died in March, 1954, of leukemia.

Mary Agla Moody was an active housewife who helped others, working for the Clover Bend schools to prepare meals. She did all the housework and often worked in the fields.

To this couple was born one son, Halbert Jones Moody, on May 17, 1920. Hal Moody attended grade schools at Lauratown, Clover Bend and rode the bus to Hoxie High School, where he graduated in 1937.

In 1939, he entered the University of Arkansas at Fayetteville and received a degree, BSBA. He served in the Navy during World War II until becoming inactive in 1946. He served as State Representative from Lawrence County in the legislature from 1947 through 1950. He was called back in 1950, during the Korean War until 1952. After that he formed the Moody Equipment and Supply Company in Little Rock, which he owned for approximately 30 years. During this time, he served as chief clerk of the House of Representatives for 12 years, was assistant secretary and secretary of the Senate from 1973 to 1994. He retired in 1995, and lives in Little Rock.

He married the former Patsy Camp from Hoxie in 1950, and they have four sons and nine grandchildren. Patsy's parents were Robert and Rubye Grissom Camp and one sister, Bobbie Carolyn, all of Hoxie, and grandparents Ed and Artie Camp and Jesse and Florence Grissom from Strangers Home and Lauratown Communities. –Hal Moody.

The Patricia C. and Hal J. Moody Family, Sept. , 1998.

MOORE-FOLLOWWILL. Robert Dent Moore Sr. and Hazel Followwill were married on April 10, 1917, in Walnut Ridge, Arkansas by Reverend Currie at the Presbyterian Church.

Robert was born at Imboden, Arkansas on July 7, 1894, the son of Reverend A. J. Moore, a Methodist Circuit Rider and Georgia Ann Dent Moore, both native Lawrence Countians. He died on September 15, 1967, in Star City, Arkansas and was buried at the Dent Cemetery at Annieville, Arkansas.

The Robert D. Moore family: Front left to right: Alyce Marie "Toots" Binzer, Hazel Moore, age 83; and Robert D. "Bud" Moore, Jr. Back left to right: Juanita Belle "Nita" Allen, Helen Lucille "Tynse" Bassett; Selma Jeannie Smith; and Jimmye Carol Long

Hazel was born at Walnut Ridge, Arkansas on December 3, 1896, to James Walter Followwill from Indiana and Lucy Pearson Rhea Followwhill from Walnut Ridge. She died on July 23, 1988, at Walnut Ridge and was buried at Lawrence Memorial Cemetery.

This union produced six children, of whom five are still living:

1. Juanita Belle, born April 12, 1918, in Wilson, Arkansas, married Thomas Brasfield Allen Sr. from Mississippi in 1938, had two sons: John Marvin, born 1940, and Thomas Brasfield Jr., born 1943. Thomas Brasfield Sr. died in 1964, and is buried at Lawrence Memorial Cemetery.

2. Helen Lucille, born October 24, 1919, in Wilson, married Jerry Bassett from Walnut Ridge on August 11, 1949, had three sons: Jerry Dudley, born 1950, Richard Barry, born 1952, and William Michael, born 1956.

3. Robert Dent Jr., born March 7, 1924, in Wilson, married Nancy Blake Ponder from Walnut Ridge, August 5, 1949, had three children: Carol, born 1950, Jane, born 1955, and Gordon Ponder, born 1959. Robert Jr. died July 28, 1998, and Nancy Ponder Moore died August 9, 1959. They are buried at Lawrence Memorial Cemetery.

4. Alyce Marie, born October 15, 1928, in Blytheville, Arkansas, married Robert Dean Binzer from Indiana on December 12, 1953, had three children: James Robert, born 1957, Charles Moore, born 1964, and Martha Joyce, born 1965.

5. Jimmye Carolyn, born November 22, 1931, in Hoxie, Arkansas, married William Melvin Long Sr. from Louisiana on August 6, 1960, had three children: Carolyn Marie, born 1962, Sara Kathryn, born 1966, and William Melvin Jr., born 1967.

6. Selma Jeanne, born December 12, 1940, at Walnut Ridge, married Edgar Harrison Smith from Minturn on February 14, 1959, had three sons: John David, born 1959, Robert Scott, born 1961, and Jeffrey Allen, born 1963.

Four of the surviving children live in Lawrence County and Alyce Marie Binzer and her family live in Madison, Indiana.

Twenty-eight great-grandchildren and three great-great-grandchildren are also descendants of this union, 11 of whom reside in Lawrence County. –Jeannie Smith.

JAMES HENRY MOORE, born in 1857, in Missouri, and his wife, Naomi Priscilla Pulliam, born 1867, in Missouri, came to Lawrence County around 1890. Their children were: Marvin, who died at age six in Missouri; Emma, born in Missouri in 1887; Clara; Bessie; and Willie Myrtle, born in Walnut Ridge, May 1, 1893.

Emma married Arthur Ponder in 1906. Their children were: Ramona (Mrs. Chalmers Clark); Andrew married Louise Rainwater; Clara married Hatley Ring. Their children were: Jeanette (Mrs. Ben Bush) and Catherine (Mrs. Sonny Doan).

Myrtle married Oscar Edmondson. Their children were: Preston Moore, born June 22, 1914; Emma Regina, October 10, 1917; and John Henry. Preston married Opal Irvin August 22, 1935. Their children were: Billy Mack and Sandra Mae. –Jean Edmonson.

ROBERT AND MARGARET MOORE.

Robert Calvin Moore, better known as Bob, was the sixth child of William Edward and Martha Moore. Born December 4, 1866, he lived most of his life in the Denton area of Lawrence County.

He married Margaret Jane Matthews on May 21, 1893, at the New Hope Baptist Church. Her father was Wiley J. Matthews and her mother was Sarah Webb, both natives of Tennessee. She was born in Arkansas on February 22, 1872.

The couple had eight children, four girls and four boys. Benjamin Beecher was born in 1894, and married Claire Buckley. Sally May was born in 1895. Everett Matthews was born in 1897, and married Loma Smith. Coye Irene was born in 1903, and Henry Lawrence was born in 1904. Vera Maude was born in 1907, and married Paul Winfield Cameron. Vena Blanche was born in 1910, and died as a small child. Alva Truman was born in 1915, and married Bonnie Gibson.

Bob Moore farmed and raised livestock, but the off season found him doing carpentry work both for himself and the neighbors. He also worked at the C. M. Sullivan Mercantile Store at Denton.

The couple was active for all their lives in the New Hope Church, where both their parents had attended, and Bob served as a deacon for many years.

Mrs. Moore, who died in 1946, was remembered in Mrs. D. J. Webb's "Denton" column in *The Times Dispatch.* She wrote, "Mrs.

Robert Calvin and Margaret Jane Matthews Moore.

Moore, better known as Aunt Mag by the younger generation, had lived a beautiful life. In her younger days when any of her neighbors were sick, she was by their bedside doing what she could for them. Her life was one that inspires all to try harder to live a better life."

When Mr. Moore died in 1951, Mrs. Webb wrote, "He had spent most of his life in this home and he had been a Christian for 61 years. He was one of the most honest, upright men I have ever known. He stood for what he felt was right, even if he had to stand alone." James L. Bland, publisher of *The Times Dispatch,* wrote in his "Frankly Speaking" column, "It was said of him that he was a man without fault, reverent, truthful and helpful."

Robert Calvin and Margaret Jane Moore were laid to rest at the New Hope Cemetery, just down the road from the church which had been a central part of their lives. –Tom Moore.

ROBERT WALKER MOORE, 1883-1959, was born in the Hopewell Community of Lawrence County. His grandparents were Robert W. Moore and Hannah Morris Darter. His parents were Moses Morris Moore and Sarah Smith. They had three children: Robert Walker, Kate and Ida, who died in her teens. Kate married Wave Verkler, Robert W. was married to Sudye Billings, 1888-1985, in Hot Springs, Arkansas, in 1908. He owned land on Spring and Black Rivers which he farmed. He was the largest hog buyer in Arkansas. He was postmaster at Black Rock for several years, a school teacher and superintendent of the Sunday School at the Methodist Church for several years. He also served on the school board.

Home of R. W. and Sudye Moore where they lived for more than 50 years. It is a three story brick (red) with basement and sleeping porch on second floor.

Sudye's parents were John H. Billings and Regga Fain, who lived in old Walnut Ridge, Arkansas. Her father was a farmer and operated a small grocery store in later life. She had two sisters, Margaret Jones and Micca Huey. She was a public school teacher as well as a Bible School teacher. Her parents were the first people in the community to put screens on their windows. Robert and Sudye lived in the Poindexter house in Black Rock where they raised seven children.

Nama Avis, 1911-1992, married William Bates Stuart of Ravenden (deceased) and they had two children: Brady and Robert Stuart of Memphis, Tennessee. Morris Moses Moore, 1913-1952, married Obduah Rafferty of Memphis. They had one son, Charles Robert, Hardy, Arkansas. Later, he married Jennie Sue Spades, deceased. Ama Henrietta Moore married Henry Bernauer. Their children are: Dr. William Bernauer and Brenda Bernauer of Oklahoma City, Oklahoma. Helen Vivian Moore married Frank Page of Memphis, deceased. They have two children: Robert Page of Nashville and Jim Page of Memphis. Robert B. Moore, 1919-1987, married Frances Taucher of Chicago, Illinois. They had four children: Marguerite Digman and Rhetta Moore, Walnut Ridge, Arkansas, Bill Moore of Black Rock and Marsha Moore, 1950-1969. Evelyn Sudye Moore married John Tucker of Hornbeak, Tennessee. They have one son, John Michael, who lives in Mississippi. John N. Moore married Kathleen Smith of Black Rock. Their children are Patricia Aikman, Paragould, Arkansas; and Morris Moore of Walnut Ridge, Arkansas.

–Mrs. John J. Tucker.

TRUMAN AND BONNIE MOORE. Truman Moore, who grew up at Denton, married Bonnie Marie Gibson of the Clear Springs Community on April 9, 1939. They both were graduates of Sloan-Hendrix Academy at Imboden. He was a member of the class of 1934, and she was in the class of 1938.

Truman's early career included teaching school at Rosebud, Oak Grove, Clear Springs and Pleasant Hill, and selling cars for Snapp Motor Company. He served as bookkeeper for John K. Gipson plantation at Lauratown, then returned to sales work with Plunkett-Jarrell Grocery in Hoxie then with Wilcoxson & Sons furniture and appliance business in Walnut Ridge.

In 1955, he entered into partnership with Paul Bowlin of Pocahontas to start a new furniture and appliance business in Walnut Ridge. Bowlin-Moore Furniture Company opened for business on September 17,

Mr. and Mrs. Truman Moore.

1955, in a building on Southwest Second which had formerly housed Piggly-Wiggly. With Truman as manager and co-owner, the business grew steadily and moved into a new building at 115 West Elm in 1960.

Bonnie, who was a full time homemaker while assisting with the business at different times during its early years, joined the staff full time in 1969. Following continued growth of the furniture business, Truman and Bonnie acquired full ownership in 1978, and renamed it Moore Furniture Company. After operating on their own for four years, they decided to retire in 1982 and sell the business to Bob and Mary Ann Cole, who eventually renamed it Cole Furniture Company.

Truman was very active in civic affairs while in business. He served a term as president of the Walnut Ridge Chamber of Commerce and a term as president of the Arkansas Furniture Association, along with other activities.

Truman and Bonnie raised four children: Frances Margaret, born in 1940; Catherine Marie, born in 1942; Harry Truman, born in 1947; and Thomas Alva, born in 1951. Because of the emphasis they placed on the importance of education, they put all four children through college. All are graduates of Arkansas State University in Jonesboro.

Frances married Doug Austin of Hoxie; Cathy married Larry Clowers of Hot Springs; Harry Truman married Linda Lou Lipscomb of Blytheville; and Tom married Darlene Flippo of Powhatan.

Truman and Bonnie enjoy four granddaughters, a grandson, a great-granddaughter, and two great-grandsons.

In retirement, the Moores enjoy various hobbies. Bonnie is interested in quilting, flower gardening and collectibles, while Truman follows his interests in real estate, yard care and reading. Throughout the years, they have been active members of the First Baptist Church of Walnut Ridge, where both have held leadership positions in Sunday School, Women's Missionary Union and Men's Early Morning Bible Class. Truman also serves as treasurer of the New Hope Cemetery Association, a special interest for him because the cemetery property was provided by Moore family ancestors in the mid 19th century. –Tom Moore.

WILLIAM EDWARD MOORE brought his family to Lawrence County about 1850, from Brunswick County, Virginia, where he was born August 12, 1822. He first came to Arkansas by horseback; then he sent back for his father and mother, Allen and Lydia, two brothers, Drury Wilson and Harvey, and Wilson's family.

In Arkansas he met Martha Ann Judkins and her family, also new arrivals from Virginia. They were married on April 7, 1853, when he was 30 and she was 19. He purchased his first parcel of land in Lawrence County on July 7, 1852, when he paid his brother, Wilson, 35 dollars for 13 acres. This property adjoined the land that Wilson and his wife, Elizabeth, earlier had deeded to the New Hope Baptist Church.

Courthouse records show that William acquired and resold numerous tracts of land in the area around Denton and toward Smithville. Among the earliest was a 40 acre tract in Section 30, which he acquired through land patent from the United States Government, dated March 1, 1855. It was signed by Franklin Pierce, President of the United States.

William Moore, like the rest of the men in the Moore family and most early pioneers of Lawrence County, made his living as a farmer. On the 1870 tax books of Lawrence County, he is listed as owner of 355 acres of land, all in Section 30.

The Moore family alliance to the New Hope Church was strong from the beginning, as evidenced by Wilson's selling seven acres to the young congregation in 1851, for a

William Edward and Martha Judkins Moore.

church site. All the Moore families and several affiliated families attended church there.

A history of the New Hope Church by Walter E. McLeod, a cousin and a historian, was published in *The Times Dispatch* on August 17, 1944, near the church's 100th anniversary. He listed many of the church's pioneer families, including the Moores, and recalled attending there as a child. He sat in the "amen corner" with his father, and he remembered, "the old graybeards" who were the pillars of the church then, William Moore, Wilson Moore and others, including Wiley Matthews, whose daughter, Margaret, later married William and Martha Moore's son, Robert.

William enlisted for Confederate service with Company F, 45th Arkansas Cavalry, but served only a short time due to his age, 43, and poor health.

Martha's mother, Sarah Judkins, wrote a letter to her niece in Virginia in 1854. Among her comments, she said Martha Ann "has made a happy choice in a companion, he is very kind and affectionate to her....M. Ann's husband had land, a good many hogs and some cattle."

The couple had 10 children. Laura Catherine married Berry Field; Henry Allen married Saphronia Dent; Sarah Elizabeth died at age four; Joseph Edward married Josephine Childress; Nathaniel Augustus married Ada James; Robert Calvin married Margaret Jane Matthews; Clara Street died at 18; Margaret Ida married S. Kent Childress; Susan Ada died at age eight; and Leonard Harvey married Florence Coop.

William and Martha acquired the home place of her parents, William Henry and Sarah Dozier Judkins, on the Smithville-Powhatan Road, and lived there many years. He died in 1890, she in 1901. –Tom Moore.

HARTMAN WILLIS MORSE FAMILY. Hartman Willis Morse was born September 17, 1919, in the river bottoms in Lake City, Arkansas, where his grandpa operated a farm. He was the son of Willis Grant and Vada Pearl Gibson Morse. He was the oldest of five children.

Hartman learned to hunt and trap as a child. He loved the woods and river. He joined the Army, but never made it into battle. He was injured and spent several months in a California hospital. Later, he returned home, where he met and married Annie Maxine Darris on July 8, 1944. Maxine was born January 9, 1926, the daughter of Al and Mary McCutchen Darris.

Hartman and Maxine moved into a cabin boat where they set up housekeeping. Maxine was raised on a cabin boat that traveled the river from Pocahontas to the mouth of White River, but mostly staying around Powhatan. She was the middle child of seven children. She often told of learning to swim so early she couldn't remember it. Her dad took shells from the river for a living. He also hunted and fished to supply food for his family.

Hartman returned to his love and great passion of hunting and fishing, but this time with a purpose. He had a family to support. Their first child, Alvita, was born April 25, 1945, on the cabin boat pulled up to the bank. Maxine always told that Hartman set on the back of the cabin boat and fished while she had a baby. Hartman said what else could he do, he couldn't help and was too nervous to do anything else.

Hartman fished on the Black River for many years. He caught and sold fish. His best friend was Bryson Waddel. He helped Bryson tend his honey bees for extra money. He dry docked his cabin boat because Maxine was afraid for her children. After he dry docked the boat, their second child was born on March 12, 1948. They named her Joyce Louise.

Hartman and Maxine Morse.

Hartman and Maxine had five more children: Nina Ann, born December 29, 1950; Brenda Sue, born February 6, 1952; and David, born October 20, 1954. After David was born, the family moved to Michigan, where Alvita died from a brain tumor at the age of 11. She is buried in Lincoln Memorial Park Cemetery in Plymouth, Michigan. The family came back home. On February 6, 1961, Tommy Gene was born.

We moved to Florida, then back to Michigan, where their last baby was born on July 31, 1962, Sandra Leora. Later, we returned home to stay. Dad bought a house in Portia, Arkansas.

Maxine died December 20, 1987, and Hartman died August 12, 1997. Both are buried in Oak Forest Cemetery in Black Rock. –*Joyce Morse.*

JOE NEELEY. Joseph Samuel "Joe" Neeley employed by Magnolia Pipeline transferred to the community of Saffell in 1950. He came as an operating engineer for the Magnolia Petroleum pipeline pumping station there. Joe was born February 19, 1905, near Keota, Oklahoma. He was the eldest son of Joseph Henry and Amanda Cagle Neeley. They had migrated to Oklahoma from Texas in the 1890s. Joe, a teenager, returned to East Texas to work with his Uncle Walter P. Vic in a machine shop near Kilgore, Texas. There he met people who were affiliated with oilfield construction, and he began to follow that trade.

Joe returned to Keota to marry Ann Rumage. His first son, Russell Nathaniel, was born there August 24, 1924. Ann was killed two years later in a runaway horse accident. Russell stayed

Joe and Mary Ellen Neeley, 1963.

Descendants of Joe Neeley: Walter, Kyle and Betty Neeley, 1992.

with his maternal grandparents until he was 10.

In 1934, Joe married Leona Welker Brock, who was born June 5, 1910, in Tuttle, Oklahoma. Leona had a son, Albert Floyd Brock, whose father was Charles Brock. Al was born February 6, 1928, at Tuttle, Oklahoma. On January 1, 1934, Joe began his tenure with Magnolia Petroleum Company, Dallas, Texas. He started by doing pipeline construction near Oklahoma City, Oklahoma. Joe, Leona, Russell and Al lived in Oklahoma City when Joe and Leona's first son was born. He arrived September 15, 1935, and was named Bobby Joe. Joe and family moved to Steward Station near Shawnee, Oklahoma in 1936. There Walter P. Neeley was born May 29, 1937. Joe's job required him to walk 82 miles each week to inspect and repair a section of six inch diameter pipeline between Steward Station and Depew Station to the north.

Bobby Joe had a tragic accident in 1942. He drowned near his home one evening. The family was distraught; subsequently Leona required complete hospitalization. She died September 17, 1993, in Ada, Oklahoma.

When World War II started Russell enlisted into the Navy. Al joined the Army after graduating from high school. Joe and Walter moved to Oklahoma City in May of 1945, to care for Joe's ailing father who died January 27, 1947. Russell died of cancer January 20, 1994.

In 1947, Joe and Leona were divorced. In 1948, Joe married Mary Ellen Wheeland, born April 10, 1928, in Oklahoma City. In 1949, Mary Ellen and Walter accompanied Joe to Little Rock, Arkansas, where the new family was transferred preceding the move to Lawrence County. Joe died following a series of strokes, October 28, 1974, in Shawnee, Oklahoma.

The descendants of Joe Neeley currently living in Lawrence County are: Walter P., his third son, and Kyle, his grandson. Walter graduated from Strawberry High in 1955, and from Oklahoma University with a B.S. in Electrical Engineering in 1961.

Walter married Betty Gene Davis, born July 3, 1941, at Smithville, on August 5, 1961, at Imboden, Arkansas. Betty is the daughter of Grover and Imogene Dailey Davis of Denton. Their families have been in Lawrence County since 1852. Betty has a B.S.E. and M.S.E. in Elementary Education from Arkansas State University; postgraduate work at the University of North Texas. Walter and Betty have one son, Kyle, who was born in Irving, Texas. Kyle was born March 18, 1979. He attended elementary and junior high in Irving, Texas and graduated from Lynn High in 1997. He is presently attending college at Arkansas State University. –*Walter Neeley.*

JOHN NEWMAN was born June 10, 1875, in Randolph County, Arkansas, near Warm Springs. He was the son of Charles and Nancy Jane Young Newman.

John's father was a Swedish immigrant and worked as a well digger. When John was small the family moved to Oregon County, Missouri, near Myrtle. Here John grew up on his family's farm. At the age of 19, John married Miss Ida Buckley and they had four daughters. Following a wagon trip to Texas, Ida became ill and died.

John moved his family to Hoxie, Arkansas, and worked at various jobs. Later, he moved his family to Minturn and worked as a hired hand. There he met a tall, shy neighbor girl, Lutisha Chesser, who was 16 years younger. Tish's mother, Lizzie, discouraged the relationship. She distrusted the tall brooding man her daughter was interest in. John and Lutisha were married on November 28, 1911, and quickly became parents of five children. In 1917, John and Tish bought a homestead, joining Tish's mother, Lizzie, near Egypt, and here they farmed and raised their family. John was a temperamental man, prone to long periods of depression and violent behavior.

My grandparents were complete opposites. She was shy and quiet and loved to read and always subscribed to a newspaper. Tish cared for her family in a loving way, with hugs and pats on the back and endless work all the while, humming a song. John loved to hunt and spent many nights in the Cache River bottoms hunting, thus helping to feed his family. Few men could work as hard and long as my Grandpa.

The family suffered tragedies through the years. Once, grandma accidently poisoned the family when someone put rat poison in a

John and Tish Chesser, taken December, 1916. Children are: standing, back: Emy Newman, baby Johnny on Tish's lap. Mable and Beulah standing in front and John Newman.

baking powder can and she used it in her baking. My dad remembered one hot day in May, 1927, he and grandpa were in the fields and they saw a tornado strike Egypt. John sent dad running to warn grandma and then he turned the mules loose and huddled under a wagon until the hail stopped. Without a cellar close, Tish gathered her children close and covered them with a feather bed and, terrified, they listened as the tornado roared over them. Afterwards, grandpa and dad set out to find the older girls who had walked to Egypt to get the mail. They were found safe at a neighbors, and the men spent the rest of the day helping survivors and picking up the dead.

Grandpa retired from farming in 1946, and he passed away on June 23, 1951. Tish lived in Wichita, Kansas, with her children part of the time and died in a gas explosion at her home there on January 11, 1959. Tish and John are buried in Lawrence Memorial Cemetery at Walnut Ridge, Arkansas.–*Barbara Newman Howard.*

JOHNIE LESLIE NEWMAN was born October 28, 1916, near Egypt, Arkansas, the son of John and Lutisha Chesser Newman.

Johnie had a distaste for school and refused to attend, so his dad put him to work on the family farm. This pleased Johnie because he loved to be outside and in the fields. Johnie always had a good horse and he rode it to the Little Brown School when there was a revival and to court Gladys Kieth. Gladys was the daughter of Jess Kieth and Susie Davis Kieth. Her father died when Gladys was two and one half and her mother married George Parker. Mr. Parker worked as a sharecropper for Johnie's dad and the youngsters played together when they were four years old. Johnie and Gladys were married on February 17, 1934, in Sedgwick, Arkansas.

The newlyweds settled into farm life and quickly started a family. Their first child, a son, was still-born October 15, 1934. A second child, Neva, was born on September 29, 1935. The following year on August 29, 1936, a second son was also still-born. On September 12, 1937, Gladys gave birth to a second daughter, Margie.

Johnie and Glady Newman, 1988.

The young family struggled during the Depression, and after hearing the glowing stories of riches in California from friends, Johnie sold his mules and equipment, moved his family into his parent's home and traveled to California with his friends.

After a few months Johnie became homesick and unable to afford the fare home, he "rode the rails" back to Arkansas. Another daughter, Barbara, was born on January 31, 1939.

Johnie moved his family into a log house on Horse Island near Bono, Arkansas. He helped clear land and sharecropped. He stated he worked from sunup to sundown for 50 cents a day and then traded it out in Russell Harrels Grocery Store.

On August 11, 1940, a third child, Jerry, was born. With a son at last, the boy quickly became the apple of his dad's eye.

Gladys later gave birth to three more children: Janet on October 3, 1942; Larry on November 4, 1943; and Lindell on September 7, 1946. Then in the spring of 1947, following a farming accident that almost cost her life Gladys miscarried twin sons. This ended her child bearing years.

The family lived on the Bramlett farm for a few years. The children remember the raccoons laying on the staircase, raccoons Johnie had killed the night before. Hunting was his passion and the weather didn't get too bad or too cold to prevent him from leaving a warm bed and going to the woods.

One fond memory was of a particular bad year and times were terrible, and one day the mailman brought a huge box from Sears Roebuck. Inside were clothes and toys and a pair of knee boots for Johnie. They had not ordered the items and tried to give them back, but was told they were ordered and paid for and would not say who had sent them. They never knew who the guardian angel was. There are sweet memories of the many nights Gladys rocked the latest baby to sleep in a straight back chair on the front porch and sang wonderful old hymns.

In 1946, Johnie's dad quit farming and he and Tish moved into Egypt, and Johnie moved his family onto the family farm. Here they remained until 1952, when he moved the family to Randolph County, at Gumstump to farm for Roy Townsend. Mr. Townsend had given Johnie his first start and now offered him a chance to farm big.

The Newmans would remain in Randolph County until 1959, when following the death of Johnie's mother, he purchased the family farm from his siblings and returned to Egypt.

On May 5, 1965, a farm accident almost took Johnie's life and did permanently take his hearing. He had a difficult time adjusting to his disability, but he continued to farm until retiring in 1977. He and Gladys sold most of the acreage and built a new home on the site. They remained here until Johnie's death on August 3, 1989.

A lot has been said about daddy, both good and bad. He was a tall handsome man, sandy haired and the palest of blue eyes. He had a sentimental streak and would cry at the drop of a hat. He had a hot temper and loved a good fist fight and his broken knuckles proved it.

Daddy never learned to read or write, but he was a whiz at math. His word was his bond. If he said something, it was the truth. He loved a poker game and had an eye for the ladies. An angel he was not.

After Johnie's death, Gladys continued to live on the farm as long as her health permitted. She died July 6, 1998, and she and Johnie and their sons are resting in the Markham Cemetery near Egypt. –Barbara Howard.

WILLIAM JESSE NICKS. Arkansas State Representative, William Jesse Nicks was a descendant of John Nicks of Guilford County, North Carolina. The history of John Nicks before 1753, is obscure, but he is known to have been one of the original members of the Nottingham Colony. Until 1750, England had difficulty colonizing North Carolina. The King of England could not entice settlers to remain there so the English Crown recalled all but one land grant - a 3000 mile strip lying below the Virginia line and extending from the Atlantic Oceans west as far as the continent went; this belonged to Lord John Carteret, Earl of Granville. As time passed, Lord Darteret gave grants to small landholders. John Nicks received a total of 640 acres.

John Nicks and his wife, Margaret Quinton, raised three sons and five daughters. The sons were John II, George and Quinton. All three served in the Revolutionary War. One recompense the government offered its soldiers for their service was land in the newly

Arkansas State Representative William Jesse Nicks.

opened territory of Tennessee. Around 1808, John II accepted this as his pay and moved his family there. One son who moved with John II was William, July 8, 1789-November 3, 1857, and wife, Sarah Pugh, born 1791, South Carolina.

William and Sarah had 13 children: Malinda, Pleasant, A. Totty, Prudence, William Jesse, Rodney Doak, James Q., Amanda, John Sebastain, Silas, Alexander Lavina and Douglas. William was one of the founders of the Christian Church in Shady Grove, Tennessee. In 1998, his gravestone is still standing in good condition in the Shady Grove Cemetery.

Dr. William Jesse Nicks, November 8, 1818-July 26, 1864, married Elizabeth Ann Puckett, February 24, 1829-1923, and moved west in about 1857-58, in a wagon train (it is assumed with other Nicks families). They crossed the Mississippi River at Bird's Point, near Cairo, Illinois. Elizabeth was treasurer of the train and went across in the first carriage. William Jesse served as captain under General Price in the Confederate Army during the Civil War. At age 16, his son, William Barrett, joined him and they surrendered at Jackson Port, Arkansas at the end of the war. They fought in the Battle of Pea Ridge. William Jesse died at his home in Howell County, Missouri from injuries received during the war.

William Barrett, 1847-1900, married Josephine Elizabeth Beaver, 1850-1899. Their children were William Jesse, John Thomas, Nancy Elizabeth, Joseph Houston, Henry Nevel, Annie and W. Ray. William Barrett and Josephine are buried in Clover Bend Cemetery. Their gravemarkers have disappeared.

William Jesse, November 6, 1871-April 1, 1916, married Victory Caldona Arnold, August 17, 1872-September 30, 1917. They are buried in Lawrence Memorial Park. William Jesse was a member of the Arkansas House of Representatives, 1915-1916. They lived in the Richwoods Community and had three children: William Joseph, 1908-1925; Dora Dean, July 30, 1910-January 11, 1947; and Trixie Josephine, August 22, 1912-April 12, 1986.

William Joseph died in his late teens, and was never married.

Trixie married Orville Knots, from Randolph County. They had two daughters Phyllis Dean Vance, September 11, 1932-January 29, 1985, and Betty Joe Lemons.

Dora Dean married Azril Thurman "Jack" Rippee, July 24, 1910-February 22, 1993, son of Edward Thurman Rippee and Effie Pearl Smith. They had six children: Thurma Lea Triplitt, Elizabeth Anne Basham, Richard Allen, Mona Karen Messenger, Dona Joe Zuckerman and Raylene Izak. Today none of the children from this union reside in Lawrence County, however, all are still living.

The Nicks/Rippee farm in Richwoods was sold to Colbert Gill in 1997. –John & Raylene Izdk.

NORRIS - HUDSON. Mary Ann (Holt) Norris, the widow of Thomas Norris, married James Franklin Hudson in Lawrence County, on November 5, 1865. He was born in Tennessee in 1838, the son of Evan and Mary Hudson. Evan and Mary, both were born in North Carolina. James was a farmer now with a ready made family and Mary Ann a loving mother. The children to this union were; Lee E. born in 1866; Mary Ellen, born in 1868; James Whitson (Whit), born in 1870 and died April 9, 1952. Whit was a farmer, Nazarene preacher and also ran orphanages in Texas and Oklahoma. He married Flora Bell Chitty. Their children were; Cleatus N., 1898 - 1930, Mary E. 1900 - ; Willie May 1902 - 1938; James Albert 1913 - 1998. Flora died in 1932 and Whit married again on September 11, 1940 to Nettie Smith. Whit, Flora and two of his sons are buried in the Antioch Cemetery, northwest of Butler, Cluster County, Oklahoma. Elijah was born in 1972; Oscar was born in 1877. Oscar was a farmer, newspaper editor and Pentecostal Holiness Preacher. He married Lena and had two known children; Marshall was born in 1908; Marion was born in 1910. Absalom Barksdale was born in 1877. Mary and James left Lawrence County before 1877 and were living in Denton County, Texas by 1880. They continued to live in

Back Row, Left to Right: Mrs. Elijah Hudson: sons Elijah, Oscar, Absalom Barksdale Hudson. Seated: Thomas (Jeff) Norris, James Franklin Hudson (1838), Mary Ann Holt, Norris Hudson (1835) and son James (Whit) Hudson in 1900.

northern counties of Texas. James died less that a year before Mary. Mary lived with her children Whit and Oscar and died July 1, 1911 in Lamasco, Fannin County, Texas. She is buried in Honey Grove Cemetery, 15 miles northwest of Bonham, Texas. Mary's son Oscar wrote a memorial tribute of his mother for his sister who couldn't come to the funeral. She loved her children, fed and nursed stray animals and loved life. She was a strong devoted Christian, happy ministering to and feeding people and worked tirelessly doing the Lord's work until the very end of her allotted time here on earth. –Nelta Dupree Evans

THOMAS "BIG TOM" AND SUSAN TOMPKINS NORRIS.

Thomas Norris, son of William "Billy" Norris, grandson of Nicholas Norris Sr. spent all of his life in Sharp County. His grandfather, Nicholas Norris Sr., was one of the first settlers on Strawberry River, in what was then Lawrence County, Missouri Territory in 1810. Nicholas was buried in the Norris Cemetery near Strawberry River, in Sharp County, Arkansas.

Photo courtesy of Newton Norris, son of Lonzo N. Norris.

The family of Thomas "Big Tom" and Susan Tompkins Norris lived in this home about two miles from Poughkeepsie, Arkansas. In the picture are the last six children of 16 children born to this couple. They are left to right: Lucian, Harmon, Walter, Maude Pernie, Dudley H., Lonzo N., Thomas and Susan Norris. Other children born to this union were Little Sissie, Charlie E., Loutishia Emaline, Martha, Dona, Carroll Jeff, Francis Marion, Albert, Bill R. and Thomas Marshall. The old homestead still stands on the Norris farm located on Strawberry River. It is now owned by the Parsley family. –Newton Norris.

OLDHAM. Henry Clay Oldham was born June 13, 1856, in Denton, Lawrence County, Arkansas, died June 17, 1928, in Eaton, Lawrence County, Arkansas. He married Sarah Mahala Ketner, daughter of Daniel Ketner and Catherine Amanda Bour December 4, 1879, in Denton. Mahala was born March 5, 1858, in Denton, died March 17, 1940, in Eaton. Both are buried at the Old Lebanon Cemetery, Eaton, Arkansas. Their children were: Leona, Thomas Henry, Jesse Marvin, Haney A., Harvey, Nettie Evia, Mollie, Virgie Jane and Alvie Daniel Oldham.

Leona Oldham, born November 23, 1880, in Eaton, died April 9, 1960, in Eaton. She married James P. Richey on July 26, 1898, in Eaton. James was born December 26, 1879, and died in 1946, in Eaton. Both are buried in the Old Lebanon Cemetery.

Thomas Henry Oldham, born January 19, 1883, in Eaton, died August 14, 1969, in Hoxie, Arkansas. He married Nora Selsor on August 20, 1905, in Oak Grove, Arkansas. Nora was born January 26, 1886, in Powhatan, Arkansas, died April 28, 1935, in Walnut Ridge, Arkansas. Thomas also

married Loma Good on May 9, 1909, in Eaton. Loma was born February 25, 1892, in Denton, died September 14, 1972, in West Memphis, Arkansas.

Jessie Marvin Oldham, born July 26, 1885, in Eaton, died February 2, 1972, in Walnut Ridge. Jessie married Fannie Carlton on January 20, 1907, in Eaton, Willie Martin on August 24, 1930, in Coffman Community, Portia, Arkansas, Mary Lawson on April 11, 1951, in Eaton, and Grace Kelly on July 20, 1968, in Lynn, Arkansas.

Haney A. Oldham was born December 29, 1888, in Eaton, Arkansas. Haney died September 23, 1972, in Pocahontas, Randolph, Arkansas. Haney married Stella Helms, daughter of Thomas Ephram Helms and Willie J. Haley on April 18, 1909, in Denton, Arkansas. Both are buried in the Old Lebanon Cemetery.

Harvey Oldham, born August 2, 1890, in Eaton. Harvey died March 3, 1974, in Black Rock. Harvey married Josie A. Richey on January 10, 1909, and Luella Frazier on July 2, 1921.

Nettie Evia Oldham, born February 14, 1893, in Lynn. She died December 22, 1988, in Walnut Ridge, Arkansas. Nettie was buried December 24, 1988, in Old Lebanon Cemetery. She married Joseph Alfred Brown (see the Parmer Sanford Brown story).

Mollie Oldham, born September 21, 1895, in Eaton, died in March, 1985, in Pine Bluff, Arkansas. Mollie Married Thurmon Frank Van Horn August 13, 1916, in Eaton.

Virgie Jane Oldham, born January 12, 1899, died January 22, 1899, in Lynn, Arkansas.

Alvie Daniel Oldham, born March 10, 1900, in Eaton. He died March 25, 1988, and was buried in Lawrence Memorial Cemetery, Walnut Ridge, Arkansas. Alvie married Ella Howard December 21, 1924, in Eaton, Arkansas. –Joey & Sherry Ethridge.

JACKSON HENDERSON OLDHAM FAMILY.

Jackson H. Oldham Sr. is the youngest son of Tyree and Nancy Oldham of Pendleton County, Kentucky. Tyree was a son of Jesse Oldham, son of Richard Oldham and Elizabeth Bayse, and Elizabeth Simpson of Madison County, Kentucky.

Jesse and Tyree are listed at Fort Boonesboro with Daniel Boone's original settlers to that area. Jesse and Tyree were with Daniel Boone when Indians attacked Fort Boonesboro in 1775. Jesse is also known as growing the first "recorded" corn crop in the state of Kentucky as found in court records in Madison County, Kentucky.

Jackson was raised on the Oldham plantation at Falmouth, Kentucky, which was once a 1000 acre tract that was purchased by Tyree Oldham in 1816, from Henry Clay. Tyree built a stately Virginia style brick home across the river in Shoemakertown about 1825. The plantation had 22 slaves as recorded in the Falmouth courthouse records. The family also ran the Oldham Ferry and the Grist Mill on the Licking River at Falmouth. The home was just torn down in the fall of 1996, because of flooding.

Jackson married Elizabeth Watson, daughter of Joseph Watson, in Kentucky and had four children: James M., born 1839; Anna O, born 1841; William, born 1844; and George Samuel Oldham, born February 1, 1845, died in 1878, in Pendleton County, Kentucky. Elizabeth died in 1845, in Pendleton County, Kentucky. George stayed in Kentucky with his mother's people. It is through George's descendants, in a deposition, we learn who Jackson's father actually was.

Jackson moved to Lawrence County, Arkansas, where his brother, William, had moved (thought by some to be his father, but most likely raised by William after his mother's death). Then he married Sarah Ann McCarroll, daughter of James McCarroll and Mary Beasley, on June 22, 1846, in Lynn, Lawrence, Arkansas. They had the

following children: Mary, 1847-1860; Thomas N., 1849-1870; Jackson Henderson Jr., May 8, 1850-1911; Martha J., 1853-1887; Sarah "Emma", 1855-1922; Henry Clay, 1856-1928 (married Sarah Mahala Ketner); and Ella D. Oldham, born 1858, died 1860-1870. Jackson Sr. served as a deputy sheriff for Lawrence county for many years and served in the New Hope Baptist Church. William, his brother, married Ann Wilkerson in Kentucky, sister to George W. Wilkerson of Lawrence County, Arkansas. William, known as a deacon church starter, and Ann moved to Phillips County, Arkansas.

After Sarah died, Jackson married her sister, Melissa McCarroll, on October 13, 1862, in Eaton, Lawrence County, Arkansas and had the following children: Mary A., born 1864; Henderson V., born 1866; and Harvey Oldham, born 1866. Jackson died of a heart attack under a tree on September 9, 1886, while looking for a man.

More information on the descendants of the Oldham family can be found in The Descendants of Nathaniel and John McCarroll written by the late John Richard McCarroll of Waco, Texas.–Allen Brown.

AZER OSBURN FAMILY. In 1852, the Azer Osburn family moved to Lawrence County, Arkansas, with first wife, Mary A. Porter. According to the 1860, census for Black River TWP, Azer Osburn was born October 19, 1832, in Marshall County, Tennessee, and died May 9, 1912, in Lynn, Arkansas. He is buried in Dry Creek Cemetery. He married Mary A. Porter on July 7, 1850, in Marshall County, Tennessee. Mary was the daughter of James Porter and Elizabeth Cavender.

Azer and Mary were the parents of nine children: James T. Osburn, July 27, 1851-June 26, 1941; he is buried in Dry Creek Cemetery; Mary J. Osburn, born January 3, 1854; Margaret E. Osburn, born May 28, 1856; Sarah H. Osburn, born October 21, 1858; she married John S. Felts on June 20, 1880; Susan C. Osburn, born September 16, 1861; she married John Lawson on May 5, 1859; Frances D. Eastbourne, born October 15, 1863; she married David Baley on August 5, 1881; Emily Osburn, born June 25, 1866; she married James Marlin Watson, September 3, 1893-December 2, 1931, in Cooke County, Texas; Rev. William Jefferson Osburn, September 1, 1868-December 2, 1843; Henry Clinton Osburn, born February 28, 1871; he married Molie E. Rogers on January 5, 1890; died March 10, 1934; he is buried at Dry Creek Cemetery at Lynn, Arkansas.

Azer Osburn married Sarah E. Ingram on November 25, 1875. They were the parents of six children: Joseph L. Osburn, born September 25, 1876; Florence G. Osburn, born July 12, 1877; Azor Edmond Osburn, born August 7, 1879; he married Leona Phillips on July 2, 1905; Theodore P. Osburn, born July 27, 1881; Riller Savannah Osburn, born May 8, 1884; she married Sam Lindsey on August 9, 1903; Isac Noble Osburn, born July 12, 1886; he married Maggie Winford on December 11, 1910.

On December 12, 1889, Azer married Mary A. Morrison in Lawrence County, Arkansas. Mary was 36 years old. They were the parents of two children: Perly Ann Osburn, born September 11, 1891; she married J. R. Pennon November 17, 1912; Tabitha May Osburn, born March 13, 1893; she married R. C. Lingo on March 14, 1909.

Emily Osburn and James Marlin Watson were the parents of the following children: Edna Marie, born August 4, 1897; Arthur Noble "Booger", born July 9, 1899; Owen Ayer "Stich", born about 1902; Pearl, born December 31, 1902; Orel Elbridge "Sach", born about 1905.

Reverend William Jefferson Osburn married Harriott Jane Pryor on August 25, 1887, in Strawberry, Arkansas. Harriott was the daughter of James Pryor and Melvine Hardin Pryor. William was first a Baptist preacher, but converted to Assembly of God; he preached at Assembly of God Church in Portia for many years; William and Harriott were the parents of 11 children: Rena Euphenia, born July 7, 1887, in Portia, Arkansas, died July 13, 1913; she is buried at Crossroad Cemetery in Portia; Ethel Lauran, born October 30, 1890; she married Talley Whittingham on November 8, 1908; died December 11, 1959; Mary Melvina, born October 5, 1882; she married first Monie Oliver Watson and second George Whitmire on September 23, 1911; died September 14, 1964; Cordia Ann, May 22, 1895; July 9, 1915, in Illinois; James William, born October 31, 1897; Essie Laura, born February 9, 1900; Floyd Owens, born September 3, 1902; he married Edith Sellers; died November 10, 1945; Lillian Beatrice, born December 3, 1904, in Tuckerman, Arkansas; died April 27, 1997; Chesley Azor, February 13, 1907, September 2, 1915; Evert Jefferson, born March 3, 1909; he married first Nola Johnson, second Euna Smith; died January 4, 1952; Bessie Lee, born January 14, 1912; she married first Robert Smith, second Herman Beasley; died about 1970.

Lillian Beatrice married Harvey Smith, a blacksmith at Black Rock. They were the parents of: Laquetia, Euphenia and Sonny. After Harvey's death, Beatrice married Jasper Higginbottom. Lillian Beatrice died when she was living in Salem, Missouri, on April 27, 1997. She is buried in Oak Forest Cemetery, Black Rock, Arkansas.

OWENS. John Elliott Owens (served as sheriff of Lawrence County) was born January 18, 1872, and died February 23, 1922, but those who have been researching his family history have yet to discover who his parents were or where he was born. We do know he had a brother, Benjamin F. Owens and a sister, Minnie.

The marriage records in the County Clerks Office, Walnut Ridge, Arkansas, state John E. Owens posted bond for marriage license to marry Mrs. Jennie Whitlow on August 18, 1894.

This marriage between John E. Owens of Minturn, Arkansas and Margaret Virginia "Jennie" Pruett Whitlow of Alicia, Lawrence County, Arkansas was solemnized on August 19, 1894. The children of this marriage were: Herbert S., born September 8, 1895; Henry Clay, born September 3, 1897; Weltia, born January 3, 1902; and Melvia Mae, born July 11, 1905.

In addition, Virginia Owens raised her son, William Henderson Whitlow, son of Forest H. Whitlow, her first husband. –Leta Owens.

SAMUEL MOODY PACE FAMILY. Samuel Moody Pace was born March 16, 1842, probably in Tennessee. He was married in 1872, in Kentucky, to Mary Susan Long. He came to Arkansas sometime after the end of the War Between the States. He lived in Independence County in 1880, later moving to the Smithville area. He and Susan were parents of three children: Richmond and Newton, twins born January 15, 1867, and a daughter, Annie Mae, born 1869. Samuel Pace served in the Civil War, Company K, Kentucky Infantry, and was injured during his service. In 1873, he married Evelene Roseanna Forrest of Missouri. They were the parents of six children who were in the Thayer, Missouri, area at the time of Sam's death in 1889. Nothing else is known of these Missouri children. S. M. Pace is buried in New Hope Cemetery near Denton, Arkansas.

A. Richmond and Newton Pace were identical twins, and often mistaken for each other. Richmond, 1867-1934, married Mary Ann Oldham

Rickey in 1888, and they are buried in New Hope Cemetery near Denton, Arkansas.

B. Newton, 1867-1931, married Fannie Florence Latimer, 1876-1951, in 1893, at Lynn, Arkansas. They lived in the Eaton-Lynn area and are buried in Old Lebanon Cemetery. Their children were:

1. Samuel Moody, 1895-1919, who died in France following World War I. He was not married. His body was returned from France and buried in Old Lebanon Cemetery.

2. John Ervie, 1897-1961, served during World War I, and was married to Flossie Farmer, 1913-1990, of the Coffman-Portia area. They had no children. They are buried in Old Lebanon Cemetery.

3. Susie May, 1901-1976, married S. Cleo Nunally and they were the parents of eight children. Susie and Cleo are buried in California.

4. Murphy Archie, 1904-1975, married Norine Walker of Lynn and they were parents of two children: Samuel Bland "Sammy", 1927-1935, and Willene who is married to Bill Jeffreys in California. Murphy and Norine are buried in California and Sammy is buried in Old Lebanon.

5. Richmond "RD", 1907-1954, served in the US Army during World War II and was never married. He died suddenly on his way to work in California. He is buried in Old Lebanon Cemetery.

6. Mary Elizabeth, 1910-1994, married Cleo Champ Stewart, 1905-1997, in 1935, and they had five children: Catherine, Jimmy, Donald, Betty and Randall. They lived all their lives in the Eaton-Denton area. They are buried in the Old Lebanon Cemetery near Eaton.

7. Pauline, stillborn in 1913, is buried in Old Lebanon Cemetery. Buried unnamed, her sister, Mary, called her Pauline. Her grave was marked much later.

8. Frances Florence, 1915-1988, left Arkansas during the 1930s, and married Fred Fick in northern California in 1937. They lived in California and southern Oregon and were hunters, trappers and guides on the rivers there. Their children are: Mary Helen, Carolyn, Jane and Fred Fick Jr.

C. Annie May Pace, 1869-1956, married Henderson V. "Bud" Oldham in 1885. They are buried in Lawrence Memorial Park in Walnut Ridge.
–Catherine Richey.

PARKER FAMILY. Ray Allen Parker and his twin sister, Ruby, were born on September 12, 1926, to George W. and Susie Davis Parker in the Big Brown Community of Lawrence County, Arkansas. Ray grew up on the family farm and attended school at Big Brown.

Ray was a headstrong boy and when he turned 16, he began to plead with his parents for permission to join the Navy, but his mother, Susie, was so frightened of the war that she tried desperately to talk him out of it. At this time, Ray's two older brothers, Roy and Frank, were both serving in the United States Army. As soon as Ray turned 17, he finally persuaded his parents to give their permission for him to enter the service. He entered the Navy on September 14, 1943, and served the next 20 years until his retirement on August 30, 1963.

During those 20 years, Ray traveled the world on his assignments and saw all the things a country boy could only dream of. Ray's military rank was S 2/C, S 1/C, PR3,

Ray and Imogene (Sackett) Parker on their wedding day.

PR2, PR1, PRCA, PRC. During his tenure he was stationed at San Diego, California, Salten Sea, Guam, Algaies NP. LA Pensacola, Florida. UC-24 US-23 NA AS Saufley Field.

Ray served on the USS Hinsoaks, USS Coral Sea, USS Midway, USS Sileorry, USS Palau, USS Philippine Sea, USS Batan and USS Barioko. He served in the Asiatic, Pacific and American Theaters.

Ray married Imogene Sackett on April 17, 1948, in Little Rock, Arkansas. They are the parents of three children. Their first child, a daughter, Rayetta, was born February 26, 1949, in Jonesboro, Arkansas and died two days later.

Their second child, Ray Allen Parker Jr., was born June 15, 1949, while the family was stationed at San Diego, California. A second son, George Wesley, was born on August 30, 1954, at USN Saufley Field, Pensacola, Florida.

Ray and Imogene Parker were divorced in 1973, and he married Linda Bennet Escue. They were later divorced also. Ray died of colon cancer on October 31, 1994, in Plano, Texas. He is buried beside his parents and brother, John, in the Aldridge Cemetery on Route 3, Walnut Ridge, Arkansas.

Imogene also remarried and divorced. She continues to live in Jonesboro, Arkansas. The Parker boys both live in the Dallas, Texas area.
–Barbara Newman Howard.

FRANK LEO PARKER was born on October 16, 1925, in the Big Brown Community of Lawrence County, Arkansas to George Washington and Susan Arminda Davis Parker. He grew up on the nearby family farm and attended school at the Big Brown school, but left school after completing the sixth grade.

At the age of 18, Frank was inducted into the United States Army and following basic training was sent to the European Theater where he served many months assigned to the 30th Combat Infantry Regiment. Frank was trained as an expert combat rifleman and spent many months on the front lines during World War II, acting as a decoy to draw out concealed enemy positions and movements.

Frank was active in the "Battle of the Rhine" and he received numerous ribbons and medals for his bravery and courage, including the African, European and Middle Eastern ribbons, two Bronze Stars and the Congressional Medal of Honor.

Frank was discharged from the military in May of 1946, and in July, 1946, he married Eleanor Songer of Sedgwick, Arkansas.

Frank Leo Parker, basic training graduation, June 1944.

The newlyweds farmed for a short time after Frank's release, but he was having a great deal of difficulty adjusting to civilian life after the horrors of the war and so in October of 1947, he reenlisted into the Army and remained until December, 1948, when he received a medical discharge.

The Parkers farmed in the Clover Bend area for a short time, then Frank moved his family to Rockford, Illinois, where for the next several years he worked at a variety of jobs. Frank Parker was a small man in stature, only five foot, three inches tall, and weighed 135 pounds, but with a fiery temper and a stern determination, he was a force to be reckoned with if he felt that he was treated unjustly or if he may have had a bit too much to drink.

Frank and Eleanor Parker are the parents of four children.

1. Ellyn, born June 6, 1950, is married to Glen Neal and lives in Edwardsville, Illinois.

2. James, born February 23, 1954, married Louise Cannavan and lives in Alton, Illinois.

3. Barbara, born March 27, 1958, married James Myers and lives in McCune, Kansas.

4. Lori, born May 6, 1962, married Charlie McDaniels. She is divorced and lives in Pearl, Illinois.

Frank and Eleanor were divorced in 1967, and Frank died of a massive coronary on October 29, 1980, and is at last at peace in the Greenpond Cemetery, Pearl, Illinois. Eleanor still lives nearby.
–Barbara Newman Howard.

GEORGE WASHINGTON PARKER was
born in the Roberts Store Community of Lawrence County, Arkansas on May 7, 1887, to Samuel Jessie and Sarah Parker. Sarah died at his birth or shortly after. Stories are told of George's premature birth and that he weighed only two and one half pounds at birth, and the family wrapped him and placed him in a shoe box then sat him on the oven door to keep him warm. How they managed to keep him alive back then was a miracle. George was raised by his sister, Ada Kisling, and her husband, Dempsey, until his father, Jessie, remarried. Soon after their marriage the Parkers moved to southern Missouri and soon afterwards George's father died and his stepmother later remarried. George told that his stepmother was mean to him and he dis-

George and Susie Parker.

liked his new home so one day he ran away and for a long period of time he walked, without shoes the long distance back to his sister's home in Lawrence County. Here he remained until his first marriage in 1914.

On August 8, 1919, George married Susie Davis Keith. Susie was a young widow with three small daughters.

The Parkers sharecropped for a time, then purchased a farm in the Big Brown area and here they raised their large family.

Their first child, Roy, was born in 1921. Roy married Aileen Stevens. He served in the United States Army during World War II with the 81st Infantry, attached to the 1st Marine Wild-Cats Division. He served in the South Pacific for 32 months. After his discharge he returned to Lawrence County and remained for several years, then he moved to Rockford, Illinois, where he remained until his death.

Jessie Mae was born in 1922. She married Fred Seels and lives in Jonesboro. Fred and their daughter, Gayle, are deceased.

Frank Leo was born in 1925, and also served with the United States Army special forces in Africa and Europe. He married Eleanor Songer and lived in Illinois for many years. He is deceased.

Ray Allen and his twin sister, Ruby, were born in 1926. He served in the United States Navy for 20 years and returned to Arkansas after his discharge. He married Imogene Sackett. He is deceased.

Ruby married Edward Tinker. They divorced and she then married Jess O'Connor. Jess is deceased and Ruby lives in Jonesboro.

Imogene was born in 1929 and married Robert Hare. He is deceased. Imogene and her children live in North Carolina.

Johnny Eugene and his twin sister, Joyce Eudene, were born in 1934. Johnny became ill and died when he was 10 years old.

Joyce married V. G. Owens and they lived in Rockford, Illinois for many years. They are divorced. She then married Robert Danner. She lives in Jonesboro.

Susie Parker could not seem to recover from the death of her son and she grew more despondent and for reasons known only to her, she took her own life on July 18, 1946. George Parker remained in the home for a time then he sold the farm and moved into Sedgwick where he remained until his death on January 9, 1949.

George, Susie, Johnny and Ray Allen Parker all rest in the Aldridge Cemetery near Egypt, Arkansas.

Submitted by Barbara Newman Howard.

RAY JAMES PARKER was born to George
and Susie A. Parker on September 29, 1921.

Ray was the eldest of eight children. He attended the Big Brown Community School and worked on his father's farm four miles east of Sedgwick, Arkansas.

He joined the C. C. Camp for a year before being drafted into the United States Army in 1943. He served with the Wild Cat Division of the 81st Infantry, attached with the first Marine Division in the South Pacific, during World War II. He was discharged in 1945, returning to Lawrence County where he married

Ray J. Parker and wife, Geneva.

Aileen Songer of Sedgwick, Arkansas.

He worked for Barnett's Refrigeration of Jonesboro, Arkansas until September of 1952, when they moved to Rockford, Illinois, where he was employed with the National Lock Company for 20 years.

Ray and Aileen were divorced in 1970. He remarried in 1978, to Geneva and moved to Belvidere, Illinois where he died November 12, 1988.

While serving in the Army, he earned every medal the Army had to offer except the Purple Heart.

While married to Aileen, they took care of his youngest sister, Joyce, after their father's death in 1949.

Ray and Aileen adopted one child, a daughter. –*Joyce Danner.*

PEACE FAMILY. In the early 1840s the Peace
family traveled up the Cherokee Trail of Tears from Alabama to southeast Missouri. They settled in a valley which they named Peace Valley, located northeast West Plains, Missouri, where Francis Marion Peace was born on April 23, 1865, to Pleasant Elgin Peace and his second wife, Mary Martha Wright Scales Peace. Francis Marion married Mary Martha Jones in 1885 and their union produced four children: Lillian Beatrice, born in 1886; Cleo, born in 1888; Earl Osmer, born in

1890; and Earnest Gervase "Dutch," born in 1894. During the Civil War, Mary Martha's father, a Confederate, was captured by the North near Powhatan, but he managed to escape on his pony. It was not until years later after their marriage, that Mary Martha found out that her husband was the soldier who had captured her father during the war.

Fruit Farm House.

In 1898 Francis and his family moved to Black Rock from Missouri to operate 294 acres planted in strawberries and peach trees. Additional land was later purchased for the farm. Francis, with the help of his brothers and cousins, cleared the land for a fruit farm. The trees were planted by hand numbering up to 40,000. This land was called the Fruit Farm and several people were employed there. When the peaches were harvested they were delivered by wagon to the Black

Francis Marion Peace, Mary, Lillian Beatrice Peace, Cleo Peace, E.G. Dutch Peace, Earl Omer Peace.

Rock Train Depot for shipping to all parts of the United States. Albert and Estella Williams, operators of the Black Rock Drug Store, on a visit to the Charlie Martin family in California, located a box of peaches at a local market. Estella remarked to her husband, Albert, that these were the most beautiful peaches she had ever seen in her life. Mrs. Williams lifted the top of the box and discovered that the peaches had been shipped from the Peace Fruit Farm in Black Rock, Arkansas.

Peaches from the Peace Fruit Farm were entered in the 1904 World's Fair in St. Louis and won the Bronze Medal. This beautiful medal is on display at the Powhatan Courthouse State, Park (courtesy of Luther and Gervase Peace of

Elva Luther Peace, wife of Dutch Peace washing at the fruit farm in 1931; born January 24, 1894, died August 14, 1990.

Memphis, Tennessee). The farm was owned by the McNair Fruit Company of St. Louis and was finally sold.

Located on the farm was a large barn, a corral and at the old spring well site a packing shed for the fruit, and other buildings. The spring site had originally been a salt lick and the well was built with large granite rocks from the quarry close to the Clay Sloan farm.

Ernest Gervase "Dutch" Peace and his wife, Elva Luther Peace, lived on the fruit farm and had two sons, Ralph Gervase and Luther Marion. Both sons grew up in Black Rock and maintained ties to the town. Mrs. Peace loved to entertain and their home was the scene for many square dances for young people.

During the early 1900s, some of the family began to cut pearl buttons and operate a grocery store, "F.M. Peace and Sons." In 1933 the family moved to Albuquerque, New Mexico.

The Peace family was very prominent in the community and gave whole heartily to the betterment of the community. –Luther Peace.

PEARSON. Thomas Pearson and his wife, Malinda White Pearson, came to Lawrence County, Arkansas, in 1846.

He was the son of Thomas and Nancy Ennette (Arnott) Pearson, born in 1821, probably in Tennessee. He married Malinda White, August 31, 1842, in Milton, Cannon County, Tennessee. She was the daughter of Stephen and Jane Bell White and was born February 18, 1822, in Sumner County, Tennessee.

After the births of their first two children, Sarah "Jane", July 8, 1844, and Elizabeth A., May 19, 1846, in Rutherford County, Tennessee, Thomas and Malinda moved to Lawrence County, Arkansas.

Two years later, the family moved to Polk County, Missouri, where William M. "Billy" was born October 5, 1848; then Thomas Pearson brought his family back to Lawrence County and on May 13, 1854, Nancy "Eliza" was born. Mary Malinda was born January 25, 1855; Simon, 1856, Martha Malissa, January, 1861, Thomas A., June 8, 1863, and Jordan, 1868.

The family is enumerated in the Big Creek Township in the 1860 census.

Thomas Pearson served with the Confederate Army in Company C., 45th Arkansas Cavalry. Likely, he only spent the last few months in the Army and may have been with General Stirling Price in his last raid into Missouri. Pearson was paroled at Jacksonport at the end of the war.

The Pearson's oldest daughter, Jane, married Wiley Croom, March 18, 1866, in Lawrence County. Croom was also a Confederate soldier, serving in Company K, 21st Arkansas. They had children: Dave, Fillmore, Ben, Mary, Ida, Susie, Annabel, Tom, Grover and Adlai. Jane Pearson Croom died May 22, 1902, in Izard County and is buried in Oxford Cemetery.

Elizabeth "Lizzie" married Isaac Whitlow, May 20, 1866, in Lawrence County. They had children: Betty, Jane, Dora, William and Ollie. Ike and Lizzie Pearson Whitlow eventually settled in the Texas Panhandle, Roberts County, where she died November 26, 1924.

Billy was born in Ebenezer, Polk County, Missouri. He married twice, first in 1868, to Mary Phillips and later to Malinda. He had children: Rebecca, James W., Martha J., Emily and Robert. No place or date of death is known, but he did live at one time in Oxford, Izard County.

Eliza married Uriah Abraham Bell, December 24, 1868, in Lawrence County. They had children: Lew, Alfred, Dick, John, Becky, Harrison and Frank. She died April 24, 1909, but the place is unknown.

Mary Pearson married the brother of her sister Lizzie's husband, John G. Whitlow, June 30, 1872, in Izard County. They had children: Sally, Malinda, Ada, Effie, Calvin, Cora, Birtie, Marvin and Audie. They moved from Izard County to Madison County and then to Cooke County, Texas. About 1905, they settled in Cleveland County, Oklahoma Territory, where they lived until their deaths. She died March 25, 1944, in Newalla, Oklahoma, and is buried in Pilgrim's Rest Cemetery.

There is no information on Thomas and Malinda's son, Simon. He may have died at an early age or at least before 1884.

Martha married Richmond W. Waggoner, probably about 1878, in Arkansas. They had children: Phineus, Oscar, Thomas, Daisy, Roxie and Ransom. Richmond Waggoner died about 1895, and soon afterward, Martha followed her brothers, John and Isaac Whitlow to Cooke County, Texas. She stayed in that area to raise her family while John continued to Oklahoma Territory and Isaac eventually settled in Roberts County, Texas. The place or date of her death has not been determined.

Thomas A. Pearson married Martha and they had children: Oscar, Thurman, Earl, Maude and Tom. There is no further record of him except that he bought the family farm in Izard County in 1884.

Another son, Jordan, also has no further records and he also may have died at an early age.

Malinda White Pearson died August 22, 1876, in Izard County, and is buried in Violet Hill Cemetery. Thomas Pearson married again, to Martha Adams. She had at least one daughter, Jessie, living with them per the 1880 census. Thomas died May 25, 1884, in Izard County and is also buried at Violet Hill Cemetery. –Leon and Ann McDonald.

ALICE PEAY. George W. Million is the son of George W. and Nancy Robinson Million. Alice is the daughter of George Washington and Elizabeth Callahan Peay, who were in Lawrence County for the 1860 census.

George W. and Alice Peay Million were the parents of six children.

1. Martha J., born 1873, married John Campbell, and John Morrow, September 30, 1891. One son, David Alfred Morrow, was born March 20, 1918.

2. William Thomas, born December 13, 1875, married first Nancy Ann Sutton, December 26, 1896, and second Cannie Riggs, October 25, 1903. He died November 9, 1910, and is buried at Sutton Baptist Church.

3. Frances "Fanny", born 1878, died 1892; buried Shiloh unmarked grave.

4. Gertie Agnes, born August 13, 1882, married William David Wagner, August 3, 1902, died July 11, 1935, and is buried Sutton.

5. Johnnie Walter, born February 27, 1884, married John Robert Carter, September 23, 1900, died August 21, 1945, and buried Oak Ridge, Kennett, Dunklin County, Missouri.

6. Lucy Belle, born February 14, 1887, died February 15, 1960, buried at Sutton.

Alice was born about 1854 at

Alice Peay and George Washington Million.

Henry County, Tennessee or possibly Calloway County, Kentucky. She died about 1889; buried in an unmarked grave Shiloh possibly at Sutton. George married Laura M. Donnell, January 5, 1890. He died about June/July, 1890. Laura wanted his money, possessions and land, but not the children. She took it to court. The children were split up among relatives, doing household chores for their upbringing. –Mary Ann Carter.

JOHN PEAY and Emily Hall are the parents of George W. (Washington/William). I just don't know if John was the son of William or his brother, George Peay of Rockingham County, North Carolina. John Peay is from Rockingham County, North Carolina. He was married March 10, 1814, to Emily Hall of Virginia. They stayed in Rockingham until before 1850, where they were found in household 82 in Henry County, Tennessee. John was 62 years and Emily was 54. They have a Susan H., born 1826, in household. Just across the Tennessee-Kentucky state line in Calloway County was George Peay and his family of five children, one son and four daughters, in household 278. He was 34 years old and Elizabeth was 32.

George was married to Elizabeth D. Callahan, November 26, 1838, in Rockingham County, North Carolina. Elizabeth was the daughter of Forrester Callahan, who also went to Calloway County, Kentucky by 1850. (I have not found where he went after 1850, or who his wife was.)

By 1860, John, Emily, George, Elizabeth and family were in Lawrence County, Arkansas. John and Emily were in household 1303 with a Emily J., born 1843, in their household. She must have been a granddaughter. George and Elizabeth were in household 1357 with eight children: William G., 20; Mary, 18; Eily J., 17; Martha, 15; Louisa, 13; Angelia, 10; Alice, seven; and Bell 5/12. John Peay either died in Lawrence County or Randolph because Emily was living with son George in 1870, Randolph County and was 72 years old. George and Elizabeth were in household 51 in 1870, Randolph County with six of their children.

William married Jane B. Dean, November 8, 1860, in Lawrence County. By 1880, George and Elizabeth's children were almost all married except for Virginia Bell who married Jessie F. Ford after 1884. She was born February 3, 1860, and died April 6, 1889, and is buried at Shiloh. It seems Jessie was married about four times. Virginia is the only Peay member of the family I have been able to find a tombstone for. I believe there are others buried in Randolph County at Shiloh. Louisa F. married Thomas Grinder/Grider, April 3, 1867. Angelia married Edwin L. McCall, November 11, 1870. Edwin was in their household in 1870 census. In 1880, they were in household 199 with three children: Samuel Hillis, born 1871; Flora R., born 1874; and Edward, born 1877. Alice L. married George Washington Million, March 17, 1872. They have three children by 1880 census. They were in household 50, Elevenpoint township, Martha, born 1873; William, born 1877; and Frances, born 1878. George W. and Elizabeth D. were in household 179 Demun township. Since there is no 1890 census and 1900, is 20 years away from 1880, I assume George and Elizabeth died in Randolph County or have moved elsewhere. They were 63 and 62 in 1880. –Mary Ann Carter.

JEFF DENNIS AND SYBLE EVANGELINE CASPER PENN. Dennis, the son of Taylor and Mattie Morgan Penn, was born February 13, 1911, at Lynn, Arkansas. He worked on the family farm while attending school at Lynn, graduating from there in 1927. At this time, Lynn's school ended at 10th grade. His mother took Dennis and Dollie to Morrilton to live so that they could attend school. While there Dennis became ill with a rare disease that almost took his life. His mother took him to Hot Springs for a series of hot baths and he was not able to return to school for several months. Later, he attended at Black Rock and was in the graduating class of 1932.

In the summer of 1932, he met Syble, who was here with her parents, Homer and Annie Boatenhammer Casper of Wauchula, Florida. They were visiting her grandparents, Jake and Emma Casper of Lynn. Dennis and Syble fell in love. She returned to finish her last year of high school, to return again the following summer to once again visit relatives. Syble had lived her younger years in Arkansas and attended school in Portia, Arkansas. The romance deepened that summer with a proposal to marry Dennis.

Jeff Dennis and Syble Evangeline Casper Penn.

Syble told the story about how Dennis kept her sitting in the hot sun in front of the Methodist church until she blistered while trying to get her to say she would marry him. They were married May 26, 1933, lived in the upstairs of his mom's home for the next year, then went to Wauchula, Florida seeking work for the next year. Their first child, Martha Ann Durham, was born while there on January 26, 1935. Soon afterwards they were on a train heading to the Penn farm. They built their first little home down what was known as the Old Military Road on the family farm. This is where their second child, Jimmy Dean Penn, was born on January 18, 1937. Gary Dennis Penn was the fourth child born January 12, 1946. The next two children were born at the clinic in Walnut Ridge. Gregory Allen Penn, born February 6, 1953, lost his life in a gun accident at the age of 26. David Byron Penn, the last child, was born July 24, 1955.

Dennis was a man of many interests in his short life here on earth. He truly loved farming in every way. He raised cattle and hogs and traded animals all over the county. He was known for building one of the first generators to produce electricity and to generate water with a windmill. He spent many years operating a grade A dairy, raising broilers and operating a sawmill. He lost his life at this sawmill, June 15, 1956, leaving his wife to raise five of the six children. Syble devoted her entire life to raising the children, loving and adoring all of the grandchildren and great-grandchildren until her death, January 9, 1997. Even though she was very busy as a mother, she still found time to earn money to help support the family by sewing for the public, working a short time at the Geurin Drive-In, cooking in the school lunchroom and even doing some substitute teaching at school. *—Martha Ann Durham.*

ROBERT E. PENN. Richard Jefferson Penn and Martha Ann Smith married in 1858, and lived at Jessup. One of their sons, Robert E. Penn, moved from their home in Jessup to Strawberry, Arkansas, where he opened the Penn Mercantile Store.

During the time that Robert E. Penn was moving to Strawberry, John A. Cathey and his wife, Sarah W. Roberts Cathey, were raising their daughter Kate Cathey. These two families were joined by the marriage of their daughter, Kate, to Robert in 1881.

In August, 1888, Robert and Kate began their own family with the birth of their first child, Maude. She married Lewis Williams and had four children: Irene Williams Wallis, Madge Williams Wright, Imogene Williams McDaniel and Clemon Williams.

In June, 1890, Robert and Kate welcomed their second daughter, Clyde, into the family. Clyde eventually married George Little and had three children. Their children were Myrl Little Andrews, Cortez Little, who died as an infant, and Unis Little Manning.

1898 - Robert E. Penn home located over by creek at Strawberry, Arkansas. Front: Clara. Back right: Clyde, Maude, John, Harvey, Robert E., Myrtle and Kate.

The first son, John Richard Penn, was born in June, 1892. John became the husband of Pearl Mize and had four children: Fred Jennings Penn, Harold Gene Penn, John Thomas Penn and Mary Katherine Penn Butterfield.

Harvey Penn became the fourth child and the second son in September, 1893. Harvey became the husband of Beulah McLaughlin and had three children: R. E. Penn and a set of twins, Betty Lou Penn Broadwater and Evelyn Sue Penn Garrett. After the death of Beulah, Harvey married Forene Jones.

March, 1895, brought another daughter, Clara, to Robert and Kate's family. Clara became the wife of Vestern Doyle and had four children: Judd Doyle, who died at the age of four, Herman Doyle, Robert Doyle and Eugene Doyle.

The youngest child of Robert and Kate was born in June, 1898, and named Myrtle. Myrtle later married Charlie Wood, but never had any children.

During his life at Strawberry, Robert operated the Penn Mercantile and also owned a sawmill and gin. He was later joined by John and Harvey as owners of the store. The sons bought and continued to operate the store when their father, Robert, retired. After several years Harvey sold his ownership to John, who continued to own and operate the store until his retirement in 1967. After the death of his wife, Pearl, John moved to Jonesboro, Arkansas, to live with his son, John Thomas Penn, until his death in 1978.

There are no surviving children of Robert E. and Kate Penn. Three of their grandchildren still live in Strawberry, Arkansas. They are: Clemon Williams, Madge Wright and Irene Wallace. They are the children of Maude Penn and Lewis Williams. *—Tom Penn.*

GEORGE WASHINGTON PERKINS FAMILY. Thirteen generations of the Perkins family have been researched. Space only allows the following 11.

1. Chauncy, born 1645, died in Perkins Estate in Upton Court, England.
2. Richard, 1663-1705, England.
3. Richard II, 1689-1772, North Carolina.
4. William, 1714, died in Kentucky.
5. John, 1770-1841, Cape Girardeau, Missouri.
6. Jesse L., 1815-1849, Wayne County, Missouri.
7. Peter, 1848-1916, married Ruey Jane Myers. Children: Etta E., 1873-1931, married Peter L. Bess.
8. George Washington, born 1868, in Bollinger County, Missouri, died 1945, in Smithville, Arkansas, married Lula Mae Winfrey. Children:
9. Ray, 1891-1942, California, married Nellie Oliver. Ethel, 1892-1931, married Grover Jones. Webster, 1894-1959, married Beatrice Deyling. Stella, 1895-1945, married Ottis McPike, divorced married E. R. Williams, died; married Don Martin. Ivy, 1897-1927, married Gladys Tomberlin. Etta, 1899-1978, married Charles Jones. Clifford, 1905-1960, married Mabel Brown, died 1937; married Vida Guthrie, died 1978. Rena, 1906-1989, married Ray Peebles.
10. Children of Ray and Nellie.
   a) Edward, 1912-1990, married Vida Gilliam.
   b) Arthur, 1916-1988, California, married Georgia Sims.
   c) Lottie Mae, born 1918, in Arizona, married Adelor Pierre Dionne.
   d) Dorothy, born 1925, in Arizona, married James Aaron Sims, divorced. Children of Ethel and Grover;
   e) Myles A., 1920-1975, married Irene Bryant.
   f) W. O., 1928-1950, married Rose Grieder.
   g) Wanda Lee, 1926-1957, married J. V. Hash.
   h) Milna Ray, born 1931, died in California, married Ethel Sterling. Children of Webster and Beatrice; Earl D., 1921-1998, married Irene Taylor.
   i) Paul Laverne, born 1922, married Bonnie Baker. Children of Stella;
   j) Chester McPike Williams married Eleanor Floch.
   k) Homer Williams died in 1958, in California, married Matilda Papooga. Children of Etta and Charles;

Front row: Clifford, George, Rena, Lula; Back row: Ethel, Ray Etta, Webster, Stella, Ivy.

l) Monroe, 1923-1995, California, married Marjorie Flippo, divorced.

m) George Wincel, born 1921, married Louise Dawson. Children of Clifford, Mabel and Vida;

n) Curtis G., born 1930, married Olivia Noles, divorced. Kenneth, January, 1932-October, 1932; Imogene, 1934-1949.

o) Iwanda, born 1935, married Joe Stone. Child by Vida; Reva Dee, married Henry Green Jr. Children of Rena and Ray;

p) Jess, 1927-1983, married Betty Lou Porter.

q) Syd, born 1945, married Jo Ann Ingram.

11a. Helen Cavagna, Bert, Jerry Wayne, Jan.

b) Marshall, Tonya Taylor.

c) Lavella Cassinelli, Mirna Estes.

d) Linda Markee, Karol Powell.

e) Stanley, Sharon Fisk, Sandra Jo Stavely.

f) Marilyn, Jerry.

g) Grover Bane, Liddie, infant.

h) Marie, Jackie, David.

i) Jo, Myra Jines, Jim.

j) Gayle Bray.

k) Christina Sobel, Eric Williams Larson.

l) LeAnne Ostrovski, Lantie, Linda Kay Delcid.

m) Annette Denton, Adriene Pinter.

n) David, Karen Croft, Cynthia Simmons, Linda Divelbiss, Lynn Kelly.

o) Darla Kellett.

p) Gale, Donna Hamaker.

q) Janet Miller, Joy Peebles.

—Bonnie Phillips.

JAMES FRANK PERRIN was born December 3, 1868, the oldest child of Jasper A. and Sarah Ellen Nations, grandson of Joab and Rebecca Churchman Perrin from Grainger County, Tennessee, and Eli/Elias and Sarah Weathers Nations. He married his first cousin, Ida Srailda Carter, daughter of Edward Franklin and Delilah Scott Carter. Ida is the granddaughter of John W. and Delilah Perrin (sister to Jasper) Carter and William and Sarah Scott. She was born February 1, 1872, married February 18, 1889. They had these children:

1. Adaline "Addie" J., born May 13, 1891, Lawrence County. She married a Conway and Hubert Woodyard. She died July 26, 1975, in Swifton, Jackson County, Arkansas.

2. Iva P., born July, 1894, married Price.

3. Ethel Mae, born February, 1897.

4. Alma L., born July 2, 1905, married Clyde Kell, died November 1, 1975, Swifton, Arkansas.

5. A set of twins.

James was a farmer. They were in household 77 in 1900, Lawrence with three children. By 1920, they had seven children, but only four were alive. They lived in household 220. Ida died September 6, 1933, and is buried at Hope Cemetery, Imboden, Lawrence County. James died December 12, 1948, and is buried next to his wife.

—Mary Ann Carter.

DANNY WALKER PHILLIPS was born August 18, 1954, in Walnut Ridge, Arkansas to Gurden Dean and Juanita Louise Culver Phillips. He learned to enjoy the outdoors as he grew up on his family's farm located on Bethel Road. He attended church nearby at New Hope Baptist Church where he accepted Jesus as Savior. He attended all 12 years of school at Lynn and graduated as valedictorian of his class on May 19, 1972. He attended his freshmen year at Southern Baptist College in Walnut Ridge, transferred to University of Central Arkansas in Conway and graduated with a BS in Biology in 1976. He also completed graduate courses at Arkansas State University.

On August 17, 1976, in the United Methodist Church of Black Rock, he married his high school sweetheart, Lesia Joy Sloan. Lesia was born December 29, 1954, at Jonesboro to Jack Mountjoy and Suzanne Cornelius Sloan. She was raised at Black Rock, attended all her school years there, and graduated as valedictorian of her class on May 19, 1972. She attended one year of college at Southern Baptist College and graduated from University of Central Arkansas with a BSE degree in Home Economics in 1976. She completed graduate courses toward certification in gifted and talented at Arkansas State University and UCA.

Danny's employment includes shift foreman at Frit Industries, graduate assistant at ASU, insurance sales, apprentice electrician. He began a career on the river in 1981, working as a deckhand for Security Barge Lines. Captain Phillips is currently relief captain on the MV Mark Aaron with American Commercial Lines. He is a man of humor who still enjoys fishing and hunting.

Seated, from left: Danny and Lesia Phillips. Standing, from left: Austin, Ryan and Clay Phillips, c. 1993.

Lesia has been employed as a teacher at Sloan-Hendrix School, Poughkeepsie School and River Valley School. She has also substituted for extended periods at Black Rock, Strawberry and Lynn schools. Other employment includes three years as Food Service Director at Southern Baptist College, jewelry clerk at Wal Mart, graduate assistant at ASU, and five years as Home Economist with the Arkansas Department of Health.

Their children include Ryan Walker, born August 6, 1978; Austin Blake, born August 18, 1980; and Clay Carson, born October 1, 1984. These three young men are the only children of their generation in the direct line of descent from George Washington Phillips to carry the Phillips name. Ryan graduated from Lynn School in 1996, as valedictorian and is pursuing a BS degree in Agriculture Business. Austin graduated as an honor student (tying for second highest GPA) from Walnut Ridge School in 1998. He is a student at ASU. Clay is an honor roll student at Lynn School. The entire family are members of New Hope Baptist Church.

The couple began their lives together in the "Jean" house just off Wasson Road. The family later lived at 408 Faculty Circle and 808 Florida Street in Walnut Ridge. They bought their first home in Black Rock at 403 Elm Street. In 1986, they bought their current abode, a ranch style rock house at 321 Bethel Road, just down the road from Danny's parents. For the school year of 1997-98, the family lived at 213 Ridgecrest Drive in Walnut Ridge. *—Lesia Sloan Phillips.*

GEORGE WASHINGTON PHILLIPS was born January 11, 1868, to William and Ninetta Hasting Phillips. George was the youngest child (except for a sister who was stillborn) of six half brothers and sisters, three stepbrothers and sisters, and seven own brothers and sisters. He was 20 when his father passed away and 22 when his mother died. He continued to live with other family members in the family home until he was married to Lucy Ann Walker on May 22, 1901, by Henry Moore.

As a child, Mrs. Phillips lived for a while at Davidsonville. Her parents were Robert and Jane Harmon Walker. Siblings include: Minnie (Mrs. John Evans), William B. and Cartwright Walker. The Phillips had the following children:

1. Pierce Ferguson, born February 26, 1902, married Mary Elizabeth Warner on December 11, 1925, in Alton, Missouri. He died January 24, 1978, and she died December 23, 1987. They operated a farm off Clear Springs Road. Their children are Betty "Jean" (Mrs. James O.) Davis, Verna Charline (Mrs. Arthur Morrison) Wilkerson and Barry Gale Phillips.

2. Lala Jane was born October 10, 1903. She married Curtis Wilson. They lived in Memphis and had no children. She died of breast cancer on August 17, 1966.

3. Louise Mable was born October 3, 1906. She married Paul Henderson. Their children are: Ronnie Lee and Elden Clay. The family operated a dairy farm off Clear Springs Road.

4. Noel Washington "Jake" was born May 8, 1908. He had a son, Herschel Lee. He married Lillian Shelma Wade on December 12, 1943, in Pocahontas. Their daughter is Sarah Lou (Sue, Mrs. Jim) Norman.

Front row: George, Russell and Lucy Phillips. Back row: Pierce, Noel, Lois and Lala Phillips, c. 1913.

5. Russell Lloyd was born January 26, 1911. He married a widow, Mrs. Addie Hoover. She had Paul Edward, Peter, Patrick, Janet and Judy. They had Jerry Lee and Glenda Louise.

6. Lennie Tennie was born June 25, 1914. She married Ernest Jones. They lived in Strawberry and had no children. She died April 27, 1986.

7. Gurden Dean was born May 15, 1919. He married Juanita Louise Culver on October 30, 1943. He is a machinist and they also operate a farm on Bethel Road 225. Their children are Gary Dewayne and Danny Walker. Danny's family information is given elsewhere.

8. Chesser Alvin "Simon" was born November 22, 1921. He married Opal Leanora Crays on August 15, 1949, in Pocahontas. They lived

in Pocahontas the majority of their life. He operated a grocery store, later he owned and operated Pocahontas Dairy. They also made investments in rental property. After selling the dairy, he worked for Sears and as an independent appliance/heating and air conditioning serviceman. Due to miscarriage, they had no children.

The Phillipses also raised two nephews, Eulysses and Jewell Evans. These boys were sons of her sister, Minnie. Mrs. Evans and another son both died of pneumonia while living in Pocahontas.

The family operated a farm (part of his father's property) on Denton Road. He built their home himself.

A story in the *Batesville Guard* tells that in the fall of 1916, Mr. Phillips was driving a team of horses that became frightened by a car and ran away, throwing him out and injuring him. Some years later, Mr. Phillips had a stroke and was bedfast maybe 10 years before he died on January 4, 1939, a week before his 71st birthday. Mrs. Phillips died of a heart attack on June 24, 1958. They are buried at Holobaugh Cemetery. –Lesia Phillips.

WILLIAM PHILLIPS FAMILY. According to family tradition, William Phillips left Tennessee during a quarantine yellow fever epidemic. He stole across the Mississippi in a rowboat between 1:00-4:00 a.m. and crossed into Arkansas. Census records and other information indicate his arrival between 1848 and 1850. In Lawrence County he rode along Stennitt Creek until the land leveled off and then homesteaded there. Legal documentation shows he acquired 240 acres in 1861. Other land entries indicate additional acquisitions of 40, 80 and 52 acres. They were all located in Township 17N, R2W. Mr. Phillips built a log home using timber from his property. The sills of the house were made from logs 30 feet in length and 16 inches square. He used wooden pegs to anchor the logs.

County clerk records of 1865, indicate he was paid $50 "for keeping part of the public records of the county two years during the war." He was also appointed constable of the Spring River Township.

He was born April 25, 1822. His brothers included John, Martin and Jim Phillips. William married Mary Permelie Armstrong, February 8, 1828-June 16, 1856, on October 21, 1847. While in Tennessee, they had their first child. The remaining children were born in Arkansas.

1. Alice E., August 11, 1848-May 21, 1926, married Jim Bryson on September 5, 1872.

2. Thomas Stevens "Tom", January 25, 1850-February 13, 1937, married Lisa Dent on December 24, 1871. Their farm was located near and across the road from Holobaugh Cemetery.

3. Tennessee "Tennie", April 11, 1851-January 1, 1932, married Green Dean on December 19, 1870.

4. Monroe Phillips, December 12, 1852-October 11, 1865.

5. Mary Permelie "Amelia", January 30, 1854-November 19, 1939, married Thomas Marion Duvall on October 25, 1874.

6. John, August 25, 1855-December 31, 1903, married Susan F. Coffman (died November 16, 1938) on February 7, 1878.

On August 23, 1857, William, a widower, remarried. Ninetta Hasting was a widow with three children: Helen married a Wayland; Franklin, born 1854 or 55; and Almeda "Meda", born 1855 or 56, married Bud Davis. Ninetta

lived from October 8, 1830, until March 6, 1890. Their children are:

1. James "Wayman", June 7, 1858-October 11, 1928, married Willie J. Ferguson.

2. Mary S., March 17, 1860-June 14, 1934, married Ab Richardson on January 19, 1878. They lived on Rowsey Road. Both died of pneumonia.

3. Lee Ann "Lena", June 23, 1862-April 2, 1927, married Henry Brady, February 21, 1884.

4. Rhoda, May 2, 1864-September 20, 1911, married Billie Dent on March 26, 1883. They lived on Rock Cove Road. She died of tuberculosis.

5. Robert H. "Bob", March 15, 1866-March 12, 1934, married Addie Phillips, daughter of Fren Phillips, on November 22, 1891.

6. George Washington, January 11, 1868-January 4, 1939, married Lucy Ann Walker on May 22, 1901. Their family history is given elsewhere.

7. Amanda Catharine was stillborn December 10, 1879.

As adults, three of the sons, Tom, Bob and George, operated, lived on and raised their families on separate sections of the farm.

The first Mrs. Phillips is buried in a cemetery in Denton on property currently owned by Jim Penn. William is buried at Bethel Cemetery off Highway 117. His son, Tom, created Mr. Phillips' tombstone. Tradition says Ninetta is also buried at Bethel Cemetery. –Lesia Sloan Phillips.

PICKETT. James Calvin Pickett was born in 1854. He married Rebecca Ann Davis in 1878, in Texas County, Missouri. They had four sons: James Lynn, Lucian, Hester, Perry and Jessie; three daughters: Jennie Pickett Turner, Lola Pickett Horn and Flora Pickett White.

James Lynn Pickett was born near Alicia, Arkansas in 1887. He married Alice "Allie" Ruth Clark of Alicia. She was the daughter of George W. Clark and Alice Neal Clark of Alicia. George Clark was the postmaster at Alicia in the early 1900s. Alice had two brothers: Henry and Georgie Clark and two half brothers: Jim Clark and Roscoe Corigan.

James Lynn Pickett and Alice Clark Pickett had one son, Lynn Almus Pickett; three daughters, Alice Geneva Pickett Taylor, Annie Urcel Pickett Mathis and Wanda Lynn McLain.

Lynn Almus Pickett married Elva Luther, daughter of Leonard and Ida Luther. They had one son, Michael and one daughter, Brenda.

Urcel Pickett married James Mathis of California. They had one son, Jimmy Lynn, and two daughters, Patsy Mathis and Barbara Mathis Dolis.

Wanda Lynn Pickett married Walt McLain. They had three stepchildren.

Alice Geneva Pickett married William "Bill" Roy Taylor of Alicia. They had two sons, Berland and Phil and two daughters, Judith Taylor Williams and Donna Taylor Dharano. –Berlan Taylor.

FREDDIE JAMES PICKNEY SR. AND FAMILY. Freddie James Pickney Sr. was born February 2, 1921, in Black Rock, Arkansas, the son of William Elijah and Allie May Propst Pickney. Freddie has lived most of his life in Lawrence County. He attended school at Black Rock, Coffman, Bosley and Shiloh. When he was 12 years old the family moved to St. Louis, Missouri. He worked in a poultry house for a year and later as a porter in a restaurant. When he was 20 years old he married Dorothy June Nibblett. She was born June 22, 1926, to Everett and Dora Williams Niblett. They had three children: Freddie James Jr., born September 26, 1942; Dorothy Diane, born Novem-

ber 2, 1944; and Sharon Kay, born November 16, 1946.

In 1943, Freddie was drafted into the Army. He served as corporal in World War II during his three year stay in the service. When he returned he and Dorothy divorced and Freddie returned to Black Rock. He and his brother, Burnis, ran a cafe in downtown Black Rock. They hired a young woman as cook, Violet Viola Lawrence Sanders. She and Freddie married on May 21, 1947. Viola was born June 21, 1924, in Hamel, Arkansas, in Randolph County, but grew up in Wild Cherry, Arkansas, in Fulton County and attended school there. She is the daughter of Richard Ruben and Martha Elizabeth Thornton Lawrence. Viola was married first to Teed Sanders of Fulton County, Arkansas, on October 4, 1941. They had one child: Donald Max Sanders, born November 1, 1943. They divorced and she and her son, Donald, came to Black Rock in 1945.

Freddie and Viola had two more children: Bobby Joe, born March 24, 1949; and Jeannette Fern, born July 28, 1951.

First row: Sharon. Second row: Freddie Jr., Freddie Sr. and Viola. Third row: Donald Max, Jeannette, Bobby Joe and Diane.

Freddie Jr. married Nancy Ruth Woodson on November 16, 1964, daughter of Wesley and Cora Woodson.

Dorothy Diane married first April 21, 1960, to Charles Burley Ludwig, born January 24, 1939, son of Earl and Vella Whitlow. Diane married second June 29, 1978, to Earl Wayne Ragsdale, born September 4, 1946, son of Marvin and Vada Ragsdale.

Sharon Kay married first May 7, 1966, to Paul Erwin Rickterkessing. She married second in 1979, to David Berlekamp. Sharon died December 5, 1990, and is buried in Oak Forest Cemetery in Black Rock.

Donald Max married July 23, 1966, to Patricia Ann Storms, born September 4, 1944, daughter of Raymond and Lena Storms.

Bobby Joe married August 13, 1967, to Elizabeth Ann Wilford, born September 25, 1948, daughter of John and Edith Wilford.

Jeannette Fern married November 9, 1968, to Jerry Wayne Darris, born September 2, 1949, son of Reverend Henry and Zelma Darris.

Freddie Sr. ran the Ozark Service Station on Highway 63 in Black Rock for about 20 years. He retired in 1983, and he and Viola and their children still live in the Black Rock area. –Freddie Pickney.¡

FREDDIE JAMES PICKNEY JR. FAMILY. Freddie James Pickney Jr., son of Freddie James Pickney Sr. and Dorothy June Niblett, daughter of Everett Niblett and Dora Bell Williams Niblett, was born September 26, 1942, in St. Louis, Missouri. He lived with his mother until she died in a car accident on September 13, 1953. He stayed a few years with his mom's sister, Clara Simmons; then moved to Black

Family of Freddie J. Pickney Jr.-(L-R) Julie, Dean, Nancy, Feddie, Scott, Tina, and Josh.

Rock to live with his dad. He graduated from Black Rock High School in 1961. No jobs were to be found in Lawrence County at that time and all of the young people were going up north to work so he left to visit his cousin and painted bridges in Wisconsin. The Vietnam war broke out and Uncle Sam started drafting all of the young guys in his age group so he decided to enlist. He is a Vietnam veteran after serving four years in the US Navy as an Interior Communications Electrician aboard the USS Coral Sea. He married November 13, 1964, to Nancy Ruth Woodson, daughter of Wesley Dee Woodson and Cora Oleta Elizabeth Tyree Woodson, born July 24, 1943. Freddie and Nancy have two sons.

1. Freddie Dan Pickney, born September 30, 1965, at Downy, California, graduated from Black Rock High School in 1983. He graduated from Arkansas School of Technology in Little Rock, Arkansas and has worked for the same company as a field engineer on copiers and micro filmers for the past 10 years. He married June 19, 1993, to Julie Ann Adams, daughter of Larry Adams and Freda Cline Adams, born in Paragould, Arkansas on June 30, 1971. Graduated from Arkansas University June 15, 1995, and is teaching at Paragould, Arkansas.

2. Daniel Scott Pickney, born January 12, 1968, at Lawrence Memorial Hospital in Walnut Ridge, Arkansas, graduated from Black Rock High School in 1986. He attended Arkansas State University for two years and is working at World of Color as a pressman and has worked for the same place for 11 years. He married August 28, 1998, to Tina Annette Maynard Leonard, daughter of Sam Reed Maynard II and Jo Ann Robinson Maynard, born in Jonesboro, Arkansas on December 27, 1967. Tina brought into the marriage one son: Joshua Lynn Leonard, born July 8, 1983, son of Timothy Lynn Leonard, grandson of Raymond Robinson and Amanda Viola Murphy Robinson and Sam and Susie Maynard.

Both Dean and Scott and families live in Craighead County. Freddie and Nancy live at Black Rock where they have made their home for 31 years. Fred has worked for the IBM Corporation for the past 21 years as an Account Customer Service Representative. –Freddie Pickney, Jr.

HARRY RUFUS PICKNEY FAMILY. Harry Rufus Pickney was born March 23, 1911, in Black Rock, Arkansas, the son of William Elijah and Allie Propst Pickney.

On July 4, 1931, Harry married Gertie Lee Emmerton Shannon, the daughter of Hade and Nervy Cebers Emmerton.

Gertie married first to Henry Shannon on July 5, 1923. Henry died April 1, 1928. Gertie and Henry had three sons.

1. William Austin Shannon, born March 4, 1925, married Loretta. Austin died January 25, 1990.

2. Elery Carl Shannon, born March 20, 1927, married first to Caroline Johnson and second to Elaine Barton.

3. Eldon L. Shannon, born December 11, 1928, married Melba Faye Meeks.

Harry and Gertie married at the Portia Picnic in Portia, Arkansas. Harry and Gertie had 11 children.

1. Harry Jr. Pickney, born February 19, 1933, died from pneumonia on April 1, 1934.

2. Allie Jane Pickney, born October 28, 1934, married July 18, 1953, to Kenneth Dale Barton.

3. Nina May Pickney, born May 1, 1937, died from infantile paralysis (polio) on September 5, 1937. It was the first case reported in Lawrence County.

4. Wanda Lee Pickney, born December 5, 1938.

5. Mary May Pickney, born March 9, 1941, married George W. Rice on June 15, 1959.

6. Ruth Willene Pickney, born January 14, 1943, married Everett H. Harmon on June 3, 1963. Willene died on August 11, 1989, at the age of 46. She is buried in Oak Forest Cemetery in Black Rock.

7. Harry Clay Pickney, born July 16, 1945, married August 13, 1965, to Sheila Jones.

8. James Vernon Pickney, born September 23, 1946, married October 2, 1961, to June Bryant.

9. Jewell "Joe" Caldwell Pickney, born July 8, 1948, married Regina.

10. Betty Ann Pickney, born October 1, 1952, married January 31, 1976, to Larry S. Monehan.

11. Ruby Sue Pickney, born August 27, 1953, married Thomas Scrape.

For a living, Harry cut wood, raised hogs and peanuts. Harry died on July 19, 1969, from a heart attack. He is buried in Oak Forest Cemetery in Black Rock. Gertie still lives in Black Rock and is 91 years old. –Lin Eagan.

WILLIAM ELIJAH PICKNEY FAMILY. William Elijah was born January 1, 1881, in Winchester, Tennessee, son of Julius and Mary Louise Yarbrough Pickney. In December of 1887, the family came to Black Rock.

William worked on the Frisco Railroad, farmed, worked at the button factory, cotton gin, sawmill and had his own sorghum mill. William was married three times.

On June 19, 1901, he married Allie Mae Propst, born September 24, 1882, in Smithville, Arkansas, the daughter of Henry Calwell and Clara May Cozort Propst. Allie died January 12, 1979, and is buried in Oak Forest Cemetery.

William and Allie had 11 children.

1. May Francis, born May 1, 1902, died August 17, 1991, married April 28, 1918, to Houston Willis, born July 3, 1897, died December 20, 1962.

2. Marvin Alexander, born November 7, 1903, died November 28, 1904.

3. Alvin Caldwell, born May 6, 1905, died December 4, 1997; married first to Peggy ??, died 1945; married second to Dottie ??, born July 20, 1919, died December 14, 1995.

4. Jewell William, born June 6, 1907, married first to Wilda ??, born May 10, 1900, died Octo-

William and Allie Pickney.

ber, 1981; married second December 24, 1983, to Elna Dowell-Gibson, born October 3, 1900.

5. Clara Marie, born May 10, 1909, died May 1, 1997; married June 26, 1926, to William Narl Nunally, born April 9, 1906, died October 14, 1985.

6. Harry Rufus, born March 23, 1911, died July 18, 1969, married July 3, 1931, to Gertie Prichard-Shannon, born 1909.

7. Lucy Levonna, born February 4, 1913, married July 29, 1929, to Aubrey Kenneth Brandon, born ???, died September 20, 1951.

8. Bessie Allie, born June 14, 1915, married September 13, 1934, to Elmer Walling, born May 3, 1903, died November 9, 1964.

9. Charles Woodrow, born May 3, 1918, died July 12, 1982, married March 15, 1945, to Naomi Diedrich, born March 15, 1912, died March, 1987.

10. Freddie James, born February 2, 1921, married first in 1941, to Dorothy June Nibblet, born June 22, 1926, died September 13, 1953; married second May 21, 1947, to Violet Viola Lawrence-Sanders, born June 21, 1924.

11. Burnis Clay, born January 19, 1925, married July 13, 1946, to Bernice Keaney, born October 30, 1924.

William married second March 5, 1928, to Virginia Victoria Dillon-Patterson, born February 19, 1892, died July 12, 1975. William and Virgie had two children.

1. Willie Marie, born June 25, 1926, married first January 9, 1946, to Larry Ross; married second July 5, 1983, to Russell Fletcher Allison.

2. Merrell Edward, born December 9, 1930, married October 20, 1966, to Margaret Ringle, born March 15, 1921, died January, 1985.

William mar-

William E. Pickney used this combination pea sheller and wood saw on his farm outside of Black Rock, Arkansas, in the early 1920s.–Diane Ragsdale.

ried third, October 10, 1950, to Florence Collins, born 1891. Bill and Florence left Lawrence County and moved to Antioch, California. William died January 24, 1963. Florence died September, 1982. Both are buried in California.

OSCAR POPE FAMILY. Oscar was the son of John Pope and Mattie Elkins. Oscar moved to Lawrence County in early life.

Susie was the daughter of Issac V. McBride and Sophrona McBride. She was born at Imboden.

Oscar and Susie had six children. They farmed at Arbor Grove.

The Pope family moved to Clover Bend in November of 1943. There were six children in the Pope family: Kathleen, Oscar Jr., Gene, Walter, Delphard and Lloyd.

They also farmed in the Clover Bend Community. The children all began school at Duvall. The Duvall district consolidated with Clover Bend in the 1941-42 school year. Gene, Walter, Delphard and Lloyd all attended the Clover Bend School.

Kathleen married Alton Schlueter. They made their home in St. Louis, Missouri. They had three girls. Kathleen died in 1981.

Oscar Jr. married Mary Moore. They also made their home in St. Louis. Oscar Jr. was inducted into the United States Army in 1944. They had two children. Oscar Jr. died in 1988.

Gene was inducted into the Army in 1943. He spent his entire Army career in the Philippines. After his Army years he returned home and graduated high school at Clover Bend. He started his college work at ASU in 1946. He majored in agriculture. He was a Veteran Agriculture teacher for three years. He married Patsy Hallmark in 1948. They have three girls. Gene and Pat are in the agriculture placement business with Agri-Associates.

Walter left Clover Bend in 1950, and began a career in the US Navy. He retired from the Navy in 1973, as a naval officer. Walter and his wife, Marilyn, live in Las Vegas, Nevada. He is presently employed as an electrical engineer. He and Marilyn have five children.

Delphard married Betty Ann Jean. He was in the Navy at the time. The Navy took them from California to Virginia. Delphard was discharged in December, 1954. He enrolled at ASU in 1955. He graduated in 1958, and began teaching Vocational Agriculture in 1958. He retired from the Area Vocational Center in Jonesboro in 1992, as a Vocational Administrator. Delphard and Betty have three children.

Lloyd married Louella Beck in 1957. They have one daughter. They made their home in St. Louis, Missouri. Lloyd is retired as a manufacturing superintendent from Barry Wehmiller County in Clayton, Missouri. Lloyd and Louella own the ALP Realtors, Inc. in Bridgeton, Missouri.–*Del Pope.*

DEWELL HERBERT PRATT was born November 25, 1921, at Richwoods in Lawrence County to Herbert and Elsie Dixon Pratt. He moved from Egypt to Clover Bend with the family in 1938. The family had obtained through a government program from the New Deal, a farm and a new house.

About that time, he went to Hope and then to Texarkana to work in the Civilian Conservation Corp and was there almost two years helping to reclaim land through a soil conservation program. He was paid eight dollars a month and sent home 22 dollars.

D. H. and Virl Pratt.

He bought his first car in 1939, selling 20 head of shoats and three sows for 125 dollars to obtain the money for the car. He went to Tug Terrels at Tuckerman and bought a 1929 A Model Ford, which he remembers was "wore out." He paid 75 dollars for the car with 50 dollars down.

Dewell returned to Clover Bend around 1940, and farmed and raised hogs for a short time. He remembered hitchhiking to Michigan and working as a mechanic 18 hours a day for 80 dollars a week.

Dewell married Virl J. Ward on March 2, 1942, and she joined him in Michigan.

By August of 1942, he had entered the military service. He served in the infantry, first division, Company A, 26 Regiment. During World War II while serving for nine months in France, England, Belgium and Germany, during the Central Europe Campaign, he was awarded a Bronze Star. He was honorably discharged in 1945, and came back to Lawrence County.

Dewell and Virl opened a grocery store at Clover Bend around 1948, and operated the store for almost three decades. The family lived in four rooms in back of the store for a short time, moving to a farm house next to the store, and then building a new house where they lived until 1995.

The store was a gathering place for many of the farmers in the winter time, where they sat around a potbellied stove and played checkers.

After closing the store, Dewell had a used car lot at Hoxie and then owned and operated Pratt's Salvage with his two sons, D. H. Jr. "Hulio" and Robert, for several years.

Hulio died suddenly January 26, 1993, when he was only 44 years old of an apparent heart attack.

Virl and Dewell moved to Hoxie in the summer of 1995. Dewell died suddenly 8, 1995. He was 73 years old.

Dewell and Hulio are buried at the Clover Bend Cemetery.

Dewell and Virl were the parents of three children: Sue Pratt Whitmire, D. H. Pratt Jr. "Hulio" and Robert L. Pratt. Sue is a teacher at Hoxie Elementary and Robert continues to operate Pratt's Salvage in Hoxie.–*Sue Pratt Whitmire.*

DEWELL HERBERT PRATT JR. D. H. Jr. or Hulio, as he was affectionately called by all his friends, was born to D. H. and Virl Pratt in 1949, at Clover Bend. He attended Clover Bend and graduated from there in 1966. He married Becky Britton from Sedgwick, but they divorced during the 1970s.

Hulio worked for a time in Sterling, Illinois, but came back to Lawrence County working for an implement dealer, farming some and eventually joining D. H. Sr. and Robert running the Pratt Salvage at Hoxie.

Hulio loved the lake and the water. He spent many hours there with a wide circle of friends. He loved to tease his nieces and nephews and I am sure they remember a big smile always on his face.

Hulio died suddenly during the night, January 26, 1993, of an apparent heart attack. He was only 44 years old. He was buried at the Clover Bend Cemetery. His father was buried beside him two years later. They are both sadly missed by their family and friends.

"Hulio" D. H. Pratt Jr. 44th Birthday.

Memories of Hulio will include his love of fishing and hunting. His sister remembers the time he stuck a knife in his knee and begged her not to tell "Mom." He gave his sis a Civil War calendar the last Christmas that he lived and it is still hanging with the January, 1993, calendar showing, the month that he died. He is so sadly missed by family and friends. –*Sue Pratt Whitmire.*

HERBERT DEWELL PRATT was born January 9, 1901, to Lonnie B. and Martha Ann Robertson Pratt at Warm Springs, Arkansas, in Randolph County. His father died when he was very young. He had one sister, Audrey Turbeyville.

Herbert married Elsie Elizabeth Dixon, January 23, 1921, at Richwoods in Lawrence County. Elsie was born at Warm Springs, January 22, 1905, to John and Ellen McElrath Dixon.

Herbert farmed at Big Brown near Egypt until 1939, when he moved with his family to Clover Bend. He became owner of a 60 acre farm and a new house through the NEW DEAL. Sometime during the 1950s, he retired from farming and rented his farm out. He then began fishing commercially and trapping. He also worked as a carpenter during that time.

Herbert D. and Elsie became the parents of six children. They are: Dewell, Vastina, H. V., Pauline, J. L., and Marilyn Sue "Pat." Dewell married Virl Ward. They became the parents of three children: Sue, D. J. Jr., and Robert Pratt. Dewell died in 1995.

Herbert Dewell Pratt.

Vastina married Cecil Smith. They farmed for many years near Sedgwick, but are now retired. They are the parents of two children: Lonnie and Connie.

H. V. Pratt married Rozella Massey. Their three children are: Pam Johnson, Alan Pratt and Karen Pratt. H. V. died in 1996. Rozella now resides in Walnut Ridge, Arkansas.

Pauline married Robert Alls. They currently reside on their farm in Missouri after living for years in Illinois. They have three children, all daughters: Shirley, Tina and Paula.

J. L. died in 1996. He has two children who still reside in Illinois where J. L. lived and worked for many years. His children are Johnny and Lisa.

Pat married Gary Permenter and they now live at Quitman near Searcy. Gary is an electrician and Pat works at Johnson Pharmacy. They have two children: Dena and Mike.

Herbert died in 1990. He is buried at Lawrence Memorial Park. Elsie is 94 years old and now resides at the Walnut Ridge Convalescent Home.

Early memories of Herbert and Elsie for many include sitting under the massive trees in their large front yard drinking ice tea in the summer. Herbert would be making a fish net which took many hours of patient handwork. None of us realized at the time what an art this was. Elsie would always have a jar of cookies made. No one ever saw the bottom of the jar. It was always full. Most of us remember Grandpa Hub chasing the grandchildren and romping with them and Granny Elsie would be cooking those wonderful meals. And we miss all of it! –*Sue Pratt Whitmire.*

VALENTINE AND CAROLINE HARGETT PRICE. "Valentine and Caroline Price traveled by covered wagon with ox team from North Carolina, with their six children to Tennessee. Then they headed west in the early 1850s, and settled in the Strawberry River near Smithville in Lawrence County, Arkansas." The parents of Valentine and John Culpepper Price were Monsieur Price, born about 1765, and Mary Robards Price, born 1765.

Their children were: Sarah E., born about 1838; Wilson, born about 1838; David A., born January 13, 1840; Charlotte P., born 1841; Lind C., born 1847; Elizabeth, born 1842; Hampton, born 1845; William H., born 1847; Mary Jane, born 1849; and Hugh Mack, born 1854; Martha S., born 1856, and Eliza A., born June 3, 1860. The last three were born in Lawrence County. Valentine and Caroline Price are buried in Old Bethel Cemetery. All dates are approximate except those stated. They attended New Hope Baptist Church of Denton, Arkansas and are listed in the Published Meeting minutes.

Sarah E. married Obadiah Rider. Wilson had three marriages: Susan Ann Davis, daughter of Ross Davis; Mary West Steadman, a widow; and Nancy Rider his last wife. There is an article about Wilson Price in Goodspeed's *Biographical Histories of NE Arkansas.* David A. had two marriages, one to Mary Blackwell in 1867, and Emily Goodwin

Fortenberry in 1880. Charlotte P. married Shepherd Chaney of North Carolina who followed her there. Elizabeth E. married Jefferson M. Field in 1873. Hampton Price married S. A. Moore in 1872. Mary Jane married William J. Holt in 1860, and George D. Nelson in 1870. Hugh Mack married Lidda A. Moore. Martha S. married George H. Betner in 1873. Eliza A. Price married David D. Davis, son of John M. and Martha McCarroll Davis, in 1878.

The known children of John Culpepper, 1800-January 25, 1862, and Charlotte Price were: Elva M. who married a Gimary; Harriet M. Price who married Jasper Ward in 1860; Jane who married William J. Holt in 1860; William C. Price, marriage unknown; Joshua G. married Mary G. Holt in 1854; Lundy C. married Elizabeth Hudson in 1852. Valentine marriage unknown. Birth dates are not known on these children, but they were listed in the Probate Papers of Culpepper Price in the "Loose Probate Papers - Lawrence County, Marion, Arkansas - Marion Start Craig."

This is a list of known Price soldiers of the Civil War from the microfilm.

38th Company A,B,C,D,G

Price, L. C., Company B, private - July 19, 1862 - Lawrence

Price, W. H. - Company D, private - July 12, 1862 - Smithville

Price, Wilson - Company D, private - July 12, 1862 - Smithville

Company H - Price, Lunday C., corporal - Enr August 4, 1862

45th

Price, Hampton, private - Company F, age 21, born North Carolina

Price, William C., private - Company F, age 18, born Illinois

Price, Wilson, private - Company F, age 29, born North Carolina

Jeri Helms Fultz - April 6, 1998

ROBERT ROY PROPST FAMILY.

Robert Roy Propst, 1921-1995, son of Robert Franklin Propst, 1881-1944, and Myrtle Alma Kidder, 1884-1957, married Carolyn Tate, born 1932, on June 4, 1949. She is the daughter of James M. and Jennie Smith Tate, descended from Thomas Jefferson Smith and Addiline Frances Etheridge, from Kentucky, and David R. Smith and Mariah Hamby, Joseph Smith and ?? Cline and Bradbrook Green, a full Cherokee Indian, on her mother's side and Lee W. Tate and Lizzie Rash Tate on her father's side. He had two sisters, Bessie Bates and Garnet Vance.

The Propst family descended from Washington Alexander Propst, 1850-1938, and Harriet Ellen Cazort, 1850-1938, both from North Carolina. The Propst and Cazort families were charter members of the Old Lebanon Church south of Powhatan. The Cazort family communion cup

Robert and Carolyn Propst - 1980.

was donated to the Powhatan Museum. Washington and Harriet's deaths occurred just a few days apart.

The family of Simeon L. Kidder, 1847-1923, and Emma Mary Cole, 1846-1927, moved to Lawrence County from Indiana in a boxcar to O'Kean, settling at Black Rock. Myrtle Kidder Propst was a small child, but well remembered the move in the boxcar with all their possessions, household goods, animals, machinery and the family members, just

before the turn of the century, probably about 1990, or shortly before.

Myrtle was an avid scholar, though not having too much formal education. She educated herself through extensive reading. A set of books she had, covering everything from algebra through economics, science and history, published in 1927, by Home High School Study Bureau of New York, is still in the family.

Robert was granted a one year scholarship to Memphis Institute of Art in Memphis after completing his eighth grade. After his year there, he spent some time with a carnival, entered the Civilian Conservation Corps, and in World War II, served in the United States Army, 1942-46, in the Pacific area. After returning from service, he reentered school and worked for a time for Karl Maloy Hardware Store in Walnut Ridge and in heavy equipment and electrical construction work. In 1951, he began farming and raising Angus cattle which he continued throughout his life. During the 1960s, and 70s, he actively promoted better cattle by offering an artificial insemination service to the area dairies and cattlemen. Many herds were greatly upgraded through this service.

They had four children: Robert Rendall "Renny," Paul David, Virginia Lea "Jen" and James Franklin "Jimmy." They reared their family on a farm three miles south of Imboden where they moved in 1959, and where Carolyn still resides.

The three sons have remained together in a helicopter related business at Black Rock.

Renny has two sons, Christopher and Michael; Jimmy has three, Blake, Clayton and Matthew. All five are presently students in the Black Rock School. Jen located in the Cape Girardeau-Jackson area of Missouri, where she married Ron Wahlers. *–Carolyn Tate Propst.*

WASHINGTON ALEXANDER PROPST FAMILY.

Washington "Wash" Alexander Propst, February 22, 1850-February 6, 1938, was born in Concord, North Carolina to Nelson Propst, October 9, 1818-1862, and Elizabeth Eddleman, born April 22, 1821, both of Concord. He died at Black Rock, Arkansas. Nelson's parents were Henry Propst Jr., December 25, 1785-January 31, 1863, and Catherine "Katie" Cress, December 4, 1787-May 2, 1856. Catherine's mother died at sea enroute to America. Dr. Henry Propst Sr., 1729-1808, was born in Gandensheim, Germany and died in Cabarrus County, North Carolina.

In 1875, Wash married Harriet Ellen Cazort, March 10, 1850-February 14, 1938, daughter of Anthony Cazort, July 6, 1810-December 2, 1878, and Mary Ann Thomason, April 20, 1811-June 24, 1871, both born in Salisbury, North Carolina and died near Smithville, Arkansas. Mary Ann was the daughter of Burgess George Thomason, September 10, 1780-September, 1844, and Sarah Edy Clary, No-

Washington Alexander Propst, 1850-1938, and Harriet Ellen Cazort, 1850-1938.

vember 24, 1776-July 28, 1852.

Six children, two of whom, Johnny and Henry, died in their teens, were born of this marriage. The other four remained around Black Rock to marry and rear their families. They were:

Robert "Bob" Franklin Propst, May 19, 1881-May 19, 1944, married Myrtle Alma Kidder, October 6, 1904.

Lurene "Bea" Ella Propst, December 31, 1882-May 30, 19??, married Joseph Andrew Corbett, May 28, 1902.

Mahalia W. Hale Propst, September 10, 1884-November 16, 1972, married James Wesley Sutton, September 1, 1909.

Sophronia Laura Ann "Phron" Propst, April 8, 1886-June 7, 1972, married Sidney Beauegard McGhehey, February 22, 1911.

The only grandchild still living in the county is Albert McGhehey of Black Rock.

Other descendants still living in the county are:

Great-grandchildren Arbie Bates, Renny, Paul and Jimmy Propst, Thomas and Bobby Vance, Lynda Verkler, Brenda Wier, and Sid McGhehey.

Great-great-grandchildren Chris, Michael, Blake, Clayton, and Matthew Propst; Omar Vance, Jeff and Eric Vance and Dawn Kopp; Tarra and Tiffany Verkler; and Eric and Shane McGhehey.

Great-great-great-grandchildren Cheyenne and Carter Vance and Michael Colson McGhehey.

When Wash died at the age of 88, Harriet, also 88, went into a coma after neighbors heard her praying to be taken also, and died a week later. They were living in the home of their son, Bob, just west of the Sebastian (Chubby) Spades home in Black Rock at the time of their deaths.

Only the hours and hours of painstaking work and dedication to details over the years of Garnet Vance, daughter of Bob and Myrtle Propst, made this history possible. *–Carolyn Tate Propst.*

PULLIAM FAMILY HISTORY.

The Pulliam family came from North Carolina, Tennessee and Oklahoma, to Ripley County, Missouri, in about 1860. They moved to Lawrence County in Arkansas in 1914, to the Moran Community. They settled around Walnut Ridge, Arkansas. William Joseph Pulliam and Martha Bell Halcomb Pulliam's children were: Ora, Jess, Layman, Oma, Otis, Elsie, Gordon Lee, Leland, Carl, Christena, Lorine and Tom.

Ora Pulliam married Eugene Gimlin. They had Ada, Edith, Ethel, Eve Jo, Raymond, Jewel, Jessie Hope and Betty. They lived near Neeleyville, Missouri.

Jess Pulliam married Emma Risenhoover. They had three sons: Gilbert, Leonard and J. R. Gilbert's wife was Arlene. They had one son, Jessie Dean. His wife is Ann. Their daughter is Nannette. J. R. married Merle Davis. They have two daughters, Beverly and Linda. Beverly married Jim Hathcock. They have one daughter, Emily. Linda married Charles Hendrix. They have one daughter, Trisha.

Oma Pulliam married Duke Burrow. They had three sons: Harold, Deloy and Jerry. They lived in Michigan.

William and Martha's remaining children at Pulliam reunion in 1989. (L to R front) Elsie Hodge, Tom Pulliam, Oma Burrow, Layman Pulliam. (Back L to R) Carl Pulliam, Christena Hager, Lorine Pulliam.

Otis Pulliam married Christina Pearce. They had one son, Donald. He married Evelyn Randolph. They had three children.

Elsie Pulliam married Cecil Hodge. They had two daughters: Betty Sue and Patsy Lou. Betty married Julian Hart. They have two daughters Julia Sue and Cynthia. Julia married Bill Montgomery. They have two daughters, Vanessa and Valerie. Vanessa Johnston has one daughter, Baily Johnston. Valerie is married to Scott Boyle and they have a son, Skyler. Cynthia is married to Jerry Warner. They have a daughter, Dana. She is married to Tracy Moore and they have a daughter, Malorie. Patsy Hodge married Carl Moore. Their children are Gary, Larry, Sherrie, Jamie and Paula. They live in Michigan.

Carl Pulliam married Deronda Hager. They had three children: Douglas, Gregory and Carla. Douglas married Linda. They have Dana and Deronda. Dana married Bob Holland and their children are Mitchell and Jacob. Deronda married Bill Schuber. They have Ben and Veronica. Gregory married Mary Lou Mercer. Carla married Jeffrey Brown. They have Matthew and Lindy. Carl and Dee lived in St. Louis, Missouri.

Gordon Lee Pulliam died at the age of eight.

Leland Pulliam went to Oklahoma.

Christena Pulliam married Lawrence Hager. They had three children: Clara Louise, Joyce and Lawrence Hager Jr. Clara Louise married Glenn Bennett. They have Suzette and Timothy. They live in Yuma, Arizona. Joyce Hager Johnson married Vernon McKay and they have Renee McKay and Jode McKay. Joyce has a son, Christopher Johnson. They live in El Cajon, California. Lawrence Hager Jr. lives in Waco, Texas.

Lorine Pulliam lives in Walnut Ridge, Arkansas. —Loyse Forehand.

TOM AND LOTTIE PULLIAM FAMILY. In
1902, Stonewall Jackson Bryant, August 9, 1871-December 17, 1949, married Ollie Broadfoor, December 23, 1882-May 21, 1952. They had 12 children, including Etta Charlottie "Lottie", May 30, 1910-November 26, 1997.

In 1927, Lottie married Walter Glen Woodard, 1907-1978. Their children were Billye Normalene and Georgia Budea Lorica.

On February 26, 1935, Lottie married Thomas "Tom" Lemuel Pulliam, February 6, 1905-December 20, 1995. Tom's parents, William Joseph Pulliam, April 13, 1874-March 15, 1953, and Martha Belle Halcomb, 1878-July 14, 1951, were married May 5, 1894. Tom was the fifth of their 12 children.

Tom and Lottie's children were Thomas Jerry, Terry Joe, Shirley Charlene "Polly" and Peggy Deronda.

Billye married Charles William "Bill" Holder. Their daughters are Debbie and Denise.

Debbie married Curt Holland. They are parents of Melissa and Joshua.

Denise married (divorced) John "Mac" Collins, died 1991. Their daughter is Christine.

Georgia married Floyd Clay Holder (Floyd and Bill's parents were Redmon and Viola Holder). Their children are Clay, Kelly and Barbara.

Barbara married Thomas Sims. Their children are Staci, Andrea and Katelyn.

Jerry married Joann Brown, daughter of Blanco and Eumeca. Their sons are Thomas and Timothy. Jerry died in 1975.

Tommy married Charlotte Harness. Cody is their son.

Tommy is now married to Rhonda Bailey. Rhonda's son is Jason.

Timmy married Verna Martin. They are parents of T. J. and Chelsea.

Terry Joe married Wilda Richey, daughter of Lester and Ruby. Their sons are Duane and Randy.

Taken at Tom and Lottie's 50th wedding anniversary celebration, February 26, 1985. Front: Lottie and Tom. Back: Shirley Turbyeville, Billye Holder, Terry Pulliam, Peggy Dame and Georgia Holder.

Duane married Jana Clay. Their son is Brandon. Duane is now married to Peggy Hunt. He adopted her daughter, Amanda.

Randy married Leisa Goldman. Their daughter is Grace Anne.

Shirley married Ray Turbyeville, son of Jack and Stella. Their children are Scott and Pamela.

Scott married Rhonda Verkler. Their children are Elaina, Thomas, Janee' and Allison.

Pam married Bill Wilcoxson. They are parents of William and Eric.

Peggy married Buel Dame, son of Charles and Aleeta. Their children are Rhonda, Andrea and Jill.

Rhonda's daughter is Morganne Dame. Rhonda married Kevin Simms. Kevin is the father of Kirk and Lindsey.

Andrea married Kevin Kapales. They are the parents of Makenzie.

Jill married Anthony Whitley. Their sons are Jacob and Austin.

Tom and Lottie farmed in the Clear Lake Community most of their married lives. A self taught barber, he would give many free haircuts to men in the community on weekends.

Descendants of Tom and Lottie living in Lawrence County in 1998, include Shirley and Ray Turbyeville, their children, Scott and Pam, and their families. Also residing in Lawrence county are Peggy and Buel Dame, and their daughter. Rhonda, and her family.

Billye and Georgia and families live in St. Louis, Missouri.

Jerry's sons and families live in Harrison, Arkansas.

Terry Joe and his family live in Jacksonville, Arkansas.

Peggy's daughters, Andrea and Jill, and families, live near Memphis, Tennessee.

—Billye Woodard Holder.

WILLIE LAYMAN PULLIAM FAMILY. Willie
Layman Pulliam came with his parents, William and Martha Halcomb Pulliam, from Missouri to Lawrence County in 1914. They farmed at what was known as the Pulliams Old Home Place at Old Walnut Ridge. He married Amy Holland in 1922. They had four children: Chester, Loyse, Anna and Vida Sue. They moved to the Clear Lake Community in 1938, where they lived until 1968, when they moved to Walnut Ridge.

Chester Pulliam married Liberty Forehand. They had two children: Dennis and Karen. Dennis married Dixie Eno. They have three children: Kevin, Steven and Lee Ann. Kevin married Kristi Washington and they have three children: Ashley, Eleanor and Caroline. They live in Jonesboro. Steven married Allison Davis and they have one son, Joshua. They live in Kentucky. Karen has one daughter, Kerri Patterson. They live in Walnut Ridge. Chester served in World War II in the Phil-

Pulliam family in January, 1972, at Layman and Amy's 50th wedding anniversary. (Front L-R) Loyse Forehand, Vida Rosselot. (Back L-R) Relton Forehand, Anna Henry, Laymn Pulliam, Amy Pulliam, Chester and Liberty Pulliam.

ippines in 1944 and 1945. He passed away in 1983.

Loyse Pulliam married Relton Forehand and they have three children: Janet, Jo Carol and Harold. Janet is married to Daryl Cox. She has a son, Jonathan Surles. They live in Little Rock, Arkansas. Jo Carol is married to Mike Phillips and they have two children: Amy and Craig. They live in Walnut Ridge. Harold is married to Teresa Boyd. He has a daughter, Cameo. They live on their farm in the Clear Lake Community.

Anna married Sammy Henry. Their children are: Kay, Brenda and Christopher. Kay is married to Jack Johnson. Her children are: Lisa Mann and Billy Combs. Lisa has two children: Heather and Brandon. Brenda is married to Douglas Parsons. They have two daughters: Stephanie and Samantha. Stephanie is married to Danny Smith and they have one son, Jordan. Samantha is married to Richard Mitchell. Brenda and Kay's families live in Pocahontas, Arkansas. Sammy was in the Army in Germany in 1952 and 1953. He passed away in 1971. They lived in Michigan for 18 years and came back to Arkansas. Christopher Henry lives in Louisiana.

Vida Sue Pulliam is married to Ralph Rosselot. She has two children: Donna and Darrell Davis. Donna is married to Larry Williams and they have one daughter, Kristie. They live at Ravenden. Darrell is married to Kathy Fortenberry. He has one daughter, Jennifer Lawson. They live in Paragould. —Relton Forehand.

BENJAMIN FRANKLIN RAGSDALE married
Sarah Ann Holder in Lawrence County on September 24, 1875.

Ben was born in Lawrence County in September, 1855. He died at the state hospital in Little Rock on April 25, 1947.

Sarah Ann Holder was born in Tennessee in 1850, and died in 1918. Sarah and Ben are both buried at Hope Cemetery, Imboden, Arkansas.

Their children, all born in Arkansas, were Lou Ann, Thomas 1879, Leona Elizabeth, 1882, William J. 1884, Robert 1888, John 1891 and Mary Sue 1892.

Lou Ann married Charlie Hoggard, Thomas married Mary Annison, Leona married Charles Reeves, William Wayland, William J. remained single, Robert married Jenny Hall, John married Flay Stratton, Mary Sue married George Weaver.

Ben's father was Calvin Ragsdale, born 1822, in Arkansas, died sometime around 1865. Ben's mother was Jane Russell, born 1828, in Indiana, died 1871, in Arkansas. They were married in Lawrence County, Arkansas, September 30, 1847. Calvin and Jane's other children were twin sons, William and Willis, born 1853, Silas 1856, Mary Ann and George.

Silas married Mary Caffle, July 13, 1878. —Nellie Cates.

RAINEY. This Rainey family lived and grew up at 123 East Walnut Street, Walnut Ridge, Arkansas. Pop was a rural mail carrier with a fair income for the 1930s depression years. He had to provide a car for the job and pay repair bills, buy tires, etc. and the remainder went for family living. Mama supplemented the family income hatching baby chicks in an incubator in our back bedroom. She also raised canaries for sale and sold fox terrier puppies. Mama had time for teaching a Sunday School class and WMU at First Baptist Church where she and Pop became members at an early age. All six siblings became members. All six children graduated from Walnut Ridge High School.

Leenell went to A & M College at Jonesboro, where she obtained a teachers certificate. Walnut Ridge hired her to teach fourth grade at age 19. She completed her degree and went during the summers to Oklahoma A & M College to finish a Masters in home economics. Leenell taught Home Economics at Melbourne School. Six months later she went to the Sheridan School to pioneer the first School Lunch and Canning Center in Arkansas. She was District School Lunch Supervisor for the State Department of Education for several years before taking a Parish Supervisor job in De Ridder, Louisiana, where she met and married Joseph S. Mitchell. They were married 20 years before she died in 1979, at the age of 66. Leenell and Joe were involved with several civic groups in Beauregard Parish and enjoyed tour group traveling and fishing.

Laura Lorine Phelps Rainey (Mama), Jack Russell Rainey, Rachel Bassett Rainey, Gilbert Somers Rainey, Russell Rainey (Pop), Martha Jane Rainey, Lorine Phelps Rainey, Leenell Virginia Rainey, July 1939.

Gilbert, at age 12, started working at the *Times Dispatch*. He married Vivian Catching and to them Pop and Mama's first grandchild, Gilbert S. Rainey Jr., was born. Martha Frances came later. Vivian worked for the telephone company in Walnut Ridge and Little Rock. Gilbert Sr. and Vivian moved to Little Rock with their family in 1947, where he was employed by Bass Printing Company. After retirement they returned to Lawrence County. Gilbert Sr. and Vivian were devoted to their church and family providing a "happy home" for them. They enjoyed traveling.

Jack, during his spare time, worked at Otis Catching Shoe Shop. He married Pat Henderson and moved to Magnolia where both his and Pat's daughters, Patsy Jane (Mama and Pop's first granddaughter) and Nancy, were born. They returned to Walnut Ridge for Jack to work at the *Times Dispatch* until he went into the Navy during World War II. He carried the mail on Route 3 and Route 1 in Walnut Ridge. Jack and Pat were also known for their many hours of fishing year round.

Martha Jane entered nursing school at Methodist Hospital in Memphis at the age of 17. After graduation, she became supervisor of Methodist Eye, Ear, Nose and Throat in Memphis, then was an industrial nurse at Newport Primary Training Air Base, before going to Big Springs General Hospital in Texas. This is where she met Harold Thomas Boyd. After Boyd was discharged he and Martha Jane were married in Walnut Ridge at the Rainey home. They lived in Kansas, Paragould, Jonesboro and then moved to Walnut Ridge in 1947, where Harold retired from AP&L and Martha Jane retired from Lawrence Memorial Hospital. Their children, Thomas Russell and Virginia Rainey, grew up in Walnut Ridge. Martha Jane and Boyd were excellent gardeners and kept a beautiful yard.

Rachel, while a senior, sacked groceries at McCarroll's store on Saturdays. During the summer, she was employed by the NYA for 15 days a month and the other 15 days she typed for Lawyer Smith and Dowell Abstract Company. Frank Massey gave her a well rounded education of legal documents, which was beneficial to her when she was appointed to work at FSA/FHA/FmHA-USDA from which she retired with 35 years of CSA service including three and one half years at Walnut Ridge and Blytheville Air Bases where she was a mechanical draftsman. She spent many years free lance drafting for the building trade in Northeast Arkansas. Rachel built and sold several duplex rentals and after about 57 years has retired. She has lived all her life at 123 East Walnut Street, being the fourth generation to own the property. She, too, was an avid fisherman, gardener and genealogist.

Lorine worked "uptown" during her school years at Sterling Store on Saturdays. She met Billie N. Anderson at the USO while he was stationed at WRAAF. Lorine married Billie at the Rainey home and later moved to Sulphur Springs, Hopkins County, Texas. Lorine and Billie's family began growing with Marynell, Rachel Ann and Neal. Lorine died in 1997, and is buried in Hopkins County, Texas. Traveling, genealogy and fishing were their loves and today Billie spends a lot of his time camping and fishing.

The Rainey family was a fun loving and happy family. They were faithful to their religion and church, industrious and stayed long with their jobs and professions. They had many family gatherings. Stories could be told for hours. The 1930s depression was hard, but it brought families close and everyone learned from the exposure. With Mama's death in 1946, the Rainey plot was started at Lawrence Memorial Park. Mama's people are buried at Clover Bend Cemetery and Pop's at Mount Zion Cemetery. Martha Jane and Rachel are the only children alive today. But, there are already three more generations of Russell and Lorine Rainey, scattered in five states. There are many blessings to count. May the next generations have as much fun and love for each other as the first two generations of 123 East Walnut Street Raineys did.

–Rachel Rainey.

JACK RUSSELL RAINEY AND PATRICIA HENDERSON RAINEY.

Jack Russell Rainey was born at 123 East Walnut Street in Walnut Ridge on May 4, 1915, the son of Russell Rainey, 1888-1966, and Laura Lorine Phelps, 1892-1946, the grandson of D. M. Rainey, about 1853-1904, Nancy Jane Bassett, 1869-1894, Zacheus Crownover Phelps, 1858-1901, and Martha Jane Brinkerhoff, 1857-1908. Like Jack's brother and four sisters, he graduated from Walnut Ridge High School in 1933. Jack loved playing football for the Bobcats, especially against archrivals - Hoxie and Pocahontas. He spent a semester at Arkan-

sas Tech, then from 1934-1937, he worked as a linotype operator at the *Times Dispatch*. On November 7, 1937, in Greenville, Missouri Jack married his high school sweetheart, Patricia Virginia Henderson.

Pat was born in the Joplin Community, Lawrence County, on October 24, 1914, the daughter of

"Jack and Pat", about 1936, Sloanville Beach on Black River.

Charles Alexander Henderson, about 1862-1937, and Myrtle Marie Vanover, 1886-1972; the granddaughter of Henry Vanover, Mollie Epley Dulaney and Eleaner Hederson (Pat's paternal grandmother unknown). Myrtle Henderson married Norman Earl Hancock of Carlyle, Illinois, 1943, in Walnut Ridge, Arkansas. After graduating from high school with Jack, Pat worked for the Rehabilitation Administration, USDA; Arkansas Power & Light; Dowell Insurance Agency; Lawrence Insurance Agency; and the Walnut Ridge Chamber of Commerce.

Jack and Pat moved to Magnolia, Arkansas where between 1938 and 1945, he worked at the *Newport Banner-News* and the *Magnolia Banner*. Patsy Jane was born on December 18, 1939, and Nancy Marie was born on June 3, 1942. Jack entered the United States Navy in 1945, serving at the Naval Training Station in San Diego, the TADCEN Receiving Station in Shoemaker, California and as the store manager on board of the USS Sepulea. He was honorably discharged in January, 1946, as a seaman second class and returned to the *Times Dispatch* where Jack worked until 1949. In that same year he became a rural mail carrier initially on Route 3 until his father, Russell Rainey, retired and Jack transferred to Russell's Route 1. Jack retired from the post office in 1977, and died of an unexpected heart attack on February 21, 1982. Pat had died on November 16, 1981, of a rare lung cancer.

The particulars are not the people. Here are Jack's words, written in 1980, describing some of their history:

"Pat's experiences at Joplin were highlighted by spelling bees and ciphering matches. During recess the girls met in the old 'two holer' outhouse and put on a talent show. Pat, being the best singer and dancer in school, promptly told one friend she couldn't carry a tune in a bucket. That girl got off the stage and really let Pat have one on the side of her jaw."

"At the Rainey house, the skillet caught fire on the old wood-burning range and mama told Gilbert, my older brother, to run get the shovel and carry the skillet out the door. After about five minutes she said, 'Jack, go get the shovel - Gilbert can't find it.' I sailed out the back door and there was Gilbert, lying on the ground and pointing his finger at something. About that time the clothesline caught me under the chin and I turned about three flips. I then knew why he never came back with the shovel."

"When we were in the tenth grade, I bought a 1/2 interest in a Model T Ford touring car for $5 which made at least two trips each week to Birdell and Current River beach, got over 20 mpg at 20 cents a gallon - and, no one ever noticed there were no license plates on it."

Jack and Pat are fondly remembered for their mutual love of fishing at all the lakes and rivers of Northeast Arkansas, her singing and dancing (the Joplin Clog), and his inability to sing anything except on occasional "Anchors Away", their many contributions to the First Baptist Church and their love of fun times with family and friends. The Rainey house at 514 SE Third Street in Walnut Ridge prided itself in being the neighborhood gathering place for flying jenny, trapeze, tire swings, softball, basketball and soccer games. Patsy and Nancy, known as the "Rainey Girls", were always in the middle of most anything musical throughout their childhood.

Jack and Pat "Meme" are remembered as the devoted grandparents of Stephanie Rainey Bost, born 1963, Leah Johnsie Bost, born 1969, the daughters of Patsy and they late John Franklin Bost III, 1939-1996; as well as to Bilijack Ray Bell, born 1972, the son of Nancy and Chip Bell. Finally, Jack and Pat are remembered for their deep love of each other.

They are buried at Lawrence Memorial Park between Pat's only sibling, Regena Henderson Spencer, 1919-1994, and Jack's parents. Patsy Jane and Larry Eugene Hollar, married 1983, live in Lenoir, North Carolina. Nancy and Chip Ray Bell, married 1965, live in Dallas, Texas. Stephanie Bost lives in Charlotte, North Carolina. Leah Bost lives in Hickory, North Carolina. Bilijack Bell lives in Atlanta, Georgia. Billijack married Lisa Dickinson of Atlanta on June 10, 2000 and they reside in Atlanta. –Chip Bell.

RUSSELL RAINEY was born near the Mt. Zion Community, the son of Daniel McLindsey and Nancy Bassett Rainey. His parents died when he was very young and he was reared by his grandmother, Laura Gilbert Bassett.

He attended the Walnut Ridge School, Arkansas College at Batesville, where he was on the 1909 baseball team and Springfield Business College. Russell was bookkeeper for Phonix Cotton Oil Company, and Rankin Hardware Store before delivering the mail for patrons on Route 1, Walnut Ridge.

He lived across the street from the First Baptist Church, where his grandmother sent him in his youth to ring the bell and build the fire for services at the church. After he married, his residence was at 123 East Walnut Street with his family for the rest of his life.

At his death in 1966, James L. Bland Jr. wrote "The mail man has gone home," said Reverend Cecil Guthrie in his closing remarks at First Baptist Church. "Getting home" was a problem when Russell Rainey began carrying the mail July 21, 1921, under Postmaster John Pinnell, because of terrible roads and poor transportation. "Pop" Rainey's family grew accustomed to the fact that he was often delayed. When Russell Rainey retired in September, 1953, he had delivered rural mail for 30 years, eight months, and served under six postmasters: Mr. Pinnell, C. W. White, B. B. Fisher, C. C. Snapp, J. J. Sharum and Jerry Bassett. His original route consisted of 18 miles of dirt road, but in 1923, he worked up mail service on old Route 3, and mail was delivered only three days a week, Monday, Wednesday and Friday.

In 1953, Russell's route consisted of 76 miles and he estimated he had driven more than one million miles delivering mail - wearing out two teams of horses, 30 new cars and five used cars. He started with a two wheel cart. When he began using cars Russell once told us, "The car would take out and I would have to walk back to town," but he always recalled with a smile, "My patrons all along the route would help me fix flats, pull me out of mudholes or go to town for the wrecker."

During the tough times of the 1930s, rural boxholders often did not have postage money for their letters (one cent to three cents), but as one man told us, "Mr. Rainey took our letters anyway and paid the postage himself." He also conducted a shopping service for his patrons, buying and delivering to them such things as plow points, hoes, harness, sewing thread and buttons.

The rural patrons would often leave hanging on the mail box a side of fresh hog ribs, backbones, sack of corn or other things and kind words.

J. L. Bland Sr. wrote, "If I were to single out one great attribute of this helpful old friend of mine, it would be, "He dedicated every waking moment of 77 years to devotion and care of his family."

His Rainey lineage goes back to Virginia in the 1700s, and is Scotch-Irish.

His descendants live in Arkansas, North Carolina, Georgia, Louisiana and Texas.–Rachel Rainey.

ANCESTORS OF RUSSELL RAINEY.
Russell Rainey, born August 1, 1888, in Mt. Zion area, Lawrence County, Arkansas, died January 7, 1966, in Walnut Ridge, Lawrence County, Arkansas. He was the son of Daniel McLindsey Rainey and Nancy Jane Bassett. He married Laura Lorine Phelps, November 21, 1910, in Warrensburg, Johnson County, Missouri. She was the daughter of Zaccheus Crownover Phelps and Martha Jane Brinkerhoff.

Children of Russell Rainey and Laura Phelps are:

Leenell Virginia Rainey, born December 31, 1911, in Walnut Ridge, Lawrence County, Arkansas, died December 8, 1978, in De Rider, Beauregart Parish, Louisiana; married Joseph Mitchell Sr.

Gilbert Somers Rainey Sr., born February 19, 1913, in Walnut Ridge, Lawrence County, Arkansas, died February 5, 1993, in Jonesboro, Craighead County, Arkansas; married Vivian Catching, May 31, 1936, in Tulsa, Tulsa County, Oklahoma.

Jack Russell Rainey, born May 4, 1914, in Walnut Ridge, Lawrence County, Arkansas, died February 21, 1982, in Walnut Ridge, Lawrence County, Arkansas; married Patricia Henderson, November 7, 1937, in Greenville, Wayne County, Missouri.

Martha Jane Rainey, born November 20, 1920, in Walnut Ridge, Lawrence County, Arkansas, married Harold Boyd January 20, 1946, in Walnut Ridge, Lawrence County, Arkansas.

Rachel Bassett Rainey, born April 21, 1923, in Walnut Ridge, Lawrence County, Arkansas.

Lorine Phelps Rainey, born February 13, 1926, in Walnut Ridge, Lawrence County, Arkansas, died May, 1997, in Route 4, Hopkins County, Sulpher Springs, Texas; married Billie Neal Anderson Sr., December 2, 1945, in Walnut Ridge, Lawrence County, Arkansas.

Daniel McLindsey Rainey, born August 1858, in Jackson County, Arkansas, died in Woodruff County, Arkansas. He was the son of Daniel P. Rainey and Barbarba Caroline Carricker. He married Nancy Jane Bassett, December 9, 1886, Lawrence County, Arkansas.

Nancy Jane Bassett, born June 3, 1869, in Breckenridge County, Kentucky, died January 1, 1894, in Lawrence County, Arkansas. She was the daughter of Alexander Bassett and Laura Gilbert.

Child of Daniel Rainey and Nancy Bassett is: Russell Rainey, born August 1, 1888.

Daniel P. Rainey, born about 1827, in Giles County, Tennessee, died in Woodruff County, Arkansas. He was the son of Henry G. Rainey and unknown. He married Barbara Caroline Carricker, May 16, 1848, in Hardeman County, Tennessee.

Barbara Caroline Carricker, born December 18, 1826, in Carbarrus County, North Carolina, died 1904, in Woodruff County, Arkansas. She was the daughter of Charles Carricker and Sarah McCommons.

A child of Daniel Rainey and Barbara Carricker is Daniel McLindsey Rainey, born August, 1858.

Henry G. Rainey, born 1786, in Dinwiddie County, Virginia, died June, 1856, in Hardeman County, Tennessee. He was the son of Daniel Rainey and Martha Patsy. He married in 1808, in Dinwiddie County, Virginia.

A child of Henry Rainey is Daniel P. Rainey, born about 1827.

Daniel Rainey, born April 3, 1753, in Sussex County, Virginia, died 1799, in Dinwiddie County, Virginia. He was the son of William Rainey Jr. and Mary Jackson. He married Martha Patsy.

A child of Daniel Rainey and Martha is Henry G. Rainey, born 1786.

William Rainey Jr., born about 1730, in Sussex County, Virginia. He was the son of William Rainey Sr. and Mary. He married Mary Jackson, born about 1730, in Sussex County, Virginia.

Child of William Rainey and Mary Jackson is: Daniel Rainey, born April 3, 1753.

William Rainey Sr. died January 7, 1765, in Sussex County, Virginia. He married Mary.

A child of William Rainey and Mary was William Rainey Jr., born about 1730.

RAINWATER. The Rainwater clan was originally from Germany. It is Rainwater folklore that they translated the German name "Regenwasser" to the English when World War I started, and it became very unpopular to be of German origin. When they translated it to the English some of the Rainwaters spelled it with an "s" on the end, but they later dropped the "s." Some of the older Rainwaters born in the early 1900s, remember their grandparents speaking in German at times. However, they never heard it spoken enough to remember how to actually speak the language. When the war started the older ones quit speaking German altogether out of fear.

The first recorded Rainwater birth in North America was in Danbury, Stokes County, North Carolina. John Rainwater was born here in 1695, after his German parents arrived by ship. John Rainwater married Mary Furrell on June 24, 1735, in Surry County, North Carolina. This couple raised a family and they had from eldest to youngest: John, James, Mary, Sarah, Molly (twin), Millie (Twin), Winney and William. These three brothers,

Rainwater Family Reunion, 1982. First row: Chuck Rainwater, Clarence Rainwater, Kayla, Misty, unknown and Lawrence Rainwater. Second row: Linda Rainwater, Betty Rainwater, Jewell Rainwater Tucker, Annie Rainwater, Edna Mae, unknown, Freda Rainwater Musser, Jason Musser. Third row: Linda's boyfriend, Imogene Rainwater, Monty's first wife, unknown, Earl Rainwater. Fourth row: Calvin Rainwater, Cecil Rainwater, Junior Waite, Bobbie Rainwater Waite, Russell Tucker, Pat Rainwater, Monty Rainwater, Don Rainwater, Richard, unknown and Derrick Rainwater.

John, James and William, are the first Rainwaters in this country according to the first United States census. Most other people came from Germany only after the beginning of the 20th century.

The early pioneer Rainwaters migrated through Tennessee to several other states such as Kentucky, Indiana, Illinois, Missouri and Alabama. About 1850, Arkansas was changed from an Indian reservation to land open for settlement, as the Indians were moved to Oklahoma. Some Rainwater families moved from surrounding states to Arkansas to Randolph, Sharp and Lawrence Counties.

Aaron and his wife, Polly (Mary Elizabeth), were born in North Carolina, and wed there on approximately March 9, 1816. This was abut the time of the great volcano eruption in Indonesia that cancelled summer that year. Summer, 1816, was like winter, so there were no crops causing famine throughout North America and Eurasia. This probably made it hard for Aaron and Polly Rainwater just starting out. Their children born in Logan County, Kentucky, were Caroline, Elizabeth, William, Mariah, Mary, Zilpha Isabella and Martha. Also, born to them in Ray County, Missouri were Margaret Emeline, Harriet, John, Malcomb and F. E. They apparently took in three of Henry and Sarah Parks Rainwater's children that were born in Tennessee-Parks Robert, Pheby and James. Hugh Rainwater of Lawrence County was also a son of this Henry and Sarah Rainwater, and Parks Robert's brother. Something must have happened to Henry and Sarah after 1825, when Pheby was born. My father-in-law, Elmer Lawrence Rainwater, 1907-1997, and Thomas Henry Rainwater, 1867-1964, both claimed to be third cousins. Both's great-grandfather was Henry!–Kenneth Rainwater.

RAINWATER. "I fought as a Reb, and I'll die a Reb. I will never betray the cause I offered to give my life for." Riley Gilmore Rainwater spoke these words, so the story goes, when refusing to sign the Oath of Amnesty at the end of the Civil War. A member of the Arkansas Division of Sterling Price's Confederate Army, he had fought in the Battle of Pea Ridge in March, 1862. On June 5, 1865, at Jacksonport, he was issued a certificate of parole "as a prisoner of the Army of Arkansas, to go to his home and there remain undisturbed."

On Christmas Eve, 1865, he married Nancy Oldham, daughter of Mary McCarroll and Thomas Oldham. Theirs was a union that would last 48 years and bring eight children. Both Riley and Nancy are buried in the Holobaugh Cemetery near the old Rainwater home place.

Riley was the son of Lawrence County pioneer Hugh Rainwater, 1814-1875, and Sarah West Rainwater, 1819-1875. Coming from Alabama to Arkansas, they settled in 1849, near Flat Creek, west of Imboden. Educated as a minister, Hugh helped start the Flat Creek Methodist Church, the first in the county, and served as a local pastor, though he did not join a Methodist conference.

Riley Gilmore and Nancy Oldham Rainwater.

Hugh and Sarah's children and spouses in order of birth included: Mary M., 1836-1917, and Thomas Guthrie; Francis Marion, 1840-1922, and Nancy Phillips Rainwater; Riley and Nancy; Elvira, born 1849, and Matthew Lindsey; Adeline, born 1852, and John Cross; Sarah E., 1856-1911, and Joseph Phillips; Jasper, 1859-1910, and Clementine Gattis Rainwater; and Thomas Joseph, 1862-1888, and Dolly Combs Rainwater.

Although most of these couples remained in the county to raise their families, this writer's ancestors are Riley Gilmore and Nancy Rainwater, who reared six of seven children (one unnamed infant died) on a farm south of Imboden, near Smithville. Four of the six married sons and daughters of J. H. Sloan Weir, begetting 38 double first cousins. (See other Weir and Rainwater stories.)

Henry, 1867-1964, married Bettie Weir, 1869-1961, in 1887. They had 11 children. Viola married Rufus Smith and had five children: Homer, Zillah, Clara, Clay and Hugh. Hugh McGuire Rainwater, 187?-1930, married Mary Louise "Lou" Weir, 1875-1957, on the same day, November 16, 1892, that Mary W. Rainwater, 1874-1943, married Robert Weir, 1872-1943. Each couple had nine children. Charles, born 1885, married Bertie Washum; they had three sons: Addison, Truell and Henry. Zillah, 1878-1980, and Burette Weir, 1878-1959, were married in 1897, and had nine children.

Charles and Bertie's youngest, Henry, married Marguerite Cooper. Their home was in downtown Walnut Ridge, where he had a jewelry store. They were Methodists. She was the church organist and he held many church positions. Their three children, Bob, Peggy and Michael, grew up in Walnut Ridge. Bob, a pharmacist, married Patty Wilcoxson. They had twins, Ross and Renee, and Tommy. Ross married Sherry Brady, Renee married John Bland, and Tommy married Valerie Eskridge. They all have children and reside in the area. –Frances Green.

HENRY RAINWATER/BETTY WEIR FAMILY.
Golden wedding anniversaries are rare. Sixtieth anniversaries are rarer still. When a couple spends 73 years together, the feat is not only rare, but quite remarkable. Thomas Henry Rainwater, 1867-1964, the oldest son of Riley and Nancy Rainwater, married Margaret Elizabeth "Bettie" Weir, 1869-1961, the oldest daughter of J. H. Sloan and Thursa Jane Moore Weir, on September 4, 1887, at her parent's home in Imboden.

Bettie and Henry spent their entire lives in Lawrence County. They settled near Wayland Springs, where eight of their 11 children were born. Later, the family moved to Imboden to be nearer to school. The couple's 11 children were: Bertha, Orville, Riley Sloan, Terry, Juddie, Elmer, Nell, Clifford, Vera, Luther and Opal.

Bertha, born 1888, married George Kent and lived in Jonesboro. Both were long time school teachers in Lawrence and Craighead Counties. They had no children.

Orville, 1890-1967, married Lizzie Wilson. They lived in Little Rock and raised four children: Robert, Sloan, James and Martha.

Riley Sloan, 1892-1979, known as R. S., was a prominent Lawrence Countian. The banker and landowner served as county school supervisor and operated a stave mill and cotton gins. He and his wife, Virginia Hatcher, made their home in Imboden and had two sons: Sloan Jr. and William Imboden. Sloan Jr. wed Sylvia Spikes. They had no children. Bill and his wife, Angie, had two children: Virginia and William I. Jr. Among Bill and Sloan's business holdings were several Holiday Inn franchises stretched across many states. They retained their father's banking interests.

The third Rainwater son, Terry, 1895-1954, married Lena Fender. Their son, Weldon T., became a doctor and practiced medicine in Jonesboro.

Juddie, 1897-1966, and his wife, Otis Linden, had three children: Linden, Justus and Annie Rose.

Elmer, born 1899, a doctor, married June Childers and had

Riley Rainwater in the 1880s, bought pelts all over the county and shipped them to furriers in the city.

Thomas William and Jeri Lynn. His second wife was Dorothy Nerud. Their children are: Dorothy Ann and Mary Alice.

Nell, born 1901, married Glenn Barger. They had a daughter, Betty Glenn.

Clifford lived in the Kansas City area. He and his wife, Louise Stewart, were the parents of a daughter, Patricia, and a son, Louis.

The only surviving child of Riley and Nancy's 11 is the ninth one, Vera, born 1905. She married Al Gunner, who died in World War II and was buried in Berlin. She lives in Springfield, Missouri, as does her son, Larry.

Luther, 1907-1973, also lived in the Springfield area. He married Ethel Thudium and they had two children: Joyce and Shirley.

Child number 11 was Opal "Happy", born 1909, who married Dick Newton and had a daughter, Phyllis, who lives in Little Rock.

Members of the Methodist Church for over 66 years, Henry and Bettie Rainwater personified Christian living. When asked at their 60th anniversary in 1947, to what they attributed their long married life, Bettie brought out a 100 year old Bible and said, "This is it." –Frances Green.

HENRY AND MARGUERITE RAINWATER.
Henry Melvin Rainwater, born in Hoxie, Arkansas on February 24, 1910, was married on December 25, 1931, to Marguerite Evelyn Cooper, born in Walnut Ridge, Arkansas on November 1, 1909. Marguerite was the daughter of Bob and Mae McCarroll Cooper of Walnut Ridge, Arkansas.

Henry and Marguerite owned a jewelry and appliance business in Walnut Ridge and Pocahontas, Arkansas from 1933 until their retirement in 1975. They raised three children, all of whom were born in Walnut Ridge, Arkansas.

Robert H. Rainwater, born February 21, 1935, now resides in Walnut Ridge, Arkansas. Peggy Mae Rainwater, born April 21, 1938, now resides in Hot Springs, Arkansas. Henry Michael Rainwater, born July 3, 1948, now resides in Bentonville, Arkansas.

Henry was active in many civic organizations and was president of the Arkansas Retail Jewelers Association for many years.

Marguerite was a talented musician and was church organist of the First United Methodist Church of Walnut Ridge and a charter member of the Walnut Ridge Schubert Club.

Henry died on March 9, 1992. Marguerite died on May 1, 1998. –Robert Rainwater.

HUGH RAINWATER/LOU WEIR FAMILY.
Hugh McGuire Rainwater, 1872-1930, married Mary Louise Weir, 1875-1957, on November 16, 1892, in a double wedding with his sister and her brother being the other couple.

House on Weir farm between Black Rock and Imboden.

Hugh and Lou settled on a farm out from Imboden. Their first child, Alva "A.W.", was born in 1895, and a daughter, Ina, came along in 1897. She lived less than two years. Everette was born in 1900. He and A. W. started school at Post Oak. Soon the family moved to Imboden near the original site of Sloan-Hendrix Academy, but continued to farm. Daughters Vida and Ida were born in 1903 and 1905. The sixth child, Harry, came in 1908, but died before his second birthday. Robert was born in 1910, Louise in 1914, and the baby, Mary, in 1916. Around that time, the family built a house on 40-80 acres south of town. Within five years, they had moved back to Imboden, where they stayed in the same house until Hugh's death. The family was active in the Methodist Church and believed in education. All but one of the surviving children graduated from Sloan-Hendrix and two became educators.

Highly respected in the county schools, A. W., died 1982, started as a coach at Walnut Ridge School, progressing to principal, then superintendent, then business manager. A. W. married Ethel Followwill in 1919. They had Jacqueline, born 1920, and Gary, born 1935. Jacqueline married William Ramsey and has a son. Gary is a dentist in Dallas and has four children.

Everette Wright, died 1989, married Faye Terrell. They lived in Paragould. Vida, died 1996, married Murrell Moore, who operated an auto repair business in Walnut Ridge in 1928. Neither Evertte nor Vida had any children. Ida, died 1983, taught English and Latin was high school librarian and student council sponsor for many years at Walnut Ridge High School. She was one of the last Latin teachers in the state. Ida never married.

Robert, died 1961, married Inez Groves. They moved to Michigan and had four children: Bobby, Linda and twins, Billee and Bonnee. Laura Louise married Andrew Ponder in 1937. She lives in Walnut Ridge, as does her sister, Mary Agnes.

Hugh and Lou Rainwater's children were among 38 double first cousins as the result of the intermarriage of their parents' brothers and sisters. –Frances Green.

RANEY FAMILY. My name is John F. Starnes of Ravenden, Lawrence County, Arkansas. My maternal grandmother, born Sarah Ann Raney in 1879, was a descendant of one of the area's first settlers. In 1816, her great-grandparents, Samuel and Margaret Raney, along with three other families, settled on Coopers Creek near Smithville. They came here from New Madrid County, Missouri. I can recall as a child her relating stories handed down through the family about the great earthquake which occurred in 1811-12 in New Madrid.

The family's oldest record of Samuel and Margaret Raney is in an old family Bible now on display at the Powhatan Courthouse Museum, which shows Samuel Raney, born August 15, 1777. He was from Virginia. In 1794, Samuel married Margaret Fortenberry, born 1779. They were the par-

ents of nine children. Their sixth child was Radford Raney, born 1812. Radford married Huldah Morris in 1835, and together they had nine children. Of this family, the sixth child was William Masten Raney, 1847-1934, who married Eliza Foster, 1849-1888. Reverend William Masten and Eliza had eight children. Their fourth child was my grandmother, Sarah Ann Raney, Gardner, Frizzell. After Eliza's death at age 39, Reverend William M. remarried and fathered another four children. Reverend Raney and both wives are buried in Dry Creek Cemetery in Lynn, Arkansas.

Sarah Ann Raney married John Lee Gardner, 1874-1904, in 1896. Of the four children born to them, the youngest was my mother, Mary Eliza Lee, 1903-1965. After the death of John Lee Gardner at age 30, my grandmother was married to Reverend M. Watt Frizzell and had two more daughters. Sarah Ann Raney, Gardner, Frizzell was a resident of Black Rock at the time of her death in 1973, at age 94.

My mother, Mary E. Lee, grew up and attended school in Black Rock. She married L. G. "Doc" Smith in 1922. One son, Joseph B. Smith was born of this marriage. J. B. still resides on the original family farm near Black Rock. Upon the death of L. G. Smith in 1932, my mother was remarried in 1933, to my father, William Henry Starnes, 1909-1971. Four children were born of this marriage: William H. Jr., Derotha V., Yvonne Lee and John Franklin. William Jr. lives in Illinois. Derotha and Yvonne are both residents of Cherokee Village, Arkansas.

My mother and father lived their entire married life near Black Rock in what is known as the Mount Vernon Community. Mother wrote the Mt. Vernon news for the county newspapers and was known for her "news", church work and community service. Dad worked for many years as an engineer for the barge lines on the Mississippi River and most of its major tributaries. During his younger life, he was a button cutter at the old Black Rock button factory. The mussel shells from which the buttons were cut were taken from the Black River.

Mary Lee Gardner Smith Starnes died in 1965, and is buried at Black Rock. William Henry Starnes died in 1971, and is buried in Clover Bend. –John F. Starnes.

ANDREW JACKSON "JACKIE" RANEY JR. FAMILY. Andrew Jackson Raney, born 1849, at Powhatan, son of Andrew Jackson Raney Sr. and Mary Steadman, married Arkansas Lee Harris, born October, 1853. They lived at Powhatan, Wheeling and Union until his death. The date of death and place of burial is unknown. Arkansas died November 24, 1930, and is buried in Shamrock, Oklahoma.

Their children were: Oscar Fowler, born July 16, 1875, in Powhatan. He married Carrie Mae Livingston, December

Seated: Arkansas Harris Raney Butler. Left to right: Ralph Cochran, Ethel Butler and May Raney Cochran.

23, 1899. He died October 22, 1947, and is buried in Springfield, Missouri. Their children were: Roy, Oscar, James, Shelby, Hubert, William, Louise and Lois.

Henry B. Raney, born 1879, in Fulton County married Sarah E. Franks.

May Raney Cochran family. Samuel, Ralph Cochran, May Raney Cochran.

Their children were: C. L., C. O., Guy, Grace, Myrt and June.

Lucy May Raney was born February 8, 1880, at Wheeling, married Samuel Mueller Cochran, born October 20, 1872, on December 2, 1900. Their son was Ralph Leland. May died August 13, 1927, and Sam died April 6, 1940. They are buried at Union.

Edgar M. Raney, born March, 1883, married Mattie Cochran. Their children were: Myrtle, Randall, Harold, Ima, Maurice and Don.

Maggie Lee Raney, born 1885, married John William Henry Everett. Their children were: Paul, Nell, Powell, Rex and Janice Everett.

After Andrew Jackson Raney died, Arkansas Harris Raney married J. M. Butler on October 1, 1890. They were the parents of: Ethel Butler and Garland Butler.

Lucy May Raney, daughter of Andrew Jackson Raney and Samuel Mueller Cochran lived at Union where he had a general store and post office. Their son, Ralph Leland, was born on September 16, 1902, at Union. He married Emma Glenn Humpries of Morriston on June 23, 1933, at Oxford. Her parents were Tollie and Elzada Humphries. Ralph operated the Cochran Country Store and was Union postmaster. He attended school at Union, Oxford and Arkansas A & M at Jonesboro. Emma was a school teacher until their marriage. Ralph died on October 22, 1972, and Emma on November 14, 1994.

Their children are: Carolyn Mae, born October 24, 1936, and Samuel Tollie, born January 4, 1940.

Carolyn graduated from Salem High School and ASTC (now UCA) and taught home economics for 12 years. She married Ben L. Atkinson on June 24, 1962. Their son, Adam Bryan, was born on April 9, 1963, and died in infancy. Ben has worked at American Greeting in Osceola for over 35 years and they live in Leachville.

Samuel Tollie married Barbara Jane Ross and their children are: David Leon, born March 27, 1959, and James Samuel, born December 12, 1961.

David Leon married Sheila Campbell, September 15, 1979. They are the parents of Amber Niccole and Ashley Niccole (twins), born January 1, 1981. Brennan David was born November 20, 1987.

James Samuel married Kathy Shrable in 1982. Twins, Kandie Elaine and Kristy Kolette, were born January 26, 1983. Shannon Rayleen was born July 7, 1986. –Carolyn Atkinson

WILLIAM MARTIN RANEY was born October 3, 1847, a son of Samuel Raney and Margaret (Fortenberry) Raney, one of the original settlers of western Lawrence County.

His first marriage was to Elizabeth Forester. They had eight children: Mary Hulda, James Thomas, Nancy Kathryn Raney, Sarah Ann, Martha Caroline, Melissa Lee, Frances Elizabeth and William Marion.

After Elizabeth died in 1888 he married Mary Ellen Mosure in 1890. Four children were born to this marriage: Charles Childers, Effie, Pearl and William. Of these four children one is still living.

Pearl married Ottis Grey and has been a widow for many years. She is a remarkable person still very active, taking care of her own housework, yard flowers and church work. She makes her home in Tuckerman, Arkansas, still living in the house she and her husband shared many years ago.

William Martin Raney and second wife, Mary Ellen (Mosure) Raney. Children, left to right: William, Charles, Effie and Pearl.

On September 24, 1999, Pearl will be 96 years old.

The Raney family reunion is held every September on the first Saturday after Labor Day. Pearl is always in attendance.–*Pearl Gray*

RATLIFF FAMILY. Most Lawrence County Ratliffs are descendants of Zack Ratliff. Mr. Ratliff's first name is spelled Zachaeus, Zacheous, Zaccheus, Zachius, Zachariah, Zachary Taylor, Zackus and Zach in various records.

Zack was born August 11, 1824, in North Carolina. His father was Elam Ratliff, born July 3, 1779, in North Carolina, died August 2, 1855, in Lawrence County, Tennessee. Elam's father was Moses Ratliff, born sometime in the early 1700s.

In 1834, Elam moved the family to Lawrence County, Tennessee. Family tradition is, shortly after his 18th birthday, Zack was given a horse and saddle and, as was the custom in some families during those times, "kicked out of the nest." He, along with two friends, migrated to Lawrence County, Arkansas. Legend has it, lacking the funds to ride the ferry across the Mississippi at Memphis, they swam the river on horseback.

Homesteading a small farm south of Imboden, Zack served in the Mexican War in 1846, and was a member of the 1st Arkansas Volunteers and the 45th Arkansas Cavalry during the Civil War. He was captured and interned at a POW camp in Jacksonport, Arkansas, where he was released at the war's end.

He married Martha Margaret Underwood, February 10, 1848, in Lawrence County. She was born September 11, 1829, died November 8, 1886, and was the daughter of James and Elizabeth Underwood of Missouri. Zack and Martha had 11 children:

1. Melissa J., born January 15, 1849, died January 21, 1899, married Amos J. Bratcher.
2. Elizabeth, born 1850.

Zack and Martha Ratliff.

3. James S., born, 1852, died 1888, married Isabell Justice.
4. Mary A. C., born 1854.
5. Carney Strong, born December 7, 1855, died February 21, 1937, married Laura Louella Dewrock.
6. David G., born March, 1858, died 1917, married Francis D. Webb.
7. Johnson McAlexander "Mack", born January 6, 1863, died April 28, 1941, married Susan Crowden, July 16, 1891.
8. William Thomas, born October, 1860, died 1927, married Harriet Campbell.
9. Louisa Josephine, born August 25, 1865, died May 26, 1950, married Isaac Lonnie Frisbee, May 10, 1887.
10. Martha Frances, born November 23, 1868, died November 11, 1946, married first Irvin Frisbee, and second John Washburn.
11. Amos John Edward, born March 17, 1872, died April 17, 1948.

Zack was a farmer and blacksmith as were most of his sons and he eventually owned a second small farm near Smithville. He died September 3, 1890, and he and Martha are buried in the Smithville Cemetery. –*Troy Ratliff*

DAVID RATLIFF FAMILY. David Ratliff was the sixth child of Zack Ratliff, a farmer and blacksmith who lived in Lawrence County from 1842, until his death in 1890.

David was born sometime in March, 1858, and died in 1917. He married Francis D. Webb, November 5, 1877, in Howell County, Missouri. By 1880, they were in Lawrence County, farming in the Spring River Township area.

They had three children. James C. was born in 1879. Their second child, Daisey E., was born July 27, 1881, and died three years later. The third child, Alta Mae Rose, was born December 14, 1889, and died in 1965, in Indiana.

James was a blacksmith in the Powhatan and Smithville area until his death in 1949. He married Dora Elizabeth White and they had seven children: James Roy, Garland Edward, Dema Avo, Earnest Troy, Lester Cleo, Josie Francis and Robie Arlando.

Garland Edward was born February 1, 1902, and married Fannie Mae Franklin, April 19, 1919. They rented farmland in Lawrence County until 1934, when they purchased 100 acres of land immediately north of Smithville from a member of the Townsend family. They later purchased an additional 100 acres and farmed both

Left to right, front row: McAlexander "Mack" Ratliff, David Ratliff. Back: James Ratliff. Photo taken at David Ratliff's blacksmith shop in Powhatan.

properties until 1954, when they moved to Jonesboro. There Garland worked for Arkansas State University until his retirement in the early 70s, when he and Fannie returned to Lawrence County and purchased a home in Walnut Ridge.

Garland often told his children stories about his childhood in Powhatan, when steamships came up the Black River. He and his friends would swim out, grab onto the big boats, and hang on until they reached Black Rock, where they would turn loose and float back down the river.

Garland died in November of 1990, and is buried in the Townsend Cemetery west of Smithville. Fannie is a resident of the Lawrence Hall Nursing Home in Walnut Ridge. –*Avo Webb*

HOWARD RATLIFF FAMILY. Willie Elsie (known as "Billye") Robins, was the ninth child of Julia Belle Alexander and William Edward Robins. She was born in Tuckerman, Arkansas, July 12, 1906, and in 1929, married James Howard Ratliff, born April 14, 1905, in Ravenden to Owen Sanders and James Thomas Ratliff. They had two children: Jerry Joe Ratliff, born March 24, 1930, outside Hoxie, Arkansas, and Ramona Jean (known as "Jeanne") Ratliff,

Dr. Jeanne Ratliff Terrell Barfield.

born October 30, 1945, in Dewitt, Arkansas, while Howard worked for the United States Department of Agriculture as Arkansas County Manager of the old "AAA" Office, since known as the ASCS. Howard retired in 1965, after over 30 years of service. Billye spent most of her life as a homemaker, dying July 24, 1957, of liver cancer in Jonesboro, Arkansas, where they had lived since 1948. Howard passed away November 18, 1976, of congestive heart failure in Jonesboro.

The Ratliffs first came to Lawrence County when Zachias Ratliff, born in Onslow County, North Carolina, rode

Howard Ratliff.

horseback from Eastern Tennessee, with a brother to settle in the area around Strawberry Township in the early 1800s.

Joe Ratliff attended Arkansas State University until he joined the Air Force in 1951, where he attended accounting school. He left them in 1954, the year before he married Nancy Ellen Watson of Paragould, Arkansas. They made their first home in Laredo, Texas, where Jerry Joe Ratliff Jr. was born on October 3, 1956. Joe moved his family to Memphis, Tennessee, where Donna Michelle Ratliff arrived on October 15, 1960, followed by Stephen Matthew Ratliff on August 29, 1965. Joe is very much the "entrepreneur" in

Billye Ratliff with two year old Joe.

the family; his main endeavor at present is Dallas Wheels of Texas, located in both Arlington and Houston, Texas. As of September, 1998, Joe has five grandchildren.

Jeanne Ratliff also attended Arkansas State University with her first husband, Terry Terrell, until they moved to Atlanta, Georgia in 1967. Terry received his BS in Pharmacy from Mercer University's Southern School of Pharmacy in 1969. Jeanne received her Doctor of Pharmacy Degree in 1987, and followed with a Post-Doctoral Fellowship in Adult Internal Medicine at the University of Georgia. She has three children: Kimberly, born December 31, 1963, in Jonesboro, Arkansas; Christopher, born July 11, 1970, in Atlanta; and Jeffrey, born August 4, 1973, in Atlanta. Divorcing Terry in 1989, she married Leon Barfield in 1991. Leon, a graduate of the FBI Academy, is a retired Atlanta police officer doing private investigative work. Jeanne practices community pharmacy and is also Adjunct Professor of Clinical Pharmacy at Mercer. Kim has two children: Timmy, born April 4, 1990; and Brittany, born March 13, 1992. Chris also has two children: Megan, born July 18, 1994; and Sean, born June 12, 1996. Kim and family live in Loganville, Georgia. Chris and family make their home in Anderson, South Carolina.

Jeffrey Terrell works as a writer for a local Atlanta newspaper. He is a graduate of Antioch College, Yellow Springs, Ohio, with a major in Economics and World Politics. He makes his home in Atlanta, Georgia, too. –Viola Meadows.

ZACHAEUS RATLIFF FAMILY.
Zachaeus Ratliff was born August 11, 1824, in Onslow County, North Carolina. He was the son of Elam Ratliff, and grandson of Moses Ratliff. On December 17, 1810, Elam bought 68 and one fourth acres of land in Lenoir County, North Carolina, from Stephen Cox for 162 pounds 10 shillings. On January 12, 1833, he sold the land to Durant Cox for 250 dollars. In 1834, the family moved to Lawrence County, Tennessee. Zachaeus left Tennessee around 1842. He settled near Strawberry, in Lawrence County, Arkansas.

On February 10, 1848, in Lawrence County, Arkansas, he married Martha Margaret, daughter of James and Elizabeth Underwood. Martha was born in Missouri in 1829. Her father was born in Virginia and her mother in Missouri. Zachaeus and Martha lived on a farm on Coopers Creek. He was a farmer and blacksmith.

When he was drafted into the Arkansas Cavalry in 1845, his job was as a blacksmith and he was responsible for keeping all the horses shoed. They had 11 children. Zachaeus taught all of his boys to be blacksmiths, an honorable profession.

1. Melissa J. Ratliff, January 15, 1849-January 21, 1899, married Amos Bratcher about 1867.

2. Elizabeth, born February, 1850, died as a child.

3. James S. Ratliff was born about 1852. He and first wife, E. Rebecca Justus, had two children, Minnie and Bascom. After her death, he married Isabelle Justus and had Whit and James Thomas. After Isabelle's death, he moved his family to Birch Tree, Missouri, where he died December, 1889. The children walked back to Smithville, Arkansas, where they were taken in by relatives.

4. Mary A. C. Ratliff was born about 1854.

5. Carney Strong Ratliff, December, 1855-February 21, 1937. He married Mary Alta Durock on March 13, 1878. They had nine children: Marlies, Lola Elizabeth, Burge, Emma, Josephine, Jay, Thursie, Mary and Della Ratliff.

6. David G. Ratliff was born March, 1858, and died in 1917. He married Francis Webb about 1877. They had three children: James Z., born September, 1878; Daisy, born July, 1881; and Alta May, born December, 1888.

7. Johnson McAlexander Ratliff, January 6, 1863-April 28, 1941. He married Susan E. Bradford around 1893.

8. William Thomas Ratliff, October, 1860-1927. He was married to Harriet Campbell.

9. Louisa Josephine Ratliff, August 25, 1865-May 26, 1950. She married Isaac Lonnie Frisbee on May 10, 1887.

10. Martha Fannie Ratliff, November 23, 1868-November, 1946. She married Irvin T. Frisbee around 1885.

11. Amos John Edward Ratliff was born May 17, 1872, and died April 17, 1948. His first wife was Annie Mason. After her death he married Minnie Dotson. They had eight children: Ethel Belle, Carrie Alicks, Clarence Edward, William Henderson, Fanny Orean, Luke, Herbert Boyce and Haywood.

By 1860, Zach's brother, Mordica Ratliff, was living in Strawberry Township. His family included his wife, Rebecca J., born in Alabama, and children: Lucy A., George W., James M. and Wiley, born in Arkansas. Mordica died in 1867, and Zachaeus was appointed guardian of his three youngest children. Zachaeus died in 1890, Martha in 1886. They are both buried in the Smithville Cemetery. (Also see Underwood and Frisbee family histories.)

RENNISON-BERRY FAMILY.
George and Josie Rennison, with children Claude, Frank, Delta, Lavena and Mary, moved to the Smithville area in 1925, from Poplar Bluff, Missouri. He bought a sawmill and made railroad ties.

In 1928, George's eldest daughter, Artie, with her husband, Frank Berry, and children, Jasper and Ozelle, moved from Mound City, Illinois, to a farm near the Pine Hill School. Another daughter, Zetter, with husband, Roy Fletcher, and children, Roxy and Sterlin, moved from Pascola, Missouri, to Smithville, where they bought a farm. After a few years they sold this farm and returned to Pascola.

About 1930/31, George sold the sawmill and moved to Sedgwick with his family and the blacksmith shop. In 1936, he bought land in the Whittaker Community and lived there until his death, August 14, 1939. He was buried in the Military Cemetery at Sedgwick.

Jasper Jack Berry.

Claude joined the Army and was stationed in Minnesota. In 1934, he returned with his family to Lawrence County, but moved to Poplar Bluff, Missouri, about 1940.

Frank Rennison joined the Army and was sent to France when World War II started. After the war he lived in St. Louis, Missouri, until his death. He was buried in Jefferson Barracks Cemetery, St. Louis, Missouri. His headstone reads: Frank Rennison, Missouri PFC Co A 1 ENGR C BN World War II Korea - August 19, 1911-April 5, 1971.

Delta married Christopher Sansoucie; Lavena married Edward Conrey; and Mary married Willard Nicholas. By the early 1940s, all of George's children, now adults, began returning to Missouri. Most of them moved on to St. Louis.

Artie Berry worked at the Small Arms Factory in St. Louis until 1947, then returned to her daughter, Ozelle's home where she died January 4, 1948. She was buried in Lawrence Memorial Cemetery at Walnut Ridge.

Ozelle married Herman Mosier. Their first home was in the Whittaker Community; their second was in the Surridge Community near Hoxie. In 1954, they moved with their children, Boyd, Nancy, Gene and Gale, to Clarkston, Michigan. Herman obtained work at the GM Chevrolet Plant in Flint. He died January 15, 1983, and was buried in the Lakeview Cemetery in Clarkston.

Jasper Berry was inducted into the US Army, January 14, 1941, at Little Rock, Arkansas. He was assigned to the 19th Coast Artillery for basic training at Ft. Roscrans, San Diego, California. He was assigned to the S-2, Intelligence Department. In 1943, Jasper was assigned to the Service Battery, 804th Field Artillery Battalion Division. In 1945, his unit was shipped to Leyte, Philippine Islands.

Jasper was honorably discharged on January 17, 1946, at St. Louis, Missouri. He entered the University of Southern California in Los Angeles where he graduated with a degree in law in 1951. In 1954, he moved to N. Las Vegas and married Lydia Hanson. Later, he moved to San Francisco. He died there January 13, 1973, from a massive heart attack and was buried in the Willamette Cemetery, Portland, Oregon. –Ozelle Mosier.

MOSES BOLING RHEA.
In 1869, Moses Rhea moved his bride and family from Salem Twp. in Greene County to his farm in Cache Twp. in Lawrence County. He and Mary Jane Slavens, his third wife and my great-grandmother, had been married May 16, in Randolph County. She was 29; he was 46. Mary was the youngest daughter of Henry and Sarah Slavens who had settled in eastern Randolph County (then Lawrence) before 1827, arriving from Smith County, Tennessee. Henry was a physician, Baptist preacher, magistrate and, with his neighbor Thomas Drew, a delegate to the Arkansas Constitutional Convention in 1835. Henry died in 1843; Sarah was probably also dead. Mary had been living with her older sister, Elizabeth Sullins, and her family whose farm was neighbor to that of Moses and first wife Sarah Lamb.

The third of 10 children of Obediah Rhea, born 1790, Brunswick County, Virginia, and Elizabeth Emma Littlepage, born 1799, Kentucky, Moses was born June 6, 1822, in Warren County, Tennessee. In 1836, Obediah moved his family to Greene County, Arkansas, except for eldest son, John, wife and baby. Tradition recounts that John's wife, not wanting to leave her home, hid their baby with a neighbor until the others had left. Obediah and Elizabeth settled near Old Bethel Methodist Church. He died about 1855, and tradition says is buried on his farm. Elizabeth died in 1868.

On February 8, 1844, Moses married Sarah Lamb, born about 1827, in Lauderdale County, Alabama. Her parents, William Lamb and Mary See, had a farm just west of Lorado. Their children were:

1. William T.
2. Marcinda married William Hennessee.
3. Obediah.
4. John married Lizzie Cooper.
5. Carah.
6. Flavious married Laura Daily.
7. Clovis.
8. Robert.
9. Thomas (Thomas could be the son of second wife, Clementine Seego, whom Moses married in 1868, after Sarah's death in 1867).

Clementine was living nearby with the family of Moses' brother, Thomas Rhea. She died in 1869, and Moses married another neighbor, Mary Slavens.

My grandfather, James Moses, was born July 11, 1870. About the time the family moved to Lawrence County. Mary died in 1871. Moses' fourth wife was Mrs. Sarah Daily. Another William

Moses Boling Rhea, 1822-1893; brother Thomas D. Rhea, 1824-1895; Elizabeth Rhea Rutherford, 1827-1900.

"Will" was born to them. Sarah's death occurred in 1876. Mrs. Ruth Kinyon became Moses' fifth and last wife. She was a remarkable lady, loved by her stepchildren and grandchildren. The First Baptist Church of Walnut Ridge was constituted in her home September 19, 1889. A plaque honoring her has been placed on her grave where she lies next to Moses in the Rhea Cemetery on his farm seven miles east of Walnut Ridge. Moses died March 27, 1893.

In addition to his farm, Moses operated an extensive freighting business and a toll bridge over Cache River. His obituary mentions building projects he and son, John, had undertaken in Walnut Ridge. John opened the Lawrence Hotel in 1877, established a livery stable, and controlled the trolley line between Walnut Ridge and Hoxie.

Moses had a colorful aspect to his character. Court records November, 1874, show Moses and son, Obe "Obediah", as having been indicted, tried and fined for "breaking the Sabbath." They were found guilty of loading turnips onto a wagon on Sunday.

Moses fought under Price during the Civil War and was in that general's raids through Missouri and Kansas. He descended from a sturdy line of Scots-Irish reaching back into Virginia (probably Albemarle/Amherst Co). His great-grandparents, Rev. John M., 1739-1814, and Mary, 1743-1814, Rhea moved their family of 10 children into eastern Tennessee. Eldest son, Moses, 1769-1830, was the executor of his father's will. Rev. John and Mary are buried in the Rhea Cemetery 10 miles from McMinnville. About 1789, Moses married Hannah Ritter. Obediah, the father of Moses, was the sixth of 10 known children of this marriage. Obediah's older brother, John, also settled in Lawrence County quite early and is buried in the Imboden Rhea Cemetery. Rhea descendants are living in Lawrence County today.
–Joan Lamb Towery.

JOSIAH VANMETER RICHARDSON was born May 16, 1806, near Elizabethtown, Hardin County, Kentucky. He is the oldest son of Ebsenzer and Hannah Van Meter Richardson. His wife, Elizabeth, is a daughter of Thomas and Mehatebel Luce Everton. She was born May 8, 1813, at Crooked Creek, Muhlenburg County, Kentucky, and died about 1870, in Arkansas. They were married July 23, 1833, near Rockport, Spencer County, Indiana. In 1844, Josiah moved his family, along with his wife's uncle, John Luce, to Arkansas, settling near Piney Fork, Evening Shade, Sharp County, Arkansas where they lived for many years. (Piney Fork might be in Sharp County now, but Josiah and John are listed in Lawrence County 1850 and 1860 census.) Josiah

and his elder sons engaged in farming. When the Civil War broke out, his two eldest sons, Jacob and Thomas, went to the call of the Confederate Army. Josiah and the rest of his family, and John Luce went to Texas for a few years. After their return, his wife, Elizabeth, died. Josiah died in his 99th year, possibly at Salem, Arkansas. Their children are: Thomas Everton, Dr., born 1935, married first Louisa Johnson, second Viola Virginia Reeves, and third Mary; he died in 1903, Independence, Arkansas; Jacob vanMeter, Dr., born 1838, married first Sarah Johnson and second Elizabeth Breckenridge; he died in 1911, Independence; Hannah Ellen, born 1840; Mehitable Ann "Hetty", born 1842, married William Richardson Carter, son of John and Matilda Richardson Carter; she died in 1919, Polk, Arkansas; Mahala Evervon, born 1943, married George Thompson; she died in 1909; Robert Ebenezer, born 1946, married first Clara Swan and second Rispah Baker; he died 1922, Fulton; David Luce, born 1850; Joanna, born 1852, married first Charles Manwaring and second William Patterson Brewer; he died 1873, Independence; Martha Elizabeth, born 1854, married first Robert Hunt and second William Patterson Brewer; she died after 1915, Independence County. *–Mary Ann Carter.*

MEHITABLE ANN "HETTY" RICHARDSON was born February 22, 1842, Luce Township, Spencer County, Indiana. She is the daughter of Josiah VanMeter and Elizabeth Everton Richardson, granddaughter of Ebzener and Hannah VanMeter Richardson and Thomas "Judge" and Mehitable Luce Everton. She is the second wife of William Richardson Carter, born about 1837, Luce Township, Spencer County, Indiana, son of John William and Matilda Richardson Carter, grandson of William and Mehitable Luce Carter and Ebzener and Hannah VanMeter Richardson. William was married first to Nancy Ann Dunn, daughter of Guilford and Martha Dunn. They were married March 9, 1858, in Randolph County, Arkansas. They had two sons, Jacob Marion, born November 17, 1895, died May 25, 1962, in Oregon County, Missouri, and John B., born January 11, 1861, Oregon County, Missouri, married Mary Jane "Polly" Hendrix, November 28, 1880, Randolph County, Arkansas. She is the daughter of Isaac Brown and Henrietta "Hettie" Rhea Hendrix.

William married Mehitable (first cousin), January 17, 1867, in Lawrence County. They had four children: Elizabeth, born April 22, 1869, married George Washington Brown, August 27, 1886; William Amos, January 1870; Nora Belle, born about 1873, married Daniel "Dan" Ragan, April 15, 1891; and Josiah Vanmeter "Joseph", born June 12, 1875, married Maude Elizabeth Walker, August 31, 1911, in Texarkana, Miller County; she died June, 1929, Texarkana. Mehitable was in household #31 in 1880, a widow and had four children. William Richardson left her and the children and moved on. He remarries and died August 25, 1893. Mehitable died 1919, near Grannis, Polk County. *–Mary Ann Carter.*

MOLLIE HENLEY BALFOUR IVIE RICHARDSON was born July 7, 1865, in Lawrence County to Dr. Andrew Balfour, 1815-1884, son of Andrew Balfour and Mary Henley of Randolph County, North Carolina. Dr. Balfour was a physician and merchant in Powhatan, originally coming to the area in the late 1840s. Mollie's mother was a Hooten. From family stories it is possible her mother may have been Eliza Jane Houghton, daughter of Edmund Houghton (originally from Massachusetts) and widow of attorney Green P. Nunn.

After Mollie's mother died, she was raised in

the John Darter family according to family stories. She also lived with the William Braswell family and his Phillips grandchildren, William, Green W., Oscar and Albert, who were apparently orphaned. Mollie lived with her father in a boarding house two years before his death, along with uncle, Samuel Dayton

Mollie Henley Balfour Ivie Richardson

Balfour and cousin, Mary. After Dr. Balfour's death in 1884, Mollie attended Huntsville Female College in Alabama graduating with a degree in business and music with honors. She received a gold medal for best all around student.

Returning to Lawrence County, Mollie married Henry Ivie, 1866-1900, in 1888, son of Benjamin Warren Ivie and Martha E. W. J. Braswell, who came to Lawrence County around 1860. Mollie and Henry had six children: Elsie, born 1889; Oscar, born 1891; Lillie May, born 1893; Madge, born 1895; Mattie, born 1897; and William, born 1900. Henry contracted pneumonia and died in December, 1900. Mollie later married William Drewry Richardson, 1853-1921, son of Edward J. Richardson. William had returned from the west where he worked as a stage coach driver, foreman on a bridge construction gang and cow puncher. William was working on the Ivie farm when Henry became sick. He promised to stay on since Mollie had her hands full caring for five children ages four months to 11 years. Mollie and William married in 1904, and became the parents of Essie Faye, born 1905.

The family moved from the farm in Denton to Black Rock when Faye entered high school. After Mr. Richardson died and Faye graduated, they moved to St. Louis where Bill was living. Economic opportunities took some of the children away from the area. Elsie married Charles Stewart, remaining to farm nearby. Oscar died of diphtheria when five years old. Lillie May attended nursing school in Memphis and married Malachy Tynan, residing in New York City. Madge married Frank Hill and then Ed Althage. They lived in St. Louis. Mattie married Homer Brown and eventually settled in Alton, Illinois. Bill married Gladys Self and worked for the Corps of Engineers moving all over the country, finally settling in San Francisco. Faye married Henry Carter and lived in Rector.

Mollie died in 1937, while visiting her daughter in New York. Her body was brought back by train and she was buried in the Oak Forest Cemetery. Mollie's descendants are spread from Alaska to Florida; none are now living in Lawrence County. *–Rita Osborne.*

WILLIAM DREWRY RICHARDSON did not believe in living his life vicariously. He was born on January 31, 1853, and spent his boyhood in Arkansas. But as an adult, he headed "out west" in search of challenge and adventure. Had he written his resume in later years, it would have included experience as a stagecoach driver, a cattle drover on a cattle drive from Texas to Kansas, and as foreman on a bridge construction gang. It was this last job that seemed to hold the greatest fascination for him even in later years after he had settled down to farming back home in Arkansas. He was especially enthusiastic about the planning and details involved in bridge construction - particularly when it, also, included watching the railroad progress through the mountainous countryside.

Mollie Balfour Richardson, Faye Richardson and William D. Richardson.

Although still robust and strong, it occurred to William that he was nearing 50 and had saved no money. Too, he yearned to be back near his family and friends near his boyhood home, so he moved back to Denton in Lawrence County, Arkansas. He found a position as a hired hand on a rugged, 240 acre farm belonging to Henry J. Ivie. On December 7, 1900, shortly after William had gone to work on the farm, Mr. Ivie died leaving a wife and five children. The youngest child was a five month old baby, the only son of the family.

Mrs. Ivie (Mollie Henley Balfour), finding herself a widow at the age of 35 with five children to support and being a graduate of one of the South's better finishing schools, had no idea of how to go about managing a farm.

Because he was a man of compassion and integrity, Mr. Richardson agreed to stay on as the farm manager. This worked out well for the Ivie family and for Williams, and four years later, on March 11, 1904, he and Mollie were married. William became the instant father of five. On September 18, 1905, a baby daughter, Essie Faye, was born to William and Mollie completing their family.

In 1946 William "Bill" Ivie penned an essay entitled, "My Dad." In the essay Bill detailed the previous information about Mr. Richardson and described him as kindly, patient, loyal and sincere. Mr. Richardson had that rare gift of giving Bill the feeling of being a treasured son as well as an equal partner in the affairs of the family.

William D. Richardson died on July 2, 1921, and is buried in the Oak Forest Cemetery in Black Rock, Arkansas.

—Doris Carter King and Richard D. Carter, grandchildren of William D. Richardson.

ELMER HORACE RICHEY FAMILY.
Elmer H. Richey, 1896-1982, was born to Johnny H. and John Ada Rainwater Richey at Eaton. In 1919, he married Alice Nora Tretenburg, 1898-1985, daughter of William and Minnie Albright Tretenburg. The parents of seven children, the Richeys were farmers and spent the earliest years of their marriage as sharecroppers, later owning a farm near Crow Creek in the Eaton Community. Children born to them were:

1. Opal Pauline, born 1920, married Vernon Parker, son of Joe Bill and Della Flemming Parker. They were the parents of Elmer Eugene, Edward Jay, Geraldine Opal, Junior Darrell, Ellen Kay, Alice Joe, Jerry Don, Billy Ray and Linda Sue. Vernon died in 1951, and Opal married Oliver Murphy. Opal has more than 20 grandchildren.

2. Coy Richey, born 1922, married Shirley Smith, daughter of Julian and Louise Hall Smith. Their children are Coy Lavon and Steven Lawrence. They have two grandchildren.

3. O. D. Richey, born 1927, married Betty Biederman, daughter of Joe and Ida Strickland Biederman of Colorado. O. D.'s family consists of twin sons, Rickey and Ronnie and a daughter,

Cathy Sue. They have two grandchildren.

4. J. D. Richey, born in April, 1925, died in May, 1925, of complications (pneumonia) of whooping cough.

5. Loyd Richey, born 1930, married Catherine Stewart, daughter of Cleo and Mary Pace Stewart. They are the parents of three sons: Johnnie Loyd, Curtis Alan and Jackie Brian. There are eight grandchildren in the family.

6. J. W. Richey, born 1934, married Elva Lee Cruse, daughter of Estell and Tressie Birmingham Cruse. Their children are Kenneth Hugh, Renee Karen, Christy and Jeannie. There are six grandchildren in the family.

7. Hazel Opha Richey, born 1937, married A. L. Hubbard, son of Lonnie and Mae McLaughlin Hubbard. Their children are Deborah, Jimmy and Paula Diane. There are four grandchildren in this family. *—Catherine Richey.*

HAMILTON W. RICHEY FAMILY.
Our first word of Hamilton W. Richey, born 1829 in Indiana, in the records in Lawrence County are in the 1850 census of the county, where he is in the household of his parents, John and Mary (Polly Woods) Richey in Spring River Twp. In 1852, he married his widowed sister-in-law, Sarah Ann Wayland Richey, who had two sons. She had married Joseph E. Richey in 1848, and he died in 1852.

Hamilton was widowed during the 1850s, and married Mary J. Wayland in 1858. (Whether she was related to Sarah Ann has not been determined.) Widowed again, Hamilton married Mattie E. Walker in 1876,

Hamilton W. Richey, 1829-1897

and she died within a few days of him in March, 1897. Between the three wives, Hamilton was the father of at least 12 children, some of whom we know nothing beyond the names listed in census records. Socrates, Henry, Johnny and Joseph, along with their little sisters, Nora M., Mattie Oma, Flora H. and Emma L. are listed as heirs of their father at his death in 1897. Joseph died before the estate was settled.

Hamilton was apparently a farmer and owned many acres of land when he died. Most of it was in the Black River Township, and located in the hills, but near the Black River bottoms, which would have been swamp land in the 1800s. He had loaned money to many people, and these loans are listed as assets in his estate.

Hamilton's son, Socrates, born 1859, was married to Mary Ann Oldham and they had one son, Oliver Jackson Richey.

Henry Richey, born 1860, married Sarah Frances McMillon (known as Fanny) and though they had several babies, none of them survived to childhood. They adopted children: Edgar Frank Richey, Della Pickett Richey and after Henry died and she was married to Drew Chappell, she adopted Melville Roberts Chappell.

Johnny Harrison Richey, born 1868, married John Ada Rainwater, daughter of Marion and Nancy Phillips Rainwater, in 1894. They were the parents of Elmer H., born 1896; Maudie L., born 1898; Clara J., born 1899; Parvin, born 1900; Juddie, born 1902; Etta, born 1906; Morris and Marvin, twins, born 1908; Mary Susan, born 1903; and Ezra H., born 1910, just a few

months before the death of his father.

Nora Richey, born 1885, married Jim Gilooly in 1902.

Oma (Mattie Aoma) Richey, born 1889, married Will Selsor in 1904.

Flora Richey, born 1892, married John McCallister in 1911.

Emma L. Richey, born 1895, married Elmer L. Selsor in 1913.

At the time of the death of H. W. and Mattie Richey in 1897, the family had just moved into a new home (two story, with three big rooms downstairs, halls between the rooms and with room upstairs for the kids to sleep). The house is near Crow Creek and was still standing in 1990.

Hamilton W. Richey served in the Confederate Army during the War Between the States. He is buried in the Old Lebanon Cemetery in the Eaton Community. His father, John Richey, 1797-1961, served with Indiana militia during the War of 1812. *—Catherine Richey.*

LOYD RICHEY FAMILY.
Loyd Richey was born in Tyronza, Poinsett Co., Arkansas on March 18, 1930. His parents were Elmer H. and Alice N. Treatenburg Richey. Catherine J. Stewart Richey was born in Leachville, Mississippi Co. Arkansas on October 26, 1937 to Cleo C. and Mary E. Pace Stewart. Loyd and Catherine were married October 28, 1955 in Rockford, Winnebago Co., Illinois. They both were born in other countries, their lives have been spent in Lawrence Co. except for a short period of time.

Loyd entered the US Army in November of 1952. He served in Fort Bliss, Texas, Japan, Korea and then back to Fort Chaffee, Arkansas and Fort Hood, Texas. He got to Korea about the time the cease fire was called, serving on the DMZ between South and North Korea. Since his military service, he has followed the occupation of farmer, with extra jobs on the side.

The family spent many years operating a dairy farm, selling whole milk to the Sugar Creek/Hills Valley Cheese plant in Batesville. There were years of growing okra, cucumbers, cotton and always there was hay to harvest.

The family includes three sons; Johnnie Loyd, born November 1957; Curtis Alan, born July 1959; and Jackie Brian, born January 1961. The boys attended their school at Lynn. Their parents attended Lebanon, Oak Grove, Oak Ridge and Lynn.

Johnnie married Mary Elizabeth Robinson, daughter of Donald and Carolyn Robinson of Houma, LA in 1984. They were married in Houma. They have two children; Stephanie Theresa and Shawn Charles. Johnnie has worked in auto repair and jobs related to auto care since before he graduated from high school. He has his own business.

Alan married Debbie Elizabeth Cureton, daughter of E.L. and Durene Mize Cureton of Houston, TX, in February of 1982. They were married in Lynn, AR. Their children are Shelby, Alan Champ and Lana Bera. Alan is an electrician and Debbie works as a substitute teacher and school helper. The children are both horsemen and are champion riders in their Horse Show Association. Sports are important, with both taking part in basketball, baseball, and softball.

Jackie married Lesa Gwen Smith, daughter of Paul and Julia V. Herring Smith in 1984 in Lynn, AR. Their children are Brian Loyd and Julia Rhandi Kaye. He married second, Martha Elizabeth Bunch, daughter of Wilson Junior and Hazel Huddleston Bunch. They are parents of Katelyn Elizabeth Richey and Corey Michael Winspear. Jackie is an auto repair technician, able to take most any engine and make it purr. Brian and Rhandi Kaye attend Deleplaine School. He enjoys hunting and fishing, and Rhandi is a champion basketball player. –Catherine Richey.

OTTO BEVILY RICHEY. Through the lineage of John Richey, there are numerous Richeys and a great many reside in Lawrence County. Because of the vast branches of this family tree, this ancestry is confined to the direct line of Otto Richey who was born, raised and married in Lawrence County and later moved to Greene County, Arkansas. John Richey was Otto's great-great-grandfather.

According to *Goodspeed's Biographical and Historical Memoirs of Northeastern Arkansas*, page 817, John Richey, born in Virginia in 1797, moved to Indiana and married Mary Polly Woods on August 8, 1817. He moved to Arkansas in 1944. John served in the War of 1812 and the militia while in Indiana. John and Mary Polly had four sons: Joseph, Gideon B., Hamilton W. and William Park Richey, all born in Indiana.

Gideon B. Richey was born 1820, and died about 1859, in Arkansas. Approximately 1840, he married Lucinda Woods. Children documented are: Mary J., Margaret E. and William Jackson David.

W. J. D., a.k.a. Little Billy, was born July 14, 1857, in Arkansas and died October 13, 1917, at Eaton, Arkansas (W. J. D. was Otto's grandfather). W. J. D. Richey married Fannie Lee Matthews on December 21, 1879, daughter of Rufus and Mary ? Webb.

William Jackson David Richey and wife, Fannie Lee Matthews Filmore and Ethel Richey.

Their children: Rufus Gideon, Malinda A., Leona L., Amanda J., Sarah E., William Tom, Oscar Filmore and Mary E.

Rufus Gideon "R. G." or "Gid" Richey was born October 3, 1880, in the Andrew Jackson Stewart house, and died at home in Powhatan, Arkansas. On November 19, 1899, R. G. Richey married Mary Isabelle "Belle" Headrick, the daughter of James Marion Headrick and Clarissa Vaughts. R. G. Richey was a farmer and a sawmill worker. He was a member and deacon of the Oak Grove Free Will Baptist Church in Eaton, Arkansas. R. G. and Belle had 14 children: Clara Lee, William Jesse, Anna Charlotte, James Leslie (died at one year), Selma Eugenia, Cleda Ella, Otto Bevily, Henry Cleo, Dessie Mae, Lester M., Clarence Burl "Red", Dorothy Dee "Dot", Mildred Kathleen and Warren Jennings.

Otto Bevily Richey was born December 6, 1909, at Eaton, Arkansas and died December 23, 1968, in Paragould, Arkansas. On February 4, 1933, Otto married Faye Etta Davis, the daughter of Carl Lucian Davis and Rittie Mae Webb, Pearson. They had 12 children: Otis Leroy, Eldrdige Levon "Bud", Charles Lindon, Ruby Irene, Bevily Eugene, Carl Rufus, Roger Dale, Rodney Gale, Martha Ann, Mada Faye, Gary Lynn and Brenda Sue. All 12 children are still living and many have children and grandchildren of their own. Faye Etta Davis Richey died on April 28, 1999.

I have fond memories of trips to relatives around the hills of Powhatan, Lynn, Eaton and Strawberry. Mom and Dad always took us to dinner on the grounds, the homecoming, or as we called it the "graveyard cleaning" at the Old Lebanon Cemetery. Many of our family are laid to rest there at that beautiful place. The heritage my parents left fill me with pride and admiration for our forefathers. It took courage and vision to leave their homelands, to explore and to make a better life for themselves. The Richey family had that spirit and was a part of the early settlement of Lawrence County, Arkansas.

–Mada Faye Richey Barrett.

W. J. D. RICHEY FAMILY. William Jackson David Richey, 1857-1917, is the son of Gideon B. and Lucinda Woods Richey. In 1879, he married Fannie Lee Matthews, 1859-1934, daughter of Rufus and Mary A. Matthews. They were the parents of nine children who all lived to adulthood but one. The children were: R. Gideon, who married Belle Headrick; Malinda A., who married Walter Oldham; Eva died as a baby; Leona (Oner), who married William Stewart; Amanda Josie, who married Harvey Oldham; Eller, who married Joe Casper; William Tom, who married Gertie King; O. Filmore, who married first Ethel Hurst and second Minnie Phillips; and Mary E., who died at age 21 of complications of measles.

"Little Billy" as WJD was known, lived off Highway 25, which was the Batesville-Powhatan Road and farmed. His death came after he had spent the day working. All these named here were married in Lawrence County and are buried at Old Lebanon Cemetery, except Filmore, who died in California and was buried there. –Catherine Richey.

WILLIAM PARK "BILLY" RICHEY FAMILY. William P. "Billy" Richey, 1840-1900, was the son of John and Mary Woods Richey and was born in Indiana. Quite young when the family came to Arkansas, he was married in 1859, to Mary Amanda "Mandy" Singleton. They lived in the Eaton Community. He served in the Civil War. Their family included six children.

1. Elizabeth Mary, born 1862, nothing more known.
2. Lewis Henry, born 1867, married Emma Evans, daughter of John Evans. They relocated to Oklahoma and are both buried there.
3. Lucinda D. "Lou", 1871-1952, married John Nicholas Beary. Their children were: Laura, John Taylor, Nettie Lee, Dollie Ollie, Dolphus Johnson, Tommy David, Mary Elizabeth "Lizzie" and Jessie Terry, as well as three who died as babies.
4. Martha Ann, 1873-1945, married Colombus Clark Chasteen. The family moved to Oklahoma and raised their family there.
5. Amanda "Josie", 1875-1904, married Rufus H. Webb, son of Reuben P. Margaret E. Richey Webb. They were the parents of a daughter, Rittie, and two sons, Dorthy and John. The children lived with their grandmother after the death of their parents.
6. James Park "Jim", 1879-1946, married Leona Oldham, daughter of Henry Clay and Mahala Ketner Oldham. Their children were: Lewis Dewitt, Amanda Mahala Richey, William "Clay" Richey, Lilly May Richey, "Henry" Jesse Richey, Elsy Lee Richey, Martha "Oma" Richey, James Wilson Richey and Ulyess Clinton Richey.
7. William "Clinton" Richey, 1882-1939, married Ethel Casper, daughter of George and Jane Ketner Casper. Their children were: William Odell, George Brooks, Jos Lewis, Homer Troy, Jesse V., Little E., Virgil Oscar, Elsie Jane and Alva and Alpha, twins.
8. Andrew "Frank" Richey, 1884-1974, married Ara Casper, daughter of George and Jane Ketner Casper. Their children were: Evia Jane, Joseph William, George Orris, Ora Amanda, Celia Belle, Ira May, John Daniel, Winnie Ann, Lewis Franklin Roy, Vernon Ruel, Elizabeth Mahalia and Clarence Otis. –Catherine Richey.

VICKIE CLARK RIDDLE daughter of Victor and Patsy Waddell Clark of Lawrence County. I married C. R. Riddle, grandson of the late Mr. and Mrs. Dan Gibson (divorced). I have three children: Kimberly Annette Riddle, age 16, Derek Clark Riddle, age 13 and Drake Andrew Clark, 10 months.

I live at Pocahontas, Arkansas and am the Manager of the Walnut Ridge branch of Pocahontas Federal Savings and Loan Association, Lawrence County.–Vickie Clark Riddle.

Left to right: front row: Derek Clark Riddle, age 13, Drake Andrew Clark, 10 months, Vickie Riddle and back Kimberly Annette Riddle, age 16.

GEORGE HATLEY RING was the son of Edward and Carrie Spence Ring, was born September 1, 1895, in Walnut Ridge, Arkansas. He attended Walnut Ridge schools. Mr. Ring was a telegraph operator and agent for the Missouri Pacific Railroad for over 50 years. He married Clara Moore of Walnut Ridge, who was also born and reared in Walnut Ridge. She was the daughter of J. H. and Naomi Pulliam Moore, landowners in Walnut Ridge. Clara Moore Ring was a teacher in the Walnut Ridge schools for many years.

Hatley and Clara Ring were the parents of two daughters: Jeanette Ring Bush and Katherine Ring Doan. Jeanette married Ben R. Bush of Alicia. Ben was administrator of the Ben R. Bush Elementary School in Walnut Ridge for 30 years and Jeanette taught high school English in Walnut Ridge. They had one son, Ben R. Bush Jr., who married Pamela Harrell and they have two daughters: Tiffany and Jordan Bush. Katherine Ring Doan married C. T. Doan Jr. and they have four sons: Clarence Tanner Doan, Hatley David Doan, Connie Rice Doan and Leonard Dale Doan. The Doans have three grandchildren: Melody, Shawn and David Doan.

Mr. and Mrs. Ring were both very active in all school and community affairs. Mr. Ring was also on the Democratic Central Committee for 50 years, a member of the Walnut Ridge school board many years. Mr. and Mrs. Ring were very active in their church, First United Methodist. –Jeanette Bush.

NOVELLE AGNES ROBINS RIGGS. My path of life started October 2, 1913. I was named Novelle Agnes Robins, the third child of Clyde Robins, born February 28, 1886, and Sarah Elizabeth Blankenship Robins, born January 30, 1889. My father was the first son born to William Edward Robins, born April 4, 1861, and Julia Bell Alexander Robins, born March 14, 1867. I had a brother and sister who died young. My mother also died leaving my sister, Mildred Alice, born July 23, 1915, and me. Our grandparents on our father's side raised us. I grew up on Hoxie Route in a community called DuVall. I attended school at DuVall and Hoxie High.

I met my husband, Claude Riggs, born February 18, 1912, and we married as high school sweethearts in 1932. We had three children: Claude Eugene "Gene" Riggs Jr., born January 17, 1933; Julia Alice "Judy" Riggs, born January 4, 1935; and John Lew "Jack" Riggs, born October 11, 1937. Then the war started in 1941. My

Claude and Novelle Riggs 50th Wedding Anniversary, 1982.

husband volunteered to serve, leaving us to keep the home fires burning. It was a hard time for all. Then in 1945, the war was over. We were still a free country. In 1948, our fourth (and last) baby arrived. We named her Sally Jane, born July 28, 1948. Claude went to work for Missouri Pacific Railroad and we moved to North Little Rock. Our children all graduated from North Little Rock High School. They are all married and we are blessed with nine grandchildren and 15 great-grandchildren.

We celebrated our 68th wedding anniversary in July. We are blessed with good health that keeps us young and spry. I have belonged to a singing group called the Sweet Adelines for 26 years and travel all over the world.

I am 85 years old and have had a wonderful life and I am very fortunate to have had such loving grandparents and an aunt (Aunt Bill) to raise me. –Novelle Riggs.

JAMES RIPPEE SR. 1770-1830, was born in North Carolina or possibly Pennsylvania. We find a James Rippee in 1800, Ashe County, North Carolina census. He was sheriff of Clay County, Kentucky, in 1819, and a surveyor. We have no information on a wife, but know that he was the father of at least 10 children.

Just before the 1840 census, there was a large migration from Brown and Lawrence Counties in Indiana and Clay, Ford and Perry Counties in Kentucky to what was then Pulaski County, Missouri. The greater portions of these pioneer families settled in the part of Pulaski that formed Laclede, which in turn formed Wright, Webster and Texas Counties in 1840. These families included Hickman, Rippee, Young, Newton, Pool, Mott, Teague and Crider.

Edd, Effie, Azril, Thara and Cleatus Rippee. Photo taken approximately 1937.

Arthur Rippee, the eighth child of James, was married to Malinda (Aunt Linny) Young, 1815-1904. Arthur Rippee's Bible shows in his old English style handwriting the following children: Harrison G., John Ervin, William, Lurany, Frances, Mary, Sarah Jane, Thomas Richard, James Buchanan and Martha Margaret.

Thomas Richard, 1855-1896, married Dora West, died 1888, daughter of J. W. and Mary, and sister of George. T. R. and Dora had two sons, William Thomas, 1884-1972, and Edward Thurman, 1888-1964. After the death of Dora, he married Mollie Katherine Robinson, January 2, 1874-September 3, 1945, daughter of John M. and Sarah J. Byrd, in 1895. T. R. and Mollie had one son, Roy Azril, September 26, 1899-March 13, 1905.

T. R. was a witness of the marriage of his

brother-in-law, Stonewall Jackson Robinson to Sarah Margaret Mitchell on July 20, 1901. His signature appears on the marriage certificate. It was after 1901, that he became ill, with what was thought to be tuberculosis. T. R. and Mollie decided to relocate to a drier climate. They sold their farm, which was mostly wooded land, to Stonewall. Thomas Richard was about 43 years old and Mollie about 28. They left for Arizona in an ox pulled covered wagon and were leading a team of horses. There was T. R., Mollie, 17 year old Will, 14 year old Edd and two year old Roy. They joined a group of four families for this journey and additional families joined the caravan along the way. As the wagon train progressed west, T. R. became increasingly weak and died in Oklahoma. He was buried on the banks of the Red River. Molly, Will, Edd and Roy returned to Lawrence County. The trip was very difficult; the ox team was slow, stubborn and unmanageable for the young men. When the animals saw a mud-hole they would take wagon and all right into it and lie down. It was a slow, tiresome journey with long delays between short distances. They ran out of money and sold their horses to finance their trip home.

Molly later married Thomas Pugh, who died after 1950, and is buried in Lawrence County.

William Thomas married Ida Lee Williams and they had seven children: Roy Thurman, 1907-1968; Robert; Reva Christine McCardy, 1921-1994; Vela May Russell, 1919; Elsie Lorrain Hall; Audra Opal Goodman; and Nadine.

Vela May is married to J. W. Russell. They live in Walnut Ridge, Arkansas. They have one son, Larry J., married to Janice Johnson, who lives in Richmond, Virginia.

Edward Thurman was married to Effie Pearl Smith, May 26, 1890-August 8, 1987, the daughter of James A. Smith and Rhoda Looney. They had four children: Azril Thurman, July 6, 1910-February 22, 1993; Thara Robinson, January 24, 1916-May; Cleatus Earl, September 14, 1927-January 23, 1997; and Dewell Edward who died in infancy.

Azril was married to Dora Dean Nicks, July 30, 1910-January 11, 1947, daughter of William Jesse Nicks and Caldona Victory Arnold. They had six children (see Nicks history). He married Wilma Smith, born 1920, in 1947, daughter of William Grundy Smith and Nellie McLeod. They had one child, Brenda Lynn.

Brenda Lynn, born April 14, 1948, married Harold Jones, born 1944, son of James G. Jones and Lelia J. Horsman. They live in Black Rock, Arkansas, and have six children. They are: Harold Blake, born 1964; Kimberly Annette, born 1965; Sheila Lynette, born 1969; Tracy Leon, born 1971; Andrea Elaine, born 1973; and Matthew Blaine, born 1980.

Azril thirdly married Margaret Norene Ball,

(L-R) Children of Fred and Louetta Robert: Louetta Crow Robert, Lillie Robert Smith, Minnie Robert Hutton, Frank Robert, Kathleen Robert Harin, Pearl Robert Hennessee, Bill Robert and Alfred Robert, 1953.

1908-1981. She is buried in Lawrence Memorial Park. Thara married Noah Rayburn Robinson from Lawrence County. They had one son, Patrick Bernard.

Cleatus married Mary Knight from Samburg, Tennessee, 1922-1998, and had three children: Pamela Kay, Gary Thomas and Cleatus Lance. –Brenda Jones.

JOSEPH ROBERT FAMILY. The Robert family originally came from France and first settled in Ohio. They moved to the Bramlett area near Egypt in the late 1880s because of their occupation. The Robert family were timber or sawmill people. They moved where the lumber was. Joseph Robert never learned English and his son, Fred, was almost a teenager when he learned.

Fred Robert married Louetta Crow in 1889 and their decadents were Lillie Robert Smith, Minnie Robert Hutton, Frank, Kathleen Robert Hurn, Pearl Robert Hennessee, Alfred and Lawrence Earl

Frank and Grace Smith Robert, 1941.

"Bill" Robert. The Company K Military Armory of Walnut Ridge is named after Bill Robert because of his 30 years of service to the military.

Frank Robert married Gracie Ann'E Smith in 1918. She was from the Imboden Community of Lawrence County. Gracie's parents were Joe and Sally Judkins Smith. Frank and Gracie's descendants include Fredie Joe Robert, Ernestine "Tommie" Robert Smith and Patsy Ann'E Robert Hicks. For many years Freddie Joe Robert was the manager of Arkansas Power and Light in Walnut Ridge. Tommie and Patsy's families still reside in the community of Hoxie-Walnut Ridge.

–Donna Hicks.

ROBERTSON FAMILY. James Robinson/Robertson and his wife, Sarah, lived in Virginia in 1785 where their son, William Robinson/Robertson was born. They moved into Tennessee where another son, Moses, was born in 1796. They were among the first settlers of Lawrence County Missouri Territory. Later in 1819 when the area became the Arkansas Territory, William Robinson/Robertson was appointed one of the commissioners to select the location of the first county seat in Lawrence County, Davidsonville, now called Old Davidsonville. James Robertson died in 1817 and his estate was settled on November 21, 1817. Estate papers indicated his heirs were his wife, Sarah, along with William Robertson, Moses Robertson, Charles Robertson, William McAdoo and wife, Benjamin Renolds and wife, Isiah Robertson, Charity Robertson and Asa Robertson.

William Robertson was magistrate of Lawrence County, commissioned on September 6, 1823. William moved to Huntsville, Texas, in

T.M. Robertson and wife, Edith Beeler Robertson.

1830 and served in the Mexican War. (Texas was for Independence.) William and his wife, Martha, had six children. He served as county surveyor in Montgomery County, Texas. He was a very religious man and was an ordained Methodist minister. His children were: Benjamin, George Washington, Sarah, Julia, Lorene and Joshua. William also served in the Anahuac Expedition in 1832. He died in 1878 at the age of 93 years.

According to the late Dr. Marion S. Craig, the Lawrence County Robinsons/Robertsons are all descendants of James Robertson. Space does not permit to list all of the descendants. Early records indicate the spelling of the family name as Robinson; later the spelling was changed to Robertson.

Thomas Mose Robertson was born in Black Rock on February 7, 1880. He was first married to Vertie Stratton in 1904 and they had three children: T.J., Doris and Vela. After Vertie's death, T.M. married Edith Beeler in 1915. Their children were: Vernon, Vergil, Shelby, Maudline, Evelyn, Sherman, Nettie, Betty Jean, Bernard, Dora and Lavelle. All 14 children grew up in the Mt. Vernon Community near Black Rock. They attended elementary school at the Mt. Vernon one room school house and later attended high school at Black Rock.

Mose was a well known farmer and highly respected community leader. Edith was a devoted mother who raised 14 children. It is a tribute to Edith that the oldest children, T.J., Doris and Vela, would never have thought from their nurturing and upbringing that she was not their biological mother. Edith taught herself to play the piano and for many years served loyally as pianist for the Mt. Vernon Church.

Mose died on July 13, 1956; however, Edith lived a long and active life remaining devoted to her children and grandchildren until her death on December 3, 1987. She was a quiet, dedicated, Christian woman whose life was exemplified in the biblical passage. "A worthy woman who can find? For her price is far above rubies. She looketh well to the ways of her household; and eateth not the bread of idleness. Her children rise, and call her blessed; her husband also, and he praiseth her." *–Evelyn Flippo.*

DORSE C. ROBERTSON.

DORSE C. ROBERTSON. 27, electrician and construction worker of Black Rock, Arkansas, had no medals to show for it and insisted he deserved none, but he was known for the many times he cheated death.

Misfortune first visited Dorse Robertson when he was only 12. His horse pitched him to a rocky creek bed, breaking his left arm. In February of 1928, while employed by the Hoosier Engineering Company at Mount Vernon, a 28 foot, 800 pound tower leg slipped from its intended mounting then dropped four feet onto his right foot, crushing practically every bone. Within six weeks, however, he was working again!

Although he worked on towers, sometimes 100 feet high, he

Dorse C. Robertson.

handled high tension wires and other electrical devices with little trouble. One of his most serious accidents, however, was on the ground. A Rocky Mountain Limited train beat him to the crossing at Seibert, Colorado, smashing his company car and leaving him unconscious for 34 days. Surgeries for six skull fractures eventually saved his life!

His next brush with death was in 1936, when influenza and spinal meningitis rendered him unconscious at St. Bernards in Jonesboro. Following treatment, he returned home within 15 days. Despite losing a month's work, he paid the hospital bill of 600 dollars.

On June 2, 1936, while helping build a WPA bridge across Spring River north of Black Rock, a faulty platform dropped him 46 feet. An ambulance took him to St. Bernards, where doctors determined only few bones remained unbroken. His spine was broken in two places, his right forearm and wrist were crushed, all bones in the left foot and ankle were crushed and broken, and two bones were broken in his right leg. Six more operations were necessary, and he was left in a cast for 80 days. Steel braces were applied after removal of the cast.

The physical torture was extensive, but the financial strain was significant also. He estimated his bills at 12,000 dollars, only part of which was paid by insurance. He wore a brace for almost a year, then sought a bone graft in his ankle. He recovered to the point of using a cane or crutches very well, but he preferred to walk without aids. His leg was left a few inches shorter than the other. He returned to the hospital and had the leg amputated about four inches below the knee so he could get an artificial leg. Within months, he became mobile again, going with friends and returning to work.

During his last year of life, he worked for REA. Previously, all of his medical troubles were caused by accidents. One night he commented to friends that he had a cold and was going to bed. The next morning he was found in his room, unconscious on the floor. After examination by doctors, he was rushed to Memphis, but never regained consciousness. The news of his death, due to pneumonia and spinal meningitis, shocked relatives and friends.

During his short life, he had sorrow and trouble. He was the "Man of Many Mishaps," a title going back to age 12. He never talked of his troubles, instead he merely went about making friends, wearing a smile and offering kind words to everyone. With loving hearts and hands he was laid to rest. *–Evelyn Robertson Flippo.*

T.J. ROBERTSON.

T.J. ROBERTSON. Thomas Jefferson, "T.J." was the eldest son of T.M. "Mose" and Vertie Stratton Robertson. He was born in Black Rock on November 10, 1906. He attended elementary school in the one room Mt. Vernon school house. He graduated from Black Rock High School and Chilocothe Business College in Chilocothe, Missouri. As a young boy he remembered traveling with his father in a covered wagon to Oklahoma to claim land. He recalled that his father was well liked by the Indians they met and that the Indians were very friendly. This trip as a young boy was only the beginning of travel around the world for T.J. as a young adult.

After college, T.J. returned home and worked for many years for the W.P.A. as foreman where he helped build many bridges in Lawrence County. He worked for the R.E.A. (Rural Electrification Administration) as an engineer in building power lines throughout Arkansas. He also served as director for R.E.A. In the 1930s T.J. was named the first manager of Craighead Electric when the multi-county

cooperative was organized.

During World War II, he became a regional official of the REA based in St. Louis, Missouri. After the war he organized his own electrical construction company, "T.J. Robertson and Company," which built lines and power stations in the United States and in several foreign countries, including Libya, Nigeria and Nepal.

T.J. Robertson in Russia reading Russian newspaper, about 1953.

T.J. was well read and he enjoyed traveling around the world spending time in China. In 1953 he was one of four men from Arkansas who were delegates to the American Exposition held in the Soviet Union at Moscow. T.J. was very active in the political campaign of former Governor Winthrop Rockefeller and was a longtime member of the Jonesboro Rotary Club.

He was married to Mildred Cox of Pocahontas of which there was no issue and his second wife was Clelia Watts Wayland of Black Rock of which there was no issue. After a successful career in construction, T.J. retired in Jonesboro and operated an office in the Citizens Bank Building. T.J. was highly respected in the Jonesboro community and will long be remembered in helping obtain better living conditions for rural Arkansas. He died on January 3, 1995, and was laid to rest in the Jonesboro Memorial Park Cemetery. *–Evelyn Robertson Flippo.*

THOMAS ZANE ROBERTSON

THOMAS ZANE ROBERTSON, 1963-1973, was a young man adult in stature and mind. He was only 10 years old when his life was taken in a tractor rollover accident near Kirkland, Illinois. His knowledge of farming and farm machinery was equal to any adult, having spent his life on the family farm working side by side with his dad. He loved farming and farm machinery. In school he was a model student and partici-

Thomas Zane Robertson, 1963-1973.

pated in many activities. In FFA and 4-H he showed his prize-winning cattle and was always a winner. He was also a member of Kirkland United Methodist Church and loved everyone.

Tom loved to come to Arkansas and visit his relatives and his dad's Arkansas farms. He was always talking about farming to everyone he met.

Thomas Zane "Tom" was the son of Bernard and Carol Robertson. He had two brothers, David and Craig, and two sisters, Elaine and Sandra.

Near Kirkland, Illinois, on Cherry Valley Road you can see the high silo for miles around that reads:

"In Loving Memory of a Fine Son"

–Miriam Flippo Smith.

JOHN E. "EDD" ROBINS AND LOIS E. CAMPBELL ROBINS.

Edd was born on July 23, 1902, third child of Louis Robins and Elvira Turnbow Robins. His roots go back to the early days of Lawrence County, through the Robins, Goodwin, Turnbow and Fortenberry families.

Lois was the eldest child of Sidney "Sid" Campbell and Mary "Hugg" Campbell. Her roots were also well established in the area, through the Campbells, Wares, Hugg and Lane families.

Ed and Lois both attended school at the Jesup Community and were childhood sweethearts. They were united in marriage on December 30 ,1923, in the home of O. C. Bowers near Calamine with Clyde Foley and Emma Young as witnesses. From this union four children were born.

Edd and Louis Robins.

1. Ed Jr. was born on November 3, 1924. He died on February 28, 1943.

2. Charles Bernard, born July 26, 1928, currently resides near Strawberry.

3. Mollie Faye, born December 18, 1932, currently resides at 57 Harmon Drive in Lebanon, Illinois.

4. Joe Keith, born November 3, 1935, currently resides in Las Vegas, Nevada.

Ed and Lois went to California as a young couple. They spent some time in Phoenix, Arizona. They returned to their roots in 1925, and lived out their days on a small farm on Reeds Creek, where they farmed, mostly with Hereford cattle and in later years with chickens. Ed died suddenly on January 24, 1987. Lois, after the passing of Ed, lived for two years in West Memphis with her son and his wife, Martha; then upon Charles' retirement, they moved back to the Strawberry Community. She passed away on June 2, 1994, at the Cave City Nursing Home. *–Charles Robins.*

JOHN LOUIS ROBINS FAMILY.

John Louis Robins was born near Smithville on September 5, 1874, to Thomas S. and Nancy Elander Goodwin Robins (see write-up on this family elsewhere in this book). Louis was raised in the Smithville area, and with the exception of two years in California, spent his entire life in and around Smithville and Jesup.

Louis was the only child of Thomas and Nancy Robins although he had several half brothers and sisters from his father's first marriage. These brothers and sisters resided in the Clover Bend and Hoxie areas of Lawrence County and near Supply in Randolph County. Nancy Goodwin died in 1876, when Louis was only two years old. It is not known what became of Thomas Robins. Louis was raised by his maternal grandparents, John and Monima Goodwin of Smithville. The Goodwins had settled in the Smithville area around 1851, from Alabama. John Goodwin was a Confederate veteran having served with an Arkansas regiment during the war.

On July 15, 1893, Louis married Elvira Turnbow, the daughter of John B. "Frank" Turnbow. John B. Turnbow served for a few months in the Confederate Army until they found out he was only 15 and they discharged him while he was in Tennessee. Elvira, usually called Viry, was a great-granddaughter of one of Lawrence County's early pioneer families, Jacob and Nancy Taylor Fortenberry. She was the granddaughter

of Taylor and Elizabeth Catron Fortenberry. Louis and Viry were the parents of nine children; two died in early childhood. The other seven were raised in Lawrence County and lived a good portion of their lives in that area.

During his lifetime, Louis Robins pursued several occupations. In his early years he

John Louis Robins

taught school (including one session at the old Shady Grove School near Jesup). During his growing up years, he helped his Grandfather Goodwin in his carpentry business which included furniture making and the building of caskets. In the early 1900s, Louis worked in the general store at Jesup, clerking for Will Penn. He later owned a small farm on the Strawberry River between Jesup and Smithville. The hill on which the farm was located was commonly referred to as "Robins Hill." This is now the Dennis Guthrie place. In 1916, Louis was elected to be the Lawrence County surveyor on a write-in vote, but declined to serve. During this time period, his Grandfather Goodwin died, as did his father-in-law, John Turnbow. Louis and Viry sold their farm on Strawberry River about 1919, and moved their family to San Bernardino, California. The family rode the train to California. They arrived in Colton and then traveled to San Bernardino. While in that city, Louis worked for the railroad repair yards.

In 1921, the Robins family returned to Jesup in Lawrence County. They later moved to a farm on Reeds Creek and farmed that land for a period of time. Through the 1920s, he carried the mail from Jesup to Eaton and back. The route was made by horse and wagon, and on most days (especially during bad weather) it would be dark by the time the mail got back from the Denton Post Office. During the 1930s, Louis worked for the US Government Farm Program by insuring that farmers stayed within their allotted cotton crops. In the late 1930s, Louis began experiencing bad health that stayed with him until he died on June 23, 1944. Elvira Robins then lived with her daughter, Maude Howard, until her death on March 8, 1956. Both are buried in Lancaster Cemetery not far from the graves of her parents, John and Martha Turnbow and her great-grandparents, Jacob and Nancy Fortenberry. Both Mr. and Mrs. Robins had been very active in the Eli Lindsey Methodist Church at Jesup.

The children of Louis and Elvira Robins all married from families of Lawrence County, and by the time of Mrs. Robin's death in 1956, had produced 11 grandchildren. Louis lived long enough to see all of them, but one. One preceded him in death by about a year. The children of Louis and Elvira are:

1. Fannie Mae Robins, the oldest of nine children. Mae was born August 1, 1894. She

Elvira Turnbow Robins.

married Roscoe O. Sullivan of Calamine on February 3, 1924, and they lived in Calamine the rest of their lives. Roscoe and Mae operated a store and the post office in Calamine for many years. There were no children born to this union. Mae died March 22, 1966, and Roscoe, February 18, 1963. Both are buried in Sullivan Cemetery in Calamine.

2. Charles Taylor Robins. Taylor was born on January 6, 1897. He married Ida Wallace on November 22, 1919. One son, Charles Taylor Jr., was born to them; and he and his wife, Janie Gryder, reside in Lubbock, Texas. Taylor and Ida spent many years living in Texas and Arizona where Taylor worked as a carpenter and in a produce warehouse. During World War I, he served in the US Navy. Taylor and Ida retired in their native Arkansas in 1975, and settled in Cave City. Ida passed away at Cave City on March 19, 1977, and Taylor died July 28, 1900, at age 93. Both are buried in Lancaster Cemetery.

3. Maude Belle Robins. Maude Robins was born September, 1899, and on January 18, 1920, married Troy Howard. Maude and Troy did not have any children, and with the exception of four or five years in California and Arizona, lived their entire lives in and around the Jesup area. Troy was a farmer and dealt in livestock. He ran a gristmill for many years at his home in Jesup. Troy passed away on October 22, 1967, and is buried in Lancaster Cemetery. Maude then moved to Cave City and lived there until her death on May 14, 1983. She is also buried in the Lancaster Cem-

Jim and Mollie Robins family. Left to right: Byron, Jim, Barbara, David, Mollie, Martha, Bob.

etery.

4. John Edward Robins. Ed Robins was born July 23, 1903. He married Lois Campbell on December 30, 1923. Ed and Lois spent most of their lives in Lawrence County, near Strawberry and Jesup. They spent a short time in California and Arizona. They farmed for many years near Reeds Creek and then retired at that location. This is very near where Ed's great-great-grandparents, Jacob and Nancy Fortenberry, settled when they came to Arkansas in 1816. Ed Robins passed away on January 24, 1987, and Lois on June 3, 1994. Both are buried in Lancaster Cemetery. Four children were born to Ed and Lois. Ed Jr., the oldest, passed away at age 20 on February 28, 1943, and is buried in Lancaster Cemetery. The other three children are: Charles Bernard, Molly Faye and Joe Keith. Bernard and Martha Ferguson Robins live in Strawberry, Molly and her husband, Hoover Guthrie, live in Lenannon, Illinois, and Joe Keith and his wife, Therese Patient Robins, also live in Strawberry.

5. Benjamin Clyde Robins. Clyde Robins was born January 15, 1906, and married Helen Avo Hillhouse on May 26, 1929. Clyde and Helen spent most of their adult lives in Phoenix, Arizona, where Clyde was employed the majority of the time as a government inspec-

tor of citrus and vegetables in Arizona, New Mexico and California. Helen was a bookkeeper and personnel manager for one of Phoenix's largest dry cleaners. Clyde and Helen were the parents of one child, Ferna, who now resides in Boulder City, Nevada with her husband, Arno Marsh. After many years of marriage, Clyde and Helen were divorced. Clyde later married a woman in Arizona whose name was also Helen, but whose last name is unknown. This marriage also ended in divorce. Clyde and Helen Hillhouse remarried, but unfortunately this lasted only seven years and they were once again divorced. Clyde then married Mary Burdine. They retired and moved back to Jesup. Mary died August 14, 1978, and was buried in Lancaster Cemetery. Clyde then sold his place in Jesup and moved to Cave City. Clyde and Helen became fast companions, but never remarried. Clyde died November 8, 1982, and is buried at Lancaster Cemetery. Helen legally changed her name to Robins and presently resides in Batesville.

6. Pearl Robins was born September 2, 1908, and married Everette Milligan on December 24, 1925. Everette and Pearl farmed a place near Jesup until about 1938, when they moved to Phoenix, Arizona. Everette was a produce manager for a retail grocer and Pearl was a manager of a major gift shop. She traveled to Los Angeles twice a year to buy merchandise for the shop. Pearl and Everette did not have any children. In 1971, they retired and moved to Cave City. They were active members of the Cave City Church of Christ. Everette passed away on April 21, 1986, and was buried in Lancaster Cemetery. Pearl now resides in Batesville where she recently celebrated her 90th birthday.

7. Leland Stanford Robins was born March 1, 1911, and died May 27, 1911. He is buried in Lancaster Cemetery next to his mother and father.

8. Lois Robins was born August 7, 1912, and died January 15, 1913. Lois is buried at Lancaster next to her family.

9. James Lowell Robins, the youngest child of Louis and Elvira Robins, was born January 5, 1914. He married Mollie Faye Andrews of Strawberry on October 9, 1935 (see E. B. Andrews family elsewhere in this book). Jim taught school for about four years from 1935, through 1938. He taught at Pleasant Hill, Strawberry, Jesup and Calamine. Following that he worked for three years for the Arkansas Department of Welfare in Walnut Ridge. He then became involved in the furniture business with the Wilcoxson's store in Walnut Ridge. Over the next 35 years, he either owned or worked in furniture stores in Arkansas, Missouri and Tennessee. In Dexter, Missouri, Jim served as city alderman for four years and both he and Mollie were very active in the First Baptist Church there. They have raised five children: Bobby Lowell, who married Patrica Gould and resides in Cape Girardeau, Missouri; Byron Louis, who married Wannetta Cave and lives in Absecon, New Jersey; Barbara Ann, who married Gerald Billions and now resides in Germantown, Tennessee; James David, who married Janis Hawk and resides in Huntsville, Alabama; and Martha Jo, who first married Denny Willis and then Joseph Ruiz, and she and Joe live in Baltimore, Maryland. Jim and Mollie retired from the furniture business in 1976, and retired to Cave City where they reside today. Jim has been active in the local Kiwanis Chapter there and both he and Mollie are active in the Eastside Baptist Church. Mollie was recently honored by her church for teaching Sunday School for over 50 years. –David Robins.

LON CRAFTON ROBINS. Lon was the fifth child of William Edward and Julia Belle Alexander Robins. He was born October 3, 1896, in the Arbor Grove area. He died March 29, 1957, in St. Louis, Missouri.

On September 24, 1912, Lon was married to Elsie Sarah Colbert, only child of William Edward Colbert and Louisa Savannah Kendrick Colbert. Elsie was born in Arbor Grove on the farm owned by her grandfather, James Franklin, and Sarah Margaret Holloway Colbert. The log cabin where Elsie was born is now in Little Rock, Arkansas at the Territorial Restoration.

Lon and Elsie had four children born on her mother's farm across the road from the present Arbor Grove Baptist Church. At one time, Methodist, Baptist and Presbyterian shared the church. Land was given for the church by Uncle Henry Allen Colbert. In 1988, the land was deeded to the Baptists.

In 1920, Lon and Elsie's family moved to Walnut Ridge into the home of Elsie's grandmother, Sarah Patience Pace Kendrick. The home burned one year later whereupon they moved to Hoxie. At the age of 22, Lon was hired by the Missouri Pacific Railroad as a fireman. In 1942, he was promoted to engineer. Lon became a Master Mason on November 23, 1922, in Hoxie, Arkansas. Later, he became a 32nd Degree Mason and Shriner in St. Louis, Missouri.

The first of their children was William Edward Robins. He had two daughters, Tosca Marie Schaver and Germaine Louisa Schaver. They married brothers. They live in Santa Rosa, California.

The second child, Robert Jackson Robins, called Bob Jack, died at 18 months of pneumonia. He is buried in the Whitlow Cemetery.

The third, Juanita Louisa Robins, married John Roy Johnson. They had one son, Lee Roy Lon Johnson.

Lee Roy married Joyce Roberta Hager. They had one son, Christopher Lon Johnson, who married Angie Norris. They have one daughter, Shelby Michael.

Lee Roy Lon Johnson later married Patsy Dean Felts. They had one son, Jay Roy Johnson. Jay married Michelle Matthews. They live in Texas. Jay and Michelle have four children: Jessica Michelle Jones, Michelle's daughter, Meagan Nichole, and twin boys, Bradley Roy and Matthew Ryan.

The fourth child, Alleen Marie Robins, married Samuel J. Hart. Their firstborn, Elsie Jane Hart, was stillborn. Their second was Simone Josephine Hart Lester. Their third, Samuel Joseph Hart, died at the age of three months of pneumonia.

Simone Josephine Hart married Don Lester. They had one child, Samuel Lester, who lives in Pontotoc, Mississippi.

Parents and children are buried in Lawrence Memorial Park in Walnut Ridge. –Jerry Gibbens.

THOMAS S. ROBINS. There are two unrelated Robins families in Lawrence County. This history concerns the Thomas S. Robins family that settled in Lawrence County in about 1868. Thomas S. Robins was born in Tennessee in 1828, and in the late 1840s, married Latesha Fallin, also of Tennessee. Around 1854, they moved to Arkansas, probably August County. There were five children born to this marriage: Virginia, Thomas E., William E., Mary Alice "Molly" and Ida. Latesha apparently died around 1867, and in 1868, Thomas S. and his children moved to Lawrence County. In February, 1874, he married Nancy Elander Goodwin, daughter of John and Monima Goodwin of Smithville. One child, John Louis Robins, was born to this union. Nancy E. Robins died in 1876. Noth-

Descendants of Thomas S. Robins and his two wives, Latesha Fallin Robins and Nancy Goodwin Robins at the Robins reunion in 1984. The reunion is held every two years at the Wayland Springs Church Camp.

ing is known as to where Thomas S. Robins lived or died after his marriage in 1874. The children of Thomas S. Robins and his two wives remained, for the most part, in and around Lawrence County and today there are many descendants still living in the county. Histories on some of these families can be found elsewhere in this book.

Thomas S. Robins is thought to be the son of Joseph and Jinny Robins of North Carolina. In 1850, this couple resided in Tennessee with children Anderson, John and William. Anderson and William later resided in Lawrence County, but little else is known of this family. Family stories indicate that Thomas S. Robins and a brother, probably Anderson, fought for the Confederate Army during the Civil War. Little is known of Thomas' first wife, Latesha Fallin. Thomas was apparently a farmer as both in Woodruff and Lawrence Counties there are records of cotton crops. In 1870, he was in partnership in a cotton gin with a Mr. Champ Stuart near the Moran plantation (this was in the area of the old Walnut Ridge Army Airfield).

The children of Thomas Robins settled in the areas of Clover Bend, Hoxie and Jesup. Virginia first married John Hawkins and then a Judge Ingram. Thomas E. married Anna Minton and then Donie Minton. William E. married Lucy Harris then Julia Alexander. Mary Alice married Ike Pope then Sash Kelley; daughter Ida died at age 10. John L. married Elvira Turnbow. The occupations of these children included teachers, farmers, justices of the peace, store clerks, surveyors and housewives. Histories for the families of William E. and John L. can be found elsewhere in this book.

Nancy Elander Goodwin Robins, second wife of Thomas S. Robins.

Descendants of Thomas S. Robins and his spouses gather every other year (next one is in 2001) for a family reunion at the Wayland Springs Church Camp near Imboden. Some of the names now affiliated with this event are Robins, Callahan, Meadows, Milligan, Johnson, Riggs, Blankenship, Billions, Ruiz, Guthrie, Ratliff, Marsh, Salyer, Howard, McGlothin, Colelough, Verges, Erwin, West, Barnett, Sullivan, Davis, O'Keefe, Faris, O'Shaughnessy, Shields, Lozano, West, Turnbow, Roberts, Morgan, King, Pitts, Lester, Pyburn, Perkins, Wolford, Knepter, Newald, Wait, Insalow, Bagby, Suydam, Whitlow and Woodyard.

–James David Robins, great-grandson of

Thomas S. and Nancy E. Robins.

WILLIAM EDWARD ROBINS FAMILY. William Edward Robins was born in Tennessee, April 15, 1861-November 24, 1941, the son of T. S. and Latisha Fallin Robins. He had two brothers and three sisters: Thomas E., Aug, Virginia, Molly and Ida. He also had a half brother, John Lewis Robins.

He first married Lucy Blanch Harris, who died in childbirth with their first child, Thomas Richard, November 20, 1882-October 18, 1957.

He married Julia Bell Alexander, March 14, 1867-June 14, 1963, on May 23, 1884. Her parents were Phobie Sharp and James Presley Alexander. Their children were: Oliver Clyde, James Coleman, Earnest, Alonzo Crafton, Lola Chloe, Molly Claye, Minor Cable, Lillie America, Willie Elsie and Hurrye.

Robins daughters. L-R: Lillie, Lola, Malli (standing), Bill.

Will, at age nine, and his older brother, Thomas E., were sent to board with a teacher, Mr. Mount, and attended school in Powhatan for two years. After Latisha died, the four youngest children, Will, Jeta, Ida and Mollie, lived with their older sister, Virginia, for a time.

In 1885, Will received homestead rights to 80 acres of land on the Rangle School Road near the John Whitlow farm. Will and Julia built their first home on this land. They later built homes in the Arbor Grove and Duvall Communities. Their children attended Rangle, Rabbit Roust and Duvall schools.

When their oldest son, Clyde, lost his first two children and his wife, Will and Julia took his two remaining children, Novelle and Mildred, ages one and two years, and raised them as their own.

Will was well known in Masonic circles. He was a 32nd Degree Mason and enjoyed a wide acquaintance in

Will and Julia Robins 55th Wedding Anniversary.

Lawrence County. He was a farmer. Other than cotton, corn and hay, they grew tobacco, a variety of fruits, watermelons, hogs, cows, mules, horses, chickens and a large vegetable and herb garden. Milk and butter were in generous supply as was beautiful honey and sorghum molasses.

Julia lost her father at age four. Her mother married again and two half brothers were born. By the time she was eight, she lost her mother. She went to live in West Plains, Missouri, with a family who had a millenery in the home. She worked and trained in this home and was quite creative in hat making. She had gone by train to Hoxie, Arkansas, to visit her Uncle Ed Sharp when she met Will Robins. Six months later, she returned and married him on May 23, 1884.

Their grandchildren are: Rudy, Lucy, Mona, Montie, Novelle, Mildred, Ruth, Leo, Ernest, Lon

Group of Will Robin's and Thomas E. Robins' families gathered at Will's home. 1910-12.

Earl, Chloe, J. C., Pauline, Paul, Bill, Bob Jack, Juanita, Alleen, Mary, Billy, Lindy, Viola, Rosemary, James, Patrick, Pug, Mickey, Willene, Mary Lou, Willoughby, John, Judy, Jerry and Jeannie.

Julia loved to read and write. She taught herself to do both. At one time they were the only family on the Hoxie route who subscribed to the *Arkansas Gazette*, a daily newspaper. She was a Presbyterian and remained so all of her 96 years.

Their home was filled with music. They had a beautiful reed pump organ. They enjoyed a lovely windup Victrola and many records for it. All their daughters could play an instrument. *–Viola Meadows.*

JOHN ROBINSON. The head of the Robinson clan was John Robinson, born in North Carolina in 1804. John's father was born in Germany. John's marriage date and spouse are unknown. His children were: Andrew J., 1830-1881, in Tennessee and John M. Robinson, 1836-1881, in Tennessee.

Pennington Byrd was born in Tennessee in 1812. He and his unknown spouse were the parents of Angelina Melvina and Sarah J. Byrd. Pennington's occupation was house carpenter.

The 1860 census shows Andrew J. Robinson was married to Angelina Melvina Byrd and living in Westpoint, Tennessee. Also living in this household was the younger sister of Angelina, Sarah J. Byrd.

During the Civil War, John M. Robinson, brother of Andrew J., served as Sergeant 2 in Company B, 23rd Regiment, Tennessee Volunteers, CSA. He was in the battles of Shiloh, Perryville, Tulloma, Franklin, and Murfreesboro and was wounded at Chickamauga. On returning home from the war, John M. Robinson married Sarah J. Byrd, the youngest daughter of Pennington Byrd and sister of Angelina. The two Robinson brothers were married to the two Byrd sisters.

By 1880, John M. and Sarah J. Byrd Robinson were the parents of Mollie K., 1874-1945; Stonewall "Stoney" Jackson, 1877-1925; Caroline "Carrie", 1879-1955; George, 1880, died during infancy.

Because of the political and economic turmoil in Tennessee following the Civil War, the Robinson and Pugh families moved west in 1880. The Pugh family and the Robinsons were related. The Rippee family joined this group. Darrel Pugh, the chronicler of the Pugh family, stated that as they journeyed west, in western Tennessee an unknown epidemic struck their party. Within a three week period, 13 members of their family died, including John Robinson Sr., his sons, Andrew, John M. and his wife, Sarah J. Byrd Robinson.

Orphans Mollie, Stoney and Carrie were assimilated into widowed Angelina's family who raised them. Leaving Lawrence County, Tennessee, sometime in the early 1880s, Angelina Melvina Byrd Robinson, widow of Andrew J. Robinson arrived in Randolph County, Arkansas, with her family of seven children and her sister's

three orphaned children in late 1881.

Angelina's family consisted of: Sarah age 13; Andrew 11; Luella, eight; Laura, nine; Thomas, six; Benjamin, two; and Mary Robinson, nine months. Her sister's orphaned children were: Mollie, seven, Stoney, three and Carrie Robinson, one in 1881. They later moved to Lawrence County. *–Lester Robinson.*

STONEY J. AND MAGGIE MITCHELL ROBINSON FAMILY. Stoney J. Robinson, son of John M. and Sarah Byrd Robinson, married Sarah Margaret "Maggie" Mitchell, a daughter of Frank and Louisa Hensley Mitchell, in Pocahontas, Arkansas, in 1900. During his prime years, Stoney was a rancher and a business associate of John L. Lester. In his final years he

Robinson family, Christmas 1935. Front: Robert E. Robinson, front row left to right: Wilma, Bessie, Mother Maggie Robinson. Back row left to right: Ethel, Lester, Waymon and Noah Robinson.

was a farmer.

Their children were: Joseph, 1902-1919; Bessie May, 1904-1984; Wilma Ruth, born 1907; Noah Raeburn, 1909-1986; Walter Waymon, 1911-1941; Ethel Pearl, 1914-1984; John, 1915-1920; Leo, 1917-1920; Lester Lawrence, born 1921; and Robert Earl Robinson, 1924-1955.

Stoney and Maggie Mitchell Robinson lived during their married life in Richwoods and Moran. Their last move was to Minturn, Arkansas, in 1918.

Stoney Robinson died in 1925, leaving his widow Maggie to raise her seven surviving children. She was a lady of patience and virtue who put her trust in God and prayed for divine guidance.

Their descendants in 1998, numbered 83 people. Stoney and Maggie's descendants have a reputation for honesty and hard work.

The three grandchildren of Stoney and Maggie Robinson presently living in Arkansas are: Wava McCarty VanWinkle in Pocahontas, Margaret McCarty Dement of Mountain Home and Philip Collins of Pocahontas. *–Lester Robinson.*

J. R. ROGERS FAMILY. Martha Jane Stubblefield was born in Oregon County, Missouri, in 1855. She was the granddaughter of Fielding Stubblefield. He, according to family history and Goodspeed, settled on the Eleven Point River in Randolph County about 1803. Martha Jane's father was Clinton Stubblefield and her mother was Margaret Looney. The family owned large parcels of land. They took part in community affairs. Fielding was one of the commissioners of the courthouse in Randolph County.

Things were changing after the Civil War when Martha J. was growing up. But, one day a young teacher came to the community. To quote his daughter, "He boarded with Clinton Stubblefield and taught school to children in the community; he began courting Martha Jane and after some time, they married." His name was Archibald Carson. His father, grandfather and great-grandfather's names were all Uriah Carson I, II and III, in North Carolina. The Uriah Carson family were Quakers.

The eldest son of Archibald and Martha Jane was J. M. Carson. He married (when she was 16) Viola Williams, daughter of Samuel and Syntha B. Nettles Williams. The paternal grandfather of Syntha Nettles

Shadrach Nettles, great-great-great-grandfather of J. R. Rogers.

was also an early settler of Arkansas. He was Shadrach Nettles.

Shadrach Nettles settled in what was then Lawrence (now Randolph) County. After the line was surveyed between Missouri and Arkansas, his house, he was told, was in Oregon County, Missouri!

Viola Shadrach's great-granddaughter, J. M. and Viola Carson had 10 children. One of their sons, Frank Carson, was a long time resident and businessman in Lawrence County. One of their daughters was Sylvia Carson Rogers, the mother of the main subject of this history.

Archibald Carson, the teacher, had become blind. He and Martha Jane, evidently, sold her land in the hills, and accord-

J. R. Roger's family taken in late 1940s, before his birth.

ing to their children, "moved to the bottoms to pick cotton." After Martha died, Viola and J. M. Carson took care of the blind father until he died. Arch and M. J. are buried in the Duty Cemetery.

If her great-grandmothers were the Southern Belles of the plantations, Sylvia had just as much fun at barn dances in Randolph and Lawrence County. Her father was usually playing the fiddle and it was usually his barn.

Sylvia married young and had one daughter. They divorced soon after. She later married Delbert Rogers and lived with him until his death in 1982. Besides her daughter, Jewelene E., Delbert and Sylvia had five children: Dalbert E., an Army veteran; Thelma M., teacher; Wanda L., a beautician; Louise M., real estate associate and writer; and J.

J. R. Rogers, Mayor of Walnut Ridge, 1994-present.

R., mayor of Walnut Ridge who lives there with his wife, Michelle and their daughter, Johnna. Dalbert Rogers was the son of Elmer and Ada Ward Rogers of Piggott and grandson of John Russell Rogers and Rebecca Caroline Rogers.

J. R.'s son, now almost 17, is also named John Russell Rogers. J. R.'s other son, Jason, died in 1991, in a car accident.

Dalbert and Sylvia raised their family in Lawrence and Randolph Counties. A big part of this time was in O'Kean, Arkansas, where at one time Dalbert was Marshall. They called him "Crip" Rogers, due to a log cutting accident when a young boy, that left him with a crippled leg.

J. R. Rogers was born June 10, 1952, to a poor family, but they always had a clean home and something to eat. Priorities were family, church, honesty and good grades in school. As with many folks, entertainment was homemade. His mother sang and played the harmonica. Quite young he resolved to play the guitar. His dedication was commendable. His desire to have his own music store was realized with more hard work and sacrifice. His delight in making people smile has always been evident, and he has been blessed with a wonderful ability to do so. His honesty is a well known fact, as was his father's. Before this became Lawrence County, Arkansas, some ancestors decided this was a good place to settle and rear their children.

J. R. is in his second term as mayor of Walnut Ridge. –*Wanda Thornton.*

ELDER ROBERT ROSS was born January 3, 1914, in Todd County, Kentucky, the son of Samuel and Judith Acock Ross. Samuel Ross died March, 1826. Judith, with her family and Acock relatives, migrated to Polk County, Missouri. Robert was a blacksmith and received his license to preach in Lawrence County, Arkansas, where he was one of the early pastors of the New Hope Baptist Church.

Robert Ross, after being duly set apart for ordination by the United Baptist Church at Providence, was duly ordained a minister of the church on the third day of November A.D. 1850. William Tatum, James Bradley and William B. Senter, Presbytery. Filed and recorded this 21st day of September A.D. 1865. H. W. Harlow, Clerk J. W. Townsend D.C.

In the history of Polk County Baptist Association of Missouri, "Eld. Robert Ross was instrumental in building up Slagle Church in Polk County, Missouri.

Usually Elder Ross was a man of few words, mild and peaceable in his habits, but when aroused he could carry his audience with him as he would tell the story of

James Thomas Ross c.1900.

the cross. His first wife died in the triumph of faith; his second wife survived him. Elder Ross died November 29, 1889." Luraney Ross died June 28, 1884. They are buried at Slagle Cemetery, Bolivar, Polk County, Missouri. The inscription on their headstone says, "Remember us as you pass by, As you are now so once was we, As we are now, so you must be, Prepare to death and follow us."

The first child of Robert and Luraney Ross was born in Kentucky, and the others in Missouri. They are: Samuel, born 1835; Margaret, born 1836; John, born 1839; William H., born 1842; James Thomas, born 1844; Robert A., born 1848; Mathias, born 1850; and Eda Ann, born 1853.

James Thomas Ross was ordained Elder by the Free Will Baptist Church at Friendship No. 2 at Scott County, Arkansas, on September 29, 1890. He married Mary Ann Hudson on December 28, 1865, at Lawrence County. Their children were: Cyndia Luraney "Lou" married William Thomas Howard; Martha Ann "Mat" married William H. Chappell; twins, Margie Alzira and Nancy; Mary E.; David Washington married Mattie Wallace; and Robert Evan married Emma Wilson, and then Minnie Ellen Casteel. In the 1910 census of Richland Twp., Yell County, Arkansas, there were eight children, but only three living. They were: Lou, Bob and Dave. James Thomas Ross died in 1917, and Mary Ann in 1911. They are buried near Waveland, Arkansas at Moore's Chapel Cemetery.

Each year a reunion is held at Havana, Arkansas for their descendants. –*Ina Lou Howard Willingham.*

CHARLES P. ROWLAND married Clara Belle Banning in Lawrence County on April 28, 1890. Charles lived in Michigan from his birth in Gratiot County on April 8, 1870, until at least 1880. Clara Banning was born in Cowden, Shelby County, Illinois, on November 27, 1870. A family story is that they met on a wagon train that was headed for Arkansas for homesteading land. They lived in Lawrence County until 1937, moving to Poplar Bluff, Missouri, where they resided until Charles' death, June 7, 1947, and Clara's death, October 27, 1959. Their children, all born in Lawrence County, were:

1. Cynthia Mable, born January 31, 1891, died 1968, in Lawrence County, married first Sidney Trott Hudson, born May, 1879, in Arkansas, died 1937, and married second Ben Davis. The Hudson children were: Mary Susan, born 1912; Clara R., born 1914; Edward Rose, born 1918; Dorotha; Paul Butler; Calvin

Charles P. Rowland and Clara Belle Banning Rowland.

Coolidge; Virginia Vaughn; and Louise, born 1935.

2. Willis B., born October 15, 1892, died about 1895.

3. John Warren, born April 28, 1893.

4. Christina Perl, born December 20, 1897.

5. Joseph Brooks Rowland, born May 17, 1900, at Black Rock, died March 2, 1977, at Pocahontas, married Beulah Leona Reeves, born September 30, 1903, at Imboden, died April 22, 1990, in Ft. Walton Beach, Florida. Their children were: Glendon Charles, born 1922; Catherine; Clarice Marie; Brooks Clifford, born 1928; Walter Hughes, born 1930; Clyde Franklin, born 1933; Nellie Sue, born 1937; Cecila Yvonne, born 1940; Paul Wayne; and Carolyn Ruth, born 1943.

6. Charles Lester, born February 3, 1903.

7. Gladys, born 1905.

8. Clarice May, born May 25, 1908.

9. Elsie, born 1911.

Charles' father was Joseph B. Rowland, born 1830, in Monroe or Tompkins County, New York, died 1910, in Lamar County, Texas. Charles' mother was Joseph's second wife, Sarah Ann Clymer, born 1848, in Clinton County, Michigan, married Joseph B. on January 1, 1866, in Gratiot County, died Gratiot County, Michigan about 1879. Joseph B. and Sarah Ann's other children, also born in Gratiot County, Michigan, were: Edward Victor, born 1866; Loren H., born October, 1872; and Jessie L., born July, 1876. Joseph married Loretta Clymer, Sarah's sister, on March 25, 1882, in Montcalm County, Michigan. They soon moved to Kansas where their only child, Leroy B., was born in 1883.

During the Civil War, Joseph B. Rowland was mustered in Company D, 26th Michigan Infantry on November 26, 1862, at age 32. Two of his brothers, Daniel, age 27, and John S., age 20, served in the same company and were both wounded in action. Joseph B. was wounded in action in July, 1864, during the siege of Petersburg. After hospitalization, he was transferred to Company B, 14th Regiment, Veterans Reserve Corps which guarded Washington, D.C. during the war.

Joseph B. Rowland's parents were David, born 1797, in Connecticut, and Mary, born 1801, in New York. Sarah Ann Clymer's parents were Isaac Clymer, born 1800, in Pennsylvania and Sarah, born 1814, in New York.

Charles P. Rowland was once rescued from a cave-in of a well he was digging. He was an outgoing person with a talent for singing. –D.N. Lee.

JOSEPH BROOKS ROWLAND.
Beulah Leona Reeves married Joseph Brooks Rowland June 29, 1921, in Lawrence County, Arkansas. Beulah was born September 30, 1903, at Imboden, Arkansas. She was the only child of five children born to Charles and Leona Reeves that lived to be an adult. Ten children were born to Beulah and Brooks. Beulah died April 22, 1990, in Florida.

Charles Hardin Reeves, Leona Ragsdale Reeves and Beulah Reeves.

Brooks was born May 17, 1900, at Black Rock, Arkansas. He was the son of Charles and Clara Rowland. He died March 2, 1977, at Pocahontas, Arkansas. Both Brooks and Beulah are buried at Black Rock Cemetery.

Charles Hardin Reeves married Leona E. Ragsdale December 25, 1902, in Lawrence County, Arkansas. Charlie was born in Arkansas in 1880. He was the son of Robert E., born 1854, in Illinois and Mandy Reeves, born 1857, in Tennessee. Charles was one of 12 children. His siblings were: John, 1882; Robert E. Jr., 1888; William, 1891; Noah, 1893; Ida, 1896; Eli, 1889; Les; Sarah; Sabery; and Minnie.

Charles was born June 4, 1880, and was killed in a tornado that hit Imboden, Arkansas on June 5, 1915.

Beulah and Leona always loved and cherished Charley's memory. Many stories of Charley and Leona were told to his grandchildren.

Leona married William Wayland at Imboden in 1918. She was widowed again after a couple of years. She died at Pocahontas, Arkansas, November, 1965.

Leona and Charley are both buried at Hope Cemetery at Imboden, Arkansas. –Nellie Cates.

FRANCIS "FRANK" ROWSEY.
Frank and Lassaphine (Lass for short) moved to Lawrence County shortly after the Civil War. They were both born in 1855, and came to Lawrence County from Tennessee. They bought a farm outside of Imboden, and made their home there. They had seven children: Georgia Maness, who died in infancy, Julia, Cora, Freeland, Emmanuel, Maude and Jayphen Young. Frank died in 1933, and Lass in 1939.

Julia married Casper Justus and had four children: Flynn, G. C., Farell, Huron and Violet. Cora married Luther McLeod and had three children: Elton, Alton and Mary. Freeland married Margie Matthews and had four children: Mary, Inez, Bud and Frank. Maude married Jim Bellamy. They had five children: Pearl, Freeland, Byron, Velma and J. J. Lastly, Jay Y., 1888-1973, married Blanche Childress, 1894-1980. They had children: Thelma, Helen, Jayetta and Billy. Jayetta lives in Walnut Ridge.

–Jay Clark, grandson of Jayetta Rowsey Clark.

DR. D.B. RUDY.
Dr. Dionysius Bodine Rudy was born in Henderson County, Kentucky, December 24, 1851, to William Robert and Jane P. Smith Rudy. He received his education in the local schools and Cairo Academy. In 1871 he commenced the study of medicine under Dr. Samuel Furman of Cairo, Kentucky. He then studied at the University of Louisville and graduated in 1875. He practiced medicine in McLean County, Kentucky, until the fall of 1876 when he moved to Sharp County, Arkansas. In 1878 he returned to the University of Louisville to continue his studies and graduated on March 1, 1879. In May 1879 he came to Lawrence County, Arkansas, and began to practice medicine. On January 11, 1880, he married Miss Anna Belle Henderson, the daughter of James and Nancy Finley Henderson. They were the parents of three children: Maud; Anna Belle who married Cleo Thomas Holt; William Bodine who married Myrtle Amanda Fisher. Mrs. Rudy died October 5, 1887, and in 1888 he married Miss Paralee Fortenberry, daughter of William and Mary Raney Fortenberry. They were the parents of the following children: James Frederick who married Nora F. Taylor; Pearl who married Charles L. Turnbow; Mary Jane "Jannie" who married Joe Morgan Raney; and Sloan who married Mary O'Bannon. Dr. Rudy died at Imboden June 16, 1944.

–Bonnie Perkins.

WILLIAM BODINE "BILL" RUDY
was born January 28, 1887, in Lawrence County, Arkansas, to Dr. D. B. and Anna Belle Henderson Rudy. His mother died when he was eight months old and he was raised by his mother's sister, Margaret and her husband, Rufus B. Hillhouse. He married Myrtle Amanda Fisher, daughter of Dr. S. L. and Mary Ellen Barnett Fisher, on April 7, 1907, and they were the parents of the following children: Hazel Lou, who married Steele B. Baker; Helen Fisher Rudy; James Vernon Rudy who married Anna Mary Johnson of Pine Bluff, Arkansas; and Mary Belle who married Warren Applen. Early in their married life they lived on the Rudy farm in Sharp County, now owned by granddaughter, Bonnie (Baker) and Lavern Perkins. The family moved to town where he worked in Hillhouse store and became a rural mail carrier. He retired in 1957.

The family was active in the Methodist Church. Mrs. Rudy died November 26, 1937. In 1963, Mr. Rudy married Mrs. Ora McKamey Guthrie, widow of Dr. T. C. Guthrie. He died June 11, 1976, and is buried in the Smithville Cemetery. –Bonnie Perkins.

William Bodine Rudy.

RUGGLES-SLOAN-BLACK FAMILIES OF LAWRENCE AND RANDOLPH COUNTIES.
Information can be found about Fergus Sloan III, Rosannah Ruggles and their children in the Lawrence County Historical Society Spring Issue of 1990, Volume 13, Number two. Rosannah Ruggles was the daughter of Comfort Ruggles and Chloe Bearss from Otsego, New York.

Missouri Caroline "Zerua" Sloan married James Seaborn Black of Black's Ferry in Randolph County, Arkansas. James Seaborn Black was a stagecoach driver and farmer. They lived in Bearden, Ouachita County, Arkansas. He died in 1857, and is buried in the Moss Cemetery. He has an above ground vault.

The children of James Seaborn and "Zerua" were: Thalia, Rosannah Eliza Ruggles, Cicero Sloan, Margaret "Maggie", Dallas, Susan, Andrew and the youngest son James Buchanan Black. "Buck" Black was only one year old when his father died. "Zerua" came to Texas sometime before 1875. She came with Cicero, Andrew, Maggie and "Buck." "Zerua" is buried in the Simmons Cemetery, Ben Franklin, Delta County, Texas. James Buchanan went back to Ouachita County, Arkansas to marry Lou Ella Richardson on October 18, 1883. She was the daughter of James L. Richardson and Letitia B. Broughton.

The children of James Buchanan Black and Lou Ella Richardson Black were: Edward Montrose "Trosie", Delmar Richardson, Maidee, James Buchanan Jr., Charles Erwin, Sloan Black and a baby girl who died young. Edward Montrose "Trosie" Black was a farmer and manager of the Co-Op Gin in Cooper, Texas. He married Ethel Eliza Barrett in 1911, at Cooper, Delta County, Texas. He passed away in 1964, and is buried in the Oaklawn Cemetery at Cooper. Ethel E. Barrett Black passed away in 1980, at the age of 94. "Trosie" and Ethel had three children: Dallas Welcome, Kathryn Ethelda and Virginia Jett Black.

Dallas Welcome Black married Lorene Moss in 1931, at Hugo, Oklahoma. Dallas Welcome and Lorene had three daughters: Sara Lou, Linda Sue and Genette Black. They moved from Delta County during World War II. Dallas left the farm to work in a defense plant. He became a jig builder and worked all over the United States. He moved back to the farm after he retired. Dallas passed away in 1977 and is buried at the Ruttan Cemetery in Delta County, Texas. Lorene moved to Shawnee, Oklahoma, to be close to her daughter, Sara Lou, and her family. Lorene died in 1990, and is buried at the Ruttan Cemetery also.

Sara Lou married Kenneth M. Epley in 1953. We live in Shawnee, Pottawatomie County, Oklahoma, and have four children who have grown up here. Our children are: Terry Kay, Sharon Louise, David William and Janet Sue Epley.

The latest descendants of the Ruggles-Sloan-Black-Epley line are our grandchildren: Andrew and Garey Knoles, Marla and Scott King, Chelsey and Chad Epley and Jillian Pasquali.

I have researched often in Lawrence and Randolph Counties and consider them to be the place of my roots.

—Sara Lou Black Epley.

JOHN WESLEY SANFORD AND ROSE ENGLISH SANFORD.

John Wesley Sanford and his wife, Rose English Sanford, migrated to Arkansas from central Kentucky sometime between 1911 and 1914. They were accompanied by Rose's two sons by a previous marriage, Van and Mac Vincent; their son, Gilbert B. Sanford, their daughter, Annie Williams, whose husband had drowned a year earlier in Kentucky and her young son, Earl Williams. They rented property known as the "Guthrie place" near Annieville. Annie Sanford Williams married Arthur Sharp and had four other children, Trula, Gerald, Albert and Mable. Gilbert went into the Army in 1917. He met and married Clara St. Clair, whose family had also come to Arkansas from Kentucky. They lived in Memphis, Tennessee for a while before moving to Williford, Arkansas. They bought property in 1923, from Jasper Justus, known as the "Old Hoffman Place." They purchased additional property called the "Helms" place in 1937, there they lived until their deaths. Clara died in 1968, Gilbert in 1975.

They reared five children, who attended Oak Hill School, in the Imboden district and Manning School in the Ravenden district. The children were:

1. Harold, born in 1919, married Loren Littlefield and lived in Dallas, Texas. They are survived by 12 children and numerous grandchildren and great-grandchildren.

2. Jessie "Jackie", born 1922, married Doyle C. Madison. They live in Del Rio, Texas and have five children and several grandchildren.

3. Julia "Judy", born in 1924, married Wayne Goff and had six children and several grandchildren. She is widowed and lives in Tyler, Texas.

4. Georgene, born in 1926, married Clyde Pickett, had eight children, has numerous grandchildren and great-grandchildren. She is the only member of the Sanford family still living in Lawrence County.

5. Lucille, born in 1928, married Charles Fooks and resides in Salisbury, Maryland. They have three children and six grandchildren.

Gilbert and Clara Sanford lived in and raised their family in Lawrence County. They have been followed by approximately 130 descendants, now living in various parts of Arkansas, Texas, Louisiana, Oklahoma, Illinois, Missouri, Arizona and Maryland.

John and Rose Sanford, Anne and Arthur, and Gilbert and Clara Sanford are buried in Parks Cemetery off Highway 115 in Western Lawrence County.

—Charles and Lucille Fooks.

SAULS FAMILY.

William "Bill" Sauls, 1848-1879, married Malanda Ham Sauls, 1848-1881, had children: Ed Sauls Sr., 1868-1893; Dee Sauls, 1872-1936; and Betty Janes Sauls, 1874-1936.

They migrated from Pike Ville, North Carolina to Kenton, Tennessee. Bill Sauls died in 1879. Malanda Ham Sauls married Nathan Venson and migrated to Walnut Ridge, Arkansas. Both died 1881. Children went to live with Biggs family in Poughkeepsie, Arkansas.

Ed Sauls Sr. married Parlee Tompkins. Sauls had Lottie P. Sauls, 1890-1973; Liza C. Sauls, 1892-1980; and Ed Sauls Jr., 1893-1995.

Ed and Olive Brightwell Sauls family. Left to right: Carmel Saul Foster, Dad Ed Sauls, Mom Olive Brightwell Sauls, Freida Sauls Lewallen. Top: J. E. Sauls, Denver O. Sauls, John Carlon Sauls, A. D. Sauls, Edna Sauls Bookout, Walnut Ridge, Arkansas, 1963.

Dee Sauls married Alice Standfield, had Mattie Sauls McGee.

Betty Jane Sauls, 1874-1936, married Charlie Wade; had Dora, Addie, Auther, War I, Myrtle, Mary, Iva.

Lottie P. Sauls, 1890-1973, married Bill Neely, 1885-1945, in 1907; had Roy, Hubert, Don, Ople, Ray, Nina, Tina, Marvlie, Billy.

Liza C. Sauls, 1892-1980, married Staten Hulett, 1892-1950. They had Thelma, Truin Charline, Syble, Oleta, Staten Jack Hulett Jr.

Ed "Bud" Sauls, 1893-1995, married Olive Brightwell, 1890-1972; had Carmel, Denver, A. D., J. E., John Carlon, Edna, Freida.

Ed Sauls Jr. moved from Poughkeepsie, Arkansas to Imboden, Arkansas in 1927; moved to Walnut Ridge, Arkansas in 1932.

Carmel Sauls, born 1914, married Leslie Foster; had Nova Sue Foster Dobbs, 1933, Joe L. Foster, 1940.

Denver O. Sauls, born 1916, married Sylvia Sue McFarland in 1945; Denver was in the Navy, 1937-1945; Chief's Gunners Mate, South Pacific World War II.

Albert Dee Sauls, born 1918, married Betty Broyles in 1946; United States Coast Guard, 1942-1946, Quarter Master, South Pacific World War II.

James E. Sauls, born 1921, married Ann Bell Holloway in 1944; United States Army, Company K, 153rd Infantry, 1941-1945, Seward, Alaska.

John Carlon Sauls, born 1924, married June Lewis in 1950; United States Army, 1943-1946, Tank Corp, Germany.

Bonnie Edna Sauls, born 1926, married Herman Bookout, 1945.

Freida Onida Sauls, born 1929, married Wallace Lewallen in 1947.

Elgen Brightwell, 1822-1898, married Elisbeth Armstrong, 1823-1850; buried Mt. Pisgah Cemetery, Poughkeepsie, Arkansas; had Letty B., 1845; Wiley O., 1846-1920; James H., 1847-1919; migrated from Meig, Tennessee to Mountain View, Arkansas, 1840.

Elgen married Mary Jane Howser; moved to Poughkeepsie, Arkansas, 1870; had Matilda E., 1852-1930; Tennessee Virginia, 1853-1923 - Ring; Nancy A., born 1854; George W., 1855-1896; Jasah S., 1856-1890; John O., born 1859; Phillesee, born 1861; William H., born 1863; Orain, born 1866; Mary K., 1868-1909 - Tom Haney.

Willeg O. Brightwell, 1846-1910, married Kathern Wells; settled in Newark, Arkansas; buried Walnut Grove Cemetery; had William Adam, born 1846; William Ralph; Aubert Edger; Helbry Houston; Glenn E.

James H. Brightwell, 1847-1919, married Nancy Thresa Gay, 1849-1893; had Mary Tenny,

1873-1898 - Dick Fortun; William Leonard, 1875-1942 - Florance Lane; Charles Nelson, 1876-1942 - Elisbeth Goff; Jennie Alma, 1878-1941 - Walter McLeod; Dudly G., 1879-1882; Ben O., 1882-1957 - Florance Norris; Sarah Cordelia, 1885-1903 - Elmer Lane; Winnie Olive, 1890-1972 - Ed Bud Sauls Jr.

Benjamin O. Brightwell moved to Imboden, Arkansas, 1924; wife: Florence; buried Hope Cemetery; had Agnus, Aneel, Ruby, Lillian, Owean Beach, Louise Beach, Avis, Allen, Maxzine, Eugine, Imogine.

—Denver O. Sauls

CHARLES FRANK SCHMIDT

was born August 25, 1895, at Pocahontas, Arkansas in Randolph County. He was the son of Joseph and Gertrude Ahrweiler Schmidt. Joseph was born January, 1851, near Kiln, Prussia. Gertrude was born August, 1858, in Prussia. They immigrated to America in March of 1882. They went directly to Pocahontas from the Port of New York.

Charles "Charlie" married Josephine Katherine Kirkemeier on June 20, 1918, at Pocahontas. Josephine was born February 11, 1900, at Caterville, Illinois. Her parents, Steven and Francis Spihlman Kirkemeier, immigrated through the Port of New Orleans in 1851.

Charlie worked at the family owned brick mill near Pocahontas, along with his father and brothers. He took over ownership for a while. He operated it for a few years, then moved to Hoxie in Lawrence County where he had a lifelong profession as a brick mason. He worked on many of the commercial buildings in Lawrence and Randolph Counties. He bricked many homes in the area. He worked on the post office building in Walnut Ridge, now the *Times Dispatch* office. He did a major portion of the brick work on the Davy Crockett Restaurant and Alamo Courts.

Charlie and Josephine had nine children.

Stephen John, born March 29, 1919, married Lena Hitt; children: Patricia Ann married Troy Sheets, children; Trisha Lee; and Alfred Dean, child: boy.

Stephen Charles married Barbara Palmer, children: Stephen John married first Dianne King, child; Andrea; married second Michelle, child: Blake; Tamberla Dawn married Steven Cox, child: Michelle.

Stanley Ray married Jewel Petero; children: Kimberly Rena and Randall Ray.

Patrick William married Joyce Green, child; Judy Faye, child: girl.

Dorothy Frances, May 23, 1921-October 24, 1924.

Virginia Louise, born February 24, 1923, married Dovie Willett, child: Linda Suzanne married Richard Daugherty.

Helen Elizabeth, born March 31, 1925, married first Fred Hefley, deceased; second Robert "Sonny" Benge, children: Ronald Dean married Debbie Bradley (divorced), children: Wesley Dean and Gregory Seth.

Timothy Ray married Janet Mosteller, children; married second Jana?; children: Michelle, Charlene, child Emil; and Audrey.

Charles Henry, born February 28, 1927, married Catherine Turner; children: Richard Charles, a twin, married Rochelle ?; children: Lindsey and Laurie.

Reginald Lester, a twin, married Cheryl ?; children: Jessica and Aaron.

Agatha Rita, born August 31, 1930, married Leroy Schultz, child: Michael Allen married Debbie Fann, children: Derrick and Jessica.

Mary Agnes, born March 28, 1933, married Walter Barrett, children: Walter Andrew "Andy" married Kathy Ellis, children; Amy married Rodney

King, child: Callie; Tony married Trisha ?, child: Taylor; and Amber.

Franklin Gene "Frankie" married first Vickie Webb, children: Tyler and Rusty; married second Pam ??.

JoAnnette married Michael Ramsey, children: Kelly and Jennifer.

Betty Jean, a twin, born March 12, 1939, married Harry Drewes, children: Pamela Jean married Craig Miller, children: Stephanie and Clayton.

Brenda Faye married John Bantz, child: Heather.

Sandra Ann married Scott Stremke, children: Sarah, Stacy and Stuart.

Judy Kaye married David Myers (divorced).

Bobby Joe, a twin, born March 12, 1939, married Sharon Gaines, children: Theresa Kaye married Michael Brinkman, children: Adam and Vanessa.

Lorita Denise married Michael Hunt, children: Melissa married Steven Darrah, child: Katelin; Jeremy and Matthew.

Marcy Ann married Jeffrey Brinkman, children: Kimberly and Michelle.

Kevin Robert married Tania Driver, children: Kevin Jr. and David.

In 1949, the Schmidt's oldest son, Steve, and his family were involved in a horrible automobile accident near Pocahontas. Steve was killed and Lena was hospitalized for several months. Remarkably, the children all survived without major injuries.

Charles Henry, the second son, died of a heart attack in 1971, in Garland, Texas.

Charlie died April 30, 1967, at home in Hoxie. Josephine died February 12, 1973, in Lakewood, California, while visiting her daughter, Virginia and her son, Bobby. Charlie, Josephine and Steven are all buried at St. Paul's Cemetery in Pocahontas. Charlie is buried in the Masonic Cemetery in Pocahontas. —Sharon Schmidt.

HOMER AND BEULAH ANN FORTENBERRY SEGRAVES.

Homer Segraves, July 28, 1898-October 3, 1988, and Beulah Ann Fortenberry, born July 9, 1902, were married June 16, 1921. They were natives of Lawrence County. Both were descendants of families who settled in Lawrence County in 1816.

Homer was the seventh of nine children of Martha "Mat" Fortenberry, 1861-1926, and Andrew Jackson "Jack" Segraves, 1860-1937. Mat was the daughter of James, 1826-1881, and Harriet Finley Fortenberry, 1826-1891, granddaughter of Jacob, 1789-1862, and Nancy Taylor Fortenberry, 1791-1850, James, 1791-1852, and Jane Dobbins Finley.

James Fortenberry was born and grew to manhood on the Jacob Fortenberry homestead on Reeds Creek. After marriage, James and Harriet settled near Strawberry River, possibly on the old Finley homestead.

Beulah was born on the Fortenberry homestead on Strawberry River between Lynn and Strawberry. She was the second child of John Taylor Fortenberry, February 5, 1870-January 5, 1911,

Beulah (Fortenberry) and Homer Segraves.

and Ellen Greene Fowler Fortenberry, February 18, 1878-January 23, 1959. Beulah's grandparents were William, 1836-1889, and Mary "Polly" Raney Fortenberry, 1840-1888, and Jim and Nancy Ann Hardin Greene. Great-grandparents were Taylor, 1813-1865, and Jane Cravens Fortenberry, 1817-1850, John, 1802-1855, and Nancy Wayland Raney.

Homer Segraves took over the operation of the old Fortenberry farm when he and Beulah moved there in 1922. They lived in the house where she was born and which had been built by her grandfather in 1874.

Homer was a progressive farmer using good farming and soil conservation practices. He was also a community and church leader.

Beulah took pride in her homemaking skills. She won ribbons at county fairs for her cooking and sewing entries.

She now lives in her home in Walnut Ridge where she and Homer moved after the farmhouse burned in 1974.

Homer and Beulah had two children: Janive, born June 15, 1924, and Don Sevier, August 27, 1926-November 14, 1959.

Don Segraves was a graduate of Strawberry High School and the University of Arkansas. He married Josephine Walling in 1947. They had three sons: Danny Joe, born March 23, 1948, James Randall, born July 21, 1951, and Donald Dwight, born December 12, 1952. At the time of his death, Don was teaching at Washington State College and working toward a doctorate.

Janive married Hubert Howard Blanchard Jr., June 14, 1946. She graduated from Strawberry High School in 1940. She holds BSHE and ME degrees from the University of Arkansas. Her professional career included Home Economist with Extension Service, a high school home economics teacher and Supervisor of Home Economics with the Arkansas Department of Education.

Hubert Blanchard Jr., born July 21, 1920, was the oldest of five children of Hubert Howard and Van Martin Blanchard. A graduate of Egypt High School he has BSA and ME degrees and Diploma for Advance Study from the University of Arkansas. He began his career in education at Strawberry. He later was Lawrence County School Supervisor, 1954-1959; Associate Executive Secretary of the Arkansas Education Association, 1959-1976; and Director of the Arkansas Teacher Retirement System, 1977-1986.

Hubert and Janive's children are Warren Martin Blanchard, born October 5, 1948, and Charles Howard Blanchard, born June 24, 1950. —Hubert Blanchard.

CHARLES ELDON SHANNON.

born December 25, 1951, in Ottawa, Illinois, lived there one year and moved to Mt. Vernon, Indiana and lived there 12 years. He attended school in Mt. Vernon, Walnut Ridge, Arkansas and graduated from Black Rock High School in May, 1969. He was in the Army and was stationed in Korea. He attended

Dianne and Charles "Chuck" Shannon.

Southern Baptist College for two years.

He was married to Sarah Dianne Brewster, September 10, 1977, in Conway, Arkansas. Dianne was born October 18, 1953, in Shreveport, Louisiana. They have no children. —Charles Shannon.

CHESTER LEE SHANNON FAMILY.

Chester Lee Shannon, son of Melba Faye Meeks Shannon and Eldon Lee Shannon, was born in Evansville, Indiana, February 17, 1960; married Ann Marlene Kennedy on June 12, 1985, in Walnut Ridge, Arkansas. Marlene was born June 12, 1965, in Fort Bragg, North Carolina. Marlene is the daughter of Marvin and Sharon Kennedy.

Chester, Marlene and Spencer Shannon.

Chester "Chet" is a teacher at Black Rock High School and coaches the boys basketball and baseball teams. Marlene is a teacher at the Walnut Ridge Elementary School. They have one son, Spencer Lee Shannon, born April 19, 1994, in Jonesboro, Arkansas. Chester and family live at Black Rock.

DEBRA LYNN SHANNON, born November 14, 1955, in Evansville, Indiana, daughter of Faye and Eldon Shannon; attended schools in Mt. Vernon, Indiana, Walnut Ridge and graduated from Black Rock High School in 1973; attended Southern Baptist College, B.R.V.T.S. and A.S.U. She resides in Pocahontas and works at B.R.A.D. Children are: Seth Shannon Clark, born August

Debbie, Seth and Paige Clark.

1, 1979, in Jonesboro, Arkansas; Paige Lynn Clark, born October 19, 1981, in Jonesboro, Arkansas.

Also: children of Preston Lee Clark, born May 12, 1956, son of Otis and Fredia Justus Clark, now deceased. —Debra Clark.

ELDON AND FAYE SHANNON. Melba Faye Meeks was born February 15, 1934, at Black Rock, Arkansas, daughter of Cecil Curtis and Johnie C. Woodson Meeks; attended Black Rock school through the 11th grade. Completed 120 class hours of instruction in General Adult Education, and obtained a certificate of equivalency of high school graduation, August 25, 1966. In 1976, attended B.R.V.T.S. and received an LPN license; worked part time until 1984. Started oil painting in 1981, attended one class and was hooked. Joined the Lawrence County China Painters in 1993, and spends more time china painting now, than oil painting.

Married to Eldon Lee Shannon, April 14, 1951, son of Gertie Lee Emerton Shannon Pickney. Eldon was born December 11, 1928, at Lauratown, Arkansas. He worked for

Eldon and Faye Shannon.

Mechling Barge Lines and Dravo Barge Lines for 40 years. He obtained his engineers license and worked in both pilot house and engine room. In 1963, bought the Ozark Service Station from Oscar Sens. Freddie Pickney was the first operator. We moved back to Arkansas in December, 1964. Moved to Walnut Ridge then built a house on Highway 63 in Black Rock. Sold the station to Charlie Cavenaugh, he put in a quick shop. In 1997, we built a house on our farm south of Black Rock near the "old red barn." The house that had been "The Three Rivers Fish House" has been demolished. We have three children.

1. See the Charles Eldon Shannon family.
2. See the Debra Lynn Shannon Clark family.
3. See the Chester Lee Shannon family.

Also, one stepson: Eldon Eugene Shannon, born October 31, 1949, in Imboden, Arkansas. Mother Ruby Schmidt. Gene lives in Huntsville, Alabama. He is in law enforcement.

He has two sons and a stepdaughter. He and his wife, Kathy live in Hazel Green, Alabama. – *Faye Shannon.*

SHARP FAMILY. Ephriam Sharp was born July 30, 1815, near Cincinnati, Ohio, and died November 17, 1898, near Strawberry, Lawrence County, Arkansas. He was the ninth child of 10 children of his father John's first marriage to Elizabeth Elston, and grandson of Isaac and Mary W(o)olverton Sharp. Ephriam's family moved to Decatur County, Indiana, when he was 12 years old, where he grew to manhood and on October 29, 1834, married the first of his four wives, Margaret Stevens. Ephriam and his younger brother, William H., moved to Van Buren County, Arkansas, about 1836. Coming to Lawrence County about 1837. They built a grist mill, cotton gin, sawmill and carding machine on Mill Creek near Evening Shade. Ephriam and Margaret had eight children: One died at birth; Samuel, born December 11, 1835, Decatur County, Indiana; John Thomas, born December 2, 1837, Decatur County; Rebecca, born May 10, 1841, Van Buren County, Arkansas; Nancy, born March 4, 1843; Harriett, born 1844; Catherine, born October 9, 1847; and Mary Ann, born 1849. The last four being born in Lawrence County, Arkansas.

Margaret died about 1853 at Evening Shade and January 8, 1854, he married Malinda Murphy. Child of this marriage was Eliza, born July 19, 1856. Malinda died January 13, 1857. On July 19, 1858, he married Elvina Godwin and the children of this marriage were Amanda, born January 24, 1863, and Mary, born August 3, 1867. Elvina died December 18, 1872. He then married Nancy Croom Smith on April 27, 1873. There were no children of this marriage and Nancy died November 7, 1898, and 10 days later Ephriam went to his last sleep on November 17, 1898.

The story of Ephriam's life can be noted in his work, wives and children, but there is another story that must be told. He was a breed of pioneers that came to the timbered and virgin land of beautiful Arkansas and carved out a new life in this frontier. Owning no slaves he remained neutral in the War Between the States, but was loyal to the Union, taking up arms against neither his state or nation. He served the state in what is called the 15th Legislature at Little Rock traveling over 100 miles on horseback to carry out his duties and carrying a single shot pistol issued him by the state for protection. It was in the 1868 Legislative session that a piece of Lawrence County was carved out to form the county of Sharp, named for "the gentleman from Lawrence," Ephriam Sharp. Ephriam wrote into the bill that the county seat would be Evening Shade, which had been his home for several years.

No history of Lawrence County could be complete without the mention of the two Sharp brothers, Ephriam and William Sharp, who, leaving their families and homes in Indiana, helped to build the new state of Arkansas, filled with promise and hardships. These two brothers left thousands of descendants that have now scattered to the four winds of the earth, each carrying a proud heritage.

I am one of the 5th generation of descendants of Ephriam.
–*Ira Sharp Dennis.*

EPHRIAM EDMON SHARP was born June 14, 1866, Lawrence County and died June 29, 1957, Lawrence County, Arkansas, was the son of Samuel and Nancy Willmuth Sharp. He was the first of five children born to this union. The other children were: John William, March 27, 1868-July 5, 1871; Charles, June 11, 1869-September 22, 1870; Mary Margaret, October 15, 1871-September 16, 1873; and Martha Canzada, February 11, 1874-1892. Ephriam was the grandson of Ephriam Sharp for whom Sharp County was named.

Ephriam's younger siblings all died within a short time of their birth, except for his younger sister, Martha Canzada. After finishing school he taught at a little school near Jesup, Arkansas, a short way from his home. At age 20 his teaching career was cut short with the death of his father, Samuel. He then took over the care of his mother and younger sister. Ephriam was now a farmer with 120 acres to manage. Early in 1887 he married his first wife, Melissa Evelyn Saffell. To this union were born eight children. He married the second time to Louella E. Bray, no children. The third marriage was to Julia Ann Elizabeth Roe. They had three children. Ephriam continued to farm the land and raised his family in Lawrence County. His children went to different states and scattered the Sharp name to different areas.

Children of Ephriam and Melissa:
1. William Wesley, November 20, 1887-February 10, 1905.
2. Mary Ann, March 25, 1890-July 8, 1890.
3. Samuel Hiram, August 3, 1891-February 21, 1912. He had married Louella Callahan, October 15, 1911.
4. Rodolph Pendleton, September 21, 1893-November 1, 1973, married Kathleen Hartsell, October 13, 1918.
a) Henry Earl married Miran Steadman and had Larry and Cherie.
b) Neil Homer married Evelyn Strickland and had Jerry and Gary.
c) Glen Edgar
d) Kathleen.
5. Cornelius Oscar, October 12, 1895-April 4, 1903, married Ruby Whinery.
a) Ephriam William married Walterine Hollingsworth Kunkle and had Kenneth and Melissa.
6. Ernest Stewart, March 16, 1???-December 27, 1965, married Thelma Wood Pruett.
7. Walter Edgar, August 31, 1901-November 22, 1957, married first Anna Lee Harris and second Twiller.
8. Homer Lloyd, October 25, 1904-September 16, 1948, married first Ruth Robins and had Billy Cole, Lona Helen and George Loyd. He married second Sarah Elizabeth Odom and had Wilma Olene, Melba Eugenia, Neil Wilson, Melissa Evelyn, Henry Lloyd, William Gail and Ira May.

Children of Ephriam and Julia Roe were:
1. James Frances, August 19, 1917-April 29, 1991.
2. Nancy Jane, born May 4, 1919, married first Patterson and had William Edmon. She married second Robert Odom and had James Robert

3. Martha Ellen, December 5, 1920-November 22, 1997, married George May and had Helen Ann, Ephriam Edmon, Mary Ellen and James Henry.

–*Ira Sharp Dennis.*

FRANCIS MARION SHARP FAMILY.
Francis Marion "Buddy" Sharp was born February 12, 1880, in Lawrence County, Arkansas. He was the son of Reverend William Thomas Sharp and Mary A. Holder and a great-grandson of Solomon Sharp, one of the earliest settlers in the Powhatan area. Buddy was both a farmer and a timber man. In August of 1903, Buddy married Mary Elizabeth Henderson in Lawrence County, Arkansas. Mary was born in Tucker, Missouri, on February 8, 1884, and was the daughter of Andrew W. Henderson and Sarah Louise Holland. Mary died October 11, 1965, in Pocahontas, Arkansas, at the age of 81. Buddy died in Randolph County, Arkansas on April 16, 1966, at the age of 86.

Buddy and Mary had the following children.

Francis Marion and Mary Elizabeth (Henderson) Sharp.

1. Homer Sharp married Thursday Bettis. Their children were: Russell, Lorazell, Ozita, Bonnie, Connie Sue and Janice.
2. Marvin Sharp married Bertha Hopper in England in 1945. Their children were: Rosemary, Irene, Ilene, Kathleen, Katherine, Marvin Jr. and Ruby Ann.
Bertha, Kathleen, Marvin Jr. and Ruby Ann were tragically killed in a fire near Pocahontas, Arkansas in 1951.
3. James Benjamin Sharp married Marie Howard. Their children were: Joan, Sandra, Eddie, Dewayne and Allen.
4. Alta Sharp married Elmer Eubanks. Their children were: J. R., Charles, Bob, Bill, Betty, Shirley and Mary.
5. Irene Sharp married Lloyd Salyards. Their children were: Don, Dallas, Mary Ann, Glenda, Jim, Phyllis and Teresa.
6. Juanita Sharp married Reverend Grady Linebaugh. Their children were: Wayne, Gale, Larry and Deborah.
7. Alma Marie Sharp married Elmer Jefferson "Jeff" Davis on October 27, 1923, in Lawrence County, Arkansas. Their children were: J. D. and Harold. J. D. Davis married Josie Neece. Their children were: Peggy, Duke, Dottie and Kay. Harold married Mildred Phillips. Their children were: Ricky, Karen and David. David married Patty G. Nipps in Randolph County, Arkansas in 1991.
8. Ernest Cleo Sharp was born in Pocahontas, Arkansas on January 29, 1921. He married Mary Lou Allen on October 25, 1943, in Costa Mesa, California. She was the daughter of Milo Everett Allen and Julia Mary O'Connor. Their children were: Linda Lou, Ernest David and Cynthia Rose. Ernest David Sharp "David Berlin" was born in Santa Ana, California on November 21, 1951. He first married Celina Marie Lobato on June 3, 1972, in Durango, Colorado. Their children were: Daniel James Sharp, born December 12, 1973, in Anchorage, Alaska (married Tiffany in June of 1997, in Maple Valley, Washington); and Lisa Kedren

Sharp, born in Anchorage, Alaska on August 8, 1975. David next married Tara Marie VanOrsdal on December 22, 1984, in Settlers Bay, Alaska. Their children were Cora Shea, born January 8, 1986, in Anchorage and Jackson Cole, born March 22, 1996, in Anchorage, Alaska. *–Dave Davis.*

SOLOMON SHARP FAMILY. Very little is known about Solomon and his wife, Amy, before 1820. He was known to reside in Lees Twp, Crawford County sometime before 1820. According to his children's census records, he was born in Tennessee around 1795. He began farming and stock raising upon his arrival to Lawrence County, Arkansas, around 1820. Their first location was on the place owned by Captain Stewart near Powhatan. Solomon and Amy had the following children, most of which were born in Spring River, Lawrence County, Arkansas.

Sitting: William Thomas and Martha (Holder) Sharp and children.

1. William M. Sharp, born about 1817.
2. John James Sharp, born about 1818. He married Louisa Turman in Flat Creek in February of 1843. He died August 2, 1846, shortly after enlisting as a soldier in the Mexican War.
3. James Ervin Sharp was born about 1821. He married Sarah Ann Long.
4. Solomon Sharp Jr. was born about 1824. He married Eva Ann Starnes.
5. David Sharp was born about 1826. He married Martha I. Smith, August 1, 1849.
6. Levi H. Sharp was born about 1828. He married Margaret McGhehey in 1849. She was the daughter of George W. McGhehey and Charlotte Vancil. Margaret died September 4, 1872, Levi married second Hannah G. Whiteon.
7. Jacob Sharp was born in 1830.
8. Rebecca Sharp was born about 1831. She married James M. Smith.
9. Polly Ann "Mary" Sharp was born about 1833.

John James, Solomon Jr. and Levi were inducted into the military June 18, 1846, in Smithville, Arkansas, and except for John James (died shortly after enlisting of sickness) served in the Mexican War and released from duty April 20, 1847.

Solomon's son, Jacob, married Mary Francis Eddy in Spring River, Lawrence County, Arkansas, October 6, 1851. His children were: Johnathan L., Sarah E., Anna A., William Thomas, Larkin, Jacob Jasper, Madison and Phineas. Jacob enlisted in the CSA, July 15, 1862, in Company G, under Colonel Shaver, 38th Arkansas Infantry Regiment. He was a private, detailed as a teamster and was in until September 24, 1863. He died in 1899.

Jacob's son, William Thomas Sharp, was born April 5, 1856. He married Martha A. Holder August 26, 1875. She was the daughter of Bledsoe Holder and Elizabeth. Their children were: Jacob

Jasper, Taylor, Moses, Ider, Girtie E., Arthur and Francis Marion Sharp (my grandfather) who married Mary Elizabeth Henderson, daughter of Andrew W. Henderson and Sarah Louise Holland.

William Thomas Sharp was ordained a priest in Mount Olive Church, October 20, 1900. William was a farmer and a Free Will Baptist minister. He died October 4, 1938, in rural Walnut Ridge, Arkansas. *–David Berlin.*

KELLEY F. "KELL" SHELTON was born March 15, 1893, near Franklin, Arkansas. His parents were Francis M. and Rebecca Watson Shelton. Kell moved to Lawrence County at an early age, living in the Strangers Home-Lauratown Community. He married Ethel Irene Pruett, daughter of William Y. and Eliza A. Maxey Pruett, also of the Strangers Home-Lauratown Community, on February 25, 1919, at Newport, Arkansas.

Mr. Shelton's first wife, Rose Mae Williams, and Mrs. Shelton's first husband, John Williams, both died during the flu outbreak of 1918.

Mr. and Mrs. Shelton owned considerable farm land around Alicia, Arkansas. They also owned and operated a service station, grocery store,

Mr. and Mrs. Kell Shelton

cafe and motel on the old Highway 67 in Alicia. Their home was in Alicia for about 50 years. Mr. Shelton died on May 14, 1965. Mrs. Shelton lived in Jonesboro for several years and died on February 23, 1996. Both were members of the Alicia Methodist Church and are buried at Strangers Home Cemetery near Alicia.

Mr. Shelton's children by his first wife were: Beulah Mae who married Carl Pruett and Lula Gertrude who married Marshall Folkers. Mrs. Shelton's only child by her first marriage was Mildred Williams who married Wilburn Watts. Their other children were: William Eugene who married Velma Chestine and Carrie Jones; Winston Neeley who married Mary Fasanella and Arvilla K. "Val"; Madalyn Elizabeth who married John F. Davidson; Morton Harlin who married Viola Hurst; Gloria Alene who married Jack Rousey; Lavida Jane who married Lloyd McCracken; Billy Ronald who married Anna Jo King; and Benny Donald who married Linda King and second Peggy Axum. *–Lavida McCracken.*

ENOCH PLEASANT SIMMONS, February 10, 1858-September 2, 1915, born in Missouri, son of David Hudelson Simmons, married Elizabeth Jane Stillwell, April 24, 1858-December 8, 1911, born in Tennessee, daughter of Daniel Stillwell. They had nine children. In 1900, the family moved to Strangers Home in Lawrence County, Arkansas where both are buried. Their children are:

1. Lula Leuvenga, February 6, 1882-October 9, 1917, and John William Capps, November 23, 1905-July, 1952, married July 19, 1906. Both are buried at Strangers Home. Their children are:
a) Mabel Nina, born October 4, 1908, married Luther Boyd, born November 23, 1905.
b) Sanford Pleasant, born July 15, 1910, and Goldie Wilburn, born February 22, 1917, married April 2, 1932.
c) Carmel Leuvenga, born May 27, 1912, and Curnel Batchelar, born May 30, 1910, married September 11, 1931.

d) Roy Hancel, born March 21, 1914, and Helen Mitchell, August 21, 1916-January 7, 1982, married December 27, 1945.

2, David Huddleston (twin) was born in 1884, married Goldie Ferguson and lived in California. Their children are: Charley, Thelma, Ruby, Arley and Jewell.

3. Dan (twin) was born in 1884, and died young.

4. D. Lawrence, August 16, 1886-October 6, 1957, married Etter Mae Counts, September 27, 1892-May 7, 1947, on March 5, 1909. Both are buried at Strangers Home. Their children are:
a) Orville Enic, November 30, 1909-January 5, 1977, married "Bill" Colvey.
b) Ruby Florence, born February 2, 1912, and Roy Clifford Dunn, December 10, 1905-October 12, 1958, married in 1944.
c) Agnes Inez, born January 10, 1914, and Floyd Rash, 1907-January 27, 1976, married October 6, 1931.
d) Mattie Alma, January 25, 1916-January 25, 1937, never married.
e) Pirley Gertrude, born March 18, 1923, married Bill Woods.
f) Alta Lucille, born June 20, 1926, and Curtis Bartlett, born April 8, 1925, married January 26, 1952.
g) Edna Mae, born November 27, 1931, and Buford L. Harbison, born March 8, 1929, married April 27, 1946.
h) Bonnie Louise, born November 29, 1934, married Robert William Luehr, born June 25, 1934.
i) Gilbert George, January 24, 1918-October 24, 1981, and Dora Lee Ditto, January 4, 1924-April 23, 1961, married November 9, 1940. Gilbert and Gladys Wooter married April 30, 1953. Gilbert and Beulah Pauline Green, born May 12, 1934, married August 23, 1955.

5. Ed died young.
6. Fred died young.
7. John Elmer, May 30, 1891-February 6, 1983.
8. George Byrd, July 7, 1894-December 18, 1984, married Minnie Lucille Alls, February 14, 1896-August 30, 1939. She is buried at Strangers Home. He is buried in Eloy, Arizona. Their children are:
a) Huey Carnelis, born January 12, 1921, and Ethel Marie Hartley, born February 8, 1924, married March 13, 1940.
b) Charles Bernard, born October 6, 1928, and Helen Clinton, May 19, 1929-April 16, 1978, married November 11, 1946.
c) Glenda Sue, born July 25, 1932, and Harry Earl Campbell, born May 10, 1930, married March 30, 1950.
d) Betty Lou, born July 25, 1932, and Gerald Archie Mousseau, born June 21, 1926, married May 24, 1952.
e) Darrell Lee, born August 4, 1935, and Betty Sue Chandler, born June 15, 1937, married March, 1956. George's second wife was Eller Braughland Owens. Their children: Donald Lee, born May 9, 1941; and Glenetta, born 1945.

9. Jarrett Mack, August 2, 1898-June 14, 1913, is buried at Strangers Home.

JOHN ELMER SIMMONS, born May 30, 1891, in Rockbridge, Missouri, the seventh child of Enoch Pleasant Simmons and Elizabeth Jane Stillwell Simmons, came to Lawrence County when nine years old. He served in World War I, having been inducted into the Army on July 1, 1918, at Walnut Ridge as a private with Company D of the 6th Infantry. He left the United States on August 24, 1918. On October 15, 1918, while serving on the front lines near the Meuse River in Verdun, France, he received a shrapnel wound of the left knee from an exploding bomb. From a field hospital he was transferred to an Army hospital at Bordeaux, France and was there from November 5, 1918, to February 11, 1919. He arrived back in the United States on February 27, 1919, and was honorably discharged on March 21, 1919, at Camp Shelby, Mississippi. On May 19, 1919, the War Department sent his brother, Lawrence, of Clover Bend a request for the name, post office address and degree of relationship of the nearest heir of John E. Simmons, Late Private Company D, 6th Infantry, who died October 14, 1918. His family also received a death certificate from the War Department. Very much alive he returned to his home (Strangers Home area), Lawrence County, Arkansas and worked in the timber cutting business and farmed. Fifty-eight years late on July 15, 1976, he was awarded a Purple Heart.

On December 5, 1922, he married Lillie Marie Sago. They had two children, Elmer Eugene and Nora Leona. They moved to Colorado in 1928, and divorced July 20, 1932. On September 6, 1934, at Littleton, Colorado, he married Nellie Mae Smith Philput, born January 4, 1906, in Kansas to Samuel Jacob Smith and Amelia Anna McBride Smith. Nellie had a daughter, Pearl Louise Philput. John and Nellie's children are: Mary Jane and John Roy. In 1950, they moved back to Alicia, Arkansas. They operated the Simmons Cafe on Old Highway 67, before moving to Shelby, Michigan in 1955. John passed away February 6, 1983, and Nellie, April 8, 1981. Both are buried at Mount Hope Cemetery, Shelby, Michigan.

Elmer Eugene, August 23, 1923-November 25, 1998, and Lorene Harris, born April 5, 1928, married March 29, 1947. Their children are John Charles, born May 22, 1949; James Michael, born August 7, 1949; and Katherine Charlene, born November 8, 1953.

Nora Leona, November 10, 1925-1995, and Willis Victor Pochon, born November 10, 1918, married May 20, 1946, at Littleton, Colorado. Their children are Ronald, born June 22, 1947; Suzanne, born November 19, 1948; and Victor, born October 21, 1951.

Mary Jane, born August 6, 1935, and Christopher John McAlee, born June 24, 1931, married June 21, 1953, at Tuckerman, Arkansas. Their children are Laura Faith, born January 4, 1959, and Christopher James, born February 16, 1964.

John Roy, born May 22, 1937, and Zella Mae Jarvis, born March 17, 1937, married January 28, 1956, at Hart, Michigan. Their children are: Roxanne Marie, born July 30, 1956; Larry Dale, born August 25, 1958; Karen Jean, born October 21, 1962; and Paul Allen, born June 25, 1968.

Pearl Louise, born March 9, 1928, and James Leonard Kay, April 28, 1911-October 25, 1995, married August 23, 1942, at Alicia, Arkansas. James Leonard was the widower of Pearl Evelyn Smith. They had two children, Nellie Mae, born August 15, 1931, at Lauratown and Bobbie Dale, born June 19, 1935, at Strangers Home. Pearl Louise and James Leonard's children are Leonard Leon, born February 16, 1944; Linda Phyllis, born September 3, 1945; Terry Richard, born February 18, 1947; and Sharon Ann, born April 19, 1949, all born in Walnut Ridge. In the 1950s, they moved to Shelby, Michigan. James Leonard is buried at Mount Hope Cemetery in Shelby. His first wife is buried at Strangers Home. –Roxanne Simmons.

SKIMAHORN FAMILY. The Skimahorns came to Lawrence County in the early 1900s. Grandpa's name was General Jack, who married Mary Lacy in Missouri. They moved to Lawrence County to raise a family. They had seven children; one was my father, Louie Tom. He married Vicy Amanda Collins, also from Missouri. They lived in Lawrence County the rest of their lives. They had 13 chil-

dren, eight boys and five girls. Two died as babies: Allan and Vicky. Otis Lee was the eldest. He has died. Also, Louie Jr. has died. That leaves Mary, Charley and Jewel, Loyd and Jim, Bill, and Louise, Ruth and Roger. After Junior died, that was the last Skimahorn in Lawrence County.

Grandpa bought the first piece of land, then Louie. They bought 40 acres; then the World War II broke out and Virgule, the youngest of grandpa's children, was called. He was killed in action in 1945, just days before the war was over. While the war was going, some of the girls' husbands were in the war also. They made it back. Grandpa lived in an old log house on his land until he died in 1946.

Louie Jr. passed away in 1982. He lived on the farm that we were all raised on. He had three children up until then. There were several Skimahorns in Lawrence County. –Mary Davies.

SKIMAHORN. Louie Jr., known to friends as JR, was born on November 18, 1939, in Lawrence County, Arkansas. He was the son of Louie Tom and Vicy Amanda Collins Skimahorn and the grandson of G. J. and Mary Lacy Skimahorn.

JR married Anna Elizabeth Martin on June 3, 1967, in Lawrence County. Anna was born on March 19, 1948, in Walnut Ridge, Arkansas. She was the daughter of Charley and Virginia Barham Martin of O'Kean, Arkansas.

Louie Tom died in 1965, and Vicy passed away two years later. Both are buried in Lawrence Memorial Cemetery. After their deaths, JR and Anna bought the family farm that was located in the Whiskerville Community of Lawrence County. JR and Anna

JR Skimahorn

farmed until his death on August 30, 1983. Anna sold the farm and she and their children moved to Walnut Ridge. Anna currently lives in Jonesboro, Arkansas, and is a respiratory therapist.

JR and Anna had three children. Their first child was born on December 8, 1968, in Walnut Ridge and was named Sonya Annette. Louie Tom Skimahorn II was born in Pocahontas, Arkansas on November 27, 1971. Amanda Virginia was born on October 2, 1977, in Jonesboro.

Sonya graduated from Walnut Ridge High School in 1987. She married Don Sparks in 1993, in O'Kean. She is a respiratory therapist and he is an emergency medical technician. They live in Paragould.

Louie Tom Skimahorn II died on June 9, 1989, from injuries sustained from a motorcycle accident. He would have been a graduate of WRHS in 1990. He wanted to become a farmer. The summer of his death, he was working on the farm of Sonny Williams.

Amanda graduated in

Louie Tom Skimahorn II

1995, from WRHS and in 1998, became a licensed practical nurse. She married Shane Martin in Marmaduke, Arkansas in 1997. Shane is a police officer in Jonesboro. They reside in Paragould, also.

Louie Tom and Vicy Amanda also had seven sons and five daughters besides JR. –Shane Marlin.

SANDY SLAYTON FAMILY. The Slayton family were Pennsylvania Dutch. They moved to the Birdell area of Pocahontas in Arkansas. A memory passed to the family by Sandy Slayton was of the Union Army moving through the area and taking his father to war and never seeing him again. Amos Josephus "A.J." was the son of Sandy Slayton. He married Myrtel Bowen in 1908, and their descendants include Paul, Lovell, Freda Slayton Hicks, Willis, Wanda Broadway and Kenneth.

Lovell Slayton resided in the Anneville Community with his wife, Margaret Graham. Their children included Darrell,

A. J. Slayton and Myrtel Bowen Slayton, 1908.

Joe and Jean Slayton Williams. Darrell and Joe were very active in the Walnut Ridge Community until their deaths. Darrell and his wife, Betty Cole Slayton, were killed in an airplane crash in 1968, with Bob and Marilyn Futrell. Jeanie Slayton married Carl Williams in the 1960s, and their descendants are Shannon Williams Wright and Todd Williams. Shannon Wright was tragically killed in the Westside School shooting in 1998. Todd lives in the Jonesboro area.

Willis Slayton retired to the Walnut Ridge area in 1980. He lived in the community until his death in 1999.

Many of these descendants have died, but Freda and Wanda still reside in the Hoxie-Walnut Ridge area. –Donna Hicks.

SLOAN. One of the first settlers of Lawrence County, Arkansas were Fergus III, 1787-1849, and Rosannah Ruggles Sloan, who came from Washington County, Missouri. They had migrated to Missouri via a wagon train with their original families from Ostego, New York, about 1810. The Sloans arrived in Lawrence in 1820, and took up land on Spring River about Opposition among the bears and panthers. Fergus built a large log house which became a gathering place for the community, especially as a place of worship for the Methodists. Fergus was a successful farmer and cattleman. He was quite literate and liked to read. Roasnnah stayed quite busy with the keeping of her household and guests. They had nine children.

1. Caroline married Sebourne Black. They moved to southern Arkansas.

2. Alexander Ruggles married Sally Janes. They moved to southern Arkansas.

3. Elizabeth D. "Eliza" married first Erwin Janes and second William B. Janes.

4. James F. Sloan married first Katie Shaver and second Margaret Raney.

5. Benjamin Brace married Susan Henderson.

6. Emma Electa "Amy" Sloan married Albert G. Stuart.

7. William Comfort married first Susan Henderson Sloan and second Elizabeth Jane Cravens.

8. Celinda Ann Sloan married Alfred Oaks.

9. Margaret Rosannah married John F. Henderson.

All of the children married and many of their descendants are still living in Lawrence County.

Fergus Sloan III died while visiting relatives in Caledonia, Missouri. He is buried in the cemetery there. Rosannah Ruggles Sloan, 1798-1860, dropped dead in the field with a bridle on her arm. She was going out to get her horse.

When Margaret Rosannan, their last child, was the bride of John F. Henderson, she was given a horse, chickens, pigs and a maid. When she and the maid were crossing Spring River on horseback, they both fell in the river and nearly drowned. She was pulled out by a Sloan servant who remembered that Margaret had a swimmy head and went to check up on her. Margaret was married five times. She was quoted as saying, "As long as the good Lord took them, she would too." In 1850, the Sloan farm and the Henderson farm were adjoining.–*Vivagene Wheezer Handley.*

SLOAN FAMILY. One of the first private transfers of land in Lawrence County was on February 15, 1814, when Samuel "Bennet" sold his "improvement right" to William Sloan to a "certain place...on the north side of Spring River and particularly known by the name of Shugar Tree Bottom (Powhatan Deed A&B).

Although William Sloan himself never moved to Arkansas, in 1819 three of his sons, Thomas, Fergus II and James, moved to Lawrence County. About 1829 when about 36 years, James moved to Clark County, Arkansas. The mother of Judge Harold Erwin is a descendant of this James Sloan. Judge Erwin resides in Newport and serves as presiding justice of the Lawrence, Sharp, Independence and Randolph Counties' circuit. After having lost three children, the brother Thomas returned to Missouri in 1831.

Lawrence County, Arkansas, pioneer Fergus Sloan III moved to the struggling territory in 1819. He was born December 16, 1787, in Lincolnton, Lincoln County, North Carolina, and died November 13, 1849, while on a visit to his relatives in Caledonia, Missouri. He was buried in the Caledonia graveyard. He married 1818 in Missouri before going to Arkansas, Roseanna Ruggles of Otsego, New York. Her parents were Comfort Ruggles and Clowie Barce who came west at the same time the Sloans did and crossed the Mississippi River together at St. Genevieve.

Fergus Sloan III took up The Shugar Tree Bottom farm on Spring River near Ravenden at a place called Opposition and there built a large substantial log house. Lawrence County was then more the home of bears, panthers and deer than that of civilized white men. He was one of the first settlers and his house was the place of worship for the settlers. The Sloans were Presbyterian, but as most of his neighbors were Methodist, he joined them in their faith.

Fergus Sloan III was a successful farmer and stockman for that day. When business permitted he was found with a book in hand. His wife lived at their old homestead until her sudden death of heart failure. She died August 9, 1860, and is buried in the graveyard at Smithville, Arkansas. One of her faithful, old slaves, Uncle "Alf," lived to be over a 100 years old, died in 1912 having seen five generations of the Sloan family in Lawrence County.

The children of Fergus Sloan III and Roseanna Ruggles were nine in number and all lived to be married. They were: Carolina married Shelbourne Black and moved to the southern part of Arkansas and had issue; Alexander married Sally Janes and moved to the southern part of Arkansas and had issue; Eliza married E. Janes (brother to Sally Janes) and had issue; James F. married first Martha "Mattie" Shaver, no issue, second Margaret "Maggie" Raney from a pioneer Arkansas family, had issue; Benjamin Barce married Su-

san Henderson, from another Arkansas pioneer family, had no issue; William Comfort married first his brother's widow, Susan Henderson, had issue, married second Elizabeth Jane Cravens, an Arkansas pioneer family, had issue; Amy married first Albert Stewart, had issue, married second Ben Holt, no issue; Ann married Alfred Oaks, no issue; Margarite married five times, first to John Henderson (Susan Henderson's brother), had issue, no issue by other unions, buried at Kingsville, Arkansas. –*Sara Black Epley.*

CLAY AND KITTY (MATTHEWS) SLOAN. Sloan was born in 1861 in Smithville, Arkansas to James F. Sloan and Margaret Raney Sloan. His family moved to Powhatan where he lived with two brothers; Frank and Dolph. Of the three sons, Dolph never married and he lived with Mrs. Sloan until his death in 1934.

Clay attended school at the Powhatan Male and Female Academy and resided in Powhatan until he left for Arkansas College at Batesville where he graduated in 1881. Mr. Sloan began teaching after his college graduation. Clay taught at the Powhatan Male and Female Academy and continued his teaching career until 1886. He also served from 1884 to 186 as County Examiner. He held the position of County Clerk from 1886 to 1890 and represented Lawrence County from 1891 to 1893 in the Arkansas House of Representatives. From 1893 to 1897 Clay was a state senator. Highly respected by his colleagues, Mr. Sloan was chosen President portempore at the close of the first session. Later he became Lt. Governor where he served for 30 days as Governor of the State of Arkansas while the present governor was out of the state. Clay was state auditor form 1879 to 1902, serving also on the Board of Charities and Commissioner of Agricultures. For many years he served as chairman of the Democratic Central Committee for Lawrence County.

Clay married Kitty Matthews, daughter of B.F. and Katherine (McIlroy) Matthews in 1888 at the Powhatan Methodist Episcopal Church, South. The couple lived at Powhatan until 1900 when they moved to Black Rock to rear four sons; Lawrence, Eugene, James F., and Ralph M. An infant son was born on February 20, 1904 and died on March 3, 1904. Lawrence Sloan married Hatz Padgett and to this union were six children; Larry, Katherine, Margaret, Mabel, Tom, and Virginia. This family lived in Strawberry. Eugene married Beatrice Lynch and had Patricia, Clay and Jimmy Gene. Eugene and Beatrice reared their children in Jonesboro.

Clay and Kitty (Matthews) Sloan in front of their home, "Clovercrest."

James F. married Snow Mountjoy and lived at Black Rock where they raised three sons: James F. III, Jack and Winston. Ralph M. married Elizabeth Morrison and to this union were three children; Ralph, Jr., James, Bobby.

Clay and Kitty were well known and respected in Lawrence County. They were successful financially as Clay was politically. Kitty preceded Clay in death on April 1, 1936 and Clay died on February 14, 1942. This fine couple was laid to rest at the Oak Forest Cemetery in Black Rock. –*David Clay Sloan.*

DANIEL FRANKLIN SLOAN, born November 30, 1956, is the third child and oldest son of Jack Mountjoy and Suzanne Cornelius Sloan. He is a lifetime resident of Lawrence County, attending all 12 years of school at Black Rock. He graduated valedictorian of his class and accepted a four year scholarship from the Army to attend the University of Arkansas at Fayetteville. While at the university, he met and married Barbara Dianne Cross, born August 2, 1958, daughter of Thomas B. and Mary L. Cross. Dianne graduated from Fayetteville High School in 1976, and also attended the University of Arkansas. Dan and Dianne were married May 12, 1979. After completing a Bachelor's degree in Agricultural Engineering, Daniel accepted a com-

From left: Sarah, Daniel, Dianne and Jeremiah Sloan.

mission in the United States Army and was assigned to the Corps of Engineers in June, 1980. After Engineer Officer Basic Course at Fort Belvoir, Virginia, he attended the Ranger School at Fort Benning, Georgia. Upon completion of Ranger School, Daniel served three years with the 249th Engineer Battalion in Karlsruhr, West Germany. While in Germany, Dianne completed a Bachelor's degree in Sociology from the University of Maryland.

Upon return to the states, the couple spent six months at Ft. Belvoir for Engineer Officer Advanced Course and then assumed command of F Company, 3rd Battalion, 4th Training Brigade at Ft. Leonardwood, Missouri. While living in Missouri, the couple's first child, Jeremiah Caleb Sloan, was born January 25, 1987. After finishing company command duties, Daniel resigned his commission and joined the Arkansas Army National Guard. He and Dianne both taught one year at Crocker Public Schools, Crocker, Missouri. Dianne completed a Masters in Education from Drury College, Springfield, Missouri, while the family lived at Fort Leonardwood.

In 1987, the couple moved from Missouri to Black Rock. They both accepted teaching jobs at Black Rock Public Schools in 1988. Dan taught math, science and physics at the school, has coached elementary basketball and Odyssey of the Mind teams and serves as Technology Coordinator. Dianne was high school Library Media Specialist from 1988 to 1994. She also taught remedial reading courses and served as Elementary Library Media Specialist for part of this time.

The Sloan's youngest child was born June 30, 1993. In fall of 1999 Sarah Asiel Sloan is currently in second grade at Black Rock. Her brother, Jeremiah, is a seventh grader and enjoys playing basketball for the school and community teams. He is a member of Boy Scout Troop 65.

Dianne currently teaches courses at Williams Baptist College in the Elementary Education Department. The family attends church at New Hope Baptist Church outside of Black Rock. Dan serves as a deacon and Dianne teaches Sunday School. Dan has served as Cub Master for Cub Scout Pack 65 for four years. He continues to serve in the Arkansas National Guard and is currently a Lt. Colonel and commander of 1st Battalion, 87th Troop Command at Camp Robinson, North Little Rock.

The family operates a three house poultry farm for Townsends, Inc. out of Batesville. Their home site was previously the home of both his parents and his grandparents, James F. and Snow Mountjoy Sloan. –*Daniel Sloan.*

EARL BABER SLOAN and his brother, Neil, bought the Bloom Brothers cotton gin in 1930. They had a very successful business partnership, built on mutual respect and affection. Individually, they operated large acreage of farmland. In 1936 Earl was awarded the title of Master Farmer by the representatives of the *Progressive Farmer* and *Southern Realist.*

Earl Sloan married Pauline "Polly" Dillport, 1903-1991, in 1924 one year after he moved on his farm seven miles northeast of Walnut Ridge, near Cache River. Jesse Andrew's grandfather lived on the farm at that time. Andrews & Sons manage this acreage today. Earl and Polly Sloan had three children - all surviving in 1999: Carolyn Baber Sloan married Swan Dowell Swindle, 1954, had issue; Earl Jr and Sara Ann Sloan married first Robert Harvey Smith Jr., 1961 had issue, married second Henry Maney Heckle, 1983 no issue. Carolyn and Swan Swindle have a daughter, Carol Sloan Swindle. Carol Sloan

Earl and Pauline Sloan were prominent residents and landowners in Walnut Ridge.

Swindle teaches at the University of Central Arkansas and is the proud mother of young Polly Caroline Swindle who was born in China (1997). Carol Sloan Swindle graduated with a B.A. from Hendrix College in Conway, Arkansas, with a M.A. from Tulane University, New Orleans, Louisiana, and a PhD. in finance from the University of Florida, Gainesville, Florida. She was employed by Entergy in New Orleans, taught at Lyons College in Batesville, Arkansas, and Lehigh University in Bethlehem, Pennsylvania, before returning to Arkansas.

Sara Ann Sloan and Robert Harvey Smith Jr., 1939-1994, had three children: Virginia "Ginny" Inez Smith married David Terry Fields, 1988 have two children Sarah Megan, 1989 and Spencer David, 1992; Sarah Elizabeth Smith married Robert Walthar Leibold Jr., 1989 have two children Nathaniel Zane, 1992 and Hannah Clare, 1995; Milton Baber Smith married Stephanie Louise Saracini, 1992, and have daughter, Lillie Kathleen, 1998.

Virginia "Ginny" Inez Smith Fields received a B.A. and a J.D. from the University of Arkansas, Fayetteville. She is admitted to practice law in Texas and Arkansas. Ginny lives with her family in Austin, Texas, where her husband, Terry, is a practicing architect. Sarah Elizabeth Leibold received a B.A. from Trinity University in San Antonio, Texas, where she now lives with her family. Her husband, Rob, works with public relations for St. Mary's University in San Antonio. Milton Baber Smith has succeeded his father as president and chief operating officer of the First National Bank of Lawrence County in Walnut Ridge, Arkansas. Both of his grandfathers, Robert Harvey Smith and Earl Baber Sloan, were associated with First National Bank of Lawrence County. Milton graduated from the Baylor School in Chattanooga, Tennessee, and received a B.A. from Southern Methodist University in Dallas, Texas. Milton Baber Smith and daughter, Lillie Kathleen, are the only direct descendants of the Frank Fowler Sloan family still living in Lawrence County. –*Sara Sloan Heckle.*

FRANK FOWLER SLOAN FAMILY. Frank Fowler Sloan was the second of the three sons of James F. Sloan and Margaret Jane Raney Sloan. He was born August 3, 1863, at Smithville, Arkansas, and moved with the family to Powhatan in 1869. His mother, widowed in 1873, married Colonel Milton Dyer Baber in 1877. At the time of his mother's remarriage, Frank Fowler was about 14 years of age. Colonel Baber brought to this family one child, a daughter Virginia "Jennie," born November 17, 1866.

The son, Frank, attended the schools at Powhatan and finished his education in 1883 with a A.B. degree from Arkansas College (now Lyons College) at Batesville. He married his stepsister, Miss Virginia "Jennie" Baber, also an Arkansas College graduate and for several years they made Powhatan their home, but in 1900 they moved to Portia to establish a home there. The railroad had come to Portia. Powhatan which was a center of trade because of river traffic began to lose importance.

Both Frank and Jennie Sloan were persons of fine intellectual endowments. Both loved to read and loved music. Mrs. Sloan taught piano for years. Frank and Jennie Sloan would combine with Clay and Kittie Sloan to form a quartet for their enjoyment and for the enjoyment of their friends.

Mr. Sloan personally directed the cultivation of his home farm near Portia and came to be regarded as one of the outstanding farmers of the county. He applied good business principles and methods to his farming and thus made it profitable, so that at the time of his death in 1927 he had acquired considerable acreage in choice farm lands.

Frank and Jennie Sloan were the parents of six sons and three daughters: Milton, Margaret, Horace 1889-1942, Leland, Victor 1893-1965, Neil 1896-1962, Earl 1899-1990, Stanley 1901-1926, Vivian 1903-198?. Milton, Margaret and Leland died as infants. Stanley Sloan inherited his parents' love of music, had a beautiful tenor voice, but he was frail and died in his 20s.

Horace Sloan loved learning and the law. He graduated from Arkansas College, B.A. 1908 from DePauw University in Greencastle, Indiana, B.A. 1909 and from the University of Chicago Law School, J.D. 1912. While at DePauw University, Horace met and later married Geraldine Smith of Winchester, Indiana. Horace Sloan established a successful law practice in Jonesboro, Arkansas. After the 1927 flood of the Mississippi River, Horace Smith wrote the text still used in Arkansas' law schools on drainage law, a two volume, *The Law of Improvement Districts in Arkansas*, 1928. Horace

and Geraldine Sloan had three children: twins Emily and Frank, born 1915 and Geraldine, born 1923. Emily married Dave Abernathy in 1935 and received her B.A. from Arkansas State College (now Arkansas State University in 1936. The Abernathys had three boys and one daughter: Dave, Bill, Frank and Emily Ann. Dave Abernathy married Harriet ?? and had two chidlren, Wesley and Day. Bill is married and has a family. Bill has a firm in Memphis that does psychological testing for fiduciary institutions. Frank is married and lives with his family in Kentucky. He teaches in college. Frank O. Sloan graduated from Northwestern University in Evanston, Illinois, and from the University of Texas Law School. Frank O. Sloan followed his father in the practice of law in Jonesboro. He married and though he had no children of his own, he adored his adopted daughter, Margaret Ann. Geraldine Sloan became an opera singer with the Philadelphia Opera Company. She married Dr. Harold Greenberg from Yonkers, New York. The Greenbergs are survived by four sons, all living in and around New York City.

Victor Sloan married Mayme Buerklin. They lived in the old Sloan home in Portia for many years. Victor and Mayme loved their home, their community and their church. For years Victor was treasurer of the City of Portia. As careful with public funds as he was with his own, after Mr. Sloan's tenure in office, the City of Portia was able to pave every street.

Neil Sloan married Imogene Robinson. They had one daughter, Gloria Francis Sloan who married Bascom Price Raney. The Raneys are survived by three sons, Neil, Bascom Clarence "Lance," Sloan and a daughter, Sara. Neil manages a portion of the Sloan-Raney land in Lawrence County. He lives in Jonesboro. Lance is a medical doctor in Jay, Florida. He and his wife, Shirley, have two daughters, Sara Abigail and Gloria Sloan Raney. Sara is married to David Howell who farms a large portion of the Sloan-Raney land in Lawrence County. The Howells live in Jonesboro where Sara has a successful art gallery. Sloan has a law degree and has been focusing on a writing career. He, too, resides in Jonesboro. –*Sara Sloan Heckle.*

JACK M. SLOAN FAMILY. Jack Mountjoy Sloan, born September 20, 1927, met his wife, Suzanne Cornelius, August 24, 1934-October 15, 1995, daughter of Vance Zeb and Ozelle Graves Cornelius of San Antonio when he was an Air Force lieutenant stationed at Lackland

The Jack Sloan family shortly after the birth of the first grandchild, Ryan Phillips, son of Lesia and Danny Phillips. Seated, left to right: Dina Durham, Jack Sloan with Ryan Phillips, Dixie Sloan. Standing, left to right: Patrick, Michael, Kelly, Suzanne, Daniel, and Jacki Sloan, and Lesia Phillips.

Air Force Base. Lt. Colonel Cornelius was stationed adjacent at Kelly Air Force Base. They married at the chapel on Kelly Field on May 27, 1953.

Their children are: Lesia Joy, born December 29, 1954. Dixie Lee Dawn, born December 12, 1955. Daniel Franklin, born November 30, 1956. Dina Gail, born April 13, 1958. Kelly Vance, born May 1, 1960. Michael Alan, born July 6, 1961. Patrick Cornelius, born August 30, 1963. Jacquelyn Suzanne, born November 3, 1971.

Lesia married Danny Walker Phillips on August 17, 1976. They have three children: "Ryan" Walker, born August 6, 1978; "Austin" Blake, born August 18, 1980; and "Clay" Carson born October 1, 1984.

Dixie married Ralph McGinnis. They divorced. Her second marriage was to Sam Moore. She has two stepsons: Randy and Sammy.

Dan married Barbara "Dianne" Cross on May 12, 1979. Their children are: "Jeremiah" Caleb, born January 25, 1987; and "Sarah" Asiel, born June 30, 1993.

Dina married William "Sloan" Durham on June 18, 1976. Their children are "Justin" Sloan, (April 27, 1980-July 2, 1997); William "Courtney", born September 13, 1983; "April" Shanel, born April 13, 1986; and Calie Blair "Kalie", born February 6, 1990.

Kelly married Tammy Copeland who had a daughter, Christina. They had a son, Skylar Vance, born April 11, 1984. They later divorced.

Mike married Sharon Kay Prater. They had a son, "Nathan" Alan, born February 25, 1983. They divorced. He married Linda Blount and had a son, "Trever" Michael, born October 28, 1991. They divorced.

Pat married Jean "Michele" Hallmark on February 16, 1985. Their children are: "Christopher" Patrick, born February 2, 1988; "Bridget" Ann, born February 24, 1997; and "Brandon" Franklin, born December 21, 1998.

Jacki married James Clay Blankenship on June 18, 1988. Their children are: Felecia "Shantel", born December 16, 1988; and "Jacob" Tyler, born October 6, 1996.

The family ancestors begin with Fergus Sloan and Rosanna Ruggles who came as a married couple from Caledonia, Missouri to near Ravenden. His son, James F. Sloan, married Margaret Jane Raney. Their son, Clay Sloan, "Big Daddy", married Catharine "Kittie" Matthews. Their son, James Franklin Sloan, (January 23, 1898-February 7, 1960,) married Snow Congdon Mountjoy, born February 15, 1902, on January 23, 1918. Their children are James Franklin III (Jamie or Jim), Jack and Winston Ivan.

Jack graduated as salutatorian from Black Rock School in 1945. He served in the Army in Japan during the Occupation, returning to earn a degree in Agriculture from the University of Arkansas in Fayetteville and a commission in the Air Force in 1951. He served in the Air Force during the Korean War.

Jack followed the footsteps of his father, managing and operating the family farms and serving on the Black Rock School Board for years. He was instrumental in the organization of Black Rock Development Corporation and Farm Service, a farm supply cooperative. He also served on the original board of directors of both companies. He is a founding and still active member of the Black Rock Lions Club. Suzanne devoted the majority of her time to her family and home and was active in charitable activities. At various times she was employed with VISTA, Olan Mills, Wal-Mart, and as a census worker. She also operated a restaurant for a time. –Lesia Sloan Phillips.

JAMES F. SLOAN was born in Lawrence County near Ravenden in 1827 and lived in the county all his life. In 1855 James F. married Martha Catherine Shaver, 1835-1855, sister of the late Colonel Robert Glenn Shaver, but of this marriage there was no issue. He was married again in 1860 to Miss Margaret Jane Raney, 1843-1933, daughter of Andrew Jackson Raney, 1815-186?. Three sons were born to James F. and Margaret Jane: Clay, 1861-1942; Frank Fowler, 1863-1927; Dolph, 1866-1933.

Mr. Sloan and his wife, Margaret Jane Raney, located on Reed's Creek, but soon moved to Smithville where he engaged for a time in the mercantile business with a Dr. L.S. Bobo. About 1859 he formed a mercantile partnership in Smithville with his younger brother, W.C. Sloan. A bridegroom when Arkansas seceded from the Union, Mr. Sloan hired a substitute to serve in his place in the Confederate forces. As the hostilities persisted, he did serve and suffered severely from the measles while in service.

After the war, in 1869 James F. and Margaret moved their family to the new county seat, Powhatan, where the following year he again engaged in the mercantile business. Powhatan was an important river town. The Sloan brothers bought cotton then shipped it by the river boats to St. Louis.

James F. Sloan died at age 46 in 1873. His poor health was attributed to exposure suffered as a confederate soldier. Prior to the war, Mr. Sloan was a Whig in politics, but after that a Democrat.

In 1877 Margaret Jane Raney Sloan was married to Colonel Milton Dyer Baber, 1837-1893, a widower with one daughter, Virginia "Jennie," 1866-1949. There were no surviving issue from this union. –Lesia Sloan Phillips.

JAMES F. SLOAN II was one of the most highly-respected and valued citizens of Northeast Arkansas and Lawrence County. Mr. Sloan was born at Powhatan on January 23, 1896 to Clay and Kitty (Matthews) Sloan. A farmer and stockman, he held extensive farming interests. His economic successes were matched or exceeded by his continuing efforts to improve the economy of

James F. Sloan, II

Lawrence County and to improve the welfare of the people. Long before the era of government restrictions on money crops, Mr. Sloan had adopted the philosophy that Lawrence County could best grow and prosper with a diversified approach to farming. He worked unceasingly toward this end by being a leader in farm organizations that urged this diversification to improve the general farm economy.

James F. Sloan had a long and creditable record of public service. He served 23 years as a member of the county ASC committee and served as chairman of the committee. He was a Mason, a Presbyterian and a veteran of World War I.

Mr. Sloan married Snow Mountjoy and from this union were three sons: James F. Sloan III of Walnut Ridge, Jack Sloan of Black Rock, and Winston Sloan of Fayetteville. The Sloans resided in Black Rock until moving to Walnut Ridge a few years before Mr. Sloan's death.

James F. Sloan II died on February 7, 1960 and is buried in the family burial plot at Oak Forest Cemetery in Black Rock. His wife, Snow Sloan, remains a resident of Walnut Ridge. The many people to whom he had been a benefactor, along with his numerous associates and friends, were extremely appreciative of the many contributions he made to the various facets of their lives. –David Clay Sloan.

PATRICK CORNELIUS SLOAN, born August 30, 1963, is the fourth son and seventh child of Jack Mountjoy and Suzanne Cornelius Sloan. Brothers and sisters: Lesia Joy Sloan Phillips, Dixie Lee Dawn Sloan Moore, Daniel Franklin Sloan, Dina Gail Sloan Durham, Kelly Vance Sloan, Michael Alan Sloan and Jacquelyn Suzanne Sloan Blankenship. Their direct line of ancestors include James Franklin Sloan, son of Clay Sloan, son of James F. Sloan, son of Fergus Sloan. Patrick attended Black Rock Schools K-12, and graduated from Black River Technical School in Pocahontas as an outstanding student in Diesel Mechanics in 1984. He has worked alongside his father on the family farm since a young child. Pat has been active in Boy Scouts of America since he began as a Cub Scout and achieved the level of Eagle Scout. He has continued his involvement acting as an adult leader in both Cub Scouts and Boy Scouts.

He married Jean "Michele" Hallmark, daughter of Hal Edward and Ruth Ann Agne Hallmark of Cash on February 16, 1985. Michele was born August 4, 1963. She attended school at Cash Elementary and Westside

From left: Patrick and Brandon Sloan, Christopher Sloan, Michelle and Bridgette Sloan.

High School. She graduated in 1982, from Delta VoTech as a licensed practical nurse. She worked for St. Bernard's Hospital for 10 years, Lawrence County Cooperative School for Exceptional Students for a year and a half.

Their children are: Christopher Patrick, born February 2, 1988; Bridget Ann, born February 4, 1997; and Brandon Franklin, born December 21, 1998. The family is part of the congregation of New Hope Baptist Church.

Their first home was north of Black Rock off of Cemetery Road. Currently, they live on and operate a poultry farm on Crow Creek off of Parker Springs Road 310. –Patrick Sloan.

SMITH FAMILY. James Smith, immigrant Smith ancestor of these Smiths, came from England to Weymouth, Massachusetts in the 1630s. The first of the Smith-Hamby family settled in Lawrence County in 1830. David R. Smith, born to Joseph and Olive Smith in West Haven (Rutland County), Vermont, March 14, 1798, reportedly left home

1908, beside the barn. Green Whitfield Smith, son Elmer, age 16 and daughter, Lula, age 14.

because he couldn't get along with his father. David's son, John, later went to Branson, Missouri for the same reason.

In Caldwell County, Kentucky, 1824, David married Mariah Hamby, born in South Carolina, 1804, to John and Bradbrook Hamby. The last name of Bradbrook believed to be a Cherokee, remains unknown,

Amos Hamby lived in Lawrence County in early 1830s, son of John and Bradbrook Hamby; pictures date unknown - born 1796.

despite, due to speculation, it was reported to the Mormon History Center as Green.

David bought Lawrence County land from Iron Mountain railroad for 15 cents per acre. He used the same cattle mark that his father used.

John Hamby gave his property to his son, Amos, in Livingston County, Kentucky in 1830, to take care of his parents from then on. John started over in Arkansas. On March 14, 1831, he registered his cattle mark. That day, Joseph Green, David and Mariah's son, was born. The David Smiths were Methodists. At age 74, David married Melissa Hillis.

Joseph Green Smith married three times and had a number of children. Some descendants still live in Lawrence County. His grandson, son of "Dock" Smith, still lives on his grandfather's farm near Black Rock.

Joseph Smith married Letitia M. Gentry, October 21, 1853. She was born in Ten-

Probably later 1940s. Elmer Ross Smith entering Black Rock School his father, Henry Elmer Smith, attended.

nessee to John Reuben Gentry and wife, Alvira Adams. John died in Randolph County, Arkansas in 1856 or 1857. Alvira and her unmarried children returned to Tennessee. John was the nephew of a Tennessee governor (in 1830s), Newton Cannon. He was a man of great integrity. He and Andrew Jackson disliked each other. Once when Cannon was a colonel under Jackson, Jackson refused to pay his men. Cannon paid them out of his own pocket.

Green Whitfield "Whit", born July 4, 1859, was the third child of Joseph and Letitia Smith. He married Joanna Perkins, granddaughter of Amos Hamby, in Dadeville, Missouri, March 11, 1887. Amos was with the Hambys who settled in Arkansas, but was in Cedar County, Missouri by 1834, where he died in 1876. Whit stayed in Missouri a few years, but returned to Black Rock, where he reared his three children. Joanna died in 1908. Their children left the area as adults.

Letitia died December 22, 1865. She is buried on the farm where her grandson lives. There was a cemetery on David's property near Black Rock. Many Smiths and Hambys are buried there, but an occupant some years ago took down the tombstones and buried them on the property.

On May 30, 1866, Joseph Green Smith married Sidda Stuard. His Bible record reveals that. There is an erroneous courthouse record that states that she married his brother (already married), Thomas Jefferson Smith, on that date.

Sidda gave Whit (date unknown) her cedar sugar keg. In 1920, he gave it to Myrtle Smith, wife of his son, Elmer. Now it belongs to Gwyndolyn Smith, Whit's granddaughter. She was two years old when Whit died, but loved him dearly, remembers much about him and many incidents that occurred.

On March 17, 1913, Whit married Ella Davis, widow. Both of his sons lived in Blytheville three blocks apart. Fred Green Smith, February 10, 1889-October 5, 1940, had a large two story home and invited them to spend their winters in Blytheville. He had one son, Fred Whitcomb, deceased. Henry Elmer, January 23, 1892-May 17, 1941, had only one child before Whit's death. Later, two others were born, Elmer Ross and Mary Evelyn, both deceased.

Whit's daughter, Lula, married William Thompson from Black Rock. They lived in Blytheville for a while, but were living in Forrest City long before Whit's death. Lula, February 4, 1894-August 2, 1973, was born in Aldrich, Missouri as were her brothers. She lived in Little Rock many years and is buried there.

The day Whit died he and Ella strung beans on their back porch. They were preparing to go on vacation. He said he was going to lie down a while. He died within a few minutes.

In the 1970s, Gwyndolyn told her mother that her memory of her grandfather on the day of his funeral was that he was in no casket, but lying on boards between two chairs. Her mother confirmed that. He was buried beside Joanna in Morris Cemetery, Bona, Missouri.

Whit denied himself much in order to leave each of his children $1,000 and a horse. Although centrally located in town, Elmer had a barn for his and Fred's horses, Dude and Duke.

Whit was not Ella's last husband. Mae Smith Justus said Ella climbed a tree to get apples for a pie when she was about 70.

AUSTIN SMITH FAMILY.
Austin's parents were Fred Winfield and Florence Cotham Smith. He had three brothers: Golie, Jim, Thomas and four sisters: Lois, Glenda, Evelyn and Bonnie.

Austin married Ernestene Robert in 1946. They have one daughter, Sherry Annett Smith Moore. She teaches home economics at Walnut Ridge High School. Sherry has one son,

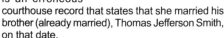

Probably made late 1893. Their daughter, born February 14, 1894, was not born yet so Fred was not ???? and not had his 2nd birthday. Whit and Joanna Smith and sons, Elmer on his father's lap and Fred beside his mother.

Jeannie Wess Moore, Phillip Moore, Ernestine Smith, Austin Smith, Sherry (Smith) Moore. Front: Mica LouAnn Moore.

Phillip F. Moore, and one daughter, Mica LouAnn Moore. Phillip is married to Jeannie Wess Moore and they live in Nashville, Tennessee. Phillip is a songwriter and

Fred and Florence Smith.

Jeannie teaches art. Mica is in college at Conway. Austin and Ernestene are retirees.
–Donna Hicks Pinkston.

DAVID R. SMITH.
Born in West Haven, Rutland County, Vermont, March 14, 1798, the son of Joseph and Olive Smith, David left Vermont in the 1820s, to make his own way in the world. Some say he had a falling out with his father, some say with another brother. The truth of the family split is now lost in antiquity. We do know he was in Caldwell County, Kentucky in 1824, because the marriage record is there for David and his first wife, Mariah Hamby. And the young David Smith family was in Arkansas by 1830, when the first census was taken. Some of their descendants have remained in Arkansas since that time and, because of the large families the Smiths had and the small population of the county as a whole, our family had intermarried with most of the early Lawrence County families.

Mariah was the daughter of William Hamby and his Cherokee wife, Bradbrook Green. The Hamby family were Tories in the Revolution while the Smiths were soundly for the new nation of America.

Children of David and Mariah are:

1. Cintha Jane Smith, born 1826, married Bethel Odom, April 25, 1860.

2. Joseph Green Smith, born March 14, 1831, Powhatan, died 1897, married first Stidda Stuard, second unknown, third Letitia Gentry, daughter of John and Elizabeth Adams Gentry.

3. Thomas Jefferson Smith, born June 11, 1833, Powhatan, died December 8, 1896, married Addiline Francis Ethridge, daughter of Stephen and Sarah Ethridge.

4. Nancy A. Smith, born 1835, married Daniel W. Rhea, July 1, 1866.

5. David Crittenden Smith, born February 10, 1837, died after 1920, married first C. A. Pyland and second Mary Ann Bottoms.

Of the above mentioned children we have more information on all of them except Cintha Jane.

The children of Joseph Green and Stidda Stuard Smith are: Nancy Emma Smith, born about 1867, died June 9, 1887; and Mat Smith.

The child of Joseph Green and unknown is: Josephine Smith, who married a Douglas.

The children of Joseph Green and Letitia Gentry Smith are: Sarah M. Smith, born July 14, 1855, married Peter J. Ballard; John Wilson Smith, born March 18, 1857, died June 22, 1926, married

Martha Elizabeth Harden, daughter of James and Tennessee Frediking Harden; Green Whitfield Smith, born July 4, 1859, died August 19, 1921, married Joanna Perkins; Fanny Smith, born about 1861; Letitia "Doc" Gentry Smith, born about 1865, married first Addie, second Mary E. Hardin; and Henrietta Smith, died September 16, 1873.

David and Mariah were members of the Methodist Episcopal Church. Well-respected in their community and believing in service to God and their fellow man, they made good citizens themselves and raised their family to be the same. Their three sons served in the Confederate Army and then came home to take care of their families and farms.

–Dale Hinshaw McMasters.

EFFIE PEARL RIPPEE SMITH was a direct descendant of Johann Heinrich Weidner, October 9, 1717-July 21, 1792, who was born in Saxe-Coburg, Germany, and Mary Catherine Muehle, May 24, 1733-August 20, 1804. Heinrich and Catherine lived in Hickory, North Carolina, and parented eight children. They were: Daniel, Henry II, Abram, Barbara, Mary, Mollie, Catherine and Elizabeth.

Henry served as Patriot in the Battle of Kings Mountain during the Revolutionary War. Today the Madison County Missouri Chapter of The Daughters of the American Revolution is named the Captain Henry Weidner Chapter.

Henry II married Sarah Shell in Lincolnton, Lincoln County, North Carolina in 1781. Sarah died in Lincolnton and Captain Henry died in Marquand, Missouri. They were the parents of Anna Marie "Mary" Weidner, who married Henry Myers, born 1768. Henry Myers and Mary were the parents of Sophia A. Myers, born about 1806, in Fredricktown, Missouri, and died in 1843, in Randolph County, Arkansas.

Sophia married Martin Miller Hogan, who was born August 28, 1801, in Hopkinsville, Kentucky and died January 26, 1894, in Randolph County. He and Sophia were married November 10, 1826, in Jackson County, North Carolina. They were the parents of Rebecca Susan Hogan, who married Nimrod Smith on February 15, 1850, in Randolph County.

Nimrod and Rebecca had five children. They were: Mary E., John, Liddia, James A. and Elizabeth. Nimrod was killed during the Civil War in Shelbyville, Tennessee on March 16, 1863. James A. Smith was born in 1856, family lore tells of his service to the Confederate Army during the Civil War, however, this researcher has not been able to find proof of service.

James A. married Rhoda Looney, daughter of Jonathan and Anna J. Jones of Lawrence County. They were the parents of Otto C., Lottie N., Effie Pearl, William A., Tola A. and Ora E.

Effie married Edward Thurman Rippee (see Rippee history) on March 18, 1908, and they had four children: Azril, Thara, Cleatus and Dewell. They lived in the Richwoods Community. Effie was an exceptional woman. In addition to her own children, she raised three half-siblings and four grandchildren after the death of their mother.

Today several descendants of the Smith family still live in and around Lawrence County. A niece, Wanda Smith Slatton,who is married to Roy, lives in Bono, and Brenda Lynn Rippee Jones, a granddaughter, who is married to Leon, lives in Black Rock. –Brenda Jones.

EVAN SMITH of Powhatan was born on September 17, 1902, near Calamine, Arkansas, in Sharp County. He was raised on a farm and by the time he was 10 years old he could feed hogs, cows, horses and mules, cut wood, plow, plant crops and put up fences. The Smith family soon

after moved to Powhatan, a busy river town. He had four brothers and three sisters.

When Evan was 15 years old he recalls seeing the United States Quapaw steamboat tied up at Powhatan. In talking with the captain of the boat, Evan was asked if he wanted to work on the boat. He went and talked

Evan Smith.

with his parents and received a note for permission to work on the snagboat. He took two pair of overalls, two or three shirts and a pair of shoes and began his work on the boat. His pay was $50 a month including board and laundry. There were nine laborers, a cook, maid and a man called "sailorboy." This experience on the boat trained him to be a fireman.

Life on the snagboat included travel as far as Poplar Bluff, Missouri, on Black River to the lock and dam at Batesville on White River. The snagboats went as far down as New Orleans and up to Memphis cleaning out the logs to keep the river channels open to all boats.

In 1922 his plans were to be off for the winter; however, he was told due to another worker's illness he was needed to stay on the job. He caught a train back to Powhatan where he married Laura Smith, no relation. When he arrived he and Laura were married at the Powhatan log house by Justice of the Peace Tom Watson. To this union was born five sons, Dempsey, Frank, Tommy, Cleatus and Jerry; and six daughters, Lois Smith Colbert, Joann Smith Drury, Bonnie Smith Richey, Mary Smith Maxwell, Geraldine Smith Davis and Pat Smith all raised in the town of Powhatan. Laura died later in 1979.

In 1925 a bridge building company arrived at Powhatan to begin construction of the Powhatan Swinging Bridge. During this period, railroads had bypassed Powhatan and people were out of work. Evan went to see the bridge superintendent and he was the first man hired. On September 25, 1925, construction began on the Powhatan Bridge and Mr. Smith was paid $6 a day for 10 hours work. The bridge spanned a quarter mile and was made from lumber cut from local saw mills. The oak floor of the bridge was three inches thick and 16-18 inches wide. Lumber was brought on an eight wheel log wagon pulled by four horses. The cable for the bridge was premeasured number nine steel wire strands. Mr. Smith used a harness to pull the strands as they were spliced and clamped together, anchor to anchor. The bridge was 350 feet from anchor to anchor and up to 90 feet high.

In 1926 the bridge was finished and as Evan was helping take down the scaffolding he fell 40 feet. He sustained a broken right leg and a 25 foot steel ball accidentally hit him; these injuries were to remain with him the rest of his life.

In 1951 a new bridge was opened at Black Rock; thus eliminating the Powhatan Bridge. Despite his injury, Evan helped dismantle the same bridge he helped to build.

Evan remained active, continued to work and had an interest in the betterment of the community. He died on April 24, 1992, at the age of 89 and is buried next to his wife at the Powhatan Cemetery. –Bonnie Smith Richey.

HARVEY EDWARDS SMITH, 1885-1935, and Nettie Goodwin Smith, 1886-1938, were originally from Smackover, Arkansas. They came to Walnut Ridge around 1923, and assumed the management of The Lawrence Hotel. They had two sons, Robert Harvey Smith, 1906-1972, and Ray C. Smith, 1907-1966.

Robert Harvey Smith married Inez Harvey, 1901-1988, of Old Walnut Ridge. They raised two children, Robert Harvey Smith Jr. and Annette Smith. Robert H. Smith Sr. was engaged in farming and was associated with the Lawrence Agency, Smith Implement, Inc. and First National Bank of Lawrence County. He was Chairman of the Board of Riceland Food and he was very active in politics on the state and national level.

Ray C. Smith married Elizabeth Gibson and they had a daughter, Mary Anne and a son, John Kay Gibson Smith. Ray married Bess Harvey, 1912-1959, and they had a daughter, Sherry Ray Smith. Ray was involved in farming, cattle and the restaurant business.

Sherry married Alfred Dunham from Walnut Ridge. They reside in El Dorado, where Alfred is a CPA and they have two sons names Robert and Nathan.

Robert Harvey Smith Jr., 1939-1994, married Sara Sloan of Walnut Ridge. Robert Harvey Smith Jr. served as President of First National Bank of Lawrence County for 27 years until his death. He was pri-

marily responsible for the bank's current building on Main Street. Robert H. Smith Jr. also managed farming and other business interests. Robert and Sara had three children: Virginia Inez is married to Terry Fields. They have two children, Sarah Megan and Spencer David and they reside in Austin, Texas. Sarah Elizabeth is married to Rob Leibold and they have two children, Nathaniel Zane and Hannah Claire. They reside in San Antonio. Milton Baber Smith is married to former Stephanie Saracini. They have a daughter, Lillie Kathleen and they live in Walnut Ridge.

Annette Smith married Tom L. Hilburn and they raised four children: Leslie, Tom, Natalie and Caroline. Tom was a practicing attorney for many years before being elected Chancery Judge, an office which he still holds. Leslie is married to Bill Morgan and they have two sons, Waylon and Nigel. They reside in Walnut Ridge. Tom is married to Karla Johnson and they have one daughter, Holly, and they live in Little Rock. Natalie is married to Jamie Smith. They have a son, Jake. They reside in Walnut Ridge. Caroline is married to Lanier Robison and they have three children: Lauren, Chase and Grace and they reside in Memphis, Tennessee. –Milton Smith.

JAMES SMITH FAMILY. James M. "Matt" Smith and his wife, Rebecca Sharp, daughter of Solomon and Amanda "Amy" Sharp, were born in Arkansas. James was born about 1825, but research has yet to indicate where he was from or his parentage. James and Amy married in Lawrence County, April 3, 1849. James enlisted during the Civil War in Powhatan, at 40 years old, joining Company G, 45th Regiment of the Arkansas Cavalry as a private. The Muster and Descriptive Roll describes James with blue eyes, dark hair, dark complexion and five foot, 10 inches. James received a veteran pension of 100 dollars when he was 80.

James and Rebecca, 1831-1890, lived north-west of Black Rock, near Stinnett Creek. The census lists James as a blacksmith, a skill carried on until today by a Smith grandson and great-great-grandson. James and Rebecca were parents of 11 children: Henry "Jake" Smith, Laura E. Thompson, Geneva "Jenny" Weir, Levi Smith, Dorah E. Smith, Sarah A. Moore Arnold, Mary E. Smith, Martha J. Weir and Solomon Smith were born in Arkansas. Two children were born in Texas between 1858-1860: Margaret "Maggie" West and Andrew Jackson Smith. Rebecca, and we believe James, are buried in Kelley Cemetery.

James and Rebecca's son, Henry "Jake" Smith, 1869-1950, raised his family across the road from his father's property. Jake married Ora Dell Chaplain and they raised 10 children (see the Chaplain family). Their children went to Pleasant Hill School, a two story "one room" school house. Eight of their children lived and raised their own families in Lawrence County.

Jake farmed approximately 160 acres, with 10 acres of fruit trees, cattle, hogs and several teams of horses for field work. He was a quiet man, tall and husky, very knowledgeable, generous and well respected. Jake was a good carpenter, often helping build houses and barns. Jake enjoyed fishing on Spring River, at the back of his property, where he caught huge catfish, sturgeon, carp and eel. Fish were strung on poles held at shoulder level, their tails dragging in the dirt. For his annual 4th of July family picnic, Jake always roasted a hog, bought 10 gallon containers of ice cream and a whole stalk of bananas for making sundaes.

Jake was the first in the area to own a car, telephone and radio for listening to the Grand Ole Opry and Lum and Abner. It's for his "driving" that Jake is most remembered. He drove his Model "T" by putting it into gear and pushing and holding the gas pedal all the way to the floor. The car would buck and jump up the hills, throwing gravel and roaring as he headed down the dirt road to town. Ora Dell never rode with him and everyone else was just as afraid to go for a ride. Jake and Ora Dell lived in their home until they died. They are buried in Kelley Cemetery. –Donna Christensen.

LEWIS DAVID SMITH married Susan Hutsell on March 3, 1907, in Lawrence County. Susan died in 1917, and he married Rosa Armenta McCord on January 6, 1918. Mr. Smith and his first wife had six children. He and wife, Rosa, had nine children. Mr. Smith was a farmer and lived outside of Hoxie until 1938, when he and his family moved to the Sedgwick area. He lived in the Sedgwick area until his death on May 6, 1957. Children are:

1. Joseph Phineas, born December 28, 1907, married Lurene Holder. He died in July of 1994. Their children are: Charles Eugene, Morgan Thomas, Norma Jean, Lewis Franklin, Ray Neil, Gary Wayne, Margaret Ann, Martha Louise and Joseph Phineas.

2. Jesse, born 1909, and died after 1910, at 18 months old.

3. Otto Turell, born June 26, 1911, married Ethel Barnes. He died in August of 1998. They had one son, Lee Roy.

4. Martha Ellen (twin), born September 25, 1913, was first married to Cecil Montgomery and then married Ernest McCafferty. She died October 18, 1992. She had six children: Thomas Truman, Rosa Aline, Joe Trulin Montgomery and Lewis Ditus, Richard, Buss McCafferty.

5. Mary Ann (twin), born September 25, 1913, married Paul Graham. Their children are: John David, Carolyn Sue, Theron Thomas and Marlin Talmadge.

6. Lavon, born in 1915, and died August 7, 1917.

Family reunion, 1992. Rosa Smith Potts is front row, third from right. Children front from left are: Raymond, Phineas, Otto, Martha, Mary and back row: Easter, Darrell, Garland, Virginia, Noble, Emmaline, Cecil, Jerry.

7. Raymond Lewis, born December 30, 1918, married Clare Lee Milgrim. He died September 9, 1995. Their children are: Patricia Ruth, Raymond Lewis and Brenda Lee.

8. Jerry Washington, born November 12, 1920, married Martha Ashlock. He died in November of 1994. Children are: Jerry Ray, Joseph Dean and Kathryn Jean (twins) and David Lee.

9. Cecil Owen, born January 14, 1923, married Vastina Pratt. Their children are: Lonnie Owen and Connie Ellen.

10. Rosa Emmaline, born February 22, 1925, married Lawrence Charles Ashlock. Their children are: Rosa Ann, Jimmy Charles and Sandra Louise.

11. Noble Harold, born August 26, 1927, married Lucille Louise Buchanan. They had one child, Charles Nelson. After Louise's death, he married Eunice Earline Hefner and they had two children: Debra Jean and Donald Wayne.

12. Virginia Ruth, born January 8, 1930, married Lloyd Bonner. Their children are: Judy Ruth and Ronnie Lloyd.

13. Garland Merrell, born July 24, 1932, married Geraldine Wilson. Their children are Roger Merrell and Donna Suzanne.

14. Darrell Ray, born April 24, 1935, married Frances Tubbs. Their children are: Lee Darrell, Gregory Howard, Frances Kaye and Lesa Faye.

15. Easter Louise, born June 16, 1939, first married Cecil Bagwell, then Karl Lemkuhl, Richard Davis and Gene Rosenblum. She had one son, Brian David Bagwell Lemkuhl.

Mrs. Rosa McCord Smith married again in 1964, to William Potts, who died in 1966. In 1998, at the age of 100, Mrs. Potts resides at the Lawrence Hall Nursing Home in Walnut Ridge. –Virginia Bonner.

MAE ADELINE THORNTON SMITH FAMILY. Mae Adeline Thornton was born July 31, 1886, in Elizabeth, Arkansas, in Fulton County, the daughter of Hosea Lee and Cora Ann Reynolds Thornton. She had one sister, Martha Elizabeth Thornton Lawrence.

Mae married first August 31, 1902, to Hardie W. Holland, born 1883. They married in Fulton County, Arkansas. They had no children.

Mae married second on February 13, 1906, to Albert Dover, born 1886, died December 8, 1931. Mae and Albert had four children:

1. Ester E., 1908-1914.

2. Chester and Hester (twins), died at birth in 1909.

3. Minnie Gertrude, born November 24, 1910; died April 5, 1984.

Mae married third to Ervin Lester Smith, born June 27, 1881; died May 31, 1959, son of George Harvey and Samantha Elizabeth Gann Smith.

Mae and Ervin had five children:

1. Lester Odis, born September 10, 1915; died July 15, 1994; married September 14, 1941, to Fay Ellen Banks.

2. Orville "Bud" Vester, born April 27, 1918; died April 2, 1977; married Bessie Burrow.

3. Martha Jane Rosetta "Eddie", born March 14, 1921; died July 5, 1980.

Ervin and Mae Smith.

4. Glesper Ogohthridge, born February 21, 1924; died October 7, 1997, married March 14, 1947; to Juanita Agnes Pittman.

5. Ervin Lester Jr. "E.L.", born June 18, 1927; died February 3, 1973.

Ervin and Mae had lived in Black Rock for over 50 years in a house behind the Black Rock School. Ervin died at the age of 77 and Mae died at the age of 90. Ervin is buried in the Elizabeth Cemetery in Elizabeth, Arkansas and Mae is buried in the Kelly Cemetery in Black Rock. –Jeanette Darris.

RAYMOND LEWIS SMITH AND CLARA LEE MILGRIM SMITH. My dad's name was Raymond Lewis Smith. He was born on December 30, 1918, in the Surrege Community of Lawrence County. He was the son of Lewis David Smith and Rosa Armenta McCord Smith. He had seven brothers and five sisters. They were: Phineas, December 28, 1907; Otto, June 16, 1911; Mary Graham, September 25, 1913; Martha McCafferty, September 25, 1913; Jerry, November 12, 1920; Cecil, January 14, 1923; Emmaline Ashlock, February 22, 1925; Noble, August 26, 1927; Virginia Bonner, January 8, 1930; Garland, July 24, 1932; Darrell, April 24, 1935; and Easter Rosenblum, June 16, 1939.

He lived in the Surrege Community until he was 20 years old; then he moved to Sedgwick, but he always cherished the community he grew up in and he visited it often. Dad worked on the family farm until November, 1941, when he entered the Army during World War II. He was a member of the 153rd Infantry. He toured several foreign countries

Raymond Lewis Smith Sr. and Clara Lee Milgrim Smith married on December 19, 1947. This picture was made in 1982.

and risked his life for our country. This was something that he thought of as an honor the rest of his life. I have always been very proud that my dad was a soldier.

After four years in the war, he returned to Sedgwick. He discovered the girl next door had grown up into a beautiful young lady. When he left she was 13; now she was 17 and soon she became his wife.

My mother was Clara Lee Milgrim Smith. She was born on February 22, 1929, in the Little Brown Community of Lawrence County. She was the daughter of Henry Dexter Milgrim and Ollie Mae Johnson Milgrim. She had two sisters, Addie Mae Milgrim Kennedy, January 31, 1925; and Jessie Ruth Milgrim Fultner, September 18, 1935. Mom's dad was a sawmill operator, so they lived in several different places because of his job. She met my dad in 1939, whenever she moved across the road from him. She always told me how handsome he was in his Army uniform. It was love at first sight, and although they had lots of hard times during the next 42 years, it was still that deep love that kept my dad by her side until the day she died on March 18, 1988.

Dad and mom were married on December 9, 1947, at Walnut Ridge. They bought a farm, one and one half miles southwest of Sedgwick on Rural Route 3 and they lived there the rest of their lives. They had three children: Patricia Ruth, October 7, 1947; Raymond Lewis Jr., October 7, 1949; and Brenda Lee, September 6, 1958.

Dad and mom are both gone now. Mom died March 18, 1988, and dad died on September 9, 1995. Although they are not with us any longer, they still live on through our family and our cherished memories of two precious parents. –Brenda Wade.

RAYMOND L. SMITH JR. Dad and mom only had three children, but our family has grown into a very large clan. Raymond, Pat and I spent our entire childhood on the same 80 acre farm. It was located one and one half miles southwest of Sedgwick on Rural Route 3, now known as Highway 228, but then it was a tree lined, gravel road.

During Pat and Raymond's childhood, dad farmed and raised cattle. They worked in the fields, especially chopping and picking cotton. They have many stories and memories of the "cotton patch." By the time I was old enough to work in the fields, dad was working at B. B. Vance's and farming mostly soybeans, so I missed all the "fun."

Pat was born on October 7, 1947. She married Gerald David Connor on January 30, 1965. He is the son of Emerson Connor and Dessie Shaffer Augustine. They have three children: Tammy Leann, September 15, 1965; Randall David, October 14, 1966; and Tonya Kaye, April 12, 1972. Tammy married Charlie Dickerson on February 7, 1987. They have a daughter, Emily Claire Dickerson, April 29, 1988. Ten years later, Tammy blessed us again with a beautiful baby girl, Katie Leann Galbreath, November 7, 1998. Tammy's family lives in Hoxie and attends church at Cache River Pentecostal Church in Sedgwick.

Randy married Richetta Fletcher on September 29, 1990. They live in Jonesboro and attend church at United Methodist Church of Jonesboro.

Tonya married Lanny Hutsell on November 23, 1990. They have two sons: Aaron Connor Hutsell, April 3, 1993; and Kaylan Doyle Hutsell, February 17, 1995. They live in Hoxie and are members of Hoxie First Baptist Church.

David and Pat are members of Cache River Pentecostal Church at Sedgwick. They live on dad's farm, 3132 Highway 228.

Raymond married Joyce Wayvon Hurn on August 30, 1968. She is the daughter of Milburn Hurn and Elsie Shelton Hurn. They have three children. Angela Reane, January 9, 1970, married Shawn Parrish on August 18, 1990. They have two daughters: Whitlee Shaye, December 6, 1990, and Leslee Anna, October 21, 1992. They live in Hoxie and attend church at First Assembly of God in Walnut Ridge.

Raymond and Wayvon's sons, Kevin Lewis, October 3, 1973, and Christopher Ray, September 11, 1974, still live at home.

Raymond and Wayvon's family attend church at Cache River Pentecostal of Sedgwick. They also live on dad's farm, 3094 Highway 228.

I married Bobby Gene Wade on June 10, 1977. He is the son of Bill Wade and Helen Dent Wade. We have two children: Bobby Jason Wade, July 27, 1979; and Brandi Lee Wade, February 24, 1983. Jason is in his third year of college and Brandi will be a junior this fall at Hoxie High School.

Our family are members of the Walnut Corner General Baptist Church, where Bobby has served as a bi-vocational pastor since 1995. We live at 267 Lawrence 702, about five miles from our family farm.

Although I do not live there anymore, I will never part with the place my parents worked so hard for and the place they both filled with love for all their family. The memories of all the good times we had there are worth more than gold. –Mrs. Bobby Wade.

The family of Raymond Lewis Smith and Clara Lee Milgrim Smith. This picture was made on Christmas Day, 1998 at the home of Bobby and Brenda Wade.

SETH THOMAS SMITH. Born September 23, 1860, in Black Rock, Seth was the fourth child and the third son of Thomas Jefferson Smith and his wife, Addiline. He married Martha Frances Shelton, August 11, 1989, in Black Rock. She was the daughter of Henry and Martha Catherine Donnell Shelton. To this union were born nine children.

1. Emma Adeline, born July, 1879, married first Wesley Barnett, second Richard Duckworth and third George M. Stanley. The only children Emma had were the Duckworths: David Warren, Graden, Elsie and Thomas G.

2. Joseph Franklin, born January, 1881, married first Cora Bell Hicks and had Carleton, Edward and Louis, and then married second Sallie Judkins and had Virgil and Gracie.

3. William Walter, born February 8, 1883 (see a separate article for this family).

4. Grover Cleveland, born March, 1885, married Effie Inze and had one son, Dolph Tinsley.

Seth Thomas Smith family, about June, 1898. Joe and Emma, Walter, Henry, Cathrine. Seth Thomas and Fannie, Shelton Smith Hatcher and Jennie.

5. Henry Crockett, born December, 1886, married Suzie Sanders and had no children.

6. Katherine Elizabeth, born February 11, 1889, married first George Smith and had one son named George, then married second John Holobaugh and had Norma, David, Joseph Green, Raymond Eugene, Clelah Virginia, Verna Mae and Howard Talmadge.

7. Thomas Hatcher, born April 5, 1893, married Helen Kell, daughter of Johnson and Martha McLaughlin Kell and had these children: Eva Inez, Gail C., Vernon K., Terrel Hershel and Beryl Thomas.

8. Virginia "Jenny" Irene, born December 20, 1897, married James Miller Tate, son of Lee and Elizabeth Rash Tate and had six children: Jewell, Chester, Edith, Mildred, Charles and Carolyn.

9. John Marvin, born June 27, 1902, married Ida Brown and had James, Verma Jean and Verlon.

Looking at the names in this family you will see that many of them are still in Lawrence County. –Dale McMasters.

THOMAS JEFFERSON SMITH. Third child and second son of David and Mariah Hamby Smith, "Jeff" Smith was born in Powhatan, Lawrence County, June 11, 1833, and died December 8, 1896. He married Addeline Frances Ethridge, May 12, 1853. She was the daughter of Stephen and Sarah Ethridge. To this union were born nine children.

1. John Ewing Smith, March 24, 1854-December 10, 1944, married first Sophia M. Jensen, second Nancy Rebecca McDaniels and third Phernetta Green Boyd. It was while John Ewing was living with his father and brother in Lawrence County in 1898, that Mormon missionaries began calling on the family and on December 29, 1898, John was baptized into that church. The next spring, April 2, 1899, Phernetta was baptized along with Zilma. Just 20 days later, after her 8th birthday, April 22, 1899, Nartha was baptized. On the first of June, 1902, Lucy was baptized, making the complete family members of the Latter Day Saints Church. It was in 1904, that John sold his holdings in Arkansas and moved to Utah.

2. William Robert Smith, November 9, 1856-December 10, 1926, married first Maggie Thomas and second Elizabeth J. Moore. Robert and Maggie had a daughter, Lenora and he and Elizabeth had Mollie Lillie, who married Andrew Gwen; Thomas Arthur, who married Sally Watts; William Frank, who married Pearl Waters; and Lou J. M. who married Tom Watts.

3. Surrena Luella Smith, January 17, 1859-February 8, 1899, married Henry Clay George and had Susan, born about 1879; Nettie, born February, 1880; Selma Naomi, born September 25, 1880; Addie, born July, 1884, married Frank Meeks; and Rose, born May, 1889.

4. Seth Thomas Smith, September 23, 1860-May 8, 1932, married Martha Frances Shelton, daughter of Henry A. and Martha Donnell Shelton (see more about this family in their own article in this book).

5. Nancy Addeline Smith, February 9, 1866-August 14, 1871.

6. Susan Jane Smith, January 15, 1868-1943, married Isaac Davidson, the son of Isaac and Cynthia Davidson. Their children were Edward Lawrence, born March 6, 1888; Rudolph, born November, 1889; and Eunice Grace, born July, 1892.

7. George Franklin Smith, September 3, 1873-April 20, 1963, married first Ellen Gwin Leather, second Addie Ross. The children of George and Ellen are: Charles Morton, born October 13, 1908, married Opal; Robert Orville, born October 23, 1912, married Josephine; and Joe, born June 3,

1916. The children of George and Addie are Homer Paul, born January 14, 1896; Oles Omer, born September 30, 1897; Carrie, born May 2, 1903; and Luther.

8. Mary Isbell Smith, August 5, 1875-February 23, 1954, married Virgil Clark. Their children are Edith and Hubert.

9. Harvin Moton Smith, August 3, 1878-January 16, 1897.

Many descendants of these people are still residing in Lawrence County.

–Dale Hinshaw McMasters.

WILLIAM GRUNDY SMITH, born November 23, 1886, and Nellie Copeland McLeod, born March 29, 1891, were married February 19, 1908, at Denton, Arkansas.

Grundy was the only son of Albert Vanburen Smith, born January 29, 1860, and Annie Catherine Pickett, born March 21, 1864. Their two daughters were Leora and Viola.

Nellie was the youngest child of Hector Murdock McLeod, born January 29, 1854, and Margaret Jane Davis, born October 25, 1860. Their other children were: Leona, W. Henry and Murdock Cornelius "Neil."

Grundy and Nellie were blessed with 12 children who were all born and raised on the family farm in Denton.

Milton Vanburen, born September 7, 1908, married Verdeanis Drum. Both are deceased.

Lucy Mildred, born September 17, 1910, married Batley Williams. Mildred lives at Lawrence Hall in Walnut Ridge.

Madge, born January 17, 1913, married Sidney O'Dell. Madge lives in a Warsaw, Indiana, nursing home.

Emmanuel Muth, born February 11, 1915, married Jewell Campbell. "Manuel" died in a car/train accident in 1977.

Eula Agnes, born June 25, 1917, married Orvel Jones. They live in Scottsdale, Arizona.

Wilma Leona, born February 18, 1920, first married Azril Rippee. In 1951, she married Howard Beavers and they still reside in the Annieville Community.

Leslie Gustavis, born July 5, 1922, married Johnnye Murphy. They reside in Jonesboro, Arkansas.

William Grundy Jr. "W. G.", born April 11, 1925, married Margaret Hall. They live in Jonesboro, Arkansas.

Alton Wright, born September 16, 1927, is married to Gail Shivley. They reside in Pocahontas, Arkansas.

Kennard Laverne, born July 5, 1930, married Virginia Glenn. They live in Metarie, Louisiana.

Raymond Corneilus, born May 29, 1933, married Jean Smith. They reside in Imboden, Arkansas.

Phyllis Gail, born January 1, 1937, first married Lowell Lawson. After his death, she then married Wendell Pegram. They live in Springdale, Arkansas.

Grundy was a farmer and also raised hogs, chickens and cows. He also made brooms and was a shoe cobbler.

Nellie was a homemaker with the endless duties of a wife and mother, but always had time for family, friends and neighbors.

Each child had chores to do including working in the fields. Long before they were grown they knew all about hard work.

The Smith family, though hard workers, also knew how to have fun. I love hearing the stories about grandmother playing the organ and granddaddy playing the fiddle with all the family gathered around singing.

Nellie died February 16, 1973. Grundy died on December 1, 1973.

In addition to their children and sons and daughters-in-law, they leave behind 37 grandchildren, countless great-grandchildren and several great-great-grandchildren to share and carry on the legacy of William Grundy and Nellie McLeod Smith. *–Brenda Jones.*

WILLIAM WALTER SMITH was born February 8, 1883, in Lawrence County and died July 8, 1958, in Lawrence County. He was the great-grandson of David R. Smith, one of the original settlers of the county who came to Arkansas in the 1820s, before it was a state. Walter was the third child and second son of Seth Thomas and Martha Frances Shelton Smith. He married Daisy Belle Hedrick, October 15, 1905, near Flat Creek. She was the daughter of Thomas Crockett and Rebecca Jane Kelley Hedrick. To this union were born 16 children.

1. Clara Lou, November 11, 1906-September 6, 1933, married James Clifton Marvel and had three children: James Clifton, Walter Thomas and Catherine.

2. Edna Irene, March 8, 1908-February 17, 1983, married first William "Bill" Bonner and had one son, Charles Edward who died when he was four; married second Richard Caron Hinshaw and had Robert Sanford, Richard Glenn, Laura Belle, John Ballard, Louis Wesley, Donald K., Milton Folbe and Arna Dale.

3. Mary Mable, October 26, 1909-September 9, 1982, married Cecil Elliott.

4. Elmo George Glenn, February 4, 1911-March 14, 1991, married Ina Lawson, daughter of Walter and Nettie Ragsdale Lawson and had one daughter, Roberta.

5. Georgia Alma, November 22, 1913-August 4, 1997, married Tom E. Propes, son of Joseph and Emma Goins Propes and had three children: Jane, Tom and Jim.

6. Fannie Bell, December 15, 1915-October 16, 1987, married Joe Propes, brother of her sister Alma's husband, and had two children, Kathryn and Bobby Joe.

7. Thomas Walter, February 2, 1917-December 29, 1918.

8. Mildred Rebecca, August 6, 1918-August 2, 1921.

9. William Sloan, born February 28, 1922, married Nancy Jo Morris, daughter of Jesse and Calla Cross Morris and had eight children: Calla, Christina, Bill, Randy, Clint, Sammy, Daniel and Lance.

10. Ruby Nell, born December 29, 1923, married James Stogsdill, son of Forest A. and Bertha Garrett Stogsdill and had four children: James A., Carol A., Michael W. and David A.

11. James Calvin, April 30, 1926-April 6, 1997, married Virginia, daughter of Robert and Dora Mayberry Lynn and had two children, Ronald and Aurelia.

12. Louis Howard, October 15, 1927-April 8, 1997, married first Ruby D. Jacobson and had Tom, Patricia and Carolyn and then married Juanita Holland and had Howard, Bill, James and Timothy.

13. Edward Earl, born July 2, 1929, married firs Aurora Camacho and had Celeste and Edward, then married Mattie Lou Turner and had Bill and Diane.

14. Wallace Wayne, born November 17, 1931, married Helen Pickett, daughter of Allen and Vesta Oliver Pickett and had Kay, Gary and Vicky.

15. Russell Laverne, July 7, 1933-March 1, 1968, married Nellie Haney and had Barbara, Russell and Brenda.

16. Cecil Allen, born March 4, 1936, married Wanda Jean, daughter of Russell and Aline Riley Skinner and had Debra, Larry, Cecelia, Pamela, Carla and Karen.

–Dale Hinshaw McMasters.

RUTHIE MONDOZIA TYREE SNEAD FAMILY. Ruthie Mondozia Tyree, daughter of George Washington Tyree and Biddy Louisa Lamb Tyree, was born December 27, 1914. She married Thomas Thedore Snead on March 1, 1931, in the old T. Verkler Place at Black Rock. Ruth and Ted had two children. They are:

1. Thomas Thedore Snead Jr., born October 25, 1931, at Lauratown, in Lawrence County, married June 7, 1953, to Patricia Maurine Johnson, born August 14, 1933. Tom and Patsy were blessed with five children.

a) Paul Thomas Snead, born August 9, 1956. He has two children: Nathan Thomas Snead, born June 13, 1983, and Amanda Gayle Snead, born November 24, 1986.

b) John Garland Snead, born February 23, 1960, married November 29, 1989, to Julie Ann Webster, born October 23, 1965. They have two children: Melissa Kay Snead, born March 22, 1990, and John Garland Snead Jr., born July 10, 1992.

c) Philip Lee Snead, born January 24, 1963, married June 25, 1982, to Deborah Kay Linton, born April 29, 1964. They have three children: Timothy Lee Snead, born April 24, 1986; Jared Ray Snead, born May 15, 1991; and Aaron Joe Snead, born October 14, 1992.

Ted and Ruth Snead.

d) Linda Maurine Snead, born September 6, 1968, married May 23, 1987, to Raymond Thomas Smith, born July 4, 1965. They have two children: Rebecca Maurine Smith, born August 8, 1991, and Zachary Thomas Smith, born January 10, 1997.

e) Jeanie Ruth Snead, born October 10, 1971, married November 5, 1994, to Anthony Derrick Shoffitt, born February 19, 1966. Thomas Thedore Snead Jr. and his wife, Patsy, make their home in Lufkin, Texas and their children live in the surrounding community.

2. Freda Alene Snead, born February 5, 1934, in Lawrence County, married Everett Mullin, August 8, 1952, and they had two children.

a) Steven Mullin, born March 11, 1953, married August 28, 1971, to Claudia Clark, born January 14, 1954. Steven and Claudia live in Salt City, Utah and they have two daughters.

Nicoel Christine Mullin, born April 1, 1972, married Kevin Garn. They had two children: Justine Garn, born January 11, 1989, and Riley Garn, born February 5, 1994. Nicoel later married Heath Hobdale.

Candace Loraine Mullin, born November 8, 1975, married Craig Biedler and they have one daughter, Samath Biedler, born January 9, 1995. Candace and family live in San Dimas, California.

b) Jeffrey Dale Mullin, born February 7, 1955, married Mary Zamora, born October 20, 1958. They have two sons, Christopher James Mullin, born April 12, 1984; and Mark Anthony Mullin, born July 12, 1987. Jeffrey and family make their home in Friendswood, Texas.

Freda now resides in Friendswood, Texas.

Thomas Thedore Snead died February 21, 1988.

Ruthie Mondozia Tyree Snead died March 13, 1998.

They are buried in Oak Forest Cemetery at Black Rock, Arkansas. *–Garland Sneed.*

SNOW HISTORY. William T. Snow, born 1809, Surry County, North Carolina, married Mary Waller in 1835; child, George Washington Snow, born 1836, Roane County, Tennessee. George married about 1857, to Mary Jane Elder. Mary Jane Elder Snow Bottom is buried at Snow Cemetery, Lawrence County. George and Mary Jane had a child, John Alonzo Snow, born 1871, Tiptonville, Tennessee. George died September, 1876, and his father, William Snow, died December, 1876. John Snow was five. Mary Jane must have been a good, strong person. Many people have told me that my great-grandfather was a fine man. Mary Jane and son buried George in Tiptonville, Tennessee. John Snow married Mary Elizabeth Cunningham. They had three children born in Lawrence County: Glenna Snow, 1896-1904; Ora Snow, 1898-1975; and Lynn Leon Snow, 1901-1984. Mary Elizabeth Cunningham Snow's parents were Henry C. Cunningham and Emily "Emma" Martin.

Ora Snow Minton had eight children in Lawrence County. Frost or Frosty Snow was grandfather Lynn's given

Lynn Leon Snow, 1901-1984.

name at birth. He preferred to be called Lynn and that is what everyone called him all his life. Like his given name, he was a jolly, happy soul and the grandchildren say he could laugh and play. I miss the twinkle of his eyes. He was a farm laborer and he was a favorite for many.

Lynn Snow met Neta-Belle Elliott and married in Walnut Ridge, Arkansas, 1928. Grandmother was born 1910, Pocahontas. I recently asked her how they met. She smiled and said, "Lynn knew of someone who lived near us and started coming over our way (the Elliott girls were around Manson) from Snow Town, and that's how we met." "I was the prettiest girl he ever saw." Lynn and NetaBelle had three girls: Nona Snow, 1930; Betty Lynn, 1933, in Lawrence County; and Janet, born 1940, Leachville, Arkansas.

Lynn, NetaBelle, their children and his parents moved to Leachville in 1936. Grandmother tells that Lynn's cousin, Clarence Overbay, told them, "it is the best farming country anywhere. There were Cunninghams all around Leachville and Harrisburg, Arkansas, Snow's too."

John Snow died 1955, his wife Mary, died 1961. They are buried in Snow Cemetery. A place they loved, Snow Community.

Grandmother recalls there were many Snows around Snow Town in the 1920s and 1930s. People moved because of work, family and friends. She recalls a Tom Bottom from Walnut Ridge who was somehow kin to John Snow. Mary Cunningham Snow had brothers around Harrisburg. Mary Elder Snow Bottom married Bill Bottom.

My parents drove us through what was Snow Town when I was young. The house my mother was born in was still standing. It has been gone a while now. It is a scattered picture in my memory. Listening to grandmother Snow I can picture a thriving community with lots of kin somewhere among them a jolly, happy soul and twinkling eyes. His children know how he came to life one day. A Lawrence County Snow Reunion is held the second Saturday of June at Crowley Ridge State Park. A quilt is raffled for upkeep of Snow Cemetery. – *Elaine McClain.*

GEORGE W. SNOW was born in Roane County, Tennessee, June 12, 1836, the son of Captain William T. and Mary Waller Snow. He married Mary Jane Elder, 1842-1930, who died and is buried in Snow Cemetery, Walnut Ridge. They were the parents of six children: Amanda "Mady" Jane, 1858-1932, who married James Henry Douglas; James "Jim" Frost, 1862-1937, who married first Margaret Ada Womble and second Ada Barker; Georgiana, born 1864, married George Douthitt; Martis "Doc" Woodrow, 1866-1953, who married first Frances "Fannie" Womble and second Cora Mae Helms; John Alonzo, 1871-1955, married Mary Elizabeth Cunningham; and William "Bill" Caswell, 1869-1937, married first Sarah Hatfield and second Margaret Shoffitt.

George was a farmer, and served as a private in his father's company in the Confederate Army. During the war, he was taken prisoner by the Union forces. When he returned from the Yankee prison, his health was broken and he died at 40 years of age.

The first time George appears in the Lake County, Tennessee court minutes is May 1, 1871, when he was elected as a school commissioner of District 1. On May 2, he was appointed a juror and on June 3, 1872, he was appointed road overseer. George was initiated into the Masonic Order on October 31, 1869, passed May 14, 1870, and raised July 14, 1870. According to the court minutes, George and Mary moved to Arkansas between July, 1872, and February 1873; however, he was home on a visit when he died September 28, 1876. He is buried in the Cronanville Cemetery, Lake County, Tennessee beside his parents.

Mary and her children remained in Arkansas and she married second Bill Bottom, by whom she had one child, Parrie Bottom, 1883-1954, who married Charles Cunningham.

–Isabelle Rogers Algee.

GEORGE W. AND MARY JANE ELDER SNOW. Most of the Snow family in Lawrence County is descended from George W. and Mary Jane Elder Snow. George, whose health had broken during the Civil War, died while visiting his parents in Lake County, Tennessee. His widow remained on their farm in Lawrence County. In 1881, she married Bill Bottom, who died in 1889.

George and Mary Jane had seven children: "Mandy", "Jim", Georgianna, Martis "Doc", "Bill", John Alonzo and George W. Our Snow family is descended from James Frost Snow. Our Snow story concentrates on his descendants.

Jim first married Margaret "Ada" Womble. Jim and Ada had Omer, "Jess", Clyde, Miggie Reemer, Roy, Dearsey, 1895-1896, and Lee. In 1900, after his first wife's death, JF married Ada D. Barker of Poinsett County. James and this Ada had Fiona, Alex Frost, Mary Lucille and "Paul." They also had several children who died young: unnamed, Amanda, Emma, Julia and Otto.

Jim gave land to all his adult sons. His obituary in 1937, says Jim "was head of one of the large clans of the Snow family that have been prominently identified with the development of this section for over a half a century."

Omer married Ardel Hilderbrandt. They had James Joseph "Joe."

"Jess" married Frances Melissa Minton. Children: Glenna Ovella, James "Leonard" and Charles Leroy.

Clyde Snow married William I. "Bill" Duty. Children: Marguerite, Ruth, Clarence "Dub", Ed and Billy.

Miggie Reemer "Mug" married Hase Ivy and later Moud Ward.

Roy Barney married Edith Lenora Mayfield. Children: Evelyn "Mardell," a boy, born and died 1921, and Ross Mayfield "Nub" who was a World War II veteran.

Lee married Ella Sue Duty. As a wedding gift to the young couple, James Frost Snow gave them 60 acres that Lee farmed and never mortgaged, even during the Depression. Lee donated part of his farm for the Snow Cemetery, where they are buried by their babies: twins Melba Louise and Bobbie B., and Wanda Raye. Alice "Geraldine" taught at an elementary school before moving to Michigan, where she married George Fuller. Randall "Max" Snow, who was manager at Memphis Funeral Home. Max and Maggie had two children: Stephen Randall, a United States Foreign Service Officer, and Kirk, who died in 1991.

Fiona "Jewell" Snow married Clarence Elmer Harris Sr., son of Benjamin Harris, husband of her sister, Mary Lucille Snow. Jewell and Clarence had Ramona, Mary Jane, Shirley, James, Helen, Clarence and Ida Bell. Jewell's second husband was "Art" Barnes.

Alex Frost first married Irby Moore. Alex and Irby had Don Earl a couple weeks before Irby died. Alex later married Lola Einlock.

Mary Lucille married Benjamin "Ben" Harris. After Ben died, she lived with Paul and Vivian in Michigan and took care of their children while they worked.

Leonard "Paul" married Vivian Blankenship. They had Ada Lou, Paula, Rebecca Sue, James Riley, Rose and Sherman Snow. After Paul died, Vivian lived in James Frost Snow's old home. – *Betty Snow.*

HARRY LEE SNOW FAMILY. Harry Lee Snow was born March 1, 1902, Moran Community, Lawrence County, and died July 10, 1984, in Pocahontas. He was born about one mile from his final resting place in the Snow Cemetery, Lawrence County. He was the first child of Martis Woodrow "Doc" Snow and Cora Helms Snow. Harry married Sylvania Jane Bellah, 1902-1989, in Datto. They lived and farmed for many years in the Giles Community. Their children were: Howard Lee "Joe" Snow, born 1925, died 1997, and buried in the Snow Cemetery; Cameron Gene Snow, born 1928; Theda Gay Snow, born 1930; Joyce Ann Snow, born 1935; Linda Kay Snow, born 1940; and Sharon Joan Snow, born 1942.

Howard married Lillian Heral. Their children were: Marilyn, born 1951; Timothy Howard, born 1953; Jonathan Bruce, born 1957; Thomas Lee, born 1972; Marilyn, married Larry McReynolds; daughters: Andrea, born 1977, married Bobby Cates, and had son, Trevor, born 1995, and lives in Pocahontas; Ashlee, born 1980, married Robert Rainwater in 1998, and Marilyn died in 1996, buried in Snow Cemetery; Tim married Sherry Jean Brooks: employed Arkla-Pocahontas: daughters: Katrina, born 1980, Dallas, Texas; Erika, born 1983, Pocahontas. Jonathan, born Rockford, Illinois, married Pamuel Sue Jarrett: employed Cole National: Children: Kyle, born 1982, Pocahontas; Stormy, born 1985, Pocahontas. Thomas is now first lieutenant in the US Army, serving in Hanau, Germany.

Gene is a 1948 graduate of Walnut Ridge High School; he served 20 years in the US Air Force and married Evelyn Massey. He lives in Trumann, Arkansas. Their children: Teresa, born 1955; Dean, born 1958; Iva Jean, born 1961; Russell Lee, born 1967. Teresa is married to Robert Roberg. Her sons: Ernesto DiVittorio II, born 1975, now first lieutenant in US Air Force. Damien DiVittorio, born 1980; Dominic DiVittorio, born 1981; Dean lives Albany, New York: has two sons, Scott, born 1978; Christopher, born 1982. Iva is married to Donnie Scroggins; her son, Justin

Harry Lee Snow family. Sons and daughters of Harry Lee Snow and Sylvania Bellah Snow. Left to right: Joyce Snow Anderson, Howard "Joe" Snow, Theda Snow Massey, Sharon Snow Barnett, Linda Snow Brooks, Cameron Gene Snow.

Carter, born 1978. Russell lives in Murfreesboro, Tennessee. He served in Desert Storm.

Theda Snow, a 1948 graduate of Walnut Ridge High School, married Billy Massey. He retired from John Deere, Moline, Illinois, after 34 years. Their sons: Roger, born 1950, died in 1994; David, born 1952; Michael, born 1953; Roger married Debra Shingledecker. His daughter, Lisa, was born 1974. In 1991, he was awarded a Civilian Award for his service with AMCCOM during Desert Storm; he is buried in National Cemetery, Rock Island, Illinois. David was Mr. Lawrence County in 1952, as he was the first baby born on January 1; he married Emily Moen; two children: Erin, born 1977; Eric, born 1982. Lives near Kansas City, Missouri; he is vice president Allied Construction Services. Michael is now married to Evalyn Knight; Children: Joshua Massey, born 1974; Melanie Massey, born 1977; Randa Dixon Johnson, born 1971; Lance Dixon, born 1974; Jennifer Linden, born 1980; Julie Linden, born 1983. He is with Fort James Paper Company, Muskogee, Oklahoma.

Joyce Ann Snow, a 1954 graduate of Walnut Ridge High School, married Robert Anderson. Bob was an electrical engineer with McDonnell-Douglas for 32 years in St. Louis. Joyce has 17 years in their library records division. Their children: Carol Ann, born 1959; Keith Alan, born 1961; Steven Aric, born 1966; Carol married Ron Stagner, now living Lenexa, Kansas. Children: Lauren, born 1983; David, born 1987. Keith married Michelle Long, O'Fallon, Missouri; Children: David, born 1989; Mathew, born 1994; Christopher, born 1998. Steve married Julie Jacobsen, Florissant, Missouri. Children: Brittani, born 1994, and Drake, born 1997.

Linda Kay Snow, a 1958 graduate of Walnut Ridge High School, is now married to Willard Brooks; she lives Maynard, and is employed at Maynard Post Office. Sons: Christopher Corbett, born 1966; Mark Corbett, born 1968; Brooks, born 1978. Chris married Lori Russell. Sons: Trent, born 1991; Samuel, born 1997 and lives in Reyno, Arkansas. Mark married Stephanie Clements and lives in Raleigh, North Carolina: daughter Serenity, born 1998. Brian graduated Maynard High School in 1997, now working as police dispatcher in Walnut Ridge.

Sharon Joan Snow, a 1960 graduate of Walnut Ridge High School, is married to Robert Barnett. She is living in Springfield, Missouri. Daughters: Lesley Lynn, born 1968; Lori Ann, born 1973; Melissa Gail, born 1975. Lesley is married to Humberto Forneron and lives in Lawrence, Kansas.

The Snow family traces its roots to Albemarle County, Virginia. John Snow Sr., 1710-1784, married Sarah. His son, Frost Snow Sr., 1730-1813, born Spotsylvania County, Virginia, lived in Surry County, North Carolina; he married Elizabeth Johnson. Their son, Thomas Snow, 1770-1818, born Albemarle County, Virginia, lived in Surry County, North Carolina; he married Elizabeth Hale, died Roane County, Tennessee. They were parents of our great-great-grandfather, William T. Snow, 1809-1876, who married Mary Waller, Roane County, Tennessee. They were parents of George W. Snow, 1836-1876, married Mary Jane Elder Snow (Bottom), 1842-1930. She is buried in Snow Cemetery. William Snow and his son, George, both served in Confederate Army. George and Mary brought their family of six to Lawrence County in 1872. Their children: Amanda Jane Douglas; James Frost; Georgiana Snow Douthit; Martis Woodrow; John and William Snow. *–Theda Snow Massey.*

JAMES "JIM" FROST SNOW was born in Hamilton County, Tennessee, October 13, 1862, son of George W. and Mary Elder Snow. He married first Margaret Ann Womble, 1866-1900, by whom he had seven children and married second Ada Barker, 1875-1961. The family says that there were 22 children in this family - several sets of twins. However, the names of only 16 have been located at this time.

Omer Carl Snow, 1885-1909, who married Artie or Ardel Hilderbrand; Lawrence "Jess" Wood Snow, 1887-1959, who married Frances Melissa Minton; Clyde Snow, who married William I. Duty; Miggie Reemer Snow, died 1911, and twin Mounger Lena; Roy Barney Snow married Edith Lenor Mayfield; Dearsey, 1895-1896, and possible a twin, Dorcie Snow; Lee Snow, born 1897, married Ella Sue Duty; Jewell Snow, 1904-1967, married first Clarence Harris Sr., second Archie "Art" Barnes; Alex Frost Snow, born 1905, and twin Amanda, 1905-1905, he married first Don Earl "Erby" Moore, second Lola Winlack; Mary Snow, born 1908, and twin Emma Louise, 1908-1912, Mary married Benjamin Harris; Julia Ray Snow, 1914-1926, and twin Otto Ray, 1914-1914; and Paul Snow, born 1915, who married Vivian Blankenship.

Jim Snow died February 25, 1937, in Lawrence County, Arkansas and is buried in the Snow Family Cemetery, Walnut Ridge, Arkansas.
–Mary Kathryn Landua.

MARTIS WOODROW "DOC" SNOW was born in Obion County (now Lake County), Tennessee in 1866, son of George W. and Mary Elder Snow. He married first November 10, 1885, Frances "Fannie" Womble, 1868-1898, by whom he had five children. Doc married second Cora Mae Helms, 1880-1957, by whom he had 11 children. They are all three buried in the Snow Cemetery, Walnut Ridge.

Doc's children were: Mary Essie, 1886-1966, who married first William Brown, second Joe Buckner, third Lee Happle Trusty; Clarence Lester, 1888-1919, married Alpha Bradley Farmer; Anna Lela, 1892-1969, who married Obediah "Obe" Dan Overbay; Johnie, 1894-1896; Mable Wade, born 1897, married James Elija Bellah; Infant daughter, 1900-1900; Harry Lee, 1902-1984, married Sylvania Jane Bellah; Claude, born 1903, married Jessie Lavalle Smith; Marvin Woodrow, born 1906, married Gladys B. Leonard; Sadie Blanche Snow, born 1907, married Mose LeMasters; Luther Melvin, twin, born 1907, married Lessie Mae Bellah; Van, born 1909, married Ernest Harber; Bradley Clinton, born 1911, married Delores Foster; Ressie, born 1913, married Lester Barnes; Cleanon, born 1916, married Wilma Arline Floyd; and Azeal, born 1919, married Max Slatton.

Martis Woodrow and his second wife, Cora Mae Helms Snow's oldest son, Harry Lee, 1902-1984, married Sylvania Jane Bellah, 1902-1989. Both are buried in the Snow Cemetery. Their children are: Howard Lee Snow, born 1925, and lives in Pocahontas, Arkansas; Gene Snow, born 1928, lives in Trumann, Arkansas; Theda Snow Massey, born 1930, lives in Pocahontas, Arkansas; Joyce Snow Anderson, born 1935, lives in Hazelwood, Missouri; Linda Snow Brooks, born 1940, lives in Maynard, Arkansas; and Sharon Snow Barnett, born 1942, lives in Springfield, Missouri.

Doc died September, 1953, in Leachville, Arkansas and is buried in the Snow Cemetery, Walnut Ridge, Arkansas.
–Lawrence W. Algee.

WILLIAM "BILL" CASWELL SNOW was born January 27, 1869, in Tiptonville, Lake County, Tennessee, son of George W. and Mary Jane Elder Snow. His family moved to Lawrence County, Arkansas between July, 1872, and February, 1873. Bill married first in Walnut Ridge, 1892, Sarah Hatfield, 1874-1897, by whom he had two sons. He married second in Pocahontas, 1901, Emma Margarett Shoffitt, 1875-1959, daughter of Jack Shoffitt, by whom he had six children.

Emma married first Robert Jones by whom she had William Edman Jones Sr., Charles "Casey" Jones and Grace Jones Binkley.

Bill's children were: George Parker Snow Sr., 1894-1944, who married Janie Hogan; James Edward "Ed" Snow, 1895-1979, who married Bettha Leeanna Doak; Mary Margaret Snow, born 1902, who married Emmett "Bud" Duty; Esther Snow, born 1904, married first George Kell, married second Albert Parris Stallings Jr.; Arthur Snow, 1906-1941, married Dorothy Brown; William Russell Snow, 1913-1974, married Loyce Smith; Martha Snow, 1915-1915, and twin David Snow, 1915-1915, both of whom are buried in Snow Cemetery, Walnut Ridge.

Bill died July 27, 1937, in Pocahontas, Arkansas and is buried in the Snow Cemetery in Walnut Ridge with his first wife, Sarah. His second wife, Emma, is buried in Masonic Cemetery in Pocahontas.
–Scarlett Ruth Algee.

CAPTAIN WILLIAM T. SNOW was born in Surry County, North Carolina, June 24, 1808, son of Thomas and Elizabeth Hale Snow. He married first, October 18, 1832, Polly Mounger, who died 1833. They had one daughter, Mary Jane, born 1833. William married, Roane County, Tennessee, January 22, 1835, Mary Waller, 1815-1894, daughter of William and Mary "Polley" Barksdale Waller. William and Mary had: George, 1836-1876, who married Mary Jane Elder and lived in Walnut Ridge; Elizabeth, 1837-1927, married Benjamin Newton Caruthers; Isaac Bird, 1839-1857; Sarah, 1841-1883, married Jacob Teenor and also lived in Arkansas; Lewis Hetsell, born 1843; James Knox Polk, 1844-1868; Tennessee Ann, 1847-1923, married James William Tipton; Emily Texas, 1849-1903, married David Watson; William, 1852-1868; Elcy Savannah, 1854-1877, married James Burrus; John Barksdale, 1857-1933, married Alice Peacock; and Laura Matilde, 1859-1912, married Wyatt Robert Algee, 1858-1924.

William was captain of Company C, 3rd (also called 2nd and 5th) Battalion, Tennessee Cavalry. Captain Billy raised and commanded a company from upper end of Hamilton County. This company was part of Ashby's 2nd Tennessee Cavalry. In about 1862, Snow, being 53 years old, had to resign his captaincy due to ill health. He then formed "Snow's Scouts." Two of his sons, George and James Knox, also served in their father's company. William remained "unreconstructed" until his death. As part of his will he states, "I wish my executors to bring suit against the United States Government for the damages for a tract of land in east Tennessee."

Before the war, William was the 3rd High Sheriff of Hamilton County. He lived on a large plantation at Snow Hill near Ooltewah. This three story house was built of bricks, handmade on the plantation, and had walls two feet thick. During the war, cannons were hauled from Chattanooga by Yankees to bombard the home, but they were unsuccessful in routing the Confederates who defended it. There were scars where the cannon balls hit, but they did not penetrate the walls.

Towards the end of the war, William and all of his children, except Elizabeth, who was married, moved to what later became Lake County. When Lake County was formed in 1870, Snow was elected the first trustee, a post he held until 1874.

He was initiated into Harmony Masonic Lodge, Tiptonville, April 4, 1867.

He was a member of Shady Grove Missionary Baptist Church. The church struggled, but in 1870, only three members remained: Captain William Snow, James Box and Nellie Thompson, a faithful black member. These three became charter members of the Tiptonville First Baptist Church.

William died December 1, 1876, and is buried in Cronanville Cemetery with his wife and five of his children.
—*Ralph Sands Algee.*

SPADES HISTORY.

John Spades came from Alsace, France prior to 1859, becoming a naturalized citizen on February 12, 1859. He was born May 26, 1839, the son of Catherine Znbad and Jacob Spades. He enlisted in the Union Army at Havana, New York, August 29, 1862, and discharged at Rutland, Virginia, June 8, 1865. His record tells us he was present at the surrender of General Lee to General Grant at Appomattox Courthouse. He was a member of Company A-89th Regiment of New York Volunteers and attained the rank of sergeant. John settled first in Elmira, New York, where he married Mary Agnes Gibbons, February 13, 1866, and soon thereafter moved to Williamsport, Pennsylvania, where all of their children were born. Mary Agnes was born in County Mayo, Ireland. Their children: Mary Jane, born July, 1867; John Gibbons, born 1869, died at age one; Sebastian Augustine, born September 18, 1872; and Catharine, born 1874. The Spades family left Williamsport in 1889, moving to Orange, Texas, where John was employed in the lumber business. They were in Galveston, Texas, in September, 1900, during the flood that took over 6000 lives. The son Sebastian rescued Mary Jane and Catherine off a rooftop into a boat during this flood. Catherine lived the remainder of her life in

Sebastian Spades, painter/decorator, Manager of Opera House in Black Rock.

the Galveston area and married William Hildenbrand. She died in the 1950s.

About 1896, John Spades and Mary Agnes moved to Black Rock, Arkansas. It is believed the lumber industry is what brought them here. Around the turn of the century there were 31 sawmills in operation in and around Black Rock. Their eldest daughter, Mary Jane, was married to John F. Bottger and they were already here with their four children, Fred, Austin, Richard and Esther. John and Mary's son, Sebastian, also came to Black Rock and on to St. Louis where he entered the United States Army, August 24, 1893, and was discharged November 23, 1896. Sebastian did return to Black Rock as he was known here in 1898. In 1898, Sebastian was deputized by the Black Rock City Marshall to assist in the arrest of a Negro who had stolen a hog. The Negro grabbed a pistol from one of the deputies, shot and killed the Marshall; shot Spades and escaped. Later, he was captured; trial was held and he was sentenced to two years in the State Penitentiary.

Sebastian married his first wife in 1899, and lived the rest of his life in Black Rock, where he died August 7, 1945. His mother, Mary Agnes, died August 21, 1896, and is buried in Oak Forest Cemetery, Black Rock. Buried beside her are Sebastian's first wife, Ethel Ripley, and three children who died in infancy. John Spades moved to St. Louis and died April 10, 1898, buried in Calvary Cemetery.

Sebastian remarried in 1910, to Pearl Judkins, a member of a distinguished family which had produced teachers, lawyers, doctors and politicians serving

Sebastian Spades.

state, county and local offices.

Sebastian known as "Chubby" and Pearl reared a large family of children, to which they were deeply devoted. Chubby worked as a painter and decorator, manager of the Opera House in Black Rock, organized and was commander of the first National Guard Company in Lawrence County. He served five terms as Mayor of Black Rock and died during his sixth term. President Roosevelt took notice of Mr. Spades election to a sixth term and Jonathan Daniels, Presidential Secretary, addressed Mr. Spades a note of congratulations which also expressed interest in the fact that three of Mr. Spades' sons were in the service, one of whom had recently been liberated from a German prison camp. A fourth son later served in Korea. The children of Pearl and Chubby Spades: Jennie Sue married Morris Moore; Mary Elizabeth married Jay H. Myers; Sebastian Augustine married Lorene Nunnally; Joseph Austin married June DeArman; Virginia Pearl married Howard Madsen; Rowena Frances married Coy Lawson; Richard Judkins married Ina Ruth Wilson; Cathryn Regina married Paul Callahan; and Michael Warren married Marjorie Mozelle Wilson.

Sebastian Augustine "Chubby" Spades was a community minded individual. Jim Bland Sr. wrote in the *Times Dispatch* at Chubby's death, "A soldier, a statesman in his understanding of the affairs of average Americans." His descendants in the county and state continue to be civic minded as they are engaged in business enterprises, the medical profession, the legal profession and as teachers and law enforcement officers. —*Richard Spades.*

WILLIAM HENRY "WILL" SPOTTS FAMILY.

In 1915, Will Spotts and his wife, Mollie, moved their family from Sharp County to the Cover Bend Community. Their children were: Owen, 13; Opal, 11; Blanche, 9; Sue, 7; Fern, 5; Willis Poe, 3; Buford, 1. Will, a prosperous farmer, rented land near the Clover Bend Cemetery. Here in 1916, the eighth child, Bernita, was born. Next, in line, Vester, known as "Buster", was born in 1919.

After farming five years on three different farms, they moved to the farm they were to occupy for the next 26 years, the "Baker Place," located on the corner one half mile north of Lauratown Store, one fourth mile west of Lauratown School, a large two story house, facing east. This road was the first gravel road built in Lawrence County. Here, Will and Mollie settled down to raising kids and cotton.

The last two children, Joe, 1922; and Irma, 1925, were born at Lauratown. Eight of the younger children attended elementary school at Lauratown. The only high schools (Walnut Ridge High and Sloan-Hendrix), were too distant to attend.

After graduating from Clover Bend School, Owen Spotts taught one term at Counce School, in the southern part of the county. He was 17 at the time. He later graduated from Sloan-Hendrix Academy in Imboden. Opal, Blanche and Sue also taught in various schools in the county.

At six feet, 235 pounds, Will Spotts was an imposing physical appearing man. He was recognized as a community leader. He served as justice of the peace and also several years as school director of Lauratown School.

Small, blonde, and blue-eyed (all 11 kids inherited the blonde hair and blue eyes), Mollie was the spiritual and educational leader of the family, seeing to it that each of her children were near the top of their class and also attended Sunday School and church when available. Lauratown was on the Strangers Home Circuit - Methodist Church - with services each fourth Sunday. All denominations worshiped in the school house. There were no church buildings. Also, all community functions were conducted in the school house.

In 1928, tragedy struck the Spotts family. Willis Poe came down with osteomyelitis, which was misdiagnosed, and almost ended his life.

Clarice's father, W. H. Spotts, 1933 at Lauratown, Arkansas, age 66 years old.

About the same time, mother Mollie contracted tuberculosis. She died in early 1930, and was buried in Clover Bend Cemetery. She was 49. Her disease would be classed as outpatient treatment today. Proper treatment was not available in the area at that time.

Will lived on at the home location until shortly before his death in 1950. He is also buried in Clover Bend Cemetery. His three youngest sons served extended time in the armed forces during World War II.

All 11 children of Will and Mollie grew to adulthood and married, producing 19 grandchildren. —*G.B. Spotts.*

STARNES. William Henry Starnes, born March 28, 1822, in Tennessee, migrated to Lawrence County and settled near Black River at what later became the town of Black Rock. He married Martha Pernecia Turman, born 1825, in 1853. Two children were born of the marriage, James Henry Henderson, 1854-1906, and Mary E. Records indicate William H. died in Lawrence County in 1859. No family records exist of the dates of death for his wife, Martha P. or his daughter Mary E. The daughter is believed to have died at age 16-17.

James Henry Henderson, the only son of William H. and Martha P., married Julia Emmaline Moor, 1860-1941, in 1880, in Lawrence County. They were the parents of seven children. William Henry, 1882-1904; Benjamin Franklin, 1884-1966; Charlie H., 1891-1967; Pernecie "Neecy", born 1897. Gertrude, Johnny N. and Walter F. died in infancy.

The Starnes farm was located three miles west of Black Rock on Highway 63, near Stennit Creek. Old-timers have told of how James Henry Henderson and Julia created quite a stir when they purchased a McCormick Thrasher. The thrashing machine was sent by boat up the White River to the Black River and on to what is now Black Rock. Two wagons with double teams were needed to haul it to the farm. This was the first such machine in that part of the county and people came from miles around to see it work. Folks came from as far away as Imboden.

James Henry Henderson Starnes died in 1906, and was buried on the family farm. Julia E. Starnes lived until 1941, and is buried in the Oak Forrest Cemetery in Black Rock.

Benjamin Franklin "Frank", the Starnes' second son, married Elizabeth Eudora "Betty" Forrester in 1906. They were the parents of 10 children which included two sets of twins. Their children were: Clyde, William Henry, Elsie, Leslie, Lorene Midge, Oliver, Paul, Pauline, Ruth and Marcelle.

William Henry, the second son of Frank and Betty Starnes was my father. He was born in 1909, and died 1971. He and my mother, Mary Lee (nee-Gardner) were married in 1933. See Gardner and Raney history. –Derotha Bates.

SID STEELE FAMILY. All the Steeles who live in Lawrence County are descendants of Tillmon and Matha Steele. They lived and farmed in the Clover Bend Community.

Sidney "Sid" William Steele was the first born, followed by daughter, Jewell Steele Lawrence and son, Ralph Steele, who served in the Navy in World War II. Ralph married Wanda Jones, also from the same area.

The Steeles were religious people and were very active in the Hopewell Community Assembly of God Church.

Sid Steele was born August 5, 1912. Christine Golden Steele was born October 22, 1915. Sid married Christina M. Golden, daughter of Arthur and Zella Alphin Golden, in 1932.

Their firstborn child was named Mary Louetta, followed by Freda Ann and Glenda Jean. Sid and Christina had a second family 11 years later when Mona Carol was born, followed by a son, Darrell Steele and the baby, Peggy June. All of the children graduated from the Clover Bend School. During that time, Sid served on the school board. Several went on to college.

At the age of 58, after the children were all out of school, Christina decided to go to college. She enrolled at Southern Baptist College, now known as Williams Baptist College, for two years and graduated from Arkansas State University in Jonesboro with a Master of Science in Education. She later taught kindergarten at the Clover Bend School until she retired.

Darrell and Peggy Steele McMillon are the only two children who still live in Lawrence County. Peggy followed in her mother's footsteps and is a teacher in the Hoxie School District. –Mary Steele Clark.

JOE B. STEELE. The Joe B. Steele family of Lawrence County traces their ancestry back eight generations to Archibald Steele, who was born in Scotland in 1728, and boarded a ship at Dublin, Ireland in 1757, bound for America. Archibald Steele and his wife, Agnes Edwards, are buried in the Presbyterian Church Cemetery near Rock Hill, South Carolina.

Private Joseph T. Steele, Joe B. Steele's grandfather, was a Confederate soldier, serving in Company B, 42nd Infantry, General Henry Heath's division, out of Senatobia, Mississippi.

On July 1, 1863, Private Joseph T. Steele was captured at Gettysburg, Pennsylvania and remained a prisoner of war at Gettysburg until his release on June 11, 1865. After his release from the Union prison, he returned to Olive Branch, Mississippi and farmed for several years before moving to Sidney, Arkansas. Joseph T. Steele died on February 26, 1902, of pneumonia after walking five miles around a frozen White River to serve on a petit jury.

Joe B. Steele's mother, Edna Lee Ball Steele, traces her ancestry to Captain Farlin Ball, who was related to and served with George Washington in the Revolutionary War. It is believed that Captain Farlin Ball was closely related to Martha Ball Washington, George Washington's mother.

Eldridge M. Ball, Joe B. Steele's maternal great-grandfather, at the age of 28, enlisted in the Confederate Army on August 27, 1862, at Camp Bragg in Northwest Arkansas. Ball was a private in Company G, 27th Arkansas. Ball, along with 500 of the 1,887 men of the 27th, deserted after the fall of Little Rock in September, 1863. He then enlisted in Company C, 4th Arkansas Mounted Infantry (Union) in late autumn of 1863. When Ball's wife had a baby in 1864, he slipped home to see her and the child. According to Union muster rolls, he was captured and hung by the enemy on May 5, 1864.

Joe B. Steele, March 13, 1923-May 13, 1998, was the son of Ernest Clyde Steele Sr. and Edna Lee Ball Steele of Sidney, Arkansas. He was a veteran of World War II, serving in the Navy for just under three years as a Signalman 3rd class. He was a master plumber, a Mason and served on the Nettleton School Board while living in the Jonesboro area. Steele moved his family to Lawrence County in January of 1962. He was an avid horse lover who raised and trained registered quarter and paint horses.

Joe B. Steele married B. Louetta Bufford of Desha, Arkansas. Louetta Bufford's parents were James Walter Bufford and Henrietta Manuel Bufford of Desha, Arkansas. She was valedictorian of her graduating class at Desha High School.

Louetta Bufford Steele was the first BRAD director of the Higginbottom Headstart Day Care when it first opened in Imboden, Arkansas in 1966.

Front: Roger Dale Steele, Louetta Bufford Steele. Back: Joe Ball Steele, Larry Joe Steele, made in Jonesboro, Arkansas, 1955.

Beginning in 1971, she served as director of the First Baptist Church Day Care in Walnut Ridge, Arkansas and retired in 1991, after being director there for 20 years.

Louetta Bufford Steele traces her ancestry back to Daniel James, 1816-1900. In 1942, Daniel and Malinda Pate James moved to Independence County from east Tennessee. The James' settlement later became known as Jamestown, which is near Batesville.

Joe B. and Louetta Steele had two sons, Larry Joe Steele, born March 31, 1946, and Roger Dale Steele, born October 11, 1950.

Larry Joe Steele married Janet A. Sayen of Little Rock, Arkansas. They have three children, Christopher Lee Steele, Jonathan Blake Steele and Jaime Louetta Steele.

Roger Dale Steele married Martha "Marty" Jane Barnes of Pocahontas, Arkansas. They have two children, Joby Baker Steele and Amanda Leigh Steele Hickman.

Joby Baker Steele married Brenda McDonald and they have three children, Payden Dale Steele, Molly Katelyn Steele and Caleb Baker Steele.

Amanda Leigh Steele married Brian Hickman of Harrison, Arkansas. –Louetta Steele & JoAnn Baker.

CLEO STEWART FAMILY. Cleo C. Stewart, October 10, 1905-November 12, 1997, is the son of Filmore and Perditta Davis Stewart. Born on the farm his grandfather, Andrew Jack Stewart, owned between Denton and Eaton, he lived most of his life within five miles of there.

He married in 1935, to Mary E. Pace, January 5, 1910-August 29, 1994, daughter of Newton and Fannie Latimer Pace. Their first years were spent in sharecropping and moving. He and Mary farmed, as most families did, raising corn, cotton, sorghum cane, and peanuts, as well as big garden which provided food for the whole year for the family. Much of the canning during early years was done in the canning kitchen which was located at Eaton. In mid 1940s, they bought a farm in the Eaton Community. After the boll weevil destroyed the cotton crops, truck crops became the family's source of income. Strawberries, okra, cucumbers, and spinach were all grown and harvested for processing plants.

There were five children born to this couple: Catherine Joyce, born in 1937, is married to Loyd Richey, son of Elmer and Alice Tretenburg Richey. They have three sons: Johnnie Loyd, Curtis Alan and Jackie Brian. They are farmers and live at Powhatan. Loyd was in Korea at the time of the truce between North and South.

Jimmy Wayne, born in 1939, is married to Linda Yastrab. Their children are: Scott Wayne James, Shelli Ann and Stephen Michael. Jim started working at Camcar in Rockford, Illinois in 1958, and they still live there. Jim was in Vietnam during the early months the US Army was deployed to that war zone.

Donald Michael, born 1942, married first Louise Barnett, second Therese Miros and third Sue Bennett. He has three children: Shannon Denise, Mary Elizabeth and Christopher Michael. Donald is a graduate of Southern Baptist College, Arkansas State University and the University of Arkansas and is a superintendent for Pulaski County Public Schools in Little Rock.

Betty Jean, born 1944, is married to James H. Denison, son of Floyd S. and Dicy A. Bell Denison. Their children are: Jami Jean, Dale and Annette. Betty has been a rural mail carrier for the postal service for many years in the Fenton, Michigan area. James worked as a tool maker in the Detroit area before retirement. James served in the US Army.

Randall Patrick was born in 1949, and served in the US Army in Germany. He worked for many years at Lake Charles State Park, a few years as park superintendent. He has worked for the past several years as an electrician in construction work. –Catherine Richey.

EMIT RAY AND MARY FRANCES COX STONE

were united in marriage, May 4, 1956. Emit was born Mach 13, 1938, to Dillion and Lena Stone of the O'Kean area. Mary Frances Cox Stone was born February 3, 1937, to Loyd Oliver and Dorothy Margaret Rice Cox of Hoxie. Mary's grandparents were Lawrence Countians, Will Ed and Mary Frances Story Cox and John Glover and Mary Melissa Hogan Rice. Mary grew up in the Owl City Community with two brothers, Jerry Dean and J. R. and graduated from Hoxie High School in 1955.

Emit and Mary Frances worked for the Cox family farm in the early years of their marriage, becoming managers in the late 1970s, of the Cox, Cox and Stone Farms. Mary also came to work as bookkeeper at Cox Implement Company when her mother retired from that position. Mary is co-owner of Cox Implement Company of Hoxie.

Mary Frances and Emit Stone have one child,

Mary Frances Cox and Emit Ray Stone, 1955.

Emit Ray Stone Jr., born January 31, 1964. Ray grew up on the farm learning farm skills from his dad and Grandpa Cox. Ray graduated salutatorian in 1982, from Hoxie High School.

On September 13, 1963, Ray Stone was united in marriage to Johnnie L. Barnhill. Ray is employed by Cox, Cox & Stone Farms. Johnnie and Ray have two children, Benjamin James, born January 26, 1989, and Ragan Mary, born June 18, 1991. Ray graduated Cum Laude in Agri Business from Arkansas State University in 1986. Johnnie graduated with honors in English from Arkansas State University in 1986.

The families worship together at First Baptist Church, Walnut Ridge. –Mary Frances Cox Stone.

EMIT RAY JR. AND JOHNNIE STONE.

Emit Ray Stone Jr. was born January 31, 1964, to Emit Ray and Mary Frances Cox Stone of the Owl City Community in Walnut Ridge. His grandparents are Loyd and Dorothy Rice Cox and Dillion and Lena Stone. Great-grandparents are Will Ed and Mary Story Cox and John and Mary Rice, all of Lawrence County.

Ray grew up on the family farm learning farming from his dad and grandfather. After graduating salutatorian in 1982, from Hoxie High School, Ray entered Arkansas State University.

On June 16, 1984, Ray and Johnnie L. Barnhill of Portia were married. Johnnie was born September 13, 1963, and is the daughter of Jerry and Jane Barnhill. She had a brother, Randy and a sister, Elaine. Johnnie grew up in the Barnhill's farming operation. After graduating with honors from Hoxie High

School in 1982, she entered Arkansas State University.

Ray graduated cum laude in 1986, with an agri business degree from Arkansas State University. Johnnie graduated with honors in 1986, with a degree in English from Arkansas State University.

Their children are Benjamin James, born January 26, 1989, and Ragan Mary, born June 18, 1991.

Ray is employed with Cox, Cox & Stone Farms. Johnnie is a stay-at-home mom. The Stone family lives on the farm. They worship at First Baptist Church, Walnut Ridge.

Johnnie and Ray Stone, Ben and Ragan, 1999.

JAMES STOTTS

and three of his brothers moved from Tennessee to the Arkansas Territory in the early 1830s. They settled just south of what is now Jonesboro. The area where they settled was first Lawrence County; then Green County was created; in 1838, Poinsett was established and then Craighead County in 1859. They stayed in the same area, but the county lines changed.

John Stotts secured a patent to a section of land four miles south of what is now Jonesboro. William settled a mile below John on old Highway Number 1. Andrew J. settled at what is now called Ridge Station and James settled in the McDaniel settlement near Christian Valley. The Stotts brothers each owned large tracts of land and were known to be great hunters. Some of the numerous members of the Stotts family later settled on Buffalo Island. But most of the later generations continued to live in or near the Jonesboro area and married into other pioneer families of Poinsett and Craighead Counties.

James Stotts was born in Wilson County, Tennessee, about 1811. His parents were Joseph Joshua and Rebecca Thomas Stotts, who moved from Wythe County, Virginia, to Tennessee sometime after 1810. James Stotts' marriage to Sarah Snoddy was recorded at the Lawrence County Courthouse December

Sarah Margaret Stotts Mays, born September 29, 1869, died March 28, 1942, daughter of John Elam Stotts and Margaret Patrick, granddaughter of James Stotts and Sarah Snoddy.

18, 1832. Her half brother, Rufus Snoddy (Rufus was listed in 1830 census of Lawrence County), signed their marriage bond. Sarah's parents were Samuel and Mary Purviance Snoddy, both from North Carolina. Her father, Samuel Snoddy, died in Arkansas, probably Lawrence County, about 1829.

James served as Poinsett County Sheriff for two terms, 1840 to 1844. He was elected state representative in 1846. The 1850 Poinsett County census list James Stotts, wife Sarah, mother-in-law Mary Snoddy, and children John Elam and Sarah Stotts. James apparently died sometime after 1855, and before the 1860 census. By 1860, the area they lived in had become part of Craighead County and Sarah Snoddy Stotts was married to Augustus Ransome. The 1860 census listed Augustus and Sarah Ransome and her children, John Elam Stotts and Sarah Stotts.

Sarah, daughter of James and Sarah Stotts, married B. M. Hopkins. They had two children, Augustus and Jodella Hopkins. B. M. died and Sarah married E. C. G. Dameron. Sarah Stotts Hopkins Dameron died September 10, 1880. Court records show that Dameron appropriated to his own use a large part of property that had been left to the Hopkins children by their mother.

John Elam Stotts, son of James and Sarah Stotts, married Margaret Missouri Patrick, December 20, 1864. Margaret's parents were Robert Newton Patrick and Margaret Fronabarger, natives of South Carolina. At the time of their marriage John had a large plantation about six miles from Jonesboro. They had four children: James Robert, Mary Florence married John Moss, Sarah Margaret married John Alexander Mays and Dora Helen married Charles Morrison.

There were two known Revolutionary soldiers that have been traced to the above mentioned families. They were: James Purivance, father of Mary Purivance Snoddy; John Fronabarger Sr., grandfather of Margaret Fronabarger Patrick.

The Stotts family and many of their descendants have contributed to the growth of Northeast Arkansas, but we must give credit to the hardy souls of an earlier era, who braved many hardships and dangers to settle the wilderness frontier that we now call our home. –Sarah Mays Dacus.

JOHN ELAM STOTTS,

born December 25, 1844, in Poinsett County, Arkansas, was the son of James Stotts and Sarah Snoddy, natives of Tennessee. James and Sarah were married in Lawrence County October 25, 1832. James and three brothers migrated from Tennessee to the territory of Arkansas in the early 1830s. They settled south of what is now Jonesboro, and at that time, part of Lawrence County. Sarah's half brother, Rufus Snoddy, was listed in the 1830 census of Lawrence County.

On December 20, 1864, John Elam married Margaret Missouri Patrick, born July 4, 1848, in Gibson County, Tennessee. Margaret was the daughter of Robert Newton Patrick and Margaret Fronabarger, natives of York County, South Carolina.

In a December, 1866, letter to his brother is Texas, Robert Patrick said, "Missouri married John Elam Stotts, a man in very good circumstances as he has a very good plantation." He also related many hardships that he had suffered during and after the Civil War. Two sons served in the Confederate Army, and one son died of measles and "camp diarrhea." He said, "The war has nearly ruined me. There are a great many northern men amongst us." He told of raiding parties, one with 1400 and another with 1200 men, that made two ravaging raids on Jonesboro. In one raid the soldiers took 1000 dollars from him. He said, "The war is ended now, it went against us. We will have to make the best of it if we can."

Margaret died September 24, 1873. John and Margaret were the parents of four children: James Robert, born 1865/66; Mary Florence Stotts, born September 15, 1867, and died July 3, 1913, married John Moss in 1887, and were parents of: Bliss; Joe; Bob Newton; Mary "May" Moss, who married Elzie Houston; Sarah Margaret Stotts, born September 29, 1869, died in

Mary Florence Stotts Moss, born 1867, died 1913. She was the daughter of John Elam Stotts and Margaret Missouri Patrick and granddaughter of James Stotts and Sarah Snoddy.

California, March 28, 1942. Sarah married John Alexander Mays and they were the parents of Edgar, Grant, Bertha and John Mays who married Allie Wood; Dora Helen Stotts married Charles Morrison and they were the parents of six children: Clyde, Mabel Ruth, Billie, Thomas Edward, Frederick Coste and Eula Morrison.

After Margaret Missouri's death, John Elam married Mrs. Cynthia Cockeral. They had three children: Altha, who married Will McDaniel; Elizabeth "Lizzie" and a son who died shortly after birth.

John Elam Stotts died September 8, 1883. Great-granddaughter, Sarah Mays Dacus, was told this story of his death. He was on his way home from Jonesboro when, at the corner of what is now Main and Nettleton, someone stepped out of the bushes and shot him. He was driving a fine team and wagon. The horses found their way home. He lived until he reached home, but the wound proved fatal. Some said he was shot by a highwayman, some said by a jealous husband. Others said that he was shot by mistake.

After John Elam's death, Cynthia Stotts married a Mr. Cowan and they had a son, Almarin Cowan. Cynthia died leaving a young son, two daughters and three stepdaughters. According to court records, Mr. Cowan sold off most of the Stotts land to support himself and his son. Bill Weaver and his wife, Mary, took Altha to live with them and Dr. Howell took Lizzie into his home.

There are many descendants of the Stotts, Moss, Houston and Mays families still living in Northeast Arkansas. Histories of some of these families can be found in *Goodspeed's History of Northeast Arkansas* published in 1890s, and in the *History of Poinsett County*, published in 1998. – *Sarah Mays Dacus and Jean Passmore.*

ALBERT G. STUART FAMILY AND THE STUART FARM SINCE 1855.

This story begins when Albert Galatin Stuart, 1834-1862, married Emmie Electa "Amy" Sloan on January 3, 1853. Not long thereafter they went to the Stuart farm on Spring River above Ravenden and on March 27, 1855, Albert G. Stuart purchased the Stuart farm from William C. Sloan. Little did they know that the Stuart family would continue to own and operate the same farm continuously for the next 144 years!

Albert was the son of William Stuart, born in 1812, and Nancy Childress Stuart, who were married in 1832. Emmie's parents were Fergus Sloan III and Rosanna Ruggles Sloan, who were married in Washington County, Missouri in 1818, and settled on Browns Creek at Ravenden.

Albert's grandfather and grandmother were Colonel William Stuart, 1785-1822, who came to Lawrence County from Christian County, Kentucky and Rebecca Kuykendall Stuart, who was a second cousin of the Revolutionary War soldier Benjamin Hardin IV, settled about three miles west of Powhatan on Flat Creek in 1816. Colonel William Stuart was wealthy with lands and tenements, Negroes and divers other goods and chattels to a large amount. He was a devout man whose home was also the home for the early Methodist preachers before a church was ever established in this part of the country including Reverend Isaac Brookfield and Reverend Jonathan Wayland.

Albert's Uncle C. "Champe" T. Stuart was the first treasurer of Lawrence County, Arkansas from 1836 to 1840, and also had a cotton gin at Davidsonville in partnership with Robert Smith.

They, William and Rebecca, were married in Christian County, Kentucky on September 15, 1798. It has been told that Colonel William Stuart's father was Reverend John Stuart from Abingdon, Virginia, who married Daniel Boone's sister and came to Kentucky with Daniel Boone and was killed by Indians in Kentucky. It has also been told

John Brady Stuart, born 1940, age 21 in this picture.

that Reverend John Stuart's father was Stephen or Biggers Stuart from Scotland. More research needs to be done to verify this.

Albert Stuart was an only child when something happened to his parents resulting in his uncle, Champs T. Stuart, asking the Lawrence County Court to appoint another uncle, Pittman C. Stuart, to be his guardian in October of 1847, as Albert was a minor. Albert and Emmie had three children. Their first child was William Washington "Pete" Stuart, 1853-1915, the Pete coming from the sound of a bird singing that flew in the house near him when he was a baby.

Their second child was Martha Ann Celinda Catherine Stuart, 1855-1924, whose first husband was Thomas W. Ball and whose second husband was Thomas J. Watts. Some family members called her Aunt Sissy. Martha is a great-grandmother to Reverend John Thomas Stoll, a Methodist minister, who presently lives at Ravenden. Their third child was Albert Stuart Jr., 1859-1880. He was the one that was informed by friends at Ravenden that the girl he had like was getting married to another man and people had gathered for the event downtown. Albert Jr. said, "I intended to marry that girl! So he quickly got on his horse and interrupted the marriage ceremony! He spoke to the girl briefly. She then got on Albert's horse with him and they rode away fast into the distance.

Emmie Stuart added another 30 acres to the farm on July 10, 1855, purchasing it also from William Comfort Sloan who was her brother. Albert Stuart sold a slave and purchased the original 228 acres for $580.

Albert Stuart and Emmie, 1836-1897 (some refer to her as Emma), were facing the Civil War soon after their children were born. The Confederates came to enlist Albert, but he was hidden under the haystack and couldn't be found! The Confederates came to the Stuart farm a second

time and this time Albert joined the Confederate Army. Emmie hid food in the cave on the farm in case the Yankees should come. Emmie had to prepare one of the slaves for burial during a time when no one else could take the responsibility. The other slaves were upset during this time. Two of the slaves names were Lewis and a girl named Cleary.

Albert died while in the Confederate Army in Georgia of stomach trouble in September, 1862, leaving his wife and three young children. Emmie Stuart's second husband was Ben Holt, but they had no children.

Albert's son, William Washington "Pete" Stuart, lived on the farm in the large log house with fireplace and cistern which still stands on the Stuart farm to the present time. He loved coon hunting and kept a large number of fox hounds on hand at all times and fed the dogs mush. Pete Stuart, strong in character, helped people to become more than what they were and was a good businessman as he owned three farms, one at Williford and one on Black River and the home place.

Pete Stuart married Jane Halstead. Jane was the type of person that you liked to be around, free and funny. Pete and Jane had three children: Emma Stuart, 1884-1916, who married Frank Stratton; John Brady Stuart, 1885-1934; and Mountie Ann Stuart, who married Claude Henderson on November 5, 1905. They lived in the Mountie house which was a small log house which still stands on the Stuart farm to the present time. Their children were: Alvin, Stuart, Harrell, Rudolph and Emma Jane. All are deceased except Rudolph, who lives in Arkansas City, Kansas.

John Brady Stuart continued to operate the Stuart farm after his father's death in 1915. Brady married Velma Lydia Bates, who was a school teacher having taught at the Dail School house and at Alicia. Velma's father was Willie Bates and her mother was Ludy Blond Henderson Bates Southworth. Her stepfather was Reverend W. S. Southworth, a Methodist Circuit Rider. Velma's grandmother was Margaret Sloan, sister of Emmie Sloan Stuart and her uncle was Will Henderson from Imboden. She was a faithful Methodist belonging to the Ravenden Methodist Church. Velma believed in saving and investing money instead of spending it on things you really don't need. She wrote a history of Ravenden.

Brady Stuart had a dynamic personality and was a front porch story teller, humanitarian and match maker, resulting in many people getting

John Brady Stuart, 1885-1934, riding his horse, Ole Dan, a fox trotting horse.

married. His advice was sought after. Much of this colorfulness came from the Halstead side of the family. Brady and Velma had three children: William Bates Stuart, 1910-1987, who continued to operate the Stuart farm after his father's death in 1934, from German measles and a weak heart. Myrtle Imogene Stuart, the second child, was born in 1913, and married the late Aubrey Wolff. Myrtle resides in the Stuart home 71 W. Nettleton in Ravenden at the present time. The Stuart home in Ravenden was built by her father in 1916, out of oak lumber from the farm. Charlie Beavers was the carpenter. Charlie said the house might blow over, but it wouldn't come apart for it was braced so well. Myrtle was a supervisor at the LaDame Laundry in Birmingham, Alabama for almost 30

205

years and is truly a good hearted, intelligent, loving person that everyone likes. She has no children, but she has been a mother to all of us.

The youngest child of Brady and Velma was Ludie Jane "Bobbie" Stuart, born in 1917, who now lives in Carbondale, Illinois with her daughter, Karen Jane Miller. Both Myrtle and Bobbie liked to get to ride on their father's horse, Ole Dan, who was a fox trotting horse when they were young girls. Bobbie was a beautiful young lady who had a dynamic personality like her father, became a hair stylist and she and Karen have traveled to many parts of the world including India and Iran. Bobbie's eldest daughter, Nan, married into the Ganon family, a very prominent family, in Dallas, Texas after graduating from Southern Methodist University. Nan was Miss Blytheville of 1958. Nan's daughter, Charlotte G. Gannon, is in hotel management in Dallas and Hawaii.

Bates Stuart operated the farm, but was also assistant postmaster at Ravenden for 16 years. He also had a wonderful personality like his father and people near the post office would raise their windows so they could hear Bates laugh as he met the patrons at the post office. His life long hobby wasn't golf, but his herd of quality Angus cattle. Bates was mayor of Ravenden and was responsible for the installation of the street lights. He won election to the board of directors of Sloan-Hendrix Academy over a prominent physician.

Bates married Nama Avis Moore, 1911-1992, in Paragould in 1937. Nama attended Hendrix College and graduated from Arkansas State and was a school teacher. She was from a prominent Lawrence County family who lived in Black Rock. Her father was R. W. "Bob" Moore, who owned much fine land on Black River, ran for Lawrence County judge and was the largest hog buyer in the state of Arkansas. Nama's mother was Sudye Billings Moore whose parents were the first to have screens over their windows in the Walnut Ridge Community. Nama also specialized in preparing fine food for the family and social events. This was her hobby. Nama believed the Methodists needed to have their own church facilities in Ravenden and took the leading part in having the Methodist Church built. She contacted many who had moved to Aurora, Illinois to find work to send money back to build the new church. Nama is listed in *Who's Who of American Methodism* in 1948. Bates and Nama were teachers in the Sunday School of the United Methodist Church for many years.

Bates and Nama had two sons: John Brady Stuart, born in 1940, and Robert Walker Stuart, born in 1946.

I, John Brady Stuart, the author of this family history with help from several sources, have continued to manage the Stuart farm since 1987, when my father lost his battle with heart trouble. I have owned the John Stuart Real Estate Company in Memphis since 1977. I married Gwen L. Thomas on October 10, 1962. As well as being a real estate broker, I have been involved in public speaking from time to time at church events, eulogies and political rallies. I ran for the Tennessee State House of Representatives in 1962, when I was only 21 years old and my wife-to-be, Gwen, and I campaigned together. I have had a lifelong interest in John Wesley, founder of the Methodist Church and have a collection of antique Methodist books dating back to Wesley's time. I was a lay delegate to the Memphis Annual Conference of the United Methodist Church for more than 20 years and have been a teacher in the Sunday School or youth group for approximately 35 years.

John Brady and Gwen have three sons, John William Stuart, born in 1968, is in real estate with the family firm in Memphis; James Wesley Stuart, born in 1974, is the father of the newest Stuart, Christopher Wesley Stuart, born February 4, 1999, who with mother, Misty Mills Stuart, live in Memphis; and Robert Thomas Stuart, born in 1985, is in the seventh grade in Memphis at Snowden School where he is on the soccer team. Robert likes to go to Spring River and the Stuart farm as well as his brothers, William and Wesley.

Robert Walker Stuart lived in Ravenden until moving to Memphis when he was six years old in 1952. Robert is a successful businessman who owns three high volume convenience stores in Memphis. He recently opened two Powertel telephone stores, one in Memphis and one in Nashville. Robert married into the Gallini and Bursi families and has two daughters: Tonya, born in 1972, and Jana, born in 1976, and Kayla Hughes, granddaughter, born in 1993. Tonya and Jana both charming young ladies, are in college at the present time, Tonya at the University of Memphis and Jana at the University of Mississippi. Robert has been a lifelong tennis player his team having won the City of Memphis and Tennessee State Team Tennis Championship several times. The Robert W. Stuart home is in Aintree Farms in Germantown, Tennessee.

In conclusion, I, John Brady Stuart, trust that the younger generations of the Stuart family will see to it that the Stuart farm continues to serve the needs of others whether it be lumber, food, hunting, fishing, a place of beauty and meditation, or hiking and may it remain in the Stuart name for another 144 years!

–*John Brady Stuart, February 12, 1999.*

HENRY EDWARD SUDDUTH FAMILY.

Henry Edward Sudduth was born in Alabama January 29, 1857, and came with his parents, David and Elizabeth Land Sudduth to Lawrence County about 1858. They were farmers.

Henry married Elizabeth LeGrand Whitlow, born May 16, 1861, Lynn, Lawrence County, on August 22, 1882, in Sharp County, Arkansas. Henry died August 30, 1930, in Los Angeles, followed by Elizabeth, January 3, 1936.

Henry and Elizabeth had seven children, all born in Lynn, Arkansas: Rebecca "Rebecie", 1884; Mildred, 1885; Henry Ellis "Eli:, October, 1890; Henrietta "Etta", August 27, 1895; Harry "David", May, 1897' Gertrude "Trudie", May, 1899; and Effie "Jessie", January 17, 1900.

Most of this family left Lawrence County during

Mr. Henry Edward Sudduth, taken around 1918, Lawrence County, Arkansas.

the 1920s, and settled in Los Angeles, California. The exception was Rebecca.

Rebecie married Marion Jackson Stewart and had 10 children. Most of the descendants from this family live in Pine Bluff, Arkansas. Mildred married William Newport in 1903, and died the same year.

Eli left Lawrence County in 1914, and joined the Army. He fought in World War I and then married Mary Delphia Lancaster, and they had one daughter, Pauline.

Henrietta married Druie Mateland Taylor in Lawrence County on November 12, 1911, and had one son, Edward Raymond Taylor. Druie died very young and "Etta" remarried in Tyronza, September 23, 1918, to Rufus "Murray" Doran. They had one son, George Trevor Doran. George fought in World War II in England and married Eileen Theresa Wyatt there. They have three children: William Murray, Donna Theresa and Peter George and nine grand-

Elizabeth Whitlow Sudduth, taken around 1918, Lawrence County, Arkansas.

children. The family has a successful stationery store in Anaheim, California.

Harry "David" married Iva Wright. They had one daughter, Sybil; Gerturde "Trudie" married Oscar Marsh and had one son, Jerry. She remarried Oscar Anderson and resided in Long Beach, California, until her death in 1956. Effie "Jessie" married Phil Zolik, had no children and died in 1986, in Los Angeles.

Henry and Elizabeth stayed in Lawrence County until the late 1920s, and then finally at the urging of their children they moved to Los Angeles, California. –*Rae Anna Ellis.*

JEFF D. SUDDUTH FAMILY.

Jared Sudduth, born 1827, in Tuscaloosa, Alabama, married August 27, 1848, to Telitha Land, daughter of Hiram and Cynthia Doster Land. Telitha died after September, 1861, in Lawrence County, Arkansas and Jared died before 1870, when his second wife, Anna B. Norman Sudduth, is in the census with the living children. Family legends says "carpetbaggers came and took Jared out and probably hung him". Children of Jared and Telitha:

John Smart Sudduth, born 1853, in Pontoc, Mississippi, married July 18, 1877, Lucy Ratliff Goings and died December 16, 1882, killed by tobacco thieves.

Mary Allen Sudduth, born about 1856, in Mississippi or Arkansas; believed to have died around 1880.

David M. Sudduth, born 1858, and died before 1870.

Jefferson Davis Sudduth, born September 19, 1861, in Lawrence/Sharp County, Arkansas and died March 20, 1949, married August 7, 1884, in Ft. Smith, Arkansas to Felonious Allen Whitlow, daughter of P. R. and Susan Benton Whitlow. Both Jeff and Felonious are buried in unmarked graves in Lawrence Memorial Cemetery.

Children of Jeff and Loni Sudduth:

Cleveland R., May 11, 1885-October 24, 1885.

Theodore T., September 8, 1886-January 13, 1912.

Lillie Mae, October 18, 1888-March 24, 1889.

William Fred, December 31, 1889-February 21, 1958, married April 11, 1920, to Arlie Jane Goff.

Edgar Melbourn, April, 1893-January 18, 1918, of flu, married December 28, 1913, to Lora Montgomery, also died during flu epidemic.

James David, October 8, 1895-February 19, 1962, married Ester Era Davis.

Marinda Vastine, born November 12, 1897, married December 20, 1914, to Fisher M. Jones; both died in 1924, along with their two oldest daughters in a car train accident. The youngest two children survived.

Jeff D. Sudduth family.

Palmon C., November 19, 1893-October 31, 1901.

Christena Octavious, June 23, 1901-January 12, 1990, married James L. Hoffman on January 21, 1922; both are buried in Lawrence Memorial Cemetery (see Hoffman).

Lura F., June 12, 1903-February 29, 1952, married January 21, 1922, to Rudolph Shipman.

Calvin Hillary, November 5-March 29, 1987, married Virgie Inez Doan, December 19, 1903-June 11, 1966, the daughter of James M. and Lela Inez Dutton Doan. Hillary is buried in Old Lebanon near his second wife, Mabel, and Aunt Virgie is buried in Detroit, Michigan.

Roy Sudduth, March 16, 1905-April 26, 1908.

Fannie, August 30, 1909-August 31, 1933, of spinal meningitis.

Baby born unknown, died March 28, 1909.

Anyone wishing further information may contact Barbara Wright Miller, 211 W. Michigan Ave., Clinton, Michigan 49236.

–Barbara Wright Miller.

ELIZABETH JANE SWAN. Elizabeth Jane Swan was born in Randolph County, Arkansas, on February 26, 1866. She was the daughter of Jonathan and Martha Jane Reece Price, former residents of Williamson County, Tennessee. Lizzie, as she was called, married John T. Chesser in Randolph County on February 15, 1885, and they are the parents of two children: Burlie C. Chesser and Etna Lutisha Chesser Newman. John T. Chesser died of a fever on April 12, 1896, and is buried in the Chesser Cemetery near Pocahontas. Lizzie was a tall, thin woman with deep set eyes and a determined attitude. She was very strong willed, but possessed a very gentle side. She never shirked from any job regardless of its difficulty. She loved horses and racing a good horse.

Lizzie married twice more and bore a third child, Virgie Mae Wann (Mrs. Clarence Ward). Lizzie later divorced Mr. Wann and she fought a custody battle for Virgie that went to the Arkansas Supreme Court. Lizzie won!

Lizzie's final marriage was to a widowed neighbor, Matt Swan, who had six young children. Wanting to make a fresh start the family moved to Lawrence County and began to farm in the Davenport Crossing area between Minturn and Alicia. In 1915,

Elizabeth Jane (Price) (Chesser) Swan.

Matt Swan became ill and later died, leaving Lizzie with eight children to care for. Later, unable to care for all the children, Lizzie allowed them to be placed in the homes of their relatives.

Lizzie's son, Burlie Chesser, graduated from high school in Pocahontas and joined his mother at Minturn.

In 1917, they bought a homestead of 120 acres near Egypt and cleared the land and built a large home and out buildings.

In 1918, Burlie was inducted into the military and Lizzie continued to farm her land alone.

Lizzie continued to make her home with Burlie after his return from military duty and after his marriage in 1924, to Miss Janie Cline.

Lizzie, like most people, lost what wealth she had during the Crash and the following Depression, but she also developed a heart condition and contracted tuberculosis. During the depression, Lizzie's large herd of cattle were taken from her and were driven into the woods and slaughtered. She was unable to keep enough to feed her family. She never seemed to recover from the hardships. Her tall frame became thinner and her eyes grew sadder and on January 22, 1937, she passed away at her home. She is buried alongside all of her children and their spouses in a family plot in Lawrence Memorial Cemetery at Walnut Ridge, Arkansas.

–Barbara Howard.

ELMER TATE FAMILY. Ruby Pearl Sanders was born January 22, 1924, to Mabel Lola Sanders and Norman "Bud" Sanders at Hoxie, Arkansas. Her siblings were: Mildred, born 1922, at Black Rock; Ray Norman, born 1925, at Jonesboro; Raymond Junior, born January, 1927, at Parkin; Roy Lee, born 1930 at Beebe; and Billy Gerald, born 1933. A brother, Robert Lee and a sister, Millie Fay died in infancy.

Her father, Norman, was born about 1880, to William Sanders and Martha Cantrell, either in Salem, Fulton County, or in Batesville, Independence County. Accounts vary. Her mother, Mable Lola Sanders, was born to James Sanders and Emma Grey in Egypt, Arkansas in 1903.

Money was hard to come by and father Norman worked at whatever was at hand to feed his family, including willow furniture making, trapping, and as a deputy sheriff in Jackson County.

Growing up as a young girl during the Depression, she recounted how difficult life was and how even simple things were appreciated, such as the time she found a jar of peanut butter after a flood, (how delicious it tasted,) the flour sack dresses her mother made for her and her sister, the toys she improvised for play, paper dolls cut out of catalogues, and a soap bubble pipe made from an empty thread spool with a bar of soap to rub across it.

Elmer Tate and Ruby Pearl Sanders Tate at the time of their marriage in 1941.

Fishing and hunting was a mainstay in the family's diet, and creating recipes for the squirrels and rabbits her father had shot was a challenge. "Making do" was a way of life for this family.

In 1941, at the age of 17, she married Elmer Tate, born 1904, in Perry County, Tennessee, in Searcy, Arkansas. To this union were born two children, Geraldine, 1945, and Earline, 1948.

Ruby left Lawrence County as a young person, but often recalled the times she and her family had when they lived there.

Elmer passed away in June of 1964, from cancer, and Ruby in June, 1985, from Lou Gehrig's Disease. *–Geraldine Wilson.*

JAMES M. TATE FAMILY. James Miller Tate, 1893-1958, married Virginia "Jennie" Irene Smith, 1897-1949, daughter of Seth Thomas Smith, 1860-1932, and Martha Fannie Shelton, 1861-1942, in 1917, at Imboden. He was a farmer in the area between Black Rock and Imboden and bought Roseland farm a mile north of Black Rock in about 1927.

At the time of their marriage, Jennie was teaching school at Post Oak School south of Imboden. A small child gave her a biscuit cutter made from a milk can which she used throughout her life. Daughter Carolyn continued using it until just recently when it collapsed, and she still has it along with the old doughboard her mother had used all her married life.

James Miller was a progressive farmer. He practiced soil conservation practices such as terracing, sodding, and ponds. All pastures were kept mowed with a sickle mower.

In 1936, he made the big decision to trade in a team of mules on his first tractor, a John Deere with lug wheels. Recently, a three page handwritten letter from W. E. McCollum of

James Miller Tate 1893-1958.

Imboden postdated March 30, 1933, detailing how to build brooders for chickens was found among old pictures. Thus, he diversified his farming to include an extensive chicken operation for the time.

He and Jennie spent endless hours promoting the Craighead Electric Co-op because he had the foresight to see how much it could save labor.

As soon as electricity became available, about 1938, he installed many things to make life easier: an electric pump for the well, washing machine, refrigerator, and electric iron. He was very frugal; lights were turned off when not in use.

They were firm believers that everyone should be able to make a living. Jewel had embarked on a dairy operation on the farm when World War II interrupted his plans. The oldest daughter, Edith, became a cosmetologist; Mildred, a registered nurse; Chester entered farming; Charles enlisted in the Navy; and Carolyn entered business training.

In 1948, James Miller purchased the first pickup baler in the county. They sent an engineer who stayed with the family for a week, going to the field each day until he figured out the problem. When he had it solved

Virginia "Jennie" Smith Tate, 1897-1949.

James M. Tate family home near Black Rock, Roseland Farm, the home place, 1949.

he went back to the factory, produced the part needed, and sent it out to be placed on the baler.

The family was active in the Black Rock Methodist Church. He was a trustee for many years during the planning and construction of the new church building in 1948.

They had six children: Jewel, Chester, Edith, Mildred, Charles, and Carolyn. Chester, who died at 36, Edith and Carolyn remained in Lawrence County. Mildred Freeman returned here to live in 1999.

Grandchildren still residing here are: Randall Tate, Elizabeth Pickney, and Renny, Paul and Jimmy Propst.

Great-grandchildren in the county are: Kellie Briner, and Christopher, Michael, Blake, Clayton and Matthew Propst.

Great-great-granddaughter, Kaitlin Tate Briner, lives in Walnut Ridge.

–Carolyn Propst.

LEE W. TATE FAMILY. Lee W. Tate, 1871-1942, married Elizabeth "Lizzie" Rash, 1869-1925, on October 2, 1892, at Imboden, Arkansas. Lee, son of James L. Tate, 1836-1921, and Marthey Ginnings, 1832-1854, of South Carolina, migrated to Arkansas where he married Lizzie Rash, who was born in Stuttgart, Germany, to Nicholas and Catherine Ann Rash. Lee settled between Black Rock and Imboden in the Clear Spring Community. He donated the rock for the Clear Spring church which is still active.

Lee and Lizzie had six children who lived to adulthood: Delbert, James Miller, Rufus Clifton "Tuff", John D., Oberia, and Bessie. Records show there was also a baby who apparently died within days of birth. All are now deceased.

Delbert, James Miller, and Tuff remained in Lawrence County where they had farming and business interests. Some of their children, Dale Smith Cavenaugh, Carolyn Propst of Black Rock, and Vera Hibbard of Portia, remained in Lawrence County to rear their families. Dale is deceased; Vera and Carolyn still reside there. Mildred Freeman returned here to live in 1999.

Great-grandchildren who are still living in the county are: Randall Tate of Imboden; Elizabeth Pickney of Black Rock; Snow Ann Burrow of Imboden; Renny, Paul, and Jimmy Propst of Black Rock; Larry Hibbard of Portia; and Mary Sue Lovelady of Walnut Ridge.

Great-great-grandchildren in the county are: Kellie Briner of Walnut Ridge; Christopher, Michael, Blake, Clayton and Matthew Propst of Black Rock; Justin Burrow of Imboden; Terry Hibbard of Portia; and Scotty, Michael and Lisa Lovelady of Walnut Ridge.

One great-great-great-granddaughter, Kaitlin Tate Briner, lives in Walnut Ridge.

–Carolyn Propst.

JAMES ARTHUR TAYLOR was born in Richland County, Illinois, in 1860, and served in the Union Army during the Civil War. He married Susan Edmondson and there were three sons: Elmer, Charlie Carlton, and Arie. During the Civil War the Iron Mountain railroad ended at Ironton, Missouri, south of St. Louis. After the war the railroad was extended to Piedmont in Wayne County, Missouri, and became the railhead for western expansion. The railroad became known as St. Louis Iron Mountain and Southern railroad. James procured timber for the railroad and moved to Eaton in Lawrence County, Arkansas, where excellent saw and rail timber abounded. He operated a general store and post office and purchased timber for the railroad.

Charlie Carlton Taylor, 1877-1949, was born in Piedmont, Missouri. He married Nancy Octavia Hedrick, 1883-1958, daughter of Thomas Crockett Hedrick (father, John Burton Hedrick; mother, Winaford Prigmore) and Rebecca Jane Kelley (father John W. Kelley; mother, Nancy Lawson), October 6, 1901, in Lawrence County, Arkansas. The children of Charlie and Octavia are:

1. Arthur Clay, 1902-1987.
2. Susan "Susie" Rebecca, 1904-1986.
3. Hazel Iola, 1906-1958.
4. James Raymond, 1908-1959.
5. Nora Violet, 1910-1997.
6. Thomas Fay, 1912-1994.
7. Junie Marie, 1914-1921.
8. Charlie Eugene, 1916-1996.
9. Nancy Audrey, 1918-1991.
10. Howard Sloan, 1920-1985.
11. Mary Ruth, born 1922.
12. Calvin Jackson, 1925-1968.

They moved to Marked Tree in the winter of 1916, to grow cotton. During the winter of 1921 they moved to the Greenfield Community north of Harrisburg, and were involved in farming. They sold out and retired in 1944.

James Raymond Taylor was born June 24, 1908, at Imboden (Clear Springs), Arkansas. He was all county athlete in Poinsett County, excelling in broad jump and baseball. Raymond married Mary Frances Shockley, 1907-1997, daughter of James Marcus Shockley, 1860-1936, and Lilly May Cromwell, 1874-1967 (father, Arthur G. Cromwell; mother, Mary J. Davis) in May, 1929. Children of Raymond and Mary are:

1. Billy Ray, born 1931.
2. Bobby Louis, 1937-1992.
3. James Gary, born 1944.
4. Jerry Wayne, born 1947.
5. Mary Ellen, born 1949.

Raymond shared a barber shop with Clay during his early married life then became involved in farming and was a horse and mule dealer. He became active in politics and served on the District Eleven school board, including a term as president. He served as City Marshall of Harrisburg and was appointed Chief of Police at Newport. He worked at Newport for many years. During those years at Newport, he maintained a farm in Randolph County and focused on raising white faced cattle until shortly before his death.

Mary Taylor was born April 1, 1907, at Harrisburg and grew up on her parent's farm in the Old Bolivar Community north of town. Her grandmother, Mary J. Davis Cromwell, born 1844, was a first cousin of Jefferson Davis, President of the Confederate States. The Cromwells and Shockleys came to Arkansas from the Altoona Community, northeast of Birmingham, Alabama. Mary made her home in Imboden in late 1949, and lived on West Third Street for 42 years until her death on March 31, 1997. She had a passion for gardening and flowers, winning many ribbons at the Lawrence County Fair.

Four of Mary's children had the privilege of attending and graduating from Sloan-Hendrix. Bobby was valedictorian of his class. All of Mary's sons graduated from college and Mary Ellen attended college. Billy and wife, Jeannine Terrell Taylor of Jonesboro live in Heber Springs, Arkansas. Gary and wife, Nancy Vickers Taylor of Ponca City, live in Ponca City, Oklahoma (sons Joseph Ryan and James Robb). Jerry and wife, Patricia Richards Taylor of Sugar Grove Illinois, live in Edmond, Oklahoma (children: Michael and Cyndi Taylor Thomas, grandson Garrett Taylor). Mary Ellen and L. D. Holladay live at Scott, Arkansas (children: Sharon Henson Garner, Todd Henson, grandchildren: Natalie Garner and Taylor Garner).

Eugene and Fay owned a farm south of Imboden after World War II until about 1951, before they moved to northern California. The only descendants of James Arthur Taylor living in Lawrence County are Beverly Waltermire, May 29, 1950, daughter of Calvin and Georgia Burton Taylor, husband, Jay and daughter, Sarah Waltermire, November 12, 1975. They live in Walnut Ridge.

Mary said it best about three weeks prior to her death in 1997, "I just don't know of a better place we could have lived." –Billy Taylor

WILLIE "PETE" TAYLOR and Hannah Madden Taylor lived in the Strangers Home Community and later moved to Alicia. They were the parents of 13 children: Jessie, Luther Woodrow, Roy, Robert "Bob", William "Bill", Eugene, who was killed in World War II, Ezekiel, and Lee Jr. Emmie Taylor Ferguson, Wonedith Foster, Floita, Louvell Taylor Duncan, and Loutrisha Taylor Cates.

Jess Taylor married Ola Fowler. They lived in the Strangers Home Community and had three children: Boyce, Bonita and Harold Dean.

Boyce Taylor, the son of Jess and Ola Taylor, married Retha Smith, daughter of Mr. and Mrs. Steven Smith of Swifton. They had one daughter, Sherry.

Bonita Taylor married Delano Tennison, son of Joe and Pearl Tennison of Hoxie and Clover Bend. They had two children: Allen and Lana.

Dean Taylor married Kay Jones, daughter of Leland and Alma Jones of Alicia. They had one son, Denny. Dean married Helen Smith from Black Rock. She was J. B. and Wencie Smith's daughter. They had one stepson, Chad, and one daughter, Pasha.

Woodrow Taylor married Rachel Marie Smith, daughter of Roy and Bessie Smith. They had three children: Annette, Bonnie Sue, and Roy Luther.

Annette Taylor married Keith Spring of Chicago. They have two children: Ricky and Dianna and four grandchildren.

Bonnie Sue Taylor married Marlin Clinton of Chicago. His parents were Joe and Hazel Clinton. They have two children: Debbie and Brett and four grandchildren.

Roy Luther Taylor married Marlyn Angus of Lockport, Illinois. They have two children: Tammie and Tina and two grandchildren.

Roy Taylor died when he was very young.

Robert "Bob" Taylor married Juanita. They had four children: Lee Wayne, Elaine and Renee and Tina.

William Roy "Bill" Taylor of Alicia married Alice Geneva Pickett. Her parents were James Lynn Pickett and Alice Ruth Clark. They had four children: Berlan LaRoy, Phil Ledel, Judith Carol, and Donna Susan.

Berlan Taylor married Linda Carolyn Downum of Clover Bend. She was the daughter of Edward "Ed" and Virginia "Lou" Downum. They had one daughter, Caroline "Cari" Narissa.

Phil Taylor married Kay Martin, daughter of Howard and Retha Martin of Wynne. They have one daughter, Holland Ledeliah.

Judy Taylor married Rickey Dale Williams, son of Johnny and Pansy Williams of Biggers. They have one son, Justin Dale Williams and one granddaughter, Jade Brean Williams.

Donna Taylor married Vett Dharans of Detroit. They had one son, Joshua Lighten.

Eugene Taylor married Cozene Foster, daughter of Mr. and Mrs. Wayne Foster of Alicia. They had one daughter, Betty Ann.

Ezekiel Taylor married Billie Caughron. They had four children: Gary, Kenny, Lisa, and Joey.

Lee Taylor Jr. married Shirley Dodd. They were the parents of Jimmy, Tommie, and Tony.

Emmie Taylor married Walter Ferguson. They had two children: Levon and Yvon Maralto.

Wonedith Taylor married Curtis Foster, son of Mr. and Mrs. Wayne Foster. They have two children: J. R. and Chloie Jean Foster Swann.

Louvell Taylor married Lehman Duncan. They are the parents of Cathy Duncan Saffell, Cindy Duncan Wood, and Felicia Duncan Baughn.

Loutrisha Taylor married Bobbie Artes. They are the parents of David and Letisha Artes. –Berlan Taylor.

JEFFERSON DAVIS TAYLOR FAMILY.

Jefferson Davis Taylor, born October 8, 1862, was probably born in Lawrence County, Arkansas. He married Clara Mary Bagley in Walnut Ridge, Arkansas, on September 1, 1889. Clara was born in Illinois, February 15, 1874.

Jefferson and Clara had five children born in Lawrence County: Druie Mateland, July 7, 1891; Freddie Ray and Nellie May, March 2, 1893; Edward Riley, July 15, 1895; William Pink, October 30, 1897. The twins and Edward died in infancy. Jefferson was a marble cutter and worked in a sawmill. He died in a sawmill accident in Neelyville, Missouri, February 2, 1899.

Druie Mateland married Henrietta Sudduth, born Lynn, Arkansas, August 27, 1895, on November 12, 1911, in Lawrence County. Henrietta was the daughter of Henry Edward Sudduth and Elizabeth LeGrand Whitlow. Druie played on the Clover Bend baseball team and traveled to

Edward Raymond Taylor, 1913-1982, Clover Bend.

games around the county. He died of malaria October 27, 1916 in Tyronza, Arkansas. Druie and Henrietta lived on a river boat on the Black River in Clover Bend where their son, Edward Raymond Taylor, October 30, 1913, was born. The Taylor family were farmers. After Druie's death, Henrietta married Rufus Murray Doran of Lynn, Arkansas and had one son, George Trevor Doran, born 1919. After Rufus' death, Henrietta moved to Los Angeles, California, and lived there the rest of her life, dying December 25, 1974, in Glendale, California.

Edward Raymond Taylor was married to Anna Arizona Russell on June 21, 1936, in Los Angeles, California. Ed was a stationery engineer, a wonderful husband and father. He was active in church, Masons and the Shrine in Los Angeles. He

Druie Mateland Taylor, 1891-1916, Lawrence County.

died May 11, 1982, while on vacation. Ed and Anna had two daughters, Wahneeta Faye, born November 28, 1939, and Raeanna Marie, born November 15, 1944, both in Los Angeles. "Neeta" is married to Gilbert C. Ramirez and has a son and daughter, Gilbert and Diane and four grandchildren. Raeanna is married to Jim Ellis and they have one daughter, Tevis Dionne. They resided in Seattle, Washington and then later, Steamboat Springs, Colorado.

William Pink married Edith Ashlock in Lawrence County, October 11, 1917, and they had four children: William, Verna Mae, Beatrice and an infant. Both Bill and his wife, Betty, live in Lawrence County and have children and grandchildren. Verna married Raymond Shreeves and has resided in Greene County for over 30 years. They had a large family, some still residing in Greene County, Arkansas and the others have spread Lawrence County roots all over the nation.

We are a God-fearing, happy, and healthy family and proud to have our roots in Lawrence County, Arkansas. If any reader has any information on this family, please write to R. Ellis, POB 880010, Steamboat Springs, Colorado 80488. –Rae Anne Ellis.

JERRY ALLAN TAYLOR FAMILY.

Jerry Allan Taylor was born in Fayetteville, Arkansas, on January 30, 1948, first child to Wilford Wasson Taylor and his wife, Doris Lorene King Taylor. The family moved to Hoxie, Arkansas, in 1949.

Jerry attended school at Hoxie High School, graduating in 1966, as Co-Valedictorian. Jerry attended Hendrix College in Conway, Arkansas, where he majored in Economics and Business. In 1968, Jerry joined the newly formed Army ROTC (Reserve Officer Training Corps) unit at Arkansas State Teachers College in Conway under a cooperative arrangement with Hendrix College. In May, 1970, Jerry graduated from Hendrix College with a Bachelor of Arts degree and a Regular Army Commission as a Second Lieutenant in the Field Artillery Branch.

On July 10, 1970, Jerry married Jean Shackelford, daughter of James William and Frances Adele Bergholm Shackelford of Helena, Arkansas, in Helena, Arkansas. Jean was also a 1970 graduate of Hendrix College. After a short stay in North Little Rock, Arkansas, Jerry and Jean moved to Fort Bragg, North Carolina, where Jerry began his Army career with the 82nd Airborne Division. Jerry continued serving in Korea, Germany, and several posts in the United States, including Oklahoma, Louisiana, Kansas, North Carolina and Virginia. He commanded at the Battery and Battalion levels, both overseas and in the states. In August, 1990, he deployed with the 82nd Airborne Division as Commander of 1st Battalion, 319th Airborne Field Artillery Regiment, to Saudi Arabia for Desert Shield/Desert Storm. Jerry returned to the United States following the end of Desert Storm in May, 1991. After attending the National War College, he was assigned to the Joint Chiefs of Staff in Washington, D.C., where he was the JCS Representative to the Strategic Arms Negotiations with the former Soviet Union in

Jerry, John, Jamie and Jean Taylor.

Geneva, Switzerland. He retired from the Army as a colonel in July, 1995.

Jerry and Jean have a son, John Wasson Taylor, born at Fort Sill, Oklahoma, November 27, 1976, and a daughter, Jamie Taylor, born at Nurenburg Military Hospital, Federal Republic of Germany, September 12, 1981. Through the years, Jerry has been active with the Boy Scouts of America, the Masons and his church or chapel wherever he lived.

Jerry currently works for the Department of State, Washington, D.C. in the area of Arms Control and Treaty Verification Compliance. He and Jean reside in Burke, Virginia. –Lorene Taylor.

TIMOTHY LEE TAYLOR was born on October 14, 1960, at Lawrence Memorial Hospital in Walnut Ridge, Arkansas, the third child to Wilford Wasson Taylor and his wife, Doris Lorene King Taylor.

Tim attended Hoxie School, graduating in 1979. In 1978, Tim began his career with KRLW Radio Station, located on Highway 412 east of Walnut Ridge.

Tim joined the 164 Airlift Group, Tennessee Air National Guard, Memphis, Tennessee, on February 8, 1980, as an Aircraft Electrician on C-130A aircraft. Tim was deployed to Howard Air Force Base, Panama during Desert Shield and Desert Storm as back fill for active duty personnel.

On November 15, 1980, Tim married Rita Kay Alls, daughter of J. Wilson and Mazie B. Alls. The wedding took place at the Hoxie United Methodist Church. Rita is a 1979 graduate of Hoxie School, graduating in the top five. Tim and Rita have two children, Leah Jo, born August 3, 1984, at the Randolph County Medical Center in Pocahontas, Arkansas, and Mark Evan, born September 13, 1987, at the Randolph County Medical Center in Pocahontas, Arkansas.

Tim has been employed by the Walnut Ridge Area Chamber of Commerce since December 31, 1989, as its Executive Director and President. Rita was employed by the Sloan Law Firm in Walnut Ridge, Arkansas for 17 years and is currently employed by the Regions Bank in Walnut Ridge, Arkansas, as a loan secretary.

Tim, Rita, Lea and Mark reside at 108 Brewer Drive in Walnut Ridge, Arkansas. –Lorene Taylor.

WILL TAYLOR FAMILY. William Stanley "Will" Taylor was born in Jesup, Arkansas, on September 12, 1888, and died in Smithville, Arkansas, July 1, 1958. He was buried in Smithville Cemetery. Will was the second of seven children born to John Wesley Taylor and Fannie McCarroll. John Wesley Taylor was born in Jesup, Arkansas, on September 14, 1851, and died in Searcy, Arkansas, December 3, 1925. He is also buried in Smithville Cemetery. Fannie McCarroll Taylor was born near Smithville on October 20, 1868. She died in Jesup, Arkansas, October 10, 1918, and was buried in Smithville Cemetery.

William Stanley was married to Vida Ann Kendall, April 16, 1911, Easter Sunday in the Smithville Methodist parsonage by Reverend F. H. Champion. Vida Ann was born in Smithville, Arkansas, on February 1, 1890. She died in Walnut Ridge, Arkansas, January 8, 1975, and was buried in Smithville Cemetery. She was the third child of Jarrett W. Kendall and Harriet Isabell Wasson. Jarrett Kendall was born in Henry County, Tennessee, October 17, 1838. Jarrett W. Kendall died in

John Wesley and Fannie (McCarroll) Taylor.

Smithville, Arkansas, September 30, 1903, and was buried in Hillhouse Cemetery. Harriet Isabell Wasson Peed Kendall was born near Smithville, Arkansas, October 4, 1850, and died in Smithville, Arkansas on February 18, 1883. She was buried in Ware Cemetery near Calamine.

Jarrett W. Kendall and Harriet Isabell Wasson Kendal, 1880.

W. S., as he was known, was a barber and cattle buyer in Smithville. Vida was a homemaker. They had two children, Zelma Inez and Wilford Wasson. Zelma Inez was born in Smithville, Arkansas, on December 29, 1912. She died October 7, 1988, and was buried in Lawrence Memorial Cemetery. Wilford Wasson was born in Smithville, Arkansas, January 23, 1922.

Wilford attended school at Smithville, Strawberry and Sloan-Hendrix Academy in Imboden. He graduated from Sloan-Hendrix in May of 1941. After graduation Wilford worked in Michigan before entering the Army on September 8, 1942. He served until December 6, 1945, with the 843rd Engineer Aviation Battalion, Company C in McCord Field, Washington and in England, France and Germany.

After being discharged from the Army, Wilford attended Arkansas State Teachers College in Conway, Arkansas, for two years. He then transferred to the University of Arkansas in Fayetteville, Arkansas, and graduated in June of 1949, with a BSE major in vocational agriculture.

William Stanley and Vida Ann Kendall Taylor, April 16, 1911.

Wilford was married in the First United Methodist Church in North Little Rock, Arkansas, on December 20, 1946. Reverend Garland C. Taylor, Wilford's uncle, performed the ceremony. Lorene was born in Pottsville, Arkansas, on June 29, 1925. She was the daughter of James Elijah King and Ethel Rackley King. James King was born in Pottsville, Arkansas, on January 28, 1895. He died in North Little Rock, Arkansas on September 16, 1977, and was buried in Rest Hills Cemetery in North Little Rock, Arkansas. Ethel Rackley King was born in Pottsville, Arkansas on October 18, 1896. She died in North Little Rock, Arkansas on June 10, 1977, and was buried in Rest Hills Cemetery in North Little Rock, Arkansas.

Lorene graduated from Pottsville High School in May of 1943. She graduated from Arkansas State Teachers College in Conway, Arkansas, in August of 1946, with a BSE major in Vocational Home Economics. Lorene taught seventh grade from 1946 to 1947, in North Little Rock Junior High School.

Wilford and Lorene moved to Hoxie, June, 1949, where Wilford was the first vocational agriculture teacher in the Hoxie School. The Hoxie FFA members and the Hoxie chapter earned several district and state honors under his leadership. Wilford also served as president of the

Lawrence County Teachers Association from 1961 until 1962. He taught at Hoxie until October of 1963, when he became the postmaster in Hoxie, retiring February, 1987.

Lorene taught in the Hoxie School System for 36 years, 28 years as a vocational home economics teacher. In the summer of 1986, Lorene was

Wilford Wasson and Lorene King Taylor, 1980.

named "Teacher of the Year" by the Arkansas Association of Vocational Home Economics Teachers.

Wilford and Lorene are members of the Hoxie United Methodist Church where each has served in leadership positions. Lorene has served as president of the United Methodist Women and Wilford has served as president of the United Methodist Men. Wilford was a charter member of the Hoxie Housing Authority, serving as a commissioner from 1964 until 1988.

Wilford and Lorene have three children: Jerry Allan, born in Fayetteville, Arkansas, on January 30, 1948; Sandra Kay, born in Fayetteville, Arkansas, on February 12, 1949; and Timothy Lee was born in Walnut Ridge, Arkansas, on October 14, 1960. –*Lorene Taylor.*

TEEL FAMILY. Most of the Lawrence County Teels are descendants of William Henry Teel and his two wives. William was born February 3, 1885. He married Cordelia Coe on November 13, 1903. They had two sons, Henry, 1904-1931, and Joe, 1905-1980. Cordelia died March 16, 1906, leaving the two babies. In 1907, William married Dollie Bell Baker, 1888-1954, daughter of William Jasper and Nancy Fletcher Baker. They lived north of Walnut Ridge, where he farmed. Later, he operated a small grocery store on Highway 67.

They had nine children, five of them while living in the Mt. Zion Community: Fred, Lela, Rubye, Opal and William Jr. "Bill." In the spring of 1919, they moved to "the Doyle place" in the Lane Community where Louise, Charlene, Freda, and Ruth were born. Some attended the Lane School.

As the children grew up and finished or gave up their schooling, they sometimes lived with older siblings or friends to be near a school or a job. Soon they established their homes, mostly in the eastern part of the county, as their parents had. Henry died at age 27 and was buried in the Kissee Cemetery at Old Walnut Ridge.

Joe married Christine Spray. They had eight children. J. W., the first, and his wife, Theresa, who live south of Hoxie, had six children: Joel, Jennifer, Tyson, Terence, Bridget and Wendy, all graduates of Hoxie High

Mama and Papa Teel, Dollie Bell Baker Teel and William Henry Teel, 1948, behind their store on Highway 67 North.

School. Geraldine married Russell Sharp and had a son, Keith. Jolene and husband, Don Morris, of Pocahontas had three children: Donnie, Ronnie and Joan. Bobby and wife, Etta Fay Ingram, of Walnut Ridge had two sons, Kenny and Denny. Velma and husband, Jim Stalnaker, of Walnut Ridge had a son, Randy. Gary and Evelyn Marlin of Walnut Ridge have a son, Michael, and a daughter, Carol Ann. Roger and Carolina Willfond of Walnut Ridge have one son, Bryan. Kathy and husband, Steve Arnold, and their daughter, Christy, live in Missouri.

Fred, 1909-1976, finished high school at Hoxie, where he played football. He married Mardell Davis. Their children included Linda Carol, 1943-1970, Norma, Jerrye and Dennis, who live out of state.

Lela, 1911-1998, first married Ike Towell. They lived north of Walnut Ridge and farmed. After he died, she married Earl Smith of Pocahontas. She had no children.

Rubye, born 1913, married Sloan Weir of Hoxie in 1933. See "The Sloan Weir Family."

Opal, born 1916, married Martie Berry and they had three daughters: Mildred, Agnes and Shirley. They moved to Kansas in the 1950s.

William Jr. "Bill", born 1919, and wife, Knowles Oldham, live in Walnut Ridge next door to their daughter, Kathryn, who married Leon Woody and had a daughter, Nicole. Son Tony and his wife, Linda, had three children: Mechelle, Heath and Natalie, all who grew up in Lawrence County. Bill, Tony and Heath farm together.

Lousie, 1921-1995, and Joe Bill Starnes were the parents of Harry, Sandra Sue and Bob of the Little Rock area.

Charlene, born 1925, married Denver Stapleton of California. They had two daughters, Sandra and Paula.

Freda, born 1927, and first husband, Phil Reisner, had a son, Ron. Then she and John Watts of Seattle had a daughter, Suzanne.

Ruth, born 1929, and husband, H. B. Holder Jr., of Walnut Ridge had two sons, Michael and Scott. Mike and Lisa Gipson of Paragould have two children, Rachel and Zachary. Scott and Becky Roberts of Walnut Ridge have a daughter, Emily.

The Teels hold a reunion every year or so to give family members the opportunity to "catch up." –*Francis Green.*

JOHN S. TERRY FAMILY was born about 1756. He served in the militia of Bedford County, Virginia, during the Revolutionary War and removed to Madison County, Kentucky, about 1784. He married Frances Gaddy, daughter of William and Susannah Dollard Gaddy, in Madison County, May 28, 1797.

The family lived in Kentucky until about 1810, and spent a few years in Illinois Territory before arriving in Lawrence County by 1820. Children of John S. and Frances Gaddy Terry were:

1. Sarah/Sally Ann Terry, born Kentucky, 1799, died May, 1870, Saline County, Arkansas; married first 1813, Illinois Territory to Robert Brazil; married second Saline County, Arkansas, October 30, 1842, to Jacob Prillaman.

2. William S. Terry, born Kentucky, about 1799, died Saline County, Arkansas, April 4, 1843; married about 1819, Elizabeth.

3. Amassa/Massy Terry, born about 1800, died about 1842; married first in Arkansas, about 1821, to Reverend Jesse James; married second Saline County, Arkansas, September 15, 1837, to Alfred Bankston; married third in Saline County, Arkansas, April 14, 1839, to William Redford.

4. Stephen S. Terry, born about 1801, died Saline County, Arkansas, 1838; married Unity.

5. George S. Terry, born Kentucky, about 1805; married first in Missouri, about 1824, to Polly W.; married second in Arkansas, about 1842, to Mary Avants.

6. Turner Shannon Terry, born about 1806, died Saline County, Arkansas, January 8, 1839; he married in Arkansas, April 17, 1836, to Caroline Matilda Bond.

7. Anna Terry, born Illinois Territory, October 26, 1813, died Arkansas, April 7, 1896; she married first in Illinois to Epaphroditus Thornburg Kendall; she married second in Arkansas, December 13, 1840, to Wade Hampton Hilton.

8. Frances/Frankie/Fanny Terry, born Illinois Territory, about 1815; she married first about 1838, Green B. Mitchell Butler; she married second in Arkansas, May 28, 1840, to William Walker.

9. Susannah Jane Terry, born Illinois Territory about 1816; she married first 1838, to Walter H. Dunbar; she married second in Arkansas, April 2, 1849, to Francis/Frank Neal.

10. James S. Terry, born Illinois Territory 1817, he died in Saline County, Arkansas 1839.

The John S. Terry family lived in Lawrence County about 10 years, but by 1830, they were in Pulaski (now Saline) County, Arkansas. John S. Terry died in Saline County in 1838. His wife, Frances Gaddy Terry, survived him and died after 1860. –Carole Mayfield.

WILLIAM ALEXANDER TERRY

WILLIAM ALEXANDER TERRY was a son of George Terry, an Englishman who came to South Carolina in 1808, and later migrated to Franklin County, Indiana. William moved to Lawrence County about June, 1850, from Tippah County, Mississippi. He bought 320 acres of land near Strangers Home in Marion Township. His wife, Mahala, and several children accompanied him. In 1852, he wrote his brother-in-law, Isaac Soper in Franklin County, Indiana, and told of the death of two of their children and of the illness in the rest of the family. He died in July, 1855, and his wife evidently preceded him in death. In his probate the local Methodist minister, R. G. Gillespie, became guardian of the minor children. John Gaston, his oldest son, wrote to his uncle in Indiana that they would have to sell most of the property, but they wanted to keep the family together. They were: John G., Thomas T., Sarah Ann (married George Forster), Lydia Mahala (married first Stephen L. Bush and second Joseph Ruffner), Nancy Jane (married Samuel Swift), Eliza Ellen (married Richard Haggard), and Martha M. (married Matthew Ballard).

George Forster, from Nurenburg, Germany, was living in Lawrence County by 1855, when John wrote his cousin in Indiana about the death of his father. He also mentioned that his sisters had beaus who were spending a lot of time visiting. "Ann's is a little Dutchman, a Mr. George Forster; he comes every other day and sometime twice every other day. Lydia's is a Mr. Henry Ruffner; he comes three times a day." His sister, Sarah Ann Terry, also included a note in the letter, addressed to Sarah Soper. She described her beau as "my little George - the best looking young man in these parts; he came from Germany five years ago; he is going to start to Texas in a few weeks with a drove of jacks to sell." Lydia did not marry her beau, but Sarah Ann did marry her little Dutchman in 1862. They bought land in Jackson County and had a large family, but only two boys and two daughters reached adulthood. The two boys died before marrying and only one daughter, Christina Joanna, never married.

George Forster died in 1889. He was buried in the family graveyard on their farm with all of his children who had died. Sarah lived until 1895. She was survived by Albert Christopher, and Kathina Regina, who was known as Aunt Kate

Forster, and Joanna Christina, who married John D. Ashley in 1891, when he came from Izard County to teach at the Possum Trot School. They lived on the Forster land and raised five children: Fallon, George, Selma, Nettie Ann and Moreau "Mo." Christina Joanna died in 1910. John D. re-married to Martha Toler, a daughter of Thomas Toler. She had been a student of his when he taught, and they had a second family of three boys, J. D., Tom and Milton. –Joanna A. Baker.

THOMASON FAMILY

THOMASON FAMILY. In 1851, many members of the Thomason family came to Lawrence County, Arkansas in a wagon train. There were many families, including George W. Thomason, who was born in 1780, in Rowan County, North Carolina, and died shortly after they arrived in Lawrence County in 1851 or 1852. He left his wife, Sarah Elizabeth Clary back home in North Carolina. She died there in 1852. The children of this couple were: Jane, born 1808, married John Craige in North Carolina; John Thomason, born 1810, married Harriet Fraley in North Carolina; Mary Ann Thomason, born 1811, married Anthony Cozort in North Carolina; Burgess Thomason, born 1812, married Nancy Barnes in North Carolina; Elizabeth H. Thomason, born 1815, married Benji Blackwell in North Carolina; Sarah M. Thomason, born 1817, married William Blackwell in North Carolina; John Casper in Arkansas; and Richard Thomason, born 1818, married Mary Elizabeth Krider in North Carolina.

George W. Thomason is buried in Old Lebanon Cemetery, beside Nancy Barnes Thomason who died in 1852. Prior to her death, she had moved her church membership from North Carolina to the New Hope Baptist Church near Denton. That was quite a distance to walk or ride to services since the family lived near Cypress Creek and their property joined where the old Lebanon Cemetery and Church are. Burgess Thomason gave the Lebanon Presbyterian Church four acres for the church. Burgess and daughter Sarah Cozorts and two families of Blackwells were all among the initial members of the church in 1852.

Mary Ann and Anthony Cozort came to Arkansas with 10 children from about age 20 down. Two more were born in Arkansas. Ten of these were girls, two were boys.

Burgess and Nancy Barnes Thomason had two living children when they arrived in Arkansas, but one died shortly after. Sarah, who was born in 1843, married Andrew Jackson Stewart and they were the parents of five chidlren: Filmore L., 1873-1972, married Ditta Davis; James T. "Jim", 1876-1950, married Etta Casper; Sarah Eugenia "Jessie", 1881-1956, married Tom Claxton; and twins, Wiley, 1887-1888, and Charles H., 1887-1970, who married Elise Ivie. Burgess married a second time to Elizabeth Stewart who was the aunt of his son-in-law, Jack Stewart. They had no children.

Elizabeth H. Thomason, 1815-1882, married Benji Blackwell and they had five children: Mary J., John Calvin, who was baptized on the day Lebanon Presbyterian Church was formed, William Scott, Joseph R., and Benji B. Blackwell.

Sarah Mahalia Thomason, 1817-1876, married first William Blackwell, and second John Casper. She was the mother of Mary A. Blackwell, Sarah Angeline Blackwell, William Joseph Blackwell, John Blackwell and George W. Casper.

All these related families lived in the Eaton Community, attended churches in the area, and most are buried in Old Lebanon Cemetery.
–Catherine Richey.

The George Thornton Family. From left, front row: G. B., Annie Dixon and George Edward Thornton and Julian. Back row: Lee, James, Felix, William, George, DeWitte, Sarah and Charlie.

THORNTON FAMILY

THORNTON FAMILY. The Lawrence County Thorntons came here from Tennessee. They were dairy people there, and when George and Annie Dixon Thornton, came here they first settled in the hills between Imboden and Smithville. The dairy business is a seven day per week job and perhaps that encouraged them to have nine boys and one girl, a baseball team, they used to say. One of them. Felix H. Thornton, who was a minister for 50 years, and perhaps is the best known of the brothers, as his ministry covered Southern Missouri, beginning at Branson where he began his preaching to Northern Arkansas where he closed that career. The children included Charlie, DeWitte, William, George, Felix, B. G., Lee, James and Julian and the girl, Sarah.

And no tale of those dairy days in the Lawrence County hills is complete without the Horse Story. In 1915, George and Annie loaded their belongings, including livestock, on a freight train (it was not unusual in those days to move this way) and among it all was a homesick horse. Soon after settling, the horse turned up missing. They trailed him to the ferry at Powhatan, where he hadn't been allowed on the ferry, so he swam Black River. The trail lead eastward and the horse was finally found back at the old homestead in Tennessee. He had traveled over 100 miles on a train, at least partly at night, but had found his way back home! A sweet four-letter word - HOME.

Incidentally, George and Annie are credited, according to the late Jim Worshum of Imboden, with bringing the first Jersey cattle to Lawrence County in about 1915.

In about 1924, they moved their dairy to Walnut Ridge to the "Russ Place" which is now where the town's swimming pool is located on NE Second Street. No one remembers how long it operated there.

This is being written by a grandson, Billy D. Thornton, son of the minister of the Thorntons, Felix H. And he figures in another interesting tidbit of the family history. When World War II broke out in 1941, he was 12 years old and was a paperboy in Hoxie for the Memphis Press-Scimitar. Being an "enterprising young man," he saw the need for newspapers at the new Army Air Base that got under construction north of Walnut Ridge that same year. For months he was the only source of daily newspapers for the entire base.

Much later, when the Bryan Funeral Home was built in Hoxie, Reverend Thornton preached the first funeral there. At retirement Reverend Thornton wrote a book about his family and the life of a Pioneer Preacher, The Call That Forces and a copy is in the files at Powhatan Courthouse. The family, Felix and Nell Moody Thornton and the children, Billy D., the late Jerry D., as well as Patsy McManners and Rosemary Peace, all appreciate this historical endeavor of Lawrence County.
–Billy D. Thornton.

THORNTON. Nancy House Thornton moved to Lawrence County, Arkansas, with her daughter and son-in-law, Pascal and Matilda Whitlow, from Hardin County, Tennessee, about 1859.

She was the daughter of John and Catherine Westmoreland House and was born in 1797, in South Carolina. In about 1814, in Spartanburg, South Carolina, she married Isaac Thornton, son of Josiah and Sarah Thornton.

By 1830, Isaac and Nancy Thornton were living in Madison County, Alabama. By 1840, they had moved to Hardin County, Tennessee. Their children included Matilda; William W., who married Susan A. Tucker and Catherine C. (Hargrave?); Sarah S., who married M. J. Alford; Isaac, who married Lucinda and Rebecca; Thursday M., who married Samuel P. Wallace; Elmira, who married Davis; Melvinia L., who married Samuel Wallace ?; and Mahala, who married William M. Mosley.

Nancy Thornton's husband, Isaac Thornton, died sometime before October 13, 1850, in Hardin County, Tennessee.

After his death and probably about 1857, Nancy and at least three of her children, plus several other families traveled together from Hardin County to Lawrence County, Arkansas. In the 1860 Lawrence County census Nancy is described as being 62 years old and living with her daughter and son-in-law, Samuel P., and Thursday Wallace in Strawberry Township. The Wallaces also had two children, Martha J., who was four years old and had been born in Tennessee, and Isaac Thomas, who was one year old and was born in Arkansas.

Samuel P. Wall served with the Confederate Army in Company A., Shaver's Arkansas Infantry from Lawrence County.

In 1870, Samuel Wallace was living in Clover Bend, Marion Township. His first wife, Thursday, had died and he may have married her sister, Melvinia. A third child, Samuel K., age one, is listed along with Martha who is 14 and Thomas I. who is 11. Nancy Thornton continued to reside with the Wallaces. She was 70 years old.

Nancy Thornton's son, Isaac, and his wife, Lucinda, were living in Marion Township of Lawrence County in 1860. Isaac and Lucinda were both 27. They had two children, Caroline, age five and Nancy, who was six months old.

In the 1870 census Isaac's wife, Lucinda, had died and he had remarried, Rebecca, age 35, an Arkansas native. His daughter, Caroline, the only one born before the family left Tennessee, was now 15. The other children listed are Nancy, age 11; Jane, age 10; Sarah, age 8; Alexander, age 6; and Dennis, who may be the child of Rebecca, was age one.

Another of Nancy Thornton's daughters, Matilda, and her husband, Pascal Whitlow, were at Strawberry Creek, Lawrence County, in the 1860 census. They had children Nancy P., who married Morgan Raney; Isaac H., who married Elizabeth Pearson; Mary A., who married Jefferson Wadley; William M.; John Granville, who married Mary Pearson; and Sarah M., who married John Grisham Mullen.

They were in Smithville, Lawrence County, in 1870. They were members of the Milligan Camp Ground Cumberland Presbyterian Church and Matilda Thornton Whitlow was probably buried there since she died in 1871. Her daughter, Sarah, and her husband, John G. Mullen, along with other members of his family, are buried there. Most of Whitlow family, including her husband Pascal, had moved to Izard County by the 1880 census.

Nancy House Thornton died between 1870 and 1880, probably somewhere in Lawrence County. She possibly is buried at Milligan Camp Ground Cemetery. –*Leon and Ann McDonald.*

PETE TODD FAMILY. John W. Todd Sr. married a Bowen in East Tennessee about 1793. To this union 10 children were born. The eighth, J. W. Todd Jr., was born in February, 1815. He married Mahala Phillips in East Tennessee in 1836. To this union two children were born: Sarah in 1838, and Peter, October 23, 1857, near Marion, Illinois. J. W. Todd Jr. operated a mercantile business in the north during the Civil War. Peter married Hester Steers in December, 1875, in Illinois. To this union six children were born: Millie, October, 1876; Joseph T., April 9, 1878; Triplet boys did not live; C. Edd, July 1883. Hester died in December, 1889, and is buried in Grand Chain, Illinois.

Pete Todd and his family, including his father, John W. Todd Jr., moved to Smithville, Arkansas in covered wagons sometime after Hester's death. John W. Todd Jr. died in 1895, and is buried in Lancaster Cemetery near Jesup.

The Pete Todd family prior to leaving Grand Chain, Illinois in late 1800s.

Pete's children were in school and their school teacher was Miss Effie May Lay, daughter of David H. and Rachel Billings Lay, of Jesup. Effie lived with and nursed her parents who had tuberculosis, commonly called "consumption." After the death of her parents, David, March 24, 1896, and Rachel, February, 18, 1898, she married Pete Todd, December 13, 1898. To this union four children were born. Fred, the first child, born February 12, 1900, died at the age of nine months and is buried at Smithville. Sula was born near Powhatan in 1902. Sula married Walter Martin and had three girls. Sula died February 11, 1946. Taddie Mamie was born near Powhatan on September 30, 1904. She married Lawrence Faulkner, son of William Samuel and Mary Adeline Davis Faulkner, on April 23, 1921. Six children were born to this union. The firstborn was Clyde William, born April 24, 1923, married Martha Sanders. No children were born to this union. After her death, he married Sally. Clyde died August 26, 1995. Joe Calvin, born May 24, 1926, married Betty Jean Chappell. To this union three children were born: Joe Maurice died at a young age, Linda Kathryn and Phillip Alan. Vivian Lucille was born April 8, 1929, and died May 14, 1929. Lawrence Jr., born September 7, 1933, married Carolyn Burns Myers. He has a stepson, Randall Wayne Myers. Mary Carolyn, born October 26, 1938, married William Edward Bilbrey Jr. To this union two daughters were born: Rita Karen and Maleta Sue. Glenda Sue, born December 1, 1940, married Stephen Michael Bierk. To this union two children were born: Todd Michael and Kelly Sue. Taddie Todd Faulkner died January 22, 1991, and is buried in the Powhatan Cemetery. Jesse, Pete and Effie Todd's youngest child was born July 4, 1913. He had one daughter, Betty Marie. Betty married James Gray.

Pete Todd died May 10, 1925, and Effie Todd died October 27, 1948. They are buried in the Powhatan Cemetery. –*Maleta Tipton.*

JOSEPH P. TOLBERT was born November, 1854, in Missouri, son of James Tolbert and Mary A. Tolbert, her last name is unknown. James was killed at the end of the Civil War and may have been a Union soldier.

Joseph married about 1874, to Julia Sophonie, last name unknown, and they are buried in the cemetery in Black Rock.

The Tolberts came to Lawrence County about 1880, from Fulton County, Arkansas and Howell County, Missouri. Children were:

Jim Tolbert, born December, 1874, Howell County, Missouri; wife's name was Polly.

Mary Melvinnie Tolbert, June 4, 1877-July 14, 1960, in Rockford, Illinois, but is buried in Lawrence Memorial Park Cemetery. "Mollie" married first to John Phaby and had one daughter, Annis Phaby, who married Joe Box. After John's death, Mollie married to Ira Lee Wright (see Wright family).

James Tolbert and son, Joseph P. Tolbert.

Ada Tolbert, February, 1880-1961, married on December 8, 1901, in Lawrence County to Charlie Dodson.

Lester J. Tolbert, born June, 1890, married about 1903, to Flora Davis.

Harvey Rex Tolbert, born October, 1892, married Mary Ovella Beasley.

William Frank Tolbert, born April 14, 1882, married September 8, 1912, to Nettie A. Creek.

Anyone wishing more information may contact Barbara Wright Miller, 211 W. Michigan Ave, Clinton, Michigan. 49236.

–Barbara Wright Miller

TONEY FAMILY. Littleberry Toney was born in 1795, in the Pendleton District of South Carolina. His parents were William and Martha Toney. William Toney also had a father named Littleberry. This latter Toney married Elizabeth Calloway.

At some point, Littleberry's parents moved to Williamson County, Tennessee. There he married Mary Wilson on February 28, 1826. We have no record of children being born. We assume she died soon after the marriage. Sometime before March 17, 1833, Littleberry and his brother, John, moved to Madison County, Missouri. He married Nancy, the daughter of the Reverend William McMurtrey on the above date. At some point, they moved to the Cape Girardeau area, not far from Madison County. A part of that area was given to Arkansas and it became Lawrence County, Arkansas.

Some time before 1846, Littleberry served as County Tax Assessor and Sheriff of Lawrence County. In about 1848, he became Clerk of the County Court. He often went by Berry or L. B. Toney.

Littleberry Toney and Nancy McMurtrey had five children. Mary Elizabeth is my ancestor. She is the only one born in Madison County, Missouri. Sarah L., William Martin, Littleberry Jr. and Elvie were all born in Lawrence County, Arkansas. Of course they were really born in the same town. Strange situation changing states without even moving.

On November 17, 1852, Littleberry Toney died. Nancy and the family probably stayed quite a few more years in Lawrence County before moving on to Yell County, Arkansas. Nancy married Samuel L. Sharp in Lawrence County on January 9, 1862, and Mary Elizabeth married John Harris in Lawrence County on October 18, 1867. They all moved to Yell County, Arkansas after 1867. Littleberry Toney's grandfather, being named Littleberry, also was called Berry. This Berry Toney and his brothers-in-law, Richard and Joseph Calloway, helped to save their best friend from the Tories in Wilkesboro, North Carolina, during the Revolutionary War. Colonel Benjamin Cleveland of Kings Mountain fame was their friend. He was traveling to visit his New River plantation on April 14, 1781. Unfortunately, Captain William Riddle, a noted Tory leader, was approaching the area. Captain Riddle was in route to the 96th District of South Carolina where a reward was paid for prisoners. Riddle had a party of six or eight men, so he felt brave enough to try to capture Colonel Cleveland. After the capture, Littleberry Toney and his brothers-in-law, the Calloways, heard about it. Right away they set out to rescue him from the Tories. They followed the trail of Riddle and his men for quite a distance and found their campsite. A great gun battle ensued and Richard Calloway was grievously injured, but eventually recovered. Anyone desiring to read the exact story can go to Draper's Manuscripts.

Our first Toney ancestor arrived from England to Virginia about 1665. His name was Edmond Toney. He traveled by ship, with another Toney male, probably his brother whose name was Peter. They settled in New Kent County, Virginia. Robert Toney of Bromesberrow in Gloucestershire, England, is an ancestor of Edmond and Peter Toney. This Robert of Bromesberrow is a descendant of the ancient Toney family of Normandy, France. These early Toneys of Normandy were related to William the Conqueror and were the hereditary Standard Bearers to the Dukes of Normandy. They came to England with Duke William and fought at the Battle of Hastings. The Toney family of Normandy came to France with the First Duke of Normandy, Rolf the Ganger. They came from Norway. The ancient Toney men of this line, as Standard Bearers to The Dukes of Normandy and then later to King William, The Conqueror of England, were obligated to marry into royalty and most of them did. Most of the women's lines of descent reach back to the Emperor Charlamayne.
–Shirley Perez.

MR. AND MRS. LUTHER TRIBBLE.
I am Patricia Clark Tribble, daughter of Victor and Patsy Waddell Clark of Lawrence County. I am married to William Luther Tribble, son of the late William Luther Tribble Sr. and the late Mary Josephine Ponder of Lawrence County. We have four children: Patrice Michele Tribble, William Luther "Trey" Tribble II, Dylan Clark Tribble and Christopher Michael Tribble who came and departed this earth August 26, 1980.

Michele is 21 and a graduate of Westside High School. Trey is eight years old and Dylan is six years; students of Westside High School.

I work at World Color at Jonesboro, Luther works for Rural Water Service of Craighead County.
–Patricia Clark Tribble.

Left to right, front row: Patricia Clark Tribble, Dylan Tribble (six years), Luther Tribble, Trey Tribble (eight years), standing Michele Tribble, age 21.

FREEMAN E. P. TRIMBLE.
Born in St. Francis County in 1845, to William and Sethena Trimble, Freeman E. P. Trimble was the grandson of Moses, born 1786, Virginia, and Anna Styers Trimble, born 1787, Tennessee, among the earliest settlers in St. Francis County. His father, William, was born in Alabama around 1818, but by 1829, the Trimbles were living in the Arkansas Territory near Caldwell, about eight miles from what would later become Forrest City. Freeman's father owned a sawmill there.

In 1861, Freeman joined Dobbin's 1st Cavalry, which later became the Fifth Arkansas Infantry; after being part of several engagements with Union forces, then hospitalized at Nashville; he was discharged in 1862, at Tupelo for being under age.

In 1872, Freeman married Arena McDonald Cook, the widow of William Cook. Arena was the daughter of James McDonald and Susannah Smith of Randolph County. Of their nine children, only four lived until 1900: Mary, born 1875, married P. Williams and second William Sailor; Minnie Cora, born 1877, married Thomas M.

Trimble sisters. Seated left: Mary; right: Minnie. Standing left: Ida; right: Ella.

Horton and second James Sagely; and twins, Ida, born 1880, married John Broome; and Savannah Ella married Emmett Pritchard.

Mary Sailor had two sons: Gus, who married Orpha Morris, who died; then Minnie Rose; and Jess, who married Louize Gooch. Minnie Horton had four children: Melvon Cornelius "Jake" and Salina by her first husband; Thomas Horton and Virginia Melford "Jack" and Leola, known as Tincey, by her second, James Sagely. In addition to his son, Roscoe, by his first wife, John and Ida Broome had three children: Roland, Lucy and Hazel. Ella and Emmett Pritchard's children were: Bessie Lee and Jesse Freeman.

Freeman Trimble and his family lived in the Richwoods Community near Clear Lake and Portia. He died around 1899, and Arena died sometime after the 1900 census and before the 1910 census. –Regina Horton.

JOHN BENJAMIN TURNBOW
was born in Middle Tennessee in 1844. According to family history he was orphaned at an early age. Some time before the Civil War he made his way to Lawrence County, Arkansas. In early 1862, he joined the 13th Arkansas Infantry as a member of Company F. In July, 1962, he was discharged from the Confederate service as a minor being under 18 years of age. At the time of his discharge, Company F was near Knoxville, Tennessee. Again, family history says that: John had put corncobs in his boots to be able to enlist and also that when he came home from the Army, he had swum the Missis-

John and Martha Turnbow sitting on the porch of their house in Jesup.

sippi in his uniform."

On November 28, 1869, John B. "Frank" Turnbow was married to Martha Jane Fortenberry, daughter of Taylor and Elizabeth Catron Fortenberry. Martha Fortenberry Turnbow was born Christmas Day 1852. In 1895, John and Martha were given, by the

John and Martha Turnbow sitting, Belle Morgan on his lap and Charley on her lap. Elvira Robins and John F. Turnbow standing; about 1890.

United States Homestead Act of 1862, 40 acres of land near Cooper Creek between Smithville and Jesup. The 1900 census indicates that John and Martha had been married 31 years and had 10 children, six of which were living at that time. The names of the four who had died are not known, but the remaining six were: John Frank, Elvira, James, Belle, Charley and Fannie. Frank's wife was named Rosa Taylor, Elvira married John L. Robins, Jim married Mollie Todd; Charley married Pearl Rudy; Bell married George Morgan; and Fannie married Robert Taylor. John Benjamin Turnbow died June 25, 1917, and Martha Jane Fortenberry Turnbow, July 19 1926. Both are buried in the Lancaster Cemetery near Strawberry. Many descendants of these families still live in Lawrence County today. –David Robins.

ANNA WANDA LEE TYREE,
daughter of Howard Ray Tyree and Beulah Leaf Tyree, was born August 19, 1930, on the island at the mouth of Spring River at Black Rock. She graduated from Caraway High School and worked for Bell Telephone Company and for 10 years she worked in Memphis as a radio dispatcher for the police department.

Wanda married for the first time on June 28, 1951, to Charles Hamblin, who was born on April 4, 1926, in Guntown, Mississippi. They had two children: Steven William Hamblin, born March 31, 1952, and Shirley Diane Hamblin, born September 21, 1953. Shirley married Danny McKinney and they have three children: Susan Blair McKinney, born August 9, 1983; John Charles McKinney, born July 17, 1985; and Joseph Witt McKinney, born April 4, 1990. Wanda's second marriage was to Gifford Dean Collinsworth from Wynne, Arkansas, born August 9, 1926. Dean was a veteran of World War II, serving in the United States Navy. He died August 8, 1988. Wanda and children live in the Hernando, Mississippi area.–Wanda Collingsworth.

CARL VERNON TYREE FAMILY.
Carl Vernon Tyree, son of Howard Ray Tyree and Beulah Leaf Tyree, was born in Lawrence County on July 28, 1936. His early childhood days were spent on a farm near Clear Lake, then later he lived in Caraway, Arkansas. He wrote a story for the Times Dispatch in 1963, called "Back When They Made Buttons," interviewing Cecil Meeks and William L. Harmon, both veteran river men. He was his own photographer and climbed a tree to get a good shot of the Main Street of Black Rock. He married Beatrice A. Ling on November 1, 1958, and they had three children.

1. Howard V. "Howie" Tyree, born June 9, 1959, married Lori Flynn in August, 1984, and they had two children: Lea Tyree, born November 4, 1986, and Arlena Tyree, born May 18, 1991. Howie and Lori were divorced in 1995, and he married in 1996, to Jan and they live in Midland, Michigan.

2. Pamela Kay Tyree, born June 6, 1964, married Arthur McArthur and they have one child, Nicole McArthur, born October 18, 1991. Pamela lives in New Hampshire.

3. Deborah L. Tyree, born July 8, 1965, who married Kevin Cleary and they have three children: Rachel Lynn Cleary, born September 19, 1983, Kevin James Cleary Jr., born February 4, 1987, and Ryan Justin Cleary, born March 20, 1990. Deborah and family live in Flint, Michigan, where she works as a registered nurse. Vernon spent many years in the newspaper business and many hours playing music, a talent the Tyree children inherited from their dad. Vernon and Beatrice were divorced in 1982, and he married the second time to Joan Carpenter on January 13, 1984. Vernon and Joan live in Fenton, Michigan. —Dan Tyree.

GEORGE WASHINGTON TYREE, son of William Scott Tyree and Docia Louisa James Tyree, was born in Myrtle, Missouri, on September 30, 1877. He married on January 23, 1909, in Lawrence County to Biddy Louise Lamb, daughter of Thomas and Sarah Elizabeth Menton Lamb, born February 19, 1891. George Washington Tyree worked at the old Roundhouse at Hoxie and at the old sawmill in Minturn. In 1909 he moved his family to Colbert, Oklahoma. In 1916, George sold almost everything he had and bought a covered wagon and a team of horses and returned to Arkansas. But on his way back one of the horses died near Broken Bow, Oklahoma, and one of the wagon wheels broke, so he sold his remaining goods and obtained passage on a train to Walnut Ridge. He share-cropped, dug shells out of Black River and fished. In 1925, he leased 40 acres of land. While he had the flu, his hired help exposed him to the mumps. The doctor mistakenly gave him quinine which caused his eardrums to burst, leaving him deaf. He had a summer cabin at Scott's

George Washington Tyree, Biddy Louisa Lamb Tyree and George's brother, Delford Tyree.

Ferry on Black River where he liked to stay. He walked up the railroad tracks to get there and when a train came he could feel the vibrations and would get off and let them pass, but one day in 1942, the United States was involved in World War II and there were a lot of troop trains moving on the tracks. As he was walking toward Black Rock, at the old Mile Post about one mile out of town he felt the vibrations and stepped off to let the train go by and when it passed, not knowing there was another train right behind it, he stepped back on the tracks in front of it and was killed. The children of George and Biddie Tyree are:

1. Leamon Tyree died a few weeks old of the hives.

2. See the Slettie Almeta Tyree Gunn family.

3. See the Howard Ray Tyree family.

4. See the Ruthie Mondozia Tyree Sneed family.

5. Cora Oleta Elizabeth Tyree. See the Wesley Dee Woodson family.

Biddy Louisa Tyree died November 8, 1918, and buried in Clark Cemetery. George Washington Tyree died June 20, 1942, and is buried in Oak Forest Cemetery, Black Rock, Arkansas. —Louise Smith.

HOWARD RAY TYREE FAMILY. Howard Ray Tyree, son of George Washington Tyree and Biddie Louisa Lamb Tyree, was born December 7, 1912, in Colbert, Oklahoma, and raised in Lawrence County. He helped his dad, who share-cropped planting cotton and corn. He attended school when and where he could. When he was 16 years old he started sharecropping for himself and married in Walnut Ridge, on October 13, 1929, to Beulah Leaf, daughter of John and Rebecca Leaf, born February 19, 1911. He loved to play the guitar and the harmonica. Ray and Beulah had 10 children.

1. Anna Wanda Lee Tyree (see the Anna Wanda Lee Tyree Collinsworth family).

2. Betty Genva Tyree, born in Lawrence County on March 24, 1932, married Ed Keeler and has six children: Danny, Brenda, Sheila, Eddie, Twilla and Dennis.

3. James Merle Tyree, born January 23, 1934, at Lauratown, married and has 11 children.

4. Carl Vernon Tyree (see the Carl Vernon Tyree family).

5. Ray Clarence "RC" Tyree, born April 21, 1938, has five children, lives in Grand Blank, Michigan.

Ray and Beulah Tyree.

6. Herman Dee Tyree, born December 11, 1939, has three children: Jo-Ann, David and Johnny. Herman lives in Flint, Michigan.

7. Velma Louise Tyree, born January 30, 1943, married Stuart Smith on October 3, 1969. Louise has five children: Ramona Leigh, Tina Louise, Roy Allen, Bethany Lynn and Robert Steven. Stuart's grandparents were Mable Robd and Glendoph Smith, his great-grandparents, John Robd and Mary Hart, came to America in 1871, from Lanconshire, Scotland. Louise and family live in Flint, Michigan.

8. Vonita Faye "Bonnie" Tyree was born March 18, 1944, married John Lienberger, has two children: Michael and Roger Dewayne. Bonnie lives in Flint, Michigan, and has worked 17 years for the Chevrolet Motor Company.

9. Lloyd Dewayne Tyree, born June 16, 1945, and died September 21, 1946.

10. Jerry Tyree born and died August 14, 1946.

Lloyd and Jerry are buried in Bowman Cemetery.

Howard Ray Tyree and Beulah moved to Flint, Michigan, in the 1950s, and retired from the General Motors Plant in Flint, Michigan, in the late 1970s, moving to Ashland, Mississippi. Beulah Leaf Tyree died September 7, 1981, of heart failure and emphysema. Howard Ray Tyree died August 1, 1991, of a heart attack. Ray and Beulah are buried in Ashland, Mississippi. —Vernon Tyree.

SLEETIE ALMETA TYREE FAMILY. Sleetie Almeta Tyree, daughter of George Washington Tyree and Biddy Louisa Lamb Tyree, was born at Black Rock, November 9, 1910. Her mother died when she was eight years old. Being the eldest child of four, Sleetie had to become a stand-in mother to her baby sister, Cora, who was only 11 months old and her little sister, Ruth, age four, and brother, Ray, at age six.

She married when she was 16 to Clarence Edward Gunn on June 8, 1927, in Manila, Arkansas. Sleetie and Clarence adopted one son

named Larry Kenneth Gunn, born June 19, 1946, and he has one son named Kenny Gunn.

Clarence Edward Gunn died October 10, 1970, and is buried in Manila, Arkansas. Larry Kenneth Gunn has made his home in Texas. Sleetie Almeta Tyree Gunn lives at Black Rock, Arkansas. —Slectic Tyree Gunn.

Sleetie Tyree Gunn and sister, Cora Woodson.

WILLIAM SCOTT TYREE FAMILY. William Scott "Bill" Tyree, son of Andrew Jackson Tyree and Nancy Nash, was born November 20, 1847, in Laclede County, Missouri. He married on March 11, 1875, to Louisa Docia James in Randolph County. They had eight children.

1. George Washington Tyree (see the George Washington Tyree family for more information).

2. Harriet E. Tyree, born in 1879.

3. Mendoza "Dozie" Bell Tyree, born May 13, 1882, married William Thomas Estes and had 11 children. The first three children were all boys and they did not live very long. Their other eight children are: Charles Estes, born October 30, 1901; George Estes, born April 26, 1903; Felix Estes, born December 17, 1904; Felix and his wife, Grace, live at Hoxie; Ona Louise Estes, born July 4, 1907, died June 20, 1970; Nelus G. Estes, born April 12, 1912, died April 23, 1939; Opal Estes, born July 22, 1915; Pearl Estes, born April 10, 1919; and Ruth Estes, born March 12, 1922, married Elgin Smith, born August 2, 1924, and they had two children: Bob Smith, born November 12, 1952, and Don Smith, born March 23, 1956. Don married Teresa Freeland and they had two children: Jason Smith, born July 28, 1984, and Allen Smith, born December 27, 1985. Elgin Smith died October 13, 1996, and Ruth Estes Smith lives in Fairborn, Ohio. Mendoza "Dozie" Bell Tyree died November 30, 1946.

4. Viola Tyree, born February of 1884.

5. Clyda Tyree, born March, 1889, died December, 1910.

6. William Tyree, born January 18, 1891, married Audie Williams, born April 2, 1908, and they had 13 children: Eugene Tyree, Mary Tyree, Joseph Tyree, Peter Tyree, Paul Tyree, William Tyree Jr., James Lloyd Tyree, Norman Tyree, Clone Tyree, Marie Tyree, Ettamae Tyree, Inez Tyree and Donna Mae Tyree. William Tyree died September 7, 1956. Audie Tyree died July 30, 1989.

The William Scott Tyree family.

7. Delford Tyree, born December 31, 1897, lived at Clover Bend for many years then moved to Minturn, married Alma Bunton and they had three children: Delford Tyree Jr., born September 10, 1929, and died April 17, 1994; Anna Bell Tyree, born May 20, 1925, married a Wheeler and she lives in Shreveport, Louisiana; and Ruby Tyree, born October 26, 1926, married a Edwards and she lives in Texas.

8. Manzie Mary Tyree, born November 18, 1894 (for more information see the William Marion Wells family). –*Ruth Smith.*

JAMES UNDERWOOD FAMILY. James Underwood, born 1804, died before November 11, 1852, in Lawrence County, Arkansas. He married Elizabeth, born 1807, in Missouri. James' father was born in Virginia and his mother in Missouri. In Lawrence County probate papers dated November 24, 1852, James was called Captain James Underwood. James enlisted in the Mexican War on June 18, 1846. His entry reads: Company C Arkansas Battalion, Infantry & MR Pvt.

They had the following children: David, born 1828, in Missouri; Jamison J., born about 1831, in Missouri; Martha Margret; Thomas, born 1837; and Sarah A., born 1841.

Martha Margret Underwood was born in 1833, in Missouri. She married Zachaeus Ratliff, son of Elam Ratliff, on February 10, 1848, in Lawrence County, Arkansas. Martha died in 1886. Zachaeus Ratliff was born on August 11, 1824, in North Carolina; he died on September 3, 1890, in Arkansas; he is buried in September, 1890, in Smithville, Arkansas Cemetery. (Also see Ratliff and Frisbee family histories.) –*J.C. Brown.*

BOSTON B. VANCE FAMILY. In December, 1914, Boston Bard "B. B." Vance and his wife, Elsie, arrived in Sedgwick, Arkansas, to make their new home. Accompanying them on the adventure were Elsie's parents and sister, Jessie, Katherine and Nettie Crader, along with the John Rhodes family. The move had been encouraged by Mary Statler Aldridge, first cousin of Jessie Crader.

The group left Glen Allen, Missouri, on different trains. Boss and John rode an immigrant car of a freight train with the livestock and household goods. Jessie accompanied the womenfolk on a passenger train.

Arriving in Sedgwick, Boss pursued farming to support the family. At the off-season he worked for the railroad as an agent and a laborer to keep the trains rolling. However, his real interest lay in the timber surrounding the area. In the early 1930s, he won a heavy-duty wagon given away at the Pitzelle's Store in Walnut Ridge. This facilitated his being able to haul the cut timber from the woods to sell. In 1937, he put together a sawmill from spare parts, thus beginning the business now known as B. B. Vance & Sons, Inc. The business grew from logging to a lumber yard, then into home building and to its present phase of commercial construction. Located in Sedgwick it expanded to the Jonesboro area in the early 1950s, and moved exclusively to Jonesboro in 1976.

Boss and Elsie's children were all born at Sedgwick: Howard, Mildred, Glenwood "Peck" Merle "Toby" and Maxine "Skeet." Each graduated from high school in Walnut Ridge. This was an important accomplishment to the parents with only grade school educations.

Howard attended Arkansas State College and taught school for several years before joining his dad in the timber business. He lives in Jonesboro and along with his wife remains active in the construction business. He married Wanda Grace Sellars in 1939, and their family consists of Gene, David and Ann.

Mildred graduated from Arkansas State College and taught in the public schools for several years before going back to the college as kindergarten teacher for the training school in 1948. She received her masters degree from Peabody College and her doctorate from the University of Texas. Returning as a professor in early childhood education, she completed her 50th year at Arkansas State University in 1998. Remaining single, she has lived in Sedgwick through the years.

Peck joined the Army Air Corps during World War II and was a German war prisoner after his airplane was shot down. Following the war, he married Charlotte Lamew and they had two children: Sam and Jeanne. He left the family business in the early 1980s, and with his son has Vance Fence Company in Sedgwick.

Toby joined the Army and served in the Pacific Theater in World War II. He married Irene Hutcheson and they had one son, Donnie. Toby managed the Sedgwick lumber yard until his death in 1975.

Skeet graduated from Arkansas State College and taught at the Sedgwick, Bono, and Hoxie schools. She married Russell Scott. Danny and Robyn were their children. Farming was their life until Russell died in 1996, and Skeet in 1997.

Elsie died in 1964, and Boss in 1976. All the deceased members of the Vance family are buried at Jonesboro Memorial Park. –*Mildred Vance.*

W. E. VERKLER JR. FAMILY. John Verkler, 1849-1896, and Ella Waples, 1859-1955, were married March 7, 1878, in Kankakee, Illinois. They had four children, including Waverly Edward Verkler, born April 23, 1881. In the mid 1880s, after the birth of Waverly Edward Verkler, John Verkler moved his family to Marked Tree, Arkansas. His sawmill business was flooded out and he moved to Black Rock, Arkansas, in Lawrence County. Here he started a sawmill business and farmed. John Verkler drowned in Spring River and his body was found 21 days later in Black River. Ella Waples Verkler married W. H. Johnson in 1916.

Waverly Edward Verkler, April 23, 1879-July 12, 1960, married Katie Moore, October 23, 1884-April 2, 1959, on October 5, 1904, at the home of the bride's parents, Moses M. and Sally Smith Moore in Black Rock. They spent their entire married life at Black Rock. He was quite active in farming and saw milling. He operated two boats on the Black River transporting logs for his sawmills. The boats "The Ruby Pearl" and the "The Reda Nell" were named after his two daughters.

Wave Ed and Katie Verkler had seven children: Jewel Thomas Verkler, October 2, 1906; John Morris Verkler, July 3, 1908-April 21, 1975; Ruby Pearl Verkler, February 9, 1910; Waverly Edward Verkler Jr., September 28, 1912-May 15, 1997; Glen Hollis Verkler, November 9, 1917; Lawrence Harold Verkler, February 11, 1923-December 7, 1983; Freda Nell Verkler, April 17, 1926. The only one of the seven children to remain in

Wave Ed Jr. and Imogene Verkler in summer of 1980, near Heber Springs, Arkansas.

Lawrence County throughout his lifetime was Wave Ed Verkler Jr., 1912-1997.

Waverly Edward Verkler Jr. was known to many people in Lawrence County as Wave Ed or W. E. He was married to Imogene Burris, August 8, 1919-November 11, 1982, on January 10, 1936. Wave Ed and Imogene Verkler had eight children: Robert "Bob" Verkler, Charles "Bud" Verkler, Harold Verkler, Darrell Verkler, Waverly Edward "Eddie" Verkler III, Sandra Verkler, Greta Verkler and Mary Verkler.

Wave Ed was involved in many civic organizations, conservation projects and businesses in Lawrence County. As a young man, he negotiated along with W. E. Sr. for the purchase of 750 acres of land along the Black River in the early 1930s. The wooded property was purchased for 1000 dollars and a boxcar load of rough cut oak lumber. It was then cleared and logged with a crosscut saw and day labor at 50 cents a day. He started the first agricultural limestone mill (Verkler Limestone Company) in Arkansas in 1939, on Stinnett Creek. Parts of the old mill are still visible today. Wave Ed owned and operated Verkler Ford Company in Black Rock until 1978. After selling this business to Cavenaugh Ford he started Verkler Supply and it is still operating in Lawrence County today.

Many descendants of Wave Ed and Imogene Verkler make their home in Lawrence County. This includes children, Bud, Darrell and Eddie Verkler, Sandra McGinnis, Greta Mondy, grandchildren, Cindy, Leslie, Mitch and Tiffany Verkler, Dana Jones, Mallory and Dylan McGinnis, Jakie Hanan Jr., Alanna, Alyssa, Elijah and Isaac Mondy, and great-grandchildren, Britney Verkler and Stanton Jones. –*Sandra McGinnis.*

SAM VINES FAMILY. Sam Vines was born 1894, to Lester, Lucindy Vines in Missouri. He was the fourth child. His mother died when he was two. He came to Walnut Ridge, Arkansas in 1908, with his brother, Henry, two sisters, Betty and Alice. He worked in timber for Bob Longmeyer of Clover Bend before going into the Army. He served in France during World War I.

He and Nora Dobbs were married June 24, 1920, at Clover Bend. In time, they had a family of seven children. They were: Walter, Alma, Cleo, Genevee, Thomas, Lee and Wayne.

In later years they moved to Doc Neece farm seven miles out of Alicia, Arkansas. We attended school at Clover Bend and Hopewell. When dad took a load of cotton to the gin, he would bring in groceries and supplies for the kids. Our only transportation was by wagon and horses. Mom shopped from Montgomery Ward catalog therefore, we did not go to town. The Depression broke out in 1929, no jobs, almost no pay for the crops of any kind. Rations were hard to manage so another move was necessary.

Back row: Walter, Alma, Cleo, Sam. Row two: Genevee, Nora, Thomas. Front: Wayne, Lee.

In 1935, dad drew a bonus from the government so they decided to sell our farm and house belongings for that change. Dad bought a 1926 Model T, a large trailer and loaded our necessities and headed west to California. We joined the thousands of the "Tent City" generation in search of a better life, leaving our Dobbs and Vines relatives in Lawrence County. Several of the younger are still there in 1999. We landed in California eight weeks later, due to delays along the way, but we did find ample work and all we children married in California.

In 1941, World War II broke out. Walter served in the Army on the Elginquin Medical Ship, with awards of good services. Cleo served in the infantry in Germany with medals of honor. He was wounded once, came home and was killed in a car wreck one month later in 1946. Lee and Thomas missed the draft, but we all worked in the shipyards to support our soldiers. Our youngest brother, Wayne, joined the Air Force out of high school, served 21 years and retired with high honors of service.

Our parents and siblings are all gone now other than Walter, the oldest and I, Alma, the second oldest. Our dad is in the military cemetery at San Bruno, near San Francisco, California. Other siblings are wherever they lived at the time of their deaths. Dad's sisters, Alice Vines Johnson and Betty Vines Hagar both married, raised their families and died around Minturn, Hoxie and Walnut Ridge. Henry Vines settled in the Delta of Mississippi around 1930-32, where he raised his family and was laid to rest there. God bless our family wherever you are.

–Alma Vines Moore and Francis Herring.

BRYSON WADDELL FAMILY.

Bryson Earnest Waddell was born in South Carolina to George Washington and Sally Peirson Waddell.

He was a twin and the youngest of five children. He lived at Hamil, Eleven Point and Black Rock before moving to Powhatan. He was married to Tola Mae McIlroy on January 2, 1923. They were parents of one daughter, Patsy, who married Victor Clark. They live in Portia and are parents of three daughters and one son.

Bryson Waddell.

Bryson Waddell and family lived many years on Powhatan. He rented the Powhatan jail and for many years operated the Waddell Honey Business with the help of his wife and daughter.

"For Pure Arkansas Honey Bees and Equipment See Bryson Waddell, Powhatan, Arkansas."

Mr. Waddell knew how to make good honey. He knew the bee operation and also the equipment. One could drive through Powhatan and see the hillside by the jail covered with beehives. Honey was shipped out to all parts of the country in barrels. It was common to go in a store and buy a jar of honey with the label "Bryson Waddell Pure Arkansas Honey."

Mr. Waddell was a well known businessman and was a member of the APIARY board. Mr. Waddell was also a fisherman.

–Patsy Waddell.

HENRY BOYD WADDELL FAMILY.

As a young man Henry Boyd Waddell came to Lawrence County in the early 1900s. He was born in Spartanburg, South Carolina, 1873-1924, and grew up there. He was a descendant of Thomas Con and Mary Tucker Waddell. This information was given by Connie Waddell Baird and Cleney Waddell Corbett to niece Edna LaMew.

Thomas Con was the father of 12 children, six sons and six daughters. Henry Boyd was the oldest. Other siblings were: Clyde, Coke, Witt, Guy, Wells, Elizabeth Jarrett, Mary Jane Jarrett, Effie Smith, Lillian Marler, Leona Henry and Anna Broady. Some of their descendants are still living in Lawrence County.

Claude and Ruby Hibbard Waddell with daughters, Edna Lea and Hope.

In the early 1900s, Henry Boyd met and married Edna Estelle Gates, 1885-1935, the daughter of George and Francis Moffett Gates. They were the parents of 10 children whose names all begin with the letter "C": Clyde married Lucille Chastain; Clarence married Lorene Ellison; Claude married Ruby Hibbard; Chester died young; Clo Viola died young; Christine died young; Clara died young; Connie married Thomas E. Baird; Cloyce married Leonard Austin, Ira Bond and Carmack Nelson; and Cleney married Herbert Corbett. All raised their families in Lawrence County.

Henry Boyd and Edna Estelle Gates Waddell.

Henry Boyd was a farmer and raised his children to know how to work hard and to appreciate the necessity of an honest occupation. Edna Estelle, true to her inner convictions, helped to instill in her children a fear of God, and a solid spiritual foundation.

Clarence Waddell served in World War II. He saw combat action in the Philippine Islands. Claude and Ruby Waddell were killed in an automobile accident in 1959. Cleney Corbett is the only one of the 10 children living. She resides at Alicia in Lawrence County.

Grandchildren living in Lawrence County are: Roger and Barbara Cude Waddell; Larry and Loretta Williams Corbett; Stanley and Sherry Smith Corbett; Dwain and Willene Fouts Austin; Joyce and Joe Crawford; Kathleen Baird Hattenhauer; Maydeen Baird Forkum; Billy and Hope Waddell Segraves; Arliss and Edna Lea Waddell LaMew; and Kelly and Joyce Howard Waddell.

Great-grandchildren living in Lawrence County are: David and Cindy Drury Segraves and family; Bobby and Cheryl Davidson Segraves and family; Tommy and Jennifer Waddell and family; Tammie H. Hester and son; Rodney Waddell; Bill and Debbie Corbett Teague and daughter; Danny and Cynthia Simmons Nichols and family; Gene and Charlotte Simmons Wheeless and family; Bryon and Tammy Phillips Simmons and family; Jason Forkum; and Phyllis Crawford. –Edna LaMew.

MINOR HARRIS WALLIS, born November 13, 1858, in Cadiz, Kentucky, died March 18, 1937, in Lawrence County, Arkansas; he is buried Jenkins Cemetery. He arrived in Arkansas in the 1870s or 1880s. He was a farmer and public servant; Clear Lake School Board Member, Justice of the Peace, Judge of Quorum Court. He married Sarah Dosie DeRosett. Their children were: Hartman, Jess, Charley Addison, and daughter, Mary Emma. Hartman married Ethyl Hullett; children, Maurice and Lavonda.

Jess married Lucy Sullivan; children, Mattie Bell, Harry Douglas, Charlotte "Jackie" of Akron, Ohio, and Jessene. Charley Addison married Manie Maggie Jean Hogan of Ravenden Springs, Arkansas; children, Addison Odell, Minor Enoc, William Joseph "Bill" of South Beloit, Illinois, Donnie Evis, Loves Park, Illinois; Waymon Willis of Rockford, Illinois; and Nancy Elizabeth Pinnon of Roscoe, Illinois.

Grandchildren of Donnie Wallis.

Mary Emma married John Henry Patterson of Pocahontas, Arkansas; their children were: Beatrice Launa, John Henry Jr. of Post Falls, Idaho; Wallis Gilbert (killed in action, Vietnam), Athel Caleb of Machesney Park, Illinois; and Sarah Jean of Rockford, Illinois.

Sarah DeRossett Wallis' sisters were Fanny, Betty; brothers Robert, Eugene, John, Newt. John's children Johnny of Hayward, California, Cathrin of Lake Tahoe, California. Newt's children: Hershel (Willie Wilkerson) Lehman (RoseBettis), Williford, Arkansas.

Maggie Jean Wallis brothers were Charley, Joseph; sisters Faye (Jack Edson). Lillie (Joe Collins). Ena (William J. "Jack" Guntharp). Josephine daughter Gwen (Vernon Hepler of Ravenden, Arkansas). –Donnie Wallis.

WARD FAMILY. Reverend Gideon and Mary Ward moved to Greene County before the 1860 census and brought several children with them. Ashley M. Ward was born in 1844, and served in the Civil War from 1862 to 1865. Ashley M. Ward is the grandfather to many Lawrence County residents.

Charley D. Ward's father, Albert E. Ward, was the son of Ashley M. Ward, 1844, and Mary. Mary died early in her life and is buried in the Finch Cemetery in Greene county. Ashley and Mary had Obedia, 1864; Mary A., 1867; Richard, 1869; Albert E., 1874; and Ada B., 1877. Ashley M. Ward married Frances Slatton Burks, born 1862, in Greene County on July 6, 1880. Frances and Ashley had Parker, Dessi, who married Charley Andrews and Amanda, who married Mark Stevens.

Albert E. Ward and Lizzie Etna Ray Ward had three children: Wizner Lee Ward, 1897, married Mable South. Wizner and Mable had three children: Max, Ola and Leatrice. Mary Hazel Ward Binkley, 1903, married Oliver Binkley. Hazel and Oliver had one child, Exie Vera, 1921. She mar-

Ward Family.

ried Jack D. Jones. Charley D. Ward, 1908, married Vedis Segraves. They are all buried in the Lawrence Memorial Cemetery.

Charley's parents were Albert Ezra Ward, 1874, and Lizzie Etna Ray Ward, 1875. Albert and Lizzie were married in 1894. Lizzie was born in Shirefield, Alabama. Albert and Lizzie were divorced and he married Ceily Collins. Albert and Lizzie are buried in the Lawrence Memorial Cemetery.

Albert E. Ward, Wizner Lee Ward and some other men played music. Albert had a band called *A. E. Ward and the PlowBoys.* In 1929, they went to Alabama to make a record. They ran out of money and sold the rights to the record to get the money to come back home. Randy Shawn Jones, the son of Exie and Jack Jones still has a copy of the record. The gift of music and entertainment still flow down the Ward family line through Exie, Lex and Charles Ray's children.

Charles Ray Ward married Joyce Crossno in 1955. They had three children: Steve, 1956; John, 1958; and Brenda, 1961. They moved to Rockford, Illinois, but returned to Arkansas in 1975, and Lawrence County in 1982. Joyce and Ray's son, John, owns B and J's Market on Main Street in Walnut Ridge, and is married to Betty Ward. Steve is married to Peggy Yates. Brenda is married to Robert Shannon. *–Donna Harris.*

CLARENCE WILLIS WARD was born to John and Bettie Ward on March 21, 1899, near Imboden, Arkansas. He lived near Egypt from the time he was a small boy.

Clarence married Virgie Wann, April 22, 1919. Clarence was 20 and Virgie was 17. Clarence farmed in the Egypt area for several years.

Then the family moved to Clover Bend around 1937. They acquired a 40 acre farm and a new house through the New Deal Community Program instituted by President Roosevelt.

Virgie died shortly after moving into their new home. By this time they had five children: Cecil, Helen, Virl, Joe and Evelyn.

Clarence married Dovie Sullens, April 4, 1940. Dovie was a widow with two daughters, Colleen and Mary Lou. Clarence and Dovie then became parents of their own children: Willis Lee, Linda Kay and Ronnie.

Clarence taught a Bible class at the nearby Church of Christ for several years. His son, Joe Ward, tells a humorous story of the family during World War II traveling to church in a car that would

Clarence Ward, Velmar Ward, Dollie Wilson, Dorothy Ward, John Ward.

not start (parts were not to be had during the war) pulled by the tractor driven by Joe.

Grandma Dovie, as all her grandchildren affectionately call her, when asked how Clarence found her over at Grubbs where she was living with her parents, laughed and said she wondered the same thing. She is a very handsome woman and a good cook, and kind to everyone, so it really wasn't must of a mystery.

Clarence died suddenly on August 16, 1952, near Paul's Switch while enroute to Jonesboro to consult a physician for treatment of heart trouble. He was 53 years old. He is buried at Lawrence Memorial Park as is Virgie. Dovie is presently in the Nursing Center at Lawrence Hall in Walnut Ridge. *–Sue Whitmire.*

GEORGE MANSON WARD was born February 5, 1850, to Benjamin F. and Eliza Jane Ward, both of Tennessee. George moved with his family from Mt. Vernon, Illinois, to Sharp County shortly after the Civil War. By that time, his father had died and Eliza had married James Mabry, a widower with children.

George worked as a farm hand for Mary Rhea, widow of John Rhea, in 1870, in Randolph County (Mud Lane, Imboden). George married a daughter, Martha Jane Rhea, November 27, 1870. The couple had two children: John Anderson, February 11, 1876, and America Ellen, September 12, 1871.

George drowned tragically during an overflow, July 5, 1878, while trying to save a calf. He is buried in the Rhea Cemetery on Muddy Road at Imboden (located on the former Herschel Davis farm).

Martha married John Odom. She died shortly after the birth of a daughter, Kate.

The children, John and Ellen, were reared by Charlie Ward, younger brother of George. *–Sue Whitmire.*

JOHN ANDERSON WARD was born February 11, 1876, to George M. and Martha Jane Rhea Ward of Randolph County. Both parents died while young, so John and Ellen were reared by Charlie Ward of Imboden.

John married Mary Elizabeth Wells "Bettie", November 15, 1896, at Old Jackson.

John was farming in the Spring River Township in 1900. By this time, they had two children, Clarence Willis and Dolla M. Velmer came along later.

Bettie died in 1935. John then married Ethel Horton and they had a daughter,

Front, from left: John Ward, Velmer Ward, Mary Elizabeth Ward. Back: Dollie Ward, Clarence Ward.

Dorothy Ward McEntire. John died at Little Rock, November 29, 1956. He was 80 years old. Bettie, John and Ethel are buried at Lawrence Memorial Park, Walnut Ridge. *–Sue Whitmire.*

LEX AND DELLA WARD. Lex V. Ward was married to Della Mae Wilson Ward in 1950. They had eight children: Donna Jean Ward, Baker, Harris, 1951; James Ray, 1952; Richard Sterling, 1955; Oliver Lex, 1956; Nena Leatrice, 1957; Jeffery Lynn, 1963; Jerold Wayne, 1966; Leigh Ann Ward Lewis, 1968.

Lex and Della lived in Walnut Ridge most of their married lives. Della was the daughter of Eph Wilson and Lela Lawhon Wilson. They lived in Rockford, Illinois in 1973, where Della was killed in a car accident. Della is buried in the Lawrence Memorial Cemetery. Lex moved his father, Charley, and mother, Vedis, to Walnut Ridge with his children in 1974. Later, some of Lex and Della's children returned to Illinois.

Donna Jean Ward married Billy Lee Baker Sr. in 1971. They had a son, Billy Lee Baker Jr., 1973. Billy Lee Baker Jr. married Lindy Debow in 1997. Donna later married Paul H. Harris from White County in 1979. They had a daughter, Jessica Paulette Harris, 1980, who is attending Crowley's Ridge College in Paragould. Donna graduated from CRC in Paragould and Harding University in Searcy. She is a special education teacher.

James Ray Ward married Fredia Simmons in 1993. James is the owner of Ward's Body Shop in Walnut Ridge since 1984.

Richard S. "Dick" Ward married Teresa White in Loves Park, Illinois. Rick has a son, Richie, 1974.

Oliver Lex "Olie" Ward served in the Marines. Olie lives in Rockford, Illinois.

Jeffery L. Ward moved to Loves Park, Illinois. Jeffery L. Ward married Jill Hughes in Loves Park, Illinois. They have three children: Ryann, Myles and Tyler.

Nena Leatrice Ward was a certified building inspector and plan reviewer for many years. She received many awards and certificates while working in the building industry. Nena has a son, Shawn Neal Downing, born 1975. Both Nena and Shawn are presently living in Lawrence County.

Jerold Wayne "Jerry" Ward married Leslie Burns from Fort Smith in 1988. They had Alex and Victoria Ward.

Leigh Ann Ward married Kenny Lewis in 1996. Leigh had a daughter, Amy Alexamae, 1991, and Rylee Ward Lewis, 1997.

Lex's parents were Charley D. Ward, 1908, and Vedis Segraves Ward, 1909. They were married in Lawrence County, 1929. Charley and Vedis had four children: Lex Vern Ward, 1931; James Albert Ward, 1933-1980; Charles Ray Ward, 1936; Ellen Ruth Ward Stout, 1939; and a baby girl who died in 1934. Charley and Vedis are buried in the Lawrence Memorial Cemetery.

Vedis' parents were Monroe Segraves and Mary Jane Jacks Segraves, buried in Randolph County. *–Donna Harris.*

Lex Ward and Della Mae Wilson on their wedding day. They were married at the Midway Assembly of God Church. Ceremony was by Brother Rorex, the preacher there at the time.

ROBERT BRYAN AND GAYLA ANN ELLIS WARDEN. Robert Bryan Warden was born April 4, 1954, to Robert F. "Bob" and Edith Sue Bryan Warden of Walnut Ridge, Arkansas. Grandparents are William Cedric and Suebelle Parks Bryan of Hoxie and Harry Clelon and Neva Elizabeth States Warden of Salem, Illinois.

Robert Bryan attended the Walnut Ridge Schools until the ninth grade when he was sent to Castle Heights Military Academy in Lebanon, Tennessee, from which he was graduated in 1972. In 1974 Robert Bryan graduated from the John

A. Gupton School of Mortuary Science of Nashville, Tennessee, and joined the staff of the Bryan Funeral Home in Hoxie, Arkansas. He became the third generation to work in the Bryan Funeral Home. In 1975, he earned his Embalmer and Funeral Director Licenses.

On December 28, 1973, Robert Bryan Warden and Gayla Ann Ellis were united in marriage. Gayla was born to Henry S. and Anna Grace Whaley Ellis on September 16, 1953. Gayla is a 1971 graduate of Walnut Ridge High School and a 1973 graduate of Southern Baptist College. Gayla joined the staff of Bryan Funeral Home in 1974. She earned her Funeral Directors License in 1979.

Robert Bryan and Gayla became managers of the Bryan Funeral Home in 1979, when Bob and Sue Warden retired from the business.

Robert Bryan, Gayla, Amanda and Chris Warden in 1985.

The Warden's children are: Amanda Michelle, born April 3, 1977; and Robert Christopher, born October 13, 1980. Amanda is a licensed EMT with a goal to become a paramedic. Chris will pursue a degree in mortuary science, making him a fourth generation at the Bryan Funeral Home. *–Jackie Cox.*

ROBERT "BOB" FRANCIS AND EDITH SUE BRYAN WARDEN.

Robert "Bob" Francis Warden moved from Salem, Illinois to Walnut Ridge as a newlywed. Bob met Edith Sue Bryan while attending Arkansas State College on a football scholarship in 1949. Bob, the first of three children born to Harry Clelon and Neva Elizabeth States Warden of Salem, Illinois, was born March 9, 1930. Edith Sue Bryan Warden, daughter of William Cedric and Suebelle Parks Bryan of Hoxie, Arkansas, was born November 28, 1931. The couple were united in marriage on July 4, 1950.

After marriage, Bob joined the staff of the Bryan Funeral Home while Edith Sue worked as a telephone operator. On January 16, 1952, Jacqueline Sue Warden was born. On April 4, 1954, Robert Bryan was born. The family moved in 1955, to Dallas, Texas, where Bob and Sue attended the Dallas Institute of Mortuary Science.

Bob and Sue Warden, 1975.

After graduation, the Wardens earned their embalmer and funeral director licenses from the Arkansas State Board of Embalmers & Funeral Directors in 1957. Bob and Sue returned to Hoxie to work in the family's business, the Bryan Funeral Home.

On August 14, 1970, Jackie married J. R. Cox of Walnut Ridge. Their children are: Matthew Blake, Brett Aaron, Blair Suzanne and Britni Sa-

Wedding Day, July 4, 1950, of Bob and Sue Bryan Warden (center) Neva and Harry Warden (left) and Suebelle and W. C. Bryan (right).

rah Cox. Their grandchildren are: Matthew Garrett Cox, Courtney Blake Cox, Madison Grace Cox and Caleb Bryan Cox.

On December 28, 1973, Robert Bryan married Gayla Ann Ellis of Walnut Ridge. Their children are Amanda Michelle and Robert Christopher.

In 1974, Robert Bryan and Gayla Warden joined the staff of the Bryan Funeral Home. Later in that same year, Mr. and Mrs. W. C. Bryan retired, leaving the business to Bob and Sue Warden. In 1992, Bob and Sue retired and the funeral service was turned over to Robert Bryan and Gayla Warden. During their retirement, Bob and Sue enjoyed traveling the world together in their RV and by plane. They were members of the First Baptist Church, Walnut Ridge. Edith Sue Warden died May 19, 1998. *–Jackie Cox.*

WARE HISTORY. In 1817, before Arkansas became a territory, Joseph Ware and Martha McKnight married in Lawrence County. Their home was in the area which later became Sharp County. Joseph was born May 12, 1792, in Greenville, South Carolina, to Samuel and Sally Ware. His father fought with the Illinois Regiment to protect St. Louis during the War of 1812. Samuel's father was William Ware of Chester County, South Carolina, around 1735-40. Martha was born January 22, 1796, in Spartanburg, South Carolina. Her parents were William M. and Nancy Thompson McKnight. Her father was born in Rowan County, North Carolina, in 1761. Known as an "Indian Fighter," he was also a Minute Man in the Revolutionary War, fighting in the battles of Musgrove's Mill and King's Mountain.

Joseph Ware died December 4, 1833; Martha died September 12, 1863. They are buried in the Ware Cemetery, Sharp County. Their children were Charles, William, Sallie, Erastus, James, Asa Park, Parker Seudecar, Nancy Jane and Mary Ann.

Charles married Susan Bandy. Their children were Margaret Campbell, Joseph, Nancy Jane Roe, Albert, Wilson, William, Ann, Charlie, Susan McLain and Martha Craig. Sallie married Abraham Peed. Parker married Elizabeth McLain (children: George, Vallie, Stacy). Nancy Jane married James Barnett

Asa Park and Elender Cartwright Ware, around 1890. They treasured "The Book."

(children: Sarah Frances, America Elizabeth, Elvira and Mag).

Asa married Elender Cartwright (children: Sarah Ellen, Mary Jane, William, Joseph, Reuben, Martha Josephine O'Neal, Margaret Louise Hazeltine Nichols and Susan Angeline Pilkenton.

Asa and Elender moved to Aurora, Missouri, in the early 1900s. He lived June 22, 1828-September 1, 1903. She lived March 1, 1829-July 19, 1912. They are buried in Zion Cemetery, Lawrence County, Missouri.

Sarah Ellen Ware married Granville King. Among their descendants were twin sons, Oscar and Roscoe, twin grandsons, and twin great-grandsons. Other children were Melar McGinnis, Margaret McGinnis, Fred, Alven, Ester Hutchinson and Asa Washington (known as Bob).

The Ware name is not heard as frequently as it was in early days. Many Ware descendants, like their forefathers, moved to new areas. However, numerous kin remain. Among them are the progeny of Sarah Ware King's twin sons. Oscar married Laura Lurie Milligan, another very early pioneer family. Some of their local descendants are Orelia Butler, Michele King, Lowell King of Cave City and Lowell's children and grandchildren. Roscoe married Alberta Louvenia "Bertie" Mobley, also related to some early pioneer families, including the Barnetts and Smiths. Roscoe and Bertie's children were Everette, Ellis, Lamon and Lorene Christenberry. Interestingly, Everette moved to North Carolina, full circle to the state of his great-great-great-great-grandfather, William Ware of the mid 1700s. Mrs. Christenberry and her daughter, Mrs. Henry (Carolyn) Gipson; Ellis' widow, Junia Thompson King and her daughter, Mrs. Stephen (Geneva) Emerson; Lamon's widow Ethel Allen King and her son, Mack, and daughter, Mrs. Alton (Dorothy) Cooper, all live on land adjoining Granville and Sarah Ware King's old homestead. Some of the local Ware descendants can point out the locations where the molasses mill and sawmill were operated and where Indians apparently once ran a thriving arrowhead-making operation. *–Geneva Emerson.*

WARNER, MAGNESS, CAZORT, HOLLOWAY HISTORY.

Thomas Jefferson Warner was born in Potosi, Washington County, Missouri, on January 6, 1820. He was one of eight children born to Stephen Warner and Ediann Cummins Warner. He and his sister, Jemina Warner Smith, and her husband, William C. Smith, settled in Lawrence County, Arkansas about 1841.

On September 9, 1843, he married Sarah Richardson, the daughter of Lambert Richardson and Nancy Beasley Richardson. Two daughters were born to this marriage: Nancy Jane on November 2, 1844, and Ediann in 1846. Sarah died in 1847, leaving him with the care of two young children. On May 2, 1851, he married Columbia Ann Lively, a widow with a small daughter, Elizabeth. Thomas and Columbia had two children: Mary Frances "Mollie", born January 24, 1856, and John Stephen, born July 16, 1863.

Elizabeth Lively married Will Perry; Nancy Jane Warner married Josiah Stephen Magness on February 10, 1872; Ediann married Charles F. Page on March 2, 1861; Mary Frances married Dr. James W. Coffman on February 20, 1876; and John Stephen Warner married Martha Elliot on December 17, 1883.

Thomas J. Warner was a carpenter and served his community and state in various ways. From 1850 through 1852, he was coroner of Lawrence County. In 1860, he captured a murderer, Daniel Hettibram, and in 1861, he volunteered to serve in the Civil War and served as a captain in Shaver's Seventh Arkansas Confederate Infantry, along with his

Family on left: Joseph Waldron, his wife, Annie and children, Annie and Clifford. Family on right: Watkins Lee Holloway, his wife, Eudora and children, Rupert and Frances. Seated: Annie Cazort Holloway and Harriet Cazort Propst. Photo taken in early 1905.

Picture taken approximately 1914. Bottom row, left to right: Ruth Warner, Edna Addie Warner, Daisy Warner, Gladys Warner and John W. Warner. Second row: Roy Warner, Andrew Jackson Warner, Jesse Lee Warner. Top row: Ora Alice Tyler Warner and Lester Warner.

BILLY JOE WARREN.

The marriage of Billy Joe Warren and Rebecca Inman, daughter of Daisy Shaver of Palestine, Arkansas, and Alvin Inman of the Ingram Community in Randolph County, Arkansas, on January 5, 1949, was the beginning of the Billy Joe Warren family.

Their children are: Danny, his wife Karen and two sons, Jacob and Joshua. Brenda, unmarried; Garry and his daughter, Jennifer, her husband Michael Henson and their three children: Dalton, Cheyenne and Jade. Billy, his wife Vivian Mitchell, two children Billy and Amanda; Patricia, unmarried; and Doris, unmarried.

Billy Joe and Rebecca Priscilla Inman Warren.

The Warren family has many ties to Lawrence County. Billy Joe was born in Hoxie on February 6, 1930, to Dock Warren and Pauline Hibbard. Dock Warren's parents were Thomas and Mary Frances Ginger Warner. Pauline's parents were John and Emmadee McMillion. All were long time residents of Lawrence County.

Billy and Rebecca Warren and Danny who was born in Sedgwick on December 29, 1950, left Arkansas in 1954, to reside in Chicago, Illinois, for the next 18 years. Brenda Joyce was born on June 28, 1955. Garry Lee was born on September 5, 1956, Billy Dale was born in Walnut Ridge at Dr. Elder's clinic on October 11, 1957; Patricia Kay was born April 8, 1959, and Doris Ann on November 22, 1961.

The family returned to Arkansas to reside in Hoxie where Mr. Warren operated the Gulf Station and Garage on Texas Street for many years.

All the children with the exception of Danny attended the Hoxie Schools. Brenda attended Crowley's Ridge College in Paragould and Patricia attended Williams Baptist College, which was then Southern Baptist College.

The Warren family's church ties include the Landmark Missionary Baptist Church in Portia, Arkansas. *–Brenda Warren.*

brother, William W. Warner, who was a member of the Drum and Fife Corps of the same unit. After a year of service, he resigned and served in the House of Representatives in Little Rock. After the war he returned to Lawrence County and served as justice of the peace. In the words of his granddaughter, Eudora Magness Holloway, "He was English, tall, medium weight, blue eyes, jolly and full of jokes and fun." His favorite song was "Pass Me Not Oh Gentle Savior." After the death of his wife, Columbia, he lived with his daughter, Nancy Jane, and her husband, Josiah Magness, until his death in the late 1890s.

Nancy Jane Warner and Josiah Magness raised a family of four daughters: Ida Bell, Eudora Etta, Ora May and Stella Rose. Ida and Ora never married. They owned a millinery shop in Black Rock and were mentioned in *Fortune 500* in the early 1900s. Eudora married

Captain Thomas Jefferson Warner and his brother, Private William W. Warner, taken during Civil War when they served as Confederate soldiers in Shaver's Seventh Arkansas Infantry.

Watkins Lee "Boy" Holloway on October 13, 1898, in the Presbyterian Church in Black Rock. Stella married Oscar Otis "Frank" Eudally.

Watkins Lee "Boy" Holloway was the son of Stephen Powers Holloway and Almedia Ann "Annie" Cazort, daughter of Anthony Cazort and Mary Ann Thomason Cazort. The Cazorts arrived in Lawrence County in 1850, with a group of about 50 families from Rowan County, North Carolina. Watkins Lee Holloway and Eudora raised a family of eight children: Rupert, Frances, Alma, Oscar, Ida Mae, Joseph, Imogene and Nancy.

Watkins Lee's sister, Annie Elizabeth Holloway, married Joseph E. "Jody" Waldron, son of William Henry Waldron and Mary M. Cook, on January 4, 1899. "Jody" and Annie Waldron's four surviving children were: Annie, Dewitt, Eula and Richard Lee "Bud." *–Alma Duty.*

ANDREW JACKSON WARNER FAMILY.

In 1900 or 1901, Andrew and Ora Tyler Warner came to Lawrence County. This young couple with their three sons: Roy, Lester and Jess, settled in farming country southeast of Hoxie.

They left parents and siblings in Vichy, Missouri. Both of Andrew's parents, Andrew A. and Charlotte Henry Warner, were German. There, Andrew J. had been a school teacher and a farmer.

The Warner's eight children that were born after moving here were: Addie, John, Gladys, Ruth, Daisy, Ralph, Ray and Lawrence. One of the children, Ralph, died as a baby. The other 10 grew up and raised families and for the most part they lived in Lawrence County. Their oldest son, Roy, married Arah Jackson. Roy and Arah had four children: Fern, Mildred, Vera and Leroy. Roy farmed his entire life and died at age 49 in 1944. Lester married Marie Wilson and their children were: Esther, Leonard, Yvonne, Raymond, Chester, John and Charlie Ray. Chester and John were twins. John died at birth. Jess married Florence Clark and they had two children: Virginia and Orville Lee. After Florence's death, Jess married Thelma Holloway and their children were: Betty, Joe, Drucilla, Helen, Melvin, Joyce and Glen. Addie married Sidney Parsons. Their children were: Charles, Chester, Beatrice, Mable, Mary, Alice, Ray, Sidney, Cheley, John and Patsy. John married Velma Murphey and their children were: Irene, Delois and John Jr. John was an Assembly of God minister for over 50 years. Gladys, their next child, married Lonel Fry, who was also an Assembly of God minister for more than 50 years. They were parents of 10 children: Lorine, Lavada, Ruby, Luczene, Shelby, Nina, Norma, Benny, Gerldine and Laurence. Lavada died at nine months of age. Laurence, Shelby, Ruby and Lorine have all died in the last six years. Ruth married Harvey Ivins, who was a minister with Church of God of Prophecy. He pastored in Canada several years. Their children were: Arthur, Daniel, Christine, Freida, Louella, Flora, Bonnie, Joyce and David. Arthur died in an accident at age seven. The next child was Daisy, who married Boyce "Toots" Burns. Their children were: Daphine, Bobby, Willis and Marvin. The Burns operated a grocery store in Walnut Ridge in the 1950s and 1960s. Ray married Lucy Binkley. Their children are: Shirley and Jerry. Lawrence married Daphine Floyd and they had one child, Billy. After Daphine's death, Lawrence married Ruth Cook. Their children are: Wendell, Laney and Tonda. Ray and Lawrence are the only two siblings of the Warner family that are still living.

The Warner family all attended church at Midway Assembly of God Church, where Ora was a charter member. Although Andrew never joined the church, he took his family and sat outside with several other men. He apparently thought his wife had enough religion for the both of them. However, shortly after Ora's death, Andrew became a Christian. *–Geraldine Brewer.*

DANNY WAYNE WARREN,

the son of Billy Joe and Rebecca Priscilla Inman Warren of Hoxie in Lawrence County, Arkansas, was born at Sedgwick, Arkansas, on December 29, 1951, having six sisters and three brothers; a set of twin girls, a girl and one boy died in infancy. The surviving children are: Danny Wayne, 1950; Brenda Joyce, 1955; Garry Lee, 1956; Billy Dale, 1957; Patricia Kay, 1959; and Doris Ann, 1961.

Having been raised in Chicago, Illinois, Danny moved to Hoxie, Arkansas, in 1974. His occupation was construction and stone work.

Danny Warner, Karen Pirtle Warren.

He wed Karen Roy Pirtle on June 21, 1981, in Hoxie, Arkansas, in a garden wedding performed by Betty Johnson.

Karen was born June 17, 1955, to Thelma and Doyle Pirtle.

Karen and Danny had two children: Jacob Richard Nathaniel, 1982; and Joshua Adam, 1985.

They remain in Hoxie making it their home with both children attending the Hoxie school system. –Brenda Warren.

DOCK WARREN, son of Thomas H. Warren and Mary Frances Ginger, was born April 8, 1893, in Fulton, Arkansas. He wed Pauline Hibbard, daughter of John E. Hibbard and Emmadee McMillion, long time residents of Lawrence County.

Dock had moved to Hoxie, Arkansas, in 1929. Later he resided in Marked Tree and Paragould, but returned to Hoxie in his later years to remain until his death in 1975.

Dock wed Pauline Hibbard on December 18, 1922, in Hoxie, Arkansas. They had five children, with a son dying at birth. The surviving children were: Mary Frances, 1923-1972; Vera Juanita, 1925-1980; Billy Joe, 1930, wed Rebecca Pirtle Inman; Barbara Ellen, 1938; and Infant son, 1944-1944.

Dock was a commercial fisherman and farmer. –Brenda Warren.

MARGARET CONNELL MCCARROLL WATSON. "Margaret" Connell McCarroll was born March 27, 1910, in Walnut Ridge, Arkansas to Dr. Horace Rudolph "Dolph" and Pearl Henry McCarroll. After graduating from Ouachita Baptist University in 1930, she attended the Sorbonne University in Paris, France, but the great depression made it impossible for her to continue studying abroad. She taught mathematics in Arkadelphia, Arkansas; mathematics and English in Walnut Ridge, Arkansas, and from January 1, 1937, through May of 1972, she taught mathematics at Pine Bluff High School. She served as Chairman of the Mathematics Department from September, 1959, through, May, 1972. She estimates that she taught over 7000 students during this time. In the meantime, she studied under a National Science Foundation Scholarship at Vanderbilt University and Auburn University in Alabama, where she completed her Master's degree. She was married in San Antonio, Texas, on June 13, 1937, to Richard Brinsley "Scrubby" Watson, who was born in Monroe, Louisiana, on July 13, 1897, and who died in Pine Bluff, Arkansas, on February 5, 1975. His father, Earnest William Watson, named him for a relative, Richard Brinsley Sheridan, 1751-1861, an Irish dramatist and orator. "Scrubby" was well known as director of the Pine Bluff High School Band, which received many awards under his leadership. His greatest honor was being selected for membership in the prestigious organization of the American Bandmasters Association. They had no children, but Scrubby had one daughter, Mildred Watson, from a former marriage. –Margaret McCarroll Watson.

WATTS FAMILY. The genealogy of the Watts family is far from complete. Family tradition has E. Manual Watts married to Nancy Oborne living in Missouri before relocating to Lawrence County. Their children were: W. W., born September 20, 1876; Dorthula Emmaline, born March 23, 1881; Albert, born 1884; Manuel Edward, born February 14, 1886; and Jessie M., born March 18, 1889.

Dorthula Emmaline Watts married Aaron Conrad Huffman and they had the following children: William Henry Huffman, born March 5, 1896; Lizetta Huffman, born April 4, 1896; Bertha Linda Huffman, born October 16, 1901; Wilma Isophene Huffman, born September 3, 1904; Charlie Shelton Huffman, born January 31, 1909; Berlie Leona Huffman, born September 13, 1914; Dovie Elizabeth Huffman, born September 25, 1917; and Hazel Juanita Huffman, born December 18, 1922. –Leta Owens.

BEN AND LOUISA WATTS FAMILY. Times were uncertain preceding the War Between the States and many families had to make hard choices concerning their loved ones and their safety. Thus, was it for Ben and Louisa Watts of Chestnut Grove, Tennessee. Ben was a farmer, but after a dispute with the landlord over the crops. Ben asked the man to buy his half of the crops, but the landlord told Ben that he would receive nothing as he would be conscripted into the Army and would not be there to harvest the crops anyway! The family loaded their belongings onto a wagon and started their journey. When they had traveled only a short distance, Ben told them he had forgotten something and must return, but would catch up with them later. Ben reportedly returned to the homestead and set fire to the house and all his crops to insure the landlord did not profit from his family's hard work!

The family moved to Southeast Missouri, back into Tennessee, then migrated to Lawrence County, Arkansas. By 1880, the family consisting of Ben, age 55, Louisa, age 43, Wilson, age 23, Thomas, age 19, George, age 18, Willie, female age 16, Martha, age 13, and Tennessee, age 11, were living in Spring River Township near the Friendship Community. Next door to the family, William, age 26, was living with his wife, Cynthia, age 27, and their four year old son, Newton Rector. Also in this household was Mary Burke, probably Cynthia's sister. According to a deed found in the Lawrence County Courthouse, Ben, William and a Board of Directors were instrumental in getting the land and helping to establish the Methodist Church South at Friendship. William was a farmer. He was loved and respected by many and affectionately called "Uncle Billy."

George married and had several children: Minnie, Lillian, Charley, Pete and Birdie. George was a horse trader and a fine fiddle player. He played at many country dances.

Wilson migrated to Texas and the family contact was lost. Martha married a Mr. Phillips of Lawrence County.

Thomas was a farmer and an avid hunter. This love to hunt drew him keeper into the hills to settle at Opposition. He married Martha Stuart Ball, widow of Thomas Ball. Martha and Mr. Ball had four children: Thomas Buster, Ludie Electes, Donna and Dalferson. Martha and Thomas Watts had six children: Hector Wan, Willie Myrtle, Benonia, Zeruiah, Sloan Fergus and Zachry. These were large families and all had to work together to survive.

Tennessee married John Bottoms on July 27, 1884. They lived and raised their family in the Portia area. She was known to all of us as "Aunt Tennie."

The Watts were a proud and hard working family. Many descendants live in Lawrence County today. –Carolyn Lawrence.

THOMAS WATTS FAMILY OF OPPOSITION Turbulent times preceding the Civil War made Ben and Louisa Watts of Chestnut Grove, Tennessee, pack their family and belongings onto a wagon to search for a less threatening place to live. One account of their leaving has Ben as a fugitive after a dispute with the landowner over crops and ending with the home place and crops being burned.

The family lived in Southeast Missouri, then Tennessee, and finally migrated to Lawrence County, Arkansas. In 1880, Ben, Louisa and their children, William, Wilson, Thomas, George, Willie, Martha and Tennessee, were living in Spring River Township south of Ravenden near the Friendship Community. Ben and Louisa died and are buried there.

Thomas Jefferson Watts was born July 28, 1861, in Missouri and died June 7, 1946, at Opposition. He was a farmer and an avid hunter. This love for hunting drew him to the hills. He homesteaded many acres of land overlooking Spring River. Today on the south side of the river are rock bluffs that carry the name "Watts Bluff."

Thomas married Martha Anne Celinda Catherine Stuart Ball, commonly called "Sissy." Martha was the widow of Thomas W. Ball. Her parents were Albert Gladstone Stuart and Emma Electa Sloan. Her maternal grandparents were Fergus and Rosanna Ruggles Sloan, illustrious citizens of the past. Martha and Thomas Ball had four children: Thomas Buster Ball, Ludia Electes Anderson, Donnie Ball Gray and Dalferson Ball.

Thomas Jefferson Watts on his 82nd birthday in 1942, at Opposition, Arkansas.

Thomas Watts and Martha had six children: Hector Wan, born 1885, married Winnie Halstead and had no children; Willie Myrtle, born 1886, never married and made her home with her sister, Zeruiah; Benonia "Bud", born 1888, married Essie Graves, whose mother, Hattie Ball, was a sister to Thomas W. Ball, and had six daughters: Opal Lawrence Swetnam, Ola Bragg, Bessie Lawrence, Florence Clements Offerman, Marvine Turnbow and Martha Hughes. All but Marvine either live in or have descendants in the Ravenden area today.

The fourth child of Thomas and Martha Watts was Zachry Haynes, born 1892. He was named after a relative and hero of the Civil War. Zack never married and lived on the family farm until his death. Sloan Ferguson Watts, born 1896, lived in Opposition, Ravenden, and Aurora, Illinois. He married Lola Holder and had four children: Glen, Gene, Virginia and James. Margaret Zeruiah "Rue", their last child, born 1898, married John L. Stoll of Benson, Illinois. He had bought land in Arkansas in 1917, and moved to Lawrence County after World War I. They had a son, John Thomas, an instructor for Sloan-Hendrix at Imboden, who married Elaine Burkhammer and raised his family and still lives at Ravenden today. –Carolyn Lawrence.

NEVIL WAYLAND. Nevil Wayland was born 1790, in Virginia. He married and had seven children: Sarah married Miller; Rebecca, born 1805, married William Raney. William and Rebecca are in household 562 in 1850 the census with three children: Thomas, 1835, Benjamin, 1837, and Margaret, 1845. Henry, born 1808; Jarret, born 1813, married Rhoda, and died 1865, in Lawrence County. They are in household 641 in 1850, Lawrence County with two children and household 1312 in 1860 with four children: George, 1836, William, 1845, Stephen Edward, 1852, Absalom, 1854, and Thomas Jefferson, 1857. Mary "Polly", born 1814, married March 5, 1835, Joseph Childers, their children are: Mary, 1855, and Sarah, 1856. Jonathan, born 1815, married

1846, Emma Ann Eddy, died 1885. They are in household 639 in 1850 with Francis Marion, born October 7, 1846, and Elisha Theodore, born November, 1847. Francis married Sarah Matthews; Elisha married Mary Alice Matthews and Mary Taylor Morris. Lucinda, born 1820, married before 1837, William Manson and had Sinclair, born in 1838. William Manson had been married before to Elizabeth Crabtree and had Rosetta, born 1836, who married Robert Forrester, stepbrother to Lucinda, September 30, 1852. William died October 28, 1839, and Lucinda married Thomas Wells. They are in household 657 in 1850 with five children: Candair, 1840, Mary, 1842, Thomas N., 1845, Louisa J., 1847, and Lucinda, 1849. They have Emily, 1851, and Andrew Turner, 1856, and Thomas died October 19, 1856, and Lucinda was again a widow. Nevil married Permelia Forrester, September 3, 1837. He died between 1840 and 1850, because Permelia was a widow by 1850. –*Mary Ann Carter.*

WEIR. Both James Adam Weir, 1819-1896, and his wife, Sarah Elizabeth Sloan Weir, 1820-1885, were born, reared, educated and married in Iredell County, North Carolina. They brought their three year old twins to Randolph County in 1845, nine years after Arkansas became a state; they settled near Imboden in 1846. They had seven other children, the first of numerous descendants who would become respected citizens of the county - educators and churchmen, businessmen and merchants, farmers and landowners.

A minister, Mr. Weir was well educated and was a Greek and Latin scholar. He taught one of the county's first subscription schools at Hopewell and helped establish the Hopewell Methodist Church.

James and Sarah Elizabeth's nine children included the North Carolina born twins sons, John Hamilton Sloan and James William McKnight; a second set of twins, George F. and Julia A.; then Sarah L. Jane, Mary Emiline, Robert S., Burett S. and one who died a young man.

James Adam Weir, patriarch of the Lawrence County Weirs.

Sarah E. died at age 65 and James at age 77. Both are buried in Holobaugh Cemetery. Many of the Lawrence County Weirs are descendants of John Hamilton Sloan Weir. –*Francis Green.*

ALVIN WEIR FAMILY. Alvin, the seventh son of Charles Burette and Zillah Rainwater Weir's nine children, and his wife, Blanche Fender, lived on a farm in the Fender area. They had three children, Anthony, Thomas and Andrea, all Walnut Ridge High School graduates. Alvin farmed and for a time operated a grocery store at Fender. Years after Blanche's death, Alvin married Virginia Collar of Walnut Ridge.

Tony, 1941-1997, married Gail Wilson of Hoxie. They lived in Walnut Ridge and had two boys, Allen and Lance, who both graduated from Walnut Ridge. Allen and his wife, Martha, own a sporting goods store in Walnut Ridge, and have three sons. Lance lives with his mother in Hoxie. Tony and his second wife, Brenda, lived near Paragould.

Tommy and his family live in Atlanta. His son, Chris, lives in Dallas. Ann married Frank Schwandegger. They have two sons, Seth and Aaron, and live in Omaha, Nebraska. –*Frances Green.*

BURETTE WEIR FAMILY. Charles Burette Weir, born September 7, 1878, son of John Hamilton Sloan and Thersa Jane Moore Weir of Imboden, married Zillah Rainwater, born October 19, 1878, youngest daughter of Riley and Nancy Rainwater, who lived on a farm near Smithville. Zillah described the early days of their 62 year marriage as the lifestyle of "gypsies." "We moved every time the weather changed," she would say. Oft-quoted as having had a baby in every house between Black Rock and Imboden, except the school and the church, she had nine children between 1898 and 1924.

Both Burette and Zillah grew up in western Lawrence County with parents who were devout churchgoers, farmers and landowners, good citizens active in their local schools and politics. They lived as their models had, greatly influencing their children and grandchildren. After Burette retired, they lived in Hoxie approximately 30 years before his death in 1959. Zillah died in 1980. Both are buried in Lawrence Memorial Park.

Their nine children grew up on both sides of Black River. Most married county residents and started families in the county, living their entire lives here. Fewer than 20 of their 150-plus descendants are county residents today. Only five grandchildren of the nine now live in the county.

The oldest, Jewel Weir, 1898-1987, married Naomi Crouch, 1904-1994. They reared five children: Earlene, Louise, Norma, Charles and Madelyn, in Pocahontas. He was a carpenter.

The second child was Virgie, 1901-1997, who lived almost her entire life in the county. She married Jewel Courtney and had four children. One of them, Jewel Snapp, and her family remained in the county.

Charles Burette and Zillah Rainwater Weir.

Taylor Weir died at age 14, and is buried at Holobaugh Cemetery.

Ina Weir, 1908-1987, married Clarence Poe. They lived in Hoxie and then in Elwood, Indiana. Their children are Alleta, born 1927, and Shirley, born 1935, both Hoxie graduates, and Linda, born 1941, and Harold, born 1943.

Cleo Weir, 1911-1969, married Evelyn Finger of Mississippi. They had two sons, Simon, born 1937, and Sammy, born 1941, both graduates of Walnut Ridge High School where Sammy was an outstanding football player. Cleo was co-owner of the Red and White Store in Walnut Ridge.

Sloan Weir, born 1913, married Rubye Teel and they reared six surviving children of eight: Charles, Cameron, Bonnie, Frances, Ruth Anne and Riley. Four live in the county.

Alvin and wife, Blanche Fender, lived on a farm in the Fender Community. They had three children: Anthony, 1941-1997, Thomas and Andrea, all Walnut Ridge High School graduates. Alvin later married Virginia Collar of Walnut Ridge.

Morris, born 1918, was a 1938 graduate of HHS and died two years later of meningitis.

Clarence Burette "Jack", 1924-1970, served in the United States Navy before marrying Myrtle Ivins of Hoxie. They moved to Rock Falls, Illinois, where they raised five sons, Corwin, Keenan, Malcolm, Greg and Kurt.

Lasting tributes in the Hoxie United Methodist Church attest today to the lives of Burette and Zillah Weir - the birch pulpit dedicated to his memory in 1961, and the pulpit Bible purchased in her memory in 1981. They are visible reminders of the faith and faithfulness of two highly revered Lawrence County citizens. –*Frances Green.*

JOHN HAMILTON SLOAN WEIR and his twin were born in North Carolina in 1842, the first of nine children. They came west to Arkansas in 1845, with their parents, James Adam and Sarah Elizabeth Sloan Wier. As a boy, J. H. Sloan worked on the family farm; then he enlisted in the Confederate Army in 1862, at age 20, and fought in battles within the state and was discharged in 1865. He signed the Oath of Amnesty in Magnolia and walked back to his Imboden home.

In 1868, J. H. Sloan married Thersa Jane Moore, daughter of Robert W. Moore, who came to Arkansas from Tennessee with his parents. They had nine children. One died in infancy, and a son, Taylor, died at age four. Of the other seven, two sons and two daughters married Rainwater brothers and sisters, all children of Riley G. Rainwater. These unions produced 45 offspring - 38 of them "double cousins" - many of whom stayed in the county to work and raise families. Remnants of these families remain in the county today. (See the other Weir and Rainwater stories in this book.)

Sloan and Thersa's oldest child, Margaret "Betty", married Henry Rainwater and bore 11 children: R. S., Bertha, Orville, Terry, Juddy, Elmer, Nell, Clifford, Luther, Vera and Opal. Af-

John Hamilton Sloan and Thursa Jane Moore Weir.

ter farming near Wayland Spring for 18 years, they moved to Imboden to be near school, and then to Hoxie in 1919.

Robert S. married Mary Rainwater. They lived on a farm near Imboden and were the parents of nine: Madge, Eula, Lillye, Nettie, Lou, Elbert, Cecil, Lora and Nancy.

Mary Louise "Lou" married Hugh Rainwater. They lived in Imboden. Of their nine children, the second, Ina, and the sixth, Harry, died as babies. Others were: Alva "A.W.", Everett, Vida, Ida, Louise, Robert and Mary.

Burette married Zillah Rainwater. They had nine children: Jewel, Virgie, Taylor, who died at 14, Ina, Cleo, Sloan, Alvin, Morris, who died at 22, and Clarence B. "Jack."

The two younger sons of J. H. Sloan, Mose and Clay, both merchants in Hoxie married Hudson sisters, Fannie and Laura. The youngest daughter, Laura, 1886-1983, married Andrew McCarroll. They had no children.

Mose, 1880-1969, and Fannie had four children. Dolphus and Mary Jane died in infancy. Clara, 1909-1989, and Nell, 1914-1960, were both teachers in the Hoxie and Walnut Ridge schools.

Both highly regarded, Clara was known statewide as an excellent choral director, and Nell was a home economics teacher, despite blindness in her last years.

Clay, 1884-1952, and Laura, 1884-1978, were married in 1905, and had three children. The oldest, Butler, 1906-1968, a postal employee in Hoxie and later in California, married Edna Rose Flavin, a teacher, and they had a son, Phillip, born 1948, who lives in Little Rock.

Marie, 1909-1943, married Herbert Keller, a United States engineer, and they lived in Hoxie. They had no children.

Clay Jr., 1915-1998, and Helen Neece, born 1921, married in 1943. As a young man, Clay worked in his father's Red and White Store, served in the United States Navy during World War II and later was manager of the Arkansas Employment Security Division for Lawrence and Randolph Counties. Helen taught school 37 years at Hoxie, retiring in 1980. They had three children. The first, Clay Weir III, born 1946, lived only three months. A daughter, Sarah Marie, born 1950, and a son, John Hamilton, born 1952, graduated from Hoxie. Sarah, a teacher, married Jack Frost in 1973, and they live in Conway. Their children are Allen, born 1982, and Kate, born 1984. John married Cathie Gilkes in 1989. They live in Harrison, where he is an investment broker and she is a music teacher. –Francis Weir.

ROB AND MARY WEIR FAMILY.
Mary West Rainwater, 1874-1943, and Robert Sloan "Rob" Weir, 1872-1943, both born in Imboden, were married in 1892. She was the daughter of Riley G. and Nancy Rainwater, and he was the son of J. H. Sloan and Thursa Jane Weir, all of western Lawrence County. They are one of four pairings of Weir and Rainwater siblings.

Rob and Mary lived near Imboden all 51 years they were married, mostly on the "Weir Farm" in a two part house with a dogtrot. The house had a large cellar under the kitchen floor and a cistern in the backyard. The living room with large fireplace was on the left side, and the right side was a parlor, often used by the nine children for courting. Both sides and a lean-to at the back served as sleeping quarters. Rob was a farmer. Like so many Weir and Rainwater relatives, they were Methodists.

They are the parents of seven sons and two daughters who gave them more than 50 grandchildren. The only child of Rob and Mary Weir still living is Lora Weir Cude of Black Rock.

The children and their spouses were Madge, 1894-1979, and Childress Moore, three children (one died); Eula, 1869-1968, and Owen Winchester, 10 children (three died); Lillye, 1897-1988, and

Lawrence Spotts, one son; Nettie, 1899-1988, and Roy Stewart, four children; Lou, 1901-1988, and Virgil VanHorn, two children; Elbert, 1904-1989, and Easter Pettyjohn, one adopted child; Cecil, 1907-1990, and Louis Beach, two daughters; Lora, born 1909, and Dee Cude, four children; and Nancy, 1912-1998, and Flynn Justus, no children.

A number of these descendants remain in the area, some fourth or fifth generation Lawrence Countians. –Frances Green.

SLOAN WEIR FAMILY.
Riley Sloan Weir was born August 9, 1913, in Imboden, the sixth child of Charles Burette and Zillah Rainwater Weir. Proud of inheriting the names of both of his pioneer grandfathers, John Hamilton Sloan Weir and Riley Gilmore Rainwater, he taught his children pride in their ancestors and regaled any who would listen with stories of his boyhood.

He grew up working on the farm with his father and attended school at Post Oak and Sloan-Hendrix Academy, but never finished. In 1933, he married Rubye Lucille Teel, daughter of William H. and Dollie Bell Baker Teel, of Walnut Ridge. Living through the Depression, they knew hard times and hard work. Sloan held a variety of jobs: grocer, dry cleaner, farmer, truck driver between crops, ginner, and like his parents, the family moved often during the early years of their marriage, as their eight children were born.

Their first, Charles Billy, was born in Hoxie in 1935. Upon graduating from Walnut Ridge High School, he farmed with the Sloans in the Arbor Grove Community. In 1955, he married Joyce Noblin of Pocahontas.

Sloan and Rubye Weir celebrated their golden wedding anniversary in 1983, at the Hoxie United Methodist Church with their children, from left: Riley, Cameron and Charles Weir; Rubye and Sloan Weir; Bonnie Martin Lindsey; Frances Green; and Ruth Anne Brand.

In 1958, father and son moved from the farm to Hoxie and Walnut Ridge. Charles and Joyce, who still live in Walnut Ridge, had Charles Billy II, born on Sloan's birthday in 1958, and Suzanne, born in 1961. Both graduated from Walnut Ridge High School and earned college degrees, Charles from the University of Arkansas and Suzanne from the University of Central Arkansas. Charles married Lynda Lee of Little Rock, and they have a son, Connor Bradley, born 1988, and daughter, Amanda, born 1990. Charles is the only grandson and Connor is the only great-grandson with the Weir surname. Suzanne and husband, Jack Morris, live in Fayetteville. They have two children, Morgan, born 1992, and Casey, born 1996.

Cameron Lee was born September 16, 1937, in Walnut Ridge. A 1955 graduate of Hoxie, he worked out of state, then moved to Walnut Ridge in 1959, when he married Sharon Self of Swifton. They had two daughters, Rochelle "Shelly" in 1970, and Deanna in 1976. Both graduated from

Walnut Ridge High School. Shelly died in a car/train accident in 1990. Deanna is a college student.

In 1939, on June 30, twins Bonnie Sue and Betty Lou were born in Hoxie. Betty lived only four days. Bonnie attended Hoxie and married Bob Martin of Hoxie in 1955. Their daughter, Penny, born 1961, graduated from Hoxie High School in 1980, and married Terry Ring in 1981. They live in Alma and have two children, Jarod, born 1985, and Breanne, born 1996. Bonnie married Don Lindsey in 1983. They lived in Walnut Ridge.

Mary Frances was born March 16, 1941, in the Fender Community. A 1959 Hoxie High School graduate, she earned a teaching degree at Arkansas State University in 1962, and married James W. Green, son of Herbert and Julia Mae Green of Hoxie. Both are retired teachers living in Hoxie. They are the parents of James W. Jr. "Jimmy", born 1963, and Gwendolyn, born 1973, who are also Hoxie graduates. Jimmy has a degree from Arkansas State University and Gwen has a BA from Lyon College and a MA from the University of Mississippi. Jimmy married Valarie Kegley of Piggott in 1990. They have two daughters, Sarah, born 1994, and Olivia, born 1996, and live in Walnut Ridge.

James Robert, born October 12, 1942, in Walnut Ridge, lived only three weeks.

Ruth Anne was born in Hoxie April 5, 1944. She married Clarence Daniel Brand of Hoxie. Both 1963 Hoxie High School graduates, they live in White Hall. Their son, Dan D., born 1967, a pilot, and his wife, Jenni of Springfield, Missouri, have a daughter, Celia Grace, born 1999. Their daughter, Katherine Lynn, born 1970, lives in Conway.

Riley Sloan Jr. was born August 17, 1951, in a Walnut Ridge clinic, the only child not born in the home. He and Vickie Wicker, both 1969 Hoxie High School graduates, were married in 1972, in Sedgwick. Their daughter, Jill, born 1977, also finished high school at Hoxie. Riley married Kathy Thomas Moss in 1988, and they live in Bono.

Sloan and Rubye have been married 65 years. She resides in Hoxie in their home of 35 years. He has been a resident of Lawrence Hall Nursing Home in Walnut Ridge for four years. He is the only surviving child of Burette and Zillah Rainwater Weir. –Frances Green.

JOHN WELLS SR. FAMILY.
John Wells Sr. and his wife, Mary "Polly" Hudspeth, were among the earliest settlers of Lawrence County. They settled on Spring River at the present location of the town of Ravenden in 1807. Wells Creek, which runs through the Opposition Community, is named for this family. John was born in Virginia in 1778, and Mary was born in North Carolina in 1774. They were married in Kentucky. John was a farmer and livestock dealer. He died in 1845, and Mary died in 1852.

Their children were:

1. William, whose wife's names was Luvenia.
2. Washington, who married Brunetta Stubblefield.
3. George H., who was unmarried.
4. John Jr., who first married Cinderella Looney and whose second wife was Elizabeth Grayson.
5. Henry G., who married Minerva Janes.
6. Emily, who first married William Capp and later married A. C. Childers.
7. Clara, who married A. J. Cravens.
8. Thomas.
9. Eliza.
10. Mary.
11. James.

This family remained prominent in the Ravenden and Powhatan areas throughout the 19th century.

The Rob Weir family, left to right, back row: Lou, Lillie, Homer Smith, Eula, Nettie and Madge. Standing between, Elbert; Seated, Rob and Mary, holding Nancy. Standing in front, Lora and Cecil.

John R. Wells, son of John Wells Jr., was born in 1838, and became a physician. He joined the Confederacy in the Civil War and reached the rank of Captain and Assistant Surgeon. After the war he settled at Powhatan, where he practiced medicine for many years. His wife was the former Nettie Stuart and they raised five children. Dr. Wells died in 1918, and is buried in Hope Cemetery at Imboden.

The John Wells Sr. family maintained a cemetery in which many family members, as well as others, were buried. This cemetery was located in Ravenden directly across First Street from the old L. W. Perry store property. Long ago the tombstones were all moved from the site and a business was erected over the old cemetery. That business is now history, also.

James T. (Texas Tom) Wells, son of William and grandson of John Sr., lived for many years on a small farm on Janes Creek, and later at Imboden. He is buried in Old Union Cemetery. His sister, Emily (known to many as Aunt Emily Lomax), lived for many years at Ravenden Springs and is buried in the Janes Cemetery near there.

A few years after the John Wells Sr. family moved to Lawrence County, a related family settled nearby in what is today Randolph County. The latter family was headed by Thomas H. Wells, who was born in South Carolina. Thomas had several sons and most of the Wells families in Randolph County and western Lawrence County today can be traced to him. The exact relationship of John Wells Sr. to Thomas H. Wells is not known.

Submitted by Don R. Brown.

JONATHAN WELLS FAMILY. Jonathan Wells was born in Kentucky, and then came to Clover Bend to live in 1882. He married Elizabeth "Lizzie" Ludwig, born in Pennsylvania in 1884. They had nine children: Anna Wells, Charles "Pet" Wells, Tommie Wells, Hattie Wells, Freddie Wells, Helen Wells, Clarence Wells, William Marion "Willie" Wells (see the William Marion Wells family) and Pearl Wells.

Pearl married Fred Smith and she wrote an article for *The Times Dispatch*, April 20, 1983, recalling the early years of Clover Bend. "In 1882, the land was a plantation owned by F. W. Tucker and her father was his farm boss. My family lived there all of their lives except for two or three months. Mr. Tucker got angry with my dad and fired him. Dad put our personal things and family into two covered wagons and left for Oklahoma. When we arrived there was an urgent message from Mr. Tucker wanting us to return at once, which we did."

Jonathan Maxie Wells and Betsy Wells.

We lived in the old house down by the school. I have picked mushrooms for Ms. French and Ms. Crawford and taken them around the corner. They always filled my basket with candy and fresh fruit. There were several colored families that lived in the vicinity. Steve Murry and family worked for Ms. French and Ms. Crawford and Luke Shockey worked for Mr. Tucker and my father. My father served the community as deputy sheriff, J. P., School Board member. The store and the post office, saw mill, cotton gin and other business buildings were on the river bank, south of where the French home now stands.

The old school (where I attended) was in session three months in summer and three months in winter, grades one through nine, with only one teacher. All the churches met in the old school on the "break." I was born, raised and married in the same house down by the old school. In 1912, my father died, leaving my mother a small farm, in front of where the school now stands. She later sold the farm and bought the house that stood near Mr. Pratt's store. The big oak tree that still stands was in our yard. She lived there until she died in 1929.

In 1914, I married Fred Smith and lived in Lawrence County all of my life, until 1975. Due to ill health, we moved to Jonesboro to be near our children. My husband passed away in 1976. I just hate to see the buildings all gone and no reminders of the aged community. –Maxine Wells.

WILLIAM MARION WELLS FAMILY. William Marion "Willie" Wells, son of Jonathan Wells and Elizabeth Ludwig, was born February 11, 1891. He was born and raised at Clover Bend. While he was attending school there, he always built the fires and rang the bell. He married Almanzie Mary Tyree, born November 18, 1894. Willie and Manzie as everyone called them had three children.

1. Jonathan Maxie Wells, born February 8, 1917, married Besty Maybelle Baldridge, born May 14, 1919. Maxie and Besty had two children.

a) Maxie Gene Wells, born January 21, 1942, married Jean McAnally and they have one daughter, Stephanie Ann Wells, born June 11, 1974, married on July 10, 1998, to Anthony Wayne Orr.

Willie Wells and Manzie Tyree Wells.

b) Ruth Ann Wells, born December 6, 1943, married William Daninger and they have one son, Dennis Daninger, born February 23, 1965.

2. Baby Wells, born November 16, 1919, and died November 17, 1919.

3. Willene Wells, born February 7, 1935, at Hopewell, attended school for the first eight years at Lindsey Switch School, which was located between Hoxie and Minturn, then graduated from Hoxie High School.

Almanzie Mary Tyree Wells died February 20, 1973. William Marion Wells died April 20, 1976. They are buried at the Hopewell Cemetery. Jonathan Maxie Wells is in the nursing home at Walnut Ridge, and his wife, Besty, lives at Hoxie. Willene Wells lives at Hoxie and goes to the nursing home everyday to help care for her brother. –Willene Wells.

FREDERICK WESTPHAL, 1888-1979 AND ANNA WELLS, 1890-1981. Born in Walnut Ridge, Arkansas, son of Charles Westphal and Sophronia Ozment Westphal, Frederick attended the Old Wing School and was an exceptionally good student. There is a group photo of these children which shows him with all the seriousness he had in his personality all his life. There is a letter he wrote as an eight year old child to Anna Wells (the little girl who came to visit next door to Frederick's home) where he tells her about his work and his textbooks. He loved them (See Correspondence record.) Frederick left school at the end of eighth grade and went to work as a carpenter with his father and Herman Cousins.

Back Row: J.G. Wells, Fred Westphal, Louis Wells. Middle: Almeda Wells, Daisy Wells, Anna Wells. Front: Trixie (?) Wells.

For a while he worked as a train man for the Rock Island Railroad (he said he stoked the engine..he was 16). Then he married Anna Wells and they moved to Hot Springs, Arkansas, where there was work building hotels, bathhouses and hospitals around 1911. In 1918 they moved to Little Rock, Arkansas, and bought a home at 2425 West 12th Street, moving into it in 1918 when their first child, Frederick Jr., was two years old. By 1919 he had a second son, Carl Wells, and his father had come to live with them. There was much work building in the Little Rock area also...Lafayette Hotel, Veterans Hospital, Army camps, cabinet work, Lonoke County Courthouse, The Majestic Hotel, Hot Springs, Arkansas. For a number of years he remodeled some of the Safeway groceries in the southern states. He also worked for Stuart McGee Construction Company and Herman McCann Construction Company. Then he got a job as foreman-designer-supervisor with Rice/Stix Construction, St. Louis, Missouri. For years until he retired, he traveled about the country supervising remodeling and construction in department stores from designs of the Rice/Stix crews. He was bonded, brought in a boxcar of tools, hired local people to work, thus never having any unpleasant union problems. He usually boarded in a private home. For about five years after he retired Rice/Stix continued to employ him anytime one of his original clients asked for him. His skills and relations with people saved his company many hundreds of dollars and hours of labor. (Only one incident of an accident is recorded...a man tried one of the power tools in a department store where the crew was remodeling, had turned off their machinery and gone to lunch. The man turned on a saw, got his hand in the way and cut off two fingers. He tried to sue the department store; Rice/Stix and lastly Frederick Westphal. Anna immediately removed all their properties from her husband's name and sat it out for over 10 years before it was settled. The man did not win his case; he had no right to touch the equipment.)

Anna Wells, 1890-1981, about five year old, Black Rock, Arkansas.

Anna Wells, oldest of seven children, was the daughter of John G. Wells and Almeda Langin

Wells. John was a grocer in Black Rock, Arkansas, and 14 terms he was mayor of Black Rock which was a prosperous river and railroad town in the 1890s. Anna graduated valedictorian of her class, receiving a gold watch for her scholarship from the Black Rock High School Board.

Her grandfather, John Langin, a farmer, traced his family back to Cape Breton Island, Canada. Of Scotch and French heritage, his people had moved in towards the Great Lakes to Ontario near New London and Woodstock. (Note: British law in 1744 demanded loyalty to the crown or leave. The French were evicted, lands, goods confiscated; people put on ships..families even separated and sailed down the coast to the colonies...all but Virginia...This began the Cajuns from French Acadia who settled in Louisiana.) Anna worked as a telephone supervisor in Hot Springs and while in Little Rock worked as a children's clothing buyer for Pheiffers Department Store. She was active in the Bandmothers Club at Little Rock High School and they all attended Asbury Methodist Church.

Anna Wells' younger sister, Lillian Wells Smith from Black Rock, Arkansas, told me about the marriage of Anna and Fred Westphal in 1911. Weddings were as important and showy then as now, but they did not have such a gala affair. Anna's parents were doubtful about a marriage into a German family in 1911. They did not say so, but as one letter which still exists written by Anna's mother states, "Papa would have been angry if Fred had not asked for your hand." But Fred had and he arrived on the morning of their wedding day with the buckboard, picked up Anna and off they went. They lived in Hot Springs, Arkansas, briefly, lived in Walnut Ridge until 1918. Their son, Frederick Jr., was born in Walnut Ridge. They bought their home in Little Rock in 1918.
–Hinda Westphal.

DALTON WHEELESS FAMILY.
Dalton John Wheeless was the only son of Jesse and Mintora Wheeless. He was born June 8, 1918, in White County, Arkansas. He died on June 13, 1997. Dalton had seven sisters. Jesse was a farmer in Randolph County and Dalton grew up working on the farm with his father.

Dalton married Ollie Landis, daughter of Tom and Eva Landis of Randolph County. The couple were married in the home of Brother J. T. Shoffit in the Dean Community on February 21, 1937. In the early years of their marriage, Dalton farmed with his father in Randolph County.

In the fall of 1943, the couple moved to Lawrence County near the Lawrence and Randolph County Line. Dalton continued to farm in that area until he retired in 1981, at the age of 63. The couple had seven children: Louise, Jimmy, Ronnie, Carolyn, Wendell, Rick and Gene. Dalton and Ollie also have 18 grandchildren and 21 great-grand-children.

Dalton and Ollie in 1937.

Dalton and Ollie in 1997, on their 60th wedding anniversary

Louise died in 1943, at the age of five. Jimmy died in 1967, at the age of 27. The remaining children all live in Lawrence or Randolph County. Mrs. Wheeless still resides in Lawrence County. –Gene Wheeless.

DARRELL GENE WHEELESS FAMILY.
Darrell Gene Wheeless is the youngest child of Dalton and Ollie Wheeless. He was born May 27, 1957, and has lived in Lawrence County his entire life. The Wheeless family was a farm family. Gene worked with his father and brothers growing soybeans, wheat, cotton and rice. Gene graduated from Walnut Ridge High School in 1975 and began farming on his own in 1980.

Gene married Charlotte Simmons West in 1990. Charlotte is the daughter of Kathleen Simmons Hattenhauer of Hoxie, Arkansas, and the late Fred Simmons. She is the youngest of five children. She grew up in Hoxie and later lived in Missouri and Kansas. Charlotte returned to Walnut Ridge in 1989 and worked at Wal-Mart while attending Williams Baptist College.

Gene and Charlotte made their home on the Lawrence and Randolph county line with their two sons, Patrick Wheeless and Nicholas West. The family was then blessed with the birth of their daughter, Jessica Austin Wheeless.

In 1994 Charlotte graduated from Williams Baptist College summa cum

The Wheeless family in 1994.

laude with a Bachelor of Science in Education degree. She now teaches fifth and sixth grade science at Walnut Ridge Public School. Charlotte was named Teacher of the Year in May 1999 and in the top five in the state later that year. Gene farms in both Lawrence and Randolph County and also raises and trains horses.

Patrick Wheeless was born February 5, 1976. He graduated from Walnut Ridge High School in 1994 and is a student at the University of Arkansas in Fayetteville. Patrick is pursuing a degree in Kinesiology. He enjoys working at Northwest Athletic Club and coaching basketball.

Nicholas West was born January 11, 1981. He graduated from Walnut Ridge High School in 1999. Nick was named Who's Who of American High School Students in both his junior and senior years. Nick attended Colorado Outdoor Adventure Guide School in Woodland Park, Colorado. Nick enjoys hunting, fishing and training horses.

Jessica Wheeless was born March 24, 1991. She is in the fourth grade at Walnut Ridge Elementary School. She was recently accepted into the Gifted and Talented Program. Jessica enjoys reading as well as taking dance and art lessons.

The Wheeless family bought a home in Powhatan in 1996 and they enjoy living in their country home. Some of their favorite activities at home include fishing in the pond, raising and riding horses, swimming in the pool, and playing with Lady, their Labrador Retriever. The family can often be seen enjoying an afternoon buggy ride in the Powhatan area. Gene also enjoys giving horse and buggy rides at various community events. –Charlotte Wheeless.

ANCESTORS AND DESCENDANTS OF ABRAM TOLLETT AND BARBARY WHITE.
Silas White was born about 1777, in Chowan County, North Carolina. He married first Elizabeth Brown, daughter of Robert Brown and Catherine, about 1799. She died before 1842. They had these children: Benjamin H. White, born 1800; Abram Tollett White, 1807-1880; Robert B. White, born about 1810; Betsy White, 1810-1820, Georgia; William, 1820-1825, Georgia; Silas White Jr., 1825-1830, Georgia; Joseph Anderson White, 1825-1830, Georgia; James, 1825-1830, Georgia; and Berry. Silas married a second time to Mary. Abram Tollett and wife, Barbary White, my great-great-grandparents, were born in Pidgeon Mountain, Georgia, and appeared in Lawrence County in the early 1850s. He was a farmer, teacher and shoemaker. He and his wife had 10 children: Mary, born 1832, Georgia; Darius, born 1836, married Nancy Amanda Gibson; Melissa, born 1838; Georgia, married James Kerr; Hannah G., born 1840, Georgia, died 1907; in Arkansas; she married first Levi Sharp, second Sterling H. Kerr; third Hugh Wells; fourth Cornelius Davis (brother of John Davis); Sarah Ann, born August 1, 1842, died August 8, 1922; she married John M. Davis (son of Ross Davis); John, born 1844; Henry Brown, born 1846, died 1870, married Dora Toler; C. Robert, born 1849, married Hannah Buckhannon; Tollett Franklin, born 1855, married Nancy Josephine Marcum; and Barbara A. White, born 1856, married Henry Phillips.

Abram T. and Barbary acquired land in 1855, and lived the rest of their lives in Lawrence County. Abram did not appear after the 1880 census, but Barbary was listed in a newspaper as being an Eastern Star member in 1910.

Silas and Elizabeth "Betsy" Brown White are my great-great-great-grandparents. Abram T. and Barbara White were the parents of my great-grandmother, Sarah Ann White Davis, the second wife of John M. Davis of Denton Township, Lawrence County. John's first wife was Martha McCarroll.

One of my great aunts, Mary Helms, daughter of Nancy Brown and David Helms, married Charles Henry White, son of C. Robert White and first wife, Hannah J. Buckhannon.

Sarah Ann White and John M. Davis had these children: Mary Adeline, 1866-1937, married Sam Faulkner; George Franklin, 1868-1942, married Cansada Bilbrey; Henryetta, 1870-1953, married first J. R. Goad, second Thomas Ephram Helms; Charles Cornelius, 1874-1920, married Floda Field; Martha Elizabeth, 1876-1913 (my grandmother), married William Cam Helms; John Melvin, 1879-1925; Susie Agnes, 1882-1967, married Daniel Webster Puckett; Elizabeth Barbara Davis, 1885-1934, married Dr. Thomas C. Guthrie.

John's home was located near the Old Bethel Cemetery in Denton, Arkansas. My cousin, Tom Helms, the son of Warren and Frances Helms, remembers going there with his dad to see the old home of John and Sarah White Davis which he says was a two story log home with four fireplaces. Old Bethel Cemetery has many of the Davis, White and McCarroll families and many early settlers of that area. –Geraldine Fultz.

WHITLOW.
Pascal Whitlow moved to Lawrence County, Arkansas, in 1859, from Hardin County, Tennessee, with several other members of his and his wife's families.

Pascal was the son of Henderson and Sarah Mitchell Whitlow and was born in 1808, in Laurens County, South Carolina. After his family moved to Hardin County, he married Mary Matilda Thornton, daughter of Isaac and Nancy House Thornton, in

1836. Once in Arkansas they first had a home on Strawberry Creek then were living at Smithville, Reeds Creek Township, by 1870.

They had seven children, all born in Tennessee, including Joshua, who was stabbed and killed with a knife in 1855, at the age of 18, as he tried to protect his sisters from a "crazy man." The other children of Pascal and Matilda Whitlow were Nancy P, who married Morgan Raney; Isaac H., who married Elizabeth Pearson; Mary A., second wife of Jefferson Wadley; William M.; John Granville, who married Mary Pearson, sister of Elizabeth; and Sarah M., who married John Grisham Mullen. All these marriages took place in Lawrence County.

Nancy and Morgan Raney had children Isaac, Esterlee, Josephene, Morris, Sarah, William and John W. Nancy was a member of the Milligan Camp Ground Cumberland Presbyterian Church as were Pascal and Matilda and their son, Isaac.

Isaac and Elizabeth Whitlow married May 20, 1866, in Lawrence County and had children: Betty, William, Jane, John, Dora and Ollie. They left Lawrence County by 1880, and lived first in Izard County, then Madison County and eventually Roberts County, Texas, where Ike died December 3, 1923.

Mary A. Whitlow was working as a housekeeper for Jefferson Wadley and his first wife, Matilda, in 1880, and at the first wife's death sometime after that date, Mary and Jeff were married. Mary did not have children of her own, but raised her stepchildren, Daniel, Martha, David and Susan.

William M. Whitlow did not come with the family to Lawrence County and may have died before the family made their migration. He never appears in their Arkansas records.

John Granville married Mary Malinda Pearson, sister of Elizabeth, both daughters of Thomas and Malinda Pearson, June 30, 1872, in Izard County, after he and his brother, Isaac, moved west. The Pearson family was also from Lawrence County. John and Mary had children: Sally, Malinda, Ada, Effie, Cora, Calvin, Birtie, Marvin and Audie. The family moved to Madison County, Arkansas, by 1895, and lived there about three years when they moved to Era, Cooke County, Texas, and eventually to Cleveland County, Oklahoma Territory, where John died January 22, 1927, and Mary died March 25, 1944. Both are buried in Pilgrim's Rest Cemetery in Newalla, Oklahoma.

Sarah M. "Sally" married John "Grisham" Mullen, son of Thomas and Rebecca Durham Mullen, September 14, 1877, in Sharp County. She died February 20, 1940, and is buried in Milligan Camp Ground Cemetery, as is Grisham.

The mother of the Whitlows, Matilda Thornton Whitlow, died about 1871, and is probably also buried in the Milligan Camp Ground Cemetery. There are more than 100 unmarked graves there and she was a long time member. Her husband, Pascal, left Lawrence County with his sons, Isaac and John, and moved first to Sharp County; then in 1880, he was living with Isaac in Franklin, Izard County. He was 69 years old at that time and in the next record of Isaac's family, 1900 in Madison County, he is no longer listed. *—Leon McDonald.*

BENJAMIN TOLBERT WHITLOW was born
to Pinkney Reeves Whitlow and Susan Marinda Benton in Smithville, Arkansas. He married Mary Ann Campbell. They were lifelong residents of Lawrence County and buried at Powhatan Cemetery. Their children were: Anna Mae, Joseph Reeves, Lehman E., Ruby Faye 1926. They were farmers, blacksmiths and grocery store owners. *– Ruby Dulaney.*

Family of Ben T. and Mary Whitlow, made in their yard in early 40s. Ben and Mary seated, left to right standing: Ruby Faye, Martha, Lehman, Joe, Opal, Mae, Clarence. Children left to right: Harold Gene Thorn, Ray Thorn, Iris Whitlow, Bly Thorn, Joe Ray Whitlow.

COLEMAN WHITLOW FAMILY. Coleman
and Henrietta Whitlow and their children came to Lawrence County in 1862, from Hardin County, Tennessee. Their children were: William, Granville, Mary, James Milton, Amanda, Sarah, Virgin and Forrest Whitlow. They lived in the vicinity of Clover Bend and later in the Arbor Grove Community working as farm laborers.

Coleman's parents were Henderson and Sally Whitlow of Hardin County, Tennessee. Coleman had a brother, Paschal, who was living in Lawrence County and their home in Hardin County was in the middle of the Civil War was the reason for leaving Tennessee and moving to Lawrence County.

William's first wife was Francis E. Wann and his second wife was Mary Dunken. Granville's first wife was Julia Boleware and his second wife was Mrs. C. B. Colbert and Mary's husband was Taylor

Coleman Whitlow.

Colbert. James Milton's first wife was Amanda Pearlee Williams, his second wife was Alice Martin, his third was Mrs. Clara Reed and his fourth was Mrs. Mary Cavanaugh. Amanda H.'s husband was Joseph Starnes and Sarah A.'s husband was John H. Grigsby. Virgin F.'s first husband was Elisha Darter and her second husband was William Long and Forrest H.'s wife was Virginia Pruett.

James Milton was born on March 13, 1854, in Hardin County, Tennessee and was married to his first wife, Amanda P. Williams, on September 8, 1878, in Lawrence County. Their children were: Sarah Elizabeth, John Henderson, Lovella, Walter W. and Eddie. James married his second wife, Alice, on September 15, 1892, and their child was Clarence Anderson. Mrs. Clara Reed was James' third wife and their only child was Cicero James and his fourth wife was Mrs. Mary Cavanaugh and they had no children. Sarah married Zack Robins, John Henderson married Lillie Robins, Zack Robins' sister and Lovella married Joe Cole. Walter W. and Eddie died at a young age. Clarence married Essie Ring and Cicero married Lura (unknown).

James M. (Uncle Bud) was a farmer in the Arbor Grove Community. Although he couldn't read or write, he acquired considerable amount of farm land in the eastern district of Lawrence County by buying land and selling it later at a profit. The original 40 acres he purchased was in 1882,

for $200 on which the Whitlow Cemetery is located and it has been in the Whitlow family since. James M. was fatally injured when he stepped out in front of a car in Walnut Ridge in November, 1935, and was buried in the Whitlow Cemetery. *–James Whitlow.*

JOHN AND LILLIE WHITLOW. John
Henderson Whitlow, son of James M. and Amanda P. Williams Whitlow and Lillie Martha Robins, daughter of Tom Emerson Robins and Alice Annie Minton Robins were married on February 8, 1903, by Elder F. M. Dover. John was born January 30, 1882, two miles northwest of Minturn in the Arbor Grove Community and Lillie was born February 16, 1883, north of Walnut Ridge in the Lane Community. The first house they lived in was an old log cabin in the Arbor Grove Community. In 1907, they bought 200 acres of land from his dad five miles southwest of Hoxie. It took 13 hard working years to pay for the farm and that is where they lived until he died, January 27, 1965. After his death, Lillie moved to Jonesboro and she passed away June 28, 1973. Their children were: Robert, Ann, Martin, Johnny, Imogene and Virginia.

Robert "Bob" married Lavinia Anderson and their children are: Cherie, Gypsy, Doris and Bobby Ray. Bob married a second time to Mary Gibson. Bob worked for the *Memphis Press Scimitar* newspaper for 45 years and was a professional boxer in the 1920s.

Ann married Bolin Irby and he was a sales manager for Cudahy Meat Packing Company in Tulsa, Oklahoma. Ann attended Sloan-Hendrix Academy where she won an academic award in her sophomore year. Their adopted children are: John and Martha.

Martin married Maxine Mitchell and their children are: Billy Wayne, Jerry and Rita. Martin was a soybean and rice farmer in the Arbor Grove Community. He started growing rice in 1940, on some land that his dad had purchased and had cleared in the 1930s.

John and Lillie Whitlow.

Johnny married Wilma Ingram and their children are: Linda, Patsy and James. Johnny was a cotton and soybean farmer farming the 200 acres his dad had bought in 1907.

Imogene "Jean" married Elbert Looney and their children are: Gary, Barbara and Bonnie. They lived in Pontiac, Michigan, where they owned donut shops serving the automotive industries. Jean's second husband was Chester Bowles of Michigan.

Virginia married N. V. "Pete" Hutchison and their children are: Jerry, Carla, Larry, David, Ronnie, Jeananne and Nita. Pete was a farm equipment salesman, tire salesman and they owned a printing company in Jonesboro.

On May 9, 1927, a tornado touched down on the Whitlow farm and damage was done to the house. They built a very nice modern house where it still stands with the large barn. It was said it was the most modern house between Hoxie and Alicia when it was built. In 1939, a windmill was put up on the farm for watering livestock and although there is no longer livestock on the farm, the windmill still pumps water to the garden and lawn.

When Lillie was small, her family moved to a farm west of Hoxie on Village Creek. In the early 1890s, some men came and did an archaeology survey and dug up some Indian skeletons and

Indian artifacts. They took the items to Chicago where they were on display at the World's Columbian Exposition in 1893. She was excited about it because the men brought coloring books for her and her brothers.

John had three fingers missing from one hand. The story was when he was raising registered Spotted Poland China swine some piglets got out of the farrowing pen. He was catching them and putting them back in the pen and the piglets were squealing. The mother sow got upset and when John hopped in the pen the sow attacked him. She was on top of him and his German Shepard dog leaped over the fence and jumped on the sow. They started fighting and that freed John and when he got out of the pen, he saw that sow had bit off three fingers. He was thankful for his dog for what he believed saved his life. –*James Whitlow.*

JOHN W. AND WILMA WHITLOW.

Johnny Wade, son of John H. and Lillie Whitlow, and Wilma Adrain Ingram, daughter of James Edward and Mary Ingram, were married on October 4, 1939, in Walnut Ridge by Julian Green, pastor of the Presbyterian Church. John was born March 4, 1912, on his parents farm five miles southwest of Hoxie and lived on the same farm all of his life. Wilma was born October 4, 1919, four miles west of Hoxie on Old Highway 63 on the Sloan farm. Their children are: Linda Kay, Pasty Lee and James Bryan.

Linda married Larry Riley on February 10, 1963, at the Arbor Grove Free Will Baptist Church. Linda and Larry live on their family farm in Bernie, Missouri where the main crops are corn, rice and soybeans. Their children are: Sharon, Jim and Jon. Their first child passed away at birth.

Pat married David Wilkins on February 23, 1964, at the Arbor Grove Free Will Baptist Church. They live in Jonesboro where Pat works for the Craighead County Farm Bureau and David is a rice and soybean farmer in the Otwell Community, south of Jonesboro. Their two sons are: Gary and Todd.

James lives in Walnut Ridge working at S-B Power Tools in the Technical Services Department. He lived 19 years in Alvin, Texas

John W. Whitlow and Wilma Whitlow, James Bryan, Patsy Lee and Linda Kay, 1953.

working as an electrician in the petrochemical industry.

Linda was born July 24, 1941, at St. Bernards Hospital in Jonesboro. Pat was born October 11, 1943, in an ambulance between Hoxie and Sedgwick with Mr. Bryan, the driver, delivering the baby. James Bryan was born February 10, 1947, at the Fairchild Clinic in Walnut Ridge and his parents named him after this grandfather and Mr. Bryan, the ambulance driver who later owned Bryan Funeral Home.

Johnny and Wilma farmed the land his dad had bought in 1907. Johnny and Wilma purchased 140 acres of that farm when his dad passed away in 1965. The other 60 acres belong to Johnny's mother, Lillie. They built a house in 1972, next to a beautiful pecan grove that his dad planted in 1927. A windmill that was erected in 1939, is located next to the pecan grove and is used to water the lawn and grove.

Johnny passed away in a Houston, Texas hospital in August, 1990. James bought the farm and Wilma is still living on the place. James had a water well put down in 1996, and 50 acres of the land was precision leveled so rice and other crops could be watered.

The Whitlows are members of the Arbor Grove Free Will Baptist Church where Johnny and Wilma served as teachers for several years and Johnny as treasurer, Sunday School superintendent and song leader.

–*James Whitlow.*

MARY ANN CAMPBELL WHITLOW

was born at Jersey ???; wife of Benjamin Tolbert Whitlow, daughter of Joseph Alexander Campbell and Margaret Ellen Ware Campbell; mother of Anna Mae, Joseph Reeve, Lehman E. and Ruby Faye Whitlow; buried at Powhatan; lifetime resident of Lawrence County. –*Ruby Dulaney.*

Ben T. and Mary Whitlow.

PINKNEY REEVES WHITLOW,

born February 8, 1827, Allen County, Kentucky, son of John W., married Susan M. Benton, born September 9, 1833, in Ohio County, Kentucky, daughter of Erasmus Benton, born September 24, 1809, Kentucky and died October 18, 1853, McLean County, Kentucky, and Elizabeth Howard Benton, born February 15, 1809, in Kentucky and died January 20, 1886, McLean County, Kentucky. Burial is in Old Buck Creek Cemetery. P. R. and Susan married on November 6, 1856, in McLean County, Kentucky. Vital statistics of that county state that P. R. Whitlow was a widower. The 1860 census lists two young sons, Volentine, born 1854 (probably son of first wife), and John W. Whitlow, born 1859. There is possibly a girl listed in the 1860 mortality schedule, Leila A. Whitlon/Whitlow, age one, who died on April 1, 1860, in an accident, who may be the child of P. R. and Susan, unproven at this time. All are deceased by the 1870 census of Lawrence County, Arkansas. P. R. Whitlow enlisted in Company A of the 15th Missouri Cavalry, in December, 1861, to June, 1865. He was wounded in his leg and in 1901, applied for and received the Arkansas Confederate Soldier Pension. The other children of P. R. and Susan Benton Whitlow are:

1. Elizabeth LaGrande Whitlow, born May 16 1861, married August 22, 1882, in Sharp County, Arkansas, to Henry Edward Sudduth, son of Elizabeth Land and David Sudduth.

2. Felonious Allen Whitlow, born October 13, 1864, married August 7, 1884, in Ft. Smith, Arkansas to Jefferson Davis Sudduth, son of Telitha Land and Jared Sudduth.

3. James Carson Whitlow, born 1867, married September 26, 1886, to Luda Ann Davis, born June 22, 1861, and died October 19, 1899, Luda Ann Davis Whitlow is buried in Price Cemetery, Lawrence County. Other's wives were: Mary V. Deeter, Myrtle Lynch, Ada Gibson, Lucy Wooding and Sena White.

4. Robert Edgar Whitlow, March 15, 1868-May 1, 1945, married August 11, 1892, to Rachel E. Hopkins.

5. Clara Malvern Whitlow, January 9, 1879-October 20, 1946, in Portia, Arkansas, married September 26, 1886, to Albert Curtis Benn.

6. Mary A. Whitlow, born February, 1871, married August 16, 1891, to John Lee Winter.

7. Erestus Eugene Whitlow, born February 22, 1872, married Nettie Hastings. After her death, he married Eva Trentham. Erestus was a minister and traveled all over. And all of his children were born in different states.

8. Martha E. Whitlow, August, 1875-August, 1944, married on January 12, 1890, to John David Foley.

9. Belle Zora Whitlow was born 1877, and died about 1920, in Newark, Arkansas. She married February 15, 1894, to John H. Nelson and married second to Christopher Graves.

10. Benjamin Tolbert Whitlow was born July 25, 1880, and died June 21, 1950. He married November 27, 1904, to Mary Ann Campbell.

Submitted by Barbara Miller.

PINKNEY REEVES WHITLOW FAMILY.

Both Pinkney Reeves Whitlow and his wife, Susan Miranda Benton, were born in Kentucky February 8, 1827, and September 9, 1833, respectively. They were married in McLean County, Kentucky November 6, 1856. Pinkney died February 27, 1911, and Susan died August 5, 1897, both in Lawrence County. They are buried in the Price Cemetery in Strawberry.

They were farmers. Ten children were born of this union, and all in Lawrence County, Arkansas.

Elizabeth LeGrand "Relsey", born May 16, 1861, married Henry Edward Sudduth; Felonious Allen, born October 31, 1864, married Jefferson Davis Sudduth; James C. Whitlow, born about 1867, married Luda Ann Davis; Robert E. Whitlow, born 1868, married Rachel Hopkins; Clara or Flora M., born February, 1870, married Albert C. Benns; Mary A., born February, 1871, married Winter Lee; Erestus U. "Ret", born 1874, married Nettie E. Hastings; Martha E. "Mattie", born August, 1875, married John Foley; Bellzora, born 1877, married John Nelson and a Mr. Graves; and Ben Whitlow, born January, 1882, married Mary Campbell.

Henry and Jefferson Sudduth were first cousins, married to sisters. Robert "Bob" Whitlow was a circuit judge in Poinsett or Lawrence County.

Pinkney Reeves Whitlow, 1827-1911.

Many descendants from this family still reside in Lawrence County. I have several great pictures of the Whitlow family and would love to share them. Please contact Raeanna Ellis, P. O. Box 880010, Steamboat Springs, Colorado 80488. Thanks! –*Raenna Ellis.*

ROBERT EUGENE WHITLOW FAMILY .

Robert Eugene "Gene" Whitlow, born October 30, 1928, in Lawrence County close to Lynn, son of Garland Mock Whitlow, born January 28, 1901, and Birtha Edith Dunlap Whitlow, born August 31, 1911. Both Garland and Birtha were born at Driftwood which is about five miles below Lynn. Gene was raised in the Riverview area and attended school at Strawberry. He married on August 21,

1953, to Nancy Anita "Neta" Stewart, born July 13, 1935, in Black Rock, daughter of Samuel Lee Stewart who was born October 12, 1901, in Missouri and Clara Leona Rice Stewart, born February 2, 1907, in Black Rock.

Gene and Neta have one son, Robert Lee "Bob" Whitlow, born March 20, 1956, in Walnut Ridge. Bob attended school at Black Rock and married Barbara Brown, born May 15, 1962, daughter of Gene "Moe" Brown and Bertice Medlock Brown. They have four children: Robert Lee Whitlow Jr., born October 10, 1977; Bridget Nicole Whitlow, born July 4, 1983; Brittney Loyd Whitlow, born October 27, 1985; and Blake Eugene Whitlow, born February 26, 1987.

Bob and family live in Black Rock. He is employed at S. B. Power Tool Company of Walnut Ridge, where he was worked for the past 16 years. Barbara is attending Arkansas State University to become a registered nurse.

Gene and Anita Whitlow.

Gene and Neta have owned their own business for 34 years, "Gene's Garage" located on the corner of Sixth and Main Street, next to their home in Black Rock. Gene has driven the Black Rock school bus for the past 20 years. Neta worked at S. B. Power Tool Company for seven years. They have been married 45 wonderful years and have spent everyone of them surrounded by their friends and loved ones in Black Rock. *–Gene Whitlow.*

H. H. "BUD" WHITMIRE. Henry H. "Bud" Whitmire, named for his grandfather, Henry Jasper Whitmire, was born on January 4, 1943, to Joe Boyd and Christene Eagan Whitmire at Strawberry. Bud married Sue Pratt Whitmire on March 26, 1962, at Clover Bend Church of Christ. Carolyn Sue Pratt Whitmire was born to Dewell and Virl Ward Pratt on January 4, 1944, at Walnut Ridge, Arkansas.

Bud entered the United States Navy right out of high school at Clover Bend, and was stationed at Whidbey Island Naval Air Station, Washington State, from 1961 to 1964. Sue joined him there in the summer of 1962, the year of the World's Fair in Seattle, Washington. Their oldest son, Michael Scott, was born there in Oak Harbor, Washington, July 13, 1963.

Bud and Sue moved back to Arkansas briefly, then to Kansas City, Kansas and Missouri, in the mid 1960s, and stayed there until 1969. While there, Bud attended Moler Barber School and Sue worked as bookkeeper and order desk clerk at Seavey Flarsheim Food Brokerage Company. Bud then worked at the Drexel McClure Barber Shop.

Bud and Sue Whitmire family. Back, left to right: Michael, Sue, Mitch, Kristy. Front, left to right: Cristy and Bud.

Back in Arkansas, Bud started working at Whiteway Barber Shop and Sue worked as a bookkeeper for Southern Baptist College, now Williams Baptist College, where they also lived. About 1970, they built a house on Highway 91, Walnut Ridge. Mitchell Shawn was born in 1970, and Bud had by that time put in a barber shop at Hoxie. Cristy Suzanne was born in October, 1973.

The move to Hoxie came in 1990, when the family bought an old house on Broad Street. By Christmas that year, Mitchell had gone off to Desert Storm and fought with ground forces there in Kuwait in 1991. Cristy finished high school at Hoxie and went off to college at Hendrix. Michael worked in Memphis, Tennessee.

Michael married Gretta Dean in 1982, and Crystal LeighAnn was born to them in 1984. Mitchell married Kristy Oldham in 1992, and Cristy married Cap Phillips in 1993.

Mitchell and Kristy have two children, Cody Mitchell and Shelby Claire and live at Ft. Campbell, Kentucky. Mitchell graduated from Arkansas State University as did Kristy. Mitchell received a commission in the United States Army. Kristy is a registered nurse.

Cristy and Cap have one son, Teague, and lived briefly in Jonesboro and then moved to Walnut Ridge. Cap farms with his family and Cristy is pursuing a physical rehabilitation degree at Arkansas State University after finishing a biology degree there. Cap graduated from Arkansas State University with a degree in agriculture.

Michael lives and works in Memphis. Crystal lives with Gretta's mother at Alicia following Gretta's tragic, premature death.

Bud still barbers and Sue has been teaching for over 20 years at Hoxie Elementary. *–Sue Whitmire.*

CARL A. WHITTAKER FAMILY. In the early 1900s, my father and mother, Carl A. and Lucinda Whittaker, moved to Alicia from Clay County. They were parents of 11 children: Earl, Opal, L. J., Ruth, Fern, Harold, Wanda, Carl Jr., Gwendolyn, Mary and Bettye. They also raised three grandchildren: Wanda, Steve and Billy.

My father worked as a mechanic, cotton ginner, veterinarian, logger, carpenter and farmer. He played the violin, French and Jews harps and was a great whistler. As a hobby he loved whittling. My mother was a great domestic worker. She loved gardening, raising flowers, sewing, quilting and crocheting. One of her pastimes was playing the organ and singing.

In the middle to late 1920s, with the family growing, I am sure my father wondered how he was going to provide for them, but, with his determination and willingness to work he always seemed to make ends meet, sometime working two jobs.

In the early 1930s, this being the depression years, things started to decline. This was the time I was born. I was allergic to most milk and was struggling to stay alive. The black lady (known as Miss Mary), who was employed by my mother to help with the domestic chores lived with her husband in a boxcar along the railroad tracks. These workers were known as the section gang. Miss Mary told my father to get goats milk for me. This he did and I began to improve. Mary's main chore was to take care of me.

When we lived in Moran, our house stood where the airport runway now is. When we lived in Portia, the team ran away with my dad, and the goat and cart ran away with Junior and Gwen. A crosstie fell from a boxcar on Billy's foot. Mary ran into a barbwire fence. While I was riding horses I was kicked by another horse and busted an ankle. I took my first dip of snuff at age of four when we lived in Portia. We had fun times when friends gath-

Left to right: Pleaz Whittaker, Della Whittaker, Leona Whittaker, John Whittaker, Lela Whittaker, Lena Whittaker, Earl Rountree. Left to right: Charlie Whittaker, Ella Whittaker, Clarence Whittaker, Stella Whittaker, Carl A. Whittaker, Fern Whittaker, Lucinda Whittaker. Carl A. and Lucinda Whittaker - father and mother, Earl Rountree and Fern Whittaker, brothers.

ered at nights and on weekends to eat, play croquet, play music and sing.

In the middle 1930s, we moved to the Will Dobbs home in Clover Bend and in 1938, my father and mother made another move to our 40 acre farm bought from the government. We thought we were rich. We had a new house, barn and other outdoor buildings, a pump on the kitchen sink and another at the barn. Most of our vegetables, fruit and meat were raised on the farm. We bought flour, sugar, coffee and some spices. We had a sorghum mill and made molasses for our use and also for others in the community.

I had three brothers who served in World War II: Fern, Harold and Carl Jr. Later, Billy served in the Korean War. We attended school at Old Clover Bend and later in the new school.

My sister, Wanda Whittaker Healey's funeral was the first funeral held in the new school auditorium in early 1939.

Miss Mary, her husband and other members of the section gang gathered at night on the loading platform near the railroad tracks and sang for the residents. We lived across the street and our front porch was always full of neighbors who came to hear them sing.

Two sayings I remember my parents trying to instill into our hears were: "The more you give the more you receive" and "Do unto others as you would have them do unto you." They were always there for us, through good times and bad. They were the greatest parents. *–Betty Claxton.*

TELEMACHUS WHITTAKER FAMILY. Telemachus Whittaker was born in Kentucky about 1824, arriving in Lawrence County about 1847. He died December 2, 1881, and is buried at Whittaker Cemetery, Lawrence County, Arkansas. According to the 1880 census, he was a farmer, father born in North Carolina, mother born in Virginia.

Telemachus' first wife is unknown. They had the following children:

Thomas William; John F.; Sarah J., born November 8, 1847, in Lawrence County, Arkansas; Josiah, born 1849, in Lawrence County, died before 1860. His wife probably died giving birth to Josiah.

Thomas William Whittaker, born April 15, 1843, in Missouri, died on May 20, 1904, in Lawrence County, Arkansas; married Malissa Whittington about 1865. Malissa was born in Tennessee about 1845, and died about 1880. Their children were: Mary E., 1866-1906, married Lindsay Ratliff; Sarah Mary Ann, 1867-1918, married James "Jim" Manning; Elizabeth, born 1869, married Clarence C. Marshall; James, born 1871, died in a mining fire in the Ozarks; Thomas, born 1873; Talamacus, born 1876; and Susan Belle Caroline, February 28, 1880-July 5, 1953, married Joshua Albert Howell.

Thomas "Tom" Henry Whittaker & Maude Mae Manning, early 1950.

Thomas William Whittaker next married Malissa A. Whittington, born 1851, in Missouri, died 1921. Their children: Thomas Jefferson, 1882-1952; John H., 1883-1949; Martha Ann, 1884-1937; William Maxie, 1888-1941; Talbert Jack, 1889-1962; Charles, 1891-1898; and Effie, 1896-1950. The Malissa Whittingtons were cousins.

John F. Whittaker, born 1845, in Missouri, died 1920; he is buried at the Whittaker Cemetery in Lawrence County, Arkansas. John's first wife is unknown. They had one child, Laura Belle, born September 10, 1872, in Lawrence County, Arkansas; died August 6, 1949, in Lawrence County. Laura married William L. Conrey September 6, 1887.

John F. also married Annie Clemons, born 1852, in Lawrence County. They had one child, Elizabeth "Lizzie", born July 12, 1879, in Lawrence County, died November 4,

Carl Whittaker and Allie Guess, about 1948.

1948, in Lawrence County. Lizzie married Oliver H. Fry September 4, 1893. Lizzie also married Harrison Cook and a Frazier.

John F. next married Laura Belle Crow on August 26, 1884. Their children: Pearl Jane, October 11, 1884-January 6, 1943, married Burton H. Meadows, March 1, 1903; Nora M., August 28, 1887-August, 1921, married Felix; Andrew Fry, November 11, 1906; Thomas Henry; Maude Whittaker, born January 28, 1892, in Lawrence County, died 1915, married Jackson H. Deen March 26, 1911; Esther Francis, born May 19, 1895, in Sedgwick, Arkansas, died February 10, 1978; buried Manning Cemetery #1, married Virgil Tell Manning March 18, 1912; Bert Corbett, born May 22, 1897, in Sedgwick, Arkansas, died May 4, 1962, Riverside, California, married Ada Belle Murphy, married Edna Pine Everson.

John F. Whittaker and Laura Belle Crow, about 1884.

Thomas Henry "Tom" Whittaker, March 29, 1889-December 9, 1964, married Maude Manning April 26, 1908. They are buried at Lawrence Memorial Park Cemetery in Walnut Ridge, Arkansas. Their children: Marie Francis married Burley Shackleford; Viola Louise married Homer Frye; Walter Ralph married Bernice Crumpler; Carol Marvin married Allie Guess; Alean Margorie (twin) married Dallo Bennett; Christine Margaret (twin) married Herbert Herzog; Bernice Stella married Les Freeman; Betty Sue married Robert Wolthoff. Carol and Walter owned and operated the Whittaker Brothers Meat Market in Walnut Ridge. Viola was a teacher at the Whittaker School.

Telemachus next married Mary Ann Hillers October 26, 1849, in Lawrence County, Arkansas. Mary Ann was born on September 5, 1832, in Illinois. Their children: Telemachus, born 1856, in Lawrence County, Arkansas. Telemachus was on the 1870 census, but was not on 1880 census; Betsy Ann Elizabeth, born December 2, 1859, in Lawrence County, died May 8, 1923, in Lawrence County; Susan B., born 1863, in Lawrence County; Bud, born 1864, in Lawrence County; Babe Whittaker, born 1868, in Lawrence County.

–Barbara W. Brown.

HAZEL EUGENE WOODSON WIER FAMILY.

Hazel Eugene Woodson, daughter of John R. Woodson and Minnie Bell Horton Woodson, born September 24, 1914, in Lawrence County, raised in the Clear Springs area, was the first one in her family to have a birth certificate because they were not started until 1914. Her brother, Clay, stood in line for hours at the courthouse in Powhatan to get her one. She attended school at Black Rock. She married Walter Barton "Bart" Wier, son of Edward Frank Wier and Angnes Barton, born July 7, 1914. Hazel first met Bart when she was 10 years old. He came to her house selling milk. Bart was a very good basketball player at Black Rock School, making all county and all district as Hazel watched his every game. They fell in love and married at an early age. They

Hazel Woodson Wier family.

moved to Detroit, Michigan, where he worked as a millwright installing conveyors for factories. They had eight children.

1. Dorothy Ann Wier, born September 22, 1933, first married Arther D. Spradlin. They had four children: Arther D., Barton Eugene, Debbie and Beverly. Dorothy married the second time to Harry L. Hajek and had one child, Tammy.

2. Norma Jean Wier, born September 16, 1936, married Leon C. Neece. They had two sons: Norman, born October 5, 1955, and Kenny, born September 19, 1958, and died October 16, 1991.

3. Joseph Edward Thomas Wier, born December 4, 1948, married Joyce McDaniel. He had three children: Shawn, Greg and Sherrle. Joseph Edward Thomas Wier died September 2, 1987.

4. Betty Bartina Wier, born March 4, 1942, married Charles Allen Young on May 16, 1959.

They had one daughter, Vickie Lynn Young, born February 2, 1961. She married Jeff Hamilton and they have two children: Jonathan Austin and Cody Matthew.

5. Patricia Sue Wier, born March 16, 1944, married Morris William Nunally on July 17, 1959. They have five children:

a) William Nelson Nunally, born October 27, 1960, married Teresa Bagwell and they have two children: Christopher Shanee and Jennifer Dawn, who has one son, William Shane Hunter.

b) Mitchel Morris Nunally, born August 17, 1963, married Robin Anglin. They have three children: Mitchel Morris Nunally Jr., Whitney Lavelle and Tisa Nichole.

c) Narl Daniel Nunally, born July 28, 1969, married Kim Ring.

d) Christie Lynn Nunally, born February 18, 1976.

e) Joseph Weston Nunally, born June 28, 1981.

6. Donna Jane Wier, born December 16, 1946, married Jim Smith. They had five children: Jimmie Ann, Jamie Lynn, Norma Shelly, Jennings L. and Jesse.

7. Wendall Ray Wier, born June 13, 1952 (twin) had three children: Linda Kay, Wendell Ray and Michael Lugo. He married the second time on November 25, 1988, to Brenda Kay Vance, daughter of J. B. and Garnet Vance, born March 30, 1957.

8. Linda Kay Wier, born and died June 13, 1952 (twin).

Walter Barton Wier died April 28, 1982.

Hazel Eugene Woodson Wier lives in Walnut Ridge, Arkansas. –Betty Young.

ALYSON RACHEL WILLIAMS.

My name is Alyson Rachel Williams. I was born in Jonesboro, Arkansas, on June 2, 1985. I have always lived in Lawrence County.

My father is Allen Darnelle Williams was born on February 21, 1962. He was born in Walnut Ridge and has lived here since.

His father is Walter Warren Williams. He was born on September 29, 1932. He was born in Lawrence County and has always lived here. His parents were Florence Irene Riddles Williams and his father is Earnest S. Williams.

Allen's mother is Bernice Emelene Price Williams. She was born on November 21, 1933. She was also born in Lawrence County and has always lived in Lawrence County. Her parents are William Jerry Price and Elzora McCall Price.

Bernice Williams and Walter Williams got a divorce in the mid 1970s. My grandmother has not remarried, but my grandfather did. He married Loreine Velora McClintock Manning Williams.

Loreine Velora McClintock Manning Williams was born March 5, 1930. She was born in Peach Orchard. She has lived in the Lawrence County area for most of her life. She did live in California for three years. Manning is part of her name because she was married before she married Walter Williams. Her husband before was Harry Manning, but he passed on. Her parents are J. R. McClintock and Erma Irene Thomas McClintock.

My mother is Terry Sue Anderson Cunningham Williams. She was born on June 2, 1958, in Chicago, Illinois. She has lived in Lawrence County for 34 years of her life. My mother was married to Jim Cunningham before she married my father. During that marriage, they had one child, my half brother, Jeremy Cunningham. He was born on March 13, 1976.

Her father is E. W. Anderson. He was born on November 22, 1924. He was born in Peach Orchard and has lived in the Lawrence County area all his life. His parents are Telfair Anderson and Alma Lindly Anderson.

Terry Sue's mother is Alice Marie Rose Thompson Anderson. She was born on January 16, 1923, in Randolph County. Alice Marie's last name was Thompson at one time because she was married to a Thompson, but they soon divorced. She has lived in this area all of her life. Her parents are Maude Elizabeth Shelton Rose and Clarence Rose.

–Alyson R. Williams - 8th grade.

"CHAMP" WILLIAMS COMES HOME.

"I'm not coming home to find my youth but to see my friends," Champ Williams said yesterday.

Williams made the comment as he arrived here on the eve of a homecoming celebration to which he is bringing lunch and gifts for all 848 townspeople.

In spite of the declaration, Williams, 69, a wealthy Orlando, Florida, restaurateur, was engulfed with boyhood memories as he drove into town to check out preparations for today's homecoming bash.

"You see that field right over there?" he said, pointing through the car window. "That's where Wilson's daddy got killed by a bull. Wilson was a friend of mine. His daddy was running across the field and the bull took out after him. He tried to climb a tree but couldn't get up in it, and the bull smashed into him."

At a small white house two blocks from the main intersection, Williams frowned and said, "This is where our old house used to be, but I believe they've torn it down. No. Wait a minute. It's just been altered and rearranged. This was all garden. I remember when our well went dry and I had to go down the hill to Drew Rice's pump. I'd carry a bucket of water back for every plant in the garden. It was tough."

The more Williams drove through the town the more he realized that going home is a journey into the past. Since he left more than 50 years ago at the age of 12, that past is a boy's past.

"Things looked much bigger when I was young," he said. "I remember the swimming hole in the river. I was 8 or 9 and it seemed like the biggest, deepest stretch of water...Now, I realize I could spit across it."

At a long low block building, Williams stopped the car. "This was Papa's blacksmith shop. I remember the Halloween some boys dismantled Papa's wagon, pulled the sections to the roof with a rope and reassembled it on the roof. My Papa came out the next morning and you'd have thought he'd been stuck with a sword."

Earlier, when passing through nearby Walnut Ridge, Williams spotted the stretch of railroad track where his father was killed in 1936. "There were two sets of tracks," he said. "Papa thought the train was on the other track. He slowed down to a walk when he reached the track the train was on."

Although Williams moved to Florida in 1923, he vividly remembers the days when his grandmother, Phereza Kincaid, ran the Southern Hotel, which he said had the best restaurant in town.

"She was one smart lady," Williams said. "She'd give you a room and three meals a day for $1.25 a day. Drummers (traveling salesmen) making the circle out of Memphis stayed at the hotel five days a week. On weekends, local people came to Sunday dinner. Everybody in town who could afford it went to eat at the Southern Hotel."

All but a tiny part of the hotel has been torn down. The remaining part serves as a private home.

"My grandfathers on both sides of the family were apparently well-to-do," Williams said. "But by the time I came along something had happened. The money was gone. After my grandmother sold the hotel and moved to Orlando she moved us, too.

"I remember being told I would have to sell my sled," he said, his eyes on some distant snowhill. "I didn't want to give up that sled, but they said there was no snow in Florida. They convinced me I'd never see snow again."

Williams' father, the village blacksmith, did not like Florida and returned home after a year or so. Williams remembered the summer he hitchhiked from Orlando to Black Rock with 15 cents in his pocket.

"You could do that then; you couldn't do it now. I stayed in Black Rock a couple of weeks and my father gave me 50 cents to hitchhike back."

Although Williams left town in humble circumstances, he is returning home flush. During the last 30 years, he has developed a highly successful restaurant business that now numbers 21 eating, drinking and snacking places in Orlando's International Airport.

"But we're the only family restaurant in a major airport in America," he said proudly. His two sons, Steve and Bruce, help run the restaurant complex, which is known as Champ's Plaza.

Florida restaurateur Champ Williams (right) is the champ of the people in his hometown.

Williams' sons, as well as his brother, Wayne; a sister, Anna Gillham, and a cousin, Willie Ann Khalial of Sacramento, will be with him today when the homecoming part unfolds at the school gymnasium.

As Williams arrived in town yesterday he was met by a large red and white banner stretched across the main intersection, reading "WELCOME HOME CHAMP."

Williams beamed. But he told Mayor Charles Penny, "That's going to have to come down. This isn't my day. It's Black Rock's day."

Penny, who fully intends to leave the banner up, replied, "Tell that to the town."

Williams grinned.

While he was standing in the street under the banner, people started coming outside to meet him. They came from the Black Rock grocery, the barber shop, the pool room and the drug store that Mayor Penny is restoring. Two or three members of the volunteer fire department said the entire fire fighting force intend to help unload Williams' Christmas truck when it arrives. The truck left Orlando as 12:30 p.m. Monday after some mechanical delays.

"Don't worry, it's going to get here," Williams said. "Am I going to have a crowd tomorrow?" he asked.

"I think we are going to have more than we can handle," the mayor said.

"Good, that's what this is all about," Williams said. "Say, Old Screw Eye, the cross-eyed marble player, is supposed to be coming. I sure want to see him again. He was the best marble shot I ever saw."

Williams grinned the grin of a man who had suddenly looked across a great gulf of years and caught a glimpse of his youth.

–Willie Ann Khalial.

SHIRLEY CHARLOTTE MEEKS WILLIAMS FAMILY.

Shirley Charlotte Meeks, daughter of Cecil Curtis Meeks and Johnie Caldonia Woodson Meeks, was born May 13, 1938, in Black Rock, Arkansas. Shirley started very young working in the fields with her mother and brothers picking cotton and watching her father cut pearl buttons out of shells from Black River. She baby-sat and worked in restaurants while attending Black Rock High School and graduated in 1957.

For the first nine years that Shirley was growing up there was this young man hanging around her home with her brothers. He was Billy Dean Williams, son of Bill R. Williams and May Propst Williams. He was born June 26, 1930, and enlisted in the United states Navy in 1947, and served for 13 years. Then he came home and married Shirley. Bill and Shirley have five children:

Bill and Shirley Williams family.

1. Tommie Jean Williams, born July 8, 1959, married Ray Lynn Richey on September 16, 1976. Tommie Jean and Ray have three sons. They are: Ray Heath Richey, born January 25, 1977, and Jason Lynn Richey, born February 18, 1978, and Nathan Dean Richey, born January 5, 1982.

2. Michael Dean Williams, born June 18, 1961, married on July 24, 1982, to Nancy Caryl Helms, daughter of Leon and Rose Helms. Mike and Nancy have two children: Ian Michael Williams, born September 30, 1988, and Tyler Dean Williams, born September 7, 1990.

3. Rosemary Williams, born and died July 12, 1962.

4. Rebecca Sue Williams, born October 12, 1963, married on June 27, 1981, to Jeff Callahan. They had one daughter, Cristin Machelli, born March 10, 1982. Becky and Eddie Jones have one son, Trevor Blake, born November 2, 1989.

5. Charlotte Ann Williams, born February 18, 1965, married Michael H. Crooms on December 8, 1980. They have two children: Rachel Crooms, born December 12, 1982, and Michael H. Crooms Jr., born April 12, 1985.

Bill has worked for the past 30 years on a riverboat in Mississippi and he and Shirley live at Black Rock next door to the house where she was born and where her mother still lives. Their children all live in Lawrence County.

Billy Dean Williams and Shirley Meeks Williams. *–Shirley Williams.*

HOUSTON LAFAYETTE "BLOCKIE" WILLIS FAMILY.

Houston "Blockie" was born July 3, 1897, in Kings Mill, Arkansas, in Sharp County, the son of William Elijah and Eliza Elva McCord Willis. Houston had one brother, Silas Wesley Willis, born February 2, 1900, and died October 6, 1959, from a heart attack. He is buried in Oak Forest Cemetery in Black Rock. In 1913, the family moved from Sharp County to Black Rock.

On April 28, 1918, he married May Francis Pickney. May was born May 1, 1902, in Black Rock, the daughter of William Elijah and Allie Propst Pickney. Houston and May had five children.

Front row from left: Hall, Houston "Blockie", May, Lucille. Back row from left: Ruby, Wilma, Vernon.

1. Ruby Louise, born June 7, 1919, married June 7, 1940, to Leonard Paul Hill, born September 1, 1917, in Black Rock. He died February 23, 1961, the son of Witt and Florence Montgomery Hill.

2. Wilma, born November 28, 1922, married August 24, 1942, to Jennings Paul Smith, born March 16, 1921, son of Max and Katie Pearle Smith.

3. Vernon, born September 23, 1925, married October 4, 1946, to Anna Mae Bryant, born November 9, 1930, daughter of Elmer and Lena Burleson Bryant.

4. Raymond Hall, born October 29, 1927, married May 8, 1948, to Glenda Sue Hall, born April 9, 1931, the daughter of Edward Morgan and Ruth Nancy King Hall.

5. Lucille, born September 25, 1930, died September 21, 1946, from the results of a car accident by the Old Lebanon Cemetery on Highway 25 one mile west of Eaton, Arkansas, in Lawrence County near the Old Lebanon Church, two days before her 16th birthday. She is buried in Oak Forest Cemetery in Black Rock.

Houston worked at the button factory in Black Rock for several years in the 1930s. He also was a mechanic and had his own trucking company, hauling people's furniture and wood.

In 1954, the family moved to Genoa, Illinois, where Houston worked in the Argo Factory and May was manager of the cafeteria. In 1960, they settled in Black Rock.

Houston was stricken with diabetes and had his left leg amputated below the knee due to an ulcer that would not heal. He died December 20, 1962, at his home in Black Rock at the age of 67.

May died August 17, 1991, in St. Bernards Hospital in Jonesboro from leukemia at the age of 89.

Both are buried in Oak Forest Cemetery in Black Rock. –Glenda Willis.

WILLMUTH FAMILY.

John E. Willmuth was born in Graves County, Kentucky, in 1840. He moved to the Hazel Grove Community in Lawrence County where he was an elder in the Baptist church. The Willmuths owned and operated a cotton gin built in 1887. The gin, operated by oxen, ginned 269 bales of cotton in 1888. Located at the mouth of Piney Creek, the gin moved to Caney Creek, then was relocated to Saffell and operated by Hollie Saffell for many years. The Willmuths also owned farm land in the area.

John E. Willmuth married Lucinda Campbell of Tennessee. They had seven children: William R., Sidney J., George W., Lawrence F., John W., Henry C. and Mary W.

Sidney J. remained in Lawrence County and operated the family cotton gin. The other children moved to various parts of the country. Sidney J. married Julia Gardner and they are the grandparents of the Willmuths residing in Lawrence County today. Sidney J. was born on September 30, 1867, and died on May 20, 1933. Julia Gardner Willmuth was born on September 21, 1871, and died on March 3, 1934. Their children are: Hattie Arlene, September 24, 1894-July 14, 1965; Hettie, September 14, 1896-February 21, 1920; Joyce Florine, November 10, 1903-January 16, 1988; Frank Kenneth "Bud", April 1, 1899-August 2, 1957; Hal Norwood "Ruben", June 22, 1905-January 26, 1993; Willie "Bill", January 23, 1910-November 12, 1993; Willene, born January 23, 1910; and Jack, August 3, 1918-April 22, 1934.

Mr. John E. Willmuth, Mrs. Owen Willmuth Cross Cowan. Mr. Sidney Willmuth, Dorothy and Howard Cross. Mrs. Cowan is a niece of Mr. Sidney Willmuth.

Hattie Willmuth married Hollie Saffell. Their children are: Billy, Tommy, Lorena Hubbard, Venita Doyle and Lana Johnson. They live near Saffell with their families and operate businesses and farms in the community.

Bud and Verna Milligan Willmuth had seven children. Pauline Howard, Mary Wanda Williams, F. K. and Murphy currently live in Lawrence County with their families. The three other children are: Charles Van of Cave City; Sue Ratliff of Conway and Brenda Moore of North Little Rock.

The children of Hal and Amy Mason Willmuth are: Harold Norwood of Walnut Ridge and Carroll V. of Strawberry. A daughter, Sydney W. Kealer, lives in Bryant.

The Willmuth family has a history of active community leadership. Carroll V. was a rural mail carrier in Lawrence County for 28 years. Harold has been a dentist in Walnut Ridge since 1965. F. K. and Carroll V. served the Strawberry School as board members for a number of years. Lorena Hubbard, Venita Doyle and Lana Johnson own and operate a fabric store and quilt shop near Saffell. F. K. and Murphy own and operate cattle farms. Harold N., Murphy and Sydney still own property that was a part of the original Willmuth farm.

The Willmuth family has been an asset to Lawrence County. John E. Willmuth began a legacy in Lawrence County over 100 years ago. –Harold Willmuth.

WILSON.

Mary Ann Parsley and Berry Herman Wilson moved to Lawrence County in 1919. They bought an 80 acre farm that was located on the corner of what is known as Clear Springs Road and Highway 63. They reared two children, Chester and Irene, on the farm. The children attended Clear Springs School. Chester died at age 14 of the flu. Irene Wilson Daniels also reared two children, Jack and Anna Lue, on the farm.

Berry Wilson was a Baptist minister and served many churches in the area as pastor during the 1920s, and 1930s. He was pastor at the Clear Springs Baptist Church before his death in 1936. Berry Wilson's parents were Amanda Lane and John A. Wilson of Sharp County, Arkansas.

Mary Ann Parsley Wilson lived on the farm from 1919 until 1974. She attended Clear Springs Baptist Church. Her parents were Martha Jane Peed and Bethel Parsley of Calamine, Arkansas.

Irene Wilson Daniels lived on the farm and reared her two children there. They also attended Clear Springs Baptist Church where she served the church in several areas. She passed away in 1965. Irene's two children, Jack and Anna Lue, graduated from Sloan-Hendrix School at Imboden, Arkansas. Jack Daniels lives on a farm near Jonesboro, Arkansas. Anna Lue Daniels Cook lives at Germantown, Tennessee. Anna Lue Cook taught third grade at Black Rock School for many years.

WILSON FAMILY.

William M. Wilson, born 1811, in Tennessee, married Elizabeth, born 1825, in Tennessee. They moved to Lawrence County, Arkansas, in 1860. He was a farmer and had 10 children: Isaac, born 1842, Missouri; William, born 1846, Missouri; Polly A., born 1848, Missouri; Nancy Jane, born 1850, Missouri; Dorcas, born 1852, Missouri; Martha E., born 1854, Missouri; Orleans E., born 1858, Missouri; James W., born 1860, Arkansas; Clara A., born 1864, Missouri; and Lavina, born 1870, Missouri.

James W. Wilson married Mary Francis Baker in 1860. Her parents were Beverly R. Baker and Samantha Ross of Randolph County, Arkansas. Beverly Baker was a corporal in Company C, 33rd Regiment Missouri in the Civil War in Randolph County, Arkansas on December 10, 1864. He was a mail carrier between Pocahontas and Imboden. He caught pneumonia and died March, 1894. Their children were: John W., November 4, 1875-January 13, 1961, Arkansas, married Hattie Buchanan; James Elijah, December 29, 1880-March 22, 1956, in Arkansas, first married Elizabeth Jane Ponder, second Zelma Cecil Finley; Lena E., August 8, 1886-July 12, 1960, in Arkansas, married Henry C. Nicholson; Grover C., May 18, 1891-May 19, 1982, in Arkansas.

James Elijah Wilson and Zelma Cecil Finley in 1930, when they married.

John W. Wilson married Hattie Buchanan and their children were: Mark H., born 1916; Marie, born 1918; Mary, born 1919; Virginia, born 1923; Joan, born 1921. They owned a general store in Newport. He was in the Spanish American War. They moved to Little Rock in 1946. He died in 1961, and she died at 105 in 1994.

Lena E. Wilson married Henry Clay Nicholson. They had seven children: Alma, Herman, Ethyl, Edgar Robert, Violet and Ralph. They lived in Jackson County, Arkansas, and died there.

Grover Wilson married Mary and they had one child: Noel. Grover had one leg amputated due to diabetes. He lived to be in his 90s, and is buried in Swifton, Arkansas.

James E. Wilson married Zelma Cecil Finley, daughter of Delia Majors and Charlie Finley of Elizabeth, Arkansas, in Van Zandt, Texas, December 25, 1930. They had three children: Cecil June, September 7, 1931; Louisiana, married Hayes Crouch; Velma Glee, born on August 8, 1935, Arkansas, died January 13, 1998, Little Rock, Arkansas; she married Dewayne Merryman; Vernon Stanley, born on August 22, 1937, Arkansas, died February 2, 1954, Little Rock, Arkansas; he married Mary Gray. Zelma died of blood poisoning during a pregnancy on December 10, 1941, in Carroll County, Arkansas, leaving James to raise the children. He never remarried and stayed in Arkansas until he died March 22, 1956, in Little Rock with diabetes.

Cecil June Wilson married Hayes W. Crouch on June 29, 1946, in England, Arkansas. They had three children: Paul W., April 26, 1947; he married Nancy Lavally; Portia A., March 26, 1949; she married first Michael Crowder, second Billy Davis; Janie D., July 9, 1950; she married Paul Knappenburger. June was a nurse, working at the VA Hospital in Little Rock until she retired in 1998. Paul owns an auto repair shop in Beeville, Texas. Portia is a hair stylist in San Angelo, Texas. Janie is a development specialist in Oxnard, California.

Portia A. Crouch married Michael Crowder in California, and had one child: Alicia, born December 3, 1970. They divorced and she married Billy Davis March 26, 1974, in Florida. They had one child: Jason W. Davis, December 3, 1974. Portia works as a hair stylist in San Angelo, Texas, and Billy is retired from General Telephone Company.
–Bill and Portia Davis.

BERRY AND MARY WILSON.

The Lady Was a Farmer. The black leather reins were wrapped around her thin waist; the wooden breaking plow handles were held in her calloused hands. Babe, the gentle plow mare, was always attuned to the wishes of the lady operating the farm equipment. They had worked together for seven seasons. It was 1943 and the lady was starting this growing season by tilling up the soil. She was adding a new crop to the farm, three acres of cotton.

Mrs. Berry Wilson would be farming under the War Production Program - 1943 Farm Plan for Arkansas. The WPP was begun during World War II by the United States Department of Agriculture to establish war crop goals. Under this program, Mrs. Wilson would be raising one acre of sweet potatoes, six acres of hay, one acre of alfalfa, one acre of Irish potatoes, seven acres of corn and three acres of cotton. The normal yield of cotton produced was 230 pounds per acre. She would be producing less than one bale.

The lady also had 17 head of cattle, including seven milk cows. She had 125 laying hens and nine hogs. A large home garden was producing. Mrs. Wilson utilized all 80 acres of her farm located in the foothills of the eastern Arkansas Ozarks, in Lawrence County.

Berry and Mary Wilson were married in 1905. He was a Baptist preacher, she was a southern lady. They bought the farm in 1919 for $3,000. There was a white two story frame house on the property and 57 of the 80 acres were cleared for crops or pasture.

The southern lady and the Baptist preacher worked side by side to make the farm into a productive operation. They built a dairy barn and operated a successful dairy business along with the corn and hay crops that they raised on the tillable land.

Berry H. and Mary Ann Parsley Wilson. They were on their way to church, 1933.

Two children, Chester and Irene, were reared on the farm. Chester died during the winter of 1923 from the flu. That was an epidemic year for the flu. Irene would mature into womanhood, marry, divorce and return to the farm to rear her own son and daughter.

In 1936 the Baptist preacher died, leaving his wife with the farm, a dairy business, crops to tend and hay to harvest, 175 laying hens, the one work horse, Babe, and a 1936 Ford that she could not drive.

Mrs. Berry Wilson did not sit long in sorrow. She took the reins of the plow horse and continued farming. During the fall of 1936, she harvested the corn crop by herself. The neighbors dropped in from time to time to help with some of the more overwhelming jobs such as hay cutting. This was a time when a horse was used to pull the mowing machine that cut the hay. A horse pulled the rake that windrowed the hay for drying and for loading the hay wagon. That same horse pulled the wagon that carried the hay to the barn. Loading and unloading the hay into the hayloft was all done by hand using a pitchfork. Hay cutting was a hard job for a man, but it was almost impossible for one lady working alone.

Mrs. Wilson found the inner strength daily to do the heavy farm work in all weather. The temperatures fell below zero in winter and climbed to the century mark in the summer. Mrs. Wilson never had a day off. Her work began at daybreak and lasted until all the day's work was completed. Other than Babe, her only companion for many years was her faithful collie. During the winter, her farm tasks became even harder. When the temperatures were below freezing for long periods, just keeping drinking water for all the livestock became a problem. Holes were chopped in the ice on the pond so the animals could drink, but those froze back quickly. Her own water was drawn from a hand-dug well.

The livestock had to be fed more hay during cold weather, when pastures were frozen. She fed dairy feed to the cows from 100 pound bags. The local feed store delivered her feed once a month in the heavy cotton bags which the lady recycled into useful items.

Mrs. Wilson heated her house and cooked her food with wood. She cut her wood in the fall. She had built a large wooden sled with runners on the bottom. She needed at least four cords of wood plus the smaller split up wood for her cooking stove. During the winter, she never let the fire go out in the large heating stove, but she built a new fire each morning in the cooking stove in the kitchen.

Mrs. Wilson bought only flour and sugar. She had her corn ground into meal at the gristmill at Powhatan, Arkansas. All her other food was raised in the garden or on the farm. Once the food was raised it was canned. Mrs. Wilson canned all the vegetables from her garden and she used the chickens she raised for meat. Her dairy cows provided her with milk, and she made her own butter, cream and cheese. She had a small refrigerator, but the freezing space was limited. She dried apples and peaches. She kept red potatoes, sweet potatoes and turnips in the cellar under the house. These kept all winter.

In the evenings, with all the farm work done, she found time for her favorite pastime - quilting. She pieced and quilted wonderful intricate designs. The quilting frames hung from the ceiling. Her beautiful handmade quilts are treasured by her grandchildren today.

She kept a worn leather Bible by her chair. She read this daily and attended church every Sunday she could, walking a mile to Clear Spring Baptist Church, where her husband had been pastor. She served as church secretary and teacher.

Spring was her favorite season. Trees burst into bloom, baby chickens were hatched, calves were born, the garden and fields were tilled and vegetables, crops and flowers were planted.

Her daughter, Irene, returned to the farm in late 1943 with her two children. Mrs. Wilson was glad to have her daughter home again. She spent many hours teaching her grandchildren the joys of farm life.

She operated the farm and lived to be 93 years old. Farm, family and church made this lady's life one of joy. She lived a simple life on the farm, and never knew a time when the farm did not need her or a time when she did not need the farm. This southern lady was my grandmother.
–Anna Lue Cook, granddaughter.

ELLA ALENE WOODSON WILSON.

Ella Alene Woodson, daughter of Wesley Dee Woodson and Cora Oleta Elizabeth Woodson, was born December 28, 1934, three days after Christmas. She was raised at the mouth of Spring River and being the eldest of eight children, watched over the little ones. "To keep us out of mama's hair, she would take us to the river bank to watch the big boats." remembers younger sister, Nancy Woodson Pickney.

Alene, age 17, moved to Kansas City, Kansas. "When Christmas came, she'd play Santa sending everyone a store bought toy and a new pair of winter shoes as it's a long walk from the mouth of Spring River to the Black Rock schoolhouse."

Eventually, she met James Alvin Wilson Sr., a brown-eyed handsome Air Force veteran with a

Alene and Jim Wilson's grandsons: Logan James Wilson Potts, age two and Jake Maxey Wilson Potts, age six.

beautiful smile. They had a lot in common. Jim came from a large family, the youngest of nine children belonging to Mr. and Mrs. Charles Ezra Wilson of Kansas City, Kansas. He was born December 22, 1930. Fireworks lit up the sky as Alene and Jim married July 4, 1957. They had two children: James Alvin Wilson Jr., born April 10, 1958, in Kansas City and Tamara Dee Wilson, born November 25, 1961, in Sun Valley, California. Both children graduated Basehor High School, Basehor, Kansas, Kansas City Community Col-

Family of Ella Alene Woodson Wilson: Alene, Jim Sr., Tamara, Daryl and Jim Jr.

lege and University of Kansas, Lawrence, Kansas. Both settled in Basehor. Jim remains single.

Tamara married Daryl Louis Potts August 5, 1988, in Bonner Springs, Kansas. Daryl, born April 10, 1959, is the son of Mr. and Mrs. Maxey D. Potts Sr., Beaumont, Texas. Daryl and Tamara have two sons born in Kansas City: Jakob Maxey Wilson Potts, born February 18 1992, and Logan James Wilson Potts, born August 4, 1995. Daryl's daughter from a previous marriage, Heather Rose Potts, was born June 22, 1982, Beaumont, Texas.

During the midwest floods of 1993, Alene and Jim celebrated their 36th wedding anniversary. A month later, Jim died suddenly of a heart attack, August 21, 1993, at age 62. "Grandpa" bestowed a cherished memory for his young grandson, Jake, just 18 months old. Those who were there remember watching Jake happily wave his chubby little hand at the sky, not paying any attention to the waiting ambulance. He told of grandpa going into a beautiful rainbow in the clouds.

The Wilson and Potts families are members of the Church of Christ. Fond childhood memories include worship at the Black Rock Church of Christ with Grandma and Grandpa Woodson; Grandpa's favorite saying, "My word is my bond."; all the holidays when even icy winter roads couldn't stop a family reunion; and just knowing Grandma Woodson's homecookin' and hugs were just around the next bend kept generation after generation coming back. –Tamara Potts.

WINCHESTER. William Winchester was born in Westminster, England, December 22, 1711, son of James and Jane Winchester, baptized January 1, 1712, in the parish church of Saint Martin-in-the-Fields, Westminster, London England.

Having an adventurous spirit and completing a good education as a surveyor, William indentured himself to a Peter Simpson of London for five years, arriving in America on board the ship "Hume", in Annapolis, Maryland, March 6, 1731. After completing his indenture, he established himself as a farmer in Baltimore County, Maryland. He married Lydia Richard, 1727-1809, in 1747. William died 1790, in Carroll County, Maryland. Their children, all inheriting the adventurous spirit of their father, all left home to seek their fortune, as soon as they were grown. Daniel married Rosanna Matthews and moved to Charleston, South Carolina where Jonathan was born, 1807-1876.

Jonathan's first wife, Rebecca Lemons, died and he then married Mary Ann Trowell in Murfreesboro, Tennessee. Their son, James Trowell Winchester, was the great-grandfather of the present day Winchesters in Lawrence County.

James Trowell Winchester, born in Oak Ridge, Tennessee, 1850-1916, died in Denton, Arkansas. Wife, Sara Ann Catherine McCarthy, born Izard County, Arkansas, 1855-1927, died Eaton, Arkansas. They were the parents of:

1. Susan Isabell Winchester, 1874-1945, married James Marion Shelton, 1872-1945, Izard County, Arkansas. Both are buried in Lawrence County, Arkansas.

2. Infant died Izard County, Arkansas.

3. Infant died Izard County, Arkansas.

4. Infant died Izard County, Arkansas.

5. Janie Arene Winchester, 1883, Izard County, Arkansas, died 1969, Walnut Ridge, Arkansas; married in Lawrence County, Arkansas, to Charlie Marion Rainwater, 1885-1959. Both are buried in Lawrence County, Arkansas.

6. John Dallas Winchester, born 1886, was preceded in death by two wives, Ada Belle Casper, 1890-1918, Winfred Casper, 1899-1923, third wife, Laura Madison Pickett, dates unknown.

7. Infant died Izard County, Arkansas.

8. William Owen Winchester, 1890, Izard County, Arkansas, died 1974, VA hospital, Memphis, Tennessee; married Eula Weir, 1896-1989, in Denton, Arkansas, 1915. Both are buried in Imboden, Arkansas.

9. Walter Isaac Winchester, born 1893, Izard County, Arkansas, died 1949, Smithville, Arkansas.

10. Oscar Morris Winchester, born Denton, Arkansas, 1895, married Clara Matthews, born 1900, Black Rock; marriage and death dates unknown.

11. Joseph Ernest Winchester, 1898, Denton, Arkansas, died 1998, Pocahontas, Arkansas; married Ester Lily Jean, born June 11, 1901, died February 17, 1993, hospital, Pocahontas, Arkansas.

The Winchester family were known to be hard working farmers, preachers and teachers.

Reverend James T. (Baptist minister) brought his family to Lawrence County where he was the pastor of New Hope Church, Denton, Arkansas, as shown in the church records. A "handshake" was a contract, not to be broken.

History lists many Winchester men who have served in the armed forces and fought for the freedom of the American people. In this century, World War I, and World War II, those listed are Oscar Morris Winchester, William Owen Winchester, Robert Owen Winchester, Almie Marion Rainwater and Jean Winchester. Jean Winchester gave his life on May 16, 1945, on Okinawa, South Pacific, World War II.

Possibly others I don't know about.
–VeTrix (Mrs. Robert) Winchester.

ALBERT SIDNEY WOOD married Mattie Higgs on April 4, 1894, in Marion County, Arkansas. Albert was born April 26, 1873, at Flippin and died May 26, 1951. Mattie was born July 4, 1875, at Yellville and died September 30, 1950. They moved from Arkansas to Texas, for a brief period about 1907, and then on to the Lawrence County area. Their children were:

1. Joseph Raymond "Ray", born October 5, 1895, at Flippin.

2. Jessie, born 1898, at Flippin.

3. Henry Bryan "Sam", born October 8, 1901, at Flippin.

4. Beulah, born January 1, 1904, at Yellville.

5. Lucy "Snow", born February, 1906, in Marion County.

6. Charley "Jack", born November 9, 1909, in Lawrence County.

7. Velma "Babe", born September 20, 1912, in Lawrence County.

"Ray" once recalled the train trip to Texas when he and Sam were about ages 12 and 6. Ray said he was wearing a knitted sweater and that Sam pulled on the cuff until it stretched, it seemed to him, about half the length of the car.

Albert Sidney was a railroad ticket agent at Minturn. Later he owned small country stores near Egypt and Hoxie. He was the seventh child of 12 born to Joseph Wood, born 1841, in Marion County, and died 1904, and Emily Summers, born 1843, in Marion County, and died 1886. On March 4, 1894,

Henry Bryan "Sam" Wood and Ruby Prewitt Wood about 1924.

Joseph married Sarah A. Williams Pickle, born March 4, 1862, Crawford, Missouri. Joseph was a Confederate soldier who served in the 27th Arkansas Infantry.

Mattie Higgs had brothers and sisters. One of Mattie's brothers practiced medicine. He once received a cadaver at the train station, took it home and boiled it so he could have a skeleton for his medical practice. Another brother, who was almost blind, tuned pianos. He died from food poisoning from eating corn from a tin can.

Albert and Mattie's third child, Henry Bryan "Sam" Wood, was married on August 3, 1924, to Ruby Ethel Prewitt, born March 6, 1905, at Hardy, and died October 12, 1990. They met as a result of Ruby making a trip from Sharp County to visit her sister "Tinny" who lived in Lawrence County. Tinny was doing the cooking for a crew of loggers who were cutting timber. Tinny's husband set up a large tent for cooking and serving. Ruby's cousin, who knew Sam Wood, introduced him to Ruby at the food tent. From that point, Ruby made additional trips to visit her sister. Sam and Ruby married in secret and both continued living at their respective parent's home. They later said that Sam needed to wait until after the harvest so he could afford to rent their own place. They had five children.

1. Joyce Mae, born August 21, 1925, at Alicia, married Edward Rose Hudson, October 12, 1941; one child, Beverly Edrath.

2. Howard Bryan "Pete", born December 26, 1927, in Lawrence county, married first Juanita Broom; children: Jacqueline and Bryan; married second Ethel Mae Dodd Simmons.

3. John Willis "Bill", born October 11, 1930, in Lawrence County, married Margaret Hendrix; children: Steven and Phillip.

4. Roberta Willene "Bertie", born January 8, 1935, in Lawrence County, married Victor Hanshaw; children: Mark and Kenneth.

5. Jerry Blake "Buck", born June 30, 1940, in Lawrence County, married Wanda Bullock; children: John and Blake. –D.N. Lee.

WOODSON. Anita Sue Woodson James, daughter of Wesley Dee Woodson and Cora Oleta Elizabeth Tyree Woodson, married Clyde Benjamin James Jr., son of Clyde Benjamin James Sr. and Willie Ruth McCall James of Portia, Arkansas, on August 30, 1963, at Black Rock, Arkansas. They were divorced in 1978.

Jobs were hard to find for a young couple in Lawrence County in 1963, so having family in Kansas, they moved there and raised a family. They were blessed with three children from this union.

1. Melody Lynette James, born March 15, 1964, in Kansas City, Kansas, married Travis Fraker on August 14, 1993, and was divorced July 16, 1997.

2. Clyde Benjamin James III was born in Kansas City, Kansas, on April 2, 1965, married Shannon Hoenker July, 1990. They were divorced a few years later. They had one daughter from this marriage, Shanna Lynn James, born November 23, 1990, at Shawnee Mission, Kansas.

Anita Sue Woodson James and her children: Melody L. James, Clyde Benny James III and Robert Wesley James.

3. Robert Wesley James, born November 13, 1968, in Northridge, California, was married to Susanna Kay Griffin, born May 1, 1976, in Kansas City, Missouri on April 25, 1998. She brought into this marriage one son, Noah Max McFarlin, born July 27, 1996, at Kansas City, Missouri.

Anita Sue Woodson James lives in Wyandotte and Clay Counties in Kansas.

ARTHUR TAYLOR WOODSON FAMILY.
Arthur Taylor Woodson, better known as Dick Woodson, was born August 8, 1902, and raised in the Mt. Vernon area near Black Rock and attended school there. He worked at the button factory when he was young; then he worked for free with Heavy Blankenship to learn the electrical trade. Later he taught his sons and grandsons. His son, David, remembers helping him at the age of 14 when the R.E.A. Electric Company first came to Black Rock in 1941. They put one pull-chain light in each middle-class household if they could afford it, and in the upper-class homes they sometimes put one wall switch light and one plug-in. He married on February 26, 1924, to Ella Etna Maxey, born in the bootheel of Marston, Missouri, on September 10, 1905. She was the daughter of Mose Henry Maxey and Nettie Jane Poindexter. Dick had five children.

Dick and Etna Woodson.

1. Richard Taylor Woodson, born November 18, 1925, married Josephine Lottie Phillips and had four children:

a) Nancy Carol Woodson, who married Luther Jerry Wallis and had two children: Deanna Laine Wallis, who married Billy Wayne Robinson, had one son Christopher Robinson, and Scott Edward Wallis, who married Amy Blyth Huddleston, one son London Scott Wallis.

b) Richard Taylor Woodson Jr. married Debbie Woodson, one son, Daniel Woodson.

c) Rebecca Jo Woodson married Ronald Jerry Johnson and had two sons, Ronald Jerry Johnson Jr. and Richard Woodson.

d) Glen David Woodson married Mary Woodson and had one daughter, Rachel.

2. David Neil Woodson, born December 8, 1928, first married Donna Belle Blansett, had two children:

a) Melonie Ann Woodson, who married Jim Smother, and had three children: Jededich, Daniel and Machaela.

b) Dallas Neil Woodson.

David married the second time to Gladys Mardell Tolbert Crooms.

3. Sarah Jane Woodson, born September 21, 1931, first married Paul P. Hall and had two children, Randy Paul and Sherry Diane; married second time to Randall Noel Freeman and had two children, Gary and Sandy.

4. Nina Jean Woodson, born July 25, 1938, first married William W. Foley, and had two children.

a) Cynthia Ann Foley, born October 23, 1957, married Donald Carson and had two children: Christina Leigh and Charles Andrew.

b) William Michael Foley, born July 4, 1959, married Sandra Cyr.

Nina married the second time to Jerry Don Truitt Sr. He brought into the marriage one son, Jerry Don Truitt Jr.

5. Clyde Henry Woodson, born November 17, 1940, married Regina Victoria Ferguson and had two daughters.

a) Regina Victoria Woodson, born November 7, 1963, married Donald Wayne Rubino and had two children: Cory Wayne and Jessica Lauren.

b) Nina Elaine Woodson, born April 8, 1967, married John Hadley and had two children: Thomas Henry Woodson and Autumn Erin Elizabeth Hadley.

Arthur Taylor "Dick" Woodson died January 20, 1976.

Ella Etna Maxey Woodson died January 28, 1979, buried in Oak Forest Cemetery. –*Nina Truitt.*

CLAY CURRY WOODSON.
I am Billy Lavon Woodson, son of Clay Curry Woodson and Edith Irene Woodson.

The picture is of my wife, Jewel, my son, Rickie, my son's wife, Adell, and their four children: Andrea, Melissa, Christopher, David and myself, Billy Lavon Woodson. –*Billy Woodson.*

The Billy Lavon Woodson family. Billy Lavon, Jewel, Rickie, Adell, Andrea, Melissa, Christopher and David Michell Woodson.

CLAY CURRY WOODSON FAMILY.
Clay Curry Woodson, son of John Riley and Minnie Bell Horton Woodson, was born October 22, 1906, in Lawrence County, Arkansas. He started working for the Frisco Railroad in June, 1932, and retired in October, 1971.

He married April 17, 1926, to Edith Irene Ward Woodson, born July 8, 1908. Clay and Irene had two sons.

1. James Carrol Woodson, born November 24, 1927, at Black Rock, Arkansas, was raised in and around Lawrence County; he was a carpenter; he married on November 13, 1948, to Kathleen Mozell Jones Woodson, born March 30, 1931, at Minturn, Arkansas. James and Kathleen had two daughters.

The Clay Curry Woodson family.

a) Linda Kay Woodson, born October 2, 1949, at Walnut Ridge, Arkansas, first married Jerry Wesley Haigwood on December 16, 1967, and had one child, Michelle Elaine Haigwood, born July 10, 1969.

Linda second married Paul Junior Combs on July 12, 1975, and had one child, Deanna Marie Combs, born October 13, 1976.

Linda and family now live in Tuckerman, Arkansas.

b) Carol Ann Woodson, born August 31, 1955, in Rockford, Illinois, married Gary Ray Shrable on August 15, 1980. Carol and Gary have two sons: Beau Tillman Shrable, born April 28, 1982, at Jonesboro, Arkansas; and Brett James Shrable, born May 27, 1986, at Jonesboro, Arkansas.

James Carrol Woodson died February 26, 1990, of colon cancer at Walnut Ridge, Arkansas. His wife, Kathleen, still lives in Lawrence County.

2. Billy Lavon Woodson, born September 16, 1932, in Lawrence County, Arkansas, married in Lawrence County, October 6, 1951, to Jewel Cobble Woodson, born on November 16, 1932. They had one son.

a) Rickie Lavon Woodson, born April 14, 1953, in West Memphis, Arkansas, married on June 16, 1978, in Aurora, Nebraska to Adell Jenson Woodson, born April 16, 1959. Rickie and Adell have four children:

Andrea Christine Woodson, born October 5, 1980, in Saratoga Springs, New York.

Melissa Ann Woodson, born January 14, 1983, at Langley Air Force Hospital, Hampton, Virginia.

Christopher Seth Woodson, born June 22, 1984, in Langley Air Force Hospital, Hampton, Virginia.

David Michell Woodson, born March 17, 1987, in Honolulu, Hawaii.

Rickie and Adell are now living in Bena, Virginia.

Billy and Jewel live in Sterling, Illinois.

Clay Curry Woodson died of bone cancer January 22, 1976. His wife, Irene, still lives in Portia, Arkansas. –*Irene Woodson.*

EARL LUCIFER WOODSON FAMILY.
Earl Lucifer Woodson, son of John Riley Woodson and Minnie Horton Woodson, was born March 23, 1904, near Clear Springs. When he was a young lad he and his brothers, Wes and Clay, walked over to their Grandpa Horton's house and worked, either driving a team of mules pulling logs to the sawmill, driving cattle to the stockyards or loading the wagon with shells to take to the button factory. Instead of money for their labor they would get either a side of beef, a ham, or a bushel of peas to take home. Earl went to school at Mt. Vernon. He later worked at the sawmill, was a cutter at the button factory and dredged gravel and crushed rocks at the gravel plant on Black River. Earl loved to play tricks. He used to eat razor blades and tuck them back in his jaw with his tongue and anyone that saw him do this, would swear that he swallowed them. This was a very neat trick. He was married on May 24, 1924, to Delia Viola Fry, born August 15, 1904, in Orgen County, Missouri. Children names are:

1. John Clyde Woodson, born July 1, 1925, died July 2, 1942.

2. Glendon Elwood Woodson, born October 20, 1926, married Louise Woodson and had two children: Kathy and Suzie. Glendon Woodson died March 24, 1954.

3. Harold James Woodson, born June 22, 1929, married Shirley Woodson and had three children: twins Berry Joe and Gary James and Michael Jeffery.

Harold Woodson died December 17, 1982.

4. Mary Retha Woodson, born January 15, 1933, married Ray Brown. Children: Jimmy Ray, Michael Lee. Mary Retha Woodson died July 5, 1951.

5. Tommy Earl Woodson, born July 20, 1935, married Janice Collins. Five children:

a) Tim Woodson - children: Danielle Lucia, Haley Elizabeth.

b) Terry Woodson married Debbie Slaugherback. Children: Christopher Thomas, Nicholas, Jade Nicole.

c) Greg Woodson married Susan.

d) Andrew Woodson married Cathy Yurko, children: Chris, Sarah

e) Kristi Woodson married Daniel Prade, children: Jake Thomas, Teddi Marie.

Earl & Dellie & Sons Charles and Ted.

6. Oties Woodson, born 1937, died 1938.

7. Charles Woodson, born March 5, 1939, married Ellen Woodson March 5, 1959. Three children:

a) Michael Wayne Woodson, born July 1, 1961, died April, 1965.

b) Jerry Don Woodson married Donna Hutcheson, children: Charles Craig, Steven Michael.

c) Darren Ray Woodson married Tammy Williams, child: Sarah Elizabeth.

8. Ted Woodson, born August 16, 1940, married Tottie Woodson, children: Lesia and Tammy.

9. Larry Woodson, born October 23, 1946, married Pat Woodson, children: Richard, Angie, Karen, Larry Don.

Earl and Dellie Woodson raised their family at Hoxie, later moving to Paragould, Arkansas.

Earl Lucifer Woodson died October 30, 1977.

Dellie Viola Fry Woodson died August 30, 1990. –*Charles Woodson.*

JAMES CARROLL WOODSON.

I am Linda Morgan, granddaughter of Clay Curry Woodson and Edith Irene Woodson. This photo of my dad and mom, James Carroll and Kathleen Woodson, was taken on their 40th wedding anniversary. –*Lynn Morgan.*

James and Kathleen Woodson 40th wedding anniversary.

JAMES WESLEY WOODSON FAMILY.

James Wesley Woodson, son of Wesley Dee Woodson and Cora Oleta Elizabeth Tyree Woodson, born February 6, 1947, at the mouth of Spring River at Black Rock. He graduated from Black Rock High School in 1965, and is a veteran of the Vietnam War, serving two years in the US Army.

He married on May 23, 1968, in Lawrence County to Parker Diane Stanley, daughter of Parker Leon Stanley and Voncile Hawkins Stanley

Family of James Wesley Woodson.

of Paragould, Arkansas. James and Diane had four children.

1. Sandra Jean Woodson, born July 1, 1969, at Walnut Ridge, Arkansas, graduated from Black Rock High School in 1987, married the first time to Larry Woodruff June 10, 1989. She divorced him December 22, 1994. She married the second time to Johnny Wilburn, November 1,1996.

2. Stacy James Woodson, born August 4, 1971, at Pocahontas, Arkansas, graduated from Black Rock High School in 1991. He is a veteran of the US Navy serving from 1990 through 1995, and is now living in Craighead County.

3. Christopher Stanley Woodson, born December 13, 1973, graduated from Black Rock, Arkansas, in 1992, and joined the US Navy soon after. He has one son, Korliss Alexander Moore, born August 26, 1995.

4. Billy Cassidy Woodson, born May 2, 1975, at Pocahontas, Arkansas, graduated from Black Rock High school in 1993. He is a veteran of the US Navy, enlisting in August, 1993. He married Carrisa Mullens on October 23, 1994, and has one son, Wesly James Woodson, born May 1, 1995, Jacksonville, Florida.

James Wesley Woodson has worked for the United Parcel Service for the past 28 years and he and Diane live in Powhatan, Arkansas. –*James Woodson.*

JOHN DEE WOODSON FAMILY.

John Dee Woodson, son of Wesley Dee Woodson and Cora Oleta Elizabeth Tyree Woodson, was born on September 15, 1936. He was raised at the mouth of Spring River, spent time as a young lad either under the water hogging for mussel shells or on the river bank helping his daddy rig his boat with crow feet (14 inch pieces of stiff wire with four hooks in four directions). These are placed four to the line and 10 lines on each side of the boat to go drag up and down the river. When they returned with their catch of the day, his mom and the other kids would have a big black vat of boiling water ready to cook the shells to could get the mussel bait out and to check for pearls. A few of the shells were called the mucket, cucumber, washboard, pimple-back, grandma and the

John Dee Woodson family.

blupper. These were sold to places in Arizona to make jewelry. Shells were all piled together in one huge pile and sold for 20 dollars a ton. In 1996, you could sell the mucket and the cucumber which were two of the main pearl bearing shells for two thousand dollars a ton.

John attended school at Black Rock. After working at the gravel pit and picking more than his share of cotton at three dollars a hundred pound, he went to Indiana; then he worked in Kansas City for two or three years at a service station during the day and as a busboy at night. He and his sister, Alene, would put their money together to pay the rent, then send the rest home so the younger brothers and sisters could finish high school. He moved to Illinois and started at the bottom of a construction company and then began working his way up, going to school at night and worked as a tool and die apprentice during the day. Years later he received his degree and started his own, Aljo Construction Company, in 1965.

He married on December 26, 1959, in Elgin, Illinois, to Sharon Lou Burke, born September 2,1941, daughter of Charles Estel Burke and Mildred Gilberta Williams. He has three children.

1. Sheldon Alan Woodson, born July 31, 1961, married October 2, 1982, to Angela Annette Bittle; three children: Shawna Elise, Joshua Alan and Micah Elizabeth.

2. Shannon Dee Woodson, born February 2, 1963, married Sandra Gail Bittle on September 16, 1988. Children are: Derek Ryan, Bailey Michelle and Matthew Logan.

3. Sherri Lee Woodson, born July 7, 1965, married David Rowlett on September 19, 1987; two children: Albrey Lee and Preston Greg.

John Dee and Sharon moved their family and business to Heber Springs, Arkansas in 1978, and still own and manage Aljo Construction Company and the Rub-A-Dub Laundromat, with the help of their two sons. –*John Woodson.*

JOHN RILEY WOODSON FAMILY.

John Riley Woodson was born in Alabama, about 1853. His mother was Mary Ann Lawson, daughter of Pryor and Rebecca Lawson. She was born in Alabama about 1828. John had an older brother, Lorenza Dow. In the late 1850s, Mary Ann Lawson Woodson and her two sons, along with her father, Pryor, her brothers, John V., Andrew and Washington, her sister, Nancy, and her husband, John William Kelly, moved to Dent County, Missouri. In the spring of 1865, the Woodsons, Lawsons and the Kellys moved to Lawrence County, Arkansas and settled in the Powhatan area.

Nancy Lawson Kelly died in 1866. Mary Ann Lawson Woodson married her sister's husband, John William Kelly on January 31, 1867, in Lawrence County; they had one son, Andrew. In 1875, John Riley Woodson married Frances Emilene Jones, daughter of James A. Jones and Lydia Ann Griffith. Lydia, born in Tennessee, 1835, daughter of David and Catherine Griffith, later married John V. Lawson on September 6, 1866, in Lawrence County. He was John Riley Woodson's uncle. John and Francis had nine children:

James Edgar "Ed" married Luvinia Moore.

Leonia "Lee" married first Oscar Phillips and second G. M. Ditto.

Estella Belle married Thomas C. Hurst.

Riley Van Daley married Alice Martin.

Pryor W. died young.

Robert Franklin Perry married Jessie Mae Fry.

Mary Florence married Robert Duckworth.

William Henry married Ivy Franks.

Percy Winkle married Ida Carter.

Francis Emilene Jones Woodson died between 1895 and 1899. Mary A. Lawson-Woodson

John R. Woodson, with congregation where he preached.

Kelly died October 8, 1882, and is buried in the Kelly Cemetery near Imboden. John Riley Woodson married Minnie Bell Horton Higgins at the age of 46 and fathered eight more children. Lawrence County is full of descendants of Lorenza and John Riley Woodson. –Cora Woodson.

LORENZA DOW WOODSON FAMILY.

Lorenza Dow Woodson was born in 1846, in Alabama. He always used the surname of Woodson, but there are two stories surrounding his birth. First, he was born out of wedlock and second, his father was an Indian named Goffer or Goforths. Indians at this time were considered incapable of understanding the legal aspects of a contract. Since obtaining a marriage license at that time was considered entering into a contract, the Indians were not allowed to obtain a marriage license, so it is possible that Lorenzo's dad and Mary A. Lawson were married by the Indian Tribal Laws. He was visited two or three times by his Indian family according to his son, Morton Wyatt Woodson. He was in the Confederate Army and was a prisoner at

Family of Lorenza Dow Woodson.

Jacksonport, Arkansas, when the war ended. Lorenza Dow Woodson married Eva Rosanna Hill on February 3, 1867, in Lawrence County. Lorenza and Rose had nine children.

1. William H. Woodson, born 1868 (twin), married Susan Slayton on September 2, 1888.
2. Asa W. Woodson, born 1868 (twin), married Catherine Fleming on July 15, 1895.
3. Morton Wyatt Woodson, born August 28, 1870, married Nellie Mae Kidder.
4. Robert T. Woodson, born 1872.
5. Mary Delilah Woodson, born September 19, 1876, married James Avis Weir.
6. Marvin Arthur Woodson, born September, 1879.
7. Daniel D. Woodson, born October, 1881, married Hattie.
8. Jessie C. Woodson, born December, 1884.
9. Martin L. Woodson, born December, 1889, married Cora L. Johnson.

Eva Rosanna Hill Woodson died March 8, 1902. Lorenza Dow Woodson was a sick man in his old age, with a bad kidney and a bad lung. He died November 29, 1899, and is buried in Oak Forest Cemetery at Black Rock. –David Woodson.

MANUEL LAVERE "ROOSTER" WOODSON FAMILY.

Manuel Lavere "Rooster" Woodson, son of John Riley Woodson and Minnie Bell Horton Woodson, born September 22, 1918, in Lawrence County, married Mary Pearl Darris Woodson September 18, 1937. Rooster and Pearl's seven children are:

1. Jewel Winston Woodson, born December 21, 1938, married Julia Diane Land, May 27, 1960. Jewel's three children are:
   a) Mary Jo Woodson Morris, born February 1, 1961. Mary Jo's children are Amy Michelle, Janet Dawn and Kimberly Jo.
   b) David Allen Woodson, who married Julie Joyce Arneson, October 6, 1984, one son, Matthew Warren.
   c) Diane Reane Woodson, born June 22, 1982.
2. Charles Henry "Porky" Woodson, born June 13, 1941, married Barbara Parker, June 1, 1961. Porky's five children are:
   a) Michael Wayne Woodson, who married Debra Diane Riggs, May 20, 1984, had three children: Michael Seth, Eric Stephen and Jennifer Michile.

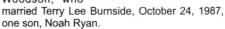

Manuel "Rooster" and Pearl Woodson.

   b) Sherry Lynn Woodson, who married Terry Lee Burnside, October 24, 1987, one son, Noah Ryan.
   c) Deborah Karen Woodson, who married Larry Scott Luther, March 23, 1991, had two children: Alesha and Hunter Scott.
   d) Sheila Sharlene Woodson, who married Marcus David Ellison, January 3, 1989, had three children: Tyler Wayne, Christian David and Dalton Allen.
   e) Charles Kevin Woodson, born August 17, 1970.
3. Paul Edward Woodson, born February 11, 1944, married Emma Faye Hoffman, February 20, 1962, had three children.
   a) Angela Woodson, who married Phillip Pickett.
   b) Beverly June Woodson, who married Guy Hill, had two children: Nathan and Candy.
   c) Tamy Ann Woodson, who married Dewayne Reese.
   Paul Woodson died April 18, 1976, at Hoxie, in a house fire, and is buried in Oak Forest Cemetery. Emma Faye Hoffman Woodson died September 20, 1966.
4. Johnny Woodson, born May 31, 1946, married Ann Gaylord, had four daughters: Lori, Linda, Lynette and Lisa. Johnny married the second time to Karen, had one son, Johnny Woodson Jr.
5. Billy Salvan Woodson, born March 5, 1949, married Carla Woodson, had two children: Connie Lynn and Billie Jean.
6. James "J. J." Woodson, born July 10, 1950, first married Diane Woodson, had two children: Shawn and Jeff. His third marriage was to Melissa Kay Spades, April 18, 1988, and had one son, Joshua.

7. Patricia Elaine Woodson, born November 11, 1954, married James F. Silar, May 1, 1971, had four children.
   a) James Franklin Silar, who married Keota Silar, one child, Brittney.
   b) Mary Belinda Silar, who married Tommy Nelson, April 11, 1992, had two children: Shannon and Justin Lee.
   c) Diana Ruth Silar married Justin Carter Gott, November 19, 1994, had two children: Christian Brook and Ashley Rebecca.
   d) David Paul Silar, who married Susan Ranee Reinertson, June 20, 1998.
   Manuel Lavere "Rooster" Woodson died March 3, 1970, in Veteran's Hospital at Memphis, Tennessee. Mary Pearl Darris Woodson died September 3, 1986. Both are buried in the Oak Forest Cemetery, Black Rock. –Manuel Woodson.

MINNIE BELL HORTON WOODSON FAMILY.

Minnie Bell Horton, born February 3, 1879, in Powhatan, Arkansas, was raised in Evening Shade, the daughter of W. A. Horton, who according to his grandchildren, real name was William Alexander Ethone Opia bonte parte Horton (the spelling may be incorrect). She had one brother, Duddly Horton, who married Jane Higgins, one half-sister, Nellie and one half-brother, Fred.

She first married when she was 16, to Elic Higgins on March 10, 1895, in Lawrence County. Elic and Minnie had one child that smothered to death trying to keep warm in the ice cold winter, as they were living in a barn, at her dad's place. Elic Higgins died between 1895 and 1899.

Her second marriage was October 23, 1899, to John Riley Woodson, son of Mary Ann Lawson. John was 46 years old and Minnie was 20. John was a farmer and a preacher. He was ordained as a minister for the Missionary Baptist Church on April 24, 1906. John and Minnie lived in the Black Rock area most of

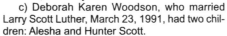
Minnie Bell Horton Woodson.

their lives, but did spend some time in Philips County, Arkansas in 1918, and lived in Wiley Township, Randolph County in 1920. John R. and Minnie Woodson's eight children are:

Ollie Magalene married Earnest Earl Lawson.
Earl Lucifer married Delia Viola Fry.
Clay Curry married Edith Irene Ward.
Johnnie Caldonia married Cecil Meeks.
Wesley Dee married Cora Oleta Elizabeth Tyree.
Hazel Eugene married Walter Barton Weir.
Leslie died young.
Manuel Lavere "Rooster" married Mary Pearl Darris.

John Riley Woodson died at Gum Stump in April or May of 1920, and is buried in nearby Duty Cemetery.

The third marriage of Minnie's was to Cleve Kirkpatrick on January 1, 1930. Minnie was known as Grannie Woodson to everyone. She used to keep her money in a tobacco pouch pinned in the pocket of her petticoat. The old-timers didn't believe in banks because of all of the bank robbers that were running around, so she buried it in old jugs or cans except what she thought they might need for a few weeks. Cleve didn't worry about money, not as long as Grannie had a coon roasting in the oven of the old wood stove and a few sweet potatoes baking. Cleve Kirkpatrick died December 10, 1963, and Minnie Woodson Kirkpatrick died April 11, 1965, home of pneumonia. They are both buried in Oak Forest Cemetery at Black Rock, Arkansas. –Daniel Pickney.

MORTON WYATT WOODSON FAMILY.

Morton Wyatt Woodson, son of Lorenza Dow Woodson and Eva Rosanna Hill Woodson, was born August 28, 1870, near Smithville, Arkansas. He was raised on 167 acres of farm land three miles out of Black Rock toward Imboden. When Morton was around 10 years of age, Jesse James was running from the law and hid out in his dad's barn. As a young lad, Morton hauled supplies for the Frisco Railway with one old mule and a wagon. He fell victim to the smallpox epidemic, probably catching it from feed bags from the riverboats, but he recovered. He went to a little school out from Black Rock, toward Imboden, dropping out in third grade to help send his brothers to a school that taught Morse code so they could work for the railroad. He watched as a few straggling Indians passed through moving on to other territories after the Trail of Tears. He grew up farming, and working the land, sawing lumber and helping to build the wall around the old Powhatan Courthouse. His name can still be seen on the stone where he wrote it many years ago.

He married March 19, 1898, Nellie Mae Kidder, born May 16, 1880, in Washauska, Indiana. Nellie traveled to Arkansas in a covered wagon with her father, Simon Kidder, and mother, Mary Emma Cole Kidder, in 1894. Mote and Nellie reared nine children.

Morel & Nellie Woodson, daughter Cliffie, sons, Carl and Dick.

1. Carlton Waynerite Woodson married Mary L. Pittman; children: Marvin, Dorthy.

2. Cliffie Hazel Woodson married first Homer Lingo, one son, Everett Lingo; married second Don Roth, three children: Nancy Joann, Mary Nell and Danny.

3. Arthur Taylor Woodson married Ella Etna Maxey.

4. Maud Woodson married first C. Green Evans; married second John Fleming.

5. Clyde Otis Woodson married Lucille Farley, three sons: Ronald Lee, Kenneth and Stephen Wayne.

6. Mildred Hallie Woodson, born August 1, 1910, married Edward Ellis Sinnings.

7. Jessie Alma Woodson, born November 3, 1917, married Leslie Delbert Carroll; two children:

a) Sabra Ann Carroll married Thomas Verkler; children: Thomas Leslie, Glen Weston.

b) Glen Jasper Carroll; children: Kristy, Sue, Gene Allen.

8. Mary Emma Woodson, born July 15, 1919, married Wilbur Isaac Blonde Martin on November 13, 1938; two daughters:

a) Linda Martin married C. H. Starnes; children: Johnny Shan and Ilyan Marie, who married Richard Bowker; children: Richard Charles and Bridget Nicole.

b) Rosemary Martin married Paul Ragsdale; children: twins, Jessica and Paul, and Rosana.

9. Glen Morton Woodson, born December 7, 1920, married Mary Childress.

Mote Woodson was well versed in the Bible, a member of the Church of Christ. Uncle Mote, as most of Black Rock knew him, was an honorable and loving man. Morton Wyatt Woodson died August 5, 1970. Nellie Mae Kidder Woodson died December 1, 1980. They are buried in Oak Forest Cemetery at Black Rock, Arkansas. –Clyde Woodson.

ROBERT WOODSON FAMILY.

Robert Franklin Perry Woodson was born February 16, 1887, at Black Rock, Arkansas. He was the son of John Riley and Frances Emilene Jones Woodson. He married Jessie Mae Fry on September 4, 1908, at Reyno, Arkansas in Randolph County. Jessie was the daughter of John Leondas and Mary A. Ladyman Fry.

Rob and Jessie's first two children, a boy and a girl, both died as infants. Melva Mae was born September 17, 1913. About 1915, Jessie gave birth to twin boys named Aubrey Hayward and Audrey Leslie. Audrey died at about 18 months of unknown causes. Coleta Muriel was born December 9, 1917, in Randolph County.

Rob and Jessie lived in Randolph County until about 1917, when they moved to Phillips County with Rob's father, John, and his family. The men worked at the button factory in Clarendon.

While they were living in Phillips County, Aubrey contracted spinal meningitis and died. He was buried at Brown's Store Community, Marvel, Arkansas.

The Woodson family moved back to Randolph County soon after the child's death. They lived in the Skaggs Community in Wiley Township.

Rob and Jessie had another daughter, Wilma Bernadine, born November 23, 1919. The family moved to Lawrence County in mid 1920.

Mary Roberta, called "Bob", was born May 6, 1921, and Olan Leondas "Buddy" was born October 30, 1924.

Rob and his family lived with Jessie's folks in Walnut Ridge on Third Street. After this house burned, they lived in the community of Pugh for a while.

They moved back to Walnut Ridge and Melva married Cecil L. Gaines. Melva and Cecil had 11 children, 10 that lived to adulthood. Melva died April 4, 1991, in Walnut Ridge.

Muriel married Mick Kizziar. They had three children. After their divorce, Muriel was married to Bill Davis. Muriel died January 10, 1982, in Walnut Ridge.

Bernadine married Grady Shaw and they had two children. They settled in Mississippi.

"Bob" married Herbert Brewer and had five children. Bob died April 11, 1981, in Walnut Ridge.

"Buddy" married Ann Loehr and settled in San Francisco, California. They had five children. Buddy died October 13, 1994, in Livermore, California.

Rob Woodson lived in Walnut Ridge until his death on June 30, 1950. Jessie died July 6, 1962, in Walnut Ridge. They are buried in Lawrence Memorial Park. –Sharon Schmidt.

THELMA JEANETT CROSSLIN WOODSON,

daughter of Wesley Dee Woodson and Cora Oleta Elizabeth Tyree Woodson, was born November 10, 1941, in the family home at the mouth of Spring River. Dr. Tibbles was the doctor.

She married Harold Mac Junyor in July of 1959, and graduated from Black Rock High School in May of 1960; she divorced Harold Mac Junyor in 1965.

She joined the US Army and met her second husband. She married July 1, 1970, to Claude Harvey Crosslin, born May 14, 1933, in Tennessee. He was also in the Army, a veteran of the Korean and Vietnam Wars and later retired from the service. They had one daughter, Pennie Claudine Crosslin, born June 12, 1974, in Kansas City, Missouri. She was raised in Florida and is attending the University of Kansas. Claude Harvey Crosslin died May of 1992, in Tampa, Florida, and is buried in Oak Forest Cemetery at Black Rock, Arkansas. Jeanett is living in Tampa, Florida where she has, for the past nine years, been in nursing, taking care of high risk babies. –Thelma Crosslin.

The family of Thelma Jeanett Crosslin Woodson.

THOMAS EUGENE WOODSON FAMILY.

Thomas Eugene Woodson, son of Wesley Dee Woodson and Cora Oleta Elizabeth Tyree Woodson, was born June 24, 1938, at the top of the largest hill in Black Rock overlooking what is now the Black River Bridge and Highway 63.

He graduated from the cotton fields and Black Rock High School in 1957; he is a veteran of the US Army, joining in July of 1957, and serving his country in Fulda Gap, West Germany and other parts of Europe. He worked in banking, accounting, quality control, management and other areas of business obtaining his business degree from several colleges around the United States by working days and going to school at night. He purchased his first company in 1983, his second company in 1986, and his third company in 1989.

His first marriage was in 1966, to Jeri Lynn Farrel of California. Tom and Jeri had one son, Timothy Eugene Woodson, born January 30, 1967, in Phoenix, Arizona. Timothy first married, Rachel Woodson, 1994, in Lawrence County; they had one son, Dakata Thomas Woodson, born June 15, 1995. Timothy married the second time to Holly Harland.

Thomas' second marriage was to Joyce Lee Gladden, June 29, 1970, in Grandview, Missouri. Tom and Joyce had one

The family of Thomas Eugene Woodson.

daughter, Windy Kathleen Woodson, born April 13, 1971. Windy married Mike Clark on September 26, 1992. Windy and Mike had two daughters: Tori Lynn Clark, born February 19, 1993, in Overton, Nebraska, and Michaela Kathleen Clark, born August 9, 1994. Windy and Mike and family now live in Wanconda, Illinois. Tim, Holly and Dakata Woodson live in Jonesboro, Arkansas, and Thomas Eugene Woodson has now retired and living the good life of hunting, fishing, golfing and playing with his grandchildren in Black Rock, Arkansas. –Thomas Woodson.

WESLEY DEE WOODSON FAMILY.

Wesley Dee Woodson, son of John Riley Woodson and Minnie Bell Horton Woodson, was born January 19, 1913, at Black Rock, Arkansas; he was raised in the Clear Springs area. Around the age of 18, he worked at the C.C. Camp at Fort Chaffee, Arkansas. He received a medical discharge and came home to Black Rock. He worked as a cutter at the button factory that was located on Highway 25 toward Powhatan. Charlie Penny was his boss. He got paid by the gallons he cut, depending on how much they weighed and how good they were.

Around 1940, he went to work for the W.P.A., getting paid one dollar and a nickel a day. He helped to rebuild the Black Rock Schoolhouse after it burned and worked on building the Black River Bridge. Later, he worked at the gravel pit. Married in 1934, to Cora Oleta Elizabeth Tyree Woodson, daughter of George Washington Tyree and Biddie Louisa Lamb, born October 6, 1917, at Clover Bend, Arkansas. Her dad was a sharecropper, moving from farm to farm, so she attended three different schools: Clear Lake, Portia and Clover Bend.

The first time she saw Wes she was walking across a field and he came riding up on a horse and asked her if she had seen his cow. When Wes and Cora were married times were hard and money was scarce, so if you had a roof over your head, your health, a pot of beans on the old potbellied wood stove, a pair of shoes and a good warm winter coat for all of your kids, you were very thankful. Wes and Cora raised their family at the

Wes and Cora Woodson

mouth of Spring River in a shotgun house built on stilts so that when Black River flooded, they wouldn't have to move out right away. Kerosene lamps were used, as there was no electricity in that area, milk was 25 cents a gallon, usually bought from Mrs. Holmes and Tom Norris came by two times a week selling 50 pound blocks of ice for 35 cents to put in the wooden icebox to keep it cold. Everyone in the family helped to put food on the table by fishing, hunting, planting a garden, digging shells, chopping or picking cotton.

Wes and Cora Woodson reared eight children. They are:

1. See Ella Alene Woodson Wilson family.
2. See John Dee Woodson family.
3. See Thomas Eugene Woodson family.
4. See Thelma Jeanett Woodson Crosslin family.
5. Nancy Woodson. See Freddie James Pickney Jr. family.
6. See Anita Sue Woodson James family.
7. See James Wesley Woodson family.
8. See Barbara Louise Woodson McNeil family.

Wes and Cora are members of the Church of Christ. Wesley Dee Woodson died August 15, 1988, and is buried in Oak Forest Cemetery. Cora lives at Black Rock, Arkansas.

WESLEY DEE WOODSON FAMILY. Barbara Louise Woodson Stone, the youngest child of Wesley Dee Woodson and Cora Oleta Elizabeth Tyree Woodson, was born in Lawrence County on April 13, 1949. She married Larry Johnie Stone, son of Johnie Stone and Pauline Stone of Portia, Arkansas, on September 16, 1967, in the Black Rock Church of Christ building. They divorced in 1974.

After leaving Black Rock the couple moved to Kansas City, Kansas, established a home and had two children. Dawn Michelle Stone was born on May 10, 1967, and Kelly Pauline Stone was born January 30, 1970. Dawn Michelle married Kevin Stubbs in 1993, and gave birth to one daughter, Taryn Marie Elizabeth Stubbs on January 12, 1994. Dawn and Kevin were divorced in late 1994. She is presently married to Gary Swain and lives in Searcy, Arkansas. She has been employed with the same office for approximately seven years as a licensed optician. Kelly Pauline Stone married once in 1989, to Michael Heggie, of Higginson, Arkansas. They lived in several different areas before divorcing in 1994. Kelly attended the School

The W.A. Horton and Minnie Woodson family taken at Bonita Springs.

of the Ozarks, in Clarksville, and also Jacksonville Community College in Florida. She received her certification as a surgical technician. She moved to Little Rock, Arkansas in 1995. On June 20, 1996, she gave birth to Kanyon Lee Edwards; father is Kerry Edwards of Little Rock.

In 1977, Barbara married Robert D. Lowert, M.D. They were married for 13 years and divorced in 1992. Barbara recently married Kenneth Mark McNeil on June 26, 1998, in Ochos Rios, Jamacia and now resides in Conway, Arkansas. Kenneth is the son of the late Joe McNeil and Margaret Nabholz McNeil, who continues to reside in Little Rock. Barbara graduated from Arkansas State University in 1977, and worked as a nurse for 24 years. She specialized in ophthalmic photography and was active in this occupation for 12 years. Barbara has recently received her real estate license and works with Century 21, Dunaway & Hart, Inc. in Conway. She has been an avid scuba diver for 11 years and is a professional skydiver with a license since 1990.

WORLOW FAMILY. The William and Catherine Hamilton Worlow family migrated from Washington County, Indiana, to Lawrence County in the 1870s, settling in the Lauratown/Clover Bend area. William and Catherine, daughter of Robinson and Elizabeth Bough Hamilton, were married on May 13, 1841, in Washington County.

They were the parents of 11 children: George Henry, Joseph, Andrew Jackson, Phoebe, John William, Elizabeth Mahuldah, Ann Eliza, Cassie, Mary, Robinson and another daughter, uncertain of name. All of the children with the exceptions of Andrew Jackson and the youngest daughter were in Lawrence County at some time between 1875 and 1900. Only one son, John William, has descendants in Lawrence County in 1998.

John William Worlow and his first wife, Charlotte Prey, were married in Martin County, Indiana, on January 20, 1875, and were the parents of Della and William "Bill." After Charlotte died on February 19, 1883, John William married Willie Catherine Woodward Harrison on June 6, 1894, in Lawrence County. Willie Catherine's parents were Franklin and Susan Percy Williams Woodward originally of Wayne County, Missouri.

John William and Willie Catherine settled in the Oak Grove community north of Sedgwick. They were the parents of nine children: Dee, Ethel, Essie, Lillie, Effie, Elsie, Joe, Hazel and Edith.

Left to right: Joe Worlow, Tom Manning, Walter Manning and John William Worlow. Writing on wagon: Sold by S. N. Pitzele & Co., Walnut Ridge, Arkansas. Picture printed by McCarroll Studio, Walnut Ridge, Arkansas. Picture was taken around 1924-1925.

John William was a cotton and corn farmer and in the off season, with hand tools and seasoned timbers, made ox yokes and bows commercially.

John William died on December 13, 1928, leaving his widow and children to carry on with the farm. In addition to raising cotton and corn, they always had a large garden, fruit trees, cows for milk and butter and chickens for eggs.

John William's and Charlotte's daughter, Della, died at an early age. Their son, William "Bill", married Cora Wicker on August 11, 1903, and they resided in Sedgwick. Bill worked for the Frisco Railroad. Their children were Mabel, Ezra "Jack", Earl "Pete", Charles "Charlie", Ruth and Minnie.

John William's and Willie Catherine's son, Dee, married Alma Meadows, daughter of George and Mary Frances Rye Meadows, on April 29, 1917, in Lawrence County. Dee and Alma eventually settled in Kansas City, Kansas, where he worked for the Missouri-Pacific Railroad. They had one son, Milton.

Daughter, Essie, married Thomas Manning on May 2, 1917, in Lawrence County. They were the parents of Walter and Tom.

Daughter, Lillie, married Frank Shackelford on September 14, 1920, in Lawrence County. They were the parents of Mildred, who died at an early age, and son, Charles.

Daughter, Effie "Doll", married Mitchell "Blackie" Baird on December 23, 1931, in Lawrence County. They were both killed in a tornado near Minturn in 1938.

Daughter, Edith, married Arthur Carter on October 30, 1939, in Lawrence County. They resided for many years in St. Louis before moving back to Lawrence County.

Ethel died as an infant, and Hazel and Elsie remained single.

Son, Joe, married Ruby Ellen Healey, daughter of Emmett and Ivie Spivey Healey on January 2, 1932, in Lawrence County. They are the parents of Joline Worlow Jones, deceased; John; Glendon; Tommie Jean; Jerry; and David.

Joe and Ruby have 13 grandchildren: John Paul Jones, Joe Glenn, Deana, Michael, Randall, Mitchell, Jeffrey, Eric, Brett, Brooke, Elise and Natalie Worlow and seven great-grandchildren: Valerie, Steven, Jacob, Benjamin, Tyler, Spencer and Meredith Worlow. –*Tommie Jean Worlow.*

JAMES L. WRIGHT was born April 15, 1864, in Missouri, according to the census, he married October 29, 1885, in Lawrence County to Susan Emily Mary Erwin, daughter of V. A. S. and Rebecca Erwin. He died November 18, 1930. She was born September 18, 1863, and died 1932; burial for both was in Lancaster Cemetery. Their children:

Charlie F. Wright, born May, 1886, married February 16, 1908, to Ester Laird.

Ira Lee Wright, December 12, 1888-January 12, 1954, married May 29, 1909, to Mary Melvinnie Tolbert Phaby, June 4, 1877-July 14, 1960; burial Lawrence Memorial. Their children: Beaulah, born May 25, 1921, and died 1950; married Leonard Hiser.

Rector Eli Wright, born September 18, 1914, in Black Rock, married November 14, 1938, to Marguerite L. Hoffman, born December 13, 1921, daughter of James L. and Christena O. Sudduth Hoffman. Children of Rector and Marguerite: Gloria Carol died at birth, Barbara Sue Miller, Larry Allen, Rebecca Eileen Foster and Victoria Lynn Wright Rapp. The Wrights live in Westland, Michigan.

Jim Wright.

Hattie I. Wright, born February, 1892, married December 3, 1911, to Jewell Pace. They moved to California.

Malinda Wright, born February, 1894, and died September 14, 1929, married October 9, 1910, to Charles Wesley Smith.

James A. Wright, born December, 1895, married March 8, 1916, to Venia "Vinnie" Doyle; moved to California.

Mary M. Wright, born March, 1898, married October 21, 1916, to Elam Watson.

John B. Wright, born about 1899, died about 1901.

Odessa Wright, born abut 1903, married Clyde King and a Huskey. –Barbara Miller.

WYATT. The Wyatt family was among the first to settle in Lawrence County. In 1815, the year Lawrence County was formed, John and Polly Trimble Wyatt and their sons, Thomas, Abraham and Reuben, traveled with a group of 15 families from Livingston County, Kentucky. This group was led by Benjamin Hardin, Revolutionary War veteran. They settled near Rosie, Arkansas, (near Batesville), which was cut off into Independence County in 1820. Court records from Davidsonville show that in 1817, John Wyatt was granted a ferry license to operate across White River at Salado Creek.

Abraham Wyatt was born in Livingston County, Kentucky, in 1798, and married Nancy Dudley in the 1820s. After her death about 1839, he migrated north to the Janes Creek area, south of Ravenden Springs, a part of Lawrence County at the time. He remarried to Polly Criswell, widow of Harmus Criswell, in 1840. He was an elder in the Cumberland Presbyterian Church and attended the 1849 presbytery in Pleasant Valley. After dying suddenly at a Portia camp meeting in 1851, his widow and youngest two daughters lived on the farm, surviving the war years by growing sugar cane and corn.

Newton Wyatt, born near Rosie in 1830, and John D. Wyatt, born in 1822, both sons of Abraham, settled on Janes Creek about the same time as Abraham. Joseph J. Wyatt, also a son of Abraham, married first Elizabeth Hudspeth, then Mary Hudspeth and lived in Randolph County. Polly A. Wyatt, daughter of Abraham, married James P. Wright, and has descendants in the Janes Creek area. John D. married Sarah Berry, a young widow, and had seven children, none of whom reached adulthood. They are all buried in the small Wyatt Cemetery, on the west bank of the creek near Ravenden Springs. Newton married twice. First to Elvira Hudspeth, who had five children: William C., John F., Joseph J., Mary and Kirk. John F. Wyatt is an ancestor through his daughter, Clara, to the Phillips family that lives near Janes Creek. Newton's second marriage was to the widow, Sarah (Hudspeth, sister to Elizabeth, Mary and Elvira) English, and produced three children: Hillis in 1868, Jim in 1869, and Betty in 1873. Betty died in 1892.

These brothers homesteaded land which was until recently still in the family. The farmstead is located on Wyatt Road, off Arkansas 90, north of Ravenden. It is on John F. Wyatt's old farm that the main Wyatt Cemetery is located. This part of Lawrence County was attached to Randolph County in 1861, thus Hillis, Jim and Betty were born in Randolph County.

Hillis Wyatt was an active member of the Imboden Methodist Church and attended the ribbon cutting of the building that now stands. He married Nannie Buster in 1890, and prospered as a farmer. The couple had six children: Vesta, Monte, Donna, Jesse, Luther and Irene. Hillis died in 1942, and Nannie died in 1945.

Vesta Wyatt Purdy, his oldest, attended Normal College at Conway, and taught many years

Front, left to right: Luther, Donna, Jesse. Middle row: Nannie and Hillis Wyatt. Back row: Monte, Vesta.

at Hoxie School, then at Lynn. She died in 1972, at the age of 81.

Jesse and Donna also attended Normal School and may have taught in the county.

Monte was born in 1894, and married Zola Edmondson in 1915. The couple farmed in the Portia bottoms and had four children of which three survived to adulthood: John Newton Wyatt of rural Walnut Ridge; Tom Wyatt of Marmaduke for many years and now of Jonesboro; and Bobby Wyatt, who lived in Murfreesboro, Tennessee, and died in 1983, at the age of 59. Monte died in 1923, of appendicitis.

Zola was a school teacher at Ponder Switch's and Sedgwick. She died in 1965.

Jesse died young, leaving a widow and son, who moved from the state after remarriage and adoption.

Jim Wyatt, Hillis' brother, married Hattie Beck and had six children: Myrtle, Earl, Malta, Julie Ernest and Bowman. Bowman has descendants in northern Lawrence County. Ernest was a veteran of World War I. –Greg Elders.

YATES. George W. Cooper, born about 1851, in Lawrence County, was the son of Barry, born January, 1830, Tennessee, and Charity Young-Cooper, born August, 1827, Tennessee. George had three sisters: Janie, Elizabeth "Sissy" and Lena, one brother: Jim, a twin to Sissy. George W. Cooper recorded a will in Lawrence County, Arkansas Territory, dated August 2, 1835.

On May 8, 1874, George W. Cooper married Mary A. "Polly" Wrenfrow, daughter of Henderson and Martha Wrenfrow. This only child, a daughter, Carra Bell, was born November 4, 1876, at what was later known as the Will Baird place near the Bradford Cemetery. Carra sBell's mother died when she was very young; therefore George took his daughter to live with his parents where they continued to live until he remarried, March 20, 1886, in Lawrence County, to Nancy J. Gideon. The children of this marriage were: Nora, who died when she was 17, May, who first married Hallmark, second Sam Rader; Elmer; and Lea, who married Sammy Ladd.

Deed records show in 1883, George W. Cooper was deeded two parcels of land from H. and Martha Wrenfrow and one from Holder and in 1903, a land patent for 83.6 acres, all in section 1, twp. 19N, R3W and section 6, twp. 19N, R2W, which joined Barry Cooper's homestead. George was a farmer, school teacher, and helped build the Iron Mountain Railroad from Newport to Walnut Ridge, Arkansas. He would sometimes take his young daughter, Carra Bell, with him when he was working at Newport.

Carra Bell Cooper married Jahue Stokely Yates, born April 12, 1870, North Carolina, son of Samuel and Jane Davis Yates, on December 14,

1893, after Jahue had gone to the Cooper home and as he stated, "saw sitting at the organ, the prettiest girl he had ever seen." To this union 12 children were born: Lonny; Ben, who married Nola Jane Baird; Virgie Lee married John Wesley Ladd; William

Jahue S. and Carra Bell Cooper-Yates.

Edgar married first Roxie Tucker and second Leatha Hill; Rufus Theodore married Eunice Hughes; Samuel Dortch married Lara Leona Hill; Bessie Marie married Walter Edison Hughes; Alma Magine married William Emert Hughes; Leo Gordon, 1910-1912; Millard Carlee, 1912-1914; Nina married Ralph McPherson; Jewel married first Barney Williford and second Henry Taylor; and Boyd, 1919-1920.

Carra Bell Cooper Yates died in Williford, Sharp County, Arkansas, August 24, 1948, having been a kind and loving daughter, farm wife, mother, grandmother. Jahue Stokely Yates died September 12, 1956. Both are buried in the Bradford Cemetery.

Alma Mazine Yates Hughes deserves special credit for preserving much of the family's history in a story she wrote in 1979. –Patsy Yates.

MRS. MARY ZALAKER AND FAMILY. It is a long journey from the sweat drenched fields of rural Austria, to the quiet little town of Walnut Ridge, in northeast Arkansas. This is the life followed by Mary Lozar Zalaker in her quest for happiness for her family.

Mary Lozar, who was born February 12, 1883, orphaned by age 6, and sent to live with an aunt in a small farming community near Graz, Austria, in central Europe. As part of a common labor force, the spring and summer days were labor intensive; workers had to be in the fields before daybreak, to begin work at first light of day. Home chores were completed after dark. Religious services at the Catholic Church were the only diversions.

At age 18, she was considered ready for marriage, which was prearranged as was the custom at that time. She had never met the groom, John Zalaker, until the day of the ceremony. Though he had been carefully chosen by family members, it was not known that he had a violent temper and penchant for alcohol, a combination that was to make Mary's future life difficult.

In 1905, their first child, John, was born, and soon after, Mary's husband migrated to the United States, locating in West Allis, Wisconsin. Two years later, he sent for his wife and child, meeting them at Ellis Island. His chosen profession in woodworking, at which he was naturally skilled, and Mary contributed to the family income by operating a boarding house. Two children were added to the family, Mary (nicknamed Mamie), February 16, 1911, and Frank, February 4, 1914.

In 1916, the family moved to a farm near Hilliard, Missouri. There on May 6, 1917, twins Peter and Paul were born. Peter died as an infant. After spending several unrewarding years attempting to farm, the family moved to Poplar Bluff, where Mrs. Zalaker did laundry work for the public, while her husband worked on the railroad. It was here the last child, Dorothy Louise, was born, February 1, 1925.

At the age of 12, the oldest son, John, had become an apprentice in a dry cleaning shop in Poplar Bluff. There he became adept in all phases

About 1920, Mrs. Mary Zalaker and oldest son, John, daughter, Mary, and two younger sons, Frank and Paul.

of the business, and in 1925, found an established dry cleaning business for sale in Walnut Ridge, Arkansas. At the age of 20, he single handedly acquired and operated this business, against all odds of being a newcomer in a close knit community of old established families with different religious and ethnic values. He purchased a small frame house, and soon sent for his mother and siblings to begin a new life free from abuse.

Mrs. Zalaker contributed to the welfare of the family by baking pastries and bread, and selling dairy and poultry products. She drew on her knowledge of wine making, and operated a li-censed and bonded winery (Arkansas #112) from 1935 to 1943. A few of the articles Mrs. Zalaker used in the operation of this cottage industry still remain and are on display at the Arkansas Historic Wine Museum, Paris, Arkansas.

The father, John Zalaker, continued to live in Poplar Bluff until early 1939, when the family was notified of his serious illness, at which time he was moved to Walnut Ridge, where he died May 9, 1939.

Daughter, Mary "Mamie" was an invalid, suffering from Parkinson's disease and died April 27, 1943, at the age of 32.

In December, 1931, Mary's son, John, married Irene Little and they later welcomed Robert Eugene Zalaker and Martha Carol Zalaker to their family. John continued to operate Zalaker's Cleaners until his retirement in 1978. He died August 6, 1981, at the age of 76.

Frank was married to Maida Maxwell, November 7, 1942, and served in World War II for three years. After his return from service, the couple moved to Memphis, where they both worked for Sears until retirement. Frank died January 6, 1982.

Paul Louis lived to young adulthood, marrying Marguerite Lenore Stinson, May 17, 1941. He answered the call to service in World War II and gave his life for his country on May 27, 1944. He was a Technical Sergeant and top turret gunner in a squadron of B17s over Germany when his plane went down over enemy territory. Though some of the crew survived and were captured, Paul lost his life trying to save the life of his companion, whose parachute had become entangled in the damaged aircraft. He was posthumously awarded the Distinguished Flying Cross, Purple Heart, Air Medal and Oak Leaf Cluster.

Mrs. Mary Zalaker.

Mary's last child, Dorothy Louise, continued to live with her mother, working at the World War II Army Air Base, later an industrial park, associated with various industries at Walnut Ridge. In June, 1948, she was married to Homer Neal Willmuth, and to this union was born a daughter, Mary Louise Willmuth, who now lives in Scottsdale, Arizona. Dorothy continues to live in Walnut Ridge, at the original site of her mother's small home, which was later moved to make space for a larger home.

Mrs. Mary Zalaker lived with her daughter and family until her death June 17, 1969, at the age of 86. All deceased members of the Zalaker family are interred in Lawrence Memorial Park Cemetery, Walnut Ridge.

—*Mrs. Dorothy Willmuth.*

239

INDEX

241

243

MASSEY 53, 100, 108, 168, 171, 200, 201
MASTEN 174
MATELAND 209
MATHIS 49, 90, 105, 166
MATNEY 113
MATTHEWS 147
MATTHEWS 23, 24, 29, 35, 36, 38, 48, 60, 76, 84, 95, 96, 101, 102, 109, 123, 127, 134, 146, 147, 150, 156, 157, 179, 183, 186, 192, 194, 221, 232
MATTIX 147
MATTOX 81
MAUPIN 155
MAXEY 190, 236
MAXIE 33
MAXWELL 106, 196, 239
MAY 78, 150, 189
MAYBERRY 199
MAYER 91
MAYFIELD 42, 200, 201, 211
MAYLAND 72
MAYNARD 45, 167
MAYO 49
MAYS 204, 205
MCALEE 191
MCALEXANDER 12, 15
MCANALLY 223
MCANVIA 112
MCARTHUR 21, 214
MCBEE 73
MCBRIDE 57, 123, 143, 167, 191
MCBRYDE 64
MCCAFFERTY 197
MCCALEB 18
MCCALISTER 81
MCCALL 35, 45, 69, 144, 163, 228, 232
MCCALLISTER 178
MCCAMBELL 83
MCCARDY 180
MCCARROLL 11, 35, 39, 57, 75, 77, 78, 80, 81, 84, 89, 90, 91, 103, 104, 107, 108, 113, 132, 136, 147, 148, 149, 150, 160, 169, 173, 209, 220, 221, 224
MCCARTHY 232
MCCARTNEY 70
MCCARTY 36, 184
MCCAULEY 123
MCCAULY 40, 57
MCCLAIN 200
MCCLAMROCH 64
MCCLANAHAN 40, 82
MCCLINTICK 53
MCCLINTOCK 228
MCCLUSKEY 80
MCCOLLUM 207
MCCOMMONS 172
MCCORD 28, 33, 197, 230
MCCORMACK 85, 86
MCCORMICK 40
MCCOY 24, 71
MCCRACKEN 190
MCCRORY 61
MCCULLAH 23
MCCULLOUGH 42
MCCULLOUGHS 11
MCCURY 25
MCCUTCHEN 88, 157
MCDANIEL 119, 164, 205, 228
MCDANIELS 135, 162, 198
MCDONALD 68, 103, 123, 163, 203, 212, 213, 225
MCDONOUGH 64
MCDOUGAL 99
MCDOWELL 87, 153
MCELRATH 168
MCELROY 82, 146, 147
MCELYEA 100
MCENTIRE 121, 123, 217
MCFARLAND 139, 187
MCGAHA 57
MCGEE 36, 47, 53, 148, 187
MCGEEHEE 103
MCGHEE 148
MCGHEHEY 24, 135, 169, 190
MCGINNESS 145
MCGINNIS 194, 215, 218

MCGINNUS 145
MCGLOTHIN 183
MCGOLDRICK 141
MCILROY 60, 192, 216
MCINTIRE 53, 127
MCKAMEY 6, 7, 44, 51, 52, 53, 59, 110, 149, 150
MCKAY 170
MCKEE 143, 144
MCKENNEY 26, 139
MCKENZIE 84
MCKIMEY 52
MCKINLEY 152
MCKINNEY 23, 43, 45, 60, 115, 122, 213
MCKINNEYS 11
MCKNELLY 118
MCKNIGHT 66, 82, 101, 108, 124, 132, 154, 218
MCLAIN 60, 166, 218
MCLAUGHINS 11
MCLAUGHLIN 35, 75, 87, 103, 104, 125, 126, 135, 138, 147, 150, 164, 178, 198
MCLEOD 10, 11, 12, 17, 28, 36, 38, 59, 62, 63, 65, 74, 87, 89, 105, 138, 140, 145, 147, 150, 151, 157, 186, 199
MCLINDSEY 172
MCMANNERS 211
MCMASTERS 141, 196, 198, 199
MCMATH 13
MCMILLEN 45
MCMILLION 219, 220
MCMILLON 119, 178, 203
MCMULLEN 122
MCMULLIN 43
MCMURTREY 212
MCNABB 69, 94
MCNEIL 237
MCNUTT 125
MCPHERSON 238
MCPIKE 45, 164
MCQUAY 134, 135, 142
MCREYNOLDS 200
MCWHIRTER 101, 129
MEACHAM 87
MEADA 88, 111
MEADOR 123
MEADORS 55
MEADOWS 6, 27, 41, 49, 52, 55, 74, 75, 76, 77, 151, 176, 183, 184, 228, 237
MEDEARIS 70
MEDLOCK 35, 45, 112, 131, 227
MEEKS 19, 80, 152, 153, 154, 167, 188, 198, 229, 235
MEGAN 193
MELFORD 213
MELIM 73
MELTON 68, 73, 104
MEMASTERS 115, 136
MENDENHALL 23
MENDOLIA 134
MENTON 214
MERCER 170
MEREDITH 49
MERIWETHER 118, 136
MERRELL 197
MERRYMAN 230
MESSENGER 159
METCALF 24, 76
MEYERS 114
MIDDLECOFF 107
MIDDLETON 23
MIDKIFF 6
MIEUX, LE 27
MILAM 76, 104
MILAN 35
MILES 138
MILGRIM 57, 197, 198
MILIGAN 45
MILLER 10, 16, 40, 41, 44, 45, 49, 50, 63, 67, 87, 89, 100, 109, 122, 129, 130, 132, 141, 149, 154, 165, 188, 196, 207, 212, 226, 237, 238
MILLIGAN 34
MILLIGAN 39, 45, 67, 128, 144, 154, 183, 218
MILLIGANS 11

MILLIKIN 37
MILLION 78, 103, 163
MILLS 73, 89, 90, 105, 117, 151, 206
MILLSAP 130
MILNER 39, 99
MINTON 42, 83, 183, 200, 201, 225
MIROS 203
MITCHELL 31, 56, 57, 58, 95, 99, 103, 104, 108, 109, 114, 149, 155, 170, 172, 180, 184, 190, 225
MITCHENER 26
MITTS 87
MIZE 28, 50, 53, 58, 90, 155, 164
MOBBS-GUTIERREZ 146
MOBLEY 218
MOEN 201
MOFFETT 216
MOIX 69
MONDOZIA 199
MONDY 215
MONEHAN 167
MONIHAN 121
MONROE 83
MONTGOMERY 95, 128, 140, 170, 197, 206, 230
MOODY 25, 39, 45, 62, 84, 125, 132, 155, 156, 211
MOON 61, 125, 130
MOONEY 94
MOOR 203
MOORE 6, 7, 19, 26, 28, 29, 31, 34, 36, 43, 45, 48, 49, 53, 64, 70, 75, 90, 96, 99, 101, 102, 106, 109, 123, 124, 131, 135, 146, 147, 150, 156, 157, 165, 167, 169, 170, 173, 174, 179, 194, 195, 198, 200, 201, 202, 206, 215, 216, 221, 222, 234
MOORES 11, 92
MOREHEAD 45
MORGAN 29, 41, 61, 92, 101, 131, 139, 163, 183, 213, 234
MORGANS 12
MORRILTON 163
MORRIS 15, 40, 48, 50, 60, 77, 92, 133, 146, 152, 174, 199, 210, 213, 221, 222, 235
MORRISON 32, 46, 81, 160, 165, 192, 204, 205
MORROW 128, 163
MORSE 88, 143, 157
MORTON 198
MOSELYS 11
MOSIER 66, 176
MOSLEY 50, 62, 212
MOSS 186, 205, 222
MOSTELLER 187
MOTES 123
MOUGHLER 124
MOUNGER 201
MOUNT 29
MOUNTJOY 192, 194
MOUSSEAU 190
MULLEN 28, 35, 48, 53, 98, 120, 121, 140, 143, 212, 225
MULLENS 100, 234
MULLIGAN 40
MULLIN 199
MULLINS 72, 84, 133, 155
MUNGLE 123
MURLEY 143
MURPHEY 40, 219
MURPHY 78, 112, 126, 167, 178, 189, 199, 228
MURRY 111, 223
MUSE 49
MYERS 11, 17, 18, 23, 24, 25, 101, 143, 146, 162, 164, 196, 202, 212

N

NABHOLZ 237
NALLEY 56
NANNA 57
NASH 214
NATION 103, 104
NATIONS 75, 77, 78, 103, 104, 165
NEAL 46, 114, 162
NEECE 29, 39, 40, 71, 88, 94, 189, 215, 222, 228

NEECES 89
NEELEY 31, 89, 158
NEELY 32, 187
NEIL 23, 45, 151
NELDON 106, 107
NELSON 58, 129, 169, 216, 226, 235
NERUD 173
NESMITH 69
NETHERCUTT 131
NETTLES 185
NEUMAN 107
NEWALD 183
NEWBERRY 46, 50, 53
NEWMAN 87, 90, 126, 135, 158, 161, 162, 207
NEWMANS 159
NEWPORT 46, 206
NEWSUM 149
NEWTON 173
NIBBLETT 166, 167
NIBLETT 166
NICHOLS 61, 216
NICHOLSON 123, 230
NICHOLSONS 39
NICKS 159, 180
NOBLIN 33, 36, 39, 77, 124, 222
NOLES 165
NORLIN 64
NORMAN 108, 165, 206
NORMANS 11
NORRIS 26, 40, 124, 126, 141, 159, 160, 183, 237
NORWOOD 128
NOSARI 99
NUNALLY 144, 161, 167, 228
NUNLEY 136
NUNN 177
NUNNALLY 89, 111, 113, 202
NUTT 73

O

O' DONNELL 127
OAKS 36, 117, 191, 192
O'BANNON 186
OBORNE 220
O'CONNOR 114, 162, 189
O'DELL 91, 199
ODOM 21, 50, 109, 189, 195, 217
O'DWYER 40
OFFERMAN 220
OGLESBY 111, 118
O'KEAN 60
O'KEEFE 183
O'LAUGHLIN 140
OLDHAM 35, 73, 106, 136, 148, 160, 161, 173, 178, 179, 210, 227
OLDHAMS 11, 89
OLIVER 40, 41, 164
O'NEAL 119, 123
O'NEALS 11
ORR 42, 50, 146, 223
ORRELL 53
ORRICK 56, 72
ORVIS 55
OSBORN 37
OSBORNE 76, 177
OSBURN 45, 46, 126, 160
O'SHAUGHNESSY 183
OSTERHUS 151
OSTROVSKI 165
OVERBAY 201
OVERSTREET 43, 123
OWEN 39, 45
OWENS 33, 49, 55, 149, 161, 162, 190, 220
OWINGS 76
OXBERRY 83
OZMENT 223

P

PACE 22, 36, 39, 83, 89, 92, 99, 161, 178, 183, 203, 238
PACK 61
PADAN 45
PADGETT 192
PAGE 73, 157, 218
PAINE 45
PALMER 46, 81, 187

SCHMIDT 107, 143, 187, 188, 189, 236
SCHNEIDER 4
SCHUBER 170
SCHUBERT 147
SCHULETER 75
SCHULTZ 40, 41, 129, 187
SCHUTZ 49
SCHWANDEGGER 221
SCOTT 6, 23, 29, 42, 53, 77, 78, 88, 107, 114, 123, 139, 154, 165, 215
SCRAPE 167
SCROGGINS 200
SCROGGS 93
SCUDDER 149
SEAGRAVES 99
SEAMANS 23
SEARS 39
SEAT 99, 147
SEAY 49
SEBURN 129
SEE 176
SEEGO 176
SEELS 135, 162
SEGRAVES 46, 47, 119, 188, 216, 217
SELEY 16
SELF 50, 177, 222
SELLARS 215
SELLERS 63, 161
SELSOR 160, 178
SELVEGE 56
SENTENEY 94, 95
SENTER 185
SETTLES 49
SEYL 153
SHACKELFORD 209, 237
SHACKLEFORD 120, 228
SHAFER 45
SHAMBLEE 73
SHANNON 51, 53, 56, 152, 154, 167, 188, 189, 217
SHARP 24, 26, 35, 45, 47, 65, 76, 89, 103, 109, 118, 122, 123, 126, 145, 155, 184, 187, 189, 190, 210, 213, 224
SHARUM 11, 16, 172
SHATZEN 103
SHAVER 59, 122, 129, 190, 191, 192, 194
SHAVERS 11
SHAW 45, 50, 56, 101, 236
SHEARON 143
SHEETS 187
SHEFFIELD 57
SHELL 6, 39, 43, 196
SHELLY 141
SHELTON 40, 47, 50, 71, 88, 190, 198, 199, 207, 229, 232
SHEPARD 76
SHEPPARD 49
SHERIDAN 220
SHERMAN 45
SHERREL 56
SHERRILL 45
SHIELDS 60, 183
SHINAULT 74
SHINGLEDECKER 201
SHINN 138
SHIREY 11
SHIVLEY 199
SHOCKEY 223
SHOCKLEY 36, 208
SHOFFIT 224
SHOFFITT 47, 199, 200, 201
SHOTWELL 12
SHRABLE 134, 174, 233
SHREEVES 209
SIDES 46, 95
SILAR 235
SIMINGTON 103
SIMMINO 65
SIMMONS 45, 56, 61, 70, 145, 165, 166, 190, 191, 216, 217, 224, 232
SIMMS 36, 170
SIMPSON 28, 48, 50, 69, 122, 141, 232
SIMS 50, 82, 164, 170
SINCLAIR 99
SINGLETON 90, 179

SINNINGS 236
SIPES 127
SISK 28, 98
SITTON 53
SKAGGS 94
SKIDMONE 145
SKIDMORE 141
SKILLERN 23
SKIMAHORN 191
SKINNER 44, 45, 199
SLATTON 65, 196, 201, 216
SLAUGHERBACK 234
SLAVENS 176, 177
SLAYDEN 17
SLAYTON 11, 36, 41, 114, 120, 124, 140, 191
SLOAN 6, 11, 25, 28, 29, 44, 48, 49, 53, 59, 60, 74, 97, 98, 103, 105, 117, 131, 146, 150, 165, 186, 187, 191, 192, 193, 194, 205, 220, 221, 222
SLUSSER 67
SMALLEY 23
SMALLWOOD 47
SMELSER 49, 151
SMITH 10, 23, 25, 28, 29, 31, 34, 35, 36, 37, 45, 46, 49, 53, 57, 61, 65, 66, 69, 75, 76, 79, 80, 82, 83, 85, 86, 87, 88, 89, 94, 95, 97, 98, 102, 103, 106, 114, 115, 119, 120, 122, 123, 125, 129, 135, 140, 141, 150, 156, 157, 159, 161, 164, 168, 169, 170, 173, 174, 178, 180, 182, 186, 189, 190, 191, 193, 194, 195, 196, 197, 198, 199, 201, 207, 208, 210, 213, 214, 216, 218, 223, 228, 230, 238
SMITHEE 36, 137
SMITHS 11, 41, 61, 92, 127
SMOTHER 233
SMOTHERMAN 81
SNAPP 43, 53, 84, 172, 221
SNEAD 11, 199
SNEED 46, 113, 199, 214
SNIPES 56
SNODDY 204
SNOW 53, 70, 84, 118, 200, 201
SNYDER 152, 153
SOBEL 165
SOMMERFELDT 121
SONGER 75, 162
SOPER 211
SOPHONIE 212
SOSSAMON 56
SOUTH 26, 216
SOUTHERN 4
SOUTHLAND 25
SOUTHWORTH 117, 205
SOVEREIGN 114
SPADES 6, 11, 23, 25, 34, 157, 202, 235
SPALDING 149
SPARKS 57, 58, 98, 154, 191
SPENCE 111, 179
SPENCER 88, 111, 172
SPICER 43
SPIHLMAN 187
SPIKES 84, 149, 173
SPINT 76
SPIVEY 114, 237
SPIVY 34
SPOTTS 29, 45, 52, 202, 222
SPRADLIN 228
SPRAY 210
SPRING 208
SPRINGER 117, 123, 124
SPRINKLE 128
SPURGEN 141
SPURLOCK 75, 103, 124
STACY 81
STAGGS 74
STAGNER 201
STAHL 50
STAINAKER 109
STALLINGS 201
STALLS 101
STALNAKER 47, 77, 210
STANDFIELD 187
STANDLEY 130
STANFORD 36

STANLEY 198, 230, 234
STAPLETON 110, 210
STARBUCK 70
STARK 40
STARKS 34
STARLING 51, 76
STARNES 25, 34, 40, 102, 174, 190, 203, 210, 225, 236
STARR 53, 83, 104, 147
STARRS 12
STATES 86, 217, 218
STATLER 55, 80, 123, 151
STAUDT 53
STAVELY 165
STEADMAN 12, 29, 30, 35, 36, 101, 134, 149, 168, 174, 189
STEELE 11, 203
STEERS 212
STEINSIEK 56
STEMAC 40
STENBERG 125
STEPHEN 68, 218
STEPHENSEN 81
STERLING 164
STEVENS 48, 49, 162, 189, 216
STEVENSON 97, 131
STEWARD 73
STEWART 4, 6, 19, 22, 33, 41, 50, 53, 79, 83, 89, 92, 102, 161, 173, 177, 178, 179, 192, 203, 206, 211, 222, 227
STILLWELL 190
STINSON 88, 239
STIVENS 143
STOCKHAM 48
STOCKTON 56
STOGSDILL 138, 199
STOKELY 61
STOKES 11, 132
STOLL 53, 205, 220
STOLP 154
STONE 23, 37, 49, 86, 165, 204, 237
STOREY 55, 56, 78
STORMS 166
STORY 45, 85, 86
STOTTS 204, 205
STOUDER 139
STOUT 123, 217
STOVALL 6, 7, 38, 45, 135, 139, 150
STRALEY 55, 56
STRATTON 35, 170, 181, 205
STRAUGHAN 47
STRAUGHN 29
STRAYHORN 50
STREET 65
STREMKE 188
STRICKLAND 148, 149, 178, 189
STRINGER 23
STUARD 195
STUART 29, 36, 48, 101, 157, 191, 205, 206, 220
STUBBLEFIELD 184, 222
STUBBS 237
STURCH 76
STYERS 213
SUDDUTH 122, 206, 207, 209, 226, 237
SUGG 118
SULLENS 217
SULLINGER 114
SULLINS 176
SULLIVAN 11, 44, 72, 127, 137, 182, 183, 216
SUMMEROUR 56
SURBUR 78
SURLES 40, 103
SURRIDGE 23
SUTTON 19, 78, 80, 124, 163, 169
SUYDAM 183
SWAIM 37
SWAIN 144, 237
SWAN 37, 177, 207
SWANN 37, 209
SWARTZLANDER 132
SWATMAN 93
SWETNAM 220
SWIFT 211
SWINDLE 23, 35, 42, 48, 87, 193
SWINK 23, 36

TANNER 77, 131
TASSEY 50
TATE 25, 169, 198, 207, 208
TATUM 185
TAYLOR 28, 36, 53, 61, 62, 64, 94, 95, 99, 101, 104, 114, 116, 117, 139, 164, 165, 166, 182, 186, 206, 208, 209, 210, 213, 238
TEAGUE 41, 87, 216
TEEL 123, 210, 221, 222
TEENOR 69, 84, 201
TELL 228
TENNESSEE 146
TENNISON 44, 52, 208
TENNY 187
TERRELL 174, 176
TERRY 210, 211
TETER 149
TETTINGHOF 121
THACKER 48, 50
THANET 55
THATCHER 138
THENNES 121
THIENES 107
THOMAS 113, 140, 206, 208
THOMASON 46, 79, 169, 211, 219
THOMISON 67, 101
THOMPSON 35, 36, 47, 57, 70, 134, 147, 148, 150, 177, 195, 197, 218, 229
THORN 45
THORNBURG 12, 29, 60
THORNBURGH 77
THORNSBURG 36, 48
THORNTON 140, 141, 166, 185, 197, 211, 212, 224
THORPE 96
THRASHER 45, 53, 139, 141
THREET 49
THRESHER 50
THUDIUM 173
THURMAN 144
TIBBELS 11
TIBBLES 62, 236
TILDON 137
TILLMAN 43
TIMBERLY 73
TINKER 41, 162
TINSLEY 52, 70, 137
TIPPETT 49
TIPTON 6, 7, 15, 30, 47, 67, 72, 101, 201, 212
TISDALE 103
TISHIE 124
TODD 100, 212, 213
TOLBERT 64, 97, 122, 212, 226, 233, 237
TOLER 211, 224
TOLLETT 224
TOLSON 4
TOMBERLIN 164
TOMLIN 124
TOMPKINS 71, 160, 187
TONEY 212, 213
TOWELL 210
TOWERY 177
TOWNSEND 11, 12, 18, 23, 24, 25, 28, 108, 125, 142, 146, 159, 175
TOWNSLEY 35, 49, 75
TOYE 130
TRACY 79
TRAIL 43
TRAMMELL 95
TREAT 68
TREATENBURG 178
TRENTHAM 34, 226
TRETENBURG 178
TRIBBLE 82, 88, 213
TRICE 110
TRIMBLE 213
TRIMMER 35
TRIPLITT 159
TROTT 93
TROTTER 139
TROUTT 32
TROWELL 232
TRUITT 233

Downtown Walnut Ridge.

Printed in the USA
CPSIA information can be obtained
at www.ICGtesting.com
JSHW060050150824
68134JS00032B/2708